C000156988

1 MONTH OF
FREE
READING

at

www.ForgottenBooks.com

By purchasing this book you are eligible for one month membership to ForgottenBooks.com, giving you unlimited access to our entire collection of over 1,000,000 titles via our web site and mobile apps.

To claim your free month visit: www.forgottenbooks.com/free917032

* Offer is valid for 45 days from date of purchase. Terms and conditions apply.

ISBN 978-0-265-96825-3
PIBN 10917032

This book is a reproduction of an important historical work. Forgotten Books uses
state-of-the-art technology to digitally reconstruct the work, preserving the original format
whilst repairing imperfections present in the aged copy. In rare cases, an imperfection in
the original, such as a blemish or missing page, may be replicated in our edition. We do,
however, repair the vast majority of imperfections successfully; any imperfections that
remain are intentionally left to preserve the state of such historical works.

Forgotten Books is a registered trademark of FB &c Ltd.
Copyright © 2018 FB &c Ltd.
FB &c Ltd, Dalton House, 60 Windsor Avenue, London, SW19 2RR.
Company number 08720141. Registered in England and Wales.

For support please visit www.forgottenbooks.com

SESSIONAL PAPERS

VOLUME 13

FIRST SESSION OF THE THIRTEENTH PARLIAMENT

OF THE

DOMINION OF CANADA

SESSION 1918

VOLUME LIII.

A11A83

DEC 12 1919

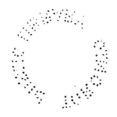

ALPHABETICAL INDEX

TO THE

SESSIONAL PAPERS

OF THE

PARLIAMENT OF CANADA

FIRST SESSION. THIRTEENTH PARLIAMENT, 1918.

3

LIST OF SESSIONAL PAPERS.

Arranged in Numerical Order, with their titles at full length; the dates when Ordered and when presented to the Houses of Parliament; the Names of the Senator or Member who moved for each Sessional Paper, and whether it is ordered to be Printed or not Printed.

CONTENTS OF VOLUME A.

Census of Prairie Provinces—Population and Agriculture—Manitoba, Saskatchewan, and Alberta, 1916.. .. ..*Printed for distribution and sessional papers.*
(This volume is bound in three parts.)

CONTENTS OF VOLUME 1.

1. Report of the Auditor General for the year ended 31st March, 1917, Volume I, Parts a, b and A to K; Volume II, Parts L to U; Volume III, Parts V to Z.   Presented by Hon. Mr. Maclean, March 20, 1918.. .. ..*Printed for distribution and sessional papers.*

1. Report of the Auditor General for the year ended 31st March, 1917, Volume IV, part ZZ. Presented by Hon. Mr. Maclean, April 22, 1918.
Printed for distribution and sessional papers.

. CONTENTS OF VOLUME 2.

2. The Public Accounts of Canada, for tht fiscal year ended 31st March, 1917.   Presented by Hon. Mr. Maclean, March 20, 1918.. .. .. ..*Printed for distribution and sessional papers.*

3. Estimates of sums required for the service of the Dominion for the year ending on the 31st March, 1919, and, in accordance with tht provisions of "The British North America Act, 1867."   Presented by Hon. Mr. Maclean, March 22, 1918.
Printed for distribution and sessional papers..

4. Supplementary Estimates of sums required for the service of the Dominion for the year ending on the 31st March, 1918, and, in accordance with the provisions of "The British North America Act, 1867."   Presented by Hon. Mr. Maclean, May 18, 1918.
Printed for distribution and sessional papers.

5. Supplementary Estimates of sums required for the service of the Dominion for the year ending on the 31st March, 1919, and in accordance with the provisions of "The British North America Act, 1867."   Presented by Hon. Mr. Maclean, May 20, 1918.
Printed for distribution and sessional papers.

CONTENTS OF VOLUME 3.

(This volume is bound in two parts.)

8. Report of the Superintendent of Insurance for the year 1917. (Vol. I.)
Printed for distribution and sessional papers.

8. Report of the Superintendent of Insurance for the year 1917. (Vol. II.)
Printed for distribution and sessional papers.

9. Abstract of Statements of Insurance Companies in Canada for the year ended 31st December, 1917. (Subject to corrections.) Presented by Hon. Mr. Maclean, May 13, 1918.

CONTENTS OF VOLUME 4.

10. Annual Report of the Trade of Canada (Imports for Consumption and Exports), for the fiscal year ended 31st March, 1917.   Presented by Sir George Foster, May 22, 1918.
Printed for distribution and sessional papers.

CONTENTS OF VOLUME 5.

CONTENTS OF VOLUME 6.

CONTENTS OF VOLUME 7.

CONTENTS OF VOLUME 8.

CONTENTS OF VOLUME 9.

CONTENTS OF VOLUME 13—*Continued.*

35. Report of the Militia Council for the Dominion of Canada, for the fiscal year ending 31st March, 1917. Presented by Hon. Mr. Mewburn, April 10, 1918.
Printed for distribution and sessional papers.

36. Report of the Department of Labour for the fiscal year ending 31st March, 1917. Presented by Hon. Mr. Crothers, March 26, 1918... ..*Printed for distribution and sessional papers.*

36a. Tenth Report of the Registrar of Boards of Concilliation and Investigation under "The Industrial Disputes Investigation Act, 1917," for the fiscal year of 1917.
Printed for distribution and sessional papers.

38. Report of the Department of the Naval Service, for the fiscal year ending 31st March, 1917. Presented by Hon. Mr. Ballantyne, March 19, 1918.
Printed for distribution and sessional papers.

38a. Supplement to the Seventh Annual Report of the Department of the Naval Service (Fisheries Branch). Contributions to Canadian Biology, being studies from the Biological Stations of Canada, 1916-17.. ... .*Printed for distribution and sessional papers.*

CONTENTS OF VOLUME 14.

39. Fiftieth Annual Report of the Fisheries Branch of the Department of the Naval Service, 1916-1917. Presented by Hon. Mr. Ballantyne, March 19, 1918.
Printed for distribution and sessional papers.

40. The Report of the Joint Librarians of Parliament. Presented by Hon. The Speaker, March 18, 1918.. .. .., ...*Not printed.*

41. Minute of Council appointing the Honourable Martin Burrell, Secretary of State; the Honourable John Dowsley Reid, Minister of Railways and Canals; the Honourable Arthur L. Sifton, Minister of Customs, and the Honourable James A Calder, Minister of Immigration and Colonization, to act with the Speaker of the House of Commons, as Commissioners for the purposes, and under the Provisions of the Eleventh Chapter of the Revised Statutes of Canada, 1906, intituled: "An Act respecting the House of Commons.". Presented by Sir Robert Borden, March 18, 1918.. .. .. ..*Not printed.*

42. Copies of Orders in Council, as follows:—
P.C. 987, dated 10th April, 1917.—Defence of Canada Order, 1917. Regulations, penalties, etc.
P.C. 1397, dated 21st May, 1917.—Regulations *re* persons employed on docks, etc. carrying matches, smoking, etc., prohibited.
P.C. 1451, dated 25th May, 1917.—Further penalties under Defence of Canada
P.C. 2277, dated 17th August, 1917.—*Re* Desertions from merchant vessels; penalties, etc.
P.C. 2769, dated 4th October, 1917.—Ship's lights: regulations, *re.*
P.C. 3306, dated 29th November, 1917.—Prohibition, sending code messages *re* merchant ships without authority.
P.C. 3307, dated 29th November, 1917.—Seamen undergoing imprisonment for desertion may be liberated for service on vessels.
P.C. 3319, dated 29th November, 1917.—Regulations *re* persons employed on docks.
P.C. 3017, dated 3rd December, 1917.—Naval authorities may authorize embarkation of explosives in merchant ships.
P.C. 3362, dated 24th December, 1917.—Transportation of explosives by railways.
P.C. 86, dated 15th January, 1918.—Competent naval authority may prescribe order in which ships may be supplied with coal.
P.C. 87, dated 17th January, 1918.—Regulation prohibiting taking of firearms, etc., from Canada by sea without permission of naval or military authority.
P.C. 91, dated 15th Janury, 1918.—Regulations providing that all British ships, 1,600 tons or over, trading to Europe and the Mediterranean must have wireless apparatus, etc.
P.C. 261, dated 1st February, 1918.—Regulation *re* carriage of explosives on passenger trains.
P.C. 282, dated 26th February, 1918, respecting the placing at the disposal of The War Trade Board the output of any factory or workshop engaged in the production of arms, ammunition, food, machinery, etc.
P.C. 524, dated 2nd of March, 1918, in substitution of Regulation Fifty-one, respecting penalties for refusing to obey any orders or rules issued under the provisions of the Defence of Canada Order, 1917.
P.C. 558, dated 8th of March, 1918, amending P.C. 987, dated 10th April, 1917.— Regulation respecting the employment of look-outs on merchant vessels of 2,500 gross tonnage and upwards.
P.C. 559, dated 8th March, 1918, respecting the exportation of goods from Canada to neutral countries. Presented by Sir Robert Borden, March 18, 1918...*Not printed.*

CONTENTS OF VOLUME 14—*Continued.*

CONTENTS OF VOLUME 14—*Continued.*

CONTENTS OF VOLUME 14—*Continued*.

CONTENTS OF VOLUME 14—*Continued.*

CONTENTS OF VOLUME 14—*Continued.*

CONTENTS OF VOLUME 14—*Continued.*

CONTENTS OF VOLUME 14—*Continued.*

CONTENTS OF VOLUME 14—*Continued.*

CONTENTS OF VOLUME 14—*Continued.*

CONTENTS OF VOLUME 14—*Continued.*

CONTENTS OF VOLUME 14—*Continued.*

P.C. 1455, 29th May, 1917. Authorizing grant of certain lands to the town of The Pas for industrial purposes.

P.C. 1471, 1st June, 1917. Setting apart certain lands in the Province of Manitoba for Indians.

P.C. 1532, 4th June, 1917. Authorizing grant of certain lands for church purposes to the Board of Management of the Church and Manse Building Fund of the Presbyterian Church in Canada for Manitoba and the Northwest.

P.C. 1533, 4th June, 1917. Vesting certain lands in His Majesty in the right of the Province of Alberta.

P.C. 1536, 5th June, 1917. Authorizing Rev. W. B. Cumming, Saskatoon, to make entry by proxy on behalf of James Grossart.

P.C. 1580, 11th June, 1917. Withdrawing certain lands which had been reserved for the Hudson's Bay Railway.

P.C. 1613, 13th June, 1917. Authorizing grant of certain lands to the town of Gimli, for cemetery purposes.

P.C. 1691, 21st June, 1917. Authorizing sale of certain lands to John Hedberg, Jasper, Alberta.

P.C. 1675, 21st June, 1917. Authorizing license of occupation to Canadian Northern Railway Company of certain lands on the Red Deer River for bridge construction purposes.

P.C. 1761, 26th June, 1917. Authorizing sale of certain lands to the Canadian Pacific Railway Company.

P.C. 1716, 26th June, 1917. Restoring the homestead entry of L. H. Roberts who died wihle on active service overseas.

P.C. 1717, 26th June, 1917. Authorizing sale of certain lands to William Rincheshen.

P.C. 1718, 26th June, 1917 Authorizing grant of certain lands for cemetery purposes to the rural municipality of Bright Sand, No. 529, Saskatchewan.

P.C. 1817, 30th June, 1917. Authorizing exchange of certain lands to Indians in lieu of lands surrendered.

P.C. 1820, 30th June, 1917. Authorizing grant of lands for church and cemetery purposes to the Bethel Evangelical Scandinavian Lutheran Congregation.

P.C. 1821, 30th June, 1917. Authorizing grant of land for cemetery purposes to the Ruthenian Greek Catholic Parish of St. Michael's in Communion with Rome, St: Martin, Manitoba.

P.C. 1866, 6th July, 1917. Dispensing with residence duties in connection with the entry of W. L. Taylor for the N.W. ¼ 13-25-1, W.P.M.

P.C. 1877, 9th July, 1917. Authorizing person on active service overseas to appoint attorney to make application for patent.

P.C. 1937, 12th July, 1917. Authorizing grant of certain lands for cemetery purposes to St. George Cemetery Company, Egremont, Alberta.

P.C. 2039, 26th July, 1917. Authorizing grant of certain lands for park purposes to the town of Drumheller, Alberta.

P.C. 2036, 27th July, 1917. Authorizing grant of land for cemetery purposes to rural municipality of Bear Lake, No. 740.

P.C. 2037, 27th July, 1917. Authorizing grant of land for church purposes to Synod of the Diocese of Qu'Appelle.

P.C. 2038, 27th July, 1917. Authorizing sale of certain lands to Diocese of Ruperts Land.

P.C. 2066, 27th July, 1917. Authorizing the cancellation of the survey of certain lands along the old Dawson Road.

P.C. 2075, 30th July, 1917. Amending Order in Council dated 29th May, 1917, with reference to the name of the Board of Trade of the town of The Pas, Manitoba.

P.C. 2076, 1st August, 1917. Authorizing regulations re timber.

P.C. 2090, 1st August, 1917. Amending forest reserve regulations.

P.C. 2108, 6th August, 1917. Authorizing certain changes in Dominion lands regulations for the protection of water-power resources.

P.C. 2109, 6th August, 1917. Authorizing license of occupation to Canadian Northern Pacific Railway Company of certain lands in the bed of the South Thompson River.

P.C. 2171, 8th August, 1917. Authorizing the disposition of certain lands for townsite purposes.

P.C. 2239, 15th August, 1917. Confirming the late C. R. Coutts in his entry for the S.E. 6-83-17 W. 6.

P.C. 2241, 18th August, 1917. Authorizing sale by auction of certain school lands.

P.C. 2258, 18th August, 1917. Authorizing the lease of certain lands to the Salts and Potash Company of Canada.

P.C. 2259, 18th August, 1917. Granting certain lands for cemetery purposes to La Corporation Episcopale Catholique Romaine de Regina.

P.C. 2226, 18th August, 1917. Transferring certain lands from Indian Affairs to Interior Department to be used for church purposes.

P.C. 2287, 18th August, 1917. Confirming the late Joe White, who died on active service overseas, in his entry for the N.E. 11-89-9 W. 4.

P.C. 2419, 1st September, 1917. Dispensing with residence duties in connection with the entry of J. L. Crawford for the N.E. 21-2-15 W. 3rd.

CONTENTS OF VOLUME 14—*Continued.*

CONTENTS OF VOLUME 14—*Continued.*

CONTENTS OF VOLUME 14—*Continued.*

CONTENTS OF VOLUME 14—*Continued.*

P.C. 8, 4th January, 1918.—Scrutineers, travelling and living expenses of defined.
P.C. 9, 4th January, 1918.—Special returning officers and clerks; remuneration of.
P.C. 10, 4th January, 1918.—Scrutineers; appointment Major Thomas Gibson, of London, Eng., in place of Brigadier-General J. F. L. Embury.
P.C. 11, 4th January, 1918.—Further regulations for carrying the Military Voters' Act, 1917, into effect.
P.C. 12, 8th January, 1918.—Payment for services of Boards of Appeal in Ontario and revising officers in Nova Scotia *re* revision of voters' lists.
P.C. 13, 4th January, 1918.—Election in Halifax; Ward 6 constituted one single polling division.
P.C. 63, 8th January, 1918.—Special returning officers and clerks; remuneration of. O.C. 4th January, 1918 (P.C. No. 9) amended.
P.C. 84, 12th January, 1918.—Special returning officers; appointment Capt. Harold Baker, C.E.F., London, Eng., in place of Lt.-Col. Nelson Spencer.
P.C. 85, 12th January, 1918.—Clerk of special returning officer; appointment Archibald Dickson, of Harrow, Eng. in place of Capt. Rippon, R.A.M.C.
P.C. 98, 16th January, 1918.—Clerk of special returning officers; appointment E. L. Ginna in place of Ainslie W. Greene.
P.C. 162, 19th January, 1918.—Resignation of R. A. Pringle as special returning officer and appointment of John W. P. Ritchie in his stead, and appointment of special returning officers and clerks.
P.C. 323, 8th February, 1918.—Length of sessions to constitute a day's work.
P.C. 396, 18th February, 1918.—Lieut. N. G. Charlton, presently in France, appointed to replace Major Powell as special returning officer.
P.C. 397, 18th February, 1918.—Edgar E. R. Chevrier appointed to replace J. A. Pinard as special returning officer.
P.C. 602, 12th March, 1918.—Proclamation of returns from overseas issued on receipt of telegraphic information. Presented by Hon. Mr. Doherty, April 15, 1918.
Not printed.

97. Return to an Order of the House of the 3rd April, 1918, for a copy of all judgments rendered up to date under the operation of the Military Service Act, 1917, by the Central Appeal Judge. Presented April 15, 1918.—*Mr. Trahan* .. ..*Not printed.*

98. Return to an Order of the House of the 20th March, 1918, for a return showing the names of all persons employed in Ottawa in the Military Service Council, their salaries and former occupations. Presented April 15, 1918.—*Mr. Devlin*.. .. ..*Not printed.*

99. Report of the Royal Commission appointed to inquire into and report upon the Pilotage System and its administration at the port of Halifax, N.S. Presented by Hon. Mr. Ballantyne, April 15, 1918.. .. ..*Not printed.*

100. Return to an Order of the Senate, dated 21st March, 1918, showing:—The details of certain totals, being the estimated cost of streets, sewers, etc., given on figures 29-30, placed between pages 96-97 of Rural Planning and Development, written by Thomas Adams, being a report published by the Commission of Conservation dated 1917. The said totals being $35,584, $26,736, $20,748 and $23,533.—*The Senate*.. .. ..*Not printed.*

101. Return to an Order of the Senate, dated 22nd March, 1918, showing:—1. The different aviation camps established by the Canadian Government and their location, with the date of their establishment. 2. The number of aviators who have gone through those camps since their establishment, and of those who have obtained their certificates. 3. The number of aviators now qualifying in each of these camps. 4. The number of accidents which happened in each of these camps, distinguishing: (a) mortal accidents; (b) serious accidents; (c) slight accidents, with their respective dates. 5. The number of machines out of commission, as a total loss or seriously damaged.—*The Senate.*
Not printed.

102. Return to an Order of the House of the 10th April, 1918, for a copy of all correspondence concerning the resignation of W. F. O'Connor, K.C., as Cost of Living Commissioner. Presented April 16, 1918.—*Mr. Lemieux*.. .. ..*Not printed.*

103. Copy of Order in Council, P.C. 758, dated 26th March, 1918, relating to the making of a contract with the Dominion Steel Corporation, Limited, for the manufacture of steel plates required in the construction of ships and boilers. Presented by Hon. Mr. Ballantyne, April 18, 1918.. .. ..*Not printed.*

104. Copy of Order in Council, P.C. 915, dated 16th April, 1918, prohibiting the press from publishing any adverse statement, report or opinion concerning the action of the allied nations in the prosecution of the war; and also prohibiting any person from publicly expressing any adverse statement, report or opinion concerning the same. Presented by Hon. Mr. Doherty, April 18, 1918.

105. Report of the Military Service Council on the administration of the Military Service Act, 1917 Presented by Hon. Mr. Doherty, April 18, 1918.

CONTENTS OF VOLUME 14—*Continued.*

CONTENTS OF VOLUME 14—Continued.

CONTENTS OF VOLUME 14—*Continued.*

127. Return to an Order of the House of the 25th March, 1918, for a return showing:—1. If any money has been paid to the Dundalk *Herald*, the Flesherton *Advance*, the Markdale *Standard*, the Durham *Chronicle*, the Grey *Review*, or the Hanover *Post* for advertising or for any other reason since 1st October, 1917. If so, how many was paid in the case of each of the papers mentioned. Presented April 29. 1918.—*Mr. Cahill.*
Not printed.

128. Return to an Order of the House of the 15th April, 1918, for a return showing:—1. The officers employed at Quebec on the staff of the Military District No. 5. 2. How long they have been connected with this. branch. 3. What service each of them is performing. 4. What salary and allowance each of them is receiving. 5. Names of those amongst them who have performed service overseas. 6. How long they have been actually at the front. 7. How long they were in the trenches. 8. To which battalion they belonged while overseas. Presented April 29, 1918.—*Mr. Power.. ..Not printed.*

129. Report of the Commissioners appointed to investigate the businesses of William Davies Co., Ltd., and Matthews-Blackwell, Ltd., dated 1st November, 1917. Presented by Hon. Mr. Crothers, May 1, 1918.

130. Return to an Order of the House of the 24th April, 1918, for a return showing the details of certain totals being the estimated cost of street sewers, etc., given on figures 29 and 30 placed between pages 96-97 of Rural Planning and Development written by Thomas Adams, being a report published by the Commission of Conservation dated 1917. The said totals being $35,584, $26,736, $20,748 and $23,533. Presented May 1, 1918.—*Mr. Lemieux.. .. ..Not printed.*

131. Statement of expenditure of the Dominion Publicity Committee in account with the Dominion Government, and in connection with the Victory Loan, 1917. Presented by Hon. Mr. Maclean, May 1, 1918.

131a. Report of Mr. A. E. Ames, Chairman of the Dominion Executive Committee of Canada, in connection with the Victory Loan, 1917. Presented by Hon. Mr. Maclean, May 1, 1918.. .. ..Not printed.*

131b. Statement showing details of remuneration paid in connection with Victory Loan. Presented by Hon. Maclean, May 11, 1918.. .. ..Not printed.*

132. Return to an Order of the House of the 3rd April, 1918, for a return showing:—1. How many local tribunals were established throughout Canada under the Military Service Act. 2. What remuneration per diem was allowed each member of such tribunal. 3. What was remuneration per day for Secretary of tribunal and also for constables or caretaker of the tribunal sessional chamber. 4. What has been the total expenditure to date on account of tribunals under the Military Service Act. 5. Whether there are any outstanding claims unpaid. Presented May 1, 1918.—*Mr. White (Victoria).*
Not printed.

133. Report of the Ninth Annual Meeting of the Commission of Conservation, Canada, November 27-28, 1917.—(*The Senate*).. .. ..Not printed.*

134. Return showing—1. Whether the building of the hospital for invalid soldiers at Ste. Anne de Bellevue is under Government control. 2. If not, through whose agency. Whether it is being built by contract or under the supervision of any public body. 3. What sum has been paid by the Government for the land where this hospital is being erected. 4. What the cost of construction will be. 5. How many invalid soldiers it will accommodate. 6. How far this hospital is from Macdonald College. 7. Whether the Government has considered the very grave inconvenience which may result from the erecting of such an institution in the vicinity of a college where hundreds of young ladies are being educated. Presented May 1, 1918.—*Mr. Boyer*   *Not printed.*

135. Return to an Order of the Senate, dated April 23. 1918, giving the following information:—The names, dates of appointments, salaries or wages of all clerks and employees of the Department of Public Printing and Stationery, under the following heads:— (a) King's Printer's staff, including advertising. (b) Printing Branch. 1. Clerks. 2. Proofreaders. 3. Typesetting rooms: Mono. Lino, Job and Parliamentary. 4. Press rooms: Platen and Cylinder. 5. Binding: Book, Pamphlet. 6. Stereotyping. 7. Map engraving. 8. Any other Departments. (c) Outside Printing Branch. (d) Accountants. (e) Stationery. (f) Distribution. (g) Mechanical staff. (h) *Canada Gazette.* (i) Caretaker. (j) Any other Departments.—(*The Senate*).. .. ..Not printed.*

136. Return showing:—1. Whether tenders have been recently submitted to the Department of Militia and Defence or to the War Purchasing Commission for a supply of Smoked Wiltshire Bacon, at Toronto, Kingston and London. 2. If so, who the tenderers are, and what their prices are, in each case. 3. To whom the contract has been awarded in each case, and at what price. Presented May 2, 1918.—*Mr. Murphy.. ..Not printed.*

CONTENTS OF VOLUME 14—*Continued.*

137. Order in Council, P.C. 26/942, dated the 19th April, 1918, with regard to remissions made under section 88 of The Indian Act, chapter 81, R.S.C. 1906, of the interest on arrears of purchase price of Park Lot No. 19, in the village of Southampton, in the County of Bruce, Ontario, amounting to $18.—(*The Senate*).. .. ..*Not printed.*

138. Order in Council, P.P. 871, dated 23rd April, 1917, being regulations for the protection of migratory game birds, migratory insectivorous and migratory non-game birds, which inhabit Canada during the whole or any part of the year, under the authority of The Migratory Bird Act, 7-8 George V, 1917.—(*The Senate*).. .. .. ..*Not printed.*

139. Return to an Order of the House of the 6th May, 1918, for a return showing :—What the gross earnings of the National Transcontinental railway were for the year ending 31st March, 1918 ; how much was earned between Moncton and Quebec, between Quebec and Cochrane Junction, between Cochrane Junction and Winnipeg, and between Lake Superior Junction and Fort William, and the amount paid by that railway to the Canadian Pacific for terminal charges at Quebec. Presented May 13, 1918.—*Mr. Lavigueur*.. .. ..*Not printed.*

140. Return to an Order of the House of the 24th April, 1918, for a copy of all correspondence, letters, telegram and other papers exchanged between the Food Controller and the Winnipeg Civic Authorities concerning cold storage conditions at Winnipeg. Presented May 13, 1918.—*Mr. Lemieux*.. .. ..*Not printed.*

141. Interim Report No. 2, Georgian Bay Canal Commission,—Wheat Prices, and a Comparative Study of United States and Canadian Markets, by W. Sanford Evans. Presented by Hon. Mr. Carvell, May 13, 1918.. *Printed for distribution and Sessional Papers.*

142. Interim Report No. 3, Georgian Bay Canal Commission—Transatlantic Passenger and Freight Traffic and Steamship Subsidies, by W. Sanford Evans. Presented by Hon. Mr. Carvel, May 13, 1918.. .. ..*Printed for distribution and Sessional Papers.*

143. Return to an Order of the House, of the 24th April, 1918, for a copy of all correspondence and petitions passed between the Prime Minister and Civil Service Federation, concerning certain appointments made in the Post Office and Customs Departments since the 17th of December, 1917. Presented May 13, 1918.—*Mr. Lemieux*..*Not printed.*

144. Return showing :—1. Whether the Government is aware that in the past sixteen months in the Cities of Winnipeg, Hamilton, Toronto, Ottawa and Montreal, the following quantities of foodstuffs, are reported to have been ordered to be destroyed as unfit for human consumption ;—(*a*) Meats : Winnipeg, 7,262 lbs.; Hamilton, 4,874 lbs.; Toronto, quantities not given in lbs., only sides, quarters, legs, etc,; Ottawa, 7,787 lbs.; Montreal, 105,898 lbs. (*b*) Poultry : Winnipeg, 11,364 lbs.; Hamilton, 8 fowl; Montreal, 2,344 lbs. (*c*) Fish : Winnipeg, 9,066 lbs.; Toronto, 74,587 lbs., weight not given, only number of packages for remainder ; Montreal, 137,903 lbs. (*d*) Vegetables : Winnipeg, 265,565 lbs.; Toronto, 5,855 lbs. cabbage, the rest weight not given, only crates, baskets, etc., also recently 48,010 lbs., or 24 tons of food unfit for human consumption ; Montreal, 13,940 lbs. (*e*) Eggs : Winnipeg, 3,013 lbs.; Hamilton, 40 doz.; Toronto, 1,050 doz., 6 tubs, 1 pail, and 8 gallons yolk. (*f*) Butter : Winnipeg, 3,374 lbs.; Hamilton, 22 lbs. (*g*) Fruit (fresh and dried) : Winnipeg, fresh, 46,375 lbs., dried, 37,207 lbs.; Hamilton, fresh, 12 baskets ; Montreal, fresh, 3,362 lbs. 2. If so, what action the Government proposes .taking to prevent a continuance of such waste. Presented May 13, 1918.—*Mr. Foster (York).*

145. Return showing :—1. Whether the Government is aware that 236,490 pounds of food were destroyed in the city of Toronto between April 4 and April 29, 1918, according to a report of one of the Departments of the Toronto City Corporation. 2. Whether the Food Controller has taken any action to stop such wholesale waste of food. 3. If so, what he has done in this particular case. Presented May 15, 1918.—*Mr. Proulx.*
Not printed.

146. Return to an Order of the House of the 22nd April, 1918, for a return showing :—1. The names of all persons employed in connections with the work of preparing the Votes and Proceedings, the Order Paper and the Journals of the House (*a*) in English, and (*b*) in French, and the salary and other remuneration paid to each. 2. The number of each of these documents printed, (*a*) in English, and (*b*) in French, and the cost of printing and binding the same for the fiscal year ending the 31st of March, 1918. Presented May 15, 1918.—*Mr. Currie*.. .. ..*Not printed.*

147. Return to an Order of the House of the 22nd April, 1918, for a return showing :—1. The names of all persons employed in connection with the work of reporting and translating in the House. 2. How long each has been so employed. 3. The rate of remuneration paid to each during the past year, with the total amount paid to each class of persons. 4. Number of copies of the Debates of the House printed during the past year, (*a*) in English, and (*b*) in French, specifying the number of the unrevised and of the revised editions, respectively. 5. The cost of printing and binding the same for each year since 1900, inclusive. 6. The amounts paid in addition to the above, in each year since 1900, inclusive, for (*a*) reporting, (*b*) translating, (*c*) typewriting, and (*d*) printing proceedings before Parliamentary Committees. Presented May 15, 1918. *Mr. Currie.*
Not printed.

CONTENTS OF VOLUME 14—*Continued.*

148. Return to an Order of the House of the 24th April, 1918, for a return showing:—1. What control the Canadian Government has over the operations of the Imperial Royal Flying Corps in Canada, and what Department of the Government would exercise this control. 2. Whether the Canadian Government has any officers or representatives on the Canadian Branch of the Imperial Flying Corps. If so, what their names are, and what positions they occupy. 3. Whether the Canadian Government intends to take over all the offices, plant, and equipment, of the Imperial Royal Flying Corps in Canada at an early date. If not, why not. How many accidents and deaths have occurred in Canada, United States and Overseas among our flying men. 5. The nature of the investigations into these accidents, and where the records are kept. 6. Whether the Government of Canada at the close of the war intends to establish and maintain a Canadian Flying Corps. If so, what preparations are under way, with this end in view. 7. How many Canadians and how many Americans, have joined the Imperial Royal Flying Corps in Canada. 8. How many mechanics are employed by the Imperial Royal Flying Corps in Canada. 9. What amount of money has been expended in Canada by the Imperial Royal Flying Corps. 10. How many Canadian Officers who have seen air service overseas are in the employ of the Imperial Royal Flying Corps in Canada. Presented May 16, 1918.—*Mr. Armstrong (Lambton).*

148a. Return to an Order of the House of the 24th April, 1918, for a return showing:—1. What status the Canadian recruits of the Royal Flying Corps have in the military affairs of Canada. 2. In the case of permanent injury or death of Canadians in the Royal Flying Corps in the discharge of their duties, what provision has been made to pension their dependents. 3. How many men came to Canada from England to establish training camps for the Royal Flying Corps; if any of these men have returned to England. If so, how many have been replaced by Canadians. 4. What comparative results were obtained in training cadets at the training camps around Toronto and the camps located in Texas. 5. Whether the Royal Flying Corps went to Texas and remained there at the expense of, and on the request of the United States Government. 6. Whether the authorities of the Royal Flying Corps were asked to give consideration to a location in British Columbia. If so, what the nature of the request was. 7. If it is not a fact that the weather conditions in Texas proved very unfavourable for flying corps training purposes. 8. What investigations of a technical character were made of the air conditions in Texas before selecting that place as a training ground for our airmen. 9. What investigations were made as to the atmospherical and climatical conditions in British Columbia regarding the locating of an air squadron training camp in that province. 10. Whether the Imperial Munitions Board took an option to lease a large area of land at Delta, near Vancouver, B.C., to establish winter training camps for the Canadian training squadrons of the Royal Flying Corps, and whether tenders were asked for materials, hangers, buildings, etc. If so, why these negotiations were dropped. 11. How many deaths in the Royal Flying Corps training camps in Texas resulted from atmospherical conditions, which are unfavourable to the successful training of aviators. 12. Whether any requests have been made to the Canadian Government for assistance to the Royal Flying Corps either through appropriation or gifts of money for training machines. If so, the nature of these requests. 13. Where the records are kept of the causes of injury or illness of Canadian cadets and mechanics of the Royal Flying Corps. 14. Whether English-born drill sergeants are exclusively employed in the training of Canadian cadets in the Royal Flying Corps in Canada. 15. What efforts have been made by the Canadian Government or individuals or organizations to develop and assist the Flying Corps in Canada, and whether the Government has extended any assistance to these individuals or organizations. 16. Whether any part of the amount of $100 provided by Order in Council for each aviator trained in Canada to defray a part of the expense incurred in training has been paid, or whether any request for payment has been made. Presented May 16, 1918.—*Mr. Armstrong (Lambton)*.. .. ..*Not printed.*

149. Second Report of the War Purchasing Commission, covering period from 1st January, 1917, to 31st March, 1918. Presntd by Sir Robert Borden, May 16, 1918.. .. ..*Not printed.*

150. Return to an Order of the Senate dated 9th May, 1918, for a return giving a statement of imports of petroleum oils and spirits (gallons, value and duty) during each of the following fiscal years ending 31st March: 1909-10-11-12-13-14-15-16-17, and for each month of the unexpired year ending 31st March, 1918.—*(The Senate)*.. ..*Not printed.*

151. Report of the Administrative Chairman of the Honourary Advisory Council for Scientific and Industrial Research 1917-18. Presented by Sir George Foster, May 17, 1918.
Not printed.

152. Return to an Address to His Excellency the Governor General, of the 13th May, 1918, for a copy of the Order in Council appointing Mr. Main Johnson and passed under the War Measures Act as mentioned by Hon. Mr. Rowell on page 1350 of *Unrevised Hansard.* Presented May 20, 1918.—*Mr. Archambault.*.. .. ..*Not printed.*

153. First Report of the Munition Resources Commission, November, 1915, to February, 1918, inclusive. Presented by Hon. Mr. Burrell, 20th May, 1918.. .. ..*Not printed.*

CONTENTS OF VOLUME 14—*Concluded.*

154. Return to an Order of the House of the 22nd April, 1918, for a return showing:—What amounts have been paid by the Government for printing or advertising to the *Globe,* Toronto, and the *Devoir,* Montreal, during each of the fiscal years ending 31st March, 1915, 1916, 1917 and 1918.   Presented May 20, 1918.—*Mr. McMaster*.... ..*Not printed.*

155. Return to an Order of the House of the 25th March, 1918, for a copy of all petitions, letters or communications of any kind either asking for or opposing the importation of coolie labour, from first of September last to date.   Presented May 20, 1918.—*Sir Wilfrid Laurier*.. .. ..*Not printed.*

156. Return to an Order of the House of the 25th March, 1918, for a copy of all memoranda and petitions by Slav subjects of Austria, naturalized in Canada, setting forth grievances and suggesting remedies.   Presented May 20, 1918.—*Sir Wilfrid Laurier.*
Not printed.

157. Return to an Order of the Senate, dated 12th April, 1918, for a return giving:—1. The name, rank, and qualifications of each of the persons, upon whose advice and recommendation, lobster hatcheries, heretofore operated in Canada by the Department of Naval Affairs, are to remain closed.   2. Copies of the reports and recommendations (or if the same are published, the references thereto in official publications), which fully disclose all the facts, reasons, and grounds, upon which the Department makes its decision to abandon the policy of operating lobster hatcheries.—(*The Senate*).
Not printed.

158. Order in Council P.C. 668, dated 25th March, 1918, *re* procedure for conferring titles of honour upon subjects of His Majesty ordinarily resident in Canada.   Presented by Sir Robert Borden, May 21, 1918.. .. ..*Not printed.*

159. Return to an Order of the House of the 2nd May, 1918, for a return showing:—1. The amount paid the Toronto *Globe* and the Toronto *Star* respectively, from 1st January, 1917, to 1st April, 1918, for all service between the said dates.   2. Whether any contract of any kind was made with either of the said newspapers between the dates mentioned for advertising, publicity, or news editorial and feature service.   3. If so, by whom said contract or contracts were made, and what the particulars are thereof.   Presented May 22, 1918.—*Mr. Murphy*.. .. ..*Not printed.*

160. Return to an Order of the House of the 8th April, 1918, for a return showing:—1. What quantity of bran, shorts, or mill feed have been exported to the United States (a) by license; (b) without license, between 1st August, 1917, and 28th February, 1918.   2. To what firms in Canada licenses to export this feed have been granted, and for what quantity in each case.   Presented May 22, 1918.—*Mr. Kay*.. .. ..*Not printed.*

161. Return to an Order of the House of the 15th May, 1918, for a return showing:—1. The total amount paid to the Journal Publishing Company of Ottawa, Limited, during the fiscal years 1912-13-14-15-16-17 inclusive, for (a) rentals; (b) printing.   2. Whether the official cheques of the Government for said rentals and printing jobs were issued directly in favour of the above company, or to P. D. Ross, Esq.   Presented May 23, 1918.—*Mr. Brouillard*.. .. ..*Not printed.*

162. Return to an Order of the House of the 16th May, 1918, for a return showing:—1. The total number of the families of soldiers deceased since the beginning of the war, who receive pensions from the Government.   2. Of this number, how many reside in Great Britain, how many reside in Canada, and how many reside elsewhere.   Presented May 23, 1918.—*Mr. Seguin*.. .. .., ...*Not printed.*

163. Report dealing with the purchase and sale of Fordson tractors by the Canada Food Board.   Presented by Hon. Mr. Crerar, May 23, 1918.. .. ..*Not printed.*

NINTH ANNUAL REPORT

CIVIL SERVICE COMMISSION OF CANADA

FOR THE YEAR ENDED
AUGUST 31
1917

PRINTED BY ORDER OF PARLIAMENT

OTTAWA
J. de LABROQUERIE TACHÉ
PRINTER TO THE KING'S MOST EXCELLENT MAJESTY
1918

[No. 31—1918.]—A½

OTTAWA, September 1, 1917.

The Honourable
 ARTHUR MEIGHEN,
  Secretary of State of Canada.

SIR,—In conformity with the provisions of section 44 of the Civil Service Amendment Act, 1908, we have the honour to submit, herewith, a report of the proceedings of the Civil Service Commission of Canada, for the year ended August 31, 1917.

We have the honour to be, sir,

Your obedient servants,

ADAM SHORTT,
M. G. LAROCHELLE,
Commissioners.

To His Excellency the Duke of Devonshire, K.G., P.C., G.C.M.G., G.C.V.O., etc., etc., Governor General and Commander in Chief of the Dominion of Canada.

MAY IT PLEASE YOUR EXCELLENCY:

The undersigned has the honour to lay before your Royal Excellency the accompanying report of the Civil Service Commission of Canada for the year ended August 31, 1917.

Respectfully submitted,

ARTHUR MEIGHEN,
Secretary of State.

OTTAWA, September 1, 1917.

CONTENTS.

INDEX.

REPORT OF THE COMMISSIONERS.

The Civil Service Commissioners hereby submit the ninth Annual Report of the proceedings of the Commission, covering the twelve months from September 1, 1916, to August 31, 1917. The tables of the appendix furnish all the required particulars as to the various examinations which were held during that year, and as to the appointments and promotions made in the Inside Service.

EXAMINATIONS.

Semi-annual examinations.—According to the regulations, the semi-annual examinations are to be held, both for the Inside and the Outside Service, in November and in May. This year, the November tests were postponed to December, in order to permit as many returned officers and soldiers as possible, to try them. In December, they took place in twenty-five Centres of the Dominion, and in May, in twenty-seven. In all, 1,627 candidates were examined, 465 for the Inside, and 1,162 for the Outside Service.

General Competitions, Inside Service.—No Second Division competitive examination took place in December, 1916, but one was held in May, 1917, for fifteen situations. Out of twenty-seven candidates, seventeen were successful, nine men and eight women.

In the Third Division competitions, which were held for 130 positions, 420 candidates were examined, 175 in December, and 245 in May. Ninety-two were successful, seven men and eighty-five women.

Eighteen candidates were also examined for the lower grades of the Inside Service. Fourteen passed.

Special Competitions.—The commission was requested to hold thirty-three special competitions of a professional and technical character for the following positions: three draughtsmen, seven technical clerks, two research chemists, one engineering chemist, one chemist, three assistant chemists, five analysts, two translators, one reporter of debates, one technical assistant, one process photographer, one patent examiner, one assistant engineer.

A number of candidates competed for these positions, and the departments to which the successful ones were assigned appear under the head of permanent appointments.

Outside Service Examinations.—Qualifying examinations were held for clerkships in the Outside Service. Two hundred and forty-four candidates were tested, 112 in December and 132 in May. Forty-nine were successful in the first test, and sixty-seven in the second.

Nine hundred and eighteen candidates were examined in the Preliminary examinations for the Outside Service, 496 in December and 422 in May. Five hundred and seventy-three passed.

Promotion Examinations—Examinations were held under regulation 20, for promotion from the Third to the Second Division. Out of eleven candidates, four were successful.

Naval Cadets Examinations—In the Naval Cadets examinations, thirty-one candidates were examined and twenty passed.

APPOINTMENTS.

Permanent Appointments, Inside Service—Of the nine men who successfully competed for the Second Division in the May examination, only one, as yet, has received a permanent appointment. Such of the others as are exempt from the military service will doubtless be appointed in due course. None of the eight successful female candidates has been appointed, but they were declared eligible for the Third Division or for temporary employment.

As above stated, ninety-two candidates were successful in the Third Division competition examination, seven men and eighty-five women. Seven men and seventy-five women were assigned to permanent positions, and the others have been assigned to temporary situations while waiting for their permanent appointment.

The successful candidates in the special competitions have been permanently appointed to the following departments: Naval Service, two draughtsmen; Mines, one assistant engineer, one engineering chemist, two research chemists, three assistant chemist; Interior, five technical clerks; Inland Revenue, five analysts; Labour, one technical clerk; Trade and Commerce, one translator; Public Works, one process photographer, one technical assistant; Agriculture, one chemist, one technical clerk.

Sixteen appointments of a professional or technical nature were made without competition under section 21 of the Act, with certificates of qualification from the Commission.

Temporary appointments—Four hundred and seventy-three temporary appointments have been made to the Inside Service. The persons appointed satisfied the commission as to their qualifications.

PROMOTIONS.

One hundred and forty-seven promotions were made in the First, Second, and Third Divisions of the Inside Service.:—

> From 3 B to 3 A..76
> " 3 A to 2 B.. 4
> " 2 B to 2 A..23
> " 2 A to 1 B..30
> " 1 B to 1 A..14

GENERAL OBSERVATIONS.

Surplus of officers in Second Division.—During the last few years, the commissioners have noticed a gradual decrease of the number of clerks assigned to the Second Division, which, according to section 5 of the Act, should be limited to the junior administrative and technical officers of the department. Somewhat congested by the automatic classification of September, 1908, further unnecessary appointments to that division could only magnify the actual surplus of its employees, and aggravate the situation. In order to obviate the inadequacy of the scale of salary of the clerks of the Third Division, the heads of the departments have been inclined to place them in the Second Division, without due regard to the nature of their duties. In fact, nearly all the successful candidates in the Second Division competitions have been assigned to mere routine work.

Inadequate salary of the Third Division.—It seems to us that the best way to deal with this difficulty would have been a proper increase of the remuneration of the clerks of the Third Division. Such has been the remedy suggested by the commission in its annual reports, and the Government appears to have reached the same conclusion, since a Bill providing for a higher scale of salary was presented to Parliament during the session of 1914.

Owing to inadequacy of the salary attached to the Third Division, the Commission has been unable to secure the required number of young men for the different departments. In a number of cases, positions intended for men had to be filled by women. On the other hand, it cannot be argued that the examinations were too difficult, since a surplus of woman have passed them successfully.

Privilege of returned officers and soldiers.—According to the Order in Council of the 16th October, 1916, the returned officers and soldiers securing the required percentages of marks, in the general competitive examinations, are to be preferred to the ordinary candidates.

Four competed in the Second and Third Division examinations, and failed Three hundred and thirteen tried the preliminary tests, and 233 passed.

Temporary appointments in connection with the war.—A very large number of temporary civil employees were appointed in connection with the war, without any reference to the commission. Greater salaries than those authorized by the Civil Service Act were paid to them, which was a source of serious inconvenience to several departments. The undersigned are of the opinion that the commission could have supplied most of them at the usual rates.

The whole respectfully submitted.

MICHEL LaROCHELLE,
ADAM SHORTT,
Commissioners.

APPENDIX

THE REGULATIONS OF THE CIVIL SERVICE COMMISSION WITH REFERENCE TO ENTRANCE TO THE SERVICE AND PROMOTION IN THE SERVICE.

(Approved by His Excellency the Governor General in Council, on the 19th April, 1909. Amendments approved on the 22nd February, 1911, the 21st March, 1913, and the 12th April, 1915.)

In accordance with section 10, clause 2, of the Civil Service Amendment Act, 1908, requiring that the duties of the Civil Service Commission "shall be performed in accordance with regulations made by the Commission, and approved by the Governor in Council," the following regulations have been prepared by the Commission:—

EXAMINATIONS FOR ENTRANCE TO THE INSIDE SERVICE.

1. In order to comply with section 13 of the Civil Service Amendment Act, which states that "except as herein otherwise provided, appointment to positions in the Inside Service under that of deputy head shall be by competitive examination, which shall be of such a nature as will determine the qualifications of candidates for the particular positions to which they are to be appointed, and shall be held by the Commission from time to time in accordance with the regulations made by it and approved by the Governor in Council," the Commission will provide for general competitive examinations for entrance to the following divisions and subdivisions of the Inside Service:—

  (a) Clerks for Subdivision B of the Third Division.
  (b) Clerks for Subdivision B of the Second Division.

2. In accordance with section 15 of the Civil Service Amendment Act, the number of competitors to be selected, for appointment to the Service, from those taking the examinations for the above divisions, shall be computed by the Commission on the basis of the reports from the several departments as to their probable requirements for the ensuing six months.

3. The general competitive examinations shall be held twice a year, in the months of May and November. Forms on which applications for these examinations shall be made will be provided by the Commission, and may be had on application to the Secretary of the Commission. Where not less than three candidates make application to take an examination at the same place, general competitive examinations shall be held at the following places: Sydney, Halifax, Yarmouth, Charlottetown, St. John, Fredericton, Moncton, Quebec, Sherbrooke, Montreal, Ottawa, Kingston, Hamilton, Toronto, London, Sault Ste. Marie, Port Arthur, Winnipeg, Brandon, Regina, Saskatoon, Calgary, Edmonton, Nelson, Vancouver and Victoria. Examinations may also be held at such other places as may be selected by the Commission for the convenience of candidates applying for examination.

(2) Where competitive examinations are required involving technical or scientific subjects and necessitating the use of scientific apparatus, it shall not be necessary to hold such examinations at each of the above places, but the Commission shall, as far as possible, arrange for at least one place in each province where such examinations may be taken.

4. Any examination may be taken in the English or French language, at the option of the candidate.

31—1½

5. A general examination for messengers, porters, sorters and packers shall be held annually in the month of May, at the same places as the general examinations for the Third and Second Divisions, and shall include the following subjects of the ordinary public school standard: Writing, spelling and the first four rules of arithmetic. The minimum percentage of qualification shall be fifty per cent on each subject and sixty per cent on the whole examination.

6. Where messengers, porters, sorters and packers require certificates of qualification and fitness under section 22 of the Civil Service Amendment Act, the Commission may require any or all of these to pass an examination which shall be as nearly as may be of the same standard as that set for those who take the general examination for entering that grade of the Service.

7. The general competitive examination for clerkships of Subdivision B of the Third Division shall include the following subjects: Writing and copying manuscripts, spelling, composition, arithmetic, geography, history, typewriting. The maximum number of marks for each subject shall be one hundred, except in the subjects of writing and copying manuscripts, for each of which the maximum number shall be fifty marks. No candidate shall be selected for appointment to a position in the Third Division who secures less than fifty per cent of the marks assigned to the subjects of spelling, composition and arithmetic and sixty per cent of the marks assigned to the whole examination. The standard of examination shall require a good general knowledge of the above subjects.

8. Candidates may take, in addition to the foregoing subjects, either or both of the subjects of stenography and book-keeping. Where candidates obtain over sixty per cent of the marks assigned to either or both of these subjects, the marks above sixty per cent may be added to the total of the marks obtained on the compulsory subjects in determining the relative standing of the candidates in the general examination.

9. Persons employed in the Civil Service, in the Third Division, may take the general competitive examination for entrance to the Second Division under the following regulations:—

(1) Such persons must be between the ages of eighteen and thirty-five years at the time of examination.

(2) Their records in the reports to be furnished under the Civil Service Amendment Act must be good.

10. To insure the availability of a sufficient number of competent typewriters and stenographers, the commission may appoint a special competitive examination for typewriters and stenographers, for Subdivision B of the Third Division, which shall include the following subjects: Typewriting, stenography, writing and copying manuscripts, spelling and composition. Successful candidates must obtain at least fifty per cent of the marks assigned to each subject and sixty per cent of the marks assigned to the whole examination.

(2) Where a sufficient number of typewriters and stenographers are not available among those who have taken the full examination for Subdivision B of the Third Division, the requirements of the departments may be supplied by appointing, in order of merit, those who have taken the special examination for typewriters and stenographers.

(3) No one appointed as the result of such special examination shall be considered as eligible for promotion to Subdivision A of the Third Division who has not subsequently qualified in the additional subjects of arithmetic, history and geography, as required for the regular examination for entrance to the Third Division.

11. Where candidates for employment as temporary clerks require certificates of qualification and fitness under section 23 of the Civil Service Amendment Act, the Commission may require any or all of these to pass an examination which shall be as nearly as may be of the same standard as that set for those who take the general examination for entering that grade of the service.

12. Candidates for the general competitive examination for clerkships of Subdivision B of the Second Division shall take all the subjects in group A of the following list, and any five in group B:—

A.—Writing, Spelling, Composition, Literature, Arithmetic.

B.—Algebra, Geometry, Physics, Chemistry, Geology (including mineralogy), Biology (animal and vegetable), French (for those taking the general examination in English), English (for those taking the general examination in French), Latin, German, History (modern), Political Science, Economics, Geography (general, physical and commercial), Philosophy (scholastic or general), Law (English or Civil).

(2) The maximum number of marks for each subject shall be one hundred, except in the subject of writing, for which the maximum number shall be fifty marks.

(3) No candidate shall be selected for appointment to a position in Subdivision B of the Second Division who secures less than forty per cent of the marks assigned to each subject in group A, and sixty per cent of the marks assigned to the whole group.

(4) No candidate shall be selected for appointment to a position in Subdivision B of the Second Division who secures less than thirty per cent of the marks assigned to each subject in group B, and forty per cent of the marks assigned to the five subjects selected.

(5) The standard of examination shall require a good general knowledge of the subjects selected from the above groups. In order that due regard may be had to the different educational systems in Canada, a curriculum shall be prepared by the Commission showing, with as much detail as possible, the ground to be covered under each of the subjects in the above groups A and B. A copy of this curriculum shall be supplied to any person on making application to the Secretary of the Commission.

13. Candidates may take, in addition to the foregoing subjects, any or all of the subjects of typewriting, stenography, and book-keeping. Where candidates obtain over sixty per cent of the marks assigned to any one or more of these subjects, the marks above sixty per cent may be added to the total of the marks obtained on the whole examination in determining the relative standing of the candidates.

14. Where the deputy head of a department applies to the Commission for a nomination to a clerkship in Subdivision B of the Third Division requiring special qualifications not covered by the general examination for that division, or for a nomination to a clerkship in Subdivision B of the Second Division requiring special qualifications in technical or scientific subjects, a special competitive examination may be provided by the Commission, instead of the general competitive examinations for either of these subdivisions. The subjects for such special examination shall be arranged between the Commission and the deputy head of such department.

15. Where the deputy head of a department applies to the Commission for a nomination to a position above that of Subdivision B of the Second Division, which requires to be filled by appointment from without the Service, the Commission shall, after consultation with the deputy head of the department in which the appointment is to be made, provide a special competitive examination or test, which may or may not involve written answers to questions, but which shall be of such a nature as to secure a person well qualified for the position to be so filled. In determining the qualifications of candidates for such positions, the examination or test shall have special reference to executive ability and tact, such special or professional training as may be required, and a successful experience in duties similar to those pertaining to the positions to be filled.

16. Where the appointment is one which is to be made under section 21 of the Civil Service Amendment Act inasmuch as the person to be appointed requires to obtain from the Commission a certificate that he possesses the requisite knowledge and ability, the Commission, with the consent and co-operation of the head and deputy head of the department in which the appointment is to be made, may arrange a form of examination or test, by which to determine whether the person is qualified. On satisfying the Commission that he is duly qualified, such person will receive the certificate of the Commission.

17. When the selection is made by the head and deputy head of the department without reference to the Commission, the Commission may make such inquiries and appoint such an examination or test to determine the qualifications of the person so nominated as it may deem necessary for an intelligent and responsible discharge of its duties.

PROMOTIONS IN THE INSIDE SERVICE.

18. A candidate who is recommended by the head of a department for promotion, other than from the Third to the Second Division, in order to receive the prescribed certificate of qualification, must satisfy the Commission of his ability to perform the duties of the position to which he is to be promoted. For this purpose the Commission, if it considers an examination necessary, may, after consultation with the deputy head of the department in which the promotion is to take place, prescribe a promotion examination, having regard to the requirements of the subdivision to which the promotion is to be made, and the special duties of the position to be filled.

19. Where there are two or more persons in the employment of a department who are eligible for promotion to any vacant position, the Commission may, at the request of the head of the department, provide a competitive promotion examination limited to those who are declared eligible for promotion. Such an examination shall have regard to the requirements of the subdivision to which the promotion is to be made, and the special duties of the position to be filled. Upon the results of this examination, if satisfactory, the Commission shall issue the required certificate of qualification.

20. Candidates, who under subsection 2 of section 26 of the Civil Service Amendment Act, 1908, are nominated by the head of a department for promotion from the Third to the Second Division must, in order to receive the prescribed certificate of qualification, satisfy the Commission that they are entitled to enter the Second Division. To this end, the Commission, after consultation with the head or deputy head of the department in which the promotion is proposed, shall prescribe a non-competitive promotion examination which, while having special reference to the requirements of the positions to be filled, shall nevertheless insure a qualification substantially equivalent to that required in the open competitive examination for entrance to the Second Division. Such non-competitive promotion examination shall include all of the subjects in group A under regulation 12, any three of the subjects in group B under regulation 12, and two papers on the work of the department in which the candidate for promotion is engaged. The minimum percentages required for passing on the subjects included in group A shall be not less than forty per cent of the marks assigned to each subject and sixty per cent of the marks assigned to the whole group. The minimum percentages required for passing on the subjects selected from group B shall be not less than thirty per cent of the marks assigned to each subject and forty per cent of the marks assigned to the three subjects, also that candidates must obtain at least fifty per cent on each of the papers on the work of the departments in which they are engaged. In the case of a candidate who does not obtain the minimum of forty per cent assigned to the three subjects

selected from group B, but who obtains an excess of marks above the minimum percentage required on each of the papers on the work of the department, such excess shall be added to the marks obtained by him on the subjects selected from group B for the purpose of estimating his percentage on the whole group. Where a candidate, who has obtained the aggregate marks required on the promotion examination, fails in one subject only, not being one of the papers on the work of the department, such candidate may, on the recommendation of the deputy head of the department, complete the examination by writing on that subject alone at the ensuing examination. The minimum standard required on such subject shall be fifty per cent if the subject is in group A, and thirty per cent if the subject is in group B. Any candidate who fails only in the total number of marks assigned to group A may, on the recommendation of the deputy head of the department, complete the examination by writing on that group alone at the ensuing examination.

21. All general competitive examinations for entrance to the Service shall be advertised in the *Canada Gazette* at least four weeks before the examinations are to take place. Special competitive examinations shall be advertised in the *Canada Gazette* at least two weeks before the examinations are to take place. Such advertisements shall state the number of positions to be competed for, the conditions to be complied with by the competitors, the subjects to be covered by any special examinations, and the places at which the examinations may be held.

22. Within one month after the publication of the results of a Civil Service examination any candidate who considers that his answer papers have not been correctly valued, may make application to the Commission to have his papers re-read. Such application must be accompanied by a fee of $3 in the case of the Third Division or lower examinations, and $5 in the case of the Second Division or higher examinations. In cases where the appeal is sustained the fee will be returned.

(2) The answer papers of all candidates at any Civil Service examination, after being valued by the examiners, shall be retained by the Commission for a period of six months from the date of publishing the results, and at the end of that period they shall be destroyed.

23. Every successful candidate, before receiving a permanent appointment to the Inside Service, must furnish the Commission with a certificate of good health, which shall be filled out on standard forms to be furnished by the Commission.

(2) There shall be appointed by the Governor in Council in each place where an examination is held one or more medical examiners, from whom such certificates shall be obtained.

(3) The fees for the health certificate shall be: For messengers, porters, sorters, packers, and for temporary clerks, two dollars ($2); for clerks of the Third Division, three dollars ($3); for clerks of the First and Second Divisions, five dollars ($5).

24. Every successful candidate, before receiving an appointment to the Inside Service, must furnish the Commission with references to at least three reputable persons who may be able to give adequate information as to the candidate's character and habits.

25. The following shall be the schedule of fees to be paid by the candidates at the several examinations held under the direction of the Commission:—

Examination for lower grade positions, a fee of................	$ 2 00
Examinations for clerkships in Subdivision B of the Third Division, a fee of...	4 00
Examinations for clerkships in Subdivision B of the Second Division, a fee of..	8 00

8 GEORGE V, A. 1918

Extra examinations which may be authorized from time to time for positions requiring special qualifications, a fee of 8 00

Promotion examinations:—

    In the Third Division.. 2 00
    To the Second Division....................................... 3 00
    In the Second Division....................................... 4 00
    For higher divisions... 5 00

(2) No fee shall be required for the privilege of taking optional subjects.

(3) The fees for the regular Third and Second Division examinations, for lower grade examinations, and for any special examinations, shall be payable by the candidates when making application for the examination. Should any candidate, after making application and paying the required fee, be unable to write on the examination, one-half the fee may be returned.

26. Copies of the reports of the " conduct and efficiency of all officers, clerks and employees below the First Division " which, in accordance with section 40 of the Civil Service Amendment Act, are required to be made in each department, shall be furnished to the Commission by the deputy heads of the various departments every three months.

(2) To insure uniformity these reports shall be made out on forms prepared by the Commission which may be procured by the departments upon requisition to the Government Stationery Office.

27. As soon as practicable, after the coming into force of these regulations, the deputy heads of the several departments shall furnish to the Commission, for the purpose of its Establishment Books, returns of the officers of their departments, with such particulars as to their past service and present employment as are provided for on the form prepared by the Commission.

28. The secretary of the Treasury Board shall notify the Commission of all changes which take place in the organization of the offices in the several departments in the Inside Service, whether these changes result from the creation of new offices, the division or combination of existing offices, or the abolition of offices; also of all changes in the personnel of the officers holding respective offices in the several departments in the Inside Service, whether these changes result from original appointment, promotion, transfer, death, resignation or dismissal.

29. The Commission shall select examiners duly qualified to prepare the necessary examination papers and to value the answers of the candidates, in connection with the general and special examinations provided for in the Civil Service Acts and in these regulations.

(2) Each of the examination papers for the First and Second Divisions of the Inside Service shall be prepared and the answers valued by two examiners.

(3) In the case of promotion examinations, and of special or technical examinations for the First and Second Divisions, as far as possible one of the two examiners shall be selected from within the department in which the appointment is to be made, and the other from without.

30. Examiners for the Inside Service shall be paid in accordance with the following scale of fees:—

    To each examiner for setting a paper for the general competitive examination for the First and Second Divisions $15 00

    Where the examination is one of a special or technical character for the First or Second Division of the Inside Service, and where not more than five candidates are taking the same examination, each examiner shall be allowed $20 for setting the paper and valuing the answers.

    To each examiner for setting a paper for the Third Division examinations................................. 10 00

To each examiner for setting a paper for the lower grade examinations.................................... 5 00

To each presiding examiner at the various centres where the examinations are held:—

Per day... 10 00

Per half day... 5 00

Where the number of candidates at any centre exceeds twenty-five, an assistant examiner may be appointed for such additional number up to twenty-five, and other additional assistants may be appointed in like proportion, where the number of candidates exceeds fifty.

To each assistant to the presiding examiner:—

Per day... $5 00

Per half day... 3 00

For valuing the answers in the case of the general competitive examinations, the compensation shall be as follows:

For each paper in the examinations for the First or Second Divisions.................................... 0 50

For each paper in the examinations for the Third Division 0 20

For each paper in the examinations for the lower grades. 0 10

OUTSIDE SERVICE EXAMINATIONS.

The Preliminary and Qualifying Examinations prescribed by the Civil Service Act for the Outside Division of the Civil Service shall be held semi-annually at the same times and places as the examinations for the Inside Division of the Civil Service and shall be conducted in like manner and governed in all respects by the rules and regulations prescribed for the examinations for the Inside Service, with the following exceptions, viz.:—

(1) The Preliminary Examination shall include the following subjects of the ordinary public school standard: Writing, spelling, and the first four rules of arithmetic. The maximum number of marks in each subject shall be one hundred. The minimum percentage for qualification shall be forty per cent in each subject and fifty per cent on the whole examination.

(2) The Qualifying Examination shall include the following subjects: Writing and copying manuscripts, spelling (including dictation), arithmetic, geography, history, and composition. The maximum number of marks for each subject shall be one hundred, excepting in the subjects of writing and copying manuscripts, for each of which the maximum number shall be fifty marks. The minimum percentage for qualification shall be forty per cent in each subject and fifty per cent on the whole examination. The standard of examination shall require a good general knowledge of the above subjects.

(3) Candidates in the Qualifying Examination who fail in one subject only, but who make the required aggregate of fifty per cent, or three hundred marks, may come up for the subject in which they failed at any one or more subsequent examinations; and, on their passing the same, the marks made in the other subjects at the previous examination will be allowed them, but candidates failing in more than one subject, or in the aggregate, if they come up for examination again must take all the subjects required.

(4) Every successful candidate at the Preliminary or Qualifying Examination will receive a certificate from the Commission.

TABLES

TABLE No. 1—Examinations, regular and special, held under the direction of the Commission.

Examination Number.	Date of Examination.	Nature of Examination.	Department.	Number of Vacancies.	Number of Candidates.	Successful Candidates.
	1916.					
628	Sept. 1	Special Lower Grade	Interior	1	1	Doris ..., Ottawa, Ont.
629	" 14	"	Interior	1	1	Wm. M. Baillie, Aylmer, Que.
630	" 27	Special Preliminary	Outside Service	1	8	See page 18.
631	" 29	Special Lower Grade	...	1	1	...
632	Oct. 4	"	Agriculture	1	1	...
633	" 6	"	Agriculture	1	1	...
634	" 6	"	Interior	1	1	Joseph Wm. Smyth, Ottawa, Ont.
635	" 12	"	Interior	1	1	Garnet Reid, Ottawa, Ont.
636	" 13	"	Agriculture	1	1	...
637	" 24	"	Agriculture	1	1	...
638	Nov. 3	"	Agriculture	1	1	... Fraleigh, St. Mary's, Ont.
639	" 8	"	Post	1	1	T. Robillard, ..., Ont.
640	" 17	"	Agriculture	1	1	Thos. L. Delaney, Ottawa, Ont.
	Dec. 1	"	...	1	1	Cecil M. ..., Ont.
641	" 4	"	...	1	1	Edith P. Kish, Ottawa, Ont.
642	" 7	"	Justice	1	1	None.
643	" 11	"	Post Office	2	2	E. G. Wills, ..., Ont.
644	" 11	"	Post Office	1	1	Sam Levin, Ottawa, Ont.
645	" 13	"	Interior Works	1	1	None.
646	" 15	"	Public Works	1	1	None.
647	" 18	Preliminary	Secretary of State	1	496	..., Ottawa, Ont.
648	" 19	Qualifying	Outside Service	1	112	See page 18.
649	" 20	Third Division	Outside Service	55	175	See page 20.
650	" 20	Special Lower Grade	Inside Service	1	1	See page 21.
	" 22	"	Interior	1	1	J. Bryan, ..., Ont.
	" 22	"	Post Office	1	1	Anna Fairbanks, ..., Ont.
		"	Secretary of State	1	1	E. Barrette, Ottawa, Ont.
	1917.					
651	Jan. 3	"	Public Works	1	1	Eugene Menard, Ottawa, Ont.
652	" 9	Reporter	Senate	1	4	None.
653	" 16	Special Lower Grade	Agriculture	1	1	Thos. I. Dives, Ottawa, Ont.
654	" 18	Translator	Trade and Commerce	1	9	S. L. E. Durantel, Montreal, Que.
655	" 25	Special Lower Grade	Public Works	1	1	O. Legault, Ottawa, Ont.

8 GEORGE V, A. 1918

TABLE No. 1.—Examinations, regular and special, held under the direction of the Commission.—*Concluded.*

Examination Number	Date of Examination	Nature of Examination	Department	Number of Vacancies	Number of Candidates	Successful Candidates
656	Jan. 29	Special Lower Grade	Public Works	1	1	None.
657	Jan. 30	"	Post Office	1	1	Lucienne Dorval, Ottawa, Ont.
658	Feb. 6	"	Mines	1	1	P. Desormeaux, Ottawa, Ont.
659	Feb. 6	"	House of Commons	1	1	Louis Boulet, Ottawa, Ont.
660	Feb. 8	"	Mines	1	1	None.
661	Feb. 17	"		1	1	J. Barry, Ottawa, Ont.
662	Feb. 24	"	Post Office	1	1	None.
663	Mar. 1	"	Post Office	1	1	None.
664	Mar. 6	Special Preliminary	Post Office		1	None.
665	Mar. 9	Special Lower Grade	Outside Service		218	Eva Carson, Ottawa, Ont. See page 22.
666	Mar. 9	"	Post Office	4	1	Helene Paradis, Levis, Que.
667	Mar. 13	"	Post Office	1	1	...e ...e, Ottawa, Ont.
668	Mar. 16	"	Post Office	1	1	Gordon S. ..., ..., Ont.
669	Mar. 23	"	Post Office	1	1	Lucy B. ..., Ottawa, Ont.
670	Mar. 26	"	Post Office	1	1	Antonio Lalonde, ..., Ont.
671	Mar. 28	"	Post Office	1	1	...ty Mulligan, Ottawa, Ont.
672	April 7	"	Post Office	1	1	E. D. ...
673	April 11	"	Interior	1	1	M. A. Kelly, Ottawa, Ont.
674	April 17	"	Post Office	1	1	Myrtle Hammond, Ottawa, Ont.
675	April 18	"	Agriculture	1	1	Lillian Pryce, Ottawa, Ont.
676	April 20	"	Post Office	1	1	None.
677	May 4	"	Library of Parliament	1	1	Albert Gagne, Hull, Que.
678	May 9	"	Interior	1	1	H. C. Stock, ..., Ont.
679	May 11	"	Interior	1	1	David A. Rice, Ottawa, Ont.
	May 11	"	Royal North west Md Police	1	1	Victor Quaglia, Ottawa, Ont.
	May 11	"	Post Office	1	1	None.
	May 11	"	Post Office		1	Charles Winneris, Ottawa, Ont.
	May 11	"	Justice	1	1	Lora Anton, Ottawa, Ont.
	May 11	"	Post Office	1	1	Francis J. Kehoe, Ottawa, Ont.
		"			1	Wilfrid Sylvester, Ottawa, Ont.
						Aurore Cousineau, Gatineau Point, Que
680	May 15	Preliminary	Post ... Service		422	See page 23.
681	May 16	Qualifying	Outside Service		132	See page 25.

No.	Date	Grade	Service			Remarks
682	15	Lower Grade	Tide Service	75	18	See page 26.
683	16	Third Division	Inside Service	15	245	See page 26.
684	14	Second Division	Inside Service		27	See page 27.
685	14	Promotion to Second Division			11	See page 27.
686	16	Naval Cadetships	Naval Service		31	See page 27.
687	25	Special Lower Grade	al Northwest Minted Police			
688	25	"	Post Office	1	1	None.
688	30	"	al Northwest Mtd Police	1	1	None.
689	1	"	Post Office	1	1	None.
690	5	"	Royal Northwest Mtd Police	1	1	Lawrence Casey, Ottawa West, Ont.
691	6	"	Royal Northwest Mtd Police	1	1	B. Monk, Ottawa, Ont.
692	6	"	Post Office	1	1	None.
693	15	"	Agriculture	1	1	J. Shillington, Ottawa, Ont.
694	19	"	Post Office	1	1	Fanny Watson, Ottawa, Ont.
	22	"	Post Office	1	1	H. A. Wilson, Ottawa, Ont.
695	25	"	al	1	1	Gladys Beatty, Ottawa, Ont.
						G. Earl Moodie, Ottawa, Ont.
696	5	"	Royal Northwest Mtd Police	1	1	None.
697	7	"	Tle and merce	1		James M. O'Regan, Ottawa, Ont.
			Royal Northwest Mtd Police			
698	7	"	Post Office	1	1	Millie Larose, Ont.
699	9	"	Tde and Commerce	1	1	Robert Pearson, Ont.
	10	"		1	1	Norman E. My, Ont.
700	10	"	Agriculture	1	1	ames Rogers, Ottawa, Ont.
701	12	"	Agriculture	1	1	J. Ont.
	13	"	al the	1	1	S. Griffiths, Ont.
702	13	"	Post Office	1	1	F. E. Calvert, Ottawa, Ont.
703	21	"	Post Office	1	1	Euphemia M. My, Ottawa, Ont.
704	25	"	Post Office	1	1	Leo Marin, Ottawa, Ont.
705	27	"	Justice	1	1	None.
706	31	"	Justice	1	1	F. O'Reilly, Ottawa, Ont.
707	2	"	Post Office	1	1	ard Falardeau, Ottawa, Ont.
708	20	"	Post Office	1	1	Elzear r, Ottawa, .
	28	"	Post Office	1	1	None.

8 GEORGE V, A. 1918

TABLE No. 2.—Number of candidates writing at the different centres at the regular examinations.

(a) DECEMBER, 1916.

Place of Examination.	Prelim-inary.	Quali-fying.	Third Division.		Total.
			Men.	Women.	
Prince Rupert	1	1	1	....	3
Nanaimo	5	....	....	....	5
Victoria	13	4	....	....	17
Vancouver	7	10	1	....	18
Nelson	1	1	....	.....:...	2
Edmonton	16	3	....	....	19
Calgary	8	3	1	2	14
Moose Jaw	15	1	....	....	16
Saskatoon	10	2	....	....	12
Regina	21	....	....	....	21
Brandon	1	2	....	....	3
Winnipeg	24	5	....	....	29
Sault Ste. Marie	....	1	....	....	1
North Bay	7	2	....	....	9
London	8	4	....	....	12
Hamilton	13	4	....	....	17
Toronto	71	20	1	3	95
Kingston	3	6	....	4	13
Ottawa	108	12	25	123	268
Montreal	111	14	1	4	130
Sherbrooke	7	1	....	1	9
Quebec	27	7	....	1	35
St. John	6	2	....	1	9
Moncton	1	....	....	....	1
Chatham	....	....	....	5	5
Charlottetown	1	4	....	....	5
Halifax	11	3	....	1	15
Total	496	112	30	145	783

SESSIONAL PAPER No. 31

TABLE No. 2.—Number of candidates writing at the different centres at the regular examinations.—Concluded.

(b) MAY, 1917.

Place of Examination.	Preliminary.	Qualifying.	Lower Grades.		Third Division.		Second Division.		Promotion to Second Division.		Naval Cadetships.	Total.
			Men.	Women.	Men.	Women.	Men.	Women.	Men.	Women.		
Prince Rupert		2										2
Victoria	9	4									3	16
Vancouver	4	6				7					2	19
Nelson		1										1
Frank	9	1										10
Edmonton	14	8										22
Calgary	35	4										39
Moose Jaw	11											11
Saskatoon	25	3										28
Regina	22	11										33
Brandon	3											3
Winnipeg	13	7										20
Wingham						7						7
London	4	5				1		3			1	14
Hamilton	8	2				2						12
St. Catherines		1									5	6
Toronto	43	16				2					3	64
Kingston	2	4	1			3						10
Brockville	2	1			1	13						17
Ottawa	76	12	1	7	21	178	15	7	11		5	333
Montreal	90	28	7			3	1				5	134
Sherbrooke	5		1			1					1	8
Quebec	33	5									2	40
St. John	2	4									1	7
Chatham						3						3
Moncton							1					1
Charlottetown	1	1			1							3
Yarmouth	1	1									1	3
Halifax	10	5	1			2					2	20
Total	422	132	11	7	23	222	17	10	11		31	886

NOTE.—A Special Preliminary Examination for returned soldiers was held on March 6th, 1917. At this examination 56 other candidates wrote, of whom 43 were successful.

8 GEORGE V, A. 1918

TABLE No. 3.—Successful candidates at the regular examinations.

NOTE.—Candidates who are marked with one star (*) have served overseas in His Majesty's Forces during the present war and have been honourably discharged therefrom, and are accordingly entitled to preferential treatment in the matter of appointment.

(a) *Special Preliminary Examination for the Outside Service, September, 1916*

IN ALPHABETICAL ORDER.

*King, William Henry.
*Lewis, Albert John.
*Allen, William Patterson.
*Montgomery, D. Gerald.
*Barnett, William Harold.
*Northfield, Thomas W.
*Gerrish, Henry.
*Wherry, Frank A.

(b) *Preliminary Examination for the Outside Service, December, 1916.*

IN ALPHABETICAL ORDER.

At *Prince Rupert, B.C.*—
Struthers, John McSkimming.

At *Nanaimo, B.C.*—
Cullen, Alexander.
McGuckie, John Martin.
Scott, Nellie G.
Sutherland, Lillis I.
Thomson, Andrew L.

At *Victoria, B.C.*—
*Abbott, George Stanley.
*Comerford, Edward Waller.
Craig, Edward H. H.
Dicks, Thomas I.
Miller, Lena.
Mackenzie, David.
Tomlinson, Fred.
*Watson, Thomas.

At *Vancouver, B.C.*—
Cucksey, Walter Lloyd.
Duke, Aylmer Earl.
Postlethwaite, Frank.

At *Nelson, B.C.*—
Cryderman, Charles Norman.

At *Edmonton, Alta.*—
Atkinson, Burton West.
Carthew, A. Isabelle.
Dixon, Geo. M.
Ellis, Elmer E.
Freeze, Harry A.
Hopkinson, Frank A.
Miller, Isabel Robertson.
Moody, Robert Wellington.
McLeod, John.
McMahon, Clark A.
McMann, Allan J. D.
Porter, Frederick A.
Wright, Helen M.

At *Calgary, Alta.*—
Gregory, William James.
Pare, Bertha Anna.
Russell, Joseph.
Samuel, Geoffrey B.

At *Moosejaw, Sask.*—
Burke, Hildred May.
Davidson, William Howard.
Ellis, Frank Butler.
Ellis, James.
Fleming, St. Clair.

Morrison, Janet Summers.
Munro, John Gordon.
McKee, Robert A.
Neal, James.

At *Saskatoon, Sask.*—
Burke, Nella M.
Murphy, Edward John.
Quinn, Edward.
Ross, Jessie M.
Shepherd, Alfred Edward.

At *Regina, Sask.*—
Chapman, George.
Eadie, James.
Harris, Samuel Thomas.
Hill, Joseph H.
Malone, Frank Patrick.
Mann, Frank.
Mowat, Hugh P.
Smith, Thomas Henry.
Wardrop, James W.

At *Winnipeg, Man.*—
Acheson, Alfred Edwin.
Curtis, Roydon H.
Dorsett, Walter.
Forbes, James C. K.
*Greenwood, C. H.
Hill, Charles Y.
Hood, E. F.
Knittel, W. R.
Little, William S.
*McDowell, Harry.
MacMartin, Percy Victor.
McNeill, James Martin.
Newman, Chas. F.
*Peden, William.
Riley, T. S.
Rowe, George Walter.
Rutherford, Ethel Marguerite.
Sparling, Edwin James.
Stenhouse, John C.

At *North Bay, Ont.*—
Beaton, Charles James.
*Ellis, Frank W.
Lindsay, Marguerite.
Redden, John Bruce.
Windrum, William J.

At *London, Ont.*—
Burns, Wm. Patrick.
Cline, Gordon Stanley.
Legg, Walter Martin.
Siebert, Wm. Arthur.
Wallace, Andrew.
Windower, William E.

TABLE No. 3—Successful candidates at the regular examinations—*Continued.*

At Hamilton, Ont.—
*Berg, Archibald.
*Graham, Thomas John James.
Hammond, Joseph R.
Johnson, William B.
Lawrence, William Ed.
*Murphy, John.
Plante, Chester Clewes.
*Siebert, Robert Arthur.
*Whiteside, William.

At Toronto, Ont.—
Bell, Irene Veronica.
Brady, Ford James.
Brown, Annie B.
Brown, Charles Holden.
Brown, Elsie Jane.
Brown, Homer Joseph.
Brown, Wallace Gordon.
Campbell, Clarence.
Cockburn, Leonard Frank.
Crossley, E. C.
Durie, Frederick David.
*Finn, Owen.
Foster, Myrtle.
Fraser, Marion E.
Garbarino, F. C.
Gauci, Francis.
Gibson, C. Ellsworth.
*Godfrey, Stanley M.
Good, Florence Agnes.
Goodwyn, Frank.
Hacker, Iona Ruth.
Harper, Henry.
Harris, Edward P.
*Harrison, William E.
Irving, John Seymour.
*Jackson, George Ernest.
*Lamble, Robert F.
Laxton, William.
Mann, Chas. Edward.
*Mesley, Ernest.
*McAllister, Oscar M.
*McCann, Jack.
McConaghy, Frank Paul.
McConnachie, Duncan.
McHugh, Michael.
Macphail, Elizabeth.
Newman, Maud.
Pearson, Kathleen.
Portch, Harold Roy.
Robinson, Edna.
Rooney, Joseph Henry.
Rolstein, Lena.
Russell, Edna.
Rutherford, Ewart Allen.
Scott, Harvey Martin.
Self, George Sherlock.
Spence, Mary.
Stanley, Reta May.
Taylor, Miriam M.
Tijou, May Martha.
Tummon, M. Percy.
Warnke, John Albert.
Wilcox, Rose Victoria.

At Ottawa, Ont.—
Barbe, Alexina Rose.
Boland, Eva.
Brown, Joseph Thomas.
Bradley, Inez.
Bulger, Francis E.
Cecile, Clemence.
Chugg, Ada Beatrice.
Cochrane, John Wilfrid.

At Ottawa, Ont.—Con.
Condon, Edmund G.
Cook, Esther Agnes B.
Cosgrove, Mary Louise.
Dea, Margaret G.
Dempsey, Catherine.
Dunn, Rose Gwendolyne.
Durham, John Thomas.
Duscet, John J.
Gibbs, Lillian May L.
Gormley, Ella Teresa.
Gray, Helen Edith K.
Hardy, Dorothy C.
Hartney, Kathleen M.
Hupp, Frank A.
Jackson, Muriel Nunn.
Kelly, John J.
Lafond, Marie L.
Lane, Ellen Eliza.
Lowry, Olive.
Manion, Daniel Joseph B.
Miller, Duncan.
Mix, Kyra Doris.
McDermott, Edward Patrick.
Nagle, Theresa.
Neville, Wm. John.
O'Neill, Arthur Thomas.
O'Neil, Wm. James.
Petepiece, Lillie E.
Purcell, Marjorie.
Regimbal, Florence.
Rogers, Hilda.
Sauve, Aline.
Spooner, Rose Ann.
Toplas, Edith.
Beauchamp, Annette.
Bergeron, Anne Marie.
Bergevin, Louise.
Berthiaume, Joseph Apolydore.
Boissonault, Marie.
Brossard, Gratienne.
Carriere, David.
Cayer, Antoinette.
Cayer, Gratia.
Charlebois, Maria.
Chartrand, Rhea.
Chene, Joseph Eugene.
Daoust, Eugenie.
Daoust, Odiana.
De Gagne, Germaine.
Deslauriers, Marie-Anne.
Dignard, Rose.
Drouin, Maria.
Dube, Rene.
Durocher, Eugenie.
Galipeau, Louisa.
Gouin, Adrienne.
Gouin, Cecile.
Groulx, Blanche.
Lafond, Marguerite.
Lafreniere, Laura.
Lahaie, Marie Aurore.
Lalonde, Aldege.
Leduc, Geraldine.
Levesque, Oscar.
Menard, Mary Clara.
Paradis, Ernest.
Periard, Alcide.
Plouffe, Dorina.
Rattey, Marie Beatrice.
Robertson, Annette.
Seguin, Jos. Elzear.
Simard, Adelaide.
Tremblay, Aline.
Trudel, Josephine.

31—2½

8 GEORGE V, A. 1918

TABLE No. 3.—Successful candidates at the regular examinations—*Continued*

At Ottawa, Ont.—Con.
Vadenais, Cecile.

At Montreal, Que.
Adducchio, Anita.
Allard, Eugene.
Auclair, Ernest.
Beauchamp, Annette.
Beaudet, Mathilde.
Beaulieu, Georges.
Bergeron, Alice.
Berthiaume, Paul.
Blouin, Josephine.
Bourcier, Lydia.
Brodeur, Alexandre.
Brunelle, J. Alphonse.
Brunelle, Hector.
Brunet, Eloi.
Campbell, Alexandre.
Canniff, Daniel Roy.
Chagnon, Marie-Anna.
Charbonneau, Georgette.
Charbonneau, Imelda.
Chouinard, Charles.
Cote, Ernest Emile.
Davin, Ernest.
DeCelles, Richmond.
Delage dit Lavigueur, Joseph.
Desjardins, Joseph Henri.
Desy, Archambault.
Dugas, Rodolphe.
Dupuis, Alexis.
Forget, Real.
Gagnon, Honore.
Gagnon, Joseph.
Geoffrion, Ernest.
Hickey, Michael John.
Holmes, Thomas.
Jarrand, Valerie.
Ladouceur, J. N.
Lapierre, Horace.
Leclerc, Gabrielle.
Lefebvre, Roger.
Lemire, Ida.
Meunier, Clement.
Minville, Esdras.
Norton, James Frederick.
Ouelette, Anne Marie.
Pepin, Jeanne.
Perras, Emilienne.
Petit, Marie Diana.
Piche, Edmond.
Piche, Wilhelmine.

At Montreal, Que.—Con.
*Poirier, Conrad J.
Portelance, Auguste.
Pouliot, Louis.
Ranger, Wm. A.
Robichaud, Andre.
Roch, Marie-Louise.
Rochon, J. Benoit.
St. Louis, Cecile.
Scott, Dorothy M.
Thibault, Antoine.
Trudeau, Severin.
Vanier, Rosario.
Vinette, Adrien.

At Sherbrooke, Que.—
Audet, Antonio.
Croteau, Wilfred William.
Lafond, Joseph David E.
Thibodeau, Berthe.

At Quebec, Que.—
Bourgault, Albert.
Couillard, Elzear.
DesPres, Louis.
Fleury, Maurice E. R.
Fortier, Yvette.
Gagnon, Maurice.
Gingras, Judith.
Martin, George.
Moffet, Jean Charles.
Paquet, Joseph Alexis.
Pelletier, Octave.
Rouleau, Wenceslas.
Simard, Henri.
Tache, Marguerite Burke.
Tardif, Albert.
Turcotte, J. Henri.

At St. John, N.B.—
*Garnett, George Kyle.

At Charlottetown, P.E.I.
Walker, William Wallace.

At Halifax, N.S.—
Bates, James Edward.
Brennan, Harold J.
Henrion, James Francis.
Purcell, Frederick James.
Smith, Effie Florence.
Weldon, Louisa Frances.

(c) *Qualifying Examination for the Outside Service, December, 1916.*

IN ALPHABETICAL ORDER.

At Prince Rupert, B.C.—
Tite, George Robert S.

At Victoria, B.C.—
Charlton, Mabel A.
Godson, Cyril Clifford.

At Vancouver, B.C.
Hodnett, Thomas Percival.
Millar, Norman Royan.
Nuttall, George,
Prendergast, Matthew Emery.
Smyth, John Douglas.

At Nelson, B.C.—
Atkins, Benjamin Richard.

At Calgary, Alta.—
Osterhout, Harold L.

At Moosejaw, Sask.—
Cole, Margaret.

At Brandon, Man.—
Schramm, Rudolph A.

At Winnipeg, Man.—
Hunter, John.
Spicer, Alfred.

At Sault Ste. Marie, Ont.—
Gibson, Stanley.

TABLE No. 3.—Successful candidates at the regular examinations—*Continued.*

At *North Bay, Ont.—*
  Gregory, Anna.

At *London, Ont.—*
  Fisher, Gordon P.
  Windover, William E.

At *Hamilton, Ont.—*
  Young, Harold W.

At *Toronto, Ont.—*
  Ault, Ralph Ross.
  Ayten, Robert Wade.
  Cochrane, Beatrice A.
  Cudworth, Samuel.
  Gibson, C. Ellsworth.
  Goodwyn, Frank.
  Kirk, Arthur.
  Lindala, Irene.
  Mogk, W. Harold.
  McGill, Gordon M.
  McGill, Roger Alexander.
  Macphail, Elizabeth.
  Smith, John Rupert.
  Street, Herman H.

At *Kingston, Ont.—*
  Birley, Violet B.
  Blair, Bessie.
  Diack, Lillian Helen.
  Gillespie, Elizabeth G.

At *Kingston, Ont.—*Con.
  Perry, Edith May.
  Revelle, Clarence.

At *Ottawa, Ont.—*
  Burke, James Martin.
  Lowry, Olive.
  Pednault, Romeo.
  Swetman, Earl C.
  Champagne, Fernand.

At *Montreal, Que.—*
  Francis Camille Hubert.
  Gareau, Anselme Edmund.
  Herbert, Alexander Lorne.
  *Herrick, Albert Edward.
  *Jordan, Malcolm.
  Picke, Edmond.
  Sarrasin, Omer.

At *Quebec, Que.—*
  Gingras, Basile.
  McDonald, Marguerite.

At *Charlottetown, P.E.I.—*
  Coyle, Frederick Arthur.
  Ferguson, James R.
  Peters, Mary Katherine.
  Procter, Gerald E.

At *Halifax, N.S.—*
  Mahoney, John Francis.

(d) *Competitive Examination for position in Subdivision B of the Third Division,
Inside Service, December, 1916.*

1. Clerks.

IN ORDER OF MERIT.

1. Langdon, Lillian L., Ottawa, Ont.
2. Davis, Mary Agnes, Ottawa, Ont.
3. Kilduff, Frances E., Ottawa, Ont.
4. Hill, Eva Luella, Ottawa, Ont.
5. Sproule, Margaret E., Toronto, Ont.

6. Cummings, Mabel M., Ottawa, Ont. ⎫
                                      ⎬Equal.
   Living, Helen Kathleen, Westboro, Ont.⎭
8. Campbell, Annie L. Deseronto, Ont.

2. Stenographers and Typewriters.

IN ORDER OF MERIT.

** 1. Cochrane, Elsie Victoria, Ottawa, Ont.
** 2. Askwith, Mary Edna, Ottawa, Ont.
** 3. McRae, Catherine M., Sudbury, Ont.
** 4. Gilbert, Viola N., Ottawa, Ont.
** 5. Gauthier, Eliane, Ottawa, Ont.
** 6. Smith, Marjorie, Ottawa, Ont.
** 7. Tierney, Elizabeth, Ottawa, Ont.
** 8. Smith, Eillen Mary, Ottawa, Ont.
** 9. Lavallee, Ethel G. W., Quebec, Que.
**10. Reid, Harold E., Ottawa, Ont.
**11. Wight, Ruby, Ottawa, Ont.
**12. Williams, Edith, Ottawa, Ont.
**13. Macdonell, Jean Laurel, Kingston, Ont.
**14. Wainman, Edna, Ottawa, Ont.

15. Perron, Flore Julienne, Montreal, Que.
16. St. Marie, Alberte, Ottawa, Ont.
17. Desilets, Marie Emelie Anna, Ottawa, Ont.
18. Doran, Lillian Irene, Ottawa, Ont.
19. Demers, Dora, Ottawa, Ont.
20. Simard, Adelaide, Ottawa, Ont.
21. McKibbin, Hazel Helen, Ottawa, Ont.
22. Beland, Beatrice, Ottawa, Ont.
23. Flanagan, Mae, Ottawa, Ont.
24. McGovern, Eva Clarissa, Ottawa, Ont.
25. McGovern, Ada Theresa, Ottawa, Ont.
26. Robertson, Dorothy Jean, Ottawa, Ont.
27. Walls, Louise, Chatham, N.B.
    **Also successful as clerks.

TABLE No. 3—Successful candidates at the regular examinations—*Continued.*

(e) *Supplementary Examination in Arithmetic, History and Geography for successful candidates at previous examinations for Stenographers and Typewriters, December, 1916.*

IN ALPHABETICAL ORDER.

Barry, Annie L.
Belisle, Marie Isabelle.
Canham, Myrtle B.
Eligh, Sarah.
Grant, Joseph Paul.

Leyden, Gertrude.
McIlmoyle, Ethel.
Macneill, Grace.
Russell, Jennie T.
Usher, Louise Marion.

(f) *Special Preliminary Examination for the Outside Service, March, 1917.*

IN ALPHABETICAL ORDER.

At Victoria, B.C.—
  *Belding, Harry B.
  *Crosswaite, Ernest.
  *Heryet, William.
  *Joplin, Albert E.
  *Wood, John Alfred.

At Vancouver, B.C.—
  *Blancard, Robert Louis.
  *Delmonico, Henry Norman.
  *Dolphin, James Edward.
  *Hepburn, Thomas Gould.
  *King, Harry.
  *McHallam, Peter.
  *Sharp, James.
  *Thomas, James William.

At Edmonton, Alta.—
  *Baird, H. R.
  Buchanan, Jessie Victoria.
  Cotton, David William.
  Dairon, Andrew.
  *Dron, Marcel.
  *Figg, E.
  Flesher, William Albert.
  Johnson, Geo. R.
  *Malloy, R.
  *MacIntosh, Duncan.
  *Neilans, John.
  Rae, Robert.
  Underwood, Edward.
  Weston, George Frederick.
  *Whitehead, Ralph.
  *Yeates, Frank.

At Calgary, Alta.—
  *Beresford, A.
  Bowler, T. E.
  *Brown, H. J. S.
  *Cadenhead, J.
  *Cole, G. H. S.
  *Conley, Henry.
  *Dakin, E. R.
  *Day, Chester R.
  *Downe, H. E.
  *Edinborough, C. E.
  *Gower, Fred.
  *Grady, John M.
  *Hawley, Edward.
  *Henderson, R. W.
  *Knights, F. W.
  *Maltby, Edward.
  *Mardon, C. H.
  *Paterson, W.
  *Rear, J. M.
  *Scott, Wm.
  *Slack, Walter S.
  *Stewart, George.

*At Calgary, Alta—*Con.
  Taylor, R. A.
  *Towers, John A.
  *Turner, John H.
  *Wells, George.

At Frank, Alta.—
  *Bunyan, Reginald.
  *Campbell, Donald.
  *Dooley, Francis.
  *Horne, John Arthur.
  *Johnson, John.
  *Lindsay, James R.
  *McCuaig, John.
  *Mack, John.
  *Mackenzie, J. C.
  *Richmond, George A.
  *Riley, Addison L.
  *Smithson, Ernest Wm.
  *Warwick, Frank.

At Moose Jaw, Sask.—
  *Algie, Albert.
  *Ashworth, Matthew William
  *Crain, C. W.
  *Borthwick, William.
  *DeLisle, Andrew James.
  *Hamilton, Campbell.
  *Kidd, Thomas W.
  *Kyle, Oliver S.
  Merrifield, W. J.
  *McAllister, James.
  *Neal, Charles William.
  *Stevenson, Louis B.
  *Swain, Edgar.

At Saskatoon, Sask.—
  Attree, Harry.
  *Baldwin, Harold.
  Clark, Albert.
  *Cook, William Henry.
  *Denholm, David.
  Enright, Melville Walter.
  *Herbert, George Henry.
  *Jobin, G. S.
  *Kennett, Ernest B.
  *Moore, William J.
  Mutch, Ewen M.
  *Pallett, Ernest Edward.
  Parry, Harold R. L.
  *Peckett, Edward.
  *Pinchin, William John.
  Pout, Maurice R.
  Rosson, A. E. W.
  *Sherwood, Howard F.
  *Yovell, William Charles.

TABLE No. 3.—Successful candidates at the regular examinations—*Continued.*

At *Regina, Sask.*—
Adamson, Wm. John Earl.
*Asals, David.
*Jolleys, Edward.
McGrath, Patrick.
*Morris, Arthur Norman.
Redman, Francis Wm.
*Reid, Robert
Ryan, H. A.
*Smith, Charles.
*Telfer, Oliver White.
*Thomas, Charles.
Wilson, Frank.

At *Winnipeg, Man.*—
*Henderson, John William.
*Murphy, Bartholomew.
*McKay, George C.
*Warsley, R. J.

At *London, Ont.*—
Cusolito, Joseph D.
*Featherstone, Frederick.
Lane, Edgar L.
McCausland, William.
Porte, Edgar Johnston.
Sage, Joseph Laurence.
*Williams, William.

At *Hamilton, Ont.*—
*Gibb, James.
Mowat, Fred.
*Shaw, Archibald McKelvie.
*Starling, James Adney.

At *Toronto, Ont.*—
*Abrahamson, Philip Allen.
*Allen, Robert A.
*Armstrong, Bernard C.
*Boal, Harry Ritchie.
*Burley, Edward.
*Cheatley, Joseph.
Clayton, William V.
*Cramm, Donald Blake.
*Crossley, Harry R.
*Donaldson, James Munroe.
*Finch, Albert B.
Harris, Wilfrid.
*Lee, Godfrey.
*Loan, Daniel M.
*Lowe, Arthur Thos.
*McDonald, Malcolm.
*Padmore, Arthur S.
*Parker, John Thomas.

At *Toronto, Ont.*—Con.
*Power, Joseph.
*Riley, William.
*Roberts, David.
*Scott, Robert.
*Tait, Roy E.
*Wakeman, Frank.
*Whitnall, Percy.
*Wilcox, Charles John.
*Whyte, Andrew.
*Young, Wm. Murray.

At *Ottawa, Ont.*—
*Marshall, Charles John.
McLaughlin, Frederick Wm.

At *Mon'real, Que.*—
*Bernard, Robert H.
· *Boothby, John Norman.
Chene, Agathe.
Coderre, Frs. Xavier.
*Colebrook, James Henry.
*Daly, John M.
Demers, Harris.
*Edgar, James V.
Ferland, Moise.
Gagnon, Achille.
Garland, Percy Edgar.
*Grant, Wilson E.
*Harris, Wm. Augustus.
*Hebert, J. Louis.
*Hudon, Joseph A.
*Jordan, Malcolm D.
Lamarre, Come.
Lapointe, Jean-Baptiste.
*Lawson, John.
*McLeod, Ross John.
Monet, Marguerite.
Paiement, Jos. Arthur.
*Powell, Walter Ernest.
*Price, Frederick L.
Proulx, Jean Baptiste.
Quesnel, Albert.
Ryan, Wm. C.
*Stephen, John M.
*Stewart, Jas. Ferguson.
St. Pierre, Benjamin.
*Townsend, John C.
Trudeau, J. Hormidas.
*Turner, Wm. B.
*Wills, Sydney Chas.
At *St. John, N.B.*—
*Duplisea, Harold J.
*Nuttall, Gordon A.

(g) *Preliminary Examination for the Outside Service, May, 1917.*

IN ALPHABETICAL ORDER.

At *Victoria, B.C.*—
*Cherry, Arthur.
Dorman, Jessie.
Drybrough, Elizabeth A.
Heaney, Margaret Jane.
*Hutchinson, Joseph F.
*McCallum, Alexander.
*Tolhurst, Charles John.

At *Vancouver, B.C.*—
Dunmore, Robert W.
Greenfield, Edith Kent.
Hill, Annie Graham.

At *Frank, Alta.*—
*Cox, Percy Jack.
*Hamlin, Donald E.
*McLay, Donald K.
*Newberry, James Walter.

At *Frank, Alta.*—Con.
*Novitski, Henry.
*Robertson, David Allen.
*Whitaker, Alfred T.
*Zela, Albert Paul.

At *Edmonton, Alta.*—
Campbell, Jessie.
Campbell, Mary.
Cunningham, Phillips G. D.
Geldert, James G.
Hindle, John.
Horswell, John.
Johnson, Harry Earl.
*Kennedy, John.
Meadows, Thomas.
Neal, Harry C.
*Starkie, Benjamin.
*Tench, Charles V.

8 GEORGE V, A. 1918

TABLE No. 3.—Successful candidates at the regular examinations.—*Continued*.

At *Calgary, Alta.*—
  *Adams, Edgar G.
  *Alford, M. T.
  *Bassenger, F.
  *Bayack, G.
  *Broadhurst, E.
  *Brown, Geo.
  *Butt, F. A.
  Cook, Alfred Chas. Ed.
  *Coupland, Wm. John.
  *Coverdale, Alfred.
  *Cox, Arthur M.
  *Ellison, D. W.
  *Heywood, J. W.
  *Hodges, F.
  *Huckell, J. T.
  *James, F. J.
  Lett, Wm. Ralph.
  *Mathieson, A.
  *Medlicott, E.
  *McKinley, A.
  *Roland, A. J. H.
  *Redshaw, A.
  *Roberts, R. H.
  *Smith, T.
  *Summers, J. A.
  *Taylor, Philip.
  *Tozer, W. G.

At *Moosejaw, Sask.*—
  Horton, Elgin F.
  Hubbs, Delbert L.
  McKay, James W.

At *Saskatoon, Sask.*—
  Campbell, Duncan.
  *Fairbairn, John Edgar.
  *Frost, George Basil.
  *Horseman, Hubert.
  *Maule, Percy.
  *Myles, David.
  Smith, F. E.
  Stewart, Cecil Raymond.
  *Tucker, Edward J.
  *Woolley, James Henry.

At *Regina, Sask.*—
  Carroll, Matthew.
  Coolican, Emma T.
  Crossett, Sylvia Muriel.
  Elliott, Luther Hugh.
  Goth, W. Meredith.
  Halleran, Cecil Calvin.
  Hicks, Burnal James.
  Howell, Robert Percival.
  Lorimer, Edwin Banks.
  Milligan, Joseph Albert.
  McDonagh, John Arthur.
  MacMath, Joseph.
  McGillivray, Annie L.
  Osborne, William.
  Ryan, George M.

At *Brandon, Man.*—
  Reed, Charlie.

At *Winnipeg, Man.*—
  "Gardner, George.
  Gardiner, James.
  Harrison, F.
  Horsley, Olive.
  Mansfield, J. W.
  *Moir, James.
  Page, Frederick S.
  "Pontifix, Russel H.

At *London, Ont.*—
  Stowe, Harry B.
  Sylvestre, Romeo E.

At *Hamilton, Ont.*—
  Hanham, James H.
  *Harper, George.

At *Toronto, Ont.*—
  Blackstone, Norman W.
  *Binny, Walter J.
  *Brooker, Clement.
  *Brown, Herman O.
  Buchan, John P.
  Buffan, Howard C.
  Bush, Elsie Mae.
  Cameron, Robert.
  d'Almeida, Joseph R. G.
  *Downey, Robert V.
  Dunlop, Alice M.
  Ellis, Thomas G.
  Flanigan, Leonard G.
  *Fleming, Frederick C.
  Fuller, John Ewing.
  Hilyer, Clarence H
  *Kerr, James.
  *Lecoq, John P.
  Lindsay, Kathleen.
  *Metzer, Albert.
  Pegley, Charles E.
  Purvis, Hilda G.
  Simon, Saul.
  *Taylor, William P.
  Santerre, A. J.
  Schause, J. F.
  Wesley, Victor E. T.
  Williamson, Lloyd C.
  Willson, James E.
  *Wood, John H.
  *Woolfenden, John.

At *Ottawa, Ont.*—
  Baker, Mrs. M. A.
  Bélanger, Blanch.
  Bélanger, Dora.
  Blondin, Joséphine.
  Bouvrette, Edna.
  Bowen, Mrs. Kate.
  Brisebois, Gracia.
  Cairns, Frederick Hugh.
  Cormier, Narcisse E.
  Couillard, Joseph Lorenzo.
  Dinel, René.
  Dormody, Cora.
  Egger, Marie Therese.
  Emond, Lauretta.
  Faught, Louise M.
  Gagnon, Angeline.
  Galipeau, Louise Irenee.
  Godin, Joseph William.
  Héroux, J. Aimé.
  *Huband, Gerald B.
  Kirke, Kathleen.
  Labelle, Lorette E.
  Laflamme, Yvonne.
  Lamothe, Leo.
  Lapointe, Albertine.
  Laroche, Yvonne.
  Lavoie, Georgianna.
  Mahoney, Mary.
  McMahon, Katherine.
  O'Hagan, Lillian B.
  Pelletier, Irene.
  Scanlon, Annie.
  Séguin, Wilfrid.
  Shuttleworth, Mrs. E.
  Simmard, Rose-Anna.
  Smith, Vera.
  Thoburn, Daisy May.
  Trumble, Anna.
  Waddell, Harold.
  Webster, Gladys Pearl.
  Whitelaw, Earl.

TABLE No. 3.—Successful candidates at the regular examinations. —*Continued.*

At Montreal, P.Q.—
Archambault, Joseph.
Beauchamp, Maria.
Beeho, Herbert Augustus.
Boucher, Annette.
Brien, Arthur.
Charbonneau, Joseph Armand L.
Charbonneau, Joseph Arthur.
Chartrand, J. H. Adelard.
Cournoyer, Jean Baptiste.
Dagenais, Marie Jeanne.
Desbiens, Adelard.
Deslauriers, Ephrem.
Dicker, Octave.
Dion, Eva.
Dion, Fédora.
Forest, Gertrude.
Geoffrion, Joseph U. A.
Gervais, Argé.
Gervais, Gaston.
Goyette, Joseph Michel L.
Gravel, Bernadette.
Guyot, Alberte.
Hottote, Alexandre.
Houde, Charles Henri.
Labelle, Joseph Léon G.
Labrosse, J. A. Georges.
Laferrière, Camille.
Lafontaine, Jos. Francis Arthur.
Languedoc, Joseph Alphonse.
Lefebvre, P. Réal.
Marchand, Joseph Albert.
Martineau, Aurèle.
Massicotte, Jean-Maurice.
Morin, Hélène.
MacDonald, John Hugh.
Ouellette, Rosaire.
Ouimet, Aldéric.
Paquette, Graziella.
Plante, L. Henri M.
Poisson, Mme. Roméo.
Prévost, Wilfrid.
Reid, Cécile.
Richardson, Anne-Marie.
Sauvé, Arthur.
St-Denis, Horaceatta.

At Montreal, Que.—Con.
Sullivan, Wm. C.
Surprenant, Maxime.
Taillefer, Marie Thérèse.
Taillefer, Rodolphe.

At Sherbrooke, P.Q.—
*Cutts, Edward Johnston.
de Lottinville, Maurice.
Maréchal, Blanche.
Tanguay, Régina.

At Quebec, P.Q.—
Bégin, Régina.
Bilodeau, Germaine.
Cogger, Dalton.
Couillard, Blanche.
Dallaire, Alexandre.
Drouin, Agénor.
Francoeur, Antonia-Diana.
Fréchette, Emérique.
Gendron, Marie Anne Berthe.
Lessard, Marie Rose.
Levesque, Emile J.
Mannix, Ellen.
Moffet, Marie Aline.
Paquet, Irène.
Pelletier, Marie Louise.
Pruneau, Aimé.
Tétu, Wilfrid.
Thibault, Charles Eugène.
Turgeon, Yvette.

At St. John, N.B.—
Cameron, Ian Donald.
Gillespie, J. H.

At Halifax, N.S.—
*Brennan, W. D.
Burns, Robert R.
Harris, Florence Mary.
Horne, Gordon Edward.
*Nowlan, William G.
Peckham, James Gordon.
Tapper, George Wm.

(h) *Qualifying Examination for the Outside Service, May, 1917.*

IN ALPHABETICAL ORDER.

At Prince Rupert, B.C.—
Davis, Allan M.
Hudson, George Eddy.

At Victoria, B.C.—
*Belding, Harry B.
*Heryet, William.

At Vancouver, B.C.—
Birmingham, Henry D'Arcy.
Gibbs, William.
*Lowry, John G.

At Frank, Alta.—
*Warrick, Frank.

At Edmonton, Alta.—
Crossland, Ernest.

At Calgary, Alta.—
*Slimming, David H.

At Saskatoon, Sask.—
*Baldwin, Harold.
*Herbert, George H.

At Regina, Sask.—
Beauchamp, Robert.
Bragg, Geo. William.
Gardner, Charles.
Goth, W. Meredith.
Munro, Fenton.
Usher, Wm. Henry.

At Winnipeg, Man.—
Dickson, Arthur Edward.
Stevenson, James.

At London, Ont.—
Jackson, Arthur.
Johnston, Pamela Iva N.
Riddle, Herbert Morton.
Trepanier, Frank A.

At St. Catherines, Ont.—
Ball, Gertrude E.

At Toronto, Ont.—
*Allen, Robert A.
*Armstrong, Bernard C.
Bush, George L.

CIVIL SERVICE COMMISSION

8 GEORGE V, A. 1918

TABLE No. 3.—Successful candidates at the regular examinations—*Continued.*

At Toronto, Ont.—Con.
  Credicott, Richard.
  *Cramm. Donald B.
  Deasy, James C.
  *Lowe, Arthur T.
  *Macdonald, Malcolm.
  *Riley, William.
  *Roberts, David.

At Kingston, Ont.—
  Coutu, Nada May.
  Hough, Mabel M.
  Loney, Luther M.

At Ottawa, Ont.—
  Cowley, J. A. E.
  Hartney, Berna M.
  Mann, Lorne A.
  Shuttleworth, Mrs. Ellen.
  Vaughn, Patrick J.
  Delage, Eugene.
  Gosselin, Gustave.

At Montreal, P.Q.—
  Cadrin, Michel.
  *Douglas, Joseph Monteith.
  Gagnon, Joseph.

At Montreal, P.Q.—Con.
  *Grant, Wilson Edwin.
  Hudon, Laetitia.
  *Jessiman, Robert Harris.
  Labeau, Adolphe Paul.
  Minville, Esdras.
  *McLeod, Ross John.
  Paradis, Louis D.
  Poupart, Georges Henri.
  Théberge, Alphonse.
  Thibault, Antoine.
  *Turner, William B.
  Vallée, Paul E. M.

At St. John, N.B.—
  Blakslee, Asa D.
  McLaughlin, Leo B.

At Charlottetown, P.E.I.—
  Curran, Wm. Stanislas.

At Halifax, N.S.—
  Harris, Florence M.
  Hennigar, Merle Frances.
  Robertson, Gerald Reid.
  Weldon, Louisa F.

(i) *General Examination for positions in the Lower Grades, Inside Service, May, 1917*

IN ORDER OF MERIT.

1. Lefebvre, Roger, Montreal, Que.
2. Portelance, Auguste, Montreal, Que.
3. Corbeil, Emilien, Montreal, Que.
4. Williamson, Mary Elisea, Ottawa, Ont.
5. Bigras, Rene, Montreal, Que.
6. Rochon, J. B., Montreal, Que.
7. Trudeau, Severin, Montreal, Que.
8. Murphy, Clarence D., Halifax, N.S.
9. Cloutier, Adrien, Cookshire, Que.
10. Vinet, Adrien, Montreal, Que.
11. Reinhardt, Mercedes, Hull, Que.
12. Gaulke, Edna Agnes, Ottawa. Ont,
13. Savage, J. T., Ottawa, Ont.
14. Hewitt, May, Ottawa, Ont.

(j) *Competitive Examination for positions in Subdivision B of the Third Division, Inside Service, May, 1917.*

1. *Clerks.*

IN ORDER OF MERIT.

1. Porter, Harriett M., Ottawa, Ont.
2. Campbell, Hazel Kathleen, Ottawa, Ont.
3. Barsalou, Dieudonne, Ottawa, Ont.
4. Wylie, Margaret, Alexandria, Ont.
5. Edgar, Muriel H., Ottawa, Ont.
6. O'Neil, Ruby F., Ottawa, Ont.
7. Clement, Marie-Antoinette, Ottawa, Ont.
8. Roe, May Gertrude, Ottawa, Ont.
9. Brown, Kathleen, Ottawa, Ont.
10. Reeve, Dorothy Vernon, Napanee, Ont.
11. Hinton, Gertrude, Ottawa, Ont. }equal.
   Buckingham, Edna, Ottawa, Ont.
13. Boyle, Harriett, Ottawa, Ont.
14. Bowers, Cora, Ottawa, Ont. } equal.
   MacFadden, Bessie I. I.
16. Joynt, Laura I., Ottawa, Ont.
17. Lewitt, Thirza E., Ottawa, Ont.
18. McCann, Maisie Aileen, Ottawa,
   Ont. } equal.
   Haskett, Robert Fletcher,
   Ottawa, Ont.
20. Maloney, Clara V., Old Chelsea, Que.
21. Alexander, Bessie, Ottawa, Ont.
22. Deveau, William Wallace, Brockville, Ont.
23. Lecovin, Harry, Ottawa, Ont.
24. Towsley, George C., Ottawa, Ont.
25. Hicks, Uriah Stephen, Ottawa, Ont.

2. *Stenographers and Typewriters.*

IN ORDER OF MERIT.

** 1. Boulais, Marguerite, Ottawa, Ont.
** 2. Bush, Marjorie N., Ottawa, Ont.
** 3. Hill, Mary E., Ottawa, Ont.
** 4. Morgan, Florence A., Ottawa, Ont.
** 5. Burgess, Stella Jeanne, Ottawa, Ont.
** 6. Gillespie, Muriel, Ottawa, Ont.
** 7. Bennett, Irene Margery, River Desert, P.Q.
** 8. Bourgault, Armande, Ottawa, Ont.
** 9. Mattice, Mary Anne, Finch, Ont.
**10. Cody, Ella, Ottawa, Ont. } equal.
**   Beaton, Ella, Ottawa, Ont.
**12. Cody, Irene, Ottawa, Ont.
**13. Kuhn, Olga Madeline, Brockville, Ont.
**14. Richer, Emeriza, Ottawa, Ont.
**15. Stewart, Claribelle, Ottawa, Ont.
**16. Warner, Daisy S., Ottawa, Ont.
**17. Lamb, Mary I., Ottawa, Ont.
**18. Leslie, A. Vivia, Westboro, Ont.
**19. Young, S. Agnes, Ottawa, Ont.
**20. Valice, Alice, Ottawa, Ont.
**21. Keenan, M. Margaret, Chatham, N.B.
**22. Duhamel, Rheta D., Ottawa, Ont.
**23. Howell, Stella, Ottawa, Ont.
24. Turriff, Edith, Ottawa, Ont.
25. Wright, Doris, Ottawa, Ont.
26. Kenny, Mabel, Ottawa, Ont.
27. Hanafin, Bernadette, Vancouver, B.C.
28. Mackenzie, Mary, Toronto, Ont. } equal.
   Gibson, Mary L., Ottawa, Ont.
30. Bailey, Helen Blanche, Ottawa, Ont.
31. Dilworth, Norah, Ottawa, Ont.
32. Viau, Marie-Rose, Ottawa, Ont.

**Also successful as clerks.

SESSIONAL PAPER No. 31

TABLE No. 3.—Successful candidates at the regular examinations.—*Concluded.*

(*k*) *Supplementary Examination in Arithmetic, History and Geography, for successful candidates at previous examinations for Stenographers and Typewriters, May, 1917.*

IN ALPHABETICAL ORDER.

Argue, Dorothy A.
Barnes, Flora Alice.
Demers, Dora.
Denison, Mabel Irene.
Fairbairn, Helen.
Fowler, Ethel Marguerite.
Gavin, Hazel Maude.

Hoar, Edith May.
Long, Alice Myrtle.
McCann, Irene Margaret.
Spence, Ethel J.
Ranger, F. Anna.
Taylor, Ellen.
Whyte, Marion Isabel.

(*l*) *Competitive Examination for positions in Subdivision B of the Second Division, Inside Service, May, 1917.*

IN ORDER OF MERIT.

1. George, Charles Willis, Ottawa, Ont.
2. Lewis, Joseph, Ottawa, Ont.
3. Zivian, Isaac, Ottawa, Ont.
4. Laishley, Wilfrid, Ottawa, Ont.
5. Daigle, Auguste E., Cocagne, N.B.
6. Lynch, John A., Ottawa, Ont.
7. Carson, Wareham S., Ottawa, Ont.
8. Bradley, Harold M., Ottawa, Ont.
9. Pringle, Alfred, Ottawa, Ont.

The following female candidates having obtained standing equivalent to those of the successful male competitors, while there are no vacancies in the Second Division to which they can be appointed, are eligible for appointment to the Third Division.

IN ORDER OF MERIT.

1. Potvin, Ethel Mary, Ottawa, Ont.
2. McDowell, Queenie B., Hyde Park, Ont.
3. Roughsedge, Mary E. K., Ottawa, Ont.
4. O'Connor, Winifred N., Ottawa, Ont.
5. Simpson, Grace Margaret, London, Ont.
6. McEvoy, Lenore K., Ottawa, Ont.
7. Richards, Rachel E., Ottawa, Ont.
8. George, Patricia B., Ottawa, Ont.

(*m*) *Non-competitive Examination for promotion to the Second Division, Inside Service, May, 1917.*

IN ALPHABETICAL ORDER.

Daly, P. J., Mining Lands and Yukon, Department of the Interior.
Graham, Hugh M., Department of Indian Affairs.
Hutton, Wm. Howard, Accounts Branch, Department of the Interior.
May, Oswald, Postal Stores Branch, Post Office Department.

(*n*) *Competitive Examination for entrance to the Royal Naval College, May, 1917*

IN ORDER OF MERIT.

1. Brock, Patrick Willet, Vancouver, B.C.
2. Crowell, Seymour Corning, Yarmouth, N.S.
3. Woollcombe, Edward Mickle, Ottawa, Ont.
4. Budden, Arthur Napier, Montreal, Que.
5. Marle, George Carlyle, Montreal, Que.
6. Pickard, Frederick L. S., Victoria, B.C.
7. Smith, Adam W. S., London, Ont.
8. Glasgow, Paul John, Toronto, Ont ⎫
   Smith, Arnold Beverley, Toronto, Ont. ⎬ Equal
10. Hague, Edward Cousins, Montreal, Que. ⎭
11. Myers, Gordon Conant, Barrie, Ont.
12. Davy, Arthur C. M., Westmount, Que.
13. Adams, Frederick Johnstone, Ottawa, Ont.
14. Kingstone, John A. C., St. Catharines, Ont.
15. Mitchell, George MacGregor, Halifax, N.S.
16. Winans, Leonard Grenville, Westmount, Que.
17. Adamson, Agar Rodney C., Toronto, Ont.
18. Mackintosh, Roland C. S. H., Guelph, Ont.
19. Lee, Edward Thurston, St. John, N.B.
20. Reynolds, Hibbert L., Halifax, N.S.

TABLE No. 4.—Candidates who were successful as a result of an appeal against the valuation of their papers, March, 1917.

Special Preliminary Examination for the Outside Service.

At Vancouver, B.C.—
King, Harry.

8 GEORGE V, A. 1918

TABLE No. 5.—Number and percentage of successful candidates at the regular examinations.

Examination.	Examined.			Successful.			Per cent successful.		
	Men.	Women.	Total.	Men.	Women.	Total.	Men.	Women.	Total.
DECEMBER 1916.									
Preliminary....................	......	....	496	......	....	323	......	....	65
Qualifying.....................	......	....	112	......	....	49	......	....	44
Third Division.................	30	145	175	1	38	39	3	26	22
MAY 1917.									
Preliminary....................	......	....	422	......	....	250	......	....	59
Qualifying.....................	......	....	132	......	....	67	......	....	51
Lower Grade....................	11	7	18	10	4	14	91	57	78
Third Division.................	23	222	245	7	50	57	30	23	23
Second Division................	17	10	27	9	8	17	53	80	63
Promotion to Second Division........	11	....	11	4	....	4	36	....	36
Naval Cadetships................	31	....	31	20	....	20	64	....	64

NOTE.—It will be observed in connection with the Third and Second Division Examinations that only sufficient candidates are declared successful to fill the vacancies in connection with which the examinations are held. It may thus happen that candidates who have obtained the prescribed percentages are not declared successful.

TABLE No. 6—Number and percentage of returned soldiers who were successful at examinations.

Examination.	Examined.	Successful.	Per cent successful.
SEPTEMBER, 1916.			
Preliminary.....................	8	8	100
DECEMBER, 1916.			
Preliminary.....................	40	22	55
Qualifying......................	6	2	33
Third Division..................	2	0	0
MARCH, 1917.			
Preliminary.....................	162	137	85
MAY, 1917.			
Preliminary.....................	103	66	64
Qualifying......................	39	19	49
Lower Grade.....................	1	1	100
Third Division..................	1	0	0
Second Division.................	1	0	0

TABLE No. 7.—Number of returned soldiers writing on examinations at the different centres.

Place of Examination	September, 1916 Preliminary	December, 1916 Preliminary	December, 1916 Qualifying	December, 1916 Third Division	March, 1917 Preliminary	May, 1917 Preliminary	May, 1917 Qualifying	May, 1917 Lower Grade	May, 1917 Third Division	May, 1917 Second Division	Total
Victoria	—	3	1	—	5	4	3	—	—	—	16
Vancouver	—	—	—	—	9	1	1	—	—	—	11
Frank	—	—	—	—	14	8	1	—	—	—	23
Edmonton	8	1	—	—	8	3	5	—	—	—	16
Calgary	—	2	—	—	24	31	1	—	—	—	65
Moosejaw	—	—	—	—	13	3	—	—	—	—	38
Saskatoon	—	—	—	—	14	17	2	—	—	—	33
Regina	—	—	—	—	11	2	—	—	—	—	13
Brandon	—	—	—	—	—	1	—	—	—	—	1
Winnipeg	—	3	1	—	4	4	4	—	—	—	16
North Bay	—	1	—	—	—	—	—	—	—	—	1
London	—	7	—	1	2	—	—	—	—	—	2
Hamilton	—	1	—	1	3	2	—	—	—	—	12
Toronto	—	7	4	—	28	19	8	1	1	1	67
Ottawa	—	1	—	—	1	—	—	—	—	—	5
Montreal	—	7	—	—	23	2	14	—	—	—	50
Sherbrooke	—	1	—	—	—	1	—	—	—	—	2
St. John	—	3	—	—	3	—	—	—	—	—	6
Charlottetown	—	—	—	—	—	1	—	—	—	—	1
Halifax	—	—	—	—	—	4	—	—	—	—	5
Total	8	40	6	2	162	103	39	1	1	1	363

8 GEORGE V, A. 1918

TABLE No. 8.—Examiners who prepared the questions and valued the answers at the examinations.

REGULAR EXAMINATIONS.

(a) *Preliminary Examinations for the Outside Service.*

Arithmetic..T. E. Clarke, B.A., Ottawa, Ont.
Spelling, English...................................William Burke, Ottawa, Ont.
French...J. A. Lajeunesse, O.M.I.
                              University of Ottawa, Ottawa, Ont.
Writing, (preparing questions) English..............C. H. Bland, B.A.,
                              Civil Service Commission, Ottawa, Ont.
          French..............J. R. A. Baril, B.A.,
                              Civil Service Commission, Ottawa, Ont.
          (valuing answers).........................J. C. Spence, B.A.,
                              Ottawa, Ont.

(b) *Qualifying Examinations for the Outside Service.*

Arithmetic......................................I. T. Norris, B.A.,
                              Ottawa, Ont.
Composition, English............................W. J. Sykes, M.A.,
                              Ottawa, Ont.
          French..............................Rev. G. Dauth, B.A.,
                              Laval University, Montreal, Que.
Copying Manuscripts, English...................W. A. Graham, B.A.,
                              Ottawa, Ont.
          French......................Rev. G. Dauth, B.A.,
                            Laval University, Montreal, Que.
Geography......................................Finlay Hood,
                              Ottawa, Ont.
History...Robert Stothers, B.A.,
                              Ottawa, Ont.
Spelling, English...............................J. E. Miller,
                              Ottawa, Ont.
          French..................................J. M. Lanos, M. Lit.,
                            Royal Military College, Kingston, Ont.
Writing, English................................W. A. Graham, B.A.,
                              Ottawa, Ont.
          French.................................Rev. G. Dauth, B.A.,
                            Laval University, Montreal, Que.

(c) *Examination for positions in the Lower Grades of the Inside Service.*

Arithmetic......................................T. E. Clarke, B.A.,
                              Ottawa, Ont.
Spelling, English...............................William Burke,
                              Ottawa, Ont.
          French....................................J. A. Lajeunesse, O.M.I.,
                            University of Ottawa, Ottawa, Ont.
Writing, (preparing questions) English..............C. H. Bland, B.A.,
                              Civil Service Commission, Ottawa, Ont.
          French..............J. R. A. Baril, B.A.,
                            Civil Service Commission, Ottawa, Ont.
          (valuing answers).........................J. C. Spence, B.A.,
                              Ottawa, Ont.

(d) *Competitive Examinations for positions in the Third Division of the Inside Service.*

Arithmetic......................................F. A. Jones, B.A.,
                              Ottawa, Ont.
Book-keeping...................................G. L. Blatch, B.A.,
                              Ottawa, Ont.
Composition, English...........................F. A. Perney,
                              Ottawa, Ont.
          French....................................J. M. Lanos, M. Lit.,
                            Royal Military College, Kingston, Ont.
Copying Manuscripts, English...................W. A. Graham, B.A.,
                              Ottawa, Ont.
          French......................J. M. Lanos, M. Lit.,
                            Royal Military College, Kingston, Ont.

Geography...A. E. Meldrum,
        Ottawa,.Ont.
History..J. H. Putman, D. Paed.,
        Ottawa, Ont.
Shorthand, English.................................R. C. Dunbar,
        Ottawa, Ont.
     French...J. R. A. Baril, B.A.,
        Civil Service Commission, Ottawa, Ont.
Spelling, English..................................J. E. Miller,
        Ottawa, Ont.
     French...J. M. Lanos, M. Lit.,
        Royal Military College, Kingston, Ont.
Typewriting, English...............................R. C. Dunbar,
        Ottawa, Ont.
     French...J. R. A. Baril, B.A.,
        Civil Service Commission, Ottawa, Ont.
Writing, English...................................W. A. Graham, B.A.,
        Ottawa, Ont.
     French...J. M. Lanos, M. Lit.,
        Royal Military College, Kingston, Ont.

(e) *Competitive Examinations for positions in the Second Division of the Inside Service.*

Algebra..S. Beatty, Ph. D., University of Toronto, and L. A.
        H. Warren, M.A., Ph. D., University of Manitoba,
Arithmetic...C. C. Jones, B.A., Ph. D., LL.D., University of New
        Brunswick, and J. Matheson, M.A., Queen's
        University.
Biology..B. A. Bensley, B.A., Ph. D., University of Toronto,
        and C. M. Derick, M.A., McGill University.
Book-keeping.......................................G. L. Blatch, B.A., Ottawa.
Chemistry..G. Dauth, B.A., Laval University, and E. Mackay,
        B.A., Ph. D., Dalhousie University.
Composition, English...............................A. E. Attwood, M.A., Ottawa.
        French..................................J. Boyon, O.M.I., University of Ottawa.
Economics..W. C. Keirstead, M.A., Ph. D., University of New
        Brunswick, and O. D. Skelton, M. A., Ph. D.,
        Queen's University.
French and English.................................G. Dauth, B.A., Laval University, and J. L. Morin.
        M.A., McGill University.
Geography..H. H. Langton, M.A., University of Toronto.
Geology..J. A.Bancroft, M.A., Ph. D., McGill University, and
        W. A. Parks, B.A., Ph. D., University of Toronto.
Geometry...S. Beatty, Ph. D., University of Toronto, and L. A.
        H. Warren, M.A., Ph. D., University of Manitoba.
German...G. H. Needler, BA.., Ph.D., University of Toronto,
        and H. Walter, M.A., Ph.D., McGill University.
History..A. E. Gosselin, M.A., Laval University, and G. M.
        Wrong, M.A., University of Toronto.
Latin..N. DeWitt, B. A., Ph. D., Victoria University and
        W. G. Sullivan, M.A., University of Saskatchewan,
Law, Civil..R. W. Lee, M.A., B.C.L., McGill University.
     English...John D. Falconbridge, Toronto.
Literature, English................................J. F. Macdonald, M.A., Queen's University, and A.
        MacMechan, B.A., Ph.D., Dalhousie University.
     French..A. E. Gosselin, M.A., Laval University.
Philosophy, General.:..............................W. Caldwell, D.Sc., McGill University, and J. Watson
        M.A., LL.D., Queen's University.
        Scholastic.............................A. E. Gosselin, M.A., Laval University.
Physics..F. H. Day, M.Sc., Royal Military College, and J. C.
        McLennan, B.A., Ph.D., University of Toronto.
Political Science..................................S. B. Leacock, Ph.D., McGill University, and O. D.
        Skelton, M.A., Ph.D., Queen's University.
Shorthand, English.................................R. C. Dunbar,
        Ottawa, Ont.
     French...J. R. A. Baril, B.A.,
        Civil Service Commission.
Spelling, English..................................F. A. Jones, B.A.,
        Ottawa, Ont.
     French...J. A. Lajeunesse, O.M.I.
        University of Ottawa.
Typewriting, English...............................R. C. Dunbar
        Ottawa Ont.
        French...J. R. A. Baril, B.A.
        Civil Service Commission.

(f) *Examination for entrance to the Royal Naval College.*

The papers for this examination were prepared by the Staff of the Royal Naval College, as follows:—

Algebra..D. V. F. Robinson.
Arithmetic...B. S. Hartley.
Drawing...R. H. Howley and C. Hartley.
English..D. V. F. Robinson and L. N. Richardson.
French...J. J. Penny.
Geography...A. G. Hatcher.
Geometry..L. N. Richardson.
German..J. J. Penny.
History...J. J. Penny.
Latin...J. J. Penny.
Science , Elementary..............................A. G. Hatcher.

SPECIAL EXAMINATIONS.

(a) *Examinations for positions in the Lower Grades of the Inside Service.*

Arithmetic, Spelling, and Writing, (English)........C. H. Bland, B. A.,
                                     Civil Service Commission.
Arithmetic, Spelling, and Writing, (French)........J. R. A. Baril, B.A.,
                                      Civil Service Commission.

(b) *Tests for positions for Temporary Stenographers and Typewriters.*

Shorthand and Typewriting, (English).............C. H. Bland, B.A.,
                                        Civil Service Commission.
Shorthand and Typewriting, (French)..... ....J. R. A. Baril, B.A.,
                                        Civil Service Commission.

TABLE No. 9.—Examiners who acted as members of the Boards of Appeals.

(a) *Preliminary and Lower Grade Examinations.*

Arithmetic, Spelling and Writing (English)........... Miss E. E. Saunders M.A.,
                                        Civil Service Commission (December). and
                            J. R. A. Baril, B.A., Civil Service Commission (May).
Arithmetic, Spelling, and Writing (French)........J. R. A. Baril, B.A., Civil Service Commission.

(b) *Qualifying Examinations.*

Arithmetic...F. A. Jones, B.A.,
                                        Ottawa, Ont.
Composition (English).............................W. A. Graham, B.A.,
                                        Ottawa, Ont.
Composition (French).............................J. M. Lanos, M. Lit.,
                                        Royal Military College, Kingston, Ont.
Copying Manuscripts (English....................F. A. Jones, B.A.,
                                        Ottawa, Ont.
        "   (French)....................J. M. Lanos, M. Lit.,
                                        Royal Military College, Kingston, Ont.
Geography, History................................J. H. Putman, D. Paed.,
                                        Ottawa, Ont....
Spelling (English).................................W. A. Graham, B.A.,
                                        Ottawa, Ont.
       (French)...............................Rev. G. Dauth, B.A.,
                                        Laval University, Montreal, Que.
Writing (English)..................................F. A. Jones, B.A.,
                                        Ottawa, Ont.
       (French)...............................J. M. Lanos, M. Lit.,
                                        Royal Military College, Kingston, Ont.

(c) *Third Division Examinations.*

Arithmetic...F. Hood,
                                        Ottawa, Ont.
Composition(English)..............................W. J. Sykes, M.A.,
                                        Ottawa, Ont.
       (French)...............................Rev. G. Dauth, B.A.,
                                        Laval University, Montreal, Que.

SESSIONAL PAPER No. 31

Copying Manuscripts (English)..................... F. Hood,
                                                 Ottawa, Ont.
              (French)..................... Rev. G. Dauth, B.A.,
                                                 Laval University, Montreal, Que.
Geography..................................... F. Hood,
                                                 Ottawa, Ont.
History.. W. J. Sykes, M.A.,
                                                 Ottawa, Ont.
Shorthand...................................... T. Bengough, C. S. R.,
                                                 Toronto, Ont.
Spelling (English).............................. W. J. Sykes, M.A.,
                                                 Ottawa, Ont.
         (French).............................. Rev. G. Dauth, B.A.,
                                                 Laval University, Montreal, Que.
Typewriting.................................... T. Bengough, C.S.R.
                                                 Toronto, Ont.
Writing (English).............................. F. Hood,
                                                 Ottawa, Ont.
        (French).............................. Rev. G. Dauth, B.A.,
                                                 Laval University, Montreal, Que.

TABLE No. 10.—Examiners under whose supervision the different examinations were conducted.

Place of Examination.	Supervisor.
(In alphabetical order).	
Brandon, Man..............	S. J. McKee, B.A., LL.D., Brandon College.
Brockville, Ont............	Rev. H. H. Bedford-Jones. M.A.
Calgary, Alta.............	E. W. Coffin, B. A., Ph. D., Principal, Normal School.
Charlottetown, P.E.I......	S. N. Robertson, M.A., LL.D., Principal, Prince of Wales College and Normal School.
Chatham, N.B.............	Rev. J. J. Pinkerton (December) and G. H. Harrison, Principal, High School (May).
Dawson, Y. T.............	T. G. Bragg, Superintendent of Schools.
Edmonton, Alta...........	Rev. J. H. Riddell, D.D., Principal, Alberta College.
Frank, Alta..............	Rev. W. T. Young.
Fredericton, N.B..........	W. T. Raymond, B.A., University of New Brunswick.
Halifax, N.S..............	Howard Murray, B.A., LL.D., Dalhousie University.
Hamilton, Ont............	R. A. Thompson, B.A., LL.D., Principal, Collegiate Institute.
Kingston, Ont............	J. F. Macdonald, M.A., Queen's University.
London, Ont..............	N. C. James, M.A., Ph. D., Western University.
Moncton, N.B.............	G. J. Oulton, Aberdeen High School.
Montreal, Que............	N. E. Wheeler, McGill University. }Associate.
	A. Dollo, Polytechnic School. }Examiners.
Moosejaw, Sask...........	J. W. Sifton, Superintendent of Schools.
Nanaimo, B.C.............	Herbert Skinner.
Nelson, B.C..............	B. P. Steeves, Principal, Normal School.
North Bay, Ont...........	P. W. Brown, Principal, High School.
Ottawa, Ont..............	C. H. Bland, B.A., Civil Service Commission.
	J. R. A. Baril, B.A., Civil Service Commission.
	S. J. Daley, Civil Service Commission.
Peterborough, Ont.........	A. Mowat, B.A., Inspector of Schools.
Port Arthur, Ont..........	Rev. C. W. Hedley, M.A.
Prince Rupert, B.C........	J. C. Brady, Principal, High School.
Quebec, Que..............	Rev. A. E. Gosselin, M.A., Rector, Laval University.
Regina, Sask.............	J. S. Huff, Principal, Normal School.
Rimouski, Que............	Rev. R. Ph. Sylvain, Principal, Rimouski Seminary.
Saskatoon, Sask..........	W. C. Murray, M.A., LL.D., President, University of Saskatchewan.
Sault Ste. Marie, Ont......	W. B. Race, B. A., Principal, High School.
Sherbrooke, Que..........	Rev. A. O. Gagnon, St. Charles Borromee Seminary.
Sorel, Que...............	Rev. Father Ignace, Mont St. Bernard Academy.
Sydney, N.S..............	A. W. Woodill, Supervisor of Schools.
St. Catharines, Ont........	A. E. Coombs. Principal, High School.
St. John, N.B............	W. M. McLean, Inspector of Schools.
Toronto, Ont.............	James Brebner, B.A., Registrar, University of Toronto.
Vancouver, B.C...........	William Burns, B.A., Principal, Normal School.
Victoria, B.C.............	Rev. J. Campbell, M.A...
Windsor, Ont.............	F. P. Gavin, B.A., Principal, Collegiate Institute.
Wingham, Ont............	G. R. Smith, B. A.,Principal, High School.
Winnipeg, Man...........	W. J. Spence, B.A., Registrar, University of Manitoba.
Yarmouth, N.S............	W. F. Kempton, Principal, Yarmouth Academy.

8 GEORGE V, A. 1918

·TABLE No. 11.—Competitions for special positions held by the Commission.

Competition Number.	Date of Advertisement.	Nature of Position.	Department.	Number of Vacancies.	Number of Competitors.	Successful Competitors.
	1916.					
275	Sept. 12	Temporary Draughtsman.	Naval Service......... (Hydrographic Survey Branch.)	2	53	*W. S. Larmour, Ottawa, Ont.
276	" 28	Technical Clerk....:	Interior................ (Topographical Survey Branch.)	1	21	J. H. Byrne, Ottawa, Ont.
277	" 30	Research Chemist..	Mines................. (Mines Branch.)	1	5	None. (Position re-advertised December, 27.)
278	Oct. 19	Analyst............	Inland Revenue........ (Laboratory.)	5	7	Geo. E. Grattan, Nobel, Ont; John A. Gunton, Toronto, Ont.; Wm. H. Hill, Guelph, Ont.; James Walker, Montreal, Que.; Wm. Campion, Ottawa, Ont.
279	Nov. 23	Clerk...............	Labour.................	1	16	No appointment made.
280	" 23	Assistant Chemist...	Mines................. (Mines Branch.)	1	7	R. J. Traill, Ottawa, Ont.
281	" 23	Translator.....•....	Trade and Commerce...	1	9	S. L. Durantel, Montreal, Que.
282	" 23	Reporter...........	Senate............... (Debates Staff.)	1	4	No selection made.
283	Dec.. 6	Assistant...........	Public Works.......... (Cement Testing Laboratory.)	1	3	J. B. Marion, Ottawa, Ont.
284	" 27	Research Chemist..	Mines................. (Mines Branch.)	1	7	Ross E. Gilmore, Montreal, Que.
285	" 27	Process Photographer.	Public Works............	1	11	Thomas G. Bell, Ottawa, Ont.
	1917.					
286	Jan. 24	Chemist...........	Agriculture............ (Experimental Farms Branch.)	1	6	No selection made.
287	April 12	Assistant..........	Agriculture............ (Cattle Division, Live Stock Branch.)	1	7	None. (Position re-advertised August 23.)
288	" 18	Clerk..............	Interior................	3	17	James Goulding, Toronto, Ont.; J. M. Douglas, Montreal, Que. ; J. B. Henshaw, Ottawa, Ont.
289	May 16	Technical Clerk.....	Interior................ (Topographical Surveys Branch.)	2	5	No selection made.
290	July 18	Map Draughtsman..	Mines................ (Geological Surveys Branch.)	1	3	No selection made.
291	" 18	Translator.........	House of Commons..... (Hansard Staff.)	1	15	J. P. A. Chevassu, Montreal, Que.
292	Aug. 9	Assistant Engineer..	Mines................. (Mines Branch.)	1	2	Karl A. Clark, Ottawa, Ont.
293	" 9	Assistant Engineering Chemist.	Mines................. (Mines Branch.)	1	4	Thos. W. Hardy, Ottawa, Ont.
294	" 9	Clerk..............	Naval Service. .... (Stores Branch.)	2	7	A. W. Smith, Toronto, Ont; F. C. Gliddon, Ottawa, Ont.
295	" 23	Assistant Chemist..	Mines.... .... (Mines Branch.)	1	3	No selection made.
296	" 23	Assistant Chemist..	Mines................. (Mines Branch.)	1		Positions re-advertised October 17, 1917.
297	" 23	Assistant..........	Agriculture............ (Cattle Division, Live Stock Branch.)	1	7	Frank G. Semple, Ottawa, Ont.
298	" 30	Patent Examiner....	Agriculture............	1	:	Hugh A. Camp'··'· ꞌ ꞌ. ··ꞏ

.   *Declined appointment.

SESSIONAL PAPER No. 31

TABLE No. 12.—Persons who have exhibited to the Commission certificates of graduation from a Canadian University or from the Royal Military College, and are, in virtue thereof, regarded as eligible for employment in the Outside Service, without examination.

Name (*In alphabetical order.*)	Degree.	University or College.
Cresse, Louis George A.	Bachelor of Law	Laval.
Gagnier, Herve	Bachelor of Arts	Laval.
Gagnon, Henri	Bachelor of Arts	Laval.
Gatien, Romuald	Bachelor of Science	Laval.
Levesque, Wilfrid	Bachelor of Science	Laval.
Moussette, John B.	Bachelor of Arts	Laval.
Paradis, Jules	Doctor of Medicine	Laval.
Parr, Ludger	Bachelor of Arts	Laval.

8 GEORGE V, A. 1918

Table No. 13.—Permanent appointments made by the Commission to positions in the Lower Grades.

(A) Selected from the general list of successful candidates.

(B) Nominated by the Departments and qualified by special examinations.

Name.	Age	Salary.	Position.	Residence when appointed.	Date of certificate.	Department.
(A).						
Arnold, Gordon L......	17	$ 500	Sorter......	Fenelon Falls, Ont..	Jan. 1, 1917.	Post Office.
Heroux, Joseph Aime...	18	500	Messenger..	Terrebonne, P.Q....	Sept. 12, 1916.	"
Legault, Ovila.........,	17	500	"	..Ottawa, Ont...	Jan. 29, 1917.	Public Works.
O'Bomsawin, George R.	17	500	"	..Pierreville, P.Q....	Dec. 21, 1916.	Post Office.
Robillard, Thomas M. J..............	17	500	"	..Ottawa, Ont.......	Nov. 6, 1916.	"
Stock, Herbert C.......	34	800	" . ..	"	May 1, 1917.	Library of Parliament.
(B).						
Bartlett, Edwin D.....	43	600	Messenger..	Ottawa, Ont........	April 1, 1917.	Post Office.
Carson, Eva Margaret..	18	600	Sorter......	North Nation Mills, P.Q..............	April 1, 1917.	"
Case, Robert Henry....	27	600	Messenger...	Gananoque, Ont....	July 1, 1917.	Interior.
Dorval, M. H. Lucienne Y..................	16	600	Sorter......	Ottawa, Ont.......	May 1, 1917	Post Office.
Desormeaux, Percy H..	19	600	Messenger...	"	July 1, 1917.	Mines.
Farrell, Yvonne........	21	500	Sorter......	"	Jan. 1, 1917.	Post Office.
Fairbanks, Anna........	27	600	"	"	April 1, 1917.	"
Greaves, Joseph........	50	600	Messenger..	"	Oct. 1, 1916.	Interior.
Gibson, Arthur J.......	38	600	" ..	Hull, P.Q.........	July 1, 1917.	"
Harty, Katherine G...	24	500	Sorter......	Ottawa, Ont.......	Oct. 1, 1916.	Post Office.
Hibbard, Harold V.....	17	500	Packer......	"	Oct. 17, 1916.	"
Hanlon, Lillian K.....	18	500	Sorter......	"	Jan. 1, 1917.	"
Horan, Gertrude Anna	17	500	Sorter......	"	Jan. 1, 1917.	"
Hudon, Emma.........	27	600	"	"	April 1, 1917.	"
Kerr, Mabel...........	21	500	Sorter......	"	Sept. 1, 1916.	"
Levin, Samuel.........	16	600	"	"	April 2, 1917.	"
Monk, John E. B......	14	600	Messenger..	"	June 25, 1917.	Royal North West Mounted Police.
McCrudden, Margaret..	30	500	Sorter......	"	Jan. 1, 1917.	Post Office.
Neville, William J.....	16	600	"	"	July 1, 1917.	Militia and Defence.
Paradis, Helene........	17	600	"	Levis, P.Q........	April 1, 1917.	Post Office.
Scott, William...........	36	600	Packer.....	Ottawa, Ont........	April 2, 1917.	Indian Affairs.
Sherwood, Lucy B.....	20	600	Sorter.....	"	July 1, 1917.	Post Office.
Turley, John...........	31	500	Messenger...	"	Jan. 1, 1917.	"
Thompson, Gordon S...	16	600	Sorter.....	"	April 2, 1917.	"
Wills, Edward Geroge..	29	600	Messenger..	Woodroffe, Ont.....	Dec. 11, 1916.	Justice.
Wiles, Norman B.......	16	500	Packer......	Ottawa, Ont........	Jan. 1, 1917.	Post Office.
Woodburn, Madge G...	32	600	Sorter......	"	June 1, 1917.	Interior.
Waddell, Harold.......	16	600	"	"	July 1, 1917.	Militia and Defence.
Walters, Anabel........	23	600	"	"	July 1, 1917.	Interior.

SESSIONAL PAPER No. 31

TABLE No. 14.—Permanent appointments made by the Commission to positions in the Third Division, as the result of open competitive examinations.

Name.	Age.	Salary.	Residence when appointed.	Date of certificate.	Department.
Askwith, Mary E............	20	700	Ottawa, Ont............	Jan. 13, 1917.	Post Office.
Bradley, Roberta R..........	16	500	Ottawa, Ont............	Mar. 14, 1917.	Agriculture.
Beaton, Ella Maud...........	19	600	Rockland, Ont.........	June 9, 1917	Trade and Commerce
Bush, Marjorie E............	19	700	Ottawa, Ont............	" 9, 1917.	Agriculture.
Bailey, Helen B.............	21	600	"	July 1, 1917.	Post Office.
Boulais, Marguerite..........	19	700	"	" 1, 1917.	Naval Service.
Bourgault, Marie A. A.......	18	600	St. Jean Port Joli, P.Q..	" 25, 1917.	Post Office.
Calder, Catherine M.........	22	600	Westboro, Ont.........	Oct. 1, 1916.	Public Works.
Carson, Wareham S..........	19	500	Waterdown, Ont.......	" 1, 1916.	Agriculture.
Craig, Annie M..............	21	750	Ottawa, Ont............	Jan. 1, 1917.	Justice.
Campbell, Annie L...........	21	500	Deseronto, Ont........	" 13, 1917.	Naval Service.
Cummings, Mrs. Mabel M....	26	600	Ottawa, Ont...........	April 2, 1917.	Naval Service.
Cochrane, Elrie V............	19	600	"	July 1, 1917.	Commission of Conservation.
Doran, Lillian I..............	20	650	"	Jan. 13, 1917.	Commission of Conservation.
Desilets, Marie E. A..........	21	500	"	" 13, 1917.	Naval Service.
Davis, Mary Agnes..........	24	500	Jockvale, Ont.........	Mar. 9, 1917.	Auditor General.
Dilworth, Norah.............	25	600	Ottawa, Ont...........	July 1, 1917.	Post Office.
Deveau, William W..........	16	600	Brockville, Ont........	" 1, 1917.	Post Office.
Duhamel, Rheta D..........	20	600	Ottawa, Ont........	" 1, 1917.	Insurance.
Edgar, Muriel H............	20	600	"	Aug. 13, 1917.	Post Office.
Fleury, Ange................	18	500	"	Oct. 1, 1916.	Marine.
Flanagan, Mary C...........	17	500	"	Jan. 13, 1917.	External Affairs.
Godfrey, Cara L.............	26	500	"	Sept. 2, 1916.	Agriculture.
Gilbert, Viola N.............	30	700	Alexandria, Ont........	Jan. 16, 1917.	Interior.
Gauthier, Marie S. E.........	18	600	Ottawa, Ont........	Mar. 7, 1917.	Agriculture.
Gillespie, Kathleen M........	22	700	"	July 1, 1917.	Interior.
Gibson, Mary L.............	19	600	"	" 1, 1917.	Interior.
Hurtubise, Arthur..........	20	700	"	Oct. 1, 1916.	Agriculture.
Hill, Mary Ethel............	17	700	"	July 1, 1917.	Inland Revenue.
Hicks, Uriah Stephen........	16	600	"	" 1, 1917	Naval Service.
Hinton, Jennie G............	23	600	"	Aug. 2, 1917.	Agriculture.
Johnson, Gertrude...........	28	500	Toronto, Ont.........	Nov. 27, 1916.	Post Office.
Kilduff, Frances E...........	18	650	Ottawa, Ont..........	Jan. 13, 1917.	Agriculture.
Kenny, Mabel...............	20	600	Embrum, Ont.........	June 9, 1917.	Agriculture.
Keenan, Marion M..........	23	600	Chatham, N.B.........	July 23, 1917.	Trade and Commerce.
Lee, Harold A. L............	19	500	Ottawa, Ont..........	Dec. 11, 1916.	Interior.
Labelle, Marie J. Y..........	20	600	Hull, P.Q............	Jan. 1, 1917.	Agriculture.
Langdon, Lillian L...........	21	800	Ottawa, Ont..........	" 24, 1917.	Interior.
Living, Helen K.............	27	700	Westboro, Ont.........	April 1, 1917.	Agriculture.
Lamb, Mary T..............	19	600	Ottawa, Ont..........	July 4, 1917.	Interior.
Lecovin, Harry..............	17	600	"	" 13, 1917.	Post Office.
Macdonell, Jean L. C........	19	500	Kingston, Ont..........	Jan. 18, 1917.	Interior.
Martin, Jean D..............	20	500	Ottawa, Ont..........	Feb. 15, 1917.	Naval Service.
Mahoney, May G............	24	600	"	April 2, 1917.	External Affairs.
MacFadden, Bessie I. I......	21	600	Carleton Place, Ont....	June 9, 1917.	Trade and Commerce.
Mattice, Mary M............	18	700	Finch, Ont...........	" 18, 1917.	Interior.
Morgan, Florence A..........	19	700	Ottawa, Ont..........	" 22, 1917.	Interior.
Murray, Adona M...........	21	600	Almonte, Ont.........	July 9, 1917.	Post Office.
McMahon, Mary............	24	500	Chatham, N.B.........	Oct. 1, 1916.	Agriculture.
McGovern, Eva C...........	19	500	Ottawa, Ont..........	Jan. 13, 1917.	Post Office.
McKibbin, Hazel H..........	23	500	"	" 13, 1917.	Post Office.
McGovern, Ada T...........	19	500	"	Feb. 1, 1917.	Post Office.
McRae, Catherine M. C......	18	700	Sudbury, Ont.........	July 1, 1917.	Trade and Commerce.
McCann, Maisie A..........	18	600	Ottawa, Ont..........	July 1, 1917.	Naval Service.
Parmalee, Ruth M...........	19	500	"	Sept. 7, 1916.	Auditor General.
Perron, Flore J..............	25	750	Montreal, P.Q.........	May 21, 1917.	Inland Revenue.
Porter, Harriett M..........	32	700	Ottawa, Ont..........	July 1, 1917.	Naval Service.
Reed, Laura M..............	23	500	North Hatley, Ont.....	Sept. 11, 1916.	Naval Service.
Robertson, Jessie E..........	19	600	Ottawa, Ont..........	Oct. 12, 1916.	Interior.
Rousseau, Marcienne........	30	500	Rimouski, P.Q.........	Jan. 4, 1917.	Post Office.
Robertson, Dorothy J........	23	500	Ottawa, Ont...........	" 13, 1917.	Naval Service.
Reid, Eleanor D.............	17	600	"	April 1, 1917.	Naval Service.
Roe, May G................	17	800	"	June 28, 1917.	Interior.
Smith, Florence Ada........	18	500	"	Sept. 16, 1916.	Post Office.

·8 GEORGE V, A. 1918

TABLE No. 14.—Permanent appointments made by the Commission to positions in the Third Division, as the result of open competitive examinations.— *Concluded.*

Name.	Age.	Salary.	Residence when appointed.	Date of certificate.	Department.
Stewart, Marion F..........	24	500	Ottawa, Ont.............	Oct. 1, 1916.	Civil Service Commission.
Spittal, Agnes G...........	18	600	"	" 1, 1916.	Agriculture.
Ste. Marie, Alberte J.......	19	500	"	Jan. 13, 1917.	Inland Revenue.
Smith, Eileen M............	16	600	"	" 13, 1917.	Agriculture.
Smith, Marjorie...........	19	650	" "	Feb. 1, 1917.	Interior.
Sayer, Amanda.............	21	500	"	" 1, 1917.	Naval Service.
Stewart, Irma C..........	18	600	"	Aug. 27, 1917.	Interior.
Tierney, Elizabeth.........	25	600	"	Feb. 1, 1917.	Interior.
Turriff, Edith.............	31	600	"	June 9, 1917.	External Affairs.
Towsley, George E........	17	600	"	July 16, 1917.	Post Office.
Woodburn, Mary G. U.....	20	600	East Aylmer, P.Q........	Oct. 12, 1916.	Interior.
Wight, Ruby..............	17	500	Ottawa, Ont.............	Jan. 16, 1917.	Interior.
Wainman, Edna A..........	19	500	"	" 22, 1917.	Interior.
Walls, Margaret Louise......	21	500	Chatham, N.B...........	" 25, 1917.	Interior.
Williams, Edith............	28	650	Cornwall, Ont............	" 25, 1917.	Interior.
Warner, Daisy S...........	20	600	Ottawa, Ont.............	June 9, 1917.	Agriculture.
Wright, Doris E. C.........	16	600	"	July 4, 1917.	Interior.
Wylie, Margaret E..........	20	600	Alexandria, Ont..........	" 28, 1917.	Post Office.

SESSIONAL PAPER No. 31

TABLE No. 15.—Permanent appointments made by the Commission to positions in the Second Division, as the result of open competitive examinations.

Name.	Age.	Salary.	Residence when appointed.	Date of certificate.		Department.
Abbott, William E.	28	1,000	Marysville, Ont.	July	1, 1917.	Customs.
Bradley, Harold M.	27	1,000	Ottawa, Ont.	"	1, 1917.	Public Works.
Deachman, John S.	19	800	Carleton Place, Ont.	Sept.	1, 1916.	Customs.
Dupont, Joseph A.	23	800	Hull, P.Q.	Mar.	30, 1917.	Trade and Commerce.
Fitzgerald, Robert R.	21	800	Charlottetown, P.E.I.	Sept.	1, 1916.	Customs.
Mackintosh, Margaret.	26	800	Madoc, Ont.	Oct.	26, 1916.	Labour.
O'Brien, Nora E.	27	1,000	Halifax, N.S.	June	5, 1917.	Labour.
Pilon, Joseph V.	20	800	Windsor, Ont.	Sept.	1, 1916.	Customs.
Petrie, Edward.	26	800	Ottawa, Ont.	Oct.	1, 1916.	Customs.
Parr, Joseph L.	23	1,000	Ottawa, Ont.	April	2, 1917.	Library of Parliament.
Raynard, Kenneth S.	22	800	"	Oct.	1, 1916.	Customs.
Younger, Lloyd R.	20	1,000	Guelph, Ont.	July	1, 1917.	Customs.

TABLE No. 16.—Permanent appointments to special positions made by the Commission as the result of open competitions.

Name.	Age.	Position.	Rank.	Date of appoint-ment.	Salary.	Residence when appointed.	Depart-ment.
Bell, Thomas Grayson..	45	Process Photogra-pher.	II B	April 17,1917	1,300	Ottawa, Ont..	Public Works.
Cantelo, Robert Charles	25	Ass't. Engineering Chemist.	II A	Oct. 17, 1916	1,600	St. Thomas, Ont.	Mines.
Durantel, Sosthene L. E.	47	Translator..........	II B	Mar.1, 1917	1,300	Montreal, P.Q	Trade and Commer-ce.
Gilmore, Ross Earlby...	28	Research Chemist..	I B	Mar. 19, 1917	2,100	Montreal, P.Q	Mines.
Marion, Jean Baptiste...	41	Ass't. in Cement Testing Labora-tory.	III B	Jan.29, 1917	800	Ottawa, Ont..	Public Works.
Traill, Robert James....	28	Ass't. Chemist......	II A	Dec. 18, 1916	1,600	Ottawa, Ont..	Mines.

SESSIONAL PAPER No. 31

TABLE No. 17.—Permanent appointments to special positions made by the Governor General in Council, on the receipt of a certificate of qualification from the Commission.

(A) After selection by open competition.

(B) After selection by the Departments, without competition.

Name.	Rank.	Salary.	Date of certificate.	Date of Order-in-Council.	Residence when appointed.	Position.	Department.
(A).							
Ball, William F...	II B	$1,200	Nov. 7, 1916	Dec.20, 1916	Jasper, Alta...	Draughtsman	Post Office.
Fisher, Ward......	I B	2,100	Sept. 30, 1916	Nov. 8, 1916	Ottawa, Ont..	Ass't Superintendent of Fisheries.	Naval Service.
Stansfield, Edgar..	I B	2,500	Oct. 6, 1916	Nov.24, 1916	"	Chief Engineering Chemist.	Mines.
(B)							
Brot, Maurice.....	II B	1,300	Sept. 1, 1916	Mar.12, 1917	Montreal, P.Q	Ass't. Analyst	In'l'd Revenue.
Breton, Joseph C...	II B	1,200	April 23, 1917	May25, 1917	Ottawa, Ont..	Clerk........	Inl'd Revenue.
Brother, George H..	II A	1,600	May 25, 1917	June 9, 1917	Toronto, Ont.	Ass't Analyst.	Inl'd Revenue.
Douglas, Robert...	II A	1,800	Oct. 1, 1916		Britannia Heights, Ont.	Secretary to the Geographic Board.	Interior.
Fournier, Jules.....	II A	1,600	Mar. 31, 1917		Ottawa, Ont..	Translator....	Senate.
Grenier, Armand..	I A	2,800	May 29, 1917	May 16,1917	Montreal,P.Q.	Civil Law Reporter.	Justice.
Gooderham, Charles B.	II B	1,300	May 30, 1917	June 21, 1917	Truro, N.S...	Ass't to the Apiarist.	Agriculture.
Gunton, John A...	II B	1,300	June 1, 1917		Simcoe, Ont..	Ass't Analyst	Inland Revenue.
Hill, William H...	II B	1,300	July 1, 1917	July 17, 1917	Ottawa, Ont..	Ass't Analyst	Inland Revenue.
Lye, Ossian G.....	II B	1,300	June 1, 1917		Toronto, Ont..	Ass't Analyst	Inland Revenue.
Marshall, John H.	II A	1,600	Jan. 1, 1917	Jan. 27, 1917	Stella, Ont....	Patent Examiner.	Agriculture.
McFall, Robert James.	I B	2,100	June 20, 1917	July 17, 1917	Minneapolis, Minn,U.S.A	To Study Canadian internal trade problems.	Trade & Commerce.
Rowat, Richard	II B	1,300	Dec. 1, 1916	Mar. 12,1917	Athelston, P.Q.	Ass't. Analyst	Inland Revenue.
Tremblay, Joseph U.	II A	1,600	Nov. 25, 1916		Ottawa, Ont..	Translator....	House of Commons.
White, Michael S..	II B	1,300	Oct. 1, 1916	Jan. 27, 1917	Ottawa, Ont..	Translator....	Interior.
Westervelt, Alexander P.	I B	2,400	April 1, 1917	April10, 1917	Clarkson, Ont	Chief of Markets Intelligence Division.	Agriculture.

8 GEORGE V, A. 1918

TABLE No. 18.—Certificates of qualification issued by the Commission for temporary employment in the Lower Grades.

(A) From the general list of successful candidates.

(B) Nominated by the Departments and qualified by special examination. ·

Department.	Name.	Salary.	Date of certificate.	Position.	Made permanent.	Depart-ment.
(A)						
Civil Service Commission	Menard, Eugene	600 00	April 2, 1917	Messenger..		
Justice	Moodie, G. Earl	600 00	June 25, 1917	"		
	O'Reilly, Francis	600 00	Aug. 1, 1917	"		
Post Office	Ranger, Eugene	500 00	Sept. 9, 1916	"		
	Lajambe, Philias	500 00	Sept. 25, 1916	Sorter		
	Levin, Sam	500 00	Dec. 12, 1916	"	April 2, 1917	P. Office.
	Mooney, Alexander F ..	500 00	Dec. 18, 1916	"		
	Thompson, Gordon S..	500 00	Mar. 19, 1917	"	April 2, 1917	P. Office.
	Shillington, John T	600 00	June 9, 1917	Messenger.		
	Casey, Lawrence	600 00	June 11, 1917	Sorter.		
	Wilson, Herbert A	600 00	June 21, 1917	Packer.		
Public Works	Menard, Eugene	500 00	Jan. 3, 1917	Messenger..		
Trade & Commerce	Dupuis, Roland	600 00	July 25, 1917	"		
(B)						
Agriculture	Ingram, Violet	500 00	Oct. 19, 1916	Sorter		
	Fraleigh, Emma	500 00	Nov. 6, 1916	"		
	Delaney, Thomas L	500 00	Nov. 14, 1916	L. G. Officer		
	Johnston, Cecil M	500 00	Nov. 21, 1916	"		
	Dives, Thomas I	600 00	Jan. 19, 1917	"		
	Manion, D. J. B	600 00	April 19, 1917	Messenger..		
	Watson. Mrs. Fanny	600 00	June 26, 1917	Sorter		
	Griffiths, Sydney	600 00	July 1, 1917	L.G. Officer		
	May, Norman C	600 00	July 12, 1917	"		
	Thomas, John Ellis	600 00	July 16, 1917	"		
Interior	Sherwood, Doris	500 00	Sept. 2, 1916	Sorter		
	McStravick, Violet	500 00	Sept. 2, 1916	"		
	Baillie, William M	500 00	Sept. 16, 1916	Messenger.		
	Smyth, Joseph W	500 00	Oct. 10, 1916	"		
	Reid, Garnet	500 00	Oct. 13, 1916	"		
	Bryan, John	500 00	Dec. 28, 1916	"		
	Mulligan, Mary J	500 00	Mar. 27, 1917	Sorter		
	Pryce, Lillian	600 00	April 2, 1917	"		
	Hammond. Myrtle	660 00	April 19, 1917	"		
	Rice, David A	600 00	May 7, 1917	Messenger..		
	Quaglia, Victor	600 00	May 14, 1917	Sorter		
Justice	Kehoe, Francis J	600 00	April 9, 1917	Messenger..		
Mines	Desormeaux, P	500 00	Feb. 7, 1917	Messenger..	July 1, 1917	Mines.
Post Office	Hudon, Emma	500 00	Oct. 19, 1916	Sorter	April 1, 1917	P.Office.
	Fairbanks, Anna	500 00	Dec. 29, 1916	"	April 1, 1917	"
	Dorval, Lucienne	500 00	Feb. 15, 1917	"	May 1, 1917	"
	Carson, Eva	500 00	Mar. 5, 1917	"	April 1, 1917	"
	Valiquette, Mrs. Olive.	500 00	Mar. 13, 1917	"		
	Rochon, Hilda	500 00	Mar. 19, 1917	"		
	Sherwood, Lucy B	500 00	Mar. 27, 1917	"	July 1, 1917	P. Office.
	Bartlett, Edwin D	500 00	Mar. 30, 1917	Messenger..	April 1, 1917	"
	Lalonde, J. J. B. Antonio	600 00	April 4, 1917	Sorter		
	Dunne, Rose G	600 00	April 23, 1917	"		
	Gagne, Albert	600 00	April 25, 1917	Messenger..		
	Kelly, Michael A	600 00	April 27, 1917	Sorter		
	Sylvester, Wilfrid	600 00	May 15, 1917	Messenger..		
	Anton, Lora J	600 00	May 19, 1917	Sorter		
	Wimperis, Charles	600 00	May 28, 1917	Packer		
	Cousineau, Aurore	600 00	June 6, 1917	Sorter		
	Falardeau, Adelard	600 00	June 18, 1917	Packer		
	Beatty, Gladys	600 00	June 28, 1917	Sorter		
	Larose, Millie	600 00	July 10, 1917	"		
	Rogers, Agnes	600 00	July 12, 1917	"		
	Calvert, Francis E	600 00	July 19, 1917	"		
Post Office	Wesley, Mrs. E. M	600 00	July 24, 1917	"		
	Fontaine, J. A	600 00	Aug. 17, 1917	"		
	Cyr, Elzear	600 00	Aug. 22, 1917	Packer.		
Secretary of State	Wood, David	500 00	Dec. 5, 1916	Messenger..		
	Barrette, Joseph L. E.	500 00	Dec. 5, 1916	"		

TABLE No. 19.—Persons assigned for temporary employment in the Third and Second Divisions under the provisions of Section 18 of the Civil Service Amendment Act, 1908.

(A) Third Division.   (B) Second Division.

Department.	Name.	Date of certificate.	Re-employed.	Department.	Made permanent.	Department.	Salary.
	(A)						$
Agriculture	Labelle, Marie J. Y.	Sept. 7, 1916			Jan. 1, 1917	Agriculture	600
	Living, Helen K.	Jan. 13, 1917			April 1, 1917	"	700
	Richer, Emerisa	Aug. 10, 1917					
Interior	Sayer, Amanda	Jan. 2, 1917			Feb. 1, 1917	Naval Service	500
Justice	Cody, Ella	June 25, 1917					
	Beland, Beatrice	June 26, 1917					
Mines	Campbell, Ethel K.	July 28, 1917					
Naval Service	Reid, Eleanor D	Feb. 20, 1917			April 1, 1917	Naval Service	600
Post Office	Demers, Dora	July 5, 1917					
	Brown, Kathleen	" 16, 1917					
Trade & Commerce	Lin, Olga M	June 23, 1917			Aug. 27, 1917	Interior	600
	Stewart, Claribel	Aug. 1, 1917					
	(B)						
Customs	Abbott, W. E.	Oct. 2, 1916			July 1, 1917	Customs	1,000
	Cumming, L. R.	" 2, 1916					
	Paynter, F. W.	" 2, 1916					
	Meldrum, W. E.	" 6, 1916					
Inland Revenue	Brunet, Raymond	Sept. 5, 1916					
Insurance	Laishley, Wilfrid	June 9, 1917					

TABLE No. 20.—Certificates of qualification issued by the Commission for temporary employment in the Third and Second Divisions under the provisions of Section 23 of the Civil Service Amendment Act, 1908, and Section 20 of the Civil Service Amendment Act, 1910.

(A) Third Division.   (B) Second Division.

Department	Name	Date of certificate	Re-employed	Department	Made permanent	Department	Salary
Agriculture	(A)						
	C[...], Ernestine	Sept. 2, 1916					
	Edmond, Sadie	Oct. 22, 1916					
	Atkinson, Catharine	Oct. 16, 1916					
	[...], Mrs. Olive A.	" 19, 1916					
	Higgins, Helen M.	" 23, 1916					
	[...], William A.	" 30, 1916					
	Hill, Gladys	Nov. 8, 1916					
	Hodgson, Nita	" 9, 1916					
	Bleeks, Carmen	" 9, 1916					
	[...], Rose	" 9, 1916					
	Spence, Dalton A.	" 11, 1916					
	Law, Margaret M.	Dec. 22, 1916					
	[...], Nellie	" 12, 1916					
	McCarthy, Theresa	Jan. 20, 1917					
	Bush, Marjorie E.	Feb. 1, 1917				June 9, 1917 Agriculture		700
	Spicer, I. M.	Mar. 5, 1917						
	[...], [...] F.	" 12, 1917						
	Burke, Evelyn	" 22, 1917						
	Presley, Annie	" 27, 1917						
	Turnbull, Edna	April 28, 1917						
	Painter, [...] F.	May 1, 1917						
	Boland, Florence	" 18, 1917						
	Kenny, Mabel	" 30, 1917				June 9, 1917 Agriculture		600
	Doran, Edith M.	June 12, 1917						
	[...], Fannie M.	" 13, 1917						
	McKenna, Elizabeth	" 14, 1917						
	Dagoonais, Ernest	" 18, 1917						
	Penman, Ethel	July 7, 1917						
	Boyle, Harriett	" 12, 1917	Aug. 10, 1917 Naval Service					
	[...], Mollie	" 14, 1917						
	[...], Eric	" 14, 1917						
	Saipe, Bertha	" 18, 1917						
	Alexander, Frank N.	Nov. 25, 1916						
Customs	Clarke, Muriel	July 16, 1917						

SESSIONAL PAPER No. 31

Department	Name	Date			Salary
External Affairs	O'Connor, Rose	Sept. 15, 1916		June 9, 1917 External Affairs	
	Brownlee, Agnes	Oct. 31, 1916			
	Turriff, Edith	Nov. 25, 1917			
	Cowick, Kathleen	Jan. 4, 1917			
	O'Brien, Daisy F.	" 24, 1917			
Governor General's Secretary	Bars, Edith	July 10, 1917			600
	Bell, Alice M.	Aug. 16, 1917			
Indian Affairs	Ste. Marie, Alberte	Oct. 2, 1916			
Inland Revenue	Pope, Ethelwyn D.	Jan. 4, 1917		Jan. 13, 1917 Inland Revenue	600
Interior	Potter, Jane C.	May 25, 1917			
	Laishley, Wilfrid	Jan. 30, 1917			
Insurance	Boyd, Mary	Feb. 14, 1917	June 9, 1917 Insurance		600
	Duhamel, R. D.	" 26, 1917			
	Renaud, Marie Blanche	Sept. 11, 1916		July 1, 1917 Insurance	
Justice	Cas, Arthur S.	" 30, 1916			
	Robertson, Dorothy	Oct. 4, 1916	Nov. 3, 1916 Naval Service	Jan. 13, 1917 Naval Service	500
	Alton, Kathleen	Nov. 16, 1916			
	Patterson, Ruby	Feb. 8, 1917			
	Parisien, Aline	Aug. 20, 1917			
	Thompson, Lily B.	Feb. 28, 1917			
Labour	Switzer, ghes E.	Mar. 8, 1917	Mar. 19, 1917 Naval Service		
	Dowd, Annie	" 17, 1917			
	Kingston, Sara G.	April 2, 1917			
Mines	Teusaw, Laura	Sept. 1, 1916			
Naval Service	Shea, Ursula Irene	" 1, 1916			
	Steele, Hilda J.	" 5, 1916			
	Murphy, May F.	" 5, 1916			
	Doyle, Adelaide	" 6, 1916			
	Donaldson, James I.	" 7, 1916			
	Idam, fke L.	" 8, 1916			
	Stonemsky, Pearl	" 8, 1916			
	Howell, Stella L.	" 9, 1916			
	Adn, Edna M.	" 25, 1916			
	Adn, Kathleen	" 26, 1916	Nov. 16, 1916 Justice		
	Dunne, ma M.	Oct. 6, 1916			
	Locke, Bessie	" 6, 1916			
	Sanderson, Freda	" 10, 1916			
	Arrett, Joseph	" 10, 1916			
	Bourdeau, Conrad H.	" 11, 1916			
	Penman, John W.	" 26, 1916			
	Schofield, Flora	" 26, 1916			
	Forhan, James	" 30, 1916			
	Webb, M. Effie	Nov. 2, 1916			
	Mer, Nettie L.	" 3, 1916			
	Robertson, Dorothy	" 6, 1916		Jan. 13, 1917 Naval Service	500
	Porter, Harriett M.	" 9, 1916		July 1, 1917 Naval Service	700
	Age, Ethel M.	" 13, 1916			
	Ward, lary G.				

TABLE No. 20.—Certificates of qualification issued by the Commission for temporary employment in the Third and Second Divisions under the provisions of Section 23 of the Civil Service Amendment Act, 1908, and Section 20 of the Civil Service Amendment Act, 1910.—*Continued.*

(A) Third Division.   (B) Second Division.

Department	Name (A)	Date of certificate	Re-employed	Department	Made permanent	Department	Salary
Naval Service	Doran, Edith M	Nov. 30, 1916	June 12, 1917	Agriculture	Jan. 13, 1917	Naval Service	500
	Campbell, Annie I	Dec. 1, 1916					
	Finlayson, Esther T	4, 1916					
	..dy, Elinne S	5, 1916					
	..dw, Eunice L	6, 1916					
	Savage, I.	6, 1916					
	Lee, Rose	6, 1916					
	Ewin, Stella M	11, 1916					
	Smith, Margaret M	18, 1916					
	Gravel, Alyce	18, 1916					
	Merkley, Alice E	26, 1916					
	Ambrose, Clara V	26, 1916					
	..fin, Ha Eliza	26, 1916					
	Daly, Margaret A	29, 1916					
	McCann, M	29, 1916			July 1, 1917	Naval Service	600
	..th, Mabelle B	Jan. 2, 1917					
	Carey, Marie Anna	2, 1917					
	Bothwell, Agnes E	7, 1917					
	Wilson, Anna E	15, 1917					
	Ball, Jennie L	17, 1917					
	McDonell, Mrs. Oscar	22, 1917					
	..dir, Benoite	22, 1917					
	..Son, ..ath	22, 1917					
	Fleming, Ella E	22, 1917					
	..th, Mary A	22, 1917					
	Latremouille, Alice	22, 1917					
	Rothwell, Lina G	22, 1917					
	Batlo, ..fin A	22, 1917					
	DesPlats, ..fio E	22, 1917					
	Bracken, Marguerite C	24, 1917					
	Larochelle, Reine	24, 1917					
	Stewart, Margaret N	24, 1917					
	Guenette, ..fin	25, 1917					

Name	Date		Department
Kingston, Sara G.	Feb. 26,	1917	April 2, 1917 Mines.
Viau, Marie Rose	" 29,	1917	" 5, 1917 Naval Service.
..., Yvonne	" 30,	1917	
..., Hildred G.	" 31,	1917	July 16, 1917 Post Office.
Ben, Kathleen	Feb. 1,	1917	
Stevens, Gwendolyn L.	" 13,	1917	
O'Neil, Ella ...	" 14,	1917	
Singleton, ... B.	" 16,	1917	
..., Irene	" 27,	1917	
Marshall, Alice	Mar. 2,	1917	
Leggett, Edgar	" 6,	1917	
Fournel, ... R.	" 14,	1917	
..., Helen A.	" 19,	1917	
Rattray, Minnie	April 2,	1917	
Switzer, Agnes E.	" 7,	1917	
Crozier, Ida M.	" 10,	1917	
Pomerville, Ida L. V.	" 12,	1917	
Bastedo, Katherine S.	" 17,	1917	
Craig, ... B.	" 25,	1917	
..., Pauline	May 2,	1917	
Fixter, Harold	" 8,	1917	
Bennett, Irene M.	" 9,	1917	
Sinclair, Mossie	" 14,	1917	
Phillips, Helena I.	" 15,	1917	
Becker, Agnes	" 21,	1917	
Gougeon, ...	" 25,	1917	
Duford, Cecile	" 28,	1917	
Lally, Irene	May 31,	1917	
McCullough, Lydia T.	June 1,	1917	
..., Mary	" 5,	1917	
Montgomery, Eva R.	" 7,	1917	
Moffatt, Ida ...	" 9,	1917	
O'Toole, Mrs. E.	" 11,	1917	
Saindon, Beatrice	" 13,	1917	
Duggan, Julia M.	" 14,	1917	
Rousseau, Margaret	" 14,	1917	
Bradford, ...	" 16,	1917	
Rolston, Eva E.	" 18,	1917	
Cameron, ... S.	" 19,	1917	
..., Margaret	" 20,	1917	
Young, Edith G.	" 21,	1917	
Blake, Lillian	" 22,	1917	
Dawson, Irene G.	" 26,	1917	
Edith, Elsie B.			
Gardiner, Mrs. Eup ...			
Noel, Aline ... ... E.			
..., Robert D.			
Beehler, Theresa			

TABLE No. 20.—Certificates of qualification issued by the Commission for temporary employment in the Third and Second Divisions under the provisions of Section 23 of the Civil Service Amendment Act, 1908, and Section 20 of the Civil Service Amendment Act, 1910.—*Continued.*

(A) Third Division.   (B) Second Division.

Department	Name	Date of certificate	Re-employed	Department	Made permanent	Department	Salary
Naval Service	(A)						
	Merry, ▮e P	June 26, 1917					
	Boyd, Florence E	" 27, 1917					
	▮, ▮ M	" 29, 1917					
	Kinch, Lyda M	July 3, 1917					
	▮y, Kathleen	" 4, 1917					
	▮e, Norma E	" 4, 1917					
	▮n, ▮a C	" 4, 1917					
	▮ve, ▮th A	" 11, 1917					
	▮n, Grace O	" 12, 1917					
	Murphy, ▮a M	" 13, 1917					
	▮d, ▮y Claire	" 14, 1917					
	Richardson, Hilary J	" 17, 1917					
	▮ell, Kathleen	" 17, 1917					
	Kerrigan, Anastasia	" 17, 1917					
	McNabb, Lena	" 18, 1917					
	▮y, Frances	" 18, 1917					
	Lyons, Margaret M	" 19, 1917					
	Croshaw, Eva	" 23, 1917					
	▮n, Dorothy L	" 23, 1917					
	▮n, Hilda	" 24, 1917					
	▮by, ▮a	" 31, 1917					
	Petepiece, Lillie E	Aug. 4, 1917					
	▮	" 10, 1917					
	▮n, Mildred	" 10, 1917					
	Lowrey, ▮rma E	" 11, 1917					
	Sheridan, Catharine A	" 20, 1917					
	▮s, Beatrice G	" 23, 1917					
	▮h, ▮ie	" 23, 1917					
Post Office	▮th, ▮ie	Sept. 5, 1916			Feb. 1, 1917	Interior	650
	Davis, Mary	" 8, 1916			Mar. 9, 1917	Auditor General	500
	Shea, Elmo Edward	" 9, 1916					
	▮n, ▮a Dee	" 18, 1916					
	▮e, J. deG	" 23, 1916					
	Lavergne, Ida	" 27, 1916					

500   600 600

Name	Date			
Lanthier, Joseph D.	Oct. 2, 1916			
McCaffr ym Mary E.	" 2, 1916			
Paradis, J sep E.	" 5, 1916			
?y, Ella T.	" 10, 1916	Aug. 7, 1917 Post office		
Chene, Joseph E.	" 16, 1916			
M, Loretta M.	" 16, 1916			
Dunham, Kathleen.	" 21, 1916			
Keilly, Magdaline.	" 30, 1916			
?by, Helen J.	" 30, 1916			
Trudel, ie A. J.	" 30, 1916			
Williamson, Mary E.	Nov. 7, 1916			
Bouvrette, Edna E.	" 7, 1916			
Eggor, Mario T.	" 9, 1916			
Liston, Ida.	" 17, 1916			
?y, Jessie.	" 17, 1916			
Kehoe, Frank J.	" 18, 1916			
?nan, Allie.	" 22, 1916			
Locke, Dorothy K.	" 23, 1916	May 11, 1917 Justice		
Gilhooly, Lena.	" 24, 1916			
Seguin, Joseph F.	" 25, 1916			
?y, ?estin T.	Dec. 4, 1916			
MacDonald, Anna B.	" 9, 1916			
Prendergast, Henriette.	" 11, 1916			
Harris, ?yl M.	" 19, 1916			
Vanasse, Claire.	" 20, 1916			
McLennan, Annie.	" 20, 1916			
Blunt, Ethel.	" 26, 1916			
Bailey, Ben B.	Jan. 7, 1917		July 1, 1917	Post Office
Dilworth, Nora.	" 10, 1917		1, 1917	Post Office
?nie, Vesta.	" 31, 1917			
Briggs, Margaret H.	" 31, 1917			
Stewart, Isabelle.	Feb. 3, 1917			
?ll, Teresa.	Mar. 1, 1917			
Cochrane, Loretta.	" 3, 1917			
?r, Jo b H.	" 6, 1917			
McCusker, Kathleen.	" 7, 1917			
?r, ?bas P.	" 12, 1917			
?r, Anna.	" 24, 1917			
Morris, Rose.	April 2, 1917			
Kirby, ?nald S.	" 7, 1917			
Powell, Fraser E.	" 12, 1917	June 13, 1917 Naval Service		
Cameron, Ida S.	" 13, 1917			
MacRostie, James R.	" 16, 1917			
Cousens, William C.	" 16, 1917			
Moreucy, Lyons J.	" 20, 1917			
Judson, Frank M.	" 20, 1917			
Cleary, Nelson W.	" 23, 1917			
Webster, Gladys P.	" 24, 1917			

Jan. 13, 1917 Post Office

TABLE No. 20.—Certificates of qualification issued by the Commission for temporary employment in the Third and Second Divisions under the provisions of Section 23 of the Civil Service Amendment Act, 1908, and Section 20 of the Civil Service Amendment Act, 1910.—*Continued.*

(A) Third Division.   (B) Second Division.

Department	Name. (A)	Date of certificate.	Re-employed.	Department.	Made permanent.	Department.	Salary.
Post Office	Craig, Mildred	April 30, 1917					
	Taylor, H ld H	May 3, 1917					
	Nutting, Bruce P	10, 1917					
	Dolan, William A	10, 1917					
	Thomas, Trevor	10, 1917					
	, David	11, 1917					
	, Earl	11, 1917					
	Lally, John P	11, 1917					
	, Randall	22, 1917					
	, Frederick J	31, 1917					
	Duggan, Kathleen	June 1, 1917					
	Slonemsky, Leo	1, 1917					
	Chevrier, Alexandre A	5, 1917					
	Mathe, Paul	5, 1917					
	Kelly, Dorothy	7, 1917					
	O'Hagan, Lillian	11, 1917					
	Lawrence, Ethel E	16, 1917					
	Poitras, Aimé	26, 1917					
	Hedges,	27, 1917					
	Champagne, Fortunat	27, 1917					
	Walsh, Ethel	29, 1917					
	Rolston, Ella G	July 3, 1917					
	Mr. Dorothy H	11, 1917					
	Shuttleworth, Mrs. Ellen	14, 1917					
	Winter, Margaret H	31, 1917					
	Pearl, Harold N	Aug. 20, 1917					
	Graham, Gra M	21, 1917					
	Léveillé, Levina	22, 1917					
	, Madge	27, 1917					
Public Works	Giard, Barbara	Dec. 26, 1916					
	O'Keefe, Gertrude	Jan. 11, 1917					
Railways and Canals	Murray,	Oct. 18, 1916					
Secretary of State	Me, Lily A	Jan. 4, 1917					
Trade and Commerce	Berton, Philip L	Sept. 1, 1916					

Name	Date		Department
W., Marion	Oct.	9, 1916	
Stewart, Katie	"	12, 1916	
Lauib, Margaret F.	"	12, 1916	
..., Mary E.	"	14, 1916	
Furlong, Lillian	"	19, 1916	
..., Louisa	Oct.	6, 1916	
Young, Edith G.	"	10, 1916	Naval Service
..., Ilda M.	"	10, 1916	June 14, 1917
DeLisle, Dora A.	"	10, 1916	Trade and Commerce
Pepper, Clara C.	"	10, 1916	May 9, 1917 Trade and Commerce
McNeely, Lily	"	10, 1916	Nov. 2, 1916 Agriculture
			July 11, 1917 Trade and Commerce
McEvoy, Lenore	"	10, 1916	May 7, 1917 Trade and Commerce
McCagherty, Pearl	"	10, 1916	
Deschamps, Delicia	"	10, 1916	
McDonald, Flora E.	"	10, 1916	
Roy, ...	"	10, 1916	
Liston, Clara C.	"	10, 1916	
Laflamme, Yvonne	"	10, 1916	
..., Margaret	"	12, 1916	
McCabe, Anna C.	"	16, 1916	
Lewis, Charlie W.	"	19, 1916	
Tomlinson, Helena R.	"	24, 1916	June 5, 1917 Naval Service
McCormick, Mabel I.	"	25, 1916	
O'Toole, Mary E.	"	30, 1916	
Fitzmaurice, ...	"	31, 1916	
Menard, ...	Nov.	3, 1916	
Clyne, Mary	"	4, 1916	
Nash, Violet	"	7, 1916	June 16, 1917 Post Office
Cummings, Bertha E.	"	8, 1916	
Lawrence, Ethel E.	"	17, 1916	
..., Chrissie	"	18, 1916	
Sauvé, Dora M.	"	20, 1916	
Craig, Pearle L.	"	20, 1916	
..., Clara	"	21, 1916	
Reinhardt, Mercedes	Dec.	6, 1916	
..., Mrs. Mary M.	Jan.	29, 1916	
Ellis, Katherine	April	3, 1917	
Walton, Edna L.	"	23, 1917	
Field, Lewis L.	"	23, 1917	
Gwin, Nellie R.	"	23, 1917	
McDonald, Theresa	"	27, 1917	
May, Gladys E.	"	30, 1917	
Cross, Dora E.	May	5, 1917	
McElroy, Lottie M.	"	8, 1917	
Bell, Esther	June	1, 1917	
Taggart, Doreene			
Allen, Vera			
Halliday, Helen C.			
McMurchy, Elizabeth			

TABLE No. 20.—Certificates of qualification issued by the Commission for temporary employment in the Third and Second Divisions under the provisions of Section 23 of the Civil Service Amendment Act, 1908, and Section 20 of the Civil Service Amendment Act, 1910.—*Concluded.*

(A) Third Division.   (B) Second Division.

Department	Name	Date of certificate	Re-employed	Department	Made permanent	Department	Salary
	(A)						
Trade and Commerce	' Gir, Wilfred	June 5, 1917					
	Evans, Gertrude B	" 5, 1917					
	Lane, Jennie V	July 11, 1917					
	Belsher, Annie F	" 12, 1917					
	Stewart,	" 12, 1917					
	B a hp ... lce Lillian	" 12, 1917					
	Sherin, Alice E	" 14, 1917					
	Moffatt, Hazelle E	" 16, 1917					
	Downing, Meryl M	" 16, 1917					
	Gélinas, Thoeodora	" 17, 1917					
	Bradley, Jessie M	" 18, 1917					
	Troy, Lela M	" 23, 1917					
	Levine, Sarah	" 31, 1917					
	Owrid, Lillian	Aug. 1, 1917					
	Thompson, Mary W	" 2, 1917					
	...dy, Teresa	" 18, 1917					
	(B)						
Finance	Renwick, Lewis	July 3, 1917					
	Savignac, Joseph A	Oct. 23, 1916					
Public Works	Farmer, Alfred S	Dec. 16, 1916					

SESSIONAL PAPER No. 31

TABLE No. 21.—Certificates of qualification issued by the Commission for temporary employment in the Third and Second Divisions, under the provisions of Sections 23 and 33 of the Civil Service Amendment Act, 1908.

(A) Third Division.   (B) Second Division.

Department.	Name.	Date of certificate.	Salary.	Position.
	(A)		$	•
Agriculture.........	Evans, Gertrude B.............	Nov. 2, 1916	720	Clerk.
	McNeely, Elexey.....,........	" 2, 1916	720	"
	Omond, Mrs. Olga H...........	" 2, 1916	720	"
	Govan, Margaret L............	Dec. 11, 1916	720	"
	Selwyn, Harley...............	" 13, 1916	700	Stenographer.
	Nathanson, Joseph N..........	May 18, 1917	800	Clerk.
Inland Revenue....	Beaulne, Mrs. Lou............	Sept. 26, 1916	800	Stenographer.
	Mirsky, Sam..................	Dec. 8, 1916	700	Clerk.
	Gordon, Marie V..............	Mar. 17, 1917	600	Stenographer.
Insurance.........	Palmer, Gertrude L...........	July 16, 1917	800	Clerk.
Justice............	Brouillette, Mrs. Laura L.....	Oct. 10, 1916	800	Stenographer.
Mines.............	Cornett, Mrs. Jean...........	Nov. 9, 1916	600	Clerk.
	Groves, Edmund...............	Dec. 11, 1916	800	"
Naval Service.....	Allen, William A.............	April 17, 1917	600	Clerk.
Trade and Commerce..........	Snider, Pearl, L.............	May 22, 1917	700	"
	(B)			
Agriculture.......	O'Sullivan, Adrienne M........	Nov. 2, 1916	900	Clerk.
	O'Gorman, Elizabeth E........	" 2, 1916	900	"
	Eby, Elizabeth V.............	" 2, 1916	900	"
	Hulburd, Ethel E.............	" 14, 1916	900	"
	Cochrane, Lilyan L...........	" 15, 1916	900	"
	Mulvaugh, Laura J............	Dec. 1, 1916	900	"
Finance...........	Cluffe, Gilbert C............	June 11, 1917	1,300	Clerk.
Inland Revenue....	Gunton, John A.....,.........	Jan. 12, 1917	1,300	Ass't. Analyst.
	Hill, William H.............	" 12, 1917	1,300	"
	Grattan, George E............	" 15, 1917	1,300	"
	Lye, Ossian G................	Feb. 10, 1917	1,300	"
	Johnson, Lawrence E..........	July 16, 1917	1,300	"
Interior...........	Gauley, Robert J. P..........	Oct. 1, 1916	1,200	Technical Clerk.
	Byrne, John H...............	Dec. 18, 1916	1,300	"
	Timm, Hannah E..............	May 9, 1917	1,300	"
	Hooper, Benjamin R..........	June 5, 1917	1,300	"
	Henshaw, Joseph B...........	July 3, 1917	1,200	Clerk.
	Goulding, James.............	" 9, 1917	1,200	"
Mines............	Forman, John H..............	May 14, 1917	1,200	Ass't. Chemist.
	Mohr, Clifford B............	" 21, 1917	1,200	"
	Rivier, Charles E...........	June 1, 1917	1,300	Translator.
	Graham, Walter F............	Aug. 15, 1917	1,200	Ass't Chemist.
	Coyne, Benedict P...........	" 20, 1917	1,200	"
	Hardy, Thomas W.............	" 20, 1917	1,500	"
Naval Service.....	Connor, William H...........	June 22, 1917	1,000	Clerk.
	Wakely, John W..............	" 23, 1917	1,000	"

TABLE No. 22.—Certificates of qualification for promotion issued by the Commission.

Department.	Name.	From.	To.	Date of Certificate.
Agriculture.........	Strachan, Esther F...	Sub-div. B of 3rd Div.	Sub-div. A of 3rd Div.	Jan. 16, 1917
	Wetmore, Marion L...	" B " 3rd "	" A " 3rd "	" 16, 1917
Auditor General.....	Lawlor, A. Margaret..	" B " 3rd "	" A " 3rd "	Oct. 3, 1916
	Raitt, Jean M........	" B " 3rd "	" A " 3rd "	Feb. 10, 1917
	Stockton, E.E.......	" B " 1st "	" A " 1st "	July 11, 1917
	Tribble, J. N........	" A " 2nd "	" B " 1st "	" 11, 1917
	McDonald, P. D.....	" A " 2nd "	" B " 1st "	" 11, 1917
Civil Service Commission.	Paynter, William J....	" B " 3rd "	" A " 3rd "	Feb. 6, 1917
Commission of Conservation.........	Beaulieu, Alice.......	" B " 3rd "	" A " 3rd "	July 12, 1917
	McElroy, Kathleen...	" B " 3rd "	" A " 3rd "	" 12, 1917
Customs...........	Bennet, Miss M. M....	" B " 3rd "	" A " 3rd "	Nov. 28, 1916
	Howard, H. A........	" B " 3rd "	" A " 3rd "	" 28, 1916
External Affairs.....	Green, A. E..........	" B " 3rd "	" A " 3rd "	Feb. 12, 1917
	Baker, F. M.........	" B " 1st "	" A " 1st "	" 16, 1917
	White, William.......	" B " 3rd "	" A " 3rd "	April 27, 1917
Finance..............	Yetts, Charles N.....	" B " 3rd "	" A " 3rd "	Jan. 16, 1917
	Fetterly, Miss E. S...	" B " 3rd "	" A " 3rd "	May 16, 1917
	Brodie, Miss C. E....	" B " 3rd "	" A " 3rd "	" 16, 1917
	Shore, Miss S. G.....	" B " 3rd "	" A " 3rd "	" 16, 1917
	Shearman, Miss G...	" B " 3rd "	" A " 3rd "	" 16, 1917
	Loughran, Miss G. D. M...............	" B " 3rd "	" A " 3rd "	" 16, 1917
	Cameron, Miss J.....	" B " 3rd "	" A " 3rd "	" 16, 1917
	Cohoon, L. B........	" A " 2nd "	" B " 1st "	June 20, 1917
	Macfarlane, James G .	" A " 2nd "	" B " 1st "	" 20, 1917
	Artz, G. J...........	" A " 2nd "	" B " 1st "	" 20, 1917
	Gullock, G. L....'....	" B " 2nd "	" A " 2nd "	" 20, 1917
	McIntyre, B. G.......	" B " 2nd "	" A " 2nd "	" 20, 1917
Governor General's Secretary.........	Walker, J. R. Mills...	" B " 2nd "	" A " 2nd "	Mar. 6, 1917
House of Commons	Desaulniers, D. L....	" B " 1st "	" A " 1st "	Feb. 5, 1917
Indian Affairs......	Graham, Hugh......	" A " 2nd "	" B " 2nd "	June 23, 1917
Inland Revenue.....	Lemay, Arthur......	" A " 2nd "	" B " 1st "	Nov. 1, 1916
	Roy, L. G...........	" A " 2nd "	" B " 1st "	Jan. 23, 1917
	Allen, A. T..........	" B " 2nd "	" A " 2nd "	" 23, 1917
	Teevens, L. P........	" B " 2nd "	" A " 2nd "	" 23, 1917
	Westman, Leroy E....	" B " 2nd "	" A " 2nd "	Feb. 27, 1917
Interior.............	Cameron, Mary......	" B " 3rd "	" A " 3rd "	Oct. 3, 1916
	Roger, William C....	" B " 2nd "	" A " 2nd "	Nov. 3, 1916
	Bazinet, Odilon G....	" B " 3rd "	" A " 3rd "	Dec. 1, 1916
	McClymont, Percy J. I.................	" B " 2nd "	" A " 2nd "	Jan. 16, 1917
	Renault, Joseph F....	" B " 3rd "	" A " 3rd "	May 3, 1917
	Story, Alice A........	" B " 3rd "	" A " 3rd "	" 12, 1917
	Turner, William J. L..	" B " 3rd "	" A " 3rd "	" 15, 1917
	Daly, P. J...........	" A " 3rd "	" B " 2nd "	June 23, 1917
	Hutton, W. H........	" A " 2nd "	" B " 2nd "	" 23, 1917
	Edey, R. K..........	" B " 3rd "	" A " 3rd "	" 28, 1917
	Leahy, Frank J.......	" B " 3rd "	" A " 3rd "	" 28, 1917
	Bedard, Beulah.......	" B " 3rd "	" A " 3rd "	" 28, 1917
	King, Mary C........	" B " 3rd "	" A " 3rd "	" 28, 1917
	Rollins, William T....	" A " 2nd "	" B " 1st "	" 29, 1917
Justice..............	Plaxton, C. P........	" A " 2nd "	" B " 1st "	May 16, 1917
	Matté, G...........	" B " 2nd "	" A " 2nd "	" 16, 1917
Labour..............	Stewart, Bryce M....	Sub-div. A of 2nd Div.	Sub-div. B of 1st Div.	Oct. 20, 1916
	Stewart, Bryce M....	" B " 1st "	" A " 1st "	June 21, 1917
Marine..............	Roy, R.............	" B " 2nd "	" B " 1st "	Sept. 28, 1916
	Lucas, H. L.........	" B " 2nd "	" A " 2nd "	" 28, 1916
	Rowan, J. T.........	" B " 2nd "	" A " 2nd "	" 28, 1916
	Hamel, A. J.........	" B " 2nd "	" A " 2nd "	" 28, 1916
	Edge. V. J..........	" A " 2nd "	" B " 1st "	" 28, 1916
	Treanor, W. C........	" A " 2nd "	" B " 1st "	Oct. 28, 1916
	Thompson, Mabel B..	" B " 3rd "	" A " 3rd "	Nov. 6, 1916
	Breen, J. A..........	" B " 3rd "	" A " 3rd "	" 24, 1916
	Lanthier, Mary E.....	" B " 3rd "	" A " 3rd "	" 24. 1916

SESSIONAL PAPER No. 31

Table No. 22.—Certificates of qualification for promotion issued by the Commission—*Continued.*

Department.	Name.	From.	To.	Date of certificate.
Marine............	McCullough, Evelyn..	Sub-div. B of 3rd Div.	Sub-div. A of 3rd Div.	Mar. 24, 1916
	Tremain, A. de B.....	" B " 1st "	" A " 1st "	April 14, 1917
	McClenaghan, J. E....	" B " 1st "	" A " 1st "	" 14, 1917
	Hawken, H. E. A....	" B " 1st "	" A " 1st "	" 14, 1917
	McDonnell, F.........	" B " 1st "	" A " 1st "	" 14, 1917
	Quinn, W. J.........	" A " 2nd "	" B " 1st "	" 14, 1917
	Dame, A. H.........	" B " 2nd "	" A " 2nd "	" 14, 1917
	O'Malley, J. R........	" B " 3rd "	" A " 3rd "	May 8, 1917
	Fairweather, Winnie..	" B " 3rd "	" A " 3rd "	June 13, 1917
Militia and Defence..	Usher, Louise M......	" B " 3rd "	" A " 3rd "	Jan. 1, 1917
	Eligh, Sarah E.......	" B " 3rd "	" A " 3rd "	" 1, 1917
	Burke, Miss M........	" B " 3rd "	" A " 3rd "	April 28, 1917
	Beard, Frank........	" B " 1st "	" A " 1st "	May 11, 1917
	Watterson, A. E......	" A " 2nd "	" B " 1st "	" 11, 1917
	Maple, H. E	" B " 2nd "	" A " 2nd . "	" 11, 1917
Mines.............	Bolton, L. L..........	" A " 2nd "	" B " 1st "	Oct. 16, 1916
	Macoun, James M.....	" B " 1st "	" A " 1st "	Mar. 2, 1917
	Rose, Bruce...........	" A " 2nd "	" B " 1st "	" 2, 1917
	Hayes, A. O..........	" A " 2nd "	" B " 1st "	" 2, 1917
	Mackay, B. R.........	" A " 2nd "	" B " 1st "	" 2, 1917
	Poitevin, Eugene.....	" B " 2nd "	" A " 2nd "	" 2, 1917
	Bleakney, Eilleen.....	" B " 3rd "	" A " 3rd "	" 2, 1917
	Moffat, Anna V..:....	" B " 3rd "	" A " 3rd "	" 2, 1917
	Salt, Lillian A........	" B " 3rd "	" A " 3rd "	" 2, 1917
	De Schmid, Hugh S..	" A " 2nd "	" B " 1st "	" 2, 1917
	Cole, L. Heber........	" A " 2nd "	" B " 1st "	" 2, 1917
	Leverin, H. A.	" A " 2nd "	" B " 1st "	" 2, 1917
	Robinson, A. H. A.....	" A " 2nd "	" B " 1st "	April 7, 1917
Naval Service......	LeBlanc, Joseph O....	" B " 2nd "	" A " 2nd "	Oct. 12, 1916
	Lyon, Mary C........	" B " 3rd "	" A " 3rd "	" 14, 1916
	White, Edith.........	" B " 3rd "	" A " 3rd "	" 14, 1916
	Lacombe, Arthur.....	" B " 3rd "	" A " 3rd "	" 14, 1916
	Fairbairn, Helen.....	" B " 3rd "	" A " 3rd "	June 12, 1917
	McVeigh, Thomas F..	" A " 2nd "	" B " 1st "	" 29, 1917
	Rush, W. A...........	" A " 2nd "	" B " 1st "	" 29, 1917
	Finlayson, Alex. C....	" A " 2nd "	" B " 1st "	" 30, 1917
Post Office.........	Arkley, Miss H. P....	" B " 3rd "	" A " 3rd "	Oct. 30, 1916
	Brown, Miss A. C....	" B " 3rd "	" A " 3rd "	" 30, 1916
	O'Hagan, A. W. S....	" B " 3rd "	" A " 3rd "	" 30, 1916
	Price, Miss E. A......	" B " 3rd "	" A " 3rd "	" 30, 1916
	Bégin, Pierre.........	" B " 3rd "	" A " 3rd "	" 30, 1916
	Denison, Miss O. E...	" B " 3rd "	" A " 3rd "	" 30, 1916
	Barrett, J. T.........	" B " 3rd "	" A " 3rd "	" 30, 1916
	Sheppard, Miss M. E..	" B " 3rd "	" A " 3rd "	" 30, 1916
	Hayes, Miss J. M.....	" B " 3rd "	" A " 3rd "	" 30, 1916
	Bailey, Miss E. H....	" B " 3rd "	" A " 3rd "	" 30, 1916
	Whelan, George......	" B " 3rd "	" A " 3rd "	" 30, 1916
	Moss, Miss M. L......	" B " 3rd "	" A " 3rd "	" 30, 1916
	Thoburn, Miss M. E..	" B " 3rd "	" A " 3rd "	" 30, 1916
	McIntosh, Miss M. C.	" B " 3rd "	" A " 3rd "	" 30, 1916
	McIntosh, Miss I. A...	" B " 3rd "	" - A " 3rd "	" 30, 1916
	Crowder, Miss E. A...	" B " 3rd "	" A " 3rd "	" 30, 1916
	Hornidge, R. F.......	" B " 3rd "	" A " 3rd "	" 30, 1916
	Morris, E. T..........	" B " 3rd "	" A " 3rd "	" 30, 1916
	Barry, N. T...........	" B " 3rd "	" A " 3rd "	" 30, 1916
	Horsley, Miss M. B...	" B " 3rd "	" A " 3rd "	" 30, 1916
	Stewart, Mary........	" B " 3rd "	" A " 3rd "	" 30, 1916
	O'Dempsey, J. A.....	" B " 3rd "	" A " 3rd "	" 30, 1916
	Hill, G. A. L.........	" B " 3rd "	" A " 3rd "	" 30, 1916
	McEachern, W. C.....	" B " 2nd "	" A " 2nd "	Nov. 25, 1916
	Fairweather, J. H.....	" B " 1st "	" A " 1st "	Jan. 19, 1917
	Macneill, Grace.......	" B " 3rd "	" A " 3rd "	" 19, 1917
	May, O...............	" A " 3rd "	" B " 2nd "	June 23, 1917
Privy Council.......	Boyce, J. F...........	" A " 2nd "	" B " 1st "	Aug. 31, 1917
Public Archives.....	*Kenny, J. F..........	" A " 2nd "	" B " 1st "	April 13, 1916
	Shortt, George E.....	" B " 2nd "	" A " 2nd "	May 29, 1917

*Omitted from Report of 1915-1916.

8 GEORGE V, A. 1918

TABLE No. 22.—Certificates of qualification for promotion issued by the Commission—*Concluded.*

Department.	Name.	From.	To.	Date of certificate.
Public Works.........	Viens, E..............	Sub-div. A of 2nd Div.	Sub-div. B of 1st Div.	Oct. 14, 1916
	Evans, John E........	" B " 3rd "	" A " 3rd "	" 28, 1916
	Mackay, C. S. A......	" A " 2nd "	" B " 1st "	Nov. 22, 1916
	Thivierge, J. O.......	" B " 2nd "	" A " 2nd "	" 28, 1916
	Dawson, H. F........	" A " 2nd "	" B " 1st "	" 28, 1916
	Hennessey, George F.	" B " 3rd "	" A " 3rd "	Dec. 15, 1916
	Plunkett, Florence....	" B " 2nd "	" A " 2nd "	Jan. 16, 1917
	Ross, Frank W........	" B " 3rd "	" A " 3rd "	May 16, 1917
	Allen, Miss M. K.....	" B " 3rd "	" A " 3rd "	June 19, 1917
Railways & Canals..	Lyons, James.........	" B " 3rd "	" A " 3rd "	Dec. 5, 1916
	Bogart, Miss L. B....	" B " 1st "	" A " 1st "	Mar. 6, 1917
	Puglsey, J. W........	" B " 3rd "	" A " 3rd "	May 3, 1917
	Mathie, Andrew H....	" B " 3rd "	" A " 3rd "	" 8, 1917
	Greenway, William J..			
Royal North West Mounted Police....	Hann, G. T..........	" B " 2nd "	" A " 2nd "	Mar. 6, 1917
Secretary of State...	Jerome, Miss M. A. P.	" B " 3rd "	" A " 3rd "	April 16, 1917
Trade and Commerce............	Archer, W. A........	" B " 3rd "	" A " 3rd "	Oct. 20, 1916
	Dumouchel, Corinne..	" B " 3rd "	" A " 3rd "	Feb. 23, 1917

EXAMINATION PAPERS

REGULAR EXAMINATIONS.

(1) Preliminary Examination for the Outside Service, November, 1916.

ARITHMETIC.

Time: $1\frac{1}{2}$ hours.

NOTE.—No marks will be allowed unless the full work is shown and the answer is correct.

Values.

9   1. Write in words: 600017; 29007763; 8293050000.

6   2. Write in figures: Nine million seven hundred thousand and seven; Forty-three billion ninety million five thousand· six hundred and twenty-five.

17   3. Add: 37889; 6976; 78749; 35986; 73887; 878; 30937; 80862; 77786; 3699; 89994; 7983.

17   4. Multiply 3968007549 by 90785.

17   5. Divide 382579167893 by 6973.

17   6. A grocer bought 20 cases of eggs, each containing 30 dozen, at 27 cents a dozen. He paid 19 cents a case to have the eggs shipped to him. He sold them at a total gain of $23.00. What price per dozen did he charge, if there were $\frac{1}{2}$ dozen unsaleable eggs in each case?

17   7. The exports of Canadian produce for May, 1915, and May, 1916, are given in the table below.
     (a) What was the total for May, 1915?
     (b) What was the total for May, 1916?
     (c) By how much did the total for May, 1916, exceed the total for May, 1915?

Canadian Produce.	May, 1915.	May, 1916.
Animal Produce.........	$ 76,033,299	$107,482,272
Agricultural Products....	135,374,932	299,035,751
The Mine.............	52,604,187	68,727,974
The Fisheries..........	19,953,656	23,103,465
The Forest............	42,896,032	52,316,834
Manufactures..........	104,589,832	261,999,746
Miscellaneous..........	980,567	7,917,394

8 GEORGE V, A. 1918

SPELLING AND DICTATION.

SPELLING.

Time: 30 minutes.

NOTE.—Copy the following, correcting the errors in spelling; 3 marks will be deducted for every misspelled word in your copy.

Value—50.

He was a man of grate forse of charactar, unflinching currage, much wurldly shreudness, with a bisness fakulty allmost amounting to genious. At one perriod, his time was ingrossed buy cevere and continuous labor, ocassioned by the organising and kondukting of his noomerous manufactories, sumtimes from fore in the morning till nine at knight. At fifty years of aje he set to work to lern english grammar and emprove himself in writing and in speling. After over-cumming every obstikle, he had the satisfakshun of reeping the reward of his interprize. He died in 1792. Be it fur good or fur eval, he was the founder in England of the modren factury sistem, a branch of endustry which has onquestonably prooved a sourse of emmence welth to endeviduals and to the nation.

He establisht noo mills, and the amount and the excellance of his produkts were such that in a short tyme he obtaned so compleat a kontrol of the trade, that he guverned the mane opperashuns of the other cottun spinners.

DICTATION.

Time: 30 minutes.

NOTE.—This paper should not be seen by the candidates. The Examiner will read over the whole extract once, and then reread it slowly and distinctly, indicating to the candidates the occurrence of each full stop. A third reading of the whole extract may be given if sufficient time remains. The whole time occupied should not be more than half an hour.

Value—50.

I turn now to see the satisfaction which comes from physical exertion, including brain-work. Everybody knows some form of activity which gives him satisfaction. It may be riding on a horse, or rowing a boat, or climbing a mountain, or tramping all day through woods or along beaches with a gun on the shoulder, or again it may be moulding a mass of white-hot metal in the glow of a furnace, or wrestling with the handles of a plunging, staggering plough, or tugging at a boat's tiller when the breeze is fresh, or bringing hay in before the shower. There is real pleasure and exhilaration in bodily exertion, particularly with companionship either of men or animals, and competition. There is pleasure in the exertion even when it is pushed to the point of fatigue, as many a sports-man knows, and this pleasure is, in good measure, independent of the attainment of any practical end. There is pleasure in mere struggle, so it be not hopeless, and in overcoming resistance, obstacles, and hardships.

WRITING.

Time: 30 minutes.

Value—100.

Copy the following extract:—

The waterways of Canada are one of the most remarkable of its geographical features. East of the Rocky Mountains, the southern part of the Dominion slopes to the north-east toward Hudson Bay; and the rivers in the south flow eastward. Thus, the Saskatchewan River, with its northern and southern branches, flows eastward into Lake Winnipeg, and thence northward by the Nelson River into Hudson Bay. On the north, the Great Plain has a northerly slope, and the Mackenzie River, with its tributaries, the Slave, Liard, Athabaska and Peace Rivers, flows into the Artic Ocean. The Mackenzie, exclusive of its tributaries, but including the Slave, Peace and Finlay Rivers, has a total length of 2,525 miles. The Yukon River in the Yukon Territory also flows northward, passing through Alaska into Behring Strait after a course of 2,300 miles. In British Columbia, the Fraser, Columbia, Skeena and Stikine Rivers flow into the Pacific Ocean.

8 GEORGE V, A. 1918

(2) Qualifying Examination for the Outside Service, November, 1916.

ARITHMETIC.

Time: $2\frac{1}{2}$ hours.

NOTE.—The first *four* questions and any *seven* from the remaining eight constitute a full paper.

Values.

12   1. Multiply $882 \cdot 876$ by $3371 \cdot 55$, and divide the product by the difference between $8340 \cdot 20$ and $7838 \cdot 79$.

6   2. Simplify $\dfrac{7\frac{1}{2}}{6\frac{2}{3}} + \left(\dfrac{11\frac{1}{2} - 2\frac{2}{5}}{11\frac{1}{2} + 2\frac{2}{5}} \times 10\frac{9}{13}\right) - 7\frac{1}{8}$.

6   3. Simplify $(64 \cdot 3 + 7 \cdot 94 - \cdot 615) \div 5 \cdot 73$.

6   4. Add 6278548; 5876394; 8967357; 2863876; 4976849; 9678438.

10   5. For what amount should a 90-day note be drawn so that when, discounted at a bank at 7% per annum; it may produce $716.98?

10·   6. What was the value when due of the following note?

> $200.00   OTTAWA, May 15, 1916.
>   Two months after date I promise to pay E. V. Colville, or order, the sum of two hundred dollars with interest at 8 per cent per annum. Value received.
>   J. M. PETERS.

10.   7. During the first year a man increased his fortune by $\frac{4}{7}$ of its value, during the second year by $\frac{1}{11}$ of this increased value, and during the third year by $\frac{2}{3}$ of its new value. It then amounted to $24300. What was its value at first?

10   8. To what sum will $3000 amount in five years at 6% per annum, compound interest?

10   9. A person has $205 in 50c. and 25c. pieces. Find the number of each, if there are 460 of both.

10   10. Find the marked price of goods which cost $34 so that the dealer may make a gain of 20% on cost after giving a discount of 15% off his marked price.

10   11. 240 lbs. of flour at 4c. a lb. were mixed with 360 lbs. at 6c. a lb. How many pounds of each kind are there in $10.40 worth of the mixture?

10   12. How many pounds of chicory at 12c. a pound must be mixed with 80 pounds of coffee at 30c. a pound to make a mixture worth 20c. a pound?

COMPOSITION.

Time: 2½ hours.

Value—100.

1. Write a composition of about 250 words on one of the following subjects:—

    (a) The greatness of Shakespeare.
    (b) The Value of a Good Education.
    (c) The Crops of 1916 in Canada.
    (d) "No one gets something for nothing."
    (e) Some Duties of a Citizen.

2. Condense into about 200 words the gist of the following passage. Give your answer in well-constructed sentences, preserving all the essential points.

This question of winter steam communication is of great importance to the people of Prince Edward Island. The prospect of obtaining it was one great reason why the people of the Island consented to Confederation. That was well understood by the people of the Island at the time of Union, and it is better understood to-day. Owing to the peculiar situation of the Island, to her insular position, and to the fact that for five months of the year her coasts are completely surrounded with ice, she could not derive any benefits from Confederation. The people of the Island were aware that the Dominion was pledged to the construction of public works of great magnitude, such as the opening of canals, the building of railways, and other work of a similar nature. They also knew that, on becoming a part of the Dominion of Canada, they would be compelled to contribute their share for the construction of those works, and unless means of communication bringing them in connection with the railway system of the Dominion, winter and summer, were secured to them, they would not be in a position to participate in the benefits which would accrue to the rest of the Dominion by the construction of these works. They, therefore, have it expressly stipulated in the terms of Confederation, that efficient steam communication, winter and summer, should be maintained by the Dominion Government for the conveyance of mails and passengers to and from the Island. Now, let us, consider for one moment how this part of the compact has been carried out. We find that for the first two years after Confederation nothing at all was done towards fulfilling this part of the contract, so far as the winter season was concerned. In the year 1876, the Government, recognizing the rights of the Island in this matter, placed the now famous *Northern Light* upon the route between George-town and Pictou. I am not going to say anything disparaging of the *Northern Light*. She was built expressly for the purpose of testing the practicability of navigating the Straits in midwinter. She was merely placed there as an experiment, and, if she has not come up to the expectations of those who took an interest in her, she has not altogether proved a failure. She has at intervals succeeded in effecting a crossing, sometimes making her trips with considerable regularity, and sometimes being for a whole week at a time locked in the ice, being unable to move in any direction. She has, however, been successful to a certain extent, and her operations have been of great benefit to those engaged in trade, as they have been enabled to receive consignments of goods that they otherwise would have to do without till spring. With regard to the carriage of mails and passengers, which is, after all, the main feature of this affair, and which is the only part of the original compact that we can insist upon having carried out, her operations have been most unsatisfactory. Even during the present winter, which has been one of the most successful seasons, it was found necessary, about the middle of January, to take the mails away from her and have them forwarded by the only route by means of which communication can be kept up with the outside world in midwinter—the Capes route. Capes Traverse and Tormentine are only separated by a strait of some nine miles in width, and experience has shown, after many attempts at other points, that this is the route which must be adopted for our winter mail service. Such being the fact, it becomes the duty of the Government to so improve this route as to make it as perfect as possible, and all their energies and means should be concentrated on this one point. At present, the crossing is effected by use of the small ice-boats, as it was before Confederation. I need not refer to the difficulties and hard-ships experienced by the brave and hardy men who have to perform this service, who are called upon in the middle of our severe winters to risk their lives in the public interest. They have been most successful in performing this duty, and, owing to their skill and ability, we are enabled to receive our mails with some degree of regularity. But the great difficulty they have to contend with is not the ice, but open water, when high winds prevail, and they have been frequently compelled to return on account of open water, without being able to effect a crossing. It is believed by parties who are competent to judge in this matter, that a small steamboat to supplement the ice-boats would perfect this service, so far as the crossing is concerned. The only thing then required to render this service complete would be to connect this ferry with the Inter-colonial and Prince Edward Island Railways. This would necessitate the construction of two short lines of railway on both sides.

GEOGRAPHY.

Time: 2 hours.

NOTE.—Candidates will take Question 1 and any *five* others.

Values.

20 1. Draw an outline map of Great Britain and Ireland, and indicate with names:
    (1) the larger coast waters;
    (2) *ten* inlets which furnish good harbours;
    (3) *four* groups of islands near the coast;
    (4) *five* celebrated university centres.

16 2. Name in order *sixteen* towns or cities on the Canadian Northern Railway from Toronto to the Pacific Coast, and *sixteen* towns or cities on the Grand Trunk Railway from Detroit to Lévis.

16 3. Write a note on India, telling about its location, its size, population, climate, and principal products.

16 4. Explain how it is that events happening in France in the afternoon may be reported in Canada in the forenoon of the same day. At what time of the day can the same events be first reported in India, in South Africa, in Australia?

16 5. Write a short note on any *four* of the following Canadian products, telling definitely from what part of Canada they come, and to what part of the world they are shipped: nickel, mica, asbestos, carborundum, graphite. Does Canada hold a peculiar place as a producer of any of these?

16 6. Indicate the course of each of the following rivers; describe the nature of the country drained by it, also its usefulness to man as a means of navigation or of power development: Red, Grand, Richelieu, Ohio, Hudson, Columbia.

16 7. What natural or artificial advantages have assisted in the growth of each of the following cities: Valleyfield, Pittsburg, Cleveland, New Westminster, Peterborough, Winnipeg, St. Louis, New York?

SESSIONAL PAPER No. 31

HISTORY.

Time: 2 hours.

NOTE.—Five questions only are to be attempted.

Value—100

1. Make a list of the chief events in the reign of Queen Anne *or* Queen Victoria. Write short accounts of any *three* of the events.
2. Explain the position and duties, in Early French Canada, of the following: the Seignior, the Intendant, the Bishop, the Governor. Write short sketches of *one* Governor and *one* Intendant.
3. Describe the Life of Jacques Cartier, and give an outline of his three voyages to Canada. What was their result?
4. Give the causes of the Peninsular War. Name the chief engagements, and indicate the parts played in it by (a) Sir John Moore, (b) the Duke of Wellington, (c) Napoleon.
5. What colonies had Britain in America before the Conquest of Canada in the Seven Years' War (1756-63)? Of what value were they to her? How were they lost, and who were the leaders in the struggle?
6. Locate the following Battlefields: Louisbourg, Ste. Foye, la Hogue, Balaclava, Plassey. Describe the *first three,* telling in each case the period the war, the commanders, and the results to the nations engaged. Give details for each battle.
7. Write notes on: Turgot, Danton, Voltaire; *or*
   Write notes on: the Coureurs des Bois; Jesuits in Canada; the Siege of Delhi; Why 1867 is an important date in Canadian History.

SPELLING AND DICTATION.

SPELLING.

Time: 30 minutes.

Value—50.

NOTE.—Copy the following, correcting the errors in spelling; 5 marks will be deducted for every misspelled word in your copy.

If this is not done, what will happen? Seperation, first of one part, then of another; weekness of each part and weekness all round. Think of the impetis that this would give to every forse that makes for cayos among the three hundred millions over whom God in His providence has placed us. The work that the British Empire has in hand is far grandir than the comparitively limmited duties with which the States are content to deal. Its problems are wider and more inspireing; yet, at the same time, the white race, that alone, so far, has proved itsself fit for self-goverment, lives by itsself, instead of being comingled with a coloured race to which only nomenal freedom is aloud. Any one who has lived either in South Africa or in the States will understand what a free hand and what an unspeakible leaverage this gives us. We nead no Force Bill to ensure us a free balot in Britain, Canada, Austrailia, or New Zeeland. Allready our suns are taking there part in interducing civillization into Africa, under the proteckshun of the flag, and in perserving the spirit of the Empyre among the teaming millions of India and south-eastern Asia, those peoples kindered to ourselves, who for centuries before had been the pray of successive spoilars. And, in this bludy war, the bonds of Empyre have been moar cloasly dron together; and the Mutherland has seen a new spirit of loyaltie and devoshun spring from her suns and dotters across the sees.

31—5

DICTATION.

Time: 30 minutes.

Value—50.

NOTE.—This paper should not be seen by the candidates. The Examiner will read over the whole extract once, and then reread it slowly and distinctly, indicating to the candidates the occurrence of each full stop. A third reading of the whole extract may be given if sufficient time remains. The whole time occupied should not be more than half an hour.

All has passed, unregretted as unseen; or, if the apathy be ever shaken off, even for an instant, it is only by what is gross, or what is extraordinary; and yet it is not in the broad and fierce manifestations of the elemental energies, not in the clash of the hail, nor the drift of the whirlwind, that the highest characters of the sublime are developed. God is not in the earthquake, nor in the fire, but in the still, small voice.

They are but the blunt and the low faculties of our nature which can only be addressed through lamp-black and lightning. It is in quiet and subdued passages of unobtrusive majesty, the deep, and the calm, and the perpetual,—that which must be sought ere it is seen, and loved ere it is understood,—things which the angels work out for us daily, and yet vary eternally, which are never wanting, and never repeated, which are to be found always, yet each found but once; it is through these that the lesson of devotion is chiefly taught, and the blessing of beauty given.

We are too often disposed to accept the superficial instead of the real; to study results and ignore causes; to be governed by external appearance; while in reality, the value of all our experiences lies in the hidden spirit or principle which actuates them.

TRANSCRIPTION AND WRITING.

Time: 1 hour.

Value—50 for each.

The candidate is required to make a neat, clean and correct copy of the manuscript handed to him with this slip, writing out all abbreviations at full length, and correcting any misspellings. The words scored through are to be omitted, and the interlineations and the marginal and other additions are to be inserted in their proper places as indicated. All changes or corrections, other than these, *will be counted as errors*. This paper will be taken as a test of writing also.

Civil Service of Canada — Qualifying Examination
Agriculture in Canada — In speak^g of
industries in England, manufactures

tr./
stet/

(naturally) (wd) be put 1st In Canada,
while manufactures are very important,
agriculture employs a larger no. of
people than any other industry. In the
early yrs. of Canada's history, farm^g
was carried on only in the south-eastern
port^n of B. N. A. — Ont., Que., & what are

;however, /
& north-west/

now the Maratime Provinces. Gradually,
the country farther west, was opened up

tr./
tr./
the forests were
cut away,

by roads & rwys, & the area of agricultural
was extended widely. In the yr 1885,
when the C. P. R. was completed, practically
the whole of the north-western port^n of
the Dom^n was thrown open to settlement.

;wh. all land is
occupied & only sold
for a high price, }
stet/

It is difficult for those liv^g in
Europe, to understand that some of the
best farm^g land on the continent of America
is to be had almost for the ask^g, by anyone who wishes to cultivate it. The
settlement of these lands is heartily encouraged
by the Govt, because a fertile soil &
great natural resources are of no service

31—5½

8 GEORGE V, A. 1918

§/ tr/
Of course, it is
important also to
get a good class of
settlers.

unless ~~there~~ are people there to cultivate
& develope them. Both Canada & the
motherland wish loyal & sturdy men
& women to take up this land & help to
build up a strong colony & natⁿ.

Anyone who will cultivate the
land in the West can get a farm

tr/   of 160 ac. free*. He can buy land also
fr. rwy. & other corporatⁿˢ at a low figure.
In Canada nearly all the farmers

; if he chooses to
exert himself for
a few yrs,

own their hold⁸, & any capable farm
labourer, may become an owner himself

✻   ; while in Northern Ont & Que. he
can procure one on nominal terms,
without any cost in some instances.

(3) Competitive Examination for Positions in Subdivision B of the Third Division, Inside Service, November, 1916.

ARITHMETIC.

Time: 2½ hours.

Value—100.

1. (a) Simplify $\frac{1}{2} \times \frac{3}{4} - \frac{1}{4}$ of $\frac{2}{3} + \frac{1}{5} \div \frac{3}{20}$.
   (b) Multiply ·0256 by 1·0071, and divide the product by 2·7975.

2. A field is 80 rods long and 20 rods wide. Find the total cost of material for a tight board fence, 6 feet high, around it, if—

   (a) the posts cost 10 cents each and are placed 11 feet apart;
   (b) the boards are one inch thick and nailed to two continuous lines of scantling, 2 inches by 4 inches;
   (c) all lumber costs $20 per M.

3. A man borrowed $800 at 5% and paid back $175 at the end of each year to pay the interest and reduce the principal. How much does he owe, after making his third payment?

4. A farmer paid $1.50 per bushel for his seed wheat and sowed 1¾ bushels per acre in a field 64 rods by 40 rods. His crop averaged 32½ bushels to the acre and sold at 98 cents per bushel. Find his net gain, if his expenses for tillage and harvesting amounted to $12.50 per acre.

5. When wheat is ground into flour, 18 per cent is lost (as bran, etc.). If the weight of bread is 133⅓ per cent of the weight of flour used in making it, how many two-pound loaves can be made from the flour obtained from 20 bushels of wheat? (60 pounds of wheat make one bushel.)

6. A man invested $5460 in 3 per cent stock at 91. He sold out 20 shares when it had risen to 93½, and the remainder when it had fallen to 85. He invested the total proceeds in 4½ per cent stock at 102. Find the change in his income.

7. $260.00   OTTAWA, 27 March, 1913.

   Three months after date, I promise to pay to the order of James Black the sum of Two Hundred and Sixty Dollars with interest at 6 per cent per annum, value received.

                                                      W. W. GREY.

   Find the value of the foregoing note when it is legally due.

8 GEORGE V, A. 1918

BOOK-KEEPING.

Time: 2½ hours.

Value—100.

1. Enter in Journal or Cash-book the following:—
    - (a) 1. Bills Receivable amounting to $800 were deposited in the bank for collection.
        2. Discounted my own note for $1,200 at bank, and left Bills Receivable amounting to $1,500 as collateral security. Discount charged, $10.
        3. Bank notifies me that $700 of notes mentioned in 1 have been paid and the remaining $100 note dishonoured.
        4. Bank informs me that $600 at the collateral notes mentioned in 2 have been paid to them, and that $200 of these notes falling due yesterday were dishonoured. The balance have not yet matured.
    - (b) Sold goods to A. Perch for $500. Received in payment his note for $300 at 3 months bearing interest at 6% ($4.50) and the balance in cash. When note came due, it was taken up with a new note at 2 months for $200 bearing interest at 6%, and the balance in cash.

2. Draw up a form of Petty Cash Book, and describe the method of keeping it. Illustrate by half a dozen entries.

3. On January 1st, 1916, H. White had a Capital of $3,250; Merchandise, $2,541; Cash on hand, $43; Cash in bank, $306; Sundry Debtors, $1,988; Bills Receivable, $2,622; Furniture and Fixtures, $500; Horse and Cart, $250. He owed Sundry Creditors $2,144, and Bills Payable, $2,856. The following business was done in January:—

Jan. 1. Bought goods from McKinley, $940.
     2. Sold goods to Richardson, $310.
     3. Issued cheque on bank to McKinley, $340.
     5. Sold goods to Thomas, $1,120.
     7. Bought goods from Drysdale, $565.
   10. Received cheque from Richardson and deposited, $300. Discount allowed to Richardson, $10.
   12. Sold goods to Rogers, $663.
   13. Received note from Thomas at 3 months, $1,120.
   14. Bought goods from Tory, $71.
   17. Bought goods from Charles B., $125.
   19. Issued cheque to Tory, $70. Discount allowed by Tory, $1.
   21. Bought from sundry creditors, goods, $1,244.
   22. Sold to sundry debtors, goods, $1,099.
   23. Received cheques from sundry debtors, $1,344. Discount allowed to debtors, $131. Deposited in bank, cheques, $1,344.
   24. Discounted note at bank, $1,120. Discount on note, $12. Issued cheques to sundry creditors, $1,672. Discounts received for cash payments, $146.

31. Issued cheque for salaries, $100. Issued cheque for rent, $150. Paid cash for coal, $10. Paid cash for gas, $4. Stock on hand at end of period, $3000.

4. Referring to Question 3: Supposing the horse and cart had been sold on credit to Smith for $200, that a new horse and cart had been bought on credit from Shaw for $350, that the rent paid ($150) was for the three months beginning January 1st, that $20 of the amount owing by sundry debtors was considered uncollectable, and that a fire insurance policy for one year had been taken out, to date from January 1st, the premium on which ($60) had not been paid; make adjustments and prepare Profit and Loss Account and Balance Sheet.

COMPOSITION.

Values. Time: 2½ hours.

10 1. Write the application called for by the following advertisement taken from an Ottawa paper:—

WANTED—A bright young man or lady for special office work. Must be first-class stenographer. Good salary to suitable person. Apply fully to Box 151, Post Office, Ottawa.

40 2. Write a letter to a friend discussing one of the following topics. The letter should contain not less than 250 words.

Why I am proud that I am a British Subject.
The value of a course of lessons in " First Aid."
It is desirable that immigrants from the Mother Country should find homes in Canada rather than in the United States.

50 3. Write in your own words and in well-constructed sentences, a synopsis of the following passage, preserving all of the essential points. This passage is from a speech delivered in the House of Commons on Nov. 21, 1910.

I join with my honourable friend who has moved this Address in congratulating both the British Empire and the American Republic upon the splendid result which has attended the deliberations of the Hague Tribunal. In submitting this vexed question to the determination of that tribunal, these two countries have given to the world an object lesson which I hope will not be forgotten. The issue of that arbitration is very creditable indeed to both countries, and I have no hesitation whatever in publicly offering my congratulations not only to the Government, but especially to my honourable friend the Minister of Justice, for the very successful issue which has been brought about by this tribunal. On some occasions in the past it may have been that difficulties arising between the United States and Canada have led to certain differences between the great Republic to the south and the Empire of which we are proud to form a part. I trust that this is not so to-day, I believe it is not so to-day and I trust that it will not be so in the future. Here lies Canada, a great and growing nation upon this continent, surrounded by very much the same conditions, confronted by very much the same problems, of those which present themselves to the people of the United States. We are bound to the British

Empire by a loyal fealty, by a warm affection, by everything which stands for the solidarity of this Empire, but we are also closely associated with the great Republic to the south of us by a constant and increasing social and commercial intercourse, and it seems to me in that way, and for that reason, that Canada should in the future come to be a bond of amity, of friendship, between the Republic and the Empire and I hope that both governments will lend themselves to the splendid movement which looks to the celebration of a centennial of peace between the Empire and the Republic. I trust that this will be done, and I join in the aspirations of those who have said that no better or more enduring monument of that centennial of peace could be established than to make continuous and permanent at all times to come that disarmament upon the great contiguous waters of both nations which has now existed for almost a century under the Treaty of 1818. That treaty, as we are all aware, is liable to be terminated on very short notice by either of the contracting parties. I believe every man in this country would like to see that condition made more enduring and permanent. In that way this Empire and the great adjoining Republic would give to the world an object lesson which is very much needed in these days of great armaments and great preparations for war; and then we might look forward to a day which may come, and which I hope will come, when the great Republic and this great Empire, acting together in the interests of humanity and civilization, can command, and will command, the peace of the world.

GEOGRAPHY.

Time: 2 hours.

Value—100.

Note.—Candidates will take Question 1 and any other *six*.

1. Draw a map of Canada and the United States, outlining and naming: (a) the *five* great physical divisions of each, (b) the *five* chief mountain-ranges of each, and (c) the provinces and states that lie along the international boundary from the Pacific Ocean to Lake Superior. .

2. Locate definitely and give in each case the leading industry of any *seven* of the following: Limerick, Paisley, Galashiels, Stoke, Bradford, Grand Mère, Trail, Summerside, and New Westminster.

3. Define, explain and give a Canadian example of each of the following: mountain-range, river-system, young valley, mature valley, drowned-valley, alluvial plain, and continental shelf.

4. By means of a sketch-map in each case, show in their proper connection, and name the rivers and lakes of the Nelson, Mackenzie, St. Lawrence, and Columbia basins, respectively.

5. What, where, and for what noted are: Bucharest, Trebizond, Piræus, Metz, Toulon, Transylvania, Trentino, Kavala, Avlona, and Dar-es-Salaam?

6. Sketch a map of the British Isles showing five chief seaports, four great manufacturing centres, three naval stations, and two leading educational centres. Indicate to which of these groups each place belongs.

7. Name and locate seven chief canals of the St. Lawrence system, and state what particular obstacle to navigation is overcome by each. .

8. Name the three leading products of (a) India, (b) Egypt, (c) South Africa, (d) Newfoundland, and (e) British West Indies.

9. (a) Draw a diagram showing the zones, their width and boundaries, and
   (b) state and explain the exact position of these boundaries and the
   exact time of the solstices and equinoxes, respectively.

HISTORY.

Time: 2 hours.

Value—100.

NOTE.—Six questions only are to attempted.

1. Give a brief account of the missions founded by the Jesuits among the Huron
   Indians.
2. Outline the political career of Lord Elgin in Canada.
3. Describe the circumstances under which the province in which you reside
   became a part of the Dominion of Canada.
4. (a) The British North America Act fixed the life of a Canadian Parliament
       at five years. Explain how it has come about that the Parliament
       which convened after the elections of September, 1911, is still
       a legally constituted authority.
   (b) Explain the composition of the Canadian Parliament, and show how
       it differs, if at all, in this respect from that of Great Britain and
       Ireland.
5. Name four Premiers of Canada since Confederation. Who chooses our
   Premier, and how is he guided in making this choice? What is a
   Premier's first important work after accepting appointment? Under
   what circumstances ought a Premier to tender his resignation?
6. (a) Write a note on the Irish Famine of 1846.
   (b) Describe briefly its political consequences.
7. Describe briefly the effect of the Napoleonic Wars on Britain's Colonial
   Empire.
8. Give a brief account of the industrial changes in England during the first
   half of the Nineteenth Century.
9. Sketch the part being played by France in the present European War.

SHORTHAND.

Value—100.

NOTE.—Both the following passages should be dictated to the candidates in a
   clear and distinct voice, at the rates indicated. No preliminary reading
   is to be given to the candidates. The bar-strokes will indicate to the
   reader his progress at the end of every fifteen seconds. Upon completion
   of the two readings, the candidates should be notified that they will be
   allowed one hour and a half for transcribing their shorthand notes in
   manuscript.

EIGHTY WORDS PER MINUTE.

The establishment of the Central Experimental Farm proved so popular
throughout the country that a demand came from farmers in 1 other parts of
Canada for the establishment of farms in the different provinces. It was
inconvenient for the farmers to 1 travel to Ottawa from many different parts
of the country; in addition to that, considering the great diversity of our 1 soil
and climate, the Central Farm could not carry out all the experiments that
would demonstrate what was the best 1 for all parts of the country. The Central
Experimental Farm, of course, carries out many experiments of all sorts in 1 con-

nection with the growing of crops, the production of stock, the cultivation of tobacco, the rotation of crops, and the 1 testing of seeds. Experiments are carried out with a view to determining what varieties of grass or vegetables will do 1 best in certain sections of the country. The Central Farm is open to the farmers of the country at all 1 times; the correspondence which it carries on with farmers from one end of Canada to the other is, I believe, 1 of enormous dimensions. The farms in the different provinces work along similar lines, though not on so large a scale. 1 They are branches of the Central Farm. They make all kinds of experiments to determine what crops should be grown 1 and how those crops can be best grown in the particular locality in which the farm in question is situated. 1

ONE HUNDRED WORDS PER MINUTE.

At no place on the American continent has potato growing reached as high a state of efficiency as it has along the St. John river, 1 in the Province of New Brunswick, and across the line, in the State of Maine. I think it is the opinion of most farmers in 1 the Maritime Provinces that spraying with Paris green is usually productive of some good. They claim that it removes the fungous growth, or what is 1 usually called rust. When I was home, the last week in January, I discussed this matter with a gentleman who told me that he had 1 sprayed his potato plants six or seven times during the summer. The spraying is done with a machine costing over $100; as the 1 machine goes along, the spray is automatically pumped under the leaves and stalks of the plant. He said that he sprayed the whole field of 1 potatoes, with the exception of half a dozen rows, and that when he came to dig them, he had a much better yield from the 1 half-dozen rows than he had from the rest of the field, which he had sprayed. I want to be quite fair in this matter; 1 I will give both sides of the case. Another gentleman told me that he sprayed all but half a dozen rows, and that he got 1 better results from the sprayed portion than from the portion which he had not sprayed; so you have evidence both ways. In my judgment, the 1 spraying does good. But the farmer knows that; he does not need information on that subject from the inspectors or from the Department of Agriculture. 1 Last year I did not spray the plants; but perhaps I will use the spray next year, because I think it may do some good. 1

SPELLING AND DICTATION.

SPELLING.

The paper set is that given on page 65.

DICTATION.

The paper set is that given on page 66.

TRANSCRIPTION AND WRITING.

Time: 1 hour.

Value—50 for each.

The candidate is required to make a neat, clean and correct copy of the manuscript handed to him with this slip, writing out all abbrevations at full length, and correcting any misspellings. The words scored through are to be omitted, and the interlineations and the marginal and other additions are to be inserted in their proper places as indicated. All changes or corrections, other than these, will be counted as errors. This paper will be taken as a test of writing also.

Civil Service of Canada - Third Div. Clerkships.

of electricity./
δ/ tr/

The introduct^n into the farm'c districts of Ont. has tended to (improve greatly) the condit^ns both in the farm-house & in the barn, & the farmer has shown himself to be fully alive to the value of efficient labour-

δ/

sav^g devices. In those places wh. it is impossible

δ/

to get electricity is not available, gasoline engines are be^g

stet/

largely used, & if tractors cost^g fr. $300 to

it is practicable/

$400 (can be placed on the market as has

δ/

been planned,) they will make a great diff^ce to the farmer in the sav^g of labour. On the land itself the farmer is becom^g awake to the necessity of employ^g modern methods,

especially tile drain^g }

& nos. of tract^n ditchers are at work in different pts. of the prov^ce. The very wet season, while it has emphasizing the need

& the probability is that next yr. will see more drain^g (done by the farmers) (than ever)

for tile drain^g, hindered the work a great deal, but, notwithstand^g, a considerable quantity of tile was laid by hand & by machine. It has been fairly well proved, especially by the experience of this yr., that wh. farms have been well drained the quality of the crops has been improved & the quantity wh. has been produced has been increased

stet/

fr. 25 to 30 %. It is very gratify^g

8 GEORGE V, A. 1918

[handwritten manuscript text]

to see how well the farm⁴ community
has *answered* ~~responded~~ to the call for recruits, &
with what vigour & cheerfulness they have
coped with the difficulties *consequent* caused by the
~~resultant~~ shortage in help. This has

tr/ been (in great measure) ~~brought about~~ *accomplished*
by extra work on the pt. of the farmers

tr/ themselves. More land was (given up also)
to pasture, & the use of improved
machinary diminished the necessity
for hired help.

δ/ ;both on their own farms & in giv⁴
δ/ *ing* assistance ~~to~~ their neighbours

TYPEWRITING.

Value—100.

Copy the following:—

Time: 30 minutes.

OTTAWA, December 24, 1915.

Dear Sir,—For some time past I have had under consideration the question of an amendment to the Bank Act authorizing the banks to take as security for advances to farmers, liens upon cattle and certain other live stock. It would seem that such liens should be registered in order that the rights of other creditors might not be prejudiced. The question, as you know, is one which has been much canvassed at successive revisions of the Bank Act, and there has been a conflict of view as to the expediency of such legislation. As it is greatly desirable at this juncture of our affairs that production should be facilitated in every way possible, I should appreciate an early expression of your views upon the following questions:—

1. Would such legislation facilitate and lead to increased advances by your bank to the stock-raising community, and would it tend to increase production?

2. Will there be during the coming year sufficient bank credits available for all the increased production possible to the Canadian agricultural and stock-raising community?

3. If the answer to (2) is in the negative, can you suggest any feasible plan for increasing the available bank credits for the purpose in view?

As I am exceedingly interested in the matter referred to, I shall be greatly obliged for a full and frank expression of your views.

Yours very truly,

W. T. WHITE,

Minister of Finance.

Now, let us compare the expenditures of Australia for 1911-12 with those of 1916-17. I take 1911-12 because that year marked the height of her prosperity, whilst 1916-17 finds her in the most crucial period in her history. In 1911-12, when she was abnormally prosperous, the surplus of her national debt took $14,114,000; the estimate for 1916-17 is $39,649,000.

	1911-12.	1916-17.
Civil Government.................	$4,463,000	$7,240,000
Department of Agriculture.........	1,379,000	4,263,000
Immigration.....................	1,079,000	1,534,000
Pensions........................	240,000	3,365,000
Militia..........................	6,868,000	5,706,000
Public Works—income............	8,621,000	18,814,000
Public Works—capital............	3,742,000	8,072,000
Steamship subsidies..............	1,918,000	2,963,000
Naval Service...................	256,000	2,250,000

The list gives us some striking contrasts from beginning to end. The total estimate for 1911-12 was $132,827,000, as against $188,981,000 for 1916-17. These figures show what a heavy burden the war has placed upon the Empire, apart altogether from the direct expenditure for military purposes.

There are two facts in this war that will ever remain salient—the gallantry of the British aristocracy, and the courage of the French democracy. It has been said—I have read it time and again before the war in books, pamphlets, reviews—that England was decadent, that her aristocracy was effete, idle, degenerate. But when the sons of the British nobility responded to the call of duty on the 4th August, 1914, when they buckled on their armour, when they rushed to the front in Artois and Champagne, when later on they were mowed down at Charleroi and Mons, mingling their blood with that of the soldiers of the Republic, I could not help thinking that they were the worthy sons of their sires, of the noblemen who wrested from King John the Magna Charta, and of the men of that aristocracy who played such a prominent part in Europe in the course of the 18th century; I could not help thinking that their chivalrous spirit was after all the best evidence that "blood will tell."

As regards the French democracy, let me quote the words of the Minister of Munitions, Mr. Thomas, one of the leaders of the Old French Labour Party: "Comrades, I am surprised to hear what is now being said. We, who have been with the colours, know all about the fatigue, the suffering, and the demoralization of French warfare; but we are to-day in the same mind as we were on the day of mobilization. I want to fight in order that my son here may never have to go to war. If I am to die, then I shall die; but I do not want him to see war. To avoid this we will make every sacrifice—our liberty, our blood, and our life."

That is the spirit of the French democracy, a spirit which is on a par with that which animates the British aristocracy.

8 GEORGE V, A. 1918

(4) Preliminary Examination for the Outside Service, May, 1917.

ARITHMETIC.

Time: 1½ hours.

NOTE.—No marks will be allowed unless the full work is shown and the answer is correct.

Values.

9   1. Write in words: 700093; 370019679; 4070900063.

6   2. Write in figures: Thirty-five million four hundred and sixty thousand seven hundred; Three billion nine hundred million fifty thousand and seven.

17   3. Add: 58868; 86987; 677898; 979; 846997; 97694; 39886; 58994; 7889; 867685; 934867; 8978.

17   4. Multiply 6739587946 by 96078.

17   5. Divide 173723639810 by 5894.

17   6. Make out a simple bill for the following: On November 4, 1916, Mr. J. Robert bought of Mr. A. Allard, 93 Chapel St., Montreal: 1 box Butter, weighing 56 lb., at 37c. a lb.; 1 quarter Beef, weighing 97 lb., at 13c. a lb.; 3 bags Flour at $4.75 a bag; 2 bags Sugar at $8.67 a bag; 6 bags Potatoes at $1.97 a bag; 3 barrels Apples at $5.85 a barrel; 2 pails Lard, each weighing 20 lb., at 19c. a lb.; 1 Cheese, weighing 78 lb., at 17c. a lb.; 24 doz. Eggs at 38c. a doz.   Find total amount of the bill.

17   7. A farmer had 70 acres of cultivated land.   There were 29 ac. of oats, 18 ac. of barley, 2 ac. of potatoes, and the rest was hay.   The oats yielded 37 bu. per ac., the barley 29 bu. per ac., the potatoes 167 bu. per ac., and the hay 2 tons per ac.   Find the total value of the crops at these price: oats, 48c. a bu.; barley, 57c. a bu.; potatoes, 93c. a bu., and hay, $11.75 a ton.

100

SPELLING AND DICTATION.

SPELLING.

Time: 30 minutes.

NOTE.—Copy the following, correcting the errors in spelling; 3 marks will be deducted for every misspelled word in your copy.

Value—50.

On the opposit side of the cleering and near the point where the brook tumbeled over sum rocks from a still hier level, sum fifty or sixtey loges rudely maid of logs, brush, and earth inturmingled were to be discovered.   They were arranged without any order and seamed to be struckted with verry

SESSIONAL PAPER No. 31

littel attenshun to their neetness or beauty. Indead, so verry inferior were they, in the two latter particulers, to the village the scout had just scene, that he began to expeckt a secund surprize no less astonishing than the formur. This expecktation was in no degree deminished when, by the doutful twillight he beheld twenty or therty forms rising from the cuvver of the tall, course grass in frunt of the loges, and then sinking agen from the site as it were to burrow in the erth. By the sudden and hastie glimpses that he caught of these figgers, they seamed more like dark, glancing spectres, or sum other unerthly beings, than creetures fashuned with the ordenary and vulger materiels of flesh and blood.

DICTATION.

Time: 30 minutes.

NOTE.—This paper should not be seen by the candidates. The Examiner will read over the whole extract once, and then reread it slowly and distinctly, indicating to the candidates the occurrence of each full stop. A third reading of the whole extract may be given if sufficient time remains. The whole time occupied should not be more than half an hour.

Value—50.

Gentleness is indeed the best test of a gentleman. A consideration for the feelings of others, for his inferiors and dependants, as well as his equals, and respect for their self-respect, will pervade the true gentleman's whole conduct. He will rather himself suffer a small injury, than by an uncharitable view of another's behaviour incur the risk of committing a great wrong. He will be tolerant of the weaknesses, the failings, and the errors of those whose advantages in life have not been equal to his own. He will be merciful even to his beast. He will not boast of his wealth, or his strength, or his gifts. He will not be puffed up by success, or unduly depressed by failure. He will not force his views upon others, but speak his mind freely when occasion calls for it. He will not confer favours with a patronizing air. He is a man from whom one may receive a favour, and that is saying a great deal in these days.

WRITING.

Time: 30 minutes.

Value—100.

Copy the following extract:—

Under the Experimental Farm Stations Act, 1886 (R.S. 1906, c. 73), were established a Central Experimental Farm at Ottawa for Ontario and Quebec, and four branch Farms: (1) for the Maritime Provinces at Nappan, Nova Scotia; (2) for Manitoba at Brandon; (3) for the Northwest Territories at Indian Head, Saskatchewan; and (4) for British Columbia at Agassiz. After these five Farms had continued in operation for twenty years, the first steps were taken toward their extension in number by the establishment of new Experimental Stations for Alberta, one at Lethbridge in 1906, and the other at Lacombe in 1907. Since this date, development in the number of Farms and Stations, and in the work carried on by them, has been rapid and continuous; and every province has now one or more Farms or Stations. In 1915, including the Central Farm at Ottawa, there were altogether 19 Farms and Stations with a total area of 8,935 acres.

8 GEORGE V, A. 1918

(5) Qualifying Examination for the Outside Service, May, 1917.

ARITHMETIC

Time: $2\frac{1}{2}$ hours.

Value—100.

NOTE.—Nine questions only are to be attempted.

1. Add 42567895; 87659476; 58796837; 49278369; 78654783; 59678954; 35893592; 63876784; 39396666, and divide the total by 87543.

2. Multiply $346 \cdot 78954$ by $5 \cdot 7984$, and substract the product from 3000.

3. Simplify $\dfrac{(\frac{1}{2} + \frac{1}{3}) \times (\frac{1}{2} + \frac{1}{6})}{(\frac{1}{2} - \frac{1}{3}) \times (\frac{1}{2} - \frac{1}{4})} + \dfrac{(\frac{1}{4} + \frac{1}{3}) \times (\frac{1}{4} + \frac{1}{3})}{(\frac{1}{2} - \frac{1}{4}) \times (\frac{1}{3} - \frac{1}{4})} - \dfrac{(\frac{1}{3} + \frac{1}{2}) \times (\frac{1}{3} + \frac{1}{6})}{(\frac{1}{2} - \frac{1}{3}) \times (\frac{1}{3} - \frac{1}{4})}$

4. A man who had \$112000 spent a part of it in buying a house, and then invested $\frac{1}{3}$ of the remainder at 4% and the other $\frac{2}{3}$ at 5%, and received \$3920 income from these latter investments. Find the price paid for the house.

5. A man ascended and descended a mountain in $2\frac{1}{2}$ hours. Going up he went $2\frac{1}{3}$ miles an hour, and coming down at $3\frac{1}{2}$ miles an hour. What is the distance to the top of the mountain?

6. To what sum will \$1530 amount at the end of 4 years at 6% per annum, compound interest?

7. A person bought 84 lbs. of tea and 56 lbs. of coffee for \$79.80. If $12\frac{1}{3}$ pounds of coffee are worth \$5.55, what is the value of a pound of tea?

8. The sum of \$250 placed at interest at 6 % per annum amounted to \$256 at the end of a certain time. What was that time?

9. A merchant wished to raise \$494 by having his 70-day note discounted at a bank at 6% per annum. For what sum should the note be drawn?

10. What is the weight of a barrel of oil, if it is known that $\frac{1}{4}$ had been sold at one time and $\frac{2}{3}$ of the remainder at another time, and after that there remained 80 lbs.in the barrel?

11. What was the value of the following note when it came due?
\$240.00.   OTTAWA. January 9th, 1917.
    Three months after date I promise to pay to S. H. Bleaker, or order, the sum of Two hundred and forty dollars, with interest at 7% per annum, value received.

A. M. FRANKLIN.

SESSIONAL PAPER No. 31

COMPOSITION.

Time: 2½ hours.

Value of each question: 50 marks.

1. Write a composition about 250 words in length on one of the following subjects:
   (a) Our debt to those who have gone to fight for us, and how we may try to repay it.
   (b) An argument in favour of having every girl take a course in domestic science in the elementary schools.
   (c) Reasons given to account for the high cost of living.
   (d) A discussion of hunting with a camera as compared with hunting with firearms.

2. Give in about 250 words in well-constructed sentences the substance of the following extract from a speech made in London to the Premiers of the self-governing Colonies:—

I pass on, then, gentleman, to the second point—the question of commercial relations, and in regard to this I wish to say what I have already stated in answer to inquiries which I received before the Conference, that every question is an open question for full and free discussion. We rule nothing out of order. We do not pretend to bar the consideration of any subject, whatever its purport may be, but we do not propose, ourselves, to formulate any proposals in the first instance. We think it is absolutely necessary in a matter of this kind which involves so many considerations of detail, that there should be in the first instance a free interchange of opinion in order that we may not put before you suggestions which perhaps we should find afterwards were altogether out of harmony with your views, but if it appears hereafter desirable, after full discussion, to make proposals, I have no doubt we shall be able to do so.

In reference to this matter, also, I am placing papers before you which will give you a very full account of the present state of trade between the Colonies and the Mother Country, and also a matter which is very important for us to consider, of the condition of trade between the United Kingdom and foreign countries; and, without going into detail, I would say there are two salient facts which appear on the surface of these fuller returns which I shall put before you. The first is this: That if we chose—that is to say, that if those whom we represent chose—the Empire might be self-sustaining. It is so wide; its products are so various, its climates so different, that there is absolutely nothing which is necessary to our existence, hardly anything which is desirable as a luxury, which can not be produced within the borders of the Empire itself. And the second salient fact is that the Empire at the present time, and especially the United Kingdom—which is the great market of the world—derives the greater part of its necessaries from foreign countries, and that it exports the largest part of its available produce—surplus produce—also to foreign countries. This trade might be the trade, the inter-imperial trade, of the Empire. It is at the present time, as I say, a trade between the Empire and foreign countries. Now, I confess that to my mind that is not a satisfactory state of things, and I hope that you will agree with me that everything which can possibly tend to the interchange of products between the different parts of the Empire is deserving of our cordial encouragement. What we desire, what His Majesty's Government has publicly stated to be the object for which they would most gladly strive, is a free interchange. If you are unable to accept that as a principle, then I

31—6

8 GEORGE V, A. 1918

ask you how far you can approach to it? If a free interchange between the
different parts of the Empire could be secured, it would then be a matter for
separate consideration altogether what should be the attitude of the Empire
as a whole, or of its separate parts, towards foreign nations. The first thing
we have to do, the thing which touches us most nearly is to consider how far
we can extend the trade between the different parts of the Empire—the reciprocal
trade.

GEOGRAPHY.

Time: 2 hours.

NOTE.—Candidates will take Question 1 and any five others.

Values.

20 1. On an outline map show the position and name of each lake, river and
       canal on the great waterway between Lake Superior and the
       Atlantic. Indicate also five places where railway cars are taken
       across from Canada to the United States by bridge, tunnel or
       ferry, naming the Canadian and the United States town or
       city connected at each crossing.

16 2. What is the size, position and population of Newfoundland? What
       are the products of its forests, its mines and its surrounding
       waters? Name and locate its three most important towns or
       cities.

16 3. Write a short paragraph on each of the following:—
       (a) The reason why the coast of Alaska has a milder climate
           than the coast of Labrador, although Alaska is farther north.
       (b) The natural advantages of the Niagara district for fruit-
           growing.
       (c) The natural advantages and the natural disadvantages of
           Hudson Bay as a waterway for the shipment of western
           grain.
       (d) The usefulness of the Ottawa River.

16 4. The dependencies of the United States are Porto Rico, Alaska, Hawaii,
       and the Phillipines. With as great accuracy as you can, give the
       location of each dependency, a description of its people, and
       make a list of from three to five of its chief products.

16 5. From what countries does Great Britain obtain her supply of wheat,
       wool, cotton, lumber, paper, gasoline, rubber, beef, horses, nickel,
       sugar, tea, coffee, silk, hemp, jute?

16 6. Locate and tell some interesting fact about each: Ypres, Plymouth,
       Vladivostock, Dingwall, Bucharest, Trebizond, Bordeaux, Faroe
       Islands, Lemberg, Bagdad, Corinth.

16 7. Name eight republics of South America with their capitals. Where are
       Falkland Islands, Barbadoes, Trinidad, British Guiana, Guaya-
       quil, Valparaiso, Para, Strait of Magellan?

HISTORY.

Time: 2 hours.

NOTE.—Five questions only are to be attempted.

Value—100.

1. Write notes on: The Hundred Associates, The Seigniors and Seigniorial Tenure, The office and duties of an Intendant, The Jesuit Order and its work in Canada.

2. How did the Hudson's Bay Company originate? What lands had it control of, and what were its powers? What profits did the company obtain, and what benefits accrued to England?

3. What is meant by the North-west Passage? Who were attracted to it and attempted to explore it? How far were they successful, and what lands were explored at the same time?

4. Who were the United Empire Loyalists? Where did they locate, and what did Britain do for them? How did they succeed in (a) Settlement, (b) Government in Upper Canada?

5. What were the causes of Papineau's Rebellion? By a rough map show the chief centres of the Rebellion, and tell how it was quelled? What became of Papineau?

6. When was Lord Elgin Governor General of Canada? Outline fully his work as Governor and point out the benefits from his rule to (a) Canada, (b) Britain.

7. What methods did Napoleon adopt to defeat Britain (a) on the sea, (b) on land? Is there any similarity between Napoleon's methods then and Germany's methods now to overthrow Britain?

SPELLING AND DICTATION.

SPELLING.

Time: 30 minutes.

Value—50.

NOTE.—Copy the following, correcting the errors in spelling; 5 marks will be deducted for every misspelled word in your copy.

I red not long ago a diahtribe by a riter who seamed very anxous to senshure exadgerrated statemeants by Canadians about there country. Not only were his owne paiges full of all sorts of inackewrasies, but many of his assurshuns were so phantastickally untrew that they were only laffed at by peapel who new the facts. Unfortunaitly, most of his readers in the Old Country were not in a possition to no all the facts, and were therefour at the mercy of his deseptions.

31—6½

8 GEORGE V, A. 1918

I have nown Canada intimaytly now for thurty years, boath by long rezidents and by repeated journies of careful investigashun from one end of the country to the other. If their is one thing I obgect to, it is exadgerrashun. Even if it were not a vise in it self, it shood be sevearly condemned as leeding to disapointment when its victoms are at last undecieved; and kno senshure is two strong for anny interrested or responsable partys "with an acks to grind" who make misleeding staitmeants too intending emmigrants or two possable purchacers of land. I have nown peapel who have been thus mislead; and.I am glad that the Canadian Government emfaticaly discountinances annything that mite lead to sutch a result.

DICTATION.

Time: 30 minutes.

Value—50.

NOTE.—This paper should not be seen by the candidates. The Examiner will read over the whole extract once, and then reread it slowly and distinctly, indicating to the candidates the occurrence of each full stop. A third reading of the whole extract may be given if sufficient time remains. The whole time occupied should not be more than half an hour.

May I be permitted, without any impropriety, to recall that it was my privilege to experience and to appreciate that courtesy, made up of dignity and grace, which was famous all the world over, but of which no one could have an appropriate opinion, unless he had been the recipient of it. In a character so complex and diversified, one may ask what was the dominant feature, what was the supreme quality, the one characteristic which marked the nature of the man. Was it his incomparable genius for finance? Was it his splendid oratorical powers? Was it his marvellous fecundity of mind? In my estimation it was not any one of these qualities. Great as they were, there was one still more marked, and if I have to give my own impression, I would say that the one trait which was dominant in his nature, which marked the man more distinctly than any other, was his intense humanity, his paramount sense of right, his abhorrence of injustice, wrong and oppression, wherever they might show themselves. Injustice, wrong, oppression acted upon him, as it were, mechanically, and aroused every fibre of his being, and from that moment to the repairing of the injustice, the undoing of the wrong, and the destruction of the oppression, he gave his mind, his heart, his soul, his whole life, with an energy, with an intensity, with a vigour paralleled by no man, unless it be the first Napoleon.

TRANSCRIPTION AND WRITING.

Time: 1 hour.

Value—50 for each.

The candidate is required to make a neat, clean and correct copy of the manuscript handed to him with this slip, writing out all abbreviations at full length, and correcting any misspellings. The words scored through are to be omitted, and the interlineations and the marginal and other additions are to be inserted in their proper places as indicated. All changes or corrections, other than these, will be counted as errors. This paper will be taken as a test of writing also.

Civil Service of Canada— Qualifying Examination

§/ tr/   It seems to be, therefore, justifiable
to state that to improve the river by
means of storage is a work of great import.,
& one upon wh. the safe navigatⁿ of
the canal appears dependant. The informatⁿ
§/   collected to date shows that there is
exist/   sufficient storage, to control the river
stet/   at ordinary spring level, & fr. the surveys
with the flows   made & informatⁿ collected, the cost
previously shown,   of the reservoirs for storage is not ex-
§/   cessive when you compare it with the
benefits derived. Their operatⁿ however,
tr/   is a questⁿ of some moment by reason
of their no. & inaccessibility, but it is
beleived that a more extended study
will develop a system by wh. this can
stet/   be done at a reasonable cost. This wd.
tr./   require probably the constⁿ of telephone
lines & some other minor work, but it is
not expected that the inaccessibility of this
for any grt. period/   country can long continue.
Aside fr. the advantages to
future navigatⁿ that can be obtained
fr. them, there are others wh. are sufficient
tr./stet/   in themselves to guarantee the constⁿ of

, if not the total ~~many of them~~. The flood of 1876 is still
no. sufficiently well remembered by those ~~who were~~ engaged in industries along the river to
tr./ state that its recurrence is feared greatly. ~~I~~ It is ~~not~~ possible to estimate what ~~the~~ in case of result⁹ damages might be ~~if there was~~ a recurrence of the flood of the magnitude of that of 1876.

tr./ The river, ~~at that time~~, particularly at Ottawa, was much less restricted, ~~&~~ the then improvements & const⁹ built since ~~that time~~ by the various power-users have no doubt
tr./ now interfered seriously with the free flow of the river.

(6) Examination for Positions in the Lower Grades, Inside Service, May, 1917.

ARITHMETIC.

Time: 1½ hours.

NOTE.—No marks will be allowed unless the full work is shown and the answer is correct.

Values.

9   1. Write in words: 400019; 9070700; 8293500009.

6   2. Write in figures: Ninety-five million five thousand six hundred and seventeen; Twenty-nine billion five hundred million four hundred and eighteen.

17   3. Add: 62794; 8995; 6786; 934895; 27683; 68897; 4678; 896787; 56883; 989; 8673; 935978.

17   4. Multiply 673098540 by 40598.

17   5. Divide 63501419912 by 8736.

17   6. Subtract 4987 × 3678 from 6872 × 3945.

17   7. A dealer bought 195 barrels of apples at $4.75 a barrel. He sold 86 barrels at $5.65 a barrel, 76 barrels at $4.95 a barrel, and the rest at $4.50 a barrel. Find his total gain.

──────

100

SPELLING AND DICTATION.

SPELLING.

The paper set is that given on page 78.

DICTATION.

The paper set is that given on page 79.

WRITING.

The paper set is that given on page 79.

8 GEORGE V, A. 1918

(7) Competitive Examination for Positions in Subdivision B of the Third Division, Inside Service, May, 1917.

ARITHMETIC.

Time: $2\frac{1}{2}$ hours.

NOTE.—Candidates will do the first question and any other six. All work must be shown.

Value—100.

1. (a) Find the G.C.M. of 148; 444; 592; 703.
   (b) Divide 152.847420 by 30.207.
   (c) Simplify $\dfrac{2\frac{1}{2}-\frac{1}{3} \text{ of } 1\frac{1}{5}+\frac{4}{5}}{\frac{2}{5}+\frac{1}{3} \text{ of } \frac{5}{8} \div \frac{4}{5} \times \frac{1}{2}\frac{2}{5}}$

2. A man commenced business with $3000 capital. The first year he gained $22\frac{1}{2}\%$, which he added to his capital; the second year he gained 30% of this new capital and put the gain into his business; the third year he lost $16\frac{2}{3}\%$ of his capital for that year. Find his net gain for the three years.

3. A fruit dealer bought 168 cases of oranges and lemons for $551.25. There were $\frac{2}{3}$ as many oranges as lemons, and the latter were worth $1.25 per case more than the former. Find the cost of each per case.

4. A contractor invested $30000 in twelve houses of equal value. He sold 4 of them at once for $3200 each and invested the proceeds at 7%. He rented 6 of the houses at $22.50 per month each, and the other two were idle. He paid taxes on $\frac{2}{3}$ of the cost of the unsold property at the rate of 14 mills on the dollar. In one year how much more did he make than if he had invested the $30000 at 7%?

5. A mason charges 27c. a square yard for plastering the walls and ceiling of four rooms. The first room is 20 feet long and 8 feet wide; the second is 18 feet long and 9 feet wide; the third is 12 feet long and 7 feet wide, and the fourth is 18 feet long and 16 feet wide. Find the total cost, each room being 12 feet high.

6. A drover bought a number of cows for $4375 and sold a number of them at $43 a head for the sum of $3655, thereby gaining on those sold $680. Find how much he must get for the remainder per head in order to gain $400 more.

7. On March 10, 1917, Wise & Co. sold an automobile for $1500 to Henry Black, who gave his note for 60 days. Wise & Co. had the note discounted immediately at the bank at 8% per annum.
   (a) Find how much money the bank paid to Wise & Co.
   (b) Write out the note given by Henry Black.

8. Green coffee when roasted losses $\frac{1}{5}$ of its weight. If a grocer buys green coffee at $25\frac{1}{4}$c. a pound and sells it at 35 c. a pound after it is roasted, what will he gain by selling 510 pounds?

BOOK-KEEPING.

Time: 2½ hours.

Value 100—.

A Syndicate of four men, A. B. C. and D was formed to purchase a business property. Each contributed $10,000.00 to the Syndicate.

The property cost them $40,000.00, clear, May 1, 1916. It was leased to T. for five years at a rental of $4,000.00 per annum, payable monthly at the end of each month. All taxes and repairs were to be paid by the Syndicate. Real Estate Agents, R. E. & Co., were appointed to act for the Landlords and collect the rentals, for which they were to be allowed commission of 3 per cent on all rents collected and paid over to the Syndicate. At the end of each quarter the members of the Syndicate were to be given credit for their share of the net revenue, excepting any odd balance which might be left over.

The following amounts were collected by R. E. & Co. from the Tenant:—

May, 1916	$ 325 00	November, 1916	$200 00
June, 1916	325 00	December, 1916	275 00
July, 1916	225 00	January, 1917	225 00
August, 1916	300 00	February, 1917	350 00
September, 1916	400 00	March, 1917	325 00
October, 1916	375 00	April, 1917	300 00

Repairs amounting to $80.75 were allowed the Tenant, to be credited on his rent account.

R. E. & Co., after deducting their commission, handed over the balance to the Syndicate, in the following amounts, which were at once deposited in the Bank to the Syndicate's credit: May, $300.00; June, $300.00; July, $200.00; August, $300.00; September, $400.00; October, $350.00; November, $200.00; December, $250.00; January, $200.00; February, $325.00; March, $300.00; April, $300.00.

The Syndicate paid the following accounts by cheque: Taxes, $840.00; Insurance, $325.00; Water Rates, $60.00; Repairs, $275.00; Expenses, $38.00; and paid each member of the Syndicate $150.00 each quarter.

Use Cash-book, Journal and Ledger, and write up the above transactions, and show accounts for the Tenant, the Landlord, the Real Estate Agents, and each of the members of the Syndicate at the end of each quarter.

Take off a Trial Balance at the end of the year.

COMPOSITION.

Values. Time: 2½ hours.

40   1. Write a letter to a newspaper or magazine discussing one of the following subjects. The letter should contain not less than 250 words.

        Safety First.
        The Returned Soldier.
        Preparation for Peace.
        Home Gardening.

30   2. Write a brief summary of the following extract from a report on the transportation of supplies from Canada to England.

The prompt action of the government in adopting my suggestion has secured to Canadian manufacturers and farmers an uninterrupted outlet for the hundreds of millions of dollars worth of War Office orders, the acceptance of which would not have been possible but for the inauguration of an economical overseas service.

Further, the fact that the transports, owing to their regularity in sailings have been in a position to handle promptly the War Office supplies, which otherwise would have occupied space on regular liners, has been of distinct advantage to the export trade of Canada, and has released to that extent ocean space for commercial tonnage. Since the inauguration of the service, not a pound of Imperial Government transport has been forwarded on regular liners.

During the period.between 28th August, 1914, and 30th April, 1915, 244,913 gross tons were handled on account of Imperial and Dominion governments.

Between, however, the 1st of May and 30th November, 1915, there was an enormous expansion—over 410,000 tons being forwarded during that period (seven months), or about 67% more than was moved in the previous eight months.

The Overseas Department is now being called upon to provide for about 125,000 gross tons of munitions, war material, and supplies per month, or approximately one and a half million tons per annum, and the tonnage is still growing.

30   3. Write in well-constructed sentences a synopsis of the following letter from a " neutral " to the London Times.

What is England going to do? This was the whispered query that I heard time and again in Germany. For I found that the possible power of Britain is more truly appreciated and understood in Germany than in any other country in Europe to-day. The great German captains of industry, who have hitherto made the success of German arms possible, seem to realize that if ever the vast industrial might of Britain, so akin to their own, is properly mobilized, if its resources are consistently and adequately exploited, if every ounce of latent energy is made available, then, no matter how great a success German arms may have achieved, no matter how firmly entrenched German troops may stand on enemy soil, the tables will turn, and German chances of final victory will fade into limbo.

I have just crossed Great Britain from one end to the other, and I have visited innumerable towns and cities. Britain at last, after more than a year's delay, is mobilized for war. Her achievement to-day far surpasses the wildest idea of the " Kolossal ". I have seen factory after factory working steadily twenty-four hours a day, seven days in the week, employing thousands of men and women making shells, shells, shells! I have seen factory after factory making aeroplanes; I have seen guns being forged under hydraulic pressure of 12,000 tons; howitzers forged out of the stoutest steel, which requires sixteen hours in a blast furnace to heat.

I have seen shell cases pressed out of the living ingot in less than five minutes, and shells forged at a speed three times as great.

I have seen men working at great forges, where gun parts are cast, straining every nerve and muscle to accomplish their difficult tasks, handling vast lumps of red-hot metal with lightning dexterity. I have seen machine-guns by the hundreds, and rifles by the thousand—all of the most careful workmanship and finish.

. The whole North country has been turned into one vast arsenal. The deep pall of fog and smoke that hangs low over the great industrial centres of the Midlands, deeper, denser than it has been for some years past, means that England has at last turned with full energy to the mighty task. The achievement is the more remarkable when it is appreciated that all this work is merely a beginning.

GEOGRAPHY.

Time: 2 hours.

NOTE.—Candidates will take Question 1 and any other six.

Value—100.

1. Draw a map of Canada from the international boundary to the 60th parallel, outlining the provinces, locating and naming the two largest cities in each, and indicating the course of the Canadian Pacific Railway.

2. Give the location of each of the following lakes, stating the slope and province in which each is found: St. John, Nipigon, Champlain, Simcoe, Temiscaming, Winnipeg, Lesser Slave, Woods, Megantic, Athabasca, Nipissing, St. Clair, Rainy, and St. Peter.

3. Name in order, with capitals, those States of the American Union bordering on the Atlantic, and state whether their respective capitals are situated inland or on the seacoast.

4. (a) Name the five chief foodstuffs and the five chief raw materials for manufacture imported by Great Britain, and state from what part of the British Empire each comes in the greatest abundance. (b) Name four chief manufactured products exported by Great Britain to Canada, and in each case name a large city in Great Britain manufacturing the product mentioned.

5. Give, in order of importance, the seven provinces of Canada that lead in the production of fish, and name the three chief varieties caught in each.

6. Sketch a map of the Atlantic Ocean north of the Equator, locating Halifax, St. John, Sydney, New York, Boston, Portland, Liverpool, Bristol, Gibraltar, Lisbon, Bordeaux, and Bermudas.

7. Name and locate in each case two chief places in Canada engaged in the production of flour, steel, paper, cottons, sugar, salt, and boots and shoes.

8. What, where and for what noted are: Drummondville, Kitchener, Revelstoke, Levis, Gowganda, Kenora, Banff, Lethbridge, Tadoussac, and Springhill.

9. What waters are connected, and what lands are separated, by each of the following straits and channels: Gibraltar, Dover, The Sound, St. George's, North, Belle Isle, Canso, Davis, Northumberland, and Juan de Fuca.

8 GEORGE V, A. 1918

HISTORY.

Time: 2 hours.

Values.

20   1. Write brief notes (not more than five lines each) on any *five* of the following: Daniel O'Connell, William Lyon Mackenzie, Mirabeau, Lord Salisbury, Marshall Ney, Lord Elgin, and George Canning.

16   2. Name the Province in which you live, and tell how its revenue for purely Provincial purposes is obtained; *or*

   Enumerate the chief sources of the revenue raised in Canada for Federal purposes.

16   3. Tabulate in concise form the chief causes that led to the Lower Canada Rebellion in 1837-38. Give a very brief account of the events of 1837 in that Province.

16   4. Describe as clearly as you can the existing situation in regard to Home Rule in Ireland; *or*

   Write a note on Irish emigration, giving the underlying causes, the chief periods of emigration, and the parts of the world most affected by this emigration.

16   5. Outline the struggle to secure responsible government in any *one* of the following: Upper Canada, Lower Canada, Nova Scotia. In your opinion, what date definitely fixes the securing of this form of government for the Canadas? Why?

16   6. Explain the following: customs duty, excise duty, preferential tariff, revenue cutter, contraband of war, interned, running a blockade, admiralty prize court; *or*

   Outline briefly the system of government as it existed in Quebec under the French regime about 1725.

100

SHORTHAND.

Time allowed for transcription of notes: 1½ hours.

EIGHTY WORDS PER MINUTE.

Value—100.

The people of Canada were beginning to think of drawing their money out of the banks in gold. We were | threatened with a condition that might have produced a panic which would almost have paralysed the energies of Canada in | this war. We were obliged to prevent the exportation and hoarding of gold. We were obliged to make bank notes | good legal tender. We were obliged to provide that Dominion notes need not be redeemed in gold. These measures were | accepted by the country. Then, we were faced almost immediately afterwards with another very serious problem. The revenues of this | country had fallen enormously immediately after the outbreak of the war. Trade was almost paralysed; importation almost stopped, and exportation | as well, and then we found ourselves confronted with a very serious condition in a very large district in Western | Canada. There was this condition confronting us: the revenues of the country were shot to pieces on the one hand, | and on the other hand there was the need for some assistance to the people in that unfortunate district. We had the alternative, to display a lack of courage and to say that, confronted by a war such as was | upon us, with reduced revenues, it would be impossible for the Government to do anything or to attack the problem | in a courageous way; or we had the other alternative of doing what we could to relieve the situation. |

ONE HUNDRED WORDS PER MINUTE.

Canada has been particularly fortunate in the character of those who have been selected to be the representatives of the royal authority. They have all | been men of great eminence, whether eminence by character or eminence by ability, and most of them have been eminent for both ability and character. | It is due to those who have occupied that high office to say, when they had fulfilled their term and the time came for them | to sever their connection with us, they carried with them the gratitude, the esteem, the respect of all classes of the community. But no Governor | General who ever left our shores was followed with so much of the blessings and the affection of the people of Canada as was His | Royal Highness the Duke of Connaught. Undoubtedly, the peculiar enthusiasm with which he was received by us when he came to preside over the destinies | of Canada was due to the fact that he belonged to the Royal Family. But he earned the gratitude and respect of the Canadian people | by his own personal qualities; his devotion to duty; his high sense of honour; his simple, affable manners; his straightforward, democratic ways. And if the | whole truth is to be told, I believe everybody will agree with me, that in the impression which he made in Canada he himself was | not the sole factor; a great deal was due also to his gracious consort, a lady who, in her high station, gave, during the time | she was with us, an example of those exalted virtues ever dear to the British heart. It is said that when asked to become Governor, | he hesitated, and that he accepted the office for a period of not more than two years. His stay was probably prolonged by the war. |

8 GEORGE V, A. 1918

SPELLING AND DICTATION.

SPELLING.

The paper set is that given on page 83.

DICTATION.

The paper set is that given on page 84.

TYPEWRITING.

Time: 30 minutes.

Value—100.

Copy the following:

Nearly fifty years ago the first Parliament of the Dominion assembled· In it were the statesmen who had brought under one government Ontario, · Quebec, Nova Scotia and New Brunswick. These men, Macdonald, Brown, Cartier, Tupper and others, whose loyalty, determination and courage laid the foundation of the present Great Dominion, have been justified in their work by the growth, solidity and importance of this country. Confederation saw four provinces, with little common interest except loyalty to the Crown, brought into union; a half century has passed and the Canada of 1867 is now a mighty empire, stretching from the Atlantic to the Pacific, one-half of North America, comprising all the British possessions on this continent except Newfoundland.

The fathers of Confederation laid the foundation of a vaster country than they believed possible at the time. Then Canada was a colony of Great Britain; to-day she is a partner in world affairs, whether of peace or war.

A little over fifty years ago representatives from the four provinces met to consummate Confederation. Then there were doubts as to the stability of the proposed union; even as to the worth of overseas Dominions to the Empire. What a change in fifty years! Within a few weeks there will be another conference in London, when representatives from the overseas Dominions will sit in the councils of the Empire determining the best policy to pursue to win victory in the great world's war, and with that victory the preservation and strengthening of the bonds of empire. What Imperial or Colonial statesmen in 1867 would have even dreamed that within such a brief period the overseas Dominions could have won a partnership in the great British Empire?

The following table shows the properties purchased:—

Vendors.	Price.	Interest.
Mrs. Campbell	$16,500.00	$ 655.00
Mrs. Benneast	5,100.00	202.46
James McKay	6,500.00	257.62
C. Grossman	6,787.00	139.66
Mrs. Ireland	4,200.00	166.65
Mrs. Beelamy	6,787.00	269.44
John McLeod	7,250.00	
James Kerr	7,000.00	273.41
Mrs. Muir	10,250.00	
Mrs. McSpadden	122,700.00	4,991.85
	$193,074.00	$ 6,956.09

A Disabled Soldiers' Training Board consists of a member of the Provincial Commission, a vocational officer and a medical man. The duties of this Board are:

(a) To consider all cases which, in the light of the medical reports, appear to be subjects for special training, and to report upon each, with suitable recommendations, to the Military Hospitals Commission.

(b) To consider from time to time reports of the progress of men undergoing training, and to make recommendations as to change of treatment or of training, or its discontinuance.

Each Provincial Employment Commission has been asked to nominate suitable persons to act as an advisory committee on the training of disabled soldiers who are eligible for re-education. The personnel of this advisory committee includes, in most instances, some person acquainted with the processes of education, an agricultural educationalist, an employer, and a labour representative.

The duties of the Provincial Advisory Committee may be summarized as follows:—

(a) To prepare, with the assistance of the vocational officer, schemes of instructions in general subjects and elementary vocational training in, or in connection with, the convalescent homes or hospitals of the province.

(b) To organize and carry out schemes as may be approved.

(c) To maintain a regular inspection, preferably through the vocational officer, of all instruction being carried on.

(d) To make a survey of the facilities at present, and from time to time, available for vocational training in public educational institutions and private workshops, farms, etc.

(e) To assist the Employment Commission by providing definite information as to the training received by men who desire assistance in obtaining employment.

(f) To appoint or approve local sub-committees on training in connection with local employment committees in centres where it appears necessary to have such committees.

(g) Generally, to advise and assist in the training of returned soldiers in every possible way.

TRANSCRIPTION AND WRITING.

Time: 1 hour.

Value—50 for each.

The candidate is required to make a neat, clean and correct copy of the manuscript handed to him with this slip, writing out all abbrevations at full length, and correcting any misspellings. The words scored through are to be omitted, and the interlineations and the marginal and other additions are to be inserted in their proper places as indicated. All changes or corrections, other than these, will be counted as errors. This paper will be taken as a test of writing also.

Cwl Service of Canada — Third Div Clerkships.
Extract from Report on Constⁿ of Georgian Bay
Canal — As a large amt. of lumber is manu-
factured at ~~the capital~~ Ottawa, the questⁿ of pass^g
saw-logs & pulp-wood down the river ~~at the~~
~~time of~~ constⁿ & after the waterway ~~canal~~ is in

tr/   operatⁿ will (here be taken up). For yrs.
saw-logs have been floated down the Ottawa
in any way ∧   in booms, without raft^g them, together ∧ — Ar-
riv^g at the head of a rapid, the boom has
§/   been opened, & the logs ~~have been~~ allowed
to plunge (in a haphazard ~~way~~ manner) over the
tr/§/   chutes. (Log slides ~~have been built~~) at a
tr./   (few pts only), & the sq. timber slides
§/   have fallen into ~~complete~~ decay, (two rafts
tr./   only) hav^g passed down dur^g the last ten yrs.
The saw-logs, drift^g over the rapids, have
in heaps ∧   piled ∧ on rocks & islands dur^g low water,
& the high water of the spring fails to float
stet/   them ∧ all off. Many logs have ~~become~~ water-soaked
& float in ~~an~~ ~~upright~~ vertically positⁿ, the end
§/   project^g just above ~~the~~ water, or float^g
unseen (perhaps) just beneath the surface.
These "dead-heads," as ~~are~~ they are called
§/   ~~them~~, cd. not be ~~allowed~~ endured in a navigible
stet/   channel, wh. they wd. be a ~~constant~~ menace

to steel boats - mov'd at full speed. When
the waterway is open, logs can't not be
,besides endanger'g⟩ allowed to float loose on its surface, for
the skin of the ⟩they may be threshed in by the screw,
boat, ⟩ break'g the propellor blades & injur'g the
tr./ machin'y. It will be necess'y, therefore,
in some form⟨ to raft the logs, & pass them through the
locks, like tows of barges.

,however,⟨ At Ottawa, pass'g them through
the canal wd. bring them below the falls,
tr./ instead of above, wh. they are received now
at the mill. ⚹

tr./ Dur'g the period of const'n,
wh. will last fr. three to five yrs., special
arrangements will be req'd to pass the
logs down to the various mills.

tr./ ⚹ It will be necess'y, therefore, to provide
smell
a lock for the passage of the rafted
tr./ logs into the basin above the dam
s/ at the Chaudiere.

8 GEORGE V, A. 1918

(8) Competitive Examination for Positions in Subdivision B of the Second Division, Inside Service, May, 1917.

ALGEBRA.

Time: $2\frac{1}{2}$ hours.

Value—100.

NOTE.—Seven questions only are to be attempted.

1. Simplify

   (a) $\quad \dfrac{a}{4} - \left[\dfrac{2c-3a}{4} - \left\{c - \dfrac{a-2c}{2} - \left(2c - \dfrac{3a+c}{2}\right)\right\}\right]$,

   (b) $\quad \dfrac{a-7a^{\frac{1}{2}}}{a-5\sqrt{a}-14} \div \left(1 + \dfrac{2}{\sqrt{a}}\right)^{-1}$

2. Express, as the product of four factors, each of the following expressions:—

   (a) $3(6x^2+5x)^2 - 10(6x^2+5x) - 8$;

   (b) $(a-b)(b^3-c^3) - (a^3-b^3)(b-c)$.

3. Solve the equations:

   (a) $\dfrac{x}{y} + \dfrac{y}{x} = 2\frac{1}{2}$

   $x+y=6$.

   (b) $x^2 - xy = 8x+3$

   $xy - y^2 = 8y - 6$.

4. (a) Find a number of two digits such that if the number is divided by the product of its digits the quotient is $5\frac{1}{3}$, and such that if 9 is substracted from the original number the order of the digits is reversed?

   (b) If $\sqrt{x}$ varies as $\sqrt[3]{y}$, and if $x = 4$ when $y = 64$, what will be the value of x when y has the value 27?

5. (a) Find the equation whose roots are the reciprocals of the roots of the equation $5x^2 - 20x + 17 = 0$.

   (b) Prove that the roots of the equation $(q^2-4pr)x^2 + 4(p+r)x - 4 = 0$ are real for all values of p, q, r, positive and negative.

6. (a) In an arithmetical progression there are 21 terms. The sum of the three middle terms is 129; and the sum of the last three terms is 237. Find the progression.

   (b) If a, b, c are three numbers in geometrical progression, prove that

   $$a^2b^2c^2\left(\dfrac{1}{a^3} + \dfrac{1}{b^3} + \dfrac{1}{c^3}\right) = a^3 + b^3 + c^3.$$

7. Find the square roots of:

   (a) $3 - \dfrac{6x}{a} - \dfrac{2a}{3x} + \dfrac{a^2}{9x^2} + \dfrac{9x^2}{a^2}$,

   (b) $19 - 4\sqrt{12}$.

8. (a) Numbers are formed by writing the six digits, 1, 2, 3, 4, 5, 6 in every possible order. How many of these numbers are greater than 560,000?

   (b) From an assembly consisting of 12 Conservatives and 9 Liberals, in how many ways can a committee of six be chosen so as to contain not more than two Liberals?

9. (a) Expand $(1-2x^3)^{\frac{3}{2}}$ as far as the fourth term, and simplify the result.

   (b) In the expansion of $(1+x)^{m+n}$ show that the coefficient of x^m and x^n are equal. Find the numerical value of this coefficient when m = 3 and n = 9.

10. (a) Show that $\log_a M^{\frac{p}{q}} = \frac{p}{q} \log_a M$.

   (b) Find the fifth root of 0·01008, having given

   $\log\ 2 = 0·3010300,$ $\log 30 = 1·4771213,$
   $\log 70 = 1·8450980,$ $\log 398·742 = 2·6006921.$

ARITHMETIC.

Time: $2\frac{1}{2}$ hours.

NOTE.—Six questions only are to be attempted. The details of the work must be given.

Value—100.

1. Reduce $\dfrac{\frac{10}{3} + \frac{4}{3} - 1 - \frac{24}{7}(\frac{4}{5} + \frac{1}{9})}{\frac{3}{2}(\frac{7}{4} - 1) - \frac{4}{3}(\frac{7}{4} - \frac{1}{10})}$ to its simplest form.

2. Compute the value of $\dfrac{1}{\sqrt{3}+1} + \dfrac{1}{\sqrt{2}-1}$ correct to four decimal places.

3. The present worth of a bill of $442.75 is $385. Find how long the bill has to run at $4\frac{1}{2}$ per cent per annum, simple interest.

4. By selling a carriage for $73.15 I should lose 5 per cent. At what price must I sell it to gain 15 per cent.

5. Find the compound interest on $8,750 for $1\frac{1}{2}$ years at $3\frac{1}{4}$ per cent per annum, payable half-yearly.

6. A person finds that he can obtain $25 more per annum by investing in $3\frac{1}{2}$ per cent stock at 96 than in 3 per cent stock at 88. How much has he to invest?

7. A could do a certain piece of work by himself in 24 days, and B could do it by himself in 36 days. If after A has worked at it 14 days B joins him, and they both work together, how soon will it be finished?

8. A merchant who sold his goods at a profit of 10 per cent found that when he allowed $2\frac{1}{2}$ per cent discount off his selling price, his business increased by one-third. Find whether his total profits were increased or diminished by adopting this plan, and in what proportion.

9. What will be the length of fence required to enclose a circular field of $3\frac{1}{4}$ acres?

10. Find to the nearest ton what weight of stone will be required to line a semi-cylindrical tunnel 30 feet in internal diameter and 120 yards long. The lining is to be 15 inches thick, and 4 per cent of the volume of the lining is to be deducted for cement. One cubic foot of the stone employed weighs 170 lbs.

8 GEORGE V, A. 1918

BIOLOGY.

Time: 2½ hours.

NOTE.—Seven questions only are to be attempted: four in the first section and three in the second.

BOTANY.

Value—100.

1. Give an account of the structure and the functions of leaves.
2. Compare underground stems with roots.
3. Describe the reserve food-materials found in seeds.
4. Write the life-history of a horsetail (*Equisetum*).
5. Discuss the decomposition of organic matter in the soil, and its relation to agriculture..
6. Write short descriptions of *three* Canadian plants, no two of which belong to the same family.

ZOOLOGY.

1. Describe the chief features of the skeleton in any common fish.
2. In what respects does the digestive system of a bird differ from that of a mammal, and how are these differences explained on a basis of habit?
3. Describe the gills and circulation of the blood in the fresh-water mussel. Why is respiration an important function?
4. Describe the plan of segmentation in the common earthworm, mentioning those organs of the body to which the segmental arrangement does not apply.
5. Discuss the importance of the conservation of wild life in Canada.

BOOK-KEEPING.

The paper set is that given on page 89.

CHEMISTRY.

Time: 2½ hours.

NOTE.—Seven questions only are to be attempted. All definite chemical reactions should be expressed by equations.

Value—100.

1. What is meant by reversible reaction? Tell what you know about chemical equilibrium and the laws which govern it.
2. What is a normal solution? How do you prepare such a solution? What weight do you use of the following substances when you make a litre of a normal solution of them: hydrochloric acid (HCl); sulphuric acid (H_2SO_4); sodium chloride ($NaCl$); calcium hydrate ($Ca(OH)_2$. *Atomic weights:* $H = 1 \cdot 008$; $O = 16$; $Cl = 35 \cdot 46$; $Na = 23$; $S = 32 \cdot 06$; $Ca = 40 \cdot 07$.
3. From what source is phosphorus obtained? By what process?
4. For what reasons do you consider the air as a mixture and not a compound?

5. How do you prepare sulphuric acid (*a*) in the laboratory, (*b*) industrially?

6. What are the chemical products of the dry distillation of wood? What do you know about methyl alcohol?

7. What is saponification? Write an equation to illustrate reactions of this type.

8. In what group of organic compounds do you place starch? What bodies contain it in nature? What is the action when it is boiled with dilute acid?

9. Describe practical means of preparing acetylene? What are its properties and uses?

10. I wish to prepare 200 litres of hydrogen bromide. How much bromine and phosphorus must I use?

$$PBr_3 + 3H_2O = PO_3H_3 + 3HBr.$$
$$P = 31 \cdot 04; \ Br = 79 \cdot 92.$$

COMPOSITION.

Time: 3 hours.

NOTE.—Candidates are advised to give attention to their writing.

Values.

30 1. Write an essay of at least five paragraphs on *one* of the following subjects:—
   (*a*) Canada's Jubilee, 1867 to 1917.
   (*b*) A Description of One of the Naval Engagements of the War.
   (*c*) A Week on the Farm.
   (*d*) Aerial Navigation.

10 2. Write in correct form a note of apology to a friend for failing to keep an appointment.

15 3. Criticise the construction of the following sentences, and rewrite in improved form:—
   (*a*) For thou art a girl as much brighter than her,
        As he is a poet sublimer than me.
   (*b*) He preferred to know the worst than to dream the best.
   (*c*) He brought a picture under his arm which he asked permission to exhibit.
   (*d*) I will have great pleasure in accepting your invitation.
   (*e*) The manager is one of those who never interferes in matters which he has no control over.

10 4. Give the literal meaning of the following derivative words, that is, show by your definitions that you know what the prefixes and affixes mean:—*submarine, immigration, co-operate, bullock, transport, precaution, insecurity, recolonize, unspeakable, gosling.*

35 5. Write in concise form the gist of the following communication. Give a heading or title to each of your paragraphs. The synopsis should contain all the salient points, and nothing that is unimportant.

The Government of the King, which has associated itself with the answer handed by the President of the French Council to the American Ambassador on behalf of all, is particularly desirous of paying tribute to the sentiment of

8 GEORGE V, A. 1918

humanity which prompted the President of the United States to send his note to the belligerent powers, and it highly esteems the friendship expressed for Belgium through his kindly intermediation. It desires as much as Mr. Woodrow Wilson to see the present war ended as soon as possible.

But the President seems to believe that the statesmen of the two opposing camps pursue the same objects of war. The example of Belgium unfortunately demonstrates that this is in no wise the fact. Belgium has never, like the Central Powers, aimed at conquests. The barbarous fashion in which the German Government has treated, and is still treating, the Belgian Nation does not permit the supposition that Germany will preoccupy herself with guaranteeing in the future the rights of the weak nations which she has not ceased to trample under foot since the war, let loose by her, began to desolate Europe. On the other hand, the Government of the King has noted with pleasure and with confidence the assurances that the United States is impatient to co-operate in the measures which will be taken after the conclusion of peace, to protect and guarantee the small nations against violence and oppression.

Previous to the German ultimatum, Belgium only aspired to live upon good terms with all her neighbours; she practised with scrupulous loyalty towards each one of them the duties imposed by her neutrality. In the same manner she has been rewarded by Germany for the confidence she placed in her. Through her, from one day to the other, without any plausible reason, her neutrality was violated, and the Chancellor of the Empire, when announcing to the Reichstag this violation of right and of treaties, was obliged to recognize the iniquity of such an act and to predetermine that it would be repaired.

But the Germans, after the occupation of Belgian territory, displayed no better observance of the rules of international law or the stipulations of the Hague Convention. They have, by taxation, as heavy as it is arbitrary, drained the resources of the country; they have intentionally ruined its industries, destroyed whole cities, put to death and imprisoned a considerable number of inhabitants. Even now, while they are loudly proclaiming their desire to put an end to the horrors of war, they increase the rigours of the occupation by deporting into servitude Belgian workmen by the thousands.

If there is a country which has a right to say that it has taken up arms to defend its existence, it is assuredly Belgium. Compelled to fight or to submit to shame, she passionately desires that an end be brought to the unprecedented sufferings of her population. But she could only accept a peace which would assure her, as well as equitable reparation, security and guarantees for the future.

The American people, since the beginning of the war, have manifested for the Belgian nation its most ardent sympathy. It is an American committee, the Committee for Relief in Belgium, which, in close union with the Government of the King and the National Committee, displays, an untiring devotion and marvellous activity in revictualling Belgium. The Government of the King is happy to avail itself of this opportunity to express its profound gratitude to the Commission for Relief as well as to the generous Americans eager to relieve the misery of the Belgian population. Finally, nowhere more than in the United States have the abductions and deportations of Belgian civilians provoked such a spontaneous movement of protest, action and indignant reproof.

These facts, entirely to the honour of the American nation, allow the Government of the King to entertain the legitimate hope that at the time of the definitive settlement of the war, the voice of the Entente powers will find in the United States a unanimous echo to claim in favour of the Belgian nation, innocent victim of German ambition and covetousness, the rank and the place which its irreproachable past, the valour of its soldiers, its fidelity to honour, and its remarkable faculties for work assigned to it among the civilized nations.

ECONOMICS.

Time: 2½ hours.

NOTE.—Six questions only are to be attempted.

Value—100.

1. (a) Define Land, Capital, Labour. (b) What arguments for and against including land and capital in the same category? (c) Do commodities have value because they embody labour, or does labour derive its value from the commodities it helps to produce?

2. Explain the banking facilities which the new Federal Reserve Banks of the United States are meant to provide, and compare with the manner in which similar needs are provided for by Canadian banks.

3. Have the experiences of the war tended to strengthen or to weaken the arguments for increased governmental regulation, supervision, or control, of industrial and commercial enterprises? Discuss.

4. (a) From what sources and on what terms are the farmers of Canada securing short-term and long-term credit? (b) What additional facilities in rural credits have the Provinces of Manitoba and Saskatchewan sought to provide?

5. (a) What are the main 'axes employed in the different Provinces for raising municipal revenues? (b) Do the experiences of our western cities justify the use of the " single " land tax for municipal taxation?

6. Outline the methods employed in recent Canadian and British war finance, (a) in the way of increased taxation, and (b) in public borrowing.

7. (a) Explain the methods employed by our Labour Department to measure increase or decrease in cost of living. (b) Indicate the advance of prices in Canada since the beginning of the war and compare with advance in other countries, and give the causes. (c) What is meant by the quantity theory of money? Apply it to this problem of advancing prices.

8. Why was it that the London Stock Exchange, the mechanism of international trade and the banking system of England were so embarrassed by the war, and how did the Imperial Government come to their relief?

9. (a) For the fiscal year of 1915 Canada imported gold coin and bullion to the value of $131,992,992. Why? and whence? (b) In the calendar year 1915 the United States imported gold to the value of $451,954,590, and for the year of 1916 to the amount of $685,990,234. Account for this great increase of gold and indicate the use being made of it, and its effect upon prices and foreign trade.

8 GEORGE V, A. 1918

10. For the last four calendar years the foreign trade of Canada (merchandise) is as follows:—

	Imports.	Exports.	Balance.
1913..........	$678,169,442	$ 460,519,246	− $217,650,196
1914..........	481,319,309	428,315,512	− $ 52,007,797
1915....,....	450,547,774	653,488,412	+ $202,940,638
1916..........	776,731,891	1,112,244,002	+ $347,713,111

(a) Account for the drop in imports after 1913, and for the recent great increase in exports. (b) What are our main markets, and what are the chief articles of export that have brought about our increase in trade? (c) How were we settling our balance in 1913, and what are we doing with our balance now?

FRENCH AND ENGLISH.

Time: 2½ hours.

Value—100.

1. *Translate into French:*

While an author is living, it is not extraordinary that mankind should form an erroneous estimate of his works. The influence which prejudice and partiality often possess over the minds of his contemporaries, is incompatible with a correct decision of his merits. It is not until time has effaced the recollection of party feelings, when the virtues and foibles of the man are forgotten, and warm emotions of friendship or resentment are no longer felt, that the merit of an author can be fairly ascertained. So variable is public opinion, which is often formed without examination, and liable to be warped by caprice, that works of real merit are frequently left for posterity to discover and admire, while the pompous efforts of impertinence and folly are the wonders of the age. The gigantic genius of Shakespeare so far surpassed the learning and penetration of his times, that his productions were then little read and less admired.

2. *Translate into English:*

On aurait beau dire que la politesse n'est qu'une enveloppe, une écorce dont l'absence n'implique pas essentiellement un vice du cœur, cette enveloppe, cette écorce est necessaire dans la société pour éviter les froissements qui peuvent se produire soit entre les personnes ordinairement étrangères les unes aux autres, soit entre des membres de même famille. Les hommes en société sont ainsi faits; nos théories ne les changent pas. Les plus belles, les plus pures qualités pourraient être méconnues et même importunes si ceux qui les possèdent, se confiant dans l'excellence du fond, négligeaient la forme. Il n'est pas permis de parler sèchement en disant des choses justes, ni de faire du bien avec des manières blessantes. La vraie politesse ne consiste pas simplement dans un attachement rigoureux aux formules cérémonieuses; elle consiste dans l'étude délicate des sentiments d'autrui et dans les égards soigneusement accordés à ces sentiments.

3. *Write a French Composition (about 200 words) on* ONE *of the following subjects:-*

Description of a Storm.
The Value of Time.
On Literary Evils.

GEOGRAPHY.

Time: 2½ hours.

Values.

5   1. (a) Explain fully how by burning damp straw a light frost may be prevented from injuring young crops or fruit-blossoms.

5   (b) How is the water-supply of a country affected by the destruction of the forests? Explain fully.

5   (c) What is the " Laurentian penneplain "? Explain each of the two words in this connection.

6   2. (a) Name the *six* largest lakes of Canada west of Lake Superior.

6   (b) Name the *six* principal rivers of New Brunswick *or* the *six* principal rivers of Manitoba. (Only one province to be taken.)

6   (c) Name the *six* largest cities or towns of Canada east of Montreal.

10   3. (a) Describe the position on the map of any *five* of the following: Athabasca Landing, Beaufort Sea, Bras d'Or Lake, Hamilton Inlet, Marble Island, Michipicaten Island, Picton, Lake St. Peter.

10   (b) Describe the boundaries of the Province of Ontario.

10   4. (a) Name *five* of the National Parks of Canada, giving the position of each on the map.

8   (b) Name the *four* principal canals of Canada other than those along the St. Lawrence River, and state what natural obstacle to navigation was avoided in each case.

9   (c) What are the principal kinds of fish caught or sold in Canada, and in what waters is each kind chiefly found?

5   5. (a) Name the *five* principal colonies lost by Germany during the present war.

9   (b) Name the countries of Europe that are still neutral in the war, and describe their position on the map.

6   (c) Name the *six* principal cities or towns of the North of England.

8 GEORGE V, A. 19˙8

GEOLOGY.

Time: 2½ hours.

NOTE.—Not more than six questions are to be attempted. The first two questions must be answered. Four of the remaining questions (3 to 8) are to be answered. Be careful to answer separately the different parts of the questions.

Values.

16   1. State the chemical composition, the crystal form, the colour, and the economic uses of each of the following minerals: (a) Pyrite, (b) Ortholclase, (c) Cassiterite, (d) Magnetite.

16   2. (a) Name and state the mineral composition of *two* rocks that might occur in a batholith.

   (b) Name and state the mineral composition of *two* rocks that might occur in a dyke.

   (c) Name and describe *one* metamorphic rock.

17   3. (a) Give proofs of the secular elevation of land: (i) In Post-Glacial time; (ii) in remote geological time.

   (b) State some evidence of the degradation of land which you have observed yourself.

17   4. (a) What rocks are characteristic of each of the following subdivisions of the Pre-Cambrian: Laurentian, Grenville, Keeweenan?

   (b) State definitely *one* locality of occurrence in Canada of each of these formations.

17   5. (a) Name *two* phyla (branches) of Invertebrate fossils that you would consider as of especial value in stratigraphic geology.

   (b) Give full reasons for your selection.

   (c) Name *two* phyla of little stratigraphic value.

   (d) Give full reasons for your selection.

17   6. (a) To what systems do the rocks of the Rocky Mountains proper belong?

   (b) When and in what manner were these ranges formed?

   (c) Name the chief passes through these ranges, and state the railway or railways which make use of each.

17   7. (a) Name some typical Cretaceous fossils.

   (b) Indicate the geographical distribution of Cretaceous rocks in Canada.

   (c) What economic products are obtained from these rocks?

17   8. Explain fully why Canada is indebted to the Glacial Age for the following:—

   (a) Water-powers.

   (b) Gravel beds far from existing waters.

   (c) The easy gradient of the National Transcontinental Railway through northern Quebec and Ontario. -

GEOMETRY.

Time: $2\frac{1}{2}$ hours.

NOTE.—Not more than seven questions are to be attempted.

Value—100.

1. (a) If two angles and a side of one triangle are equal respectively to two angles and the corresponding side of another triangle, the triangles are equal in all respects.

   (b) If two isosceles triangles are erected on the same or opposite sides of a common base, prove that the line joining the vertices bisects the vertical angles of the triangles, and is perpendicular to and bisects the common base.

2. (a) A quadrilateral which has two opposite sides equal and parallel must be a parallelogram.

   (b) ABCD is a parallelogram, and X, Y are the middle points of the sides AD, BC. If Z is a point on XY, or XY produced, show that the triangle AZB is one-quarter of the parallelogram ABCD.

3. (a) Prove that triangles on the same base and between the same parallels are equal in area. What is this area in terms of the length of the base and the distance apart of the parallels?

   (b) Bisect a triangle by a straight line passing through a given point in one of its sides.

4. (a) The sum of the squares on two sides of a triangle is equal to twice the square on half the base together with twice the square on the median to the base.

   (b) In any quadrilateral the sum of the squares on the sides equals the sum of the squares on the diagonals together with four times the square on the line joining the middle points of the diagonals.

5. (a) Equal chords of a circle are equidistant from the centre.

   (b) In a given circle draw a chord which shall be equal in length to one given straight line (not greater than the diameter) and parallel to another.

6. (a) The opposite angles of any quadrilateral inscribed in a circle are together equal to two right angles.

   (b) ABC is a triangle. P, Q, R are points on BC, CA, AB, respectively. Show that the circles described about the triangles AQR, BRP and CPQ meet in a point.

7. (a) Construct a square equal in area to a given rectangle.

   (b) Describe a circle to touch a given circle, and to touch a given straight line at a given point.

8. (a) To describe the escribed circle of the triangle ABC which touches the side BC and the other two sides produced.

   (b) Derive an expression for the radius of the escribed circle in terms of the sides and the area of the triangle.

9. (a) The areas of similar triangles are proportional to the squares on corresponding sides.

   (b) ABC and ADE are secants to a circle from a point A outside the circle. Show that $\dfrac{\triangle \text{ABE}}{\triangle \text{ADC}} = \dfrac{\text{BE}^2}{\text{DC}^2}$.

10. (a) If from the vertical angle of a triangle a straight line is drawn perpendicular to the base, the rectangle contained by the sides of the triangle is equal to the rectangle contained by the perpendicular and the diameter of the circumcircle.

    (b) Construct a triangle, having given the base, the vertical angle and the rectangle contained by the sides.

8 GEORGE V, A. 1918

MODERN HISTORY.

Time: 2½ hours.

Value—100.

NOTE.—Six questions only are to be attempted.

1. Explain how the war began which resulted in the first siege of Louisbourg, and how it ended.
2. Outline the career of William Pitt, Earl of Chatham.
3. Explain how the first Republic came to be founded in France, and why the King was executed.
4. Why was the Peace of Amiens not enduring?
5. Why did Napoleon fall?
6. How did Free Trade come about in England?
7. Why did Canada not join the revolted Colonies in the American Revolution?
8. On what would you base the claim that Montcalm was a great general?
9. Indicate the place of Simcoe in the history of Upper Canada.
10. Explain the circumstances which brought Manitoba and British Columbia into the Canadian federation.

LATIN.

Time: 2½ hours.

NOTE.—Candidates will translate two only of the three following extracts, answering the questions appended to the extracts selected.

Value—100.

Translate:

I. Labienus etiam, cum Caesaris copias despiceret et Pompei consilium laudaret, "Noli", inquit, "existimare, Pompei, hunc esse exercitum, qui Galliam, Germaniamque vicerit. Omnibus interfui proeliis neque temere incognitam rem pronuntio. Minima pars illius exercitus superest: magna pars periit, quod accidere tot proeliis necesse fuit; multos pestilentia consumpsit, multi domum discesserunt, multi sunt relicti in Italia. An non audistis ex eis, qui per causam valetudinis remanserunt, cohortes Brundisi esse factas? Ac tamen quod fuit roboris duobus proeliis superioribus interiit." Haec, cum dixisset, iuravit se nisi victorem in castra non reversurum, reliquosque ut idem facerent, hortatus est.

(*a*) Parse, giving the principal parts of the verbs: *periit, audistis, remanserunt, reversurum.* (*b*) Explain the term *cohors.* (*c*) What mood is *vicerit,* and why? (*d*) What case is *proeliis* (*omnibus interfui proeliis*), and why? (*e*) What case is *Brundisi?*

II. Hac re audita, barbarus, nihil doli subesse ratus, postridie loco sibi a benissimo, hostibus opportunissimo, adeo angusto mari conflixit, ut eius multitudo navium explicari (explicare = *to deploy into line*) non potuerit. Victus ergo est magis consilio Themistoclis quam armis Graeciae. Hic quamquam male rem gesserat, tamen tantas habebat copias relictas, ut etiam cum his superare posset hostes. Itaque Themistocles veritus ne bellare perseveraret, certiorem eum fecit id agi, ut pons, quem ille in Hellesponto fecerat, dissolveretur, ac reditu in Asiam excluderetur, idque ei persuasit. Itaque in Asiam reversus est seque a Themistocle non superatum sed conservatum judicavit.

(a) Parse, giving the principal parts of the verbs: *ratus, conflixit, gesserat, dissolveretur.* (b) What kind of genitive is *doli?* (c) Comment on the mood of *fecerat.* (d) What kind of ablative is *consilio?* (e) What is the accusative singular of *mari?*

III.
> Aeneas scopulum interea conscendit et omnem
> Prospectum late pelago petit, Anthea si quem
> Iactatum vento videat Phrygiasque biremes,
> Aut Capyn, aut celsis in puppibus arma Caici.
> Navem in conspectu nullam, tres litore cervos
> Prospicit errantes; hos tota armenta sequuntur
> A tergo, et longum per valles pascitur agmen.
> Constitit hic arcumque manu celeresque sagittas
> Corripuit, fidus quae tela gerebat Achates,
> Ductoresque ipsos primum, capita alta ferentes
> Cornibus arboreis, sternit, tum vulgus et omnem
> Miscet agens telis nemora inter frondea turbam.

(a) Parse, giving the principal parts of the verbs: *pascitur, constitit, corripuit, gerebat, nemora.* (b) Comment on the termination of the accusative *Anthea* (c) Comment on the use of *quem* in l. 2. (d) Scan. l. 3.

IV. *Translate into Latin* SIX *only of the following sentences:—*
1. With such words the generals used to exhort their men.
2. Let us enter the city in order that we may dwell there.
3. Have you not told all these things to your wise friends?
4. Cæsar ordered the camp to be fortified with a rampart.
5. I am afraid that they may not come on the fifth day.
6. Having learnt these things, we retreated at once to Rome.
7. The lieutenant told the general that all our men had been killed.
8. He asked me when I had returned home.
9. If you send me the books, I shall read them with care.
10. To err is human, to forgive divine.
11. He is so foolish that he can never do a wise thing.
12. It is the duty of all citizens to fight bravely and spare the conquered.

V. *Candidates will attempt* ONE *only of these groups of questions:*

A. (a) What do you mean by a semi-deponent verb? Give three examples. (b) Give the genitive singular of: *alter, senex, bos, respublica, dives;* and the genitive plural of: *genus, ars.* (c) Give Latin sentences illustrating the use of the supine in -*um*, and of the supine in -*u*. (d) Write the Latin for: *11, 15, 28, 400.*

B. (a) Give the comparative and superlative of: *acer, pius, male.* (b) Distinguish in meaning between: *quidam, quisquis, quisque, quisquam.* (c) What verbs in Latin govern the genitive? (d) Give the gender of: *iter, fons, pelagus, aestas.* (e) Parse: *esto, duxere, superasset.* Give three perfects in Latin which have a present meaning.

C. (a) From what verbs do the following perfects come: *quaesivi, questus sum, finxi, fixi, vici, vixi, vinxi?* (b) Write Latin sentences containing examples of: ablative of manner, ablative of price, ablative of description. (c) What cases do the following prepositions govern: *ob, penes, coram?* (d) Give the meaning of the following nouns when they are used in the plural: *finis, vis, littera, aedes.*

8 GEORGE V, A. 1918

ENGLISH LAW.

Time: 2½ hours.

NOTE.—Eight questions only are to be attempted.

Value—100.

1. Describe briefly the procedure relating to a preliminary enquiry held under the provisions of the Criminal Code in the case of a person accused of a crime.

2. Define (*a*) burglary, (*b*) house-breaking, (*c*) robbery.

3. What power have the Dominion Parliament and the provincial legislatures, respectively, to legislate on the subject of education?

4. Indicate briefly to what extent the system of government established by the British North America Act, 1867, is similar in principle to that of the United Kingdom, and to what extent it is similar in principle to that of the United States of America.

5. B draws on A a bill of exchange payable to C at a named place three months after date. C presents the bill, obtains A's acceptance, and endorses and delivers the bill to D. D endorses and delivers the bill to E. Explain briefly the rights and liabilities of A, B, C, D, and E, respectively.

6. Define a cheque, and explain in what respects it differs from a bill of exchange.

7. The Bank Act forbids a bank to lend money or make advances on the security of any goods, wares and merchandise. Outline the exceptions to this prohibition.

8. Explain what is meant by conditions and warranties, respectively, in connection with a sale of goods. What are the remedies of the buyer in case of breach?

9. What is stoppage *in transitu?* How may the right be exercised? When does the transit end for this purpose?

10. A and B carry on business as partners and become indebted to **X**. Then B retires from the partnership. A and C form a partnership and agree to pay the debts of the old firm and to indemnify B against liability in respect of such debts. These facts become known to **X**. Whom is **X** entitled to sue for the debt? Reasons.

11. What is meant by the statement that an act or contract is *ultra vires* of a company? Illustrate.

12. A company is incorporated with an authorized capital of $50,000, divided into 500 shares. A desires to become a shareholder to the extent of ten shares. In what ways can he do so? What will be the amount of his liability to the creditors of the company?

SESSIONAL PAPER No. 31

LITERATURE (ENGLISH).

Time: 2½ hours.

Note.—Candidates will take Question 9 and any *five* of the others.

Value—100.

1. Write brief notes explaining the importance in English Literature of any *three* of the following: John Wyclif, Sir John Mandeville, Sir Thomas More, William Tyndale, Sir Thomas Malory, William Caxton.

2. Name *three* English dramatists contemporary with Shakespeare, and give a brief sketch of the life and work of any *one* of them.

3. Tell briefly the story of Milton's life. Name his chief poems and prose works. Give such an account of any *one* poem as would enable a person who had not read it to get an adequate idea of its subject and style.

4. Name *three* poets and *three* prose writers who did·their chief work between 1660 and 1744. Give a list of the works of *one* from each group, with brief explanatory notes on the chief works you mention.

5. Write explanatory and descriptive notes on any *three* of the following:
   · Johnson's *Dictionary*, Percy's *Reliques*, Macpherson's *Ossian*, Richardson's *Pamela*, Thomson's *The Seasons*, and Swift's *Gulliver's Travels*.

6. Write notes on any *two* of the following, naming their chief works and explaining their importance in English Literature: Coleridge, Charles Lamb, De Quincey, Jane Austen, Hazlitt.

7. Name what you consider the *four* greatest poets and *four* greatest prose writers (excluding novelists) of the Victorian Age. Describe *one* important work of *one* poet and *one* work of *one* prose writer in your list.

8. Name *five* great novelists of the Victorian Age and *two* novels of each of them. Give a brief sketch of the life of any *one*.

9.   To Shakespeare, 1916.

> With *what white wrath must turn thy bones*,
> What stern amazement *flame thy dust*,
> To feel so near this England's heart
> The outrage of the assassin's thrust.
>
> But surely, too, thou art consoled,—
> Who knewest thy stalwart breed so well,—
> To see us rise from sloth and go,
> *Plain and unbragging*, through this hell.
>
> And surely, too, thou art *assured!*
> Hark how that grim and gathering beat
> Draws *upwards from the ends of earth*—
> The tramp, *tramp of thy kindred's feet!*

(a) Explain the italicised parts.
(b) What is the probable reference in lines 3 and 4?·
(c) What appropriateness is there in a patriotic poem to Shakespeare, and in the date 1916?

8 GEORGE V, A. 1918

PHILOSOPHY (GENERAL).

Time: 2½ hours.

NOTE.—Seven questions only are to be attempted.

Value—100.

1. What is meant by Methodical Doubt in the Philosophy of Descartes, and how is it distinguished from the doubt of the Skeptics?

2. "That there is a God may be demonstrated solely from the consideration that there is involved in our knowledge of Him the necessity of His Being or existence." Explain the demonstration of the existence of God to which Descartes here refers, and estimate its value.

3. Compare the main principles of Descartes and Spinoza.

4. "The Monads have no windows by which anything can enter or emerge." Explain this saying. How does Leibnitz seek to show that his theory of Monads proves the individuality of all real things?

5. State and examine the distinction drawn by Kant between the Categories of the understanding and the Ideas of reason.

6. Illustrate "Weber's Law" by examples. How does Fechner interpret the facts upon which it is based?

7. What is the relation of habits to the nerve-centres? How does an habitual act differ from a purely voluntary act. Give some practical rules for the formation of new habits.

8. Distinguish between perception and sensation, and also between emotion and instinct.

9. Discuss the problem as to the comparative value of the following theories of punishment: the preventive theory, the reformatory theory, and the retributive theory.

10. "The end of morality is pleasure." "To make pleasure the end is to destroy morality." Contrast these two theories of conduct and give your own view.

11. What is the function in the moral life that great art subserves? Discuss the view that the presentation of ideals is a "criticism of life."

PHYSICS

Time: 2½ hours.

NOTE.—Eight questions only are to be attempted.

Value—100.

1. Define the units dyne, gramme, foot-pound.
   If one inch is equal to 2·54 centimetres, find the number of litres in one cubic foot.

2. A straight, uniform lever, whose length is 5 feet and weight 10 lb, has its fulcrum at one end. Weights of 2 and 4 lb are fastened to it at distances of 1 foot and 3 feet, respectively from the fulcrum, and it is kept horizontal by a force at the other end. Find this force, and also the reaction of the fulcrum.

3. Explain what is meant by the parallelogram of forces.

The base of an inclined plane is 4 feet and the height 3 feet. A force of 8 lb weight parallel to the plane will just prevent a mass of 20 lb weight from sliding down. Find the coefficient of friction.

4. Explain the principle of (1) a siphon and (2) a barometer.

A body of specific gravity 5· weighs 20 grams in a vacuum. What will this body weigh when immersed in water?

5. What is meant by (1) *boiling point*, (2) *latent heat of vaporisation*, and (3) *relative humidity?*

How would you show that heat is a form of energy?

Describe an experiment to illustrate (1) conduction, (2) convection, and (3) radiation of heat.

6. If the weight of 1 litre of air at O° C. and 76 cm. of mercury pressure be 1·293 grams, find the weight of air in a room 20 x 10 x 4 meters, when the temperature is 15° C. and the pressure 74 cm. of mercury?

7. What is meant by *refractive index?*

An object 2 inches long is placed 8 inches in front of a convex lens of 4-inch focal length. Find by means of a diagram the position and length of the image.

8. What are some of the more common ocular defects? How may each of them be remedied?

How would you show that it is possible to recombine light of different colours in such a way as to produce white light?

9. Explain *acoustical resonance, interference*, and the production of *beats.*

A stretched string 4 feet long is in unison with a tuning-fork which vibrates 256 times a second. What will be the rate of vibration of the string when it has been shortened 6 inches, the tension remaining the same?

10. What is meant by *Magnetic Dip*, and by *Declination?*

Make a sketch of the configuration of the lines of force for two bar magnets (with poles marked) placed near each other in any relative position you choose.

11. Describe some form of voltaic cell.

Explain the action of the astatic galvanometer.

What are Faraday's Laws of Electrolysis?

12. Explain what is meant by induced currents.

How would you use an induction coil to produce cathode rays and Röntgen rays?

POLITICAL SCIENCE.

Time: 2½ hours.

NOTE.—Five questions only are to be attempted.

Value—100.

1. Explain the terms: sovereignty; state; society; separation of powers; responsible government; the referendum; laissez-faire; electoral college; neutrality; neutralization.

2. Describe the composition and powers of the Cabinet in the United Kingdom in normal times. What changes have recently been effected?

31—8

3. Write brief notes on the following:—

    Proportional Representation.
    The Imperial Conference.
    The Committee System in the French Parliament.

4. In what different ways may constitutions be amended formally? In what other ways may change come about? What is the method of formal change in each of the following: the United Kingdom, France, the United States, Australia, South Africa, Canada, a Canadian province?

5. Explain the terms: federal government; unitary government; parliamentary or cabinet government; presidential or non-parliamentary government; and classify any *fifteen* states of Europe and North America according to these categories.

6. Write notes on the following, giving illustrations from the present war:—
    Treaties of guarantee against invasion.
    The authority of the rules of international law.
    The Law of Contraband and the Doctrine of Continuous Voyage.

7. Outline the form of government of any *two* of the states of Continental Europe.

8. What subjects are assigned to the Dominion in the division of legislative powers, and what to the provinces? What are the portfolios in the Dominion Government, and what are the chief duties assigned to each minister?

9. What is meant by the principle of nationality? In what parts of Europe is it not in force to-day? In what different ways could it be given effect? What other considerations will have to be borne in mind when the map of Europe is redrawn?

10. Write notes on any *five* of the following, stating the place and period in which each lived, naming his most important works and stating briefly the theory or theories for which he is noted: Hobbes, Burke, Rousseau, Maine, Machiavelli, Spencer, Paine, Locke.

SHORTHAND.

The paper set is that given on page 93.

SPELLING AND DICTATION.

SPELLING.

Time: 30 minutes.

NOTE.—Copy the following, correcting the errors in spelling; 5 marks will be deducted for every misspelled word in your copy.

Value—50.

One of the first sirprises awaiting the turist from the Northren Hemisfere, when he visits the remoat contenants of the Southren Pacific, is to find that Australia and New Zealand may not be gruped as two ilands of like apperence, differing manely in size; near naibors which may be treated as a unit. New

Zealand is nerely twice as far from Austalia as Bermuda is from New York, and in climat and vegatation the two dominions are as unlike as Norway and South Carolina.

Australia is in no sense inferier to New Zealand in geografic intrest, but lofty peeks, profound canions, and active volcanose, all found in New Zealand, are lacking; its rivers are unimpresive, and its permeneht lakes small and few in number. Uneek vegatation of remarkible variaty and beuty, animal life of by-gone geollogicel pereods, and an aborigenel populashun, the lowest in the skale of human beings, stand out as feetures distincly Australian. It is the land of the strange and cureus, unlike any other on earth. Its isolation has kept out the animals of other countries and allowed speces of old geollogic ages to persist; it has resulted also in the continuence of plant forms there that have lost the race for existance in other contenants. The great animal grupes which develloped in geollogicel pereods before the land briges to other countries had been distroyed, are reppresented in Australia.

DICTATION.

Time: 30 minutes.

NOTE.—This paper should not be seen by the candidates. The Examiner will read over the whole extract once, and then reread it slowly and distinctly, indicating to the candidates the occurrence of each full stop. A third reading of the whole extract may be given if sufficient time remains. The whole time occupied should not be more than half an hour.

Value—50.

To untutored man, provided only with implements of stone, the facilities presented by the great copper regions of Lake Superior for the beginnings of a knowledge of mineralogy were peculiarly available. The water-worn stone from the beach, patiently ground to an edge, made his axe and tomahawk; the bones of the deer pointed his spear or were wrought into fish-hooks, and the shale or flint was chipped and ground into his arrow-head after a pattern used in every primitive age. But besides such materials of universal occurrence, the primitive occupant of the shores of Lake Superior found there a stone possessed of some very peculiar virtues. It could not only be wrought to an edge without liability to fracture, but it was malleable, and could be hammered out into many new and convenient shapes. This was the copper, found in the rocks of that region in inexhaustible quantities in a pure metallic state. In other rich mineral regions, as in those of Cornwall and Devon, the principal source of this metal is from ores, which require both labour and skill to fit them for economic purposes. But in the copper region of Lake Superior, the native metal occurs in enormous masses, weighing hundreds of tons; and loose blocks have been found lying detached on the surface in sufficient quantities to supply all the wants of the nomad hunter.

TYPEWRITING.

The paper set is that given on page 94.

DEPARTMENT

OF

PUBLIC PRINTING *and* STATIONERY

ANNUAL REPORT

FOR THE FISCAL YEAR ENDED MARCH 31

1917

PRINTED BY ORDER OF PARLIAMENT

OTTAWA
J. DE LABROQUERIE TACHÉ
PRINTER TO THE KING'S MOST EXCELLENT MAJESTY
1918

[No. 32—1918]

To His Excellency the Duke of Devonshire, K.G., P.C., G.C.M.G., G.C.V.O., etc.,
etc., Governor General and Commander in Chief of the Dominion of Canada.

SIR,—The undersigned has the honour to present to Your Excellency the Annual Report of the Department of Public Printing and Stationery for the year ended March 31, 1917.

I have the honour to be, sir,

Your Excellency's most obedient servant,

MARTIN BURRELL,
Secretary of State.

March, 1918.

32—1½

OTTAWA, March, 1918.

Hon. MARTIN BURRELL,
　　　　Secretary of State.

SIR,—I have the honour to submit the Annual Report of the Department of Public Printing and Stationery for the year ended March 31, 1917.

I have the honour to be, sir,

Your obedient servant,

J. DE L. TACHÉ,
King's Printer and Controller of Stationery.

Department of Public Printing and Stationery

1914==1918

Roll of Honour

EMPLOYEES ENLISTED

FOR OVERSEAS MILITARY SERVICE

Name.	Rank.	Unit.
Annable, J. H.	Pte.	207th " Ottawa-Carleton " Batt.
Austin, W. N.	Pte.	257th Const. Batt.
(1) Archibald, W. G.	Gunner	51st Battery, C.F.A.
Balcomb, George	Gunner	23rd Battery, C.F.A.
Balcomb, Wm.	Pte.	Ammunition Column.
(1) Baril, W.	Sgt.	5th C. F. Eng.
Batterton, Dom.	Gunner	73rd Battery, C.F.A.
(3) Bergeron, M. A.	Lieut.	Reinforcing Draft, 22nd Batt.
(2) Bouchard, W. E.	Gunner	21st Battery, C.F.A.
(3) Boucher, Geo. John	Pte.	5th Div. Ammunition Column.
Boudreault, Emery	Gunner	73rd Battery, C.F.A.
(3) Branch, Alfred W.	Pte.	38th " Royal Ottawa " Batt.
(1) Brien, Jos. H.	Pte.	257th Const. Batt.
(1) Brisebois, R.	Gunner	23rd Battery, C.F.A.
(1) Brulé, Hector	Pte.	1st Batt.
(2) Budreo, R. C.	Pte.	207th " Ottawa-Carleton " Batt.
Bullis, E. J.	Pte.	80th Batt.
Burnett, William	Gunner	73rd Battery, C.F.A.
(1) Burps, Gregory	Pte.	59th Batt.
(1) Butler, John	Gunner	23rd Battery, C.F.A.
(3) Butlin, Arthur	Bandsman	146th Batt.
Cain, Walter O.	Pte.	230th Forestry Batt.
Cain, Wm.	Pte.	257th Const. Batt.
Cairncross, Jas.	Trumpeter	8th C.M.R.
Carrier, Georges	Gunner	73rd Battery, C.F.A.
(1) Chapdelaine, Aimé	Sub. Lieut.	Royal Flying Corps.
Cowtan, Chas.	Pte.	257th Const. Batt.
Cunningham, W. A.	Cpl.	C.A.S.C.
Curry, Stanley R.	Pte.	2nd Ottawa Depot Batt.
(4) Dagenais, H. A. R.	Lieut.	150th " Canadien-Francais " Batt.
(1) DeMontigny, J. I. G.T.	Cpl.	22nd " Canadien-Francais " Batt.
(3) Dempsey, Wm.	Pte.	77th Batt.
DeNiverville, Albert	Sub. Lieut.	Royal Flying Corps.
(3) Depocas, Louis L.	Gunner	73rd Battery, C.F.A.
Desrivières, J. A.	Dvr.	Imperial Transport.
Doherty, W.	Pte.	77th Batt.
(3) (1) Donovan, W. J.	Sgt.	77th Batt.
DuVal, Iréné	Sub. Lieut.	Royal Naval Air Service.
Foisy, Joseph	Gunner	74th Battery, C.F.A.
(1) Foley, J. H.	Lieut.	199th " Irish Rangers."
(1) Globensky, L. E. M.	Pte.	38th " Royal Ottawa " Batt.
Graham, Roland M.	Pte.	5th Div. Ammunition Column.
(1) Haydon, J. A. P.	Sgt.	77th Batt.
(3) Hazel, Wm. J.	Gunner	73rd Battery, C.F.A.
Howe, Frederick H.	Pte.	1st Ontario Depot Batt.
Labelle, J. H.	Gunner	73rd Battery, C.F.A.
Lamoureux, S. A.	Pte.	230th Forestry Batt.

Name.	Rank.	Unit.
(1) Landles, Wm.	Pte.	Queen's Field Ambulance.
Langley, Harry	Pte.	257th Const. Batt.
Lapierre, A. J.	Pte.	224th Forestry Batt.
(2) Leduc, Romuald	Sub. Lieut.	Royal Flying Corps.
Leek, John	Pte.	257th Const. Batt.
Lefebvre, P. A.	Pte.	77th Batt.
Le Feuvre, S. G.	Pte.	238th Forestry Batt.
Lemieux, Jos. A.	Pte.	224th Forestry Batt.
Macdonald, A. H.	Capt.	230th Forestry Batt.
Maloney, T. L.	Pte.	C.A.S.C.
(3) Mann, J. H.	Gunner	73rd Battery, C.F.A.
Meade, M. F.	Pte.	257th Const. Batt.
Miller, R. C.	Pte.	207th " Ottawa-Carleton " Batt.
(3) Montminy, Arcadius	Pte.	207th " Ottawa-Carleton " Batt.
Moreau, Joseph.	Gunner	74th Battery.
McCadden, T.	Pte.	77th Batt.
McCartney, S.	Pte.	238th Forestry Batt.
(3) (1) McDonald, D.	Pte.	C.A.S.C.
(1) McGovern, H. F.	Pte.	Remount Division.
(2) McGovern, Wm. M.	Pte.	8th C.M.R.
(3) McGuire, E. J.	Pte.	C.A.S.C.
McStravick, P.	Pte.	156th Batt.
O'Connor, P. J.	Pte.	5th Ammunition Column.
O'Neil, W.	Pte.	Ammunition Column.
(3) Parent, Aristide	Pte.	230th Forestry Batt.
Parmelee, Rotus E.	Pte.	Engineers' Signal Corps.
Pasch, A. C.	Pte.	224th Forestry Batt.
(1) Paynter, C. S.	Gunner	23rd Battery, C.F.A.
Paynter, J. J.	Sgt.	23rd Battery, C.F.A.
(3) Price, C. J. F.	Lieut.	224th Forestry Batt.
Proulx, Gaston	Pte.	5th Div. Ammunition Column.
(1) Rainey, C. E.	Sgt.	" Princess Patricia."
Ralph, Robert	Gunner	73rd Battery, C.F.A.
(3) Richer, Hector	Pte.	230th (Voltigeurs) Batt.
Robertson, A. W.	Pte.	207th " Ottawa-Carleton " Batt.
(3) Root, Edward J.	Gunner	74th Battery, C.F.A.
Ross, Donald	Pte.	Queen's Field Ambulance.
(3) Sanderson, A. E.	Pte.	238th Forestry Batt.
Schau, Andrew	Pte.	77th Batt.
Schingh, J. E.	Lieut.	Reinforcing Draft, 24th Batt.
Sculthorpe, A. W.	Pte.	257th Const. Batt.
Sirois, H. Auguste	Pte.	1st Quebec Depot Batt.
(3) Smith, W. L.	Bandsman	207th " Ottawa-Carleton " Batt.
Sunderland, H.	Pte.	257th Const. Batt.
(3) Thomas, Frederick R.	Pte.	257th Const. Batt.
Tierney, J. J.	Pte.	199th " Irish Rangers " Batt.
Tighe, James	Pte.	77th Batt.
Twyman, T. G.	Gunner	23rd Battery, C.F.A.
(3) Ward, Geo. J.	Pte.	77th Batt.
Woods, M. W.	Gunner	23rd Battery, C.F.A.

LIST OF EMPLOYEES ENLISTED FOR MILITARY SERVICE IN CANADA.

Allard, W. L.	Lt.-Col.	Recruiting Officer, M.D. No. 3.
Botham, Charles H.	Signalman	Royal Navy Can. Vol. Reserve.
(3) Cameron, P. A.	Bandsman	108th " Selkirk " Batt.
deErnsted, Auguste	W. O.	Royal Navy Can. Vol. Reserve.
(3) Fallis, R. W.	Bandsman	108th " Selkirk " Batt.
(3) Fallis, W. J.	Bandsman	108th " Selkirk " Batt.
Guthaus, F. J.	Sergeant	Instruction Sergeant, M.D. No. 3.
Lesieur, Eugene	W. O.	Royal Navy Can. Vol. Reserve.
Peachy, Maurice	Seaman	Royal Navy Can. Vol. Reserve.
(3) Smith, Francis Ed.	Carpenter	Royal Navy Can. Vol. Reserve.
Taylor, William L.	Signalman.	Royal Navy Can. Vol. Reserve.

(1) Wounded.   (3) Returned to civil duties.
(2) Killed.   (4) Resigned.

Recorded to March 31, 1918.

ACCOUNTANT'S BRANCH.

OTTAWA, November, 1917

J. de L. TACHÉ, Esq.,
   King's Printer and Controller of Stationery.

SIR,—I have the honour to submit the following report of the transactions of this branch of the department for the fiscal year ending March 31, 1917. Complete details of the financial operations of the department will be found under the following heads:—

1. General Financial Statement for the year.

2. Letter of Credit Account.

3. King's Printer's Advance Account.

4. Printing Branch Account and comparative statements.

5. Stationery Branch Account and comparative statements.

6. Expenditure on Appropriations and detail of same.

7. *Canada Gazette*, comparative statement of Revenue and Expenditure.

8. Casual Revenue Account.

9. Audit of Intercolonial and Prince Edward Island Railways Printing Accounts.

10. Government Newspaper Advertising Accounts.

Respectfully submitted,

J. A. FRIGON,
Chief Accountant.

Dr.

1. GENERAL FINANCIAL STATEMENT FOR THE FISCAL YEAR ENDING MARCH 31, 1917.   Dr.

	Printing Branch.		Stationery Branch.		Casual Revenue Receipts.	Appropriation Credits.	Total.
	Letter of Credit Receipts.	Work completed and chargeable to Departments.	Letter of Credit Receipts.	Goods purchased and chargeable to Departments.			
	$ cts.	$ cts.	$ cts.	$ cts.	$ cts.	$ cts.	$ cts.
KING'S PRINTER'S ADVANCE ACCOUNT.							
Advances to Printing Branch account by letter of credit..... $ 2,398,636 74							
Less refunds..... 668 14							
$ 2,397,968 60							
Advances to Printing Branch Account by bills of exchange..... 107 31							
Advances to Printing Branch account by cheques on New York..... 3,984 56	2,402,060 47						2,402,060 47
Advances to Stationery Branch account by letter of credit..... $ 1,967,789 27							
Less refunds..... 46 26							
$ 1,967,743 01							
Advances to Stationery Branch Account by bills of exchange..... 37,312 48							
Less refunds..... 31 05							
$ 37,281 38							
Advances to Stationery Branch account by cheques on New York..... 30,713 22							
Less refunds..... 1 50							
$ 30,711 72			2,035,736 11				2,035,736 11
Printing, binding, etc., chargeable to departments.		933,249 50					
Printing, etc., ordered outside and chargeable to departments.		544,196 63					
Paper stock from stationery used on above work.		924,468 70					

Item						Total
Linotype and monotype dross sold to public					1,338 03	
Empty spools sold to public					34 07	
Paper stock saved in Press room and sold to Stationery Br'ch					1,121 90	
Total	2,402,060 47				2,035,736 11	2,404,408 83
Stationery, etc., chargeable to departments			1,943,379 79			
Total			1,943,379 79			1,943,379 79
CASUAL REVENUE ACCOUNT.						
Proceeds of sales—						
Parliamentary publications to departments		4,259 63				
" " public		8,316 07				
Canada Gazette, advertising and subscriptions		37,562 78				
Voters' lists to public		141 70				
Waste paper, empty cases, etc., to public		6,282 00				
Excess of revenue over expenditure in Printing Branch account		2,348 36				
Profit on Stationery Branch account		116,073 48				
Total		174,984 02				174,984 02
APPROPRIATIONS.						
Gratuities				2,498 07		
Civil Government salaries				70,662 50		
" contingencies				10,300 00		
Printing, binding, and distributing the annual statutes				16,000 00		
Contingent expenses in connection with the voters' lists				10,600 00		
Plant—New				50,000 00		
Plant—Renewals				7,000 00		
Miscellaneous printing				150,000 00		
Canada Gazette				21,000 00		
Distribution of parliamentary documents				45,000 00		
Total				383,060 57		383,060 57
Grand total						9,343,629 79

Cr.   Cr.

1. GENERAL FINANCIAL STATEMENT—Concluded.

	PRINTING BRANCH		STATIONERY BRANCH		Casual Revenue Deposits.	Appropriation Expenditure.	Total.
	Letter of Credit Expenditure.	Receipts from Departments.	Letter of Credit Expenditure.	Receipts from Departments.			
	$ cts.	$ cts.	$ cts.	$ cts.	$ cts.	$ cts.	$ cts.
KING'S PRINTER'S ADVANCE ACCOUNT.							
Expenditure on Printing Branch account—							
Wages........................	858,612 72						
Printing material............	72,392 74						
Paper stock..................	906,761 69						
Miscellaneous expense........	13,886 59						
Outside work................	550,406 73						
Total.................							2,402,060 47
Expenditure on Stationery Branch account—							
Goods, stationery, etc........			1,872,549 09				
Wages.......................			96,656 27				
Miscellaneous expense........			66,530 75				
Total.................							2,035,736 11
Deposits to credit of Dominion Government—							
Sales of printing, etc. to departments..		2,401,914 83					
" linotype and monotype dross..		1,338 03					
" empty spools..........		34 07					
" paper stock saved and on hand in Press room, on March 31, 1917.......		1,121 90					
Total.................							2,404,408 83
Sales of stationery, etc., to departments.......				1,943,379 79			
Total.................				1,943,379 79			1,943,379 79

CASUAL REVENUE.

Deposits to credit of Dominion Government—					
Sales of Parliamentary publications to departments	4,259 63				
" Parliamentary publications to public	8,316 07				
" Canada Gazette advertising and ...	37,562 78				
" voters' lists to public	141 70				
" waste paper, empty ... etc., to public	6,282 00				
Entry :—					
Excess of revenue over ... in Printing Branch account transferred to credit of Casual Revenue account	2,348 36				
Profit on Stationery Branch account transferred to credit of ... Revenue account	116,073 48				
Total					174,984 02

APPROPRIATIONS.

Expenditure—					
Civil Government salaries		2,498 07			
" contingencies		58,803 50			
Printing, binding and distributing the annual statutes		10,206 17			
Contingent ... in connection with the voters' lists		15,561 75			
Plant—New		10,598 33			
Plant—Renewals		37,335 81			
Miscellaneous printing		6,995 62			
... ...		149,991 42			
		20,995 69			
Distribution of parliamentary documents		44,992 33			
Total					358,028 69
Unexpended balances—					
Civil Government salaries		11,859 00			
" contingencies		93 83			
Printing, binding and distributing the annual statutes		438 25			
Contingent expenses in connection with the voters' lists		1 67			
Plant—New		12,614 19			
Plant—Renewals		4 38			
Miscellaneous printing		8 58			
Canada Gazette		4 31			
Distribution of parliamentary documents		7 67			
Total					25,031 88
Grand total	174,984 02	383,060 57	1,943,379 79	2,035,736 11	2,404,408 83	2,402,060 47	9,343,629 79

2. LETTER OF CREDIT ACCOUNT.

Total amount received by letter of credit for the fiscal year ending March 31, 1917..........$	4,646,117 55
Total amount received by bills of exchange..	37,419 74
Total amount received by cheques on New York......................................	41,527 19
	$ 4,725,064 48

Detail, by accounts, of net expenditure drawn on above amounts—

Printing Branch account...	$ 2,402,060 47	
Stationery Branch account..	2,035,736 11	
Printing, binding, and distributing the annual statutes...................	15,561 75	
Contingent expenses in connection with the voters' lists...............	10,598 33	
Plant, New...	37,385 81	
Plant, Renewals..	6,995 62	
Canada Gazette..	20,995 69	
Miscellaneous printing..	149,991 42	
Distribution of parliamentary documents.............................	44,992 33	
	$ 4,724,317 53	

Refunds, deposited to credit of respective accounts—

Printing Branch account...$	668 14	
Stationery Branch account...	78 81	
		746 95
		$ 4,725,064 48

3. KING'S PRINTER'S ADVANCE ACCOUNT.

Advances to King's Printer during the fiscal year 1916-17—

For Printing Branch account.......................................$	2,402,728 61	
For Stationery Branch account......................................	2,035,814 92	
		$ 4,438,543 53
Amount received for printing, etc., in excess of expenditure on the same....................		2,348 36
Amount received for stationery, etc., profit on account..............................		116,073 48
		$ 4,556,965 37

Deposits to credit of Receiver General, made by the King's Printer to cover advances during the fiscal year 1916-17—

Amount received from departments and Parliament for printing, etc....$	2,401,914 83	
Amount received by Printing Branch from Stationery Branch for sale of printing paper...	1,121 90	
Amount from sale of dross..	1,338 03	
Amount from sale of empty spools...................................	34 07	
		$ 2,404,408 83
Amount of refunds—Printing Branch......................................		668 14
		$ 2,405,076 97
Amount received from departments and Parliament for stationery, etc......$	1,943,379 79	
Amount of refunds—Stationery Branch...................................	78 81	
		$ 1,943,458 60
Amount by which the stock of Stationery Branch was increased during the fiscal year 1916-17..		208,429 80
		$ 4,556,965 37

STATEMENT of Printing, Lithographing, etc., and Paper supplied to Departments and Parliament for the Fiscal Year ending March 31, 1917.

Department.	Outside Work.	Inside Printing, Binding, etc.	Paper.	Total.
	$ cts.	$ cts.	$ cts.	$ cts.
Agriculture	58,149 67	87,246 07	147,910 49	293,306 23
Archives	3,023 50	5,215 99	5,327 38	13,566 87
Auditor General	108 55	969 07	836 97	1,914 59
Canadian Government Railways	1,126 59	4,246 85	4,227 43	9,600 87
Canadian Munition Resources Commission		8 41	1 79	10 20
Civil Service Commissioners	316 40	1,614 20	797 45	2,728 05
Clerk of the Crown in Chancery	847 03	2,992 44	5,871 83	9,711 30
Commission of Conservation	59 50	20 03	7 46	86 99
Commission of Inquiry, Railways and Transportat'n.		70 08	´ 42 07	112 15
Customs	6,261 39	19,325 70	30,116 18	55,703 27
Departments generally	50 00	99 79	81 68	231 47
Dominion Police	124 09	750 57	1,206 05	2,080 71
Economic and Development Commission		55 78	31 26	87 04
Exchequer Court		993 44	193 76	1,187 20
External Affairs	3,717 35	3,429 25	1,619 70	8,766 30
Finance	4,213 17	12,532 15	25,461 50	42,206 82
General Consulting Engineer		2 99		2 99
Governor General's Secretary	145 85	603 96	871 45	1,621 26
House of Commons	16,672 72	209,110 28	25,233 61	251,016 61
Immigration	10,368 04	6,357 25	4,294 01	21,019 30
Indian Affairs	227 71	3,235 54	1,690 46	5,153 71
Inland Revenue	2,460 26	21,815 14	10,031 68	34,307 08
Insurance	33 05	11,843 58	3,632 85	15,509 48
Interior	42,886 21	48,350 19	33,661 05	124,897 45
International Joint Commission	1,076 07		121 60	1,197 67
Internment Operations Office	8 00	60 90	348 25	417 15
Justice	147 30	1,704 55	992 51	2,844 36
Labour	21,272 52	2,845 03	2,399 46	26,517 01
Library of Parliament	36 50	6,561 82	29 42	6,627 74
Marine	11,574 93	18,480 51	11,353 91	41,409 35
Military Hospitals Commission	355 98	1,949 50	3,017 87	5,323 35
Militia and Defence	154,241 00	127,355 47	325,233 66	606,830 13
Mines	77,718 56	11,362 12	23,897 59	112,978 27
Miscellaneous printing	15,363 88	92,801 05	44,262 19	·152,427 12
National Gallery of Canada		10 98	4 62	15 60
National Service Commission	998 45	4,089 14	11,930 24	17,017 83
Naval Service	19,297 16	40,794 36	28,959 66	89,051 18
Penitentiaries	113 55	1,032 96	485 76	1,632 27
Pension Commissioners	301 40	1,387 92	4,400 89	6,090 21
Post Office	49,089 80	52,203 89	74,530 07	175,823 76
Privy Council	43 10	1,200 65	1,374 93	2,618 68
Public Printing and Stationery	10,040 57	40,592 76	21,519 95	72,153 28
Public Works	3,302 43	10,168 71	8,936 64	22,407 78
Railways and Canals	539 19	3,763 86	3,006 32	7,309 37
Railway Commsision	141 13	2,491 53	872 31	3,504 97
Royal Commission re Fuse Contracts		5,226 48	692 49	5,918 97
Royal Commission re War Supplies		1,215 17	72 52	1,287 69
Royal Mint		49 86	184 04	233 90
Royal North-West Mounted Police	418 19	2,307 26	2,818 36	5,543 81
Secretary of State	6,667 34	17,857 68	12,540 49	37,065 51
Senate of Canada		5,278 87	346 11	5,624 98
Supreme Court		338 50	184 76	523 26
Trade and Commerce	17,797 83	31,783 32	33,361 78	82,942 93
Transcontinental Railway Commission	22 80	160 35	43 75	226 90
War Purchasing Commission	2,837 87	7,285 55	3,398 44	13,521 86
Total	544,196 63	933,249 50	924,468 70	2,401,914 83

COMPARATIVE STATEMENT of Printing, Binding, Lithographing, etc., and Paper supplied to Departments and Parliament for the last five fiscal years: 1912–1913, 1913–1914, 1914–1915, 1915–1916, and 1916–1917.

Department.	1912–13.	1913–14.	1914–15.	1915–16.	1916–17.
	$ cts.	$ cts.	$ cts.	$ cts.	$ cts.
Agriculture	97,384 62	126,833 99	142,255 05	174,876 62	293,306 23
Archives		6,297 51	2,692 95	4,968 69	13,566 87
Auditor General	1,137 14	3,053 69	1,928 99	1,552 67	1,914 59
Canadian Government Railways	7,342 60	5,981 86	6,866 02	6,140 19	9,600 87
Canadian Munition Resources Commission					10 20
Civil Service Commissioners	1,680 42	3,137 80	3,352 70	3,185 60	2,728 05
Clerk of the Crown in Chancery	1,202 20	5,374 56	1,196 83	4,989 48	9,711 30
Commission of Conservation	45 54	56 08	87 24	116 52	86 99
Commission of Inquiry, Railways and Transportation					112 15
Customs	45,887 42	56,889 28	64,346 87	56,144 27	55,703 27
Departments Generally	299 40	157 39	40 02	277 03	231 47
Dominion Police	760 02	908 75	2,446 08	1,448 96	2,080 71
Economic and Development Comm'n					87 04
Exchequer Court	663 41	948 44	1,776 83	409 68	1,187 20
External Affairs	2,959 70	2,406 28	4,321 68	7,203 60	8,766 30
Finance	5,084 19	7,209 48	6,980 96	13,774 26	42,206 82
General Consulting Engineer	8 47				2 99
Governor General's Secretary	2,003 19	1,421 76	1,529 14	1,422 87	1,621 26
House of Commons	281,764 62	368,705 53	372,584 69	362,475 34	251,016 61
Immigration	78,181 81	78,937 71	20,630 46	16,554 71	21,019 30
Indian Affairs	5,961 91	6,303 00	7,256 58	6,157 46	5,153 71
Inland Revenue	18,345 23	22,292 06	26,967 94	28,765 91	34,307 08
Insurance	8,247 27	9,179 33	11,655 09	10,840 80	15,509 48
Interior	83,507 26	128,340 19	160,069 85	139,193 50	124,897 45
International Joint Commission	49 58		55 51	10,167 82	1,197 67
Internment Operations Office					417 15
Justice	4,398 27	2,225 08	3,798 95	3,468 26	2,844 36
Labour	23,589 95	38,493 22	31,256 19	29,654 55	26,517 01
Library of Parliament	4,398 49	3,615 79	5,615 19	4,873 50	6,627 74
Marine	56,434 96	48,625 14	43,532 28	36,773 64	41,409 35
Military Hospitals Commission					5,323 35
Militia and Defence	53,439 74	67,408 17	134,345 79	345,645 14	606,830 13
Mines	57,242 59	131,001 59	157,910 93	134,907 09	112,978 27
Miscellaneous Printing	100,586 32	93,574 92	166,944 11	129,772 61	152,427 12
National Gallery of Canada					15 60
National Service Commission					17,047 05
Naval Service	20,507 15	18,242 47	44,309 49	68,535 56	89,051 18
Penitentiaries	1,572 51	2,026 23	1,883 95	1,525 19	1,632 27
Pension Commissioners					6,090 21
Post Office	159,476 48	172,704 24	171,132 15	168,684 98	175,823 76
Privy Council	1,135 09	1,033 84	1,293 92	1,663 86	2,589 46
Public Printing and Stationery	49,408 78	62,377 79	60,637 06	72,023 76	72,153 28
Public Service Commission	577 99				
Public Works	30,388 29	44,400 32	41,798 00	26,796 09	22,407 78
Railways and Canals	9,989 55	15,082 90	15,362 42	10,486 53	7,309 37
Railway Commission	2,369 41	3,357 66	2,988 75	2,361 15	3,504 97
Royal Commission re Fuse Contracts					5,918 97
Royal Commission re War Supplies					1,287 69
Royal Mint	426 66	433 74	159 31	150 97	233 90
Royal Northwest Mounted Police	3,908 77	4,945 13	6,252 20	7,345 55	5,543 81
Secretary of State	11,850 97	6,629 21	17,287 13	19,573 93	37,065 51
Senate of Canada	5,829 67	7,536 97	9,683 23	5,252 76	5,624 98
Supreme Court	1,334 14	1,813 45	1,359 15	1,045 96	523 26
Trade and Commerce	33,389 57	36,380 04	51,044 47	59,200 07	82,942 93
Transcontinental Railway Commission	98 97	708 47	54 44	201 36	226 90
War Purchasing Commission				543 91	13,521 86
Total	1,274,870 28	1,597,051 06	1,807,390 59	1,981,152 40	2,401,914 83

5. STATIONERY BRANCH ACCOUNT.

Inventory, April 1, 1916..		$	224,362 14
Amount of goods purchased during fiscal year 1916–17—			
Canadian and American..	$ 1,835,267 71		
British and Foreign..	37,281 38		
		1,872,549 09	
Amount of other expenditures during fiscal year 1916–17—			
Wages..	$ 96,656 27		
Customs duties and brokerage.......................................	17,780 97		
Freight, etc..	48,749 78		
		163,187 02	
Amount received for goods issued in excess of expenditure on the same....................		116,073 48	
		$ 2,376,171 73	

Amount of goods issued to departments and Parliament during fiscal year 1916–17.........	$ 1,943,379 79		
Inventory, March 31, 1917...	432,791 94		
	$ 2,376,171 73		

The stock of goods on hand has been increased during the fiscal year to the amount, $208,429.80

8 GEORGE V, A. 1918

STATEMENT of Goods purchased and Goods issued to Departments and Parliament in each month for the fiscal year ending March 31, 1917.

Month.	Goods Purchased.			Goods Issued.
	British and Foreign.		Canadian and American.	
	£ s. d.	$ cts.	$ cts.	$ cts.
1916.				
April....................................	....	....	69,650 30	97,355 12
May.....................................	523 17 0	2,549 40	128,552 11	138,084 99
June....................................	....	....	156,963 47	136,000 99
July....................................	1,291 10 10	6,285 51	167,227 80	136,213 72
August.................................	....	....	96,129 37	147,788 41
September..............................	826 1 4	4,020 19	156,592 04	161,637 17
October................................	823 13 11	4,008 65	164,906 53	176,260 37
November...............................	487 15 4	2,373 80	188,074 61	154,286 12
December...............................	861 0 0	4,190 20	143,129 14	163,300 83
1917.				
January................................	446 8 6	2.172 60	129,698 06	172,702 31
February...............................	997 8 9	4,854 20	167,697 74	184,597 64
March..................................	1,409 3 1	6,857 88	266,660 45	275,152 12
	7,666 18 9	37,312 43		
Amount of Canadian and American purchases.........	....	....	1,835,281 62	
Amount of British and Foreign purchases.............	....	....	37,312 43	
			1,872,594 05	
Refunds on goods purchased......................	....	....	44 96	
Totals of goods purchased and of goods issued........	....	....	1,872,549 09	1,943,379 79

SESSIONAL PAPER No. 32

COMPARATIVE Statement of amount of Goods issued to Departments and Parliament for the last five fiscal years, 1912-13, 1913-14, 1914-15, 1915-16, and, 1916-17.

Department.	1912–13.	1913–14.	1914–15.	1915–16.	1916–17.
	$ cts.	$ cts.	$ cts.	$ cts.	$ cts.
Agriculture............................	18,463 12	29,760 29	25,439 47	26,809 13	36,646 37
Archives.............................		2,113 95	2,380 62	984 95	1,325 66
Auditor General......................	2,811 98	3,628 64	3,492 83	3,600 45	4,966 07
Canadian Government Railways........	16,889 54	24,593 76	22,777 22	2,360 90	39,973 90
Canadian Munitions Resources Commission............................				88 70	223 31
Civil Service Commission..............	1,020 09	1,549 79	1,368 31	768 17	412 51
Clerk of the Crown in Chancery........	941 09	294 51	230 70	1,128 89	66 05
Commission of Conservation..........	10 02				
Commission of Inquiry, Railways and Transportation.......................					122 22
Customs.............................	29,788 59	38,889 03	35,223 85	27,577 83	35,800 97
Departments Generally................	767 42	571 40	770 39	820 46	1,260 34
Dominion Police......................	541 02	567 88	1,764 06	961 70	1,121 94
Economic and Development Commission					184 78
Exchequer Court......................	371 12	211 61	181 29	628 47	444 55
External Affairs......................	1,340 44	1,238 93	2,127 98	2,310 73	2,416 67
Finance..............................	3,522 10	5,877 64	4,181 88	7,263 66	22,536 97
General Consulting Engineer...........	91 68	89 16	73 02	60 05	65 97
Governor General's Secretary..........	1,293 94	1,802 78	1,803 52	1,410 79	1,932 10
House of Commons....................	13,963 00	17,620 78	16,504 33	26,950 08	29,359 21
Immigration.........................	9,939 47	12,416 38	8,802 03	8,921 72	6,538 10
Indian Affairs.......................	12,481 82	15,982 50	17,224 14	17,983 06	16,982 36
Inland Revenue......................	6,323 16	7,474 62	8,940 10	10,699 69	10,083 29
Insurance...........................	967 91	1,637 25	1,484 02	1,805 53	3,583 40
Interior.............................	64,683 34	81,690 86	75,839 46	61,392 20	74,388 35
International Joint Commission........	152 75	31 92	23 67	13 50	33 00
Internment Operations Office.........				4 40	2,222 81
Justice..............................	4,049 65	5,896 20	11,492 36	5,917 61	5,140 96
Labour..............................	2,628 51	3,195 06	1,630 00	1,314 30	1,451 28
Library of Parliament.................	309 34	333 09	280 84	591 72	869 33
Marine..............................	23,082 60	31,968 04	24,005 77	15,221 00	17,348 24
Military Hospitals Commission........					8,433 93
Militia and Defence...................	38,444 28	49,738 30	103,201 76	227,648 29	375,478 41
Mines...............................	12,535 52	24,949 05	13,183 80	8,951 58	9,039 52
National Gallery of Canada............					65 63
National Service Commission..........					17,204 54
Naval Service........................	11,034 56	11,584 97	29,129 88	38,203 67	39,622 01
Penitentiaries.......................	2,631 66	2,373 22	1,612 33	1,726 86	1,903 82
Pension Commissioners...............					27,145 06
Post Office..........................	100,988 15	136,938 37	116,822 81	87,670 89	108,795 21
Privy Council........................	1,946 76	1,908 73	2,384 72	1,689 93	2,538 11
Public Printing and Stationery........	443,843 44	501,328 22	428,492 15	567,642 27	936,272 31
Public Service Commission............	129 85				
Public Works........................	45,653 16	65,387 08	54,029 05	36,237 30	29,892 75
Railways and Canals..................	14,741 48	26,673 47	22,142 70	15,481 94	12,647 18
Railway Commission..................	7,619 67	6,755 01	5,612 16	3,512 24	4,877 81
Royal Mint..........................	168 45	242 89	227 77	267 93	372 30
Royal Northwest Mounted Police......	7,040 09	11,246 35	15,742 88	10,948 40	12,220 55
Secretary of State....................	7,533 23	6,204 77	7,736 18	6,875 09	6,579 53
Senate of Canada....................	6,331 79	11,079 67	9,515 25	7,828 22	12,339 14
Supreme Court.......................	1,195 48	1,034 97	986 26	1,133 13	1,222 34
Trade and Commerce.................	12,351 84	6,604 27	5,358 95	8,505 77	19,431 74
Transcontinental Railway Commission.	1,238 76	944 46	222 54	129 92	239 04
War Purchasing Commission...........					558 15
Total.................	931,861 87	1,154,429 87	1,084,443 05	1,273,292 12	1,943,379 79

6. DETAIL OF EXPENDITURE OF APPROPRIATIONS.

Appropriation—Gratuities..$ 2,498 07
Detail of expenditure, death gratuities paid to widows or legal representatives of—
  Miss Grace Madden, bindery hand, died April 16, 1916................$ 63 98
  J. G. Simard, linotype machinist, died June 21, 1916..................   207 00
  John Campbell, hand compositor, died August 1, 1916................   172 92
  Wm. Bambrick, labourer, died August 31, 1916......................   129 69
  W. Emmanuel Bouchard, pressfeeder, killed at the front, September
    15, 1916...   129 53
  Napoléon Perrault, bookbinder, died October 2, 1916................   177 92
  John B. Manson, pressman, died October 11, 1916...................   181 56
  Mrs. M. O'Meara, charwoman, died October 29, 1916................   53 00
  C. W. Spearman, hand compositor, died November 17, 1916..........   172 92
  A. Dupont, hand compositor, died November 20, 1916...............   177 92
  Joseph Roger, assistant foreman, press room, died December 26, 1916.   213 51
  Adjutor Desrochers, hand compositor, died February 5, 1917.........   170 62
  Wilfrid Bouvrette, proofreader, died February 9, 1917..............   169 77
  Wm. C. Thomas, clerk, died February 24, 1917.....................   170 61
  Fred. Roxborough, bookbinder, died February 27, 1917.............   170 62
  Abraham Dallaire, labourer, died February 5, 1917................   136 50
        Total...————$ 2,498 07

Appropriation—Civil Government Salaries.....................................$ 70,662 50

Detail of expenditure—
  Salaries paid during the year......................................$ 58,803 50
  Unexpended balance... 11,859 00
                                                                    ————$ 70,662 50

Appropriation—Civil Government Contingencies................................$ 10,300 00
Detail of expenditure—
  Charwomen and cleaning...$ 3,500 45
  Office printing... 2,482 08
  Office stationery... 2,961 00
  Travelling expenses..   791 09
  Cab hire and street car fares.....................................   181 50
  Postage..   70 00
  Advertising...   130 58
  Newspapers and periodicals.......................................   80 42
  Sundries...   9 05
                                                                    $ 10,206 17
  Unexpended balance...   93 83
                                                                    ————$ 10,300 00

Appropriation—Plant, New..$ 50,000 00

Detail of expenditure—
  Hand composing rooms..$ 4,980 72
  Monotype room..   1,098 17
  Linotype room...   447 74
  Stereotype room...   6 99
  Press room...   6,894 58
  Bindery—
    Book..$ 7,463 62
    Pamphlet...   702 42
    Loose leaf..   14 00
                                                                   ————
                                                                    8,180 04
  Die stamping room...   39 67
  Map engraving room..   219 53
  Departments generally... 1,278 86
  Chief mechanic's room...   854 38
  Offices..   1,147 29
  Storekeeper's stock.. 11,265 68
  Customs duties...$ 858 40
  Brokerage..   20 00
                                                                   ————
                                                                    878 40
  Freight, etc..   93 76
        Total...$ 37,385 81
  Unexpended balance.. 12,614 19
                                                                    ————$ 50,000 00

Appropriation, Plant, Renewals...$ 7,000 00

Detail of expenditure—

Hand composing rooms...$	474 13	
Monotype room...	1,504 49	
Linotype room..	1,146 49	
Stereotype room..	79 06	
Press room...	353 32	
Bindery—		
Book...$ 669 50		
Pamphlet................................... 403 43		
Loose Leaf................................. 74 00		
	1,146 93	
Die stamping room..	58 40	
Map engraving room..	88 76	
Departments generally..	132 92	
Chief mechanic's room..	895 31	
Offices...	126 58	
Storekeeper's stock...	726 06	
Customs duties................................$ 141 36		
Brokerage..................................... 36 95		
	178 31	
Freight, etc..	84 86	
Total...$	6,995 62	
Unexpended balance..	4 38	
		7,000 00

Appropriation—Miscellaneous Printing....................................$ 150,000 00

Detail of expenditure—

Agriculture...$	49,650 74	
Auditor General..	19,066 03	
Archives...	996 13	
Civil Service Commission..	247 54	
Clerk of the Crown in Chancery.....................................	5 86	
Customs...	5,981 69	
External Affairs..	27 29	
Finance..	1,032 40	
Indian Affairs..	819 35	
Inland Revenue..	1,159 40	
Insurance..	1,612 36	
Interior..	10,618 40	
Labour...	2,010 98	
Marine...	5,532 25	
Militia and Defence..	48 60	
Mines..	2,067 52	
Naval Service..	1,521 09	
Penitentiaries..	279 15	
Public Printing and Stationery......................................	24,155 87	
Public Works...	3,139 32	
Railways and Canals..	3,791 33	
Railway Commission..	2,091 90	
Royal Northwest Mounted Police....................................	636 10	
Secretary of State..	572 50	
Trade and Commerce...	12,927 62	
	$ 149,991 42	
Unexpended balance..	8 58	
		150,000 00

Appropriation—Canada Gazette..$ 21,000 00

Detail of expenditure—

Printing of *The Canada Gazette*...........................$ 14,087 19		
Paper used for above..................................... 4,088 93		
Editing and translating................................... 2,658 00		
	$ 20,834 12	
Office printing..	11 57	
Postage..	150 00	
Total...$	20,995 69	
Unexpended balance..	4 31	
		21,000 00

Appropriation—Distribution of Parliamentary Documents...............................$ 45,000 00

Detail of expenditure—
    Office printing...$ 2,763 37
    Office stationery...   6,987 95
    Postage...   870 00
    Express and freight.......................................   305 25
    Salaries...   34,065 76

        Total...$ 44,992 33
Unexpended balance...   7.67
                                     —$ 45,000 00

Appropriation—Printing, binding and distributing the Annual Statutes........................$ 16,000 00

Detail of expenditure—
    Printing and binding......................................$ 15,560 06
    Office printing...   1 69

                                  $ 15,561 75
Unexpended balance...   438 25
                                     —$ 16,000 00

Appropriation—Contingent expenses in connection with the voters' lists.........................$ 10,600 00

Detail of expenditure—
    Printing of voters' lists...................................$ 2,288 01
    Office printing...   109 76
    Office stationery...   1,265 56
    Salaries...   6,903 26
    Express and freight.......................................   31 74

        Total...$ 10,598 33
Unexpended balance...   1 67
                                     —$ 10,600 00

7. " CANADA GAZETTE."

COMPARATIVE STATEMENT of Receipts and Expenditure on account of *Canada Gazette* from the year 1874 to the fiscal year ending March 31, 1917.

Year.	EXPENDITURE.					REVENUE.			
	Copies Gratis.	Subscribers.	Paper.	Printing and Distribution	Translation.	Subscriptions.	Advertising	Loss.	Gain.
			$ cts.	$ cts.	$ cts.	$ cts.	$ cts.	$ cts.	$ cts.
1874....	1,045	77	1,142 17	2,416 40	119 45	242 20	931 43	2,494 59	....
1875....	1,077	85	1,177 17	2,144 00	135 55	242 80	943 74	2,635 13	....
1876....	1,049	88	1,195 98	2,301 51	184 80	241 80	578 41	2,836 11	....
1877....	1,084	81	1,292 25	2,323 45	141 80	224 75	681 62	2,743 13	....
1878....	1,108	79	1,016 65	2,139 48	125 80	268 40	683 47	2,318 53	....
1879....	1,115	85	1,195 21	2,293 81	123 90	246 50	739 82	2,613 60	....
1880....	1,170	70	1,208 48	2,307 72	106 30	243 90	862 38	2,538 09	....
1881....	1,251	68	1,197 38	2,132 20	137 40	253 65	1,028 04	2,085 29	....
1882....	1,238	92	1,360 61	2,261 85	197 60	378 44	2,706 28	735 34	....
1883....	1,250	109	1,414 24	2,181 48	215 30	367 25	2,181 53	1,262 24	....
1884....	1,290	85	1,428 16	2,219 00	148 24	414 67	6,658 12	1,727 48	....
1885...	1,321	69	1,404 76	2,243 43	169 44	169 45	289 35	2,363 14	....
1886....	1,318	77	1,683 88	2,241 65	72 20	299 70	2,020 82	1,576 21	....
1887....	1,366	84	1,979 21	2,537 79	389 10	321 40	2,831 04	1,571 66	....
1888....	1,369	81	2,164 85	2,933 57	349 80	307 35	2,909 72	2,231 15	....
1889....	1,367	83	1,883 83	2,859 19	103 60	308 60	4,637 49	....	99 47
1890....	1,429	71	1,758 50	3,128 36	204 00	487 95	2,777 03	1,825 88	....
1891....	1,436	84	1,492 62	2,060 45	211 85	324 18	3,309 65	331 70	....
1892....	1,439	86	1,480 19	2,069 36	188 98	313 47	3,436 32	....	11 26
1893....	1,426	84	1,485 71	2,826 07	240 54	306 50	4,612 37	....	366 55
1894....	1,418	82	1,181 66	2,485 08	265 10	298 73	3,545 87	89 24	....
1895....	1,425	75	1,153 87	2,704 36	232 50	281 65	4,015 64	....	206 56
1896....	1,428	72	1,129 52	3,007 00	259 75	276 65	4,673 69	....	559 07
1897....	1,492	83	1,129 07	3,003 51	245 40	298 55	4,992 94	....	913 51
1898....	1,438	87	1,450 21	3,803 11	337 10	312 70	5,574 45	....	296 73
1899....	1,486	89	940 43	3,273 01	255 30	329 95	3,948 65	190 14	....
1900....	1,529	96	1,092 72	3,640 17	289 50	350 00	4,679 98	....	7 59
1901....	1,528	97	1,349 79	4,267 81	256 60	329 65	4,370 82	1,173 73	....
1902....	1,553	97	1,430 89	3,858 22	284 00	361 80	4,451 39	759 92	....
1903....	1,545	105	1,315 56	3,999 78	253 60	371 85	5,667 65	....	470 56
1904....	1,559	116	1,427 48	4,368 81	309 80	430 40	4,523 25	1,152 44	....
1905....	1,573	177	1,684 85	6,125 57	364 80	604 12	6,997 50	573 60	....
1906....	1,559	191	1,629 58	6,909 57	460 85	750 00	7,644 35	605 65	....
1907....	1,616	184	1,322 63	4,248 17	329 20	524 27	6,821 20	....	1,445 47
1908....	1,625	200	1,805 72	7,484 48	709 80	762 15	8,472 51	765 34	....
1909....	1,665	185	2,053 45	7,319 99	587 60	721 20	8,684 40	555 44	....
1910....	1,692	208	2,158 56	6,983 10	815 80	775 25	14,219 41	....	4,037 20
1911....	1,725	250	2,548 44	9,532 19	918 55	949 85	15,844 95	....	3,795 62
1912....	1,742	258	2,943 28	9,600 27	438 60	979 15	21,077 11	....	9,074 11
1913....	1,754	271	4,385 03	19,349 44	*3,261 07	1,034 20	30,804 59	....	4,843 25
1914....	1,791	284	2,720 73	15,477 24	*3,842 06	1,090 05	23,062 88	....	2,112 80
1915....	1,907	293	4,502 28	22,597 68	*4,202 56	1,121 45	18,322 04	11,441 02	....
1916....	1,901	424	3,018 22	14,978 79	*2,905 34	1,505 58	28,357 80	....	8,961 03
1917...	991	484	4,088 93	14,248 76	*2,658 00	1,677 20	35,885 58	....	16,567 09

*Translating and editing.

8 GEORGE V, A. 1918

8. CASUAL REVENUE ACCOUNT.

DETAIL of proceeds of Casual Revenue sales made during the fiscal year ending March 31, 1917.

Sales of parliamentary publications to departments and Parliament............$	4,259 63	
Sales of parliamentary publications to the public................................	8,316 07	
		$ 12,575 70⁻
Sales of *Canada Gazette* and of advertising.................................$	35,885 58	
Sales of subscriptions..	1,677 20	
		37,562 78
Sales of voters' lists..		141 70
Sales of waste paper and empty cases..		6,282 00
Sales of printing to departments and Parliament—		
Amount received in excess of expenditure during the fiscal year 1916–17................		2,348 36
Sales of stationery to departments and Parliament—		
Amount received in excess of expenditure during the fiscal year 1916–17................		116,073 48
Total...	$	174,984 02

9. RAILWAY PRINTING AUDIT.

The amount of accounts audited at this department during the fiscal year ending March 31, 1917, for printing, binding, lithographing, etc., for the Canadian Government Railways, was $188,774.31. These accounts being paid by the railways for which the printing is done, the amount is not included in the statement of receipts and expenditure of this department.

Below is a statement of the total amount of accounts audited by this department, from 1890-91 to 1916-17.

Fiscal Year.	Amount.	Increase.	Decrease.
	$ cts.	$ cts.	$ cts.
1890–91..	49,021 53	....	....
1900–01..	59,268 59	10,247 06	....
1910–11..	95,976 55	36,707 96	....
1911–12..	104,026 24	8,049 69	....
1912–13..	110,528 56	6,502 32	....
1913–14..	148,575 51	38,046 95	....
1914–15..	141,631 99	....	6,943 52
1915–16..	140,156 30	....	1,475 69
1916–17..	188,774 31	48,618 01	....

SESSIONAL PAPER No. 32

10. GOVERNMENT NEWSPAPER ADVERTISING.

The total amount certified by this department for government advertising during the fiscal year ending March 31, 1917, was $295,694.98, the details of which are set forth in a statement on page 20. These accounts being paid by the several departments for which the advertising is done, the amount is not included in the statement of receipts and expenditure of this department.

The number of advertising accounts audited was 11,688; and of circulars issued 2,231.

There was, moreover, a considerable amount of correspondence in connection therewith.

Below is a statement of the total amount of advertising accounts audited by this department from the year 1876 to the fiscal year ending March 31, 1917, inclusive.

CALENDAR YEARS.		FISCAL YEARS.	
1876	$ 12,529 27	1898–1899	$ 27,699 72
1877	12,751 56	1899–1900	46,317 74
1878	20,583 77	1900–1901	50,790 40
1879	39,676 60	1901–1902	53,850 75
1880	63,092 50	1902–1903	41,078 02
1881	30,015 44	1903–1904	57,898 72
1882	50,604 71	1904–1905	102,848 11
1883	30,149 31	1905–1906	107,812 56
1884	39,401 48	1906–1907	89,329 77
1885	33,782 53	(March 31)	
1886	25,102 83	1907–1908	141,200 45
1887	48,596 03	1908–1909	156,673 50
1888	44,520 30	1909–1910	102,841 15
1889	35,939 47	1910–1911	144,081 66
1890	26,102 48	1911–1912	166,224 26
1891	27,519 59	1912–1913	204,762 87
1892	24,819 54	1913–1914	247,477 61
1893	26,704 27	1914–1915	200,441 19
1894	26,423 72	1915–1916	210,818 48
1895	27,424 68	1916–1917	295,694 98
1896	30,760 76		
1897	35,138 54		
'1898 (6 mos. to June 30, 1898)	16,312 58		

AUDIT OF GOVERNMENT ADVERTISING in Newspapers for fiscal year ending March 31, 1917.

Department	Ontario	Quebec	Nova Scotia	New Brunswick	Prince Edward Island	Manitoba	Alberta	Saskatchewan	British Columbia	Yukon	Other Countries	Total
	$ cts.	$ cts.	$ cts.	$ cts.	$ cts.	$ cts.	$ cts.	$ cts.	$ cts.	$ cts.	$ cts.	$ cts.
Agriculture	15,420 64	4,973 89	1,639 28	1,282 59	254 40	5,201 42	3,453 57	4,284 90	3,833 42			40,344 11
Canadian Government Railways	7,224 43	8,736 61	1,298 92	2,136 70	521 00	152 95	64 80	75 20	72 00		1,362 32	21,432 93
Customs	243 30	281 13	17 50	13 84		280 20			24 00			1,047 97
External Affairs		25 00										49 00
Finance	27,015 89	13,290 94	3,357 88	2,387 63	471 08	6,570 76	5,172 44	5,980 78	6,280 58			70,527 98
Governor General's Secretary	54 25											54 25
House of Commons	34 50	204 61	30 00	25 50	29 40		46 80	47 40	17 50			435 71
Indian Affairs	1,685 19	421 12	71 80	45 60		315 74	407 96	386 38	16 50			3,350 29
Interior	12,773 78	8,952 04	2,128 10	1,339 46	573 80	7,079 48	5,221 27	6,348 54	7,897 04	2,292 00		54,605 51
Inland Revenue	7 20											7 20
Justice	150 00											150 00
Labour	377 88	4 90										3,761 94
Marine	12,153 69	2,755 47	2,315 56	864 48	68 77	484 09	606 60	284 42	130 45			20,083 28
Militia and Defence	466 72	352 80	1,405 18	597 40	1,149 31				647 12			
Mines	352 80		107 50	308 46	48 96				91 65			1,018 67
National Service	5,334 82	2,220 02	404 52	1,304 72	325 61	1,382 86	862 56	1,096 36	1,000 02			12,658 58
Naval Service	7,479 76	4,922 18	2,591 80	1,095 54	776 30	818 50	501 61	425 46	1,977 57	17 25		20,347 21
Post Office	7,339 42	7,163 12	1,455 58	1,135 10	179 39	595 69	1,049 13	230 00	234 76			19,956 79
Public Printing and Stationery	83 60	56 88										140 48
Public Works	7,218 02	6,460 57	751 76	312 45	57 50	681 24	711 05	313 59	984 47	30 00		18,465 19
Railways and Canals	2,349 42	1,657 01	588 96			118 24						5,083 84
Royal N.W.M. Police	112 50					76 10	267 24	386 00				841 84
Senate							40 00					40 00
Trade and Commerce	135 43	0 75				1,156 03						1,292 21
Transcontinental Railway												
Total	107,650 44	62,478 94	18,164 34	12,849 47	4,455 53	24,913 56	18,405 03	19,859 03	23,207 08	2,339 25	1,362 32	295,694 98

PRINTING BRANCH.

J. DE L. TACHÉ, Esq.,
King's Printer and Controller of Stationery.

SIR,—I have the honour to submit a report of the work executed for Parliament and the various departments in the Government Printing Bureau during the fiscal year ending March 31, 1917, contained in the following tabulated statements:—

1. Annual reports.
2. Supplementary reports.
3. Routine Parliamentary work.
4. House of Commons and Senate Debates.
5. Statutes.
6. *Canada Gazette.*
7. Voters' lists.
8. Pamphlet and miscellaneous book-work.
9. Statement of other letterpress departmental work by departments.
10. Halftone plates or other insertions in annual and supplementary reports.
11. Statement of books bound.
12. Pads made.
13. Making and stamping of prepaid Post Office envelopes.
14. Die stamping of letter and note headings, and envelopes.
15. Loose leaf work.
16. Comparative statement of presswork.

In addition to the divisions of work covered by the foregoing statements there are the map engraving and stereotyping divisions.

The work of the map engraving division consists of the engraving of maps, charts, etc., of various sizes, on copper, making changes and additions to existing plates, printing transfers for lithographers, engraving and printing personal cards, and engraving plates on steel for die stamping. The cost of operating this division during the year 1916–17 amounted to $28,922.08.

The work of the stereotyping division consists of the making of matrices and stereotype plates for printing, making alterations to existing plates, casting and refining metal for the linotype division, and the manufacture of some metal equipment for use in the typesetting divisions. The cost of operation for the year 1916–17 amounted to $13,948.73.

Respectfully submitted,

FRED. BOARDMAN,
Superintendent of Printing.

OTTAWA, November 5, 1917.

19

8 GEORGE V, A. 1918

TABLE No. 1.—Statement showing the Work on Annual Reports to Parliament, Year 1916-17.

Title of Document.	Number of Copies.	Number of Pages.	Total Number of Printed Pages.	Distribution.				Cost.
				Parliament.	Department.	Stock.	Sess. Papers.	$ cts.
Agriculture, 1915–16 (English)	3,735	120	448,200	2,100	1,000	35	600	616 16
Agriculture, 1915–16 (French)	740	122	90,280	375	150	15	200	658 78
Adulteration of Food, 1915–16 (English)	3,235	604	1,953,940	2,100	500	35	600	1,405 95
Adulteration of Food, 1915–16 (French)	840	606	509,040	375	250	15	200	934 69
Auditor General, 1914–15 (French)	905	2,966	2,684,230	375	250	30	250	16,175 32
Bank Shareholders, 1915 (English and French)	3,690	612	2,258,280	2,350	300	60	980	3,620 00
Civil Service Commission, 1914–15 (French)	1,130	148	167,240	375	300	205	250	579 68
Civil Service List, 1915 (French)	830	748	620,840	375	100	105	250	2,766 30
Civil Service List, 1916 (English and French)	5,685	556	3,160,860	2,475	1,200	1,210	800	4,647 76
Criminal Statistics, 1914–15 (English and French)	4,035	444	1,791,540	2,475	700	60	800	2,317 30
Estimates of Canada, Supplementary, 1916 (English)	3,915	8	31,320	2,275	600	310	730	91 42
Estimates of Canada, Supplementary, 1915–16 (French)	730	8	5,840	375		105	250	24 46
Estimates of Canada, Supplementary, 1917 (English)	3,910	8	31,280	2,400	600	310	600	70 14
Estimates of Canada, Supplementary, 1916–17 (French)	680	8	5,440	375		105	200	36 61
Estimates of Canada, Supplementary, 1916–17 (English)	3,915	2	7,830	2,275	600	310	730	7 86
Estimates of Canada, Supplementary, 1916–17 (French)	730	2	1,460	375		105	250	3 36
Estimates of Canada, Supplementary, 1916–17 (English)	3,915	12	46,980	2,275	600	310	730	120 94
Estimates of Canada, Further Supplementary, 1916–17 (French)	730	12	8,760	375		105	250	56 01
Estimates of Canada, Further Supplementary, 1916–17 (English)	3,915	2	7,830	2,275	600	310	730	10 01
Estimates of Canada, Further Supplementary, 1916–17 (French)	730	2	1,460	375		105	250	3 07
Estimates of Canada, Further Supplementary, 1917–18 (English)	3,910	96	375,360	2,490	600	310	600	959 17
...of Canada, 1917–18 (English)	680	96	65,280	375		105	200	339 52
...of Canada, 19–18 (French)	3,235	236	763,466	2,190	500	35	600	2,100 10
Excise, 1915–16 (English)	840	236	198,240	375	250	15	200	927 95
Excise, 1915–16 (French)	50,840	1,240	62,917,600	1,975	48,000	35	730	44,239 80
Experimental Farms, 1914–15, Vols. I and II (English)	10,640	1,270	13,512,800	375	10,000	15	250	15,678 29
Experimental Farms, 1914–15, Vols. I and II (French)	666	32	21,280	375	25	15	250	95 86
External Affairs, 1914–15 (French)	2,935	40	117,400	2,100	200	35	600	209 62
External Affairs, 1915–16 (English)	615	40	24,600	375	25	15	200	147 52
External Affairs, 1916 (French)	3,990	500	1,995,000	2,100	1,250	40	600	3,775 18
Fisheries, 1915–16 (English)	845	506	437,570	375	250	20	200	2,282 39
Fisheries, 1915–16 (French)	3,400	478	1,625,200	2,100	665	35	600	3,205 74
Indian Affairs, 1915–16 (English)	625	488	305,000	375	35	15	200	1,828 20
Indian Affairs, 1916 (French)	9,865	800	7,892,000	1,975	7,100	60	720	6,765 35
Insurance Report, 1915, Vol. I (English)	1,530	810	1,239,300	375	900	5	600	3,240 78
Insurance Report, 1915, Vol. I (French)	8,860	820	7,265,200	2,100	6,700	60	600	7,102 94
Insurance Report, 1915, Vol. II (English)	1,280	834	1,067,520	375	700	5	200	3,514 81
Insurance Report, 1915, Vol. II (French)	14,315	218	3,120,670	1,975	11,500	110	730	2,007 20
Insurance Abstract, 1915 (English)	655	220	144,100	375		30	250	880 39
Insurance ..., 1915 (...)	1,145	720	824,400	375	500	20	250	3,141 38
Interior, 1916 +6 (English)	3,735	592	2,211,120	2,100	1,000	35	600	3,340 79

Interior, 1915–16 (French)	1,090	608	662,720	375	500	15	200	2,643 69
Marine, 1915 (French)	890	386	343,540	375	250	15	250	2,186 34
Marine, 1915–16 (English)	3,475	288	1,000,800	2,100	750	25	600	1,227 34
Marine, 1916	840	304	255,360	375	250	15	250	1,768 93
Militia Council, 1915–16 (French)	840	52	43,680	375	200	15	250	170 98
Militia Council, 1915–16 (English)	3,210	36	115,560	2,100	500	10	600	206 54
Naval Service, 1915–16 (English)	3,485	104	362,440	375	750	35	600	545 93
Naval Service, 1916 (French)	840	108	90,722	1,975	250	35	200	435 46
Penitentiaries, 1914–15	3,240	228	738,720	375	500	15	730	1,382 12
Penitentiaries, 1914–15 (French)	690	232	160,080	2,300	50	110	250	895 98
Postmaster General, 1916 (English)	3,285	532	1,813,320	375	475	25	600	3,882 13
Postmaster General, 1916 (French)	690	552	380,880	375	90	15	200	2,926 13
Public ... 1914–15 (French)	690	272	187,680	2,400	50	10	250	914 07
Public ... 1915–16 (English)	3,510	272	954,720	375	500	5	600	1,525 95
Public ... 1916 (French)	630	272	171,360	2,100	50	20	250	1,016 82
Public Works, 1914–15 (French)	795	1,070	850,650	2,100	150	35	600	4,789 59
Public Works, 1915–16 (English)	2,985	812	2,423,820	375	250	60	600	4,919 56
... 1916 (English)	3,160	232	733,120	375	400	15	250	1,194 41
Railways and Canals, 1914–15 (French)	890	500	445,000	1,975	250	35	600	2,426 27
Railways and Canals, 1915–16 (English)	3,935	510	2,006,850	1,975	1,200	35	730	2,410 00
Railway Commission, 1914–15	4,740	472	2,237,280	375	2,000	15	250	2,438 02
Railway ... 1915 (French)	1,140	508	579,120	375	500	10	250	1,353 41
Royal N... M... Police, 1915–16 (French)	940	296	278,240	2,100	300	15	600	1,464 37
Royal ... Mounted Police, 1915–16 (English)	3,410	384	1,309,440	375	700	10	250	1,619 20
Summary of ... 1914 (French)	1,640	258	423,120	475	1,000	15	250	2,453 79
Trade and ... 1913–14, Part V (French)	1,050	418	438,900	1,975	300	25	730	871 70
Trade and ... 1915, Part V (English)	4,240	328	1,390,720	1,975	1,500	35	730	3,553 41
Trade and ... 1915, Part VI (French)	3,415	132	450,780	2,100	650	60	600	1,953 92
Trade and ... 1914–15, Part VII (English)	3,385	560	1,895,600	375	650	35	250	695 26
Trade and ... 1914–15, Part I (French)	890	708	630,120	375	250	15	250	1,053 08
Trade and ... 1915, Part II (French)	890	200	178,000	375	250	15	250	406 44
Trade and ... 1915, Part IV (French)	715	320	284,800	375	75	15	250	1,323 49
Trade and ... 1915, Part V (French)	740	96	68,640	375	150	15	600	534 60
Trade and ... 1914–15, Part VI (French)	640	328	242,720	375	50	35	200	7,701 30
Trade and ... 1916, Part I (English)	4,385	132	84,480	2,100	1,650	35	600	1,040 48
Trade and Commerce, 1916, Part II (English)	4,535	1,002	4,393,770	2,100	1,800	15	600	2,106 46
... and ... 1916, Part III	3,735	200	907,000	2,100	1,000	210	200	610 26
... and ... 1916, Part II (French)	840	320	1,195,200	375	250	30	600	4,65 45
... 191 516 (English)	3,735	200	168,000	2,100	825	15	250	2,764 30
... and N... 191 –16 (French)	665	772	2,883,420	375	60	15	600	216 15
... Railway Commission, 1915 (French)	640	772	513,380	375		15	500	117 49
... Railway Commission, 906	3,015	46	29,440	2,100	300	15	200	81 04
... Railway Commission, 1915–16 (French)	590	24	72,360	2,350		60	200	3,810 42
Unclaimed Bank Balances, 1915 (English and French)	3,690	24	14,160	2,100	300	35	980	672 46
... (English)	3,615	668	2,464,920	2,100	750	15	730	292 65
... and M... 1916 (French)	840	76	274,740	375	250		200	
		76	63,840					
Totals	**270,680**	**33,972**	**157,158,980**	**105,800**	**120,575**	**6,235**	**38,070**	**229,615 84**
Totals (March 31, 1916)	**325,365**	**39,356**	**210,007,404**	**112,600**	**162,060**	**6,905**	**43,600**	**255,812 79**

TABLE No. 2.—Statement showing the Work on Supplementary Reports to Parliament, Year 1916-17.

Title of Document.	Number of Copies.	Number of Pages.	Total Number of Printed Pages.	Distribution.				Cost.
				Parliament.	Department.	Stock.	Sess. Papers.	$ cts.
Agricultural Instruction Act, 1914-15 (English).	8,290	216	1,790,640	1,975	5,550	35	730	1,523 91
... of ..., (French).	3,110	782	2,432,020	1,975	500	35	600	6,071 81
British ... Hydrographic Survey, 1914 (French).	640	552	353,280	375		15	250	1,855 79
Board of Visitors to Royal Military College, 1915-16 (English).	3,210	12	38,520	2,100	500	10	600	83 53
... 1915 (English).	3,740	108	403,920	1,975	1,000	35	730	456 53
... 1915 (French).	840	108	90,720	375		15	250	413 83
... Officer, 1914-15 (English).	3,265	16	52,240	1,975	500	60	730	92 10
... Medical Officer, 1914-15 (French).	605	16	9,680	375		30	200	61 54
Contribution to Canadian Biology, 1914-15 (French).	590	194	114,460	375		15	200	822 78
Dairy and Cold Storage, 1915 (French).	17,140	112	1,919,680	1,975	16,500	15	730	1,155 80
Express Statistics, 1914-15 (English).	3,340	26	86,840	1,975	600	35	730	143 74
Express Statistics, 1914-15 (French).	840	26	21,840	375	200	15	980	103 93
Fifth ..., 1911, Vol. VI (English and French).	3,340	536	3,505,440	2,350	3,000	210	730	4,015 81
Geographic Board, 1915 (...).	6,540	274	983,660	1,975	850	35	250	997 67
Geographic Board, 1914-15 (French).	3,590	298	341,210	375	500	20	800	978 82
List of Vessels, 1915 (English and French).	1,145	230	933,800	2,475	750	35	730	2,009 02
Ottawa River ..., 1914-15 (English).	4,060	608	1,985,120	1,975	500	60	800	3,730 81
Ottawa River ..., 1915 (French).	3,265	612	452,880	375	150	15	730	1,656 41
Progress Report of the Manitoba Hydrographic Survey, 1912-13-14 (English).	740	304	1,592,960	1,975	2,500	35	200	2,818 19
Progress Report of the Manitoba Hydrographic Survey, 1912-13-14 (French).	5,240	308	197,120	375		15	730	1,094 75
Railway Statistics, 1914-15 (English).	640	266	1,048,040	1,975	1,200	35	250	1,293 88
Railway Statistics, 1914-15 (French).	3,940	266	223,440	1,975		15	730	960 36
Steamboat ..., 1914-15 (English).	3,490	168	586,320	1,975	750	35	250	911 51
Steamboat ..., 1914-15 (French).	890	168	149,520	375	250	15	730	1,136 39
..., 1915-16 (English and French).	4,060	160	649,600	2,475	750	35	800	1,267 05
Telephone Statistics, 1914-15 (English).	3,340	88	293,920	1,975	600	35	730	381 17
Telephone Statistics, 1915 (French).	840	88	73,920	375	200	15	250	199 81
..., 1914-15 (English).	3,340	24	80,160	1,975	600	35	730	103 00
Topographical Surveys, 1914-15 (English).	840	24	20,160	1,975	200	15	250	87 23
Topographical Surveys, 1915 (French).	5,240	218	1,142,320	1,975	2,500	35	250	1,65. 01
Trade and ..., ...ly Report:—	1,090	228	248,520	375	500	15	200	955 36
December.............. 1915.	2,085	386	804,810	1,100	975	10		1,521 75

1916.								
January	1,885	328	618,280	1,100	775	10		1,350 43
February	1,885	340	640,900	1,100	775	10		1,371 70
March	1,885	398	750,230	1,100	775	10		1,389 31
April	1,810	370	669,700	1,100	700	10		1,693 92
May	1,810	362	635,220	1,100	700	10		1,675 26
June	1,810	408	738,480	1,100	700	10		1,792 19
July	1,810	364	658,840	1,100	700	10		1,640 94
August	1,810	362	655,220	1,100	700	10		1,617 42
September	1,810	384	695,040	1,100	700	10		1,624 81
October	1,810	386	698,660	1,100	700	10		1,789 27
November	1,810	340	615,400	1,100	700	10		1,566 39
Trade and Navigation, Revised Monthly Statements:—								
1916.								
January	1,860	552	1,026,720	1,200	600	60		1,307 46
February	1,860	552	1,026,720	1,200	600	60		1,341 13
March	1,860	552	1,026,720	1,200	600	60		1,318 98
April	1,860	552	1,026,720	1,200	600	60		1,486 49
May	1,680	552	1,026,720	1,200	600	60		1,454 29
June	1,860	552	1,026,720	1,200	600	60		1,378 99
July	1,860	552	1,026,720	1,200	600	60		1,448 36
August	1,860	552	1,026,720	1,200	600	60		1,517 25
September	1,860	552	1,026,730	1,200	600	60		1,444 88
October	1,860	552	1,026,720	1,200	600	60		1,486 20
November	1,860	552	1,026,720	1,200	600	60		1,471 75
December	1,860	552	1,026,720	1,200	600	60		1,555 88
1917.								
January	1,860	552	1,026,720	1,200	600	60		1,602 69
Veterinary Director General, 1914-15 (English)	9,740	148	1,441,520	1,975	7,000	35	730	1,439 45
Veterinary Director General, 1914-15 (French)	590	136	80,240	375		15	200	538 31
Totals	155,470	18,924	44,891,850	71,475	65,250	1,975	16,770	78,858 04
Totals (March 31, 1916)	222,085	19,508	60,799,190	67,950	136,575	1,840	15,720	87,488 44

8 GEORGE V, A. 1918

TABLE No. 3.—Statement showing the Routine Parliamentary work, Year 1916–17.

Title of Document.	Number of Copies.	Number of Pages.	Distribution.			
			Parlia- ment.	Depart- ment.	Stock.	Sess. Papers.
Votes and Proceedings.........{English.	2,485*	594	2,485	....	....	....
French	590*	592	590	....	....	....
Orders of the Day.............{English	1,025*	832	1,025	....	....	....
French	230*	826	230	....	....	....
Public Bills (Commons and{English	2,435*	284	2,435	....	....	....
Senate). French	445*	300	445	....	....	....
Private Bills (Commons and{English	1,135*	96	1,135	....	....	....
Senate). French	320*	108	320	....	....	....
Third Reading Bills (Com-{English	535*	176	535	....	....	....
mons). French	185*	212	185	....	....	....
Third Reading Bills (Senate).{English	710*	48	710	....	....	....
French	220*	22	220	....	....	....
Returns (for distribution or{English	19,900	822	9,310	6,000	470	4,120
Sessional Papers, either or{French	13,315	1,352	4,855	4,250	310	3,900
both; aggregate).						
Divorce cases (aggregate).............	3,200	146	3,200	....	....	....
Printing of various Committee sittings						
(aggregate).......................	10,850	2,940	10,850	....	....	....
House of CommonsJournals,1916{English	730	548	....	....	....	730
sixth session, 12th Parliament {French	250	522	....	....	....	250
Appendix No. 4, 1915 (French).........	260	1,572	....	....	10	250
No. 1, 1916 (English).......	780	628	....	....	50	730
No. 1, 1916 (French).......	260	664	....	....	10	250
No. 3, 1916 (English).......	25,780	308	25,000	....	50	730
No. 3, 1916 (French).......	210	336	....	....	10	200
No. 4, 1916 (English).......	2,880	200	2,100	....	50	730
No. 4, 1916 (French).......	760	208	500	....	10	250
Senate Journals, 1916, sixth{English	730	360	....	....	....	730
session, 12th Parliament......{French	250	352	....	....	....	250
Totals..............................	90,470	15,048	66,130	10,250	970	13,120
Totals (March 31, 1916)..........	80,445	15,818	68,915	....	....	11,530

*The quantities given are those ordered, for each issue, at the opening of Parliament. For a few issues these were increased.

TABLE No. 4.—Statement showing the work on the House of Commons and Senate Debates, Year 1916–17.

Title of Document.	Number of Copies.	Number of Pages.	Total Number of Printed Pages.	Distribution.				Cost.
				House of Commons	Senate.	Binding.	Stock.	$ cts.
House of Commons Debates, 1916 (sixth session, 12th Parliament)—								
Unrevised Edition (English)	3,775	2,954	10,471,810	3,165			610	11,307 49
Unrevised Edition (French)	640	2,830	1,806,000	430			210	9,714 61
Revised Edition, 4 vols. (English)	1,516	4,402	6,669,030	626		690	200	640 91
Revised Edition, 4 vols. (French)	285	4,686	1,335,510	75		175	35	605 62
Senate Debates, 1916 (sixth session, 12th Parliament)—								
Unrevised Edition (English)	2,065	498	1,028,370		1,850		215	1,656 58
Unrevised Edition (French)	45	682	30,690		25		20	1,964 53
Revised Edition (English)	560	614	343,840			500	60	1,334 17
Revised Edition (French)	110	670	73,700			100	10	816 47
Totals	8,996	17,336	21,758,950	4,296	1,875	1,465	1,360	42,140 38
Totals (March 31, 1916)	8,991	14,830	21,164,708	4,296	1,875	1,460	1,360	38,551 49
Speeches: Extra copies ordered by Members and Senators (aggregate)	137,600	582	2,607,900					1,156 98

8 GEORGE V, A. 1918

TABLE No. 5.—Statement showing the work on the Statutes, Year 1916–17.

Title of Document.	Number of Copies.	Number of Pages.	Total Number of Printed Pages.	Cost.
THE STATUTES.				
7 George V—Sixth Session, 12th Parliament.				$ cts.
Volume 1, 1916 (English)	7,096	466	3,306,736	6,911 97
Volume 2, 1916 (English)	6,196	362	2,242,952	
Volume 1, 1916 (French)	2,001	430	860,430	2,967 43
Volume 2, 1916 (French)	1,151	288	331,488	
Totals	16,444	1,546	6,741,606	9,879 40
Totals (March 31, 1916)	15,050	1,770	6,897,500	9,532 91

TABLE No. 6.—Statement showing the work on the *Canada Gazette,* Year 1916–17.

Title of Document.	Aggregate Annual Issue.	Number of Pages in Volume.
Canada Gazette	164,500	4,978
Canada Gazette (March 31, 1916)	186,875	4,778

TABLE No. 7.—Statement showing the work on the Voters' Lists, Year 1916–17.

Title of Document.	Number of Copies.	Number of Pages.
Voters' Lists—9 constituencies	1,400	440
Voters' Lists (March 31, 1916)	3,665	1,850

TABLE No. 8.—Return of Pamphlet and Miscellaneous Book-work, Year 1916-17
(copies and pages aggregate).

Description.	Number of Copies.	Number of Pages.	Total Number of Printed Pages.
Agriculture—			
Testing of Milk, Cream and Dairy By-Products (Bulletin No. 45)	85,000	24	2,040,000
Observations of the Migration of Warble Larvæ through the Tissues (Bulletin No. 22)	1,000	16	16,000
A Further Contribution on the Biology of Hypoderma Lincatum (Bulletin No. 21)	1,000	16	16,000
The Cabbage Root Maggot and Its Control in Canada (Bulletin No. 12)	40,000	60	2,400,000
The Grimsby Precooling and Experimental Fruit Storage Warehouse (Bulletin No. 47)	11,000	16	176,000
Precooling Shipment and Cold Siorage of Tender Fruit (Bulletin No. 48)	11,000	36	396,000
Practical Assistance to Wool Growers in the Marketing of their Wool Clips (Pamphlet No. 7, 2nd edition)	50,000	20	1,000,000
The Army Cutworm (Bulletin No. 13)	10,000	32	320,000
Publications Available for Distribution	5,000	12	60,000
Fruit Crop Report (5 issues)	75,000	40	602,600
The Care, San tat on and Feeding of Foxes in Captivity (Bulletin No. 20)	2,000	20	40,000
The Canadian Record of Performance for Pure-Bred Dairy Cattle (Report No. 8)	15,000	88	1,320,000
Finish the Feeders in Canada—Keep the Heifers at Home (Pamphlet No. 20)	150,000	8	1,200,000
Distribution of Pure Bred Male Animals by the Live Stock Branch (Booklet No. 3)	10,000	24	240,000
Distribution of Pure Bred Male Animals by the Live Stock Branch (Booklet No. 3, 2nd edition)	5,000	24	120,000
The Bacon Hog and the British Market—" Production and Thrift" (Pamphlet No. 21)	150,000	16	2,400,000
Spraying for Insects Affecting Apple Orchards in Nova Scotia (Circular No. 8)	10,000	16	160,000
Bulletin of Foreign Agricultural Intelligence; from February, 1916 to November, 1916 (10 issues)	148,180	868	15,011,120
Canadian Patent Office Record, February, 1916, to November, 1916 (10 issues)	12,000	4,096	4,915,200
Index to Vol. XLIII, Canadian Patent Office Record	1,200	104	124,800
Rules and Forms of the Canadian Patent Office (Revised and Amended)	5,000	32	160,000
" The Patent Act " (R.S.C., 1906)	5,000	24	120,000
Les criblures de grain et résultats des essais d'alimentation	21,000	48	1,008,000
L'avortement épizootique (extrait du feuillet No. 108 du Ministère britannique de l'Agriculture et des Pêcheries)	1,000	8	8,000
" Acte des brevets " (S.R.C., 1906)	500	24	12,000
L'essai du lait, de la crème et des sous-produits du lait au moyen du proc. dé Babcock (bulletin No. 45)	2,500	50	125,000
Soin, hygiène et alimentation des renards en captivité (bulletin No. 20)	2,000	20	40,000
La préparation des oeufs pour la vente (bulletin No. 16)	50,000	24	1,200 000
Civil Service Commission—			
Ninth Meeting of the National Assembly of Civil Service Commissions— Programme	500	8	4,000
Miscellaneous Information	500	8	4,000
Information respecting Outside Service Examinations	2,000	16	32,000
Ninth Meeting of the National Assembly of Civil Service Commissions—Report of Proceedings	300	176	52,800
The Scientific Work of the Government (Paper read before the Ninth Meeeting of the National Assembly of Civil Service Commissions, by Dr. Otto Klotz)	200	12	2,400
Renseignements concernant les examens du Service civil	1,500	64	96,000
Clerk of the Crown in Chancery—			
Résumé of General Elections, 1896, 1900, 1904, 1908, 1911 and By-Elections held between July, 1896, and January, 1916	500	124	62,000
The Dominion Elections Act with Schedule of Forms (Chap. 6, R.S.C., 1906)	23,000	140	3,220,000
Ontario Oaths (Forms 14, 17, 18 and 19)	1,000	8	8,000
Carried forward	908,880	6,322	38,711,920

TABLE No. 8.—Return of Pamphlet and Miscellaneous Book-work, Year 1916-17
(copies and pages aggregate)—*Continued.*

Description.	Number of Copies.	Number of Pages.	Total Number of Printed Pages.
Brought forward..	908,880	6,322	38,711,920
Customs—			
Memorandum (Confidential)...............................	24	16	384
Memorandum No. 2015-B—War Measures..................	6,000	24	144,000
List of Ports with Outports and Preventive Stations (Corrected to 1st July, 1916)...	2,500	52	130,000
List of Forms (Corrected to 1st July, 1916).....................	1,500	16	24,000
Classification of Exports...................................	200	8	1,600
Memorandum (Confidential)...............................	400	56	22,400
Memorandum (Confidential)...............................	300	90	27,000
Financial Report, 1915-16.................................	105	288	30,240
Experimental Farms—			
Late Blight and Rot of Potatoes (Circular No. 10)...............	200,000	16	3,200,000
Seasonable Hints (Nos. 5, 6 and 7)........................	935,000	48	14,960,000
Soil Fertility—Its Economic Maintenance and Increase (Bulletin No. 27, Second series)...................................	10,000	16	160,000
Bees and How to Keep them (Bulletin No. 26, second series)......	50,000	56	2,800,000
Tobacco Growing in Canada (Bulletin No. 25, second series)......	10,000	32	320,000
Asparagus, Celery and Onion Culture (Pamphlet No. 5)..........	10,000	8	80,000
A Review of the Status and Possibilities of Flax Production and Manipulation in Canada..................................	10,000	32	320,000
Feeding for Beef in Alberta (Bulletin No. 30, second series).........	10,000	40	400,000
The Apple in Canada—Its Cultivation and Improvement (Bulletin No. 86)...	110,000	136	14,960,000
Extracts from Annual Report, 1914-15:			
Report of the Director....................................	60,000	90	5,400,000
Field Husbandry, Division of..............................	60,000	186	11,160,000
Chemistry...	53,500	82	4,387,000
Horticulture...	60,000	288	17,280,000
Cereals...	60,000	84	5,040,000
Animal Husbandry.......................................	60,000	220	13,200,000
Forage Plants...	60,000	86	5,160,000
Poultry...	53,000	52	2,756,000
Tobacco..	53,000	58	3,074,000
Bees...	54,000	24	1,296,000
Botany...	54,000	42	2,268,000
Experimental Stations:			
Charlottetown, P.E.I......................................	250	52	13,000
Fredericton, N.B...	250	40	10,000
Nappan, N.S..	250	64	16,000
Kentville, N.S...	250	56	14,000
Ste. Anne de la Pocatière, Qué............................	50	20	1,000
Cap Rouge, Qué...	100	48	4,800
Lennoxville, Qué...	150	8	1,200
Brandon, Man...	250	84	21,000
Indian Head, Sask..	250	64	16,000
Rosthern, Sask...	250	32	8,000
Scott, Sask..	250	32	8,000
Lethbridge, Alberta......................................	250	52	13,000
Lacombe, Alberta..	250	48	12,000
Agassiz, B.C..	250	88	22,000
Inverness, B.C...	250	20	5,000
Sidney, B.C...	250	16	4,000
Rapport de l'Entomologiste du Dominion, 1914-15................	5,000	44	220,000
Culture du ginseng, des champignons et du melon................	5,000	8	40,000
Conseils pour la saison (Nos. 5, 6 et 7)........................	246,435	48	3,942,960
L'industrie de la canneberge—Ses possibilités au Canada..........	2,000	32	64,000
Les abeilles et la conduite du rucher (Bulletin No. 26, deuxième série)...	15,000	64	960,000
Extraits du rapport annuel, 1914-15:			
Rapport du Directeur.....................................	17,000	92	1,564,000
Culture du sol—Service de la..............................	17,000	188	3,196,000
Chimie...	15,500	88	1,364,000
Carried forward..	3,218,894	9,756	158,832,504

SESSIONAL PAPER No. 32

TABLE No. 8.—Return of Pamphlet and Miscellaneous Book-work, Year 1916-17
(copies and pages aggregate)—*Continued.*

Description.	Number of Copies.	Number of Pages.	Total Number of Printed Pages.
Brought forward.	3,218,894	9,756	158,832,504
Experimental Farms—Concluded.			
Extracts from Annual Report, 1914-15—*Concluded.*			
Horticulture	17,000	298	5,066,000
Céréales	17,000	84	1,428,000
Elevage	17,000	224	3,808,000
Plantes fourragères	17,000	88	1,496,000
Aviculture	16,000	56	896,000
Tabacs	16,000	60	960,000
Apiculture	16,000	26	416,000
Botanique	16,000	44	704,000
Stations expérimentales:			
Québec—Centre	150	48	7,200
Québec—Est	200	20	4,000
Cantons de l'est	100	8	800
External Affairs—			
Passport requirements of Foreign Countries	10,000	8	80,000
Confidential Papers (13 different documents)	700	464	17,450
Exchequer Court—			
Reports of the Exchequer Court of Canada:—			
No. 4, Vol. 15	1,000	136	136,000
No. 1, Vol. 16	1,000	192	192,000
Governor General—			
Military Inspection and Western Tour by Field Marshal His Royal Highness the Duke of Connaught	150	32	4,800
Finance—			
List of Insurance Companies, April 1, 1916	550	12	6,600
Loan and Trust Companies, Annual Statements for 1915	500	72	36,000
Supply Bill, 1916, Schedules A and B	500	40	20,000
Supply Bill, 1916, Schedules A, B and C	500	44	22,000
Consolidation of Appropriation Acts Nos. 1 and 2, 1916-17	500	34	17,000
An Act to levy a tax on business profits.	18,000	16	288,000
Decayed Pilots Fund Account	150	16	2,400
List of Insurance Companies, July 1, 1916	550	12	6,600
Superannuation, Judges' Salaries and Pensions	30	12	360
List of Insurance Companies, Sept. 30, 1916	500	12	6,000
List of Insurance Companies, Dec. 30, 1916	500	8	4,000
List of Securities held by Insurance Companies (as at December 31, 1916)	700	140	98,000
Canada's Need for Greater National Saving	10,000	8	80,000
Canada's Need for Greater National Saving (2nd edition)	5,000	8	40,000
Supply Bill, 1917	500	32	16,000
Tables of Values	500	132	66,000
Loi portant prélèvement d'une taxe sur les profits d'affaires	4,000	16	64,000
Devoir national de l'épargne au Canada	3,000	8	24,000
House of Commons—			
Analytical Index, Commons Debates, 1915	690	84	57,960
Discrepancy on Price of Fish	500	64	32,000
Index to Votes and Proceedings, 1916	250	64	16,000
Analytical Index, Commons Debates, 1916	690	128	88,320
Reports and Returns—Session 1917	300	8	2,400
Unrevised Debates of various dates (extra copies, aggregate)	3,200	548	197,200
An Address delivered by Mr. John Bright, Dominion Live Stock Commissioner	37,500	18	675,000
Royal Commission on Shell Contracts—Report	24,000	32	768,000
Royal Commission on Shell Contracts—Minutes of Evidence (Parts I and II)	1,000	1,710	1,710,000
General Index to House of Commons Journals, 1904-15	800	928	742,400
Carried forward	3,479,104	15,750	179,134,994

8 GEORGE V, A. 1918

TABLE No. 8.—Return of Pamphlet and Miscellaneous Book-work, Year 1916-17
(copies and pages aggregate)—*Continued.*

Description.	Number of Copies.	Number of Pages.	Total Number of Printed Pages.
Brought forward..	3,479,104	15,750	179,134,994
House of Commons—Concluded.			
Select Standing Committees of House of Commons, 1917 (Seventh Session, 12th Parliament)......................................	600	12	7,200
List of Members and Committees, 1917.........................	600	48	28,800
Index Analytique des Débats de la 5ème session du 12ème parlement	150	192	28,800
Commission Royale des contrats pour obus—Rapport.............	1,000	32	32,000
Index des Procès-Verbaux, 1916................................	75	50	3,750
Discours prononcé par Monsieur John Bright, Commissaire fédéral de l'industrie animale............................	12,500	18	225,000
Indian Affairs—			
List of Lots for Sale in the Wild Lands........................	200	8	1,600
Regulations respecting the Education of Indian Children.........	500	8	4,000
Inland Revenue—			
Official List of Licensed Manufacturers........................	850	68	57,800
Elevator Scale Equipment (2 issues)...........................	5,000	8	40,000
Weights and Measures—Inspectors' Handbook, 1916..............	300	76	22,800
Official List of Bulletins—Issued to September, 1916...........	1,000	16	16,000
Weights and Measures Act and Regulations, 1914-15.............	200	136	27,200
Bulletins:—			
Malt Extracts (No. 326).................................	4,000	24	96,000
Turpentine, as a Paint Material (No. 331).................	4,000	32	128,000
Formalin (No. 333).....................................	4,000	12	48,000
Butter (No. 334).......................................	4,000	20	80,000
Cream of Tartar (No. 335)..............................	4,000	24	96,000
Tincture of Ginger (No. 336)............................	4,000	12	48,000
Lemon Flavouring Extract (No. 337).....................	4,000	36	144,000
Sausages (No. 338).....................................	4,000	20	80,000
Sweet Spirit of Nitre (No. 339).........................	4,000	12	48,000
Ground Coffee (No. 340)................................	4,000	40	160,000
Household Ammonia (No. 341)...........................	4,000	24	96,000
Liquid Extract of Nux Vomica (No. 342).................	5,000	4	20,000
Sugar (No. 343)..	5,000	36	180,000
Spirit of Camphor (No. 344)............................	4,000	24	96,000
Evaporated Milk (No. 345).............................	4,000	16	64,000
Chocolate Candy (No. 346).............................	4,000	20	80,000
Fertilizers for 1916 (No. 347)..........................	5,000	48	240,000
Maple Sugar (No. 348)..................................	5,000	28	140,000
Mace (No. 349)..	5,000	16	80,000
Feed Flour (No. 350)...................................	5,000	20	100,000
Bay Rum, Florida Water, etc, (No. 351).................	5,000	16	80,000
Evaporated Fruits and Vegetables (No. 352).............	5,000	28	140,000
Temperance Beer (No. 353).............................	5,000	20	100,000
Gluten Flour, etc. (No. 354)............................	5,000	12	60,000
Bran (No. 355)..	5,000	28	140,000
Aspirin Tablets (No. 356)..............................	5,000	8	40,000
Canned Tomatoes (No. 357).............................	5,000	32	160,000
Cassia (No. 358).......................................	5,000	24	120,000
Tea (No. 359)...	5,000	36	180,000
Baking Powder (No. 360)...............................	5,000	28	140,000
Prepared Mustard (No. 361)............................	5,000	20	100,000
Gasolene (No. 362).....................................	5,000	16	80,000
Malt Extract for Bakers' Use (No. 363).................	5,000	12	60,000
Tabac et cigares (Cir. G. 155)...............................	5,000	8	40,000
Bulletins:—			
Sirop d'érable (No. 325)................................	500	32	16,000
Extraits de Malt (No. 326).............................	500	24	12,000
Huile à salade (No. 328)...............................	500	24	12,000
Orge mondé et orge perlé (No. 329).....................	500	28	14,000
Céréales préparées (No. 330)..........................	500	8	4,000
Térébentine, comme substance employée dans la peinture (No. 331)..	500	28	14,000
Carried forward...................................	3,661,079	17,322	183,165,944

TABLE No. 8.—Return of Pamphlet and Miscellaneous Book-work, Year 1916-17
(copies and pages aggregate)—*Continued.*

Description.	Number of Copies.	Number of Pages.	Total Number of Printed Pages.
Brought forward...	3,661,079	17,322	183,165,944
Inland Revenue—Concluded. ·			
Bulletins—*Continued.*			
Huile de lin crue (No. 332).................................	500	32	16,000
Formaline (No. 333).......................................	500	12	6,000
Beurre (No. 334)...	500	20	10,000
Crème de tartre (No. 335).................................	500	24	12,000
Teinture de gingembre (No. 336)..........................	500	12	6,000
Extrait aromatisant de citron (No. 337)....................	500	36	18,000
Saucisse (No. 338)..	500	20	10,000
Ether nitreux alcoolisé (No. 339).........................	500	12	6,000
Café moulu (No. 340).....................................	500	40	20,000
Ammoniaque domestique (No. 341)........................	500	24	12,000
Extrait liquide de noix vomique (No. 342).................	500	8	4,000
Sucre (No. 343)..	500	36	18,000
Alcool camphré—*spiritus camphoræ* (No. 344).............	500	24	12,000
Lait évaporé (No. 345)....................................	500	16	8,000
Bonbons au chocolat (No. 346)............................	500	20	10,000
Engrais pour 1916 (No. 347)..............................	500	48	24,000
Sirop d'érable (No. 348)..................................	500	28	14,000
Macis (No. 349)..	500	16	8,000
Bay rum, eau de Floride, etc. (No. 351)...................	500	16	8,000
Farine de gluten, etc. (No. 354)..........................	500	12	6,000
Tablettes d'aspirine (No. 356)............................	500	8	4,000
Interior—			
General Instructions for Taking Levels....................	200	8	1,600
Regulations Governing Water Power Rights in the Provinces of Manitoba, Saskatchewan, Alberta and the Northwest Territories..	1,000	16	16,000
Index to Orders in Council, 1911..........................	30	88	2,640
Irrigation Surveys and Inspections, 1915..................	2,500	72	180,000
Dominion Parks Motor Regulations........................	2,000	16	32,000
Levelling Operations......................................	2,000	368	736,000
Facts and Figures, 1916...................................	3,000	32	96,000
Yukon Grazing and Hay Regulations......................	1,500	8	12,000
Memo. of Information for the Guidance of Applicants for Water Rights, etc......................................	5,000	8	40,000
Timber Regulations, Yukon Territory.....................	2,000	8	16,000
Petroleum and Natural Gas Lease.........................	4,000	12	48,000
Memorandum for the Prime Minister......................	30	8	240
Water Power Regulations.................................	3,000	72	216,000
Triangulation of the Railway Belt of British Columbia......	1,000	94	94,000
List of Publications and Maps.............................	1,000	12	12,000
Canadian Woods for Structural Timber....................	20,000	48	960,000
Irrigation Surveys and Inspections, 1916..................	2,500	88	220,000
Dominion Lands Act and Amendments.....................	3,000	68	204,000
List of School Lands for Sale:			
Moosejaw, Sask...	2,500	8	20,000
Indian Head, Sask......................................	2,500	8	20,000
Vulcan, Alberta...	2,500	8	20,000
Carmangay, Alberta.....................................	2,500	8	20,000
Munson, Alberta..	2,500	12	30,000
Kindersley, Sask..	2,500	12	30,000
Glenella, Man...	2,500	8	20,000
Kamsack. Sask..	2,500	8	20,000
Dauphin, Man...	2,500	8	20,000
Biggar, Sask..	2,500	8	20,000
Rossburn, Man..	2,500	8	20,000
Blaine Lake, Sask.......................................	2,500	8	20,000
Provost, Sask...	2,500	12	30,000
Chinook, Alberta..	2,500	20	50,000
Redvers, Sask...	2,500	8	20,000
Broadview, Sask..	2,500	8	20,000
Moosomin, Sask...	2,500	8	20,000
Carried forward..	3,767,839	18,972	186,684,424

8 GEORGE V, A. 1918

TABLE No. 8.—Return of Pamphlet and Miscellaneous Book-work, Year 1916-17
(copies and pages aggregate)—*Continued.*

Description.	Number of Copies.	Number of Pages.	Total Number of Printed Pages.
Brought forward..................................	3,767,839	18,972	186,684,424
Interior—Continued.			
Instructions for the Erection of Boundary Monuments on Surveys of Dominion Lands...	500	8	4,000
Instructions for the Preparation of Plans *re* Provisions of the Irrigation Act...	3,000	12	36,000
Instructions for the Submission of Drainage Applications..........	1,500	2	3,000
Publications of the Dominion Observatory (Nos. 6 and 7, Vol. III)	2,000	100	100,000
Potash Regulations................................	1,000	16	16,000
Extracts from Annual Report, 1914–15:			
Juvenile Immigration (Part of Part II)....................	3,000	32	96,000
Commission of Dominion Parks (Part V)...................	2,500	80	200,000
Director of Forestry (Part VI)........................	2,000	100	200,000
Canadian Hydraulic Power Development (Parts XII and XIII)..	1,000	56	56,000
Extracts from Annual Report, 1915–16:			
Dominion Lands (Part I)............................	500	194	97,000
Immigration (Part II).............................	2,000	96	192,000
Director of Forestry (Part VI).......................	2,000	96	192,000
Dominion Water Powers (Part VIII)....................	2,500	228	570,000
Roll of Honour (List of Employees, Inside Service, enlisted for Overseas Duty)..................................	1,000	8	8,000
Extracts from Reports on Townships:			
East of the Principal Meridian and East of the Second Meridian East......................................	1,000	24	24,000
West of the Principal and Second Meridian................	1,000	28	28,000
West of the Third and Fourth Meridians.................	1,000	48	48,000
West of the Fifth and Sixth Meridians...................	1,000	80	80,000
In the Railway Belt, British Columbia...................	1,000	36	36,000
1 to 16, West of the Second Meridian...................	1,500	160	240,000
East and West of the Principal Meridian.................	1,000	32	32,000
West of the Second and Third Meridians.................	1,000	24	24,000
West of the Fifth and Sixth Meridians..................	1,000	56	56,000
West of the Fourth Meridian.........................	1,000	24	24,000
In the Railway Belt, British Columbia..................	1,000	40	40,000
Forest Products of Canada:			
Lumber, Lath and Shingles, 1914 (Bulletin No. 56)..........	6,000	64	384,000
Lumber, Lath and Shingles, 1914 (Bulletin No. 57)..........	500	82	41,000
Lumber, Lath and Shingles, 1915 (Bulletin No. 58A)........	1,000	32	32,000
Lumber, Lath and Shingles, 1915 (Bulletin No. 58A)........	4,000	32	128,000
Pulpwood, 1915 (Bulletin No. 58B).....................	2,000	12	24,000
Poles and Cross-Ties (Bulletin No. 58 C).................	2,000	10	20,000
Dominion Forest Officers' Manual—General Order No. 8—Property Description, Adjustments and Methods of use of the Six-inch Micrometer Block Survey Reiterating Transit Theodolite 1912 Pattern.......................................	500	66	33,000
Alphabetical List of Seed Grain, etc. (18 issues)............	9,000	1,232	616,000
Instructions Regarding the Preparation of Plans to be Filed under the Provision of the Irrigation Act......................	3,000	12	36,000
Geographical Publications of the Department of the Interior......	1,500	12	18,000
Produits des Forêts du Canada, 1914 (Bulletin No. 57)..........	2,500	64	160,000
Justice—			
In the Exchequer Court of Canada—Notes of Argument..........	25	76	1,900
In the Supreme Court of Canada—On Appeal from the Court of Appeal of British Columbia...........................	50	128	6,400
Royal Commission *re* War Supplies (6 issues)................	4,500	278	214,000
Exchequer Court of Canada—In Prize—"The Leonor"...........	125	16	2,000
The Canadian Criminal Identification Bureau................	500	8	4,000
Labour—			
United Brotherhood of Carpenters and Joiners (Extract).........	200	16	3,200
Labour Organizations in Canada—Fifth Annual Report..........	5,500	232	1,276,000
Carried forward................................	3,847,739	22,952	192,113,924

SESSIONAL PAPER No. 32

TABLE No. 8.—Return of Pamphlet and Miscellaneous Book-work, Year 1916-17
(copies and pages aggregate)—*Continued.*

Description.	Number of Copies.	Number of Pages.	Total Number of Printed Pages.
Brought forward..	4,847,739	22,952	192,113,924
Marine and Fisheries—			
Index to Notice to Mariners, 1915..............................	800	24	19,200
List of Lights and Fog Signals—Atlantic Coast, 1916..............	1,900	328	623,200
Inland Waters, 1916..............	800	164	131,200
Pacific Coast, 1916................	1,000	64	64,000
Atlantic Coast, 1917...............	2,000	328	656,000
List of Buoys, Beacons and Day Marks on the Pacific Coast, 1916.	1,000	88	88,000
Toronto Magnetical Observations, 1914.........................	300	34	10,200
Amendments to By-Laws of the Pilotage District of Quebec........	50	8	400
Meteorological Tables, 1913...................................	1,200	632	758,400
Discipline on Canadian Government Vessels....................	100	8	800
International Rules of the Road...............................	500	22	11,000
Index to Notices to Mariners, 1916...........................	800	24	19,200
Rules of the Road for the Great Lakes.........................	2,000	20	40,000
Meteorological Tables, 1914...................................	1,200	652	782,400
Supplement to List of Vessels (11 issues)	3,500	92	29,600
Règlements pour l'inspection des Chaudières et Machines des navires à vapeur...	500	80	40,000
Règlements pour la gouverne des hâvres publics.................	500	28	14,000
Militia and Defence—			
Rifle and Musketry Exercises for the Ross Rifle, 1915............	50,000	48	2,400,000
List of Casualties, C.E.F., October 7 to December 31, 1915........	20,000	160	3,200,000
Description and Action of Colt Automatic Gun....'..............	15,000	32	480,000
Report of the Halifax Military Lands Board, 1915...............	100	176	17,600
Regulations for the Canadian Officers Training Corps, 1916....'..	10,000	28	280,000
Scale of Equipment for Field Artillery Batteries...........'....	5,000	16	80,000
Regulations for Magazines and Care of War Matériel.............	300	16	4,800
Instructions *re* Organization, etc., C.E.F. Units, 1916..........	20,000	32	64,000
Instructions for Practice, Horse, Field and Heavy Artillery.......	1,000	48	48,000
Instructions for Assembling and Fitting the Pattern 1916, Dismounted Equipment...	5,000	16	80,000
Scale of Equipment for Infantry Battalions.....................	2,000	16	32,000
Section Gun Drill..	500	16	8,000
Regulations for Canadian Ordnance, etc.......................	800	16	12,800
Instructions respecting Troop Trains..........................	2,500	12	30,000
Amendments to "Instructions *re* Organization, etc., C.E.F. Units, 1916"...	20,000	18	360,000
Index to Militia Daily Orders, 1915...........................	6,800	144	979,200
Financial Instructions and Allowances for the Expeditionary Force, 1916..	15,000	144	2,160,000
List of Casualties, Jan. 1 to March 13, 1916....................	20,000	84	1,680,000
Bayonet Fighting and Physical Training........................	5,000	24	120,000
Supplementary Physical Training Tables, 1916..................	10,000	24	240,000
Bayonet Training (Provisional)................................	10,000	34	340,000
Canadian Manual of Military Cooking.........................	3,980	68	270,640
Regulations for the Canadian Army Veterinary Service..........	500	52	26,000
Draft of Proposed Report of Economic Commission..............	50	20	1,000
Standing Orders—Signal Training Depot C.E.F................	2,000	16	32,000
Regulations for Magazines and Care of War Matériel............	1,500	16	24,000
Defensive Measures against Gas Attacks.......................	1,500	20	30,000
Report of the War Purchasing Commissioners (3 Vols.)...........	3,000	2,084	6,252,000
Royal Flying Corps..	25,000	8	200,000
Physical Training—Special Tables, 1917.......................	5,000	32	160,000
Quarterly Militia List, 1916 (4 issues)........................	32,600	4,344	35,351,400
Amendments to "Regulations for Magazines and Care of War Matériel, 1913"...	300	24	7,200
Military Hospitals Commission—Special Bulletin...............	3,000	112	336,000
Military Hospitals Commission Bulletin.......................	18,000	8	144,000
Amendments to "Instructions Governing Organization and Administration, C.E.F. Units, 1916"..........................	20,000	32	640,000
Physical Training Vocabulary.................................	3,000	8	24,000
Fighting Tuberculosis—Written for Canadian Soldiers...........	25,000	24	600,000
Carried forward.....................................	4,229,369	33,520	252,116,164

TABLE No. 8.—Return of Pamphlet and Miscellaneous Book-work, Year 1916-17
(copies and pages aggregate)—*Continued.*

Description.	Number of Copies.	Number of Pages.	Total Number of Printed Pages.
Brought forward..............................	4,229,369	33,520	252,116,164
Militia and Defence—Concluded.			
Amendments to "Instructions Governing Organization and Administration, C.E.F. Units, 1916"..........................	20,000	24	480,000
National Organization for War (by Stephen Leacock)	201,450	12	2,417,400
Index to General Orders, 1915....................	7,700	456	3,511,200
Memo. re European War.....................	2,000	106	348,000
Militia General Orders, 1916–17 (aggregate)......................	582,735	1,426	9,451,160
Bureau du Service National du Canada—Directeurs et règlements.	100	8	800
Ordres généraux de la milice, 1916–17 (au total)...................	48,000	1,240	744,400
Mines—			
Canada Mines Act...........	100	120	12,000
Catalogue des oiseaux canadiens...............................	1,500	938	1,407,000
Naval Service—			
Tide Tables for the Pacific Coast, 1918...........................	18,000	64	1,152,000
Tides at the Head of the Bay of Fundy......................	3,000	36	108,000
Pelagic Sealing Commission—Return...........................	1,000	64	64,000
A few Hints on Oyster Culture.....................	2,000	40	80,000
Regulations respecting Royal Naval Air Service...............	500	8	4,000
Instructions respecting the Use of Wireless Telegraphy...........	100	20	2,000
Physical and Medical Examination.................	200	16	3,200
List of Canadian Government Ships, 1916.......................	150	68	10,200
Instructions for Transport Service at Headquarters..............	25	48	1,200
Supplementary Instructions for Use of Wireless Telegraphy.......	100	24	2,400
Tide Tables for the Eastern Coast of Canada, 1918...............	8,000	64	512,000
Admiralty Regulations.........................	50	40	2,000
Tabulation of Lobster measurement, 1916......................	100	36	3,600
List of Printed Forms.......................	500	12	6,000
Tide Tables for the Pacific Coast, 1917....	15,000	64	960,000
Tide Tables for St. John, N.B. (Bay of Fundy, 1917)............	15,000	24	360,000
Tide Tables for Vancouver and Sand Head, B.C., 1917..........	12,000	48	576,000
Canadian Monthly Orders (aggregate)...........................	2,175	224	38,050
Merchant Vessels.......................	75	56	4,200
Report of the International Waterways Commission, 1915........	1,500	290	435,000
Instructions respecting Military Transports...................	100	32	3,200
Physical and Medical Examination...........................	500	16	8,000
Confidential documents (3)........	200	34	2,350
Instructions respecting the Use of Wireless Telegraphy...........	25	16	400
Instructions respecting Recruiting.................	200	12	2,400
St. Lawrence Pilot—Below Quebec................	500	216	108,000
Confidential Weekly Orders (aggregate)......................	4,575	1,590	143,800
Index to Confidential Weekly Orders.................	100	12	1,200
Tide Tables for Nelson, Hudson Bay, 1919..................	500	8	4,000
Report on Herring Fishing Operations of Steamer "Thirty-Three" with drift Nets, 1916....	600	12	7,200
Instructions for Reporting Officers in Canada...................	40	92	3,680
Index to Canadian Monthly Orders, 1914....................	100	16	1,600
Index to Canadian Monthly Orders, 1916....................	100	18	1,800
Naval Intelligence report (aggregate)..................	525	202	7,850
Bulletin of Sea Fishery Statistics (aggregate).................	24,600	268	549,400
Confidential Navy List (aggregate)............	785	256	32,560
Réglements de pêche spéciaux—Ile du Prince-Edouard............	500	32	16,000
Nouvelle-Ecosse............	500	56	28,000
Nouveau-Brunswick...............	500	42	21,000
Manitoba..................	100	32	3,200
Alberta..................	100	32	3,200
Colombie-Britannique...............	100	34	3,400
Yukon..................	100	28	2,800
Ontario...............	100	30	3,000
Volontaires de la réserve de la Marine royale canadienne..........	3,000	8	24,000
Carried forward................................	5,210,879	42,190	275,794,014

SESSIONAL PAPER No. 32

TABLE No. 8.—Return of Pamphlet and Miscellaneous Book-work, Year 1916-17
(copies and pages aggregate)—*Continued.*

Description.	Number of Copies.	Number of Pages.	Total Number of Printed Pages.
Brought forward...............................	5,210,879	42,190	275,794,014
Post Office—			
Saskatchewan Distribution List, 1916............................	1,700	160	272,000
Parcel Post Regulations..	25,000	16	400,000
Instructions to Railway Mail Clerks............................	15,000	52	780,000
Appendix K (Extract from Postmaster General's Report, 1915–16).	20	32	640
Pro-German Correspondence.....................................	3,500	20	70,000
Confidential Circulars to Postmasters (3)......................	12,000	92	388,000
Schedule of Mail Trains (5 issues)............................	7,700	864	1,129,600
Distribution List for British Columbia, 1917..................	1,250	106	132,500
Monthly Supplement to Postal Guide, 1916–17 (12 issues)........	231,750	110	2,122,800
Monthly Money Order Circular, 1916–17 (12 issues).............	56,600	138	611,600
Supplément mensuel au guide officiel du service postal canadien, 1916–17 (12 publications).................	54,150	120	509,800
Circulaire mensuelle des mandats-poste, 1916–17 (12 publications)..	13,800	138	158,700
Public Works—			
Telephone Directory—Senate and House of Commons............	1,000	16	16,000
International Joint Commission—In the Matter of the Application of the International Lumber Commission.......................	50	8	400
General Rules for Caretakers..................................	400	12	4,800
Extracts from Annual Report, 1915–16:			
Report of the Chief Engineer..............................	100	414	41,400
Report of the Chief Architect.............................	50	112	5,600
Collection of Revenue.....................................	50	24	1,200
Report on Dredging..	50	156	7,800
Report of the Superintendent of Telegraphs................	200	122	24,400
Privy Council—			
Economic and Developing Commission—Interim Report..........	100	24	2,400
Canada at War—Speech delivered by the Right Hon. Robert Laird Borden, K.C., P.C., G.C.M.G., in New York City...........	20,000	12	240,000
National Service Board of Canada—Directors and Regulations....	500	8	4,000
Memorandum re Colonial Imperial Conference....................	500	28	14,000
Bureau du Service National du Canada—Directeurs et règlements.	200	8	1,600
Public Printing and Stationery—			
An Act to Levy a Tax on Business Profits (4 issues)............	2,350	80	29,800
Memorandum regarding the Reduction of the Cost of Publications	50	8	400
An Act to Amend the Bank Act..................................	5,000	4	20,000
Proceedings of Royal Commission re War Supplies (2 issues)......	200	248	24,800
Printing Bureau Rates in Effect July 1, 1916..................	500	8	4,000
List of Annual Reports.......................................	1,200	4	4,800
Index to Private Acts, 1867–1916.............................	200	92	18,400
Various Acts reprinted for Stock (aggregate)..................	77,575	3,190	7,828,840
Price List of Government Publications.........................	1,000	82	82,000
Criminal Code with Amendments................................	2,000	810	1,620,000
Report of Joint Commission on Printing of Parliament..........	1,000	16	16,000
Alphabetical List of Employees (Jan. 1, 1917).................	25	56	1,400
Supply Bill No. 1..	100	32	3,200
Judgments, Orders, etc.—Board of Railway Commissioners (2 issues)...	400	192	44,000
Commons Debates of various dates (aggregate)...................	1,700	680	223,600
Index to Canada Gazette, Vol. XLIX...........................	2,100	66	138,600
Report of A. D. Watson, Actuary of the Dominion..............	25	8	200
Débats de la Chambre des Communes de différentes dates (au total)...	2,300	724	331,600
Rapport de A. D. Watson, actuaire du Dominion................	25	8	200
Statuts revisés du Canada et modifications, 1907–1916.........	1,000	830	830,000
Index des lois privées du Canada, 1867–1916	200	100	20,000
Railways and Canals—			
Report on the Welland Ship Canal, 1915.......................	300	18	5,400
Information and Tariff Charges re Government Grain Elevators..	1,000	16	16,000
Welland Ship Canal (Extract from Annual Report, 1916)..........	300	20	6,000
Carried forward...............................	5,757,099	52,274	294,002,494

8 GEORGE V, A. 1918

Table No. 8.—Return of Pamphlet and Miscellaneous Book-work, Year 1916-17 (copies and pages aggregate)—*Concluded.*

Description.	Number of Copies.	Number of Pages.	Total Number of Printed Pages.
Brought forward........	5,757,094	52,274	294,002,494
Railway Commission—			
Decisions, etc........	2,000	68	136,000
Index to Vol. V of Judgments, Orders, etc........	600	20	12,000
Judgments, Orders, etc. (26 issues)........	15,725	656	488,300
Secretary of State—			
Regulations respecting Applications under the Dominion Company's Act........	1,000	24	24,000
The Bonanza Creek Gold Mining Co........	1,000	32	32,000
Confidential document........	3,000	12	36,000
War Proclamations, Orders in Council, etc........	5,000	784	.3,920,000
Appendix to Archives Report, 1915........	500	476	23,800
The Canadian Northwest—Its Early Development........	200	452	90,400
Evidence before the Royal Commission *re* Purchase of War Supplies, etc. (Vols. I, II and III)........	1,500	2,740	4,110,000
Consolidated Orders respecting Trading with the Enemy........	1,000	20	20,000
Consolidated Orders respecting Censorship........	5,000	10	50,000
List of Ordinances........	200	12	2,400
Ordinances made and Passed by the Governor and Council of the Province of Quebec, 1763-1791........	300	12	3,600
Programme—Soirée musicale en aide au 230ième Voltigeurs canadiens-francais........	800	12	9,600
Catalogue des pamphlets, journaux et rapports déposés aux archives publiques du Canada, 1611-1867........	500	476	23,800
Senate—			
List of Newspapers, 1916........	30	40	1,200
List of Senators, 1916..:........	200	12	2,400
List of Senators, 1917........	300	12	3,600
·List of Senators and Committees, 1917........	300	20	6,000
Trade and Commerce—			
Canada—The Country of the Twentieth Century........	6,000	288	1,728,000
Annual Review—Commercial Intelligence Service, 1915........	6,650	136	904,400
Instructions to Commissioners and Enumerators........	1,600	48	76,800
Confidential document........	12,000	8	96,000
List of Licensed Elevators, etc........	1,500	116	174,000
Rules and Regulations made by the Board of Grain Commissioners for Canada........	100	24	2,400
Exhibition of Enemy Samples........	6,000	8	48,000
Outlined Plan for National Trade and Commerce Convention.....	10,000	56	560,000
Grain Inspection in Canada........	10,000	64	640,000
Imports, etc.—Statement No. 19........	50	16	800
A National System of Statistics........	100	16	1,600
Index to Weekly Bulletin (July to December, 1916)........	6,900	28	193,200
Grades of Grain Growers in Western Canada........	1,000	8	8,000
List of Licensed Elevators and Warehouses........	1,500	132	198,000
Timber Import Trade of Australia........	8,000	80	640,000
British Prohibited Import List........	500	8	4,000
Report of the Deputy Minister........	1,000	20	20,000
The Canada Grain Act (2 issues)........	1,000	192	960,000
Weekly Bulletin (53 issues)........	356,610	3,148	21,693,460
Index to Weekly Bulletin (January 1 to June 30, 1916)........	6,300	32	201,600
Synopsis of the Laws of the Dominion of Canada *re* Sale of Food and other Commodities........	20,000	16	320,000
Census and Statistics Monthly, 1916-17 (12 issues)........	79,800	338	2,181,200
Instructions aux commissaires et recenseurs........	1,600	52	83,200
Statistique mensuelle (12 publications)........	13,800	348	390,200
Index de la Statistique mensuelle, 1912-13, Vols. V et VI........	1,500	16	24,000
Totals........	6,349,764	63,362	334,146,454
Totals (March 31, 1916)........	6,997,740	59,164	*399,944,540

*Last year's total should have read 399,944,540, instead of 493,431,680.

SESSIONAL PAPER No. 32

TABLE No. 9.—Statement of other Letterpress Departmental Work for the Fiscal Year 1916–17.

Department.	Envelopes.	Copies other Work.
Agriculture	1,491,625	2,764,110
Auditor General	28,000	21,925
Civil Service Commission	50,000	138,590
Clerk of the Crown in Chancery	383,325	223,960
Customs	1,228,485	7,180,460
Experimental Farms	3,401,175	4,785,350
External Affairs	22,250	117,585
Finance	703,840	5,539,985
Governor General	8,000	19,055
House of Commons	10,425	150,350
Indian Affairs	110,675	411,900
Inland Revenue	352,050	2,429,805
Interior	1,463,445	5,492,135
Justice	109,700	412,045
Labour	184,215	93,695
Library of Parliament	5,000	4,000
Marine and Fisheries	499,475	1,468,480
Militia and Defence	3,970,350	30,253,915
Mines	138,510	270,400
Naval Service	841,150	3,176,145
Post Office	8,552,810	38,712,591
Privy Council	207,160	564,000
Public Printing and Stationery	839,975	1,568,695
Public Works	493,325	1,659,555
Railways and Canals	251,110	433,330
Railway Commission	57,000	161,050
Royal Mint	12,000	22,000
Royal Northwest Mounted Police	233,000	410,680
Secretary of State	135,225	169,450
Senate	82,750	115,100
Trade and Commerce	713,600	1,564,050
Totals	26,579,650	110,334,391
Totals (March 31, 1916)	25,625,645	108,507,130

8 GEORGE V, A. 1918

TABLE No. 10.—Statement showing the Number of Half-tone Plates or other Insertions in Annual and Supplementary Reports during the Fiscal Year 1916–17.

Title of Document.	Number of Plates.	Number of Copies of Reports.	Total Plates Inserted.
Archives of Canada, 1914–15 (English).............................	2	3,110	6,220
Contributions to Canadian Biology, 1914–15 (French)..............	11	590	6,490
Experimental Farm, 1914–15 (English) Vols. I and II...............	98	50,750	4,973,500
Experimental Farm, 1914–15 (French).............................	98	10,640	1,042,720
Fisheries, 1915–16 (English)......................................	3	3,990	11,970
Fisheries, 1915–16 (French).......................................	3	840	2,520
Hydrographic Surveys, 1912–13–14 (French).......................	9	640	5,760
Hydrographic Surveys, 1912–13–14 (English)......................	9	5,240	47,160
Public Works, 1914–15 (French)...................................	12	795	9,540
Railways and Canals, 1914–15 (French)............................	64	890	56,960
Railways and Canals, 1915–16 (English)...........................	33	3,935	129,855
Royal Northwest Mounted Police, 1915–16 (English)...............	17	3,210	54,570
Summary of Mines, 1914 (French).................................	16	1,640	26,240
Topographical Surveys, 1914–15 (English).........................	10	5,240	52,400
Topographical Surveys, 1914–15 (French)..........................	10	1,090	10,900
Trade and Commerce, 1914–15 Part V (English)....................	4	4,240	16,960
Trade and Commerce, 1914–15, Part V (French)...................	4	740	2,960
Veterinary Director General, 1914–15 (English)....................	16	9,740	155,840
Veterinary Director General, 1914–15 (French)....................	16	590	9,440
Totals...	435	107,910	6,622,005
Totals (March 31, 1916).............................	956	160,550	9,397,865

SESSIONAL PAPER No. 32

TABLE No. 11.—Statement of Books Bound during the Fiscal Year 1916-17.

Departments.	Full Leather.	Half Leather.	Quarter Leather.	Cloth.
Agriculture	26	629	151	2,244
Auditor General		183	2	
Civil Service Commission		3		204
Clerk of the Crown in Chancery	2	7		500
Customs	11	1,739	468	3,570
Experimental Farms	7	161	10	28
External Affairs	4	46	26	1
Finance	501	569	117	13,069
Governor General	10	10	1	6
House of Commons	25	580	22	31,551
Indian Affairs	8	503	62	840
Inland Revenue	12	1,341	517	7,056
Interior	298	1,232	1,097	14,498
Justice	39	776	2	619
Labour		6	24	81
Library of Parliament		1,413	2	
Marine and Fisheries	3	149	72	740
Militia and Defence	118	3,773	22,672	79,672
Mines	4	634	16	2,602
Naval Service	190	429	719	6,706
Post Office	600	3,242	4,565	17,104
Privy Council	2	11	1	26
Public Printing and Stationery	6	143	146	1,014
Public Works	7	258	807	5,702
Railways and Canals	6	145	224	846
Railway Commission	4	25		125
Royal Northwest Mounted Police	48	105	31	509
Secretary of State	11	167	8	120
Senate	1	606	12	1,097
Trade and Commerce		63	50	6,126
Totals	1,943	18,948	31,824	196,656
Totals (March 31, 1916)	11,827	17,051	28,628	246,436

8 GEORGE V, A. 1918

TABLE No. 12.—Statement showing the Number of Pads made during the Fiscal Year 1916–17.

Department.	Quantity.
Agriculture..........	10,677
Auditor General..........	112
Customs..........	16,224
External Affairs..........	210
Finance..........	3,767
House of Commons..........	1,535
Indian Affairs..........	2,948
Inland Revenue..........	1,826
Interior..........	16,865
Justice..........	1,714
Labour..........	160
Marine and Fisheries..........	2,724
Militia and Defence..........	85,169
Mines..........	243
Naval Service..........	10,810
Post Office..........	8,628
Public Printing and Stationery..........	282,558
Public Works..........	9,596
Railways and Canals..........	1,073
Railway Commission..........	500
Royal Northwest Mounted Police..........	600
Senate..........	1,100
Trade and Commerce..........	4,762
Total..........	463,801
Total (March 31, 1916)..........	245,049.

TABLE No. 13.—Statement showing the Number of Prepaid Post Office Envelopes Made and Stamped during the Fiscal Year 1916-17.

	Quantity Made and Stamped.
One cent Envelopes	700,000
Two cent Envelopes	2,800,000
Total	3,500,000
Total (March 31, 1916)	4,125,000

TABLE No. 14.—Statement showing the Die Stamping of Letter and Note Headings and Envelopes during the Fiscal Year 1916-17.

Department.	Foolscap, Half-Cap, Letter and Half Letter.	Note and Half Note.	Envelopes.	Number of Impressions
Agriculture	20,000	500	16,750	37,250
Civil Service Commission	10,000			10,000
Customs	27,500		40,000	67,500
External Affairs	29,400	3,500	3,000	35,900
Finance	20,000		5,000	25,000
Governor General	24,000	28,400	35,750	88,150
House of Commons	34,000	11,000	38,000	83,000
Indian Affairs	5,000	500		5,500
Inland Revenue	60,000		56,000	116,000
Interior	59,200	1,250	46,000	106,450
Justice	83,475	6,000	48,500	137,975
Labour	70,000		23,500	93,500
Marine and Fisheries	28,000		5,000	33,000
Militia and Defence	946,500	61,500	365,500	1,373,500
Mines	13,000			13,000
Naval Service	145,000		2,500	147,500
Post Office	50,000	2,500	32,000	84,500
Privy Council	228,250	2,000	29,250	259,500
Public Printing and Stationery	27,000	7,000	319,000	353,000
Public Works	48,000	3,000	16,000	67,000
Railways and Canals	26,000	7,000	5,000	38,000
Railway Commission	37,000		8,000	45,000
Royal Mint	5,000		7,000	12,000
Royal Northwest Mounted Police		6,000	10,000	16,000
Secretary of State	52,000	11,500	20,000	83,500
Senate	43,000	27,360	10,100	80,460
Trade and Commerce	52,000	2,500	1,500	56,000
Totals	2,143,325	181,510	1,143,350	3,468,185
Totals (March 31, 1916)	1,414,700	104,015	2,043,455	3,562,170

8 GEORGE V, A. 1918

TABLE No. 15.—Statement showing the Loose-leaf Work during the Fiscal Year 1916–17.

Department.	Binders.	Loose Leaves.	Index Leaves.	Index Cards.
Agriculture	124	100,350	....	73,180
Auditor General	3	54,475	732	....
Civil Service Commission	....	500	....	4,000
Customs	64	209,300	3,839	....
Experimental Farms	4	....	....	....
External Affairs	8	2,550	1,369	49,000
Finance	33	71,770	732	119,500
Governor General	....	....	26	....
House of Commons	....	....	....	3,000
Indian Affairs	7	5,900	48	....
Inland Revenue	22	50,800	32	5,000
Interior	389	197,858	14,086	74,110
Justice	7	2,600	508	1,000
Labour	2	200	58	3,700
Library of Parliament	....	500	....	....
Marine and Fisheries	169	128,060	3,063	27,500
Militia and Defence	4,121	1,300,105	14,220	1,620,180
Mines	73	46,180	436	12,000
Naval Service	183	112,330	264	56,350
Post Office	91	59,060	831	14,200
Privy Council	....	....	500	....
Public Printing and Stationery	91	151,011	4,204	623,400
Public Works	1,364	31,790	851	7,000
Railways and Canals	1,408	225,400	8,527	1,600
Railway Commission	18	6,000	840	....
Royal Northwest Mounted Police	19	....	....	....
Secretary of State	5	1,420	30	1,000
Senate	1,950	2,500	58,015	....
Trade and Commerce	1,177	238,265	654	10,000
Totals	11,332	2,998,924	113,865	2,705,720
Totals (March 31, 1916)	4,240	2,855,119	61,773	2,748,725

TABLE No. 16.—Comparative Statement of the Number of Letterpress Impressions for the last Five Fiscal Years.

Years.	Impressions.
1912–13	86,582,643
1913–14	87,473,093
1914–15	93,925,493
1915–16	102,934,861
1916–17	103,367,779

OUTSIDE PRINTING SERVICE BRANCH.

The following is a report of the work executed for Parliament and the various departments in outside printing establishments during the fiscal year ending March 31, 1917.   The numbers below correspond to the serial numbers of the tables in the report of the Superintendent of Printing.

1 and 2. Annual and Supplementary Reports.

8. Pamphlet and miscellaneous book-work.

9. Other letterpress departmental work.

11. Books bound.

12. Pads made.

14. Die-Stamping.

15. Loose-leaf work.

17. Lithographed maps, plans, cheques and forms.

18. Halftones, linecuts, electros, and dies made.

8 GEORGE V, A. 1918

TABLE No. 1.—Statement showing the Work on Annual Reports to Parliament, Year 1916-17.

Title of Document.	Number of Copies.	Number of Pages.	Total Number of Printed Pages.	Distribution.				Cost.
				Parliament.	Department.	Stock.	Sess. Papers.	$ cts.
Geological Survey Summary, 1915 (English)	7,740	332	2,569,680	1,975	5,000	35	730	2,566 93
Geological Survey Summary, 1915 (French)	2,140	298	637,720	375	1,500	15	250	1,488 99
Labour, 1915-16 (English)	3,735	122	455,670	2,100	1,000	35	600	1,226 72
Labour, 1915-16 (French)	1,090	128	139,520	375	500	15	200	871 37
Summary of Mines, 1915 (English)	5,735	238	1,364,930	2,100	3,000	35	600	2,166 46
Registrar of Boards of Conciliation and Investigation, 1915-16 (English)	4,365	204	890,460	2,100	1,500	35	730	1,764 87
Registrar of Boards of Conciliation and Investigation, 1915-16 (French)	1,090	222	241,980	375	500	15	200	1,459 69
Totals	25,895	1,544	6,299,960	9,400	13,000	185	3,310	11,545 03

TABLE No. 2.—Statement showing the Work on Supplementary Reports to Parliament, Year 1916-17.

Title of Document.	Number of Copies.	Number of Pages.	Total Number of Printed Pages.	Distribution.				Cost.
				Parliament.	Department.	Stock.	Sess. Papers.	$ cts.
Contributions to Canadian Biology, 1911-14, Vol. II (French)	940	248	233,120	475	200	15	250	818 91
Handbook of Indians of Canada, 1912 (French)	1,645	786	1,292,970	475	800	120	250	7,580 28
Hydrometric Surveys (Stream Measurements), 1914 (French)	640	510	326,400	375		15	250	3,912 19
Hydrometric Surveys (Stream Measurements), 1915 (English)	6,290	508	3,195,320	2,100	3,500	60	630	9,375 09
Totals	11,567	2,052	5,047,810	3,425	4,500	210	1,380	21,686 47

SESSIONAL PAPER No. 32

TABLE No. 8.—Return of Pamphlet and Miscellaneous Book-work, Year 1916-17
(copies and pages aggregate).

Description.	Number of Copies.	Number of Pages.	Total Number of Printed Pages.
Agriculture—			
Sheep Husbandry in Canada..............................	20,300	128	2,598,400
Production and Thrift...........	20,000	250	5,000,000
The School Garden, as regarded and carried on in the different provinces...................	25,000	64	1,600,000
The Protection of Migratory Birds in Canada..............	500	8	4,000
The "Egg Case Plan" and its use...............	30,000	16	480,000
Production and Market............	125,000	16	2,000,000
A New Species of Platypus from British Columbia..........	400	8	3,200
A New Species of the Family Ipidas (Coleoptera)............	400	16	6,400
The Entomological Record for 1915.........	600	40	24,000
Locust Control Work with Poisoned Baits in Eastern Canada, 1915	600	8	4,800
The Ancestry of Insects............	400	16	6,400
The Protection of Migatory Birds in Canada (2nd edition)........	5,000	8	40,000
Agriculture in Canada...........	1,000	78	78,000
Agricultural Gazette of Canada, 1916, Vol. 3 (9 issues)...........	42,900	870	4,150,000
Agricultural Gazette of Canada, 1917, Vol. 4 (3 issues)..........	15,400	246	1,363,500
Production, économie—Le livre de guerre du cultivateur, 1916....	5,000	254	1,270,000
Le jardin scolaire, comment les différentes provinces le comprennent, et le conduisent...........	8,000	64	512,000
L'essai du lait, de la crême et des sous-produits du lait au moyen du procédé Babcock...........	20,000	32	640,000
La chèvre Angora.........	25,000	24	600,000
L'amputation de la queue...........	25,000	12	300,000
Conseils aux débutants...........	25,000	16	400,000
Les avantages du lavage...........	25,000	4	100,000
Plan d'un poulailler de ponte permanent...........	25,000	4	100,000
Distribution de reproducteurs mâles de race pure...........	5,125	20	102,500
La Gazette agricole du Canada, 1916, Vol. 3 (9 éditions)...........	9,000	874	874,000
La Gazette agricole du Canada, 1917, Vol. 4 (3 éditions)..........	3,000	256	256,000
Index au Vol. II de la Gazette agricole du Canada, 1915..........	1,000	34	34,000
Experimental Farms—			
Bees and How to Keep Them..........	50,000	56	2,800,000
Ginseng, Mushroom and Melon Culture..........	10,000	8	80,000
The Cranberry Industry—Its Possibilities in Canada..........	5,000	32	160,000
Dr. Montizambert's Report (Extract from Annual)..........	200	32	6,400
Flax for Fibre—Its Cultivation and Handling..........	50,000	24	1,200,000
Gopher Destruction...........	100,000	8	800,000
A Review of the Status and Possibilities of Flax Production in Canada...........	2,000	32	64,000
A New Species of Tortrix of Economic Importance from Newfoundland...........	500	10	5,000
Insect Behaviour as a Factor in Applied Entomology..........	500	12	6,000
La jambe noire de la pomme de terre...........	45,000	16	720,000
La fertilité du sol—Moyens économiques de la maintenir et de l'augmenter...........	2,000	16	32,000
La destruction du gaufre...........	3,000	8	24,000
Le lin pour la filasse—Culture-et manipulation...........	10,000	24	240,000
Interior—			
Extracts from Reports on Townships 33 to 38 West of the Principal Meridian...........	1,500	84	126,000
Atlas of Canada, 1916...........	50,000	68	3,400,000
Supplement to Homestead Maps of Manitoba, Saskatchewan, etc..	25,000	16	400,000
Handbook for the Information of the Public...........	75,000	32	2,400,000
The Peace River Country...........	10,000	48	480,000
Water Powers of Canada...........	3,000	370	1,110,000
Western Canada Irrigation Association—Proceedings of the Ninth Annual Convention, 1915...........	3,000	250	750,000
Practical Irrigation Hints for Alberta...........	2,000	16	32,000
Alfalfa growing—Address delivered by Mr. Don H. Bark........	2,000	16	32,000
The Athabaska Country...........	10,000	36	360,000
Handbook of Information for Intending Settlers...........	25,000	32	800,000
The Yukon Territory...........	3,500	248	868,000
Carried forward...........	951,825	4,860	39,442,600

8 GEORGE V, A. 1918

TABLE No. 8.—Return of Pamphlet and Miscellaneous Book-work, Year 1916-17
(copies and pages aggregate)—*Continued.*

Description.	Number of Copies.	Number of Pages.	Total Number of Printed Pages.
Brought forward....................................	951,825	4,860	39,442,600
Interior—Concluded.			
Province of New Brunswick.............................	30,000	16	480,000
Description of Surveyed Townships in the Peace River District...	5,000	262	1,310,000
Report of the Dominion Water Power Branch, 1915-16...........	2,500	198	495,000
Atlas du Canada, 1916...	25,000	68	1,700,000
Labour—			
Labour Gazette, Nos. 4 to 12, Vol. XVI and Nos. 1 to 3, Vol. XVII	132,550	1,062	11,742,500
Index to Vol. XIV, Labour Gazette.............................	10,600	20	212,000
Canadian Legislation Concerning Industrial Disputes.............	1,000	8	8,000
Industrial Training and Technical Education.....................	1,000	16	16,000
The Rise in Prices and the Cost of Living in Canada, 1900–1914....	2,500	84	210,000
Wholesale Prices in Canada, 1915...........................	3,000	332	996,000
La Gazette du travail, Nos. 4 a 12, Vol. XVI, et Nos. 1 a 3, Vol. XVII...	24,500	1,184	136,800
Marine and Fisheries—			
Phenological Observations, Canada, 1915.......................	200	16	3,200
Monthly Record of Meteorological Observations, 1916, (10 issues)..	12,100	686	830,300
Militia and Defence—			
First Aid to the Injured....................................	124,325	80	9,946,000
Manual of Infantry Training, 1916....:......................	100,000	76	7,600,000
Infantry Training for Use of Canadian Militia, 1915...............	498,000	74	36,852,000
Rules for the Management of Garrison and Regimental Dry Canteen in Canada...	10,000	36	360,000
Order of Divine Service at Camp of Instruction..................	102,000	16	1,632,000
Physical Training—Special Tables, 1916........................	10,000	24	240,000
Instructions Governing Organization and Administration.........	20,000	110	2,200 000
Report on the Examination for Admission to the Royal Military College of Canada, 1916........................	1,200	36	43,200
First Aid to the Injured (2nd edition)........................	5,000	72	360,000
Nominal Rolls, C.E.F., viz.—			
Divisional Cyclists....................................	10,000	8	80,000
2nd Divisional Ammunition Column......................	10,000	12	120,000
7th Canadian Field Artillery Brigade....:...............	10,000	24	240,000
40th Battalion..	10,000	36	360,000
3rd Divisional Supply Column..........................	10,000	12	120,000
2nd Divisional Remount Depot..........................	10,000	12	120,000
3rd Divisional Canadian Engineers......................	10,000	16	160,000
23rd Battalion..	10,000	20	200,000
88th Battalion..	10,000	24	240,000
46th Battalion..	10,000	12	120,000
51st Battalion..	10,000	36	360,000
2nd Divisional Engineers..............................	10,000	16	160,000
47th Battalion..	10,000	40	400,000
49th Battalion..	10,000	20	200,000
42nd Battalion:......................................	10,000	20	200,000
22nd Battalion..	10,000	24	240,000
39th Battalion..	10,000	24	240,000
Eaton's Machine Gun Battery..........................	10,000	8	80,000
24th Battalion..	10,000	24	240,000
46th Battalion..	10,000	24	240,000
44th Battalion..	10,000	42	420,000
5th Brigade..	10,000	20	200,000
28th Battalion..	10,000	24	240,000
Nursing Sisters.......................................	10,000	4	40,000
No. 3 Casualty Clearing Station........................	10,000	4	40,000
Duchess of Connaught Red Cross Hospital..............	10,000	4	40,000
3rd Divisional Signal Co..............................	10,000	8	80,000
6th Canadian Field Artillery Brigade...................	10,000	20	200,000
43rd Battalion..	10,000	24	240,000
29th Battalion..	10,000	24	240,000
Carried forward...............................	2,372,300	9,922	122,675,600

SESSIONAL PAPER No. 32

TABLE No. 8.—Return of Pamphlet and Miscellaneous Book-work, Year 1916-17 (copies and pages aggregate)—*Continued.*

Description.	Number of Copies.	Number of Pages.	Total Number of Printed Pages.
Brought forward..	2,372,300	9,922	122,675,600
Militia and Defence—Continued.			
Nominal Rolls—*Concluded.*			
Second Divisional Train, C.A.S.C............................	10,000	12	120,000
9th Brigade..	10,000	16	160,000
4th Brigade..	10,000	20	200,000
2nd, 2rd, 4th and 5th University Companies.................	10,000	24	240,000
Nos. 1, 2 and 3 Field Ambulance............................	10,000	20	200,000
73rd Battalion...	10,000	24	240,000
74th Battalion...	10,000	28	280,000
33rd Battalion...	10,000	32	320,000
64th Battalion...	10,000	24	240,000
50th Battalion...	10,000	12	120,000
No. 3 General Hospital.....................................	10,000	8	80,000
78th Battalion...	10,000	28	280,000
34th Battalion...	10,000	36	360,000
58th Battalion...	10,000	28	280,000
3rd Divisional Ammunition Column..........................	10,000	12	120,000
2nd Divisional Signal Company.............................	10,000	8	80,000
2nd Divisional Cyclist Corps..............................	10,000	8	80,000
60th Battalion...	10,000	28	280,000
38th Battalion...	10,000	32	320,000
3rd Divisional Ammunition Sub-Park........................	10,000	8	80,000
4th Divisional Ammunition Sub-Park........................	10,000	8	80,000
2nd Divisional Ammunition Column..........................	10,000	12	120,000
59th Battalion...	10,000	32	320,000
62nd Battalion...	10,000	28	280,000
37th Battalion...	10,000	36	360,000
55th Battalion...	10,000	28	280,000
71st Battalion...	10,000	28	280,000
54th Battalion...	10,000	36	360,000
70th Battalion...	10,000	20	200,000
72nd Battalion...	10,000	24	240,000
65th Battalion...	10,000	28	280,000
91st Battalion...	10,000	20	200,000
2nd, 3rd, 4th and 5th University Companies, P.P.C.L.I. Rein-			
forcements...	10,000	24	240,000
68th Battalion...	10,000	28	280,000
4th Divisional Train, C.A.S.C.............................	10,000	12	120,000
104th Battalion..	10,000	24	240,000
Canadian Army Dental Corps................................	20,000	8	160,000
7th Regiment C.M.R.......................................	10,000	4	40,000
Signalling Section Canadian Engineers......................	10,000	4	40,000
8th Canadian Field Artillery Brigade.......................	10,000	16	160,000
2nd Divisional Ammunition Park, C.A.S.C...................	10,000	12	120,000
2nd Reserve Park..	10,000	8	80,000
66th Battalion...	10,000	28	280,000
10th Brigade, Canadian Field Artillery.....................	10,000	16	160,000
90th Battalion...	10,000	24	240,000
3rd Divisional Train, C.A.S.C.............................	10,000	12	120,000
80th Battalion...	10,000	24	240,000
77th Battalion...	10,000	28	280,000
103rd Battalion..	10,000	20	200,000
81st Battalion...	10,000	24	240,000
95th Battalion...	10,000	24	240,000
87th Battalion...	10,000	24	240,000
53rd Battalion...	10,000	32	320,000
76th Battalion...	10,000	28	280,000
No. 2 Tunnelling Company..................................	10,000	8	80,000
8th Regiment, Canadian Mounted Rifles.....................	10,000	20	200,000
110th Battalion..	10,000	16	160,000
Mines—			
Bibliography of Canadian Geology, 1914....................	100	28	2,800
Description of the Laboratories of the Mines Branch..........	4,000	132	528,000
Carried forward	2,956,400	11,258	135,046,400

8 GEORGE V, A. 1918

TABLE No. 8.—Return of Pamphlet and Miscellaneous Book-work, Year 1916-17
(copies and pages aggregate)—*Continued.*

Description.	Number of Copies.	Number of Pages.	Total Number of Printed Pages.
Brought forward............................	2,956,400	11,258	135,046,400
*Mines—*Continued.			
Mineral Production of Canada, 1914.....................	4,000	362	1,448,000
Peat Bogs and Peat Industry of Canada, 1913-14.................	3,000	210	630,000
Zoology (Extract from Geological Survey Summary, 1915).........	200	16	3,200
Wheaton District, Southern Yukon (extract from Geological Survey Summary, 1915)................................	2,000	16	32,000
Journal of American Folk-Lore...........................	600	150	90,000
Upper Ordovician Formation in Ontario and Quebec.............	3,500	204	714,000
The Trent Valley Outlet of Lake Algonquin.....................	2,500	24	60,000
Geology of Graham Islands, B.C....	3,500	172	602,000
Late Pleistocene Oscillations of Sea-level in the Ottawa Valley...	2,500	16	40,000
An Exploration of the Tazin and Taltson Rivers, Northwest Territories........................	4,000	132	528,000
Geology of a Portion of the Flathead Coal Area, British Columbia	3,000	64	192,000
Geology of Nanaimo Map Area............................	750	156	117,000
Iroquois Foods and Food Preparation........................	2,500	244	610,000
Magnetic Properties of Cobalt and Fe2 Co.....................	5,000	44	220,000
An Investigation of the Coals of Canada......................	4,600	194	892,400
List of Mines in Canada, 1916............................	1,500	12	18,000
List of Metal Mines and Smelters in Canada, 1916..............	2,500	16	40,000
Feldspar in Canada....................................	5,000	152	760,000
Wood Mountain Willowbunch Coal Area, Sask.................	3,500	114	399,000
Production of Spelter in Canada, 1916......................	4,000	64	256,000
Pœdeumias and the Mesonacidœ, etc........................	250	10	2,500
Road Material Surveys, 1914 (in 5 Parts)....................	3,000	260	780,000
Road Material Surveys, 1914, Parts I, III and IV..............	500	142	71,000
Road Material Surveys, 1914, Parts I and V..................	500	222	111,000
Road Material Surveys, 1914, Parts I and III.................	500	90	45,000
Lime Perspective in Aboriginal American Culture—A Study in Method...............................	2,000	102	204,000
Ganoid Fishes from near Banff, Alberta.....................	400	12	4,800
The Production of Iron and Steel in Canada, 1915...............	2,000	56	112,000
Part of the District of Lake St. John, Quebec.................	3,000	96	288,000
A General Summary of the Mineral Production of Canada, 1915..	2,000	48	96,000
The Physical Properties of the Metal Cobalt..................	1,000	58	58,000
Cobalt Alloys with Non-Corrosive Properties..................	5,000	62	310,000
Oil and Gas Fields of Ontario and Quebec....................	1,500	254	381,000
The Production of Coal and Coke in Canada, 1915..............	2,000	42	84,000
Ymir Mining Camp, British Columbia.......................	3,500	194	679,000
Onaping Map Area....................................	3,500	166	581,000
Peat, Lignite and Coal.................................	5,000	282	141,000
The Anticosti Island Faunas.............................	3,000	38	114,000
Clay and Shale Deposits of the Western Provinces..............	4,000	172	688,000
Production of Cement, Lime, Clay Products, Stone and other Structural Material in Canada.........................	2,500	62	155,000
Building Stones of Canada, Vol. IV........................	4,000	468	1,872,000
Production of Copper, Gold, Lead, Nickel, Silver, Zinc, and other Metals in Canada, 1915............................	2,500	82	205,000
Products and By-Products of Coal..........................	1,000	64	64,000
The Flora of Canada...................................	3,000	16	48,000
Preliminary Report of the Mineral Production of Canada, 1916...	6,000	28	168,000
The Labrador Eskimo..................................	3,000	254	762,000
Régions aurifères de la Nouvelle-Ecosse.....................	750	380	285,000
Rapport sur les pierres de construction et d'ornement du Canada, Vol. II...........................	750	356	267,000
Région d'Arisaig, Antigonish, Nouvelle-Ecosse................	1,500	180	270,000
Archéologie. La collection archéologique du sud de l'intérieur de la Colombie-Britannique............................	750	66	49,500
Rapport préliminaire sur les dépôts d'argile et de schistes de la province de Québec................................	1,500	232	348,000
Les dépôts d'argile et de schistes des provinces de l'ouest.........	1,500	86	129,000
Les formations huroniennes de la région Timiskaming, Canada....	750	32	24,000
Quelques mythes et contes des Objibwa du sud-est d'Ontario.....	500	110	55,000
Rapport sur les pierrres de construction et d'ornement du Canada, Vol. III.........................	750	350	262,500
Carried forward..................................	3,087,150	18,692	152,412,300

SESSIONAL PAPER No. 32

TABLE No. 8.—Return of Pamphlet and Miscellaneous Book-work, Year 1916-17 (copies and pages aggregate)—*Concluded.*

Description.	Number of Copies.	Number of Pages.	Total Number of Printed Pages.
Brought forward......................................	3,087,150	18,692	152,412,300
Mines—Concluded.'			
Géologie et gisements minéraux du district de Tulamen, Colombie-Britannique..	750	180	135,000
Publications en français du ministère des Mines, (parues depuis le catalogue de juillet, 1914)..................................	1,640	8	13,120
Rapport annuel de la production minérale au Canada, 1914.........	750	362	271,500
District Upper White River, Yukon.........................	750	200	150,000
La production du fer et de l'acier au Canada, pendant l'année civile 1912..	750	40	30,000
Bassins houillers de la Colombie-Britannique..................	1,500	350	525,000
Le district férifère de Moose-Mountain, Ontario.................	750	20	15,000
Les puits artésiens de Montréal.............................	1,500	166	249,000
Congrès Géologique 1913—Liste des livrets guides:			
No. 1, Vol. I. Excursion dans l'est de la province de Québec et des Provinces Maritimes. Première partie...........	5,000	220	1,100,000
No. 1, Vol. II. Excursion dans l'est de la province de Québec et des Provinces Maritimes. Deuxième partie...........	5,000	192	960,000
No. 2, Vol. III. Excursion dans les cantons de l'Est de Québec et dans la partie est d'Ontario........................	5,000	144	720,000
No. 3, Vol. IV. Excursion aux environs de Montréal et d'Ottawa..	5,000	176	880,000
No. 4, Vol. V. Excursion dans le sud-ouest d'Ontario..........	5,000	140	700,000
No. 5, Vol. VI. Excursion dans la presqu'île occidentale de l'Ontario et de l'Ile Manitoulin........................	5,000	106	530,000
No. 6, Vol. VII. Excursion dans les environs de Toronto, de Muskoka et Madoc.................................	5,000	72	360,000
No. 7, Vol. VIII. Excursion à Sudbury, à Cobalt et Porcupine.	5,000	160	800,000
No. 8, Vol. IX. Excursion transcontinentale C-1, de Toronto à Victoria et retour, par les chemins de fer Canadian Pacific et Canadian Northern. Première partie................	5,000	108	540,000
No. 8, Vol. X. Excursion transcontinentale C-1, de Toronto à Victoria et retour, par les chemins de fer Canadian Pacific et Canadian Northern. Deuxième partie................	5,000	186	930,000
No. 8, Vol. XI. Excursion transcontinentale C-1, de Toronto à Victoria et retour, par les chemins de fer Canadian Pacific et Canadian Northern. Troisième partie...............	5,000	120	600,000
No. 9, Vol. XII. Excursion transcontinentale C-2, de Toronto à Victoria et retour, par les chemins de fer Canadian Pacific et Transcontinental National......................	5,000	172	860,000
No. 10, Vol. XIII. Excursion dans le nord de la Colombie-Britannique, dans le territoire du Yukon et le long de la Côte Nord du Pacifique.............................	5,000	196	980,000
Naval Service—			
Royal Naval College Calendar, 1916.........................	500	72	36,000
Royal Naval College Calendar, 1917.........................	1,000	54	54,000
Public Printing and Stationery—			
Chapters 14, 19 and 21, 6-7 George V, reprinted for stock.........	15,000	12	180,000
Railways and Canals—			
Information and Tariff Charges as to the Government Grain Elevators......................................	300	10	3,000
Secretary of State—			
Programme—Entertainment in Aid of the Ottawa and Ottawa Valley Branch of the Canadian Red Cross Society...........	3,000	16	48,000
Alleged German Outrages (Report)........................	55,000	64	3,520,000
Alleged German Outrages (Evidence)......................	55,000	372	20,460,000
Trade and Commerce—			
Statistical Year Book of Canada, 1914......................	10,200	716	7,303,200
Annuaire du Canada, 1914................................	2,050	720	1,476,000
Totals.......................................	3,303,390	24,046	196,841,120

8 GEORGE V, A. 1918

TABLE No. 9.—Statement of other Letterpress Departmental Work for the Fiscal Year 1916-17.

Department.	Envelopes.	Copies other Work.
Agriculture...............	....	2,265,005
Civil Service Commission...............	....	2,550
Clerk of the Crown in Chancery...............	....	290,040
Customs...............	20,000	5,495,470
Experimental Farms...............	....	5,222,725
External Affairs...............	....	30,000
Finance...............	4,000	279,700
House of Commons...............	5,000	....
Indian Affairs...............	....	80,400
Inland Revenue...............	....	1,433,610
Interior...............	270,000	1,232,880
Justice...............	....	127,500
Labour...............	20,000	36,925
Marine and Fisheries...............	35,000	771,400
Militia and Defence...............	440,640	46,316,905
Mines...............	....	30,840
Naval Service...............	61,700	1,233,910
Post Office...............	128,880	32,615,625
Privy Council...............	....	200
Public Printing and Stationery...............	....	65,300
Public Works...............	....	1,693,100
Railways and Canals...............	....	250
Railway Commission...............	....	6,000
Royal Northwest Mounted Police...............	....	217,000
Secretary of State...............	....	4,000
Senate...............	1,200	33,000
Trade and Commerce...............	176,000	976,550
Totals...............	1,162,420	100,460,885

TABLE No. 11.—Statement of Books Bound during the Fiscal Year 1916-17.

Departments.	Full Leather.	Half Leather.	Quarter Leather.	Cloth.
Agriculture...............	....	....	50	98
Customs...............	....	30	....	3
External Affairs...............	....	....	....	5,935
Finance...............	....	28	26	....
House of Commons...............	....	....	5	....
Indian Affairs...............	....	....	....	504
Inland Revenue...............	....	100	....	....
Interior...............	....	2,066	....	6,300
Justice...............	50	....	....	....
Marine and Fisheries...............	60	....	....	2,000
Militia and Defence...............	....	1,099	7,543	226,356
Mines...............	....	3	....	300
Naval Service...............	....	....	320	650
Post Office...............	....	....	7,860	16,920
Trade and Commerce...............	....	....	....	112,585
Totals...............	110	3,326	15,804	371,651

TABLE No. 12'—Statement showing the Number of Pads made during the Fiscal Year 1916-17.

Department.	Quantity.
Agriculture	29,959
Finance	627
Indian Affairs	500
Interior	8,052
Justice	550
Marine and Fisheries	609
Militia and Defence	122,526
Naval Service	4,526
Post Office	166,840
Public Works	16,762
Railway Commission	250
Royal Northwest Mounted Police	1,200
Trade and Commerce	1,400
Total	353,801

TABLE No. 14.—Statement showing the Die Stamping of Letter and Note Headings and Envelopes during the Fiscal Year 1916-17.

Department.	Foolscap, Half Cap, Letter and Half Letter.	Note and Half Note.	Envelopes.	Number of Impressions.
Governor General		2,000	3,000	5,000
House of Commons	2,000	700	6,000	8,700
Interior	15,000			15,000
Justice		500		500
Militia and Defence	475,000			475,000
Post Office	2,550			2,550
Public Printing and Stationery	190,875	175,000	617,000	982,875
Public Works	2,000			2,000
Railways and Canals		3,105		3,105
Royal Northwest Mounted Police	3,000			3,000
Senate		1,000	1,250	2,250
Totals	690,425	182,305	627,250	1,499,980

TABLE No. 15.—Statement showing the Loose-leaf work performed during the Fiscal Year 1916-17.

Department.	Binders.	Loose Leaves.	Index Leaves.	Index Cards.
Auditor General		500		4,211
External Affairs			200	24,000
Indian Affairs		2,000		500
Interior	15	10,250		
Marine and Fisheries	1	1,000	29	6,500
Militia and Defence	187	424,595	220	243,690
Mines				1,700
Naval Service		5,000		2,000
Post Office				2,370
Public Printing and Stationery		2,250		
Public Works	2	500		2,110
Trade and Commerce		110,000		
Totals	205	556,095	449	287,081

8 GEORGE V, A. 1918

TABLE No. 17.—Statement giving the Number of Maps, Plans, Cheques and Forms Lithográphed during the Fiscal Year 1916-17.

Department.	Maps and Plans.	Cheques and Forms.
Agriculture	75	5,854,240
Civil Service Commission		200
Customs		149,655
Experimental Farms	2,200	200
External Affairs		17,885
Finance		68,265
Governor General		3,590
House of Commons	1,050	17,460
Indian Affairs		10,000
Inland Revenue		139,030
Interior	511,296	1,243,275
Justice		41,900
Labour		7,570
Library of Parliament		1,200
Marine and Fisheries	225,435	138,010
Militia and Defence	1,900	7,735,460
Mines	393,935	114,710
Naval Service	11,460	202,669
Post Office		193,160
Privy Council		500
Public Printing and Stationery		4,644,735
Public Works	14,000	169,525
Railways and Canals		396,965
Railway Commission		2,000
Royal Northwest Mounted Police		32,765
Secretary of State		6,500
Senate		7,175
Trade and Commerce	42,750	1,101,795
Totals	1,204,101	22,300,439

TABLE No. 18.—Statement showing the Number of Halftones, Line Cuts, Electros and Dies made during the Fiscal Year 1916-17.

Department.	Halftones.	Line Cuts.	Electros.	Dies.
Agriculture	323	3,267	247	
Civil Service Commission	6	6		
Customs			64	
Experimental Farms	128	91	910	
Finance			152	
House of Commons		20		
Indian Affairs			22	
Inland Revenue	2	29	38	3
Interior	336	145	181	
Justice				2
Labour		4	1	
Marine and Fisheries		15	35	1
Militia and Defence	39	51	1,111	5
Mines	483	285	23	
Naval Service	24	35	63	
Post Office		12	407	3
Privy Council		3	55	2
Public Printing and Stationery		7	86	5
Public Works	35	40	35	1
Railways and Canals	36	11	28	2
Railway Commission			10	
Royal Northwest Mounted Police			16	
Secretary of State		93	7	
Senate		1	2	2
Trade and Commerce	184	125	58	
Totals	1,596	4,240	3,551	26

STATIONERY BRANCH.

OFFICE OF THE SUPERINTENDENT OF STATIONERY.

OTTAWA, February 26, 1918.

J. de L. TACHE, Esq.,
King's Printer and Controller of Stationery.

SIR,—I have the honour to submit for your information a general statement of the accounts of this branch from April 1, 1916, to March 31, 1917, as follows, viz.:—

(A) Value of goods brought forward April 1, 1916..........................$	224,362 14
Value of goods received, April 1, 1916, to March 31, 1917................	1,939,078 84
Wages, etc., charged against stock.....................................	96,657 27
Balance profit...	116,073 48
	$ 2,376,171 73

By goods issued to departments..$	1,036,618 30
Work Book Account—Printing and Sundry Printing Supplies, Printing Branch...	906,761 49
Stock on hand, verified March 31, 1917.................................	432,791 94
	$ 2,376,171 73

B—COMPARATIVE STATEMENT of the issue of goods to the several Departments of the Civil Service from April 1, 1915, to March 31, 1916, and for the year ending March 31, 1917.

Departments.	Issued in 1915–16.	Issued in 1916–17.	Increase in 1916–17.	Decrease in 1916–17.
	$ cts.	$ cts.	$ cts.	$ cts.
Agriculture	26,809 13	35,646 37	8,837 24	
Archives	984 95	1,325 66	340 71	
Auditor General	3,600 45	4,966 07	1,365 62	
Clerk of Crown in Chancery	1,128 89	66 05		1,062 84
Civil Service Commission	768 17	412 51		355 66
Customs	27,577 83	35,800 97	8,223 14	
Canadian Government Railways	23,739 82	40,212 94	16,473 12	
Departments Generally	820 46	1,260 34	439 88	
Dominion Police	961 70	1,121 94	160 24	
Exchequer Court	628 47	444 55		183 92
External Affairs	2,310 73	2,416 67	105 94	
Finance	6,107 40	22,536 97	16,429 57	
Governor General's Office and Government House	1,410 79	1,932 10	521 31	
House of Commons	26,950 08	29,359 21	2,409 13	
Immigration	8,921 72	6,106 68		2,815 04
Interior	61,378 27	74,804 88	13,426 61	
Indian Affairs and School Supplies	17,983 06	16,982 36		1,000 70
Inland Revenue	10,699 69	10,083 29		616 40
Insurance	1,805 53	3,583 40	1,777 87	
Justice	5,917 61	5,140 96		776 65
Labour	1,314 30	1,451 28	136 98	
Library of Parliament	591 72	869 33	277 61	
Marine and Fisheries	15,221 00	17,348 24	2,127 24	
Militia and Defence	226,392 98	375,478 41	149,085 43	
Mines	8,951 58	9,039 52	87 94	
Naval Service	38,203 67	39,622 01	1,418 34	
Penitentiaries	1,726 86	1,903 82	176 96	
Post Office	87,670 89	108,795 21	21,124 32	
Privy Council	1,749 98	2,604 08	854 10	
Public Printing and Stationery	16,893 80	29,510 82	12,617 02	
" Work Book	550,748 47	906,761 49	356,013 02	
Public Works	36,237 30	29,958 38		6,278 92
Railways and Canals	15,481 94	12,647 18		2,834 76
Railway Commission	3,512 24	4,877 81	1,365 57	
Royal Mint	267 93	372 30	104 37	
R.N.W.M. Police	10,948 40	12,220 55	1,272 15	
Secretary of State	6,875 09	6,579 53		295 56
Senate of Canada	7,828 22	12,339 14	4,510 92	
Supreme Court	1,133 13	1,222 34	89 21	
Trade and Commerce	8,505 77	19,431 74	10,925 97	
Military Hospital Commission	446 09	8,433 93	7,987 84	
Internment Operations	4 40	2,222 81	2,218 41	
Economic Commission	809 22	184 78		624 44
War Purchasing Commission	993 94	558 15		435 79
Canadian Munition Resources Commission	88 70	223 31	134 61	
North West Territorial Commission	13 93	14 89	0 96	
International Joint Commission	13 50	33 00	19 50	
Board of Pension Commissioners		27,145 06	27,145 06	
National Service Commission		17,204 54	17,204 54	
Commission of Enquiry, Railway Trans		122 22	122 22	
Shell Committee	25 50			25 50
Imperial Munition Board	136 82			136 82
Total issued to Departments	1,273,292 12	1,943,379 79		
Increase for Departments			687,530 67	
Decrease for Departments				17,443 00
Stock on hand, verified March 31, 1917		432,791 94	17,443 00	
Net Total		2,376,171 73		
Net Increase			670,087 67	

SESSIONAL PAPER No. 32

C—COMPARATIVE STATEMENT of Business transacted in the Stationery Office from 1886–7 (the first year that the Bureau was handed over to the King's Printer), and subsequent years up to 1916–17.

Year.	Goods received.	Goods sent out.	Demands	Letters received.	Letters sent out.	Packages despatched by Mail.	Packages and cases despatched by rail and Exp.	Paper and envelopes supplied to Printing Branch for work.
	$ cts.	$ cts.						$ cts.
1886–7......	128,463 16	132,313 88	10,297	948	3,243	4,389	102	64,528 18
1887–8......	183,731 61	186,832 56	11,251	959	3,712	3,733	168	65,264 38
1888–9......	192,101 36	185,895 04	11,591	1,175	4,020	3,979	185	87,384 95
1889–90.....	180,747 14	176,273 58	13,708	1,411	5,939	3,330	444	88,651 46
1890–1......	185,089 29	193,035 51	15,220	1,547	6,483	3,967	463	92,394 87
1891–2......	218,485 69	219,749 90	17,694	1,827	6,711	4,728	1,794	118,964 74
1892–3......	228,100 38	225,401 37	17,855	2,403	6,869	5,317	2,118	118,983 22
1893–4......	191,838 69	205,873 33	16,901	2,488	6,951	6,153	2,111	101,315 59
1894–5......	190,840 65	195,769 83	17,857	3,404	8,178	5,883	2,017	97,100 38
1895–6......	197,592 91	199,538 62	18,899	3,675	9,132	6,730	1,469	98,045 34
1896–7......	205,051 35	214,061 82	20,756	3,804	9,406	9,244	1,022	93,114 84
1897–8......	230,497 06	625,116 44	21,772	5,367	11,457	12,521	1,170	117,312 10
1898–9......	218,088 17	236,988 62	21,047	4,640	13,059	11,343	1,217	113,706 19
1899–1900...	232,017 96	252,100 23	21,928	5,984	13,277	14,129	1,060	110,049 48
1900–1......	302,766 26	301,495 95	23,227	6,856	13,689	16,382	1,038	142,421 20
1901–2......	296,721 64	288,782 90	23,086	6,204	15,292	15,191	805	115,597 91
1902–3......	280,414 42	303,160 80	23,148	6,707	15,630	16,288	412	122,530 50
1903–4......	385,810 93	352,993 61	25,752	8,539	19,389	21,263	689	140,772 33
1904–5:.....	438,232 96	427,783 74	28,003	8,439	19,229	22,822	1,102	162,787 26
1905–6...... 9 months	463,515 73	448,388 08	28,808	7,851	18,459	29,653	1,182	157,823 76
1906–7......	390,043 40	369,592 34	22,355	6,979	15,363	27,403	661	120,308 65
1907–8......	588,786 87	580,027 75	31,858	11,007	23,115	45,628	3,129	216,093 73
1908–9......	635,340 20	613,516 45	33,298	12,539	23,059	21,247	804	225,508 23
1909–10.....	599,226 80	592,902 55	36,164	13,801	23,260	53,723	1,011	222,442 62
1910–11.....	541,366 74	621,049 48	39,068	12,368	23,528	27,541	1,089	258,877 63
1911–12.....	716,868 55	774,561 30	43,753	16,091	23,247	21,601	1,307	176,654 23
1912–13.....	890,025 90	931,861 87	43,477	16,173	23,990	....	1,842	306,687 70
1913–14.....	1,123,953 58	1,154,429 87	46,598	13,627	26,962	....	2,565	361,947 03
1914–15.....	1,007,036 23	1,084,443 05	47,416	8,669	*29,994	*3,352	3,483	397,273 76
1915–16.....	1,148,242 24	1,273,292 12	48,759	8,168	*7,007	*2,673	6,019	550,748 47
1916–17.....	1,939,078 84	1,943,379 79	49,978	8,695	*36,405	*1,664	9,922	906,761 49

*Exclusive of Distribution Branch.

The expenditure of this branch shows an increase of $790,836.60 compared with 1915–16. (See statement B.) During the year requisitions on the office have reached 49,978; 8,695 letters were received and 36,405 were mailed; packages despatched by mail 1,664; and packages and cases despatched by rail, 9,922.

J. O. PATENAUDE,
Superintendent of Stationery.

8 GEORGE V, A. 1918

DISTRIBUTION of the Statutes of Canada being 7 and 8 George V, Seventh Session of the Twelfth Parliament.

LIST No. 1—BOUND IN CLOTH.

To whom sent.	Volumes 1 and 2.	
	English.	French.
Parliament of Canada.		
His Excellency the Governor General..........	2	....
Cabinet Ministers..........	22	2
Senators..........	88	22
Members of the House of Commons..........	125	40
Total..........	237	64
Departmental Lists.		
Judges, Supreme Court..........	6	4
Judges, Exchequer Court..........	2	1
Departments..........	99	12
Department of Justice for agents..........	75	....
Library of Parliament..........	40	10
Deputy Ministers..........	96	7
Totals..........	318	34
Ontario.		
Provincial Government..........	15	....
Judges..........	94	....
Clerk, Admiralty Court..........	1	....
Officials, Osgoode Hall..........	10	....
Police Magistrates..........	141	....
Sheriffs..........	41	....
Clerks of the Peace..........	47	....
Clerks, County Courts..........	45	....
Libraries and Colleges..........	14	....
Law Associations..........	28	....
Commissioner of Police..........	1	....
Mayors of City Corporations..........	9	....
City, Town and County Corporations..........	233	....
Newspapers..........	46	1
Total..........	725	1
Quebec.		
Provincial Government..........	11	18
Judges..........	53	31
Clerk Vice-Admiralty Court..........	1	1
Judges' Chambers..........	9	2
Advocates' Libraries..........	11	15
Clerk, Sessions of the Peace..........	2	2
Recorders..........	5	8
Stipendiary Magistrates..........	3	11
Sheriffs..........	4	18
Prothonotaries..........	7	15
Clerks of the Peace..........	5	5
Libraries, Universities and Colleges..........	12	21
Mayors of Cities..........	6	6
City and County Corporations..........	20	55
Harbour Commissioners..........	2	2
Clerks, Circuit Courts..........	15	53
Clerks, District Courts..........	1	1
Clerk of the Crown..........	2	3
Newspapers..........	5	9
Total..........	174	276

SESSIONAL PAPER No. 32

DISTRIBUTION of the Statutes of Canada, 1917—*Continued.*

LIST No. 1—BOUND IN CLOTH—Continued.

To whom sent.	Volumes 1 and 2	
	English.	French.
Nova Scotia.		
Provincial Government....	10	....
Judges....	15	....
Registrar, Vice-Admiralty Court....	1	....
Prothonotaries....	18	....
Judges' Chambers....	1	....
Sheriffs....	18	....
Clerks, County Courts....	19	....
City, Town and County Corporations....	40	....
Libraries and Colleges....	4	....
Harbour Commissioners....	1	....
Police Magistrates....	2	....
Newspapers....	10	....
Total....	139	....
New Brunswick.		
Provincial Government....	13	....
Judges....	13	....
Registrar, Vice-Admiralty Court....	1	....
Judges' Chambers....	1	....
Clerks, County Courts....	11	....
Clerks, Circuit Courts....	8	....
Mayors of Cities....	2	....
Sheriffs....	14	....
City, Town and County Corporations....	23	....
Libraries and Colleges....	3	....
Newspapers....	7	....
Total....	96	....
Prince Edward Island.		
Legislative Library....	4	....
Provincial Government....	8	....
Judges....	7	....
Stipendiary Magistrates....	3	....
Prothonotaries....	3	....
Sheriffs....	3	....
Judges' Chambers....	1	....
Clerks of Courts....	3	....
Mayor of City....	1	....
City and Town Corporations....	2	....
Clerk of The Crown....	1	....
Law Society....	2	....
Newspapers....	4	....
Total....	42	....
Manitoba.		
Provincial Government....	10	....
Judges....	20	....
Clerks, County Court....	13	....
Police Magistrates....	1	1
Sheriffs....	6	....
Prothonotaries....	1	....
Mayor and City Clerk....	1	....
Libraries and Colleges....	10	....
Newspapers....	6	....
Total....	68	1

8 GEORGE V, A. 1918

DISTRIBUTION of the Statutes of Canada, 1917—*Continued.*

LIST No. 1—BOUND IN CLOTH—Concluded.

To whom sent.	Volumes 1 and 2.	
	English.	French.
British Columbia.		
Provincial Government	11	....
Judges	24	....
Clerks, County Court	7	....
Registrar, Supreme Court	1	....
Judges' Chambers	1	....
City and County Corporations	3	....
Stipendiary Magistrates	21	....
Sheriffs	7	....
Libraries and Colleges	8	....
Newspapers	13	....
Total	96	....
Alberta.		
Provincial Government	10	....
Judges	21	....
Clerks, Supreme Court	6	....
Sheriffs	4	....
Libraries and Colleges	17	....
Newspapers	7	....
Police Magistrates	3	....
Total	68	....
Saskatchewan.		
Provincial Government	12	....
Judges	22	....
Clerks, Supreme Court	4	....
Judges' Chambers	1	....
Sheriffs	4	....
Libraries and Colleges	12	....
Newspapers	7	....
City Corporations	1	....
Police Magistrates	2	....
Total	65	....
Yukon District.		
The Commissioner	1	....
Judges	1	....
Officer Commanding the R.N.W.M.P.	2	....
Sheriffs	1	....
Clerk of the Court	2	....
Officials	24	....
Police Magistrates	1	....
	32	....

SESSIONAL PAPER No. 32

DISTRIBUTION of the Statutes of Canada, 1917—*Continued.*

LIST No. 2—BOUND IN FULL CALF.

To whom sent.	Volumes 1 and 2.	
	English.	French.
His Excellency the Governor General..	1	....
Their Honours the Lieutenant Governors......................................	10	1
Cabinet Ministers...	20	2
Privy Councillors (not otherwise entitled)...................................	40	16
Judges and Registrars, Supreme Court..	6	2
Library and Judges' Chambers, Supreme Court.................................	2	2
Judges and Registrars, Exchequer Court......................................	3	1
United States Secretary of State..	1	....
United States Attorney General..	1	....
United States Library of Congress...	1	1
The Prefect of Propaganda...	....	1
Canadian College, Rome...	....	1
British Legation, Washington..	2	2
Deputy Ministers and Chief Officers...	36	....
British Government..	34	....
Colonial Governments...	27	....
Total..	184	29

RECAPITULATION.

BOUND IN CLOTH.

To whom sent.	Volume 1.		Volume 2.		Volumes 1 and 2.	
	English.	French.	English.	French.	English.	French.
Parliament of Canada..................	....	....	....	....	237	64
Departmental List.....................	....	....	....	....	318	34
Ontario...............................	....	....	....	....	725	1
Quebec................................	....	....	....	....	174	275
Nova Scotia...........................	....	....	....	....	139	....
New Brunswick.........................	....	....	....	....	96	....
Prince Edward Island..................	....	....	....	....	42	....
Manitoba..............................	....	....	....	....	68	1
British Columbia......................	....	....	....	....	96	....
Alberta...............................	....	....	....	....	68	....
Saskatchewan..........................	....	....	....	....	65	....
Yukon District........................	....	....	....	....	32	....
Miscellaneous.........................	....	....	....	....	56	....
Sales.................................	....	....	....	....	1,245	2
Balance on hand.......................	760	700	2	1	1,977	706
Total ordered....................	760	700	2	1	5,338	1,083

8 GEORGE V, A. 1918

DISTRIBUTION of the Statutes of Canada, 1917—*Concluded.*

BOUND IN HALF CALF.

To whom sent.	Volumes 1 and 2.	
	English.	French.
Sales..	10	2
Balance in stock..	65	13
Total ordered..	75	15

BOUND IN FULL CALF.

To whom sent.	Volume 1.		Volume 2.		Volumes 1 and 2.	
	English.	French.	English.	French.	English.	French.
Authorized by Order in Council........	2	1	2	1	184	29
Sales....................................	....	....	....	....	3	....
Miscellaneous...........................	....	....	....	....	3	1
Balance on hand........................	....	....	....	....	135	70
Total ordered.................	2	1	2	1	345	100

REPORT

OF THE

SECRETARY OF STATE

FOR

EXTERNAL AFFAIRS

FOR THE

YEAR ENDED MARCH 31

1917

PRINTED BY ORDER OF PARLIAMENT

OTTAWA
J. DE LABROQUERIE TACHÉ
PRINTER TO THE KING'S MOST EXCELLENT MAJESTY
1918

[No. 33—1918]

To His Excellency the Duke of Devonshire, K.G., P.C., G.C.M.G., G.C.V.O., etc., etc.,
Governor General and Commander in Chief of the Dominion of Canada.

MY LORD DUKE,—

I have the honour to lay before Your Excellency the annual report of the Department of External Affairs for the year 1916-17.

I have the honour to be, My Lord Duke,
Your Grace's obedient servant,

R. L. BORDEN,
Secretary of State for External Affairs.

REPORT OF THE UNDER-SECRETARY OF STATE FOR EXTERNAL AFFAIRS.

To The Right Honourable
    Sir ROBERT BORDEN, G.C.M.G.,
        Secretary of State for External Affairs,
           Ottawa.

SIR,—I have the honour to submit my customary report in regard to the business of this department for the annual period 1916–17.

The numerous and complex questions arising from the Great European War continue to provide the subject-matter of the bulk of the correspondence of the year.

Germany's adoption of the policy of unrestricted destruction of merchant vessels, within zones defined by her, brought about a severance of diplomatic relations on the part of the United States, and a state of war was formally proclaimed by the President on the 6th April, 1917. This action of the United States was promptly followed by a severance of relations with Germany by Cuba, Brazil, and Bolivia.

The Dominions Royal Commission resumed its sittings in Canada in August, 1916, starting at Montreal, proceeding westward to Prince Rupert, and returning via Victoria and Vancouver eastward across the continent to Quebec. Sessions were held at all important centres. A fifth interim report, summarizing the information obtained on this tour, was published in February, 1917. The full and final report covering all the commission's operations was issued in March, 1917.

From March to May, 1917, marking a fresh development in the constitutional history of the British Empire, there sat at 10 Downing street, London, for the first time, the Imperial War Cabinet. This new body, over which the Prime Minister of the United Kingdom presided, consisted of the members of the War Cabinet of the United Kingdom, the Prime Minister of each Dominion or in his place a Minister deputed for the purpose, the Secretary of State for India, representing India, and other members of the Government of the United Kingdom specially concerned with Imperial affairs. The Imperial War Cabinet dealt with problems concerned with the effective prosecution of the war, and the terms on which peace might be made. In the end it was decided and announced that an Imperial Cabinet should be held annually to discuss foreign affairs and other aspects of Imperial policy (see Debates, House of Commons, Canada, Session 1917, vol. ii, pp. 1525–40; vol. iii, pp. 2354–5). At the same time, though sitting on alternate days, the Imperial War Conference, which is to be regarded as a special war meeting of the Imperial Conference of previous years enlarged by the inclusion in its membership, for the first time, of representatives from India, met at the Colonial Office under the chairmanship of the Secretary of State for the Colonies. The Imperial War Conference dealt with questions of common concern relating more especially to post-war conditions of an economic and constitutional nature. Canada's representatives at the Imperial War Conference were Sir Robert Borden, Sir George Perley, Mr. Rogers, and Mr. Hazen. Unfortunately, owing to unavoidable causes, Australia was unable to send representatives to the Imperial War Cabinet and Imperial War Conference of 1917.

Turning to matters concerning relations with the United States, it might be mentioned that the ratifications of the Migratory Birds Convention, con-

8 GEORGE V, A. 1918

cluded on the 16th August, 1916, were duly exchanged at Washington on the 7th December, 1916, and an Act confirming it was passed by the Canadian Parliament in August, 1917.

Reference may further be made to questions arising with the United States Government under the Boundary Waters Treaty, which have been adjusted by the International Joint Commission: (a) Application was made to the commission by the United States Government for the approval of certain improvements in the St. Clair river at Port Huron, involving a deepening of the channel. and the construction of a submerged weir. Canada being ready to agree to the proposed improvements conditionally upon the taking of adequate measures to protect Canadian interests, the approval of the commission was given on the 18th May, 1917, subject to Canada's conditions being met. (b) The final report of the commission on the Lake of the Woods reference was made on the 18th May, 1917. A level for the waters of the lake was recommended, which it was considered would be of the widest advantage to the various interests concerned, and compensation for damages to lands overflowed by the raising of the water suggested. A scheme was further outlined for controlling and regulating the flow of the waters, so that the desired level might be maintained. (c) The International Lumber Company, an American Corporation, applied for the approval of certain booms in the Rainy river at International Falls, and on the 3rd October, 1917, such approval was granted; it being laid down that the booms should follow lines indicated by the United States Secretary of War, and steps being taken to safeguard rights on the Canadian side of the boundary line.

TREATY OF COMMERCE AND NAVIGATION WITH PORTUGAL, 12TH AUGUST, 1914.

At the request of the Canadian Government, notice of Canada's adhesion to the above treaty was given on the 16th May, 1917, His Majesty's Government in a communication to the Portuguese Government having previously recorded their view that article 6 of the treaty, relating to the importation into the United Kingdom and the sale therein of port and madeira wines, referred only to the United Kingdom, and that the application of the treaty to any of His Majesty's dominions did not involve the application of the article referred to.

PELAGIC SEALING.

Notification was received from the Russian Government that the killing of seals on the Commander islands, which had been prohibited in 1912, would be resumed in 1917, this involving the revival of Canada's right to share of the take.

The danger attending travel across the submarine zones has made it necessary for the Canadian Government severely to restrict such travel in the case of women and children. It has been arranged to allow it only in special circumstances, approved by a Sub-Committee of the Privy Council, as justifying exceptional treatment. The measures connected with the carrying out of this procedure have added very considerably to the work of the passport office.

I gladly take the opportunity of expressing my satisfaction with the zealous and efficient manner in which the members of the staff have discharged their several duties.

I have the honour to be, sir,

Your obedient servant,

JOSEPH POPE,
Under-Secretary of State for External Affairs.

OTTAWA, October 15, 1917.

APPENDIX A.

ALPHABETICAL LIST of Foreign Consuls, Vice-Consuls, Consular Agents and Commercial Agents in the Dominion, according to the latest information supplied to the Department of External Affairs.

Name.	Designation.	Country.	Residence.	When Appointed.
Allison, M.A.	Consul	Portugal	St. John, N.B.	1903
Andre, L. A. E.	Consular Agent	France	Winnipeg, Man.	1907
Angwin, J. G.	Vice-Consul	Sweden	Sydney, N.S.	1906
Bailey, A. D.	Vice-Consul	United States	St. John, N.B.	1916
Barattieri, di San Pietro, Count G.	Consular Agent	Italy	Winnipeg, Man.	1910
Barranco y Fernandez C.	Consul	Cuba	St. John, N.B.	1914
Beebe, H.·S.	Consular Agent	United States	Beebe Jct., Que.	1909
Bell, C. N.	Consul	Guatemala	Winnipeg, Man.	1896
Bell, G. E.	Vice-Consul	United States	Calgary, Alta.	1916
Bergstrom, D.	Consul General	Sweden	Montreal	1916
Bisson, D.	Consular Agent	United States	Paspebiac, Que.	1899
Black, W. A.	Consul	Panama	Halifax, N.S.	1910
Black, W. A.	Vice-Consul	Netherlands	Halifax, N.S.	1911
Blair, F. N.	Acting Vice-Consul	Portugal	Rimouski, Que.	1913
Bonin, C. E.	Consul General	France	Montreal, Que.	1912
Borlase, G. E.	Vice-Consul	United States	Sherbrooke, Que.	1899
Botkin, T.	Consul	United States	Campbellton, N.B.	1907
Bouillon, E. A. A.	Commercial Agent	Brazil	Paspebiac, Que.	1899
Bourget, A.	Consular Agent	France	Regina, Sask.	1910
Bourgoin, George	Vice-Consul	Brazil	Montreal, Que.	1911
Boynton, D.	Vice and Deputy Consul.	United States	Sydney, N.S.	1916
Bradley, W. H.	Consul General	United States	Montreal. Que.	1907
Brady, J. R.	Vice-Consul	United States	Hamilton, Ont.	1916
Brandt, J. F.	Vice-Consul	Norway	Prince Rupert, B.C.	1912
Brookfield, J.	Consul	Dominican Republic.	Montreal, Que.	1915
Brown, R. N.	Vice-Consul	United States	Yarmouth, N.S.	1915
Bunols, J. E.	Consul General	Dominican Republic.	Montreal, Que.	1913
Burlingham, W. B.	Vice-Consul	United States	Sault Ste. Marie, Ont.	1916
Call, B. N.	Consular Agent	United States	Newcastle, N.B.	1904
Campbell, G. D.	Consul	Cuba	Weymouth, N.S.	1913
Canellas y. Martio, F.	Consul	Cuba	Montreal, Que.	1915
Carbray, T. J.	Vice-Consul	Argentine Republic.	Quebec, Que.	1908
Chater, D.	Vice and Deputy Consul.	United States	Windsor, Ont.	1904
Chao Tsong Tian	Vice-Consul	China	Ottawa, Ont.	1913
Clinton, G. W.	Consular Agent	United States	Cumberland, B.C.	1899
Clum, H. D.	Consul	United States	Calgary, Alta.	1916
Conant, H. A.	Consul	United States	Windsor, Ont.	1905
Cox, H.	Consular Agent	United States	Edmonton, Alta.	1915
Cresse, L. G. A., K.C.	Honorary Consul	Guatemala	Montreal and Quebec.	1913
Cruz, Don Manuel Garcia y.	Consul	Spain	Montreal, Que.	1911
Culver, H. S.	Consul	United States	St. John, N.B.	1910
Cummings, E. A.	Vice-Consul	United States	Moncton, N.B.	1916
Curren, A. E.	Consul	Belgium	Halifax, N.S.	1889
Curren, A. E.	Commercial Agent	Brazil	Halifax, N.S.	1913
Davies, J. R.	Vice-Consul	Sweden	Pictou, N.S.	1884
Davison, Francis.	Vice-Consul	Portugal	Bridgewater, N.S.	1905
Davison, J. McG.	Vice-Consul	Sweden	Halifax, N.S.	1906
de Castri, C.	Consular Agent	Italy	Fernie, B.C.	1913
de Clerval, M.	Consular Agent	France	Calgary, Alta.	1911
Defries, R. L.	Consul	Honduras	Toronto, Ont.	1913
de Jardin, G.	Vice-Consul	Belgium	Forget, Sask.	1911
DeLamater, I.	Vice-Consul	United States	Fort William and Pt. Arthur, Ont.	1916
de Likatscheff, S.	Consul General for the Dominion of Canada.	Russia	Montreal, Que.	1914

ALPHABETICAL LIST of Foreign Consuls, Vice-Consuls, Consular Agents and
Commercial Agents, etc.—*Continued*

Name.	Designation.	Country.	Residence.	When Appointed
Denison, F. C	Consul	United States	Prescott, Ont	1915
de Olivares, José	Consul	United States	Hamilton, Ont	1915
de Saint Victor, R	Consular Agent	France	Quebec, Que	1913
De Sola, C. I	Consul	Belgium	Montreal, Que	1911
De Wolf, J. E	Vice-Consul	Mexico	Halifax, N.S	1906
Dorsey, W. Roderick	Consul	United States	Quebec, Que	1917
Dow, E. A	Consul	United States	Fort William and Pt. Arthur, Ont	1917
Drummond, G. E	Consul General	Denmark	Montreal, Que	1910
Dubuc, A	Consul	Belgium	Winnipeg, Man	1905
Duggan, F. M	Vice-Consul	Sweden	Quebec, Que	1910
Eakins, A. W	Consul	Cuba	Yarmouth, N.S	1907
Edwards, M. B	Vice-Consul	Sweden	St. John, N.B	1913
Emanuels, E. J	Consul	Brazil	Vancouver, B.C	1915
Erzinger, J	Consul	Switzerland	Winnipeg, Man	1913
Estrada, J de	Vice-Consul	Uruguay	Toronto, Ont	1914
Falardeau, A	Consul	Peru	Quebec, Que	1916
Fisher, T. M	Vice-Consul	United States	Halifax, N.S	1917
Folger, H. S	Vice-Consul	United States	Kingston, Ont	1908
Foster, J. G	Consul General	United States	Ottawa, Ont	1903
Francis, A. P. O	Consular Agent	France	Victoria, B.C	1910
Francklyn, G. E	Consular Agent	France	Halifax, N.S	1881
Fraser, G. B	Consular Agent	Spain	Chatham, N.B	1880
Frechette, O	Acting Vice-Consul	Spain	Quebec, Que	1898
Frechette, O	Consul	Chile	Quebec, Que	1885
Frechette, O	Consul General	Colombia	Quebec, Que	1909
Frechette, O	Consul	Portugal	Quebec, Que	1908
Freeman, C. M	Consul	United States	Sydney, N.S	1911
Fryling, A	Vice-Consul	Netherlands	Calgary, Alta	1915
Futcher, F. A	Vice-Consul	Norway	Victoria and Chemainus, B.C	1907
Garrett, Alonzo B	Consul	United States	St. Stephen, N.B	1917
Gerez, A	Consul General	Argentine Republic	Ottawa, Ont	1916
Gintzburger, S	Consul	Switzerland	Vancouver, B.C	1913
Gonnason, A	Consul	Sweden	Victoria, B.C	1911
Goor, M	Consul General	Belgium	Ottawa, Ont	1913
Gordon, J. A	Vice-Consul	Argentine Republic	Montreal, Que	1908
Gorman, P	Vice-Consul	United States	Montreal, Que	1886
Grassi, G	Consular Agent	Italy	Sault Ste Marie, Ont	1914
Gunn, F	Vice-Consul	Norway	Quebec, Que	1906
Hackett, W	Vice-Consul	Norway	North Sydney, N.S	1910
Hackett, W	Vice-Consul	Portugal	North Sydney, N.S	1910
Hamel, H. C	Consular Agent	United States	Cabano, Que	1913
Hammond, J. W	Vice-Consul	United States	Fredericton, N.B	1916
Hamon, W	Vice-Consul	Brazil	Paspebiac, Que	1882
Hanson, G. M	Consul	United States	Prince Rupert, B.C	1916
Hart, A. W	Consular Agent	United States	Cape Canso, N.S	1885
Hart, G. R	Vice-Consul	Brazil	Halifax, N.S	1893
Hatheway, F	Consular Agent	France	St. John, N.B	1910
Hatheway, W. F	Consul	Guatemala	St. John, N.B	1898
Heard, W. W	Vice and Dep. Consul	United States	Quebec, Que	1915
Hechler, Henry	Consul	Liberia	Halifax, N.S	1903
Heubach, Claude	Vice-Consul	Mexico	Winnipeg, Man	1916
Heward, S. B	Vice-Consul	Netherlands	Montreal, Que	1879
Hutchinson, G A	Vice-Consul	Sweden	Richibucto, N.B	1911
Isaacs, C	Vice-Consul	United States	Montreal, Que	1916
Istel, A	Consular Agent	France	Vancouver, B.C	1913
Jarvis, C.E.L	Vice-Consul	Brazil	St. John, N.B	1896
Jarvis, M. M	Commercial Agent	Brazil	St. John, N.B	1901
Johnson, E. G	Vice-Consul	United States	Vancouver, B.C	1915
Johnston, F. S. S	Consul	United States	Kingston, Ont	1910
Johnston, Jesse H	Consul	United States	Regina, Sask	1917
Johnston, M. P	Consular Agent	United States	Lethbridge, Alta	1913
Jones, W. G	Vice-Consul	Spain	Halifax, N.S	1894
Kelly, M. A	Vice-Consul	Norway	Campbellton, N.B	1916
Kerman, W. S	Vice-Consul	Brazil	Toronto, Ont	1916

ALPHABETICAL LIST of Foreign Consuls, Vice-Consuls, Consular Agents and Commercial Agents, etc.—*Continued.*

Name.	Designation.	Country.	Residence.	When Appointed.
Kerr, Geo	Vice-Consul	Sweden	Toronto, Ont	1910
King, J	Vice-Consul	Belgium	Fort William, Ont	1913
Koren, F	Consul, with jurisdiction over the whole of the Dominion of Canada	Norway	Montreal, Que	1911
Labbie, A. P	Consular Agent	United States	St. Leonards, N.B	1916
Lacroix, Ed	Consular Agent	France	North Sydney, N.S	1909
LeBoutillier, C. S	Vice-Consul	Brazil	Gaspé, Que	1876
LeBoutillier, C. S	Acting Vice-Consul	Portugal	Gaspé Basin, Que	1895
LeGros, P. E	Commercial Agent	Brazil	Gaspé, Que	1900
Leonard, C. F	Consular Agent	United States	Peterborough, Ont	1910
LeQuesne, J. C	Acting Vice-Consul	Portugal	Paspebiac, Que	1898
Levasseur, T	Vice-Consul	Brazil	Quebec, Que	1902
LeVatte, H. C. V	Consular Agent	United States	Louisburg, N.S	1898
Linnell, I. N	Vice-Consul	United States	Vancouver, B.C	1916
Lin Shihyuan	Consul	China	Vancouver, B.C	1913
Longhi, G. P	Consular Agent	Italy	Calgary, Alta	1915
Long, T	Consul	Colombia	Toronto, Ont	1916
Mack, J. M	Consular Agent	United States	Liverpool, N.S	1896
Mahy, J. E	Consul	Belgium	Quebec, Que	1916
Maitland, R. R	Consul	Honduras	Vancouver, B.C	1913
Marino, E	Consular Agent	Italy	Fort William, Ont	1912
Marker, C. P	Vice-Consul	Denmark	Calgary, Alta	1910
Marsh, O. G	Consul	United States	Ottawa, Ont	1915
Martin, H	Consul	Belgium	Edmonton, Alta	1917
Martin, Henri	Consul General	Switzerland	Montreal, Que	1913
Martin, C. W	Consul	United States	Toronto, Ont	1916
Masi, N	Consular Agent	Italy	Vancouver, B.C	1915
Mason, T. J	Commercial Agent	Brazil	Toronto, Ont	1917
Mathers, H. I	Vice-Consul	Russia	Halifax, N.S	1899
Mathers, H. I	Consul	Denmark	Halifax, N.S	1906
Mathers, H. I	Consul	Norway	Halifax, N.S	1906
Mersereau, C. M	Consular Agent	United States	Bathurst, N.B	1915
Miles, Henry	Consul	Paraguay	Montreal, Que	1902
Milner, J. B	Consul	United States	Niagara Falls, Ont	1916
Mitchell, W. A	Vice-Consul	Mexico	Toronto, Ont	1901
Montyn, W. V	Vice-Consul	Netherlands	Winnipeg, Man	1914
Morang, G. N	Consul	Guatemala	Toronto, Ont	1896
Morissette, J. B	Commercial Agent	Brazil	Quebec, Que	1904
Morris, M. P	Consul	Panama	Vancouver, B.C	1906
Morris, M. P	Consul General	Chile	Vancouver, B.C	1897
Morris, M. P	Vice-Consul	Mexico	Vancouver, B.C	1914
Mosher, R. B	Consul	United States	Victoria, B.C	1915
Mullin, D	Consul	Belgium	St. John, N.B	1908
Munoz y. Rieva, Jose A	Consul	Cuba	Toronto, Ont	1915
Munro, W. A	Vice-Consul	United States	Cornwall, Ont	1915
Murphy, John	Vice-Consul	United States	Prescott, Ont	1917
Murphy, W. B	Consular Agent	United States	Arnprior, Ont	1909
Murray, Robert	Vice-Consul	Sweden	Chatham and Newcastle, N.B.	1910
MacMillan, F	Vice-Consul	Sweden	Sheet Harbour, N.S	1882
MacQuillan, J	Consul General	Ecuador	Vancouver, B.C	1898
MacRae, K. J	Vice-Consul	Norway	St. John, N.B	1914
McCulley, S. U	Vice-Consul	Denmark	Chatham, N.B	1913
McLaughlin, C	Consular Agent	Italy	St. John, N.B	1886
McLean, H. H	Vice-Consul	Argentine Republic	St. John, N.B	1908
Neale, F. E	Vice-Consul	Norway	Chatham, N.B	1909
Neville, J	Vice-Consul	Uruguay	Halifax, N.S	1913
Neville, J. A	Vice-Consul	Argentine Republic	Halifax, N.S	1908
Newcombe, R. M	Vice-Consul	United States	Victoria, B.C	1914
Nicholls, F	Consul	Portugal	Toronto, Ont	1906
Nobel, O. K	Vice-Consul	Denmark	Montreal, Que	1911
Nolan, J. A	Vice-Consul	Sweden	Calgary, Alta	1901
Nordbye, Dr. F. A	Vice-Consul	Norway	Camrose, Alta	1916
Nordheimer, A	Consul General	Netherlands	Toronto, Ont	1902
Numano, Y	Consul General	Japan	Ottawa, Ont	1916
Oland, S. C	Consul	Chile	Halifax, N.S	1914

8 GEORGE V, A. 1918

ALPHABETICAL LIST of Foreign Consuls, Vice-Consuls, Consular Agents and Commercial Agents, etc.—*Continued.*

Name.	Designation.	Country.	Residence.	When Appointed.
Olson, Albert	Vice-Consul	Sweden	Regina, Sask	1916
Owen, J. M	Consular Agent	United States	Annapolis, N.S	1872
Owen, W. H	Consular Agent	United States	Bridgewater, N.S	1872
Owen, W. H	Consul	Cuba	Bridgewater, N.S	1905
Oxley, F. H	Consul	Portugal	Halifax, N.S	1898
Oxley, H	Honorary Consul	Portugal	Halifax, N.S	1916
Pashley, J. H	Consular Agent	United States	Nanaimo, B.C	1906
Petry, W. H	Vice-Consul	Denmark	Quebec, Que	1911
Philpot, J	Consular Agent	United States	Port Hawkesbury and Mulgrave, N.S	1916
Pickles, F. W	Vice-Consul	Argentine Republic	Annapolis, N.S	1910
Pierce, W. A	Consul	United States	Charlottetown, P.E.I.	1916
Pirmez, R	Consul	Belgium	Calgary, Alta	1912
Planta, A. E	Vice-Consul	Norway	Nanaimo, B.C	1907
Pollock, J. R	Vice-Consul	United States	Fernie, B.C	1908
Prescott, J. W	Consular Agent	Brazil	Vancouver, B.C	1916
Printz, C. J. P	Vice-Consul	Norway	Toronto, Ont	1908
Quann, W. P	Consular Agent	United States	Kenora, Ont	1916
Radford, Wm. G	Vice-Consul	Sweden	Dawson, Y.T	1910
Ragosine, W	Consul	Russia	Vancouver, B.C	1916
Rairden, B. S	Consul	United States	Riviere du Loup, Que.	1916
Rasmusen, Bertil M	Consul	United States	Fernie, B.C	1917
Raynaud, L	Consul-Chancelier	France	Montreal, Que	1911
Richardson, E. V	Consul	United States	Moncton, N.B	1916
Robertson, P	Vice-Consul	Argentine Republic	Toronto, Ont	1913
Rochereau, de la Sablière, C	Consul	Belgium	Toronto, Ont	1904
Rochereau, de la Sablière, C. E	Consular Agent	France	Toronto, Ont	1908
Rogers, W. A	Vice-Consul	United States	Campbellton, N.B	1916
Ross, P. W. T	Consul	Uruguay	Montreal, Que	1915
Ross, T. P	Vice-Consul	Netherlands	Quebec, Que	1910
Ross, W. A	Acting Vice-Consul	Denmark	St. John, N.B	1916
Rousseau, A. M	Consular Agent	United States	White Horse, Y.T	1916
Routh, F. C	Consul	Portugal	Montreal, Que	1911
Rudolf, D. J	Consular Agent	United States	Lunenburg, N.S	1907
Ryder, F. M	Consul General	United States	Winnipeg, Man	1915
Ryerson, Jas	Consular Agent	United States	Galt, Ont	1899
Salgado, S. G	Vice-Consul	Cuba	Halifax, N.S	1915
Sanford, H. M	Vice-Consul	United States	Ottawa, Ont	1898
Shotts, G. W	Consul	United States	Sault Ste. Marie, Ont.	1906
Sinclair, N	Consular Agent	United States	Summerside, P.E.I	1907
Slater, F. C	Consul	United States	Sarnia, Ont	1906
Smith, H. J	Vice-Consul	Sweden	Winnipeg, Man	1904
Snowball, R. A	Consular Agent	France	Chatham, N.B	1902
Somerville, J. G	Vice-Consul	United States	Niagara Falls, Ont	1914
Soot, H. R	Vice-Consul	Norway	Winnipeg, Man	1909
Sorensen, C	Vice-Consul	Norway	Port Arthur, Ont	1914
Sorensen, C	Vice-Consul	Norway	Fort William, Ont	1914
Stable, N. Perez	Consul General	Cuba	Halifax, N.S	1914
Stahlschmidt, C. B	Consul	Norway	Vancouver, B.C	1907
Strickland, C. L	Vice-Consul	United States	Charlottetown, P.E.I	1911
Sutliff, L. G	Vice-Consul	United States	Winnipeg, Man	1915
Taggart, G. R	Consul	United States	Cornwall, Ont	1912
Tamayo, P	Consul	Mexico	Toronto, Ont	1912
Tanguay, E. G	Vice-Consul	Paraguay	Quebec, Que	1914
Taylor, T. M	Consul	Guatemala	Vancouver, B.C	1916
Terrero, Don L	Consul General	Venezuela	Ottawa, Ont	1913
Terry, W. S	Consul	Belgium	Victoria, B.C	1912
Thierry, F	Consul	Panama	Montreal, Que	1915
Thompson, J. Enoch	Consul	Spain	Toronto, Ont	1900
Thompson, J. Enoch	Consul	Panama	Toronto, Ont	1905
Thomson, P. W	Consul	Panama	St. John, N.B	1905
Thomson, P. W	Consul	Netherlands	St. John, N.B	1905
Thorgeirsson, O. S	Vice-Consul	Denmark	Winnipeg, Man	1914
Tovell, D. S	Vice-Consul	United States	Toronto, Ont	1904
Ukita, S	Consul	Japan	Vancouver, B.C	1917

SESSIONAL PAPER No. 33

ALPHABETICAL LIST of Foreign Consuls, Vice-Consuls, Consular Agents and Commercial Agents, etc.—*Concluded.*

Name.	Designation.	Country.	Residence.	When Appointed.
Van Roggen, M. A.	Vice-Consul	Netherlands	Vancouver, B.C.	1910
Vroom, C. N.	Vice and Dep. Consul	United States	St. Stephen, N.B.	1895
Waagen, C. B. N.	Vice-Consul	Norway	Calgary, Alta.	1916
Wakefield, E. C.	Consular Agent	United States	North Bay, Ont.	1906
Walsh, J. C.	Consul General	Greece	Montreal, Que.	1915
Ward, W. A.	Vice-Consul	Denmark	Vancouver, B.C.	1909
Waterous, C. A.	Consul	Chile	Brantford, Ont.	1908
Watson, F. C.	Vice-Consul	United States	Sarnia, Ont.	1914
Watson, J. C.	Consul	United States	Yarmouth, N.S.:	1916
Watt, G.	Consular Agent	Italy	Chatham, N.B.	1886
Wedmore, P. W.	Vice-Consul	Spain	St. John, N.B.	1912
West, G. N.	Consul General	United States	Vancouver, B.C.	1916
White, H. G.	Consul	Peru	Vancouver, B.C.	1914
Whitehead, J. M.	Consul	Belgium	Vancouver, B.C.	1907
Whitman, F. C.	Consul	Cuba	Annapolis, N.S.	1904
Winch, R. V.	Vice-Consul	Sweden	Vancouver, B.C.	1906
Wolf (de), J. E.	Vice-Consul	Mexico	Halifax, N.S.	1906
Woodward, C. G.	Consul	United States	Vancouver, B.C.	1911
Yang, Shuwen	Consul General	China	Ottawa, Ont.	1913
Yeigh, F.	Vice-Consul	Paraguay	Toronto, Ont.	1903
Young, J. A.	Vice-Consul	Norway	Sydney, N.S.	1911
Young, E. E.	Consul General	United States	Halifax, N.S.	1913
Zaniewsky, H.	Vice Consul	Russia	Montreal, Que.	1916
Zunini, Cavalier L.	Consul General	Italy	Montreal, Que.	1915

APPENDIX B.

ALPHABETICAL LIST of Foreign Countries represented in Canada by Consuls, Vice-Consuls, Consular Agents and Commercial Agents, according to the latest information supplied to the Department of External Affairs.

Country.	Place.	Name.	Designation.	When Appointed.
Argentine Republic....	Annapolis, N.S............	Pickles, F. W.........	Vice-Consul..........	1910
	Halifax, N.S.............	Neville, J. A.........	Vice-Consul..........	1908
	Ottawa, Ont.............	Gerez, A.............	Consul General.......	1916
	Montreal, Que...........	Gordon, J. A.........	Vice-Consul..........	1908
	Quebec, Que............	Carbray, T. J.........	Vice-Consul..........	1908
	St. John, N.B...........	McLean, H. H........	Vice-Consul..........	1908
	Toronto, Ont............	Robertson, P.........	Vice-Consul..........	1913
Belgium...............	Calgary, Alta...........	Pirmez, R............	Consul...............	1912
	Edmonton, Alta........	Martin, H............	Consul...............	1917
	Forget, Sask............	de Jardin, G.........	Vice-Consul..........	1911
	Fort William, Ont.......	King, J.............	Vice-Consul..........	1913
	Halifax, N.S............	Curren, A. E.........	Consul...............	1889
	Montreal, Que...........	De Sola, C. I....:....	Consul...............	1911
	Ottawa, Ont............	Goor, M.............	Consul General......	1913
	Quebec, Que............	Mahy, J. E..........	Consul...............	1916
	St. John, N.B...........	Mullin, D............	Consul...............	1908
	Toronto, Ont............	Rochereau de la Sablière, C.........	Consul...............	1904
	Vancouver, B.C.........	Whitehead, J. M......	Consul...............	1907
	Victoria, B.C...........	Terry, W. S..........	Consul...............	1912
	Winnipeg, Man.........	Dubuc, A............	Consul...............	1905
Brazil.................	Gaspé, Que.............	LeGros, P. E.........	Commercial Agent....	1900
	Gaspé, Que.............	LeBoutillier, C. S.....	Vice-Consul..........	1876
	Halifax, N.S............	Hart, G. R.	Vice-Consul..........	1893
	Halifax, N.S............	Curren, A. E.........	Commercial Agent....	1913
	Montreal, Que...........	Bourgoin, George.....	Vice-Consul..........	1911
	Paspebiac, Que..........	Bouillon, E. A. A.....	Commercial Agent....	1899
	Paspebiac, Que..........	Hamon, W............	Vice-Consul..........	1882
	Quebec, Que............	Levasseur, T.........	Vice-Consul..........	1902
	Quebec, Que............	Morissette, J. B......	Commercial Agent....	1904
	St. John, N.B...........	Jarvis, C. E. L.......	Vice-Consul..........	1896
	St. John, N.B...........	Jarvis, M. M.........	Commercial Agent....	1901
	Toronto, Ont............	Kerman, W. S........	Vice-Consul..........	1916
	Toronto, Ont............	Mason, T. J..........	Commercial Agent....	1917
	Vancouver, B.C.........	Emanuels, E. J.......	Consul...............	1915
	Vancouver, B.C.........	Prescott, J. W........	Commercial Agent....	1916
Chile.................	Brantford, Ont..........	Waterous, C. A.......	Consul...............	1908
	Halifax, N.S............	Oland, S. C..........	Consul...............	1914
	Quebec, Que............	Frechette, O.........	Consul...............	1885
	Vancouver, B.C.........	Morris, M. P.........	Consul General......	1897
China................	Ottawa, Ont............	Yang Shuwen.........	Consul General......	1913
	Ottawa, Ont............	Chao Tsong Tian.....	Vice-Consul..........	1913
	Vancouver, B.C.........	Lin Shihyuan.........	Consul...............	1913
Colombia.............	Quebec, Que............	Frechette, O.........	Consul General.......	1909
	Toronto, Ont............	Long, T....:.........	Consul...............	1916
Corea*.				
Cuba.................	Annapolis, N.S..........	Whitman, F. C.......	Consul...............	1904
	Bridgewater, N.S........	Owen, W. H.........	Consul...............	1905
	Halifax, N.S............	Stable, N. Perez......	Consul General.......	1914
	Halifax, N.S............	Salgado, S. G........	Vice-Consul..........	1915
	Montreal, Que...........	Canellas y. Martio, F.	Consul...............	1915
	St. John, N.B...........	Barranco y Fernandez, C.................	Consul...............	1914
	Toronto, Ont............	Munoz y Rieva, Jose A	Consul...............	1915

*Represented by Japanese Consuls.

ALPHABETICAL LIST of Foreign Countries represented by Consuls, Vice-Consuls, Consular Agents and Commercial Agents, etc.—*Continued.*

Country.	Place.	Name.	Designation.	When Appointed.
Cuba—*Con*.	Weymouth, N.S.	Campbell, G. D.	Consul	1913
	Yarmouth, N.S.	Eakins, A. W.	Consul	1907
Denmark	Calgary, Alta.	Marker, C. P.	Vice-Consul	1910
	Chatham, N.B.	McCulley, S. U.	Vice-Consul	1913
	Halifax, N.S.	Mathers, H. I.	Consul	1906
	Montreal, Que.	Drummond, G. E.	Consul General	1910
	Montreal, Que.	Nobel, O. K.	Vice-Consul	1911
	Quebec, Que.	Petry, W. H.	Vice-Consul	1911
	St. John, N.B.	Ross, W. A.	Acting Vice-Consul	1916
	Vancouver, B.C.	Ward, W. A.	Vice-Consul	1909
	Winnipeg, Man.	Thorgeirsson, O. S.	Vice-Consul	1914
Dominican Republic	Montreal, Que. *	Bunols, J. E.	Consul General	1914
	Montreal, Que.	Brookfield, J.	Consul	1915
Ecuador	Vancouver, B.C.	MacQuillan, J.	Consul General	1898
France	Calgary, Alta.	deClerval, M.	Consular Agent	1911
	Chatham, N.B.	Snowball, R. A.	Consular Agent	1902
	Halifax, N.S.	Francklyn, G. E.	Consular Agent	1881
	Montreal, Que.	Bonin, C. E.	Consul General	1912
	Montreal, Que.	Raynaud, L.	Consular Chancelier	1911
	Quebec, Que.	de Saint Victor, R.	Consular Agent	1913
	Regina, Sask.	Bourget, A.	Consular Agent	1910
	North Sydney, N.S.	Lacroix, Ed.	Consular Agent	1909
	St. John, N.B.	Hatheway, F.	Consular Agent	1910
	Toronto, Ont.	Rochereau de la Sabliere, C.E.	Consular Agent	1908
	Vancouver, B.C.	Istel, A.	Consular Agent	1913
	Victoria, B.C.	Francis, A. P. O.	Consular Agent	1910
	Winnipeg, Man.	Andre, L. A. E.	Consular Agent	1907
Greece	Montreal, Que.	Walsh, J. C.	Consul General	1915
Guatemala	Montreal, Que.	Cresse, L. G. A., K.C.	Honorary Consul	1913
	Quebec, Que.	Cresse, L. G. A., K.C.	Honorary Consul	1913
	St. John, N.B.	Hatheway, W. F.	Consul	1898
	Toronto, Ont.	Morang, G. N.	Consul	1896
	Vancouver, B.C.	Taylor, T. M.	Consul	1916
	Winnipeg, Man.	Bell, C. N.	Consul	1896
Honduras	Toronto, Ont.	Defries, R. L.	Consul	1913
	Vancouver, B.C.	Maitland, R. R.	Consul	1913
Italy	Calgary, Alta.	Longhi, G. P.	Consular Agent	1915
	Chatham, N.B.	Watt, G.	Consular Agent	1886
	Fernie, B.C.	de Castri, C.	Consular Agent	1913
	Fort William, Ont.	Marino, E.	Consular Agent	1912
	Montreal, Que.	Zunini, Cavalier L.	Consul General	1915
	St. John, N.B.	McLaughlin, C.	Consular Agent	1886
	Sault Ste. Marie, Ont.	Grassi, G.	Consular Agent	1914
	Winnipeg, Man.	Barattieri di San Pietro, Count G.	Consular Agent	1910
	Vancouver, B.C.	Masi, N.	Consular Agent	1915
Japan	Ottawa, Ont.	Numano, Y.	Consul General	1916
	Vancouver, B.C.	Ukita, S.	Consul	1917
Liberia	Halifax, N.S.	Hechler, Henry	Consul	1903
*Luxemburg.				
Mexico	Halifax, N.S.	DeWolf, J. E.	Vice-Consul	1906
	Toronto, Ont.	Tamayo, P.	Consul	1912
	Toronto, Ont.	Mitchell, W. A.	Vice-Consul	1901
	Vancouver, B.C.	Morris, M. P.	Vice-Consul	1914
	Winnipeg, Man.	Heubach, Claude.	Vice-Consul	1916
Netherlands	Calgary, Alta.	Fryling, A.	Vice-Consul	1915
	Halifax, N.S.	Black, W. A.	Vice-Consul	1911
	Montreal, Que.	Heward, S. B.	Vice-Consul	1879
	Quebec, Que.	Ross, T. P.	Vice-Consul	1910
	St. John, N.B.	Thomson, P. W.	Consul	1905
	Toronto, Ont.	Nordheimer, A.	Consul-General	1902
	Vancouver, B.C.	Van Roggen, M. A.	Vice-Consul	1910
	Winnipeg, Man.	Montyn, W. V.	Vice-Consul	1914

*Represented by Consuls of the Netherlands.

8 GEORGE V, A. 1918

ALPHABETICAL LIST of Foreign Countries represented by Consuls, Vice-Consuls,
Consular Agents and Commercial Agents, etc.—*Continued.*

Country.	Place.	Name.	Designation.	When Appointed.
Norway	Calgary, Alta	Waagen, C. B. N	Vice-Consul	1916
	Campbellton, N.B	Kelly, M. A	Vice-Consul	1916
	Camrose., Alta	Nordbye, Dr. F. A	Vice-Consul	1916
	Chatham, N.B	Neale, F. E	Vice-Consul	1909
	Chemainus, B.C	Futcher, F. A	Vice-Consul	1907
	Fort William, Ont	Sorensen, C	Vice-Consul	1914
	Halifax, N.S	Mathers, H. I	Consul	1906
	Montreal, Que	Koren, F	Consul with jurisdiction over the whole of the Dominion of Canada	1911
	Nanaimo, B.C	Planta, A. E	Vice-Consul	1907
	North Sydney, N.S	Hackett, W	Vice-Consul	1910
	Port Arthur, Ont	Sorensen, C	Vice-Consul	1914
	Prince Rupert, B.C	Brandt, J. F	Vice-Consul	1912
	Quebec, Que	Gunn, F	Vice-Consul	1906
	St. John, N.B	MacRae, K. J	Vice-Consul	1914
	Sydney, N.S	Young, J. A	Vice-Consul	1911
	Toronto, Ont	Printz, C. J. P	Vice-Consul	1908
	Vancouver, B.C	Stahlschmidt, C. B	Consul	1907
	Victoria, B.C	Futcher, F. A	Vice-Consul	1907
	Winnipeg, Man	Soot, H. R	Vice-Consul	1909
Panama	Halifax, N.S	Black, W. A	Consul	1910
	Montreal, Que	Thierry, F	Consul	1915
	St. John, N.B	Thomson, P. W	Consul	1905
	Toronto, Ont	Thompson, J. Enoch	Consul	1905
	Vancouver, B.C	Morris, M. P	Consul	1906
Paraguay	Montreal, Que	Miles, Henry	Consul	1902
	Quebec, Que	Tanguay, E. G	Vice-Consul	1914
	Toronto, Ont	Yeigh, F	Vice-Consul	1903
Peru	Quebec, Que	Falardeau, A	Consul	1916
	Vancouver, B.C	White, H. G	Consul	1914
Portugal	Bridgewater, N.S	Davison, Francis	Vice-Consul	1905
	Gaspe Basin, Que	LeBoutillier, C. S	Acting Vice-Consul	1895
	Halifax, N.S	Oxley, F. H	Consul	1898
	Halifax, N.S	Oxley, H	Honorary Consul	1916
	Montreal, Que	Routh, F. C	Consul	1911
	North Sydney, N.S	Hackett, W	Vice-Consul	1910
	Paspebiac, Que	Le Quesne, J. C	Acting Vice-Consul	1898
	Quebec, Que	Frechette, O	Consul	1908
	Rimouski, Que	Blair, F. N	Acting Vice-Consul	1913
	St. John, N.B	Allison, M. A	Consul	1903
	Toronto, Ont	Nicholls, F	Consul	1906
Russia	Halifax, N.S	Mathers, H. I	Vice-Consul	1899
	Montreal, Que	de Likatscheff, S	Consul General for the Dominion of Canada	1914
	Montreal, Que	Zaniewsky, H	Vice-Consul	1916
	Vancouver, B.C	Ragosine, W	Consul	1916
Spain	Chatham, N.B	Fraser, G. B	Consular Agent	1880
	Halifax, N.S	Jones, W. G	Vice-Consul	1894
	Montreal, Que	Cruz, Don Manuel Garcia y	Consul	1911
	Quebec, Que	Frechette, O	Acting Vice-Consul	1898
	St. John, N.B	Wedmore, P. W	Vice-Consul	1912
	Toronto, Ont	Thompson, J. Enoch	Consul	1900
Sweden	Calgary, Alta	Nolan, J. A	Vice-Consul	1901
	Chatham, N.B	Murray, Robert	Vice-Consul	1910
	Dawson, Y.T	Radford, Wm. G	Vice-Consul	1910
	Halifax, N.S	Davison, J. McG	Vice-Consul	1906
	Montreal, Que	Bergstrom, D	Consul-General	1916
	Newcastle, N.B	Murray, Robert	Vice-Consul	1910
	Pictou, N.S	Davies, J. R	Vice-Consul	1884
	Quebec, Que	Duggan, F. M	Vice-Consul	1910
	Regina, Sask	Olson, Albert	Vice-Consul	1916
	Richibucto, N.B	Hutchinson, G. A	Vice-Consul	1911
	Sheet Harbour, N.S	MacMillan, F	Vice-Consul	1882
	Sydney, N.S	Angwin, J. G	Vice-Consul	1906

ALPHABETICAL LIST of Foreign Countries represented by Consuls, Vice-Consuls, Consular Agents and Commercial Agents, etc.—*Continued.*

Country.	Place.	Name.	Designation.	When Appointed.
Sweden—*Con*	St. John, N.B	Edwards, M. B	Vice-Consul	1913
	Toronto, Ont	Kerr, Geo:	Vice-Consul	1910
	Vancouver, B.C	Winch, R. V	Vice-Consul	1906
	Victoria, B.C	Gonnason, A	Consul	1911
	Winnipeg, Man	Smith, H. J	Vice-Consul	1904
Switzerland	Montreal, Que	Martin, Henri	Consul General	1913
	Winnipeg, Man	Erzinger, J	Consul	1913
	Vancouver, B.C	Gintzburger, S	Consul	1913
United States	Annapolis, N.S	Owen, J. M	Consular Agent	1872
	Arnprior, Ont	Murphy, W. B	Consular Agent	1909
	Bathurst, N.B	Mersereau, C. M	Consular Agent	1915
	Beebe Jct., Que	Beebe, H. S	Consular Agent	1909
	Bridgewater, N.S	Owen, W. H	Consular Agent	1872
	Cabano, Que	Hamel, H. C	Consular Agent	1913
	Calgary, Alta	Clum, H. D	Consul	1916
	Calgary, Alta	Bell, G. E	Vice-Consul	1916
	Campbellton, N.B	Botkin, T	Consul	1907
	Campbellton, N.B	Rogers, W. A	Vice-Consul	1916
	Cape Canso, N.S	Hart, A. W	Consular Agent	1885
	Charlottetown, P.E.I	Pierce, W. A	Consul	1916
	Charlottetown, P.E.I	Strickland, C. L	Vice-Consul	1911
	Cornwall, Ont	Munro, W. A	Vice-Consul	1915
	Cornwall, Ont	Taggart, G. R	Consul	1912
	Cumberland, B.C	Clinton, G. W	Consular Agent	1899
	Edmonton, Alta	Cox, H	Consular Agent	1915
	Fernie, B.C	Rasmusen, Bertil M	Consul	1917
	Fernie, B.C	Pollock, J. R	Vice-Consul	1908
	Fort William, Ont	De Lamater, I	Vice-Consul	1916
	Fort William, Ont	Dow, E. A	Consul	1917
	Fredericton, N.B	Hammond, J. W	Vice-Consul	1916
	Galt, Ont	Ryerson, James	Consular Agent	1899
	Halifax, N.S	Fisher, T. M	Vice-Consul	1917
	Halifax, N.S	Young, E. E	Consul General	1913
	Hamilton, Ont	de Olivares, José	Consul	1915
	Hamilton, Ont	Brady, J. R	Vice-Consul	1916
	Kenora, Ont	Quann, W. P	Consular Agent	1916
	Kingston, Ont	Johnston, F. S. S	Consul	1910
	Kingston, Ont	Folger, H. S:	Vice-Consul	1908
	Lethbridge, Alta	Johnston, M..P	Consular Agent	1913
	Liverpool, N.S	Mack, J. M	Consular Agent	1896
	Louisburg, N.S	LeVatte, H. C. V	Consular Agent	1898
	Lunenburg, N.S	Rudolf, D. J	Consular Agent	1907
	Moncton, N.B	Richardson, E. V	Consul	1916
	Moncton,-N.B	Cummings, E. A	Vice Consul	1916
	Montreal, Que	Bradley, W. H	Consul General	1907
	Montreal, Que	Gorman, P	Vice-Consul	1886
	Montreal, Que	Isaacs, C	Vice-Consul	1916
	Nanaimo, B.C	Pashley, J. H	Consular Agent	1906
	Newcastle, N.B	Call, B. N	Consular Agent	1904
	Niagara Falls, Ont	Milner, J. B	Consul	1916
	Niagara Falls, Ont	Somerville, J. G	Vice-Consul	1914
	North Bay, Ont	Wakefield, E. C	Consular Agent	1906
	Ottawa, Ont	Foster, J. G	Consul General	1903
	Ottawa, Ont	Sanford, H. M	Vice-Consul	1898
	Ottawa, Ont	Marsh, O. G	Consul	1915
	Paspebiac, Que	Bisson, D	Consular Agent	1899
	Peterborough, Ont	Leonard, C. F	Consular Agent	1910
	Port Arthur, Ont	De Lamater, I	Vice-Consul	1916
	Port Arthur, Ont	Dow, E. A	Consul	1917
	Port Hawkesbury and Mulgrave, N.S	Philpot, J	Consular Agent	1916
	Prescott, Ont	Denison, F. C	Consul	1915
	Prescott, Ont	Murphy, John	Vice-Consul	1917
	Prince Rupert, B.C	Hanson, G. M	Consul	1916
	Quebec, Que	Dorsey, W. Roderick	Consul	1917
	Quebec, Que	Heard, W. W	Vice and Dep. Consul	1915
	Rivière du Loup	Rairden, B. S	Consul	1916

8 GEORGE V, A. 1918

ALPHABETICAL LIST of Foreign Countries represented by Consuls, Vice-Consuls, Consular Agents, and Commercial Agents, etc.—*Concluded.*

Country.	Place.	Name.	Designation.	When Appointed.
United States—*Con*	Regina, Sask	Johnston, Jesse H	Consul	1917
	Sarnia, Ont	Slater, F. C	Consul	1906
	Sarnia, Ont	Watson, F. C	Vice-Consul	1914
	Sault Ste. Marie, Ont	Shotts, G. W	Consul:	1906
	Sault Ste. Marie, Ont	Burlingham, W. B	Vice-Consul	1916
	Sherbrooke, Que	Borlase, G. E	Vice-Consul	1899
	Summerside, P.E.I	Sinclair, N	Consular Agent	1907
	Sydney, N. S	Freeman, C. M	Consul	1911
	Sydney, N. S	Boynton, D	Vice and Dep. Consul.	1916
	St. John, N.B	Culver, H. S	Consul	1910
	St. John, N.B	Bailey, A. D	Vice-Consul	1916
	St. Leonards, N.B	Labbie, A. P	Consular Agent	1916
	St. Stephen, N.B	Vroom, C. N	Vice and Dep. Consul.	1895
	St. Stephen, N.B	Garrett, Alonzo B	Consul	1917
	Toronto, Ont	Martin, C. W	Consul	1916
	Toronto, Ont	Tovell, D. S	Vice-Consul	1904
	Vancouver, B.C	West, G. N	Consul General	1916
	Vancouver, B.C	Woodward, C. G	Consul	1911
	Vancouver, B.C	Linnell, I. N	Vice-Consul	1916
	Vancouver, B.C	Johnson, E. G	Vice-Consul	1915
	Victoria, B.C	Mosher, R. B	Consul	1915
	Victoria, B.C	Newcomb, R. M	Vice-Consul	1914
	White Horse, Yukon	Rousseau, A. M	Consular Agent	1916
	Windsor, Ont	Conant, H. A	Consul	1905
	Windsor, Ont	Chater, D	Vice and Dep. Consul.	1904
	Winnipeg, Man	Ryder, F. M	Consul General	1915
	Winnipeg, Man	Sutliff, L. G	Vice-Consul	1915
	Yarmouth, N.S	Watson, J. C	Consul	1916
	Yarmouth, N.S	Brown, R. N	Vice-Consul	1915
Uruguay	Halifax, N.S	Neville, J	Vice-Consul	1913
	Montreal, Que	Ross, P. W. T	Consul	1915
	Toronto, Ont	Estrada, J. de	Vice-Consul	1914
Venezuela	Ottawa, Ont	Terrero, Don L	Consul General	1913

REPORT

OF THE

INSPECTOR OF PENITENTIARIES

FOR THE

FISCAL YEAR ENDED MARCH 31

1917

PRINTED BY ORDER OF PARLIAMENT

OTTAWA
J. DE LABROQUERIE TACHÉ
PRINTER TO THE KING'S MOST EXCELLENT MAJESTY
1918

[No. 34—1918.]

To His Excellency the Duke of Devonshire, K.G., P.C. G.C.M.G., G.C.V.O, &c,. &c., &c., Governor General and Commander in Chief of the Dominion of Canada.

MAY IT PLEASE YOUR EXCELLENCY:—

I have the honour to lay before Your Excellency the Annual Report of the Inspectors of Penitentiaries for the fiscal year ended March 31, 1917, made by them in pursuance of the provisions of section 19 of the Penitentiary Act.

I have the honour to be, Sir,

Your Excellency's most obedient servant,

CHAS. J. DOHERTY,
Minister of Justice.

CONTENTS.

REPORT

OF THE

INSPECTORS OF PENITENTIARIES

FOR THE FISCAL YEAR 1916-17.

To the Hon. C. J. DOHERTY, K.C.,
  Minister of Justice.

SIR,—I have the honour to submit herewith statistics and reports regarding the operation of the penitentiaries for the fiscal year ended March 31, 1917.

The number of convicts at the close of the fiscal year was 1,694, as compared with 2,118 at the close of the previous fiscal year. There were 35 female convicts, as compared with 37 at the close of the previous year. The average daily population was 1,938, as against 2,074 during the previous year.

The following table shows the movement of population at the several penitentiaries:—

—	Kingston.	St. Vincent de Paul.	Dorchester.	Manitoba.	British Columbia.	Alberta.	Saskatchewan.	Total.
In custody April 1, 1916	596	477	238	155	330	192	130	2,118
Received.								
From jails	148	202	98	32	51	56	39	626
By transfer...................	9	....	....	....	1	....	....	10
By forfeiture of parole..........	1	2	5	....	....	3	....	11
By revocation of license..........	10	10	5	2	2	2	....	31
From reformatories	....	....	1	....	....	....	....	1
From military courts	....	....	2	....	....	....	....	2
Recaptured	....	....	....	....	1	....	....	1
Returned by Order of Court......	....	....	....	....	1	....	....	1
Discharged.								
Expiry of sentence	134	76	44	27	68	31	28	408
Parole	127	138	66	53	56	53	33	526
Deportation..	21	9	3	8	27	3	5	76
Death	2	5	....	2	2	1	....	12
Pardon........................	4	29	25	3	1	2	1	65
Transfer	....	4	....	2	1	1	1	9
Order of Court	1	1	....	....	1	1	....	4
Returned to Provincial authorities.	....	1	....	....	....	1	2	4
Escapes	....	....	....	2	1	....	....	3
Remaining March 31, 1917. . .	475	428	211	92	229	160	99	1,694

8 GEORGE V, A. 1918

Health.—The surgeons report that the institutions have been free from any epidemic, and that sanitary conditions are good. The number of convicts in hospital at the close of the year is as follows:—

Kingston	9
St. Vincent de Paul	3
Dorchester	4
Manitoba	2
British Columbia	2
Alberta	1
Saskatchewan	0
Total	21

Female Convicts.—The small number of female delinquents—50 per cent of whom come from one province—would suggest the propriety of arranging for their custody and maintenance at the Mercer reformatory, or some other well-regulated female prison under provincial control. The ward at Kingston penitentiary, where female delinquents from all Canada are now centralized, is admirably managed by intelligent and faithful matrons, but it is obvious that reformatory influences could be exercised more efficiently in an institution specially designed for that class of offenders.

Farm Operations.—About fifteen hundred acres were under cultivation during the year, with varying results according to climatic conditions in the different parts of the country in which the institutions are situated. The following table shows the value of the products and the net profit at each prison during the fiscal year:—

Penitentiary.	Value of Products.	Net Profit.
	$	$
Kingston	10,246	1,222
St. Vincent de Paul	9,315	970
Dorchester	6,742	2,570
Manitoba	11,185	2,544
British Columbia	7,014	753
Alberta	4,464	2,028
Saskatchewan	10,733	2,046
Total	59,699	12,133

The value of the farm productions and the net profits that are increasing gradually year by year will no doubt expand rapidly, since the wardens have been reminded of the necessity of making the industry the paramount one during existing world conditions. Except at Kingston and British Columbia penitentiaries, the reserves are excellent land for agricultural purposes.

NATIONALITY (Place of birth).

British—

Canada	936
England	126
Ireland	41
Scotland	24
India	7
Newfoundland	6
Other British countries	9
	1,149

NATIONALITY (Place of birth).—*Continued.*

Foreign—
United States..	182
Austria-Hungary..	104
Russia..	74
Italy..	61
China..	32
Germany..	17
Sweden..	12
France..	8
Roumania..	8
Turkey..	7
Japan..	6
Greece..	6
Norway..	6
Other foreign countries..	22
	545

1,694

CREEDS.

Christian—
Roman Catholic..	841
Anglican..	266
Methodist..	169
Presbyterian..	155
Baptist..	78
Lutheran..	51
Greek Catholic..	42
Other Christian creeds..	18
	1,620

Non-Christian—
Buddhist..	33
Hebrew..	23
Other non-Christian creeds..	10
No creed..	8
	74

1,694

AGE.

Under 20 years..	141
20-30 years..	714
30-40 "	473
40-50 "	241
50-60 "	99
Over 60 years..	26
Total	1,694

SOCIAL HABITS.

Abstainers..	299
Temperate..	837
Intemperate..	558
Total..	1,694

CIVIL CONDITION.

Single..	1,028
Married..	589
Widowed..	77
Total	1,694

RACIAL.

White..	1,553
Coloured..	56
Indian..	20
" halfbreed..	21
Mongolian..	38
East Indian..	6
Total	1,694

8 GEORGE V, A. 1918

EXPENDITURE — 1916-17,

—	Gross Expenditure.	Revenue.	Net Expenditure.
	$ cts.	$ cts.	$ cts.
Kingston	214,815 22	17,995 94	196,819 28
St. Vincent de Paul	192,032 47	8,704 37	183,328 10
Dorchester	109,451 84	10,059 89	99,391 95
Manitoba	74,284 12	7,576 21	66,707 91
British Columbia	116,225 55	5,075 86	111,149 69
Alberta	96,412 64	5,972 02	90,440 62
Saskatchewan	105,262 11	8,078 38	97,183 73
Totals	908,483 95	63,462 67	845,021 28

COMPARATIVE STATEMENT OF NET OUTLAY.

—	1914–15.	1915–16.	1916–17.
	$ cts.	$ cts.	$ cts.
Kingston	176,478 38	190,269 17	196,819 28
St. Vincent de Paul	159,475 56	161,867 83	183,328 10
Dorchester	89,126 59	91,003 84	99,391 95
Manitoba	72,385 56	77,058 09	66,707 91
British Columbia	127,661 16	124,042 94	111,149 69
Alberta	95,815 07	94,056 28	90,440 62
Saskatchewan	88,228 09	115,830 33	97,183 73
Totals	809,170 41	854,128 48	845,021 28
Average daily population	1,989	2,074	1,938

COMPARATIVE COST PER CAPITA.

—	Kingston.	St. Vincent de Paul.	Dorchester.	Manitoba.	British Columbia.	Alberta.	Saskatchewan.
	$ cts.	$ cts.	$ cts.	$ cts.	$ cts.	$ cts.	$ cts.
Staff	188 55	179 20	228 99	401 60	219 93	303 66	363 47
Maintenance of convicts	95 85	81 36	81 70	76 99	76 59	81 14	76 17
Discharge expenses	9 15	7 78	7 29	17 24	12 90	11 66	10 45
Working expenses	51 10	67 68	47 37	92 96	31 74	29 17	87 86
Industries	19 71	18 69	32 03	16 12	16 45	24 00	34 95
Lands, buildings and equipment	17 59	40 97	50 04	23 54	47 08	78 23	308 42
Miscellaneous	4 33	1 39	1 15	9 51	41	4 25	1 10
Deduct revenue per capita	33 33	18 60	43 36	65 31	17 68	32 63	72 13
Net cost per capita	352 95	378 47	405 21	572 67	387 42	499 48	810 29

SESSIONAL PAPER No. 34

ACTUAL COST.

Supplies on hand April 1, 1916.. .. ..$	166,497 00	
Gross expenditure 1916-17..	908,484 00	
		1,074,981 00
Deduct—		
Supplies on hand March 31, 1917..	205,485 00	
Estimated value of labour on production of		
capital and revenue..	75,000 00	
		280,485 00
Net cost..		794,496 00
Cost per caput..		409 96
Cost per caput per diem..		1 12

COMPARATIVE SUMMARY.

	1915.	1916.	1917.
	$ cts.	$ cts.	$ cts.
Gross expenditure ....:	856,208 00	898,900 00	908,484 00
Net expenditure..	809,170 00	854,128 00	845,021 00
Actual cost...	776,554 00	808,707 00	794,496 00
Cost per caput	390 42	389 93	409 96
Cost per caput per diem........	1 07	1 07	1 12
Average daily population..............................	1,989	2,074	1,938

1867---1917.

As the fiscal year under review is the semi-centennial of the Dominion of Canada, it may not be inappropriate to review the history and progress of our penal institutions during that perior. It is gratifying to note that Canada is a pioneer in penological reform, being the first country to incorporate a provision in its constitution that penal-class convicts be segregated and placed under distinctly separate authority. The provision that penal-class prisoners (those serving two years or more) should be placed in institutions under federal control, while all others, including misdemeanants, prisoners awaiting trial, and parties held as witnesses should be under provincial control, shows the wisdom and foresight of the statesmen who drafted the British North America Act. It is only of recent years that other states and countries have awakened to the necessity for like provision, and in some states and countries you will still find penal-class convicts herded with delinquents that are held for minor offences.

The number of penal-class prisoners in custody on December 31, 1867, was 972, of whom 64 were females. These were located as follows:—

Kingston, Ont..	907
St. John, N.B...	27
Halifax, N.S..	38

On March 31, 1917, the convict population of the four original provinces was 1,096, an increase of less than 13 per cent in fifty years.

The population of the penitentiaries of Canada on March 31, 1917, was 1,694, of whom 35 were females. In 1867 there was one convict to each 3,586 inhabitants. In 1917 there was one convict to each 4,254 inhabitants. When one realizes the

8 GEORGE V, A. 1918

extension of the country—the increased population—the influx of immigrants, many of whom were unaccustomed to rigid penal laws—the relative increase of population in cities and towns where crime is more easily accomplished, and the fact of the extension of our penal code to hundreds of acts that were formerly not illegal or punishable, the results are eminently satisfactory and are a tribute to the manner in which our penal institutions have been administered.

Actual results speak more effectively than either the hysterical shrieks of theoretical critics or the plaintive wail of super-humanitarians, who are suffering from abnormal development of the bowels of compassion.

It was apparently the policy of the Fathers of Confederation to establish interprovincial penitentiaries, whereby several provinces would be served by one institution. At the union, the Kingston penitentiary served for the purposes of Ontario and Quebec, and steps were taken for the centralization of penal class convicts in the Maritime Provinces at Dorchester, N.B., to replace the institutions at Halifax and St. John. The first departure from this policy was in 1873, when a property was acquired (which had formerly been used as a provincial reformatory) from the provincial government of Quebec, and the penitentiary of St. Vincent de Paul was proclaimed a penitentiary for the province of Quebec. The language question was no doubt urged as a reason for the severance, but it has not removed the diversity of tongues at either institution. It is to be feared that the recently deceased patronage evil was the potent factor in determining the departure from the original policy. If, as a substitute solution, a central penitentiary had been established in the Coteau-Cornwall district, where there is abundance of arable land, it would have saved the country millions of dollars, and would have been convenient equally to both provinces concerned. It would also have removed the institutions to a point far from the local urban interference and intermeddling that have crippled the efficiency and economic management of both of the existing penitentiaries.

In the western provinces the departure from the original policy is more marked and even less justifiable. A separate institution for British Columbia is warranted for physical reasons, but the smaller penitentiaries at Edmonton, Prince Albert, and Stony Mountain could be amalgamated in one central institution, with every possible advantage. The overhead charges in the maintenance of a penal institution, and especially the staff charges, which constitute about 50 per cent of the whole expenditure, would be reduced materially by the suggested change. It is safe to estimate that the annual expenditure would be reduced at least 30 per cent. The valuable reserves attached to the existing prisons would, if disposed of, more than meet the expenditure involved, the annual expenditure would be materially reduced and efficiency promoted by the centralization suggested.

Administrative system.—The system adopted in 1867 was a board of commissioners, but it was soon found that there was no concerted action or interest taken, and that the whole work devolved on the secretary, who, by frequently visiting the prisons, conferring with the wardens and other officers and generally studying conditions, obtained a practical knowledge of prison matters that served as a substitute for similar action by the commissioners. On the occasion of their periodical meetings the commissioners did the only sensible thing they could do by "rubber-stamping" the suggestions of their secretary.

In 1875 this unsatisfactory condition resulted in the abolition of the Board of Commissioners and the vesting of practically all their powers and duties in the secretary under the title of inspector of penitentiaries. In 1901 a second inspector was appointed. The system adopted in 1875 is still continued. It is amusing to note that expert advisers within the past few years have recommended the adoption of the system of control by a board of commissioners as a "modern prison reform," in evident ignorance of the fact that the suggested system was tried and found wanting years ago, and that for forty years it has been obsolete.

Structural improvements.—The structural conditions in 1867 were open to severe criticism. The cells were extremely small, ill-ventilated and difficult of supervision. Important improvements have been made, especially since the structural work of the institutions has been carried on through this department by convict labour, under the direction of our own officers. The cell dormitories constructed during the past twenty-five years are not really cells, but alcoves facing well-lighted and thoroughly ventilated corridors, and protected by a barrier of polished steel across the entire front of the alcove that impedes neither light nor ventilation. In the rear wall of the alcoves are upper and lower ventilators connecting with a central ventilating chamber that extends to the roof of the building. The cells or alcoves are fitted with folding bed and table, running water and sanitary closets and wash basins. On each range or row extending the entire length of the block there is a Marechal locking bar that enables an officer by a simple turn of the wrist to lock or unlock any or all of the prisoners on the range in a few seconds. I know of no prisons in any country that combine convenience, security, and comfort in like degree. The ill-ventilated and ill-lighted cells that characterized the prisons of 1867 have all been replaced, and the general introduction of electric lighting since that date, replacing gas or oil lamps, has added materially to the proper ventilation and sanitary condition of the dormitories.

Separate cells.—In this connection it may be noted that the policy of single or separate cell accommodation—that is, a separate cell for each convict—has been in operation in our penitentiaries since 1867, and has been strictly adhered to. The necessity for this is too obvious to require explanation. It is sufficient to state that men who come to us after having been "reformed" in institutions where the dual cell or the open dormitory system is in use, very frankly admit their having seen and participated in practices at those institutions that are not conducive to morality. Not infrequently these men show their appreciation of the safety and decency that the penitentiary cells afford.

Prison farms.—During the past few years a great deal has been said and written regarding the introduction of prison farms as a modern prison reform. This reform has been in operation at the Canadian penitentiaries for fifty years, and has afforded remunerative and healthful employment to such of the penal class criminals as can with reasonable safety be employed outside the walls. The restriction imposed by climatic conditions in this country necessitates the provision of other suitable employment during more than half the year, but the farming operations, as an auxiliary industry, have been a boon to prison management.

There are four principles that are discussed by penologists as modern reforms, which have been in practice in Canada for the past fifty years. These are:—

(1) Segregation of the penal class in separate institutions and under separate management.

(2) A separate cell for each convict.

(3) Prison farms operated by convict labour.

(4) Remission of sentence for good conduct and industry. The provision for remission of sentence was enlarged in 1886. Formerly five days per month was the limit allowed, but, in 1886 the allowance was increased so that long term convicts can shorten the penalty by approximately one third of the entire original sentence. It is applicable to all classes of convicts, irrespective of the length of the sentence.

The consideration of systems and practices that have been tried and abandoned for cause may be of some interest:—

(1) The reason for the abolition of the system of control by a Board of Commissioners has already been referred to.

8 GEORGE V, A. 1918

(2) The sub-classification of penal class convicts. This was tried and was in operation from 1886 until 1896. The classification was necessarily arbitrary and divided the convicts into three grades. The higher grade or prison aristocracy were designated by a star and clothed in plain civilian grey; the second grade or bourgoise represented the middle class and floated between the two extremes. Their clothing was an indistinct checked cloth; the third grade or common herd were clothed in a distinct checked suit, similar to that now in use for all convicts.

As the classification was based on prison conduct, it followed that the first grade included nearly all life prisoners, recidivists and many who were under sentence for brutal and unnatural crimes, while the lower grades had many young convicts convicted of comparatively minor crimes, whose reckless disregard of prison rules deprived them of the privileges of a higher grade. These men attributed their degraded position to discrimination and personal antipathy on the part of the warden, and were generally sincere in the belief, although it had no foundation in fact to justify it. The first class assumed their grade as a right, and showed no appreciation of it as a privilege. Aside from the bitterness and envy that the classification produced, the only appreciable effect on the institution was the abnormal number of escapes and attempts at escape that characterized the period in which the practice continued. The convicts concerned were, with few exceptions, of the prison aristocracy or first grade, and it is obvious that the prospect of success suggested by their civilian dress was to a great extent responsible for the evasions. The number of escapes and attempts during the few years the practice continued are, in the aggregate, greater than those that have occurred in the succeeding two decades. The successful classification of criminals involves their incarceration in separate institutions—the classification to be made by the court by which they are sentenced rather than by prison officials.

(3) *The elimination of tobacco.*—The practice of furnishing this luxury to convicts at public expense was one of the abuses that ante-dated Confederation, and was not abolished until 1897. Not more than 20 per cent of the men were habitual chewers when admitted, but all claimed to be such in order that they might have an article of commercial value with which to traffic within the prison. Weak officers were supplied by convicts, who were thus immune from report whatever prison offence they committed. The tobacco ration was stored and sold through dishonest officers in exchange for liquor, drugs, etc. It was also used between convicts as payment for unnatural and immoral practices. The dormitory cells and workshops were rendered unclean and unsanitary by the tobacco-chewing industry and, daily, complaints were made as to the quality and quantity supplied. It has been suggested by ill-informed persons that its re-introduction would be an incentive to good conduct and industry—in other words, that the convicts should be bribed to behave—but those who have had experience in prison management, when it was permitted, know that in such cases the convict regards the privilege as a right, and if for cause it is attempted to deprive him of it, he would make it a serious grievance, and, as a matter of fact, his fellow convicts would supply him with larger quantities than he was deprived of. The elimination of the practice has greatly improved the sanitary condition of the prisons, and has in many cases enabled the men to break a useless and filthy habit.

The parole system.—Of all the various improvements that have been effected, the license or parole system has been the most important, and its successful operation is a just cause of satisfaction to those who have been responsible for its administration. In conjunction with the remission system, it is the greatest and all-sufficient incentive to good conduct and industry. It has been in operation since 1899, and of the thousands who have been released on license, 94 per cent have completed their sen-

SESSIONAL PAPER No. 34

tences under the rigid conditions of life that the terms of the license impose. This success has been due largely to the intelligent and sympathetic supervision of the officer in charge.

The granting of petty privileges and perquisites to convicts as a bribe to induce good behaviour is inconsistent with the object for which prisons are established, and is puerile and ineffective as an inducement to permanent reformation. When a man is given the implement of remission by which he can curtail his sentence, and the key to liberty provided by the prospect of parole, he has every inducement to reform that he requires or expects.

The policy followed by those who have been charged with the administration of Canadian penitentiaries has been to avoid theoretical and impractical experiments, and to carry out such improvements as experience and common sense have dictated, and the result as shown by actual facts invites comparison with the results effected by other systems and policies in any other country. Much of this success is due to the loyalty and intelligence of the successive wardens, whose general devotion to duty is worthy of the highest praise.

Respectfully submitted,

DOUGLAS STEWART,
Inspector.

APPENDIX A.—REPORT OF THE DOMINION PAROLE OFFICER.

Mr. W. P. Archibald, parole officer, reports as follows:—

During the past year 838 cases have been received and reported on by the parole office, entailing a thorough investigation, embracing the antecedents and the general character of the prisoner applying for the clemency of a parole; employment and environment is also considered in event of their release. Communication is kept up with prisoners on parole, and when a man is out of employment or applies for a change of occupation the matter is adjusted to suit the prisoner when considered advisable. I am pleased to report that those who have been released on parole during the year are industriously inclined, and have been doing their very best to earn an honest living. From the statistical report I find that a little over 2 per cent of the entire number reporting have lapsed into crime. This is, I think, an excellent showing, demonstrating beyond doubt the possibility of the men and women released conditionally to reinstate themselves in the community in which they have offended, and becoming respected and self-respecting citizens.

From police reports, I am informed that those released on parole during the year have been reporting well. I also beg to state that during my visits to the various centres of the Dominion I found them suitably employed and living within their license. In exceptional cases only have complaints been made about their general conduct.

Since the outbreak of the war, 422 men who had been released on parole volunteered for overseas service and were accepted by the military authorities. Considering the 400,000 men (approximate figures) who have responded to the call of the nation, this is, of course, not a very large percentage, but I am pleased to report that the men who have gone to the front have done exceptionally well. Some have risen from the ranks to commissioned officership; others have been mentioned in despatches for bravery and distinguished conduct, subsequently receiving the Distinguished Service Medal.

It has never been considered judicious by those in authority to release men in a wholesale manner for the purpose of enlistment; only in cases of desertion or minor offences have men been released to rejoin their regiments. While some enthusiasts have advocated the emptying of penal institutions in Canada in order to fill up the ranks at the front, it is a source of gratification that these suggestions have not been considered seriously.

No just cause has been given for the argument of slackers or the disloyal elements in our country that criminals have been released indiscriminately for the purpose of enlistment. The great majority of those released during the year had served a substantial portion of their sentences in custody. No doubt the excellent showing in the percentage of men doing well has much to do with the aforementioned fact.

I would again mention and pay tribute to the men who have gone to the front and have given their service freely. In some cases they have made the supreme sacrifice for their country. Notwithstanding the fact that these men have had a fault and were punished, who, with a human heart, would even mention the past under these circumstances. Their blood mingles with other heroes of our nation who have fallen with their faces to the foe, and they now lie buried in the mother earth of France. What more could mortals do to win back their honour and the esteem of their fellow men?

The tabulated statements reveal a little over 5 per cent have not complied with the conditions of their license, principally by failure to report, and have had their licenses revoked in consequence.

TABULATED STATEMENT FOR YEAR ENDING MARCH 31, 1917.

Prisoners Released on Parole—		Revocations. Per cent.	Forfeitures. Per cent.	Total Loss. Per cent.
Kingston..	126	10 or 7.93	1 or .79	11 or 8.7
St. Vincent de Paul..	138	10 or 7.24	2 or 2.17	13 or 9.4
Dorchester.. .. .. ♠	66	5 or 7.57 -	5 or 7.57	10 or 15.15
Manitoba..	55	2 or 3.6	....	2 or 3.6
British Columbia..	56	2 or 3.5	....	2 or 3.5
Alberta..	55	2 or 3.7	3 or 5.5	5 or 9.2
Saskatchewan..	33	....	....	....
Total, penitentiaries..	529	31 or 5.86	12 or 2.27	43 or 8.1
Jails, etc..	528	18 or 3.4	....	18 or 3.4
Ontario reformatory.. ..	102	7 or 6.86	1 or .98	8 or 7.8
Total, jails and reformatories.. ..	630	25 or 3.96	1 or .15	26 or 4.1
Grand total..	1,159	56 or 4.8	13 or 1.1	69 or 5.9

Since the inception of the Parole Act in the year of 1899, I have published the total figures furnished by the Dominion police office, and the following statement is rendered up to the year ending March 31, 1917, by their office. The figures demonstrate the fact that 4,931 persons were released on parole from the peitentiaries during the eighteen years' operation. From reformatories and other prisons of the Dominion 5,283 persons have been released on parole, making a total of 10,214 paroles granted. From this number, 374 licenses have been revoked for non-compliance with condition of license, or 3·66 per cent. The number of licenses forfeited for subsequent convictions is 260, or 2·53 per cent, making the sum total of losses to the system 634, or 6·19 per cent. A slight decrease is perceptible from this year's figures in comparison with those of preceding years. Eight thousand seven hundred and eleven persons have conmpleted their sentences on probation, while those who have not yet completed their probation is 869. The above figures furnish the best criterion in judging or summing up the effective work of the parole system, as the revocations and forfeiture figures must naturally merge into the preceding year's statistics.

That 8,711 persons have completed their probation on parole and are now enjoying full citizenship is a very gratifying fact indeed, and of vital interest to those who are interested in redemptive work of any character. The figures as a whole are very satisfactory.

APPENDIX B.—WARDEN'S REPORTS.

KINGSTON.

Robert R. Creighton, warden, reports as follows:—

At the beginning of the year the population was 596; there were received 168 and discharged 289 during the year, leaving a population of 475 at its close; the average being 540.

The marked decrease is, in my opinion, due to two causes—the war and prohibition.

The opportunity offered by the war to exercise the love for excitement and adventure has no doubt appealed to a certain class of restless spirits that under normal

8 GEORGE V, A. 1918

conditions help to swell the population of this and similar institutions, and has induced them to join the colours.

That the extensive use of intoxicants is the cause, either directly or indirectly, of a certain amount of crime must, I think, be generally admitted, and so far as its use is properly controlled so far will it help to keep many a poor unfortunate out of places of this kind.

During the summer months much-needed repairing and pointing was done to the farm buildings and walls; the condition of one of the stone barns was such that a new end had to be built on.

The extension to the boundary wall was plastered on the inside with cement, thus completing that work.

The old and unsightly picket fence on Palace street, extending from King to Union streets and along the latter to the eastern boundary of the reserve, was removed and replaced with a woven wire one, having cement posts and cut-stone gate posts. It has added wonderfully to the appearance of the property, and I would strongly recommend that as it becomes necessary to replace other portions of the fencing the same material be used.

A properly constructed tile drain has been made on King street, extending along the prison enclosure, and the cinder path which has done duty for so many years has been replaced by a well-constructed cement walk. As soon as the season permits, it is the intention to regrade the hill; when this is completed, and with some other minor improvements made, it will impart to the front of the institution a well-kept look that was lacking before.

The interior of the north wing has been removed down to the ground floor, and the building is almost ready for reconstruction as a cell block. Unless conditions demand that the work be proceded with more rapidly, it is the intention to reserve work on this building for the season of the year when work out of doors cannot be carried on.

The building operations planned for the summer include a new smokestack for the boiler-house, the present one being too small to furnish the necessary draft for the proper running of the boilers, and a reconstruction of a portion of the wharf, which is to have a cut-stone face, backed with cement.

The installation of electric light in the hospital, in progress at the time of my last report, has been completed. It adds much to the comfort of the patients, who before were without light in their cells, and better conditions generally for the officers in the performance of their duties.

A well-lighted operating room, properly equipped for performing operations, has been provided, the building painted throughout and renovated where necessary.

During the year a new electric pump was installed at the water's edge, which, during the season when the water is high, gives entire satisfaction and keeps the place well supplied; when the water is low, however, it does not work so satisfactorily owing to the fact that it does not receive an adequate supply of water; this we hope to remedy during the summer by a readjustment of the intake pipe.

The Smith-Vale steam pump has been overhauled and put in good working order. It is now attached to another intake pipe, and gives much better satisfaction than it did before the change was made; so that, under ordinary conditions, we are now in a much better position as regards the water supply than we were a year ago, when it was the cause of much anxiety.

Thanks to the continued interest in our tailor and shoe shops by Major Dillon, Supply Officer for Internment Operations, and to an unusually large order for clothing from the Department of Indian Affairs, these departments of the institution have been working to their full capacity during the year. I trust these may be but the forerunner of still larger orders.

Owing to a most unfavourable season, in common with the rest of the farming community, our crops were far below the average, and consequently the farm does not make as good a showing as usual. We harvested, however, with the exception of potatoes, enough vegetables to meet our own requirements up to the present.

The piggery continues to show good returns. After supplying the steward with all the pork required for the institution, we had a considerable quantity for sale, which was disposed of at an unusually high price.

The general health of the inmates has been good; we have been free from epidemics, and there has been comparatively little illness of any kind.

There were two deaths, one from paraplegia and the other from uremic coma; both these cases would have resulted fatally under any conditions.

I regret to say there were two serious accidents during the year; as the result of one, the arm of the man who was injured had to be amputated at the shoulder joint. The other, a broken ankle, is, I am glad to report, nearly well again.

Detailed reports of the unfortunate occurrences were sent you at the time they occurred.

The conduct of the prisoners has, on the whole, been good, and the discipline up to the average.

ST. VINCENT DE PAUL.

G. S. Malepart, warden, reports as follows:—

At the beginning of the year the population was 477; there were received 204 and discharged 258, leaving a population of 423 at the close of the year.

During the year 80 feet of the boundary was completed, and the coping on the whole front wall, about 900 feet, has been put in place. Owing to a very dangerous bulge in the wall on the east side, I found it necessary to take down nearly 200 feet within 5 feet of the grade, and rebuild the same. The old wall has also been pointed with good strong cement mortar.

A division fence between the adjoining property and the warden grounds was removed and a cement fence was erected in place of same, with a fine cresting, which adds greatly to the appearance of both properties.

A small stone building was erected in rear of the boiler-room for the housing of the hose trucks, and a tower provided for the drying of the hose after use.

The government block tenements were all put in a good shape, and it should cease to cause trouble for some time, beyond the minor repairs caused by the ordinary wear and tear.

The glasses in the top of the dome's roof were renewed, and that portion of the structure made water-tight.

The erection and completion of a water tower has been in operation for the past three months, and is giving a good and efficient service.

The installation of new closets in the hospital has been done.

New lead cable for the electrical plant from power-house to the pump and village has been erected.

The removal of the old tanks from the attic of the administration building and the installation of a new force pump in boiler-house has been done.

The installation of a new locking apparatus for the north wing, replacing the one previously in position, has been performed.

The completion of the plumbing in the new kitchen, and extension for heating the gate, the store, and the piggery has also been done.

The discipline of the prison has been good.

34—2

DORCHESTER.

A. B. Pipes, warden, reports as follows:—

During the year the building operations were: the extension of the boundary wall, which was completed in the early autumn, and the starting of work on the new reservoir, which we expect to see finished this season.

We had one escape and recapture, a full account of which was forwarded you at the time. I am pleased to report that on the whole the conduct of the prisoners has been good, and the discipline maintained.

MANITOBA.

W. R. Grahame, warden, reports as follows:—

The movement of convicts for the year has been as follows: Remaining at midnight, March 31, 1916, 155; received during the year, 189; discharged, 97; remaining at close of year, 92. The daily average during the year was 116.

From the foregoing statement it will be seen that there has been a decrease in population as compared with the former year, owing chiefly, no doubt, to the gigantic struggle in which the Empire is engaged at the present time in Europe.

Two convicts escaped on July 21, 1916, from the farm yard. One had served a previous sentence of two years, and had only three months to serve to complete his second term; the other had completed one year of a two-years' sentence.

Farming operations were carried on successfully during the year; a considerable quantity of potatoes, oats, and pork was sold, and everything put in readiness for a vigorous effort during the coming season.

The reinforced cement floor in the storeroom adjoining the shops has been completed; the new heating arrangements which were installed in the new shops have proved satisfactory.

During the coming summer we shall be able to furnish employment for the whole of our population on work that is urgently required to be done.

I am pleased to say that the discipline of the institution has been good.

I cannot close without mentioning the untiring efforts of Major Sims, of the Salvation Army, in looking after the welfare of men discharged or paroled from here; also the Territorial singers of the Army, who, by their singing at our Divine services on several occasions, have justly merited the hearty appreciation extended to them by all who heard them.

BRITISH COLUMBIA.

John C. Brown, warden, reports as follows:—

Notwithstanding the comparative failure of the oat crop, common all over the district, the farm has had a successful year. Roots and garden vegetables were very good—the potato crop being the heaviest in the history of the penitentiary—and the piggery also had a successful year. Partly because of large crops, and partly because of the decrease in prison population, we had a considerable surplus of potatoes and pork for sale, and also a fair quantity of garden vegetables.

The work of bringing the prison "up to date" has gone on steadily during the year. The new cell wing has been completed, and now holds all the prisoners in custody, except a few in the hospital. The modern cell accommodation here is now almost equal to the largest number of prisoners ever in confinement in this penitentiary at any time, and therefore considerably in excess of present requirements. This fact enables us to give exclusive attention to other improvements, and we have begun the construction of a building which will have a modern kitchen on the ground floor and a fine hospital in the second and third stories. We hope to make rapid progress with this during the summer.

The outstanding feature in the history of the year is the great decrease in prison population. This is the third time I have been able to report a decrease. The figures are: Prisoners in penitentiary: March 31, 1915, 349; March 31, 1916, 328; March 31, 1917, 227. This does not include two men on our books who are confined in the provincial hospital for the insane. March 31, 1914, saw 376 prisoners within the penitentiary walls, so that the war years have brought a most notable decrease, and to a considerable extent that decrease is the direct result of the war. The "boom times" of 1912 and 1913 largely increased the population of the province, and the depression which followed left it with a stranded surplus unable to find employment and equally unable to return to distant homes. Of these, when the war came, thousands enlisted, as well as thousands of others who were comfortably settled in various employments, so that it speedily became true that the employer was looking for labour rather than labour looking for an employer, thus curing that condition of " no work and no money " which leads so many into petty crime.

Only one officer of the penitentiary enlisted during the year; but the staff generally has kept up contributions to the patriotic and other war funds with commendable regularity and liberality.

There were two deaths during the year, both from tuberculosis. One, a Chinaman, was sent to the hospital almost immediately after he was received; the other, an Indian, contracted the disease while in prison.

There was one (temporary) escape. A prisoner working at the outskirts of the reserve ran away and was not recaptured for several hours.

The new heating system was in use during a considerable part of the winter. It appears to be entirely satisfactory.

The Salvation Army officer in charge of that branch of the Army's work continues faithfully and successfully to look after the interests of discharged prisoners.

ALBERTA.

J. C. Ponsford, warden, reports as follows:—

From the report of the movement of convicts it will be seen that the population of this penitentiary decreased 32 during the year. The reduction in the population I attribute almost wholly to the European war, as many men who formerly followed an indolent and criminal career were induced to enlist in the various expeditionary forces which were recruited from the province of Alberta. From various sources I have received information where quite a number of ex-convicts from this institution have been killed or wounded, and of many others who are serving with the colours and are doing their bit on the battlefields of France.

Two of the permanent officers of this penitentiary were granted extended leave of absence, and enlisted in the 78th Artillery for overseas service.

The operations of the farm during the year were very successful, showing a profit of $2,028.54 on the small amount of land under cultivation, being a little less than 45 acres.

We built, during the year, a new brick stable and machinery building. The stable will accommodate ten horses, and is modern in all respects. This was a much-needed improvement, and adds materially to the appearance of the surroundings.

I very much regret having to mention in this report the death of Convict Cohen. The cause of death was toxæmia, caused by an ambolism occluding the abdominal artery, causing gangrene. Otherwise the health of the convicts was above the average. The only accident of the year was a broken wrist bone to Convict Zehentmeier.

We had two escapes during the year, both of which were recaptured within a very short time of their escaping.

SASKATCHEWAN.

W. J. Macleod, warden, reports as follows:—

There were 130 prisoners in custody at the beginning of the year; received, 39; discharged, 70; remaining in custody at close of year, 99, including three convicts in the provincial hospital for the insane. The daily average for the year was 112.

I am pleased to report that we have completed the cells on the east side of our new cell block, which gives us accommodation for 104 prisoners. We moved the prisoners over there this month, and they were very glad to be removed from the temporary cells in which they have been since this institution opened. Our new cell block is, indeed, a great improvement, being bright, well lighted, well heated, and with first-class ventilation. We are now working on the cells on the west side in our new block, squaring up the piers and walls, and plastering. We have torn down the wooden cells in the old portion of the old cell wing, but have left the cells in the new extension so that if our population increases before the west side of the new cell block is finished we will have plenty of accommodation.

During the past summer we drove piles for the foundation and built a new boiler house, 40 feet by 40 feet with a 75-foot brick chimney, and installed two high-pressure boilers, 66 inches by 14 feet, with which we heated our new cell block. We also installed the heating system in new cell block, and am pleased to state that when steam was turned on there was not a leak, and all traps, etc., were in first-class working order. We also wired all cells and the corridor in new cell block, putting all wires in conduits, and when the electricity was turned on everything was most satisfactory. We also put down the floor and foundation walls for a coal storage, 40 feet by 30 feet, built onto the east side of boiler-house, and put up temporary wooden walls and a roof over it, in which we stored our winter's supply of coal. We also built a concrete duct from boiler-house to new cell block and shops' building for steam and water pipes. We were only able to get the floor and walls poured before cold weather set in, and had to put a temporary top over it for the winter months. We installed a watchman's electric clock, with stations in shops building, hospital, new cell block, and boiler-house. We will put stations in yard during the coming summer. Our plumbers are now busy connecting up closets and wash bowls in cells to sewage system in duct, and we expect to have them in working order in a few weeks.

We took up 250 feet of 6-inch sewer pipe from in front of shops' building to fence, and laid a 9-inch pipe in its place. This 6-inch pipe carried sewage from shops' building, hospital, and stable, and was continually giving us trouble, as it was altogether too small for the amount of sewage going through it. It connected with a 9-inch pipe near the fence, which runs down to sewage beds.

Last fall we drove down steel sheet piling for a new well, 30 feet by 10 feet, outside of south fence, and dug well down some 19 feet, and when we finished we had 11 feet of water. This piling has still some three or four feet to go yet, and has to be cut for suction pipe and bored for sand points. The water which we got is nice and clear, and should be first class for drinking and cooking purposes.

We also drove piles and poured cement for four foundation piers for our new 80,000-gallon water tower. We put these piers down 8 feet and they are 10 feet 6 inches by 8 feet 6 inches at base, and 2 feet by 2 feet at top, and also put in one pier at centre for water pipe to rest on. The water-tank contractor's crew worked some ten or twelve days in December on tank and put up three of the legs which holds tank, and then had to stop work owing to cold weather. They are to start work again in April.

A year ago last winter our stable walls were covered some inches thick with frost, and made our stable very damp; so during last summer we plastered the stable so as to get an air space and thus avoid this dampness. I think we will have to put in steam heat at each end of stable, as during the very severe weather it is very cold.

. We installed a new steam hot-water heater, which furnishes hot water for laundry and kitchen. This is a great improvement, as before we had to heat our water for laundry, bathing, and kitchen with hot-water fronts in ranges, and at times laundry work and bathing of convicts would have to stop, waiting for hot water.

Considering the season, we had very good results from our farm. We had 301 acres under crop and about 75 acres which we summer-fallowed. Out of our crop we shipped two carloads of potatoes and one carload of oats to the penitentiary at Kingston last fall, and this spring we sold 4,320 bushels of oats to farmers in this district. We have plenty of oats left for seed and feed. We have 79 hogs all in fairly good condition after the very severe winter. In this connection I beg to draw your attention to the fact that we are badly in want of a proper building in which to keep our pigs. At present they are kept in pens built of poles and covered with straw, and, as you can imagine, it is some trouble to give them water and soft feed with the thermometer hanging around from 30 to 60 below zero for days at a time. The feed and water simply freezes solid in their troughs before it can be eaten.

We have cut and hauled some 85 cords of wood off our farm for use in burning bricks next fall. This about cleans up all the wood worth cutting on the farm.

We hauled enough gravel and sand during the winter from our reserve across the river for all building purposes for the coming summer.

We made about 131,000 bricks during the past summer, which, with what we have on hand, will be enough for all buildings which we intend to put up this coming summer.

The health and conduct of all convicts has been very good during the past year.

We have eight officers on active service, whose positions are being held for them, and a number of other officers have resigned from the staff and enlisted.

APPENDIX C.—CRIME STATISTICS.

MOVEMENT OF CONVICTS FOR THE PAST TEN YEARS.

KINGSTON.

Years.	Remaining at beginning of year.	Admitted.	Discharged.	Remaining at end of year.	Daily average.
1907-08	458	181	151	488	463
1908-09	488	245	163	570	535
1909-10	570	203	215	558	571
1910-11	558	176	232	502	520
1911-12	502	182	190	494	487
1912-13	494	208	186	516	498
1913-14	516	199	204	511	499
1914-15	511	277	229	559	530
1915-16	559	245	208	596	570
1916-17	596	168	289	475	540

ST. VINCENT DE PAUL.

Years.	In custody at beginning of the Year.	Admitted during the Year.	Total.	Discharged during the Year.	Remaining at end of Year.	Daily Average.
1907-08	402	174	576	175	401	392
1908-09	401	280	681	171	510	457
1909-10	510	224	734	201	533	536
1910-11	533	190	723	247	476	498
1911-12	476	180	656	214	442	461
1912-13	442	165	607	202	405	417
1913-14	405	194	599	198	401	392
1914-15	401	207	608	161	447	417
1915-16	447	220	667	190	477	457
1916-17	477	204	681	262	428	468

DORCHESTER.

Years.	Admitted.	Discharged.	Remaining at end of Year.	Daily Average.
1907-08	120	79	235	211
1908-09	119	108	246	240
1909-10	118	118	246	234
1910-11	119	110	255	250
1911-12	82	117	220	231
1912-13	100	125	195	209
1913-14	114	78	231	210
1914-15	117	113	235	225
1915-16	113	110	238	240
1916-17	111	138	211	232

MANITOBA.

Years.	In custody at beginning of the Year.	Admitted during the Year.	Total.	Discharged during the Year.	Remaining at end of the Year.	Daily Average.
1907-08	175	42	217	97	120	140
1908-09	120	77	197	53	144	129
1909-10	144	84	228	63	165	158
1910-11	165	90	255	82	173	163
1911-12	173	95	268	85	183	174
1912 13	183	97	280	80	200	186
1913-14	200	76	276	104	172	181
1914-15	172	87	259	92	167	162
1915-16	167	77	244	89	155	164
1916-17	155	34	189	97	92	116

SESSIONAL PAPER No. 34

BRITISH COLUMBIA.

Years.	In custody at beginning of the Year.	Admitted during the Year.	Total.	Discharged during the Year.	Remaining at end of the Year.	Daily Average.
1907–08.................	137	84	221	69	152	142
1908–09.....	152	113	265	61	204	178
1909–10.	204	93	297	88	209	213
1910–11..................	209	145	354	94	260	226
1911–12.	260	168	428	97	331	290
1912–13.	331	175	506	115	351	345
1913–14.....	351	179	530	153	377	370
1914–15.	377	163	540	191	349	355
1915–16.	349	131	480	150	330	337
1916–17..:................	330	56	386	157	229	287

ALBERTA.

Years.	In custody at beginning of the Year.	Admitted during the Year.	Total.	Discharged during the Year.	Remaining at end of the Year.	Daily Average.
1907–08.	57	48	105	25	80	70
1908–09.....	80	60	140	49	91	86
1909–10..................	91	107	198	50	148	112
1910–11..................	148	118	266	67	199	177
1911–12..................	199	99	298	131	167	168
1912–13.	167	120	287	81	206	180
1913–14..................	206	98	304	101	203	195
1914–15.....	203	101	304	129	175	175
1915–16..................	175	107	282	90	192	181
1916–17..................	192	61	253	93	160	183

SASKATCHEWAN.

Years.	In custody at beginning of the Year.	Admitted during the Year.	Total.	Discharged during the Year.	Remaining at end of the Year.	Daily Average.
1912–13...........	58	65	123	28	95	76
1913–14..................	95	68	163	55	108	101
1914–15..................	108	75	183	51	132	125
1915–16.....	132	43	175	45	130	125
1916–17.................	130	39	169	70	99	112

APPENDIX D.—REVENUE STATEMENT.

SUMMARY OF REVENUE

Kingston.. ... .$	17,995 94
St. Vincent de Paul..	8,704 37
Dorchester..	10,059 89
Manitoba..	7,576 21
British Columbia..	5,075 86
Alberta..	5,972 02
Saskatchewan..	8,078 38
$	63,462 67

8 GEORGE V, A. 1918

APPENDIX E.—EXPENDITURE STATEMENT.

KINGSTON.

Staff—		
Salaries and retiring allowances..	$96,454 65	
Uniforms and mess..	5,536 67	
		$101,991 32
Maintenance of Convicts—		
Rations..	35,477 82	
Clothing and Hospital..	16,622 96	
		52,100 78
Discharge Expenses—		
Freedom suits and allowances..	5,109 52	
		5,109 52
Working Expenses—		
Heat, light and water..	16,300 48	
Maintenance of buildings and machinery..	9,028 66	
Chapels, schools and library..	421 05	
Office expenses..	1,472 58	
		27,222 77
Industries—		
Farm..	2,751 84	
Trade shops .. .. `..	14,332 19	
		17,084 03
Prison Equipment—		
Machinery..	4,800 55	
Furnishing..	1,447 05	
Utensils and vehicles..	455 32	
Land, buildings and walls..	2,267 91	
		8,970 83
Miscellaneous—		
Advertising and travel..	631 05	
Special	1,704 92	
		2,335 97
		214,815 22

ST. VINCENT DE PAUL.

Staff—		
Salaries and retiring allowances..	79,823 29	
Uniforms and mess..	4,251 51	
		84,074 80
Maintenance of Convicts—		
Rations..	27,866 33	
Clothing and Hospital..	15,407 78	
		43,274 11
Discharge Expenses—		
Freedom suits and allowances..	4,019 01	
Transfer and Interment..	65 15	
		4,084 16
Working Expenses—		
Heat, light and water..	22,307 52	
Maintenance of buildings and machinery..	12,888 42	
Chapels, schools and library..	260 50	
Office expenses..	1,162 38	
		36,618 82
Industries—		
Farm..	1,312 19	
Trade shops	2,795 13	
		4,107 32
Prison Equipment—		
Machinery.. .. .. `.. ..	529 65	
Furnishing..	1,139 38	
Utensils and vehicles..	1,468 21	
Land, buildings and walls..	16,084 68	
		19,221 92
Miscellaneous—		
Advertising and travel..	184 80	
Special..	466 54	
		651 34
		192,032 47

DORCHESTER.

Staff—
- Salaries and retiring allowances.. .. .. | $50,939 80
  Uniforms and mess.. .. .. | 1,922 27 | | $52,862 07

Maintenance of Convicts—
  Rations.. .. .. | 12,951 51
  Clothing and Hospital.. .. .. | 6,890 50 | | 19,842 01

Discharge Expenses—
  Freedom suits and allowances.. .. .. | 1,984 42 | | 1,984 42

Working Expenses—
  Heat, light and water.. .. .. | 7,944 62
  Maintenance of buildings and machinery.. .. | 3,974 90
  Chapels, schools and library.. .. .. | 544 45
  Office expenses.. .. .. | 612 15 | | 13,076 12

Industries—
  Farm.. .. .. | 3,200 37
  Trade shops.. .. .. | 5,024 60 | | 8,224 97

Prison Equipment—
  Machinery.. .. .. | 1,653 31
  Furnishing.. .. .. | 839 62
  Utensils and vehicles.. .. .. | 580 73
  Land, buildings and walls.. .. .. | 10,122 52 | | 13,196 18

Miscellaneous—
  Advertising and travel.. .. .. | 207 52
  Special.. .. .. | 58 55 | | 266 07

| | | 109,451 84

● MANITOBA.

Staff—
  Salaries and retiring allowances.. .. .. .. | 39,699 19
  Uniforms and mess.. .. .. | 2,462 02
  Living allowance .. .. | 3,941 79 | | 46,103 00

Maintenance of Convicts—
  Rations.. .. .. | 4,788 26
  Clothing and Hospital.. .. .. | 4,170 42 | | 8,958 68

Discharge Expenses—
  Freedom suits and allowances.. .. .. | 2,055 32
  Transfer and Interment.. .. .. | 246 40 | | 2,301 72

Working Expenses—
  Heat, light and water.. .. .. | 7,725 19
  Maintenance of buildings and machinery.. .. .. | 2,316 76
  Chapels, schools and library.. .. .. | 191 45
  Office expenses.. .. .. | 414 68 | | 10,648 08

Industries—
  Farm.. .. .. | 1,225 71
  Trade shops.. .. .. | 1,704 61 | | 2,930 32

Prison Equipment—
  Machinery.. .. .. | 604 85
  Furnishing.. .. .. | 233 91
  Utensils and vehicles.. .. .. | 230 79
  Land, buildings and walls.. .. .. | 1,169 26 | | 2,238 81

Miscellaneous—
  Advertising and travel.. .. .. | 66 60
  Special.. .. .. | 1,036 91 | | 1,103 51

| | | 74,284 12

8 GEORGE V, A. 1918

BRITISH COLUMBIA.

Staff—

Salaries and retiring allowances..	$54,219 61	
Uniforms and mess..	3,667 65	
Living allowance..	5,470 58	
		$63,357 84

Maintenance of Convicts—

Rations..	13,994 39	
Clothing and Hospital..	· 7,365 24	
		21,359 63

Discharge Expenses—

Freedom suits and allowances..	3,093 61	
Transfer and Interment..	342 20	
		3,435 81

Working Expenses—

Heat, light and water..	5,396 78	
Maintenance of buildings and machinery..	3,183 57	
Chapels, schools and library..	293 03	
Office expenses..	724 71	
		9,598 09

Industries—

Farm..	2,382 40	
Trade shops..	1,989 10	
		4,371 50

Prison Equipment—

Machinery..	2,817 10	
Furnishing..	574 80	
Utensils and vehicles..	690 84	
Land, buildings and walls..	9,902 39	
		13,985 13

Miscellaneous—

Advertising and travel..	39 75	
Special..	77 80	
		117 55
		116,225 55

ALBERTA.

Staff—

Salaries and retiring allowances..	45,444 11	
Uniforms and mess....	5,340 41	
Living allowance..	4,464 22	
		55,248 74

Maintenance of Convicts—

Rations.. .. ·..	10,198 50	
Clothing and Hospital..	4,433 29	
		14,631 79

Discharge Expenses—

Freedom suits and allowances..	1,825 39	
Transfer and Interment..	608 90	
		2,434 29

Working Expenses—

Heat, light and water..	2,122 68	
Maintenance of buildings and machinery..	1,735 79	
Chapels, schools and library..	108 57	
Office expenses..	660 57	
		4,627 61

Industries—

Farm..	⸗ 651 80	
Trade shops..	3,195 80	
Coal mine..	456 81	
		4,804 41

Prison Equipment—

Machinery..	59 08	
Furnishing..	616 93	
Utensils and vehicles..	577 12	
Land, buildings and walls..	13,134 44	
		14,387 57

Miscellaneous—

Advertising and travel..	191 60	
Special	586 63	
		778 23
		96,412 64

SASKATCHEWAN.

Staff—		
Salaries and retiring allowances..	$34,479 11	
Uniforms and mess..	3,101 19	
Living allowance..	3,204 13	
		$40,784 43
Maintenance of Convicts—		
Rations..	6,076 57	
Clothing and Hospital..	2,956 22	
		9,032 79
Discharge Expenses—		
Freedom suits and allowances..	1,345 71	
Transfer and Interment..	231 30	
		1,577 01
Working Expenses—		
Heat, light and water..	5,222 50	
Maintenance of buildings and machinery.. ..	1,879 14	
Chapels, schools and library..	247 01	
Office expenses..	763 79	
		8,112 44
Industries—		
Farm..	2,814 49	
Trade shops..	1,770 75	
		4,585 24
Prison Equipment—		
Machinery.. .. .., ...	4,172 03	
Furnishing..	81 40	
Utensils and vehicles..	985 57	
Land, buildings and walls..	35,807 75	
		41,046 75
Miscellaneous—		
Special..	123 45	
		123 45
		105,262 11

PENITENTIARIES GENERAL.

Salary of purchasing agent, 12 months	3,100 00	
Salary of Miss Grant, 12 months..	752 00	
Salary of Miss Brill, 9 months..	454 20	
Salary of Mrs. McLean, 2 months..	100 00	
Postage..	143 00	
Stationery..	22 20	
Printing..	18 38	
Telephones..	54 45	
		4,644 23
Assistance to paroled convicts..	....	42 08
Sundries	....	37 67
		4,723 98

REPORT

OF

THE MILITIA COUNCIL

FOR THE

DOMINION OF CANADA

FOR THE

FISCAL YEAR ENDING MARCH 31

1917

PRINTED BY ORDER OF PARLIAMENT

OTTAWA
J. DE LABROQUERIE TACHÉ
PRINTER TO THE KING'S MOST EXCELLENT MAJESTY
1918

No. 35—1918]

To His Excellency the Duke of Devonshire, K.G., P.C., G.C.M.G., G.C.V.O., etc., etc.,
Governor General and Commander in Chief of the Dominion of Canada.

MAY IT PLEASE YOUR EXCELLENCY:

The undersigned has the honour to present to Your Excellency the report of the Militia Council for the fiscal year ending March 31, 1917.

Respectfully submitted,

S. C. MEWBURN, Major-General,
Minister of Militia and Defence.

DEPARTMENT OF MILITIA AND DEFENCE,
Ottawa, January 25, 1918.

CONTENTS.

ANNUAL REPORT

OF

THE MILITIA COUNCIL

Year Ending March 31, 1917.

The following statements and reports for the year ending March 31, 1917, are submitted, viz.:—

1. Financial Statements for the twelve months ending March 31, 1917. Appendix A.

2. Statement showing changes in the strength of the Permanent Force from April 1, 1916, to March 31, 1917.   Appendix B.

3. Statements showing: Number of officers appointed to the Permanent Staff and Force; number of officers appointed to the Active Militia (non-permanent), and number of warrants issued during year ending March 31, 1917. Appendix C.

4. Statement of Certificates issued during the year 1916–17.   Appendix D.

5. Report of the Commandant, Royal Military College, for year 1916–17. Report of the Board of Visitors, Royal Military College, 1917.   Appendix E.

6. Report of the Superintendent of the Dominion Arsenal for year 1916–17. Appendix F.

E. F. JARVIS,

Secretary, Militia Council.

APPENDIX A.

The following are statements showing:—

1. Appropriation Accounts.

2. Allowances paid to Active Militia in the various Districts.

3. Showing Expenditure by Stations on account of Pay and Allowances of the Permanent Force.

4. Statement of Expenditure on account of Pay and Allowances of Officers and Warrant Officers of the Permanent Force.

5. Statement of Expenditure on account of Pay and Allowances of Officers and Warrant Officers of the Permanent Force with details of expenditure by stations.

6. Statement of Expenditure on account of Pay and Allowances of N.C.O's. and men of the Permanent Force.

7. Statement of Expenditure on account of Pay and Allowances of N.C.O's. and men of the Permanent Force with details of expenditure by stations.

8. Expenditure on account of Officers and men of the Active (non-permanent) Militia attending Schools of Instruction.

9. Militia and Defence Revenue.

10. Comparative Statement of Expenditure for the ten years 1907–8 to 1916–17.

11. Expenditure on account of War Appropriation to March 31, 1917.

12. Table of Changes in the strength of the Permanent Force.

STATEMENT No. 1.—Appropriation Accounts, 1916–17.

Name of Grant.	Amount of Grant. $ cts.	Expenditure. $ cts.	Grant Unused. $ cts.	Grant Exceeded. $ cts.	Remarks.
Allowances, Active Militia	100,000 00	47,573 02	52,426 98		No camps being held, allowances reduced 50 per cent.
Annual Drill					No appropriation voted.
Cadet Services	100,000 00	80,310 97	19,689 03		(Owing to the continuance of the war only a small proportion of this appropriation was used.)
Clothing and Necessaries	800,000 00	39,191 27	760,808 73		
Contingencies	60,000 00	23,213 64	36,786 36		Telephone tolls, etc. charged to War Appropriation.
Customs Dues	100,000 00	68,780 50	31,219 50		Duties on C.E.F. Supplies charged to War Appropriation.
Departmental Library	1,000 00	640 55	359 45		All expenditure except salaries of staff charged to War Appropriation.
Dominion Arsenal	100,000 00	29,924 13	70,075 87		Construction of permanent works curtailed owing to War.
Engineer Services and Works	500,000 00	396,894 97	103,105 03		
Grants to Associations and Bands	83,000 00	7,980 90	75,019 10		There were practically no bands, and all other expenditures under this appropriation were greatly decreased owing to the War.
H.Q. and District Staffs	218,765 00	208,301 58	10,463 42		
Maintenance, Military Properties	180,000 00	164,166 27	15,833 73		No appropriation voted.
Ordnance Arms, Lands, etc					By arrangement with the Department of the Auditor General this over expenditure was to have been charged to War Appropriation but in the meantime the Department of Finance closed the accounts of the fiscal year and the transfer of the charge could not be effected.
Permanent Force	2,300,000 00	2,396,182 90		96,182 90	
Printing and Stationery	70,000 00	70,000 00			
Royal Military College	160,000 00	147,576 00	12,424 00		
Salaries and Wages	260,000 00	205,801 33	54,198 67		Owing to the continuance of the war the additional expenditure provided for under this appropriation did not accrue.

STATEMENT No. 1.—Appropriation Accounts, 1916-17—*Concluded.*

Name of Grant.	Amount of Grant.	Expenditure.	Grant Unused.	Grant Exceeded.	Remarks.
Militia and Defence.	$ cts.	$ cts.	$ cts.	$ cts.	
Schools of Instruction	150,000 00	81,383 54	68,616 46		Owing to the War the expenses in connection with many of the classes held were charged to War Appropriation.
Topographical Surveys	40,000 00	31,274 32	8,725 68		The greater part of the transportation during the year was due to the war and charged accordingly.
Transport and Freight	175,000 00	43,922 52	131,077 48		
Training Areas	200,000 00	224,623 05		24,623 05	*See remarks re Overdraft "Perm. Force" and foot note.
Warlike Stores	100,000 00	15,753 32	84,246 68		The stores purchased were chiefly in connection with the war and charged to War Appropriation.
	5,697,765 00	4,283,494 78	1,535,076 17	120,805 95	
War Appropriation		298,291,030 66			

Name of Grant.	Amount of Grant.	Expenditure.		Grant unused.
		Militia.	Pension Board Commission.	
Pensions.				
European War	3,000,000 00	1,068,920 10	1,378,454 93	552,624 97
Act 1901 (Statutory)	90,000 00	47,037 61	40,562 44	2,399 95
Rebellion 1885 and General	20,000 00	9,578 46	10,034 75	386 79
Fenian Raid	2,000 00	808 90	658 90	532 20
Pay by Statute.				
Chief of General Staff				
Inspector General				
Adjutant General		18,290 12		
Quartermaster General				
Master General of Ordnance				
Militia Revenue		57,503 61		
Casual Revenue				

Properties Sold.	Balance of proceeds of sale brought for'd. from 1915-16.	Expenditure, 1916-17.	Balance of proceeds of sale to be carried forward to 1917-18.
Barracks, Toronto..................................	144 15	....	144 15
St. Helen's Island, Montreal..........................	19,783 10	....	19,783 10
Fort Osborne Barrack Site, Winnipeg..................	62,947 27	....	62,947 27
	82,874 52	....	82,874 52

* During the fiscal year, expenditure was made out of this vote for compensation for timber cutting rights to parties on land expropriated for Petawawa Camp grounds. To this the Auditor General took exception and an appropriation to cover these payments amounting to $38,355.75 was provided by Parliament this present Session. This appropriation more than offsets the overdraft.

EMENT No. 2.—Allowances paid to Active Militia in the various Districts during the financial year 1916-17.

District.	Command Pay and Drill Instruction.	Care of Arms.	Postage.	Stationery.	Efficiency Grants C.O.T.C.	Refund for Stores charged as deficient or returned.	Gross Amount.	Less Deductions and Deficiencies.	Net Expenditure.
	$ cts.	$ cts.	$ cts.	$ cts.	$ cts.	$ cts.	$ cts.	$ cts.	$ cts.
No. 1		120 77	28 20			330 14	479 11	19 32	459 79
2	5,610 19	5,524 00	863 13	19 90		2,110 82	14,128 04	1,037 79	13,090 25
3	2,006 50	1,500 00	260 00			94 10	3,860 60	566 58	3,294 02
4	5,956 14	2,148 75	661 45	1 95	6,010 00	284 85	15,063 14	1,208 87	13,854 27
5	2,029 30	1,194 36	297 50	108 64		68 64	3,698 44	212 48	3,485 96
6	4,495 41	1,687 90	613 50	32 40	210 00	54 33	7,093 54	282 67	6,810 87
10					2,191 25		2,191 25		2,191 25
11	558 20	50 00		5 85		19 18	633 23	188 51	444 72
13	2,779 52	2,309 17	364 38			2 32	5,455 39	1,513 50	3,941 89
Totals	23,435 26	14,534 95	3,088 16	168 74	8,411 25	2,964 38	52,602 74	5,029 72	47,573 02

SESSIONAL PAPER No. 35

STATEMENT No. 3.—Showing Expenditure by Stations on account of Pay and Allowances of the Permanent Force for the year 1916–17.

Station.	Strength, all ranks, March 31, 1916.	Strength, all ranks, March 31, 1917.	Pay and Allowances, Officers and Warrant Officers.	Pay and Allowances N.C.O's and Men.	Total Pay and Allowances.
			$ cts.	$ cts.	$ cts.
London..........................	92	62	18,679 18	42,100 46	60,797 64
Toronto..........................	271	169	71,094 29	87,699 80	158,794 09
Kingston..........................	309	170	46,729 81	78,491 54	125,221 35
Ottawa..........................	176	372	74,962 93	242,138 63	317,101 56
Montreal..........................	48	54	41,096 98	29,414 84	70,511 82
St. Jean, P.Q........................	2	2	....	2,100 67	2,100 67
Quebec..........................	316	269	108,135 39	128,900 08	237,035 47
Halifax..........................	1,197	716	124,487 94	327,261 97	451,749 91
St. John, N.B......................	9	9	2,084 00	6,916 95	9,000 95
Winnipeg..........................	168	288	24,177 20	146,838 72	171,015 92
Esquimalt..........................	266	297	41,064 56	181,868 67	222,933 23
Calgary..........................	24	63	14,952 73	35,634 12	50,586 85
Regina..........................	....	35	6,324 38	5,383 03	11,707 41
Abroad..........................	1	5	4,043 60	2,573 65	6,617 25
Miscellaneous........................	....	....	....	25' 140 99	25,140 99
Totals..........................	2,879	2,511	577,850 99	1,342,464 12	1,920,315 11

8 GEORGE V, A. 1918

STATEMENT No. 4.—Statement of Expenditure on account of Pay and Allowances of Officers and Warrant Officers of Permanent Force for year ending March 31, 1917. Details of Expenditure by Corps.

Corps	Pay — Ordinary	Pay — Abroad	Allowances — Lodging	Allowances — Ration	Allowances — Fuel	Allowances — Light	Allowances — Servant	Allowances — Western	Allowances — Other	Allowances — Abroad	Total Allowances	Total Pay and Allowances	Credit to Public and Refunds	Net Expenditure
	$ cts.	$ cts.	$ cts.	$ cts.	$ cts.	$ cts.	$ cts.	$ cts.	$ cts.	$ cts.	$ cts.	$ cts.	$ cts.	$ cts.
Roy. Can. Dgns.	10,361 70		554 40	1,051 25	169 15	48 30			322 24		2,145 34	12,507 04	21 33	12,485 71
Lord Strath. Horse (R. C.)	5,629 73		700 00	108 00	177 84	31 26		545 92	1,733 11		3,296 13	8,925 86	33 77	8,892 09
Royal Can. Horse Artillery	13,869 56		2,786 90	977 49	785 32	227 88			5 89		4,783 48	18,653 04		18,653 04
Royal Can. Garrison Artillery	47,661 71		6,151 76	3,057 46	1,509 04	649 38	384 89	661 88	3,120 47		15,534 88	63,196 59	718 43	62,478 16
Royal Canadian Engineers	53,335 74		11,953 02	3,998 78	3,133 44	969 55	2,944 47	1,059 25	2,545 38		26,603 89	79,939 63	4,514 91	75,424 72
Royal Canadian Regiment	18,550 20		2,690 06	1,222 75	714 15	359 79		755 31	324 10		6,066 16	24,616 36	936 65	23,679 71
Can. Per. Army Service Corps	48,375 99		10,481 85	3,535 25	2,847 31	850 98	2,563 36	269 02	1,987 29		22,535 06	70,911 05	2,649 80	68,261 16
Permanent Army Medical Corps	46,608 15		9,975 80	2,597 94	2,511 41	756 39	2,121 69	310 14	3,127 32		21,400 69	68,098 84	2,596 58	65,502 26
Can. Per. Army Vet. Corps	8,896 97		2,441 76	558 76	605 21	181 80	364 71		507 43		4,659 67	13,556 64	216 77	13,339 87
Can. Ordnance Corps	74,693 70	1,662 48	16,719 57	5,058 13	4,599 46	1,287 59	3,234 35	1,448 40	2,357 69	1,109 62	35,814 81	112,170 99	5,047 06	107,123 93
Canadian Army Pay Corps	30,266 71		8,182 58	1,918 08	2,084 47	571 51	1,581 50	739 85	707 61		15,785 60	46,052 31	2,389 65	43,662 66
Corps of Military Staff Clerks	19,734 55		5,328 81	1,688 79	1,525 06	418 50	725 33	327 54	466 91		10,480 94	30,215 49	671 42	29,544 07
Instructional Cadre	17,219 76		4,498 32	1,324 06	1,224 84	343 63	659 29	150 00	210 68		8,410 82	25,630 58	440 72	25,189 86
School of Signalling	2,088 00		499 70	170 75	138 10	41 04	170 50	15 48	38 72		1,074 29	3,162 29		3,162 29
School of Musketry	6,053 96		1,506 56	501 72	425 40	123 32	408 62	15 48	365 82		3,346 92	9,400 88	12 08	9,388 80
Miscellaneous	6,596 00	1,076 83	1,576 45	380 50	418 34	110 77	388 00	133 65	197 35	194 67	3,399 73	11,072 56	9 90	11,062 66
Totals	410,032 43	2,739 31	86,047 54	28,149 71	22,868 54	6,971 69	15,546 71	6,431 92	18,018 01	1,304 29	185,338 41	598,110 15	20,259 16	577,850 99

STATEMENT No. 5.—Statement of Expenditure on account of Pay and Allowances of Officers and Warrant Officers of Permanent Force for year ending March 31, 1917. Details of Expenditure at each Station.

Stations	Pay Ordinary	Pay Abroad	Allowances Lodging	Ration	Fuel	Light	Servant	Western	Other	Abroad	Total Allowances	Total Pay and Allowances	Credit to Public and Refunds	Net Expenditure
	$ cts.	$ cts.	$ cts.	$ cts.	$ cts.	$ cts.	$ cts.	$ cts.	$ cts.	$ cts.	$ cts.	$ cts.	$ cts.	$ cts.
London, Ont...	12,888 87		3,286 15	1,122 25	883 08	287 01	840 50		417 93		6,816 92	19,705 79	1,008 61	18,697 18
Toronto, Ont...	50,275 05		10,186 10	3,716 97	2,668 51	797 60	2,236 30		2,941 59		22,547 07	72,822 12	1,727 83	71,094 29
Kingston, Ont...	34,035 16		7,522 90	2,238 00	2,000 61	581 23	981 00		823 32		14,147 06	48,182 22	1,452 41	46,729 81
...s., Ont...	55,814 25		12,585 28	4,244 87	3,551 55	1,061 21	2,790 86		2,183 07		26,406 84	82,221 09	7,258 16	74,962 93
Montreal, Que...	29,273 68		7,216 21	2,092 43	1,034 00	572 66	1,324 04		879 78		14,019 12	43,292 80	2,195 82	41,096 98
Quebec, Que...	77,507 34		15,150 14	5,319 94	4,230 79	1,279 43	3,374 16		2,698 63		32,053 09	109,560 43	1,425 04	108,135 39
Halifax, N.S...	94,445 80		15,140 70	5,770 25	4,096 47	1,516 72	2,181 50		2,955 93		31,661 57	126,107 37	1,619 43	124,487 94
St. John, N.B...	1,875 00			45 75	42 00		91 25		30 00		209 00	2,084 00		2,084 00
Winnipeg, Man...	14,682 61		4,610 00	845 75	1,241 43	212 20	423 00	1,586 38	1,981 88		10,900 64	25,583 25	1,406 05	24,177 20
....alt, B.C...	27,466 62		5,110 28	1,892 25	912 39	437 03	605 60	3,499 89	2,346 75		14,804 19	42,270 81	1,206 25	41,064 56
Regina, Sask...	3,772 50		1,655 05	283 25	435 10	76 30	223 75	493 11	330 33		3,502 89	7,275 39	951 01	6,324 38
Calgary, Ala...	7,995 55		3,604 73	578 00	872 61	160 30	474 75	852 54	422 80		6,965 73	14,961 28	8 55	14,952 73
England ⎫ Abroad		2,739 31								1,304 29	1,304 29	4,043 60		4,043 60
India ⎬														
Australia ⎭														
$	410,032 43	2,739 31	86,047 54	28,149 71	22,868 54	6,971 69	15,546 71	6,431 92	18,018 01	1,304 29	185,338 41	598,110 15	20,259 16	577,850 99

STATEMENT No. 6.—Statement of Expenditure on account of Pay and Allowances of N.C.O's and Men of the Permanent Force for the year ending March 31, 1917. Details of Expenditure, by Corps.

Corps	Regimental Pay	Deferred Pay	Proficiency Artillery Engineer and Corps Pay	Extra Duty Pay	Other Credits	Total Pay	Total Allowances	Total pay and Allowances	Deduct charges credited to Public	Net Expenditure
R yd Canadian Dragoons	13,357 43	94 52	222 30	262 90	1 84	13,978 99	8,054 39	22,033 38	401 11	21,632 27
Royal ?an Dragoons Inst. Cadre	563 10		27 30			620 40	637 20	1,257 60		1,257 60
?d Strathcona's Horse (R.C.)	38,608 10	29 49	121 80	737 10	49 14	39,545 63	43,193 30	82,738 93	1,625 32	81,113 61
Royal ?an ?e Artillery	16,434 70	659 76	684 10	797 45	0 90	18,676 91	11,479 16	30,056 07	152 47	29,903 60
Royal Canadian Garrison Artillery	90,899 17	4,682 96	9,578 25	5,003 15	239 87	110,402 70	65,535 70	175,938 40	2,219 89	173,718 51
Royal Canadian Engineers	95,466 95	1,101 96	37,563 60	841 50	475 32	135,449 33	61,218 00	196,667 33	2,893 20	193,774 13
Royal Canadian R gi?nt	43,584 94	949 51	1,306 25	2,076 10	28 20	47,945 00	47,475 29	95,420 29	976 86	94,443 43
Royal Canadian Regiment Inst. Cadre	24,429 62	77 43	1,560 00	459 30	31 52	26,557 87	15,383 46	41,941 33	212 72	41,728 61
?adia ?Permanent Army Service Corps	72,005 48	736 27	17,810 55	3,174 10	106 15	93,832 55	51,573 36	145,405 91	1,470 95	143,934 96
Permanent Army ?al Corps	34,276 64	409 11	5,898 25	1,722 85	371 67	32,668 52	20,090 24	52,764 76	302 82	52,461 94
Canadian Permanent Army Veterinary Corps										
Canadian ?dce Corps	1,109 00		337 50			1,446 50	860 67	2,307 17	0 32	2,306 85
Corps of Military Staff Cl	118,245 65	2,716 81	28,327 55	6,716 05	99 18	156,105 24	144,488 44	300,593 68	1,554 22	299,039 46
?os of Military Staff Clerks (Section "B")	52,205 91		10 90	695 10	132 82	53,044 73	44,940 79	97,985 72	551 29	97,434 43
?an Army Pay ?g	17,777 88		12 60	91 25	10 95	17,892 68	14,865 09	32,757 77	221 88	32,535 89
Physical Training Instructors	38,396 13		4,329 40	272 75	0 08	22,998 36	16,339 08	39,337 44	58 00	39,279 44
Musketry Staff	2,645 20	5 66	164 10	18 45		2,833 41	3,274 47	6,107 88	0 05	6,107 83
Signalling Staff	930 90					930 90	1,341 62	2,272 52		2,272 52
High Commissioner	771 90	24 78	27 20	35 80		859 68	1,057 57	1,917 25	112 85	1,804 40
Men on loan (1)	1,670 65					1,670 65	903 00	2,573 65		2,573 65
?ns Pension Fund N.C.O's and	508 66					508 66		508 66		508 66
Miscellaneous (2)				24,632 33		24,632 33		24,632 33		24,632 33
Totals	633,958 01	11,487 56	107,971 65	47,636 18	1,547 64	802,501 04	552,717 03	1,355,218 07	12,753 95	1,342,464 12

(1) Contributions by the Dominion Government towards the Pension Fund of N.C.O's and Men of the Regular Army on loan in Canada.

(2) Extra Duty Pay of Military Working Parties and of Departmental Corps at various Stations.

STATEMENT No. 7.—Statement of Expenditure on account of Pay and Allowances of N.C.O's and Men of the Permanent Force for the year ending March 31, 1917. Details of Expenditure at each Station.

Stations.	Total Pay.	Allowances.								Total Allowances	Total Pay and Allowances	Less charges credited to Public.	Net Pay and Allowances
		Lodging.	Rations.	Fuel.	Light.	Medical.	Special Western.	Other.	Clothing.				
	$ cts.	$ cts.	$ cts.	$ cts.	$ cts.	$ cts.	$ cts.	$ cts.	$ cts.	$ cts.	$ cts.	$ cts.	$ cts.
London.	24,080 82	7,405 20	4,788 75	2,986 78	905 20			744 70	1,416 60	18,247 23	42,328 05	227 59	42,100 46
Toronto.	53,258 28	15,195 30	8,146 50	6,185 56	1,894 55	212 33		423 99	2,969 09	35,027 32	88,285 60	585 80	87,699 80
Kingston.	46,519 47	12,881 91	8,017 25	5,249 16	1,588 89	667 43	145 25	639 05	3,237 80	32,426 74	78,946 21	454 67	78,491 54
Ottawa.	140,460 25	41,917 62	26,317 65	17,121 21	5,065 78	4,882 83		1,072 62	6,292 23	102,669 94	243,130 19	991 56	242,138 63
St. Jean, Que.	17,388 33	5,151 00	3,044 50	2,111 03	635 71	506 23	32 83	357 92	401 85	12,241 07	29,629 40	214 56	29,414 84
	1,202 80	292 00	456 25	120 00	36 00			1 67		905 92	2,108 72	8 05	2,100 67
Quebec.	85,480 80	19,333 10	11,092 70	7,872 12	2,403 44		65 77	444 49	4,118 85	45,330 51	130,811 31	1,911 23	128,900 08
Halifax.	235,985 63	41,623 35	22,078 25	17,116 70	5,117 38	157 02	753 47	1,747 48	7,865 02	96,301 71	332,287 34	5,025 37	327,261 97
St. John, N.B.	4,064 35	1,313 15	518 25	540 00	161 37				219 42	2,909 21	6,973 56	56 61	6,916 95
Winipeg.	67,889 99	35,916 05	11,782 00	12,520 53	2,288 30		14,656 65	1,927 74	1,705 86	80,797 13	148,687 12	1,848 40	146,838 72
Esquimalt.	49,421 00	23,433 79	8,430 50	4,659 62	1,400 06		10,201 45	475 85	1,593 14	50,194 41	99,615 41	770 63	98,844 73
Victoria.	32,957 90	26,463 44	7,395 70	5,151 29	1,567 86		9,474 61	154 29	314 61	50,521 80	83,479 70	455 76	83,023 94
Regina.	2,124 65	1,401 40	485 75	519 31	97 05	19 97	385 06	101 65	280 53	3,290 72	5,415 37	32 34	5,383 03
Calgary.	14,855 13	10,067 34	3,419 75	3,366 73	684 64	628 71	2,402 69	73 25	308 21	20,950 32	35,805 45	171 33	35,634 12
Pensions Pension Fund N.C.O's and Men on Loan. (1)	508 66										508 66		508 66
High Commissioner.	1,670 65									903 00	2,573 65		2,573 65
Miscellaneous. (2)	24,632 33										24,632 33		24,632 33
	802,501 04	242,394 65	115,973 80	85,520 14	23,846 23	7,074 52	38,117 78	8,163 70	30,723 21	552,717 03	1,355,218 07	12,753 95	1,342,464 1

(1) Contributions by the Dominion Government towards Pension Fund of N.C.O's and Men of the Regular Army on loan in Canada.
(2) Extra Duty Pay of Militia Working Parties and of Departmental Corps at the various stations.

8 GEORGE V, A. 1918

STATEMENT No. 8.—Expenditure on account of Officers and Men of the Active (non-permanent) Militia, attending Schools of Instruction, 1916–17.

(Numbers shown do not include those attending without expense to the public.)

Corps, etc.	Place.	NUMBERS TRAINED.			Cost.
		Officers.	N.C.O's, and Men.	Total.	
					$ cts.
Cavalry............................	Toronto................	72	11	83	3,401 25
Artillery...........................	Quebec................	85	....	85	3,893 00
"	Halifax...............	328	7	335·	14,428 75
"	Esquimalt............	33	8	41	2,040 50
Infantry...........................	London...............	505	211	716	19,945 70
"	Toronto..............	......	100	100	900 00
"	Esquimalt............	389	10	399	5,505 20
"	Halifax...............	597	8	605	20,540 32
Army Service Corps............	Quebec...............	129	....	129	5,991 00
Army Medical Corps...........	Halifax...............	27	3	30	793 20
Musketry..........................	Victoria..............	71	42	113	1,495 00
"	Halifax...............	10	....	10	578 00
Totals........................	....	2,246	400	2,646	79,511 92

	M.D. 1..$	18 39
	M.D. 2...	23 20
Travelling expenses, Officers and Men of	M.D. 3...	6 75
the Active Militia, to and from Schools of	M.D. 4...	Nil.
Instruction. Also includes Travelling	M.D. 5...	802 14
Expenses and Subsistence Allowance to	M.D. 6...	498 04
Instructors, Permanent Force.	M.D. 10..	Nil.
	M.D. 11..	825 90
	M.D. 13..	Nil.

$ 81,686 34

Deduct expenditure 1915–16 paid from 1916–17 Funds.......................... 1,548 25

$ 80,138 09

STATEMENT No 9.—REVENUE, 1916–17.

Militia Revenue..$	90,163 58
Royal Military College..	41,645 97
Casual Revenue..	11,949 33
Militia Pensions..	25,495 07

$ 169,253 95

Sale of Ammunition and Stores..	37,485 34
Rents of Military Properties..	4,387 57
Miscellaneous Revenues..	48,290 67

$ 90,163 58

Fines and Forfeitures...	573 12
Retirement Fund...	686 94

STATEMENT No. 10.—Comparative Statement of Expenditure for the Ten Years 1907–8 to 1916–17.

	1907-8.	1908-9.	1909-10.	1910-11.	1911-12.	1912-13.	1913-14.	1914-15.	1915-16.	1916-17.
	$	$	$	$	$	$	$	$	$	$
...les for Drill Instruction, Care of Arms, and										
Postage	70,239	115,003	66,565	104,446	83,867	85,474	101,904	66,513	68,643	45,573
Annual Drill	1,084,499	1,304,796	796,608	1,089,694	1,169,068	1,719,257	1,830,034	1,875,944		
Cadet Corps					35,947	93,723	392,207	327,679	84,972	80,311
Clothing and Necessaries	399,919	371,866	374,670	373,960	475,175	508,788	699,572	510,810		39,191
Contingencies, including Guards of Honour, Escorts and Salutes	24,807	35,010	30,364	34,979	39,920	47,674	49,957	36,557	31,670	23,214
Customs Dues	143,622	95,177	36,696	180,880	143,069	34,494	47,630	115,791	26,004	68,780
Departmental Library	968	1,050	938	755	975	1,010	1,055	1,113	985	641
Dominion Arsenal	341,083	275,936	259,524	280,034	236,790	325,863	358,315	265,262	299,678	29,924
Engineer Services	325,913	316,819	274,807	353,966	487,222	791,895	1,452,729	1,111,196	690,755	396,895
Grants towards construction of City Regimental Armouries				65,000		12,000				
Grants to Artillery and Rifle Associations and to Regimental Bands	49,278	51,085	53,187	54,985	56,270	64,315	79,506	73,605	47,878	7,981
Gratuities and Compassionate Allowances	26,879	2,513	2,375	3,970	2,551	2,170	4,300	15,190	500	
Maintenance of Military Properties	70,062	75,000	74,067	79,961	80,937	88,925	107,214	209,231	175,053	164,166
Pay of ... General and Military ..., Roll (Statutory)	21,600	21,600	21,600	21,600	21,600	21,600	21,600	15,161	18,450	18,290
Pay of Headquarters Staff	58,797	57,732	52,717	59,589	66,178	78,617	74,002	72,050	74,956	84,766
Pay of Division and District Staffs	77,272	74,860	84,719	76,430	99,300	115,844	123,772	107,410	109,241	123,536
Permanent Force—Pay, Provisions, and Supplies	1,826,258	1,787,851	1,758,005	1,845,386	1,946,636	2,200,183	2,198,453	2,114,493	2,116,245	2,396,183
Printing and Stationery	50,430	43,704	39,999	60,003	53,489	59,828	72,209	69,880	70,000	70,000
Royal Military College	92,145	108,496	95,934	127,036	134,949	131,241	149,039	153,987	135,685	147,576
Salaries and wages of Civil Employees	98,979	95,703	79,822	153,018	155,645	170,700	197,823	243,936	232,797	205,801
Schools of Instruction, Pay of Active Militia attending	40,127	32,183	50,967	80,007	70,041	77,765	97,847	164,669	178,898	81,384
Topographical Survey	23,716	28,414	23,140	26,260	24,714	35,055	39,059	35,038	25,440	31,274
Transport and Freight	109,980	112,313	101,634	124,281	138,230	175,034	199,247	208,774	60,567	43,923
Warlike Stores	554,200	231,998	342,406	334,548	531,332	683,080	703,375	496,867		15,753
Coronation Contingents					134,835					
Training Areas										
Miscellaneous small Services	7,000	350	600	6,318	21,047	17,202	6,508	234,592	233,085	224,623
Expenditure ... under the six following sub-heads was charged to ... Account up to ... inclusive, and to Revenue since then:—										
Ordnance, ..., Tents, ..., and	703,750	612,997	323,281	370,469	649,276	572,486	967,804	593,167		
Equipment generally, excepting ..., Saddl...ry and Harness	92,570	110,984	47,427	103,753	6,713	942	103,732	146,066		
Saddlery and Harness	57,098	77,858	204,770	150,230	110,468	100,000	217,419	219,077		
Clothing—Reserve stock and outfitting new units										

STATEMENT No. 10.—Comparative Statement of Expenditure for the Ten Years 1907–8 to 1916–17.—*Concluded.*

	1907-8	1908-9	1909-10	1910-11	1911-12	1912-13	1913-14	1914-15	1915-16	1916-17
	$	$	$	$	$	$	$	$	$	$
Ross Rifles, spare parts, bayonets, scabbards, arm chests, and Inspection	214,143	317,478	561,123	585,190	419,937	552,073	640,613	478,543	4,681,502	4,301,785
Dominion Arsenal, for reserve ammunition	75,000									
Lands and construction of new Rifle Ranges	155,344	126,030	63,369	162,773	183,703	341,208	51,237	29,216		
Total Ordnance, Equipment, Lands, etc.	1,297,905	1,245,347	1,299,970	1,372,405	1,370,097	1,566,709	1,980,805	1,466,069		
Total Militia Expenditure	6,795,678	6,484,806	5,921,314	6,909,211	7,579,884	9,112,376	10,998,162	9,991,817	160,433,416	298,291,031
War Expenditure								53,176,614	160,433,416	298,291,031
Aid to Civil Power (Statutory and recoverable from Municipalities)	410		58,613	13,678	716	78			25	
Toronto Barracks, Special Account				63,026	2,012	148,889	187,857	68,800		
Winnipeg Barracks, Special Account				123,000		137,053	45	87,708		
Point St. Charles Armoury				17,500						
Montreal Barracks site						180,000		217		
Transferred from Public Works Dept.						940	221,849	19,722		
Pensions—Rebellion, 1837-8	160	120	80	80	80	40				
Pensions—Fenian Raids	1,935	1,508	1,937	1,710	1,828	1,822	1,788	2,819	1,896	1,408
Pensions—Northwest Rebellion and general	16,283	12,733	16,760	17,628	17,118	17,689	17,834	20,227	21,164	19,613
Pensions—Pension Act, 1901	19,981	26,873	27,003	38,483	45,698	50,470	70,940	79,845	82,877	87,600
Pensions—European War									307,693	2,447,375
Total Pensions	38,359	41,234	45,780	57,901	64,724	70,021	90,562	102,891	413,630	2,556,056
Civil Government Salaries	63,104	101,039	126,726	130,732	137,251	146,718	157,137	168,545	172,534	173,798
Civil Government, Contingencies	11,994	13,884	13,500	10,086	11,962	22,029	27,997	20,216	28,351	19,488
Total, Civil Government	75,098	114,923	140,226	140,818	149,214	168,747	185,134	188,761	200,885	193,286
Revenue Received—										
Militia	39,809	29,791	31,783	44,259	59,829	51,359	36,641	64,831	192,300	90,104
Casual	1,174	130	2,742	1,390	1,806	2,691	1,790	1,625	41,318	11,949
Royal Military College	23,209	28,019	29,154	31,650	34,286	36,785	36,817	32,047	35,142	41,646
Pension Act, 1901	19,596	21,196	21,742	23,347	25,209	28,393	30,714	27,282	23,513	25,495
Total Revenue	83,788	79,136	85,421	100,646	121,130	119,228	105,962	125,785	292,273	169,254

SESSIONAL PAPER No. 35

STATEMENT No. 11.—Statement of Expenditure on account of War Appropriation to March 31, 1917.

Particulars.	Paid out in Canada from 1st April, 1916, to 31st March, 1917.	Paid out in London, Eng. from 1st April, 1916, to 31st March, 1917.	Total.
	$ cts.	$ cts.	$ cts.
Clothing (except boots)............................	13,927,957 68	701,477 18	14,629,434 86
Boots and repairs to boots.........................	3,282,480 83	328,303 46	3,610,784 29
Necessaries (kit bags and articles of kit)............	803,984 73	....	803,984 73
Accoutrements....................................	1,515,657 87	245,749 25	1,761,407 12
Binoculars, telescopes, prismatic compasses, etc.......	381,200 96	17,250 75	398,451 71
Saddlery and horse equipment.......	762,382 08	12,494 36	774,876 44
Motor trucks, ambulances, and other vehicles........	1,837,340 64	436,125 46	2,273,466 10
Ross Rifle Co.—rifles and bayonets..................	4,064,797 83	....	4,064,797 83
Machine guns and spare parts......................	2,123,272 95	36,575 75	2,159,848 70
Stores (furniture, bedding, utensils, etc.).............	4,363,079 39	538,839 35	4,901,918 74
Total for equipment.....	33,062,154 96	2,316,815 56	35,378,970 52
Dominion Arsenal (from War Vote).................	1,340,486 19	....	1,340,486 19
Lindsay Arsenal (Supplies).........................	213,585 04	....	213,585 04
Dominion Cartridge Co.,—Ammunition.............	1,785,336 91	....	1,785,336.91
Ammunition from other sources.....................	147,898 09	3,424 25	151,322 34
Total Ammunition and Material.........	3,487,306 23	3,424 25	3,490,730 48
Lindsay Arsenal—Site............................	3,933 26	....	3,933 26
" —Construction.................	622,548 69	....	622,548 69
" —Machinery........................	578,700 84	....	578,700 84
Borden Camp—Land................................	137,981 29	....	137,981 29
Total Land and Buildings.................	1,343,164 08	....	1,343,164 08
Pay and Allowances (includes subsistence, rations, and assigned pay).....................................	92,484,996 77	67,619,916 62	160,104,913 39
Maintenance of troops in France....................	....	41,366,666 07	41,366,666 67
Separation Allowances............................	22,218,076 96	4,142,312 88	26,360,389 84
Outfit Allowances................................	868,040 94	1,214,294 52	2,082,335 46
Engineers Services and Works......................	2,624,705 36	1,125,441 90	3,750,147 26
Purchase of Remounts, expenses of purchases, etc.....	256,459 77	3,184,301 87	3,440,761 64
Drugs and Surgical Instruments....................	598,296 67	*1,541,180 70	2,139,477 37
Travelling and Transport—Ocean...................	3,808,704 91	3,763 87	3,812,468 78
" " —Land...................	7,279,330 44	153,694 37	7,433,024 81
Forage and Stabling...............................	387,056 11	757,298 30	1,144,354 41
Pay, etc., of Censors..............................	123,277 50	....	123,277 50
Pay of civil employees............................	1,732,800 35	473,553 43	2,206,353 78
Rent, water, fuel and light........................	1,166,670 59	654,673 53	1,821,344 12
Funeral expenses.................................	39,343 83	10,378 33	49,722 16
Recruiting (Medical examination, attestation and advertising).....................................	59,412 92	1,540 25	60,953 17
Telegrams, telephones (including rental) cablegrams, and postage.................................	388,160 07	49,054 90	437,214 97
Printing and Stationery...........................	808,224 79	153,016 06	961,240 85
Conservancy and Contingencies.....................	283,293 73	42,359 29	325,653 02
Customs dues.....................................	434,909 16	....	434,909 16
Overseas balances unrecovered and in adjustment.....	....	22,957 22	22,957 22
Total Miscellaneous Payments...........	135,561,760 87	122,516,404 71	258,078,165 58
	173,454,386 14	124,836,644 52	298,291,030 66
Expended prior to 1st April, 1916.........	167,308,820 64	46,301,209 33	213,610,029 97
Totals........................	340,763,206 78	171,137,853 85	511,901,060 63

*Includes Medical Equipment.

APPENDIX B

The following table shows the changes in the strength of the Permanent Force from April 1, 1916, to March 31, 1917.

Corps.	Officers and Warrant Officers, effective 1-4-16.	N.C.O's and Men, effective 1-4-16.	Increases during Year.				Decreases during the Year.											Officers, Warrant Officers, N.C.O's and Men Effective 31-3-17.		
			Transfers from other corps.	Enlisted.	Re-enlisted.	Rejoined from desertion.	By purchase	Time expired.	Unsuitable.	Misconduct.	Medically unfit.	Other causes.	Deserted.	Deceased.	Transfers to other Corps, etc.	Promotions to Warrant Rank.	Officers.	Warrant Officers.	N.C.O's and men.
Royal Canadian Dragoons	14	54	8		4				4	1		2	1		28	1	7	2	35
Royal Canadian Dragoons Ins. Cadre		2	2														1	1	1
Lord Strathcona's Horse (R.C.)	8	151		156	60	1	1	43	43	1	13		9	1	106		7		195
Lord Strathcona's Horse (R.C.) Ins. Cadre																			
Royal Canadian Horse Artillery	10	257	10	1				2	1	2		1		1	208		15	5	45
Royal Canadian Garrison Artillery	40	384	44	58	2	5		8	3	4	4	5	12	1	188		32	10	274
Royal Canadian Engineers	29	381	84	239		3	1	1	3	16	14	6	12	4	260		19	12	389
Royal Canadian Regiment	17	311	62	101	1			3	3	1	6	2	5	2	280		6	1	175
Royal Canadian Regiment Ins. Cadre		57	10														10	10	47
Canadian Permanent Army Service Corps	27	235	18	67				1	8	9	4	4	2		41	1	20	8	250
Permanent Army Medical Corps	12	87	10	8				1	1	1		1	1		22		7	2	78
Canadian Permanent Army Veterinary Corps	2	3															2	1	2
Canadian Ordnance Corps	54	398	44	70	5			6	1	4	4	8	4		75	1	30	22	417
Canadian Army Pay Corps	23	38	10	6								5					20	4	43
Corps of Military Staff Clerks	14	92	10	23			1	1							10		8	17	99
Corps of Military Staff Clerks (Early Service Section "B")	2	40	10	19											11		1	1	57
Physical Training Instructors		7																	4
Musketry Staff	5	1		1											2		5	1	2
Signalling Staff	3		2												17		1		1
Militia Officers attached for duty	95																78		
Officers and N.C.O's in England and Abroad	2	4													1		1		4
Officers and N.C.O's on loan from British Army	12	6	2														12		8
Totals	369	2,510	314	749	72	12	5	23	67	43	41	28	46		1,253	3	282	103	2,126
	2,879																**2,511**		

The following Officers, Warrant Officers, Non-commissioned Officers and Men of the Permanent Force are paid from votes other than "Permanent Force Pay" and are not included in the above statement: 8 Officers, 1 Warrant Officer and 12 N.C.O's and Men are paid from the Royal Military College, and 4 N.C.O's and Men are paid from Topographical Survey. Average strength maintained during financial year 1916-17 was 2,352.

SESSIONAL PAPER No. 35

APPENDIX C.

NUMBER OF APPOINTMENTS TO PERMANENT STAFF AND PERMANENT FORCE, APRIL 1, 1916, TO MARCH 31, 1917.

Permanent Staff	7
Royal Canadian Dragoons	9
Lord Strathcona's Horse	4
Royal Canadian Artillery	18
Royal Canadian Engineers	4
Royal Canadian Regiment	2
Canadian Permanent Army Service Corps	5
Canadian Ordnance Corps	13
Corps of Military Staff Clerks	4
Canadian School of Musketry Corps	2
Total	68

NUMBER OF APPOINTMENTS TO THE ACTIVE MILITIA APRIL 1, 1916, TO MARCH 31, 1917.

Cavalry	382
Artillery	388
Engineers	190
Corps of Guides	29
Canadian Officers' Training Corps	88
Infantry	1,630
Canadian Army Service Corps	52
Army Medical Corps	690
Nursing Sisters, A.M.C.	678
Canadian Army Dental Corps	204
Canadian Army Veterinary Corps	55
Canadian Postal Corps	1
Corps of School Cadet Instructors	27
Canadian Militia, General List	341
Temporary Appointments, General List	723
Reserve of Officers	7
Reserve Militia	92
Total	5,577

WARRANTS GRANTED DURING THE PERIOD APRIL 1, 1916, TO MARCH 31, 1917.

Granted	79
Temporary	8

8 GEORGE V, A. 1918

APPENDIX D.

RETURN of Certificates granted Officers between

Name of School and Place Obtained.	CAVALRY.			ARTILLERY.			INFANTRY.		
	Field Officer.	Captain.	Lieut.	Field Officer.	Captain.	Lieut.	Field Officer.	Captain.	Lieut.
R. S. of C., Toronto	3	8	110			1			1
R. S. of A., Kingston					11	303			12
" Quebec						46			
" Halifax			1	3	8	118			1
" Esquimalt			1	1	1	17			8
R. S. of I., Halifax	5	16	31	3	7	11	61	170	237
" Esquimalt	12	35	53		2	5	77	95	209
R.M.C. Qualifications									
Provl. S. of Cavalry	7	11	37						2
" Artillery						1			
" Engineers								1	
" Infantry	57	153	324	2	4	18	377	878	2,020
" A.M.C.		1							
" C.A.S.C.			1			1			9
" C.A.V.C.									
Sch. of Signalling			10			4		1	82
" Musketry	6	6	85	1	1	7	27	47	466
B. of Ex. Equitation		1	36	2		13	18	89	470
Musk.—Machine Guns		1	47			10	2	10	350
Qr. Mr's. Duties									
Mechanical Transport						1			8
Partials Granted									
C.O.T.C. Candidates									
C.S.C.I. Grade "A"									
Probationers									
Totals	90	232	736	12	34	556	562	1,291	3,875

SESSIONAL PAPER No. 35

April 1, 1916, and March 31, 1917.

R.M.C. Cadets	C.O.T.C.			Engineers			C. of Guides		Army Medical Corps				C.A.S.C.			C.A.V.C.			Cadets	Total
	Field Officer	Captain	Lieut.	Field Officer	Captain	Lieut.	Captain	Lieut.	Field Officer	Captain	Lieut.	Nursing Sister	Field Officer	Captain	Lieut.	Field Officer	Captain	Lieut.	C.S.C.I.	
								6												129
																				326
44																				90
			1				1	4												137
																				28
	5	7	5			3	1	3												565
	1	1	1			4	2	1	1						2					501
3																				3
																				57
																				1
				3	15	119														138
	9	55	64		11	26	7	30	1	4	2		1	4	5					4,052
						1			4	365		54								425
														7	112					130
																3	4	6		13
		1	8					1							1					108
2		3	19			1		1							3					675
	1	11	22		1	142		6		12	81		1	1	111			1		1,019
2			8					3												433
											8									8
															25					34
																				378
																				771
																			72	72
																				1,790
51	16	78	128	3	27	295	12	55	6	381	91	54	2	12	259	3	4	7	72	11,883

2 Captains and 7 Lieutenants, C.A.D.C., qualified in Equitation............................. 9

Officers total...11,892

N.C.O's. total... 9,291
Physical Training... 3,508

Grand Total..24,691

8 GEORGE V, A. 1918

RETURN of N.C.O's Certificates granted at Royal and Provisional Schools between April 1, 1916, and March 31, 1917.

Name of Schools.	Bomb-ardiers.	Cor-porals.	Ser-geants.	Staff Sergts.	Buglers	Equit-ation.	Q.M.-Sergts.	Artifi-cers.	Bomb-ing	Trench War-fare.	Machine Gun.	Instructors.	Sig-nall'g.	Total.
Royal Schools of Cavalry		17	12			1								30
Royal Schools of Artillery	65	56	426		32		3							582
R y l Schools of Engineers														115
Royal Schools of Intry		171	655											826
Prov'l Schools of		5	12											17
Prov'l Schools of Engineers		3	122											125
Prov'l Schools of Infantry		1,515	3,498	1	36		2							5,049
Por'l Schools of A.M.C		9	40											52
Prov'l Schools of A.S.C			12											12
Halifax School of Ordnance			25											25
Bd. of Examiners Equitation						4								4
Schools of Signalling													1,551	1,551
Sls of Musketry								115			227	92		319
Trench Warfare										157				157
Schools of Bombing									427					427
Totals	66	1,776	4,802	1	68	5	5	115	427	157	227	92	1,551	9,291

Military District No. 1, London	147
" 2, Toronto	2,991
" 3, Kingston	454
" 4, Montreal	86
" 5, Quebec	Nil.
" 6, Halifax	566
" 10, Winnipeg	1,158
" 11, Victoria	823
" 12, Regina	157
" 13, Calgary	1,039
Schools of Signalling	1,551
Schools of Musketry	319
Grand total	9,291

APPENDIX E.

ANNUAL REPORT OF THE COMMANDANT ROYAL MILITARY COLLEGE OF CANADA, 1916-7.

SPECIAL WAR COMMISSIONS.

No diminution has been shown this last year in the eagerness of the Gentlemen Cadets to obtain Commissions at the earliest possible opportunity, and this magnificent spirit is worthy of the finest traditions of the College.

During the last year the following Commissions have been granted:—

Imperial Army	26
Canadian Permanent Force	21
Canadian Overseas Contingents	9
Total	56

The total number of Commissions granted direct from the College since the war commenced, and up till December 31, 1916, is as follows:—

Imperial Army	98
Canadian Permanent Force	89
Canadian Overseas Contingents	59
Total	246

Between 700 and 800 graduates and ex-cadets of the College are fighting in the various theatres of operations, and of these I deeply regret to report seventy-six have made the supreme sacrifice. Two graduates are commanding Canadian Divisions at the present time.

Up to date the services of graduates and ex-cadets have been recognized by the bestowal of 130 decorations, not including quite a number of Foreign Orders. The number of " Mentions in Despatches " is also very large.

This short résumé of the College's share in the present campaign emphasizes the high sense of duty which has always been the chief characteristic of the Gentlemen Cadets.

DISCIPLINE.

The discipline of the College continues to be excellent.

A fine spirit of *esprit de corps* is very noticeable amongst the Gentlemen Cadets.

The N.C.O's—necessarily inexperienced as they are—have helped the Staff considerably.

ATTENDANCE.

At the commencement of the College term in August, 1916, a recruit class of ninety-five were admitted, making the total number of Gentlemen Cadets in residence one hundred and thirty-nine. Both of these totals constitute College records.

In November, 1916, nineteen cadets of the Senior Class were granted Commissions; in January, 1917, one, and in March last, seven.

The present total of Gentlemen Cadets in residence is one hundred and four. Of these, ten will be leaving at the end of May, fifty at the end of July, and the balance will be eligible for Commissions at the end of the year.

SUPERIOR STAFF.

Several important changes have taken place on the College Staff since the last visit of the Board of Visitors.

May 10, 1916, Professor I. E. Martin, the Senior Professor and Head of the Scientific Department, was appointed to act as Director of Studies.

At the end of the present session Lieut.-Col. S. A. Thompson, Professor of Tactics and Topography, will be leaving the College, on the expiration of his period of appointment. I am much indebted to him for his valuable services.

Major M. V. Plummer, Royal Artillery, the Acting Professor of Artillery, and a graduate of the College, left the Staff at the end of the last session. At the urgent request of the authorities he had volunteered in 1915 to remain for an extra year, and I have nothing but praise for his high sense of duty and his help during the period he was at the College.

August 1, 1916, Captain H. C. Wotherspoon, 46th Regiment, Canadian Militia—who was unfit for active service—was appointed as Acting Staff Adjutant.

Capt. H. H. Lawson, Canadian Field Artillery—a graduate of this College—was appointed Instructor of Survey on November 1, 1916.

Professor R. O. Sweezy, Acting Professor of Survey, owing to pressure of private business, asked to be relieved of his duties at the end of last October.

I regret exceedingly to have to report that towards the end of 1916 it became necessary for Prof. A. Laird, the Professor of English, to tender his resignation owing to a breakdown in health. To the great sorrow of all ranks he died on May 10 last.

Mr. W. R. P. Bridger, M.A., was appointed Instructor in Mathematics, and came to the College from the staff of Trinity College School, Port Hope, on January 1, 1917.

Captain C. C. Adams, M.C., Royal Engineers, was appointed as Instructor in Military Engineering and Signalling, and reported at the College November 23, 1916.

Capt. B. F. Rhodes, M.C., Royal Field Artillery, was appointed Instructor in Artillery, and took over his duties on January 12, 1917.

I am very deeply grateful to the Staff, both Superior and Subordinate, for their never failing readiness to co-operate in all matters relative to the efficiency and welfare of the Gentlemen Cadets.

SUBORDINATE STAFF.

There have been a few changes amongst the Subordinate Staff.

Company Serg.-Major E. Shuter, Coldstream Guards, was appointed to the Staff June 30, 1916, as Assistant Instructor in Drill and Gymnastics.

I much regret to have to report that on January 30, 1917, Servant F. W. Anson died of pneumonia. He had been on the College Staff for over nineteen years and had won the admiration and respect of the College by his high sense of duty.

Sergt.-Major F. Ruffell, Royal Canadian Engineers, left the College at the end of April, on the termination of his engagement.

SESSIONAL PAPER No. 35

PENSIONS TO CIVIL MEMBERS OF THE SUPERIOR STAFF.

A scheme of pay for the Civil permanent members of this Staff was recommended in your last report, and has been adopted. This scheme was drafted with regard to classification and remuneration in such a manner as to place the Staff here on a level with that of the Universities in Canada, with which Institutions we are in competition for the services of the best men available.

In order to make positions on this Staff as attractive as those in other Canadian Educational Institutions I feel that equal consideration must be offered with respect to retirement from the Staff with a view to efficiency, and as our Universities have each a pension scheme under the Carnegie Foundation, I think that we should also be provided with one suitable to our situation. I wish to submit the following for consideration and, I hope, approval, that it may be incorporated into the Royal Military College Act by authority of the Governor General in Council, as was the scheme of pay so recently adopted.

The scheme for retirement is identical with that which was approved by the Board of Visitors for 1909, and this approval was re-affirmed by the Board of 1912, and for the same reasons I hope will be endorsed by the present Board for immediate action.

PROPOSED SCHEME FOR PENSIONS ON RETIREMENT.

A member of the Superior Staff of the Royal Military College, not otherwise provided for, may be retired to promote the efficiency of the Staff, under the following conditions:—

(a) If he has reached the age of fifty years, and the duration of his services has been ten years or more, he shall receive an annuity, for life, of 50 per cent of the annual salary he was enjoying at the time of his retirement, with an additional 2 per cent of such salary for each year's service over and above ten, but the maximum annuity shall not exceed 70 per cent of the salary at the time of retirement.

(b) If he is under fifty years of age on retirement, with at least ten years' service, he shall receive an annuity—as before described—less 2 per cent of the salary for each year he is under fifty.

(c) If the duration of his services has been less than ten years, he shall receive for each year's service a gratuity of one-tenth of his annual salary at the time of his retirement.

(d) In case of voluntary retirement, with the approval of the Government, the gratuity will be as previously stated herein, but the annuity will be subject to a reduction of 20 per cent if the retiring member of the Staff has not reached the age of fifty.

(e) The widow of a member of the Staff, to whom she has been married at least ten years before his retirement, shall receive one-half of the allowances which would have gone to her husband if he had retired at the time of his death, or which he was enjoying at the time.

(f) Annuities shall be paid in monthly instalments, clear of all taxes and deductions, whatsoever, imposed under any Act of Parliament of Canada.

MEDICAL ARRANGEMENTS.

On July 15, 1916, Lieut.-Col. R. J. Gardiner, was appointed Medical Officer of the College in the place of Major R. K. Kilborn, deceased.

The College this year has been singularly unlucky in infectious diseases. Measles, scarlatina, and mumps have all contributed cases to the Hospital. Measles has been especially troublesome, but it was of a very mild form.

8 GEORGE V, A. 1918

The general health of the Gentlemen Cadets otherwise has been excellent.

STATISTICS OF PHYSICAL DEVELOPMENT OF CADETS.

Recruit Class. Date of Inspection.	AVERAGE INDIVIDUAL INCREASES SINCE LAST MEASUREMENT.						
	No. in Class.	Average Age.	Height.	Weight.	Chest.	Forearm.	Upper Arm.
August, 1916...............	92	17·11	5·8¼	134½	33	10½	11
May, 1917........:........	91	18·8	5·8½	144	34	10¾	11¾
Increase from August, 1916, to May, 1917...............	....	·9	¼	9½	1	¼	¾

RIDING.

Since my last report I am pleased to say the much needed Riding School has been completed and is in full use. Previous to its erection, riding, during the winter months was, to all intents and purposes, impossible.

Major W. F. Ingpen is in charge, assisted by Capt. B. F. Rhodes, M.C., R.F.A. Under these two Officers the Gentlemen Cadets are rapidly improving in a very marked degree.

The personnel of the Riding Establishment have carried out their duties very satisfactorily.

R.M.C. REGULATIONS.

I have submitted many recommendations for amending the existing Regulations of the College, and I hope they will receive official sanction.

The recommendations include one to make the course at the College a period of four years—as it was prior to 1896. The re-adoption of this period would necessitate the lowering of the present minimum age limit by one year.

There are so many points in favour of the increased period of one year that I hope most careful consideration will be given the whole subject and that it will finally be approved.

ENTRANCE EXAMINATION SYLLABUS.

After a consulation with several of the principals of the schools whose candidates enter the College, I applied for and obtained permission to alter the syllabus of subjects for the Examination for admission.

The alterations made are as follows, and will come into force this year:—

> The papers in General Knowledge and Chemistry were abolished from the compulsory subjects, and Latin, which had hitherto been voluntary, was made compulsory.
> Geometrical Drawing, Free-hand Drawing, and Drill were abolished as Voluntary Subjects.

Thus the number of papers were reduced from fifteen to ten and all the papers are now compulsory. The change was much needed and the results obtained in future will, I think, give the examiners a better idea of the academic standing of the candidates for admission.

I consider the minimum qualifying percentage for the subjects of the examination for admission (which is at present 33 per cent) should be raised to conform with that required for matriculation. The existing percentage is easy to obtain and gives the examiner little scope in his subject.

ATTACHMENT OF GENTLEMEN CADETS TO THE PERMANENT FORCE.

The system of attaching Gentlemen Cadets to branches of the service in the Permanent Force they will eventually join is being continued with good results.

Last year the Cadets went to Petawawa for six weeks and greatly benefited by the practical experience in Artillery. This year similar approval has again been given.

MESSING.

Owing to the difficulty of obtaining male labour it was considered necessary to employ female labour in the College kitchen. The experiment has been an unqualified success and it is not too much to say the messing has very materially improved in quality and cooking.

Mrs. Douglas, who is in charge of the Kitchen Staff, is a very efficient house-keeper and the kitchen premises are a model of cleanliness.

The cost of Messing per head per diem is sixty cents.

BUILDINGS.

I would again like to bring to notice the very urgent need for additional class room accommodation. We have now some 120 to 130 Cadets working, messing, and spending their recreation hours in a building that was originally, I believe, intended to accommodate fifty-six Cadets.

I am well aware that war contingencies are very pressing but I respectfully urge that the needs of the rising generation are also very important, and that as the College is rapidly increasing in size, popularity, and usefulness, the urgent necessity of keeping pace with this increase becomes more apparent daily.

UNIFORM AND CLOTHING.

Since my last report the new uniform—approved of last year—has been adopted. A certain amount of criticism has been levelled at the mixture of blue undress worn with the British Warm Greatcoats. It should be borne in mind, however, that in pre-war days this was in accordance with the Dress Regulations.

A change of uniform is nearly always unpopular until the necessity of it becomes apparent.

I quite agree that khaki service dress looks better with a khaki greatcoat, and I see no reason why an Officer's pattern khaki service dress should not be adopted. If, however, it is, the blue undress should be abolished to avoid extra expense and a plethora of " Orders of Dress."

Although the Tunic and Mess Dress have not been issued since the war began, I think it would be a great mistake to abolish them and hope to see them again introduced after the war is over.

The articles of uniform necessary for a Gentleman Cadet are as follows:—

1 Full dress (i.e., tunic).
2 suits of khaki service dress or blue.
1 Mess dress.
1 Rain Coat.
1 British Warm Coat.
1 or two pairs of riding breeches.

The college clothing contract for the past year has been more satisfactory but delay in the issue of clothing is bound to occur so long as the increasingly. large contract is left to one firm.   I still consider the contract should be divided up, as I recommended in my report for last year, and three or four firms employed to complete it.

INDOOR IMPROVEMENTS.

A chlorinating filtration plant has been installed in the Power house and has so far worked fairly satisfactorily.   The alum filter occasionally got out of order, but now that the chlorinating plant has been added the bacteriological analysis of the water has improved.

The rooms in the dormitories have been furnished with new tables and chests-of-drawers—a much needed improvement.

The old desks and chairs in the Class rooms, which had been in use for a very long period have all been replaced by new ones.

The Commandant's Quarters have been renovated and put into a sound state of repairs.

OUTDOOR IMPROVEMENTS.

The scheme to turn the precincts of Fort Frederick into a vegetable garden has been found impracticable owing to the insufficient depth of surface soil.

The planting of ornamental trees still continues and I hope to extend the system of flower beds.

Since last year a cart roadway has been made leading from the lower entrance drive to the back of the Educational, Building.   This will prevent the necessity of tradesmen's carts using the front drive.

The adoption of the hydro-electric power system would remove the many unsightly poles and overhead wires that exist at present.

VISITORS.

His Royal Highness the Duke of Connaught paid his farewell visit as Governor General on the 21st September, 1916.

Mr. F. B. McCurdy, Parliamentary Secretary to the Department of Militia and Defence, and the Adjutant General, visited the College on the 28th September 1916.

Lieut. Peckhoff, French Foreign Legion, visited the College on November 20th, 1916.

His Excellency the Duke of Devonshire, Governor General, visited the College on May 7th last.

Many graduates from the front have also come during the last year.

C. N. PERREAU, Colonel, General Staff,

Commandant, Royal Military College of Canada.

KINGSTON, 24th May, 1917.

SESSIONAL PAPER No. 35

ROYAL MILITARY COLLEGE—REPORT OF THE BOARD OF VISITORS, 1917.

The Board assembled at the Royal Military College, Kingston, Ont., at 3.30 p.m., on Friday the 25th day of May, 1917.

PRESENT:

Chairman—Major-Gen. W. E. Hodgins, Acting Adjutant-General.

Members—The Rt. Hon. Lord Shaughnessy, K.C.V.O.,
  Major-Gen. E. W. Wilson, G.O.C. M.D. No. 4 (for Lt.-Col. H. J.
  Lamb, D.S.O., overseas),
  Col. R. A. Helmer, Director General of Musketry (for the Chief
  of the General Staff).
Secretary—Capt. J. S. Chenay for Col. C. S. MacInnes, D.A.G.

The following members were unavoidably absent:—

  Major-Gen. W. Gwatkin, C.B., Chief of the General Staff.
  Hon.-Lt.-Col. The Rev. Monsignor Dauth.
  Hon.-Col. R. A. Falconer, C.M.G., M.A., LL.D., D. Litt., President
  of the University of Toronto.
  Major-General S. C. Mewburn, Director General Canadian Defence
  Force.
  Lt.-Col. C. W. Rowley.
  Rt. Rev. C. F. Worrell, D.D., D.C.L., Archbishop of Nova Scotia.

The Board, having assembled, proceeded to interview the Commandant, Col. C. N. Perreau, Royal Dublin Fusiliers, and discussed with him the various matters which he brought before them. The Board also had personal interviews with members of the military and civil staffs and with gentlemen cadets, also inspected the cadets at drill, physical training, riding, bayonet fighting, machine gun practice and bombing.

The grounds and building were also carefully inspected and the working of the various departments inquired into.

GENERAL REMARKS.

The members of the Board of Visitors were particularly impressed by the deplorable shortage of anything like adequate class-room accommodation and the erection of a suitable building providing the necessary number of class-rooms, the space for scientific and technical training and a general gathering place for the gentlemen cadets, as outlined in this report, is earnestly urged. The lamentable lack of sufficient dormitory accommodation is also apparent and the necessary additional space should be provided as soon as possible.

The Board desire to place on record the following expression of appreciation by the Rt. Hon. Lord Shaughnessy, K.C.V.O., on the occasion of his first visit to the Royal Military College:—

  " If I may be permitted, as an individual member of the Board who is paying his first visit to the Royal Military College, I should like to express my appreciation of the discipline, training in all branches, cleanliness and fine morale that were in evidence throughout.

35—3

" While I have a theory as to the manner in which the educational system may be broadened so as to increase the efficiency of the College as a national training school, I have a strong conviction that, as conducted at present, the College is a most valuable asset in the national life of Canada."

The Board also desire to bring to notice the splendid part which graduates of the Royal Military College are taking in the present war. Since the present war commenced, 246 commissions in the Imperial and Canadian Service have been granted to graduates and there are between 700 and 800 graduates now serving in the various theatres of operations, two of whom are commanding Canadian Divisions. The large number of decorations won by graduates gives evidence of the excellent service rendered by them. It is with the deepest regret that the Board records the fact that seventy-six graduates have already made the extreme sacrifice during the present war

DIRECTOR OF STUDIES.

The Board considered the question of the confirmation of the appointment of a Director of Studies and of the emoluments which should be authorized for this appointment, and are of the opinion that the practical results obtained justify the confirmation of the appointment, and the granting of an allowance in lieu of quarters, fuel and light, in addition to first grade salary, to place the appointment on a higher plane than that of Professor.

The Board therefore recommends the confirmation of the appointment and the payment of an annual allowance of $665 in lieu of house, fuel and light.

PENSIONS TO CIVIL MEMBERS OF THE SUPERIOR STAFF.

The question of pensions for the civil members of the staff was carefully considered. The Commandant recommended endorsation of the scheme approved by the Board of Visitors in 1909 and 1912, but after an examination of this scheme and all other suggestions submitted, the Board strongly recommends that all civil members of the superior staff of the Royal Military College should be given temporary rank in the Canadian Militia, while holding their appointments, and that on retirement they elect to accept either a Militia pension, subject to payment of necessary deductions, or a gratuity as at present.

QUALIFYING PERCENTAGE, ENTRANCE EXAMINATION.

The Board discussed the question of increasing the qualifying percentage in the subjects of the Entrance Examination, and, as a result, are of the opinion that the percentage required to qualify in each subject should be increased from 33 per cent to 50 per cent, and the percentage on the whole examination should be raised to 60 per cent.

The Board therefore recommend that the qualifying percentages set forth above should be approved.

UNIFORM.

At the suggestion of the Commandant the Board considered the advisability of adopting khaki in place of blue undress uniform but recommended that this question be allowed to stand until next year.

SESSIONAL PAPER No. 35

RE-ADOPTION OF A FOUR YEARS' COURSE.

The question of re-adopting a four years' course of instruction, with the necessary corollary of a reduction in the age limit on entering, was given careful consideration, but the Board is not prepared to recommend this change at present.

CLOTHING.

The Board is of the opinion that action should be taken to overcome the great delays which now arise in the supply of uniform to the Cadets. Under the present system, cadets never have their complete kits before Christmas and sometimes not even before Easter. This is entirely unsatisfactory and should be remedied at once.

After carefully considering various suggestions, the Board beg to recommend that, in order to ensure uniformity and avoid the great delays which now occur, arrangements should be at once made for the issue, by the Canadian Ordnance Corps, of the requisite supplies of uniform for the Cadets, such to be issued on repayment.

This is the only arrangement which, in the opinion of the Board, would satisfactorily settle the matter.

DISCIPLINE.

The Board begs to report that the high standard of discipline which has existed in previous years has been fully maintained. No serious offences have been reported.

DRILL, PHYSICAL TRAINING, ETC.

The inspection of the Cadets in drill and physical training was most satisfactory and reflects much credit upon the instructors, Hon.-Lieut. S. C. Cutbush and Company Sgt.-Major E. Shuter, Coldstream Guards. The practical instruction in Machine-gun Work, Bayonet Fighting and Bombing has produced excellent results and will be most useful to the Cadets.

EQUITATION.

The Board is pleased to note the great improvement in riding which has been made possible by the erection of the much-needed Riding School. Riding Instruction during the winter is now possible and the instructors, Major W. F. Ingpén and Capt. B.·F. Rhodes, M.C., have made good use of the increased facilities for instruction.

MESSING.

No complaints were received concerning the messing of the Cadets, which, owing to the scarcity of male labour, is now carried out by a staff of female employees, in charge of Mrs. Douglas, who has proven herself most efficient. The kitchen and pantry have been re-modelled and supplied with up-to-date apparatus. Everything was found scrupulously clean and in excellent shape.

The cost of messing is 60 cents per head per diem and the quality and cooking is reported as having materially improved this year.

8 GEORGE V, A. 1918

INCREASED ACCOMMODATION.

The Board consider that a very urgent need for increased class accommodation exists and that immediate action to provide this accommodation and to lay out a definite plan for the future expansion of the College should be taken. During the past year it has been constantly necessary to refuse candidates for admission to the College, owing to lack of accommodation and the large number of Cadets in attendance this year made it necessary to divide the classes into two, thus imposing a double amount of work upon the staff.

The limited accommodation has also made it impossible to carry out the desired amount of practical instructions in physics, chemistry and mechanics, the value of which has been made so apparent during the present war. No addition to the Education Building has been made since the establishment of the College, and the number of Cadets attending is greatly in excess of what it was intended for.

It is therefore recommended that an extension to the Educational Building, to provide additional class-room and laboratory accommodation, workshops for mechanical and military engineering, increased facilities for library and reading rooms, and more extended scientific training should be authorized at once as a War Measure.

The Board also found the present Dormitory accommodation taxed to the utmost and consider that additional accommodation is absolutely necessary unless the number of Cadets admitted each term is to be limited. The Board recommend that provision should at once be made for an addition to the new Dormitory Building.

Respectfully submitted,

W. E. HODGINS, Major-General, Acting Adjutant General.

Chairman Board of Visitors.

SHAUGHNESSY,

E. W. WILSON, Major-General,

G.O.C. M.D. No. 4.

R. A. HELMER, Colonel,

Director General of Musketry.

Members, Board of Visitors.

APPENDIX F.

REPORT OF THE SUPERINTENDENT, DOMINION ARSENAL, FOR THE YEAR ENDING DECEMBER 31, 1917.

The Superintendent of the Dominion Arsenal reports as follows:—

EMPLOYEES.

The average number of employees throughout the year was 858.

STATEMENTS.

1. Appropriation Account.   4. Assets and Liabilities.

2. Customs Account.   5. Capital Account.

3. Details of Net Expenditure.   6. Indirect Expenditure.

APPROPRIATION AND EXPENDITURE ACCOUNT, 1916–17.

Credits..$	1,383,482 17	
Refunds..	82,926 88	
Transfer Warrant...	153 84	
		$ 1,466,562 89

Net Expenditure...$	1,384,153 09	
Headquarter's erroneous charge against Dominion Arsenal.........	15,643 00	
" " " "	234 96	
" " " · "	190 00	
" " " "	449 10	
Balance in Bank deposited to the credit of the Receiver General on 31st March, 1917..	65,871 37	
Cash Balance deposited to the credit of the Receiver General on 31st March, 1917..	21 37	
		$ 1,466,562 89

CUSTOMS ACCOUNT IN 1916–17.

(Not chargeable against Dominion Arsenal vote.)

Credits received... ....$	46,500 00	

Custom Dues paid and charged against Capital and Production Accounts:........$	42,064 65	
Amount unexpended deposited to the credit of the Receiver General on 31st March, 1917..	4,435 35	
	$	46,500 00

DETAILS OF EXPENDITURE, 1916–17.

Wages	$ 487,865 40
Wages, "Special Service"	6,783 00
Salaries	22,749 53
Material	807,035 27
Telegrams, telephones and postage	602 59
Freight	1,482 25
Equipment, general (pulleys, hangers, shafting, etc)	11,418 57
Printing and Stationery	2,109 41
Electricity and gas	21,722 60
Cartage and cabs	6,139 39
Belting	1,574 48
Machinery	7,634 06
Travelling expenses	2,460 21
Miscellaneous	221 93
Medicines	273 88
Office fixtures, etc	410 68
Snow removal	673 60
Suspense Account	911 50
Water supply	1,912 00
Tools	122 55
Advances for travelling expenses	50 19
	$1,384,153 09

STATEMENT OF ASSETS AND LIABILITIES, MARCH 31, 1917.

	Dr. Liabilities.	Cr. Assets.
	$ cts.	$ cts.
Real Estate, (factory stores and office buildings)	....	174,489 91
Belting	....	2,242 66
Department of Militia and Defence (amount to credit of)	898,608 31	
Equipment, general (shafting, hangers, pulleys, etc.)	....	20,108 19
Machinery	....	147,867 14
Office furniture, fixtures, etc	....	971 54
Material	....	309,630 12
Suspense Account (amount in store charge and not paid, or else paid for and not yet received)	1,818 37	
Tools, loose	....	484 08
Accounts payable	25,856 27	
Accounts receivable	....	1,573 23
Semi-manufactures (work in course of completion)	....	268,916 08
	926,282 95	926,282 95

CAPITAL ACCOUNT, 1916–17—BUILDINGS, MACHINERY, ETC.

	$ cts.	$ cts.
To Balance Account:—		
For net Capital on 1st April, 1916—		
Buildings	162,554 81	
Machinery	141,810 11	
Tools	456 31	
Equipment, general	7,984 08	
Belting	1,645 08	
Office furniture, fixtures, etc.	579 75	
Dominion Arsenal (Lindsay)	11,773 20	
		326,803 34
To Accruement in 1916–17—		
On Machinery	4,257 16	
" Buildings (repairs and maintenance)	18,534 15	
" Tools	122 55	
" Equipment, general	15,355 34	
" Office furniture, fixtures, etc.	429 78	
" Belting	1,584 07	
" Dominion Arsenal (Lindsay)	38,778 36	
		425,864 75

	$ cts.	$ cts.
By Indirect Expenditure Account:—		
For Depreciation in 1916–17 on—		
Buildings	6,599 05	
Machinery	18,200 13	
Tools	94 78	
Equipment, general	3,231 23	
Belting	986 49	
Office furniture, fixtures, etc.	37 99	
		29,149 67
By Balance Account:—		
For Net ... on 31st March, 1917—		
Buildings		174,489 91
Machinery		147,867 14
Tools		484 08
Equipment, general		20,108 19
Belting ... fixtures, etc.		2,242 66
Office ... fixtures ...		971 54
Union Arsenal		50,551 56
(This account is now transferred to account of the		
D ... of Militia and Defence).		
		425,864 75

8 GEORGE V, A. 1918

Statement of Indirect Expenditure, 1916–17.

Expenditure on the following services, not charged to any special work:—

Salaries...$		20,431 81
Wages...		21,118 39
Wages, "Special Service"...		6,783 00
Material..		3,500 38
Electricity and gas...		366 73
Travelling expenses..		1,154 92
Cartage and cabs...		1,980 24
Printing and Stationery...		1,608 67
Telegrams, telephones and postage............................		455 02
Miscellaneous..		204 43
Medicines..		273 88
Customs dues...		651 45
Freight...		161 30
Snow removal...		673 60
Water supply..		52 00

Repairs to heating system and electric light wires:—

Wages...$	1,341 86		
Material, etc..	329 35		
			1,671 21

From Capital Account:—

3 per cent depreciation on	Buildings.................................$	5,014 75		
10 " "	Machinery...............................	14,473 26		
20 " "	Tools......................................	94 78		
50 " "	Belting...................................	986 49		
30 " "	Equipment..............................	3,230 28		
5 " "	Office fixtures.........................	37 99		
				23,837 55

	84,924 58
Less—amount taken in relief of indirect expenditure................................	7,754 08
	$ 77,170 50

Note.—This amount, together with indirect expenditure of each factory, has been distributed as a general percentage on direct labour, in each factory, as shown below:—

Workshop...	39·50	per cent.
Cartridge Factory..	30·31	"
Rolling Mill..	31·19	"
Shell Factory..	80·10	"
Carpenter's Shop..	21·54	"
Tool Room...	40·60	"
Charger Plant...	106·68	"
Laboratory...	48·10	"
Examining Room..	14·86	"
18-pr. Plant..	47·60	"

REPORT

OF THE

DEPARTMENT OF LABOUR

FOR THE

Fiscal Year ending March 31, 1917

PRINTED BY ORDER OF PARLIAMENT

OTTAWA
J. DE LABROQUERIE TACHÉ
PRINTER TO THE KING'S MOST EXCELLENT MAJESTY
1918

[No. 36—1918]

To His Excellency the Duke of Devonshire, K.G., P.C., G.C.M.G., G.C.V.O., etc.,
etc., Governor General and Commander in Chief of the Dominion of Canada.

MAY IT PLEASE YOUR EXCELLENCY:

The undersigned has the honour to forward to Your Excellency the accompanying report of the Deputy Minister on the work of the Department of Labour of the Dominion of Canada for the fiscal year ended March 31, 1917, all of which is respectfully submitted.

T. W. CROTHERS,
Minister of Labour.

36—1½

CONTENTS

REPORT OF THE DEPUTY MINISTER OF· LABOUR

FOR THE

FISCAL YEAR ENDED MARCH 31, 1917

To the Hon. T. W. CROTHERS, K.C., M.P.,
    Minister of Labour.

SIR,—I have the honour to submit a report on the work of the Department of Labour for the fiscal year ended March 31, 1917.

The world war has continued to affect many aspects of departmental work, especially in so far as concerns its connection with industrial disputes and the collection of information as to food prices, wages, etc. The return for the year as to the number of disputes, time losses, etc., is less satisfactory than that for the preceding year, which was the lowest on the departmental record, but shows, none the less, the comparative absence in Canada of the industrial unrest which was markedly prevalent during the few years immediately preceding the war, and which has persisted in many countries. The increasing cost of living continued to be a main ground of argument for increased wages, and judging by the relative rarity of prolonged or disastrous strikes the point has been freely conceded. Numerous wage increases have been made by employers voluntarily, and in other cases adjustments have been effected after entirely amicable negotiations. Officers of the department have been able in many cases to assist the parties in reaching a conclusion in these difficult matters, sometimes by correspondence and at other times by personal mediation. A chapter of the report gives some particulars on this point.

About the usual proportion of disputes have been dealt with under the terms of the Industrial Disputes Investigation Act, the registrar's report of proceedings under this statute appearing as usual as an appendix to the annual report.

The reports issued annually by the department on (1) Prices, and (2) Labour Organization in Canada, have appeared during the year.

The *Labour Gazette* has been published from month to month. While there has been no marked departure from the lines followed in the past, certain natural developments and improvements have been suggested and are indicated in a chapter devoted to the publication.

The Combines Investigation Act is administered under the authority of the Minister of Labour, but there have been during the year no proceedings under its provisions. The aim of this statute, it will be remembered, is to prevent undue enhancement of prices.

The rapid rise in cost of certain lines of food and other necessities of life caused the enactment, on the recommendation of the Minister of Labour, and under the War Measures Act, of an Order in Council intended to permit effective action where a price appeared to be unreasonably high, or to deal with other aspects of the situation in any way distressing to the public, and the Order in Council has been administered during the year under the minister's authority.

I have the honour to be, sir,

Your obedient servant,

F. A. ACLAND,
Deputy Minister of Labour.

DEPARTMENT OF LABOUR,
    Ottawa.   5

I. CONCILIATION **PROCEEDINGS.**

Much work is done by officers of the department by way of conciliation with respect to disputes of which word reaches the Minister or information is otherwise received, and the efforts thus made are frequently effective in preventing a threatened strike or, where a strike has actually occurred, in bringing the strike to a conclusion. This duty falls most frequently to officers who make it their special work, but on several occasions valuable assistance has been also rendered by correspondents of the *Labour Gazette* at industrial centres where the services of a special officer have not been available. There are at present five officers whose time is specially given to the work of conciliation, and who have become specially effective in the territories in which they are best known and in the industries with which they have been brought chiefly into contact. The officers in question are as follows: Mr. J. D. McNiven, who since 1911 has been stationed at Vancouver; Mr. F. W. Harrison, who since 1916 has been stationed at Calgary; Mr. T. Bertrand, who was appointed shortly after the close of the fiscal year, and who resides in Montreal; and Messrs. W. D. Killins and E. N. Compton, who are resident at Ottawa. Mr. McNiven's territory embraces the province of British Columbia, including the island of Vancouver. Mr. Harrison, at Calgary, is required to keep in touch, so far as possible, with the Prairie Provinces; a former officer, Mr. H. S. Hood, was resident in Winnipeg, but he having resigned no officer has been for the present appointed for that district, and Mr. Harrison may be called upon to come so far east as Winnipeg. Mr. Bertrand, established at Montreal, works chiefly in the province of Quebec, and may be called upon to visit the Maritime Provinces. Messrs. Killins and Compton, stationed at Ottawa, are sent to such places as may require their presence, but their activities are largely in Ontario, other duties occupying that portion of their time spent at Ottawa. The correspondents of the *Labour Gazette* who have during the year rendered assistance in conciliation work are the following: Miss Marion Findlay, Toronto; Mr. Frederick Urry, Port Arthur; Mr. John Moffatt, Sydney; Mr. Hugh Sweeney, Hamilton; and Mr. J. A. Killingsworth, St. Thomas.

There is no advantage in setting forth the details of the numerous disputes which come before the department in the course of a year, and where strikes are prevented. Where strikes are not prevented the disputes are reported in the strikes record. Where the dispute comes within the scope of the Industrial Disputes Investigation Act, and the strike is averted by procedure under that statute, the statement of the case appears in the record of the Registrar of Boards of Conciliation and Investigation. In many of the disputes where a settlement is secured by conciliation, and no strike takes place, the advantage lies, as a rule, in giving the matter as little publicity as possible, as a result of which the best work achieved in this direction often becomes known only to the chief representatives of the disputants themselves and to the Minister. In the appended lists are enumerated the disputes in which mediation work was done during the year, together with the briefest intimation of the nature of the dispute and the result of intervention:—

(1) The Acadia Coal Company, Limited, New Glasgow, N.S. Men had gone on strike on wage question. They returned to work and called for Board of Conciliation under Industrial Disputes Investigation Act, by which means the dispute was definitely arranged.

(2) Halifax Graving Dock, Halifax, N.S., and machinists. Wages demand; compromise effected.

(3) Halifax, boilermaking industry. Demand for wage increase; compromise effected.

(4) Welland Ship Canal at Thorold, Ontario. Strike of operating engineers threatened; agreement effected between the contractor and union officials.

(5) Algoma Steel Corporation, Sault Ste. Marie, Ontario. Dispute concerning alleged unfair dismissal of union officer, also as to wages and hours of work; wages increase conceded and other matters arranged.

(6) Ross Rifle Factory, Quebec City. Dispute concerning wage reductions and alleged unfair replacement of men by women; satisfactory arrangement effected.

(7) Quebec Railway, Light, Heat and Power Company, Quebec City. Alleged discrimination against union members and misinterpretation of award made under Industrial Disputes Investigation Act; adjustment effected.

(8) Buckley-Drouin Company and William Scully, Limited, clothing manufacturers, Montreal. Alleged subcontracting of government work infringing contract governing same; infringements of contract apparently unintentional and trouble adjusted.

(9) Grand Trunk Railway Shops, Stratford, Ontario. Strike threatened over alleged discrimination against union employees in staff reduction; matter arranged amicably.

(10) Dominion Coal Company Collieries, Cape Breton. Strike in No. 1 Mine, Dominion. Two unions in existence. Men returned to work and application made by each union for Board of Conciliation. Unions concerned not being in agreement Royal Commission appointed and dispute satisfactorily arranged.

(11) Confederation Construction Company, Welland Canal. Demand for new schedule with increased wages, strike being threatened; dispute arranged without cessation of work.

(12) Welland Ship Canal, Thorold. Sudden strike of labourers for increased wages. Work shortly resumed at former wage.

(13) Dominion Coal Company, St. John, N.B. Threatened strike on part of coal handlers; wages dispute; matters amicably arranged.

(14) John Inglis Company, Limited, Toronto. Complaints against arbitrary action on part of new superintendent, also wage dispute; short strike occurred; wage increase granted and other grievances adjusted.

(15) Peterborough, munitions factory. Question of overtime and hours, employees claiming a lockout; difficulties adjusted after a strike of two days.

(16) Halifax Ocean Terminals. Various wage difficulties with contractors adjusted and strike prevented.

(17) Simpson Knitting Mills, Toronto. Dispute growing out of misunderstanding *re* alterations which required temporary suspension of work; difficulties satisfactorily adjusted.

(18) Canada Steel Foundry, Limited, Welland, Ontario. Alleged unfair discharge of union officials and question of overtime pay; compromise effected.

(19) Dominion Transport Company and Shedden Forwarding Company, Montreal. Demand for wage increase; employees on strike for two weeks when compromise effected.

(20) Aetna Chemical Company and Westinghouse, Church, Kerr Company, Drummondville, P.Q. Dispute regarding wages; adjustment effected.

(21) John W. Peck Factory, Montreal. Wages dispute resulting in strike lasting two weeks, when agreement reached by negotiations.

(22) Newcastle, N.B., and neighbouring places. Lumber loaders on strike for higher wages; wage increase granted and dispute ended.

(23) Thetford Mines, P.Q. Dispute as to wages and working conditions between various asbestos mining operators and employees, the dispute including

8 GEORGE V, A. 1918

also alleged unfair use of enemy alien labour; application for Board of Conciliation, but machinery of statute not applicable because the several employers not in concert; men on strike for between two and three weeks; inquiry made under Royal Commission, which arranged satisfactory working agreement.

(24) Montreal Light, Heat and Power Company. Dispute as to wages; application made for Board of Conciliation but dispute adjusted by negotiations.

(25) Grain Elevators at Port Arthur and Fort William. Many elevator operators concerned; question of wages and conditions of work; men on strike for few days when working arrangement effected.

(26) Railway Cartage Companies and teamsters, Winnipeg. Dispute regarding wages; men on strike for few days when wage concessions made and dispute ended.

(27) National Transcontinental Railway, Transcona, Manitoba. Machinists on strike because of dispute growing out of alleged unfair employment of improvers to do machinists' work, compromise effected and dispute ended after week's strike.

(28) Pulp and Paper Company, Fort Frances, Ontario. Dispute as to wages and hours; employees on strike for a week when adjustment effected.

(29) Port Arthur Examining Warehouse contract. Wage claims against contractor satisfactorily adjusted.

(30) Canadian Pacific freight truckers, Calgary, Alberta. Wages dispute; employees on strike for few days when agreement effected.

(31) Edmonton, Dunvegan and British Columbia Railway. Dispute with train employees as to wage rates and working rules. Application made for Board of Conciliation under Industrial Disputes Investigation Act but dispute adjusted by mediation.

(32) American Bank Note Company, Ottawa. Wages and conditions of work; employees in press-room specially concerned; satisfactory working arrangements effected.

(33) Northern Power Company, Edmonton, Alberta. Dispute as to annual leave of certain employees; matter arranged without cessation of work.

(34) Saskatchewan Bridge and Iron Works, Moosejaw. Dispute as to alleged unfair use of unskilled labour to do skilled work; adjustment effected.

(35) Electric Railway Company, Moosejaw. Dispute as to wages and working conditions; matter referred later to Board of Conciliation; no cessation of work.

(36) Buckeye Machine Company, Limited, Calgary, Alberta. Demand for signed agreement and alleged improper use of specialists on machine work; a strike which lasted ten days, when agreement effected.

(37) Electric Railway, Edmonton, Alberta. Dispute regarding union recognition, also terms of new schedule; application for Conciliation Board made but working agreement effected by mediation.

(38) New Westminster, B.C. Electrical workers employed by city went on strike for new agreement; municipality refused compromise.

(39) Vancouver dairies. Drivers on strike because of dispute as to working conditions; drivers' places filled and strike proved ineffective.

(40) Esquimalt and Nanaimo Railway Company. Mechanics at Victoria, B.C., demanded new wage schedule; agreement reached by negotiations.

(41) Yarrows, Limited, and boilermakers and iron shipbuilders employed in the shipyard at Esquimalt, B.C. Dispute as to wages and hours; succession of strikes, which extended to Navy Yard and several machine shops and which lasted over three weeks; employees' demands conceded.

(42) Consolidated Mining and Smelting Company of Canada, Limited, and metal miners at Trail and Rossland, B.C. Dispute as to wages and genera

SESSIONAL PAPER No. 36

working conditions; application made by miners at each point for Board of Conciliation and Investigation but dispute adjusted by negotiations; no cessation of work.

(43) British Columbia Electric Railway Company, Limited, and linemen, etc. Dispute concerning wage schedule and working conditions, resulting in strike which lasted about four weeks; sympathetic strike threatened by street railway men, who also made certain demands; both disputes satisfactorily adjusted.

(44) British Columbia Telephone Company, Limited, and electrical workers. Agreement effected between company and union officials.

(45) Pacific Coast Coal Mines, Limited, at South Wellington, B.C. Wages dispute; men on strike for few days when wage concessions made.

(46) J. Leckie Company, Limited, boot and shoe manufacturers, Vancouver, B.C., and employees working on small government contracts. Dispute as to wages; agreement effected after week's strike.

(47) Navy Yard, Esquimalt, B.C. Demand by machinists for higher wages, strike being threatened; wage increase granted.

(48) Marconi Wireless Telegraph Company of Canada and wireless operators on Pacific Coast steamship service. Dispute as to wages and living conditions; matter referred finally to Board of Conciliation and Investigation; no cessation of work.

(49) Canadian Collieries (Dunsmuir), Limited. Miners at Extension and Cumberland, B.C., demanded wage increase; compromise effected.

(50) Victoria dock works and cement workers. Alleged discrimination against certain employees; matter amicably adjusted.

(51) Coal miners in Crow's Nest Pass region demanded wages in excess of those named in unexpired agreement. Some cessation of work occurred but efforts of departmental officers assisted largely in lessening the area and duration of the disagreement.

(52) Machinists, toolmakers, etc., employed in Toronto and Hamilton, largely on munitions work, demanded improved conditions as to wages and hours. Departmental officers assisted in effecting working agreements in some cases and, later, an investigation was made by a Royal Commission. Machinists and toolmakers in Hamilton were on strike for some months.

8 GEORGE V, A. 1918

II. THE LABOUR GAZETTE.

The *Labour Gazette* is published in both English and French, which necessitates the keeping of separate mailing lists, and the printing of all notices and forms in both languages. The number of paid subscriptions to the *Gazette* received during the past fiscal year was 5,001, the total paid circulation on the 31st March, 1917, being 6,124. All subscriptions were promptly entered, and remittances acknowledged. The customary subscription notices and renewal forms were forwarded from month to month, and mailing lists corrected and revised as occasion required. In addition to maintaining the regular list of subscribers, many sample copies were sent out from the department during the year. In connection with the circulation of the *Labour Gazette* for the twelve months ended March 31, 1917, 3,431 letters were received and acknowledged, 2,579 of which had reference to subscriptions to the *Labour Gazette*, 285 to a change of address on the part of subscribers, and 567 to other matters. For the same period, 8,728 pieces of mail matter were despatched from the circulation branch, representing communications containing notices, accounts, or receipts for subscriptions, and other communications in connection with the circulation of the *Gazette;* 928 parcels were also forwarded from the branch. During the fiscal year 1916-17, the average monthly circulation of the *Labour Gazette* was 11,909 copies, of which 6,344 were on account of paid circulation, and 5,565 to persons on the free and exchange lists. The circulation of the *Gazette* at the close of the fiscal year was as follows:—Annual Subscriptions, 6,124; Free and Exchanged Distribution, 5,634.

The following summary shows, by provinces the number of paid subscriptions to the *Labour Gazette* at the end of the fiscal year: Nova Scotia, 697; New Brunswick, 280; Prince Edward Island, 48; Quebec, 1,694; Ontario, 2,173; Manitoba, 299; Saskatchewan, 198; Alberta, 258; British Columbia, 317; The British Empire (other than Canada) 58; Foreign Countries, 102; Total, 6,124.

Under the head of copies of the *Labour Gazette* sent as exchanges are included *Labour Gazette* sent to public departments of the Governments, both federal and provincial, and to the publishers of trade papers and labour journals, in exchange for their publications. On the free list are included copies sent to members of both Houses of Parliament, commercial agents, immigration agents, public libraries, boards of trade, libraries of educational institutions, local newspapers, and the officers of organizations who supply from time to time information requested by the department.

Revenue.—The revenue of the *Labour Gazette* is derived from the sale of single and bound copies, and from annual subscriptions. Single copies are supplied at the rate of 3 cents each, or 20 cents per dozen. Bound volumes of the *Gazette*, including the issues of each year, are sold at the rate of 75 cents per copy. The annual subscription rate is 20 cents, or when more than 12 copies are taken by the same person or institution, 15 cents. The receipts from subscriptions, and from the sale of single and bound copies of the *Gazette* during the fiscal year 1916-17 shows a net revenue of $996.80.

III. THE FAIR WAGES BRANCH.

The Fair Wages branch of the department has to do with the administration of the fair wages policy of the Dominion Government, which is based on a resolution of the House of Commons adopted in the session of 1900, as follows:—

That it be resolved, that all Government contracts should contain such conditions as will prevent abuses, which may arise from the sub-letting of such contracts, and that every effort should be made to secure the payment of such wages as are generally accepted as current in each trade for competent workmen in the district where the work is carried out, and that this House cordially concurs in such policy, and deems it the duty of the Government to take immediate steps to give effect thereto.

It is hereby declared that the work to which the foregoing policy shall apply includes not only work undertaken by the Government itself, but also all works aided by grant of Dominion public funds.

Additional force was given to the fair wages resolution in the revision of the Railway Act in 1903, by the insertion in that statute of a section requiring the payment of current rates of wages to all workmen engaged in the construction of any line of railway towards which the Parliament of Canada has voted financial aid by way of subsidy or guarantee.

An Order in Council was adopted on August 30, 1907, "to more effectively further the purpose of the fair wages resolution of the House of Commons of Canada, of March, 1900," by the insertion of the following clauses in all government contracts to which the said resolution applies:—

1. Contractors shall post in a conspicuous place on the public works under construction, the schedule of wages inserted in their contracts for the protection of the workmen employed.

2. Contractors shall keep a record of payments made to workmen in their employ, the books or documents containing such record shall be open for inspection by the Fair Wages Officers of the Government at any time it may be expedient to the Minister of Labour to have the same inspected.

In connection with proposed works of construction a fair wages schedule setting forth the minimum wage rates and the hours of labour to be observed is prepared in advance and embodied in the contract. The practice is to prepare these schedules as they are required. For this purpose one of the fair wages officers of the department usually visits the locality in which the work is to be performed and ascertains, by inquiry from both employers and workmen, the scale of remuneration and the hours of labour generally prevailing in the district for the various classes of labour required.

In other cases a general clause is inserted in the contract, the terms of which are as follows:—

All mechanics, labourers or other persons who perform labour in the construction of the work hereby contracted for, shall be paid such wages as are generally accepted as current from time to time during the continuance of the contract for competent workmen in the district in which the work is being performed, and if there is no current rate in such district, then a fair and reasonable rate, and shall not be required to work for longer hours than those fixed by the custom of the trade in the district where the work is carried on, except for the protection of life or property, or in the case of other emergencies. In the event of a dispute arising as to what is the current or a fair and reasonable rate of wages or what are

8 GEORGE V, A. 1918

the current hours fixed by the custom of the trade it shall be determined by the Minister of Labour, whose decision shall be final.

These conditions shall extend and apply to moneys payable for the use or hire of horses or teams, and the persons entitled to payment for the use or hire of horses or teams shall have the like right in respect of moneys owing to them as if such moneys were payable to them in respect of wages.

In the event of default being made in payment of any money owing in respect of wages of any mechanic, labourer or other person employed on the said work, and if a claim therefor is filed in the office of the Minister of......................, and proof thereof satisfactory to the Minister is furnished, the Minister may pay such claim out of any moneys at any time payable by His Majesty under such contract, and the amounts so paid shall be deemed payments to the company.

The company shall post in a conspicuous place on the works under construction the general clause above mentioned for the protection of the workmen employed.

The company shall keep a record of payments made to workmen in its employ, and the books or documents containing such record shall be open for inspection by the fair wages officers of the Government at any time it may be expedient to the Minister of Labour to have the same inspected.

Fair wage conditions are also inserted in contracts for the manufacture of certain classes of government supplies, and in contracts for all railway construction to which the Dominion Parliament has granted financial aid, either by way of subsidy or guarantee.

The Department of Labour is also frequently consulted by other departments of the government regarding the wage rates to be observed in connection with work undertaken on the day labour plan.

The number of fair wages schedules prepared by the Department of Labour during the year for insertion in government contracts was greatly reduced on account of the reduction in the government construction operations consequent on the continuance of the European war, work of this nature for the Federal authorities throughout the year being mainly confined to works already in progress and to operations connected with Canada's part in the war. The total number of fair wages schedules prepared during the year was sixty-eight, being the smallest number prepared in any year since 1901–2. The sixty-eight schedules referred to were divided among the different departments of the government as follows: Public Works, 28; Railways and Canals, 14; Militia and Defence, 8; Interior, 9; Naval Service, 7; Marine and Fisheries, 1; and Indian Affairs, 1.

Fair wage conditions were also inserted in a number of contracts connected with the manufacture of military supplies and materials to the order of the Dominion Government.

TABLES RELATING TO FAIR WAGES SCHEDULES.

The following tables relate to Fair Wages Schedules prepared by the officers of the department during the fiscal year 1916-17, also during previous years, and show the different departments controlling the contracts concerned and the locality and value of the contract.

SCHEDULES BY PROVINCES.—TABLE showing, by provinces, the Fair Wages Schedules prepared, 1916-17.

DEPARTMENT OF GOVERNMENT.	Nova Scotia.	New Brunswick.	Prince Edward Island.	Quebec.	Ontario.	Manitoba.	Saskatchewan and Alberta.	British Columbia.	Yukon.	Total.
Public Works	3	3	1	5	10	......	4	2	......	28
Railways and Canals	1	2	1	6	2	2	......	......	......	14
Militia and Defence	......	......	......	1	7.	......	......	......	......	8
Naval Service	3	......	......	1	1	......	......	2	......	7
Indian Affairs	......	......	......	......	1	......	......	......	......	1
Marine and Fisheries	......	......	......	......	......	1	......	......	......	1
Interior	......	......	......	......	......	......	7	2	......	9
Total	7	5	2	14	21	2	11	6	......	68

FAIR WAGES SCHEDULES 1900-1917.—SCHEDULES prepared covering period from July 1900, to March, 1917, inclusive.

DEPARTMENT OF GOVERNMENT.	1900-1	1901-2	1902-3	1903-4	1904-5	1905-6	1906-7	1907-8	1908-9	1909-10	1910-11	1911-12	1912-13	1913-14	1914-15	1915-16	1916-17	Total.
Public Works	63	13	11	116	72	41	.53	95	125	43	190	156	201	327	155	84	28	1,773
Railways and Canals	....	1	50	89	153	95	84	93	163	79	48	54	77	120	25	11	14	1,156
Marine and Fisheries	....	17	12	18	21	8	10	23	18	14	14	41	24	45	36	17	1	319
Other Departments	....	....	....	....	2	3	3	11	14	12	23	39	82	60	34	10	25	318
Total	63	31	73	223	248	147	150	222	320	148	275	290	384	552	250	122	68	3,566

8 GEORGE V, A. 1918

Post Office Department Contracts, 1916-17.—Lists of supplies furnished the Post Office Department by contract, or otherwise, under conditions for the protection of the labour employed, which were approved of by the Department of Labour, 1916-17.

Name of Order.	Amount of Order.
Making metal dating stamps and type and other hand stamps and brass crown seals......	$ 7,137 32
Making and repairing rubber dating stamps and type, also other stamps...................	1,264 30
Supplying stamping material and repairing stamping pads...............................	10,266 23
Making and repairing post office scales...	485 75
Supplying mail bags...	36,723 90
Repairing mail bags...	36,370 24
Making and repairing mail locks and supplying mail bags fittings......................	56,212 78
Supplying street letter boxes and railway mail clerks' tin travelling boxes and repairing portable letter boxes, parcel receptacles and railway mail clerks' tin travelling boxes..	3,303 20
Making and repairing miscellaneous articles of Postal Stores............................	813 83
Making and supplying articles of official uniform......................................	73,006 41
Repairing, lettering and numbering parcel post hampers................................	275 95
Total..	$ 225,859 91

FAIR WAGES SCHEDULES prepared for the Department of Public Works, 1916–17, showing name of locality concerned, etc.

Nature of Work.	Locality.	Date at which schedule supplied by Department.	Date of Contract.	Amount of Contract.	Issue of *Labour Gazette* in which schedule published. Vol.	Page.
Boarding house, Dominion Govt. Forestry Farm	Sutherland, Sask	May 4, '16	June 24, 1916	$3,665 00	XVI	1501
Customs examining warehouse, Front St.	Toronto, Ont	" 9, '16	No contract.		XVI	1501
Riding school, Royal Military College	Kingston, Ont	" 15, '16	July 24, 1916	$20,000 00 Additional concrete $8 per c. yd additional facing $10 per cu. yd.		
Wharf and warehouse	Gagetown, N.B.	" 16, '16	No contract.			
Improvements to, and completion of protection dyke	Napierville, Que.	June 5, '16	No contract.			
Drill hall	Calgary, Alta.	" 16, '16	September 29, 1916	$282,051 45 Additional concrete, $9.25 per cu. yd.		
Parliament Buildings	Ottawa, Ont	" 20, '16	September.29, 1916	8% up to $4,000,000 7% further $1,000,000. No commission above $5,000,000	XVI	1773
Extension to wharf (cribwork)	Oiler, Que.	" 23, '16	No contract.			
Barn, Experimental Farm	Lennoxville, Que.	" 27, '16	September 24, 1916	$9,474 00 Additional work unit prices.	XVI	1659
Reconstruction of East pier, (pile, crib and ate), (concrete)	Pt. t sy, Ont.	July 14, '16	November 2, 1916	Schedule prices.		
Fire proofing, etc., of per tory of East Block, Parliament Buildings	Pt. Burwell, Ont	" 14, '16	No contract.			
3rd sm of jetty at mouth of Fraser River	Ottawa, Ont.	" 21, '16	"			
Extension to breakwater (cribwork)	Steveston, B.C.	" 24, '16	"			
Extension to wt breakwater, (pile, crib and concrete)	Short Beach, N.S.	" 31, '16	"			
Flat building at tal Experimental Farm	Pt. Stanley, Ont.	Aug. 3, '16	November 2, 1916	Schedule prices.	XVI	1864
Breakwater (cribwork)	Ottawa, Ont.	" 8, '16	October 19, 1916	$9,895 00	XVI	1771
Breakwater (pile and cribwork)	e Dauphin, N.S	" 12, '16	No contract.			
t s for R. N W d Police.	Bay Fortune, P.E.I.	" 21, '16	"			
Breakwater	Calgary, Alta.	" 21, '16	"			
Reconstruction of West pier (crib and concrete)	Nault's Point, N.S.	" 31, '16	"			
Public building (wood and concrete foundation)	Pt. Dover, Ont.		October 30, 1916	$9,757 00 Excavation $1 per cu. yd., concrete foundation walls, including forms, $12 per cu. yd.	XVI	1864
	Ashcroft, B.C					
Railway bridge over sluiceway, St. Charles River	Quebec, Que.	Sept. 21, '16	No contract.			
Wooden shed	St. John, N.B	" 21, '16	"			

FAIR WAGES SCHEDULES prepared for the Department of Public Works, 1916–17, showing name of locality concerned etc.—*Continued.*

Nature of Work.	Locality.	Date at which schedule supplied by Department.	Date of contract.	Amount of Contract.	Issue of *Labour Gazette* in which schedule published.	
					Vol.	Page.
Shed in rear of Postal Station "A"	Montreal, Que.	Sept. 21, '16	January 11, 1917	$7,490 00 Excavation, $1.30 per cu. yd., concrete foundation, including forms, $8.50 per cu. yd.	XVII	165
Public building	Sydenham, Ont.	Oct. 2, '16	No contract.			
"	Three Rivers, Que.	Nov. 10, '16	February 22, 1917	$87,500 00	XVII	223
3rd section of North jetty and 1st section of South jetty at mouth of Fraser River	Steveston, B.C	Dec. 28, '16	No contract.			

FAIR WAGES SCHEDULES prepared for the Department of Indian Affairs, 1916–17, showing name of locality concerned, etc.

Small stucco building on Indian Reserve	Caughnawaga, Que.	June 15, '16	No contract.			

FAIR WAGES SCHEDULES prepared for the Department of Militia and Defence, 1916–17, showing name of locality concerned, etc.

Building trades	Ottawa, Ont.	Apr. 12, '16	No contract.			
"	Barriefield Camp, Kingston Dist., Ont.	May 8, '16	May 8, 1916.			
Construction of camp near	Angus, Ont.	" 18, '16	April 22, 1916.	$12,010 00 Cost plus percentage basis.		
Construction of cartridge factory	Lindsay, Ont.	" 18, '16	April 26, 1916.	$16,500 00 Cost plus percentage basis.		
Building trades	Quebec, Que.	June 7, '16	June 27, 1916.			
"	Ottawa, Ont.	July 5, '16	No contract.			
"	Toronto, Ont.	Mar. 15, '17	"			
"	Hamilton, Ont.	" 21, '17	"			

FAIR WAGES SCHEDULES prepared for the Department of Interior, 1916-17, showing name of locality concerned, etc.

Description	Locality	Date	Remarks
Certain work at Revelstoke Park	Revelstoke, B.C.	May 8, '16	No. contract.
" Yoho and Glacier Parks	Field, B.C.	" 8, '16	"
" Rocky Mountain Park	Banff, Alta.	" 28, '16	"
" Jasper Park	Jasper, Alta.	Oct. 6, '16	"
" Buffalo Park	Wainwright, Alta.	" 6, '16	"
" Elk Island Park	Lamont, Alta.	" 6, '16	"
" Waterton Park	Waterton, Alta.	" 6, '16	"
Farm labourers' rates, Buffalo Park	Wainwright, Alta.	Nov. 6, '16	"
" " Elk Island Park	Lamont, Alta.	" 6, '16	"

FAIR WAGES SCHEDULES prepared for the Department of Naval Service, 1916-17, showing name of locality concerned, etc.

Description	Locality	Date	Contract	Vol.	Amount	No.
Certain trades	Halifax, N.S.	May 17, '16	No contract.			
Fish hatchery	Kingsville, Ont.	June 6, '16	June 30, 1916.			
Base for crane at H. M. C. dockyard	Halifax, N.S.	Aug. 19, '16	September 19, 1916.	XVI	$11,560 00 $1,540 00	1658
Various trades, dockyard	Esquimalt, B.C.	Sept. 11, '16	No contract			
Alterations and additions to the Naval College	Halifax, N.S.	Oct. 27, '16	November 10, 1916.		$12,745 00	
Workshop for Radiotelegraph branch	Esquimalt, B.C.	Feb. 1, '17	No contract.			
Six steel screw trawlers, for Canadian Govt.	Montreal, Que., and Toronto, Ont.	Feb. 12, '17	February 27, 1916.		Time and percentage basis.	

FAIR WAGES SCHEDULES prepared for the Department of Railways and Canals, 1916-17, showing name of locality concerned, etc.

Description	Locality	Date	Contract	Vol.	Amount	No.
Construction under subsidy of a branch line from a point on the Edmonton, Dunvegan and British Columbia Railway through Grand Prairie District, Alberta, for a distance of sixty miles		June 27, '16	July 12, 1916.	XVI	$384,000 00	1502
Manufacture and erection of the steel superstructure and timber floor of the Kettle Rapids Bridge on the Hudson Bay Railway at the crossing of the Nelson River, 332 miles from Le Pas, Manitoba		" 28, '16	July 14, 1916.	XVI	Schedule rates.	1502
Erection of a station, water tank, engine house, transfer platform, standpipe, pit, ash pit and turntable foundations, for the car ferry terminal at	Carleton Point, P.E.I.	July 3, '16	August 1, 1916.	XVI	Schedule rts.	1586
Repairs to Southerly end of elevator mooring dock	Pt. Colborne, Ont.	Aug. 4, '16	August 22, 1916.	XVI	New span $19,600	1306
Erection of Ragged Rapids bridge on line of C.N.R.	Trent Canal, Ont.	" 31, '16	September 9, 1916.		Old span, 3,500	
Three water tanks on Dartmouth to Deane Branch of T.C.R.	East Lawrencetown, Meaghers Grant, and Upper Musquodoboit, N.S.	Sept. 1, '16	November 15, 1916.	XVI	Bulk sum price, $2,574 each, schedule rates for backfill foundation, excavation and concrete.	1866

8 GEORGE V, A. 1918

FAIR WAGES SCHEDULES prepared for the Department of Railways and Canals, 1916–17, showing name of locality concerned, etc.—*Continued.*

Nature of Work.	Locality.	Date at which schedule supplied by Department.	Date of Contract.	Amount of Contract.	Issue of *Labour Gazette* in which schedule published. Vol.	Page.
Line of railway in Province of New Brunswick, in connection with subsidy agreement with St. John and Quebec Railway Co.						
Ice house extensions	Chaudiere Jct., Que.	Sept. 28, '16	No contract.			
		Dec. 6, '16	March 27, 1917	Bulk sum price, $2,000 schedule rates for additional.	XVII	303
	Riviere du Loup, Que.	6, '16	No contract.			
	Mont-Joli, Que.	6, '16	March 1, 1917	Bulk sum price, of $2,150 schedule rates for additional.	XVII	303
	Edmunston, N.B.	6, '16	No contract.			
	Cape Tormentine, N.B.	6, '16	"			
	Stellarton, N.S.	6, '16	"			
Superstructure of a grain elevator	Transcona, Man.	20, '16	October 10, 1916	Bulk sum price of $22,823. Schedule rates for wooden piles driven.	XVI	1773
No. 5 station on I.C.R.	St. John, N.B.	20, '16	No contract.			
"	St. Anselme, Que.	20, '16	"			
Tank	Glendyne, Que.	23, '16	"			
Yard office	Chaudiere Jct., Que.	23, '16	"			
Substructure of the Gaspereau River bridge on the Sackville Sub-Division of the I.C.R.	New Brunswick.	Feb. 6, '17	"			

FAIR WAGES SCHEDULE prepared for the Department of Marine and Fisheries, 1916–17, showing name of locality concerned, etc.

Buoy service, Detroit river and Lake Erie	District of Amherstburg, Ont.	Mar. 15, '17	No contract.			

FAIR WAGES COMPLAINTS INVESTIGATED BY THE DEPARTMENT OF LABOUR
DURING THE FISCAL YEAR ENDED MARCH 31, 1917.

Attention was given by the Fair Wages Branch of the Department of
Labour during the year to a number of complaints of non-observance of fair
wages conditions on government contracts. These complaints related mainly
to wages, hours, and conditions of employment. Some of them were disposed
of by correspondence; in most cases, however, investigation by one of the fair
wages officers of the department was necessary to establish the facts. Where
the complaints proved, on inquiry, to be well founded, steps were taken by the
Department of Labour looking to the enforcement of the contract conditions.
The investigations by the fair wages officers included a number of very important
works in course of construction at various points throughout the Dominion, among
which might be mentioned the ocean terminals dock at Halifax, harbour improvements at Toronto, wharves and ocean piers at Victoria, government elevators at Calgary and Vancouver, customs house at Ottawa, and the centre
block of the Parliament Buildings at Ottawa. In a few cases complaints
came from employees under the direct control of some branch of the
government service, and at the request of the department concerned an investigation was made by an officer of the Department of Labour, whose report was
transmitted to the officials having authority in the matter. The details of
these complaints are given in the table published herewith.

In addition to the foregoing, a number of inspections were made of many
factories both in Eastern and Western Canada in which munitions and military
supplies were being manufactured, and an effort was made to co-operate as far
as possible with the Imperial authorities in securing due observance of the
labour conditions embodied in military contracts.

TABLE of Fair Wages Complaints on Government Works and Disposition thereof during the fiscal year ending March 31, 1917.

Complaint received.	Locality and Public Work.	Department affected.	Subject of Investigation.	Disposition.
June 1, '16; Jan. 12, '16; Feb. 4, '16	Burlington, Ont. Revetment wall.	Public Works	Alleged non-payment of current rate to foreman in charge of derricks and scows; and non-payment of fair wages schedule rates to carpenters and labourers.	Investigation was made by a fair wages officer, who reported that he had been unable to examine the contractor's books. The matter was taken up with the Department of Public Works, and a sum sufficient to cover the claims was withheld from the contract price.
Mar. 22, '16	Calgary, Alberta. Government elevator.	Trade and Commerce.	Alleged non-payment of fair wages schedule rate to a watchman.	At the time this complaint was made the contract had been completed and the firm of contractors was dissolved. It was found, however, that the wage paid was not unduly low.
Mar. 23, '16; April 20, '16	Montreal-Hawkesbury. Construction of Canadian Northern Ontario Railway.	Railways and Canals.	Alleged non-acceptance of sub-contractor's cheques by bank.	The matter was taken up with the Department of Railways and Canals. Cheques in settlement were issued by the general contractor and forwarded by the Department of Labour to the claimants.
Mar. '16; Mar. 25, '16; May 15, '16; May 29, '16; June 1, '16; June 8, '16; Oct. 27, '16	Vancouver, B.C. Government elevator.	Trade and Commerce.	Alleged non-payment of current rate to watchmen; and non-payment of fair wages schedule rates to painters, sheet metal worker, electrician, and electrician's helper.	Investigations by a fair wages officer resulted in a satisfactory adjustment of the several claims.
Mar. '16; May '16; June '16	Ottawa, Ont. Customs house.	Public Works	Alleged non-payment of fair wages schedule rates to plasterers' labourers; also that tuck pointing was not being done by masons.	Investigation by a fair wages officer resulted in an adjustment of the wage claims with the exception of one which was not well-founded. The matter of tuck pointing was taken up with the Department of Public Works and adjusted in conformity with the local custom.
April 4, '16; May 22, '16; Nov. 28, '16; Nov. 31, '16; Jan. 12, '17; Feb.	Victoria, B.C. Wharf and ocean piers.	Public Works	Alleged unequal division of work between shifts of cement workers; non-payment of current rate to steel workers; non-payment of fair wages schedule rates to tug boat captain, carpenters, and labourers; wages of deck hands; excessive hours of labour; Sunday work; and system of holding back pay.	The matter was taken up with the Department of Public Works. As the result of investigations by a fair wage officer the cement workers' complaint was adjusted, the labourers' claims were settled, the steel workers' rate was increased to the union rate but claims for arrears were not allowed as the men, when hired, had little or no experience. It was found that the deck hands were receiving fair wages. Recommendations were made for the settlement of other claims but at the close of the fiscal year these matters had not been disposed of.
April 14, '16; May 4, '16; Aug. 14, '16; Sept. 18, '16; Jan. 22, '17	Halifax, N.S. Ocean terminals dock.	Railways and Canals.	Alleged operations of locomotives by unqualified men and under-manning of same; non-payment of fair wages schedule rates to carpenters and iron workers; improper classification of carpenter as labourer; and excessive hours of labour of firemen.	As the terminals road crossed the Intercolonial Railway at Halifax the complaint regarding the operation of locomotives was referred to the management of the Canadian Government Railways. Inquiry showed that the locomotives were not under-manned but that unqualified iron had been employed in cases of emergency. It was stated that in future this would not be done. Investigation by a fair wages officer resulted in a settlement of the carpenters' claims. The complaints of the iron worker and the firemen were reported to be not well-founded.
May 6, '16	Toronto, Ont. Harbour improvements.	Public Works	Alleged excessive hours of labour and non-payment of overtime rate to carpenters.	The matter was taken up with the Department of Public Works and a settlement of the claims was made.
June 24, '16	Triple Island, B.C. Lighthouse.	Marine and Fisheries.	That rates and hours specified for carpenters in the fair wages schedule were not those current in the district.	Investigation showed that the rates and hours were those prevailing at the time the schedule was prepared.

Date	No.	Place	Department	Nature of complaint	Remarks
May, Aug, Sept, Sept, Nov, Mar.	18, '16; 4, '16; 11, '16; 27, '16; 15, '16; 15, '17	Welland Canal.	Railways and Canals.	Alleged non-payment of engineers for work performed on engines outside of regular working hours; non-payment of fair wages schedule rates to carpenters, foremen and dredge engineers; non-payment of wages to a number of workmen; and classification of men working on electric and steam pumps and cement mixers.	Investigations by fair wages officers and correspondence resulted in a number of wage claims being adjusted, others were found to be not well-founded. An agreement was entered into between the contractors for section No. 3 and the steam and operating engineers. The complaint re non-payment of wages to certain workmen was not substantiated. It was decided to leave the classification of the men working on electric and steam pumps and cement mixers in abeyance as the work was closing down. Assistance was given in connection with an agreement entered into between the contractors for section No. 3 and the machinists, and in connection also with a strike of labourers. Settlements were reported of a number of claims which had been investigated during the previous year.
Sept, Nov, Jan.	6, '16; 16, '16; 17, '17	Ottawa, Ont. Parliament Buildings.	Public Works.	Regarding requests of stonecutters, toolsmiths and teamsters for increased wages; also dismissal of a stonecutter.	The matter was taken up with the Department of Public Works, and an investigation was made by the Department of Labour. A satisfactory arrangement as to wages was reached, and the dismissed stonecutter was re-employed.
Oct.	3, '16	Toronto, Ont. Refitting Exhibition Building for military use.	Militia and Defence.	That contractor was not adhering to current rates and hours for carpenters.	The matter was taken up with the Department of Militia and Defence. It was stated that there was no contract with the contractor named.
Oct.	3, '16	Toronto, Ont. Section of Union Station.	Public Works.	That there was no fair wages clause in the contract; and that carpenters were required to work longer hours than those current in the district without payment of overtime rate.	The matter was taken up with the Department of Public Works. It was stated that the work was under the authority of the Toronto Terminals Railway Company. On completion of the work the Government intended to take over a portion of the building for postal purposes.
Oct.	30, '16	Parry Sound, Ont. Marine Agency.	Marine and Fisheries.	That certain classes of labour were not receiving the current rate of wages.	Inquiry by the Department of Labour showed that the rates asked for were fair and reasonable. This information was transmitted to the Department of Marine and Fisheries under whose control the work was carried on.
Nov.	1, '16	Edmonton, Alberta. Armoury.	Public Works.	Alleged non-payment to two workmen for labour and material furnished to a sub-contractor.	The matter was taken up with the Department of Public Works. The claimants were advised to forward their claims direct to the general contractor, final payment having been made for the contract.
Nov.	25, '16	Regina, Sask. Floor in post office.	Public Works.	Alleged employment of alien enemies as carpenters and under-payment to them of current rates.	The matter was taken up with the Department of Public Works. The complaints were reported to be not well-founded.
Dec.	13, '16	Ottawa, Ont. Flax barn at Central Experimental Farm.	Public Works.	Alleged non-payment of fair wages schedule rate to carpenters.	Investigation by a fair wages officer resulted in a settlement of the claims.
Dec.	14, '16	Halifax, N.S. Dockyard.	Naval Service.	That boilermakers and helpers employed by the Department of the Naval Service should receive the increase granted to men employed in contract shops.	At the request of the Department of the Naval Service an inquiry was made as to conditions prevailing in Halifax for the classes mentioned. It was found that boilermakers and helpers employed by other firms were receiving higher wages than those employed at the Dockyard. This information was transmitted to the Department of the Naval Service.
Dec.	16, '16	Lachine Canal. Government Yards.	Railways and Canals.	Alleged non-payment of current rates to carpenters and joiners.	This matter was under the jurisdiction of the Department of Railways and Canals and was, therefore, transferred to that Department for attention.
Dec.	19, '16	Moncton, N.B. Bridge across Petitcodiac River.		Alleged unfair treatment of compressed air workers in matter of transportation charges.	The matter was referred to the Provincial Government of New Brunswick, by whom the work was controlled.
Mar.	22, '17	St. John, N.B. Railway section work.	Railways and Canals.	Alleged insufficient wages paid to extra gang section of maintenance of way men.	The matter was referred to the management of the Canadian Government Railways. The Department was later informed that an increase had been granted to the men concerned.

IV. STATISTICS.

The change in labour conditions brought about by the war and the industrial readjustments involved, have greatly increased the demands upon the statistical work of the department, especially in the prices and wages sections. Owing to the rapid advance in prices, employers and employees have frequently availed themselves of the statistics collected and published by the department on wages rates and cost of living. The work of the government in connection with food control and soldiers' pensions has also given rise to new demands for cost-of-living data. While endeavouring to meet these requirements it has been necessary to keep in mind the change in industrial conditions which will follow the close of the war, when there will be a demand for statistical data in the field of employment and unemployment.

PRICES.

The work on retail and wholesale prices has been somewhat expanded owing to the increased importance of such statistics in the recent steep and rapid rise in prices. As at the beginning of the war, quotations of retail prices were obtained weekly instead of once a month in the sixty cities in which the department has correspondents. Quotations of wholesale prices have been obtained in more markets than formerly, and in some cases more frequently. The weekly budgets of family expenditure on foods, fuel, etc., proved to be of much interest as showing the relative changes in the cost of living in Canada. Information as to price movements in other countries has been secured more extensively, and as government control of prices developed throughout the world, it became necessary to extend the work on this section considerably, thus making available to some extent the experience of other countries in regulating prices and controlling supplies. Special articles on various aspects of prices were published in the *Labour Gazette* from time to time.

WAGES.

After some years of effort the department has been able to compile a fairly satisfactory record of wage rates in representative establishments in all the more important industries. This is supplemented by a record of union rates in the different trades of the principal industrial centres. It is hoped that some sections of the wage record will soon be ready for publication. During the year much information on wages was furnished employers and employees, chiefly for use in negotiations for new wage agreements. Changes in wages and hours reported to the department are summarized monthly, and treated in some detail quarterly, in the *Labour Gazette*.

STRIKES AND LOCKOUTS.

The compilation of statistics of industrial disputes followed closely the lines adopted in former years. A statement of disputes in existence and of new disputes beginning in the month appears in each issue of the *Labour Gazette*, and an annual statement is also prepared for publication in the *Labour Gazette* and in the department's annual report. In this compilation disputes are classi-fied by provinces, industries, magnitude (as shown by numbers of employees involved and time loss), causes, and results and method of settlement. Reports of proceedings under the Industrial Disputes Investigation Act also appear in the *Labour Gazette* and in the annual report. During the year work was begun on a special report on Strikes and Lockouts in Canada 1901–16. In the report on this subject for the period 1901–12, issued in 1913, it was indicated that the department planned to issue similar reports periodically supplementary to the statements on industrial disputes appearing in the *Labour Gazette* and in the annual report of the department. The earlier report gave special attention to the quinquennial periods 1901–05 and 1906–10; the report now being prepared gives special tables for the succeeding quinquennium. Comparisons are made with the statistics of industrial disputes for the periods 1901–05 and 1906–10, and in addition a brief survey is given of industrial disputes during the sixteen years covered by the departmental record. The report should be ready for distribution towards the end of the year 1917.

EMPLOYMENT AND UNEMPLOYMENT.

A system of monthly reports from employment offices has been estabished which gives some information as to the condition of the labour market throughout the country. All the provincial and municipal employment bureaus, and the more important voluntary agencies, report monthly the number of vacancies notified to them and the number of persons placed. An arrangement has been made with the Immigration Branch, which supervises private employment offices, by which similar reports are received from all such offices in the chief centres of labour distribution. A compilation of these employment bureau reports is presented monthly in the *Labour Gazette*. The volume of employment in the building trades is reflected in some degree by a monthly table showing the value of building permits issued in thirty-five cities. As a beginning in the establishment of some measure of public employment, reports are being received monthly from fourteen city corporations showing the number of workers temporarily employed and the amount of wages paid such workers in the first pay-roll period of two weeks in the month. A quarterly table also appears in the *Labour Gazette* showing the number and percentage of members of trade unions unemployed on the last day of the quarters. The reports received from trade union secretaries on this subject cover from 70 to 80 per cent of the total trade union membership of the country.

INDUSTRIAL ACCIDENTS.

To the end of the fiscal year no change was made in the presentation of statistics of industrial accidents in the *Labour Gazette*, but the annual statement in this report is given in more condensed form than in previous years. The effort to compile and publish industrial accident statistics has been attended by many difficulties. The department has had to depend for its information chiefly upon provincial sources, and the task of securing the data on the same basis from all the provinces has presented many problems. Even within the individual province the field has been divided between factory and mines inspectors, railway boards and bureaus of labour, and recently further complexity has come in several provinces through the entrance of workmen's compensation boards into the field of industrial accident statistics. The compilation of a monthly statement of non-fatal accidents has presented the further difficulty that such accidents are often reported two or three months after the date of their occurrence. In these circumstances the record cannot be complete, but the department believes that, despite the difficulties, improvement is being effected steadily. The co-operation of the provincial workmen's compensation boards promises to contribute much to this end.

8 GEORGE V, A. 1918

Labour Legislation.

Work was begun during the year in a new field—the compilation of labour laws enacted by the Dominion and Provincial Governments.   It is proposed to issue annually a volume giving the text of all the labour laws passed during the year, with a brief survey of the trend in labour legislation.   The first volume to be issued will be that for the year 1916, on which some progress has been made. As a starting point for the annual reports on this subject the department has in contemplation a special report covering all the labour laws of Canada to the end of 1915, this to be followed, at intervals of a few years, by special reports consolidating the annual reports of the preceding years.

V. INDUSTRIAL DISPUTES IN CANADA DURING 1916.

In 1916 there were in existence seventy-five disputes, involving a time loss of 208,277 working days. There was some increase in the amount of industrial unrest as compared with 1915, in which year forty-three disputes, involving a time loss of 106,149 days were recorded. However, 1915 stands first in the sixteen years of the record as a year of industrial peace, and 1916 stands third from the standpoint of time loss and fifth from the standpoint of the number of disputes (table I). Seventy-four strikes, involving 270 employers and 21,057 workpeople and a time loss of 207,577 days were recorded as having actually commenced in 1916. One strike, that of boilermakers and iron shipbuilders at Esquimalt, B.C., was carried over from 1915.

From the standpoint of time loss, August was the month of greatest industrial disturbance, with 19 per cent of the time loss in the year (table II). November had 16 per cent of the time loss, and May 13.2 per cent. From the standpoint of the number of disputes, November was the month of greatest industrial unrest, with 17.6 per cent of the disputes which commenced during the year. May had 16.2 per cent of the disputes, and July 12.1 per cent. Fifty-four per cent of the time loss and 46 per cent of the disputes occurred in the four months, May to August.

DISPUTES BY PROVINCES.

Prince Edward Island was the only province in which no disputes were recorded during the year, although both Nova Scotia and New Brunswick had only one dispute (table III). Industrial unrest was greatest in Ontario, which province had 44 per cent of the strikes and 30 per cent of the time loss during the year. Quebec had 17 per cent of the disputes and 25 per cent of the time loss, and British Columbia 13 per cent of the disputes and 23 per cent of the time loss. British Columbia stands first as to the number of employees affected, on account of the large numbers of miners involved in strikes in the Crowsnest Pass district.

DISPUTES BY INDUSTRIES.

From the standpoint of time loss, industrial unrest was greatest in mining and quarrying, which industry is charged with 42 per cent of the total time loss in the year (table IV). Metals, machinery, and shipbuilding, 16 per cent of the time loss, and transportation 13 per cent. The number of strikes in transportation, nineteen, was also larger than in any other group, and there were fifteen disputes in metals, machinery, and shipbuilding, eleven in the clothing trades, and ten in mining and quarrying.

MAGNITUDE OF DISPUTES.

Number of Employees involved.—As in previous years, most of the disputes affect comparatively small numbers of employees. In almost half the total number, 45 per cent, less than 100 employees were involved, and 75 per cent of the cases the employees affected numbered less than 250. In table V it will be noted that the 100–250 classification had a larger percentage of the disputes than any other, but that the 250–500 classification had the greatest percentage of time loss.

Number of working days lost.—In the majority of the disputes also the time loss was small. In about 55 per cent of the cases the number of working days lost was less than 1,000 (table VI). A few large disputes contributed the greater part of the loss of time, about 62 per cent of the total number of working days lost being due to the ten disputes in each of which 5,000 or more days were lost.

8 GEORGE V, A. 1918

Industries and Duration.

The great majority of the disputes during the year were of short duration (table VII). Of the sixty-eight disputes settled during the year, twenty-one or 31 per cent were settled in five days or less, and forty or almost 59 per cent were settled in less than ten days. Only five disputes were in existence more than thirty days. Of these, two were in building and construction; one in metal, machinery, and shipbuilding; one in transportation; and one in the miscellaneous group.

Causes and Results of Disputes.

Fifty disputes, or 66 per cent of the total number in existence in the year involving 82 per cent of the time loss were due solely to the question of wages (table VIII). In forty-seven of these disputes the object was an increase in wages and in three cases to prevent a reduction in wages. Seven disputes, or about 9 per cent of the total, involving 25 per cent of the time loss, were due to demands for increases in wages and for other changes. In three disputes the object was recognition of the union, and there were eleven disputes from all other causes.

As to results, thirty of the disputes or 40 per cent of the total resulted in favour of employees, fifteen disputes or 20 per cent of the total in favour of employers, twenty-two disputes or 29 per cent were compromised, and in eight disputes or 11 per cent the result was indefinite. In the fifty-four cases in which the demand for higher wages was the cause of dispute the employees were fully successful in twenty, or 37 per cent of the total, and partially successful in nineteen cases or 35 per cent of the total. They were also successful in three of the four disputes for shorter hours, and in the three disputes to prevent wage reductions they were successful in two cases.

Methods of Settlement.

The majority of the disputes in the year were settled by negotiations between the parties, or by mediation—forty-one disputes being settled by negotiations and sixteen by mediation (table IX). One dispute was settled by reference under the Industrial Disputes Investigation Act. In five cases the strikers returned to work on the employers' terms, and in four cases the strikers were replaced.

SESSIONAL PAPER No. 36

TABLE I.—Record of Industrial Disputes by Years.

Year.	No. of Disputes.		No. involved.		Time loss in Working days.
	In existence in the year.	Beginning in the year.	Employers.	Employees.	
1901	104	104	273	28,086	632,311
1902	121	121	420	12,264	120,940
1903	146	146	927	50,041	1,226,500
1904	99	99	575	16,482	265,004
1905	89	88	437	16,223	217,244
1906	141	141	1,015	26,050	359,797
1907	149	144	825	36,624	621,962
1908	68	65	175	25,293	708,285
1909	69	68	397	17,332	871,845
1910	84	82	1,335	21,280	718,635
1911	99	96	475	30,094	2,046,650
1912	150	148	989	40,511	1,099,208
1913	113	106	1,015	39,536	1,287,678
1914	44	40	205	8,678	430,054
1915	43	38	96	9,140	106,149
1916	75	74	271	21,157	208,277
Total	1,594	1,560	9,430	398,391	10,920,539

TABLE II.—Industrial Disputes, 1916—By Months.

Month.	Disputes in existence in each month.	Disputes commencing in each month.		Disputes in existence in each month.			
		No.	Per centage of total.	Number Employers involved.	Number of Employees affected.	Time loss.	
						Working days.	Per centage of total.
January	2	1	1·3	2	127	781	·4
February	7	6	8·1	10	964	10,539	5·0
March	7	5	6·7	10	881	14,677	7·0
April	8	6	8·1	8	1,939	18,646	9·0
May	16	12	16·2	47	3,444	27,546	13·2
June	10	5	6·8	75	1,901	24,635	11·8
July	16	9	12·1	72	4,872	21,497	10·3
August	15	8	10·8	69	2,733	39,359	19·0
September	9	3	4·1	150	724	3,646	1·8
October	7	3	4·1	46	189	959	·5
November	16	13	17·6	59	6,469	33,469	16·0
December	11	3	4·1	54	1,308	12,523	6·0
Total		74	100			208,277	100

DEPARTMENT OF LABOUR

8 GEORGE V, A. 1918

TABLE III.—Industrial Disputes, 1916, by Provinces.

Province.	DISPUTES.		NUMBER INVOLVED.		TIME LOSS.	
	No.	Per cent of total.	Employers.	Employees.	Days.	Per cent of total.
Nova Scotia..............	1	1·3	1	1,188	20,196	9·7
New Brunswick............	1	1·3	1	200	2,800	1·3
Quebec...................	13	17·3	117	3,605	52,770	25·4
Ontario..................	33	44·0	105	4,619	62,686	30·1
Manitoba.................	7	9·3	14	775	10,361	5·0
Saskatchewan.............	6	8·0	13	441	1,875	·9
Alberta..................	4	5·3	7	494	8,974	4·3
British Columbia.........	10	13·3	13	9,835	48,615	23·3
Total..............	75	100	271	21,157	208,277	100

TABLE IV.—Industrial Disputes, 1916, by Industries.

Trade or Industry.	DISPUTES.		NUMBER INVOLVED.		TIME LOSS.	
	No.	Per cent of total.	Employers.	Employees.	Days.	Per cent of total.
Fishing.......................						
Lumbering.....................						
Mining and quarrying..........	10	13·3	14	11,814	88,634	42·6
Building and construction.....	7	9·3	42	210	4,124	2·0
Metal, machinery and shipbuilding	15	20·0	44	2,683	33,133	16·0
Woodworking trades............	1	1·3	1	275	1,875	·9
Printing and allied trades.....						
Textile trades................						
Clothing trades...............	11	14·7	11	1,176	19,341	9·3
Food, tobacco and liquor preparation.......	7	9·3	19	1,201	22·977	11·0
Leather.......................						
Transportation................	19	25·3	33	2,340	27,288	13·0
Public and civic employees....						
Miscellaneous trades..........	2	2·7	104	353	3,245	1·5
Unskilled labour..............	3	4·0	3	805	7,660	3·7
Total......................	75	100	271	21,157	208,277	100

SESSIONAL PAPER No. 36

TABLE V.—Industrial Disputes, 1916, by Numbers of Employees Involved.

Number of Employees involved.	DISPUTES.		NUMBER INVOLVED.		TIME LOSS.	
	No.	Per centage of total.	Employ- ers.	Employ- ees.	Working days.	Per centage of total.
5,000 employees and upwards..............	1	1·3	1	5,000	20,000	9·6
2,500 to 5,000.............................	1	1·3	1	3,630	21,620	10·4
1,000 to 2,500.............................	1	1·3	1	1,188	20,196	9·7
500 to 1,000.............................	4	5·3	38	2,800	38,166	18·3
250 to 500.............................	12	16·0	121	3,961	48,488	23·3
100 to 250.............................	22	29·3	28	3,318	45,053	21·6
50 to 100.............................	10	13·3	21	625	6,048	2·9
25 to 50.............................	15	20·0	51	491	7,441	3·6
Under 25 employees.......................	9	12·0	9	144	1,265	·6
Total................................	75	100	271	21,157	208,277	100

TABLE VI.—Industrial Disputes, 1916, by Time Loss.

Number of Working Days Lost.	DISPUTES.		NUMBER INVOLVED.		TIME LOSS.	
	No.	Per centage of total.	Employ- ers.	Employ- ees.	Working days.	Per centage of total.
15,000 and under 25,000....................	4	5·3	8	10,718	77,116	37·0
10,000 and under 15,000....................	2	2·7	31	1,170	24,126	11·6
5,000 and under 10,000....................	4	5·3	10	1,368	28,209	13·5
2,500 and under 5,000....................	12	16·0	15	2,726	44,741	21·5
1,500 and under 2,500....................	5	6·7	117	1,212	9,504	4·5
1,000 and under 1,500....................	7	9·3	27	·833	8,370	4·0
500 and under 1,000....................	14	18·7	23	2,037	10,319	5·0
250 and under 500....................	11	14·7	23	668	3,796	1·8
100 and under 250....................	11	14·7	12	347	1,874	·9
Under 100 days........................	4	5·3	4	53	222	·1
Strike in which no time was lost by employ- ees................................	1	1·3	·1	25	....	....
Total.............................	75	100	271	21,157	208,277	100

8 GEORGE V, A. 1918

TABLE VII.—Industrial Disputes, 1916.—By Industries and Duration.

Trade or Industry	5 days or less				6-10 days				11-15 days				16-20 days				21-30 days				Over 30 days				Unsettled				Total			
	No. of disputes	Employers	Employees	Days	No. of disputes	Employers	Employees	Days	No. of disputes	Employers	Employees	Days	No. of disputes	Employers	Employees	Days	No. of disputes	Employers	Employees	Days	No. of disputes	Employers	Employees	Days	No. of disputes	Employers	Employees	Days	No. of disputes	Employers	Employees	Days
Fishing	4	4	5482	21378	2	2	3644	21760	1	1	200	2800	3	7	2488	42696													10	14	11814	88634
Lumbering					2	5	54	512	2	8	55	710									2	15	60	1836	1	14	41	1066	7	42	210	4124
Mining	4	4	710	2830	5	5	447	3229	2	2	412	4944	1	1	325	2400	1	1	39	1014	1	1	150	4950	1	30	800	13766	15	44	2883	33133
Building, engineering and shipbuilding	1	1	375	1875																									1	1	375	1875
Metal, engineering and shipbuilding	3	3	194	956	2	2	95	595	2	2	62	805	2	2	278	5032	1	1	370	10360					1	1	177	1593	11	11	1176	19341
Woodworking																																
Printing and allied trades																																
Textile																																
Clothing																																
Food, also and liquor preparation					2	11	420	1910					1	1	130	2600	1	1	105	2730					3	6	546	15737	7	19	1201	22977
Leather																																
Transportation	9	10	778	2914	4	11	307	1416	2	6	853	10089	1	1	22	440	1	1	55	1155	1	3	200	7400	1	1	125	3874	19	33	2340	27288
Public and civic employees					1	100	300	1800													1	4	53	1445					2	104	353	3245
Miscellaneous trades																																
Unskilled labour					1	1	600	3600					1	1	150	2850	1	1	55	1210									3	3	805	7660
Total	21	22	7530	29953	19	137	5867	34822	9	19	1582	19348	9	13	3393	56018	5	5	624	16469	5	23	463	15631	7	52	1689	36036	75	271	21157	208277

TABLE VIII.—Industrial Disputes, 1916—By Causes and Results.

Cause or Object.	In favour of employees.				In favour of employers.				Compromise.				Indefinite.				Total.			
	No. of disputes.	No. of employers involved.	No. of employees affected.	Time loss in working days.	No. of disputes.	No. of employers involved.	No. of employees affected.	Time loss in working days.	No. of disputes.	No. of employers involved.	No. of employees affected.	Time loss in working days.	No. of disputes.	No. of employers involved.	No. of employees affected.	Time loss in working days.	No. of disputes.	No. of employers involved.	No. of employees affected.	Time loss in working days.
Increase in wages	14	37	2,653	36,786	9	13	1,682	17,980	18	28	7,106	64,426	6	22	5,712	40,677	47	100	17,153	159,869
Increase in wages and other changes	6	14	473	4,625					1	1	100	700					7	15	573	5,325
For shorter hours	3	102	650	4,200									1	30	800	13,766	4	132	1,450	17,966
Reduction of wages	2	3	410	10,560					1	1	27	324					3	4	437	10,884
Recognition of union	1	1	250	4,500					1	1	150	300	1	1	177	1,593	3	3	577	6,393
Employment of particular persons					2	2	230	3,400									2	2	230	3,400
Discharge of employees					2	2	110	750									2	2	110	750
Employment of non-unionists	1	1	260	780													1	1	260	780
Unclassified	3	6	239	1,787	2	5	101	934	1	1	27	189					6	12	367	2,910
Total	30	164	4,935	63,238	15	22	2,123	23,064	22	32	7,410	65,939	8	53	6,689	56,036	75	271	21,157	208,277

8 GEORGE V, A. 1918

TABLE IX.—Industrial Disputes, 1916—By Methods of Settlement.

Trade or Industry	Negotiations between the parties		Conciliation or mediation		Reference to Board under Ind. D. I. Act.		Return to work on employers' terms.		Replacement of strikers.		Otherwise, including indefinite or unsettled.		Total.	
	No. of disputes.	No. of employees affected.	No. of disputes.	No. of employees affected.	No. of disputes.	No. of employees affected.	No. of disputes.	No. of employees affected.	No. of disputes.	No. of employees affected.	No. of disputes.	No. of employees affected.	No. of disputes.	No. of employees affected.
Fishing														
Lumbering														
Mining and quarrying	3	357	6	10,269	1	1,188							10	11,814
Building and construction	5	144	1	25							1	41	7	210
Metal, machinery and shipbuilding	6	536	4	792			2	485	1	10	2	1,060	15	2,883
Woodworking trades			1	375									1	375
Printing and allied trades														
Textile trades														
Clothing trades	8	953	2	46							1	177	11	1,176
Food, tobacco and liquor preparation	4	655									3	546	7	1,201
Leather														
Transportation	12	1,575	2	408			1	50	3	182	1	125	19	2,340
Public and civic employees														
Miscellaneous trades	2	353											2	353
Unskilled labour	1	55					2	750					3	805
Total	41	4,628	16	11,915	1	1,188	5	1,285	4	192	8	1,949	75	21,157

VI. INDUSTRIAL ACCIDENTS IN CANADA IN 1916.

The tables on industrial accidents in Canada, which follow, are given in more condensed form than in previous years. As has been pointed out in previous reports the statement does not undertake to cover all the industrial accidents which occurred in the year. While in some provinces different departments and bureaus receive reports of industrial accidents and overlapping of these agencies has to be guarded against, there are, on the other hand, some sections of the field of industry not covered adequately, if at all, by any agency. From year to year, however, the department has been able to report improvement both as to the extent of the field covered and the accuracy of the statistics, and the increase in the total number of accidents shown in the 1916 record is mainly due to improvement in the method of reporting. Arrangements have been made for the co-operation of the Workmen's Compensation Boards in the provinces of Nova Scotia, Ontario, Manitoba and British Columbia, and it is hoped that with the assistance of these bodies the record in the coming year will give a more satisfactory view of the hazards of industry in Canada. The department is indebted to the following agencies for statements of industrial accidents reported to them; The Board of Railway Commissioners of Canada, the Department of Public Works and Mines in Nova Scotia, The Provincial Factory Inspector of New Brunswick, the Bureau of Mines of Quebec, the Bureau of Mines and the Provincial Factory Inspectors' Office of Ontario, the Temiskaming and Northern Ontario Railway Commission, the Ontario Railway and Municipal Board, the Bureau of Labour of Manitoba, the Chief Inspector of Mines of Alberta, the Department of Mines and the Provincial Factory Inspector of British Columbia.

According to the record, there were 9,462 industrial accidents in 1916, of which 950 were fatal and 8,512 non-fatal, as compared with 5,785 accidents— 836 fatal and 4,949 non-fatal, in the record for 1915. Among the industries and occupations, steam railway service was first as to fatal accidents, with 252 or 26·5 per cent of the total. In this group also there were 1,802 non-fatal accidents, or 21·2 per cent of the total. The metal, engineering, and shipbuilding group had the greatest number of non-fatal accidents—2,826 or 33·2 per cent of the total. Ten per cent of the fatal accidents were charged to this group. The mining industry had 159 or 16·7 per cent of the fatal accidents, and 1,759 or 20·7 per cent of the non-fatal accidents. As 1,308 non-fatal accidents were reported by the Ontario Bureau of Mines without information as to cause it has been necessary to omit these reports from the classification.

The most serious cause of accidents in the year was "falling objects," to which were due 165 fatal and 1,450 non-fatal accidents. "Struck by or caught between cars and locomotives" was next in importance, with 130 fatal and 219 non-fatal accidents; accordingly, 37 per cent of the accidents due to this cause were fatal. Eighty-nine fatal and 735 non-fatal accidents were due to "falls of persons," 76 fatal and 220 non-fatal accidents to "wrecks and collisions," and 71 fatal and 1,315 non-fatal accidents to "machinery."

In agriculture the principal cause of accidents was farm machinery, to which 17 fatal and 50 non-fatal accidents were due. In fishing, 12 deaths were caused by drowning. Of the 58 fatal accidents in lumbering, 31 were due to "falling objects"; this cause was also responsible for 21 non-fatal accidents in lumbering. In mines, metalliferous works, and quarries, 65 fatal and 169 non-fatal accidents were caused by "falling objects," 24 fatal and 90 non-fatal accidents by "mine and quarry ears," and 33 fatal and 9 non-fatal accidents by "explosives." "Locomotives and cars" caused 3 fatal and 2 non-fatal accidents in railway,

36—3

8 GEORGE V, A. 1918

canal, and harbour construction. In building and construction the great majority of the accidents were due to falls—"falls of persons" and "falls of persons due to collapse of scaffolds" accounting for 38 fatal and 130 non-fatal accidents, in a total of 55 fatal and 237 non-fatal accidents in the group. In the metal, engineering, and shipbuilding trades several causes were important. Twenty-one fatal and 45 non-fatal accidents were due to "electricity", 18 fatal and 221 non-fatal accidents to "falls of persons." 16 fatal and 702 non-fatal accidents to "machinery," and 14 fatal and 708 non-fatal accidents to "falling objects.' In the woodworking trades there were several causes to which one fatal accident was charged, but "machinery" ranked first as a cause of non-fatal accidents, accounting for 102 in a total of 156. There were no fatal accidents in the printing and clothing trades, but "machinery" ranked first in both as a cause of non-fatal accidents, accounting for 18 in a total of 22 in printing, and 24 in a total of 41 in clothing. Two of the 3 fatal accidents in textiles were caused by "falls of persons," and 46 of the 64 non-fatal accidents were caused by "machinery." In food, tobacco, and liquors, 22 fatal and 13 non-fatal accidents were due to "conflagrations." Five fatal and 11 non-fatal accidents were reported in leather, of which 2 fatal and 2 non-fatal were due to "falls of persons". The three principal causes of accidents in the steam railway service were "struck by or caught between cars and locomotives," which caused 130 fatal and 212 non-fatal accidents; "wrecks and collisions" which caused 76 fatal and 206 non-fatal accidents, and "falls from or in locomotives or cars," which caused 27 fatal and 311 non-fatal accidents. In electric railway service, "falls from or in locomotives or ears" accounted for 4 fatal and 8 non-fatal accidents in a total of 5 fatal and 58 non-fatal accidents. In navigation 10 deaths were caused by "drowning," and there were 9 fatal and 26 non-fatal accidents due to "falls of persons." "Animal-drawn vehicles" was the most serious cause in the miscellaneous transport group, accounting for 23 of the 51 fatal accidents and for 123 of the 309 non-fatal accidents. Among public and civic employees there were 5 fatal and 182 non-fatal accidents, of which 2 fatal and 25 non-fatal accidents were charged to "falling objects." In miscellaneous skilled trades there were three important causes "explosives" accounting for 19 fatal and 35 non-fatal accidents, "falls of persons" for 13 fatal and 67 non-fatal accidents and "machinery" for 11 fatal and 164 non-fatal accidents. In the unskilled labour group, "falling objects" caused 14 fatal and 34 non-fatal accidents in a total of 36 fatal and 102 non-fatal accidents.

SESSIONAL PAPER No. 36

FATAL and NON-FATAL Industrial Accidents, in the Calendar Year 1916.

Industry or Occupation.	ACCIDENTS.			
	Fatal.		Non-fatal.	
	Number.	Percentage of total.	Number.	Percentage of total.
Agriculture...	59	6·2	116	1·4
Fishing...	14	1·5	....	....
Lumbering..	58	6·1	178	2·1
Mines, metalliferous works and quarries............	159	16·7	(*a*) 1,759	20·7
Railway, canal and harbour construction............	8	·8	15	·2
Building and construction..........................	55	5·8	237	2·8
Metal, engineering and ship building...............	95	10·	2,826	33·2
Woodworking trades.................................	5	·5	156	1·8
Printing and allied trades.........................	....	....	22	·3
Clothing trades....................................	....	....	41	·5
Textile trades.....................................	3	·3	64	·8
Food and tobacco and liquor preparation............	35	3·7	128	1·5
Leather trades.....................................	5	·5	11	·1
Transportation:				
Steam railway service.............................	252	26·5	1,802	21·2
Electric railway service..........................	5	·5	58	·7
Navigation..	25	2·6	46	·5
Miscellaneous transport...........................	51	5·4	309	3·6
Public and civic employees........................	5	·5	182	2·1
Miscellaneous skilled trades.......................	80	8·4	460	5·4
Unskilled labour...................................	36	3·8	102	1·2
Total...	950	100	8,512	100·

(*a*) 1,308 reported unclassified by Bureau of Mines, Ontario.

8 GEORGE V, A. 1918

FATAL and NON-FATAL Industrial Accidents in 1916, by Industries and Causes.

Causes.	Agriculture Fatal	Agriculture Non-fatal	Fishing Fatal	Fishing Non-fatal	Lumbering Fatal	Lumbering Non-fatal	Mines, metalliferous works and quarries Fatal	Mines, metalliferous works and quarries Non-fatal	Railway, canal and harbour construction Fatal	Railway, canal and harbour construction Non-fatal	Building and construction Fatal	Building and construction Non-fatal	Metal, engineering and ship building trades Fatal	Metal, engineering and ship building trades Non-fatal	Wood-working trades Fatal	Wood-working trades Non-fatal	Printing and allied trades Fatal	Printing and allied trades Non-fatal	Clothing Fatal	Clothing Non-fatal	Textile Fatal	Textile Non-fatal
Machinery	17	50			11	99	5	16		2	2	12	16	702	1	102		18		24	1	46
Animal-drawn vehicles	11	16			1	4								2								
Motor-driven vehicles	10	15			31	21	65	169	2	6	8	52	14	708	1	19		3		2	2	2
Falling objects	7	12			2	10	8	42	1	2	20	96	18	221	1	6				6		5
Falls of persons due to collapse of scaffolds											18	34										
Flying chips	2	1			4	15	2	30		2		5	7	243	1	17				1		2
Objects being handled					1	11	1	9				5		132		2				1		1
Slipping on or striking against objects						2		9				3		62						1		
Sharp objects								4						88								
Horses	6	5						25		2												
Other animals	5	10							3													
Locomotives and cars	1	2			1		7	8				1	3	44		3						
Steam and electric railway cars																1						
Struck by or caught between cars and locomotives																		1				
Falls from or in locomotives or cars																						1
Setting or releasing hand brakes						7	1	11			3	7	1	131		3						4
Hand tools		3				6	10	40				9	8	87		1				4		2
Hoisting apparatus and conveyors						1								15								
Boiler and steam power apparatus												2		4								
Rail and track appliances								90				3	1	57		2				1		1
Mine and quarry cars	1	1	1				24	1	1			4	2	207								
Hand trucks, lorries and barrows					1	2		7		1				3	1	1						1
Hand, motor cars and velocipedes											1			24		3		1				
Hot substances and flames		1					23	9						2								
Conflagrations																						
Explosives	1	1	1						1	1												
Corrosive substances																						

SESSIONAL PAPER No. 36

	59	116	14	58	178	150	³451	8	15	55	237	952,826	5	156	22	41	3	64
Poisonous substances																		
Drowning			12	6		1		1										
Lightning			1								1							
Suffocation						2												
Asphyxiation						3				3	2	21		2				
...ly						7	1					1		45				
Blood poisoning														18				
Lead poisoning														5				
Doors														16				
Firearms										1		1						
Heat prostration														2				
Frost bite																		
Exposure to cold																		
Assault																		
Sliding down fire station pole																		
Fire fighting tools and appliances																		
Hawser and other ropes on vessels																		
Crushed between vessel and wharf														4				
Sprain																		

¹Farm machinery.   ²Horses and mules.   ³Not including 1,308 non-fatal accidents reported unclassified by Ontario Bureau of Mines.

8 GEORGE V, A. 1918

FATAL and NON-FATAL, Industrial Accidents in 1916, by Industries and Causes—*Concluded.*

Causes.	Food, Tobacco and liquor preparation. Fatal.	Non-fatal.	Leather. Fatal.	Non-fatal.	Steam railway service. Fatal.	Non-fatal.	Electric railway service. Fatal.	Non-fatal.	Navigation. Fatal.	Non-fatal.	Miscellaneous transport. Fatal.	Non-fatal.	Public and civic employees. Fatal.	Non-fatal.	Miscellaneous skilled trades. Fatal.	Non-fatal.	Unskilled labour. Fatal.	Non-fatal.	Total. Fatal.	Non-fatal.
Machinery	.	32	1	7	1	34				1	23	123		31	11	164	3	0	71	1,315
Animal-drawn vehicles	.	.			1							16		14	1	1	1	1	37	178
Motor-driven vehicles	3	13			3	218	1	17		3	7	56	2	25	4	73	14	34	1	42
Falling objects	2	11	2		1	140		13		26		31		32	13	67	3	19	165	1,450
Falls of persons due to collapse of scaffold								4	0										89	735
Flying objects		1			1	71					4	2		1		9		7	18	34
Objects being handled		4			1	83					1	9		2	2	7	2	7	25	400
Slipping on or striking against objects		10						2				3							2	271
Sharp objects					1	90								5		8		4	2	194
Horses						14								10		6			0	129
Other animals																			6	10
Locomotives and cars								2			4	28		11	2				11	40
Steam and electric railway cars						103						7							12	123
Struck by or caught ... cars and locomotives																			7	49
Falls ... and locomotives or cars					130	212		7						2	2		2	3	130	219
...ts and collisions					27	311	4	8											31	319
Setting or releasing hand brakes					76	206		14											76	220
Hand tols	17			1		93		2				1		1	17		2		0	2
Hoisting apparatus and conveyors					2	19				3	4	26	1		11	13	5		3	293
Boiler and steam apparatus	1	2			1										1				42	220
Railway track appliances	1					25		1		3				2		19	3		3	72
Mine and quarry cars						26				1										32
Hand trucks, lorries and wheelbarrows																				90
Hand, motor cars and velocipedes	3	3				11					4	4				8	1	1	24	91
Hot substances and flames		5			6	36				2				14	2			2	6	36
						31													6	277

SESSIONAL PAPER No. 36

Conflagrations	22													13		1	10	40	34
Explosives														6			3	97	48
Corrosive substances														4				17	1
Poisonous substances									1					5	1			5	39
Drowning																		0	2
Lightning							10											0	10
Suffocation					1		3											6	40
Asphyxiation		2		1		1	1	2	2	2	9		1		1		2	9	1
Electricity							1							2			1	61	0
Blood poisoning							5											25	1
Lead poisoning																		5	0
Doors					17													33	1
Firearms																		1	3
Heat prostration						3		1		1				2				6	0
Frost bite					9													4	0
Exposure to																		9	0
Assault																		1	0
Sliding down fire station pole																		4	0
Fire fighting tools and appliances																		8	0
Hawser and other ropes on vessels									3									3	0
...en vessel and wharf									1									1	0
Sprain																		10	0
	35	128	5	11	252	1,802	5	58	25	40	51	309	5	132	80	460	36	102	950	7,204

¹ Motor and horse driven vehicles.

8 GEORGE V, A. 1918

FATAL AND NON-FATAL INDUSTRIAL ACCIDENTS IN CANADA, 1904–1916.

Trades.	1904 Fatal	1904 Non-fatal	1905 Fatal	1905 Non-fatal	1906 Fatal	1906 Non-fatal	1907 Fatal	1907 Non-fatal	1908 Fatal	1908 Non-fatal	1909 Fatal	1909 Non-fatal	1910 Fatal	1910 Non-fatal	1911 Fatal	1911 Non-fatal	1912 Fatal	1912 Non-fatal	1913 Fatal	1913 Non-fatal	1914 Fatal	1914 Non-fatal	1915 Fatal	1915 Non-fatal	1916 Fatal	1916 Non-fatal
Agriculture	103	121	132	241	159	236	209	295	223	291	256	374	227	314	140	197	61	145	80	167	73	111	94	141	59	116
Fishing and hunting	16	1	13	1	15	3	17	4	37	7	34	7	33	7	24	2	18	1	12	1	22	1	26	1	5	1
Lumbering	60	120	75	155	119	156	129	138	113	115	130	181	110	116	71	111	54	111	80	199	11	101	53	118	58	178
Mines, metalliferous works and quarries	103	117	70	135	119	167	181	226	148	187	160	147	180	182	104	34	90	619	216	1,147	356	976	169	969	159	1,308
Railway, canal and harbour construction	43	140	46	131	69	262	33	211	46	219	38	245	62	233	49	210	94	298	149	58	51	47	14	15	8	15
Building and construction	74	383	66	434	68	562	154	570	63	364	77	482	89	513	81	401	94	1,526	98	556	90	1,098	42	1,259	35	827
Metal engineering and shipbuilding trades	12	154	8	150	4	133		138	7	116		158		160	10	115	103	185	127	213	10	127	86	123	56	156
Woodworking trades		9	1	19		17		23		12		16	9	37		14	9	20	9	29		22	9	18	2	22
Printing and allied trades	3	21	3	36	2	19	1	24	1	16	3	16	4	19	2	15	5	13	3	9	3	11	1	12		41
Clothing	3	23	3	38	3	46	3	41	2	37	3	35	17	30	5	17	8	41	6	16	10	40	20	66	3	64
Textile	6	55	9	76	20	79	18	73	14	63	9	85	71	71	10	43	81	81	2	69		73		96	35	127
Food, tobacco and liquor preparation	2	4	6	7	3	13		3	5	5	2	9	3	11		12	15	12	9	2	4		2	9	5	11
Leather																										
Transportation:																										
Steam railway service	272	348	219	321	252	323	342	337	326	316	283	293	287	332	178	281	332	1,831	348	1,724	187	279	117	1,693	252	1,802
Electric railway service													5	34	5	34	14	66	15	85	13	68	4	51	5	58
Navigation	113	168	138	85	117	61	100	74	84	62	95	91	85	63	96	39	60	62	123	100	235	96	50	40	25	46
Miscellaneous transport			140	234	45	178	55	193	54	132	50	178	53	178	44	156	45	203	52	283	49	201	30	218	51	309
Public and civic employees		7	5	6	66	19	62	80	19	55	12	91	30	134	19	83	15	266	31	199	15	223	25	162	5	182
Miscellaneous skilled trades	41	178	71	159	56	226	62	168	61	156	54	152	75	135	71	113	51	225	58	947	44	185	45	239	80	460
Unskilled labour	30	119	57	143	43	142	34	154	71	130	64	123	92	166	89	134	97	165	59	256	96	259	47	142	36	102
Total	890	1,071	1,043	2,362	1,089	2,689	1,353	2,752	1,272	2,277	1,279	2,718	1,390	2,697	1,084	2,146	1,220	5,780	1,500	7,195	1,381	5,301	836	4,049	950	8,512

TENTH REPORT

OF THE

REGISTRAR OF BOARDS OF CONCILIATION AND INVESTIGATION

OF

PROCEEDINGS UNDER THE INDUSTRIAL DISPUTES INVESTIGATION ACT, 1907

FOR THE
FISCAL YEAR ENDING MARCH 31,
1917

(Being an Appendix to the Annual Report of the Department of Labour for the same period.)

PRINTED BY ORDER OF PARLIAMENT.

OTTAWA
J. de LABROQUERIE TACHÉ
PRINTER TO THE KING'S MOST EXCELLENT MAJESTY
1918

[No. 36a—1918]

●

To the Hon. T. W. CROTHERS, B.A., K.C.,
    Minister of Labour.

SIR,—I have the honour to submit a Report of Proceedings under the
Industrial Disputes Investigation Act, 1907, for the fiscal year ended March 31'
1917.

F. A. ACLAND,

Registrar of Boards of Conciliation
and Investigation.

CONTENTS.

Industrial Disputes Investigation Act, 1907.

TENTH ANNUAL REPORT OF PROCEEDINGS, BEING FOR
THE FISCAL YEAR ENDING MARCH 31, 1917.

I. INTRODUCTORY CHAPTER.

The administration of the Industrial Disputes Investigation Act, 1907, presented during the year no feature calling for special comment. Thirty-six applications were received and twenty boards were established. The proportion of boards to applications was smaller than usual, many of the disputes having been, after reference to the department, arranged amicably without the establishment of a board; in several such cases the adjustment was effected with the aid of a departmental officer. In other cases, where the machinery of the statute was not found applicable, the dispute was referred to a Royal Commission and the threatened strike was averted, save in one case where, before the inquiry could commence, a strike, fortunately destined to be of brief duration, was declared. One other strike only occurred during the year in cases referred and this was of minor importance in an industrial sense. Several of the disputes dealt with involved large bodies of employees and powerful unions.

Reference was made in the report of last year to the extension of the scope of the Act by Order in Council under the War Measures Act to disputes in all industries engaged in war work. The amendment has remained in effect and during the year one board was established in connection with a dispute which involved war work, renewed negotiations between the parties rendering, however, inquiry by the board unnecessary.

Disputes affecting railway industries were more numerous than usual; but while fourteen applications were received, it became necessary only to establish six boards. No strike occurred in the industries concerned.

Street railway disputes caused six applications; five boards were established and all the disputes were satisfactorily arranged.

No very important dispute in the coal-mining industry came before a board during the year, but shortly before the close of the fiscal period applications were received from different sections of the employees of an eastern coal company; the employees being in this case divided as between two unions, the dispute was referred to a Royal Commission. This action was subsequent to the close of the year, but it is satisfactory to be able to add that the efforts of the commission were successful in adjusting the dispute. In the Crowsnest Pass region there was considerable friction and some loss of time from strikes. No procedure under the Industrial Disputes Investigation Act took place. Work was being carried on under an agreement effective until March 31, 1917, but the increasing cost of living caused demands from the men for increased wages. Officers of the department assisted in the adjustments which were effected. The agreement terminated simultaneously with the fiscal year, and a strike followed, which lasted for about three months, the Government, in June, appointing a Director of Coal Operations with extensive powers over the affected district.

8 GEORGE V, A. 1918

Several disputes affecting telegraph and express workers were dealt with during the year and were in all cases satisfactorily arranged.

The Act continued during the year to be the occasion of much inquiry and discussion in the United States. Communications received indicate frequent inter-school and inter-college debates on various phases of the question of industrial disputes and their settlement, in connection with some aspect of which the department is requested to furnish information as to the operations of the Industrial Disputes Investigation Act. Two investigators from the United States, Mr. Ben. M. Selekman, of the Russell Sage Foundation, and Mr. B. M. Squires, a special agent of the United States Bureau of Labour Statistics, visited the Capital and made inquiries in some detail. Their reports on the subject recognize the extent to which the administration of the statute is interwoven with the conciliation work of the department, but the investigators seemed dubious of the value of such a law in the United States.

Investigators have sometimes made the criticism that the tables printed in the annual statements of proceedings under the statute do not take note of strikes in disputes which fall obviously within the scope of the statute yet have not been dealt with under the Act. The statement is correct. The report being one of proceedings under the Industrial Disputes Investigation Act, 1907, disputes which have not been the occasion of any such proceedings fall, properly speaking, outside the scope of the report. All strikes are enumerated in the departmental record and are mentioned in the *Labour Gazette* and in the annual report of the department. In the present report, to meet this objection, tables have been included showing, for the ten years covering the life of the statute, the number of strikes in industries falling within the scope of the statute and not dealt with under its provisions, also strikes in a number of cases where the applicability of the Act is perhaps doubtful. The further criticism may be offered—has been, in fact, made—that there should be a positive ruling as to this point, so that every strike or lockout may be classified precisely, by an investigator, as lawful or unlawful; in the administration of the Act, however, it has not appeared that the course suggested would be in any way helpful to the object mainly sought, namely, the settlement of industrial disputes so far as possible without strike or lockout. Two series of tables have been, therefore, prepared. One series contains statistics as to strikes arising out of disputes which fall clearly within the jurisdiction of the statute, and without regard to the question if such disputes have been dealt with under the statute; the second series deals with disputes as to which the applicability of the statute is uncertain. Disputes of the class last mentioned have been rarely of a nature to affect closely the public welfare, this fact obviously increasing the difficulty in regarding as a public utility the industries to which they may respectively relate. It should be noted that as to many of these disputes the agencies and officers of the department have been at the disposal of the parties concerned and have been, in numerous instances, helpfully employed.

In past years it has been the practice to include in the annual report of the registrar the text of each report received during the year from a Board of Conciliation and Investigation; this is, in fact, required by the provisions of the Industrial Disputes Investigation Act. In the present report statistical details on an ample scale are printed as to each dispute dealt with by a board during the fiscal year, but the text of the findings is not included. The text of the several findings has been already printed in the *Labour Gazette*, and it has been decided to refrain from reprinting it in the present report. This course is also believed to be in harmony with the recommendations of the Editorial Committee on Governmental Publications appointed to inquire into

SESSIONAL PAPER No. 36a

such matters, the object specially aimed at being, as it is understood, a reduction of expenditures so far as this is possible without injury to the public interests. Those pursuing investigations concerning the operations of the Industrial Disputes Investigation Act may sometimes find a certain inconvenience in the omission of the text of the findings of the various boards, but if the text of a particular report is specially desired, a copy of the report can be, as a rule, procured by application to the department.

The present report contains further a statistical summary of proceedings under the statute from its inception, March 22, 1907, to the close of the fiscal year, March 31, 1917, affording thus a complete view of its operations during the decennium covering its existence.

II. SUMMARY TABLES RESPECTING PROCEEDINGS UNDER THE INDUSTRIAL DISPUTES INVESTIGATION ACT, 1907.

[The tables presented on the following pages are arranged in several divisions, viz.: (i) showing proceedings by industries concerned, from April 1, 1916, to March 31, 1917; (ii) showing proceedings by industries concerned, from March 22, 1907, to March 31, 1917; (iii) showing by fiscal years, 1907-17, number of disputes dealt with; (iv) showing by calendar years 1907–17 number of disputes dealt with; (v) containing statistical summary of each year's operations under the statute since its enactment, March 22, 1907; (vi) showing all strikes (and lockouts) in mines and public utilities during the ten years March 22, 1907, to March 31, 1917, whether or not there were proceedings under the Industrial Disputes Investigation Act, 1907; (vii) showing strikes in cases where applicability of Industrial Disputes Investigation Act was doubtful.]

8 GEORGE V, A. 1918

INDUSTRIAL DISPUTES INVESTIGATION ACT, 1907.

I. TABLE showing Proceedings by Industries from April 1, 1916, to March 31, 1917.

Industries affected.	No. of Disputes referred under Act.	No. of Strikes not averted or ended
Disputes affecting Mines and Public Utilities:—		
(1) Mines:—		
(a) Coal	3	0
(b) Metal	3	0
(c) Asbestos	1	0
Total, Mines	7	0
(2) Transportation and Communication:—		
(a) Railways	15	1
(b) Street railways	6	0
(c) Express	2	0
(d) Shipping	1	0
(e) Telegraphs	3	0
Total, Transportation and Communication	´27	1
(3) Light and power	1	0
(4) Municipal work	2	0
Total, Mines and Public Utilities	37	1

   * The proceedings under the Act during the year include one case in which certain proceedings had taken place during the preceding year, namely: a dispute between the Toronto, Hamilton and Buffalo Railway Company and employees engaged in the company's locomotive and car department at Hamilton, Ont.

   At the close of March, 1917, results were still pending in connection with seven applications, namely: (1) application made on behalf of commercial telegraphers employed by the Canadian Pacific Railway Company; (2) application made on behalf of employees of the Canadian Express Company on lines west of North Bay, Ont.; (3) application made on behalf of wireless operators on Pacific Coast Steamship Service employed by the Marconi Wireless Telegraph Company of Canada, Limited; (4) application made on behalf of certain employees of the Dominion Coal Company, Limited; (5) application made on behalf of certain employees of the Canadian Northern Railway Company on lines from Port Arthur to Winnipeg; (6) application made on behalf of certain employees of the Corporation of the City of Vancouver; and (7) application made on behalf of certain employees of the Dominion Coal Company, Limited.

SESSIONAL PAPER No. 36a

INDUSTRIAL DISPUTES INVESTIGATION ACT, 1907.

II. TABLE showing Proceedings by Industries from March 22, 1907, to March 31, 1917.

Industries affected.	No. of Disputes referred under Act.	No. of Strikes not averted or ended.
I. Disputes affecting Mines and Public Utilities:—		
(1) Mines—		
(a) Coal	46	6
(b) Metal	16	5
(c) Asbestos	1	0
Total, Mines	63	11
(2) Transportation and Communication:—		
(a) Railways	89	7
(b) Street railways	27	2
(c) Express	2	0
(d) Shipping	12	0
(e) Telegraphs	5	0
(f) Telephones	2	0
Total, Transportation and Communication	137	9
(3) Light and power	4	0
(4) Municipal work	11	1
Total, Mines and Public Utilities	215	21
II. Disputes affecting other than Mines and Public Utilities	12	0
Total, all classes	227	21

At the close of March, 1917, results were still pending in connection with seven applications, namely: (1) application made on behalf of commercial telegraphers employed by the Canadian Pacific Railway Company; (2) application made on behalf of employees of the Canadian Express Company on lines west of North Bay, Ont.; (3) application made on behalf of wireless operators on Pacific Coast Steamship Service employed by the Marconi Wireless Telegraph Company of Canada, Limited; (4) application made on behalf of certain employees of the Dominion Coal Company, Limited; (5) application made on behalf of certain employees of the Canadian Northern Railway Company on lines from Port Arthur to Winnipeg; (6) application made on behalf of certain employees of the Corporation of the City of Vancouver; and (7) application made on behalf of certain employees of the Dominion Coal Company, Limited.

DEPARTMENT OF LABOUR

8 GEORGE V, A. 1918

INDUSTRIAL DISPUTES INVESTIGATION ACT, 1907.

III. TABLE showing by fiscal years, 1907–1917, Number of Disputes dealt with.

	1907–08	1908–09	1909–10	1910–11	1911–12	1912–13	1913–14	1914–15	1915–16	1916–17	Total.
Number of applications............	34	21	27	24	18	21	16	16	14	36	227
Number of boards granted.........	31	19	25	19	15	17	15	17	11	20	189
Number of disputes where strike not averted (or ended)...........	1	1	4	4	4	4	0	1	1	1	21

(The figures contained in the above table may be thought to show discrepancies as compared with those appearing in the yearly summaries. A closer examination will, however, show the statements of both classes to be in agreement A complete statement of proceedings for a year must show all disputes dealt with during the fiscal year. The figures of the yearly statement include therefore disputes carried over from the previous year and which are counted in the summary of that year's proceedings. Thus the same dispute may properly figure in the annual statement for each of two years. In the statistical recapitulation covering several years, as above, it is necessary that no disputes shall be counted more than once and account is taken of the number of applications received during the year and thus brought within the purview of the statute.)

INDUSTRIAL DISPUTES INVESTIGATION ACT, 1907.

IV. TABLE showing by calendar years, 1907–1917, Number of Disputes dealt with.

	*1907 9 mos.	1908	1909	1910	1911	1912	1913	1914	1915	1916	†1917 3 mos.	Total.
Number of applications...............	25	27	22	28	21	16	18	18	15	29	8	227
Number of boards granted...........	22	25	21	23	16	16	15	18	12	16	5	189
Number of disputes where strike not averted (or ended)................	1	1	4	4	4	3	1	1	1	1	0	21

*The Act became law on March 22, 1907, so that the proceedings cover nine months only.

†To the end of the financial year, March 31.

(The remarks at the foot of the preceding table apply equally to apparent discrepancies as between the above summary by calendar years and yearly summaries of proceedings.)

INDUSTRIAL DISPUTES INVESTIGATION ACT, 1907.

V. STATISTICS Summaries of Operations for Each Year, 1907–1917.

In the succeeding pages will be found a statistical summary of the operations of the Industrial Disputes Investigation Act for each fiscal year since the inception of the Act, March 22, 1907.

INDUSTRIAL DISPUTES INVESTIGATION ACT, 1907.—PROCEEDINGS, 1907–08.

STATEMENT of Application for Boards of Conciliation and Investigation and of Proceedings thereunder from March 22, 1907, to March 31, 1908.

A.—MINES, AGENCIES OF TRANSPORTATION AND COMUNICATION, AND OTHER PUBLIC SERVICE UTILITIES.

1. Appointed by the Minster, under Section 1, of the I. D. I. Act, on recommendation from party concerned.
2. Appointed by the Minister, under Section 8, Sub-section 2, of the I. D. I. Act, in the absence of a recommendation from party concerned.
3. Appointed by the Minister, under Section 8, Sub-section 3, of the I. D. I. Act, on the joint recommendation of the two members first appointed.
4. Appointed by the Minister, under Section 8, Sub-section 4, of the I. D. I. Act, in the absence of a joint recommendation by the two members first appointed.

I. MINING AND SMELTING INDUSTRY.

1. COAL MINES.

Date of receipt of application.	Parties to Dispute.	Party making application.	Locality.	No. persons affected.	Nature of dispute.	Names of Members of Board: (c) Chairman; (e) Employer; (m) Men.	Date on which Board was constituted.	Date of receipt of report of Board.	Result of Reference.
April 8, 1907	(*)Cumberland Ry. & Coal Co. and employ-ees.	Employees	Springhill, N.S.	1,700	Concerning employment of non-union workmen.				On April 1, employees went on strike. It was alleged by employees that they were under impression that the mines of Nova Scotia were exempt from provisions of Act. When it was explained that the Act applied to all Canada, employees returned to work April 8. Difficulty amicably settled. No Board constituted.
April 9, 1907	(*)Canada West Coal and Coke Co. and em-ployees.	Employees	Taber, Alta	150	Concerning hours of la-bour.				On April 1, employer locked out employees. Employer alleged that this was done in ignorance of provisions of Act. When informed of provisions of Act by department, mines were re-opened on April 18. Subsequently an amicable settlement was effected through intervention of Mr. J. D. McNiven, fair wages officer of department. No Board constituted.

(*) It is important to note in connection with these disputes that the Industrial Disputes Investigation Act was not assented to till March 22, 1907. It was some weeks later before copies of the Act were available for distribution. Its provisions in consequence were not fully known by the parties at the time these disputes occurred.

INDUSTRIAL DISPUTES INVESTIGATION ACT, 1907.—PROCEEDINGS, 1907-08.—*Continued.*

I. MINING AND SMELTING INDUSTRY—*Continued.*

1 COAL MINES.—*Continued.*

Date of receipt of application.	Parties to Dispute.	Party making application.	Locality.	No. persons affected.	Nature of dispute.	Names of Members of Board; (c) Chairman; (e) Employer; (m) Men.	Date on which Board was constituted.	Date of receipt of report of Board.	Result of Reference.
April 9, 1907	*Western Coal Operators Association and employees.	Employees....	....	....	Concerning terms of joint agreement including wages schedule and other conditions of employment.	Sir Wm. Mulock, K.C., M.G. (c) 4; J. L. Parker (e) 1; L. P. Eckstein (m) 1.	April 22, 1907	May 29, 1907	Employees went on strike in the several mines while proceedings were pending in connection with the establishment of the Boards of Conciliation and while men, in consequence, it was alleged, of misunderstandings which arose with ignorance of the provisions of the Act. The Deputy Minister of Labour left for Fernie on April 19, to explain to the parties the provisions of the law. While in Fernie, the parties consented to his acting as a conciliator under the Conciliation Act, and an agreement was effected on May 4. The Boards convened at Fernie on April 30, but adjourned proceedings pending investigations by the Deputy Minister. On May 6, the Boards reconvened to receive from the parties a formal statement that the differences had been adjusted, a further cessation of work being thereby averted. An important feature of the settlement was the establishment of a standing committee of union men, the employers and employees, to which future differences were to be referred.
	Canadian American Coal and Coke Co.		Frank, Alta....	250....					
	Crowsnest Pass Coal Co.		Fernie, Coal Creek, Michel, B.C.	1,800....					
	International Coal & Coke Co.		Coleman, Alta....	370....					
	West Canadian Collieries, Ltd.		Lille and Bellevue..	350....					
	Breckenridge and Land Coal Co.		Lundbreck, Alta....	125....		Sir Wm. Mulock, K.C. M.G. (c) 4; F. B. Smith (m) 1; L. P. Eckstein (m) 1.			
	H. W. McNeill Coal Co.		Canmore, Alta....	300....					
	Pacific Coal Co....		Bankhead, Alta....	400....					

Date of application	Parties	Locality	No. affected	Nature of dispute	Board	Date of reference	Date of report	Remarks
May 8 1907	Cumberland Ry. and Coal Co. and employees.	Springhill, N.S.	1,700	Concerning payment for work in counter levels and stone in pillar work.	The Hon. Mr. Justice Graham (c) 3; P. S. Archibald (x) 1. R. B. Murray (m) 1.	May 17, 1907	July 13, 1907	Board, being unable to effect a settlement by ... presented a report signed by the Chairman and Mr. ... Minority report was ... by the ... The strike which was threatened prior to the application for Board on May 8 was averted for the ... but took ... on August 1, ... until ... 31, when the employees returned to ... on the conditions recommended in the report of the Board.
May 27, 1907	Alberta Ry. and Irrigation Coal Co. and employees of coal mines.	Lethbridge, Alta.	400	Concerning conditions of employment.				Amicable settlement including agreement as to conditions of employment and establishment of a standing committee of conciliation effected between parties while Board was in process of constitution, strike being thereby averted.
July 12, 1907	Cumberland Ry. and Coal Co. and employees.	Springhill, N.S.	1,700	Concerning wages and other conditions of employment.	His Honour Judge Patterson (c) 4; P. S. Archibald (x) 1; R. B. Murray (m) 1.	July 27, 1907	Sept. 21, 1907	Employees ... a strike on August 1, in ... to question of payment for ... in pillar work, having ... to ... of the Board ... May 17 to deal with ... of this strike proceedings ... until September 9. The Board ... for two days, and ... an ... report. The strike ended on October 31, the ... returning to work on ... conditions recommended in the report of the first Board.
Sept. 11, 1907	Hillcrest Coal and Coke Co., Ltd., and employees.	Hillcrest, Alta.	70	Concerning wages and other conditions of employment.	Hon. W. C. Fisher (c) 4; J. R. McDonald (x); F. H. Sherman (m) 1	Sept. 24, 1907	Nov. 4, 1907	The report of the Board was accompanied by a minority report by Mr. Sherman. Though neither report was formally accepted by the parties, settlement was reached in consequence of the inquiry by the Board, and a strike thereby averted.
Sept. 16, 1907	Hosmer Mines and employees.	Hosmer, B.C.	100	Concerning wages and other conditions of employment.	His Honour Judge Wilson (c) 4; F. B. Smith (a) 1; F. H. Sherman (m) 1	Sept. 30, 1907	Oct. 21, 1907	The Board presented a unanimous report, which though not formally accepted by the parties, formed the basis of an agreement subsequently reached by them and reported to the Department, a strike being thereby averted.

*Applications for a Board were received also from the employers, parties to this dispute.

INDUSTRIAL DISPUTES INVESTIGATION ACT, 1907.—PROCEEDINGS, 1907-08.—*Continued.*

I. MINING AND SMELTING INDUSTRY—*Continued.*

1. COAL MINES—*Concluded.*

Date of receipt of application.	Parties to Dispute.	Party making application.	Locality.	No. persons affected.	Nature of dispute.	Names of Members of Board: (c) Chairman; (s) Employer; (m) Men.	Date on which Board was constituted.	Date of receipt of report of Board.	Result of Reference.
Nov. 5, 1907	Canada West Coal and Coke Co. and employees.	Employees	Taber, Alta	150	Concerning wages, hours and other conditions of employment.	Hon. Mr. Justice Stuart (c) 4; S. A. Jones (s) 1; F. H. Sherman (m) 1	Nov. 20, 1907	Dec. 20, 1907	Differences adjusted, and agreement concluded before Board, dating from December 9, 1907, until March 31, 1909, a strike being thereby averted.
Nov. 5, 1907	Domestic Coal Co. and employees.	Employees	Taber, Alta	50	Concerning wages, hours and other conditions of employment.	Hon. Mr. Justice Stuart (c) 4; R. Duggan (s) 1; F. H. Sherman (m) 1.	Nov. 20, 1907	Dec. 28, 1907	Differences adjusted, and agreement concluded before Board, dating from December 9, 1907, until March 31, 1909, a strike being thereby averted.
Nov. 5, 1907	Duggan, Huntrods and Co. and employees.	Employees	Taber, Alta	40	Concerning wages, hours and other conditions of employment.	Hon. Mr. Justice Stuart (c) 4; J. Shorthouse (s) 1; F. H. Sherman (m) 1.	Nov. 20, 1907	Dec. 28, 1907	Differences adjusted, and agreement concluded before Board, dating from December 9, 1907, until March 31, 1909, a strike being thereby averted.
Nov. 12, 1907	Strathcona Coal Co. and employees.	Employees	Edmonton, Alta	40	Concerning wages, hours and other conditions of employment.	G. Montgomery (c) 3; F. L. Otter (s) 1; F. H. Sherman (m) 1.	Dec. 2, 1907	Dec. 28, 1907	Differences adjusted, and agreement concluded before Board, dating from September 23, 1907, until March 31, 1909, a strike thereby being averted.
Nov. 21, 1907	Cumberland Ry. and Coal Co. and employees.	Employees	Springhill, N.S.	1,700	Concerning wages and other conditions of employment.	His Honour Judge Patterson (c) 4; R. B. Murray (m) 1; Hiram Donkin (s) 1.	Dec. 24, 1907	Jan. 21, 1908	The Board presented a unanimous report, which the employees expressed a willingness to accept. No further cessation of work took place.
Jan. 4, 1908	Dominion Coal Co., Ltd., and members of the Provincial Workmen's Association.	Employees	Dominion, C.B.	7,000	Concerning wages and conditions of employment.	Prof. A. Shortt (c) 4; J. Dix Fraser (s) 1; Dr. A. Kendal, M.P. P., (m)	Feb. 18, 1908	Mar. 23, 1908	Differences adjusted, and an agreement concluded before the Board, effective from March 16, 1909, to December 31, 1909, strike being thereby averted.

Date	Parties	Applied by	Locality	No. affected	Matter in dispute	Board	Date	Date of report	Remarks
Feb. 10, 1908	John Marsh, John Howells, Stevens Brothers, coal mine operators, dealt with as a whole, and employees.	Employers	Woodpecker, Alta.	100	Concerning wages and conditions of employment.	Hon. Mr. Justice Stuart (c) 3; W. E. Bullock (e) 1; F. H. Sherman (m) 1.	Feb. 25, 1908	April 6, 1908	The report of the Board stated that the Act did not apply in this case, the mines having closed down for lack of orders before the investigation occurred. A wage scale was, however, recommended. The report was accompanied by a minority report, making other recommendations.
Mar. 16, 1908	Western Dominion Collieries, Ltd., and employees.	Employees	Taylorton, Sask.	90	Concerning wages and hours.	His Honour Judge Myers (c) 4; J. O. Hannah (e) 1; F. H. Sherman (m) 1.	April 10, 1908	May 5, 1908	Differences adjusted and agreement concluded before Board, effective from May 1, 1908, to May 1, 1909, a strike being thereby averted.
Mar. 16, 1908	Manitoba and Saskatchewan Coal Co., Ltd., and employees.	Employees	Bienfait, Sask.	50	Concerning wages and hours.	His Honour Judge Dawson (c) 4; G. C. Crowe (e) 1; F. H. Sherman (m) 1.	April 22, 1908	Dec. 8, 1908	The report in this case appears, as represented to the Department, to have been mislaid by one of the members of the Board and an unusual delay occurred thereon in its presentation. The Board disagreed in its findings, but no cessation of work was reported.
Mar. 25, 1908	Cumberland Ry. and Coal Co., Ltd., and employees.	Employees	Springhill, N.S.	1,600	Concerning wages	His Honour Judge Wallace (c) 4; Hon. John Armstrong (e) 2; R. B. Murray (m) 1.	April 29, 1908	May 26, 1908	The report found against the claims of the men, and was accompanied by a minority report, finding generally, but not wholly, in favour of the men. The employees declared the minority report acceptable to them. No cessation of work was reported.

2. METAL MINES.

Date	Parties	Applied by	Locality	No. affected	Matter in dispute	Board	Date	Date of report	Remarks
Sept. 12, 1907	Canadian Consolidated Mining & Smelting Co. and employees.	Employees	Moyie, B.C.	400	Concerning wages and hours.	His Honour Judge Wilson (c) 3; J. A. Harvey (e) 1; S. S. Taylor, K.C. (m) 1.	Sept. 23, 1907	Dec. 28, 1907	The Board, after the inquiry into mining conditions in British ..., the report, ... a unanimous ... of ... application ... to the ... mining ... in the province of British ... A ... and based on the ... was effected ... the company and is ... and a strike thereby ... The inquiry, moreover, had the effect of influencing ... of other differences in the industry in other parts of the province.

INDUSTRIAL DISPUTES INVESTIGATION ACT, 1907.—PROCEEDINGS, 1907-08.—*Continued.*

I. MINING AND SMELTING INDUSTRY—*Concluded.*

2. METAL MINES—*Concluded.*

Date of receipt of application.	Parties to Dispute.	Party making application.	Locality.	No. persons affected.	Nature of dispute.	Names of Members of Board: (c) Chairman; (e) Employer; (w) Men.	Date on which Board was constituted.	Date of receipt of report of Board.	Result of Reference.
Dec. 9, 1907	McKinley-Darragh Mining Co., Ltd., and its employees.	Employees	Cobalt, Ont.	120	Concerning wages.	Prof. A. Shortt (c); E. C. Kingswell (e); John A. Welch (w).	Dec. 21, 1907	Jan. 22, 1908	A unanimous report was presented by the Board, making recommendations for the settlement of the dispute. The findings of the Board were not formally accepted by the parties, but the investigation by the Board is believed to have been beneficial to the camp as a whole and no cessation of work was reported.
Jan. 9, 1908	Temiskaming and Hudson Bay Mining Co., Ltd., and its employees	Employees	Cobalt, Ont.	50	Concerning wages and hours.	Prof. S. J. Maclean (c); M. F. Purssaville (e); C. B. Duke (w).	Jan. 31, 1908	Feb. 13, 1908	Unanimous report was presented by Board, making recommendations for the settlement of the dispute. The findings of the Board were accepted by the men, but not by the company. No cessation of work was, however, reported.

II. TRANSPORTATION AND COMMUNICATION.

1. RAILWAYS.

Date of receipt of application.	Parties to Dispute.	Party making application.	Locality.	No. persons affected.	Nature of dispute.	Names of Members of Board: (c) Chairman; (e) Employer; (w) Men.	Date on which Board was constituted.	Date of receipt of report of Board.	Result of Reference.
April 20, 1907	Grand Trunk Ry. Co. of Canada and machinists.	Employees	Montreal, Toronto, Ottawa, Stratford, etc.	400	Concerning schedule involving wages, hours, apprenticeship, reinstatement of former employees, etc.	Prof. A. Shortt (c); W. Nesbitt, K.C. (e); J. G. O'Donoghue (w).	May 4, 1907	May 21, 1907	Differences adjusted, and agreement concluded before Board for period of one year from May 1, strike being thereby averted.
June 27, 1907	Grand Trunk Ry. Co. of Canada and its locomotive engineers.	Employees	Montreal, Toronto, Ottawa, Stratford, etc.	1,300	Concerning schedule of wages and rules.	Prof. A. Shortt (c); W. Nesbitt, K.C. (e); J. Cardell (w).	July 18, 1907	Aug. 16, 1907	Differences adjusted, and agreement for three years concluded before Board, a strike being thereby averted.

Date	Parties		Location	No.	Nature of dispute	Board	Date	Date	Result
July 10, 1907	Intercolonial Ry. of Canada and freight handlers in its employ at Halifax, N.S.	Employees	Halifax, N.S.	250	Concerning wages and classification of employees.	Prof. W. Murray, (c) 3; Henry Holgate (s) 1; R. E. Finn, M.P. (m) 1.	July 23, 1907	Aug. 12, 1907	On June 29, ... strike, and when ... parties ... of Act ... the differences under the Act, and ... work. On the ... of ... parties, ... were under ... Conciliation and Labour Act, ... and a ... ment effected, the terms of ... ... were ... ... to the ... ... at St. John, N.B., as well as at Halifax, N.S., and ... ... of work ... ... averted.
Sept. 5, 1907	Canadian Pacific Railway Company and railroad telegraphers	Employees	On all lines of Canadian Pacific Railway in Canada.	1,656	Concerning schedule of wages and rules of employment.	Prof. A. Shortt, (c) 3; W. Nesbitt, K. C., (s) 1; J. G. O'Donoghue, (m) 1.	Sept. 16, 1907	Oct. 12, 1907	Differences adjusted, and an agreement concluded before Board, dating from October 1, a strike being thereby averted.
Nov. 19, 1907	Grand Trunk Railway Company and railroad telegraphers.	Employer	Montreal, Que.	300	Concerning wages and other conditions of employment.	Prof. A. Shortt, (c) 3; W. Nesbitt, K. C., (s) 1; J. G. O'Donoghue, (m) 1.	Nov. 30, 1907	Jan. 23, 1908	Differences adjusted, and agreement concluded before Board, dating from January 1, 1908, a strike being thereby averted.
Nov. 22, 1907	Canadian Pacific Railway Company and carmen employed by Company on western lines.	Employer	Western lines.	1,215	Concerning wages and hours.	Prof. Odlum, (c) 3; A. M. Nanton, (s) 1; J. H. McVety, (m) 1.	Nov. 26, 1907	Dec. 23, 1907	The Board presented a unanimous report recommending a basis of settlement which was subsequently, in correspondence with the Department, accepted by both parties, and a strike thereby averted.
Dec. 19, 1907	Canadian Northern Railway Company and firemen, enginemen and hostlers in its employ.	Employees	Winnipeg and territory along Canadian Northern Railway.	359	Concerning relations of union to employer.	Prof. A. Shortt, (c) 4; F. H. Richardson, (s) 1; J. G. O'Donoghue, (m) 1.	Jan. 8, 1908	Jan. 25, 1908	Differences amicably adjusted before the Board and a strike thereby averted.
Jan. 8, 1908	Grand Trunk Railway Company and carmen in its employ.	Employees	Grand Trunk Railway System.	800	Concerning wages and conditions of labour.	Prof. A. Shortt, (c) 3; Wallace Nesbitt (s) 1; J. G. O'Donoghue. (m) 1.	Jan. 28, 1908	Feb. 28, 1908	Differences amicably adjusted before the Board and a strike thereby averted.

INDUSTRIAL DISPUTES INVESTIGATION ACT, 1907.—PROCEEDINGS, 1907–08.—*Continued.*

II. TRANSPORTATION AND COMMUNICATION—*Concluded.*

2.—STREET RAILWAYS.

Date of receipt of application.	Parties to Dispute.	Party making application.	Locality.	No. persons affected.	Nature of dispute.	Names of Members of Board: (c) Chairman; (E) Employer; (M) Men.	Date on which Board was constituted.	Date of receipt of report of Board.	Result of Reference.
Jan. 31, 1908	Hamilton and Dundas Railway Company and Hamilton Radial Railway Company, and Hamilton, & Burlington Railway Company and employees.	Employees	Hamilton, Ont.	120	Concerning relations of union to employing companies.	His Honour Judge Monck, (c) 4; Wm. Bell, K.C. (E) 1; J. G. O'Donoghue, (M) 1.	Feb. 17, 1908	April 8, 1908	Report of the Board was opposed to the claims of the men and was sustained by a minority, but eventually M. O'Donoghue, was sustaining the claims of the men. Neither party was able to bring about a cessation, and no understanding between the parties, and no cessation of which was made.

3. SHIPPING.

*May 15, 1907	Shipping Federation of Canada and longshoremen of Montreal.	Employers	Montreal, Que.	1,500	Demand for increase in wages.	Archbishop Bruchesi, (c) 3; G. W. Stephens, (E) 1; Jos. Ainey, (M) 1.	June 7, 1907	June 17, 190	On May 13, all men went on strike, ... provisions of Act, and applications ... on My 18 the ... on ... Board. On My 15, Mr. F. A. ... the then Secretary of the Department, went to ... As ... the result of ... Industrial Disputes Investigation Act, and a ... was ... by the ... of a Board. A unanimous ... was ... at ... of the ... covering the employment for the ... as of 1907 and 1908.
*May 25, 1907	Shipping Federation of Canada, Canadian Pacific Railway Company and longshoremen of Montreal.	Employees	Montreal, Que.	1,600	Demand for increase in wages.				

| May 31, 1907 | Furnes Withy Company, Cunard & Company, Pickford, Black & Company and longshoremen. | Employers | Halifax, N.S. | 500 | Concerning wages. Increase of 5 cents per hour demanded by men, 2½ cents offered by companies, but refused. | James Hall, (E) 1; Philip King, (M) 1. | | | The Union did not formally accept the recommendations of the Board, but the members, with the exception of a few, signed individual agreements with the employers, based upon the recommendations of the Board, and a further cessation of work was thereby averted. |
| Mar. 6, 1908 | Dominion Marine Association and Seamen's Union. | Employees | Kingston, Ont., & ports of Great Lakes. | 460 | Concerning wages and conditions of employment. | Prof. A. Shortt, (c) 3; Jas. Stewart, (E) 2; John A. Flett, (M) 1. | April 1, 1908 | April 14, 1908 | On May 26, strike, alleging … of the … visions of the … DuBreuil, Fair Wages Officer of the … A Board … DuBreuil lending the good offices of the Department as a concili… in the … blishment of the … Differences amicably arranged before the Board and strike thereby averted. |

*The two applications here recorded are regarded as one in the tabular statement.

INDUSTRIAL DISPUTES INVESTIGATION ACT, 1907.—PROCEEDINGS, 1907–08.—*Concluded.*

B.—INDUSTRIES OTHER THAN MINES, AGENCIES OF TRANSPORTATION AND COMMUNICATION, AND OTHER PUBLIC UTILITIES.*

Date of receipt of application.	Parties to Dispute.	Party making application.	Locality.	No. persons affected.	Nature of dispute.	Names of Members of Board; (c) Chairman; (E) Employer; (M) Men.	Date on which Board was constituted.	Date of receipt of report of Board.	Result of Reference.
Aug. 28 1907	Montreal Cotton Company and employees.	Employees	Valleyfield, Que....	2,200	Concerning conditions and wages.	Hon. Mr. Justice Fortin, (c) 4; Duncan McCormick, K.C., (E) 1; W. Paquette, (M) 1.	Sept. 4, 1907	Sept. 24, 1907	The employees went on strike on August 13, and the good offices of the Department were requested with a view to effecting a settlement, Mr. F. A. Acland, the then

secretary of the Department, and Mr. V. DuBreuil, Fair Wages Officer, visited the scene of the dispute and explained the provisions of the Act to the parties, with special reference to the sections enabling a dispute in any industry other than that of a mine or public utility to be referred, by mutual agreement between the disputing parties, to a Board of Conciliation and Investigation. As a result of the explanations and efforts at conciliation on the part of the officers of the Department, an application for a Board was forwarded to the Minister, the employees in the meantime returning to work on August 26. The Board was duly established, with the result that the differences were adjusted and an agreement concluded before the Board dating from September 17, 1907, to be effective until May 4, 1908, and thereafter until either side be given a written notice of cancellation of the same. A feature of the agreement was the establishment of a permanent Committee of Conciliation to which it was agreed that all subsequent disputes should be referred.

*These disputes were referred to a Board of Conciliation and Investigation under section 63 of the Act, which provides that "in the event of a dispute arising in any industry or trade other than such as may be included under the provisions of this Act, and such dispute threatens to result in a lockout or strike, or has actually resulted in a lockout or strike, either of the parties may agree, in writing, to allow such dispute to be referred to a Board of Conciliation and Investigation, to be constituted under the provisions of this Act," etc. Applications referring to disputes in this class of industry were received also in the cases of W. A. Marsh & Company, Boots and Shoe Manufacturers, Quebec; the Rosamond Woollen Company, Almonte, Ont.; the Eastern Townships Manufacturing Company, St. Hyacinthe, Que.; L'Association Internationale des Ouvriers en Fourrures, Montreal; Davidson Manufacturing Company, Montreal, and A. Gravel Lumber Company, Etchemin, Que.; but the parties concerned not agreeing to refer the differences for adjustment according to the provisions of the Act, no action was taken by the Minister.

INDUSTRIAL DISPUTES INVESTIGATION ACT, 1907.—PROCEEDINGS, 1908-09.

STATEMENT of Applications for Boards of Conciliation and Investigation and of Proceedings thereunder from April 1, 1908, to March 31, 1909.

A.—MINES, AGENCIES OF TRANSPORTATION AND COMMUNICATION, AND OTHER PUBLIC SERVICE UTILITIES.

1. Appointed by the Minister, under Section 8, sub-section 1, of the I. D. I. Act, on recommendation from party concerned.
2. Appointed by the Minister, under Section 8, Sub-section 2, of the I. D. I. Act, in the absence of a recommendation from party concerned.
3. Appointed by the Minister, under Section 8, Sub-section 3, of the I. D. I. Act, on the joint recommendation of the two members first appointed.
4. Appointed by the Minister, under Section 8, Sub-section 3, of the I. D. I. Act, in the absence of a joint recommendation by the two members first appointed.

I. MINING AND SMELTING INDUSTRY.

I. COAL MINES.

Date of receipt of application.	Parties to Dispute.	Party making application.	Locality.	No. persons affected.	Nature of dispute.	Names of Members of Board; (c) Chairman; (E) Employer; (M) Men.	Date on which Board was constituted.	Date of receipt of report of Board.	Result of Reference.
May 2, 1908	Standard Coal Co. and employees.	Employees.	Edmonton, Alta.	20	Concerning wages and conditions of labour.	His Honour Judge Taylor (c) 4; F. H. Smith (E) 1; F. H. Sherman (M) 1.	June 19, 1908	July 22, 1908	Company had previously made an agreement individually with employees. Representative of men was willing to take agreement for what it was worth, but would not enter into same on behalf of union. Board decided to leave the existing agreement intact, and this arrangement appears to have been satisfactory, a strike being thereby averted.
May 12, 1908	Nova Scotia Steel and Coal Co. and employees.	Employees.	North Sydney, N.S.	1,750	Concerning wages and conditions of labour.	Prof. A. Shortt (c) 3; Dr. D. Allison (E) 2; J. W. Maddin (M) 1.	June 19, 1908	Aug. 1, 1908	An agreement concluded before the Board on all points, and a strike thereby averted.
May 14, 1908	International Coal and Coke Co. and employees.	Employees.	Westville, N.S.	800	Concerning wages and conditions of labour.				No Board was established in this case, the parties having come to an amicable agreement, subsequent to forwarding the application, a strike being thereby averted.
May 15, 1908	Arcadia Coal Co. and employees.	Employees.	Stellarton, N.S.	800	Concerning wages and conditions of labour.				No Board was established in this case, the parties having come to an amicable agreement subsequent to forwarding the application, a strike being thereby averted.

INDUSTRIAL DISPUTES INVESTIGATION ACT, 1907.—PROCEEDINGS, 1908-09.—*Continued.*

I. MINING AND SMELTING INDUSTRY.—*Concluded.*

1. COAL MINES.—*Concluded.*

Date of receipt of application.	Parties to Dispute.	Party making application.	Locality.	No. persons affected.	Nature of dispute.	Names of Members of Board: (c) Chairman; (e) Employer; (m) Men.	Date on which Board was constituted.	Date of receipt of report of Board.	Result of Reference.
May 18, 1908	Port Hood and Richmond Ry. Coal Co. and employees.	Employees	Port Hood, N.S.	300	Concerning wages and conditions of labour.	His Honour Judge McGillivray (c) 3; Geo. S. Campbell (e) 1; Jas. Macdonald (m) 1.	June 8, 1908	July 2, 1908	A unanimous report was made by the Board with recommendations for a settlement of all differences, which is understood to have been accepted as a basis of working operations, a strike being thereby averted.
July 2, 1908	Maritime Coal Railway and Power Co., Ltd. and employees.	Employees	Chignecto, N.S.	200	Concerning wages and conditions of labour.	Rev Chas. Wilson (c) 1; B. Barnhill (e) 1; R. B. Murray (m) 1.	July 6, 1908	July 27, 1908	An agreement was effected before the Board on all the points at issue and covering the period of two years from July 31, 1908, a strike being thereby averted.
Oct. 19, 1908	Galbraith Coal Co., Ltd., and employees.	Employees	Lundbreck, Alta.	30	Concerning wages and conditions of labour.	Chas. Simister (c) 3; B. Smith, C. E. (e) 1; Jas. A. McDonald (m) 1.	Nov. 25, 1908	Dec. 14, 1908	The Board presented a unanimous report recommending a basis of settlement, which was subsequently, in correspondence with the department, accepted by both parties to the dispute, a strike being thereby averted.
Mar. 4, 1909	Dominion Coal Co. and employees, members of United Mine Workers of America.	Employees	Glace Bay, N.S.	3,000	Alleged discrimination against members of United Mine Workers of America.	His Honour Judge Wallace (c) 4; S. Campbell (e) 2; Daniel McDougall (m) 1.	Mar. 22, 1909		Proceedings unfinished.

2. METAL MINES.

Date of receipt of application.	Parties to Dispute.	Party making application.	Locality.	No. persons affected.	Nature of dispute.	Names of Members of Board: (c) Chairman; (e) Employer; (m) Men.	Date on which Board was constituted.	Date of receipt of report of Board.	Result of Reference.
July 20, 1908	Cobalt Central Mining Co., Ltd., and employees.	Employees	Cobalt, Ont.	105	Concerning wages and hours.	Prof. S. J. Maclean (c) 4; F. Falconbridge (e) 1; C. B. Duke (m) 1.	Aug. 22, 1908	Aug. 29, 1908	Unanimous report presented by Board making recommendations for the settlement of the dispute, and no cessation of work reported.

II. TRANSPORTATION AND COMMUNICATION.

1. RAILWAYS.

Date	Parties		Railway	No.	Nature of dispute	Board	Date of reference	Date of report	Remarks
April 28, 1908	Canadian Pacific Ry. Co. and various trades in its mechanical department.	Employees	C.P.R. system	8,000	Concerning wages and conditions of labour.	P. A. Macdonald (c) 4; C. F. Fullerton (s) 1; G. F. Galt (s) 2*; Jas. Somerville (M) 1.	May 13, 1908	July 16, 1908	The Board did not present a unanimous report, Mr. Somerville presenting a minority report. The Board made certain recommendations for settlement of dispute, which were accepted by company with some demur. Men refused to accept findings of Board and ceased work on August 5. They returned to work on October 5, accepting finally recommendations of Board.
May 14, 1908	Intercolonial Railway of Canada and Station Freight Clerks' Union, Nos. 1 and 2 of Halifax, N.S., and St. John, N.B.	Employees	Halifax, N.S., and St. John, N.B.		Concerning wages and conditions of labour.	His Honour Judge McGibbon (c) 4; H. Holgate, C. E. (s) 1; J. G. O'Donoghue (M) 1;** R. E. Finn (M) 1.**	Sept. 8, 1908	Oct. 6, 1908	The ...
May 29, 1908	Canadian Pacific Ry. and railway telegraphers in its employ	Employees	C.P.R. system	1,605	Concerning alleged wrongful dismissal of certain employees.	Hon. Mr. Justice Fortin (c) 4; Campbell, K. C. (s) 1; W. T. J. Lee (M) 1.	June 17, 1908	Sept. 26, 1908	A ...
Aug. 21, 1908	Canadian Northern Ry. Co. and carmen on its Lake St. John Division.	Employees	Lake St. John Division Canadian Northern Ry.	49	Concerning wages and conditions of labour.	Ludovic Brunet, (c) 3; E. A. Evans (s) 1; P. J. Jobin (M) 1; A. Chartrain (M) †	Sept. 30, 1908	Nov. 19, 1908	A ...
Aug. 22, 1908	Canadian Pacific Ry. Co. and firemen and engineers in its employ.	Employees	C.P.R. system	7,000	Concerning alleged wrongful dismissal of certain employees.	Hon. Judge Fortin (c) 3; W. Nesbitt, K.C. (s) 1; J. G. O'Donoghue (M) 1.	Jan. 5, 1909	Jan. 25, 1909	A unanimous report ...
Aug. 22, 1908	Canadian Northern Ry. Co. and locomotive engineers in its employ.	Employees	Canadian Northern Ry. system.	341	Concerning wages and conditions of labour.	His Honour Judge Gunn (c) 4; F. H. Richardson (s) 1; J. Harvey Hall (M) 1.	Sept. 14, 1908	Nov. 16, 1908	A ...

*Mr. Fullerton, finding himself at an early stage of the proceedings unable to agree with his colleagues, resigned from the Board, and the company declining to make a further recommendation, the Minister appointed Mr. Galt without recommendation.

**Owing to inability of Mr. R. E. Finn to act as member of Board, Mr. J. G. O'Donoghue was appointed in his stead.

† Owing to inability of A. Chartrain to act as member of the Board, P. J. Jobin was appointed in his stead.

INDUSTRIAL DISPUTES INVESTIGATION ACT, 1907.—PROCEEDINGS, 1908-09.—*Concluded.*

II. TRANSPORTATION AND COMMUNICATION.—*Concluded.*

1. RAILWAYS.—*Concluded.*

Date of receipt of application.	Parties to Dispute.	Party making application.	Locality.	No. persons affected.	Nature of dispute.	Names of Members of Board: (c) Chairman; (s) Employer; (w) Men.	Date on which Board was constituted.	Date of receipt of report of Board.	Result of Reference.
Dec. 26, 1908	Kingston and Pembroke Ry. Co. and employees, members of Order of Railroad Telegraphers.	Employees	Kingston & Pembroke Ry. system.	19 dir... 1,500 indir.	Concerning wages and conditions of labour.	His Honour Judge Gunn (c) 4; K. C. (s) Whiting, J.; I. G. O'Donoghue (w) 1.	Jan. 15, 1909	....	Proceedings unfinished.
Dec. 29, 1908	Great Northwestern Telegraph Co. and certain Railroad Telegraphers on Michigan Central Ry. system.	Employees	Michigan Central Ry. system.	75	Abolition of commission by commercial business on Michigan Central Ry. System by Great Northwestern Telegraph Co., without due notice.	Judge McGibbon (c); 4; J. F. Mackay (s) 2; J. G. O'Donoghue (w) 1.	Feb. 8, 1909	Mar. 22, 1909	*[text garbled]* ... before the Board, ... in favour of ... to the Board ... The ... being in an agreement, is under ... to such a ... was ...

2. STREET RAILWAYS.

Date of receipt of application.	Parties to Dispute.	Party making application.	Locality.	No. persons affected.	Nature of dispute.	Names of Members of Board: (c) Chairman; (s) Employer; (w) Men.	Date on which Board was constituted.	Date of receipt of report of Board.	Result of Reference.
May 8, 1908	Ottawa Electric Ry. and its employees.	Employees	Ottawa, Ont.	256	Concerning wages and conditions of labour.	Prof. A. Shortt (c) 4; G. F. Henderson (s) 1; J. G. O'Donoghue (w) 1.	May 22, 1908	June 15, 1908	Differences amicably arranged before the Board and strike thereby averted.
Sept. 3, 1908	Quebec, Light, Heat and Power Co. and its street railway employes.	Employees	Quebec, Que.	116	Concerning alleged wrongful dismissal of certain employees.	W. H. Moore (c) 1; Omer Brunel (w) 1.		Oct. 6, 1908	The two members of the Board appointed respectively on the nomination of employing company and employees presented a joint statement making certain recommendations for a settlement of the disputed points, which recommendations were accepted by both parties to the dispute as a settlement of the differences, a strike being thereby averted.

3. TEAMSTERS.

Date	Company	Parties	Place	Number	Subject	Board	Date	Date	Result
Feb. 10, 1909	Manitoba Cartage Co., Ltd.	Employees	Winnipeg, Man.	40 dir. 260 indir.	Concerning alleged discrimination against men connected with the Union.	Revv. Dr. C. W. Gordon (c) 3; Prof. R. Cochrane (e) 2; T. J. Murray (m) 1.	Mar. 2, 1909		Proceedings unfinished.

B.—INDUSTRIES OTHER THAN MINES, AGENCIES OF TRANSPORTATION AND COMMUNICATION AND OTHER PUBLIC UTILITIES.*

Date	Company	Parties	Place	Number	Subject	Board	Date	Date	Result
Dec. 17, 1908	The John Ritchie Co., Ltd., and certain employees (lasters).	Employees & employers.	Quebec, Que.	300	Concerning introduction of certain machine and wages.	Dr. Chas. Cote (c) 3; Félix Marois (e) 1; Z. Berube (m) 1.	Dec. 31, 1908	Feb. 17, 1909	An agreement was concluded before the Board covering all matters in dispute, effective from February 12, 1909, to May 1, 1910, a strike being thereby averted.

*These disputes were referred to a Board of Conciliation and Investigation under Section 63 of the Act, which provides that "in the event of a dispute arising in any industry or trade other than such as may be included under the provisions of this act and such dispute threatens to result in a lockout or strike, or has actually resulted in a lockout or strike, either of the parties may agree, in writing, to allow such dispute to be referred to a Board of Conciliation and Investigation, to be constituted under the provisions of this Act," etc.

INDUSTRIAL DISPUTES INVESTIGATION ACT, 1907.—PROCEEDINGS, 1909–10.

STATEMENT of Applications for Boards of Conciliation and Investigation and of Proceedings thereunder from April 1, 1909, to March 31, 1910.

A.—MINES, AGENCIES OF TRANSPORTATION AND COMMUNICATION, AND OTHER PUBLIC SERVICE UTILITIES.

1. Appointed by the Minister, under Section 8, Sub-section 1, of the I. D. I. Act, on recommendation from party concerned.
2. Appointed by the Minister, under Section 8, Sub-section 2, of the I. D. I. Act, in the absence of a recommendation from party concerned.
3. Appointed by the Minister, under Section 8, Sub-section 3, of the I. D. I. Act, on the joint recommendation of the two members first appointed.
4. Appointed by the Minister, under Section 8, Sub-section 4, of the I. D. I. Act, in the absence of a joint recommendation by the two members first appointed.

I. MINING AND SMELTING INDUSTRY.

1. COAL MINES.

Date of receipt of application.	Parties to Dispute.	Party making application.	Locality.	No. persons affected.	Nature of dispute.	Names of Members of Board; (c) Chairman; (e) Employer; (w) Men.	Date on which Board was constituted.	Date of receipt of report of Board.	Result of Reference.
Mar. 4, 1909	Dominion Coal Co. and employees, members of United Mine Workers of America.	Employees	Glace Bay, C.B.	3,000	Alleged discrimination against certain employees, members of United Mine Workers of America.	His Honour Judge Wallace (c) 4; G. S. Campbell (e) 2; Daniel McDougall (w) 1.	Mar. 22, 1909	April 16, 1909	*[illegible]*
April 13, 1909	Nicola Valley Coal and Coke Co. and employees.	Employees	Middlesboro, B.C.	150	Alleged discrimination against certain employees.	His Honour Judge P. S. Lampman (c) 3; Thos. Kiddie (e); Thos. Chas. Brooke (w) 1.	May 7, 1909	June 3, June 11, June 18, 1909	*[illegible]*

Date of reference	Parties		Place	No.	Subject of dispute	Board	Date of report	Remarks
April 26, 1909	Nova Scotia Steel and Coal Co., Ltd., and employees.	Employees	Sydney Mines, C.B.	340	Wages and conditions of labour, and recognition of United Mine Workers of America.	His Honour Judge J. P. Chipman (c) 4; His Honour Judge MacGillivray (s) 2; D. McDougall (w) 1. June 23, 1909	July 23, 1909	The report of the Board was accompanied by a minority report, signed by Mr. D. McDougall, member appointed on behalf of the employees. The report of the Board found against the claims of the employees. There was, however, no cessation of work, the threatened strike being averted.
May 8, 1909	Western Canadian Coal Operators... By: ... and Irrigation Co.; H. W. ... Electric ... Canadian Collieries, Ltd.; ... Coal and ... Co., Ltd., and ...	Operators	Lethbridge, Coleman, Lille, Blairhead, Hillcrest, Bellevue, Passburg, Canmore and Taber, Alta., Hosmer and Frank, B.C.	2,100	Wages and conditions of labour.	Rev. Hugh Grant (c) 4; Colin Macleod (s) 1; F. H. Sherman (w) 1. May 15, 1909	June 21, June 23, 1909	The report of the Board was signed by Mr. Colin Macleod, with was, however, ... that of the Board. The report was ... ly ... ed by Mr. party, but contents ... the ... and ...
May 10, 1909	Cumberland Railway and Coal Co. and employees.	Employees	Springhill, N.S.	1,500	Wages and conditions of labour and recognition of United Mine Workers of America.	Hon. Mr. Justice Longley (c) 3; Chas. Archibald (s) 2; E. B. Paul (w) 1. June 5, 1909	July 23, 1909	The report of the B and was accompanied by a minority report, signed by Mr. E. B. Paul, the ... member appointed on ... of the ... The Board's findings were substantially in favour of the company. The award was not, ... accepted by the employees, and strike which resulted in the closing down of the company's mines until early in the month of ... 1910, when ... were resumed on a limited scale.
June 15, 1909	Canada West Coal Co. and employees.	Employer	Taber, Alta.	300	Wages and conditions of labour.	His Honour Judge R. Winter (c) 3; Colin Macleod (s) 1; W. C. Simmons (w) 1. July 3, 1909	July 19, 1909	A unanimous report was presented by the Board, making recommendations for the settlement of the dispute. An agreement based on the findings of the Board was subsequently signed by the parties concerned effective from July 30, 1909, to March 31, 1911. The employees who had been on strike from April 23, returned to work on July 30.

INDUSTRIAL DISPUTES INVESTIGATION ACT, 1907.—PROCEEDINGS, 1909-10.—*Continued.*

1. MINING AND SMELTING INDUSTRY.—*Concluded.*

1. COAL MINES.—*Concluded.*

Date of receipt of application.	Parties to Dispute.	Party making application.	Locality.	No. persons affected.	Nature of dispute.	Names of Members of Board: (c) Chairman; (e) Employer; (m) Men.	Date on which Board was constituted.	Date of receipt of report of Board.	Result of Reference.
Nov. 18, 1909	Edmonton Standard Coal Co., Ltd., and employees	Employer	Edmonton, Alta.	75	Wages and dismissal of employees.	Geo. F. Cunningham (c) 3; Frank B. Smith (e) 1; Clement Stubbs (m) 1.	Dec. 2, 1909	Dec. 27, 1909	A ... report was presented by the Board, making certain recommendations for the settlement of the dispute, which were ... by the ... concerned, a strike ... thereby ...
Dec. 2, 1909	James W. Blain, contractor for output of Cardiff Coal Co., Ltd., and employees.	Employer	Cardiff, Alta.	60 dir. 15 indir.	Wages and conditions of employment.				Proceedings in ... with the application were discontinued in view of an agreement being reached by the parties concerned.
Jan. 5, 1910	Alberta Coal Mining Co. and employees.	Employer	Cardiff, Alta.	35 dir. 25 indir.	Wages and conditions of employment.	R. G. Duggan (c) 3; J. O. Hannah (e) 1; Clement Stubbs (m) 1.	Jan. 17, 1910		Proceedings unfinished.

2. METAL MINES.

Date of receipt of application.	Parties to Dispute.	Party making application.	Locality.	No. persons affected.	Nature of dispute.	Names of Members of Board: (c) Chairman; (e) Employer; (m) Men.	Date on which Board was constituted.	Date of receipt of report of Board.	Result of Reference.
April 5, 1909	British Columbia Copper Co. and employees.	Employees	Greenwood, B.C.	225	Alleged discrimination against certain employees.	His Honour Judge P. E. Wilson (c) 1; Edward Cronyn (e) 1; John McInnis (m) 1.	April 20, 1909	May 29, June 3, June 11, 1909	Three separate ... were presented in this case, the company expressing willingness to accept ... of the chairman as a basis of set ... , while the men accepted the ... of Mr. John McInnis. The men declared a strike on June 28, ... continued until July 24.
Jan. 8, 1910	British Columbia Copper Co. and employees.	Employer	Greenwood, B.C.	350	Employees' unwillingness to work with non-union men.	J. H. Senkler (c) 4; John A. Mara (e) 1; John McInnis (m) 1.	Jan. 10, 1910	Mar. 29, 1910	The rep of the Board was accompanied by a minority report signed by Mr. John McInnis. The Board's rep ... was substantially in favour of the ... The employees concerned being unwilling to concur in the ... of the Board, a strike was de... on ... 19, and continued until May 14, when the employ y en ... had to ... ... on ... of Board's award.

II. TRANSPORTATION AND COMMUNICATION.

1. RAILWAYS.

Date	Parties		System	Number	Subject	Board	Date reference	Date	Result
Dec. 26, 1908	Kingston and Pembroke Ry. Co., and employees, members of Order of Railroad Telegraphers.	Employees	Kingston - Pembroke Ry. System.	19 dir. 1,600 indir.	Wages and conditions of labour.	His Honour Judge Gunn (c) 4; J. L. Whiting, K. C. (e) 1; J. G. O'Donoghue (m) 1.	Jan. 15, 1909	April 22, 1909	A unanimous report was presented by the Board, which made certain recommendations for the settlement of dispute. The report, with recommendations, was accepted subsequently by both parties, a strike being thereby averted.
May 7, 1909	Canadian Pacific Ry. Co., and railroad telegraphers in its employ.	Employees	Canadian Pacific Ry. lines.	1,600......	Concerning alleged unfair dismissal and breach of contract.	Hon. Mr. Justice Fortin (c) 4; Wallace Nesbitt, K.C. (e) 1; W. T. J. Lee (m) 1.	May 29, 1909	June 11, 1909	A unanimous report was presented by the Board, making certain recommendations for the settlement of the dispute, which were subsequently in correspondence with the department, accepted by both parties concerned, a strike being thereby averted.
June 3, 1909	Grand Trunk Pacific Ry. Co., and engineers, firemen, conductors, brakemen, baggagemen and yardmen in its employ.	Employees	Grand Trunk Pacific lines.	300........	Wages and conditions of labour.	Hon. R. P. Sutherland, M.P. (c) 3; F. H. McGuigan (e) 1; J. G. O'Donoghue (m) 1.	June 24, 1909	Aug. 14, 1909	A unanimous report was presented by the Board, making certain recommendations for the settlement of the dispute and no cessation of work occurred, the threatened strike being averted.
June 8, 1909	Canadian Northern Ry. Co., and its maintenance-of-way employees	Employees	Canadian Northern Ry. lines west of Port Arthur.	1,100 dir. 700 indir.	Wages and conditions of labour.	His Honour Judge M. Myers (c) 4; W. J. Christie (e) 1; J. G. O'Donoghue (m) 1.	June 24, 1909	July 21, 1909	The report of the Board was accompanied by a minority report, signed by Mr. W. Christie. The findings of the Board were subsequently accepted by both parties to the dispute, a strike being thereby averted.
Aug. 11, 1909	Intercolonial Railway of Canada and its round-house employees.	Employees	Halifax, N.S.	20 dir. 1,000 indir.	Employers' alleged discrimination against certain employees.	Sir Geo. Garneau (c) 4; Jas. M. Gilmour (e) 1; Aaron A. R. Mosher (m) 1.	Sept. 25, 1909	Nov. 17, 1909	A unanimous report was presented by the Board, making certain recommendations for the settlement of the dispute. The findings of the Board were subsequently accepted by both parties to the dispute, a strike being thereby averted.
Oct. 2, 1909	Intercolonial Railway of Canada and machinists and fitters in its employ.	Employees	Intercolonial system.	363 dir. 43 indir.	Concerning dismissal of certain employees and alleged violation of contract.	His Honour Judge John A. Barron (c) 4; Jas. H. Gilmour (e) 1; J. G. O'Donoghue (m) 1.	Oct. 19, 1909	Dec. 8, 1909	A unanimous report was presented by the Board, making certain recommendations for the settlement of the dispute, which were accepted by both parties concerned, a strike being thereby averted.

33a—3

INDUSTRIAL DISPUTES INVESTIGATION ACT, 1907.—PROCEEDINGS, 1909-10.—*Continued.*

II. TRANSPORTATION AND COMMUNICATION.—*Continued.*

1. RAILWAYS.—*Concluded.*

Date of receipt of application.	Parties to Dispute.	Party making application.	Locality.	No. persons affected.	Nature of dispute.	Names of Members of Board: (c) Chairman; (E) Employer; (M) Men.	Date on which Board was constituted.	Date of receipt of report of Board.	Result of Reference.
Dec. 3, 1909	Grand Trunk Ry. Co. and conductors and telegraphers and station agents in its employ.	Employees...	Grand Trunk Ry. lines, east of Detroit, Mich.	260	Wages, advertising of vacancies, etc.	J. E. Atkinson (c) 4; Wallace Nesbitt, K.C. (E) 1; W. T. J. Lee (M) 1.	Dec. 21, 1909	Feb. 24, 1910	A report was presented which was unanimous on certain of the matters in dispute, Mr. Wallace Nesbitt, K.C., member appointed on behalf of the company, dissenting from the views of the other members on two points. At the close of the year the department was in communication with the parties to the dispute. No cessation of work occurred.
Mar. 17, 1910	Canadian Pacific Ry. Co. and conductors, baggagemen, brakemen and yardmen in its employ.	Employees...	C.P.R. lines...	4,360	Wages and conditions of employment.	J. E. Atkinson (c) 4; Wallace Nesbitt, K.C. (E) 1; J. G. O'Donoghue (M) 1.	Mar. 18, 1910	....	Proceedings unfinished.
Mar. 17, 1910	Grand Trunk Ry. Co. and conductors, baggagemen, brakemen and yardmen in its employ.	Employees...	G.T.R. lines...	3,017	Wages and conditions of employment.	Wallace Nesbitt, K.C. (E) 1; J. G. O'Donoghue (M) 1.	Mar. 18, 1910	....	Proceedings unfinished.
Mar. 17, 1910	Toronto, Hamilton & Buffalo Ry. Co. and conductors, baggagemen, brakemen and yardmen in its employ.	Employees...	Toronto, Hamilton, and Buffalo Ry. lines.	101	Wages and conditions of employment.	F. H. McCuigan (E) 1; J. G. O'Donoghue (M) 1.	Mar. 18, 1910	....	Proceedings unfinished.
Mar. 19, 1910	Grand Trunk Pacific Ry. Co. and its telegraph and station employees.	Employees...	Grand Trunk Pacific lines.	75	Rules and rates of pay.	W. T. J. Lee (M) 1...	Mar. 30, 1910	....	Proceedings unfinished.
Mar. 22, 1910	Dominion Atlantic Ry. Co. and employees.	Employees...	Kentville, N.S...	4 dir. 25 indir.	Terms of employment and dismissal of certain employees.				Proceedings unfinished.

2. STREET RAILWAY.

April 20, 1909	Winnipeg Electric Ry. Co. and employees.	Employees	Winnipeg, Man.	600	Concerning wages and conditions of labour.	Rev. C. W. Gordon, D.D. (c) 4; W. J. Christie (m) 1; J. G. O'Donoghue (m) 1.	May 10, 1909	June 1, 1909	A unanimous report was presented by the Board, accompanied by an agreement covering all points in dispute and effective from May 1, 1909, to May 1, 1911, a strike being thereby averted.

3. FREIGHT HANDLERS.

May 17, 1909	Canadian Pacific Ry. Co. and freight handlers in its employ.	Employees	Owen Sound, Ont.	250	Concerning wages	Donald Ross (c) 4; Wallace Nesbitt, K.C. (e) 1; J. G. O'Donoghue (m) 1.	June 2, 1909	June 17, 1909	A strike of freight handlers employed by the Canadian Pacific Railway Company at Owen Sound, and continued until May 7 and continued until May 10, when application was made for the appointment of a Board under the Industrial Disputes Investigation Act, to which the dispute was referred for adjustment. The report of the Board was accompanied by a minority report by Mr. O'Donoghue. The report of the Board was accepted by the parties to the dispute, further cessation of work being thereby averted.
Aug. 18, 1909	Canadian Pacific Ry. Co. and freight handlers in its employ.	Employees	Fort William, Ont.	700	Concerning wages and conditions of labour.	S. C. Young (c) 3; W. J. Christie (e) 1; W. T. Rankin (m) 1.	Aug. 20, 1909	Aug. 30, 1909	A strike of freight handlers employed by the Canadian Pacific Railway Company at Fort William occurred on August 9, and continued until August 16, when application was made for the establishment of a Board under the Industrial Disputes Investigation Act, to which the dispute was referred for adjustment. In the report it was stated that the employees were not informed of the terms of this Act when the strike was declared. A unanimous report was presented by the Board, making certain recommendations for the settlement of the dispute, which were accepted by the parties concerned, a further cessation of work being thereby averted.

INDUSTRIAL DISPUTES INVESTIGATION ACT, 1907.—PROCEEDINGS, 1909–10.—*Concluded.*

II. TRANSPORTATION AND COMMUNICATION.—*Concluded.*

4. LONGSHOREMEN.

Date of receipt of application.	Parties to Dispute.	Party making application.	Locality.	No. persons affected.	Nature of dispute.	Names of Members of Board: (c) Chairman; (E) Employer; (M) Men.	Date on which Board was constituted.	Date of receipt of report of Board.	Result of Reference.
Mar. 14, 1910	Allan Line; Donaldson Line; Thomson o Line; Leyland Line; Star-Dominion Line; Canada Line; South African Line; Mexican Line; Wheeler Liners; Black Diamond Line; Head Line; Canadian Pacific Railway Line; and all other owners of steamships plying to Montreal and Syndicated Longshoremen of Montreal.	Employees	Montreal, Que.	1,800	Wages and conditions of employment.	Wm. Lyall (E) 1; Gustave Francq (M) 1.	Mar. 24, 1910	....	Proceedings unfinished.

5. TEAMSTERS.

Date of receipt of application.	Parties to Dispute.	Party making application.	Locality.	No. persons affected.	Nature of dispute.	Names of Members of Board: (c) Chairman; (E) Employer; (M) Men.	Date on which Board was constituted.	Date of receipt of report of Board.	Result of Reference.
Feb. 10, 1909	Manitoba Cartage Co. Ltd.	Employees	Winnipeg, Man.	40 dir. 200 indir.	Alleged discrimination against men connected with Union.	Rev. Dr. C. W. Gordon (c) 3; Prof. R. Cochrane (E) 2; T. J. Murray (M) 1.	Mar. 2, 1909	April 1, 1909	A unanimous report was presented by the Board, making recommendations for the settlement of the dispute. The report was not accepted by the company, but the inquiry had the effect of improving the conditions and bringing about an understanding so that the threatened strike was averted.

III. MUNICIPAL PUBLIC UTILITIES.

July 8, 1909	Corporation of Saskatoon, Sask., and labourers in its employ.	Ssaskatoon, Sask.	Employees.	150 dir. 150 indir.	Concerning wages and conditions of labour.	E. J. Mellicke (c) 4; Alex. Smith (e) 1; E. Stephenson (m) 1.	Aug. 4, 1909	Sept. 9, 1909	A report was presented by the chairman and Mr. Alex. Smith, making certain recommendations for the settlement of the dispute, and stating also that an agreement had been reached on all points except the establishment of a minimum wage scale and recognition of the employees' union. No cessation of work was reported.

B.—INDUSTRIES OTHER THAN MINES, AGENCIES OF TRANSPORTATION AND COMMUNICATION AND OTHER PUBLIC UTILITIES.

April 27, 1909	Dominion Textile Co., and mule spinners in its employ.	Montreal, Que.	Employees.	70 dir. 3,000 indir.	Concerning wages and conditions of labour.	Hon. Mr. Justice Fortin (c) 3; F. G. Daniels (e) 1; A. A. Gibeault (m) 1.	May 7, 1909	May 25, 1909	A unanimous report was presented by the Board, making certain recommendations for the settlement of the dispute, which were accepted by both parties concerned a strike being thereby averted.

INDUSTRIAL DISPUTES INVESTIGATION ACT, 1907.—PROCEEDINGS, 1910–11.

STATEMENT of Applications for Boards of Conciliation and Investigation and of Proceedings thereunder from April 1, 1910, to March 31, 1911.

A.—MINES, AGENCIES OF TRANSPORTATION AND COMMUNICATION AND OTHER PUBLIC SERVICE UTILITIES.

1. Appointed by the Minister, under Section 8, Sub-section 1, of the I. D. I. Act, on recommendation from party concerned.
2. Appointed by the Minister, under Section 8, Sub-section 2, of the I. D. I. Act, in the absence of a recommendation from party concerned.
3. Appointed by the Minister, under Section 8, Sub-section 3, of the I. D. I. Act, on the joint recommendation of the two members first appointed.
4. Appointed by the Minister, under Section 8, Sub-section 4, of the I. D. I. Act, in the absence of a joint recommendation by the two members first appointed.

I. MINING AND SMELTING INDUSTRY.

1. COAL MINES.

Date of receipt of application.	Parties to Dispute.	Party making application.	Locality.	No. persons affected.	Nature of dispute.	Names of Members of Board: (c) Chairman; (e) Employer; (m) Men.	Date on which Board was constituted.	Date of receipt of report of Board.	Result of Reference.
Jan. 5, 1910	Alberta Coal Mining Co. and employees.	Employer	Cardiff, Alta.	35 dir. 25 indir.	Concerning wages and conditions of employment.	R. G. Duggan (c) 3; J. O. Hannah (e) 1; Clement Stubbs (m) 1.	Jan. 17, 1910	April 2, 1910	A unanimous report was presented by the Board making certain recommendations for the settlement of the dispute, which were understood to have been accepted by both parties concerned, a strike being thereby averted.
April 18, 1910	Canadian - American Coal and Coke Co. and employees, members of Frank, Local No. 1263 U.M.W.A.	Employer	Frank, Alta.	262	Concerning making of new agreement and recognition of U. M. W. A.	I. S. G. VanWart (c) 4; Colin MacLeod (e) 1; Clement Stubbs (m) 1.	April 29, 1910	June 4, 1910	Settlement arrived at by chairman without Board being formally convened; settlement effective to March 31, 1911.
Oct. 26, 1910	Crowsnest Pass Coal Co. Ltd. and employees, members of District No. 18, U.M.W.A.	Employees	Fernie, B.C.	3,000	Concerning alleged breach of agreement and increased charge for special train.	I. S. G. VanWart (c) 3; W. S. Lane (e) 1; Clement Stubbs (m) 1.	Nov. 18, 1910	Feb. 18, 1911	Board effected settlement which was understood to be acceptable to both parties concerned, a strike being thereby averted.
Jan. 16, 1911	North Atlantic Collieries Co., Ltd. and employees, members of Local Union, No. 2173, District No. 26, U.M.W.A.	Employees	Port Morien, N.S.	110 dir. 150 indir.	Concerning reduction in wages and conditions of employment.	Prof. Robt. Magill (c) 4; Duncan G. MacDonald (e) 2; Alexander McKinnon (m) 1.	Mar. 9, 1911	Mar. 23, 1911	During proceedings for establishment of Board, company went into liquidation and mines were accordingly closed down.

II. TRANSPORTATION AND COMMUNICATION.

1. RAILWAYS.

Date	Parties	Locality	Nature	Board	Date referred	Date reported	Result
Jan. 7, 1911	The Wettlaufer Silver Mining Co., Ltd., and certain employees. Employees...	South Lorrain, Ont. 35 dir. 30 indir.	Concerning reduction in wages.	George Ritchie (c) 4; R. F. Taylor (e) 1; Chas. H. Lowthian (w) 1.	Feb. 20, 1911	Feb. 28, 1911	A unanimous report was presented by the Board making certain recommendations for settlement of dispute. No cessation of work occurred.
Mar. 17, 1910	Toronto, Hamilton and Buffalo Ry. Co., and its conductors, baggagemen, brakemen, and yardmen. Employees...	All lines of T. H. & B. Ry. 101...	Concerning employees' demand for increased compensation and improved conditions.	J. E. Atkinson (c) 4; F. H. McGuigan (e) 1; J. G. O'Donoghue (w) 1.	April 6, 1910	...	... parties concerned without Board having been convened. The terms of ... of his ... were to ... the terms of ... in the C.P.R. and its ... in train and yard ...
Mar. 17, 1910	Canadian Pacific Ry. Co., and its conductors, baggagemen, brakemen and yardmen. Employees...	All lines of C.P. Ry. 4,360...	Concerning employees' demand for increased compensation and improved conditions.	J. E. Atkinson (c) 4; Wallace Nesbitt (e) 1; J. G. O'Donoghue (w) 1.	Mar. 31, 1910	June 22, 1910	Report of Board was ... by a minority report signed by Mr. J. G. O'Donoghue, ... on the ... of the ... the reports ... concerned, which ... to continue in ... until terminated by ... fifty days ... be in writing ... similar to, but in ... particulars ... the terms of ... the Board, and ... said to ... correspond ... in ... standard ... and ... on a ... of the principal railway ... in the Eastern States.
Mar. 17, 1910	Grand Trunk Ry. Co., and its conductors, baggagemen, brakemen and yardmen. Employees...	All lines of G.T.R. 3,017...	Concerning employees' demand for increased compensation and improved conditions.	J. E. Atkinson (c) 4; Wallace Nesbitt (e) 1; J. G. O'Donoghue (w) 1.	April 6, 1910	June 22, 1910	Report of Board was ... by a majority, ... signed by Mr. Wallace Nesbitt, K.C., ... of the company. Upon ... the reports ... the company and ... of the employees ... The negotiations were continued up till July 18. ... a strike was ... of the ... of ... August 2. Strike continued up till ... it was announced that a ... had ... arrived at ... intervention, ... strike ... off.

INDUSTRIAL DISPUTES INVESTIGATION ACT, 1907.—PROCEEDINGS, 1910-11.—*Continued.*

II. TRANSPORTATION AND COMMUNICATION—*Continued.*

1. RAILWAYS—*Continued.*

Date of receipt of application.	Parties to Dispute.	Party making application.	Locality.	No. persons affected.	Nature of dispute.	Names of Members of Board; (c) Chairman; (e) Employer; (m) Men.	Date on which Board was constituted.	Date of receipt of report of Board.	Result of Reference.
Mar. 19, 1910	Grand Trunk Pacific Ry. Co. and telegraph and station employees.	Employees	G.T.P. lines	75	Concerning rules and rates of pay.	His Honour Judge McGibbon (c) 3; Donald Ross (e) 2; W. T. J. Lee (m) 1.	April 22, 1910	July 7, 1910	A unanimous report was presented by the Board, which made certain recommendations for the settlement of the dispute. No cessation of work occurred.
Mar. 22, 1910	Dominion Atlantic Ry. Co. and employees.	Employees	Kentville, N.S.	4 dir. 25 indir.	Concerning terms of employment and dismissal of certain employees.	Honourable John N. Armstrong (c) 4; McCallum Grant (e) 2; Aaron A. R. Mosher (m) 1.	April 29, 1910	May 12, 1910	Report of Board was accompanied by a minority report signed by Mr. Aaron A. R. Mosher, member appointed on behalf of the employees, which was accepted by them. The department was informed by the company that there would be no discrimination on its part between union and non-union men. No cessation of work occurred.
May 2, 1910	Canadian Northern Ry. Co. and its blacksmiths, members of Blacksmiths' Railway Union No. 147.	Employees	Winnipeg, Man.	30	Concerning demand for new working agreement, increased wages and shorter hours.				No Board established, settlement having been arrived at between the parties concerned.
May 2, 1910	Canadian Northern Ry. Co. and its blacksmiths, members of Blacksmiths' Helpers Lodge No. 335	Employees	Winnipeg, Man.	Between 30 and 40.	Concerning demand for new working agreement, increased wages and shorter hours.				No Board established, settlement having been arrived at between the parties concerned.
May 2, 1910	Canadian Northern Ry. Co. and its machinists, members of Fort Garry Lodge No. 189, International Association of Machinists.	Employees	Winnipeg, Man.	325	Concerning demand for new working agreement and increased wages.				No Board established, settlement having been arrived at between the parties concerned.
May 2, 1910	Canadian Northern Ry. Co. and its machinists' helpers, members of Federal Union, No. 4.	Employees	Winnipeg, Man.	57	Concerning demand for new working agreement, increased wages and shorter hours.				No Board established, settlement having been arrived at between the parties concerned.

Date	Parties	Applicant	Locality	No.	Nature of dispute	Board	Date	Date	Remarks
May 2,	Canadian Northern Ry. Co. and 14 moulders, members of Moulders' Union No. 174.	Employees	Winnipeg, Man.	13	Concerning demand for new working agreement, increased wages and shorter hours.				No Board established, settlement having been arrived at between the parties concerned.
May 2, 1910	Canadian Northern Ry. Co. and certain employees, members of Railway Carmen, Northern Star No. 371, and Plumbers, Gas and Steamfitters Union, No. 49.	Employees	Winnipeg, Man.	432	Concerning demand for new working agreement, increased wages and shorter hours.	Wm. Elliott Macara (c) 3; David H. Cooper (e); Philip C. Locke (m) 1.	May 23, 1910	June 28, 1910	Board presented a unanimous report making certain recommendations for a settlement. Award was not accepted by employees concerned, some of whom declared strike on July 7. Strike continued until September 27, when the men returned to work on the terms of the Board's award.
May 2, 1910	Canadian Northern Ry. Co. and its boilermakers, boilermakers' specialists and boilermakers' helpers, members of Boilermakers and Iron Ship Builders of ..., Fort Garry, No. 451, and Boilermakers, Iron Ship Builders and Helpers, No. 212.	Employees	Winnipeg, Man.	170	Concerning demand for new working agreement, increased wages and shorter hours.	David H. Cooper (e) 1.			Pending, establishment of Board a settlement was arrived at between parties concerned.
June 21, 1910	Intercolonial Prince Edward Island Railways and telegraphers, train ... agents, ... of Order of Rail ... Tel ...	Employees	Canadian Government railway system.	490	Concerning proposed amendments to schedule and alleged mistreatment of certain employees.	His Honour Judge John A. Barron (c) 3; J. H. Gilmour (e) 1; J. G. O'Donoghue (m) 1.	Jan. 4, 1911	Feb. 20, 1911	Establishment of Board was postponed owing to ... of a conference ... Government Railways Board ... concerned. ... was received ... no settlement having ... ... making ... ... the Government ... ing Board and by the ...
June 28, 1910	Grand Trunk Ry. Co. and brass workers in Montreal, members of Brass Workers' Local 320.	Employees	Montreal, Que.	24	Concerning demand for minimum rate of 30 cents per hour.	A. G. B. Claxton (c) 4; Wm. Aird (e) 1; C. Rodier (m) 1.	July 13, 1910	July 30, Aug. 2, 1910	Report of Board was accompanied by a minority report, signed by Mr. Wm. Aird, member appointed on behalf of the company. Report was accepted by the employees concerned. No cessation of work occurred.
Sept. 3, 1910	Canadian Pacific Ry. Co. and maintenance of way employees.	Employees	C.P.R. system in Canada.	4,000.	Concerning demand for increased wages and revision of schedule.	His Honour Judge D. McGibbon (c) 4; F. H. McGuigan (e) 1; W. T. J. Lee (m) 1.	Sept. 21, 1910	Mar. 1, Mar. 4, 1911	Report of Board was accompanied by a minority report signed by Mr. F. H. McGuigan, member appointed on behalf of the company. Department was informed that the majority report was accepted by company and employees concerned.

INDUSTRIAL DISPUTES INVESTIGATION ACT, 1907.—PROCEEDINGS, 1910–11.—*Continued.*

II. TRANSPORTATION AND COMMUNICATION—*Continued.*

RAILWAYS—*Concluded.*

Date of receipt of application.	Parties to Dispute.	Party making application.	Locality.	No. persons affected.	Nature of dispute.	Names of Members of Board: (c) Chairman; (e) Employer; (M) Men.	Date on which Board was constituted.	Date of receipt of report of Board.	Result of Reference.
Sept. 3, 1910	Grand Trunk Pacific Ry. Co. and maintenance-of-way employees.	Employees	Whole system of G.T.P. Ry.	1,000	Concerning demand for increased wages and revision of schedule.	His Honour Judge D. McGibbon (c) 3; J. W. Dawsey (e) 1; W. T. J. Lee (M) 1.	Sept. 21, 1910	Jan. 7, 1911	Report of Board was accompanied by a minority report signed by Mr. J. W. Dawsey, member appointed on behalf of the company. Report was accepted on behalf of employees concerned. The company, however, declined to be bound by the Board findings. No cessation of work occurred.
Sept. 3, 1910	Canadian Northern Ry. Co. and maintenance-of-way employees.	Employees	C.N.R. system in Canada.	1,800	Concerning demand for increased wages, and revision of schedule.	His Honour Judge D. McGibbon (c) 3; F. H. McGuigan (e) W. T. J. Lee (M) 1.	Sept. 22, 1910	Mar. 2, Mar. 10, 1911	Report of Board was accompanied by a minority report signed by Mr. F. H. McGuigan, member appointed on behalf of the company. Employees accepted Board findings. Company, however, declined to be bound by the same, but accepted instead the minority report. No cessation of work occurred.
Feb. 10, 1911	Kingston and Pembroke Ry. Co. and firemen and hostlers members of the Brotherhood of Locomotive Firemen and Enginemen.	Employees	Kingston, Ont.	11 dir. 20 indir.	Concerning demand for increased wages and revision of rules.				Department advised parties concerned that further effort should be made to effect settlement and on March 11, 1911, was informed that an amicable agreement had been arrived at.

2. STREET RAILWAYS.

July 5, 1910	Toronto Ry. Co. and employees, members of Toronto Railway Employees' Union, No. 113.	Employees	Toronto, Ont.	1,800	Concerning demand for new working agreement.	His Honour Judge John A. Barron (c) 3; J. P. Mulharkoy (e) J. G. O'Donoghue (M) 1.	July 16, 1910	Aug. 30, 1910	A unanimous report was presented by Board making certain recommendations for settlement of dispute, which were accepted by both parties concerned.

| Aug. 22, 1910 | Briti h ... trie Ry. 6. and linemen, members of Local M. 213, Brotherhood of Electrical Workers. | Elec-Employees... | Vancouver and vicinity. | 50 | Concerning demand for dismissal of foreman of linemen. | A. E. Beck (r) 1; Jas. H. McVety (m) 1. | .... | Sept. 12, 1910 | Constitution of Board not completed, the parties concerned having arrived at a settlement of the matters in dispute. |
| Oct. 22, 1910 | Winnipeg Electric Ry. 6 and conductors and ... men, members of Amalgamated Association of Street and ... Railway Employees of America, ...al No. 99. | Employees... | Winnipeg, Man. | 603 | Concerning alleged discrimination against certain employees, members of Amalgamated Association of Street and Electric Railway Employees. | W. J. Christie (c) 3; Capt. Wm. Robinson (r) 1; L. L. Pelletier (m) 1. | Nov. 11, 1910 | Dec. 13, Dec. 15, 1910 | Report of Board was accompanied by a ... ty report signed by Mr. L. L. Pell ...r, member appointed on the recommendation of the empl ...ees concerned. Employees ceased work on December 16, 10, to enforce their ... for reinstatement of four ... A ... was effected ... with the ... of Citizens' Committee, by ... strike was terminated on December 31, 10. |

3. SHIPPING.

| Mar. 14, 1910 | Allan Line, Donaldson Line, Thomson Line, ... Line, White Star Dominion Line, Canada Line, S uth Africa ...e, Mexican Line, Manchester ...ars, Black Diamond Line, ... Line, ... Railway Line, and all ...ther owners of steamships navigating to Montreal and Syndicated Longshoremen of Montreal. | Employees... | Montreal, Que. | 1,800 | Concerning wages and conditions of employment. | Honourable Mr. Justice T. Fortin (c) 4; Wm. Lyell (r) 1.; Gustave Francq (m) 1. | April 7, 1910 | April 20, 1910 | A unanimous report was presented by the Board, making certain recommendations for the settlement of the dispute, which were accepted by both parties concerned, an agreement being entered into effective for a period of five years. In connection with the same a permanent Board of Conciliation was established to settle such grievances as might from time to time be complained of. |
| Aug. 8, 1910 | Allan Line, Donaldson Line, Thomson Line, ... Line, White Star Dominion Line, Canada Line, South ...ica Line, ...ter ...ers, Black Diamond Line, Head Line, Canadian Pacific Railway Line and all ...ther owners of vessels navigating in the Port of Montreal, and the Ship ...rs of the Port of Montreal. | Employees... | Montreal, Que. | 200 | Concerning wages, hours and conditions of employment. | W. D. Lighthall (c) 4; J. Herbert Lauer (g) 1; Geo. Poliquin (m) 1. | Aug. 22, 1910 | Sept. 16, Sept. 17, 1910 | R p t. of Board was accompanied by a ...ty report signed by Mr. J. Herbert ...air ...ber ...and on the recommendation of the Shipping Federation of ...da. The report was accepta ...le to the employees concerned; the shipping ...nion addressed to the department, expressed themselves as ...ble to ...pt the majority report. No ...tion of work occurred. |

INDUSTRIAL DISPUTES INVESTIGATION ACT, 1907.—PROCEEDINGS, 1910-11.—Concluded.

II. TRANSPORTATION AND COMMUNICATION—Concluded.

3. SHIPPING—Conclu ed.

Date of receipt of application.	Parties to Dispute.	Party making application.	Locality.	No. persons affected.	Nature of dispute.	Names of Members of Board; (c) Chairman; (E) Employer; (M) Men.	Date on which Board was constituted.	Date of receipt of report of Board.	Result of Reference.
Sept. 10, 1910	Canadian Pacific Steamship Co. and its employees commonly known as deckhands, at Vancouver and Victoria, members of the Sailors Union of the Pacific.	Employees	Vancouver and Victoria, B.C.	80 dir. 50 indir.	Concerning wages, hours and conditions of employment.	His Honour Judge W. W. P. McInnes (c) 3; G. E. McCrossan (E); J. H. McVety (M) 1.	Oct. 27, 1910	Nov. 28, 1910	A unanimous report was presented by Board making certain recommendations for the settlement of the dispute, which were accepted by the employees concerned. The company maintained that it had no dispute with its employees and that, therefore, no action on its part was necessary. No cessation of work occurred.

4. COMMERCIAL TELEGRAPHERS.

Date of receipt of application.	Parties to Dispute.	Party making application.	Locality.	No. persons affected.	Nature of dispute.	Names of Members of Board; (c) Chairman; (E) Employer; (M) Men.	Date on which Board was constituted.	Date of receipt of report of Board.	Result of Reference.
June 23, 1910	Canadian Pacific Ry. Co. and commercial telegraphers, members of Commercial Telegraphers' Union of America.	Employees	Commercial Telegraph lines of C.P.R.	600	Concerning wages and conditions of employment.	J. E. Duval (c) 3; F. H. McGuigan (E) 1; D. Campbell (M) 1.	July 7, 1910	July 25, 1910	A unanimous report was presented by Board in which it was stated that an agreement was concluded between the parties concerned on all points at issue.
Mar. 3, 1911	Great North Western Telegraph Co. of Canada and telegraphers, members of Commercial Telegraphers' Union of America.	Employees	All offices operated by the G.N.W. Telegraph Co. of Canada.	300 dir. 1,100 indir.	Concerning wages and conditions of employment.	Hon. Mr. Justice J. V. Teetzel (c) 3; Frederick H. Markey (E) 1; D. Campbell (M) 1.	Mar. 30, 1911		Proceedings unfinished.

INDUSTRIAL DISPUTES INVESTIGATION ACT, 1907.—PROCEEDINGS, 1911–12.

STATEMENT of Application for Boards of Conciliation and Investigation and of Proceedings thereunder, from April 1, 1911, to March 31, 1912.

A.—MINES, AGENCIES OF TRANSPORTATION AND COMMUNICATION AND OTHER PUBLIC UTILITIES.

1. Appointed by the Minister, under Section 8, Subsection 1, of the I. D. I. Act, on recommendation from party concerned.
2. Appointed by the Minister, under Section 8, Subsection 2, of the I. D. I. Act, in the absence of a recommendation from party concerned.
3. Appointed by the Minister, under Section 8, Subsection 3, of the I. D. I. Act, on the joint recommendation of the two members first appointed.
4. Appointed by the Minister, under Section 8, Subsection 4, of the I. D. I. Act, in the absence of a joint recommendation by the two members first appointed.

I. MINING AND SMELTING INDUSTRY.

1. COAL MINES.

Date of receipt of application.	Parties to Dispute.	Party making application.	Locality.	No. persons affected.	Nature of dispute.	Names of Members of Board: (c) Chairman; (e) Employer; (m) Men.	Date on which Board was constituted.	Date of receipt of report of Board.	Result of Reference.
April 13, 1911	Western Coal Operators' Association and employees, members of District No. 18, United Mine Workers of America.	Employees	Eastern British Columbia and Southern Alberta.	6,000 dir.; an indefinite number indir.	Concerning making of new agreement.	Rev. C. W. Gordon, D.D. (c) 1; Colin Macleod (e) 1; A. J. Carter (m) 1.	April 21, 1911	July 10, July 11, 1911	The employees concerned in this dispute ceased work on March 31, 19, on the termination of a two ars' agreement. wth the employing was. A Board was established by request of the es on April 18. The Board's report was ed by a ... ity report by Mr. Carter. The ... ers signified their willingness to ... tite an ... nt along the general lines suggested by the Board in its majority report; the es on the ther hand, ... ng the minority report of Mr. Carter. The majority of the mines remained closed down until the middle of November, ... en a ... nt was signed by the parties concerned effective to March 31, 1915.

INDUSTRIAL DISPUTES INVESTIGATION ACT, 1907.—PROCEEDINGS, 1911-12.—*Continued.*

I. MINING AND SMELTING INDUSTRY—*Concluded.*

1. COAL MINES—*Concluded.*

Date of receipt of application.	Parties to Dispute.	Party making application.	Locality.	No. persons affected.	Nature of dispute.	Names of Members of Board: (c) Chairman; (e) Employer; (m) Men.	Date on which Board was constituted.	Date of receipt of report of Board.	Result of Reference.
Oct. 23, 1911	Alberta Coal Mining Co., Ltd., and employees.	Employer	Cardiff, Alta.	80	Concerning wages and conditions of employment.	J. Norman Fraser (c) 3; O. Hannub (e) 1; Clement Stubbs. (m) 1.	Nov. 27, 1911	Dec. 21, 1911	Report was signed by all three members of the Board with slight objections noted by MM. Hannah and Stubbs. After the award of the Board had been communicated to both parties concerned there was a cessation of work for a few days. The department was later informed that a settlement had been reached on the basis of the Board's findings, and work resumed.

2. METAL MINES.

Date of receipt of application.	Parties to Dispute.	Party making application.	Locality.	No. persons affected.	Nature of dispute.	Names of Members of Board.	Date on which Board was constituted.	Date of receipt of report of Board.	Result of Reference.
May 25, 1911	Hudson Bay Mining Co., Ltd., and employees, members Gowganda Miners' Union No. 154, W.F.M.	Employees	Gowganda, Ont.	30	Concerning reduction in wages.	George Ritchie, K.C. (c) 4; Prof. John Sharp (e) 1; Duncan J. McDonell (m) 1.	June 9, 1911	July 10, 1911	Report of Board was accompanied by minority report signed by Mr. McDonell. The employees, being unwilling to accept the Board report, declared a strike, of which no formal settlement was reported. Operations were resumed in the company's mine at the end of July.

II. TRANSPORTATION AND COMMUNICATION.

1. RAILWAYS.

Date of receipt of application.	Parties to Dispute.	Party making application.	Locality.	No. persons affected.	Nature of dispute.	Names of Members of Board.	Date on which Board was constituted.	Date of receipt of report of Board.	Result of Reference.
May 11, 1911	Michigan Central Ry. Co. and sectionmen.	Employees	St. Thomas, Ont.	1,200 to 1,400	Concerning proposed reduction in wages.				The employees concerned in this dispute ceased work on May 1, on account of a proposed reduction in their rate of pay. Application was later made by the employees for the establishment of a Board. Whilst communications were passing between the department and the employees an officer of the department proceeded to St. Thomas at the Minister's request,

Date	Parties		Location	Concerning	Number affected	Board	Referred	Reported	Result
									for the purpose of conferring with the parties concerned. As a result the company restored the scale of wages which had existed prior to May 1, 1911, and announced its willingness to re-engage those who had ceased work.
May 17, 1911	Canadian Northern Coal and Ore Dock Co. Ltd., and employees, members of Coal Handlers' Union No. 319.	Employees	Port Arthur, Ont.	Concerning wages and conditions of employment.	150 dir. 200 indir.	His Honour Judge John McKay (c) 3; George F. Horrigan (s) 1; Andrew Boyd (M) 1.	June 2, 1911	June 19, 1911	A unanimous report was presented by the Board in which it stated that a settlement had been effected of all points at issue, an agreement effective from May 1, 1911, to April 30, 1912, having been signed by both parties.
May 17, 1911	Quebec and Lake St. John Ry. Co., and carmen, members of the Brotherhood of Railway Carmen of America.	Employees	Quebec, Que.	Concerning wages and conditions of employment.	80 dir. 15 indir.				Whilst proceedings looking to the establishment of a Board were in progress, the department was informed that a settlement had been reached on the various points at issue.
July 18, 1911	Grand Trunk Ry. Co. and machinists, members of the International Association of Machinists.	Employees	G.T.R. System	Concerning demand for a new schedule of rules and rates of pay.	2,000 dir. 6,000 indir.	Hon. Mr. Justice J. V. Teetzel (c) 3; Hon. Wallace Nesbitt, K.C. (R) 1; J. G. O'Donoghue (M) 1.	Oct. 11, 1911	Oct. 23, 1911	Report was signed by all three members of the Board, Mr. O'Donoghue, however, dissenting in certain particulars: Department was informed that the findings of the Board were not acceptable to the employees concerned. No cessation of work, however, occurred.
July 31, 1911	*Grand Trunk Pacific Ry. Co., and machinists, members of the Inter. Association of Machinists.	Employees	G.T.P. Ry. System	Concerning wages, hours, and conditions of employment, also demand for schedule.	150	Dr. J. W. Sparling, (c) 4; Rev. J. L. Gordon† (s) 2; Thos. J. Murray, (M) 1.	Oct. 12, 1911	Oct. 28, 1911	A ... the Board ... was favourable to the employees concerned and was accepted on ... half. The company, in a ... letter dated ... ember 2, declined to accept the Board's findings. On ... ober 6, the company's ... at Edmonton and Rivers were closed down, and the ... concerned declared a strike on ... 10, ... continued until December 13, 1912, when an agreement was reach d by the parties ...
Aug. 8, 1911	*Grand Trunk Pacific Ry. Co. and boilermakers, members of the Inter. Brotherhood of Boilermakers, Iron Shipbuilders and Helpers of America.	Employees	G.T.P. System	Concerning wages, hours and conditions of employment; also demand for schedule.	150				

*The two applications here recorded are regarded as one in the tabular statement.
†Honourable Wallace Nesbitt, K.C., was at first appointed a member of the Board, but, being unable to act, withdrew on October 5.

INDUSTRIAL DISPUTES INVESTIGATION ACT, 1907.—PROCEEDINGS, 1911-12.—Continued.

II. TRANSPORTATION AND COMMUNICATION.—Concluded.

1. RAILWAYS—Concluded.

Date of receipt of application.	Parties to Dispute.	Party making application.	Locality.	No. persons affected.	Nature of dispute.	Names of Members of Board: (C) Chairman; (E) Employer; (M) Men.	Date on which Board was constituted.	Date of receipt of report of Board.	Result of Reference.
Sept. 11, 1911	Canadian Pacific Ry. Co., and various employees of the Canadian Brotherhood of Railroad Employees.	Employees	Calgary and Medicine Hat, Alta.	6,500 dir. 6,500 indir.	Concerning alleged discrimination against members of union.	John Anthony McDonald (M) l.			Proceedings discontinued.
Nov. 14, 1911	Quebec Central Ry. Co. and station employees, members of the Order of Railroad Telegraphers.	Employees	Quebec Central Ry. lines.	70	Concerning demand for a new schedule of rules and rates of pay.				Pending establishment of Board a settlement was reached.
Dec. 12, 1911	Michigan Central Ry. Co. and station employees and key men and one operators, and tower men, members of the Order of Railroad re.	Employees	M.C.R. lines in Canada.	115 dir. 3,000 indir.	Concerning demand for the adoption of certain amendments to the existing schedule.	Peter McDonald (c) 4; J. E. Duval (E) l; J. G. O'Donoghue (M) l.	Jan. 17, 1912	Mar. 12, 1912	Report of Board was accompanied by a minority report signed by Mr. Duval. As a result of the inquiry the company granted an increase of wages and made certain modifications in its rules governing the employment of its station agents, telegraphers, etc. No cessation of work occurred.
Dec. 29, 1911	Pere Marquette Ry. Co. and maintenance-of-way men, members of the Inter. Brotherhood of Maintenance-of-Way Employees.	Employees	Buffalo Division of the Pere Marquette Ry.	140	Concerning wages, hours, and demand for a set of rules governing both the foregoing.	Hon. Chief Justice Sir Glenholme Falconbridge (c) 3; Hon. Wallace Nesbitt, K.C. (E) 1; J G. O'Donoghue. (M) l.	Jan. 20, 1912	Feb. 19, 1912	A unanimous report was presented by the Board, making certain recommendations for the settlement of the dispute, which were accepted by both parties concerned.
Mar. 11, 1912	Canadian Pacific Ry. Co., and clerks and railway clerks, members of Winnipeg Division, No. 177, Brotherhood of Railroad Freight Handlers and Railway Clerks.	Employees	Winnipeg, Man.	220 dir. 230 indir.	Concerning alleged discrimination by company against members of the union.	Chas. P. Fullerton, (E) 2; Thos. J. Murray, (M) l.			At the close of the fiscal year the Board had not been completed by the appointment of a chairman.

2. STREET RAILWAYS.

Date	Parties		Location	No. affected	Subject	Board	Date	Result
June 19, 1911	Montreal Street Ry. Co. and employees, members of the Amalgamated Association of Street and Electric Railway Employees of America No. 328.	Employees....	Montreal, Que....	30 dir. 1,970 indir.	Concerning dismissal of certain employees and alleged discrimination against them as members of union.	Hon. Justice Thos. Portin (c) 4; J. L. Perron, K.C. (E) 1; Charlemange Rodier (M) 1.	Aug. 11, 1911.	Board restrained from proceeding by order of out pending determination of an application by the company to the Superior Court for a writ of ... declaring the Industrial Disputes Investigation Act to be ultra vires.

3. COMMERCIAL TELEGRAPHY.

Date	Parties		Location	No. affected	Subject	Board	Date	Date	Result
Mar. 3, 1911	Great North Western Telegraph Co. of Canada and telegraphers, members of the Commercial Telegraphers' Union of America.	Employees....	All offices operated by the G.N.W. Telegraph Co. of Canada.	200 dir. 1,100 indir.	Concerning wages and conditions of employment; also alleged discrimination against members of the union.	Hon. Mr. Justice J. V. Teetzel (c) 3; Frederick H. Markey (E) 1; D. Campbell (M) 1.	Mar. 30, 1911	July 17, 1911	Report of Board was signed by all three members, Mr. Markey and Mr Campbell, however, each dissenting on one point. The findings of the Board were accepted by both parties concerned.

4. TELEPHONES.

Date	Parties		Location	No. affected	Subject	Board	Date	Date	Result
Sept. 6, 1911	British Columbia Telephone Co., and employees, members of Local Union 213, Inter. Brotherhood of Electrical Workers.	Employees....	Lines of the B. C. Telephone Co.	220	Concerning wages and company's attitude toward union men.	John H. Senkler, K.C. (c) 3; William M. Barker (E) 1; Chas. Enright (M) 1.	Oct. 6, 1911	Nov. 28, 1911	Report of Board was accompanied by a minority report signed by Mr. Barker. The department was not informed of the acceptance or non-acceptance by either party of the Board's findings. No cessation of work, however, occurred.

III. MUNICIPAL PUBLIC UTILITIES.

Date	Parties		Location	No. affected	Subject	Board	Date	Date	Result
May 27, 1911	Cities of Port Arthur and Fort William, Ont., and electrical workers, members of Inter. Brotherhood of Electrical Workers of America, Local Union No. 339.	Employees....	Port Arthur and Fort William, Ont.	32 dir. 66 indir.	Concerning wages and hours.	Rev. S. C. Murray, D.D., (c) 3; J. Dix. Fraser (E) 1; C. W. Foster (M) 1.	June 8, 1911	July 3, 1911	A unanimous report was presented by the Board in which it was stated that an agreement had been signed by both cities and their electrical workers, the agreement being effective for one year, from June 1, 1911.
May 29, 1911	City of Edmonton, Alta. and electrical workers, members of Inter. Brotherhood of Electrical Workers of America, Local Union No. 544.	Employees....	Edmonton, Alta....	35	Concerning wages and conditions of employment.	Hon. Mr. Justice H. C. Taylor (c) 3; Arthur W. Ormsby (E) 1; W. Symonds (M) 1.	June 9, 1911	July 5, 1911	A unanimous report was presented by the Board in which it was stated that a schedule of wages and a set of rules for each department had been drawn up and accepted by both parties to the dispute, effective from July 1, 1911, to May 1, 1913.

INDUSTRIAL DISPUTES INVESTIGATION ACT, 1907.—PROCEEDINGS, 1911-12.—*Concluded.*

B.—INDUSTRIES OTHER THAN MINES, AGENCIES OF TRANSPORTATION AND COMMUNICATION, AND OTHER PUBLIC UTILITIES.

Date of receipt of application.	Parties to Dispute.	Party making application.	Locality.	No. persons affected.	Nature of dispute.	Names of Members of Board; (c) Chairman; (e) Employer; (m) Men.	Date on which Board was constituted.	Date of receipt of report of Board.	Result of Reference.
April 3, 1911	John Ritchie Co., Ltd., William A. Marsh Co., Ltd., Gale Bros. and J. M. Stobo, boot and shoe manufacturers, Quebec, and employees.	Employees....	Quebec, Que......	68 dir...... 875 indir.	Concerning wages......	Dr. G. W. Jolicoeur (c) 3; Felix Marois (e) 1; Joseph Alphonse Langlois (m) 1.	April 24, 1911	June 26, 1911	A unanimous report was presented by the Board, making certain recommendations for the settlement of the dispute. It was understood that the Board's findings were accepted by the parties concerned.

INDUSTRIAL DISPUTES INVESTIGATION ACT, 1907.—PROCEEDINGS, 1912-13.

STATEMENT of Applications for Boards of Conciliation and Investigation and of Proceedings thereunder from April 1, 1912, to March 31, 1913.

A.—MINES, AGENCIES OF TRANSPORTATION AND COMMUNICATION AND OTHER PUBLIC SERVICE UTILITIES.

1. Appointed by the Minister, under Section 8, Sub-section 1, of the I. D. I. Act, on recommendation from party concerned.
2. Appointed by the Minister, under Section 8, Sub-section 2, of the I. D. I. Act, in the absence of a recommendation from party concerned.
3. Appointed by the Minister, under Section 8, Sub-section 3, of the I. D. I. Act, on the joint recommendation of the two members first appointed.
4. Appointed by the Minister, under Section 8, Sub-section 4, of the I. D. I. Act, in the absence of a joint recommendation by the two members first appointed.

I. MINING AND SMELTING INDUSTRY.

1. COAL MINES.

Date of receipt of application.	Parties to Dispute.	Party making application.	Locality.	No. persons affected.	Nature of dispute.	Names of Members of Board; (c) Chairman; (E) Employer; (M) Men.	Date on which Board was constituted.	Date of receipt of report of Board.	Result of Reference.
June 4, 1912	Inverness Railway and Coal Co. and miners in its employ.	Employees	Inverness, N.S.	500	Concerning wages, conditions of employment, and retention of dues for the Provincial Workmen's Association.	Finlay MacDonald (c) 4; Major W. Ernest Thompson (E) 1; James Cameron Waters (M) 1.	Aug. 21, 1912	Oct. 9, 1912	A unanimous report was presented by the Board, in which it was stated that an agreement had been reached by the parties concerned.

2. METAL MINES.

Date of receipt of application.	Parties to Dispute.	Party making application.	Locality.	No. persons affected.	Nature of dispute.	Names of Members of Board; (c) Chairman; (E) Employer; (M) Men.	Date on which Board was constituted.	Date of receipt of report of Board.	Result of Reference.
July 3, 1912	Britannia Mining and Smelting Co. and employees, members of Britannia Miners' Union.	Employees	Britannia Mines, B.C.	300	Concerning wages, conditions of employment and recognition of union.	Jas. A. Harvey, K.C. (c) 4; W. Ernest Burns (E) 1; George Heatherton (M) 1.	Aug. 6, 1912	Sept. 16, 1912	Report of B and was ... a ... ity report signed by Mr. Burns. The ... es concerned accepted the award of the B ard, but the company declined to do so. Mining operations were continued until February 18. ... the alleged dismissal by the company of one of the union officials brought the existing dis... tion to a head and a strike was ..., which had not been terminated at the end of the fiscal year.

36a—4½

INDUSTRIAL DISPUTES INVESTIGATION ACT, 1907.—PROCEEDINGS, 1912-13.—Continued.

I. MINING AND SMELTING INDUSTRY—Concluded.

2. METAL MINES—Concluded.

Date of receipt of application.	Parties to Dispute.	Party making application.	Locality	No. persons affected.	Nature of dispute.	Names of Members of Board: (g) Chairman; (E) Employer; (M) Men.	Date on which Board was constituted.	Date of receipt of report of Board.	Result of Reference.
*July 20, 1912	McEnaney Mines, Ltd., and employees, members of Porcupine Miners' Union No. 145, W.F.M.	Employees	Porcupine, Ont	40 dir. 1,000 indir.	Concerning proposed reduction in wages.	Peter McDonald (g) 4; H.E.T. Haultain(E)1; Wm. C. Thompson (M) 1.	Aug. 23, 1912	Nov. 7, Oct. 21, 1912	Report of Board was accompanied by a minority report signed by Mr. Thompson. The majority report was not acceptable to the employees concerned, and on November 15 a strike was declared, which was practically ended on June 21, 1913, an arrangement having been made by which, although the strike was not officially called off, the men were permitted by the Union to return to work.
*July 26, 1912	McIntyre-Porcupine Mines, Ltd., Jupiter Mines, Ltd., Vipond Porcupine Mines,Ltd., and Plenaurum Mines, Ltd., and employees, members of Porcupine Miners' Union No. 145, W.F.M.	Employees	Porcupine, Ont	225 dir. 1,000 indir.	Concerning proposed reduction in wages.				
†Nov. 30, 1912	Fort Steele Mining & Smelting Co. and employees, members of Kimberley Miners' Union No. 100, W.F.M	Employees	Kimberley, B.C	140	Concerning wages.				
†Dec. 3, 1912	Standard Silver Lead Mining Co., Ltd., Van Roi Mines, Ltd., Silverton Mines, Limited and employees, members of Silverton Miners' Union No. 95, W. F.M.	Employees	Silverton, B.C	325 dir. 50 indir.	Concerning wages.				
†Dec. 3, 1912	Queens Mines, Inc., and employees, members of Ymir Miners' Union No. 85, W.F.M.	Employees	Sheep Creek, B.C.	45 dir. 300 indir.	Concerning wages.	W. S. Bullock Web- ster (g) 3; Chas. K. Hamilton (E) 1; J. N. Bennett (M) 1.	Dec. 21, 1912	Feb. 4, Jan. 27, 1913	Report of Board was accompanied by a minority report signed by Mr. Bennett. The majority report of the Board found against the demands of the employees.

Date	Applicant		Location	No. affected	Nature of dispute	Board	Date referred	Date of report	Result
†Dec. 9, 1912	Lucky Jim Zinc Mine, Ltd., Rambler Cariboo Mines, Surprise Mine, Hope Mine, Noble Five Mines, Richmond Eureka Mines and Idaho-Alamo Mines, and employees, members of Sandon Miners' Union No. 81, W.F.M.	Employees	West Kootenay, B.C.	210 dir. 90 indir.	Concerning wages				
†Dec. 10, 1912	Blue Bell Mine, No. 1 Mine, Highland Mine, Hope Mine, Silver Horde Mine, Molly Gibson Mine, Eureka Mine, *Poorman Mine, and employees, members of Nelson Miners' Union No. 96, W.F.M.	Employees	Nelson, B.C.	300	Concerning wages				

II. TRANSPORTATION AND COMMUNICATION.

1. RAILWAYS.

Date	Applicant		Location	No. affected	Nature of dispute	Board	Date referred	Date of report	Result
Mar. 11, 1912	Canadian Pacific Ry. Co., and freight handlers and clerks, members of Winnipeg Division No. 177, Brotherhood of Railroad Freight Handlers and Railway Clerks.	Employees	Winnipeg, Man.	220 dir. 220 indir.	Concerning alleged discrimination by company against members of the union and dismissals.	Hon. Mr. Justice H.A. Robson (c) 4; Chas. P. Fullerton (e) 2; Thos. J. Murray (m) I.	April 3, 1912	May 3, 1912	A unanimous report was presented by the Board, in which it was stated that the company had re-employed all the employees who wished to return to work.
April 29, 1912	Canadian Northern Ry. Co. and Train Service Organizations.	Employees	C.N.R. lines	2,000	Concerning the proposed displacement of train crews of the Canadian Northern Ry. by the Midland Ry. Co. which had acquired running rights over the Canadian Northern line from Winnipeg to Emerson	R. Max Denistoun (e) I; L. L. Peltier (m) I.			Pending the final constitution of the Board a satisfactory arrangement was arrived at by the parties concerned.

*The two applications here recorded are regarded as one in the tabular statement.
†The five applications here recorded are regarded as one in the tabular statement,

INDUSTRIAL DISPUTES INVESTIGATION ACT, 1907.—PROCEEDINGS, 1912-13.—*Continued.*

II. TRANSPORTATION AND COMMUNICATION—*Continued.*

1. RAILWAYS—*Concluded.*

Date of receipt of application.	Parties to Dispute.	Party making application.	Locality.	No. persons affected.	Nature of dispute.	Names of Members of Board: (c) Chairman; (E) Employer; (M) Men.	Date on which Board was constituted.	Date of receipt of report of Board.	Result of Reference.
May 8, 1912.	Canadian Northern Coal and Ore Dock Co., Ltd., and coal handlers, most of whom were members of Coal Handlers' Local No. 319.	Employees...	Port Arthur, Ont...	90...	Concerning alleged breach of agreement by company, also concerning wages, recognition of union, and demand for yearly conference between company and employees.	His Honour Judge John McKay (c) 4; George F. Horrigan (E) 1; Frederick Urry (M) 1.	May 22, 1912	July 19, July 22, 1912	Report of Board was accompanied by a minority report signed by Mr. Urry. The majority report of the Board was in favour of the company. The employees refused to accept same and declared a strike on July 29, which continued until August 5, when an agreement was reached which provided for certain increases in pay and the reinstatement of certain former employees.
June 28, 1912	Canadian Pacific Ry. Co., and employees in station and telegraph service, members of the Order of Railroad Telegraphers.	Employees...	C. P. R. system...	1,800 dir...; 8,000 indir.	Concerning wages and amendment of conditions of service.	Peter McDonald (c) 4; J. E. Duval (E) 1; J. G. O'Donoghue (M) 1.	July 22, Sept. 6, 1912	Sept. 4, 1912	Report of B... was accompanied by a minority report signed by Mr. J. G. ... The ... rep ... was accepted by the ... any but was ... by the employees concerned. As a result of further conferences ... the parties an ... was reached, effective, regarding wages ... 1, 1912, and ... overtime rules and other ... from ... 1, 12. The threatened strike was thereby averted.
Nov. 21, 1912	Canadian Pacific Ry. Co., and freight handlers, freight clerks, etc., members of the Canadian Brotherhood of Railroad Employees.	Employees...	Ottawa Division of the C.P.R. Port Arthur and Fort William.	1,300 dir.; 15000 indir.	Concerning alleged unfair dismissals and refusal of company to negotiate with employees respecting schedule of rules and rate of pay.	His Honour Judge D. McGibbon (c) 4; J. E. Duval (E) 1; J. A. McDonald (M) 1.	Nov. 28, 1912	Dec. 11, 1912	Report of Board was accompanied by a minority report signed by Mr. Duval. Prior to the date of the application the employees had gone on strike and remained out from November 1 until February 1, when the department was informed that an agreement had been reached by the parties concerned and the employees accordingly resumed work.

Date	Company	Parties	Location	No. affected	Nature of dispute	Board	Date	Result
Dec. 1912	Intercolonial Ry. of Canada and locomotive engineers, members of the Brotherhood of LocomotiveEngineers.	Employees...	I. C. R. lines........	8 dir. 350 indir.	Concerning demand for reinstatement of certain employ ees and for payment for time lost to those who had been suspended.			Proceedings under Act were stayed pending further negotiations between the Government Railways Managing Board and the Brotherhood of Locomotive Engineers. No further action by the Department was necessary.
Jan. 31, 1913	Imperial and Prince Edward Island Railways, and certain employees, members of the Inter. Association of Machinists, Inter. Association of Blacksmiths and Helpers, Brotherhood of Railway Carmen of America, Inter. Association of Boilermakers, and Inter. Association of Boilermakers Help rs.	Employees.	I. C. and P. E. I. Railway lines.	1,500.......	Concerning employee s' demand for adoption of schedules and for an eight hour day.			Proceedings under Act were stayed pending negotiations between the Minister of Railways and Canals and a committee of the employees concerned, which resulted in a settlement of the matters in dispute.
Mar. 11, 1913	Canadian Northern Ry. Co. and certain employees, members of the Order of Railway Conductors.	Employees....	C. N. R. lines....	450 dir. 2,200 indir.	Concerning employees' demands for various changes in existing schedule, including wages, hours and working conditions.	Hon. Mr. Justice A. Haggart (c) 3; Wm. Cross (e) 1; J. Harvey Hall (m) 1	Mar. 29, 1913	Proceedings unfinished.
Mar. 31, 1913	Canadian Pacific Ry. Co. and certain employees, members of the Brotherhood of Locomotive Firemen and Enginemen.	Employees.	Alberta Division of C.P.R.	2,659 dir. 7,000 indir.	Concerning alleged breach of agreement by company.			Proceedings unfinished.

2. STREET RAILWAYS.

Date	Company	Parties	Location	No. affected	Nature of dispute	Board	Date	Result
May 9, 1912	Ottawa Electric Ry. Co. and employees, members of Division No. 279, Amalgamated Association of Street and Electric Ry. Employees of America.	Employees....	Ottawa, Ont........	425........	Concerning refusal of company to accept terms proposed by the employees asking for increased wages, shorter hours and improved working conditions.	Hon. Mr. Justice J. M. McDougall (c) 4; Travers Lewis, K.C. (e) 1; P. M. Draper (m) 1.	May 18, 1912	June 13, 1912	A unanimous report was presented by the Board making certain recommendations for the settlement of the dispute, which were accepted by both parties concerned.
July 18, 1912	Halifax Electric Tramway Co. and employees, members of Division No. 508, Amalgamated Association of Street and Electric Ry. Employees of America.	Employees...	Halifax, N.S........	125 dir. 501 indir.	Concerning wages and conditions of employment as set forth in schedule submitted.	His Honour Judge W. B. Wallace (c) 3; George S. Campbell (e) 1; John T. Joy (m) 1.	Aug. 1, 1912	Aug. 22, 1912	A unanimous report was presented by the Board embodying the terms of an agreement which had been arrived at by the parties concerned.

INDUSTRIAL DISPUTES INVESTIGATION ACT, 1907.—PROCEEDINGS, 1912-13.—*Concluded.*

II. TRANSPORTATION AND COMMUNICATION—*Concluded.*

2.—STREET RAILWAYS—*Concluded.*

Date of receipt of application.	Parties to Dispute.	Party making application.	Locality.	No. persons affected.	Nature of dispute.	Names of Members of Board: (c) Chairman; (e) Employer; (m) Men.	Date on which Board was constituted.	Date of receipt of report of Board.	Result of Reference.
Aug. 29, 1912	Que Railway, Light, Heat and Power Co. and street railway employees, members of Fraternite Nationale No. 1, Employes de Tramway.	Employees	Quebec, Que	231 dir. 30 indir.	Concerning wages, recognition of union and reinstatement of certain employees.	Hon. Mr. Justice C. E. Dorion (c) 3; J. L. Perron (e) 1; J. P. N. Simard (m) I	Sept. 25, 1912	Dec. 12, 1912	A unanimous report was presented by the Board, embodying an agreement signed by both parties concerned.
Sept. 16, 1912	Hull Electric Ry. Co. and members of Division No. 591, Amalgamated Association of Street & Electric Railway Employees of America.	Employees	Hull, Que	68 dir. 74 indir.	Concerning wages and conditions of employment.	Peter McDonald (c) 4; George D. Kelly (e) 1; George C. Wright, (m) I.	Oct. 1, 1912	Nov. 2, 1912	A unanimous report was presented by the Board, making certain recommendations for the settlement of the dispute which were accepted by both parties concerned.
Sept. 25, 1912	Cities of Port Arthur and Fort William and employees in street railway service.	Employees	Port Arthur and Fort William, Ont.	72 dir. Most of industrial workers in the two cities indirectly.	Concerning alleged breach of agreement and alleged unsatisfactory investigation of charges.	George H. Rapsey (c) 3; Wm. P. Cooke (e) 1; Frederick Urry (m) I.	Oct. 7, 1912	Dec. 16, 1912	The report was signed by all three members of the Board, Mr. Urry, however, dissenting in one particular. At a meeting of the Joint Board of Management a resolution was adopted accepting the findings of the Board.

3. SHIPPING.

Sept. 11, 1912	Certain Steamship Companies doing business at the port of Halifax, viz. Pickford and Black, Furness-Withy Co., T. A. S. De Wolfe and Son, Canada Atlantic and Plant SS. Co., Royal Co., and employees, members of Halifax Longshoremen's Association.	Employees	Halifax, N.S.	500	Concerning wages	His Honour Judge W. B. Wallace (c) 3; George A. McKenzie (e) 1; Arthur M. Hoare (m) I.	Sept. 21, 1912	Oct. 15, 1912	A unanimous report was presented by the Board, in which it was stated that an agreement had been arrived at by both parties concerned, effective from October 15, 1912 to December 31, 1913.

4. TELEPHONES.

Date	Parties		Location	No. affected	Nature of dispute	Board	Dates	Result
Mar. 17, 1913	British Columbia Telephone Co. and employees, members of Local Union No. 213 Inter. Brotherhood of Electrical Workers.	Employer	Lines of British Columbia Telephone Co.	320	Concerning wages and conditions of employment.			Through the good offices of the department, conferences were arranged between the officials of the company and a committee of the men, who had ceased work on March 15. These conferences resulted in a settlement of the main points at issue. The men returned to work on March 24.

III. MUNICIPAL PUBLIC UTILITIES.

Date	Parties		Location	No. affected	Nature of dispute	Board	Result
Mar. 14, 1913	...ion of the City of ... other and certain employees, being scavengers, waterworks employees, and maintenance and ... the ... Civic Employees' Union and ...ion of Ind.carriers, Building and ... Labourers.	Employees	Vancouver, B.C.	1,300 dir. 1,300 indir.	Concerning wages of waterworks men, also alleged discrimination against union men.	H. O. Alexander (g) 1; George E. McCrossan (m) l.	At the close of the fiscal year the Board had not been completed by the appointment of a chairman.

B. INDUSTRIES OTHER THAN MINES, AGENCIES OF TRANSPORTATION AND COMMUNICATION, AND OTHER PUBLIC SERVICE UTILITIES.

Date	Parties		Location	No. affected	Nature of dispute	Board	Dates	Result
Jan. 9, 1913	...wa Car Co., Ltd., ...es, ...s and helpers, members of Lodge No. 412, Inter. Association of Machinists and Lodge No. 446, Inter. Brotherhood of Blacksmiths and Helpers.	Employees	Ottawa, Ont.	69	Concerning wages and hours.	Harnett P. Hill (c) 3; George F. Henderson (e) l; James Cameron Watters (m) l.	Jan. 11, 1913 Jan. 17, 1913	A unanimous report was presented by the Board, embodying an agreement signed by both parties to the dispute, effective for one year from January 17, 1913.

INDUSTRIAL DISPUTES INVESTIGATION ACT, 1907.—PROCEEDINGS, 1913-14.

STATEMENT of Applications for Boards of Conciliation and Investigation and of Proceedings thereunder from April 1, 1913, to March 31, 1914.

A.—MINES, AGENCIES OF TRANSPORTATION AND COMMUNICATION AND OTHER PUBLIC SERVICE UTILITIES.

1. Appointed by the Minister, under Section 8, Sub-section 1, of the I.D.I. Act, on recommendation from party concerned.
2. Appointed by the Minister, under Section 8, Sub-section 2, of the I.D.I. Act, in the absence of a recommendation from party concerned.
3. Appointed by the Minister, under Section 8, Sub-section 3, of the I.D.I. Act, on the joint recommendation of the two members first appointed.
4. Appointed by the Minister, under Section 8, Sub-section 4, of the I.D.I. Act, in the absence of a joint recommendation by the two members first appointed.

I. MINING AND SMELTING INDUSTRY.

1. COAL MINES.

Date of receipt of application.	Parties to Dispute.	Party making application.	Locality.	No. persons affected.	Nature of dispute.	Names of Members of Board: (c) Chairman; (e) Employer; (m) Men.	Date on which Board was constituted.	Date of receipt of report of Board.	Result of Reference.
May 26, 1913	Acadia Coal Co., Ltd. and employees, some of them being members of Local Unions No. 351 and No. 1726, United Mine Workers of America.	Employees	Stellarton, N.S.	1,125 dir.; 260 indir.	Concerning demand for increased wages, recognition of United Mine Workers of America and reinstatement of certain former employees alleged to have been dismissed for their connection therewith.	Hon. John N. Armstrong (c) 3; W. H. Chase (e) 1; J. C. Watters, (m) 1.	June 20, 1913	July 14, 1913	A unanimous report was presented by the Board, in which it was stated that an amicable settlement of all matters in dispute had been effected.

II. TRANSPORTATION AND COMMUNICATION.

1. RAILWAYS.

Date of receipt of application.	Parties to Dispute.	Party making application.	Locality.	No. persons affected.	Nature of dispute.	Names of Members of Board: (c) Chairman; (e) Employer; (m) Men.	Date on which Board was constituted.	Date of receipt of report of Board.	Result of Reference.
Mar. 11, 1913	Canadian Northern Railway Co. and Conductors, members of the Order of Railway Conductors.	Employees	C.N.R. lines	350 dir.; 2,200 indir.	Concerning employees' demands for various changes in existing schedule, including wages, hours and working conditions.	Hon. Mr. Justice A. Haggart (c) 3; Wm. Cross (e) 1; J. Harvey Hall, (m) 1.	Mar. 29, 1913	April 25, 1913	Report of Board was accompanied by a minority report signed by Mr. Cross. Mr. Hall, whilst signing the majority report, submitted a statement of points on which he differed from the chairman. No cessation of work occurred.

Date	Parties to dispute	Location	Applicant	Number affected	Nature of dispute	Board	Date of reference	Date of report	Remarks
Mar. 31, 1913	Canadian Pacific Railway Co. and certain employees, members of the Brotherhood of Locomotive Firemen and Enginemen.	Alberta Division of C.P.R.	Employees	2,650 dir., 7,000 indir.	Concerning alleged breach of agreement by Company re promotions.	Prof. Adam Shortt (c); J. H. Wellington (e) 1; David Campbell (w) 1.	April 15, 1913	Oct. 21, 1913	Report of Board was ... by a minority report signed by Mr. ... The majority report ... that ... ... of Locomotive ... the Engineers and the ... hood of Locomotive ... and Enginemen. A conference ... be ... Co., at ... with ... was ... ... men or ... al ... ers of rail ... ... of all ... his ... sity or further ... by the Board.
July 7, 1913	Halifax and South-Western Railway Co. and certain employees, members of the Canadian Brotherhood of Railroad employees.	Bridgewater, N.S.	Employees	34 dir., 5 indir.	Concerning wages and conditions of employment as per schedule submitted.	A. B. Crosby (c) 3; Major W. Ernest Thompson (e) 1; Jno. A. McDonald (w) 1.	Aug. 12, 1913	Sept. 8, 1913	A unanimous report was presented by the Board, embodying the terms of an agreement signed on behalf of both parties to the dispute, effective for one year from June 1, 1913.
July 30, 1913	Grand Trunk Railway Co. & Maintenance-of-Way employees, members of the International Brotherhood of Maintenance-of-Way Employees.	G.T.R. lines in Canada.	Employees	3,000	Concerning wages.	His Honour Judge R. D. Gunn (c) 3; F. H. McGuigan (e); G. D. Robertson (w) 1.	Aug. 27, 1913	Sept. 20, 1913	A unanimous report was presented by the Board, making certain recommendations for the settlement of the dispute, which were accepted by both parties concerned.
Aug. 7, 1913	... Central Railway Co., and ... the ... employees, ... the of Rail... ... of Railway ... Bro... ... of Blacksmith ... and Helpers and International Brotherhood of Boilermakers, Iron Shipbuilders & Helpers.	Sherbrooke, Que.	Employees	149 dir., 40 indir.	Concerning wages and conditions of employment.				Pending establishment of Board a satisfactory arrangement was arrived at by the parties concerned.
Aug. 25, 1913	Grand Trunk Railway Co. and station and ... of ... the Order of Railroad Telegraphers.	G. T. R. lines in Canada.	Employees	1,300	Concerning wages and conditions of employment, as per schedule submitted.	His Honour Judge R. D. Gunn (c) 3; H. McGuigan (e); J. G. O'Donoghue (w) 1.	Sept. 11, 1913	Nov. 25, 1913	Report of Board was signed by all three members, Mr. O'Donoghue dissenting, however, on one or two points. The award was accepted by both parties concerned.

INDUSTRIAL DISPUTES INVESTIGATION ACT, 1907.—PROCEEDINGS, 1913 14.—*Continued.*

II. TRANSPORTATION AND COMMUNICATION—*continued.*

1. RAILWAYS—*Concluded.*

Date of receipt of application.	Parties to Dispute.	Party making application.	Locality.	No. persons affected.	Nature of dispute.	Names of Members of Board: (c) Chairman; (e) Employer; (m) Men.	Date which Board was constituted.	Date of receipt of report of Board.	Result of Reference.
Oct. 25, 1913	Canadian Pacific Ry. Co. and certain employees, members of International Brotherhood of Maintenance-of-Way Employees.	Employees...	C.P.R. System	5,000...	Concerning wages and Company's interpretation of schedule of rules.	Hon. Mr. Chief Justice Meredith (c) 4; W. N. Tilley (e) 1; Henry Irwin (m) 1.	Dec. 5, 1913	Jan. 21, 1914	Report of Board was accompanied by a minority report signed by Mr. Irwin. The majority report contained a recommendation to the effect that both sides should withdraw for the present their claims for changes in rules and rates. This recommendation was agreed to by both parties concerned.
Nov. 20, 1913	Grand Trunk Pacific Railway 6, and members and boiler-makers of No. 484 and 559, and Lodge No. 529, International Brotherhood of Boilermakers & Iron Ship-builders.	Employees...	G.T.P. System	700 dir.... 1,000 indir.	Concerning wages and conditions of employment.	Hon. Mr. Justice A. Hazzard (c) 4; Wm. Cross (e) 1; Thos. J. Murray (m) 1.	Dec. 6, 1913		Proceedings unfinished.
Jan. 9, 1914	Canadian Northern Ry. Co. and employees, members of International Brotherhood of Maintenance of Way Employees.	Employees...	C.N.R. lines	1,800 dir... 3,000 to 4,000 indir.	Concerning wages........	His Honour Judge R. D. Gunn (c) 3; W. N. Tilley (e) 1; Henry Irwin (m) 1.	March 5, 1914		Proceedings unfinished.
Jan. 9, 1914	Grand Trunk Pacific Railway Co. and employees, members of International Brotherhood of Maintenance-of-Way Employees.	Employees...	G.T.P. Ry. lines...	1,800 dir... 2,500 indir.	Concerning wages........	His Honour Judge R. D. Gunn (c) 3; F. H. McGuigan (e) 1; Henry Irwin (m) 1.	Jan. 30, 1914	Feb. 23, Feb. 26, 1914	Report of Board was accompanied by a minority report signed by Mr. Irwin. The recommendations contained in the majority report were accepted by both parties to the dispute.

Date	Parties	Employer	Locality	Nature of dispute	Board	Reference	Report	Result
Mar. 31, 1914	Canadian Pacific Ry. Employees, Co. and conductors, trainmen and yard-men, members of Order of Railway Conductors and Brotherhood of Railroad Trainmen.	C. P. R. Western lines.		3,000 dir. 2,700 indir.	Concerning demand for revision of schedule governing wages and conditions of employment.			Proceedings unfinished.

2. STREET RAILWAYS.

| June 25, 1913 | British Columbia Electric Railway Co. and employees, members of L. and Divisions No. 101 Vancouver, No. 99 Victoria, No. 134 New Westminster. Amalgamated Association of Street and Electric Railway Employees of America. | Employees | Vancouver, Victoria and New Westminster, B.C. | 2,000 dir. about 300 indir. | Concerning demand for new agreement of wages and working conditions. | Hon. Mr. Justice Denis Murphy (c) 3; H. O. Alexander (E) 1; M. B. Cotsworth (M) 1. | July 4, 1913 | Aug. 21, Sept. 3, 1913 | Members of Board were un in t h findings regarding rules but differed on the upon of wage rate wage in submitted with the majority and ity reports. The minority report was and by Mr. Cotsworth. As the of the investigation an agreement was entered into by b th parties to the dispute. |

| Mar. 9, 1914 | British Columbia Electric Railw Co. and empl ye 90 members of al Division No. 101 Vancouver, No. 109 Vi and No. 134 New Westminster. Amalgamated Association of Street and Electric Railway Employees of America. | Employees | Vancouver, Victoria and New Westminster, B.C. | 137 dir. 1,563 indir. | Concerning Company's interpretation of certain sections of existing agreement. | Hon. Mr. Justice W. A. Macdonald (c) 4; John Elliott (E) 1; Jas. H. McVety (M) 1. | Mar. 27, 1914 | | Proceedings unfinished. |

3. SHIPPING.

INDUSTRIAL DISPUTES INVESTIGATION ACT, 1907.—PROCEEDINGS, 1913-14.—*Concluded.*

II. TRANSPORTATION AND COMMUNICATION—*Concluded.*

3. SHIPPING.—*Concluded.*

Date of receipt of application.	Parties to Dispute.	Party making application.	Locality.	No. persons affected.	Nature of dispute.	Names of Members of Board: (c) Chairman; (e) Employer; (m) Men.	Date on which Board was constituted.	Date of receipt of report of Board.	Result of Reference.
Oct. 14, 1913	Certain Ship Companies trading to Port of St. John, N.B., the Allan Line, C.P.R. Steamship Lines, Dominion Coal Co., Elder Dempster and Co., the Withy and Co., Head Line, New Zealand Shipping Co., Robert Reford Co., Ltd. (Donaldon Line) and longshoremen, most of them, being members of Local N. 273, International Longshoremen's Association, local handlers and trimmers employed by the Dominion Coal Co., members of Local No. 180, International Longshoremen's Association.	Employers....	St. John, N.B......	1,040......	Concerning wages, hours and conditions of employment.	Walter E. Foster (c); John E. Moore (e); J. E. Tighe (m) 1.	Oct. 22, 1913	Nov. 14, Nov. 21, 1913	A unanimous report was presented by the Board, making certain recommendations for the settlement of the dispute. This report concerned all interests except the Dominion Coal Co. and its employees, a reference being made in this case. In the former case the Shipping Companies and employees concerned bound themselves under Section 62 of the Act to take by the award. In the latter case the award was also unanimous and was by both parties concerned.
Dec. 12, 1913	Certain Steamship Companies trading to the Port of St. John, N.B., comprising Allan Line, C.P.R. Ship and Railway Lines, Head Line, Furness and Manchester Lines, New Zealand Shipping Co., Elder Dempster & Co., Robert Reford & Co., Donaldson Line, C. N. R. Line, and Red Cross Line, and marine warehouse, freight checkers, members of Marine Warehouse Freight	Employees....	St. John, N.B......	225 dir. 1,600 indir.	Concerning wages, hours and conditions of employment.	G. Fred. Fisher (c) 3; Jos. R. Stone (e) 2; John E. Moore (m) 1.	Jan. 8, 1914	Feb. 7, 1914	A unanimous report was presented by the Board, making certain recommendations for the settlement of the dispute. The award was declared acceptable to the employees concerned, but was not accepted by the shipping companies. No cessation of work occurred.

III. MUNICIPAL PUBLIC UTILITIES.

Date	Parties	Locality	Number affected	Nature of dispute	Board	Dates	Result
Mar. 14, 1913	Checkers' Union, Local No. 825, International Longshoremen's Association.						
	...on of the City of Vancouver and certain ...o...yees, being ...s, scavengers, ...k employees and maintenance and con... ...en, members of ...lic Em... ...es' Union and ...l of International Union of ... Building and ...	Vancouver, B.C.	1,200 dir. 1,200 indir.	Concerning wages of waterworks men, also alleged discrimination against union men.	Hon. Mr. Justice Denis Murphy (c) 3; H. O. Alexander, (E) 1; Geo. E. McCrossman (M) 1.	April 5, 1913; May 14, 1913	A unanimous report was presented by the Board, making certain recommendations for the settlement of the dispute. The award was accepted by the Corporation of the City of Vancouver and was understood to be acceptable also to the employees concerned.

B.—INDUSTRIES OTHER THAN MINES, AGENCIES OF TRANSPORTATION AND COMMUNICATION, AND OTHER PUBLIC FACILITIES.

Date	Parties	Locality	Number affected	Nature of dispute	Board	Dates	Result
April 5, 1913	Certain Boot and Shoe Employees. Manufacturers of the City of Quebec, namely, J. H. Larochelle, W. A. Marsh & Co., J. Ritchie & Co., and O. Goulet and employees, members of La Fraternité Nationale des Cordonniers - Machinistes de Quebec.	Quebec, Que.	25 dir. 500 indir.	Concerning wages and alleged breach of agreement.	Hon. C. Cyrias Pelletier (c) 4; Felix Marois (E) 7; Gauthier Hébert (M) 1.	April 28, 1913; June 2, June 18, 1913	Report of Board was accompanied by a minority report signed by Mr. Hébert. The award was declared acceptable to the Companies concerned. The employees, however, refused to accept same. No general cessation of work occurred.

8 GEORGE V, A. 1918

INDUSTRIAL DISPUTES INVESTIGATION ACT, 1907.—PROCEEDINGS, 1914-15.

STATEMENT of Applications for Boards of Conciliation and Investigation and of Proceedings thereunder from April 1, 1914, to March 31, 1915.

A. MINES, AGENCIES OF TRANSPORTATION AND COMMUNICATION AND OTHER PUBLIC SERVICE UTILITIES.

1. Appointed by the Minister, under Section 8, Sub-section 1, of the I.D.I. Act, on recommendation from party concerned.
2. Appointed by the Minister, under Section 8, Sub-section 2, of the I.D.I. Act, in the absence of a recommendation from party concerned.
3. Appointed by the Minister, under Section 8, Sub-section 3, of the I.D.I. Act, on the joint recommendation of the two members first appointed.
4. Appointed by the Minister, under Section 8, Sub-section 4, of the I.D.I. Act, in the absence of a joint recommendation by the two members first appointed.

I. MINING AND SMELTING INDUSTRY.

1. METAL MINES.

Date of receipt of application.	Parties to Dispute.	Party making application.	Locality.	No. persons affected.	Nature of dispute.	Names of Members of Board: (c) Chairman; (E) Employer; (M) Men.	Date on which Board was constituted.	Date of receipt of report of Board.	Result of Reference.
July. 16, 1914	Temiskaming Mining Co and miners, surface labourers and millmen members of Cobalt Miners' Union No. 146 W.F.M.	Employees	Cobalt, Ont.	125	Concerning proposed reduction of wages.	His Honour Judge A. A. Mulufly (c) 4; R. P. Rogers (E) 1; Jas. Dogue (M) 1.	Aug. 1, 1914	Sept. 3, Sept. 11, 1914	Prior to the investigation the Company had ceased operations owing to conditions caused by the war. The Board presented two reports the minority report being signed by Mr. Dogue. The Board recommended certain improvements in conditions, to take effect when work was resumed.
Oct. 8, 1914	Miller Lake O'Brien Mine and employees, members of Gowganda Miners' Union No. 154, W.F.M.	Employees	Gowganda, Ont.	50 dir.. 100 indir..	Concerning proposed reduction of wages, conditions of employment and alleged discrimination against members of Union.	His Hon. Judge A. A. Mulufly (c) 4; R. H. James (E) 1; Robt. A. Allen (M) 1.	Nov. 5, 1914	Nov. 27, Nov. 30, 1914	Report of Board was recommended by a minority report signed by Mr. Allen. The Board recommended that the employees should accept the reduced rates until the return of normal conditions. No cessation of work occurred.

II. TRANSPORTATION AND COMMUNICATION.

1. RAILWAYS.

Date	Parties	Company	Number affected	Subject	Board	Date of reference	Date of report	Remarks
Nov. 20, 1913	Grand Trunk Pacific Railway Co. and machinists and boilermakers, members of Nos. 484 and 559, and of Lodge No. 89, and members of Brotherhood of Boilermakers and Iron Ship Builders.	G.T.P. System	700 dir., 1,000 indir.	Concerning wages and conditions of employment.	Hon. Mr. Justice A. Haggart (c) 4, Wm. Cross (e) 1, Thos. J. Murray (m) 1.	Dec. 6, 1913	April 14, 1914	Report of Board was accompanied by a minority report signed by Mr. Cross. The award was declared acceptable to the employees concerned, but was not accepted by the Company. No cessation of work occurred.
Jan. 9, 1914	Canadian Northern Railway Co. and employees, members of the Brotherhood of Maintenance of Way Men.	C.N.R. lines	1,800 dir., 3,000 to 4,000 indir.	Concerning wages.	His Honour Judge R. D. Gunn (c) 3, W. N. Tilley (e) 1, Henry Irwin (m) 1.	March 5, 1914	June 11, July 13, 1914	Report of Board was accompanied by a minority report signed by Mr. Irwin. The Board recommended that no change should be made in the rates of wages paid to the employees concerned. This was agreed to by both parties.
March 31, 1914	Canadian Pacific Railway Co. and conductors, trainmen and yardmen, members of Order of Railway Conductors and Brotherhood of Railroad Trainmen.	C.P.R. Western lines.	3,000 dir., 2,700 indir.	Concerning demand for revision of schedule governing wages and conditions of employment.	His Honour Judge R. D. Gunn (c) 4, Isaac Pitblado (e), D. Campbell (m), 1.	April 20, 1914	August 5, 1914	Report of Board was accompanied by a minority report signed by Mr. Pitblado, Mr. Pitblado, whilst signing the report, made some reservations which he set forth in a separate statement. The employees refused to accept award and asked that the schedule in force might be continued. To this the Company subsequently agreed.
April 22, 1914	Michigan Central Railroad Co. and employees, being train despatchers, station agents, etc., members of Order of Railroad Telegraphers.	M.C.R. lines in Canada.	115 dir., 3,000 indir.	Concerning wages and conditions of employment.	His Honour Judge Colin G. Snider (c) 4, Rodger Black (e) 1, David Campbell (m) 1.	May 12, 1914	June 19, 1914	Report of Board was signed by all three members, Mr. Black, however, dissenting on one or two points. Following the report of the Board negotiations took place between the Company and the employees concerned, which resulted in a settlement of all points at issue.

2. STREET RAILWAYS.

Date	Parties	Company	Number affected	Subject	Board	Date of reference	Date of report	Remarks
March 9, 1914	British Columbia Electric Railway Co. and employees, members of Local Division No. 101 Vancouver, No. 109 Victoria, and No. 134 New Westminster Amalgamated Association of Street and Electric Railway Employees of America.	Vancouver, Victoria and New Westminster, B.C.	137 dir., 1,563 indir.	Concerning Company's interpretation of certain sections of agreement.	Hon. Mr. Justice W. A. Macdonald (c) 4, John Elliot (e) 1, Jas. H. McVety (m) 1.	March 27, 1914	June 5, 1914	Report of Board was accompanied by a minority report signed by Mr. Elliot. Through the efforts of Mr. McNiven, one of the officers of the Department of Labour, conferences were subsequently held which resulted in a satisfactory arrangement.

INDUSTRIAL DISPUTES INVESTIGATION ACT, 1907.—PROCEEDINGS, 1914-15.—*Continued.*

II. TRANSPORTATION AND COMMUNICATION—*Concluded.*

2. STREET RAILWAYS—*Concluded.*

Date of receipt of application.	Parties to Dispute.	Party making application.	Locality.	No. persons affected.	Nature of dispute.	Names of Members of Board: (c) Chairman; (e) Employer; (w) Men.	Date on which Board was constituted.	Date of receipt of report of Board.	Result of Reference.
June 6, 1914	St. John Railway Co. and employees, members of Division No. 663, Amalgamated Association of Street and Electric Railway Employees of America.	Employees	St. John, N.B.	90 dir. 60 indir.	Concerning alleged discrimination against a member of the Union.	Robert L. Hayes (c)3; His Honour Judge J. G. Forbes (e), 2; Jas. L. Sugrue (w),1.	June 22, 1914	July 8, 1914	A unanimous report was presented by the Board, making certain recommendations for the settlement of the dispute. The Company refused to accept the award, and a strike of the employees followed, which continued from July 22 to July 24, when an agreement was entered into by both parties concerned.
July 2, 1914	Ottawa Electric Railway Co. and employees, members of Division No. 279, Amalgamated Association of Street and Electric Railway Employees of America.	Employees	Ottawa, Ont.	450	Concerning wages, hours, and recognition of Union.	A. E. Fripp, M.P. (w), 1.			Proceedings discontinued, an agreement having been reached by both parties concerned, effective to June 30, 1916.

III. LIGHT AND POWER.

Date of receipt of application.	Parties to Dispute.	Party making application.	Locality.	No. persons affected.	Nature of dispute.	Names of Members of Board: (c) Chairman; (e) Employer; (w) Men.	Date on which Board was constituted.	Date of receipt of report of Board.	Result of Reference.
May 2, 1914	Toronto Electric Light Co. and Toronto Railway Co. and electrical workers, members of Local No. 353, International Brotherhood of Electrical Workers.	Employees	Toronto, Ont.	300	Concerning wages, hours, conditions of employment and alleged discrimination against members of Union.	His Honour Judge D. McGibbon (c) 3; H. H. Dewart, K.C. (e) 1; J. G. O'Donoghue, (w) 1.	May 12, 1914	July 28, 1914	Report of Board in the case of the Toronto Electric Light Company was accompanied by a minority report, signed by Mr. Dewart. Negotiations resulted in a settlement of the dispute, thus obviating the necessity for any action in connection with the dispute between the Toronto Railway Co. and employees.
June 18, 1914	Dominion Iron and Steel Co. and electrical workers, members of Local No. 293, International Brotherhood of Electrical Workers.	Employees	Sydney, N.S.	55 dir. 2,000 to 3,000 indir.	Concerning alleged discrimination against members of Union.	Rev. I. W. MacMillan (c) 3; W. H. Chase (e) 1; Arthur S. Kendall, M.D. (w) 1.	July 14, 1914	Aug. 15, 1914	A unanimous report was presented by the Board, accompanied by an agreement signed on behalf of both parties concerned.

Date	Parties		Location	No. affected	Subject	Board	Reference	Report	Result
July 15, 1914	Dominion Power and Transmission Co., Ltd. and electrical workers, members of Local No. 390, International Brotherhood of Electrical Workers, and others.	Employees	Hamilton, Ont.	18 dir. 14 indir.	Concerning wages, hours and conditions of employment.	His Honour Judge L. B. C. Livingstone (c) 4; C. F. Maxwell (e) 2; John B. Pegg (w) 1.	Aug. 10, 1914	Aug. 28, 1914	Report of Board stated that on the request of both parties concerned the investigation was not proceeded with.

IV. MUNICIPAL PUBLIC UTILITIES.

Date	Parties		Location	No. affected	Subject	Board	Reference	Report	Result
May 9, 1914	Toronto Hydro-Electric System and electrical workers and members of Local No. 353, International Brotherhood of Electrical Workers.	Employees	Toronto, Ont.	200 dir. 55 indir.	Concerning wages, hours, conditions of employment, and alleged discrimination against members of Union.	His Honour Judge Colin G. Snider (c) 4; F. W. Wegenast (e) 1; Fred. Bancroft (w) 1.	May 27, 1914	June 10, 1914	Report was signed by the Chairman and Mr. Bancroft and embodied a schedule of wages and working conditions which were recommended to become effective from May 1, 1914. Mr. Wegenast did not concur in the award. The findings were accepted by both parties concerned.
June 4, 1914	London Hydro-Electric ... trial workers, m... bers of ... No. 120, ... Brother... ... of ... Wn.	Employees	London, Ont.	26 dir. 11 indir.	Concerning wages and conditions of employment.	John Jacobs (w) 1			Proceedings discontinued at the request of both parties concerned.
Oct. 13, 1914	City of Edmonton and employees in telephone, ... light and street railway ... No. ... therhood of ... Workers and ... power house employees	Employees	Edmonton, Alta.	255 dir. 55 indir.	Concerning alleged reduction of wages, without required notice.	Hon. Mr. Justice J. D. Hyndman (c) 3; Kenneth W. MacKenzie (e) 1; John B. Pegg (w) 1.	March 11, 1915	March 23, 1915	Prior to the investigation agreements were ... ed into between the ... en of Edmonton and the ... es in the telephone, electric light and ... at railway depart- ments. The Board, therefore, ... lt only with the ... es of the ... er house ... The e- port was signed by all three mem- bers, Mr. Pegg, ... er, dissent- ing on one point. The ... ard was a- ... ed by b th parties a- ... rad.
Mar. 9, 1915	City of Calgary and elec- trical workers, mem- bers of Local No. 348, International Brother- hood of Electrical Workers.	Employees	Calgary, Alta.	30	Concerning proposed re- duction of wages and termination of agree- ment.	R. A. Brown (e) 1; John B. Pegg (w) 1.			Proceedings unfinished.

INDUSTRIAL DISPUTES INVESTIGATION ACT, 1907.—PROCEEDINGS, 1914-15—*Concluded.*

B.—*INDUSTRIES OTHER THAN MINES, AGENCIES OF TRANSPORTATION AND COMMUNICATION, AND OTHER PUBLIC UTILITIES.*

Date of receipt of application.	Parties to Dispute.	Party making application.	Locality.	No. persons affected.	Nature of dispute.	Names of Members of Board: (c) Chairman; (e) Employer; (w) Men.	Date on which Board was constituted.	Date of receipt of report of Board.	Result of Reference.
May 7, 1914	Ottawa Car Manufacturing Co., Ltd., and machinists and boilermakers, members of Lodge No. 412, International Association of Machinists.	Employees	Ottawa, Ont.	75	Concerning wages and conditions of employment.	Hamnett P. Hill (c) 3; Geo. F. Henderson, K.C. (e) 1; J. C. Watters (w) 1.	May 9, 1914	May 29, 1914	A unanimous report was presented by the Board, accompanied by an agreement entered into by both parties.
June 15, 1914	Certain Montreal Contractors and their respective employees, being carpenters and joiners, members of the United Brotherhood of Carpenters and Joiners of America.	Employees	Montreal, Que.	500	Concerning alleged refusal of employers to comply with agreement of 1912.	Hon. Mr. Justice J. Beaudin (c) 4; John á York (e) 1; Gustave Francq (w) 1.	June 23, 1914	July 21, 1915	Report of Board was unanimous and was accompanied by a memorandum of agreement signed on behalf of both parties concerned, effective to June 1, 1917. A strike had occurred on June 1, which continued until June 15, when through the efforts of an officer of the Department of Labour the differences in question were referred for adjustment under section 63 of the Act.
Dec. 8, 1914	J. D. Adair & Co., Ltd., Contractors, and employees, being workmen employed in the Edmonton, Dunvegan and British Columbia Railway boat at Edmonton, Alta.	Employees	Edmonton, Alta.	127	Concerning reduction of wages.	Hon. Mr. Justice J. D. Hyndman (c) 3; O. M. Biggar, K.C. (e) 1; Wm. MacAdams (w) 1.	Jan. 4, 1915		Proceedings unfinished.
Jan. 14, 1915	J. D. McArthur & Co., Ltd., Contractors, and employees, including train men on the Edmonton, Dunvegan and British Columbia Railway and the Alberta and Great Waterways Railway.	Employees	Edmonton, Dunvegan and British Columbia Railway and the Alberta and Great Waterways Railway.		Concerning reduction of wages.	S. A. Dickson (c) 4; O. M. Biggar, K.C., (e) 1; D. Campbell (w) 1.	March 16, 1915		Proceedings unfinished.

INDUSTRIAL DISPUTES INVESTIGATION ACT, 1907.—PROCEEDINGS, 1915–16.

STATEMENT of Applications for Boards of Conciliation and Investigation and of Proceedings thereunder from April 1, 1915, to March 31, 1916.

A.—MINES, AGENCIES OF TRANSPORTATION AND COMMUNICATION AND OTHER PUBLIC SERVICE UTILITIES.

1.   Appointed by the Minister, under Section 8, Sub-section 1, of the I.D.I. Act, on recommendation from party concerned.
2.   Appointed by the Minister, under Section 8, Sub-section 2, of the I.D.I. Act, in the absence of a recommendation from party concerned.
3.   Appointed by the Minister, under Section 8, Sub-section 3, of the I.D.I. Act, on the joint recommendation of the two members first appointed.
4.   Appointed by the Minister, under Section 8, Sub-section 4, of the I.D.I. Act, in the absence of a joint recommendation by the two members first appointed.

I. MINING AND SMELTING INDUSTRY.

1. Coal Mines.

Date of receipt of application.	Parties to Dispute.	Party making application.	Locality.	No. persons affected.	Nature of dispute.	Names of Members of Board: (c) Chairman; (e) Employer; (m) Men.	Date on which Board was constituted.	Date of receipt of report of Board.	Result of Reference.
Aug. 19, 1915	Intercolonial Coal Mining Co., Ltd., and employees.	Employees...	Westville, N.S...	366...	Concerning wages......	His Honour Judge W. B. Wallace, (c) 3; John MacKeen, (e) 1; Simon Lott, (m) 1.	Sept. 1, 1915	Sept. 17, 1915	A unanimous report was presented by the Board, making certain recommendations for the settlement of the dispute, which were accepted by both parties concerned.
Nov. 20, 1915	Acadia Coal Co., Ltd., and employees.	Employees...	Stellarton, N.S ...	430...	Concerning scews......	His Honour Judge W. B. Wallace, (c) 3; Wm. W. Chase, (e) 1; Simon Lott, (m) 1.	Nov. 30, 1915.	Dec. 13, 1915	A unanimous report was presented by the Board making certain recommendations for the settlement of the dispute. The award was accepted by the company and was understood to be acceptable also to the employees concerned, the impending strike being hereby averted.

II.—TRANSPORTATION AND COMMUNICATION.

1. Railways.

Date of receipt of application.	Parties to Dispute.	Party making application.	Locality.	No. persons affected.	Nature of dispute.	Names of Members of Board	Date on which Board was constituted.	Date of receipt of report of Board.	Result of Reference.
April 16, 1915	Canadian Northern Railway Co. and employees, members of Order of Railway Conductors, Brotherhood of Railroad Trainmen, and Order of Railroad Telegraphers.	Employees...	Lines of Canadian Northern Ontario, Bay of Quinte, and B. W. and N. W. Railways.	300 dir.; 4,000 indir.	Concerning wages and conditions of employment.				On request of both parties concerned the application was not proceeded with, the matters in dispute having been settled by negotiation.

INDUSTRIAL DISPUTES INVESTIGATION ACT, 1907.—PROCEEDINGS, 1915-16.—Continued.

II. TRANSPORTATION AND COMMUNICATION—Continued.

1. RAILWAYS—Concluded.

Date of receipt of application.	Parties to Dispute.	Party making application.	Locality.	No. persons affected.	Nature of dispute.	Names of Members of Board: (c) Chairman; (E) Employer; (M) Men.	Date on which Board was constituted.	Date of receipt of report of Board.	Result of Reference.
May 17, 1915	Canadian Northern Railway Co. and employees on its eastern lines, members of Brotherhood of Locomotive Engineers and Brotherhood of Locomotive Firemen and Enginemen.	Employees	Merged lines of Canadian Northern Railway east of Port Arthur, Ont.	407 dir.; 1,120 indir.	Concerning employees' demand for same rates and rules in force west of Great Lakes.	His Honour Judge Emerson Coatsworth, (c) 4; P. H. McGuigan, (E)1; D. Campbell (M) 1.	June 21, 1915	Oct. 22, 1915	A unanimous report was presented by the Board, accompanied by a proposed schedule of rules and rules effective from November 1, 1915. The award was accepted by the employees concerned and was later accepted by the Company.
June 28, 1915	Grand Trunk Pacific Railway Co. and employees, members of International Brotherhood of Maintenance-of-Way Employees.	Employees	Lines of Grand Trunk Pacific Railway.	1,800 dir.; 1,400 indir.	Concerning termination of working agreement and proposed reduction of wages.				Pending the establishment of a Board the application was withdrawn to permit of further negotiations which resulted in the Company deferring the proposed reduction.
Feb. 28, 1916	Toronto, Hamilton and Buffalo Railway Co. and employees in locomotive and car department, members of T. H. and B. System Federation No. 36, International Association of Machinists and Helpers No. 414, International Brotherhood of Iron Ship Builders and Helpers No. 421, International Brotherhood of Blacksmiths and Helpers No. 330, and Brotherhood of Railway Carmen of America No. 94.	Employees	Hamilton, Ont.	105 dir.; 12 indir.	Concerning wages, hours and conditions of employment.	His Honour Judge Colin G. Snider, (c) 4; Geo. S. Kerr, K.C., (E) 1; Jas. Simpson, (M) 1.	Mar. 28, 1916		Proceedings unfinished.

2. STREET RAILWAYS.

Date	Parties	Party	Locality	Employees affected	Nature of dispute	Board	Reference	Report	Result
June 29, 1915	British Columbia Electric Railway Co. and employees, members of Local Divisions No. 101 Vancouver, No. 109 Victoria, and No. 134 New Westminster. Amalgamated Association of Street and Electric Railway Employees of America.	Employer	Vancouver, Victoria, and New Westminster, B.C.	1,058 dir. 156 indir.	Concerning proposed reductions in wages and changes in working conditions.	Honourable Mr. Justice W. A. Macdonald, (c) 4; A. G. McCandless, (e) 1; Jas. H. McVety, (w) 1.	July 8, 1915	Sept. 7, 1915	Report of Board was accompanied by a minority report signed by Mr. McVety. The Company accepted the award but the employees refused to do so. Through the efforts of one of the Departmental officers conferences were arranged between the parties concerned which resulted in an agreement being reached which disposed of all points at issue.
July 19, 1915	British Columbia Electric Railway Co. and employees, members of Local Unions No. 213 Vancouver, No. 230 Victoria and No. 558 New Westminster. International Brotherhood of Electrical Workers.	Employees	Vancouver, Victoria and New Westminster, B.C.	150	Concerning wages, hours, conditions of employment and alleged unfair dismissals.	Honourable Mr. Justice W. A. Macdonald, (c) 4; Jas. A. Harvey, K.C. (e) 2; Edmund H. Morrison, (w) 1.	Aug. 14, 1915	Sept. 15, 1915	A unanimous report was presented by the Board and was accompanied by a proposed schedule of rules and rates effective for two years from September 15, 1915. The award was declared acceptable to the employees concerned but was not accepted by the Company.
Aug. 30, 1915	City of Edmonton and employees, members of Local Division No. 569, Amalgamated Association of Street and Electric Railway Employees of America.	Employees	Edmonton, Alberta.	250	Concerning cancellation of agreement.				Pending the establishment of a Board the Department was informed that the dispute had been adjusted, an agreement having been entered into by both parties concerned.
Nov. 11, 1915	City of Edmonton and employees, members of Local Division No. 569, Amalgamated Association of Street and Electric Railway Employees of America.	Employees	Edmonton, Alberta.	6 dir. 220 indir.	Concerning alleged discrimination against members of Union, resulting in a number of dismissals.	Frank Ford, K. C., (c) 3; J. E. Wallbridge, (e) 1; Wm. MacAdams, (w) 1.	Dec. 20, 1915	Mar. 11, 1916	A unanimous report was presented by the Board and was accompanied by an agreement between the parties concerned, disposing of all points at issue except the case of a dismissal, the agreement providing, however, that the Board decision on this point should be final. The finding was to the effect that this suspension should be substituted for dismissal.

INDUSTRIAL DISPUTES INVESTIGATION ACT, 1907.—PROCEEDINGS, 1915–16.—*Concluded.*

TRANSPORTATION AND COMMUNICATION.—*Concluded.*

3. SHIPPING.

Date of receipt of application.	Parties to Dispute.	Party making application.	Locality.	No. persons affected.	Nature of dispute.	Names of Members of Board: (c) Chairman; (e) Employer; (m) Men.	Date on which Board was constituted.	Date of receipt of report of Board.	Result of Reference.
Dec. 20, 1915	Certain Steamship Companies ... to the Port of St. John, N.B., comprising Allan Line, C. P. R. Steamship Lines, ... Dempster and Co., ... Line, New Zealand Shipping Co., Furness Line, ... L i n e, ... Withy and Co.) ... Redford ... Donaldson Line, and Royal Mail Steam Packet Co., ... H. S. ... and Sons ... H. W. Parlee, ... dores and contractors, and Wm. Thomson and Co., Ltd., J. E. Knight and Co., W. M. MacKay, Ltd., Geo. McKean and Co., Ltd., J. B. and ... R. C. Elkin, and Alexander ..., ... brokers and ... ad ... members of Long... tion of St. John.	Employees...	St. John, N.B.	1,135...	Concerning wages, hours, and conditions of employment.	W. E. Foster, (c) 1; J. H. Leuer, (e) 1; J. E. Tighe, (m) 1.	Jan. 1, 1916	Jan. 24, 1916	A unanimous report was presented by the Board, embodying the terms of a proposed agreement effective from January 18, 1916, until December 1, 1919. The award was accepted by the employees and was also declared acceptable on behalf of most of the employers.

III. MUNICIPAL PUBLIC UTILITIES.

Mar. 9, 1915	City of Calgary and electrical workers, members of Local No. 348, International Brotherhood of Electrical Workers.	Employees...	Calgary, Alta...	30.........	Concerning proposed reduction of wages and termination of agreement.	Col. G. E. Sanders, (c) 3; R. A. Brown, (e) 1; John B. Pegg, (m) 1.	April 2, 1915	May 5, 1915	A unanimous report was presented by the Board, accompanied by an agreement entered into by both parties concerned.

| May 26, 1915 | Toronto Hydro-Electric Commission and electrical workers, members of Local No. 353, International Brotherhood of Electrical Workers. | Employees... | Toronto, Ont... | 175 dir., 25 indir. | Concerning wages and conditions of employment. | His Honour Judge Emerson Coatsworth, (c) 4; F. Erichsen Brown, (E) 1; Fred. Bancroft, (M) 1. | 2, July 1915 | Aug. 13, Aug. 20, 1915 | Report of Board was accompanied by a minority report signed by Mr. Brown. The employees signified their acceptance of the majority report. The Commissioners, however, refused to accept the majority report and a strike of the employees took place on November 2, 1915, which continued until November 23, 1915, when the employees returned to work substantially on the terms of the minority report. |

B.—INDUSTRIES OTHER THAN MINES, AGENCIES OF TRANSPORTATION AND COMMUNICATION, AND OTHER PUBLIC UTILITIES.

Dec. 8, 1914	J. D. [...] & Co., [...] and wrkmen [...] emp[...]ed in the Edmonton, Dunvegan and British Columbia Railway Shops at [...] Edmonton, [...].	Employees...	Edmonton, Alberta.	127	Concerning reduction of wages.	Honourable Mr. Justice J. D. Hyndman, (c) 3; O. M. Biggar, K.C., (E) 1; Wm. MacAdams, (M)1.	4, Jan. 1915	May 20, 1915	A unanimous report was presented by the Board in which it was stated that both parties had agreed to abide by the report. The dispute was accordingly settled.
Jan. 14, 1915	J. D. McArthur & Co., Ltd., [...] and [...] train [...] on the Edmonton, Dunvegan & [...] Railway and the [...] Railway and the [...] Waterways Railway.	Employees...	Edmonton, Dunvegan, and British Columbia Railway and the Alberta and Great Waterways Railway.		Concerning reduction of wages.	S. A. Dickson, (c) 4; O. M. Biggar, K.C., (E)1; D. Campbell, (M).	Mar. 16, 1915	April 19, 1915	A unanimous report was presented by the Board, recommending the restoration of the wages paid prior to the reduction of November 1, 1914. The award was accepted by both parties concerned.
May 28, 1915	Ottawa Car Manufacturing Co., Ltd., and machinists, members of Lodge No. 412, International Association of Machinists.	Employees...	Ottawa, Ont...	100	Concerning wages and conditions of employment.	Hannett P. Hill, (c) 3; Geo. F. Henderson, K.C., (E) 1; Jas. Simpson, (M) 1.	May 29, 1915	June 17, 1915	Report of Board was signed by all three members, Mr. Simpson dissenting on one point. The report was accompanied by an agreement entered into by both parties concerned.
Aug. 19, 1915	Nova Scotia Steel and Coal Co., Ltd., and Eastern Car Co., Ltd., and employees engaged in the manufacture of munitions of war.	Employees...	New Glasgow and Trenton, N.S.	2,000	Concerning reduction of wages.	His Honour Judge Emerson Coatsworth, (c) 4; Col. B. A. Weston, (E) 1; R. H. Murray, (M) 1.	Sept. 1, 1915	Sept. 27, 1915	Prior to the [...]tion the employ-es [...] gone out on strike. Both parties were [...]ed to [...] their [...] [...] [...] Sec. 63 to a Board and the [...] [...]t to work. The [...]ingly [...] report of the Board was [...] and [...] [...] of all matters in [...] [...], an [...] [...] having [...] previously signed [...]ing the de-sion of the Board [...] [...] th parties until the end of the war, or as long as the [...] [...]ed on munitions work.

INDUSTRIAL DISPUTES INVESTIGATION ACT, 1907.—PROCEEDINGS, 1916-17.

STATEMENT of Applications for Boards of Conciliation and Investigation and of Proceedings thereunder from April 1, 1916, to March 31, 1917.

MINES, AGENCIES OF TRANSPORTATION AND COMMUNICATION AND OTHER PUBLIC SERVICE UTILITIES.

1. Appointed by the Minister, under Section 8, Sub-section 1, of the I. D. I. Act, on recommendation from party concerned.
2. Appointed by the Minister, under Section 8, Sub-section 2, of the I. D. I. Act, in the absence of a recommendation from party concerned.
3. Appointed by the Minister, under Section 8, Sub-section 3, of the I. D. I. Act, on the joint recommendation of the two members first appointed.
4. Appointed by the Minister, under Section 8, Sub-section 4, of the I. D. I. Act, in the absence of a joint recommendation by the two members first appointed.

I. MINING AND SMELTING INDUSTRY.

1. COAL MINES.

Date of receipt of application.	Parties to Dispute.	Party making application.	Locality.	No. persons affected.	Nature of dispute.	Names of Members of Board: (c) Chairman; (E) Employer; (M) Men.	Date on which Board was constituted.	Date of receipt of report of Board.	Result of Reference.
May 10, 1916	Acadia Coal Co., Ltd., and employees.	Employees	Stellarton, N.S.	1,000	Concerning wages, hours and conditions of employment.	His Honour Judge E. Coatsworth, (c) 4; W. H. Chase, (E) 1; R. H. Murray, (M) 1.	May 22, 1916	June 5, 1916	The men struck on April 18, but returned to work on May 8, having decided to apply for a Board. The Board presented a unanimous report. It was stated on behalf of the men that they had agreed to be bound by the decision of the Board but the Department was not informed as to the Company's acceptance or rejection of the award. No further cessation of work occurred.
Mar. 10, 1917	Dominion Coal Co., Ltd., and certain employees, a portion of whom were held to be members of the United Mine Workers of this club.	Employees	Glace Bay, N.S.	1,500 dir.; 4,000 indir.	Concerning wages and alleged discrimination against union members.	....	....	....	This dispute was made the subject of an inquiry by one of the officers of the Department, resulting in an adjustment of some of the matters in dispute. Proceedings were, however, unfinished at the close of the fiscal year.
Mar. 31, 1917	Dominion Coal Co., Ltd., and certain employees, members of the Provincial Workmen's Association.	Employees	Glace Bay, N.S.	5,000	Concerning wages and conditions of employment.	....	....	....	This dispute practically is the same as the preceding, though the the application is from different applicants, the employees being divided between two unions. Proceedings unfinished.

2. METAL MINES.

Date	Parties		Location	No. affected	Matter in dispute	Board	Result
May 29, 1916	Consolidated Mining and Smelting Co. of Canada, Ltd., and employees, members of Trail Mill and Smeltermen's Union, No. 105, Western Federation of Miners.	Employees	Trail, B.C.	1,200 dir. 50 indir.	Concerning wages, hours and conditions of employment.	A. C. Flumerfelt, (m) 1. David Rees, (w) 1.	... the final ... was arrived at by the ... Departmental ... the Pacific ... in bringing ... but this result. We has dis... ... clearly ... fallen within ... Act to ...
June 12, 1916	Consolidated Mining and Smelting Co. of Canada, Ltd. and Le Roi No. 2, Ltd., and employees, members of Rossland Miners' Union, No. 38, Western Federation of Miners.	Employees	Rossland, B.C.	800	Concerning wages		It was agreed that the Board established at Trail should also deal with this dispute. As in the former case, Board procedure was unnecessary. A settlement was arrived at by the parties concerned, the Departmental officer resident on the Pacific coast having visited the locality and assisted in bringing about this result.
June 24, 1916	Various Mining Companies operating in Cobalt Camp and vicinity and employees, members of Cobalt Miners' Union, No. 146, Western Federation of Miners.	Employees	Cobalt Camp, Ont., and vicinity.	2,200	Concerning wages and conditions of employment.		In view of the fact that the dispute affected various companies whose consent could not be obtained to the establishment of a single Board as requested by the employees, it was decided that the dispute did not come within the provisions of the Act, but an inquiry into the matters in dispute was made by a Royal Commission. No cessation of work occurred.

3. ASBESTOS MINES.

Date	Parties		Location	No. affected	Matter in dispute	Board	Result
July 21, 1916	Asbestos Corporation, Johnson Mines, Jacob Mining Co., Ltd., Bell Asbestos Mines, Ltd., and Martin-Bennett, Ltd., and employees, members of Local Union, No. 143, Western Federation of Miners.	Employees	Thetford Mines, Que.	900 dir. 500 dir.	Concerning wages and Union recognition		In view of the fact ... the dispute ... could ... of a single Board ... but the ... Act ... an inquiry ... R ... effected; ... gone on ... gation

INDUSTRIAL DISPUTES INVESTIGATION ACT, 1907.—PROCEEDINGS, 1916-17.—*Continued.*

II. TRANSPORTATION AND COMMUNICATION.

1. RAILWAYS.

Date of receipt of application.	Parties to Dispute.	Party making application.	Locality.	No. persons affected.	Nature of dispute.	Names of Members of Board: (c) Chairman; (e) Employer; (m) Men.	Date on which Board was constituted.	Date of receipt of report of Board.	Result of Reference.
Feb. 28, 1916	Toronto, Hamilton and Buffalo Railway Co., ... and empl y ees in ... and car department, ... of T. H. & B. System, Federation No. 36, International Association of Machinists and Helpers No. 414, International Brotherhood of Iron ... and Helpers No. 421, International Brotherhood of Blacksmiths and Helpers No. 330, and Brotherhood of Railw y Carmen of America No. 94.	Employees	Hamilton, Ont.	105 dir., 12 indir.	Concerning demand for the adoption of a schedule of rules and rates.	His Honour Judge Colin G. Snider, (c); Geo. S. Kerr, K.C. (e); James Simpson, (m)	Mar. 28, 1916	May 1, 1916	A unanimous report was presented by the Board making certain recommendations for the settlement of the dispute. The findings were not accepted by either party concerned and a strike of the employees occurred on May 20, 1916, which had not been officially called off at the close of the fiscal year. It was understood, however, that the strikers had obtained work elsewhere.
April 13, 1916	Canadian Pa if n Railway G. and freight handlers, ... thrs of Local No. 12, Brotherhood of Railroad Freight Handlers.	Employees	Winnipeg, Man.	200 dir., 1,000 indir.	Concerning wages, conditions of employment and recognition of Union.				Pending the establishment of a Board a settlement was arrived at by the parties concerned.
June 2, 1916	Edmonton, Dunvegan & British Columbia Ry., ... and Great Waterways Railway, and ... al Canada Railway and maintenance of way empl y ees members of ... tional Brotherhood of Maintenance of Way ... ees.	Employees	Lines of Edmonton, Dunvegan & British Columbia Ry., Great Waterways Railway and Central Canada Ry.	300 dir., 600 indir.	Concerning wages, hours and conditions of employment.				Pending the establishment of a Board an agreement was entered into by the parties concerned, one of the Departmental officers resident in the West having visited Edmonton and assisted in bringing about this result.
June 8, 1916	Hfax and South Western Railway Co. and ... ees, members of Canadian Brotherhood of Railroad Employees.	Employees	Lines of Halifax and South Western Railway.	175	Concerning wages, hours and conditions of employment.				Pending the establishment of a Board a settlement was arrived at by the parties concerned.

Date	Parties	Locality	Number affected	Nature of dispute	Board	Reference	Report	Remarks
July 3, 1916	Canadian Northern Ry. Co. and employees, members of International Brotherhood of Maintenance of Way Employees.	Lines of the Canadian Northern Ry. East of Port Arthur.	1,000 dir... 3,000 indir.	Concerning wages, hours and conditions of employment.	His Honour Judge R. D. Gunn, (c) 3; F. H. Richardson, (e) 1; G. D. Robertson (w) 1.	Aug. 19, 1916	Oct. 21, Nov. 2, 1916	Report of Board was accompanied by a minority report signed by Mr. Richardson. The employees accepted the award. Subsequent negotiations between the parties concerned resulted in a settlement on the basis of the Board award.
Aug. 15, 1916	Algoma Central Railway and Hudson Bay Railway Co. and conductors, baggagemen, brakemen and yardmen, members of Order of Railway Conductors and Brotherhood of Railroad Trainmen.	Sault Ste Marie, Ont.	45 dir... 150 indir.	Concerning wages and conditions of employment.	His Honour Judge Colin G. Snider, (c) 3; F. H. McGuigan, (e) 1; D. Campbell, (w) 1.	Aug. 29, 1916	Sept. 14, 1916	A unanimous report was presented by the Board, accompanied by an agreement entered into by the parties concerned.
Aug. 15, 1916	Canadian Government Railways and shop trades, members of International Brotherhood of Machinists, International Bro. of Blacksmiths and Helpers, Brotherhood of Railway Carmen of America, International Brotherhood of Boiler makers and Helpers, International Association of Steamfitters and International Brotherhood of Electrical Workers.	Lines of Canadian Government Railways.	3,000	Concerning wages, hours and conditions of employment.				Proceedings in connection with the establishment of a Board were held in abeyance to permit of negotiations between the parties concerned. No further action by the Department was requested.
Aug. 17, 1916	Grand Trunk Railway Co. and maintenance of way employees, members of International Brotherhood of Maintenance of Way Employees.	Lines of Grand Trunk Railway.	3,200	Concerning wages.	His Honour Judge R. D. Gunn, (c) 3; F. H. McGuigan, (e) 1; G. D. Robertson, (w) 1.	Aug. 25, 1916	Oct. 21, Oct. 25, 1916	Report was accompanied by a minority report signed by Mr. McGuigan. The award was accepted by the parties concerned and the dispute was accordingly settled.
Aug. 31, 1916	Fredericton and Grand Lake Railway and New Brunswick Coal and Railway and firemen, conductors, brakemen and yardmen, members of Bro. of Locomotive Engineers and Brotherhood of Railroad Trainmen.	Fredericton, N.B.	20	Concerning wages and conditions of employment.	His Honour Judge R. D. Gunn, (c) 4; C. D. Richards, (a) 2; G. D. Robertson, (w) 1.	Nov. 2, 1916	Nov. 25, 1916	Report of Board was signed by all three members, Mr. Richards, however dissenting on one point. The report included a proposed schedule of rates and rules. The Company declared its willingness to accept the finding of Mr. Richards and the employees subsequently agreed to do likewise. The dispute was thus satisfactorily settled.

INDUSTRIAL DISPUTES INVESTIGATION ACT, 1907.—PROCEEDINGS, 1916-17.—*Continued.*

II. TRANSPORTATION AND COMMUNICATION—*Continued.*

1. RAILWAYS—*Concluded.*

Date of receipt of application.	Parties to Dispute.	Party making application.	Locality.	No. persons affected.	Nature of dispute.	Names of Members of Board: (c) Chairman; (e) Employer; (w) Men.	Date on which Board was constituted.	Date of receipt of report of Board.	Result of Reference.
Sept. 19, 1916	Canadian Pacific Ry. Co. and maintenance of way employees, members of International Brotherhood of Maintenance of Way Employees.	Employees	Lines of Canadian Pacific Railway.	6,000 dir. 17,000 indir.	Concerning wages and conditions of employment.				Proceedings in connection with the establishment of a Board were held in abeyance to permit of negotiations between the parties concerned which resulted in a settlement of the matters in dispute.
Oct. 7, 1916	Canadian Northern Ry. Co. and maintenance of way employees, members of International Brotherhood of Maintenance of Way employees.	Employees	Lines of Canadian Northern Railway west of Fort William.	3,000 dir. 2,000 indir.	Concerning wages and conditions of employment.	E. L. Taylor, K.C. (c) 4; Wm. Cross, (w) i; D. Campbell, (w) i.	Nov. 2, 1916	Dec. 11, 1916	A unanimous report was presented by the Board, accompanied by an agreement which had been entered into by the parties concerned.
Oct. 23, 1916	Canadian Pacific Railway Co. and conductors and trainmen, members of Order of Railway Conductors and Brotherhood of Railroad Trainmen.	Employer	Lines of Canadian Pacific Railway.	7,000 dir. 60,000 indir.	Concerning wages and conditions of employment.				Pending the establishment of a Board, the Dominion Government, through the Prime Minister and the Minister of Labour, pressed for a resumption of negotiations between the parties concerned. Mr. G. D. Robertson acted as a mediator. As a result the proposed strike was called off and an agreement was entered into which disposed of all matters in dispute.
Nov. 27, 1916	Pere Marquette Railroad Co. and maintenance of way employees	Employees	Canadian Division of Pere Marquette Railroad.	120 dir. 500 indir.	Concerning wages.	G. D. Robertson (w)1			Pending the completion of the Board, an agreement was entered into by the parties concerned.

Date	Parties	Location	Subject	No. affected	Board	Date referred	Date reported	Result
Mar. 27, 1917	Canadian Pacific Ry. G. and empl y... and... train, yard, station and maintenance of way service, members of Brotherhood of Locomotive Engineers, Order of Railway Conductors, Brotherhood of Railroad Trainmen, Brotherhood of Locomotive Firemen and Enginemen, Order of Railroad Telegraphers and International Bro. of Maintenance of Way Employees. Employees.	Lines of Canadian Pacific Railway.	Concerning supervision of an engineer.	10,000	E. L. Taylor, K.C. (c) 4; I. Pitblado, K.C. (e) 1; D. Campbell, (m) 1.	Feb. 19, 1917	Mar. 12, 1917	A unanimous report was presented by the board accompanied by a memorandum of settlement signed by the parties concerned.
Mar. 26, 1917	Canadian Northern Ry. Co. and clerks, stenographers, baggagemen and carcheckers, members of Canadian Brotherhood of Railroad Employees.	Lines of Canadian Northern Railway from Port Arthur to Winnipeg.	Concerning wages and conditions of employment.	95 dir. 25 indir.	...	...	...	Proceedings unfinished at the close of the fiscal year.

2. STREET RAILWAYS.

Date	Parties	Location	Subject	No. affected	Board	Date referred	Date reported	Result
May 11, 1916	Brantford Municipal Ry. ...on and street railway empl yees. ...bers of Division No. 685, Amalgamated Association of Street and Electric Railway Empl y ...f Am ri...	Brantford, Ont.	Concerning wages, conditions of employment and demand for agreement.	27 dir. 5 indir.	His Honour Judge Colin G. Snider (c) 4; F. W. Frank (x) 1; Jos. Gibbons (m) 1.	May 23, 1916	June 6, 1916	A unanimous report was presented by the Board, accompanied by a memorandum of settlement signed by the parties concerned.
June 27, 1916	Ottawa Electric Railway G. and street railway employees. ...Union No. 279, Amalgamated Association of Street and Electric Railway Em... ...es f America.	Ottawa, Ont.	Concerning wages, hours, conditions of employment and alleged discrimination against Union members.	500	Hannett P. Hill (c) 3; G. F. Henderson (e) 1; A. E. Fripp (m) 1.	July 4, 1916	July 12, 1916	A unanimous report was presented by the Board, accompanied by an agreement entered into by the parties concerned.
Sept. 2, 1916	City of Edmonton and street railway employees, members of Division No. 569, Amalgamated Association of Street and ...c Railway E... ...of America.	Edmonton, Alta.	Concerning renewal of agreement.	250	...	...	...	Pending the establishment of a Board an agreement was entered into by the parties concerned, one of the Departmental officers resident in the West having visited Edmonton and assisted in bringing about this result.

INDUSTRIAL DISPUTES INVESTIGATION ACT, 1907.—PROCEEDINGS, 1916-17.—*Continued.*

II. TRANSPORTATION AND COMMUNICATION—*Continued.*

2. STREET RAILWAYS—*Concluded.*

Date of receipt of application.	Parties to Dispute.	Party making application.	Locality.	No. persons affected.	Nature of dispute.	Names of Members of Board: (c) Chairman; (E) Employer; (M) Men.	Date on which Board was constituted.	Date of receipt of report of Board.	Result of Reference.
Sept. 4, 1916	Quebec Railway, Lights, Heat and Power Co., Ltd., and street railway employees, members of Fraternité Nationale des Employés de Tramways de Quebec.	Employees	Quebec, Que	260 dir. 305 indir.	Concerning wages and conditions of employment.	Hon. Mr. Justice C. E. Dorion (c) 3; Antonin Galipeault (E) 1; Hector Laferte (M) 1.	Oct. 13, 1916	Dec. 8, 1916	A unanimous report was presented by the Board, embodying the terms of a proposed agreement. The award was accepted by the parties concerned.
Sept. 5, 1916	Moose Jaw Electric Ry. Co., Ltd., and street railway employees, members of Division No. 614, Amalgamated Association of Street and Electric Railway Employees of America.	Employees	Moose Jaw, Sask.	36	Concerning wages, hours, conditions of employment and Union recognition.	J. H. Wellington (c) 4; Jas. Thomson (E) 1; Jas. Somerville (M) 1.	Sept. 27, 1916	Oct. 17, 1916	Report of Board was accompanied by a minority report signed by Mr. Thomson. The employees declared their willingness on account of the war to accept the award but the Company declined to do so. No cessation of work occurred.
Sept. 27	Sandwich, Windsor and Amherstburg Railway Co. and Windsor and Tecumseh Railway and street railway employees, members of Amalgamated Association of Street and Electric Railway Employees of America.	Employees	Windsor, Ont.	150	Concerning wages, hours, and conditions of employment.	His Honour Judge Jno. O. Drumgole (c) 4; Ernest G. Henderson (E) 1; Magnus Sinclair (M) 1.	Oct. 11, 1916	Nov. 9, Nov. 10, 1916	Report of Board was signed by all three members, Mr. Sinclair, however, submitting an additional report on the question of the recognition of the Amalgamated Association of Street and Electric Railway Employees of America. The report was accompanied by an agreement entered into by the parties concerned.

3. EXPRESS.

Date of receipt of application.	Parties to Dispute.	Party making application.	Locality.	No. persons affected.	Nature of dispute.	Names of Members of Board: (c) Chairman; (E) Employer; (M) Men.	Date on which Board was constituted.	Date of receipt of report of Board.	Result of Reference.
Dec. 11, 1916	Canadian Northern Express Co. and employees, members of Canadian Brotherhood of Railroad Employees.	Employees	Lines and places of operation in Canada.	300	Concerning wages, conditions of employment, and alleged discrimination against Union members.	John T. Haig (g) 2; D. Campbell (M) 1.			Pending the completion of the Board a settlement of the matters in dispute was arrived at by the parties concerned.

Date	Parties	Applicant	Locality	No. affected	Subject	Board	Date of reference	Result
Jan. 27, 1917	Canadian Express Co. and employees, members of Canadian Brotherhood of Railroad Employees.	Employees	Lines west of North Bay, Ont.	100	Concerning wages, conditions of employment, and alleged discrimination against Union members.	E. L. Taylor, K.C. (c); John T. Haig (x); D. Campbell (x) 1.	Feb. 17, 1917	Proceedings unfinished at the close of the fiscal year.
4. SHIPPING.								
Nov. 18, 1916	Dominion Coal Co., Ltd., and coal handlers, members of Coal Handlers' Union, No. 810, International Longshoremen's Association.	Employer	St. John, N.B.	50 dir. 1,000 indir.	Concerning wages			Pending the establishment of a Board an agreement was entered into by the parties concerned.
5. TELEGRAPHS.								
July 13, 1916	Great North Western Telegraph Co. of Canada and telegraphers, members of Great North Western Division No. 43, Commercial Telegraphers' Union of America.	Employees	Great North Western telegraph system.	325 dir. 1,800 indir.	Concerning wages, hours and conditions of employment.	His Honour Judge Colin G. Snider (c) 3.; F. H. McGuigan (x) 2.; D. Campbell (x) 1.	Aug. 8, 1916 Aug. 23, 1916	A unanimous report was presented the Board, accompanied by an agreement entered into by the parties concerned.
Feb. 14, 1917	Canadian Pacific Railway Co. and commercial telegraphers, members of Commercial Telegraphers' Union of America.	Employees	Lines of Canadian Pacific Railway Co.'s telegraph.	700 dir. 2,200 indir.	Concerning dismissal	E. L. Taylor, K.C. (c) 4.; John T. Haig (x) 2.; J. C. Rooney (x) 1.	Mar. 1, 1917	Proceedings unfinished at the close of the fiscal year.
Mar. 5, 1917	Marconi Wireless Telegraph Co. of Canada, Ltd., and operators on Pacific Coast Steamship service.	Employees	Vancouver, B.C.	23	Concerning wages and conditions of employment.	R. R. Maitland (c) 3.; Matthew J. Barr (x) 1.; Jas. H. McVety (x) 1.	Mar. 24, 1917	Proceedings unfinished at the close of the fiscal year.
III. LIGHT AND POWER.								
June 6, 1916	Montreal Light, Heat & Power Co. and electrical workers, members of Local Union No. 492, International Brotherhood of Electrical Workers.	Employees	Montreal, Que.	250 dir. 1,000 indir.	Concerning wages, hours, and conditions of employment.			Pending the establishment of a Board a settlement of the matters in dispute was arrived at by the parties concerned.

INDUSTRIAL DISPUTES INVESTIGATION ACT, 1907.—PROCEEDINGS, 1916–17.—*Concluded.*

IV. MUNICIPAL PUBLIC UTILITIES.

Date of receipt of application.	Parties to Dispute.	Party making application.	Locality.	No. persons affected.	Nature of dispute.	Names of Members of Board: (c) Chairman; (b) Employer; (m) Men.	Date on which Board was constituted.	Date of receipt of report of Board.	Result of Reference.
Nov. 30, 1916	City of Ottawa and waterworks employees, members of Federal Labour Union No. 15.	Employees	Ottawa, Ont.	45	Concerning wages.	Hannett P. Hill (c) 3; G. A. Crain (e) 1; J. C. Waters (m) 1.	Dec. 11, 1916	Dec. 22, 1916	A unanimous report was presented by the Board, with certain recommendations for the settlement of the dispute. The award was declared acceptable to the employees concerned and was understood to be acceptable to the Corporation of Ottawa.
Mar. 29, 1917	City of Vancouver and teamsters, labourers, etc., employed by the the Street Cleaning, Scavenging, Waterworks, Sewer and General Maintenance Departments, members of Civic Employees' Union.	Employees	Vancouver, B.C.	400	Concerning wages, appointment of foremen, and alleged discrimination against Union members.				Proceedings unfinished at the close of the fiscal year.

INDUSTRIAL DISPUTES INVESTIGATION ACT, 1907.

VI—Statement showing all Strikes in Mines and Public Utilities, 1907–17.

[In this table are recorded all strikes (or lockouts) in mines and public utilities occurring during the period 1907–17. All these strikes have been reported in the strike record of the Department of Labour, as printed in the annual departmental report. In the statements, however, of proceedings under the Industrial Disputes Investigation Act, it has been customary to record only strikes which have occurred after the disputes concerned have been dealt with by a Board of Conciliation and Investigation. In the present table strikes of the class last indicated are also included (see column III), thus rendering the statement complete. These tables are printed in response to many demands.]

1907 (FROM MARCH 22).

Industry.	I			II			III			Total.		
	No application for Board received.			Strike before or after application but ended before constitution of Board or by Board inquiry.			Strike not averted nor ended by Board inquiry.					
	No. disputes.	No. employees affected.	Approximate time losses in working days.	No. disputes.	No. employees affected.	Approximate time losses in working days.	No. disputes.	No. employees affected.	Approximate time losses in working days.	No. disputes.	No. employees affected.	Approximate time losses in working days.
Mines and Quarries—												
Coal	4	1,831	5,910	3	5,300	74,550	1	1,250	98,750	8	8,381	179,210
Metal	2	3,050	14,900							2	3,050	14,900
Quarry	1	53	689							1	53	689
	7	4,934	21,499	3	5,300	74,550	1	1,250	98,750	11	11,484	194,799
Transportation and Communication—												
Railways	3	890	5,990	1	55	385				4	945	6,375
Shipping	1	1,000	10,000	2	2,100	15,700				3	3,100	25,700
Cartage (railway freight)	4	652	2,577							4	652	2,577
Telegraphs	1	75	750							1	75	750
	9	2,617	19,317	3	2,155	16,085				12	4,772	35,402
Light and Power	1	75	375							1	75	376
Total	17	7,626	41,191	6	7,455	90,635	1	1,250	98,750	24	16,331	230,576

STRIKES IN MINES AND PUBLIC UTILITIES, 1907-17.—*Continued.*

Industry	I. No application for Board received.			II. Strike before or after application but ended before constitution of Board or by Board inquiry.			III. Strike not averted nor ended by Board inquiry.			Total.		
	No. disputes.	No. employees affected.	Approximate time losses in working days.	No. disputes.	No. employees affected.	Approximate time losses in working days.	No. disputes.	No. employees affected.	Approximate time losses in working days.	No. disputes.	No. employees affected.	Approximate time losses in working days.
1908												
Mines—												
Coal	4	3,406	17,358	2	375	1,576				6	3,781	18,963
Metal	2	58	788							2	58	788
Total	6	3,464	18,176	2	375	1,576				8	3,839	19,751
Transportation and Communication—												
Railways	3	390	1,480				1	8,000	424,000	4	8,390	425,480
Shipping	1	50	50							1	50	50
Total	4	440	1,530				1	8,000	424,000	5	8,440	425,530
Total	10	3,904	19,706	2	375	1,576	1	8,000	424,000	13	12,279	445,281
1909												
Mines—												
Coal	3	1,430	22,962	3	2,875	187,875	3	4,350	499,250	9	8,655	710,087
Metal	1	140	1,120				1	225	4,950	1	225	4,950
Asbestos										1	140	1,120
Total	4	1,570	24,082	3	2,875	187,875	4	4,575	504,200	11	9,020	716,157
Transportation and Communication—												
Railways				2	950	4,700				2	950	4,700
Shipping	2	265	2,780							2	265	2,780
Total	2	265	2,780	2	950	4,700				4	1,216	7,480
Total	6	1,835	26,862	5	3,825	192,575	4	4,575	504,200	15	10,235	723,637

1910

	No.	Empl.	$	No.	Empl.	$	No.	Empl.	$	No.	Empl.	Total $
Mines and Quarries—												
Coal				1	234	7,956	1	*1,700	*360,000	1	1,934	367,956
Metal							1	380	9,120	1	380	9,120
Quarry	1	24	24							1	24	24
Total	1	24	24	1	234	7,956	2	2,080	369,120	3	2,338	377,100
Transportation and Communication—												
Railways	2	45	140				2	3,100	73,500	4	3,145	73,640
Street railways							1	550	7,150	1	550	7,150
Shipping	1	125	125							1	125	125
Total	3	170	265				3	3,650	80,660	6	3,820	80,915
Total	4	194	289	1	234	7,956	4	5,730	449,770	9	6,158	458,015

1911

	No.	Empl.	$	No.	Empl.	$	No.	Empl.	$	No.	Empl.	Total $
Mines—												
Coal	2	1,500	8,850	2	234	3,950	2	*8,080	*1,580,480	6	9,814	1,593,280
Metal							1	30	1,170	1	30	1,170
Total	2	1,500	8,850	2	234	3,950	3	8,110	1,581,650	7	9,844	1,594,450
Transportation and Communication—												
Railways	3	297	2,453	1	1,400	28,000	1	300	21,000	5	1,997	51,453
Shipping	3	2,170	6,500							3	2,170	6,500
Total	6	2,467	8,953	1	1,400	28,000	1	300	21,000	8	4,167	57,953
Light and Power	1	60	120							1	60	120
Total	9	4,027	17,923	3	1,634	31,950	4	8,410	1,602,650	16	14,071	1,652,523

1912

	No.	Empl.	$	No.	Empl.	$	No.	Empl.	$	No.	Empl.	Total $
Mines—												
Coal	2	3,060	37,740							2	3,060	37,740
Metal	2	364	2,828				1	*1,200	*46,800	3	1,564	49,628
Asbestos	1	450	1,800							1	450	1,800
Total	5	3,874	42,368				1	1,200	46,800	6	5,074	89,168
Transportation and Communication—												
Railways	6	2,148	10,926				2	*1,550	*70,000	8	3,698	80,926
Street railways	1	75	375							1	75	375
Shipping	1	100	300							1	100	300
Cartage (railway freight)	1	40	80							1	40	80
Total	9	2,363	11,681				2	1,550	70,000	11	3,913	81,681
Light and Power				1	165	1,650				1	165	1,650
Total	14	6,237	54,049	1	165	1,650	3	2,750	116,800	18	9,152	172,499

STRIKES IN MINES AND PUBLIC UTILITIES, 1907-17.—Concluded.

1913

Industry	I. No application for Board Received			II. Strike before or after application but ended before constitution of Board or by Board inquiry			III. Strike not averted nor ended by Board inquiry			Total		
	No. disputes	No. employees affected	Approximate time losses in working days	No. disputes	No. employees affected	Approximate time losses in working days	No. disputes	No. employees affected	Approximate time losses in working days	No. disputes	No. employees affected	Approximate time losses in working days
Mines and Quarries—												
Coal	1	*3,537	*589,036							1	3,537	589,036
Metal							1	*1,000	*105,800	1	1,000	105,800
Asbestos	1	400	1,000							1	400	1,000
Quarry	1	514	7,660							1	514	7,660
	3	4,451	597,696				1	1,000	105,800	4	5,451	703,496
Transportation and Communication—												
Railways	1	400	4,000				1	*500	*13,500	1	900	17,500
Street railways	2	285	2,910							2	285	2,910
Shipping	1	18	36							1	18	36
Cartage (railway freight)	2	700	3,500							2	700	3,600
Telephones				1	200	1,400				1	200	1,400
	6	1,403	10,446	1	200	1,400	1	500	13,500	7	2,103	25,346
Light and Power (including municipal electrical work)	5	615	4,865							5	615	4,865
Total	14	6,469	613,007	1	200	1,400	1	1,500	119,300	16	8,169	733,707

1914

Industry	I. No application for Board Received			II. Strike before or after application but ended before constitution of Board or by Board inquiry			III. Strike not averted nor ended by Board inquiry			Total		
	No. disputes	No. employees affected	Approximate time losses in working days	No. disputes	No. employees affected	Approximate time losses in working days	No. disputes	No. employees affected	Approximate time losses in working days	No. disputes	No. employees affected	Approximate time losses in working days
Mines—												
Coal	1	*1,900	*169,050							1	1,900	169,050
Metal	1	75	150							1	75	150
	2	1,975	169,200							2	1,975	169,200
Transportation and Communication—												
Street railways							1	150	300	1	150	300
Light and Power (including municipal electrical work)	2	82	2,312							2	82	2,312
Total	4	2,057	171,512				1	150	300	5	2,207	171,812

1915

Industry	No.	Employees affected	Time losses	No.	Employees affected	Time losses	No.	Employees affected	Time losses
Mines—									
Coal	4	1,482	7,894	1	350	1,400	5	1,832	9,294
Asbestos	1	2,500	7,500				1	2,500	7,500
	5	3,982	15,394	1	350	1,400	6	4,332	16,794
Transportation and Communication—									
Shipping	4	1,140	19,360				4	1,140	19,360
Light and Power (municipal electrical work)				1	126	2,394	1	126	2,394
Total	9	5,122	34,754	2	476	3,794	11	5,598	38,548

1916

Industry	No.	Employees affected	Time losses	No.	Employees affected	Time losses	No.	Employees affected	Time losses
Mines—									
Coal	9	10,914	73,334				9	10,914	73,334
Asbestos				†1	900	15,300	1	900	15,300
	9	10,914	73,334	1	900	15,300	10	11,814	88,634
Transportation and Communication—									
Railways	8	593	2,984	1	125	3,874	9	718	6,858
Street railways	2	155	1,855				2	155	1,855
Cartage (railway freight)	5	1,117	17,695				5	1,117	17,695
	15	1,865	22,534	1	125	3,874	16	1,990	26,408
War Work (since Mar. 23)	8	2,039	21,528				8	2,039	21,528
Total	32	14,818	117,396	2	1,025	19,174	34	15,843	136,570

1917 (To Mar. 31.)

Industry	No.	Employees affected	Time losses	No.	Employees affected	Time losses	No.	Employees affected	Time losses
Mines—									
Coal	4	6,500	80,140				4	6,500	80,140
Light and Power	1	44	220				1	44	220
War Work	7	*1,426	*17,161				7	1,426	17,161
Total	12	7,970	97,521				12	7,970	97,521

†This dispute was referred under the Act but was investigated by a Royal Commission.

*Disputes are counted in the year in which they began but where the strike continued beyond that year the employees affected and the time losses are added to each year until the termination of the strike. These figures therefore include employees affected and time losses in connection with disputes beginning prior to the year named.

INDUSTRIAL DISPUTES INVESTIGATION ACT, 1907.

VII—Strikes in Industries not clearly within the scope of the Industrial Disputes Investigation Act, 1907.

I. No. OF DISPUTES.

Trade or Class of Labour	1907 from Mar. 22	1908	1909	1910	1911	1912	1913	1914	1915	1916	1917 to Mar. 31	Total
Shipbuilders	2	1		1	1	1	2	1	2	2		13
Bridge workers								1				3
Car builders			1	1	2	1	1	1				8
Lumber scowmen	1	4	3		1	1	2			1		17
Railway construction and tunnel workers	1	1				6	1					6
Steel railway construction workers and other labourers	1			1	1	1	1					3
Dock construction workers and other labourers										1		1
Harbour work labourers												1
Canal construction workers												21
Civic labourers (including contract work)	4	3	4	1	2	4	1			1	1	21
Teamsters (including civic work)	2	2	2		4	2	1			1		14
Cab drivers	1											1
Dairy drivers										2		1
Electrical workers (including Provincial workers)	2		2		2	3	4		1	2		15
Telephone linemen (Provincial)					1	2						3
Elevator grain shovellers												1
Total	14	11	13	4	14	22	15	3	3	10	1	110

II. No. OF EMPLOYEES AFFECTED.

Trade or Class of Labour	1907 from Mar. 22	1908	1909	1910	1911	1912	1913	1914	1915	1916	1917 to Mar. 31	Total
Shipbuilders	299	458		27	115	10	195	175	140	490*		1,909
Bridge workers								36	8*			36
Car builders			160	138	1,400	55	290	30				2,081
Lumber scowmen	80					200	450*					730
Railway construction and tunnel workers	50	1,245	778		135	9,494	1,900					13,592
Street railway construction workers and other labourers	400	85	250	36	30	60	600			25		1,425
Dock construction workers and other labourers						250						311
Harbour work labourers							500			600		500
Civic construction workers												600
Civic labourers (including contract work)	186	365	165	18	260	1,250	250		100	40	50	2,644
Teamsters (including civic work)	60	42	240		820	360	14					4,476
Cab drivers	250											250
Dairy drivers										210		210
Electrical workers (including Provincial workers)	41		125		200	258	347			80	41*	1,092
Telephone linemen (Provincial)					100	150						250
Elevator grain shovellers										200		200
Total	1,366	2,195	1,718	219	3,060	11,977	4,546	241	248	1,645	91	27,306

SESSIONAL PAPER No. 36a

III. APPROXIMATE TIME LOSSES IN WORKING DAYS.

Trade or Class of Labour.	1907 from Mar. 22.	1908.	1909.	1910.	1911.	1912.	1913.	1914.	1915.	1916.	1917 to Mar. 31.	Total.
Shipbuilders	18,000	35,724		135	805	60	2,940	1,925	6,880	5,650*		72,119
Bridge workers								72				72
Car builders			3,520	1,100	10,800	275	5,780	5,634	816*			27,925
Lumber scowmen	240					200	2,450*					2,890*
Railway construction and tunnel workers	50	2,565	3,384		270	442,774	11,400					460,443
Street railway construction workers and other labourers	800	170	500		30	60	1,200					2,760
Dock construction workers and other labourers				180		1,250				350		1,780
Harbour work labourers							1,700					1,700
Canal construction workers										3,600		3,600
Civic labourers (including contract work)	588	1,105	315	18	6,030	4,250	500		400		750	13,956
Teamsters (including civic work)	270	42	2,320		27,540	520	42			200		30,934
Cab drivers	4,250											4,250
Dairy drivers										660		660
Electrical workers (including Provincial workers)	1,350		6,400		2,700	4,014	3,314			2,080	3,157*	23,015
Telephone linemen (Provincial)					100	600						700
Elevator grain shovellers										720		720
Total	25,548	39,606	16,439	1,433	48,275	454,003	29,326	7,631	8,096	13,260	3,907	647,524

*Disputes are counted in the year in which they began but where the strike continued beyond that year that year the employees affected and the time losses are added to each year until the termination of the strike. These figures therefore include employees affected and time losses in connection with disputes beginning prior to the year named.

.   -

.   -

III. SUMMARY STATEMENTS RESPECTING PROCEEDINGS UNDER INDUSTRIAL DISPUTES INVESTIGATION ACT, 1907, DURING THE FISCAL YEAR ENDED MARCH 31, 1917.

I.—Application from Locomotive and Car Department Employees of the Toronto, Hamilton and Buffalo Railway Company, being Members of T. H. & B. System Federation No. 36, etc.—Board established.—Unanimous Report by Board.—Employees ceased Work.

Application received—February 28, 1916.
Parties concerned—(1) Employer—Toronto, Hamilton and Buffalo Railway Company. (2) Employees—workmen in locomotive and car department at Hamilton, Ont., being members of Toronto, Hamilton and Buffalo System Federation No. 36, International Association of Machinists and Helpers No. 414, International Brotherhood of Boilermakers, Iron Shipbuilders and Helpers No. 421, International Brotherhood of Blacksmiths and Helpers No. 330, and Brotherhood of Railway Carmen of America No. 94.
Applicants—Employees.
Nature of industry concerned—Railway shop work.
Nature of dispute—Concerning employees' demand for adoption by the Company of a schedule of rates and rules.
Number of employees affected—Directly, 105; indirectly, 12.
Date of constitution of Board—March 28, 1916.
Membership of Board—His Honour Judge Colin G. Snider, Hamilton, chairman; Mr. Geo. S. Kerr, K.C., Hamilton, for employer; Mr. Jas. Simpson, Toronto, for employees. Chairman appointed in the absence of a joint recommendation from the other Board members.
Report received—May 1, 1916.
Result of inquiry—The Board presented a unanimous report, with recommendations for the settlement of the dispute. The findings of the Board were declared unsatisfactory to both parties concerned, and the employees went out on strike on May 20, 1916, giving as their reason " the management of the Company delaying and refusing to grant a schedule of agreement to shop employees." The strike had not been officially called off at the close of the fiscal year, but it was understood that the strikers had obtained work elsewhere and that industrial conditions had ceased to be affected thereby.

II.—Application from Freight Handlers at Winnipeg employed by the Canadian Pacific Railway Company, being Members of Local No. 12, Brotherhood of Railroad Freight Handlers.—No Board established, Settlement having been effected by negotiation.

Application received—April 13, 1916.
Parties concerned—(1) Employer—Canadian Pacific Railway Company. (2) Employees—freight handlers employed at Winnipeg, being members of Local No. 12, Brotherhood of Railroad Freight Handlers.
Applicants—Employees.
Nature of industry concerned—Railway freight handling.
Nature of dispute—Wages, conditions of employment, and recognition of Union.
Number of employees affected—Directly, 200; indirectly, 1,000.

During procedure looking to the establishment of a Board of Conciliation and Investigation, the Department received word that direct negotiations had brought about a settlement of the dispute.

———

III.—APPLICATION FROM STREET RAILWAY WORKERS EMPLOYED BY THE BRANT-
FORD MUNICIPAL RAILWAY COMMISSION, BEING MEMBERS OF DIVISION
No. 685, AMALGAMATED ASSOCIATION OF STREET AND ELECTRIC RAIL-
WAY EMPLOYEES OF AMERICA.—BOARD ESTABLISHED.—UNANIMOUS
REPORT BY BOARD.—SETTLEMENT EFFECTED.

Application received—May 11, 1916.
Parties concerned—(1) Employer—Brantford Municipal Railway Commission.
(2) Employees—street railway workers, being members of Division No.
685, Amalgamated Association of Street and Electric Railway Employees
of America.
Applicants—Employees.
Nature of industry concerned—Street railway work.
Nature of dispute—Wages, conditions of employment, and demand for agree-
ment.
Number of employees affected—Directly, 27; indirectly, 5.
Date of constitution of Board—May 23, 1916.
Membership of Board—His Honour Judge Colin G. Snider, Hamilton, chairman; Mr. F. W. Frank, Brantford, for employer; and Mr. Jos. Gibbons,
Toronto, for employees. Chairman appointed in the absence of a joint
recommendation from the other Board members.
Report received—June 6, 1916.
Result of inquiry—The Board presented a unanimous report, which included
a memorandum of settlement signed on behalf of both parties concerned,
effective for one year from June 1, 1916. The dispute was accordingly
settled.

———

IV.—APPLICATION FROM EMPLOYEES OF THE ACADIA COAL COMPANY, LIMITED,
AT STELLARTON, N.S.—BOARD ESTABLISHED.—UNANIMOUS REPORT BY
BOARD.—NO FURTHER CESSATION OF WORK REPORTED.

Application received—May 10, 1916.
Parties concerned—(1) Employer—Acadia Coal Company, Limited. (2) Em-
ployees—coal miners at Stellarton, N.S.
Applicants—Employees.
Nature of industry concerned—Coal mining.
Nature of dispute—Wages, hours and conditions of employment.
Number of employees affected—1,000.
Date of constitution of Board—May 22, 1916.
Membership of Board—His Honour Judge E. Coatsworth, Toronto, chairman;
Mr. W. H. Chase, Wolfville, N.S., for employer; and Mr. R. H. Murray,
Halifax, for employees. Chairman appointed in the absence of a joint
recommendation from the other Board members.
Report received—June 5, 1916.
Result of inquiry—The men had gone out on strike on April 18, but returned
to work on May 8, having decided to apply for a Board. The Board
presented a unanimous report, and the dispute disappeared.

SESSIONAL PAPER No. 36a

V.—APPLICATION FROM EMPLOYEES OF THE CONSOLIDATED MINING AND SMELTING COMPANY OF CANADA, LIMITED, AT TRAIL, B.C., BEING MEMBERS OF TRAIL MILL AND SMELTERMEN'S UNION No. 105, W.F.M. —BOARD NOT COMPLETED, SETTLEMENT HAVING BEEN EFFECTED BY NEGOTIATION.

Application received—May 29, 1916.

Parties concerned—(1) Employer—Consolidated Mining and Smelting Company of Canada, Limited. (2) Employees—miners at Trail, B.C., being members of Trail Mill and Smeltermen's Union No. 105, W.F.M.

Applicants—Employees.

Nature of industry concerned—Metal mining.

Nature of dispute—Wages, hours, and conditions of employment.

Number of employees affected—Directly, 1,200; indirectly, 50.

A Board was established by the Minister on June 9, 1916, and Messrs. A. C. Flumerfelt, Victoria, and David Rees, Fernie, were appointed as for the employer and the employees respectively. At this stage Mr. J. D. McNiven, the Departmental Fair Wages Officer resident at Vancouver, was instructed to proceed to the locality and assist in bringing about a settlement. Through his efforts conferences were arranged between the parties concerned, which resulted in the men's acceptance of a compromise offer made by the company. No further action by the Department was necessary.

VI.—APPLICATION FROM MAINTENANCE OF WAY EMPLOYEES OF THE EDMONTON, DUNVEGAN AND BRITISH COLUMBIA RAILWAY, ALBERTA AND GREAT WATERWAYS RAILWAY, AND CENTRAL CANADA RAILWAY, BEING MEMBERS OF INTERNATIONAL BROTHERHOOD OF MAINTENANCE OF WAY EMPLOYEES.—NO BOARD ESTABLISHED, SETTLEMENT HAVING BEEN EFFECTED BY NEGOTIATION.

Application received—June 2, 1916.

Parties concerned—(1) Employer—Edmonton, Dunvegan and British Columbia Railway, Alberta and Great Waterways Railway, and Central Canada Railway. (2) Employees—maintenance of way men employed on the territory covered by these railways, being members of the International Brotherhood of Maintenance of Way Employees.

Applicants—Employees.

Nature of industry concerned—Railway maintenance.

Nature of dispute—Wages, hours, conditions of employment.

Number of employees affected—Directly, 300; indirectly, 600.

During procedure looking to the establishment of a Board of Conciliation and Investigation the Department was informed that through the good offices of Mr. F. E. Harrison, one of the Departmental officers resident in the West, conferences were arranged between the parties concerned which resulted in an agreement being reached, effective from July 1, 1916.

8 GEORGE V, A. 1918

VII.—Application from Electrical Workers employed by the Montreal Light, Heat and Power Company, being Members of Local No. 492, International Brotherhood of Electrical Workers.—No Board established, Settlement having been effected by Negotiation.

Application received—June 6, 1916.
Parties concerned—(1) Employer—Montreal Light, Heat and Power Company. (2) Employees—electrical workers (outside men), being members of Local No. 492, International Brotherhood of Electrical Workers.
Applicants—Employees.
Nature of industry concerned—Electrical work.
Nature of dispute—Wages, hours, and conditions of employment.
Number of employees affected—Directly, 250; indirectly, 1,000.

No Board was established in·this case, a settlement having been brought about by negotiation between the parties concerned.

———

VIII.—Application from Employees of the Halifax and South Western Railway Company, being Members of the Canadian Brotherhood of Railroad Employees.—No Board established, Settlement having been effected by Negotiation.

Application received—June 8, 1916.
Parties concerned—(1) Employer—Halifax and South Western Railway Company. (2) Employees—maintenance of way men and shop men, being members of the Canadian Brotherhood of Railroad Employees.
Applicants—Employees.
Nature of industry concerned—Railway maintenance and shop work.
Nature of dispute—Wages, hours, and conditions of employment.
Number of employees affected—175.

No ·Board was established in this case, a settlement having been brought about by negotiation between the parties concerned.

———

IX.—Application from Employees of the Consolidated Mining and Smelting Company of Canada, Limited, and Le Roi No. 2, Limited, at Rossland, B.C., being Members of Rossland Miners' Union No. 38, W. F. M.—No Board established, Settlement having been effected by Negotiation.

Application received—June 12, 1916.
Parties concerned—(1) Employer—Consolidated Mining and Smelting Company of Canada, Limited, and Le Roi No. 2, Limited. (2) Employees—miners ·at Rossland, B.C., being members of Rossland Miners' Union No. 38, W. F. M.
Applicants—Employees.
Nature of industry concerned—Metal mining.
Nature of dispute—Wages.
Number of employees affected—800·
It was agreed that the Board established at Trail, B.C., should also deal with this dispute. As in the former case, however, Board procedure was unnecessary. Mr. J. D. McNiven, the Departmental officer who assisted in the

settlement of the dispute at Trail, was instructed to proceed to Rossland with a view to using the good offices of the Department of Labour towards bringing about an amicable adjustment of the dispute in the latter place. Through his efforts conferences were arranged between the parties concerned, which resulted in a settlement being arrived at. The application was accordingly withdrawn, a resolution to this effect being passed by the Rossland Miners' Union and expressing also appreciation of the part taken by Mr. McNiven.

X.—APPLICATION FROM EMPLOYEES OF VARIOUS MINING COMPANIES OPERATING IN COBALT CAMP AND VICINITY, BEING MEMBERS OF COBALT MINERS' UNION No. 146, WESTERN FEDERATION OF MINERS.—INVESTIGATION BY ROYAL COMMISSION.

Application received—June 24, 1916.
Parties concerned—(1) Employers—Forty-two Mining Companies operating in Cobalt Camp and vicinity. (2) Employees, members of Cobalt Miners' Union No. 146, Western Federation of Miners.
Applicants—Employees.
Nature of industry concerned—Metal mining.
Nature of dispute—Wages and conditions of employment.
Number of employees affected—2,200.

In view of the fact that the dispute affected various Companies whose consent could not be obtained to the establishment of a single Board, as requested by the employees, it was decided that the dispute did not come within the provisions of the statute, but an inquiry into the matters in dispute was made by a Royal Commission.

XI.—APPLICATION FROM EMPLOYEES OF THE OTTAWA ELECTRIC RAILWAY COMPANY, BEING MEMBERS OF DIVISION No. 279, AMALGAMATED ASSOCIATION OF STREET AND ELECTRIC RAILWAY EMPLOYEES OF AMERICA. —BOARD ESTABLISHED.—UNANIMOUS REPORT BY BOARD.—SETTLEMENT EFFECTED.

Application received—June 27, 1916.
Parties concerned—(1) Employer—Ottawa Electric Railway Company. (2) Employees, members of Division No. 279, Amalgamated Association of Street and Electric Railway Employees of America.
Applicants—Employees.
Nature of industry concerned—Street railway operation, and shop and shed work.
Nature of dispute—Wages, hours, and conditions of employment; also alleged discrimination against union members.
Number of employees affected—500.
Date of constitution of Board—July 4, 1916.
Membership of Board—Mr. Hamnett P. Hill, Ottawa, chairman; Mr. G. F. Henderson, Ottawa, for employer; Mr. A. E. Fripp, Ottawa, for employees. Chairman appointed on the joint recommendation of the other Board members.
Report received—July 12, 1916.
Result of inquiry—The Board presented a unanimous report, to which was appended a copy of an agreement signed on behalf of both parties concerned, effective from July 10, 1916, until June 30, 1918, and thereafter unless notice is given of desired change thirty days prior to the end of any year. The dispute was accordingly settled.

36a—7

8 GEORGE V, A. 1918

XII.—Application from Maintenance of Way Employees of the Canadian Northern Railway Company east of Port Arthur, being Members of the International Brotherhood of Maintenance of Way Employees.—Board established.—Settlement on basis of Board Report.

Application received—July 3, 1916.
Parties concerned—(1) Employer—Canadian Northern Railway Company. (2) Employees—maintenance of way department employees, including trackmen, bridge and building employees and water supply employees, on the Company's lines east of Port Arthur, being members of the International Brotherhood of Maintenance of Way Employees.
Applicants—Employees.
Nature of industry concerned—Railway maintenance.
Nature of dispute—Wages, hours, and conditions of employment.
Number of employees affected—Directly, 1,000; indirectly, 3,000.
Date of constitution of Board—August 19, 1916.
Membership of Board—His Honour Judge R. D. Gunn, Ottawa, chairman; Mr. F. H. Richardson, Toronto, for employer; Mr. G. D. Robertson, Welland, for employees. Chairman appointed on the joint recommendation of the other Board members.
Report received—October 21, 1916.
                    November 2, 1916. (Minority report.)
Result of inquiry—Two reports were presented in this matter, the minority report being signed by Mr. Richardson. The findings were declared acceptable to the employees concerned; the Company, however, declined to accept the award as it stood, but expressed a willingness to meet the employees with a view to adjusting the matter. This conference resulted in the acceptance by the Company of the award with one slight amendment. The dispute was thus satisfactorily settled.

XIII.—Application from Telegraphers in the employ of the Great North Western Telegraph Company of Canada, being Members of Great North Western Division No. 43, Commercial Telegraphers' Union of America.—Board established.—Unanimous Report by Board.—Settlement effected.

Application received—July 13, 1916.
Parties concerned—(1) Employer—The Great North Western Telegraph Company of Canada. (2) Employees—telegraphers, being members of Great North Western Division No. 43, Commercial Telegraphers' Union of America.
Applicants—Employees.
Natrue of industry concerned—Commercial telegraphy.
Nature of dispute—Wages, hours and conditions of employment.
Number of employees affected—Directly, 325; indirectly, 1,800.
Date of constitution of Board—August 8, 1916.
Membership of Board—His Honour Judge Colin G. Snider, Hamilton, chairman; Mr. F. H. McGuigan, Toronto, for employers; Mr. D. Campbell, Winnipeg, for employees. Chairman appointed on the joint recommendation of the other Board members.
Report received—August 23, 1916.
Result of inquiry—Report of Board was unanimous and included schedules of rules and rates which had been agreed upon by both parties concerned. The dispute was thus satisfactorily settled.

SESSIONAL PAPER No. 36a

XIV.—Application from Employees of various Mining Companies oper-
ating at Thetford Mines, Que., being Members of Local Union
No. 143, Western Federation of Miners.—Investigation by
Royal Commission.

Application received—July 21, 1916.

Parties concerned—(1) Employers—Asbestos Corporation of Canada, Limited,
Johnson Mines, Jacob Mining Company, Limited, Bell Asbestos Mines,
Limited, and Martin-Bennett, Limited. (2) Employees, members of
Local Union No. 143, Western Federation of Miners.

Applicants—Employees.

Nature of industry concerned—Asbestos mining.

Nature of dispute—Wages and recognition of union.

Number of employees affected—Directly, 900; indirectly, 500.

The employees in this case were divided as between two Unions, only one
Union being represented by the applicants for a Board; while, on the other
hand, the employers concerned were several in number and no recommendation
in common could be secured. Under the circumstances the machinery of the
Industrial Disputes Investigation Act could not be effectively applied, and an
inquiry was made before a Royal Commission. As a result of the inquiry, a
settlement was effected, and the men, who had gone on strike prior to the
investigation, returned to work.

XV.—Application from Conductors, Baggagemen, Brakemen, and Yard-
men in the Employ of the Algoma Central and Hudson Bay
Railway Company, being Members of the Order of Railway
Conductors and the Brotherhood of Railroad Trainmen.—
Board established.—Unanimous Report by Board.—Settlement
effected.

Application received—August 15, 1916.

Parties concerned—(1) Employer—Algoma Central and Hudson Bay Railway
Company. (2) Employees—conductors, baggagemen, brakemen, and
yardmen, being members of the Order of Railway Conductors and the
Brotherhood of Railroad Trainmen.

Applicants—Employees.

Nature of industry concerned—Railway operation.

Nature of dispute—Wages and conditions of employment.

Number of employees affected—Directly, 45; indirectly, 150.

Date of constitution of Board—August 29, 1916.

Membership of Board—His Honour Judge Colin G. Snider, Hamilton, chairman; Mr. F. H. McGuigan, Toronto, for employer; Mr. D. Campbell,
Winnipeg, for employees. Chairman appointed on the joint recommendation of the other Board members.

Report received—September 14, 1916.

Result of inquiry—Report of Board was unanimous and included an agreement
which had been drawn up and signed by both parties concerned, effective
from September 1, 1916, and thereafter until terminated by thirty days'
notice in writing by either party to the other.

8 GEORGE V, A. 1918

XVI.—Application from Federated Shop Trades in the Employ of the Canadian Government Railways.—No Board established, settlement having been effected by negotiation.

Application received—August 15, 1916.

Parties concerned—(1) Employer—Canadian Government Railways. (2) Employees—federated shop trades, being members of International Association of Machinists, International Brotherhood of Blacksmiths and Helpers, Brotherhood of Railway Carmen of America, International Brotherhood of Boilermakers and Helpers, International Association of Steamfitters and Plumbers, and International Brotherhood of Electrical Workers.

Applicants—Employees.

Nature of industry concerned—Railway shop work.

Nature of dispute—Wages, hours, and conditions of employment.

Number of employees affected—3,000.

No Board was established in this case. Proceedings in connection therewith were held in abeyance to permit of negotiations between the parties interested, and no further action by the Department was necessary.

XVII.—Application from Maintenance of Way Employees of the Grand Trunk Railway Company, being Members of the International Brotherhood of Maintenance of Way Employees.—Board established.—Settlement effected.

Application received—August 17, 1916.

Parties concerned—(1) Employer—Grand Trunk Railway Company. (2) Employees—maintenance of way men, being members of the International Brotherhood of Maintenance of Way Employees.

Applicants—Employees.

Nature of industry concerned—Railway maintenance.

Nature of dispute—Wages.

Number of employees affected—3,200.

Date of constitution of Board—August 25, 1916.

Membership of Board—His Honour Judge R. D. Gunn, Ottawa, chairman; Mr. F. H. McGuigan, Toronto, for employer; Mr. G. D. Robertson, Welland, for employees. Chairman appointed on the joint recommendation of the other Board members.

Report received—October 21, 1916.

October 25, 1916. (Minority report.)

Result of inquiry—Two reports were presented in this case, the minority report being signed by Mr. McGuigan. The award was accepted by both parties concerned and the dispute accordingly settled.

SESSIONAL PAPER No. 36a

XVIII.—APPLICATION FROM ENGINEERS, FIREMEN, CONDUCTORS, BRAKEMEN, AND YARDMEN IN THE EMPLOY OF THE FREDERICTON AND GRAND LAKE COAL AND RAILWAY COMPANY AND NEW BRUNSWICK COAL AND RAILWAY, BEING MEMBERS OF THE BROTHERHOOD OF LOCOMOTIVE ENGINEERS AND THE BROTHERHOOD OF RAILROAD TRAINMEN.—BOARD ESTABLISHED.—SETTLEMENT EFFECTED.

Application received—August 31, 1916.
Parties concerned—(1) Employer—Fredericton and Grand Lake Coal and Railway Company, and New Brunswick Coal and Railway. (2) Employees—engineers, firemen, conductors, brakemen, and yardmen, being members of the Brotherhood of Locomotive Engineers and the Brotherhood of Railroad Trainmen.
Applicants—Employees.
Nature of industry concerned—Railway operation.
Nature of dispute—Wages and conditions of emlpoyment.
Number of employees affected—20.
Date of constitution of Board—November 2, 1916.
Membership of Board—His Honour Judge R. D. Gunn, Ottawa, chairman ; Mr. Chas. D. Richards, Fredericton, for employer; and Mr. G. D. Robertson, Welland, for employees. Chairman appointed by the Minister in the absence of any joint recommendation from the other Board members.
Report received—November 25, 1916.
Result of inquiry—The report was signed by all three members of the Board, Mr. Richards, however, noting his objection to the clause providing for a mileage basis. A schedule of rules and rates was drawn up and submitted as part of the report, the rates to be effective from July 1, 1916, and the rules from December 1, 1916. The Company expressed its willingness to accept the award of Mr. Richards, and the employees subsequently agreed to do likewise. The dispute was thus satisfactorily settled.

XIX.—APPLICATION FROM STREET RAILWAY EMPLOYEES OF THE CORPORATION OF THE CITY OF EDMONTON, BEING MEMBERS OF LOCAL DIVISION No. 569, AMALGAMATED ASSOCIATION OF STREET AND ELECTRIC RAILWAY EMPLOYEES OF AMERICA.—NO BOARD ESTABLISHED, SETTLEMENT BEING EFFECTED BY NEGOTIATION.

Application received—September 2, 1916.
Parties concerned—(1) Employer—Corporation of the City of Edmonton. (2) Employees—street railway workers on the Edmonton Radial Railway, being members of Division No. 569, Amalgamated Association of Street and Electric Railway Employees of America.
Applicants—Employees.
Nature of industry concerned—Street railway operation.
Nature of dispute—Alleged unwillingness of civic authorities to negotiate *re* renewal of agreement.
Number of employees affected—250.

No Board was established in this case. Mr. F. E. Harrison, the Departmental officer resident in Calgary, was instructed to proceed to Edmonton for the purpose of using the good offices of the Department in endeavouring to effect a settlement. Conferences were accordingly arranged, which resulted in an agreement being reached by the parties concerned, which disposed of all points at issue. -

XX.—APPLICATION FROM STREET RAILWAY EMPLOYEES OF THE QUEBEC
RAILWAY, LIGHT, HEAT AND POWER COMPANY, BEING MEMBERS OF
FRATERNITÉ NATIONALE DES EMPLOYÉS DE TRAMWAY DE QUÉBEC.—
BOARD ESTABLISHED.—UNANIMOUS REPORT BY BOARD.—SETTLEMENT
EFFECTED.

Application received—September 4, 1916.
Parties concerned—(1) Employer—Quebec Railway, Light, Heat and Power
Company. (2) Employees—conductors and motormen, being members
of Fraternite Nationale des Employes de Tramway de Quebec.
Applicants—Employees.
Nature of industry concerned—Street railway operation.
Nature of dispute—Wages and conditions of employment.
Number of employees affected—Directly, 260; indirectly 305.
Date of constitution of Board—October 13, 1916.
Membership of Board—Honourable Mr. Justice C. E. Dorion, Quebec, chair-
man; Mr. Antonin Galipeault, Quebec, for employer; Mr. Hector Laferte,
Quebec, for employees. Chairman appointed on the joint recommendation
of the other Board members.
Report received—December 8, 1916.
Result of inquiry—The Board presented a unanimous report, embodying the
terms of a proposed agreement to be effective for three years from
December 1, 1916. The award was accepted by both parties concerned.

XXI.—APPLICATION FROM CONDUCTORS AND MOTORMEN IN THE EMPLOY OF
THE MOOSE JAW ELECTRIC RAILWAY COMPANY, LIMITED, BEING
MEMBERS OF DIVISION No. 614, AMALGAMATED ASSOCIATION OF STREET
AND ELECTRIC RAILWAY EMPLOYEES OF AMERICA.—BOARD ESTAB-
LISHED.—NO CESSATION OF WORK REPORTED.

Application received—September 5, 1916.
Parties concerned—(1) Employer—Moose Jaw Electric Railway Company,
Limited. (2) Employees—conductors and motormen, being members
of Division No. 614, Amalgamated Association of Street and Electric
Railway Employees of America.
Applicants—Employees.
Nature of industry concerned—Street railway operation.
Nature of dispute—Wages, hours, conditions of employment and recognition
of Union.
Number of employees affected—36.
Date of constitution of Board—September 27, 1916.
Membership of Board—Mr. John H. Wellington, Moose Jaw, chairman; Mr.
James Thomson, Moose Jaw, for employer; Mr. Jas. Somerville, Moose
Jaw, for employees. Chairman appointed by the Minister in the absence
of a joint recommendation from the other Board members.
Report received—October 17, 1916.
October 17, 1916. (Minority report.)
Result of inquiry—Two reports were presented in this matter, the minority
report being signed by Mr. Thomson. The employees expressed their
willingness, in view of war conditions, to accept the award, but the
Company declined to do so. No cessation of work, however, was re-
ported.

XXII.—APPLICATION FROM MAINTENANCE OF WAY EMPLOYEES OF THE
CANADIAN PACIFIC RAILWAY COMPANY, BEING MEMBERS OF INTER-
NATIONAL BROTHERHOOD OF MAINTENANCE OF WAY EMPLOYEES.—
NO BOARD ESTABLISHED, SETTLEMENT HAVING BEEN EFFECTED BY
NEGOTIATION.

Application received—September 19, 1916.

Parties concerned—(1) Employer—Canadian Pacific Railway Company. (2)
Employees—maintenance of way men, being members of the International Brotherhood of Maintenance of Way Employees.

Applicants—Employees.
Nature of industry concerned—Railway maintenance.
Nature of dispute—Wages and conditions of employment.
Number of employees affected—Directly, 6,000; indirectly, 17,000.

No Board was established in this case. Proceedings in connection therewith were held in abeyance to permit of negotiations between the parties
interested, which resulted in a settlement of the matters in dispute.

———

XXIII.—APPLICATION FROM STREET RAILWAY EMPLOYEES OF THE SANDWICH,
WINDSOR AND AMHERSTBURG RAILWAY COMPANY AND THE WINDSOR
AND TECUMSEH RAILWAY, BEING MEMBERS OF AMALGAMATED
ASSOCIATION OF STREET AND ELECTRIC RAILWAY EMPLOYEES OF
AMERICA.—BOARD ESTABLISHED.—SETTLEMENT EFFECTED.

Application received—September 27, 1916.

Parties concerned—(1) Employer—Sandwich, Windsor and Amherstburg Rail-
way and Windsor and Tecumseh Railway. (2) Employees—street railway
men, being members of the Amalgamated Association of Street and Elec-
tric Railway Employees of America.
Applicants—Employees.
Nature of industry concerned—Street railway work.
Nature of dispute—Wages, hours, and conditions of employment.
Number of employees affected—150.
Date of constitution of Board—October 11, 1916.

Membership of Board—His Honour Judge John O. Drumgole, Windsor, Ont.,
chairman; Mr. Ernest G. Henderson, Windsor, Ont., for employer; Mr.
Magnus Sinclair, Toronto, for employees. Chairman appointed by the
Minister in the absence of a joint recommendation from the other Board
members.

Report received—November 9, 1916.
November 10, 1916. (Minority report.)

Result of inquiry—The report was signed by all three members of the Board,
Mr. Sinclair, however, submitting an additional report on the question
of the recognition of the Amalgamated Association of Street and Electric
Railway Employees of America. The report was accompanied by an
agreement signed on behalf of both parties concerned, effective from
October 1, 1916, to April 1, 1918. The dispute was thus satisfactorily
settled.

8 GEORGE V, A. 1918

XXIV.—Application from Maintenance of Way Employees of . the Canadian Northern Railway on its lines in Canada West of Fort William, being Members of the International Brotherhood of Maintenance of Way Employees.—Board established.—Unanimous Report by Board.—Settlement effected.

Application received—October 7, 1916.

Parties concerned—(1) Employer—Canadian Northern Railway Company. (2) Employees—maintenance of way men employed on the Company's lines in Canada west of Fort William, being members of the International Brotherhood of Maintenance of Way Employees.

Applicants—Employees.

Nature of industry concerned—Railway maintenance.

Nature of dispute—Wages and conditions of employment.

Number of employees affected—Directly, 3,000; indirectly, 2,000.

Date of constitution of Board—November 2, 1916.

Membership of Board—Mr. E. L. Taylor, K.C., Winnipeg, chairman; Mr. Wm. Cross, Winnipeg, for employer; Mr. D. Campbell, Winnipeg, for employees. Chairman appointed by the Minister in the absence of a joint recommendation from the other Board members.

Report received—December 11, 1916.

Result of inquiry—Report of Board was unanimous and included an agreement which had been drawn up and signed by both parties concerned, effective from November 1, 1916, and thereafter until terminated by sixty days' notice by either party to the other. The dispute was thus satisfactorily settled.

XXV.—Application from Canadian Pacific Railway Company.—No Board established.—Settlement having been effected by Negotiation.

Application received—October 23, 1916.

Parties concerned—(1) Employer—Canadian Pacific Railway Company. (2) Employees—conductors and trainmen, being members of the Order of Railway Conductors and the Brotherhood of Railroad Trainmen.

Applicant—Employer.

Nature of industry concerned—Railway operation.

Nature of dispute—Wages and conditions of employment.

Number of employees affected—Directly, 7,000; indirectly, 50,000.

No Board was established in this case. The dispute originated in a demand made upon the Company in September, 1913, for the acceptance of a new schedule of agreement. No settlement resulting from direct negotiations, an application was made by the employees in March, 1914, for a Board of Conciliation and Investigation, which was established in April. The Board award was not acceptable to the employees. While, however, the action to be taken by the respective parties remained uncertain, war broke out. The employees, in view of the war conditions, were averse to pressing to the point of a strike opposition to the Board award and asked that existing conditions should continue; to this the Company agreed.. In October, 1916, the employees renewed the demands of 1914 and a strike seemed to be threatened, the employees contending that the Act had been complied with by the Board inquiry of 1914. The Company made application for a Board. The Dominion Government,. through the Prime Minister and the Minister of Labour, pressed for a resumption of negotiations. Mr. G. D. Robertson, of Welland, Ont., well known as a leader in trade union ranks, also acted as a mediator. On October 25 it was announced that an agreement had been reached, and the threatened strike was averted.

XXVI.—APPLICATION FROM DOMINION COAL COMPANY, LIMITED.—NO BOARD
  ESTABLISHED, SETTLEMENT-HAVING BEEN EFFECTED BY NEGOTIATION.

Application received—November 18, 1916.
Parties concerned—(1) Employer—Dominion Coal Company, Limited. (2)
  - Employees—coal handlers at St. John, N.B., being members of Coal
  Handlers' Union No. 810, International Longshoremen's Association.
Applicant—Employer.
Nature of industry concerned—Shipping.
Nature of dispute—Wages.
Number of employees affected—Directly, 50; indirectly, 1,000.

No Board was established in this case. Negotiations between the parties
concerned resulted in an agreement being signed and the dispute was thus
satisfactorily settled.

———

XXVII.—APPLICATION FROM MAINTENANCE OF WAY EMPLOYEES ON THE
  CANADIAN DIVISION OF THE PERE MARQUETTE RAILROAD.—
  PENDING COMPLETION OF BOARD A SETTLEMENT WAS ARRIVED AT.

Application received—November 27, 1916.
Parties concerned—(1) Employer—Pere Marquette Railroad Company. (2)
  Employees—maintenance of way men employed on the Canadian Division
  of the Pere Marquette Railroad.
Applicants—Employees.
Nature of industry concerned—Railway maintenance.
Nature of dispute—Wages.
Number of employees affected—Directly, 120; indirectly, 500.

A Board was established in this case on December 11, 1916, Mr. G. D.
Robertson, Welland, Ont., being appointed a member thereof on the recommendation of the employees. At this stage the Department was informed
that an agreement had been reached by the parties concerned, effective from
December 15, 1916. No further action was therefore necessary.

———

XXVIII.—APPLICATION FROM WATERWORKS EMPLOYEES OF THE CORPORATION
  OF THE CITY OF OTTAWA, BEING MEMBERS OF FEDERAL LABOUR
  UNION No. 15.—BOARD ESTABLISHED.—UNANIMOUS REPORT BY
  BOARD.—NO CESSATION OF WORK OCCURRED.

Application received—November 30, 1916·
Parties concerned—(1) Employer—Corporation of the City of Ottawa. (2) Em-
  ployees—waterworks men, being members of Federal Labour Union
  No. 15.
Applicants—Employees.
Nature of industry concerned—Municipal waterworks.
Nature of dispute—Wages.
Number of employees affected—45.
Date of constitution of Board—December 11, 1916.
Membership of Board—Mr. Hamnett P. Hill, Ottawa, chairman; Mr. G. A.
  Crain, Ottawa, for employer; Mr. J. C. Watters, Ottawa, for employees.
  Chairman appointed on the joint recommendation of the other Board
  members.

Report received—December 22, 1916.
Result of inquiry—Report of Board was unanimous and recommended certain
   increases to take effect from December 1, 1916.   The award was accepted
   on behalf of the employees concerned and was understood to be acceptable also to the Corporation of the City of Ottawa.

XXIX.—APPLICATION FROM EMPLOYEES OF THE CANADIAN NORTHERN
      EXPRESS COMPANY, BEING MEMBERS OF THE CANADIAN BROTHER-
      HOOD OF RAILROAD EMPLOYEES.—PENDING COMPLETION OF BOARD
      A SETTLEMENT WAS ARRIVED AT.

Application received—December 11, 1916.
Parties concerned—(1) Employer—Canadian Northern Express Company. (2)
   Employees, members of the Canadian Brotherhood of Railroad Em-
   ployees.
Applicants—Employees.
Nature of industry concerned—Transportation.
Nature of dispute—Wages and conditions of employment; also alleged unjust
   · dismissal of union members.
Number of employees affected—300.

   A Board was established in this case on January 9, 1917, Messrs. John T.
Haig and D. Campbell, both of Winnipeg, being appointed members thereof
as for the employer and the employees respectively.   Whilst steps were
being taken looking to the appointment of a chairman, the Department was
informed that the dispute had been settled by negotiations between the
parties concerned.   No further action was therefore necessary.

XXX.—APPLICATION FROM EMPLOYEES OF THE CANADIAN EXPRESS COMPANY
      ON ITS LINES WEST OF NORTH BAY, ONT., BEING MEMBERS OF
      THE CANADIAN BROTHERHOOD OF RAILROAD EMPLOYEES.—BOARD
      ESTABLISHED.—PROCEEDINGS UNFINISHED AT END OF FISCAL YEAR.

Application received—January 27, 1917.
Parties concerned—(1) Employer—Canadian Express Company. (2) Employees
   on Company's lines west of North Bay, Ont., members of the Canadian
   ·   Brotherhood of Railroad Employees.
Applicants—Employees.
Nature of industry concerned—Transportation.
Nature of dispute—Wages and conditions of employment; also alleged unjust
   dismissal of union members.
Number of employees affected—100.
Date of constitution of Board—February 17, 1917.
Membership of Board—Mr. E. L. Taylor, K.C., Winnipeg, chairman; Mr.
   John T. Haig, Winnipeg, for employer; Mr. D. Campbell, Winnipeg,
   for employees.   Chairman appointed by the Minister in the absence
   of a joint recommendation from the other Board members.

   At the close of the fiscal year the investigation by the Board had not been
completed.

SESSIONAL PAPER No. 36a

XXXI.—Application from Certain Employees of the Canadian Pacific Railway Company engaged in Engine, Train, Yard, Station, and Maintenance of Way Service, being Members of the Brotherhood of Locomotive Engineers, Order of Railway Conductors, Brotherhood of Railroad Trainmen, Brotherhood of Locomotive Firemen and Enginemen, Order of Railroad Telegraphers and International Brotherhood of Maintenance of Way Employees.—Board established.—Unanimous Report by Board.—Settlement effected.

Application received—February 3, 1917.
Parties concerned—(1) Employer—Canadian Pacific Railway Company. (2) Employees engaged in engine, train, yard, station, and maintenance of way service, members of the Brotherhood of Locomotive Engineers, Order of Railway Conductors, Brotherhood of Railroad Trainmen, Brotherhood of Locomotive Firemen and Enginemen, Order of Railroad Telegraphers and International Brotherhood of Maintenance of Way Employees.
Applicants—Employees.
Nature of industry concerned—Railway operation and maintenance.
Nature of dispute—Alleged wrongful suspension of an engineer and Company's refusal to pay him for time lost.
Number of employees affected—19,000.
Date of constitution of Board—February 19, 1917.
Membership of Board—Mr. E. L. Taylor, K.C., Winnipeg, chairman; Mr. I. Pitblado, K.C., Winnipeg, for employer; Mr. D. Campbell, Winnipeg, for employees. Chairman appointed by the Minister in the absence of a joint recommendation from the other Board members.
Report received—March 12, 1917.
Result of inquiry—Report of Board was unanimous and was accompanied by a memorandum of settlement signed by both parties concerned. The dispute was thus satisfactorily settled.

XXXII.—Application from Commercial Telegraphers employed by the Canadian Pacific Railway Company, being Members of the Commercial Telegraphers' Union of America.—Board established.—Proceedings unfinished at end of Fiscal Year.

Application received—February 14, 1917.
Parties concerned—(1) Employer—Canadian Pacific Railway Company. (2) Employees—commercial telegraphers, being members of the Commercial Telegraphers' Union of America.
Applicants—Employees.
Nature of industry concerned—Commercial telegraphy.
Nature of dispute—Alleged unjust dismissal of employee and Company's refusal to reinstate and reimburse him.
Number of employees affected—Directly, 700; indirectly, 2,200.
Date of Constitution of Board—March 1, 1917.
Membership of Board—Mr. E. L. Taylor, K.C., Winnipeg, chairman; Mr. John T. Haig, Winnipeg, for employer; Mr. J. C. Rooney, Ottawa, for employees. Chairman appointed by the Minister in the absence of a joint recommendation from the other Board members.

Proceedings were unfinished at the close of the fiscal year.

8 GEORGE V, A. 1918

XXXIII.—APPLICATION FROM WIRELESS OPERATORS ON THE PACIFIC COAST STEAMSHIP SERVICE EMPLOYED BY THE MARCONI WIRELESS TELEGRAPH COMPANY OF CANADA, LIMITED.—BOARD ESTABLISHED.—PROCEEDINGS UNFINISHED AT END OF FISCAL YEAR.

Application received.—March 5, 1917.

Parties concerned—(1) Employer—Marconi Wireless Telegraph Company of Canada, Limited. (2) Employees—wireless operators on the Pacific Coast Steamship service.

Applicants—Employees.

Nature of industry concerned—Wireless telegraphy.

Nature of dispute—Wages and conditions of employment.

Number of employees affected—23.

Date of constitution of Board—March 24, 1917.

Membership of Board—Mr. R. R. Maitland, Vancouver, chairman; Mr. Matthew J. Barr, Vancouver, for employer; Mr. Jas. H. McVety, Vancouver, for employees. Chairman appointed on the joint recommendation of the other Board members.

At the close of the fiscal year the investigation by the Board had not been completed.

XXXIV.—APPLICATION FROM CERTAIN EMPLOYEES OF THE DOMINION COAL COMPANY, LIMITED, A NUMBER OF THEM BEING MEMBERS OF THE UNITED MINE WORKERS OF NOVA SCOTIA.—INVESTIGATION MADE BY ONE OF THE DEPARTMENTAL OFFICERS.—PROCEEDINGS UNFINISHED AT END OF FISCAL YEAR.

Application received—March 10, 1917.

Parties concerned—(1) Employer—Dominion Coal Company, Limited. (2) Employees—coal miners, mine workers, etc., employed at Glace Bay, N.S., a number of whom were declared to be members of the United Mine Workers of Nova Scotia.

Applicants—Employees.

Nature of industry concerned—Coal mining.

Nature of dispute—Wages and alleged discrimination against union members.

Number of employees affected—Directly, 1,500; indirectly, 4,000.

This dispute was made the subject of an inquiry by one of the officers of the Department, resulting in an adjustment of some of the matters in dispute. A separate application was subsequently received from those employees who were members of the Provincial Workmen's Association. The matter had not been disposed of at the close of the fiscal year, but looking slightly beyond the fiscal term, it may be stated that the situation was met by the appointment of a Royal Commission, which succeeded in arranging a working agreement acceptable to the Company and the workmen in both organizations.

SESSIONAL PAPER No. 36a

XXXV.—APPLICATION FROM CLERKS, STENOGRAPHERS, BAGGAGEMEN, AND CAR CHECKERS EMPLOYED BY THE CANADIAN NORTHERN RAILWAY COMPANY ON ITS LINES FROM PORT ARTHUR TO WINNIPEG, BEING MEMBERS OF THE CANADIAN BROTHERHOOD OF RAILROAD EMPLOYEES.—PROCEEDINGS UNFINISHED AT END OF FISCAL YEAR.

Application received—March 26, 1917.
Parties concerned—(1) Employer—Canadian Northern Railway Company. (2 Employees—clerks, stenographers, baggagemen, and car checkers employed on the Company's lines from Port Arthur to Winnipeg, being members of the Canadian Brotherhood of Railroad Employees.
Applicants—Employees.
Nature of industry concerned—Railway office and station work.
Nature of dispute—Wages and conditions of employment.
Number of employees affected—Directly, 95; indirectly, 25.

Proceedings were unfinished at the close of the fiscal year.

———

XXXVI.—APPLICATION FROM CERTAIN EMPLOYEES OF THE CORPORATION OF THE CITY OF VANCOUVER, BEING MEMBERS OF CIVIC EMPLOYEES' UNION.—PROCEEDINGS UNFINISHED AT END OF FISCAL YEAR.

Application received—March 29, 1917.
Parties concerned—(1) Employer—Corporation of the City of Vancouver. (2) Employees—teamsters, labourers, etc., employed by the Street Cleaning, Scavenging, Waterworks, Sewer, and General Maintenance Departments, being members of Civic Employees' Union.
Applicants—Employees.
Nature of industry concerned—Municipal work.
Nature of dispute—Wages, appointment of foremen, and alleged discrimination against union members.
Number of employees affected—400.

Proceedings were unfinished at the close of the fiscal year.

———

XXXVII.—APPLICATION FROM CERTAIN EMPLOYEES OF THE DOMINION COAL COMPANY, LIMITED, BEING MEMBERS OF THE PROVINCIAL WORKMEN'S ASSOCIATION.—PROCEEDINGS UNFINISHED AT END OF FISCAL YEAR.

Application received—March 31, 1917.
Parties concerned—(1) Employer—Dominion Coal Company, Limited. (2) Employees—coal miners, mine workers, etc., employed at Glace Bay, N.S., being members of the Provincial Workmen's Association.
Applicants—Employees.
Nature of industry concerned—Coal mining.
Nature of dispute—Wages and conditions of employment.
Number of employees affected—5,000.

8 GEORGE V, A. 1918

This application followed one which was received in the Department on March 10, 1917, from certain other employees of the Dominion Coal Company, Limited, a number of whom were declared to be members of the United Mine Workers of Nova Scotia. An investigation by one of the officers of the Department had resulted in clearing up a number of differences between the parties concerned. The matter had not been disposed of at the close of the fiscal year, but, looking slightly beyond the fiscal term, it may be stated that the situation was met by the appointment of a Royal Commission, which succeeded in arranging a working agreement acceptable to the Company and the workmen in both organizations.

REPORT

OF THE

DEPARTMENT OF THE NAVAL SERVICE

FOR THE

FISCAL YEAR ENDING MARCH 31, 1917

PRINTED BY ORDER OF PARLIAMENT

OTTAWA
J. DE LABROQUERIE TACHÉ
PRINTER TO THE KING'S MOST EXCELLENT MAJESTY
1917

[No. 38--1918]—A½.

To His Excellency the Duke of Devonshire, K.G., P.C., G.C.M.G., G.C.V.O., etc., etc., Governor General and Commander in Chief of the Dominion of Canada.

MAY IT PLEASE YOUR EXCELLENCY:

I have the honour to submit herewith for the information of Your Excellency and the Parliament of Canada, the Seventh Annual Report of the Department of the Naval Service, being for the year ended March 31, 1917, except the Fisheries Branch, reported in a separate publication.

I have the honour to be,

Your Excellency's most obedient servant,

J. D. HAZEN,
Minister of the Naval Service.

CONTENTS.

REPORT

OF THE

DEPARTMENT OF THE NAVAL SERVICE

FOR THE

FISCAL YEAR ENDING MARCH 31, 1917

OTTAWA, September 25, 1917.

Hon. J. D. HAZEN,
Minister of the Naval Service,
Ottawa, Ont.

SIR,—I have the honour to report on the Department of the Naval Service for the year ending March 31, 1917, under the following headings:—

1. Naval Service.
2. Survey of Tides and Currents.
3. Hydrographic Survey.
4. Canadian Arctic Expedition.
5. Radio Telegraphs.
6. Fisheries Protection.
7. Life Saving Service.
8. Stores.
9. Expenditures.

1. NAVAL SERVICE.

H.M.C. NAVY.

During the past year the requisite number of personnel for manning H.M.C. Ships and Establishments has been maintained by the entry of men with previous naval experience, and by the employment of Royal Naval Canadian Volunteer Reserve officers and men.

H.M.C.S. *Niobe* is still utilized at Halifax as a depot ship, and also acts as parent ship for patrol vessels based on Halifax.

·H.M.C.S. *Rainbow,* as well as submarines *C.C. I, C.C. II* and their parent ship *Shearwater,* have been continuously employed on the west coast on important duties in connection with war operations. All these vessels have been under orders of the Imperial Senior Naval Officer at Esquimalt.

A large number of other vessels, both Government and private, have been utilized, particularly on the east coast, in connection with the naval defence, mine-sweeping, patrols, examination service, and other necessary work.

The Canadian Coast Patrol, recently established, has been placed under direction of Commodore Sir Charles H. Coke, K.C.V.O., lent to the Canadian Navy from the Imperial Government. He acts under orders from this department.

The Royal Naval Canadian Volunteer Reserve officers and men continue to do valuable work ashore and afloat in H.M.C. Ships and Establishments, on both the Atlantic and Pacific coasts.

NAVAL DOCKYARDS.

With respect to the Naval dockyards, both establishments have been worked to the full output, a considerable amount of overtime having been worked. The nature of the work done has been practically all repairs.

Halifax is being used as the base for vessels of the North Atlantic fleet which has been lately strengthened; the dockyard is being used for carrying out repairs to these vessels and keeping them in going order.

At Esquimalt yard work has been carried out on Imperial vessels, as well as those of the Canadian service. The floating dock at Prince Rupert has been assembled under great difficulties, and three large armed auxiliary cruisers have been docked and put in a state of repair, after having been badly damaged by grounding.

The total amount of money paid per month in wages for the two yards is approximately 400 per cent more than that customary to be paid for the same period prior to the war.

In addition to the repairs to the vessels of the fighting fleet, the dockyards are carrying out the large number of small items of repairs needed to the various vessels now employed for auxiliary purposes for patrol and other defensive work of the coasts.

The number of patrol vessels has been materially increased during the past four months. Alterations have had to be made in these vessels to adapt them for patrol service.

Having regard to the facilities available, this work has been carried out satisfactorily. Considerable overtime has been necessary in order to expedite the completion of the repairs.

Subsidiary work in the nature of repairs and refits of the various vessels belonging to the different branches of the Naval Service have been undertaken during the year, and repairs of vessels of other departments of the Government have also been effected. Repairs to buildings and plant incidental to the up-keep of the establishment in accordance with conditions of transfer have also been completed.

NAVAL STAFF OFFICE.

The Naval Staff Office has continued to carry on its work in a satisfactory manner. The work of this branch of the service is continually increasing in importance.

ROYAL NAVAL COLLEGE.

The cadets in the college and the midshipmen at sea, in both Canadian and Imperial ships, continue to be well reported upon and to give satisfaction to their superior officers. Fourteen cadets were entered after the cadetship entry examination in May, 1916.

The fourteen midshipmen who entered the College in January, 1911, have been promoted to Acting Lieutenant. All these officers are now serving in the Royal Navy.

RECRUITING.

The Dominion Government offered to place at the disposal of the Admiralty a number of men belonging to the Royal Naval Canadian Volunteer Reserve, which offer was accepted by the Imperial Authorities.

An Overseas Division of the R.N.C.V.R. was accordingly established and recruiting offices were opened throughout Canada, to enter men in that division of the service. A provincial committee was appointed for each province, under which sub-committees were organized at the principal centres; each committee was provided with a paid secretary. The sub-committees were responsible to the provincial committee, which, in turn, was responsible to the Department of the Naval Service.

The members of all the different committees gave their services gratuitously, and they spared no efforts to advance the work of recruiting. The department wishes to express its appreciation for the valuable work done by the members of these committees.

Recruiting commenced in the fall of 1916. Up to the 31st March, 1917, 1,331 men were entered in the R.N.C.V.R. Overseas Division for service in the Royal Navy, of whom 1,188 have been sent overseas.

These men receive the same rates of pay as men of the same standing in the Royal Canadian Navy. They are actually paid the same rates as men of their standing in the Royal Navy whilst they are serving in Imperial ships, the difference between their Imperial and Canadian pay being placed to their credit, payable to them upon their discharge from the R.N.C.V.R. or their return to Canada, or paid to their dependents.

Commander F. P. Armstrong, with a recruiting committee, came to Canada in April, 1916, to recruit for the Royal Naval Volunteer Reserve Auxiliary Patrol (Motor Boat) Service; 264 Sub-Lieutenants, 52 chief motor mechanics, and 60 motor mechanics were entered by Commander Armstrong up to the 30th August, 1916, when recruiting was discontinued. Recruiting for this service was carried out by the Imperial Authorities.

The department has continued to enter officers for the Royal Naval Air Service. Up to the end of the fiscal year 1916-17, 382 officers have been entered. Since the 20th July, 1916, candidates have not been required to obtain their Aero Club certificates before proceeding to England.

The report of Admiral C. E. Kingsmill, on the Naval Service, may be found at page 1.

8 GEORGE V, A. 1918

2. TIDAL AND CURRENT SURVEY.

The work of this Survey has been satisfactorily conducted throughout the past year. Tidal observations were carried on at some stations during the summer months and at others during the whole year. The determination of mean sea-level was also carried forward at many points on the east and west coast, and the investigation of currents in the different passes begun in previous years was continued and new work of a similar nature was undertaken in several other passes, particularly on the west coast.

Six principal tide stations on the east coast and five on the west coast were operated during the whole year. A number of subsidiary stations were operated during the summer on both coasts. From the reduction of the observations taken at these stations, tidal constants are obtained upon which predictions of tides for publication in the tide tables are made. By extending the scope of these stations, greater accuracy for the time of the tides over an ever-increasing area of navigable waters is being obtained.

The improvement of the tidal records for the Pacific coast was given special attention last year, as a result of which the tide tables for Port Simpson, Prince Rupert, and Vancouver, as well as for the navigable passes of the west coast will be rendered much more accurate.

As the lighthouse at Sand Heads was replaced by a lightship it became necessary to close down the tidal station there, which hitherto had been used as a base for calculations in the strait of Georgia, and had been operated by the lighthouse-keeper. A new station at point Atkinson in the strait of Georgia, which is found to correspond to Sand Heads, was opened and has proved a satisfactory substitute for the former base. The observations taken will enable the earlier records from Sand Heads to be enlarged upon and improved. New stations were also established at the north end of the strait of Georgia and at points opposite the north end of Vancouver island. The object of these stations is to obtain further observations as a basis for the revision of the tidal data for that region.

On the east coast, new tidal observations were taken at the head of the bay of Fundy and along the north coast of Prince Edward island. The results obtained in the bay of Fundy were compared with simultaneous observations taken at St. John, N.B., and the complete results of the work will be published in a special report entitled, "Tides at the head of the bay of Fundy".

On Prince Edward island tide gauges were operated at Tignish, Alberton, Malpeque, Rustico, St. Peters, and Naufrage. The tide in this region is of a special nature as there are times when only one high water and one low water in the day are pronounced. The observations taken at the above-mentioned places were compared with the St. Paul island station, and the results as well as an explanation of the peculiarities of the tide will be given in the tide tables for 1918. This information will be valuable in determining the nature of the tides in the lower half of the gulf of St. Lawrence. It will also be of great assistance to the mariners desiring to seek shelter in the various ports along the coast in bad weather.

SESSIONAL PAPER No. 38

Through co-operation with the Hydrographic Survey, tidal observations were obtained for further points on the lower St. Lawrence at Grand Mechins and Godbout. These observations will be useful to connect previous records for the gulf of St. Lawrence with the St. Lawrence river.

The work of investigating the currents of the gut of Canso, begun in 1915, was continued during the summer of 1916. The behaviour of the current as thus ascertained is fully explained in the report of the Tidal and Current Survey appended hereto, and in the 1918 tide tables.

On the west coast, the method of calculating slack water in Seymour narrows was greatly improved. Previously these calculations were made on a very intricate and technical basis. With the new method, equally accurate results are obtained and the possibility of error in calculation is greatly eliminated. Improvements in the calculations for Active pass were also made, as well as for Porlier pass and for Wellbore channel.

All the information obtained with reference to these passes, besides serving the purposes of navigation in general, are valuable to the coal transportation and lumber interests operating in the localities. The information which enables these commercial interests to know the variations of tides and currents, the exact time when passes and river entrances are navigable, and the direction and force of the currents, is essential to them. This information is published in the tide tables and in pamphlets. For the convenience of commercial establishments, it is also supplied to them upon request, prior to its regular publication in the tide tables, etc., thus supplying them with advance information.

In Hudson bay and in James bay, the tidal observations taken closely correspond with the predictions already made, which proves that the method employed is closely accurate. The information will be useful to any business interests operating there, as well as to the Hudson bay railway in connection with its terminals.

Considerable work was done to reduce the observations taken by members of the Canadian Arctic Expedition at different points in the Arctic. The results will add substantially to our knowledge of the tide in these regions, although the rise of the tide is very small in the waters explored.

The determination of mean sea-level carried on by this survey at the principal tide stations has proven very useful to the Public Works department in connection with their geodetic work. By connecting the tide levels referred to the bench-marks of the survey as well as to the Admiralty bench-marks results published by that department have been greatly enhanced.

By reference to these bench-marks the Dominion Observatory have also obtained a reliable basis for their extended levels, references being available at Halifax, Yarmouth, and Vancouver. The departments of Railways and Canals and Public Works have also been supplied with information on tide levels and extreme tides in connection with the various railway construction works being carried out.

The complete information obtained from the various activities of this branch is published annually in the tide tables and in a series of reports on currents. A summary of operations for the year, is given in the report of the Superintendent of the Tidal and Current survey at page 3.

8 GEORGE V, A. 1918

3. HYDROGRAPHIC SURVEY.

The duties of the Hydrographic Survey are to investigate the different navigable waters in Canada, to take soundings of and chart the different courses through the rivers and along the coasts, and to survey and chart the different harbours and harbour entrances.

During the past year seven parties were engaged in carrying on the different surveys.

HALIFAX HARBOUR, ETC.

A party under Captain Anderson, in the steamer *Acadia*, were employed in re-sounding the approach to Halifax harbour and the area off the coast between Egg island and Pennant point. All the main shoals marked on Admiralty chart were re-examined; some of these shoals had less water over them than shown on the charts, while others marked on the charts could not be located. Notices to Mariners giving the results of the work have been published.

The main triangulation of 1916 was extended to the northeastward as far as Liscomb harbour, and to the southeastward as far as Port Medway.

BEDFORD BASIN AND LOCKPORT HARBOUR.

Bedford basin was re-surveyed and a new chart of it is under preparation. Lockport harbour was also examined, and new shoals located at its entrance.

Observations for magnetic declination were taken at important points along the coast.

On the 24th November, the *Acadia* having been laid up, the staff returned to Ottawa.

New charts for Bedford basin and for that part of the coast from Egg island to Pennant point, including Halifax harbour, will be published at an early date.

PACIFIC COAST SURVEY.

The Pacific Coast Survey party, in charge of Lieut.-Commander P. C. Musgrave, in C.G.S. *Lillooet*, set out from Esquimalt on the 10th April.

The season's operations were carried out in the vicinity of Queen Charlotte islands. On the way north an examination of Retreat cove in Trincomali channel and of Millbank sound was carried out.

Additional surveying of Alice arm was carried out between the 26th April and the 27 May, when the ship proceeded on her regular work at Queen Charlotte islands.

In June, soundings were taken in the west aproach to 'Dixon entrance, and work was then proceeded with in Hecate strait and near Queen Charlotte city.

In October the party returned to Alice arm, where the survey of the inlet was completed.

During the season an examination of Skidgate channel was also made.

The party returned to Esquimalt, where the *Lillooet* was laid up on the 4th November.

SESSIONAL PAPER No. 38

Valuable assistance was received from the Geodetic Survey, which supplied astronomical positions as groundwork for the Hydrographic Survey charts.

LOWER ST. LAWRENCE.

The Lower St. Lawrence Survey party, in charge of Mr. Charles Savary, in C.G.S. *Cartier*, continued the main triangulation of the south shore of the St. Lawrence as far east as Marten river, and on the north shore as far as Egg Island lighthouse.

As a result of the season's work, a new chart, taking in both shores of the St. Lawrence river, entitled "Pointe Des Monts to Father Point" will be published shortly.

The survey terminated early in November.

LAKE SUPERIOR PARTY NO. 1.

Mr. H. D. Parizeau, in C.G.S. *La Canadienne*, set out for Nipigon bay on the 4th May. A survey of this bay was carried on until the 13th September, when the party moved to Black bay. In entering Black bay the vessel ran aground and was badly injured. She was placed in the dry dock at Port Arthur, where repairs were carried out. As by the time the vessel was repaired the season was too far advanced to return to Black bay, the party worked in the vicinity of Port Arthur and Fort William until the 21st October. They then proceeded to Owen Sound, where the vessel was laid up for the winter.

As a result of the season's work, a chart of Nipigon bay will be published shortly.

LAKE SUPERIOR PARTY NO. 2.

Mr. G. A. Bachand, in C.G.S. *Bayfield* carried on work from Otter Head eastward along the shore in connection with the Michipicoten survey. They continued work in this vicinity until the 25th October, when bad weather obliged them to discontinue work for the season. They then returned to Owen Sound, where the vessel was laid up.

A new chart entitled "Michipicoten Island to Oiseau Bay" will be published from the information obtained by this survey during 1915-16.

KINGSTON HARBOUR.

Mr. Paul Jobin, and assistants, with the use of a gasolene launch, carried on the re-survey of the entrance to Kingston harbour. He was unable to complete this survey, and it will therefore be necessary to continue it during the summer of 1917.

AUTOMATIC GAUGES.

Mr. Charles Price was entrusted with the work of looking after the automatic gauges on the Great Lakes and St. Lawrence river. Eleven gauges on

8 GEORGE V, A. 1918·

the Great Lakes and eighteen on the St. Lawrence river were operated. At Sorel and Pointe Claire the gauges are operated throughout the year. Difficulty was experienced in obtaining reliable men to take readings of the different gauges operated.

The report of the Chief Hydrographer on the work of the Hydrographic Survey for the past year may be found at page 11.

4. CANADIAN ARCTIC EXPEDITION.

The Canadian Arctic Expedition set out for the North in 1913. Owing to the varied nature of the work to be carried out, and the vast area to be covered, it was decided to divide the expedition into two parties; the Northern and the Southern divisions. The Northern division was to explore the hitherto unknown parts of Beaufort sea, and carry on investigations on the northern islands; they were also to search for new land and to definitely locate any found.

NORTHERN DIVISION.

The members of the Northern division set out in C.G.S. *Karluk.* They were to proceed to Banks island or Prince Patrick island, where a base was to be established. Shortly after passing Point Barrow, however, the vessel became ice-bound and was carried eastward far down the northern coast, as far as Thetis island, where the drifting of the ice ceased. As it appeared that the vessel was frozen in for the winter, Mr. Stefansson, accompanied by Mr. B. M. McConnell, George H. Wilkins, and D. Jenness, set out for the mainland on a hunting trip. During their absence, the vessel with the remainder of the Northern division was carried away and drifted until the 11th January, when it was crushed by the ice, and sunk. In endeavouring to reach Herald island, eight members of the party lost their lives. The remainder, numbering nine men, including Capt. R. A. Bartlett, succeeded in reaching Wrangel island. Captain Bartlett journeyed on foot over the ice to the Siberian coast, and thence to Alaska in the *Herman*, where he was able to communicate with the outside world, to have relief ships sent. The shipwrecked men were taken from Wrangel island by the schooners *King* and *Wing*, and transferred to the United States revenue cutter *Bear*, which landed them at Victoria.

When Mr. Stefansson and his companions found that their vessel had been carried away, they journeyed along the northern coast to Collinson point, where the Southern division of the expedition was established. Although Mr. Stefansson was not aware of the *Karluk's* fate, he realized that the vessel would not be available to assist in the work of the Northern division. He therefore made arrangements to journey on foot over the ice to explore unknown parts of Beaufort sea, it being understood that a vessel would be sent to Banks island in the summer of 1914, provided he did not return before the breaking up of the ice. On his trip across Beaufort sea, Mr. Stefansson covered an area which was hitherto very little known. The party was carried eastward by the drift of the ice to near the 140th meridian, which they followed north to 72° 53' 23" north.

During their journey over the ice, soundings were taken at short intervals, particularly in the vicinity of the outer edge of the continental shelf. Owing to the breaking up of the ice, they were compelled to make for land and arrived at Norway island on the 24th June, 1914. They spent the summer on northern Banks island, until September, when they journeyed south to Kellett, where Geo. Wilkins, who had come north with the *Mary Sachs*, was met. A base was established at Kellett from which Mr. Stefansson made a journey to De Salis bay across southern Banks island early in December, to locate Eskimos in the vicinity of Prince of Wales strait. Failing to locate them, he returned to Kellett, where arrangements for a trip northward were completed. Early in February, 1915, the ice party, composed of Vilhjalmur Stefansson, Storker Storkerson, Ole Andreason, and Charles Thomsen, set out northward, following the west coast of Banks island as far as cape Alfred. From cape Alfred they set out across the ice in a northwesterly direction, taking similar observations as they advanced as had been taken on the ice journey over Beaufort sea the previous year. On both these journeys it was ascertained that no land exists for a considerable distance on either side of the area over which they travelled. As the ice in Beaufort sea began to break up on the 28th April, they were obliged to discontinue the ice expedition for the season of 1915, and make for land, They arrived at Lands End, Prince Patrick island, and followed its shore northeast to cape McClintock. A survey of the shore was made during this journey. From cape McClintock they again set out over the ice in a northerly direction. On the 18th June, three days after setting out, land unmarked on any chart was seen. The ice party landed on the shore of the new land, at the southwestern entrance of a bay about twenty miles in width. They crossed the entrance of this bay, and proceeded along the shore for a distance of about twenty miles. From observations taken from neighbouring hills, the land appeared to be extensive, hills appearing blue in the distance having been seen. A considerable number of animals, including seals, caribou, foxes, etc., were found in the vicinity. Owing to the lateness of the season, the party were obliged to hasten back to Kellett, without making any more extensive investigations. The party arrived at Kellett on the 8th August.

Mr. Stefansson went in the *Poler Bear* to Baillie island to despatch and receive mail and to obtain the services of another vessel. After leaving instructions for the *"North Star"* to go to Kellett as soon as possible, he returned to Banks island. On the 3rd September, 1915, the *Polar Bear*, which was purchased for the use of the expedition, set out along the west coast of Banks island. Ice, however, prevented the vessel from going farther than cape Kellett. It was decided, therefore, to endeavour to go north through Prince of Wales strait on the east coast of Banks island. They were able to go only as far as Princess Royal islands, where they were obliged to winter.

In the fall of 1915, a considerable part of the hitherto unmapped shoreline of Victoria island was completed. Several trips, including a journey across southern Banks island to Kellett, were made. On the journey to Kellett much useful and interesting information with reference to the overland route across southern Banks island was obtained. Upon arrival at Kellett, Mr. Stefansson

38—B

8 GEORGE V, A. 1918

decided to carry out the next year's journeys from there, and on the 6th January 1916, sent a party to the *Polar Bear* to inform the members at that base of the arrangements made. This party, however, experienced great difficulties in reaching the *Polar Bear*, so that instructions were received too late to be carried out. Under the circumstances, Mr. Storkerson, in charge of the *Polar Bear* base, decided to proceed north to the new land, where he began to carry on survey work. When the *Polar Bear* party failed to arrive within a reasonable time at cape Alfred, which was the place of rendezvous, Mr. Stefansson undertook to locate them, and found out that they had gone to the new land. The Stefansson party left cape Ross for the new land on the 19th April, 1916, and met Mr. Storkerson on the 3rd May at cape James Murray. From this point, the last mail from the expedition received in the department was despatched. The work of the Northern expedition for the season 1916-17 gives promise of producing very favourable results.

The further reports of the different expeditions carried on and also details of the new land discovered, are awaited with great interest.

SOUTHERN DIVISION.

The ice conditions which proved so disastrous to the first efforts of the Northern division, and which caused the destruction of C.G.S. *Karluk*, prevented the members of the Southern division from proceeding farther than Collinson point, Alaska. Their two vessels, the *Alaska* and *Mary Sachs*, were put in winter quarters, and the party established a base there.

During the winter and spring, up to the opening of navigation, the work of the expedition was carried out along the coast of Canada as far as the Mackenzie River delta, their operations being limited to geological and meteorological work, the carrying on of a survey from Demarkation point to Herschel island, an examination of Herschel Island river, and the survey of the west branch of the Mackenzie river delta. Upon the opening of navigation, the party, with the use of the above-named vessels, proceeded along the north coast of Canada eastward, through Amundsen gulf, and Dolphin and Union strait, to a point almost directly south of Sutton and Liston islands. There they entered a small harbour unmarked on the charts, which is well protected and gives good anchorage. They named it Bernard harbour, and established a base for carrying on the work of the Southern division.

During the two years following, up to the 13th July, 1916, the regular work of the division was carried out very successfully, and a survey of the mainland coast in detail from Alaska, Yukon Territory, international boundary, to the Mackenzie river, was completed.

A traverse of the Firth river, Y.T., was made, and the east and west branches of the Mackenzie river delta and the mainland coast from the west side of Darnley bay to a point well down in Bathurst inlet, as well as a large number of islands in Coronation gulf and Bathurst inlet, were surveyed. Hornaday river, Crocker river, Rae river, Tree river, and many others hitherto unexplored, were traversed, and an examination of the territory around the mouth of

Hood river was carried out. An examination was also made of Collinson point harbour, Bernard harbour, Chantry island, and the country immediately surrounding these places. Maps of all the districts named are in preparation.

The geological features of all areas covered have been carefully investigated, and the relations of the different formations have been studied in detail at the most important points of contact. As a result of the geological investigation, detailed particulars and an estimation of the available copper-bearing rocks in a new area hitherto very slightly known in the Bathurst inlet region, have been obtained. In the branches of ethnology and anthropology, extensive collections of specimens were taken from Arctic Alaska, Coronation gulf, Dolphin and Union strait, and Victoria island. Gramophone records of Eskimo folk lore, language, dance songs, and shamanistic performances, with careful transcriptions and translations, were made. A careful study of the languages and vocabularies, manners, social and religious customs, games, amusements, and general culture of the Eskimo was also made.

In the departments of marine, biology, entomology, and botany, careful studies were made at all points visited, and the life-histories of the arctic insects, animals, and plants were investigated. Specimens of the arctic plants, animals and insects were also obtained. In mammalogy and ornithology, fairly complete collections were made in the regions traversed; 619 specimens of birds, including 73 species, were obtained. The collections of mammals numbers 431 specimens, including 22 species.

Meteorological observations with barograph; thermograph; maximum; minimum, and standard thermometers; mercurial barometer, and anomometer were carried out during the three years. Trial observations were taken at Collinson point, Demarkation point, and Bernard harbour.

Upon the completion of their activities, the Southern division sailed from Bernard harbour, on the 13th July, 1916. At Young point, heavy ice was encountered, and the party were held up for four days. They worked their way through the ice on the 21st July, and followed an open lead outside of the ice, pressing along the south side of Amundsen gulf and Dolphin and Union strait. This ice did not extend farther west than the Crocker river, after which the ocean was comparatively free. At Bailley island, several Eskimos attached to the party were discharged, having been paid chiefly in stores. Herschel island was reached on the 28th July, where the surplus stores from the *Alaska* were left in care of the Royal Northwest Mounted Police, for the use of the Northern division should they be required. At Herschel island, also, the services of additional Eskimos were dispensed with. West of this point, heavy ice was encountered, from the international boundary to point Barrow. Nome was reached on the 15th August, 1916. After unloading the specimens, the vessel was hauled up on the beach, and left in charge of the Alaska Lighterage and Commercial Co. The specimens were shipped by the regular steamship route to Ottawa, via Seattle. The members of the expedition left Nome for Seattle on the 27th August.

38—B½

8 GEORGE V, A. 1918

Upon their arrival at Ottawa, the different members of the Southern division immediately began work upon the preparation of their reports. A very large number of specimens, hitherto unknown, were brought out. It was necessary to have these arranged, grouped, and catalogued. In order to carry out the work, the assistance of eminent specialists, both from Canada and from outside countries, was required. For the purpose of distributing these specimens among specialists who would be likely to give them the best attention, and obtain the fullest information available, a committee of scientists, composed of Dr. R. M. Anderson, of the Expedition; Prof. E. E. Prince, Dominion Commissioner of Fisheries; Prof. A. B. McCallum, Dominion Entomologist; Dr. C. Gordon Hewitt; and Mr. James Macoun, of the Geological Survey, was appointed. This committee has already begun the work of distributing the specimens.

A report of the activities of the northern division of the expedition may be found at page 22.

A detailed report of the activities of the Southern division by Dr. R. M. Anderson, may be found at page 28.

5. RADIOTELEGRAPH BRANCH.

During last year 156 radiotelegraph stations were in operation. Owing to the war, the Coast stations have been maintained on a war basis.

Following is comparative statement of business handled during 1915-16 and 1916-17:—

Service.	1915–16.		1916–17.		Increase or decrease.	
	Messages.	Words.	Messages.	Words.	Messages.	Words.
East Coast	45,195	846,020	37,835	704,469	7,360	Decrease. 159,551
Great Lakes	13,617	259,366	16,521	311,800	2,904	Increase. 52,434
West Coast	95,648	1,103,395	121,126	1,732,420	26,172	Increase. 629,025
Hudson Bay	7,617	570,281	6,264	392,154	1,353	Decrease. 178,127
Total	161,477	2,797,062	181,740	3,140,843	20,263	Increase. 343,781

The radiotelegraph stations on the east coast and Great Lakes are operated by the Marconi Wireless Telegraph Company, under contract, for the department. The west coast stations are operated directly by the department, and the Hudson Bay stations are operated by the department for the department of Railways and Canals.

The revenue derived from this service shows a very gratifying increase over last year, observing that the war has greatly diminished the business carried on by wireless.

The following statement gives the revenue collected last year as compared with 1915-16:—

Locality.	1915–16.	1916–17.	Increase or decrease.
	\$ cts.	\$ cts.	\$ cts.
East Coast	1,022 33	987 67	Decrease 34 66
Great Lakes	78 16	107 90	Increase 29 74
West Coast	7,394 50	15,635 76	Increase 8,243 26
Total	8,494 99	16,731 33	Net Increase 8,236.34

In addition to carrying on the work of operating the different radiotelegraph stations, the branch also undertakes the examination of wireless operators and the licensing of all radio sets on land and on Canadian ships. Owing to the very secret nature of a considerable part of the work handled by the wireless operators, it was deemed advisable to make them amenable to naval discipline. The rank of wireless operator, R.N.C.V.R., was accordingly established in which all wireless operators in the Canadian Naval Service have been entered.

During the past year 135 operators were examined, including eight re-examinations, of which sixty-four were successful. Eight holders of certificates of proficiency were successful in examinations for the operation of other equipments, and their certificates were amended accordingly.

The policy of the department to bring the radiotelegraph stations under the ownership of the Government was further advanced during the past year by the purchase of the North Sydney station from the Marconi Wireless Company.

The value of an efficient wireless service was further demonstrated by the valuable services rendered to vessels in distress which resulted in the saving of many lives and much property.

In continuance of the department policy of keeping the stations thoroughly up to date, improvements and additions were made at the following stations:—

West Coast: Cape Lazo, Dead Tree Point, Estevan, Gonzales Hill, Pachena, Point Grey, and Triangle Island.

East Coast: North Sydney.

Great Lakes: Point Edward, Port Burwell, Headquarters, Ottawa.

The radio regulations were amended during the past year to prohibit the working of ship stations while in harbour, to limit the ship stations to the use of a 600-meter wave length, and to debar all except British subjects of British parentage from entering the service. The department has also to equip numerous Admiralty transports with radiotelegraph apparatus, and to carry out the inspection of same.

The total personnel of the government radiotelegraph service, including the officers at the headquarters office, is 165.

The report of the General Superintendent of Radiotelegraph is appended at page 71.

6. FISHERIES PROTECTION SERVICE.

The following vessels belonging to the Fisheries Protection Service were in commission during the fiscal year 1916-17; *Canada, Curlew, Constance, Petrel, Gulnare, Vigilant, Galiano, Masaspina,* and *Restless.*

Owing to the urgent need of vessels for patrol service and examination service in connection with the defence of the Canadian coasts, the *Canada, Constance, Gulnare,* and *Restless* were utilized by the Naval Service, and were not available for Fisheries Protection duties at any time during the year. They maintained a close watch for illegal fishing, however, whilst on Naval Patrol Service.

These vessels, as well as the other Fisheries Protection ships, were, however, used to carry out the inspection of the life-saving stations along the east and west coasts and on the Great Lakes, when they were in the vicinity of the stations. requiring inspection.

The *Curlew* was utilized, except for short periods, when its services were required for war work, in patrolling the fisheries grounds of the bay of Fundy.

During the season assistance was rendered by the ship to the ss. *Tyne,* ashore near Grand Manan. It also searched unsuccessfully for the barge *Mule* adrift in the bay of Fundy. It towed to safety the ss. *J. L. Cann* from the dangerous position off Briar island. With the aid of the *Curlew* the schooner *W. H. Mason,* which sank in deep water at the entrance of St. Mary's bay, was located, as was also an uncharted rock, off Whitehead island. During the winter, the vessel kept the ice in St. Andrew's harbour broken up, thereby enabling navigation to be carried · on.

The *Petrel,* when not on Naval Service, carried out its regular Fisheries Protection duties along the southwest coast of Nova Scotia. The Naval work, however, required the services of the vessel for the greater part of the year.

C.G.S. *Vigilant* was engaged in patrolling the international boundary line in lakes Ontario and Erie throughout the summer of 1916. The ship was laid up at Port Dover on December 23, 1916. During the season the vessel steamed 5,818 miles, and seized 618 nets.

The *Malaspina* was utilized throughout the year, alternately on Fisheries Protection and Naval Service work. Whilst on Fisheries Protection work it was also used to inspect the life-saving and radiotelegraph stations on the west coast. The vessel was also utilized to lay a cable from Leonard island to Vancouver island. Whilst patrolling the ship seized the motor-boat *Greg* for an infraction of the fisheries laws, and handed it over to the Marine Agency at Victoria.

The *Galiano* was on Fisheries Protection duties throughout the year, except for short periods when she was required for examination service. The chief areas patrolled were the fishing grounds in the vicinity of Hecate strait and Barclay sound. This vessel was also used in carrying out the inspection of the radiotelegraph stations on the west coast.

The C.G.S. *Fispa,* a fisheries launch, was placed on fisheries patrol service in the vicinity of Prince Rupert. · Although too light for patrolling the open sea,

SESSIONAL PAPER No. 38

the *Fispa* did good work in the straits from November to April, when it was returned to the Chief Inspector of Fisheries at New Westminster.

The report of the Director of the Naval Service on the Fisheries Protection Service may be found at page 89.

7. THE LIFE SAVING SERVICE.

The Life-saving Service of Canada has been established for the purpose of saving the lives of those in danger at sea, and for rescuing those on board wrecked vessels along the coasts of Canada. Stations, equipped with life boats manned by trained men, have been built at points along the coasts where navigation is difficult and where wrecks are most prevalent. These stations are not equipped for saving vessels or cargoes but, when practicable, after those on board have been taken off, salving operations are carried out.

This department also undertakes to reward bravery for life-saving at sea, but not along the coasts and in rivers. Cases of the latter should be brought to the attention of the Royal Canadian Humane Association, Hamilton, Ont.

With each succeeding year, as the fishermen equip themselves with modern motor-boats, and the ocean-going ships become larger, the necessity for the life-saving stations at present in operation is becoming less. In most cases fishermen are able to render each other better assistance than the service can provide. For this reason, the question of doing away with some of the least useful stations is being considered.

During the past year the method of inspecting the stations has been revised. The work of inspection was formerly carried out by one inspector. It was considered that the inspections could be equally well done by the officers of the Fisheries Protection vessels patrolling the district. The new system was adopted during the past year, and has proved highly satisfactory.

During the fiscal year 1916-17, thirty-seven stations were in operation, of which twenty-four are located on the east coast, three on the west coast, and ten on the Great Lakes. Five of these stations have permanent crews on duty throughout the year, six have permanent crews on duty during the season of navigation, and the remainder have volunteer crews who drill twice a month and are called out in case of a wreck.

On the east coast, assistance was rendered to disabled vessels or motor-boats by the crews of the stations at Bay View, Canso, Cheticamp, Clark's Harbour, Herring Cove, Seal Island, Brier Island, and Whitehead. The boat at Whitehead was destroyed while going to the assistance of the schooner *J. W. Margerson*. Assistance was also rendered by the crews from Cape Tormentine, Little Wood Island, and Richibucto.

On the Great Lakes the crews from Point Pelee, Port Hope, and Toronto were called out. The Toronto crew's activities were confined to Toronto harbour and they were not called upon to render assistance out in the lake during the year. The Toronto crew, in addition to helping fifty-three different vessels, also gave assistance in cases of drowning, the station being equipped with a pulmotor.

The Bamfield and Ucluelet stations on the west coast also gave assistance to vessels in distress.

The report of the Director of the Naval Service on the Life Saving Service is appended at page 94.

8. STORES BRANCH.

The activities of the Stores Branch of the department are divided into three sections, namely: the Purchasing and Contract, the Storekeeping, and the Transportation.

PURCHASING AND CONTRACT SECTION.

This section is responsible for the purchase of all supplies required by Canadian Naval Ships and Establishments, Imperial and Allied vessels calling on Canadian ports, and for supplies required by the other branches of the department. It also attends to the charter of vessels, contracts for construction of new works, buildings, etc., and to the installations required in connection therewith.

During the past year, owing to the increased demand for materials for war purposes, and the difficulty of obtaining same, the work of the branch was rendered much more difficult than previously, but through the energy of the officers and the co-operation of the Canadian manufacturers and dealers, the supplies and equipment were kept up to requirements.

The total liability incurred during the last fiscal year amounts to $7,605,019. A considerable portion of this amount was expended on behalf of the Imperial and Allied Governments and is recoverable.

STOREKEEPING SECTION.

The storekeeping section is responsible for the distribution of supplies to Canadian Ships and Establishments, to Imperial and Allied vessels calling on Canadian ports. This work entails the keeping of a large reserve stock of supplies on hand. This stock is maintained at the Naval bases at Halifax and Esquimalt.

The activities of the Storekeeping section have expanded greatly during the past year, owing to the increase in the number of vessels requiring supplies, the difficulty of obtaining certain materials, and the necessity of substitution in such cases. The reserve stock has, however, been successfully maintained throughout the year.

The total value of receipt of stores at Halifax dockyard for the past year was $805,282, and at Esquimalt $570,496. The issues of stores to Ships and Establishments at Halifax amounted to $592,926, and at Esquimalt $411,270. In addition to the above activities, this branch has also supplied Allied ships and transports sailing from Canada with coal and fuel oil. The total receipts of steaming coal for the year at Halifax dockyard amounted to 78,575 tons, and at Esquimalt 31,711 tons. The issues at Halifax were 77,733 tons, and at Esquimalt 29,626 tons. In addition, the following quantities of Canadian coal were handled on direct issue to ships from contractors: Halifax and the east coast, 138,509 tons; Esquimalt and the west coast, 16,545 tons. At Halifax, 107,000 gallons of fuel oil were handled, and at Esquimalt 23,943 gallons.

TRANSPORTATION.

The overseas transport service has, during the past year, very successfully carried out its work of transporting supplies, etc., overseas. The Director of Overseas Transport is responsible for the shipping of overseas supplies; this entails making all arrangements for railway transportation of such supplies, and the loading of same on transports. The Naval Service department is responsible for the procuring of suitable transports, their routing, and keeping the British Admiralty informed as to their movements. The railway companies of Canada have greatly facilitated the work of transportation by their earnest co-operation.

During the past fiscal year, under the direction of the Transport Service, 386 sailings, comprising 2,429,829 tons, cleared from Canadian ports. In the year 1915-16 there were 198 sailings, comprising 970,911 tons. Although the demands on transportation have been very heavy, the service has been able to meet it, and the large quantities of supplies for shipment were handled with practically no delay.

The report of the Director of Stores is appended at page 97.

EXPENDITURES.

The total expenditure of the Naval Service department during the fiscal year 1916–17 was $16,416,839.36. Out of this amount $4,242,489.99 were expended from the regular appropriations and $4,761,991.96 out of the war appropriation; $7,412,357.41 were expended on account of the Imperial and Allied Governments, which amount is recoverable.

GENERAL

I have much pleasure in expressing my satisfaction at the efficient manner in which officers of the department have carried out their duties during the year.

I have the honour to be, sir.

Your obedient servant.

G. J. DESBARATS,
Deputy Minister.

8 GEORGE V, A. 1918

OTTAWA July 21st 1917.

The Deputy Minister,
        Department of the Naval Service,
                Ottawa, Ont.

SIR, I have the honour to submit herewith a financial statement showing the expenditure under the various appropriations, and the revenue received by the Department during the fiscal year ended March 31st, 1917.

The expenditure on account of H.M.C.S. *Niobe*, H.M.C.S. *Rainbow*, the submarines, and other vessels engaged in the defence of our coasts, the Royal Canadian Naval Hospital (Halifax) and extraordinary expenditures for the dockyards at Halifax and Esquimalt have been charged to war appropriation. The ordinary expenditure for the upkeep and maintenance of the Royal Naval College, Halifax and Esquimalt dockyards has been charged to Naval Service appropriation.

A statement of stores supplied, work done and advances made on behalf of the British, French, Italian, Russian Governments, and others, is also submitted. These disbursements amount during the fiscal year 1916–17 to $6,517, 816.80, and to this should be added the sum of $718,400.73 transferred from fiscal year 1915–16, thus making a grand total of $7,236,217.53 debited against the Allies, etc., during fiscal year 1916–17. Credits and cash received during the year amount to $7,078,825.70, leaving an outstanding balance of $157,391.83, which is not included in the amounts charged to War or Naval Appropriations, but carried forward in Suspense to the fiscal year 1917–18.

                    I have the honour to be, sir,
                            Your obedient servant,

                    L. J. BEAUSOLEIL
                            Chief Accountant.

STATEMENT of jobs completed in the workshops and stores supplied by the Halifax and Esquimalt dockyards during fiscal year 1916-17.

Service.	Halifax.	Esquimalt.
	$ cts.	$ cts.
Naval Service	560,621 15	264,284 17
Fisheries Protection Service	28,413 21	32,900 30
Hydrographic Surveys	11,579 65	5,828 42
Life Saving Service	1,670 71	3,257 99
Radiotelegraph Service	3,114 65	2,312 42
Fishery Patrol Service	5,058 02	1,236 33
British Admiralty	247,647 82	404,778 43
French Admiralty	4,171 10	
Italian Government	1,678 48	
Department of Marine		2,423 87
Department of Militia and Defence		404 49
Sundries	1,821 87	9,173 10
	(A)865,776 66	726,599 52
(B) Wages paid	168,100 05	274,897 53
Salaries	32,588 97	40,172 52
(C) Stores issued	683,906 22	416,167 61

(B) and (C) included in (A).

SESSIONAL PAPER No. 33

STATEMENT of appropriation accounts for fiscal year 1916-17.

Service.	Appropriation.	Expenditure.	Balance unexpended.
	$ cts.	$ cts.	$ cts.
Naval Service...	1,000,000 00	578,580 57	421,419 43
Fisheries Protection Service...............................	375,000 00	110,317 26	264,682 74
Hydrographic Surveys.....................................	290,000 00	223,846 53	66,153 47
Radiotelegraph Service....................................	295,000 00	182,536 39	112,463 61
Tidal Service...	35,000 00	19,465 77	15,534 23
Patrol of the Northern Waters of Canada..................	50,000 00	20,333 75	29,666 25
New Fisheries Protection Steamers.........................	30,000 00	....	30,000 00
Rewards for Saving Life, including Life Saving Service......	125,400 00	99,150 09	26,249 91
	2,200,400 00	1,234,230 36	966,169 64
Fisheries—			
Salaries and Disbursements of Fishery Officers..........	305,000 00	243,878 02	61,121 98
Building Fishways and Clearing rivers...................	30,000 00	4,564 78	25,435 22
Legal and Incidental expenses..........................	4,000 00	3,027 16	972 84
Canadian Fisheries Museum............................	8,000 00	5,248 56	2,751 44
Oyster Culture..	6,000 00	5,003 74	996 26
Cold Storage and transportation of fish.................	125,000 00	80,042 33	44,957 67
Dogfish Reduction Works..............................	60,000 00	31,472 82	28,527 18
Services of Customs Officers *re Modus Vivendi* Licenses..	900 00	364 20	535 80
Fisheries Intelligence Bureau..........................	5,000 00	3,877 84	1,122 16
Fisheries Patrol Service...............................	190,000 00	157,412 73	32,587 27
Fisheries Exhibit (Toronto Exhibition).................	10,000 00	8,594 09	1,405 91
Fish Breeding establishments..........................	400,000 00	275,166 53	124,833 47
Inspection of Canned and Pickled fish..................	25,000 00	12,007 96	12,992 04
Building Fisheries Patrol boats........................	30,000 00	33,495 13	*3,495 13
Compassionate allowances..............................	3,000 00	3,000 00	....
Marine Biological stations and investigations...........	26,000 00	26,000 00	....
	1,227,900 00	893,155 89	334,744 11
Civil Government Salaries...............................	180,950 00	155,237 37	25,712 63
Contingencies..	50,000 00	46,829 63	3,170 37
	230,950 00	202,067 00	28,883 00
Fishing Bounty..	160,000 00	159,999 80	0 20

*Grant exceeded.

RECAPITULATION.

Naval Service...	2,200,400 00	1,234,230 36	966,169 64
Fisheries...	1,227,900 00	893,155 89	334,744 11
Civil Government...	180,950 00	155,237 37	25,712 63
Contingencies...	50,000 00	46,829 63	3,170 37
Fishing Bounty...	160,000 00	159,999 80	0 20
	3,819,250 00	2,489,453 05	1,329,796 95

	$ cts.	$ cts.		
War Appropriation:—				
Disbursements.............	10,324,145 99			
Carried from 1915–16.......	718,400 73			
Gross expenditure....................		11,042,546 72		
Less:—				
Re-imbursements and				
Credits................ $ 7,078,825 70				
Transferred to 1917–18...... 157,391 83	7,236,217 53			
Net expenditure.......................			3,806,329 19	
Imperial Government (Special Account)....................			260,000 00	
Total expenditure fiscal year 1916–17...........			6,555,782 24	

SESSIONAL PAPER No. 38

STATEMENT showing amounts outstanding in respect to stores supplied, work done and advances made, etc., at end of fiscal year 1916-17.

SUSPENSE ACCOUNTS.

	Debits.	Credits.	Balance Transferred to 1917–18.
	$ cts.	$ cts.	$ cts.
British Admiralty	6,510,688 47	6,395,692 01	114,996 46
French Admiralty	84,024 56	64,248 78	19,775 78
Italian Government	2,948 95		2,948 95
Russian Government	6,842 65		6,842 65
Japanese Government	1,447 23	1,447 23	
War Office	26,946 46	26,946 46	
Commonwealth of Australia	70,385 59	70,375 84	9 75
Department of Militia and Defence	402,871 15	402,528 74	342 41
Miscellaneous	130,062 47	117,586 64	12,475 83
	7,236,217 53	7,078,825 70	157,391 83

STATEMENT of revenue of the Department of the Naval Service for fiscal year ended March 31, 1917.

	$ cts.	$ cts.
Royal Naval College—College fees (26 Cadets)		2,600 00
Fisheries Revenue		98,629 67
Modus Vivendi (Licenses to *U.S.* fishing vessels)		5,680 50
Casual Revenue		26,379 07
Miscellaneous Revenue		760 32
Wireless Apparatus Licenses		214 25
Wireless Operators Examination fees		147 00
Radiotelegraph Revenue:—		
Alert Bay Station	472 10	
Cape Lazo Station	589 56	
Dead Tree Point Station	547 03	
Digby Island Station	2,613 44	
Estevan Point Station	1,635 53	
Gonzales Hill Station	3,398 03	
Ikeda Head Station	355 96	
Pachena Point Station	127 20	
Point Grey Station	2,358 49	
Triangle Island Station	3,533 42	
Malaspina Station	5 96	
Galiano Station	4 17	
Camperdown Station	293 50	
North Sydney Station	223 66	
Sable Island Station	107 67	
Magdalen Islands Station	362 84	
Midland Station	9 60	
Point Edward Station	28 57	
Port Arthur Station	18 05	
Port Burwell Station	8 28	
Sault Ste. Marie Station	27 52	
Tobermory Station	4 56	
Toronto Station	11 32	16,741 46
		151,152 27

SESSIONAL PAPER No. 33

FISHERIES REVENUE for fiscal year ended March 31, 1917.

Province.	Amount Collected.	Refunds.	Net Amount.
	$ cts.	$ cts.	$ cts.
Ontario...	808 70	....	808 70
Quebec...	6,981 14	....	6,981 14
New Brunswick..	15,137 19	....	15,137 19
Nova Scotia...	7,178 70	2 00	7,176 70
Prince Edward Island.................................	3,605 18	8 00	3,597 18
Manitoba..	8,252 27	....	8,252 27
Saskatchewan...	3,103 25	....	3,103 25
Alberta...	5,993 40	23 00	5,970 40
British Columbia......................................	47,330 84	3 00	47,327 84
Yukon...	275 00	....	275 00
	98,665 67	36 00	98,629 67
Modus Vivendi Licenses.............................	5,680 50	....	5,680 50
			104,310 17

STATEMENT of expenditure under the war appropriation for fiscal year ended March 31, 1917.

Ship or Establishment.	Pay and Allowances.	Stores and Allowances.	Medical Services.	Subsistence of Prisoners.	Recruiting Expenses.	Repairs and Maintenance.	Purchase of Ships and Alterations.	New Ships Building.	Works, Lands, Buildings.	Misc. Effective Services.	Non-Effective Pay and Separation Allowances.	Charter of Vessels.	Total.
	$ cts.	$ cts.	$ cts.	$ cts.	$ cts.	$ cts.	$ cts.	$ cts.	$ cts.	$ cts.	$ cts.	$ cts.	$ cts.
H.M.C.S. "Niobe"	223,925 42	273,685 06	1,733 44	149 40	367 73	19,965 90				25,954 34	1,687 96		547,461 25
H.M.C.S. "Rainbow"	150,625 87	67,467 70	1,930 37	252 55		37,167 45				5,008 33	2,092 99		264,545 26
Submarines and Depot.	91,569 98	56,872 41	2,106 75	85 45	6,446 63	34,662 17				7,505 44	480 76		193,283 96
H.M.C.S. "Shearwater" (Shore Depot)	93,942 20	87,931 30	2,192 70	483 55						5,936 89	470 78		197,413 05
H.M.C.S. "Shearwater" (Ship).						5,352 76							5,352 76
H.M.C.S. "Diana" (Depot).	Credit 8 70	821 25	7 50	28 50						676 66			1,525 21
H.M.C.S. "Canada"	37,634 37	29,775 68	210 42	8 10		13,283 12				1,429 63			82,341 32
H.M.C.S. "Margaret"	40,156 94	36,222 28	234 49			16,187 72				1,530 41			94,331 84
H.M.C.S. "Florence"	9,690 04	9,320 62	153 50			7,730 93				2,548 63			29,443 72
H.M.C.S. "Hochelaga"	34,664 90	32,334 06	159 96			10,214 29				1,211 44			78,584 65
H.M.C.S. "Stradacona"	35,065 04	30,298 85	189 39			11,262 57				1,561 05			78,366 90
H.M.C.S. "Grilse"	25,613 01	18,571 85	179 47			14,520 66				1,335 76			60,220 75
H.M.C.S. "Acadia"	8,801 25	12,478 55				5,541 71				114 28			26,935 79
H.M.C.S. "Tuna"	1,228 15	8,703 41				29,225 55				995 20			40,152 31
H.M.C.S. "Speedy"	6,878 95	5,369 72				2,703 24				370 03			15,121 94
Hopper Barge No. 2.	5,364 09	11,331 21				2,402 23				1,141 23			20,238 76
Patrol Vessel No. 1.							109,378 03						109,378 03
Patrol Vessel No. 2.							109,229 28						109,229 28
Patrol Vessel No. 3.							109,547 53						109,547 53
Patrol Vessel No. 4.							109,705 06						109,705 06
Patrol Vessel No. 5.							109,406 16						109,406 16
6 Steel Trawlers (Polson).								200,234 29					200,234 29
Barrington and N. Sydney W/S.									2,775 99				2,775 99
Halifax Dockyard.		880 83				22,575 00			1,750 00				25,205 83
Esquimalt Dockyard.		593 31											593 31

Atlantic Coast Defence	118,219 63	105,049 75			18,873 63		72,692 11			284,502 65		599,606 04
Pacific Coast Defence	36,955 46	31,053 03	288 27		14,140 84		5,884 02			3,596 94		91,630 29
R.C.N. Hospital		2 40				10,620 87	13 45					10,636 72
R.N.C.V.R. Overseas Division	102,126 53	110,761 38		79,249 57			58,683 32	17,291 19				368,111 99
Headquarters	49,107 95	49 12	24 69	8,382 61			14,467 23					63,648 99
General Account		57,682 59			5,660 32		161,640 55	159,034 66				392,400 73
	1,071,351 08	967,256 36	9,390 95	1,007 55	94,446 54	271,471 09	547,266 06	200,234 29	15,146 86	370,700 00	181,067 34	288,099 59	4,037,437 71

Less Credits:—
H.M.C.S. "Niobe" Guns and gun mountings	175,497 79
H.M.S. "Protesilaus" Refund by B. Admiralty	28,009 69
Hopper Barge No. 2. Water delivered to Sundry Vessels	19,267 72
War Donations (Thos. Robb Esq.)	8,333 32
Net Expenditure	3,806,329 19

STATEMENT of expenditure under the naval appropriation for fiscal year ended March 31, 1917.

	Royal Naval College.	Halifax Dockyard.	Esquimalt Dockyard.	H.M.C.S. "Niobe".	Head Quarters.	General Account.	Total.
	$ cts.	$ cts.	$ cts.	$ cts.	$ cts.	$ cts.	$ cts.
Pay and Allowances............	50,031 28	....	211 10	5,039 19	16,006 06	6,668 45	71,287 63
Stores and Allowances........	15,912 94	166,485 89	246,937 58	....	1,342 98	....	437,367 84
Medical Services..............	258 62	18 28	35 00	....	286 50	....	628 40
Cadets Misc. Expenses........	925 88	....	....	....	....	....	925 88
Repairs and Maintenance......	5,581 12	66,823 82	83,328 23	....	....	....	155,733 17
Works, Lands, Buildings......	10,282 81	1,280 02	3,208 91	....	....	....	11,562 83
Misc. Effective Services......	12,694 91	2,184 80	....	200 00	400 65	1,077 24	19,566 51
Non-Effective Pay............	498 80	....	....	....	....	....	698 80
Depreciation.................	....	....	4,134 43	....	....	....	4,134 43
	96,216 36	236,792 81	337,855 25	5,239 19	18,036 19	7,765 09	701,905 49
Less credits:—							
Percentage on Stores........	....	18,783 51	39,263 95	....	....	....	58,047 46
Percentage on Labour........	....	8,613 59	50,468 92	....	....	....	59,082 51
Arisings....................	....	6,194 95	....	....	....	....	6,194 95
Net Expenditure.........	96,216 36	203,200 76	248,122 38	5,239 19	5,236 19	7,765 69	578,580 57

OTTAWA, APRIL 1, 1917.

The Deputy Minister,
    Department of the Naval Service,
        Ottawa, Canada.

SIR,—I have the honour to report regarding the Naval Service, for the fiscal year ending 31st March, 1917.

The progress, both mental and physical, of the cadets at the Royal Naval College at Halifax still proves Lost satisfactory. An examination for the entry of cadets to the college was held in May, 1916, and fourteen cadets were entered. The officers of the college continue to report most favourably on the cadets, and the midshipmen who have been serving in ships of the Royal Navy, H.M.C. ships *Niobe*, *Rainbow*, submarines *C.C.1.* and *C.C.2*, and patrol vessels, have also been most favourably reported upon and proved themselves capable and efficient. The fourteen midshipmen who entered the college in January, 1911, have been promoted to acting lieutenant. All these officers are now serving in the Royal Navy.

The requisite number of the personnel for the manning of all H.M.C. Ships and Establishments has been maintained by the entry of men with previous naval experience, and by the employment of R.N.C.V.R. officers and men.

H.M.C.S. *Niobe* continues to be employed as a depot ship at Halifax, and has also been parent ship for vessels employed on patrol work.

H.M.C.S. *Rainbow* has been continuously employed on the west coast in trade protection and other important duties, under the orders of the Imperial Senior Naval Officer of that station.

The two submarines and their parent ship, the *Shearwater*, have been actively employed for the defence of the British Columbian coasts.

A large number of other vessels, both governmental and private, are being utilized in connection with the naval defence of the coasts on such duties as examination service, mine-sweeping, patrols, and other necessary work.

Commodore Sir Charles H. Coke, K.C.V.O., recently arrived in Canada, having been lent by the Imperial Government to take charge of the Atlantic patrol, acting under the orders of this department.

The Naval Volunteers continue to do good work ashore and afloat, a considerable number serving continuously in H.M. and H.M.C. ships and vessels, both on the Atlantic and Pacific coasts of the Dominion.

Captain the Honourable R. Guinness, R.N.V.R., arrived in Canada in May, 1916, for the purpose of recruiting for the Royal Navy; however, it was decided, mainly on account of the comparatively low rates of pay in force in the Royal Navy, that this was not practicable, and the Dominion Government offered to divert to the Naval Service part of the quota which would otherwise be contributed to the Army, and to allow these men Canadian rates of pay, the men being enrolled as Canadian Naval Volunteers and placed at the disposal of the Admiralty.

This offer was accepted by the Imperial Government, and up to date, 1331 men have been enrolled in the R.N.C.V.R. (Overseas Division), of whom 1188 have actually been sent overseas.

The recruiting for this division was carried out entirely by this department, Captain Guinness assisting by holding recruiting meetings throughout the Dominion.

8 GEORGE V, A. 1918

The selection of candidates for the Royal Naval Air Service had continued, and a total of 382 officers has been entered for this service. Those entered since 20th July, 1916, have not been required to obtain their Aero Club certificates before going to England.

Commander F. P. Armstrong, with a recruiting committee, arrived in Canada in April, 1916, for the purpose of entering officers and men for the Auxiliary Patrol (motor-boat) service. The following gives the total numbers entered by him in Canada:—

Sub-lieutenants............................ 264
Chief motor mechanics...................... 52
Motor mechanics............................ 60

Commander Armstrong left Vancouver for New Zealand on the 30th August, 1916.

The duties and work carried out by the Naval Staff Office continue to increase in magnitude and importance, and have been carried out in a very satisfactory manner.

I have the honour to be, sir,
          Your obedient servant,

C. E. KINGSMILL, Admiral,
     Director of the Naval Service.   '

SURVEY OF TIDES AND CURRENTS.

DEPARTMENT OF THE NAVAL SERVICE,
OTTAWA, March 31, 1917.

The Deputy Minister,
    Department of the Naval Service,
        Ottawa.

SIR,—I have the honour to submit the following report regarding the Survey of Tides and Currents during the twelve months ending March 31, 1917.

One direction in which considerable progress has been made is in the methods of calculation for slack water; the improvements being based upon the experience gained in correlating the current with the tide in a number of different straits and narrows, both in eastern Canada and on the Pacific coast. Some new methods resulting from the investigations made have been applied with success to the calculation of slack water in the passes of the Pacific coast; and this will contribute to the greater accuracy of the tide tables published in future years. The general work of the Survey has been continued without interruption, and further observations of the tides or currents have been carried out during the summer season on both coasts, as well as in Hudson bay.

PRINCIPAL TIDAL STATIONS.

The six principal stations in eastern Canada and five in British Columbia have been maintained in continuous operation throughout the year. The observations obtained from these stations, after careful reduction, are submitted to harmonic analysis, by which tidal constants are obtained as a basis for the calculation of the tide tables. The data for the purpose are thus improved as additional years of tidal record are obtained. As the work of this character was done for the benefit of eastern Canada last year, it was carried forward to improve the tidal constants for the Pacific coast during the present year. Four complete years of tidal record from Clayoquot were submitted to analysis, two years from port Simpson, two years from Prince Rupert, and one year from Vancouver. Also two complete years of tidal record from point Atkinson were reduced; this being a new station for the strait of Georgia, which is found to be practically identical with Sand Heads. The observations at Sand Heads were obtained in the early years of this Survey at the lighthouse there, which has since been removed and replaced by a lightship. These further observations at point Atkinson will enable the observations to be carried forward for a longer period. This work of reduction and analysis will improve, therefore, the accuracy of the tide tables for the ports mentioned, and this will be a distinct advantage as it is from the tide tables at Clayoquot, Sand Heads, and port Simpson, that the various tables of slack water are calculated.

FURTHER TIDAL OBSERVATIONS OBTAINED.

During last season, tidal observations in eastern Canada were obtained at the head of the bay of Fundy and along the north coast of Prince Edward island. On the Pacific coast a tidal station was established at the farthest available point at the north end of the strait of Georgia and also at points in the channels opposite the north end of Vancouver island, to obtain a basis for the revision of the tidal data in that region, especially in Johnstone strait, where the heaviest traffic takes place.

Bay of Fundy.—The highest tides of the bay of Fundy are known to occur in Cumberland basin, and in Cobequid bay at the eastern end of Minas basin. Fairly extended observations were taken in Cumberland basin during the surveys for the Baie Verte canal in 1870. It appeared, however, from preliminary comparisons of such data as were available, that the tide is higher in Cobequid bay. The upper part of this bay is obstructed with sand bars; and a point was therefore selected at Burntcoat head, which is as far up as the whole tide can be measured at any one locality. There is no wharf at this point, or other artificial facilities, for the erection of a registering tide gauge, so that the observations were taken by direct levelling or by scale readings. The results were compared with simultaneous observations at the principal station for the bay of Fundy, situated at St. John, N.B. The observations in Cumberland basin, which are broken and imperfect, were also carefully reduced for comparison; and some results were also obtained from observations taken for part of a month in 1859 in Noel bay, during the Admiralty surveys for the chart. This bay is within a few miles of Burntcoat head.

The results of this work need not be enlarged upon as they will be given in a special report entitled: "Tides at the head of the bay of Fundy". A full discussion of the behaviour of the tide at this locality at the extreme head of the bay is there given. The data arrived at will throw light upon the features of the tide throughout the bay of Fundy, and will add to our knowledge of tides in general.

Prince Edward island; North Coast.—A series of tide gauges were erected along the north coast of Prince Edward island to obtain simultaneous observations throughout this region. It was desirable to obtain this while the principal station at St. Paul island is still in good working order, as it is one of the most difficult stations to maintain, and the tides of this coast must be referred to it. The points selected for tidal stations were Tignish, Alberton, Malpeque in Richmond bay, Rustico, St. Pierre and Naufrage.

The tide is quite special in its character on this coast, as there are times when only one high water and one low water in the day are pronounced, the other two being effaced. At these times the tide becomes diurnal. There was much difficulty in reducing the observations satisfactorily, but a full explanation of the nature of the tide will be given in the tide tables. The information obtained also enables the characteristics of the tide throughout the southern half of the gulf of St. Lawrence to be more adequately described.

The rise of the tide on this coast is of much value to vessels; especially in heavy weather, as the harbours are largely used for refuge, and most of them have bars across the mouth. A vessel can thus enter more safely at high water during a storm. It is thus always convenient and sometimes necessary for a mariner to know the time of high water.

These observations have also enabled a consistent series of low-water datums to be determined along this coast. This will be of service to the Public Works department for dredging and for harbour improvements.

Lower St. Lawrence.—By co-operation with the Hydrographic Survey, observations were continued at Grand Mechins and Godbout, this latter being practically the same as Point des Monts, the true dividing point between the gulf of St. Lawrence and the estuary. Good results have been obtained from these observations, which will serve as a connecting link between the estuary of the St. Lawrence and the observations obtained in 1910 along the north shore of the gulf from bay of Seven Islands eastward.

Pacific Coast.—In the region of Johnstone strait, through which heavy traffic passes not only from Vancouver to Prince Rupert but also from the Puget Sound ports to Alaska, observations of the tide were obtained in 1900 at Alert bay, Blinkinshop, and Chatham point. These observations were obtained by the survey staff of H.M.S. *Egeria*, and they should properly be referred to Port Simpson; but no observations there in that year were available. A special tide table for comparison was therefore calculated for port Simpson for the year 1900, based on the tidal constants which have been derived from seven years of tidal record there. The comparison enabled tidal differences with port Simpson to be obtained for these three localities. As a further basis for this region, a registering tide gauge was erected at the mouth of Salmon river, twenty-two miles north-west of Chatham point. At this locality, simultaneous observations with the permanent station at port Simpson were obtained during five months. In this way, the tidal data for the whole region from Seymour narrows to Alert bay were carefully revised.

Observations were obtained for the first time at two localities on the back channels off the main line of navigation, namely, at a point in the vicinity of Forward harbour and at Shoal bay at the main angle of Cordero channel, between Bute inlet and Loughborough inlet. The further tidal data thus obtained will be of benefit to the local steamers which have ports of call in this region.

The observations obtained in co-operation with the Hydrographic Survey have afforded improved data for Ocean Falls in Cousins inlet, which has been recently surveyed; and also for Queen Charlotte and Shingle bay in Skidegate inlet, Queen Charlotte islands. A tide gauge supplied to that Survey was erected last season at Granby bay in Observatory inlet, which is rapidly developing as a mining centre. This will enable the time and height of the tide to be known there, with reference to port Simpson.

INVESTIGATION OF THE CURRENTS.

The gut of Canso.—Observations of the turn of the current in this strait were continued during the past season, from May to November. They were taken by the captain of the Ferry steamer *Scotia* assisted by his first officer. After the experience of the previous season, it was possible to get more satisfactory observations and to make them more continuous during the night. Owing to the complex nature of the current, it was found best to plot these observations in the form of a diagram; and from this, a very thorough digest was made, in view of the different variations which the current presents.

The general characteristics and the varying behaviour of this current were found to be in accord with the explanations already given in the tide tables. The longer series of observations enabled more definite values to be obtained for the different elements which go to make up the behaviour which the current actually shows. There is a large inequality in the flow of the current in the two directions which follows the declination of the moon, and this is further complicated by a dominant flow in one direction. It is thus only when the moon is near the equator that it is possible to obtain any satisfactory correlation with the time of the tide. An investigation of this relation was undertaken, however, as it is valuable in showing the best methods by which such problems can be treated. As a final result, it was found that the turn of the currents accords with the time of half tide rising and falling at St. Paul island. This relation with half tide, that is, with the moment midway between the time of high water and low water, or between low water and high water, is an instructive result, as it indicates a principle which may be applicable elsewhere. It is also instructive to know that the current in this strait is related to the tide at St. Paul island which is exactly opposite the gut at the other end of Cape Breton island. It has been found elsewhere that the turn of the current in a strait behind an island is in accord

8 GEORGE V, A. 1918

with the tide on the outside of the island. Such relations indicate the manner in which currents in other regions may be dealt with, in order to calculate the time of slack water for the benefit of the mariner. In this case, the most practical result of the investigation is an explanation of the behaviour of the current so that the navigator may know what to expect.

Seymour Narrows.—From the experience gained in the cases above described, and the successful result which was obtained for Seymour inlet as explained in last year's report, an endeavour was made on similar lines to obtain a better basis for the calculation of slack water in Seymour narrows. After an extended series of trials, a remarkably constant relation was obtained between the time of slack water and half tide; the moment of half tide being half way between high water at Sand Heads in the strait of Georgia and low water at port Simpson. This method applies to the calculation of low-water slack, for which a complex method has been used in calculating the slack water tables during the last three years. It is a declination method, and is described in outline in the tide tables, and although quite satisfactory in itself, it involves an elaborate technique which has to be followed with great care to avoid accidental errors, which would be large if they occurred. The new method of calculation from the time of half tide as above mentioned is simpler, in being straightforward. The reason for the accuracy of the result which it gives is that the variation due to the change in the moon's declination is balanced out by the relative changes in the tides themselves instead of being based on the moon's change in position. By disposing of this variation, which is the most troublesome one to deal with, it becomes possible to apply a correction to take up the variation from springs to neaps. This correction can be applied to both high-water and low-water slack.

These two methods were thoroughly tested out by calculating slack water for three months in the year 1913 and comparing the results with the time of slack water as actually observed. The ultimate advantage obtained may be summed up by saying that this method is quite as accurate as the former declination method and that it eliminates the chance of errors in the calculation. This explanation may also serve to show the advantage that may result from the investigation of the behaviour of all classes of currents in different regions, in the improvement of methods of calculation.

Active Pass.—This pass is the most important of those which lead between the Gulf islands, as it is the one chiefly used by ocean-going vessels between Vancouver and Victoria. The behaviour of the current is more subject to variation than in the other passes, because of its being near to the south end of the chain of Gulf islands. Further observations of slack water in this pass were begun last May and will be continued throughout the winter. Some improvements have already been obtained, in the calculation values for slack water in the tide tables.

It has now been ascertained that a marked improvement in the calculations can be gained by referring high-water slack in this pass to the tide of the open Pacific at Clayoquot and low-water slack to the tide in the strait of Georgia. It has also been found advisable in the case of low-water slack to distinguish the half tide from lower low water; and although this involves considerably more labour in the calculation, it gives a distinctly better result. In the case of high-water slack, the only change allowed for is the annual variation in the values during the successive months of the year. When the present observations are completed, the calculation values will be revised, however, to make them as accurate as possible, and thus to improve the slack water tables.

Similar methods for Porlier pass have been used for the first time in the calculation for the tide tables of 1918. These two passes serve as standard ones from which the time of slack water in the other passes between the Gulf islands can be obtained by a difference of time. This system of referring one pass to another gives better results than if the time of slack water were obtained with reference to the time of the tide. It is also quite as convenient to the navigator to apply the differences to a table of slack water as to a tide table.

Wellbore channel.—This channel forms an entrance to the eastern passages leading to the Yuculta, which are preferred in the lumber traffic as the most convenient route. Observations of the time of slack water in Whirlpool rapids in Wellbore channel were therefore undertaken during last season from June to November. It was found that the time of slack water in this rapid can be referred to Seymour narrows, in the same way as several other tidal rapids in that region. This information will be of much value to the lumber industry which is developing in that region, as it is only possible, in towing rafts, to pass during slack water.

HUDSON BAY AND THE ARCTIC OCEAN.

Further observations were obtained at Nelson during last season. These were supervised by the wireless operator. The results have enabled the calculations for that port to be improved, and the small changes which the observations show to be necessary, indicate that the present basis of calculation is closely accurate.

Tidal data for James bay have now been obtained for two islands near the head of the bay, and for Moose factory. These two islands have been used as bases for the work of the Hydrographic Survey; and the tidal information was obtained by co-operation with that survey, in supplying it with the necessary outfit. Good data for the tide will thus be available for any railway terminals, or other works which may be contemplated in James bay.

During the progress of the Stefansson expedition, praiseworthy endeavours were made to obtain tidal information at several points in the Arctic ocean. In the vicinity of cape Kellett, simultaneous observations were obtained for a few days at a time at the cape and at a point twenty miles north. Also along the north coast of the main land, tidal observations were obtained at Collinson point, Martin point, and Demarkation point, as well as at Bernard harbour in Union strait.

The difficulty in dealing with these observations is that the tide in these open regions is usually less than one foot in range, and seldom as much as $1\frac{1}{2}$ feet, except in Union strait, where it occasionally exceeds 2 feet. Although the observations were perseveringly taken every 15 minutes day and night for several days at a time, the results that can be obtained from them are rather indefinite. The time of high and low water is necessarily uncertain. Careful abstracts and reductions have been made, however, in the endeavour to determine the establishment at these points, and the range at spring and neap tides. A knowledge of the establishment would be valuable if trustworthy in the circumstances, as it would show the direction in which the tide progresses in the open waters of the Arctic ocean.

INFORMATION SUPPLIED.

As this Survey becomes more widely known, a large number of requests are received for information. Some of these can be met by sending reports or other published information; but in reply to a number of requests it is necessary to work out special data. The new information obtained by this Survey is also communicated to the Hydrographer to the British Navy, to afford improvements in the data for Canada which are published in the British tide tables. Advance information is often communicated also to owners of vessels and

8 GEORGE V, A. 1918

fishing establishments in the regions where further information has been obtained during the season. This reaches them before it can be issued in the tide tables.

The determinations of mean sea-level, made by this Survey at several of the principal tidal stations, have been communicated to the Deputy Head of the Commission of Conservation for his new edition of "Altitudes in Canada." An abstract of the results of these determinations is given, in the introduction to this work, for Halifax, St. John, N.B., Quebec, Victoria, Vancouver and Prince Rupert. This indicated the bases of the altitudes, as they are all referred to mean-sea-level.

The extended levels of the Geodetic Branch of the Public Works Department are run on lines which make frequent connection with the shore between Halifax and Quebec. The benchmarks of the Tidal Survey, as well as some Admiralty bench-marks are thus connected with this system of levels. The Tidal Survey has accordingly supplied the tide levels for a number of localities in this region, which enhances the value of the forthcoming publication of these geodetic levels, as well as affording the corresponding advantage of connecting together the bench-marks of the Tidal Survey which originally were isolated and unconnected.

A similar service has been rendered in connection with the precise levelling of the Dominion observatory; in affording correct determinations of mean sea-level at Halifax, Yarmouth and Vancouver, on the two coasts, as a correct basis for extended levels. The true value of mean sea-level, as determined from continuous observations of the tide during a number of years, is thus proving of value in these levelling operations.

Special information on tide levels and extreme tides has also been deduced during the year from the tidal records now available, to meet the immediate requirements of railway engineers and district engineers of the Public Works Department, in regions in which they are interested.

Accuracy of the Tide Tables.—To test the degree of accuracy that the tide tables have now attained, comparisons have been made between the tables and the tides as actually observed during 1916. This series of comparisons comprised three of the harbours and reference stations in eastern Canada, and five on the Pacific coast. The deduction from these comparisons showed: (1) the average amount of error during the month, and of improvement on former years obtained by the further analysis of tidal record; and (2) any tendency in the tides as calculated for the tide tables, to be early or late on the average. Valuable indications are thus obtained regarding progress made.

PUBLICATION.

Eastern coasts of Canada.—The tide tables for this coast are issued in three editions. One is a complete edition containing all tidal information, and now amounting to 8,000 copies. The other two are abridged editions of pocket size, one for Quebec and the St. Lawrence and the other for St. John and the bay of Fundy. These two editions have now been increased to 21,000, as there are many navigators as well as fishermen who require local information and do not need the complete edition.

Tidal information for Quebec and the St. Lawrence is supplied to the Marine Department for its publication for the ship channel between Montreal and Father Point. This is especially intended for the pilot service. Tidal information for the summer season is also sent locally to three of the summer resorts on the lower St. Lawrence for the convenience of those who frequent these.

Pacific coast.—The circulation of the tide tables on this coast continues to increase. The complete edition for the coast is now 15,000 copies; and an abridged edition for the southern part of British Columbia has been increased to 12,000. This abridgement supplies a large demand for local tide tables for Vancouver, the Fraser river, and the passes in that vicinity. This is found very convenient and serviceable by all classes from pilots to fishermen and for motor-boat traffic.

The tide tables on the Pacific coast are appreciated by the lumber industry and the coal trade, in addition to their direct service to ordinary navigation. The tables are also much used by fishermen, as the best catch is often taken during some special stage of the tide.

The various editions of the tide tables are supplied without charge to the steamship companies, and to all applicants for them. They are largely circulated through the agencies of the Marine Department, the custom offices, pilot and shipping offices. A large proportion of them are mailed individually, and many are sent in reply to requests received.

Republication in Great Britain.—In the general tide tables issued by the British Admiralty there are tide tables for eight important harbours in eastern Canada and the Pacific coast. These are St. John, Halifax, Father Point, and Quebec; and on the Pacific coast Victoria, Sand Heads, Clayoquot and port Simpson. With these tables, tidal differences are given which extend their use to numerous other ports.

Hudson Bay.—Tide tables for Nelson in Hudson bay are published for the months of July to October. The method by which these are calculated has been explained above. The height of the tide is referred to the chart datum. In these tables tidal data are given for Churchill as well as several points in James bay, which have been recently added from new observations obtained there. These tables also include data for six points in the length of Hudson strait, and Ungava bay. The chief matter which is of practical importance there, is the time of the tide, to afford a basis for comparison with the strong tidal streams in this strait. These streams are due to the great rise of the tide, which is from 20 to 35 feet.

Bay of Fundy.—Under the heading of publications may be mentioned the report on " The tides at the head of the bay of Fundy," as already explained herein. This report, now in press, consists of twenty-one pages of text with twelve pages of tables, and two plates comprising a map and a plan. This report will cover information for which requests are often received.

STAFF.

The staff of this Survey for the office and field work, comprises only four in addition to the superintendent, together with the outside tidal observers who number six in eastern Canada and five on the Pacific coast at the permanent tidal stations. In addition to these, several others are employed locally in the summer season, in the observation of tides or currents; and considerable information is also obtained through co-operation with other Surveys, as already explained.

In the field last season, Mr. S. C. Hayden supervised the observation of the currents in the passes of British Columbia, the erection of tide gauges, fitting out the observers, and also inspecting the tidal stations on that coast. In Eastern Canada, Mr. H. W. Jones supervised the erection of the series of summer stations on the north coast of Prince Edward island; and carried out the important repairs to the tide gauge at St. Paul island, in reconstructing the crib work which protects it, and strengthening it with concrete. He also inspected those of the

8 GEORGE V, A. 1918

principal stations which required it.   On the bay of Fundy, Mr. R. B. Lee assisted the superintendent in the observations and levelling which form the basis for the special report above mentioned.

During the winter season, the tidal record from the principal stations which accumulates in summer requires attention; and the reduction of this record and its preparation for analysis has to be made.   The observations at the summer stations have also to be dealt with, and the slack water observations in the passes and narrows require to be brought to practical shape for calculation purposes, or to afford improved data for mariners.   There is also the calculation and publication of five sets of tide tables to be carried out during the winter months.   This is done by the same staff as above mentioned, with the assistance of Miss S. L. Howell in the reduction and computations, as well as carrying on the correspondence and attending to the office work in the summer season when most of the staff are away.

I have the honour to be, sir,
Your obedient servant,

W. BELL DAWSON,
Superintendent of Tidal Surveys.

HYDROGRAPHIC SURVEY.

DEPARTMENT OF THE NAVAL SERVICE,
April 1, 1917.

The Deputy Minister,
Department of Naval Service.
Ottawa.

SIR,—I have the honour to submit my report on the work of the Hydrographic Survey during the fiscal year 1916-17. During the year no additions were made to the equipments of the surveys, but all the vessels have been kept in the usual good condition. The following members of the staff have obtained leave and joined the Overseas Forces, namely, Messrs. J. A. Turner; O. R. Parker, R.N.R.; F. Delaute; C. B. R. MacDonald; Norman Wilson; Clifford Smith and W. J. Miller. Commander John Knight, R.N., of the pacific Coast Survey has accepted a commission on the Canadian cruiser *Rainbow*, and Mr. H. Lawson has accepted an appointment as instructor in the Royal Military College, Kingston. The positions held by these officers have not been filled.

The following parties were in the field during the summer of 1916:—

First.—The Atlantic Coast Survey, under Captain Anderson, with the steamer *Acadia*, working off the approach to Halifax harbour.

Second.—The Pacific Coast Survey under Lieutenant-Commander P. C. Musgrave, R.N., with the steamer *Lillooet*, working around the Queen Charlotte islands, British Columbia.

Third.—The Lower St. Lawrence Survey under Mr. Charles Savary, with the steamer *Cartier*, working in the mouth of the St. Lawrence river.

Fourth.—The Lake Superior Survey No. 1 under Mr. H. D. Parizeau, with the steamer *La Canadienne*, in Nipigon bay, lake Superior;

Fifth.—The Lake Superior Survey No. 2 under Mr. G. A. Bachand, with the steamer *Bayfield*, working around Michipicoten island, lake Superior;

Sixth.—The Kingston Harbour Survey under Mr. Paul Jobin, with a launch and shore party working at the entrance to Kingston harbour;

Seventh.—The automatic gauges under Mr. Charles Price, superintending the working of the automatic gauges on the Great Lakes and in the St. Lawrence river.

ATLANTIC COAST SURVEY.

The *Acadia* was again fitted out for service at H.M.C. Dockyard, Halifax, and commissioned on the 15th of June.

The work of this party consisted in re-sounding the approach to Halifax harbour, using the Admiralty charts for bases, or the area off that portion of the coast between Egg island and Pennant point. The soundings were carried off shore a distance of 20 miles, and as close inshore as was safe for the navigation of the ship. All the main shoals shown on the Admiralty charts were re-examined, and upon many of them was found considerably less water, whilst in other cases no trace of some of the shoals marked could be found. About two dozen uncharted rocks were located, and Notices to Mariners issued.

The main triangulation of 1916 was extended to the northeastward as far as Liscomb harbour, and to the southwestward as far as port Medway, an extreme distance of 115 miles. Bases about a mile long were measured at each of these harbours, and the agreement with the triangulated lengths was very close.

8 GEORGE V, A. 1918

In the spring a re-survey of Bedford basin was started, and completed during the summer. A new chart on a good scale of this important basin will shortly be issued.

During the season an examination was made of Lockport harbour, and additional shoals found in the entrance to it.

As opportunity offered, observations for magnetic declination were obtained with a Unifilar magnetometer at the following points:—

Station.	Locality.	Latitude.	Longitude	Date.	Declination.
Sand point.............	Shelburne harbour......	N. 43–42..	W. 65–19..	October.....	19–40·0 West.
Krout point............	LaHave river..........	" 44–17..	" 64–20..	"	21–00·0 "
Hubbards cove.........	St. Margarets bay......	" 44–38..	" 64–03..	September .	21–52·8 "
West entrance..........	Jeddore harbour.......	" 44–43..	" 63–01..	" ..	22–37·9 "
MacNab island........	Halifax harbour........	" 44–37..	" 63–32..	August.....	22–10·6 "
Near Back Lt. H......	Sambro harbour........	" 44–28..	" 63–36..	" ..	21–53·4 "
Day cove..............	Ship harbour..........	" 44–45..	" 62–49..	September .	22–38·2 "
Monahan I.............	Sheet harbour........	" 44–51..	" 62–32..	November..	23–05·0 "
Pye point.............	Liscomb harbour.......	" 45–01..	" 62–01..	" ..	23–30·0 "

Captain Anderson reports that the weather for surveying was exceptionally bad; while not very stormy, very much fog prevailed. Owing to fog and snow and rain, during fifty-four days out of the season of five months, nothing could be accomplished.

The season was brought to a close and the steamer laid up at H.M.C. Dockyard, Halifax, on the 24th of November. On the following day the crew were paid off and the staff returned to Ottawa. The staff for the season consisted of Assistants R. J. Fraser, L. C. Prittie, and J. L. Foreman.

As a result of the season's work the following new charts will be issued:—

"Bedford basin," including the Narrows, on a scale of six inches to one nautical mile;

"Egg island to Pennant point" including Halifax harbour on a scale of eight thousand feet to the inch. For this chart recourse has been taken to the Admiralty charts of the neighbourhood for topography and inshore soundings.

PACIFIC COAST SURVEY.

The steamer *Lillooet* was fitted out at H.M.C. Dockyard, Esquimalt, B.C., and commissioned for service on the 10th of April.

On the passage north, examination was made of Retreat cove in Trincomali channel, and also of Millbank sound, where some additional traversing of the shore-line was carried out and a hunt made for the position of the rock marked "P.D." on the Admiralty chart. The hunt was unsuccessful, so that if the rock does exist, its position has not been determined.

Additional surveying of Alice arm was commenced on the 26th of April, it being the extension of the work done on the chart "Granby bay and approaches." The survey was continued until the 27th of May, and the ship resumed her regular work at Queen Charlotte islands early in June. During the month, sounding was carried off the west side of Queen Charlotte islands in the western approach to Dixon entrance. For the balance of the fine weather, or until the middle of September, work proceeded in Hecate strait and in the neighbourhood of Queen Charlotte city.

On the latter date the party returned to Alice arm, resumed operations and completed the survey of the inlet by the 28th of October. Esquimalt was reached on the 4th of November, where the steamer was laid up and the crew paid off.

In connection with this report, Captain Musgrave expresses his gratitude to the Geodetic Survey of Canada for the great assistance they have given him in connecting his stations with those of its main triangulation and thus giving accurate astronomical positions as groundwork for the Hydrographic Survey charts. In this way, good determinations have been obtained of Prince Rupert, of Granby bay and Alice arm.

A careful examination was made of the east and west narrows of Skidegate channel which gives easy access for fishing vessels operating from Prince Rupert to the fishing grounds west of Queen Charlotte islands. Were some dredging done in these narrows the channel would be much improved.

Owing to Commander Knight and Messrs. Turner and Parker going on active service, the staff of this party was reduced to one assistant, Mr. Davies, so that the usual amount of work was not obtained. It was also necessary to leave the schooner *Naden* out of commission at New Westminster.

LOWER ST. LAWRENCE.

The steamer *Cartier* was fitted out at the Marine Department Agency at Quebec and went into commission on the 8th of May, in charge of Mr. Charles Savary, and Assistants Messrs. Edward Ghysens, M. A. MacKinnon, and E. B. MacColl.

During the season the main triangulation of the south shore was extended as far east as Marten river, and on the north shore to Egg island lighthouse.

As a result of the season's work the survey reached as far east as pointe Des Monts and a new chart entitled " Pointe Des Monts to Father Point " taking in both shores of the St. Lawrence river is about ready for the printer.

The party returned to Quebec about the first week in November and the crew were paid off.

LAKE SUPERIOR PARTY NO. 1.

The steamer *La Canadienne* was fitted out at Owen Sound, and with Mr. H. D. Parizeau and his assistants, Messrs. F. R. Mortimer and H. L. Leadman, left that port on the 4th of May and proceeded to lake Superior, where the survey of Nipigon bay was started on the 12th of May and continued until the 13th of September. On the latter date the party moved to Black bay, but, unfortunately in entering ran aground and by the time the steamer was docked and repaired in the dry-dock at Port Arthur, it was too late to resume operations, which were transferred to Port Arthur and Fort William and continued until the 21st of October, when the steamer left for Owen Sound, arriving on the 5th of November, when the crew were paid off.

On the way east, several shoals that had been reported as omitted from the charts were examined and their positions determined, so that they can be charted. As a result of the season's work an excellent chart of Nipigon bay is now ready for the printer, and will be issued before the opening of navigation 1918.

LAKE SUPERIOR PARTY NO. 2.

The steamer *Bayfield* was fitted out at the Marine Department depot, Prescott, and commissioned on the 1st of May, 1916. Mr. G. A. Bachand, with his assistants, Messrs. J. U. Beauchemin and W. K. Willis, proceeded to lake Superior to take up the work where it was dropped by Mr. Parizeau in the autumn of 1915. Work around Otter head and along the shore to the eastward of it was undertaken in connection with the survey of the shores of Michipicoten island, and continued until the 25th of October, when, owing to bad weather and trouble with the boiler of the steamer, it was deemed advisable to discontinue and proceed to Owen Sound, where the party arrived on the 27th of October.

8 GEORGE V, A. 1918

As a result of the season's work, coupled with some of Mr. Parizeau's work in 1915, a new chart entitled " Michipicoten island to Oiseau bay " has been handed to the King's Printer, and in addition to this, an excellent plan has been made of Quebec harbour, Michipicoten island. I regret to say that both Mr. Parizeau and Mr. Bachand report that work was greatly hindered during the season by lack of crew. The men were very hard to get, wages were high, and they were difficult to handle. I am afraid that due to the unsettled condition of the country, we will have great difficulty in making good headway.

KINGSTON HARBOUR.

Mr. Paul Jobin was supplied with a gasolene launch and instructed to undertake the re-survey of the entrance to Kingston harbour. He arrived at Kingston on the 18th of May, and was joined by an assistant, Mr. LeRoy T. Bowes. He also had difficulties obtaining men, but eventually settled down to very good work, but was unable to complete the work outlined for him. This work will be continued in the coming season, and a chart issued in the spring of 1918.

AUTOMATIC GAUGES.

The work of looking after the automatic gauges on the Great Lakes and St. Lawrence river as far east as Cap Rouge in is charge of Mr. Charles Price who has been assisted by Mr. C. F. Hannington, C.E., and Mr. A. R. Lee.

The following eleven gauges were operated during 1916 on the Great Lakes:

Port Arthur	Lake Superior	Jan.	1	to	Dec. 31.
Michipicoten harbour	"	June	15	"	31
Sault Ste. Marie	Above locks	Jan.	1	"	31.
Sault Ste. Marie	Below locks	Jan..	1	"	31.
Collingwood	Georgian bay	Jan.	1	"	31.
Goderich	Lake Huron	June	1	"	16.
Ile Aux Peches	Detroit river	Jan.	1	"	31.
Fighting island		Jan.	1	"	31.
Port Colburne	Lake Erie	Jan.	1	"	31.
Port Dalhousie	Lake Ontario	May	29	"	15.
Kingston	"	Jan.	1	"	31.

During 1916 the following eighteen gauges were operated on the lower St. Lawrence river:—

Pointe Claire	Lake St. Louis	Jan.	1	to	Dec. 31.
Verdun	St. Lawrence river	"	1	"	31.
Montreal (foot of lock 1)	" "	April	28	"	23.
Laurier pier, Montreal (new)	" "	July	24	"	22.
Longue pointe	" "	May	1	"	22.
Varennes	" "	April	28	to	Nov. 27.
Verchères	" "	"	27	to	Dec. 22.
Lanoraie	" "	May.	1	to	Nov. 25.
Sorel	" "	April	19	to	Dec. 31.
Range Light No. 2	Lake St. Peter	May	10	to	Nov. 19.
Nicolet river (new)	" "	Aug.	28	"	23.
Three Rivers	St. Lawrence river	April	20	"	27.
Batiscan	" "	May	3	"	25.
Cap à la Roche	" "	"	5	"	24.
Richelieu Rapids	" "	"	20	"	25.
Pointe Platon	" "	"	5	"	14.
Neuville	" "	"	6	"	16.
St. Nicholas	" "	"	8	"	25.

The gauges at Sorel and Pointe Claire are now being maintained during the whole year, and the gauges at Montreal (foot of Lock No. 1) Laurier pier, Longue Pointe, and Verchères, were operated until December 22, 1916, when a sudden raise of water made it necessary to remove them before being flooded. During the past winter there were also two staff gauge readings taken each day at Verdun and Laurier pier.

The seven gauges from Three Rivers to St. Nicholas, inclusive, are compiled by half hourly readings, and the time and elevation of high and low is also tab-

SESSIONAL PAPER No. 38

ulated. The work connected with tabulating the records from each of these automatic gauges equals that required by fully four of the regular gauges compiled by hourly readings only.

All gauges are installed and operated from wharves, except at the Nicolet river and the Richelieu rapids. For these two gauges it was necessary to drive piles and erect a platform to work from.

The main difficulty in operating the gauges is in obtaining reliable men as attendants. The lack of care by an attendant often causes the loss of readings and sometimes the breaking down of the gauge itself.

ISSUE OF CHARTS.

During the past year the following new charts were issued from this office:—

```
106  "Peninsula harbour and port Munro."
 68  "Kingston to Deseronto" (bay of Quinte).
 69  "Deseronto to Presqu'ile (bay of Quinte).
 95  "Meldrum point to St. Joseph island."
310  "Fisher channel and Cousins inlet."
311  "Harbours in Queen Charlotte islands."
 84  "Parry Sound and approaches."
 85  "McCoy islands to Collins inlet."
 89  "Penetanguishene harbour."
312  "Granby bay and approaches."
407  "Anchorages in Hudson strait."
 62  "Newcastle harbour to Toronto."
104  "Oiseau bay to Copper island."
210  "Bersimis river to Bic island."
209  "Saguenay river, St. Fulgence to Shipshaw."
```

The following new editions of former issues of charts have been published:—

```
207  "Malbaie to Goose island."
 50  "Lake St. Louis."
 52  "Lake St. Francis" (eastern portion).
 53  "Lake St. Francis" (western portion).
 94  "Little Current."
204  "Bic island to White island."
 86  "Georgian bay to Clapperton island."
  7  "Ile Aux Foins to ile de Grace."
  8  "Head of lake St. Peter."
 16  "Ste. Emmelie to Deschambault."
 19  "St. Antoine to St. Augustin."
 21  "Quebec harbour."
```

The Survey is engaged in the preparation of sets of thirty charts each, of the edition published by the late International Waterways Commission, showing the boundary between St. Regis, Quebec, and Pigeon bay. Owing to various difficulties this work has not made as good headway as it should have done, but it is hoped that it will be completed during the summer. The following of the charts were published during the year:—

```
 1  "St. Lawrence river, St. Regis to Dickinson landing."
20  "General chart of lake Huron."
22  "North channel and St. Marys river, Potagannissing bay to foot of Mud lake."
28  "General chart of lake Superior,—Whitefish point to Pigeon bay."
```

The following works have been issued to the public:—

```
"St. Lawrence Pilot,—Below Quebec" (new edition);
"Report of the International Waterways Commission" describing the boundary line between
    St. Regis, Quebec, and Pigeon bay.
```

In closing this report I have to express my thanks to all the members of the staff for the valuable service they have rendered during the past year.

I have the honour to be, sir,
Your obedient servant,

WM. J. STEWART,
Hydrographer.

MONTHLY MEAN water surface elevations of "Great lakes" for 1916, by automatic water gauges, and referred to mean sea level.

Location.		Jan.	Feb.	Mar.	April.	May.	June.	July.	Aug.	Sept.	Oct.	Nov.	Dec.	Mean.
		Feet.	Feet.	Feet.	Feet.	Feet.	Feet.	Feet.	Feet.	Feet.	Feet.	Feet.	Feet.	Feet.
Lake Superior	Port Arthur	602·48	602·42	602·22	602·33	603·01	603·50	603·78	603·75	603·83	603·60	603·40	603·09	603·12
St. Mary's river	Above Locks	601·85	601·74	601·43	601·70	602·33	602·75	603·00	603·02	603·02	602·73	602·61	602·27	602·37
	Below Locks	581·83	582·06	582·09	581·90	582·02	582·74	582·89	583·17	583·32	583·35	583·08	582·62	582·62
Georgian bay	Collingwood	579·37	579·51	579·33	579·84	580·43	580·81	581·09	581·07	580·92	580·67	580·70	580·60	580·36
Lake Huron	Goderich						580·91	581·16	581·12	580·04	580·73	580·76	580·74 till 16	580·91
Detroit river	Isle aux Peches	574·37	574·06	573·66	574·57	575·12	575·63	575·67	575·42	574·99	574·68	574·46	574·86	574·79
	Fighting island	573·68	573·65	573·45	574·04	574·51	575·01	575·07	574·80	574·36	574·02	573·76	574·14	574·21
Lake Erie	Port Colborne	571·89	571·93	571·53	572·18	572·62	·573·00	573·02	572·58	572·20	571·84	571·70	571·71	572·18
Lake Ontario	Port Dalhousie						247·89	247·92	247·29	246·57	245·95	245·62	245·38 till 15	246·66
	Kingston	244·99	245·22	245·21	245·83	247·07	247·78	247·83	247·25	246·60	246·00	245·60	245·30	246·22

SESSIONAL PAPER No. 38

DAILY MEAN water surface elevations of lake St. Louis, at Pointe Claire, Que. for 1916, elevations are above mean sea-level and are referred to C.B.M. CCCCIII on S.E. corner of R.C. Church. Elevation 83.95.

Day.	Jan.	Feb.	Mar.	April.	May.	June.	July.	Aug.	Sept.	Oct.	Nov.	Dec.
1	68·23	69·45	68·81	70·28	71·98	72·04	70·67	69·36	68·63	68·17	68·34	68·12
2	68·39	69·14*	69·11	70·80	72·07	71·94	70·62	69·24	68·57	68·14	68·34	68·09
3	68·60	69·20	68·95	71·26	72·10*	71·84	70·59	69·17	68·49	68·12	68·34	68·09
4	68·60	69·00	68·71	71·27	72·21*	71·85	70·56	69·17	68·49	68·09	68·30	68·02
5	68·80	68·92	68·46	71·09	72·24	71·86	70·47	69·15	68·49	68·07	68·10	67·98
6	68·80	68·94	68·42	70·99	72·30	71·82	70·40	69·12	68·42	68·05	68·05	68·15
7	69·21	68·88	68·21	71·06	72·33	71·66	70·34	69·10	68·39	68·04	68·06	68·32
8	69·49	68·86	68·12	70·93	72·36	71·48	70·27	69·06	68·39	68·03	68·07	68·37
9	69·49	68·97	68·02	70·75	72·36	71·41	70·16	69·12	68·40	67·98	68·14	68·19
10	69·60	69·03	67·89	70·71	72·32	71·48	70·07	69·26	68·37	67·97*	68·22	68·29
11	69·46	69·24	67·88	70·85	72·30	71·45	70·00	69·25	68·33	....	68·22	68·41
12	69·20	69·40	68·05	71·09	72·31	71·44	69·97	69·14	68·35	67·89	68·19	68·38
13	69·25	69·10	67·93	71·15*	72·20	71·37	70·01	69·06	68·06	63·89*	68·02*	68·28
14	69·30	68·93	67·77	71·23a	72·06	71·26	69·97	69·04	68·38	67·91*	67·87	68·22
15	69·33	68·96	67·79	71·19a	71·87	71·20	69·82	69·02	68·36	67·93	67·85	68·21
16	69·26	68·96	67·86	71·16a	71·69	71·14	69·78	69·00	68·36	67·95	67·86	68·22
17	69·10	68·85	67·87	71·37a	71·78	71·33	69·87	68·94	68·34	67·99	67·92	68·28
18	69·01	68·56	67·97	71·49a	72·42	71·61	69·86	68·90	68·33	68·05	67·97	68·62
19	68·75	68·00	68·27	71·60a	73·12	71·72	69·78	68·88	68·33	67·93	68·04	68·88
20	68·75	67·87	68·23	71·74a	73·39	71·91	69·74	68·84	68·30	67·86*	68·07	68·98
21	68·97	68·23	67·91	71·51a	73·44	71·93	69·71	68·84	68·29	68·03	68·05	68·96
22	68·49	68·63	67·83	71·16*	73·30	71·74	69·67	68·81	68·29	68·16	67·96	69·05
23	68·25	68·73	67·82	71·29	73·14	71·56	69·62	68·78	68·29	68·24	67·93	68·92
24	68·55	68·76	67·70	71·84*	73·01	71·36	69·63	68·76	68·28	68·26	68·03	68·79
25	68·63	68·64	67·63	71·88	72·90	71·22	69·62	68·72	68·25	68·23	68·09	68·96
26	68·39	68·50	67·53	71·90	72·78	71·17	69·59	68·73	68·25	63·29	67·97	69·15
27	68·39	68·20	67·49	71·87	72·59	71·06	69·55	68·72	68·22	68·41	68·08	69·30
28	68·53	68·11	67·53	71·87	72·42	70·95	69·54	68·72	68·18	68·46*	68·25	69·41
29	68·90	68·28	67·87	71·89	72·31	70·83	69·39	68·69	68·16	68·41	68·15	69·66
30	69·14	....	68·66	71·91	72·21	70·74	69·39	68·66	68·18	68·38	68·10	69·87
31	69·32	....	69·55	....	72·14	....	69·42	68·64	....	68·39	....	70·13
Mean	68·91	68·77	68·12	71·30	72·44	71·48	69·94	68·96	68·35	68·11	68·08	68·66

DAILY MEAN water surface elevations of lower St. Lawrence river, at Verdun, Que for 1916. Elevations are above mean sea-level and are referred to B.M. "V" on Bennett's house opposite wharf. Elevation 58.07.

Day.	Jan.	Feb.	Mar.	April.	May.	June.	July.	Aug.	Sept.	Oct.	Nov.	Dec.
1	34·81	39·81	42·81a	43·48a	35·95a	36·08	35·43a	34·85	34·53	34·28	34·38	34·47a
2	35·06	39·78	43·31a	44·60a	36·04a	36·03	35·45a	34·79	34·52	34·29	34·41	34·43a
3	35·11	39·69	43·81a	45·56a	36·08a	35·97	35·45a	34·74	34·47	34·30	34·39	34·38a
4	35·10	39·63	44·43a	44·93a	36·28a	35·95	35·45a	34·75	34·44	34·29	34·37	34·38a
5	35·03	39·61	44·68a	44·39a	36·33a	35·98	35·45a	34·74	34·47	34·28	34·29	34·38a
6	35·04	39·70	44·43a	44·89a	36·37a	35·97	35·37a	34·68	34·45	34·28	34·29	34·38a
7	35·11	39·91	44·06a	44·31a	36·37a	35·89	35·37a	34·69	34·44	34·27	34·29	34·47a
8	35·12	40·23	43·98a	44·06a	36·37a	35·80	35·33a	34·69	34·44	34·21	34·29	34·47a
9	35·14	40·57	44·06a	43·97a	36·37a	35·76	35·28a	34·72	34·45	34·24	34·33	34·55a
10	35·15	40·00*	44·14a	43·97a	36·28a	35·77	35·28a	34·79*	34·40	34·25	34·37	34·55a
11	36·07	....	44·06a	42·89a	36·28a	35·74	35·20a	34·77	34·42	34·21	34·37	34·55a
12	36·58*	....	44·06a	41·02a	36·28a	35·75	35·20a	34·73	34·44	34·20	34·33	34·55a
13	35·87	....	44·39a	40·77a	36·28a	35·73	35·11a	34·65	34·45	34·24	34·27	34·63a
14	36·40	....	44·31a	40·89a	36·24a	35·66	35·13a	34·69	34·45	34·24	34·22	34·72a
15	38·24	41·89a	44·23a	41·27a	36·20a	35·64	35·13a	34·68	34·44	34·21	34·22	34·72a
16	39·95	42·15a	44·48a	....	35·90*	35·59	35·09a	34·69	34·43	34·26	34·22	34·92a
17	41·26	42·06a	44·31a	....	35·92	35·67	35·09a	34·67	34·39	34·27	34·23	35·05a
18	41·62	41·99a	44·15a	38·20a	36·24	35·81	35·09a	34·64	34·42	34·30	34·25	35·22a
19	41·60	41·79a	44·31a	37·47a	36·63	35·90	35·05*	34·62	34·41	34·25	34·29	35·55a
20	41·52	41·89a	44·56a	36·70a	36·84	36·00	35·02	34·55	34·39	34·23	34·29	35·83a
21	41·14	42·44a	44·93a	36·28a	36·87	36·04	35·00	34·59	34·40	34·30	34·29	35·88a
22	41·34	42·85a	44·77a	36·08a	36·83	35·96	34·97	34·61	34·39	34·35	34·26	35·88a
23	40·45	42·98a	44·56a	36·12a	36·79	35·84	34·90	34·59	34·38	34·38	34·22	35·88a
24	39·78	42·89a	44·64	36·28a	36·64	35·72	34·95	34·59	34·34	34·38	34·27	36·01a
25	39·80	42·73a	44·77a	36·28a	36·59	35·59	34·96	34·57	34·35	34·34	34·34	35·59a
26	39·88	42·89a	44·56a	36·12a	36·52	35·59	34·94	34·56	34·34	34·41	34·34	38·42a
27	39·75	42·95a	44·43a	36·03a	36·39	35·56	34·91	34·54*	34·32	34·44	34·34	40·05a
28	39·76	42·49a	43·93a	35·95a	36·26	35·52*	34·89	34·57*	34·45	34·34	34·34	....
29	39·74	42·81a	43·75a	35·98a	36·21	35·53a	34·83	34·55	34·33	34·42	34·33	42·17a
30	39·71	....	43·60a	36·03a	36·16	35·51a	34·78	34·54	34·34	34·42	34·27*	42·17a
31	39·72	....	43·39a	....	36·15	....	34·85	34·54	....	34·43	....	42·17a
Mean	38·09	41·44	44·19a	40·16a	36·34	35·79	35·13	34·66	34·41	34·31	34·30	36·05a

*Denotes mean of less than twenty-four hourly readings. a Denotes mean of two staff Gauge readings.

8 GEORGE V, A. 1918

DAILY MEAN water surface elevations of lower St. Lawrence river, at Montreal (foot of Lachine canal) Que. for 1916.   Elevations are above mean sea-level and are referred to B.M. 637., Elevation 36.46.

Day.	Jan.	Feb.	Mar.	April.	May.	June.	July.	Aug.	Sept.	Oct.	Nov.	Dec.
1	21·06				26·92	26·55	23·99	21·76	20·46	20·05	20·83	20·56
2	22·32				26·96	26·35	23·81	21·55	20·53	20·01	20·72	20·50
3	23·59				27·21	26·08	24·09	21·37	20·34	19·98	20·69	20·35
4	23·82				27·14	26·12	24·11	21·37	20·25	19·91	20·56	20·25
5	24·79				27·19	26·16	23·86	21·34	20·42	19·74	20·46	20·22
6	26·49				27·21	26·39	23·57	21·36	20·32	19·69	20·23	20·32
7	27·02				27·17	26·36	23·41	21·22	20·25	19·63	20·27	20·68
8	28·26*				27·12	26·18	23·34	21·25	20·23	19·51	20·26	20·75
9	29·10				27·08	26·05	23·13	21·62	20·28	19·75	20·24	20·72
10	30·55				26·90	26·03	22·92	21·50	20·19	19·67	20·36	20·62
11					26·51	25·89	22·72	21·55	20·18	19·57	20·41	20·83
12					26·57	25·68	22·59	21·52	20·17	19·61	20·41	21·18
13					26·51	25·48	22·63	21·41	20·24	19·52	20·41	20·80
14					26·33	25·27	22·67	21·33	20·38	19·86	20·33	20·53
15					26·30	24·92	22·49	21·30	20·42	19·60	20·04	20·60
16					26·14	24·89	22·27	21·28	20·35	19·82	19·97	21·07
17					26·39	25·28	22·54	21·24	20·13	20·17	19·94	21·54
18					26·95	25·71	22·69	21·13	20·11	20·08	19·80	22·26
19					27·82	25·84	22·63	21·04	20·10	20·00	19·75	23·46
20					28·28	26·03	22·51	20·87	20·00	19·99	19·97	24·79
21					28·51	26·18	22·41	20·80	19·91	19·94	19·91	26·17
22					28·48	26·05	22·24	20·77	19·87	20·14	19·62	27·20
23					28·15	25·74	22·06	20·67	19·97	20·36	19·67	27·97*
24					28·08	25·41	22·00	20·65	19·89	20·50	19·65	
25					27·94	25·00	21·92	20·52	19·96	20·45	19·98	
26					27·71	24·81	21·87	20·52	19·92	20·33	20·02	
27					27·47	24·69	21·92	20·47	19·85	20·67	20·04	
28					27·09	24·54	21·86	20·52	19·87	20·83	20·32	
29				26·75*	26·89	24·36	21·64	20·47	19·96	20·80	20·64	
30				26·85	26·81	24·20	21·54	20·48	20·19	20·79	20·55	
31					26·81		21·68	20·52		20·94		
Mean					27·13	25·61	22·68	21·07	20·16	20·06	20·20	21·88

DAILY MEAN water surface elevations of lower St. Lawrence river, at Laurier Pier (Montreal, Que.) for 1916.   Elevations are above mean sea-level and are referred to B.M. 637.   Elevation. 36.46.

Day.	Jan.	Feb.	Mar.	April.	May.	June.	July.	Aug.	Sept.	Oct.	Nov.	Dec.
1								20·59	19·99	18·99	19·72	19·45
2								20·39	19·37	18·94	19·58	19·40
3								20·20	19·23	18·90	19·55	19·34
4								20·19	19·12	18·82	19·50	19·20
5								20·17	19·28	18·64	19·36	19·18
6								20·21	19·19	18·59	19·13	19·18
7								20·05	19·10	18·51	19·17	19·57
8								20·08	19·08	18·37	19·15	19·66
9								20·47	19·13	18·61	19·10	19·68
10								20·32	19·10	18·51	19·20	19·54
11								20·38	19·07	18·43	19·39	19·72
12								20·36	19·03	18·50	19·31	20·12
13								20·30	19·11	18·39	19·29	19·75
14								20·17	19·25	18·74	19·26	19·48
15								20·16	19·30	18·49	18·97	19·53
16								20·13	19·25	18·68	18·90	20·08
17								20·09	19·04	19·04	18·83	20·69
18								19·99	19·00	18·96	18·66	21·51
19								19·90	18·98	18·89	18·58	22·76
20								19·75	18·86	18·88	18·82	24·21
21								19·65	18·77	18·81	18·77	25·68
22								19·59	18·73	19·00	18·51	26·49*
23								19·47	18·83	19·22	18·52	
24					20·74*			19·46	18·79	19·36	18·48	
25					20·68			19·32	18·83	19·32	18·77	
26					20·74			19·35	18·80	19·15	18·87	
27					20·68			19·32	18·73	19·51	18·88	
28					20·47			19·34	19·75	19·69	19·16	
29					20·37			19·30	18·85	19·71	19·56	
30					20·49			19·31	19·09	19·68	19·47	
31								19·35		19·82		
Mean					20·16			19·91	19·03	18·94	19·08	20·65

*Denotes mean of less than twenty-four hourly readings.

SESSIONAL PAPER No. 38

DAILY MEAN water surface elevations of lower St. Lawrence river, at Longue Pointe, Que., for 1916. Elevations are above mean sea-level and are referred to copper plug B.M. in S.E. corner of Asylum pump house. Elevation 40.477.

Day.	Jan.	Feb.	Mar.	April.	May.	June.	July.	Aug.	Sept.	Oct.	Nov.	Dec.
1	20·20				25·77	25·23	22·53	20·29	19·01	18·73	19·54	19·30
2	21·59				25·76	25·02	20·38	20·10	19·09	18·67	19·38	19·25
3	22·89				26·00	24·75	22·65	19·91	18·95	18·63	19·34	19·14
4	23·13				25·93	24·80	22·68	19·91	18·84	18·55	19·22	19·03
5	24·14				25·99	24·82	22·43	19·89	18·90	18·38	19·14	18·99
6	25·84				26·01	25·06	22·15	19·91	18·91	18·29	18·91	19·01
7	26·16				25·96	25·07	21·94	19·76	18·82	18·23	18·95	19·39
8	26·37				25·90	24·92	21·87	19·78	18·80	18·12	18·93	19·49
9	26·88				25·80	24·79	21·67	20·18	18·86	18·35	18·90	19·51
10	27·16				25·62	24·77	21·43	20·03	18·82	18·27	18·98	29·39
11					25·16	24·61	21·22	20·10	18·80	18·18	19·06	19·54
12					25·18	24·36	21·06	20·09	18·76	18·25	19·09	19·91
13					25·15	24·12	21·11	20·02	18·82	18·19	19·06	19·60
14					24·99	23·91	21·15	19·90	18·96	18·50	19·07	19·33
15					24·99	23·57	21·01	19·89	19·03	18·27	18·78	19·36
16					24·83	23·50	20·88	19·85	18·96	18·44	18·70	
17					25·11	23·89	21·12	19·81	18·76	18·82	18·61	
18					25·67	24·34	21·33	19·70	18·70	18·73	18·45	
19					26·52	24·43	21·27	19·62	18·08	18·66	18·36	
20					27·08	24·62	21·13	19·46	18·56	18·67	18·56	24·14
21					27·26	24·77	21·01	19·35	18·47	18·59	18·51	25·00
22					27·23	24·63	20·85	19·30	18·44	18·78	18·23	26·50*
23					26·90	24·33	20·66	19·20	18·54	19·00	18·25	
24					26·81	24·00	20·56	19·18	18·50	19·14	18·24	
25					26·67	23·58	20·46	19·04	18·55	19·12	18·54	
26					26·42	23·36	20·40	19·06	18·51	18·94	18·57	
27					26·19	23·21	20·45	19·05	18·45	19·29	18·61	
28					25·83	23·06	20·39	19·07	18·48	19·48	18·99	
29					25·57	22·88	20·20	19·02	18·58	19·50	19·40	
30					25·49	22·72	20·10	19·03	18·81	19·48	19·33	
31					25·48		20·20	19·08		19·61		
Mean					25·91	24·24	21·23	19·63	18·75	18·71	18·86	20·36

DAILY MEAN water surface elevations of lower St. Lawrence river, at Varennes, Que., for 1916. Elevations are above mean sea-level and are referred to crow's foot B.M. on stone wall in rear of wharf. Elevation 31.97.

Day.	Jan.	Feb.	Mar.	April.	May.	June.	July.	Aug.	Sept.	Oct.	Nov.	Dec.
1					24·57	23·91	21·05	18·63*	17·32	17·19	18·09	
2					24·63*	23·71	20·88	18·44*	17·31	17·12	17·89	
3					24·80	23·47	21·16	18·32	17·26	17·06	17·83	
4					24·73	23·47	21·22	18·31	17·13	16·97	17·70	
5					24·77	23·49	20·97	18·29	17·26	16·75	17·63	
6					24·77	23·77	20·66	18·30	17·25	16·64	17·39	
7					24·73	23·83	20·43	18·14	17·15	16·59	17·43	
8					24·64	23·68	20·32	18·14	17·10	16·45	17·42	
9					24·53	23·54	20·13	18·56	17·16	16·68	17·38	
10					24·33	23·49	19·89	18·43	17·17	16·64	17·42	
11					23·87	23·31	19·68	18·52	17·15	16·56	17·53	
12					23·85*	23·04	19·49	18·51	17·10	16·67	17·59	
13					23·80	22·78	19·51	18·46	17·15	16·57	17·55	
14					23·67	22·56	19·56	18·32	17·30	16·87	17·57	
15					23·66	22·27	19·45	18·32	17·40	16·67	17·30	
16					23·52*	22·16	19·33	18·27	17·35	16·81	17·17	
17					23·85*	22·52	19·58	18·24	17·16	17·24	17·05	
18					24·35*	22·98	19·82	18·13	17·04	17·17	16·84	
19					25·34*	23·07	19·80	18·02	17·00	17·13	16·68	
20					25·77	23·24	19·61	17·84	16·87	17·14	16·89	
21					25·95	23·39	19·46	17·68	16·77	17·05	16·87	
22					25·93	23·25	19·28	17·61	16·72	17·21	16·57	
23					25·64	22·97	19·07	17·48	16·81	17·43	16·57	
24					25·53	22·61	18·94	16·47	17·33	16·86	17·03	.A.....
25					25·37	22·20	18·82	17·33	16·85	17·41	16·94	
26					25·11	21·94	18·75	17·35	16·85	17·41	16·94	
27					24·88	21·77	18·78	17·34	16·81	17·78	16·94	
28				24·36*	24·52	21·61	18·74	17·35	16·89	17·99		
29				24·37	24·26	21·41	18·58	17·32	16·99	18·07		
30				24·51	24·16	21·23	18·44	17·31	17·20	18·04		
31					24·14		18·51	17·38		18·16		
Mean					24·63	22·89	19·67	17·99	17·08	17·14	17·25	

*Denotes mean of less than twenty-four hourly readings.

8 GEORGE V, A. 1918

DAILY MEAN water surface elevations of lower St. Lawrence river, at Verchères, Que., for 1916. Elevations are above mean sea-level and are referred to crow's foot B.M. on old windmill near wharf. Elevation 30.78.

Day.	Jan.	Feb.	Mar.	April.	May.	June.	July.	Aug.	Sept.	Oct.	Nov.	Dec.
1					23·44	22·71	19·78	17·30	16·02	15·98	16·89	16·63
2					23·43	22·52	19·62	17·15	16·09	15·92	16·67	16·60
3					23·61	22·29	19·91	16·96	15·97	15·82	16·57	16·40
4					23·55	22·25	19·97	16·97	15·86	15·72	16·42	16·26
5					23·60	22·28	19·73	16·97	15·99	15·50	16·36	16·21
6					23·57	22·58	19·41	17·97	15·95	15·36	16·13	16·21
7					23·50	22·66	19·16	16·80	15·85	15·29	16·17	16·55
8					23·41	22·54	19·05	16·78	15·78	15·17	16·18	16·66
9					23·27	22·38	18·84	17·25	15·85	15·40	16·15	16·77
10					23·06	22·30	18·58	17·10	15·88	15·38	16·18	16·62
11					22·61	22·09	18·35	17·21	15·89	15·32	16·31	16·67
12					22·51	21·80	18·17	17·22	15·84	15·45	16·32	17·12
13					22·47	21·55	18·20	17·17	15·92	15·39	16·31	16·88
14					22·35	21·35	18·26	17·04	16·08	15·66	16·36	16·58
15					22·34	21·08	18·18	17·06	16·19	15·46	16·08	16·57
16					22·27	20·96	18·09	17·00	16·12	15·59	15·92	16·96
17					22·61	21·27	18·34	16·95	15·92	16·02	15·78	17·67
18					23·12	21·69	18·64	16·84	15·77	15·93	15·51	18·87
19					23·91	21·79	18·61	16·72	15·70	15·88	15·29	20·43
20					24·45	21·97	18·42	16·54	15·56	15·91	15·49	22·22
21					24·66	22·0J	18·23	16·35	15·44	15·81	15·48	23·88
22					24·69	21·96	18·03	16·25	15·42	15·95	15·22	24·69•
23					24·44	21·69	17·79	16·13	15·54	16·16	15·22	......
24					24·28	21·35	17·63	16·10	15·54	16·34	15·30	......
25					24·12	20·94	17·50	15·96	15·61	16·39	15·51	......
26					23·85	20·65	17·40	16·00	15·59	16·17	15·69	......
27				23·19•	23·64	20·47	17·43	16·00	15·56	16·50	15·76	......
28				23·20	23·29	20·30	17·39	16·03	15·61	16·70	16·10	......
39				23·25	23·01	20·13	17·25	16·00	15·73	16·81	16·66	......
20				23·39	22·91	19·96	17·12	16·00	15·97	16·81	16·67	......
31					22·91	......	17·18	16·07		16·91		......
Mean					23·38	21·65	18·40	16·67	15·81	15·89	16·02	17·88

DAILY MEAN water surface elevations of lower St. Lawrence river, at Lanoraie Que., for 1916. Elevations are above mean sea-level and are referred to B.M. top of iron pin in hydrographic station at approach to wharf. Elevation 37.399.

Day.	Jan.	Feb.	Mar.	April.	May.	June.	July.	Aug.	Sept.	Oct.	Nov.	Dec.
1					21·84•	20·94	18·00	15·53	14·31	14·45	15·34	
2					21·80	20·76	17·89	15·40	14·36	14·37	15·09	......
3					21·92	20·57	18·14	15·19	14·26	14·23	14·92	......
4					21·87	20·47	18·21	15·17	14·12	14·11	14·78	......
5					21·92	20·54	18·01	15·20	14·22	13·87	14·68	......
6					21·87	20·86	17·69	15·18	14·19	13·66	14·46	......
7					21·78	20·98	17·42	14·99	14·10	13·60	14·52	......
8					21·66	20·91	17·27	14·97	14·03	13·49	14·57	......
9					21·47	20·72	17·06	15·41	14·11	13·67	14·56	......
10					21·24	20·58	16·80	15·35	14·18	13·74	14·56	......
11					20·81	20·33	16·51	15·50	14·23	13·72	14·67	......
12					20·61	20·03	16·41	15·54	14·21	13·87	14·67	......
13					20·56	19·78	16·41	15·50	14·30	13·84	14·64	......
14					20·48	19·61	16·49	15·38	14·46	14·03	14·72	......
15					20·46	19·39	16·45	15·44	14·60	13·93	14·48	......
16					20·44	19·25	16·41	15·38	14·52	13·99	14·26	......
17					20·82	19·46	16·69	15·31	14·32	14·42		......
18					21·31	19·85	17·07	15·19	14·11	14·37		......
19					22·05	19·96	17·04	15·04	13·96	14·31		......
20					22·56	20·12	16·83	14·84	13·80	14·35	13·67•	......
21					22·79	20·22	16·59	14·58	13·67	14·29	13·64	......
22					22·82	20·11	16·36	14·44	13·65	14·36	13·40	......
23					22·61	19·87	16·08	14·31	13·79	14·54	13·39	......
24					22·41	19·55	15·87	14·27	13·84	14·73	13·57	......
25					22·21	19·17	15·72	14·15	13·92	14·83	13·73	......
26					21·97	18·85	15·61	14·19	13·90	14·62		......
27					21·76	18·64	15·62	14·22	13·91	14·89		......
28					21·43	18·48	15·60	14·27	13·98	15·11		......
29					21·17	18·33	15·50	14·25	14·11	15·25		......
30					21·05	18·16	15·37	14·25	14·36	15·27		......
31					21·08	......	15·39	14·33		15·33		......
Mean					21·57	19·88	16·66	14·93	14·12	14·30	14·39	......

•Denotes mean of less than twenty-four hourly readings.

SESSIONAL PAPER No. 38

DAILY MEAN water surface elevations of lower St. Lawrence river, at Sorel, Que., for 1916. Elevations are above mean sea-level and are referred to C.B.M., MCCCVII on N.W. side of entrance to Post Office. Elevation, 46.80

Day.	Jan.	Feb.	Mar.	April.	May.	June.	July.	Aug.	Sept.	Oct.	Nov.	Dec.
1					21·15	20·26	17·37	14·97	13·86	14·05	14·86	14·76
2					21·16	20·08	17·27	14·89	13·90	13·97	14·62	14·71
3					21·24	19·89	17·50	14·70	13·81	13·82	14·42	14·49
4					21·18	19·77	17·56	14·58	13·66	13·68	14·25	14·30
5					21·21	19·87	17·40	14·74	13·74	13·44	14·15	14·25
6					21·17	20·19	17·09	14·69	13·73	13·21	13·95	14·31
7					21·07	20·31	16·80	14·51	13·63	13·15	14·02	14·53
8					20·92	20·27	16·64	14·49	13·57	13·05	14·04	14·66
9					20·72	20·07	16·44	14·89	13·65	13·21	14·10	14·81
10					20·48	19·89	16·20	14·86	13·73	13·32	14·07	14·66
11					20·06	19·63	15·97	15·02	13·78	13·30	14·17	14·64
12					19·83	19·35	15·80	15·07	13·79	13·45	14·13	14·97
13					19·78	19·10	15·82	15·05	13·88	13·46	14·13	14·96
14					19·72	18·95	15·90	14·94	14·03	13·64	14·19	14·64
15					19·71	18·75	15·89	14·99	14·17	13·50	14·00	14·55
16					19·70	18·62	15·85	14·94	14·12	13·56	13·77	15·36
17					20·07	18·77	16·16	14·86	13·89	13·98	13·50	16·41
18					20·56	19·10	16·57	14·75	13·67	13·93	13·20	17·05
19				20·77*	21·27	19·26	16·52	14·59	13·51	13·85	12·93	16·99
20				20·72	21·76	19·39	16·30	14·39	13·34	13·88	13·08	16·85
21				20·70	21·98	19·49	16·05	14·11	13·20	13·84	13·11	16·87
22				21·28	22·05	19·39	15·81	13·96	13·19	13·89	12·89	17·09
23				20·95	21·85	19·16	15·52	13·83	13·33	14·06	12·91	17·62
24				20·82	21·64	18·86	15·30	13·79	13·41	14·24	13·10	17·56
25				20·76	21·43	18·50	15·15	13·69	13·49	14·36	13·29	17·37
26				20·80	21·19	18·19	15·02	13·72	13·47	14·17	13·56	17·53
27				20·84	20·99	17·86	15·03	13·76	13·48	14·40	13·66	17·11
28				20·86	20·69	17·80	15·02	13·81	13·58	14·61	13·98	17·47
29				20·94	20·45	17·65	14·93	13·79	13·73	14·74	14·65	17·40
30				21·08	20·32	17·50	14·81	13·79	13·94	14·78	14·80	17·40
31					20·35		14·82	13·88		14·84		17·27
Mean					20·83	19·20	16·08	14·46	13·68	13·85	13·85	15·88

DAILY MEAN water surface elevations of lake St. Peter, at Range Light No. 2, for 1916. Elevations are above mean sea-level and are referred to brass plug B.M. on north side of pier. Elevation, 18.33 (W.S. Transfer of 1916).

Day	Jan.	Feb.	Mar.	April.	May.	June.	July.	Aug.	Sept.	Oct.	Nov.	Dec.
1					19·08		16·03	13·37*	12·39		13·65*	
2					18·87		15·95	13·40*	12·42		13·48	
3					18·71		16·05	13·22	12·31		13·18	
4					18·57		16·19	13·19	12·12		12·96	
5					18·72		16·07	13·29	12·11		12·78	
6					18·98		15·75	13·15	12·14		12·71	
7					19·09		15·45	12·97	12·06		12·78	
8					19·03		15·22	12·94	12·02	11·55*	12·90	
9					18·85		15·02	13·23	12·11	11·69	12·98	
10					19·24*	18·58	14·77	13·36	12·21	11·94	12·96	
11					19·01	18·37	14·57	13·54	12·30	11·93	12·95	
12					18·66	18·10	14·42	13·68	12·39	12·09	12·96	
13					18·55	17·88	14·39	13·65	12·49	12·18	12·80	
14					18·45	17·72	14·50	13·60	12·62	12·30	12·89	
15					18·41	17·57	14·52	13·68	12·82	12·25	12·81	
16					18·42	17·43	14·54	13·58	12·78	12·20	12·48	
17					18·65	17·51	14·80	13·47	12·49	12·59	12·17	
18					19·39	17·83	15·28	13·34	12·21	12·61	11·90	
19					20·11	18·06	15·24	13·13	11·96	12·40*	11·60*	
20					20·54	18·16	15·02	12·90	11·72	12·52*		
21					20·83	18·25	14·70	12·55	11·58*	12·62		
22					20·88	18·14	14·43	12·35	11·61*	12·58		
23					20·74	17·91	14·10	12·23	11·78	12·73		
24					20·46	17·58	13·83	12·18	11·89	12·93		
25					20·23	17·25	13·67	12·11	11·97	13·10		
26					19·99	16·90	13·52	12·12	11·97	13·11		
27					19·75	16·62	13·48	12·24	12·00*	13·16		
28					19·49	16·45	13·49	12·29		13·37		
29					19·26	16·30	13·47	12·31		13·50		
30					19·10	16·16	13·34	12·29		13·58		
31					19·11		13·31	12·39		13·67*		
Mean					19·47	17·96	14·68	12·96	12·17	12·61	12·79	

*Denotes mean of less than twenty-four hourly readings.

CANADIAN ARCTIC EXPEDITION.

The Canadian Arctic Expedition, under the leadership of Vilhjalmur Stefansson, set out for the Arctic regions on the 20th July, 1913.

The work planned comprised the exploration of Beaufort sea, the investigation of animal life in the areas covered, and the taking of soundings over the regions explored. The expedition was also to ascertain if lands hitherto unknown exist, and to definitely mark any found. The investigating and areal mapping of the copper-bearing and associated rocks of the mainland between cape Parry and Kent peninsula for approximately one hundred miles inland, and of the southern and eastern shores of Victoria island were also to be undertaken.

The work was so varied both in the nature of the investigations and the area to be explored that it was decided to divide the expedition into two parties; one, known as the Northern division, to carry out the Beaufort sea work; the other, known as the Southern division, to work on the coast survey.

SOUTHERN DIVISION.

The Southern division have completed the work and have returned from the north. A complete report of operations by Dr. R. M. Anderson, executive head of the Southern division, is appended hereto.

NORTHERN DIVISION.

The Northern division, in C.G.S. *Karluk*, sailed from Nome, Alaska, on the 20th July, 1913. Shortly after rounding point Barrow the vessel became icebound. It was carried eastward along the coast to near Thetis island, where it became stationary and was apparently frozen in for the winter. Mr. Stefansson, accompanied by B. M. McConnell, George H. Wilkins, and D. Jenness, set out on a hunting trip to the mainland. During their absence the vessel was carried away and the hunting party were obliged to make their way westward along the coast to Collinson point, where they joined the Southern division, who were wintering there.

The *Karluk* was carried far to the westward, and on the 11th January, 1914, was crushed by the ice, and sank. The men in the vessel transferred supplies, ammunition and other necessities to the quarters prepared on the ice, and they settled down in their igloos to await the return of the light.

Some of the men were not satisfied with the inaction of life in the camp, and expressed a desire to set out for land, dimly visible in the Arctic twilight. Two parties were therefore formed, each composed of four men, and set out for land, the first party on the 21st January and the second on the 5th February. These men have not since been heard from, and have been given up for lost.

When the light had improved the remaining members set out for land and succeeded in reaching Wrangel island. Through the efforts of Captain R. A. Bartlett, who journeyed on foot to the Siberian coast and thence to East cape, to get in touch with the outside world, a relief expedition was organized and the men were rescued from the island.

The following men were lost in attempting to reach Wrangel island: Charles Barker, John Brady, Alex. Anderson, A. King, Dr. F. MacKay, James Murray, H. Beauchat, and T. S. Morris. B. Mamen and G. Malloch died from nephritis on Wrangel island, and George Breddy was accidentally shot.

The survivors were John Munro, R. Williamson, W. McKinley, F. E. Maurer, John Hadley, R. Templeman, H. Williams and E. F. Chafe.

ICE EXPEDITIONS.

Immediately upon his arrival at Collinson point, Mr. Stefansson began preparations for a trip on foot over Beaufort sea to the north. Although the fate of the *Karluk* was not then known, he realized that, owing to ice conditions, the party therein would probably be unable to carry out the exploration work. He purchased the *North Star*, partly for the supplies which went with the vessel, and also for the use of the vessel itself.   .

On the 22nd March, 1914, the ice party, composed of V. Stefansson, Storker T. Storkerson, and Aurnout Castel, set out. Their intention was to continue as far out across the ice as circumstances would permit and, if possible, to land on Banks or Prince Patrick island, where they would spend the summer. In the event of their failing to return before the break up of the ice, a vessel was to be sent to Banks island during the summer.   ⟍

On the journey across the ice the party covered an area previously unexplored, and travelled as far to the west of Banks island as safety would permit. When the ice began to break up, toward the end of April, the party were obliged to make for land. They landed on Norway island on the northwest coast of Banks island on the 25th June.

The summer was spent in mapping the coast line of Northern Banks island and in carrying on investigations in the interior of the island, up the "Wilkins" river; this river empties near Norway island.   ⟍

In September, 1914, the party travelled south to Kellett, where George H. Wilkins and a party in the *Mary Sachs*, sent north with supplies were met. A winter base was established at Kellett, and the *Sachs* was beached. The Vessel was considerably damaged on the way north, and required repairs.

On the 22nd December, 1914, Mr. Stefansson, accompanied by an Eskimo, Natkusiak, made a journey across southern Banks island to DeSalis bay to locate any Eskimos wintering in that vicinity. Before leaving he gave instructions to the party at Kellett to prepare for an ice trip over Beaufort sea, to begin early in February. He arrived at DeSalis bay on the 3rd January, 1915, and crossing over Prince of Wales strait followed the shore of Victoria island for some miles. Finding no indications of the presence of Eskimos he returned to Kellett, arriving on the 27th January.

Preparations for the ice trip having been almost completed during his absence, the few remaining details were arranged, and the party, composed of V. Stefansson, Storker Storkerson, Ole Andreasen, and Charles Thomsen set out north for cape Alfred early in February, following the west coast of Banks island. From cape Alfred they journeyed in a northwesterly direction until the 26th April, when the break up of the ice obliged them to make for Prince Patrick island. They landed on Prince Patrick island near Land's End, and thence followed the shore northeast to cape McClintock. They proceeded for three days north from this point, when land unmarked on the charts was discovered. A complete report, giving details of the journey, is contained in the Naval Service Annual Report of March 31, 1916. Owing to the lateness of the season and the necessity for arranging the next season's work, the party set out on the return journey without carrying on any extensive investigations. They arrived at Kellett on the 8th August.

On the 19th August the *Polar Bear*, in charge of Captain Lane, arrived at Kellett. As the services of a vessel were urgently required by the Northern division (the *Mary Sachs* had not been relaunched), Mr. Stefansson purchased the *Bear*, and set out for Baillie island. Upon arrival there he left instructions for the *North Star*, for which Mr. Wilkins had gone to the base of the Southern party on foot early in the spring, to go to Banks island without communicating with him. He returned to Kellett, whence he set out for the north in the *Bear* on the 3rd September.

8 GEORGE V, A. 1918

It was intended at first to land at Kellett and proceed north along the west coast of Banks island. Up to this time, since late July, the coast had been kept free from ice by prevailing easterly winds, but on the 3rd September the wind changed and blew from the northwest, with a heavy fall of snow. Upon reaching cape Kellett it was seen that the ice was coming in, and the party took shelter behind the cape for the night. By the morning the ice was pressed close to the west coast, debarring further progress. Fearing that with a slight change of the wind they might be shut in, Mr. Stefansson decided to make an attempt to get north through Prince of Wales strait, along the east coast of Banks island. It has since been learned that the freeze-up on the west coast of Banks island came on the 6th September, and the ice did not leave the coast until the spring of 1916.

A course was set for Nelson head, which was rounded on the night of the 4-5th September and the vessel proceeded north into the straits. South of N. Latitude 72° only scattered ice was encountered, but north of 72° there were large packs of heavy ice called "paleocrystic", that is, ice that has lasted through several summers, during which time it has been freed from most or all of its salt and become hard and glare. On September 5 there was a strong southeast wind which kept the water along the Victoria island coast free of ice, and on the night of the 5th the party took shelter near the land just south of Deans Dundas bay. On the 6th September considerable time was lost in navigating through scattered ice, and during the afternoon the wind changed to the west, bringing down heavy masses of ice from the Banks island side. They were able to proceed only as far as Princess Royal island, where the vessel was tied up for the winter and the party prepared to make their winter quarters there.

As soon as it was decided to winter near Princess Royal island the party set out to obtain as much caribou meat as possible, but as it was past the season for caribou, which had already gone south, only twenty-three were obtained. All the drift-wood that could be found within 15 miles on either side of the winter quarters was gathered. A base was established some 10 miles southwest of Armstrong point. This base was in an ideal location to complete the mapping of the northeast coast of Victoria island. Mr. Stefansson instructed Storker Storkerson to undertake this survey as soon as the ice would become frozen over sufficiently to enable them to travel.

The land east of the base near Armstrong point is high and rocky, so that crossing it by sled in the early fall would not be practicable. The survey party were therefore obliged to wait until Melville sound north of Peel point froze over, which did not happen until the middle of October.

On the 10th October the party left camp, Storkerson and Herman Kilian to make the complete trip, Noice and Andreasen for the supporting party. At Hornby point on the 24th October the supporting party turned back. Storkerson and Kilian returned on the 4th December without having been able to quite complete the work, but an effort was to be made to complete it in the spring of 1916.

During the survey the chief difficulties encountered were darkness and continual gales. At one point the party were stormbound for twelve successive days by a head gale which the dogs would not face. Drawings of the hitherto unexplored coast line covered were made by Mr. Storkerson, and will be published with the final report of operations.

Mr. Stefansson himself made several trips during the autumn of 1915. The first trip was for hunting purposes, on which he was accompanied by natives, whom he established in a sealing camp at Hay point. Later on this camp was moved to Ramsay island, and in November he made a trip south, following the curves of the coast until he found a party of Eskimos, numbering about one hundred, in Minto inlet, south across the neck of land from the foot of Walker bay. Two of the Eskimos returned with the party to the *Polar Bear*, Captain Gonzales later made a trip to the village for trading purposes, but considerable difficulty arose owing to the natives not having been accustomed to dealing with white men. Unfortunately, the natives contracted severe colds about the same time that the party from the *Polar Bear* visited them, and they superstitiously attributed their sickness to the presence of the white men. Should any of them die from cold or hunger resulting through their being unable to obtain game through illness, their white visitors would be blamed and the natives would refuse to trade further with them. Mr. Stefansson, however, did all in his power to overcome this friction between the natives and the *Polar Bear* party, and no serious results occurred.

On the 1st December, Mr. Stefansson left Ramsay Island hunting camp for Kellett. The chief purpose of this trip was to get two sleds which Captain Beneard was making for use on the ice trip the following spring. The party consisted of Stefansson, Noice, Martin Kilian, and an Eskimo. On the first part of the journey many difficulties were encountered. The party intended to follow the south coast of Banks island around as far as DeSalis bay and thence cross to the west coast by practically the same route as that used by Mr. Stefansson the previous winter in his journey across southern Banks island. Before reaching the Banks island coast, however, they broke the runner of one of the sleds, thus making it necessary to put a double load on the remaining sled. In order to avoid a second accident of this nature they decided to cross overland the whole way, as the going was smoother than on the sea ice. On this journey they were further handicapped by the death of their best dog. This dog was capable of drawing three hundred pounds, while the average dog is capable of drawing only between two hundred and two hundred and fifty pounds. In Mr. Stefansson's opinion the ice journeys for the summer of 1916 would be considerably shortened by the loss of this animal.

On the journey across Banks island it was ascertained that the map, as given in Admiralty chart No. 2118, is somewhat out on the southeast coast. This chart calls for a width of about thirteen miles due west between Ramsay island and Banks island, while in reality the distance is at least twenty-five miles. The error seems to be that this whole portion of Banks island should be moved north on the map until Milne point is nearly where Schuyler point is now placed. The party climbed the slope of Banks island from the first bay indicated north of Milne point. There really is no bay there, but only the low land at the mouth of a small river. They ascended the valley of this river for about ten miles. After the first four miles the river runs through a narrow and crooked ravine. Although the grade is considerable, the party were unable owing to the fog and blizzard, to obtain a definite idea of the exact elevation. Mr. Stefansson, however, judged that within ten miles from the coast they had attained an elevation of over four thousand feet. The journey across Banks island entailed a great amount of climbing up and down hills. The party finally came down into a river valley some seven or eight miles back of DeSalis bay. From the point where they came to it this river runs about south into the bay, but following up stream they went first north then northwest and finally about west some ten or twelve miles until the valley widened into a continuous flat, which extends to the ocean some forty-five miles southeast from the tip of cape Kellett. The slope of this flat is to the east until within some fifteen miles of the west coast. It is from one to four miles wide and is flanked by hills rising three hundred to five hundred feet over the lowland. For the last fifteen miles there is a river flanked by low banks, which are apparently water-swept each spring. This river comes into a small bay without any abrupt descent, so the party did not at first realize that they had reached the sea. On this journey it was found that by following this route there is a pass from DeSalis bay east through the high southern part of Banks

8 GEORGE V, A. 1918

island without ascending to a height of more than three hundred feet. Although the actual elevations were not obtained, the knowledge of this pass will be of great value to any one needing to cross Banks island. The total distance, following the river that flows into DeSalis bay, is about thirty-five or forty- miles.

Upon their arrival at Kellett the party found all well at that base. They were told that the *North Star* was unable to proceed more than twenty miles beyond Norway island on the west coast of Banks island, as the ice north of that point did not move during the whole summer of 1915.

On the 6th January, Mr. Stefansson sent Thomsen, Noice, and Knight across Banks island to DeSalis bay en route to the *Polar Bear*, near Armstrong point. On the way they were to close up the hunting camps at Ramsay island. Thomsen carried a letter of instruction to Storkerson to assemble such things in the way of an outfit for the ice journey as were not provided by the *North Star* or *Sachs* and bring them with two dog teams to cape Alfred.

In the meantime the party at cape Kellett, under the immediate super-vision of Mr. Stefansson, prepared for the journey to cape Alfred. These plans unfortunately did not materialize owing, in the first place, to delays experienced by Thomsen and party, who did not arrive at the *Polar Bear* until the first of February. These delays were caused by bad weather which prevented the party finding Ramsay island. For about five days they were in plain sight of it had the weather been clear. They also encountered open water about four miles beyond Milne point, which obliged them to considerably lengthen the trail. Storkerson, at the *Polar Bear*, had in the meantime much trouble getting from Mercy bay the sleds cached there the previous year. The chief obstacle was the mountainous character of the intervening land, which was practically uncrossable in the midwinter darkness, and through the roughness of the ice between point Russell and Mercy bay when that route was later adopted.

When Storkerson received the instructions sent by Mr. Stefansson the dogs were in poor condition for travel. On the journey up to point Russell in an endeavour to carry out the instructions received from Stefansson, Stork-erson lost several dogs, which rendered continuation of the journey practically impossible. As he erroneously considered that Mr. Stefansson would prefer the failure of the ice trip to the failure to explore the new land, and as he con-sidered that both could not be carried out with the dogs in such poor condition, he took upon himself to alter the plans and instead of going west started for the new land. Upon arrival, he commenced investigation of the new land, sending a sled in charge of Hermann Kilian to Mercy bay with a letter of information for Stefansson, which he would pick up on his way east.

In the meantime Mr. Stefansson and party were waiting for the arrival of Storkerson at cape Alfred. While they were waiting, hunting camps were established around cape Alfred in order to provide fresh meat for the ice trips planned. The party waited until the 7th March, when the season was already late to start on the ice. By this time considerable anxiety was felt on account of the non-arrival of Storkerson, as it was feared that Thomsen had failed to reach the *Bear* with instructions for him. On the 7th March, Stefansson started for Mercy bay to learn whether any of the men had visited the bay. The remainder of the party busied themselves in carrying supplies east to be used in the new-land work. The *Star* was temporarily abandoned and the party belonging to her were sent to Melville island to assist in the new-land work.

On the 20th March the Stefansson party met Castel a little east of cape McClure. He reported that he had been unable to recognize any point on the coast from the chart; that he had reached a bay which he thought might be Mercy bay and had gone ten miles into it, but finding no trace of sleds, and the dog feed having given out, he returned.

From Castel's observations and those of other parties it appears that for forty-five or fifty miles west of Mercy bay no point on the chart could be identified by the contour of' the coast as shown on Admiralty chart No. 2118. It appears that the big bay shown by chart No. 2118 as just east of cape McClure does not exist, although there is a bay of considerable size about six miles west of Mercy bay. This unmarked bay is the one from which Castel turned back. On the west side of it he cached a fifty-gallon drum of kerosene which was intended generally for the use of the Eskimos of Melville island in the summer of 1916. On meeting Castel, who had seen no trace of Storkerson, Mr. Stefansson gave up hope of his arrival, and sent orders to cape Alfred to break camp and commence moving to Melville island.

He also left instructions that when established on Melville island the party were to put up dried meat for the winter supply.

At Mercy bay the letter left by Storkerson, explaining the reason for the change in plans, was found. From this letter Mr. Stefansson understood that by proceeding to cape Ross, Melville island, he could get in touch with Mr. Storkerson through men stationed there to protect supplies, or through travelling parties.

Mr. Stefansson, accompanied by Wilkins, Castel, Kilian, Natkusiak, and Emiu, with three sleds, accordingly proceeded to cape Ross, arriving there on the 13th April. The party found the remains of a camp, a small cache and a note from Storkerson saying he had gone towards the head of Liddon gulf, but there was little or no information which would aid them in co-operating with him.

As there has been a heavy fall of snow the party could not tell, from following the trail, how many sleds Storkerson had. It was therefore impossible to determine if he intended to return to cape Ross or proceed to the new land. Under the circumstances, Mr. Stefansson decided that the best plan would be to send one sled in charge of Natkusiak to the head of Liddon gulf, where the dogs could be well fed and rested, while he himself would make a quick journey back along the trail leading to the *Polar Bear* until they would come across information which would guide them. Before they proceeded far, however, they were met by Herman Kilian, who had come directly from the Storkerson party. Kilian reported that Storkerson, with Thomsen, Andreasen, Noice, and Illun had left the head of Liddon gulf on the 14th April for the new land, intending to keep on advancing and to map as much country as possible so as to be home at the *Polar Bear* on the 10th July. Mr. Stefansson therefore decided to overtake Storkerson if possible as he planned to land at the north end of Melville island between the 15th and 20th July, which meant that his season of exploration work would be at least one month longer than Storkerson's. In case the new land proved extensive he did not purpose returning to Melville island, giving the whole summer to exploration work.

The party in charge of Stefansson left cape Ross for the north on the 19th April. They reached the head of the gulf in three days, crossed the portage near point Nias, and arrived at the new land on the 2nd May at the same point as the previous year. They met Storkerson on the 3rd May at cape James Murray, which appears to be the southwest corner of the new land. Arrangements were immediately made to carry out exploration and charting work. Thomsen, with one team, was sent to Kellett to carry scientific specimens from the *North Star* to the *Mary Sachs*, and also to carry the reports of the expedition to Kellett in order that they might be sent out by the first ship calling there.

The department has received no later reports from Mr. Stefansson. It is expected that a complete survey of the newly discovered land will be made, and that journeys over the ice to the west, covering parts of Beaufort sea hitherto unvisited, may be carried out. It would appear that Mr. Stefansson does not intend to leave the region until every detail of the work planned has been completed.

8 GEORGE V, A. 1918

THE CANADIAN ARCTIC EXPEDITION OF 1913.

REPORT OF THE SOUTHERN DIVISION.

The Deputy Minister,
    Department of the Naval Service,
        Ottawa.

SIR,—I have the honour to submit a report upon the work of the Southern Division of the Canadian Arctic Expedition of 1913-16.

The Canadian Arctic Expedition of 1913-16 was planned to work in two comparatively distant and distinct fields, and the nature of the investigations to be undertaken was so varied that the expedition was divided into two parties.

The Northern party, under command of Mr. Vilhjalmur Stefansson, were to explore the Beaufort sea and also carry on investigations into the animal life of this region and take soundings in the districts investigated. They were also to ascertain if islands hitherto unknown exist, and to definitely mark any found. This division of the expedition was thus to confine its work largely to the oceans and archipelagos north of Alaska and the Western Arctic region of Canada.

The work of the Southern party, under my direction, was to be confined more exclusively to the Arctic mainland and adjacent islands, as set forth in the following instructions:—

"The relative importance of the investigations for this party are: (1) geological, (2) geographical, (3) anthropological, (4) biological, (5) photographical.

"The work of the Southern party shall be primarily the investigation and areal mapping of the copper-bearing and associated rocks of the mainland between cape Parry and Kent peninsula and for approximately one hundred miles inland and on southern and eastern Victorialand.

"The work undertaken by these parties should be of a high order for this class of exploration, and should mark a distinct advance over previous work. To secure such results the geological and topographical sub-parties should follow closely the regular scheme for field parties engaged in reconnaissance work adopted by the Geological Survey. In working from the base depot, these parties should be practically complete distinct and independent units. . . . The anthropological work shall consist of ethnological and archaeological research. . . . The biological work shall consist of marine and terrestrial biology, etc., etc."

The chief of the southern party, as executive head, must afford every reasonable facility as circumstances permit to enable these sub-parties to carry out the above important work."

Ample provision was made for the scientific work of the party by selecting competent specialists for each branch of science to be studied, and providing them with all necessary instruments and such equipment and provisions as had by experience been found most suitable for use under the climatic conditions expected. The scientific staff of the Southern party as originally organized was as follows: Geologist, John J. O'Neill, of Ottawa, who had specialized in Pre-Cambrian geology and copper rocks; topographers, Kenneth G. Chipman and John R. Cox, men of several years' experience in the topographical division of the Geological Survey; anthropologists, D. Jenness, of New Zealand, an Oxford man with field experience in ethnology in New Guinea, and M. Henri Beuchat, of Paris, a writer of note on American archaeology; marine biologist, entomologist, and botanist, F. Johansen, a former member of the Danish East-Greenland Expedition of 1906-08 under Mylius Ericksen and later entomologist for the United States Department of Agriculture; meteorologist and magnetician, William Laird McKinlay, of Glasgow; photographer and cinematographer, George H. Wilkins, of Adelaide, Australia; mammalogist and ornithologist, Dr. Rudolph Martin Anderson, of the Victoria Memorial Museum of Ottawa. The latter, having had several years previous experience in exploratory work in Arctic, Alaska, Yukon Territory, and the Northwest Territories, was appointed to take charge of the Southern party in the absence of Mr. Stefansson.

Owing to the unavoidable complications arising from the unfortunate drift and loss of the *Karluk*, M. Beuchat and Mr. McKinlay were unable to join the Southern party at Herschel island as contemplated, and Mr. Wilkins was only able to be with the Southern party for a part of the time. Mr. Jenness was able to cover much of the ethnological work as planned, by taking over part of M. Beuchat's field, and by division of labour of the whole party complete meteorological records were kept for nearly three years. The magnetic instruments were lost on the *Karluk*, and consequently that branch of science is lacking in the final results.

As the expedition was not formally taken up by the Dominion Government until February, 1913, the time was rather short for assembling the multitude of articles of supply and equipment required. Although most of the members of the scientific staff were members of the Geological Survey, the general direction of the expedition was in the hands of the Department of the Naval Service. With the exception of technical instruments and equipment supplied to certain members by the Geological Survey, practically the whole of the equipment, including provisions, clothing, field gear, etc., was supplied by the Department of the Naval Service.

Some difficulty was experienced in obtaining large quantities of pemmican, dehydrated vegetables, and other condensed foods on short notice, and a vast assortment of miscellaneous goods had to be provided, "everything from a needle to an anchor," as there was no certainty of being able for three years to replenish articles consumed or left behind. Practically everything requisitioned was assembled at H.M.C. Dockyard, Esquimalt, B.C., in June, 1913. The expedition is under great obligation to Mr. J. A. Wilson, Director of Stores, Department of the Naval Service, Ottawa, and to Mr. George Philips, Naval Store Officer, Esquimalt, B.C., for their efficiency and care in seeing that articles for the expedition were supplied promptly and of excellent quality, both at the start of the expedition and later, as well as for encouragement and friendly and intelligent co-operation with the work of the expedition outside of the extent of their official duties. George J. Desbarats, C.M.G., Deputy Minister, Department of the Naval Service, is also to be thanked for continued interest and prompt attention to the work and needs of the expedition throughout more than three years of our absence in the north. Through their efforts the Canadian Arctic Expedition was probably as completely and well equipped as any expedition that has ever gone into the north.

Most of the members of both the Northern and Southern parties of the expedition, with a large part of the equipment and supplies, sailed from Esquimalt, B.C., June 17, 1913, on the steam-whaler *Karluk*, which had been purchased for the use of the Northern party. Additional supplies were shipped from Victoria and Seattle to Nome on one of the Alaska Steamship Company's vessels. The *Karluk* arrived safely at Nome on July 9. The gasolene schooner *Alaska*, which had been built in 1912 for the Bering Sea trade and to carry the United States mail to Kotzebue sound, had been under option for the use of the Southern party, and was purchased at Nome, Alaska. Its dimensions were: Length, 57 feet 5 inches; draught, 6 feet 6 inches; gross tonnage, 50; beam, 17 feet; construction, wooden auxiliary schooner; 50 horse-power standard gas engine.

Considerable additional supplies and equipment, including reindeer skins and skin clothing, sleds, dogs, distillate, coal oil, and a large supply of dried dog salmon, were obtained for the expedition at Nome. As the numbers of the party had been much increased over the originally planned number, with correspondingly increased equipment, the gasolene schooner *Mary Sachs* was also purchased in Nome as an auxiliary vessel for both parties. The *Mary Sachs* had the following dimensions: Length, 56 feet 6 inches; draught, 5 feet 6 inches; beam, 18 feet 1 inch; gross tonnage, 41; construction, wooden, gasolene, screw vessel; 30 horse-power Union gas engine.

The *Karluk* and *Mary Sachs* sailed from Nome July 20, and calling at port Clarence, sailed from there July 27. The C. G. S. *Alaska* left Nome on July 19, arriving at Teller, Alaska, July 24. Here it was found necessary to dismantle and overhaul the engine and put on a better propeller before proceeding farther. This involved discharging and reloading cargo, and the *Alaska* did not get away from port Clarence before August 11, rounded point Barrow August 20, and passed Flaxman island September 6. No ice was met until we were near the Seahorse islands, a little south of Barrow, Alaska, but east of point Barrow the prevailing westerly and northwesterly winds had packed the ice along the shore, so that there was very little open water anywhere. For the first time since 1888, when the whalers began going in to Herschel island annually, no vessel from the west was able to get in to Herschel island, and some small vessels which had spent the preceding winter east of Herschel island were unable to go out. The vessels caught between Herschel island included the 247-ton steamer *Karluk*, belonging to the expedition, the 420-ton steamwhaler *Belvedere*, the gasolene schooners *Polar Bear, Anna Olga, Elvira,* and *North Star*, the *Alaska* and *Mary Sachs* of the expedition, and the *Teddy Bear* east of the Mackenzie river. Of these the *Elvira* was crushed and sank in October, 1913, near Humphrey point, Alaska, and the *Karluk* drifted west and sank northeast of Wrangell island in January, 1914.

The ice encountered in Beaufort sea in 1913 was too heavy to be bucked successfully by any vessel, no matter of what strength of hull or power of engines. There are no true icebergs in the western Arctic ocean, such as are broken off from the peripheral glaciers of Greenland or the Antarctic continent. The immense sheets of flat ice which are formed, however, crack extensively with the rise and fall of the tides. These tide-cracks frequently open widely or close abruptly by the force of the winds, crushing the edges of the floe like glass, and forcing up great blocks to form pressure-ridges which may be 30 to 40 feet high. Snow-drifts fill up the crevices of the ridge, and as the snow melts and settles in the spring, the whole becomes cemented into a floe that is too massive to thaw in a single short summer season, and may last over for several years.

These large masses of ice in the shoal waters off the north coast of Alaska and Canada, if not too thick and numerous, are to a certain extent an advantage to small vessels, as they cut down the swell in heavy weather, and often ground in comparatively deep water some distance from shore, allowing vessels of small draught on a harbourless coast to tie up behind them, sheltered from winds and from ice crushing from outside. By creeping slowly along the shore, moving ahead a little whenever the wind and tide loosened and shifted the ice a little along the coast, the *Alaska* and the *Mary Sachs* succeeded in getting as far ahead as Collinson point, 69° 59' N. Lat., 144° 50' W. Long., in

Camden bay, on the north coast of Alaska, about ninety miles west of the Alaska-Yukon Territory international boundary, and decided to go into winter quarters at Collinson point on September 10, three or four days before the freeze-up.

The *Alaska* and *Mary Sachs* secured a sheltered harbour in a small bay behind the Collinson point sandspit; the vessels were unloaded, and the men secured comfortable quarters for the winter in a large log-house built of driftwood. Large quantities of Mackenzie river driftwood on all the beaches of the north Alaska coast furnish abundant fuel. The cariboo have been largely exterminated along this section of the coast, but some mountain sheep and cariboo meat was secured from inland Eskimos, and large numbers of ptarmigan and fish were obtained in season. The health of all members of the party was excellent throughout the year, the only illness or casualty being that of Andre Noram, cook of the *Mary Sachs*, who became insane, with symptoms indicating paresis, and committed suicide by shooting, April 16, 1914, at Collinson point.

Although it was a disappointment to the members of the party to be held up by the ice before getting into Canadian territory, the time was improved by the men in becoming used to Arctic conditions—the methods of sledging with dogs, camping, and taking scientific observations at low temperatures. A large number of astronomical observations, solar and stellar, and a series of lunar occultations were taken at Collinson point, during the winter, for astronomical position and variation of compass and chronometer. An automatic tide-registering machine was kept in commission for a considerable time, meteorological records were kept up, and various collections were made. A snow-house makes a very good observatory, but at low temperatures great care must be exercised in handling delicate instruments, as the faintest breadth or even the insensible perspiration from a bare hand near the instrument will coat lenses and metal work with a film of frost crystals. Even guns are left out of doors all winter because if brought inside they become immediately coated with a thick mass of hoar-frost and ice, which takes a long time to melt, thoroughly wets the weapon inside and out as it melts, and rusts it badly if it is not taken entirely apart and thoroughly cleaned and oiled.

Desiring to begin work in Canadian territory as soon as possible, J. J. O'Neill started from Collinson point with a dog-driver and assistant in February, to begin geological work by a reconnaissance of Firth river (more generally known locally as Herschel island river), coming from the Endicott mountains near the international boundary and emptying into the Arctic ocean near Herschel island. This was carried out successfully, as well as a geological reconnaissance of Herschel island.[1]

K. G. Chipman and John R. Cox left Collinson point on March 16 and proceeded to Demarcation point. A series of solar observations for chronometer ratings were taken at the international boundary monument, the 141st meridian of west longitude. A stop was again made at the boundary when the party was sailing out, August 4, 1916, to get time sights again at the same place over twenty-eight months later. The coast line was surveyed to the eastward, tying in Herschel island with the surveys of the Alaska-Yukon International Boundary Survey of 1912. Mr. Cox then joined Mr. O'Neill in completing the topographical work on Firth river, and completed the coast survey by sled to Escape reef at the western edge of the Mackenzie river delta, where a gasolene launch was in readiness to work in the delta as soon as the river broke out.

Mr. Chipman and Mr. O'Neill later in the spring did some geological work in the Black Mountain district west of the Mackenzie delta until the river broke out about June 1. They then proceeded by whaleboat through the east branch of the Mackenzie, charting it as far as the south end of Richard island, after

---

[1] Summary Rep. Geol. Surv., Dept. of Mines, for 1914. Ottawa, 1915, pp. 112–115, 148–149.
Ibid., 1916, pp. 236–237.

8 GEORGE V, A. 1918

which they proceeded to Arctic Red river and to fort McPherson near the mouth of Peel river, to pick up some consignments which came down by one of the Mackenzie river steamers. A launch which had been purchased for Mr. Chipman's survey party could not be made to run, and not as much territory was covered as expected, but with an expert sailor of the delta as guide, the utmost advantage was got from the whaleboat, and large portions of the middle and east branches were mapped, with a number of cut-off channels and smaller channels used in winter sled or summer whaleboat travel. At the same time Mr. Cox, with competent Eskimo guides, surveyed the west or Aklavik branch of the delta from Akpavachiak or Escape reef up to the mouth of Peel river. Astronomical positions were determined at Arctic Red river and fort McPherson and at several points in the delta, tying the work of the boundary survey with the work of previous explorers in the lower Mackenzie and Peel river country.[1]

There is a good 6-foot channel over the shoals around Tent island, near the mouth of the west branch of the Mackenzie delta, and passing these there is a deeper channel as far south as the outlet of Great Slave lake. Passing shoals of about five feet depth at that place, there is a deep channel again as far south as fort Smith, at the foot of the Grand rapids of the Slave river, 60° North latitude, near the northern boundary of Alberta. The channel into the east branch of the Mackenzie delta is also deep enough for fair-sized schooners, and the new Hudson's Bay Company's post at Kittigazuit on the east side of the delta southeast of Richard island is supplied from Herschel island by this route. The middle channel of the delta was not completely surveyed for lack of time, as the boat survey parties were obliged to meet the *Alaska* at Herschel island early in August to go east of the Mackenzie into the Coronation gulf region, where the main work of the Southern party was planned to be done.

Mr. D. Jenness, after coming ashore with Mr. V. Stefansson from the *Karluk* in September, 1913, had spent most of the winter in doing linguistic work among the Eskimos in the point Barrow region. Towards spring he came east to Collinson point and did ethnological and archaeological work from Collinson point to Demarcation point in the spring, later in the summer carrying on some extensive archaeological excavations at Barter island, Alaska, making large collections in the ruins at the site of the ancient trading rendezvous between the Mackenzie Eskimos and the western Alaskan Eskimos. Mr. F. Johansen made extensive collections of plants and insects, rearing many species of insects to study their life-histories and development. Some marine dredging was also done. During the fall and winter Chipman and Cox had prepared a map of the harbour at Collinson point and vicinity on the scale of $\frac{1}{21600}$, extending it inland to include some ten square miles of tundra, with 20-foot contours. The harbour was thoroughly sounded. It is not suitable for large vessels, carrying only about seven feet of water at the entrance, but is deeper inside of the lagoon. Vessels of somewhat larger size may obtain shelter by going behind some of the small islands in the chain extending west from Flaxman island. Further extended work along this section of the coast was not undertaken by the Canadian Arctic Expedition, for the reason that the well-known explorer and geologist, Mr. Ernest deKoven Leffingwell, who first came to Flaxman island on the Mikkelsen-Leffingwell Expedition in 1906, had spent most of his time from 1906 to 1914 with headquarters at Flaxman island, working on the geology of the Arctic coast of Alaska, and had prepared a very minute and accurate map of the coast, channels, and islands of the section from the Colville delta east, including a very complete series of soundings of all the channels. These charts and geological results are now in course of publication by the United States Geological

---

[1] Summary Rep. Geol. Survey, Dept. of Mines, for 1914. Ottawa, 1915, pp. 148–149.
Ibid., Report for 1915. Ottawa, 1916, pp. 237–239.

Survey, but the expedition was very much aided in 1913-14 by information received and tracings of unpublished charts kindly loaned to us by Mr. Leffingwell for our work on the Alaskan coast.

During the spring and summer of 1914, the routine and executive work of the southern party devolved upon me, including the apportionment of supplies and equipment for three vessels. The 10-ton gasolene schooner *North Star* had been purchased by Mr. Stefansson from its owner, Capt. M. Anderson, who was wintering in Clarence bay, a little east of Demarcation point. As a consequence, the time for zoological field work and the preparation of specimens was limited; nevertheless, 212 birds representing 52 species, and 77 mammals representing 13 species were collected and preserved. Nests and eggs of many of the species of breeding birds were also collected.[1]

The expedition vessels *Alaska* and *Mary Sachs* left Collinson point on July 25, 1914, the first day that the ice moved off the beach far enough to let us out of the harbour. The vessels had been free of the ice inside of the harbour since July 7. After some delays occasioned by ice, which was thick and close to the beach around Martin point, Icy reef, and Demarcation point, the *Alaska* reached Herschel island 69° 34′ N. Lat., 138° 54′ W. Long., August 5, and the *Mary Sachs* a few hours later. The *North Star* had got in from Clarence bay a little before. These expedition vessels were the first vessels to come into Canadian waters in the western Arctic flying the Canadian flag. The steam-whaler *Belvedere*, of Seattle, which had taken on a quantity of auxiliary supplies, coal, distillate, etc., from Nome in 1913 for the expedition, and had been compelled to winter in the ice a little off shore west of Icy reef, had come through safely and landed our stores at Herschel island about the last of July.

Herschel island is quite a busy place in July and August. Eskimo-owned and sailed boats, to the number of twenty-five or more, whaleboats, and perhaps a dozen two-masted Mackenzie-built schooners, were assembled here to trade with incoming ships. With the recent decline in the whaling industry in the western Arctic, and smaller probability of ships wintering at Herschel island, the Eskimos from the Mackenzie delta and from the westward have a still greater incentive to be at the island to trade during the short open season. In 1915, one year after the expedition went in, the Hudson's Bay Company started an innovation by spreading out on to the Arctic coast, and established a western Arctic district headquarters at Herschel island and another post 150 miles east of the Mackenzie river at cape Bathurst (Baillie islands), 70° 35′ N. Lat., 128° 05′ W. Long. Another post has been established at Kittigazuit (the point Encounter of Sir John Richardson) on the eastern edge of the Mackenzie delta, and the site of one of the largest villages of the Mackenzie Eskimos. In 1916, the Hudson's Bay Company moved 400 miles farther east along the coast and established another new post at the station just vacated by the Southern party of the Canadian Arctic Expedition at Bernard harbour, Dolphin and Union strait, 68° 47′ N. 114° 50′ W. These new posts of the company are supplied by a gasolene motor schooner, the *Fort McPherson*, from the large storehouses at Herschel island, stocked by chartered ships sent up from Vancouver, B.C. It is to be assumed that the commercial prospects of this region in the fur-trading line are of considerable importance. The presence of trading posts in hitherto untouched regions will facilitate the more detailed exploring and prospecting of districts which were formerly impossible except to specially equipped expeditions.

As previously reported,[2] Mr. Stefansson, after his separation from the *Karluk*, had established a base camp at Martin point, Alaska, with supplies

---

[1] Summary Report Geol. Survey, Dept. of Mines, for 1914. Ottawa, 1915, pp. 163-167.
[2] Report of the Dept. of the Naval Service for the fiscal year ending March 31, 1916. Ottawa, 1916, pp. 16-19, 71-75.

8 GEORGE V, A. 1918

obtained from Collinson point, and from the *Belvedere* and *North Star* outfits, and started north from Martin point on March 22, 1914, on an ice-exploring expedition over Beaufort sea. The three men of the support party returned to land at Kamarkak, about 30 miles west of Herschel island on April 16, bringing the news that Mr. Stefansson and his two sailor companions, Storker Storkerson and Ole Andreasen, were going ahead fifteen days more travel before attempting to return, with the possibility of trying to push across the ice to Banks island in case conditions were favourable. As there were a much greater number of vessels and people than usual located at frequent intervals along the coast from Herschel island to point Barrow that season, the party would have been soon heard from if they had returned to the mainland in the spring or summer. As no further news was heard from the ice party, it was evident from knowledge of their plans that they had gone on towards Banks island.

The schooner *Mary Sachs*, under command of Mr. George H. Wilkins, with a full equipment of provisions, distillate, oil, etc., for two years or more, sledges, dogs, and a large gasolene launch, started from Herschel island for Banks island on August 11, and as we learned in the following spring, had met Mr. Stefansson's party near cape Kellett early in September, very soon after the vessel reached Banks island. Of course no word of this could reach the outside world until over a year later, causing considerable anxiety, as the three men of the ice party were generally supposed to have been lost for a year and a half. Having connected with the vessel with its supplies and exploring equipment, the activities of the Northern party during the remainder of 1914-15 were engaged in operations in the region of Banks island, Prince Patrick island, and Melville island. Advices received in the summer of 1916 indicated that the party was intending to remain in the north for at least another year. The *Mary Sachs* was still at cape Kellett, the *North Star* had joined the Northern party in 1915 and was hauled up on the northwest coast of Banks island, and the *Polar Bear*, a large schooner which was purchased in 1915, was wintering near the Princess Royal islands, in Prince of Wales strait, with the intention of moving on to Winter harbour, Melville island, for the winter of 1916-17.

While at Herschel island in August, 1914, we learned from SS. *Herman* of San Francisco, of Capt. Robert Bartlett's remarkable ice-journey from Wrangell island to Siberia, and his safe arrival at St. Michael's, Alaska, to bring relief for the shipwrecked *Karluk* survivors on Wrangell island, but it was not until November 9, 1915, that we got any more news from the outside world, and learned of the loss of eight members of the *Karluk* party on the ice, and the death of three more on Wrangell island, at the same time that we learned of the great European war, which had been going on for over fifteen months.

The schooners *Alaska* and *North Star* sailed east from Herschel island, August, 17, 1914, and were delayed a little by heavy ice in Mackenzie bay between Herschel island and Shingle point. Very little ice was found east of Shingle point, on the western edge of the Mackenzie delta, and we reached Baillie island August 21, finding that the *Mary Sachs* had gone on from there towards Banks island. Leaving Baillie island at noon of August 22, we anchored in Bernard harbour, Dolphin and Union strait, in the evening of August 24, and the *North Star* arrived on August 25. We had smooth sailing on summer seas east of Baillie island, free from ice except for a little loose bay-ice in Dolphin and Union strait.

At Baillie island we had met the little gasolene schooner *Teddy Bear*, going out under sail after spending five years in the Arctic. This vessel, which I had formerly met in Coronation gulf in 1911, was the first pioneer trading vessel to come in east of cape Parry. The *Teddy Bear* was commanded, engineered, and sailed by a young French-Canadian named Joseph F. Bernard, a native of Tignish, P.E.I., who had sailed from Nome in 1909 with one white companion to search for new fields for trapping and trading. His companion had been frozen to death the first winter near Barter island, Alaska, and in 1910 Captain Bernard had gone on alone with a few Eskimos for crew and wintered a little east of the mouth of the Coppermine river. The next year he came out as far as the civilized Eskimo village at cape Bathurst, where he wintered. Without going home, he turned east again in 1912 and spent one winter in a harbour on the south side of Dolphin and Union strait, about sixteen miles south of Liston and Sutton islands, and a little west of Chantry island; the next winter in Lady Richardson bay, southwestern Victoria island, coming out in 1914 after voyaging for five years. His harbour in Dolphin and Union strait, being the first good harbour for nearly 200 miles east of Pierce point, was used as a base station for two years, 1914-16, by the Southern party of the Canadian Arctic Expedition and named by us Bernard harbour, partly in honour of Captain Bernard's pioneer energy in discovering its suitability and using it as a ship station and in recognition of his unusual kindness and rectitude as a pioneer of trade in an uncivilized and unexploited land.

Bernard harbour was chosen by us for its strategic advantages for working the coast both to the west (from cape Parry) and to the east (into Coronation gulf), as well as its nearness to Victoria island (about 35 miles north across the strait). It was about as far east as driftwood could be found in reasonable amounts for fuel.

After discharging the cargoes of the *Alaska* and the *North Star*, and replacing a broken propeller on the *Alaska*, I finally started west with *Alaska* again on September 6, with the intention of getting some driftwood timber from farther west, as well as some more coal from our cache at Baillie island. The members of the scientific staff, with Mr. Chipman in charge, were left at Bernard harbour, to put up winter quarters, with some Eskimo assistants. Capt. D. Sweeney, Mr. D. W. Blue, engineer, Mr. A. Castel, J. Sullivan, cook; Mike, the Eskimo assistant engineer, and Ikey Bolt, a point Hope Eskimo sailor, went west with me on the *Alaska*. Finding weather conditions very favourable at Baillie island, and no ice reported to the westward, it seemed well to go on to Herschel island, to bring on additional coal and oil, and additional supplies which had been expected to arrive from the westward during the summer. The *Alaska* reached Herschel island again September 11. The *Ruby*, which was expected with supplies from the west, had not arrived, and after loading some stores from our reserve stock at Herschel island, on the *Alaska*, we started east again on the morning of September 13.

The *Alaska* came back to Baillie island on the night of September 15, in the midst of a northwest gale, with frequent snow-squalls, and spray freezing on the decks and rigging. The storm kept rising for the next two days, the worst storm of the season, and did not abate until noon of September 19. There was a very high storm tide, rising about 4 or 5 feet at Baillie island, the waters of Liverpool bay seeming to have been piled up by the northwest gale and forced out between the Baillie islands and the mainland. The distillate drums and coal sacks which had been landed on the beach in the summer were half buried by the sand washed up, and we had to dig them out. Quantities of large ice had come in from the northwest during the big storm, but we tried to go out on the morning of September 20.

In trying to turn around in our narrow anchorage, the bow of the *Alaska* ran slightly in the mud. We tried to kedge her off, but with the falling of the westerly wind, the storm tide fell rapidly, and we were soon settled hard aground. The whole cargo had to be discharged and the schooner finally floated free again on the evening of September 24. As the nights were getting very dark at this season of the year with the moon gone, and considerable heavy ice was coming in from the northward, with young ice forming thick and slushy at times, it was a precarious matter to sail at night with a small vessel. In the summer time, with daylight all night, a vessel can tie up to the ice, but it is a different matter

8 GEORGE V, A. 1918

in the autumn when the ice is moving in the dark.   From the outlook at Baillie island, with at least three days more delay loading ship from the beach in a dory, it seemed doubtful that we could get east of cape Parry, or possibly Pierce point, and there are no harbours beyond that nearer than Bernard harbour.   As we did not have much to bring back to Bernard harbour, and nothing that was absolutely necessary, the advantage in getting back there with the *Alaska* did not seem commensurate with the risk involved to the vessel, so I decided to put the boat into winter quarters at Baillie island, or rather into the harbour behind the end of the Cape Bathurst sandspit.   The *Alaska* had to go to Herschel island the next summer (1915) anyhow for supplies and mail, and had a better chance of getting out early from Baillie island than from farther east.   The scientific staff, with their supplies and equipment, and the *North Star* were already favourably located at their desired base, and I knew that I could join them by sledge as soon as ice travelling was good.   There was a fair amount of supplies on the *Alaska* for the men who were to remain as ship-keepers during the winter.   Two fresh whale carcasses on the beach near the ship provided an abundance of dog-food and also attracted a number of polar bears and multitudes of white foxes to the vicinity.   Fifteen polar bears were killed by the men on the *Alaska* before I started east on November 20, the skins kept for specimens and the meat frozen and stored away.   A number of seals and ducks were killed in the autumn, and seals were killed frequently during the winter.

On November 20, 1914, I started to go from the *Alaska* at cape Bathurst to the winter base of the Southern party on Dolphin and Union strait, an approximate distance of about 400 miles, accompanied by Aarnout Castel (sailing master of the *North Star*), James Sullivan (cook of the *Alaska*), and the Eskimo, Ikey Bolt taking one Nome sled and seven dogs.   We followed the west side of Franklin bay 90 miles to Langton bay.   The only inhabitants on the shores of Franklin bay that winter were two families of Mackenzie Eskimos who had taken a small schooner belonging to the Hudson's Bay Company from the Mackenzie river, to the mouth of Horton river, where they were wintering.   This vessel went back to the Mackenzie, the following summer.   The sailing schooner *Rosie H.*, which has been permanently in the Arctic for many years, was wintering at Booth island (cape Parry) with one white man and several Herschel island people. We did not go around cape Parry, but shortened our distance considerably by crossing the portage at the south end of the Parry peninsula, from Langton bay to Darnley bay.   The yawl *Argo* came in from northern Alaska with two white trappers and their families, to the southwest corner of Darnley bay in 1913 and remained until 1915.   On the southeast side of Darnley bay we passed the house of Capt. Christian Klengenberg, an ex-whaler with his family, and another house belonging to an Eskimo family which had come in from Alaska on the *Argo*. Klengenberg's young son and daughter had a temporary trapping camp a little east of cape Lyon, and east of that there were no inhabitants west of Dolphin and Union strait.   East of Baillie island there are no permanent residents, and the western Eskimos make only casual excursions into the territory.

The *North Star* had made a cache of provisions and coal oil at Pierce point in the fall, and we took some supplies from it on this trip.   We did not know whether we should find driftwood enough for fuel at all points along the coast on the 200 miles between Pierce point and Bernard harbour, and expected to use a "Primus" coal oil stove part of the time.   However, we found enough driftwood, for fuel at every camp site along the coast, and put up piles of wood at various points so that there would be no danger of having the wood covered with heavy ice before we should pass along the coast in the spring.   On December 10, behind Keat's point, we met Kenneth G. Chipman and John J. O'Neill with a sled.   They had left Bernard harbour November 19, to make a preliminary topographical and geological reconnaissance as far west as Pierce point, in preparation for the coming spring's work, as well as to look for the whereabouts of the

Alaska. They had found the weather very unfavourable for survey work, being foggy earlier in the season, and storms and blizzards prevailing later. They had been held in camp for six days straight when we met them, with strong head wind and blizzard, while we had been able to travel part of the time with fair wind, which makes a tremendous difference. They turned around and accompanied us to the eastward. We found open water pretty close to the shore all along from cape Lyon to Clifton point, and at Deas Thompson point the ice had recently broken away from the cliffs and we had to make a detour around over the hills. We were delayed two days by a blizzard near Wise point, and reached the winter quarters of the main party about noon, December 25. Travel had been rather slow, principally on account of the shortness of the days at that time of the year, between 69° and 70° North. It was barely light enough to see a trail at 9 a.m., and it was dark about 3 p.m. on clear days, while the period of daylight was considerably shorter on cloudy and foggy days. The temperature in general was warmer than usual at that season, not going below zero Fahrenheit at any time of observation during the first two weeks of December, 1914, and an occasion rising to 25° above zero Fahrenheit. Before leaving Baillie island we had a cold snap, the thermometer reaching 31° below zero on November 7. Coming east from cape Lyon the prevailing wind was favourable, from the northwest. The freeze-up in 1914 occurred at cape Bathurst about September 30, and at Bernard harbour about October 16.

Everything was in good shape at Bernard harbour, the winter quarters of the most of the Southern party. A frame house had been built, covered partially with boards and partially with canvas, and the whole sodded over in the autumn. Enough small driftwood had been picked up in autumn to last for fuel until Christmas, and more was hauled later in the winter, and pieced out by a sparing use of coal. East of cape Bexley there is very little large driftwood on the beaches, on the points around Cockburn point, east of cape Bexley, there is quite a quantity of small pieces of wood, and quite a bit on Chantry island, but very little east of Chantry island of any kind.

About thirty seals had been killed at Bernard harbour in the autumn, by shooting at the edge of the ice in the western method, but only four caribou were killed. The great herds of caribou which usually cross the strait near this point from Victoria island to the mainland, did not pass near Bernard harbour in 1914. The Victoria island Eskimos who visited the station later, said that the reason the caribou did not cross here this autumn was on account of the late freezing of Dolphin and Union strait. The caribou came down in large numbers to the south coast of Victoria island north of here, and as the strait was not frozen so that they could cross over, they moved eastward along the south coast of Victoria island and crossed some distance to the eastward. The Eskimos on the Victoria island side north and east of Bernard harbour killed large numbers of the caribou in the autumn, and we were able to purchase all the frozen caribou meat we needed as soon as the Eskimos could haul it across, and later, after the Eskimos' winter sealing, by spearing through the ice, had commenced, we were able to buy all the fresh seal meat we needed for dog-food or table use.

During February and March, 1915, Mr. Aarnout Castel and myself made a toboggan trip from Bernard harbour across the west end of Coronation gulf, up the Coppermine river, to Dismal lake, and across to the Dease river, northeast of Great Bear lake. We were much delayed by soft snow amongst rough, jagged ice on the Coppermine, and our dogs were too exhausted to be able to proceed very far through the very deep, soft snow on Dease river, so we had to turn back to the coast without making connections with any white man or Indians on Great Bear lake to take out our winter's mail. We reached Bernard harbour again April 1, and a little later the mail was sent out along the coast to the *Alaska* at Baillie island.

8 GEORGE V, A. 1918

On the Coppermine river, around Dismal lake, on the Horton river (south of Franklin bay), and to a less extent farther west, we have often noted the large proportion of dead spruce trees near the northern limit of timber. In some areas about 90 per cent of the trees are dead, in districts which show little or no evidence of forest fires. Mr. F. Johansen and Mr. D. Jenness accompanied our inland trip as far as the edge of the timber-line on the Coppermine, near the Sandstone rapid. Mr. Johansen made a careful study of forest conditions here and found that practically all the dead trees which were examined showed traces of the ravages of bark-beetles, three species of them being found. This knowledge may be of value to northern forestry.

The programme for the spring's work had been planned before going inland. Mr. John R. Cox, with an assistant, started in March and made a careful survey of the coast along the south side of Dolphin and Union strait from Chantry island east to cape Krusenstern and as far south as Lockyer point. Starting again in April, he carried the survey around the west end of Coronation gulf, including Basil Hall bay and the north side of Back inlet, as far as the mouth of Rae river. Rae river was ascended and carefully surveyed for about 70 miles, until it forked into two small creeks. Large willows were found at rather frequent intervals on Rae river after getting some way from the coast, but no spruce or other timber. After reaching the head of Rae river, Mr. Cox's party made a six-day portage across country with their sled, striking the Arctic coast on the south side of Stapylton bay. Numbers of caribou were seen migrating steadily northward during their work on the Rae river and the trip to the coast, and they had no difficulty in killing a caribou whenever they needed meat. Mr. Cox then surveyed the section of the coast from Young point (the western end of Stapylton bay) east to the home station, reaching Bernard harbour May 25. He found that South bay, southwest of cape Bexley, was somewhat deeper in extent than we had supposed, and that Stapylton bay is not as deep as the existing charts make it appear. The rock exposures on Rae river were the prevailing dolomite and limestone of the region, with diabase near the mouth of the river. At cape Kendall, a little north of the mouth of the river, high diabase cliffs are found overlying sandy limestones.

Mr. Kenneth G. Chipman and Dr. John J. O'Neill started on the western survey from Bernard harbour on March 17, 1915, going direct to the west end of Darnley bay and working east. Connecting with the previous surveys of the Parry peninsula, the survey was carried east during April, the season being much further advanced than it was farther east during the same period. As there are no rock exposures near the coast near the south side of Darnley bay, Dr. O'Neill was able to remain on the east side of the bay to carry on geological investigations in more detail, while Mr. Chipman completed the topographic work on the southwest part of the bay.

The southern part of Darnley bay had never been surveyed before and only imperfectly explored. Two fairly large rivers flow into the south and southeast sides of the bay, the most southern of which seems to have been visited by Mr. A. J. Stone[1] while on a short trip after muskoxen from the whaling ships which were wintering in Langton bay in 1898, and indicated by him on a rather inaccurate sketch-map as Hornaday river. As the river is approximately identifiable, and has no discoverable local name, it seems proper that the name Hornaday river should be retained for this river, in honour of the well-known advocate of Wild Life Conservation in the United States and Canada. For the southeastern river we propose the name Brock river, in honour of the patriotic and capable geologist, Major R. W. Brock, former Director of the Geological Survey, to whose active interest in Northern geology the organization of the geological and topographical sections of the expedition are largely due. Dr.

---

[1] Stone, A. J. Some Results of a Natural History Journey to Northern B.C., Alaska, and N.W.T. Bull. Amer. Mus. Nat. Hist., Vol. XIII, vi, New York, 1900, pp. 63–67.

O'Neill.ascended this river for some distance, and made a good geological section of the country. Inland on the east side of Darnley bay he found beach gravels and terraces above 500 feet, and everywhere east of that point the country for some distance from the coast is of the same type. From Darnley bay to the east of Deas Thompson point there are a number of high points which have received the name of mountains, but no definite system of range is apparent. The highest of these points (Mount Davy) is between the Croker and Inman rivers. The coast has a well-defined shore-line of rock or boulders and gravel.[1] None of the rivers flowing to the coast east of Darnley bay extend any great distance inland, for their valleys are small, and both valleys and beds indicate a very heavy run-off in a short time. The Croker is the largest river, with its delta built out a short distance, and occupies a triangular valley some 4 miles wide at the coast, and extending inland for 3 or 4 miles. The river spreads out over its delta, and none of its channels are very definite. The beds of this and other rivers are composed of heavy boulders, and the quick run-off is further indicated by the continuous sandbars built across their mouths when the river is low in summer and fall.[2]

The coast-line .as traversed from cape Lyon eastward was found to be somewhat more straight than the former charts give it, but this is apparently due to the practical impossibility of sketching a coast-line accurately on a hurried boat-passage some distance off-shore, with infrequent landings. This method has given the result that many of the so-called points on this coast are not salient projections of the coast line. More often the charted points and capes are high land or rock cliffs with low land on either side. This gives the higher places the appearance of points or capes when viewed from a distance. Our method of locating control points at frequent intervals by latitude, longitude, and azimuth observations, traversing between these points by frequent compass sights and pacing all the intervening shore-line, will undoubtedly give a more accurate map, although the former maps of this section of the coast are really very good considering the conditions under which they were made. No serious rectification was necessary until we came to Stapylton bay and eastward of that point. Mr. Chipman regards the whole country surveyed as evidently a portion of the coastal plain described by Tyrrell,[3] which west of Hudson bay reaches an elevation of 500·to 600 feet, and varies in width from 75 to 300 miles. Numerous fossil shells are found along the beach terraces. West of Chantry island fossils were collected from the 15-foot and 30-foot horizons. These fossils may be duplicated on the present strand-line. Near the mouth of Inman river, fossil shells were found in numbers up to 170 feet above sea-level.

Dr. O'Neill reports the country rock,[4] at least as far west as Clifton point, as a light grey to buff-coloured dolomite, sometimes with interbedded grey chert, and frequently containing fragments and nodules of the same. Ripple-marking and what seems to be mud-cracks were seen in some layers. A concretionary structure is quite common. The beds vary in thickness from a fraction of an inch to a few feet, and in grain from very fine to quite coarse and crystalline. They have a dip of about 10 degrees, a few degrees north of west. About 15 miles east of De Witt Clinton point there is a cliff of conglomerate 40 feet in height with an 8-foot capping of sandstone. The conglomerate is made up almost entirely of pebbles of quartzite and chert, and has a few small seams of buff-coloured sandstone interbedded with it. . The overlying sandstone is coarse-

[1] Chipman, K.G. Summary Report of Geol. Survey, Dept. of Mines, for the year 1915. Ottawa, 1916, p. 245.

[2] Summary Report of the Geol. Survey, Dept. of Mines, for the calendar year 1915. Ottawa, 1916, p. 245.

[3] Tyrrell, J. B. Report of the Doobaunt, Kazan and Ferguson rivers, vol. 9, p. 158.

[4] Summary Report of the Geol. Survey, Dept. of Mines, for the calendar year 1915. Ottawa, 1916, pp. 239–241.

8 GEORGE V, A. 1918

grained and weathers reddish-brown. About DeWitt Clinton point there are cliffs of very dark grey limestone 40 to 50 feet high, with beds 3 or 4 feet thick, and with a few thin beds of light grey limestone. At one place fine-grained diabase cuts through the limestone and spreads out as a capping on the cliff. The hills about here are covered with a mantle of alluvium, resembling glacial morainic material, which weathers to a buff colour on the surface. It is at least 30 feet in thickness. About Deas Thompson point there are cliffs of limestone 30 feet in height, dark-coloured at the base and lighter grey above, thin-bedded, and with encrustations of gypsum along seams and in fissures. Keats point is made up of coarse, reddish-coloured sandy dolomite. There are two distinct sets of glacial striae in the vicinity of Chantry island, one set running east and west (true), and the younger set running north 77 degrees east (true).

In an examination of the rocks from the foot of Darnley bay to cape Krusenstern, no evidence of the existence of copper was seen. A series of sediments is intruded by sills, or sheets of diabase at intervals from 20 miles south of cape Lyon to DeWitt Clinton point; no diabase is then seen again until one nears cape Kendall on the west side of Coronation gulf; north of Back inlet.

After returning from the inland trip up the Coppermine, I started west from Bernard harbour April 21 to reinforce the western survey party, meeting Chipman and O'Neill coming east near Deas Thompson point on Amundsen gulf. The Eskimos, Ikey and Palaiyak, who were with the party, were sent on to Baillie island with the mail, and to help on the *Alaska*, while I returned eastward again with the survey party. Owing to the extremely short-handed condition in which the Southern party was situated and the large amount of work planned for the coming summer, it was impracticable for me to return to Baillie island and return to Herschel island again with the *Alaska*, as I had intended. Instructions were forwarded to Capt. Daniel Sweeney of the *Alaska* at Baillie island, and he carried out the summer's work of the vessel very creditably and carefully, bringing in the mail, and a good load of additional provisions and coal from Herschel island. The ice left the beach at Baillie island, at 5 a.m., July 10, 1915, according to Captain Sweeney's report, and the *Alaska* got out of the harbour at 9 p.m., reaching Herschel island July 13. The first vessel to reach Herschel island from the outside was the *Polar Bear*, which arrived August 3; the *Ruby*, which brought in stores for the Canadian Arctic Expedition arrived August 14. The *Alaska* was loaded and left Herschel island to go east again August 22, reached Baillie island in the evening of August 23, left Baillie island in company with the missionary boat *Atkoon* of Collingwood, and the schooner *El Sueno*, arriving at Bernard harbour September 5, 1915. The *El Sueno* arrived September 7, bringing in a small amount of auxiliary supplies for the Southern party, and at once went west again to winter at Pierce point, for the purpose of trapping. The *Atkoon* was blown up on the shore between Clifton Point and the mouth of Croker river, but the vessel was apparently uninjured, and the missionaries established a winter camp there.

Our western survey party reached the station at Bernard harbour on May 24, 1915, one week ahead of our scheduled time. We had decided upon the date June 1 as the time for the sledge-survey parties to be back at the station, to avoid being troubled by the breaking out of the rivers. The unusually mild weather during the month of May facilitated our work very much. The skies were usually clear, and conditions good for travelling and taking observations. The weather was very warm and the snow thawing fast around Croker river May 16, but east of that point the season was more backward, and at Bernard harbour the ground was completely snow-covered until after the first of June. The snowfall is not very deep in this region, however, and after the snow really starts melting, it practically disappears from the land within a very few days, except the remains of deep snowdrifts in gullies and on the shady side of hills.

From the experience of the topographers of the Southern party of the expedition this spring, and in the year preceding and the year following, it was found that very little accurate topographical surveying on the lines laid down for us, 10 miles to the inch, with control stations at frequent intervals, could be done before the middle of March at the latitude we were working (from 67° 30′ to 70° approximately). Some compass lines could be run before that time, where salient points were already located, but earlier than the middle of March the sun is too near the horizon to get satisfactory observations, on account of the great refraction near the horizon. Blizzards and clouded skies were so frequent early in the spring that calculated occultations of stars and planetary satellites could only rarely be observed at a stationary observatory, and such observations were of little use in field work, and by the latter part of March the daylight period was so nearly continuous that there was no opportunity for other than solar observations after that season.

On May 21, 1915, Mr. George H. Wilkins arrived at Bernard harbour, accompanied by James R. Crawford, discharged as engineer of the Northern party's schooner *Mary Sachs*, and one Eskimo, named Billy Natkusiak. They had come from the winter quarters of the *Mary Sachs* near cape Kellett, Banks island, making the trip in about twenty-five days, across the southern end of Banks island, Prince of Wales strait, Prince Albert sound, and Dolphin and Union strait. Mr. Wilkins had found the Stefansson party safe near cape Kellett the summer before, and had come to make some arrangements to take the *North Star* to Banks island or Prince Patrick island as an auxiliary for further advanced party for proposed more extended work of the Northern party. The plans for the work of the Southern party had been based on the certainty of having the *North Star* for the summer's work in Coronation gulf, as the *Alaska* was at Baillie island, and bound to go to Herschel island before coming in again. It was finally arranged that the *North Star* should first lay down some provision depots in Coronation gulf and take the gasolene launch and outfit as far east as cape Barrow, and then go west to Herschel island, and later to Banks island.

Mr. Wilkins had lost his cinematograph outfit on the *Karluk*, but had obtained another cinematograph camera and a few thousand feet of film from the engineer of the wrecked schooner *Elvira* in 1914. He made a short trip on the ice of Coronation gulf and secured studies of Eskimo life in camps on the ice, and later in the season, views of their summer camps, fishing scenes, and home life and habits. About 2,000 feet of cinematograph film was exposed, most of which was ultimately developed and found to be of good quality. Mr. Wilkins made a very good series of portrait studies of most of the local Eskimos (Dolphin and Union strait), men, women, and children, in full view and in profile, for Mr. Jenness's ethnological work. He also made good photographs of growing plants, insects, etc., for the botanist and entomologist, and many photographs of birds, mammals, etc., in their natural habitat; pictures of great scientific as well as artistic value.

The expedition had always prided itself on being thoroughly prepared and equipped to take the field and work at any season and under any conditions. These problems of equipment may be roughly covered under four heads: (*a*) Winter and early spring sledging with tent or snow-house, using either wood, alcohol, Primus coal-oil stove, or native blubber-lamp; (*b*) late spring and early summer, prepared for either land or water travel; (*c*) summer travel with boat or canoe; and (*d*) overland packing by men and dogs in summer.

The western survey parties having finished their work late in May, it became necessary to start early summer work at once to the eastward. In Coronation gulf the ice was still solid in June, but there was the possibility of cracks and leads to cross as the season advanced, and boat-work after the break-up of the ice. The Northern party of the expedition had made good use of waterproof tarpaulins in constructing sled-rafts to cross leads, being

8 GEORGE V, A. 1918

unable to haul canoes over rough ice, but of course this made no provision for travel after the break-up of the ice. Our problems were somewhat different, as in Coronation gulf the ice was comparatively smooth. We took a large point Barrow whaling umiak, about 28.15 feet in length, and 6 feet beam, covered with heavy bearded-seal skins, and strengthened the stern timbers to provide for the adjustment of an Evinrude detachable gasolene motor, which proved to be a very valuable auxiliary. The canoe could be lifted by two men and placed on a low, ivory-shod boat-sled, which could be hauled in the spring by four or five dogs, carrying several hundred pounds of baggage inside of the boat. If necessary to cross a lead, the umiak could be unshipped and launched in a few minutes, and if the ice should break, the canoe would be launched automatically, already loaded. Later in the season, the umiak proved its worth by carrying two or three men, three dogs, and a thousand pounds or more of provisions, gasolene, and camp gear, making 5 to 6 miles per hour, and weathering some pretty heavy seas. It could be beached on any kind of coast in a hurry, by rolling it up on inflated sealskin " pokes," a great advantage when exploring a coast whose harbours are unknown; and a sudden breeze speedily raises a dangerous lop, as it does in Coronation gulf. The umiak is also a very useful boat among ice-floes, as it is practically unstovable and can be easily and quickly hauled upon or over an ice-cake, and it will also stand bumping over the boulders on a river-bottom which might prove disastrous to a wooden boat. The weight of a wooden boat of sufficient size would also be an insuperable obstacle to transportation by sled. For inland work in the Coronation gulf region, recourse must be had to packing in the summer, as most of the streams are too small and rapid to be navigable for any distance. The survey parties were supplied with condensed rations, and had dog pack-saddles for their largest and strongest dogs. Three or four good dogs can pack all the necessary provisions for a small party for several days.

On June 9, 1915, John R. Cox, topographer, and J. J. O'Neill, geologist, started eastward from Bernard harbour with the umiak on a boat-sled, taking also another large sled-load of provisions, supplies, and gasolene. They had as assistant for the early summer an intelligent Alaskan Eskimo, Billy Nátkusiak, who had been with me in the region several years before, and also as an experiment, a family of Coppermine Eskimos (a man named Mupfa, with a wife and child). We had heretofore little success in getting any useful service from the local aborigines, who have little or no idea of serving or working for anyone. It seemed necessary, however, to engage somebody to look after the sledge dogs, or part of them, after the surveying party should have to take to boat work, and this native engaged to help in the spring and look after our dogs during the summer at a fishing-place on one of the rivers on the south side of Coronation gulf. The man Mupfa turned out to be a very capable, intelligent man, and willing to learn, and carried out his agreement for the summer very creditably, and rendered loyal service to the expedition for the remainder of the next year. The party was to proceed by sled to Tree river, or the Annielik (in Gray's bay); during the early summer to work geologically up some of the rivers in that region, moving gradually along the coast to cape Barrow, 68° 01' N., 110° 09' W., the western extremity of Bathurst inlet, where Mr. Chipman and I would meet them with the *North Star* about the first of August, if possible, bringing the gasolene launch and additional supplies.

At cape Barrow, the circumstances of the season and the condition in which we found the party and the boats at that time, would determine the extent of the survey which we could make of Bathurst inlet during the latter part of the summer. It was planned to finish up as much as possible of the eastern end of our assigned territory during the summer of 1915, leaving the region nearer home (around the mouth of the Coppermine river) for the early autumn or coming spring, when the unfinished ends could be worked to better advantage from the base station. During the early summer of 1915, Mr. K. G. Chipman began a stadimeter survey of the region about Bernard harbour, with 20-foot contours. Mr. F. Johansen did some dredging for marine life in the inner and outer harbours, and completed his collections of the plants and insects of the region, while my own collections of birds and mammals was considerably increased. Considerable quantities of salmon trout were sun dried for winter dog-food, and some caribou meat was also dried for our own consumption. The few families of Eskimos who remained about during the early summer caught and dried large numbers of lake trout, catching them with hooks through the ice in June and early in July, and spearing and gaffing large numbers of salmon trout which were impounded in stone weirs when they started to run up the streams in July. By the last of July all the local Eskimos had departed on their summer packing expeditions to look for caribou inland.

The summer of 1915 was very late and cold, and the ice melted very slowly. The *North Star* had started to leak badly during the winter, and we finally succeeded in getting the vessel free from the ice and hauled up on top of the ice in the harbour July 7, and caulked her thoroughly. A few days later the ice had melted enough to drop the vessel into the water again, and on July 20 all the ice was out of the harbour. Bay ice disappears with wonderful rapidity at that season, the hot sunshine cutting away the top almost visibly, the ice floating up as it melts, and when it finally disintegrates into small pieces which touch the water on all sides, soon disappears absolutely. After the harbour and the large bay south of Chantry island were free of ice, Dolphin and Union strait was pretty full of ice. Broad leads opened up outside for a little, but the ice seemed pretty solid to the eastward. A steady, strong northwest wind for a week, practically a gale for three or four days, kept driving the ice down into and blocking up Dolphin and Union strait, and in the early part of August, between Bernard harbour and the Liston and Sutton islands, the strait was packed full of rough, heaped-up blocks of ice, where we had only smooth bay ice all the previous winter.

After being held for nearly two weeks after the break-up of the ice by heavy ice packed into Dolphin and Union strait by continued westerly winds, a spell of easterly wind started the ice moving westward again, and we worked the *North Star* out through the ice east of Chantry island August 9, finding the ice slowly moving westward. We were unable to get by the south side of Lambert island after going about half-way, finding the south side of the strait pretty well packed with ice, and went back around the west end of Lambert island to the north side of the island, passing over some dangerous rocky shoals extending for some distance off the west end of Lambert island, 6 feet of water 400 to 500 yards off shore. There is also a series of rocky islands and reefs off the east end of Lambert island. We passed cape Krusenstern in the evening of August 10, and passed through the Duke of York archipelago during the night, finding very little ice after passing cape Krusenstern, and Coronation gulf entirely free of ice to the eastward. We reached port Epworth, the splendid harbour at the mouth of Tree river, 67° 46′ N., 111° 59′ W., and found a large stone beacon on the island at the mouth of the harbour, with a cache and a note signed by J. J. O'Neill and J. R. Cox stating that they had been working in that region until July 30, when the ice moved off the coast allowing them to proceed eastward. They had gone on east to cape Barrow, where we found another beacon on August 12, stating that they had reached that point August 2. They had been delayed by head winds, and we soon found the party camped in a little bay just east of cape Barrow. The *North Star* put down a large cache of provisions at port Epworth, consisting of flour, rice, pemmican, sugar, and gasolene for the two motor-boats; and another cache at cape Barrow for use during the summer of 1915 and the possibility of sledge work in the spring of 1916. The *North Star* at once started back to the westward, on August 12,

8 GEORGE V, A. 1918

having been delayed only three days after getting out of the harbour in making the eastern trip. Having a stiff fair breeze behind her, the *North Star* was back at Bernard harbour within twenty-four hours, and finding all the ice had moved to the westward, kept on going and soon reached Baillie island. The party who went west on the *North Star* consisted of George H. Wilkins, commanding; A. Castel; James R. Crawford (discharged at Baillie island to go out on schooner *Ruby*); and the Eskimo, Billy Natkusiak. The party remaining at cape Barrow consisted of four men, K. G. Chipman, J. R. Cox, J. J. O'Neill, and myself, with one 20-foot wooden gasolene launch with 7-horsepower Gray motor, and the skin-umiak with Evinrude motor.

Cox and O'Neill, with their Eskimo assistants, had left Barnard harbour June 9, hauling the skin umiak on a boat sled, and crossed Coronation gulf direct from cape Krusenstern to the mouth of the Tree river (port Epworth), being delayed by only one large crack in the ice, about 30 feet wide. The season was much further advanced around Tree river than it was at Bernard harbour and the ice was soon cut away around the mouth of the river. Large quantities of fish were caught after the opening of the bay, and in addition to what were used by the party and their large bunch of dogs, over 500 pounds of fish were dried, baled and put *en cache* on the island at the mouth of the harbour for autumn use. Wolverines are surprisingly abundant on the coast in this region, and unless provisions and stores are cached on islands they are apt to suffer from the ravages of these brutes during the summer. Tree river was explored for some distance inland on a packing expedition in July. Like all the other streams in this region (in the granite area) it has rapids, cascades, and falls a few miles from its mouth. It abounds in fish in the summer-time, and several families of Eskimos usually spend the summer at the first cascade, catching fish by spear, hook, and raking with a sort of double gaff-hook. Salmon trout and two species of white-fish are largely caught in the rivers, while large lake trout are caught in nearly every lake of any size. The country a little back from the mouth of Tree river is dotted with innumerable clear lakes, basins in the granite, and the vegetation, particularly in the flowering plants, is richer than the average condition in the Arctic. A good collection of plants was made here during the early summer. Tree river has two large branches, one of which is said to rise near the east bank of the Coppermine. This western branch of Tree river is said to have spruce trees near its source. The scenery around port Epworth is quite striking, vertical cliffs of dark-coloured diabase, with long talus slopes, rising to a height of 600 feet above sea-level on either side of the harbour. A long ridge of dolomite runs west from the mouth of the river, about five miles back from the island at the entrance of the harbour of port Epworth. The island at the entrance of the harbour is black shale at the base, overlain with diabase. About five miles south of the mouth of Tree river a ridge of rounded granite mountains runs to the south and east side of the river, the highest peak noticeable, about ten miles back from the entrance of the harbour, being 1,090 feet above sea-level. It is interesting to note that about half a mile east of the mouth of Tree river, there are small crevices or pockets in the granite which are filled with the soft potstone (a talc chlorite schist), much used by the Eskimos of this region for making the stone blubber-lamps which are universally used by them, and also for making stone cooking pots. The use of the cumbersome, heavy, and fragile stone pots, however, is very rapidly declining, owing to the much greater convenience of tin, iron, and copper-ware which are being introduced in trade. There is no known potstone quarry west of Tree river, and most of the stone utensils come from there although the Eskimos informed us that there are also some smaller stone deposits on the Utkusikaluk, flowing into Gray bay, and somewhere around cape Barrow.

According to.Dr. O'Neill,[1] the islands in Coronation gulf, on a line southeast from cape Krusenstern to port Epworth, are all of diabase; no amygdaloid was seen, but some of the islands are cut by narrow veins of calcite which contain small patches of chalcocite. While making a second trip through these islands in May, 1916, I was impressed by the rugged formation of these islands, including many of the islands of the Duke of York archipelago. The group known to the Eskimos as Pauneyaktok, about 20 miles southeast from cape Krusenstern, are typical of the group, having precipitous cliffs of diabase running up to 200 feet in height, facing to the south and southeast, and sloping down to the water's edge on the north and northwest sides. Underneath the diabase of one of these islands, I noticed an exposure of sedimentary rock, a series of alternate layers of black and reddish strata about one inch thick, merging into a tick, flesh-coloured stratum. The base of the islands is very seldom visible, being hidden by talus slopes from 10 to 40 feet high.

"The coast from port Epworth to Grey's bay is diabase cutting grey shale or red sandstone, which immediately underlies the shale; no amygdaloid nor copper is in evidence in this diabase, of which the upper part has been removed by erosion. The Laurentian granite comes to within 3 miles of the coast at the Kógluktualuk or Tree river, and its western contact with younger sediments extends almost true south for over 30 miles. The northern border of this granite parallels the coast to the west end of Gray's bay; it forms the southern shore of Gray's bay and the whole coast from that place to the east side of cape Barrow."—(O'Neill.)

Cape Barrow, 68° 01' N., 110° 09' W., or Han-in-nek, as it is called by the Eskimos, is a mountainous granitic region, but is not nearly so high as stated by Franklin in 1821[2]. He says: "The higher parts attain an elevation of 1,400 and 1,500 feet and the whole is entirely destitute of vegetation."

In 1915 we found the height of the highest of the granite ridges to be 340 feet above the sea-level, by aneroid, and although the hills have a barren appearance on their summits and slopes, careful inspection shows many bright green patches in little valleys and gullies where soil has collected, as well as in basins in the rocks, around the little lakes—green grass, low dwarf willow, deep tundra moss, cotton-grass or "nigger-head" tussocks (the *têtes des femmes* of the northern Indians and voyageurs) heather growing luxuriantly in many shelving rocks, and about ten species of flowering plants in bloom close to our camp on August 13. The summits of the granite ridges were usually covered with gray lichens. In this region we were often deceived by great reddish areas on cliffs, giving the appearance of a ferruginous rock, but upon closer examination proving to be only a dense coat of red lichens.

After the return of the *North Star* to the westward, Chipman, Cox, O'Neill, and myself continued the survey east from cape Barrow with the small launch, umiak, and a Peterborough canoe. It turned out that this plan cut down to some extent as originally planned, as we had to lie over a good many days on account of stormy weather and high winds when we could not use the small boats, and might have gone ahead or anchored in more favourable place with the *North Star*. With the small boats we had to find a very small and very well-protected harbour for each night's camp. We were also prevented from getting back to the station before the freeze-up, as the almost continuous heavy weather late in the autumn prevented us from travelling a large part of the time with the small boats. The Evinrude motor did good service in the early part of the season on the umiak, and the two boats were able to work to some extent independently, by having one boat make more prolonged stops at the most

[1] Summary Report of the Geological Survey, Dept. of Mines, for the calendar year 1915. Ottawa, 1916, pp. 241.

[2] Narrative of a Journey to the Shores of the Polar Sea, in the years 1819, 20, 21, and 22. By John Franklin, Captain R.N., F.R.S., and Commander of the Expedition. London, John Murray, Albemarle Street. MDCCXXIII.

8 GEORGE V, A. 1918

interesting points for geological work, while the launch could keep running more or less continuously on the coast traverse.   In the latter part of August, the Evin-rude motor on the umiak gave out, and as we were not prepared to re-babbitt the bearings, which had been cut out by some grit, we had to lay the umiak up for a while near Kater point, Arctic sound, as it reduced the speed of the launch about a mile per hour to tow the umiak, and the winds were not steady enough to keep up by sailing.   With the umiak out of commission, Mr. Chipman found it necessary to stay in the vicinity of Kater point for about three weeks, and this cut down the topographic work considerably.

Previous to this the coast survey had been completed in detail from cape Barrow, around Detention harbour (a rather large bay nearly hidden by a large island nearly hiding the entrance; with a deep channel behind except at one narrow point near the eastern exit, where it narrows to about 100 yards in width and only one fathom of water).   An investigation was made of the islands along the coast here and farther south in Moore bay.   The islands from Gray's bay east were little granite outliners here and there near the coast, but north of Moore bay, and lying two or three miles outside of the Detention Harbour islands, are some rather large islands, called Nu-a-ho'-ngak by the Eskimos. The latter islands are stratified dolomite, cut by a large dike of diabase, which also runs inland on the mainland here.   Moore bay is rather larger than indicated by the charts, with a rather deeper extension to the southeast and a number of high diabase islands.   We found our first native copper *in situ* in cracks in the diabase on an island in Moore bay.   Small veins of galena (lead sulphide, Pb. S.) were observed in cracks in the granite at Galena point, just east of Detention harbour.   There is a river of fair size flowing into the southwestern point of Moore bay.

From Kater point, O'Neill, Cox, and I continued to carry on the survey with the launch down the west side of Arctic sound.   Some difficulty was experienced in finding a channel into the mouth of Hood river through a number of low sandy islands at the mouth of the river, on account of a heavy sea running at the time.   After entering the river we found a deep channel, 9 or 10 feet deep, following the high-cut bank along the south side of the river for 3 or 4 miles from its mouth.   At the first large bend, the channel shifts to the left (west) bank, where there is a small exposure of quartzite at the water's edge, overlain by a thick deposit of light-coloured sandy clay.   Willows on the bank here were 5 or 6 feet high, one inch or more in diameter, and quite a bit of dead willow in among them.   Considerable willow drift was found on the banks, affording more fuel than was usual in this region.   Going up stream from the quartzite bend, the channel gradually swung across to the other bank, but we had no difficulty following the deep channel (over 9 feet) by watching the colour of the water, which was grey over the shoals.   We could take the launch up only to the first cascade of the Hood river, and camped there on August 27, making an inland reconnaissance in the direction of the James river.   The steep clay banks of the river are about 100 feet high at the first cascade, with a level grassy bench extending back about half a mile to a ridge of fine, red sandstone, cut on the southwest side by a dike of coarse-grained basalt, with a broad grassy valley beyond.   The next ridge was quartzite, succeeded by another grassy valley. A herd of thirty-four caribou was found here, and one fat young bull killed to replenish our meat supply.   A single lone bull had been seen and killed at Kater point a few days before.   A little farther on O'Neill struck an outcrop of granite, pegmatite, and mica schist in the valley, and established the continuity of the granite extending from Detention harbour and Moore bay down to Hood river.   Going out of the river again the coast of Arctic sound was followed to its bottom.   A fine large specimen of the Barren Ground bear was killed at the south end of Baillie's cove, the extreme bottom of Arctic sound, where he was found digging roots from the sandy soil near the mouth of a small creek.

The east side of Arctic sound is formed by one side of Banks peninsula (Tikerayuk, or " the forefinger," of the Eskimos), its most northern point being point Wollaston. Native copper was found in amygdules on both sides of Banks peninsula. Running down the east side of Banks peninsula we expected from inspection of the chart to find a passage out through Franklin's so-called Brown's channel,[1] but found that the channel was a blind one, comparatively straight, with another peninsula, shorter than Banks peninsula, on the east side. The southerly portion of this hitherto uncharted sound is fringed for several miles on its west side by high cliffs of grey dolomite. Rather steep slopes of dirt and gravel lead up from the beach in about half a mile to 490 feet elevation. From the top of this slope, nearly vertical cliffs rise to a height of 870 feet above sea-level; composed of heavy strata of dolomite, with a heavy capping of diabase, much striated on the upper surface. Ascending to the top of these cliffs, a small creek was seen to run into the bottom of the sound from a lake about five miles inland, in a broad grassy valley to the southwest. We followed the coast around a series of long, narrow fiords, peninsulas, and small islands east of here, finding the coast line very slow and difficult to work out, being very much cut up in the region tentatively indicated by Franklin as Goulburn island, the latter being really a series of long peninsulas southeast of Banks peninsula. Having struck a considerable copper-bearing area in Bathurst inlet, it was thought better to make a detailed geological sheet of this important area than to attempt to make a complete survey of the bottom of Bathurst inlet outside of the copper area. We accordingly followed the southern boundary of the diabase area across to Kannuyuk (Copper) island, a large island in Bathurst inlet, south of the Barry islands, opposite Fowler bay, on the east side of Bathurst inlet. Driftwood was very scarce east of Kater point, but by picking up every small piece we saw on the beaches, we usually managed to carry enough in the boats to last us a day or two. Bird and animal life was remarkably scarce along the coast. Caribou signs were seen occasionally, and fresh tracks on some of the islands. A very fine large bull caribou was killed on Kannuyuk island, Bathurst inlet, by Mr. Cox on September 3. Numbers of gulls were nesting in rookeries near point Wollaston and on the south side of the Barry islands.

The Barry islands, instead of a single island, are really a group of large islands. The most easterly, called Ekullialuk, the Barry island of Franklin, is properly two large islands, separated by a bay or sound 4½ miles long and 2 or 3 miles wide, running north and south and opening to the north through a deep channel about one-quarter of a mile wide. This bay has several sharp, deep bays indenting its south shore, and several little stony islands near the shore. Cruising along the south side of the big island, along the foot of the precipitous cliffs of diabase, overlying red quartzite, we found an opening into the wall, through a channel about one-quarter of a mile long, one-eighth of a mile wide at the south end and about 100 yards wide at the north end, with a strong tide rip running to the southward when we passed through. In exploring the interior of the bay, we found Sir John Franklin's portage, discovered on his return boat voyage in August, 1821,[2] a passage between walls of almost perpendicular diabase about 100 feet high, but closed by a low, narrow gravelly isthmus about 30 yards across, across which he had to portage his canoes. There are in reality two isthmuses, separated by an " island " of steep rock, the western gravel isthmus being about 100 yards across, and the other narrower. As Franklin did not happen to strike the narrow, open channel about half a mile farther east, he assumed that the whole was a single island. Just northwest of the Ekullialuk

[1] Narrative of Journey to Polar Sea, in 1819–22. By John Franklin, Capt., R.N., etc. London, 1823, p. 375.
[2] Journey to Shores of Polar Sea, in years 1819, 20, 21, and 22, by John Franklin, p. 395.

islands, and separated by another narrow, deep channel is a large island called Adligaq, and north of Adligaq and extending some distance to the northeast of point Wollaston, is the large island called Igloruallig. The northeast tip of this group of islands approaches close to point Everitt on the east side of Bathurst inlet. The region around point Everitt is known as Umingmuktor, and is the centre of a fairly large group of Eskimos called Uminguktogmiut. The Eskimos who frequent the southern and western parts of Bathurst inlet are mostly Kilusiktogmiut, and this region in general is known as Kilusiktok.

As the season was getting advanced, we felt impelled to turn back from Ekullialuk (Barry island), Bathurst inlet, on September 8, 1915, without going to the bottom of Bathurst inlet. The geological results had been encouraging, for two large areas, each of several square miles in extent, were discovered, in which the native copper is widely distributed, and much valuable geological knowledge had been gained in tracing the contact of the basalts with the granites and sedimentaries throughout the region. The plan was made to complete the detailed mapping of the copper-bearing area by sledge the following spring by one party, while another party should fill in the gaps remaining in the coast survey west of Bathurst inlet. We were delayed by heavy weather from the evening of September 9 to the morning of September 14 on Adligaq island. On the 14th we succeeded in running as far as Cheere islands, at the entrance to Arctic sound, where a gale held us until the morning of the 16th, when we succeeded in slipping across to Kater point, where we joined Mr. Chipman. Here we were delayed for eight days, storm-bound in the fine little land-locked harbour. Strong northwesterly winds prevailed, with heavy snowfall and freezing weather. The ground was snow-covered, drifting to 4 or 5 feet in depth in the lee of bluffs and in gullies, while ice on small freshwater ponds was about three inches thick. The temperature of the air during this period ranged from 25° to 31° F., but the sea-water did not get down to freezing during our stay at Kater point, although we were anxiously watching for signs of slush ice. The 24th of September was warmer and quiet, and we succeeded in reaching cape Barrow that evening. Although the weather was otherwise fair, high winds kept us at cape Barrow until September 28. On the night of the 26th, young ice formed for the first time across the little harbour, but about half of it melted or floated out during the day. On the morning of the 28th the launch was run out through about 50 yards of young ice to clear a road to the open water outside. In doing this the ice sawed long holes through both sides of the boat about midships, the boat being only sheathed with tin forward. We were obliged to unload and haul the boat up on the beach high enough to clear the holes, so that we could patch it with tarred canvass and tin. We finally left the harbour at 10.45 a.m. and followed the coast pretty closely to the westward, keeping behind the very numerous small granite islands when possible, and cutting across the mouths of the numerous narrow bays and inlets with which the coast is indented. About 2.30 p.m. we were compelled to stop near the eastern end of Gray's bay, as the wind was too strong to cross the bay ahead. On the 29th we went ahead and entered the mouth of Wentzell (or Utkusikaluk) river a little after 1 p.m. There was a sandbar island at the middle of the entrance of the river and a 4-foot shoal in the channel, but after crossing this the river was 9 or 10 feet deep, with a width of about 100 yards. The coast near the mouth of the river is composed of fine sand mostly, supporting a little grass, wild barley, etc. Small granite outcrops show here and there, and there is a very rugged-looking range of hills two or three miles inland. We stayed only a short time in the river, catching two fine whitefish in a net while we were waiting. The river was rather muddy, but no ice was seen.

At 3.30 the wind moderated a little and we started ahead again, heading for a long point to the westward. The breeze freshening, we soon struck a heavy swell and shipped much spray. Running in towards the low shore, we struck muddy water about one mile from shore and soon sighted some low sand islands at the mouth of the Kogluktuaryuk river. We tried to enter the eastern channel but grounded, and had to turn back and enter the middle channel. Quite a bit of loose, slushy ice was floating down stream and bunching up along the sides of the river mouth. Numerous fish were jumping out of the water. We found the river frozen completely across about 500 yards upstream. High, steep, black earth or clay banks begin about half a mile from the mouth of the river, running back probably two or three miles to the rocky hills.' The roar of large water-falls could be heard from the mouth of the river. As the situation did not look favourable for camping, with no wood and a good prospect of a sudden freeze-up, we ran out of the Kogluktuaryuk, which is about south of the middle of Franklin's Hepburn island (known as Igluhugyuk to the Eskimos), and pushing ahead, camped long after dark on a small island off the mouth of the Annielik river (incorrectly indicated on Hanbury's map[1] as the Unialik). The Annielik river flows into the deep southwest corner of Grays' bay. The muddy water from the Annielik discoloured the waters of the bay for one or two miles from its mouth, and young ice was forming in crystals on the surface of the water in the evening, in calm places in the bay.

Leaving the mouth of the Annielik early in the morning of September 30, we passed the high sandstone cliffs on the west side of Gray's bay and reached a point about 15 miles east of port Epworth at 11 a.m. We were compelled to stop until 3.20 p.m. on account of a stiff breeze springing up, and reached port Epworth harbour, near our cache, about 8 p.m., at which time it was pretty dark. As the freeze-up of Coronation gulf was impending, we decided to stop at Tree river and return to the winter base at Bernard harbour with sleds. Stormy weather followed for four days and the young ice in the harbour was pretty thick on October 6.

We had taken our three best dogs with us on the boats during the summer, for use in packing trips inland and for tracking boats if necessary. Seven dogs and two sleds had been left in charge of some Eskimos at the first rapids about five miles from the mouth of the river, when Cox and O'Neill left this place July 30. We found that the natives had taken good care of our dogs, and the large fish-cache on the harbour island was intact, although wolverines had broken into the rock cache on the mainland and spilled out some flour and rice. Our natives here had just killed a number of fat caribou, and as by frequently dropping a net for fish, shooting caribou, Arctic hares, and other game when needed during the summer, we had been enabled to keep a large stock of reserve provisions on hand, we had no hardship in waiting at Tree river for about three weeks, until the ice of Coronation gulf became strong enough for us to start for home October 27, without following all the indentations of the coast. The Eskimo family which had accompanied Cox and O'Neill to Tree river in June accompanied us back to Bernard harbour. We reached the station November 9, 1915, and on that date received the first mail and news from the outside world that we had received for fifteen months.

Mr. D. Jenness, ethnologist of the Southern party, arrived at Bernard harbour on November 8, 1915, after having been with the Eskimos on Victoria island since April 13, 1915. He had started out with a small band of Eskimos, of whom the chief man, a middle-aged man named Ikpukhuaq, was engaged by Mr. Jenness as a helper. These Eskimos fulfilled all their promises and obligations to Mr. Jenness in a very kindly and creditable manner during the whole time he was with them. They spent most of the summer in the Colville hills in southern Victoria island, and did not go to Prince Albert sound, as had been anticipated. A few Prince Albert Sound Eskimos came to visit them in the spring, however. The party were moving most of the time, following the caribou, and

---

[1] Hanbury, David T. Sport and Travel in the Northland of Canada. London, 1904.

38—4

8 GEORGE V, A. 1918

supplementing the caribou to some extent with fish caught in the lakes. They did not suffer from lack of food during the summer, but experienced considerable discomfort from being without fuel for either cooking or warming themselves for a good part of the time. Many districts visited did not afford a sufficient quantity even of dwarf willow or heather to make fires, and the people were obliged to eat their meat and fish in a raw state oftener than desirable. Mr. Jenness, however, had some very interesting experiences, and obtained a good understanding of the language, habits, folk-lore, and viewpoints on life in general, such as can only be obtained by continued intimate relations. During the winter he supplemented this with intensive studies of the winter snow-houses life, and many gramophone records of songs, shamanistic performances, and the like. Finger-prints of many of the people were recorded, and many of their string-games, or cats'-cradles were recorded.

The C.G.S. *Alaska* had arrived at Bernard harbour on September 5, 1915, after going from Baillie island to Herschel island for the mail and supplies. After discharging cargo, the *Alaska* went back west to Stapylton bay to look for drift-wood, as the amount of coal brought in was smaller than had been expected. Mr. Frits Johansen, marine biologist, had been in charge of the Bernard harbour station since the *North Star* had left on August 9, with only the cook and Patsy Klengenberg, interpreter, to help him. Mr. Johansen, who had been authorized, if conditions were possible, to do some dredging work on the *Alaska* after her return, accompanied the *Alaska* on the trip to Stapylton bay. He got some valuable deep soundings and dredgings in Dolphin and Union strait, down to a depth of 50 fathoms, and obtained a quantity of specimens from greater depths than he had been able to reach before. Mr. Johansen made continued studies of the fresh-water life of the ponds and lakes in the vicinity of the station, and made fairly complete collections of the flora and insect life. In the autumn he completed a series of soundings of the outer and inner harbours here, by means of holes through the young ice, in continuation of work begun in the autumn of 1914. The lines were run over the ice between islands and points of the main-land, with the soundings at paced distances, from 30 to 250 feet apart. The result was the finding of very interesting hydrographic conditions, the maximum depth inside of the islands being 12 fathoms. This information was of particular value in connection with his other marine investigations, and added materially to the topographic map of the harbour. Mr. Johansen also did some other hydrographic work in the neighbouring fresh-water lakes, by taking soundings through the young ice in the autumn.

The barren-ground caribou began to migrate across Dolphin and Union strait shortly after our return from the east, and were coming in fairly large numbers by November 15, 1915. About forty were taken before the end of the month (including about ten brought by Mr. Jenness from the south side of Victoria island), so a plentiful supply of fresh meat was on hand all winter. Salmon trout were also taken in some numbers up to the middle of December in nets set under the ice of the lakes near the station.

Captain Sweeney brought in the news that Mr. Daniel Wallace Blue, chief engineer of the C.G.S. *Alaska*, died at Baillie island, N.W.T., on May 2, 1915, after an illness of ten days. He had been troubled somewhat in the latter part of the winter by what Captain Sweeney thought was incipient scurvy. About the only noticeable symptom was that when his legs were punched with the finger, the indentations remained for a short time. Captain Sweeney and some of the natives at Baillie island had the same symptoms to some extent, as did also a trapper named Fred. Jacobsen who wintered around Liverpool bay, and Captain McIntyre and Mr. Arey on the *Argo* in Darnley bay. Mr. Jacobsen came over to Baillie island in the spring, and Mr. Blue accompanied him on a sled trip along the coast, after ptarmigan. They were all improving in condition as spring approached. A few days later, Mr. Jacobsen brought Mr. Blue back on the sled, suffering from a severe congestion of the lungs. The pneumonic symptoms kept getting worse, and Mr. Blue died May 2. He was buried on cape Bathurst. Mr. Blue was one of the original crew shipped on the *Alaska* at Nome. He was a native of Ayrshire, Scotland, about 30 years old, and learned the steam engineering trade in Glasgow. He had lived in Alaska since 1906, and had followed the placer-mining industry (both prospecting and operating) on Copper river, Tanana, Nome, and Kobuk, Alaska. There was no other illness among the members of the Southern party, during the year 1915, except a slight illness of Mr. Jenness while he was spending the summer with the Eskimos on Victoria island.

Tidal observations were taken at Bernard harbour for a time in the spring of 1915, with the automatic tide-registering machine, but not very successfully, as the machine had a habit of stopping too frequently, and was finally discarded. In December, 1915, we secured tidal records continuously for one week, from December 4 to December 11; we erected a snow-house on the ice of Dolphin and Union strait, outside of the harbour islands, set up a long, graduated pole on the sea-bottom, and read the height of the tide every half hour, day and night, and at intervals of ten minutes or oftener around the periods of high and low tides. The maximum rise of tide recorded was about $2\frac{1}{2}$ feet.

Only three or four families of Eskimos were around Bernard harbour in the late summer and early autumn of 1915, but about the middle of November they began to come up from the Coppermine River region, and from the south coast of Victoria island, until about 125 were living in a snow-house village on the beach near the station. Most of them stayed around for about three weeks, living principally on caribou meat, while their women were engaged in making new caribou-skin garments for the winter. All this work had to be done on land, as the natives of this region have superstitious taboos which forbid them dressing caribou-skins or making new caribou-skin garments while living on the ice. This was a happy time of the year for them, and there was singing and dancing going on most of the time. In the early part of December, when their new winter clothing was completed, and their stocks of frozen meat, dried meat, and fish began to run low, they all moved out to the vicinity of Liston and Sutton islands, in the middle of Dolphin and Union strait, about 16 miles north of Bernard harbour. The people build snow-houses on the ice there, and live practically exclusively on seals for the rest of the winter.

A good collection of mammals and birds was made around Bernard harbour in the spring and summer, and Mr. Jenness brought back a few zoological specimens from Victoria island. In the late summer I collected specimens at various points in the Bathurst inlet region. A good series of barren-ground caribou were collected during the autumn migration south from Victoria island. Some caribou specimens were obtained during the spring migration, some young fawns in June, and three good summer specimens, while we were in the eastern region. Specimens of fish were also taken whenever possible.

January and February, 1916, were spent by the geological and topographical men mostly in working up their field notes and preparing for the spring work. Mr. Jenness spent most of the winter at the large Eskimo sealing village near the Okullit (Liston and Sutton) islands, pursuing his ethnological studies. I made a trip to the first timber on the Coppermine river with some of the hunters in January and February, and a quantity of caribou meat was brought back to replenish the house supply, as well as a few specimens. Caribou were found to be fairly plentiful down to the coast near the mouth of the Coppermine river, and we also saw one small herd south of cape Lambert. Caribou are not often seen near the coast of Dolphin and Union strait in winter. The natives in this region spend the winter sealing through the ice, and at the present time do not molest the caribou from November until April.

8 GEORGE V, A. 1918

At the outset of this trip, in January, I sent two of the Coronation gulf natives, named Mupfa and Kohoktak, in the employ of the expedition, to haul by sledge a quantity of provisions from the station at Bernard harbour to port Epworth, Coronation gulf, which was to serve as an outfitting base for Mr. Chipman's projected survey of the south side of Coronation gulf from the mouth of Rae river east to cape Barrow and for the return trip of the two or three sledges which would be working in the Bathurst inlet area until late in the spring of 1916. These two Eskimos, with their families, faithfully hauled and cached the goods safely, and on their return trip brought back to Bernard harbour several boxes of specimens which had been cached at port Epworth in the autumn. That spot was particularly favourable for making secure caches on account of the massive flat slabs of heavy shale lying loose on the island, affording ready material for making vermin-proof caches. Wolverines are surprisingly numerous on the coasts and islands of this region, far from the nearest timbered country, and nothing edible can be left long without being securely protected from them.

I returned to Bernard harbour from the Coppermine river trip on February 27, having been gone a little over a month. It had been arranged that K. G. Chipman should start on March 1 to make a survey of Croker river before starting the eastern work. This seems to be without doubt the largest river between Darnley bay and Coronation gulf, and nothing but its mouth had been put on the charts previously. I decided that I would accompany Mr. Chipman on this trip, which was of interest not only as giving an important geological section into the heart of the barren ground half-way between Mr. O'Neill's reconnaissance from Darnley bay, and Mr. Cox's traverse from the head of Rae river to Stapylton bay, but might also throw more light on animal distribution, particularly of the muskox. Owing to stormy weather we did not get away from Bernard harbour until March 6, and reached the mouth of Croker river on March 15. Near Clifton point we spent a night at " Camp Necessity," a little cabin built in the fall of 1915, by Rev. H. Girling, of the Anglican mission service, and his assistants, Mr. G. E. Merritt, of St. John, N.B., and Mr. W. H. B. Hoare, of Ottawa. They had intended to come farther east, but had been cast up with their little schooner nearly a hunderd miles west of the Eskimos they were intending to work among. Their schooner was apparently uninjured, and they expected to move in to Dolphin and Union strait in the summer of 1916, and establish a mission at Bernard harbour. The present western range of the Copper Eskimos extends usually to cape Bexley or South bay; west of that point is a 200-mile stretch of coast to cape Lyon permanently uninhabited, and usually uninhabited west to cape Bathurst, about 400 miles.

Croker river[1] has a broad delta, forming a triangle nearly equilateral, with base about 5 miles across at the coast, and apex about five miles inland, where the river emerges from a rampart of low hills. After leaving the hills, the river follows many devious channels, through many gravelly and stony bars and islands. There were a few small domes caused by ice rising up, but no recent signs of water flowing. The river seemed to be frozen to the bottom all the way up, so far as we could observe. The river is 60 to 70 yards wide where it emerges from the first rock (dolomite) cliffs about five miles from the coast. The cliffs a little inside the first bend of the river are about 60 feet high; they are composed of stratified dolomite, yellowish on the surface, but grayish on freshly broken surfaces, with some lighter-coloured bands, and lenses of calcite. The canyon walls on both sides became gradually higher inland, from 100 to 150 feet, vertical on both sides in most places. The river maintains a uniform width of about 60 yards, narrowing in one place to about 40 yards. Heavy snowdrifts overhung the west bank in many places (due to the prevailing winds), and there had been avalanches in places, making barrier ridges of very hard, ice-like, angular-

---

[1] Summary Report of the Geological Survey for 1916. Ottawa, 1917.

fractured snowblocks extending most of the way, and sometimes entirely, across the river. The river continually makes very short, sharp bends, but its general course is northerly. There are no tributary creeks entering the lower course of the river. At very frequent intervals the sides, walls, and brink of the canyon are castellated, or split vertically into sharp, angular, pointed pillars, spires, and minarets. One straight pillar in a bend of the river, was about 40 feet high and not over 3 feet thick at the base.

About 12 miles from the mouth of the river, and nearly 8 miles up the canyon, there is a broadening of the river where a large creek comes from the southeast, splitting to send a branch around a large, picturesque, pyramidal rock island about 300 feet high, before entering the river. This was the first place where we were able to get up out of the canyon and Mr. Chipman and I climbed to the top of the hill by cutting some niches and steps in the snowbanks. The top of the canyon walls were found to be 310 feet above the river, by aneroid, and the top of the ridge behind, 350 feet above the level of the river. We could see quite a bit of land on both sides of the river, and it appeared to be smooth, rolling upland. A little above this creek, the river narrowed abruptly to a gateway about 18 feet wide and over 300 feet high, and a little farther on to another gateway about 36 feet wide. Beyond this the river was wider, but the gorge was so much obstructed by avalanche barricades of icy-hard snowblocks that it was scarcely possible to take a loaded sled over them, so we decided to camp there, cache all but four days provisions, and scout ahead with a very light sled.

Before going farther up the river, we explored the tributary creek, got out of the creek canyon about 2 miles up and went up on the hills. The deep canyon of the river, cut down more than 300 feet through the dolomite, is not visible at a distance of more than half a mile. The country slopes gradually north to the coast of Amunsdsen gulf. The river canyon was seen to make a series of intricate bends a little above the creek, the loops coming nearly together. A little farther up, the river has quite a steep descent, with some rapids, if not waterfalls. The snowdrifts and ice barriers were so deep, however, in most places that it was impossible to see the character of the river. In some stretches of the river, progress was made only by climbing over one rugged hill of snow blocks, descending 20 or 30 feet into a deep pit, and immediately ascending another ridge, like working through pressure-ridge sea ice. We frequently had to boost and lift the sled up over ridges by main strength, and take the dogs out of harness to let the sled down. The rock strata are horizontal in most places, with some slight local variations of not more than 4 or 5 degrees. Quartz geodes, with brown and transparent crystals of topaz were frequent.

After going about 20 miles in the canyon, we came out suddenly on a snow-covered, hilly country, and at the mouth of a large creek coming from a northerly direction, about seven miles from mount Davy. A short distance south of the big canyon, there is another little canyon about three-quarters of a mile long and 20 to 30 feet deep, cut through dolomite overlain with gravelly knolls. At the upper end of the little gorge, the river cliffs are overlain with a sort of mud conglomerate—fragments of dolomite, granite and diabase, imbedded in yellowish-grey mud or clay. The tops of all the hills are covered with small stones, little angular, fragments of dolomite, and a few boulders of granite and diabase. The ground is very barren everywhere, and gravelly where exposed through the thin crust of snow on the hill tops; no ground willows were seen on the hills, and only very scanty grass. Very rarely a single little sprig or two of willow would be found to have a foothold in a sheltered crevice in the bank of the river valley.

Mr. Chipman went to the top of mount Davy, which is the most conspicuous landmark from the coast from Inman river to some distance west of Croker river. He saw no rock exposures, the mountain being a hemispherical mound of gravel about 200 feet above the general level of the surrounding plain. Mount

8 GEORGE V, A. 1918

Davy has an elevation of about 2,000 feet above sea-level by aneroid, agreeing very closely with its height as determined by triangulation from the coast. Some hills to the southward seemed to be higher than mount Davy. The Croker river valley extends comparatively straight to the south from this point for 10 or 15 miles. The hills south and southwest form a rather rugged-looking range, running approximately east and west. They are similar in appearance to the rather steep gravel ridges and knolls common along this coast, and no rock exposures could be seen. Above the little upper canyon, the river is rather broad for a distance, looking like a lake, and on the east side of this expansion is a low, broad, stony and gravelly flat. The only signs of life seen on the whole river trip were an Arctic fox track near mount Davy, a few Arctic hare tracks, and one hare which we killed. One raven was seen near the mouth of the river. We later learned from the missionaries that a few caribou came down to the coast a little east of here in the month of May. In 1915 we saw four caribou in May near Wise point, and one small bunch near Young point, but from the tracks it was evident that caribou were very scarce on the coast west of cape Bexley. The coast of this region seems to be too barren to afford sufficient pasturage for large numbers of caribou at any season. No signs of muskox were seen on the trip. We returned to the coast March 24, and reached Bernard harbour April 2. The coldest weather of the winter was recorded while we were in camp up the Croker river, 46 degrees below zero Fahrenheit at 6 a.m., March 21. The thermometer rose to 9 degrees below zero at 4.30 the same day. The minimum temperature at Bernard harbour the same day was 38 below zero, and the maximum 23 below zero.

D. Jenness, ethnologist of the expedition, accompanied by Mr. H. Girling, and Patsy Klengenberg, interpreter and assistant, left Bernard harbour February 15, and returned late in March. They visited a number of Eskimo villages on the ice of Coronation gulf east of cape Krusenstern (Nuvuk), near Tree river (Kogluktualuk); and near Hepburn island (Igluhugyuk), meeting a good many Eskimos that had not been seen before, and gaining considerable information in regard to the Kiluskitogmiut, who inhabit the Arctic sound and Bathurst inlet region usually in summer; the Havuktogmiut, from the central part of the coast of southern Victoria island; the Ekalluktogmiut, from farther east than the Havuktogmiut; and the Umingmuktogmiut from the eastern part of the Bathurst inlet region, and the Asiagmiut, from the same region and the eastern part of the Kent peninsula. They visited several villages on the ice as far east as cape Barrow. A number of the eastern Eskimos came to the Bernard harbour station about the same time that Mr. Jenness returned, and many interesting gramophone records of the language and dialects were obtained. Earlier in the winter some Eskimos came from a greater distance to visit the station, notably a man named Kakshavik or Kakshavinna, calling himself a Pallirmiut, from the northwestern side of Hudson bay. He claimed to have come from a timbered country far to the eastward, and had traded at a white man's post, from his description apparently in the region of Baker lake or the Kazan river.

F. Johansen, naturalist, with Ovayuak (Eskimo) for companion, made a trip along the south shore of Victoria island, leaving the station March 6, and returning April 11, 1916. They crossed by way of the Liston and Sutton islands, Lady Franklin point, visited the Miles islands, and went along the Richardson islands as far as Murray point on the south shore of Victoria island. No Eskimos were seen except one group camped on the ice near cape Murray. He made such botanical collections as were possible at that season, took a few zoological specimens, and a number of specimens of rock at various points along the south shore of Victoria island. A few caribou were seen on southern Victoria island on March 19 and 21. The most important results of his trip were a number of species of fossil corals collected on one corner of Liston island in Dolphin and Union strait, as recognizable fossils are very hard to find in that whole region.

After his return, Mr. Johansen spent the rest of the season in completing his biological investigations near Bernard harbour, and in packing specimens and equipment preparatory to going out. His collections of plants and insects were practically complete for the region, and he made considerable additions to his collections and studies of fishes and marine and fresh-water invertebrates.

John J. O'Neill, geologist, and John R. Cox, topographer, started from Bernard harbour on March 17, 1916, to continue the survey of the copper-bearing area in the Bathurst inlet region. They took two sleds with them, so that they could work separately when desirable, and provisions for about ten weeks. They had for assistants, Ikey Bolt, an English-speaking point Hope Eskimo who had been with the expedition for over two years, and a Coronation gulf Eskimo with his family. Both the man and his wife had proved very useful in working, and they were familiar with the Bathurst inlet territory. O'Neill and Cox succeeded in cleaning up the work pretty well as planned. Tracing the southern contact or the copper-bearing diabase with the older rocks to Kannuyuk island, it was not thought advisable to waste the limited time at the disposal of the party in running a coast survey line to the southern tip of Bathurst inlet (which runs some distance south of the Arctic circle), and the time was spent in making a more complete geological sheet of the mainland and islands in the upper northwestern portion of Bathurst inlet. Over 200 islands were mapped in the region generally covered in the charts by Chapman, Lewes, and Marcet islands. The group consists of many small rocky islands which at a little distance have the appearance of forming a continuous coast line.

They found practically no game in that region in March and the early part of April, and no natives living much south of cape Barrow at that season. The natives say that the sealing is very poor in Bathurst inlet in winter and the people have to go out on the ice farther north and west in Coronation gulf. The season in Bathurst inlet seemed to be much later than it was in Dolphin and Union strait in 1916, as the seals did not begin to come up on the surface of the ice in Bathurst inlet until about May 20. The provisions of the party held out well, as they obtained plenty of caribou after the end of April. For fuel they used mostly distillate from the cape Barrow cache, burning it in Primus stoves, but later in the spring used dwarf willows from some of the islands. Early in the season they found the Eskimo snow-house and blubber-lamp useful and comfortable on occasion.

The work of O'Neill and Cox in March, April, and May, 1916, completed the survey east of cape Barrow practically as planned. Mr. O'Neill summarizes the results of the work in that region as follows:[1] " The copper-bearing rocks in Bathurst inlet occur on most of the islands west of a line running northwest-southeast from the east side of Lewes island, and north of Kannuyuk island. They cover most of the Banks peninsula and the western mainland shore from the mouth of Hood river to Moore bay, extending as much as 5 or 6 miles inland from the coast. These rocks are amygdaloids and form several successive layers which represent progressive, intermittent effusions of lava. Nearly all of them are impregnated with native copper over wide areas. The copper occurs in veins and in amygdules, and is disseminated as pepper throughout the groundmass. I have made a very conservative estimate of the amount of this copper-bearing rock (in which I actually saw native copper) and it seems that two billion (2×10^8) tons is well within the limit. It will be necessary to wait for analyses, and for the plotting of the map to give a close estimate of value of these deposits."

Kenneth G. Chipman, with Eskimo camp assistants, and Corporal W. V. Bruce, R.N.W.M.P., as voluntary aide, left Bernard harbour on April 12, 1916, to finish the survey of the south side of Coronation gulf east from the mouth

---

[1] Summary report of the Geological Survey for 1916, Ottawa 1917.

8 GEORGE V, A. 1918

of Rae river (where John R. Cox left off in 1915) to cape Barrow. Mr. Chipman completed the survey up to cape Barrow by May 20. The Bathurst inlet survey parties were met here at an appointed rendezvous, and we all went west together to the mouth of the Coppermine river.

After returning from the Croker river survey trip, I spent some time at the station arranging for the spring work and getting all accumulated zoological specimens taken care of before warm weather should set in, and finally started east with a sled and one Eskimo boy as an assistant, to make a trip into the Arctic sound and Bathurst inlet region to investigate the occurrence of the muskox, and other distributional problems of the fauna, as well as look up and assist the various surveying parties on their return. Mr. J. E. Hoff, chief engineer of the *Alaska*, with Mike, his Siberian Eskimo assistant engineer, went along as far as the mouth of Tree river, where they took out the launch motor and the Evinrude motor, and hauled them back to Bernard harbour. The hull of the launch was abandoned as it was badly worn and cut up, and the skin umiak was left for the last sled party to take back. The skin cover of the umiak had been removed the previous autumn, folded up and placed in a cache of slate slabs to protect it from vermin during the winter, and only needed to be soaked up and stretched over the canoe-frame again. The skin umiak is a very practicable means of crossing leads in the early summer, and I considered it advisable to have it on board the *Alaska* in case of accident in ice-crushes when travelling to point Barrow. The umiak is light and may be readily hauled over the ice where a wooden boat would be stoven.

The snow began to melt on the land much earlier than we had anticipated, being pretty soft by May 19, and I could not make the projected inland trip south of Arctic sound. I met O'Neill and Cox in Bathurst inlet, east of point Wollaston, and returned to cape Barrow with them, meeting Mr. Chipman's party again on May 21. There was much water on the ice around cape Barrow May 21, and much slushy snow and water until we got back to Tree river. We remained at the island at the entrance of the harbour from 3.45 a.m., May 25, until 10.30 p.m., May 27, putting the umiak in shape and getting some dog pack-saddles made for Mr. Chipman. Mr. Chipman had met the Royal North-west Mounted Police patrol from Great Bear lake near the mouth of the Coppermine river early in the month, and arrangements had been made that he should go back to Great Bear lake overland with Mr. D'Arcy Arden, who had come down with the police patrol. Mr. Chipman wanted to go out by the overland route because his work here was finished, and the prospect was good that he could get out a little sooner by fort Norman and the Mackenzie river, and it was desirable to have news of the Southern party's condition and welfare get outside, in case the remainder of the party on the *Alaska* should be prevented by ship-wreck or ice conditions from getting out by way of point Barrow and Nome, Alaska. Mr. Chipman reached the end of the telegraph line at Peace river crossing on August 18, and Ottawa about the end of the month.

It was evident that Franklin was labouring under a misapprehension when he applied the name of Tree river to the river flowing into port Epworth. The Eskimos call this river Kogluktualuk (river with big rapids.[1] In describing his interview with the aged Eskimo Terreganoeuck, or the White Fox, near the mouth of the Coppermine river, June 16, 1821, he says: " He had no know-ledge of the coast to the eastward beyond the next river, which he called Nappa-arktok-towock, or Tree river." Franklin accordingly charted the next river which we observed as Tree river, about 65 miles east of the mouth of the Copper-mine. The old Eskimo was evidently referring to the small river which they still call Naparktoktuak (na-park-tok—spruce tree), flowing out through steep clay hills about 10 miles east of the Coppermine. I crossed this stream in the

---

[1] Narative of a journey to the shores of the Polar Sea, in the years 1819, 1820, 1821 and 1822 by John Franklyn, Captain, R.N., F.R.S., and Commander of the Expedition. London, 1823, p. 352.

spring of 1911 while making a portage from the mouth of the small Kogaryuak river (18 miles east of the Coppermine) to Bloody fall, and found a few small spruce growing in the valley within 10 miles of the coast, several miles north of the northern limit of trees on the Coppermine river itself.

Sending one large sled load of specimens with some of our Eskimos directly from port Epworth to Bernard harbour via cape Krusenstern, we started west at 10.30 p.m., May 27. West of port Epworth we found that most of the melted snow water had drained off through cracks in the ice, making sled travel much better. The section of the coast from the Coppermine river to port Epworth as mapped by Mr. Chipman in 1916, lies substantially as indicated on the old charts. The only rivers of any consequence are the big Kogaryuak, emptying about 25 miles west of port Epworth, and a smaller stream, also called Kogaryuak by the natives, flowing into Coronation gulf about 18 miles east of the Coppermine. In 1910-11, Capt. Jos. F. Bernard wintered inside the mouth of the latter river with the schooner *Teddy Bear*, drawing about 6 feet of water. All these rivers have falls or rapids a few miles from the coast. East of port Epworth, considerable rectification of the chart was made around Gray's bay, locating the Annielik, Koguktuaryuk, and Utkusikaluk (Wentzell) rivers, and several long narrow inlets and many granite islands between Gray's bay and cape Barrow. A point of interest was the great length of the inlet at Inman harbour, a very deep, narrow fjord, the bottom of which is separated by a low portage of half a mile from another deep inlet running in from the east side of cape Barrow, between cape Barrow and Detention harbour, nearly making an island of the cape Barrow peninsula. For the convenience of future travellers, we have adhered to the policy of retaining the native place names where these can be ascertained, but as this inlet seems to be unnamed, we propose the name Desbarats inlet, in honour of the Deputy Minister, Department of the Naval Service, who directed the general affairs of the expedition, and to whose careful and continued attention and interest the members of all the parties are deeply indebted.

The united sledge parties returned together along the coast as far as the mouth of the Coppermine river, which was reached on the morning of May 31. The river was open to its mouth, and was flooding the ice for about half a mile outside of its mouth. About 125 Eskimos were encamped a little west of the mouth of the river, on the southeast shore of Richardson bay. Most of them were preparing to start packing overland to Dismal lake and Dease river, although two or three families were intending to spend the summer hunting caribou around the Rae river, and three or four of the least enterprising families and some older people were intending to spend the summer spearing fish at the rapids of Bloody fall, about nine miles from the mouth of the river. Mr. Chipman and Mr. Arden left the mouth of the Coppermine river on June 1, to pack across country to Great Bear lake with some good pack dogs, while the rest of our party started at the same time to the station at Bernard harbour, going a little out of the way to re-examine some geological formations at cape Kendall and cape Hearne, on the west side of Coronation gulf. Part of the way we had to wade through about one foot of water on the ice, but after passing north of cape Hearne, the weather turned cooler and froze a crust on the fresh water which was on top of the sea ice, strong enough to bear up our sleds, and travelling was more easy. Considerable stretches of open water were seen south and west of Lambert island June 5 and 6. The ice is said to be very thin there even in winter and opens up very early in the spring. Great numbers of Pacific and King Eider ducks were seen in the water and on the ice at the water's edge. We reached Bernard harbour June 6, and found everybody well except Captain Sweeney, who had injured his hand while working on the ship. The wound became infected and his arm was badly swollen and had to be operated on several times, so that he did not recover the use of it for several weeks.

Mr. George H. Wilkins, with the Herschel island Eskimo Palaiyak, reached Bernard harbour on June 15, 1916, having comé by sled from the headquarters of the Northern division of the expedition, near the Princess Royal islands, Prince of Wales strait, coming down the southern part of that strait, and crossing Minto inlet, Prince Albert sound, and Dolphin and Union strait. Mr. Wilkins brought news of the safety of the three vessels of the Northern party, and of the progress of their operations up to May 5, 1916. The *Mary Sachs* was still at cape Kellett, southwestern Banks island, where she had been hauled up since 1914, in charge of Capt. Peter Bernard, with some Eskimo assistants. The *North Star* had been hauled safely up on a small island north of Robillard island on the northwest coast of Banks island in the autumn of 1915, and the crew had gone over to join the *Polar Bear* party in the winter. The *Polar Bear* had attempted to go up through Prince of Wales strait on the east side of Banks island, but was unable to get beyond Armstrong point, and wintered between Armstrong point and the Princess Royal islands. At the time Mr. Wilkins left in May, Mr. Stefansson contemplated carrying on his travels on the northern islands until 1917, the *Polar Bear* having been directed to move its base to Winter harbour, Melville island, to spend the winter of 1916-17, with the possibility of the party remaining in the Arctic until 1918. The Northern party was stated to have provisions for one or two years more, and were killing and storing away large numbers of caribou and muskoxen on Melville island in the spring of 1916. Quite a number of their engaged western Eskimo hunters had been sent up to Melville island early in the spring to shoot caribou and muskoxen for the party's meat supply.

The remainder of June and the early part of July were spent in completing collections in the vicinity of Bernard harbour, and assembling and packing specimens, stores, and equipment for shipment out of the Arctic. Space had to be economized on the *Alaska* going out, as far as Herschel island, as we had to bring out twenty-seven people on the small schooner, viz., eleven white men, including six members of the scientific staff, a crew of three, and two members of the Royal Northwest Mounted Police; fourteen Eskimo employees, seven men, three women, and four children; and two Eskimos held by the Mounted Police for homicide. In addition to this we had to take the Eskimos' personal camp gear and dogs, stores for paying off native employees at Baillie island and Herschel island, and enough reserve provisions to provide for the wintering of as many men as might remain with the *Alaska* to take care of the vessel and bring her out the next year in case we should be prevented by ice conditions from sailing from Dolphin and Union strait to Nome in the summer and autumn of 1916. I also thought it necessary, for the same reason, to keep the skin umiak, two sleds, and two teams of dogs on board at least as far as point Barrow, Alaska.

In September, 1915, Corporal W. V. Bruce, R.N.W.M.P., came in from Herschel island, Y.T., on the return trip of the C.G.S. *Alaska*, to work on the case of the disappearance of Father Rouvier, O.M.I., and Father LeRoux, O.M.I., from the Mission at fort Norman, who had gone into the country northeast of Great Bear lake in 1913, and had not been heard of since.[1] Corporal Bruce had spent the winter working on the case, and with the assistance of various members of the expedition, gained considerable information and recovered a quantity of the personal effects of the missing fathers as well as some property which presumably belonged to Messrs. Radford and Street, who were killed by Eskimos in Bathurst inlet in 1912. In May, 1916, Inspector Charles D. LaNauze, of the Great Bear lake patrol,[1] came down to Coronation gulf with a party from his winter quarters near old fort Confidence on Dease river, and in the same month the police made prisoners of the two Eskimos, Sinnisiak and Uluksuk,

---

[1] Report of the R.N.W.M.P. for 1916. 7 George V., Sessional Paper No. 28. A. 1917. Ottawa.

SESSIONAL PAPER No. 38

who had killed the priests. Uluksuk was taken on one of the islands near the mouth of the Coppermine river, and Sinnisiak was taken on the south coast of Victoria island. Both prisoners were taken to Bernard harbour, and in July we took Inspector LaNauze and Corporal Bruce out as passengers on the *Alaska* from Bernard harbour to Herschel island. All relations of the Royal Northwest Mounted Police with the expedition have been most cordial, and while with the expedition, both Inspector LaNauze and Corporal Bruce did everything they could as volunteer assistants in whatever work was going on. The members of the expedition have also had many courtesies and much assistance in their work from Inspector J. W. Phillips, who was in command of the R.N.W.M.P. detachments at Herschel island and fort McPherson from 1913 to 1916, and from the members of his command, for which we are very appreciative.

The *Alaska* left a large permanent cache of provisions in the house formerly occupied by the Southern party at Bernard harbour, in case any parties should come down from the Northern party during the next winter. The house was left in custody of the Rev. H. Girling, who wintered near Clifton point with the mission schooner *Atkoon*, and intended to establish a mission station at Bernard harbour in the summer of 1916. This ensured our cache being protected from marauding natives.

The Hudson's Bay Company's schooner *Fort McPherson*, with Mr. W. G. Phillips in charge, sailed from Herschel island July 28, 1916, after our arrival there, for the purpose of establishing a permanent trading post for the company at Bernard harbour. As there are now trading posts of the Hudson's Bay Company at Herschel island, at Kittigazuit (east branch of the Mackenzie delta), at Baillie island, and Bernard harbour (the latter post having been satisfactorily established, from later advices), any parties from the Northern party of the expedition who may come to the mainland coast east of Herschel island will have little difficulty in getting provisions. The larger part of the Canadian Arctic Expedition stores remaining at Herschel island were mostly landed by the *Ruby* in 1915, after the *Alaska* had taken her required stores and sailed east again in 1915, and Mr. Stefansson's vessels had also taken what they were able to carry.

The work of loading the *Alaska* was begun in the summer of 1916 as soon as the vessel was loose from the ice in which she had been frozen all winter, and we succeeded in getting out of Bernard harbour much earlier than was anticipated. In the summer of 1915, prolonged northwesterly winds in the latter part of July had caused a local jam of ice in Dolphin and Union strait, and the *North Star* was not able to get away from Bernard harbour until August 9. The *Alaska*, with all members of the Southern party on board, left our headquarters for the past two years, at Bernard harbour, 7.30 p.m., July 13, 1916, and after working through some loose areas of bay ice, reached the vicinity of Young point on July 17. Here we met with masses of heavy floating ice, too heavy for us to make progress through. We were delayed near Young point for several days, tying up to heavy grounded cakes of ice along the beach, and were obliged to shift our position frequently, because the ice floes behind which we were sheltered shifted their position frequently as the tide rose and fell. The smooth rock bottom along the coast in this region prevented the big ice masses from grounding as hard and fast as they are accustomed to do on the mud and sand bottoms which are found west of cape Bathurst.

We got under way again in the evening of July 21, and worked out into a broad lead of open water outside the strip of loose, moving masses of ice which was pressing down along the mainland shore of the south side of Amundsen gulf and Dolphin and Union strait. After getting through this shore ice, we found it did not extend much west of Croker river, and that the ocean was practically open to the westward. We reached Pierce point harbour about midnight on

8 GEORGE V, A. 1918

July 23, crossed Darnley bay and reached cape Parry on the morning of July 24. We stopped at cape Parry for a short time to get a time observation, and then went ahead across Franklin bay, reaching cape Bathurst at 10.05 p.m. the same evening. The Eskimo village and the new trading station of the Hudson's Bay Company, the most northerly trading post in Canada (70° 35′ north, 128° 05′ west) is at the tip of the long sandspit running west from cape Bathurst, about half a mile east of the east end of Baillie island.

At Baillie island, I discharged and paid off Ikey Bolt or Angatitsiak (point Hope Eskimo), Mungalina (Baillie island Eskimo), and Patsy Klengenberg, interpreter and general assistant. The latter, the 17-year-old son of Capt. Christian Klengenberg, is an extraordinarily intelligent and resourceful young man, a very capable hunter and traveller, showed great aptitude in the collection and preparation of specimens, and is probably the best qualified Eskimo interpreter in the country, being familiar with all the dialects from point Barrow to Coronation gulf. The people who left at Baillie island were paid principally in stores. There was a heavy northwest gale while we were in the shelter of the cape Bathurst sandspit on July 25 and 26. We left Baillie island at 7 p.m., July 26, and reached Herschel island 2.30 p.m., July 28, having been bothered very little by ice anywhere west of Croker river.

At Herschel island I landed some surplus stores from the *Alaska*, including 1,050 pounds of pemmican, 250 pounds rolled oats, 1 barrel beef, 412 pounds tobacco, and some miscellaneous equipment, storing them with the other expedition stores at Herschel island, in charge of the Royal Northwest Mounted Police, retaining on board the *Alaska* enough provisions to winter a certain number of men in case the vessel should be caught again by ice on the north coast of Alaska. I made as complete a survey of Canadian Arctic Expedition stores at Herschel island as the time would permit. The provisions there at the time we left, exclusive of a certain amount set aside to be shipped to Banks island, were as follows:—

	Pounds.
Rolled oats, 108 50-lb. cases	5,400
Sugar, granulated, 6 50-lb. boxes	300
" 5 200-lb. boxes	1,000
" 20 100-lb. brls	2,000
Dog biscuit, 11 50-lb. cases	550
Cracklings, 55 50-lb. cases	2,750
Rice, mostly brown, 36 50-lb. cases	1,800
Beef, 1 brl	100
Total	13,900

Acting in consultation with Mr. George H. Wilkins, who had recently come down from the Northern party, and was conversant with their resources and their needs, we set aside certain provisions, and other equipment, amounting to about two tons weight, and requested the commander of the R. N. W. M. P. detachment at Herschel island to try to get any whaling or trading ship which might come in during the summer of 1916, and intended to cruise in the vicinity of cape Kellett, Banks island, to take these goods on board and try to land them for the Northern party of the expedition at cape Kellett, Banks island, securing as good rates for this freighting as he could. I have later received information from the police at Herschel island, that the selected goods were taken by Capt. C. T. Pedersen, steamship *Herman*, of San Francisco, and landed at cape Kellett, Banks island, in the latter part of August, 1916. Capt. Pedersen made the very reasonable rate of $50 per ton for two tons from Herschel island to cape Kellett. It was also stated that Capt. P. Bernard of the *Mary Sachs* had purchased a considerable quantity of additional supplies from the *Herman*. The stores which were shipped from Herschel island to cape Kellett included:—

	Pounds.
Pemmican, man, 17 50-lb. cases...	850
,, dog, 4 50-lb. cases...	200
Cracklings, 20 50-lb. cases..	1,000
Rolled oats, 6 50-lb. cases...	300
Brown rice, 6 50-lb. cases..	300
Sounding wire, 1 coil.	
Miscellaneous equipment.	
Mail for the Northern party.	

I am informed that Capt. Peter Bernard intended to make a sled trip from cape Kellett to Winter harbour, Melville island, in the fall of 1916 to bring up the mail which was sent in during the summer of 1916 to the Northern party.

At Herschel island, Yukon Territory, I discharged and paid off the remaining Eskimos in the employ of the Southern party, including Mike and his wife; Ambrose Aganvigak and his wife Unalina; Adam Ovayuak; and Silas Palaiyak; paying them as far as possible in stores remaining on the *Alaska*, and partially in cash. The *Alaska* left Herschel island for the westward on August 3, 1916, at which date no ship had yet arrived at Herschel island from the westward. We had on board nine men: Daniel Sweeney, sailing master; J. E. Hoff, chief engineer; James Sullivan, cook; scientific staff consisting of J. J. O'Neill, geologist; J. R. Cox, topographer; D. Jenness, ethnologist; F. Johansen, biologist; George H. Wilkins, cinematographer and photographer; and Rudolph M. Anderson, zoologist, in command.

Very little ice had been seen east of Herschel island, but we soon found it pretty heavy a little west of the island, although loose and moving freely, practically all the way west from the international boundary (141st meridian) to point Barrow, Alaska. We stopped long enough at the international boundary monument to get a time sight. One ship was seen on the way in, the *Herman*, but we could not speak to her as she was in the moving ice outside of Cross island, Alaska, on August 5, 1916, while we were inside of the chain of islands which includes Cross island. On account of the heavy ice outside, we again availed ourselves of the knowledge of the very excellent detailed sounding and charting done recently by Mr. E. deK. Leffingwell, and went into the inside passage behind the chain of low, sandy islands west of Flaxman island, coming out again between Midway island and Return reef. The channel inside of these islands is rather shoal, but is valuable for vessels drawing not more than two fathoms. A vessel of that draught could come in behind Flaxman island, but shoals prevent a vessel drawing more than 5 or 6 feet going out through the channel between the east end of Flaxman island and the mainland, that channel being shoal and foul from silt deposited by the Canning river. The pack ice was pretty heavy around point Barrow, and we had some difficulty in getting through, but after passing cape Smyth, about five miles southwest of point Barrow, no more ice was seen.

We left cape Smyth, which is the site of the village, including trading station, mission, government school, and the post office of Barrow, Alaska, the most northerly United States post office, on August 8, 1916. No ice was encountered south of cape Smyth, and we had a good run down to point Hope, where we stopped for a short time on August 10. Continuing across the outside of Kotzebue sound, we reached cape Prince of Wales and passed through Bering strait into Bering sea at the beginning of a heavy, prolonged northwest gale, on the evening of August 11, 1916. As the gale continued we were obliged to anchor for some time under the bluffs at cape York and Tin City, and again behind Sledge island, reaching Nome roadstead about 5 a.m., August 15, 1916.

The *Alaska* had not been leaking at all before passing point Barrow, but after passing that point began to leak badly around the stuffing-box; this

8 GEORGE V, A. 1918

necessitated considerable pumping to keep the engine room from being flooded and put out of commission. Although the weather was a little rough when we reached Nome, I succeeded in getting the cargo of specimens and stores lightered ashore that day and put on the wharf of the Alaska Lighterage and Commercial Company. It was too rough to make any repairs on the vessel, and as the weather was rougher the next day, August 16, the *Alaska* was compelled to run 16 miles over to the shelter of Sledge island again. Three sailors had been temporarily engaged upon our arrival at Nome, and the six members of the scientific staff were relieved from seaman's duty and allowed to go ashore. They had all been doing watch as deck officers from Bernard harbour to Herschel island with our Eskimo crew, and from Herschel island to Nome the duties had been much heavier. The storm abated somewhat on August 18, and the *Alaska* returned to the roadstead, but the surf was still too heavy to make a landing. The *Alaska* was ultimately hauled up high and dry on the beach at Nome and left in the charge of the Alaska Lighterage and Commercial Company for final disposal by the Department of the Naval Service. The vessel was in good shape, except for the engines, the leakage around the stuffing-box being a trifling matter, which could be readily repaired when the vessel was hauled up.

The extensive collections made by the party in geology and mineralogy, ethnology, and archaeology, terrestrial and marine biology, botany and photography, and the records and papers of the Southern party, were thus landed safely at Nome. As it was considered much safer to ship the results of our three years' work out by the regular freight and passenger service from Nome than to risk taking them down on the north Pacific to Victoria on a small schooner like the *Alaska* in the autumn season, all the collections, scientific instruments, and what equipment was worth shipping back, was trans-shipped to Seattle on the steamship *Northwestern*, of the Alaska Steamship Company. The members of the party also took passage to Seattle on the same steamer, leaving Nome August 27, and reaching Seattle via the inside passage on September 11, 1916. All collections had been safely received in Ottawa by the end of October, 1916.

To summarize: The scientific work of the Southern party was completed substantially as outlined in our plans of last year, and although some time was lost on account of adverse ice conditions in 1913, all members of the party feel that in the main the results of their work, for the past two years at least, have been as satisfactory and extensive as they anticipated, considering the difficulties which are to be encountered in working in such remote fields.

The two topographers of the Southern party, Kenneth G. Chipman and John R. Cox, have completed the survey of the mainland coast in detail, on the scale of 10 miles to the inch, from the Alaska-Yukon Territory international boundary (the 141st meridian) to the Mackenzie river, made a traverse of Firth river, Y.T., surveyed the eastern and western branches of the Mackenzie delta, and the mainland coast from the west side of Darnley bay (on the Cape Parry peninsula) to a point well down in Bathurst inlet (south of Kannuyuk island), including a large number of islands in the Coronation gulf and Bathurst inlet regions, all on the same scale. Several of the hitherto unexplored rivers in this region have been traversed, including Hornaday river flowing into the south side of Darnley bay, Croker river flowing into the Amundsen gulf, Rae river flowing into the west side and Tree river (Kogluktualuk) flowing into the south side of Coronation gulf, and an examination made of the territory around the mouth of Hood river flowing into Arctic sound. Collinson point harbour, and about 10 square miles surrounding it, and Bernard harbour, Chantry island, and the country immediately surrounding these places have been surveyed on the scale of $\frac{1}{24000}$, and mapped with 20-foot contours. The geological features have been investigated by J. J. O'Neill, and the relations of the different formations studied in detail at the most important points of contact.

The most important result of the geological investigations was the detailed mapping and estimation of the available copper-bearing rock in a great new area hitherto very slightly known in the Bathurst inlet region. So far as analysed, the ore is low-grade, but further prospecting may locate veins and richer areas to render mining operations more profitable. Isolated nuggets of float copper of considerable size are found in the region. Galena was found by the party, and other minerals doubtless occur. The whole region forms a great copper reservoir for Canada, and will no doubt be utilized in the future, when transporation problems are solved, as they are not farther north than paying properties in Alaska and Norway, and much farther south than working mines in Spitzbergen. The climate is not too bad; there is a summer of about four months, and the snowfall is light in winter.

D. Jenness, ethnologist and anthropologist of the party, has made extensive ethnological collections, from Arctic Alaska as well as in the Coronation gulf, Dolphin and Union strait, and Victoria island region, and also about one hundred gramophone records of folklore, language, dance songs, and shamanistic performances, with careful transcriptions and translations of them. He has made a collection of cats'-cradle games from the different Eskimo tribes, numbering over one hundred and forty. Their language and vocabularies, the manners, social and religious customs, games, amusements, and general culture have been carefully studied and the information recorded. With the present rapid advance of civilized ideas and customs into this particular region, it is certain that much of this information could not be obtained at a later time. The habits of the Eskimos are changing with a rapidity which is astonishing to those not conversant with the situation; improved weapons and methods of trapping reduce the game and compel shifting of tribal localities, while from the history of the past, it seems very likely that contact with the fringe of civilization will rapidly decimate the numbers of the Copper Eskimos as it has done to the Eskimos farther west.

F. Johansen, marine biologist, entomologist, and botanist, has made extensive collections in all these branches, from Arctic Alaska and Canada. He has succeeded in rearing and working out the hitherto unknown life-histories of a number of little-known Arctic insects, and made many interesting and successful sea dredgings and soundings. George H. Wilkins has made many studies with camera and cinematograph, making over one thousand film and glass plate negatives and about 9,000 feet of cinematograph exposures, of Eskimo life, natural-history objects, and Arctic scenery and topography. All the members of the scientific staff made numbers of photographs also to illustrate their work.

In mammalogy and ornithology; fairly complete collections were made in the regions traversed, although the difficulties of transportation and the pressure of other duties often prevented the obtaining of as large series as might be desirable. The collection of birds numbers six hundred and nineteen (619) specimens, including seventy-three (73) species. The collection of mammals numbers four hundred and thirty-one (431) specimens, including twenty-two (22) species and probably several more subspecies. It is not possible to tell without more detailed examination whether any new forms are represented, but many specimens represent seasonal changes of plumage and pelage which are rare in collections, and the specimens taken will largely extend the geographical range of a number of species. This branch of the work was in charge of R. M. Anderson, but all members of the expedition aided materially in bringing in specimens and notes.

A mere list of the different groups represented in the expedition's biological collections indicates something of their scope:—

Mammals, birds, fishes, insects, plants, crustaceans, echinoderms, sponges, cirripedes or barnacles, molluscs, hydroid zoophytes, medusæ and ctenophores, alcyonarians and actinians, algæ, protozoa (foraminifera and radiolaria), plankton, sporozoa, diatoms, infusoria, pteropods, cephalopods, decapods, phyllopods, copepods, schizopods, amphipods, isopods, pantopods, annelids, platyhelminthes, rotatoria, nematodes, nemertines, malacostraca, bryozoa, ascidians, peridiniales, ostracods, hirudinea chaetognatha, polychaeta.

On the biological side, to arrange for having the different groups worked up and the reports adequately published, an Arctic Biological Committee has been appointed jointly by the Department of the Naval Service and the Geological Survey, with the Dominion Commissioner of Fisheries, Prof. E. E. Prince, as chairman; Prof. A. B. MacCallum, of Toronto; the Dominion Entomologist, Dr. C. Gordon Hewitt; Mr. James Macoun, botanist, of the Geological Survey and R. M. Anderson, representing the expedition and the zoological division of the survey. The specimens to be worked up represent over forty distinct groups, each of which will require a separate chapter or report. Some of the larger groups, such as the insects, have been divided among several different men, mostly in the entomological division of the Department of Agriculture. A great many of these collections represent specimens of groups which have never been collected anywhere in the western Arctic area, and practically all of them are from districts and localities which are practically unrepresented in collections anywhere, from regions never visited before by a collector.

As far as possible these collections are being worked up by Canadian specialists, but some groups have necessarily been sent away because there was no satisfactory material in Canada for comparison. The Smithsonian Institution is well supplied with Alaskan Arctic material in some groups, and the British Museum with material from various Arctic expeditions, while the Greenland region is best represented by Danish and Norwegian collections, consequently a number of groups of specimens are being sent to some of those countries for determination. When the collections have been properly determined and worked up, Canada's museum will have a good start in the representation of the production and content of a very large area that has hitherto been very poorly represented. The specimens are being placed in the hands of the best available specialists, and these men have shown a gratifying willingness to do what they can to help unravel the problems presented so that we have satisfaction in knowing that such additions to knowledge as were obtained by the Canadian Arctic Expedition of 1913-16 may soon be made available to the public of Canada and to the world.

Full meteorological observations were kept up for three years, with barograph, thermograph; maximum, minimum, and standard thermometers; mercurial barometer, and anomometer. Tidal observations were taken for some time at Collinson point, Alaska; at Demarcation point, and at Bernard harbour, Dolphin and Union strait.

The Geological Survey, Department of Mines, is attending to the computing and plotting of the maps surveyed, in its Topographical Division, and the technical geological and ethnological reports in the Geological and Anthropological Divisions, respectively. Full reports of the various scientific activities of the members of the Southern division of the Canadian Arctic Expedition of 1913-16 are in course of preparation, and will be transmitted to the various departments as soon as completed.

I have the honour to be sir,
Your obedient servant,

RUDOLPH MARTIN ANDERSON,
Chief of the Southern Division of the
Canadian Arctic Expedition of 1913-1916.

Zoologist, The Geological Survey,
Ottawa.

A R C T I C

O C E A N

McClintock Chan...

e Sound

C M'Cli...

ice Alfre

Whumut
Kannagput Isl.
Inlet

Copp...

P...

Alaska and adjacent
regions, 1853-54

Island

Pt...

Post

I KON

K O N

Red Mine

Ted Cape

Cape ...
Point Belcher Islands
Wainwright Inlet
Icy Cape Smyth
Peard Say
Point Franklin
Cape Lisburne
Cape Thompson
Cape Krusenstern
Point Hope
...th Cape

H A L A S K A

Bering Strait
Cape Prince of Wales
Kotzebue
Sound
Cape ...
Grantley ...
Port ...
Clarence
Teller

Nome

Sledge
Island

Norton

PACI

OC

Report of George H. Wilkins on the Topographical and Geographical Work carried out by him in connection with the Canadian Arctic Expedition.

The Deputy Minister,
 Department of the Naval Service,
  Ottawa.

Sir,—I beg to report the following information on the Topographical and Geographical work carried out by me during my journeys in connection with the Canadian Arctic Expedition.

This report is mostly confined to observations made on Banks island and the vicinity for the other parts visited were either covered by the Topographers of the Expedition or by others of the party previous to my traverse.

In 1914, when proceeding in the *Mary Sachs* to meet Mr. Stefansson, we approached Banks island in a fog and the first sight of the coast that we obtained was in the vicinity of cape Lambton, which is a blunted point rising abruptly from the water to a height of fifty feet or more and shelving back about a hundred yards to rise again almost perpendicularly to almost 800 feet. The cliffs and mountains beyond were barren and rugged in appearance from the south; deeply scarred by ravines and studded here and there with boulders.

As we proceeded along the coast to the northwest we drew away from the higher cliffs and the mountains receded to undulating hills of a thousand feet or more in height. Numerous small but rapid streams had been noticed coursing through the ravines, and about fifteen miles northwest from the cape a fair-sized river enters the sea through a narrow valley. The source of this river is evidently in the mountains back of Nelson head, but for a mile or so along the coast it runs from west to east. Two ranges of hills extend parallel to the coast towards cape Kellett, intersected here and there by rivers cutting through them to the sea. We found Thesiger Bay to be more like two bays than one and we could not see cape Kellett until around a point some 17 miles from there.

The southwest coastline ends for the most part in cut-banks which are gradually washing away into the sea each summer, but here and there along the coast there are sandspits sheltering lagoon mouthed creeks or rivers. Once around the point in Thesiger bay one sees two islands not marked as yet on the Admiralty chart 2118, and a semi-circular sandspit reaching out towards them from the mainland. Behind the islands and the sandspit is good shelter for a boat of shallow draft, and we used a ten-foot channel close beside the sandspit to get into shelter.

Stretching inland from behind the islands is a narrow bay about two miles deep and it seems likely that there is a channel to get into this from the south side of the islands, but we had not time to sound these waters.

Cape Kellett is not at all like what one would expect from the chart. The sloping hills end much more abruptly and form a much less conspicuous hook, although a half-moon shaped sandspit does extend out in the nature indicated for three miles or so and half a mile in width. Behind this there is also shelter from a southwest and southeast wind, but from observation it seems that if there is ice about it will pack tightly on the cape and severely hamper any vessel trying to get out.

Another thing that makes this point very troublesome to navigate is the strong set of the current from north to southeast around the cape. It has

—5

8 GEORGE V, A. 1918

always had the same direction when I have had the opportunity to observe it, but we were unable to make sufficient observations to prove that this is always so.

From cape Kellett northward the land recedes to form a shallow bay as indicated on the map, and emptying into it is a broad but shallow river which has its source amongst the hills behind cape Lambton. Along this bay, and as a matter of fact the greater part of the western coast the beach is low and broken up by numerous lagoons whose waters lap the tundra at high tide. Long estuaries at intervals stretch in towards the rolling hills beyond. Following up the coast one comes to Worth point and from here on the place marked Haswell point long lagoons edged by sandspits border the land. Haswell point itself is really an island and both north and south of it another island will be noticed.

From Haswell point to Meek point the map is fairly accurate except that there is scarcely so deep a bight so close to the former; it is more in the middle distance. Terror island lies directly off Meek point and lies most east and west. For three miles past here the coast runs north of east but then turns south to form a bight in an inlet ten miles wide and fifteen or more deep which is not charted on the map. From Wolley point on towards cape Collins, lagoons are found most all the way, and from here onward the map is so incorrect that it is difficult to refer to it at all. Burnett bay does not exist but in its place is the low flat delta of a fair-sized river across the mouth of which lies an island, fifteen miles long and five hundred feet high at the highest point. Norway island is more off the place marked Pennell point and from here north the coast does not recede so much as one would think from off the shore for the hills beyond the flat land take the direction indicated on the chart.

Robilliard island seems about correct but from here onward in the direction of cape Alfred, a chain of islands extends all the way. There are but two Gore islands in the position indicated by the chart but the largest point of land at cape Prince Alfred is an island leaving a pointed sandspit for the cape. A conspicuous round topped hill can be noticed a mile or so south of the real cape. It is only fair to remark that when travelling from the north to the south from cape Alfred and some distance off-shore that the land has the appearance indicated by the chart. About twenty miles northeast along the coast from cape Alfred a low sandy island stretching across the mouth of a deep fiord would seem to make a good harbour for a boat. We had not time to sound this place but a few odd cakes of ice amongst the smooth would suggest a channel of at least twenty feet in depth.

About cape Clifford a river bed about two miles wide cuts through the hills from the high plateau behind and forms a break in the range which gradually increases in height from cape Alfred. About three miles further along another branch of the same river runs into the sea, making the intervening section practically an island. On the southwest branch of this river, and near the coast there is a beacon, but we could not find any trace of a record having been left.

Another few miles along the coast another small river enters the sea through steep-sided banks and on the banks of this river and about seven miles inland I found seams of coal. There is scarcely a distinctive point in the vicinity of cape Wrottesly, but just thereabouts there is a large lagoon, the outside barrier of which is a very low and inconspicuous sandspit. However the coast turns in a more easterly direction with a gradual change as far as cape McClure. Cape McClure is bold and precipitous and somewhat resembles cape Lambton in appearance. Here again the map is very deceptive for one cannot find a conspicuous point where cape Crozier is marked on the map, and although the coast turns almost south it does not make any westing but bends gradually towards cape Clifton, then some eight miles west of Providence point one finds a bay some three miles wide and ten miles deep, into the bottom of which empties a large river which Mr. Stefansson and his party followed in the summer of 1915 and will doubtless describe. I did not traverse the coast from Mercy bay to John Russel point, but from this point to Milne point the coast line seems fairly accurate.

In general topography Banks island has the appearance of a high range of' hills, whose peak is about 2,000 feet high and is within forty miles of Nelson head. The range runs from Nelson head to cape McClure ending abruptly at each end, with a high plateau in the centre of the island, but this a little lower than either end. On the western side it slopes gradually down towards the sea and the greatest watershed is in that direction. On the eastern side from Nelson head to Johnson bay the land slopes steeply down and the whole north-. west corner is hilly. Numerous small lakes dot the landscape and several' large ones ten miles long and two or more miles wide were found. One is eight miles inland directly opposite Armstrong point, and another a few miles north-west of that. Another is a few miles inland from Thesiger bay. We had no means of getting at their depths.

When following the Victoria land coast along the Prince of Wales straits one notices that Dean Dundas bay is not so deep by about five miles as it is mapped. Ramsay island would appear to be a good deal further south than it is marked, and the straits in this vicinity seem wider, but as we had no sextant with us we could not locate our positions accurately. The western coast of. Victoria island is fairly low until one comes to Walker bay. From here mount Phayre is a very conspicuous round-topped hill. Cape Wollaston itself is low, but a high-cut bank a few miles east looms up noticeably. From Holman island one can see mount Arrowsmith, but not the island charted in the sound. This we found to be really two islands much more in the centre of the mouth of Prince Albert sound than charted. Cape Kendall is undoubtedly an island, and the high cliffs near point Williams are conspicuous. No sign was seen of Clerk island although we passed several times in that locality.

Ice Conditions.—The ice conditions met with on the *Karluk* during 1913 have no doubt been reported on.

The rivers had broken out by May 23, 1914, in the vicinity of point Barrow, but I was able to travel from that place by sled leaving on May 25—to Clarence lagoon in Canadian territory reaching the latter place on June 14. Travelling for the greater part of the distance at that time of the year was very uncomfortable owing to the waters of the rivers having flooded the smooth lagoon ice, and consequently forcing us to travel off shore over the rough pack ice. Even here the water had soaked under the crust of snow and on warm days one would repeatedly break through. On other occasions it was necessary to travel through the water which was often so deep that the dogs had to swim. and the men push the sled.

The season at point Barrow in 1914 when we left was equally as much advanced as that at Collinson point when we arrived here on June 5th, but during the next few days at this place the snow disappeared very rapidly. At Clarence lagoon on the 14th most of the snow had disappeared from the. ground, the water had melted holes in the ice and the solid ice had risen and was comparatively dry once more. Around the river mouths it was honey-combed and rotten, but off shore the travelling was fairly good. It was impossible to get on to lagoon ice or lakes at this time of the year in this vicinity for the fringe of open water round the edges, but we continued to travel on the sea ice until June 20th. The first general movement in the ice along the beach was on June 29th when it piled up on the sandspits to a height of twenty feet or more. The lagoon was clear of ice by July 6th and we were able to navigate the *Mary Sachs*. After several days of northeast wind the ice opened and scattered on the 18th, but it settled back again when the wind failed the next day. By the 23rd it had opened up again and we went out of the lagoon and proceeded to Herschel island having little difficulty with the ice.

38—5½

8 GEORGE V, A. 1918

One large steam whaler had reached the island from a little further down the coast some two days earlier, and another came in three days later. The Mackenzie river boats were late, however, and did not reach the island until August 7th, having been held up by pack ice to the eastward. Leaving Herschel island on the 4th we passed through scattered floes until we reached Richard island and here we were held up by the ice for two days. A westerly wind shifted it along the beach ahead of us and we reached the Baillie islands without much trouble with the ice. East of here the straights seemed packed with ice, but a few days of easterly wind cleared it out and we proceeded to Pierce point and across to Banks island in open water. Westerly winds had set in again by the time we reached this coast and had packed the ice in along the coast and in Thesiger bay. However as we neared cape Kellett on Aug. 26th, it appeared as though the ice had never left the beach in this vicinity. However one or two small rivers had melted out the ice to some extent and after a great deal of bucking and manœuvering we brought the schooner in beside the beach on Sept. 1st. Young ice had been forming each night for several nights and cementing the older floes together, and around cape Kellett and as far west as we could see, there was solid floe ice. To the south and away to the north we could see the streaks of water sky, but there were no means of reaching it.

On September 10th, during a storm, the ice cleared away from the beach leaving the southern and western coasts free for navigation. However the main pack ice never shifted far off the western coast, but remained off shore; while the sea froze over solid enough to travel on by the 21st. Cracks and open leads of water appeared to the south and west of cape Kellett at intervals during the winter, but the ice had little motion. Travelling along the whole west coast of Banks island one could see that there had been open water there during the fall, for there was little old ice near the beach. On the north coast from cape Alfred the ice was much broken up and we had evidence of much motion in the ice during the winter as far east as cape McClure.

During the months of February and March of both 1915 and 1916, and, as a matter of fact, at intervals all through the winter, there were leads of open water in the vicinity of cape Alfred. The general drift of the ice in this vicinity was towards the west, but the same floes that went out would sometimes drift back again. At cape Kellett by the 1st of May, 1915, the sandspits were bare of snow, but during the early part of May the snow on the inland slopes was hard and made a good surface for travelling over. In fact, the ice and snow conditions remained excellent for travelling over until we reached the Dolphin and Union straits on the 21st of May, en route from Kellett, Banks island to Bernard harbour. Along the coast from here and across the Coronation gulf to the mouth of the Coppermine river the travelling was good until the 1st of June.

The season seemed particularly late in that vicintiy in 1915 and on the 21st of June there were still three feet of snow in drifts around the tents and many patches on the land. It was the 20th of July before we could move the boat in the harbour and not until the 9th of August that we could proceed along the coast to Coronation gulf. We had some trouble in getting through the straits past Lambert island but once in the gulf we had clear water as far east as cape Barrow. Leaving cape Barrow on the 11th of August, we reached Baillie island on the 11th without having encountered any ice on the way. On the 16th we crossed the straits to cape Kellett in the *North Star* without trouble and found the Banks island southeast coast practically clear of ice. The heavy pack was never far from the western shore. Starting from cape Kellett on the 26th we proceeded north close to the beach, but it was only on account of the shallow draft of our vessel—4 feet, 6 inches—that we were able to pass between the heavy pack and the beach, as far as Norway island. At this place and further north the ice was still solid on the beach, and only moved out for a few miles

SESSIONAL PAPER No. 38

further for the next few days. By the 20th of August, we had reached just north of Robilliard island but further north than here the ice never left the beach in 1915.

A westerly wind drove the pack inshore along the coast as far as we could see and by the 10th of September we could walk anywhere across the frozen sea. It would seem that in only exceptionally years that a boat could proceed along the whole west coast of Banks island for the ice does not appear to move far off the shore, and the open season is so very short in any case. During 1916 I was able to travel from Armstrong point to Coronation gulf, leaving the former place on June 1st, and arriving at the latter on June 13th; but this was just about as late as one could have travelled that year, and even then we had to use a sled raft to cross a number of the tide cracks. Most of the way we travelled through six inches or more of pen water and across the Dolphin and Union straits the ice was very thin and rotten. 1916 was a very much earlier season in this vicinity than 1915, for we took a boat from the same position as the year before some four weeks earlier.

In 1914 Banks island was covered with snow for the winter on the 12th of September, although it had been snowed over and melted off a day or two before. In 1915 the ground was covered at cape Prince Alfred by the 8th of September.

Fuel on Banks island.—There is a little driftwood to be found on the east, west and south coasts of Banks island, but none at all, except a few chips, on the north coast. On any part there is scarcely enough to keep a big camp fire going for a twelve-month within a stretch of fifteen miles and more often not so much. During the summer there is an abundance of heather to be found on the inland slopes but very little willow. Wood is sometimes found many miles inland projecting from the banks of rivers and even on the hilltops, but this is not to be depended on for fuel. The coal deposits near the northern coasts may prove useful, judging from the samples taken, for they would burn well when lighted on a primus stove. We had no means of testing it in a camp stove. However, one is always well advised to carry fuel oil in strong containers when travelling about the island.

Game, Fish, etc.—Caribou may be found on Banks island at each season of the year, but they are comparatively scarce at all times and need a deal of hunting for. They are in their prime from September until the end of November, but are hardly worth killing during March, April, May and part of June. Their skins are not so satisfactory as those of the mainland caribou, or the domestic deer for clothes although they can be used.

Seals are fairly numerous near the shore of all the islands and can most always be obtained at Nelson head, cape Kellett and cape Alfred during the winter in the leads that form in the ice. In the spring they can be shot while on the ice asleep, but this is not by any means an easy matter for they are difficult to approach. In the summer they seem to float if they are killed quite dead, and the wound is not too large, but late in the fall they float more readily.

Polar bears are comparatively numerous along the coast, although their presence may have been due in the neighbourhood of cape Kellett to a stranded whale carcass. Along the north and south coasts the open leads of water no doubt keep them near the land, and many are found travelling along the Prince of Wales straits. The Eskimo hunt them each year in the vicinity of Nelson head, and during the early spring one man told me that he had followed a bear so far out on the ice that he had seen the land on the other side of the straits.

Ducks and white geese are very numerous around cape Kellett in the spring and may be on the other part of the island for all we know. During the summer the white geese especially can be driven about in flocks when they are moulting and killed like sheep. At this time of the year they are not so very fat and are much better if killed earlier in the season. Curiously enough from some 250 geese that were killed at cape Kellett during the summer of 1915, only one was found to be a female and only one egg was found during the season.

8 GEORGE V, A. 1918

Ptarmigan are fairly numerous on the coasts in early spring, but not so plentiful as on the mainland. Many schools of fish were seen swimming in the water and the Eskimo tell us that they are plentiful in the large lakes on the island. We had a net set from a sandspit but only caught one fish. The women caught several dozen Tom-cod through the ice one fall, but we had not time to give the fishing much attention. On Victoria island the fish are very plentiful in lakes and the local Eskimo seem to catch a lot in spring and fall.

Clothing.—We found the native method of dressing with fur clothes next the skin to be most suitable for extensive travel, although when frequent changes can be had, woollen clothes are very comfortable. I also found a woollen mask that fitted closely to the face having two holes for the eyes and one for the mouth and nose, a great protection from the frosty wind. It is essential, however, that this garment should fit tightly to the face, and also that the edges of the openings are far enough away from the nose and mouth to prevent the breath melting the hoar frost which forms outside and making ice. Although I travelled at times under severe conditions I never had a frost bite on the face while using the woollen face-mask.

I found fur socks most serviceable and comfortable if a very thin woollen sock was worn next to the feet, but the care of the feet in the Arctic is a personal equation differing with each individual. Polar bear skin or domestic sheepskin mittens are most satisfactory in comparatively warm weather, but in very cold weather we found nothing that was entirely satisfactory if one was going a long journey without the chance to dry one's clothes. Well-fitting dog or wolf skin, covered with canvas, are about the best.

Winter Travel along the west coast of Banks island.—It is quite possible to travel along the coast in winter, although the temperature might average —25 degrees F. or more, and the sun does not appear for two months. However, on the western coast of the island it is more difficult than in most places, for the land is so low-lying that by lantern light it is difficult to tell when one is wandering inland and the only means of knowing in most cases is by digging through the snow at frequent intervals to see if one is still on the sea ice.

Snow Houses.—We found the building of snow houses practicable from the middle of October to the middle of May, and much preferred to live in them than tents. Their greatest drawback is perhaps the length of time they take to build. A house 12 feet in diameter, big enough to accommodate seven people can scarcely be put in condition to live in, in less than two hours by four men. It more often takes three hours, depending on the quality of the snow with which one has to build. Once the principle is grasped it requires but little skill to build a house of snow, but quite a deal of art and skill are required to build a perfect dome-shaped one, which type is by far the best.

Dog Sickness.—Dog sickness of a kind peculiar to the Polar regions is always a worry to the Arctic traveller. It attacks the dogs most frequently in spring time, although we had one dog die of it in winter. The symptoms, though generally alike, differ with each individual attacked. Persistent mournful howling and a restlessness were usually the first symptoms noticed, and the dog would then gnaw anything which it could reach. This would be followed in a few hours by apparent paralysis of the muscles of the throat. While no inflammation was noticeable, it was impossible for the dog to swallow a morsel of food, even if it was placed in the mouth. The dog was evidently in great pain and could not rest. In two days their eyes would be glazed and sunken and the next day they would invariably die.

I am, sir, your obedient servant,

GEO. H. WILKINS,
Photographer.

ANNUAL REPORT OF THE RADIOTELEGRAPH BRANCH, 1916-17.

The Deputy Minister,
    Department of the Naval Service,
        Ottawa.

· · SIR,—I have the honour to present herewith the annual report of the Radiotelegraph Branch for the fiscal year ending the 31st March, 1917.

The total number of stations in operation in the Dominion and on ships registered therein is as follows:—

Government Commercial Stations	1
Coast Stations	42
Government Ship Stations	24
Licensed Ship Stations	76
Public Commercial Stations	3
Private Commercial Stations	3
Radiotelegraph Training Schools	2
Licensed Experimental Stations	5
Total	156

The following list shows the location of the land and coast stations in Canada, their range, call signals, owners and by whom they are operated:—

COAST STATIONS for Communication with Ships.

EAST COAST.

Name.	Where situated.	Owned by.	Operated by.	Range in nautical miles.	Call Signal.
Belle Isle, Nfld	Belle Isle Straits	Dominion Government.	Marconi Wireless Tel. Co. of Canada.	250	VCM
Pt. Amour, Nfld	" "	" "	" "	150	VCL
Pt. Riche, Nfld	Gulf of St. Lawrence	" "	" "	250	VCH
Harrington, P.Q	"	" "	" "	150	VCJ
Heath Pt., P.Q	Gulf of St. Lawrence (Anticosti Isld.)	" "	" "	250	VCI
Cape Ray, Nfld	Cabot Straits	" "	" "	350	VCR
Cape Race, Nfld	North Atlantic	" "	" "	400	VCE
Grindstone Island, P.Q	Gulf of St. Lawrence (Magdalen Isld.)	" "	" "	200	VCN
Fame Pt., P.Q	Gulf of St. Lawrence	" "	" "	250	VCG
Clarke City, P.Q	"	" "	" "	250	VCK
Father Pt., P.Q	River St. Lawrence	" "	" "	250	VCF
Grosse Isle, P.Q	"	" "	" "	100	VCD
Quebec, P.Q	"	" "	" "	150	VCC
Three Rivers, P.Q	"	" "	" "	150	VCB
Montreal, P.Q	"	" "	" "	200	VCA
Cape Sable, N.S	North Atlantic	" "	" "	250	VCU
Partridge Isld,. St. John, N.B	Entrance St. John Harbour, N.B.	" "	" "	250	VCV
Cape Bear, P.E.I	Northumberland Strait.	" "	" "	150	VCP
Camperdown, N.S	Entrance to Halifax Harbour.	" "	" "	250	VCS
Sable Island, N.S	North Atlantic	" "	" "	300	VCT
Halifax, N.S	Halifax Dockyard	" "	Department of the Naval Service.	100	VAA
Pictou, N.S	Northumberland Strait.	Marconi Wireless Tel. Co. of Canada.	Marconi Wireless Tel. Co. of Canada.	100	VCQ
North Sydney, C.B	North Sydney, C.B	Dominion Government.	"	100	VCO

8 GEORGE V, A. 1918

COAST STATIONS for Communication with Ships—*Concluded.*

GREAT LAKES.

Name.	Where Situated.	Owned by.	Operated by.	Range in nautical miles.	Call Signal.
Port Arthur, Ont..............	Port Arthur, Ont........	Dominion Government.	Marconi Wireless Tel. Co. of Canada...	350	VBA
Sault Ste. Marie, Ont........	Sault Ste. Marie, Ont...	" ..	" ..	350	VBB
Tobermory, Ont.............	Entrance Georgian Bay.	" ..	" ..	350	VBD
Midland, Ont.................	Georgian Bay..........	" ..	" ..	350	VBC
Point Edward, Ont...........	Lake Huron............	" ..	" ..	350	VBE
Port Burwell, Ont...........	Lake Erie.............	" ..	" ..	350	VBF
Toronto, Ont.................	Toronto Island, Ont....	" ..	" ..	350	VBG
Kingston, Ont...............	Barriefield Common...	" ..	" ..	350	VBH

WEST COAST.

Name.	Where Situated.	Owned by.	Operated by.	Range	Call
Gonzales Hill, B.C. (Victoria).	Victoria, B.C..........	Dominion Government.	Department of the Naval Service.	250	VAK
Pt. Grey, B.C. (Vancouver)...	Entrance Vancouver Harbour.	" ..	" ..	150	VAB
Cape Lazo, B.C.............	Strait Georgia, near Comox, B.C.	" ..	" ..	350	VAC
Pachena Pt., B.C...........	West Coast Vancouver Isld.	" ..	" ..	500	VAD
Estevan Pt., B.C............	" " .	" ..	" ..	500	VAE
Triangle Isld, B.C...........	South of Hecate Str....	" ..	" ..	450	VAG
Ikeda Head, B.C............	South of Moresby Island Q.C.I.	" ..	" ..	250	VAI
Dead Tree Pt., B.C..........	South of Graham Isld., Q.C.I.	" ...	" ..	200	VAH
Digby Island, B.C., Prince Rupert.	Digby Isld., Entrance Prince Rupert Har.	" ..	" ..	250	VAJ
Alert Bay, B.C..............	Cormorant Isld., B.C...	" ..	" ..	350	VAF

HUDSON BAY.

Name.	Where Situated.	Owned by.	Operated by.	Range	Call
Port Nelson..................	Hudson Bay...........	Dominion Government.	Department of the Naval Service.	750	VBN

LAND STATIONS.

Name.	Where Situated.	Owned by.	Operated by.	Range	Call
Le Pas, Man.................	For communication with Port Nelson only.	Dominion Government.	Department of the Naval Service.	750	VBM

SESSIONAL PAPER No. 38

LICENSED Commercial Stations.

Name.	Where Situated.	Owned by.	Operated by.	Range in nautical miles.	Call Signal.
Public Commercial.					
Glace Bay, C.B..............	Near Glace Bay, C.B...	Marconi Wireless Tel. Co. of Can., Ltd	Owners.......	3,000	GB.
Louisburg, C.B..............	Cape Breton...........	"	"	Reception only	
Newcastle, N.B..............	New Brunswick.........	Universal Radio Synd.	"	2,500	CL
Private Commercial.					
Ocean Falls, B.C.............	Ocean Falls, B.C.......	Ocean Falls...	Owners.......	150	CD
Powell River, B.C...........	Powell River, B.C......	Powell River Co...	"	30	CH
Granby Bay.................	Granby Bay...........	Granby Co. S. M. & P. Co.	"	150	CZ

Name.	Where Situated.	Owned by.	Call Signal.
Marconi Test Room...........	Rodney St., Montreal...	Marconi Wireless Telegraph Co. of Canada, Ltd.	XWA
R. M.C . Kingston............	Kingston, Ont.........	R. M. C. Kingston.................	XWC
Barriefield Camp............	Barriefield, Ont........	D. S. O., 3rd M. D..............	XWD
Niagara Camp...............	Niagara, Ont..........	D.S.O., 2nd M.D................	XWE
Camp Borden...............	Camp Borden, Ont.....	D.S.O., 2nd M.D................	XWF

RADIOTELEGRAPH Training Schools.

Name.	Where Situated.	Call Signal.
Dominion Telegraph & Wireless Institute.....................	Vancouver, B.C..........	Licensed for reception only.
Columbia College of Wireless.............................	Victoria, B.C...........	

AMATEUR Radiotelegraph Stations.

All amateur stations were closed down at the outbreak of hostilities.

LICENSED SHIP STATIONS.

The following list shows the vessels of Canadian register which are equipped with radiotelegraph apparatus, their call signal and by whom they are owned and operated:—

Name of Ship.	Port of Registry.	Name of Owners.	Name of Company operating the Station.	Call Signal.
SS. Assiniboia	Montreal, P.Q	Can. Pacific Railway	Marconi Wireless Tel. Co. of Can	VGI
" Alberta	"	"	"	VFQ
" Athabaska	"	"	"	VGG
" Manitoba	"	"	"	VGH
" Keewatin	"	"	"	VGC
" Boston	Yarmouth, N.S	"	"	VFS
" Hamonic	Collingwood, Ont	Northern Nav. Co	"	VGD
" Huronic	"	"	"	VGE
" Province	Port Arthur, Ont	Great Lakes Towing and wrecking Company	"	VFR
" Empire	"	"	"	VFP
" Salvor	Victoria, B.C	B.C. Salvage Co	Owners	VFV
" Prince Albert	Prince Rupert, B.C	Grand Trunk Pac. Ry.	"	VFL
" Prince John	"	"	"	VFM
" Florence	Toronto, Ont	T. Eaton	"	VFT
" Princess Beatrice	Victoria, B.C	Can. Pacific Railway.	M. W. T. Co. of C	VFC
" Princess Charlotte	"	"	"	VFE
" Princess May	Vancouver, B.C	"	"	VFH
" Princess Royal	Victoria, B.C	"	"	VFG
" Tees	"	"	"	VFK
" Camosun	Vancouver, B.C	Union Steamship Co	Owners	VFZ
" Princess Adelaide	Victoria, B.C	Can. Pacific Railway.	Marconi Wireless Tel. Co. of Canada.	VFA
" Princess Mary	"	"	"	VFB
" Princess Alice	"	"	"	VFD
" Princess Ena	"	"	"	VFJ
" Princess Sophia	"	"	"	VFI
" Lord Strathcona	Quebec, P.Q	Quebec Salvage Co	"	VFX
" Royal George	Toronto, Ont	Canadian Northern SS	"	VGA
" Chelohsin	Vancouver, B.C	Union Steamship Co	Owners	VGN
" Prince Arthur	Yarmouth, N.S	Boston and Yarmouth SS. Co.	Marconi Wireless Tel. Co. of Canada.	VGJ
" Prince George	"	"	"	VGK
" Halifax	Halifax, N.S	C. A. Plant SS. Co	"	VGP
" Douglas H. Thomas	Sydney, C.B	Dom. Coal Co	"	VGR
" Princess Maquinna	Victoria, B.C	Can. Pacific Railway.	"	VGT
Car Ferry "Ontario No.1"	Montreal, P.Q	Ont. Car. Ferry Co	Owners	VGU
SS. Noronic	Port Arthur, Ont	Northern Nav. Co	Marconi Wireless Tel. Co. of Canada	VGW
" Seal	Windsor, N.S	Halifax Trading and Sealing Co.	"	VGV
" Deliverance	Liverpool, N.S	Southern Salvage Co	M. W. T. Co	VFO
" Bessie Dollar	Victoria, B.C	Dollar SS. Lines	Owners	VFF
" Venture	Vancouver, B.C	Union SS. Co	"	VGX
" Yarmouth	Yarmouth, N.S	C.P.R	M. W. T. Co	VGY
" Princess Patricia	Victoria, B.C	"	Owners	VGZ
SS. Dalhousie City	Toronto, Ont	N. St. C. & T. N. Co.	M. W. T. Co	VEA
" Corona	"	C. SS. Lines	"	VEB
" Kingston	"	"	"	VEC
" Toronto	"	"	"	VED
" Hazel Dollar	Victoria, B.C	Dollar SS. Lines	"	VEE
" Chippewa	Toronto, Ont	"	"	VEH
SS. Garden City	Toronto, Ont	N. St. C. & T. N. Co.	M. W. T. Co	VEI
" Chicora	Halifax, N.S	C. SS. Lines	"	VEJ
" Macassa	Hamilton, Ont	"	"	VEK
" Cayuga	Toronto, Ont	"	"	VEL
" Cascapedia	Quebec, P.Q	"	"	VEO
Tug "Harrison"	Owen Sound, Ont	J. Harrison & Sons	"	VFY
Car Ferry "Ontario No. 2"	Montreal, P.Q	Ont. Car. Ferry Co	Owners	VER
SS. Imperoyal	Sarnia, Ont	Inperial Oil Co	M. W. T. Co	VGM
" Armonia	Montreal, P.Q	R. Lawrence Smith	"	VES

LICENSED SHIP STATIONS—*Concluded.*

Name of Ship.	Port of Registry.	Name of Owners.	Name of Company operating the Station.	Call Signal.
SS. Turret Crown	Newcastle, G.B	Coastwise SS. & Barge Co	Owners	ZDH
" Luzblanca	Toronto, Ont	Imp. Oil Co	M. W. T. Co	VEU
SY. Aquilo	Vancouver, B.C	B. D. Rogers	Owners	VFU
SS. Sable I	Windsor, N.S	J. A. Farquahar	M. W. T. Co	MTZ
SS. G. R. Crowe	Toronto, Ont	G. R. Crowe SS. Co	"	VET
Tug Pilot	Victoria, B.C	B. C. Salvage Co	Owners	VEV
SS. Glenshee	Midland, Ont	Gt. Lakes Transp. Co	M. W. T. Co	VEW
" Charlton	Windsor, Ont	Victoria Harbour Lumber Co	"	VEX
" Reginald	Sarnia, Ont	"	"	VEY
" Freshfield	Montreal, P.Q	R. Lawrence Smith Co	"	VEZ
SS. Harold Dollar	Victoria, B.C	Dollar SS. Lines	M. W. T. Co	VCY
" James Reid	Sarnia, Ont	Reid wrecking Co	"	VCZ
" Schoolcraft	Midland, Ont	Manley Chew	"	VAU
" Manxman	Montreal, P.Q	R. Lawrence Smith Co	"	GDZ
" Sellasia	St. John, N.B	W. Thompson & Co	Dept. Naval Service	ZIR
" Royalite	Sarnia, Ont	Imperial Oil Co	M. W. T. Co	VBQ
" Sarnolite	"	"	"	VBR
" Iocolite	"	"	"	VBS
" Mina Brea	Toronto, Ont	Inth Petroleum Co	Owners	VAP
" Njord	Sydney, N.S	Murray & Crawford Line	M. W. T. Co	VAO

GOVERNMENT STEAMERS EQUIPPED WITH RADIOTELEGRAPH INSTALLATIONS. OPERATED by the Department of the Naval Service.

Name.	Range.	Call Signal.
H.M.C.S. *Niobe*	400 miles	VDA
" *Rainbow*	250 "	VDB
C. G. S. *Canada*	150 "	VDC
" *Acadia*	200 "	VDT
" *Malaspina*	200 "	VDU
" *Galiano*	200 "	VDV

OPERATED by the Department of Marine and Fisheries.

Name.	Range.	Call Signal.
C. G. S. *Stanley*	150 miles.	VDE
" *Lady Laurier*	150 "	VDF
" *Aberdeen*	100 "	VDG
" *Druid*	100 "	VDH
" *Montcalm*	150 "	VDJ
" *Lady Grey*	100 "	VDL
" *Quadra*	100 "	VDM
" *Estevan*	200 "	VDN
" *Dollard*	150 "	VDO
" *Newington*	100 "	VDP
" *Lurcher Lightship*	100 "	VDR
" *Simcoe*	100 "	VDS
" *Aranmore*	200 "	VDQ
" *Prince Edward Island*	100 "	VBY

OPERATED by the Department of Railways and Canals.

Name.	Range.	Call Signal.
C. G. S. *Durley Chine*	200 miles.	VDQ
" *Sheba*	200 "	VDZ

OPERATED by the Post Office Department.

Name.	Range.	Call Signal.
C. G. S., *Lady Evelyn*	100 miles.	VDX

OPERATED by the Customs Department.

Name.	Range.	Call Signal.
C. G. S. *Margaret*	200 miles.	VDW

OPERATION OF THE COAST STATION SERVICES.

The coast station services have been maintained on a war basis throughout the year. The amount of business handled by the east coast system shows a decrease from last year's business, amounting to 7,360 messages, containing 159,551 words.

The great lakes system (operated by the Marconi Wireless Telegraph Company of Canada, Limited, under contract) shows an increase of 2,904 messages containing 52,434 words.

The west coast system (operated directly by this department) shows an increase of 26,072 messages, containing 629,025 words.

The Hudson Bay system (operated for the department of the Railways and Canals by this department) shows a decrease of 1,353 messages containing 178,127 words.

Table No. 1 shows a comparative statement of the business handled by the different systems during the past seven years.

TABLE No. 1.—Comparative Statement of Business handled by the Radiotelegraph Systems during the last seven years.

Service.	1910-11.		1911-12.		1912-13.		1913-14.		1914-15.		1915-16.		1916-17.		Comparison with 1915-16.		
	Mes-sages.	Words.	Mes-sages.	Words.	Mes-sages.	Words.	Mes-sages.	Words.	Mes-sages.	Words.	Mes-sages.	Words.	Mes-sages.	Words.	Increase or Decrease.	Mes-sages.	Words.
East Coast	71,594	1,179,434	119,049	1,824,450	153,843	2,704,411	145,605	2,443,145	59,846	1,196,512	45,195	864,020	37,835	704,460	Decrease.	7,360	159,551
Great Lakes	Nil.	....	1,043	17,095	2,750	52,422	9,601	219,786	15,785	326,505	13,617	259,366	16,521	311,800	Increase..	2,904	52,434
West Coast	48,074	647,461	76,158	997,900	115,494	1,518,926	157,354	2,206,331	98,386	1,532,526	95,048	1,103,395	121,120	1,732,420	Increase..	26,072	629,025
Hudson Bay	....	....	....	....	....	....	....	....	5,259	325,961	7,617	570,281	6,264	392,154	Decrease..	1,353	178,127
Totals	119,668	1,826,895	196,250	2,839,445	272,087	4,275,759	312,560	4,869,262	179,276	3,381,504	161,477	2,797,062	181,740	3,140,843	Net Inc.	20,263	343,781

8 GEORGE V, A. 1918

REVENUE.

The total revenue collected during the year amounted to $16,731.33 against $8,494.99 in 1915-16.

The west coast service shows an increase of $8,241.26, the Great Lakes an increase of $29.74 and the East Coast a decrease of $34.66.

TABLE No. 2.—Shows a comparative statement of revenue received by the Coast Station services during the past eight years.

	1909-10	1910-11	1911-12	1912-13	1913-14	1914-15	1915-16	1916-17
	$ cts.	$ cts.	$ cts.	$ cts.	$ cts.	$ cts.	$ cts.	$ cts.
East Coast	Nil.	Nil.	229 57	475 00	318 42	322 99	1,022 33	987 67
Great Lakes	Nil.	Nil.	Nil.	17 08	27 55	85 92	78 16	107 90
West Coast	Nil.	3,108 63	4,484,77	9,928 40	15,992 70	11,329 44	7,394 50	15,635 76
Totals	Nil.	3,108 63	4,714 34	10,420 48	16,338 67	11,738 35	8,494 99	16,731 33

EXAMINATION FOR CERTIFICATE OF PROFICIENCY IN RADIOTELEGRAPHY.

135 operators were examined during the year, including 8 re-examinations. 64 candidates were successful and 71 failed.

The following list shows the names of the successful candidates for Certificate of Proficiency in Radiotelegraphy:—

Number of Certificate.	Date of Certificate.	Name.	Grade of Certificate.	Where Examination held.
142	April 3rd 1916.	Wood, E.	1st Class Ship	Halifax, N.S.
143	May 9th 1916.	Tricker, Wm.	1st "	Victoria, B.C.
144	April 13th 1916.	Wood, L. P.	1st "	Halifax, N.S.
145	" 29th 1916.	Baird, A. M.	1st "	Vancouver, B.C.
146	May 25th 1916.	Maggs, S. A.	1st "	Halifax, N.S.
147	" 2nd 1916.	Rogers, B. D.	2nd "	Victoria, B.C.
148	" 6th 1916.	Atkins, J. L.	1st "	Victoria, B.C.
149	June 16th 1916.	Hooper, W. A.	1st "	Victoria, B.C.
150	" 28th 1916.	Rosebrugh. D. W.	1st "	Halifax, N.S.
151	" 16th 1916.	Shephard, L. A.	1st "	Vancouver, B.C.
152	" 16th 1916.	Webster, C. R.	1st "	Vancouver, B.C.
153	" 16th 1916.	Hardy, D. J.	1st "	Vancouver, B.C.
154	July 13th 1916.	Gulland, F. M.	1st "	Victoria, B.C.
155	" 13th 1916.	Stobart, T. P.	1st "	Victoria, B.C.
156	" 13th 1196.	Cooper, J. K.	1st "	Victoria, B.C.
157	" 25th 1916.	Twinn, B. L.	1st "	Halifax, N.S.
158	Sept. 21st 1916.	Pottle, W. R.	1st "	Halifax, N.S.
159	" 25th 1916.	McLean, S. A.	1st "	Halifax, N.S.
160	" 9th 1916.	Arundel, B.	1st "	Vancouver, B.C.
161	" 22nd 1916.	Scott, R. B. Y.	1st "	Toronto, Ont.
162	" 22nd 1916.	Shepherd, R. A.	1st "	Toronto, Ont.
163	" 14th 1916.	Rennie, R. F.	1st Class Coast	Tobermory, Ont.
164	" 13th 1916.	Tetley, W. J.	1st "	Tobermory, Ont.
165	Oct. 2nd 1916.	Paint, O. F.	1st Class Ship	Victoria, B.C.
166	" 16th 1916.	McWilliams, J. R.	1st "	Victoria, B.C.
167	Sept. 22nd 1916.	Price, A. V.	1st "	Toronto, Ont.
168	Jan. 16th 1917.	McClure, J. S.	1st "	Victoria, B.C.

SESSIONAL PAPER No. 38

Number of Certificate.	Date of Certificate.	Name.	Grade of Certificate.	Where Examination held.
169.........	Nov. 20th 1916.	Begin, J. G. O........	1st Class Ship...........	Ottawa, Ont.
170.........	Aug. 24th 1916.	Bround, E. M.......	1st "	Halifax, N. S.
171.........	Nov. 20th 1916.	Allen, R. O........	1st "	Halifax, N.S.
172.........	" 20th 1916.	Bennett, E. G........	1st "	Halifax, N.S.
173.........	" 28th 1916.	Greenhill, D. C......	1st "	Ottawa, Ont.
174.........	" 16th 1916.	Harris, C. K........	1st "	Vancouver, B.C.
175.........	" 28th 1916.	Smith, H. E........	1st "	Ottawa, Ont.
176.........	" 29th 1916.	Edwards, G. A......	1st "	Halifax, N.S.
177.........	Jan. 5th 1917.	Bent, R. A........	1st "	Halifax, N.S.
178.........	" 10th 1917.	Moulton, W. S......	1st "	Halifax, N.S.
179.........	" 22nd 1917.	McKenzie, H. B......	1st "	Halifax, N.S.
180.........	" 24th 1917.	Peter, A. G........	1st "	Halifax, N. S.
181.........	" 23rd 1917.	Roberts, Stanley.....	1st "	Halifax, N.S.
182.........	" 16th 1917.	Walsh, H. E........	1st Class Coast.....	Halifax, N.S.
183.........	" 29th 1917.	Macken, M. H......	1st Class Ship...	Halifax, N.S.
184.........	Feb. 3rd 1917.	Woodhead, C. F.....	1st "	Halifax, N.S.
185.........	Jan. 31st 1917.	McGrady, H. G.....	1st "	Vancouver, B.C.
186.........	Feb. 7th 1917.	Rycroft, H........	1st "	Halifax, N.S.
187.........	" 7th 1917.	Pape, O. J........	1st "	Halifax, N.S.
188.........	Jan. 30th 1917.	Berry, T. V........	1st "	Vancouver, B.C.
189.........	Feb. 8th 1917.	Allen, H. D........	2nd "	Victoria, B.C.
190.........	Jan. 24th 1917.	Westland, H. L. G....	1st "	Halifax, N.S.
191.........	Feb. 12th 1917.	Heath, C. G........	1st "	Halifax, N.S.
192.........	" 7th 1917.	Dennett, J. H....	1st "	Halifax, N.S.
193.........	" 19th 1917.	Moore, W. J. E.....	1st Class Coast.	Halifax, N. S.
194.........	" 21st 1917.	Wallace, J. M........	1st Class Ship........	Halifax, N.S.
195.........	Mar. 2nd 1917.	Harris, A. K. W.....	1st "	Victoria, B.C.
196.........	" 14th 1917.	Bishop, P........	1st "	Halifax, N.S.
197.........	" 19th 1917.	Filtness, A. W.....	1st "	Vancouver, B.C.
198.........	" 30th 1917.	Ellison, J. H........	1st "	Ottawa, Ont.
199.........	April 3rd 1917.	Moor, H. H........	1st "	Ottawa, Ont.
200.........	Mar. 19th 1917.	Hodgson, E........	2nd "	Vancouver, B.C.
201.........	" 19th 1917.	Young, C. W.......	1st "	Vancouver, B.C.
202.........	" 19th 1917.	Robinson, D. M.....	1st "	Vancouver, B.C.
203.........	" 19th 1917.	Spowart, A. A........	2nd "	Vancouver, B.C.
204.........	" 7th 1917.	Holmes, J. A........	1st Class Coast.	Halifax, N.S.
205.........	Jan. 12th 1917.	Green, A. A........	1st Class Ship.........	Victoria, B.C.

The following holders of certificates of proficiency in radiotelegraphy passed a successful examination in the operation of other equipments and have had their original certificates amended accordingly.

No. of Certificate.	Name.	Additional Equipment.
58................................	Emmerson, R G........	½ K.W., 1½ K.W. and 5 K.W Ship Stations.
13................................	Lemieux, J. E. O........	5½ K.W. Coast Station.
193................................	Moore, W. J. E........	1·7 K.W. Ship Station.
90................................	Taylor, Fred...........	5½ K.W. Coast Station.
10................................	Argue, A. E...........	10 K.W. Coast Station.
76................................	Hayman, E. D.........	10 K.W. Coast Station.
80................................	Spracklin, C. R........	10 K.W. Coast Station.

TABLE No. 3.—Detailed Statement of Business handled by the ten stations on the West Coast operated by this Department.

Name of Station.	Private Business to and from Ships.		Private Business between Stations.		Business to and from Government Ships.		Government business between Stations.		Service Messages.		Retransmitted Messages.		Cost of Maintenance.	Revenue.
	Messages.	Words.	Messages.	Words.	Messages.	Words.	Messages.	Words.	Messages.	Words.	Messages.	Words.	$ cts.	$ cts.
Gonzales Hill (Victoria)	1,410	21,476	8,245	130,774	473	20,580	7,155	113,682	17,703	187,025	1,142	10,863	5,047 58	3,398 03
Pachena Point	266	3,764	19	220	131	6,542	436	1,666	2,105	17,874	229	4,728	3,014 98	127 20
Estevan Point	2,674	36,381	38	543	93	3,236	438	2,278	3,956	32,073	1,696	26,895	5,105 35	1,635 53
Dead Tree Point	6	53	1,768	47,789	15	669	9	199	2,153	16,579			1,876 40	547 03
Ikeda Head	28	388	550	9,325	20	844	13	250	1,736	11,354	88	1,633	1,294 51	355 90
Triangle Island	1,599	23,264	3,703	78,493	130	5,952	797	5,501	6,249	62,279	9,709	12,364	3,525 88	3,538 42
Point Grey	902	13,315	2,747	101,426	56	1,491	394	1,296	4,443	92,880	445	2,310	4,227 90	2,358 49
Digby Island (Pr. Rupert)	1,220	17,201	6,819	114,141	275	11,178	1,397	14,734	3,367	31,332	2	48	5,062 85	2,613 44
Cape Lazo	792	12,243	52	888	190	8,637	377	942	2,594	24,261	74	1,045	4,517 94	589 56
Alert Bay	436	6,349	392	5,397	45	1,999	29	403	2,065	17,839	5	187	4,092 86	472 10
District Office at Victoria														
General Account (including charter of steamers)													5,943 19	
Esquimalt Workshop, etc.													5,623 49	
Totals	9,333	134,434	24,333	488,996	1,428	61,128	11,045	140,951	46,371	493,496	28,610	413,415	51,332 93	15,635 76

Total number of messages handled 1,211 20
Total number of words handled 17,324 20
Total cost of maintenance of stations (including office workshop, etc.) .... $ 51,332 93
Total Revenue 15,635 76

TABLE No. 4.—Detailed Statement of Business handled by the Eight Stations on the Great Lakes, owned by the Department of the Naval Service, and operated by the Marconi Wireless Telegraph Company of Canada, Limited.

Name of Station.	Private Business to and from Ships.		Private Business between Stations.		Business to and from Government Ships.		Government business between Stations.		Service Messages.		Retransmitted Messages.		Cost of Maintenance.	Government percentage of Revenue.
	Messages.	Words.	Messages.	Words.	Messages.	Words.	Messages.	Words.	Messages.	Words.	Messages.	Words.	$ cts.	$ cts.
Port Arthur	1,018	17,095	112	1,876	226	4,979	2	60	200	2,190	97	2,034	3,500 00	18 05
Sault Ste. Marie	1,745	33,207	57	640	406	11,857	4	121	138	3,770	1,007	20,075	3,500 00	27 52
Tobermory	12	313	162	2,932	219	6,338	25	278	574	4,718	987	19,017	3,500 00	4 56
Midland	911	15,193	89	1,852	277	8,850	6	134	231	3,617	706	12,812	3,500 24	9 60
Point Edward	1,059	17,786	316	6,688	37	1,130	1	60	817	11,661	957	23,238	3,540 00	28 57
Port Burwell	512	6,283	14	218	152	2,986			77	1,862	35	787	3,501 33	8 28
Toronto	733	11,174	143	3,103	10	238	15	327	2,361	48,416	71	1,885	3,500 00	11 32
Kingston													3,503 09	
Totals	5,990	101,051	893	17,309	1,327	36,378	53	980	4,398	76,234	3,860	79,848	28,044 66	107 90

Total number of messages handled................ 16,531
Total number of words handled................ 311,800
Total cost of maintenance................ 28,044 66
Total revenue................ $ 107 90

38—6

TABLE No. 5.—Detailed Statement of Business handled by the Twenty-one Stations in the Gulf and River St. Lawrence and East Coast owned by this Department, partly operated by the Department and partly operated by the Marconi Wireless Telegraph Co., of Canada, Limited, under contract.

Name of Station.	Private Business to and from Ships.		Private Business between Stations.		Business to and from Government Ships.		Government business between Stations.		Service Messages.		Retransmitted Messages.		Cost of Maintenance.	Government percentage of Revenue.
	Messages.	Words.	Messages.	Words.	Messages.	Words.	Messages.	Words.	Messages.	Words.	Messages.	Words.	$ cts.	$ cts.
Cape Sable	298	4,748			555	12,463	197	3,183	7	136	5	67	2,619 02	
Partridge Island (St. John, N.B.)	5,498	83,328			1,286	20,879	17	290	313	4,110	437	7,069	3,514 15	
Cape Race	34	575	5	112	82	1,585	69	835	82	1,788	589	8,211	3,500 00	
Grindstone Island	4	98	804	19,945	225	4,454	47	510	41	619	795	30,940	1,497 86	362 84
Cape Bear			21	631	40	591	145	2,532	15	134	354	5,602	2,500 00	
Point Riche	5	77	1	45	91	1,904	23	486	118	2,926	472	6,963	3,816 74	
*Point Amour	2	67	511	7,924	141	4,517	496	4,184	127	3,606	3,893	79,586	3,500 00	
†Belle Isle	578	8,788	139	2,630	194	3,542	28	410	185	3,827	190	3,183	4,500 00	
Cape Ray			125	1,806									3,500 00	
Harrington	35	920											2,500 00	
Heath Point	464	10,812	78	1,873	100	1,694	162	3,943	126	2,451	3,282	58,998	3,500 00	
Fame Point			468	10,169	367	7,832	126	3,006	795	836	14	251	3,500 00	
Clarke City	295	5,681											3,500 00	
Father Point					2,018	37,967			51	579			2,500 00	
Grosse Isle	278	4,687	10	128	266	6,669	376	5,980	17	236	13	260	2,500 00	
Quebec	9	144	5	79	407	5,767	532	13,595	21	485	179	4,348	3,500 00	
Three Rivers	341	6,122	3	46	752	16,795			127	2,777	85	1,617	3,500 00	
Montreal			2	19	238	5,635	1	11	30	561	432	8,473		
Sable Island	182	3,038	1	33	82	1,961	1,164	15,709	150	3,321	12	182	4,521 01	107 67
Camperdown (Halifax)	214	3,138	1	9	87	1,811	1,023	14,232	207	2,654	452	7,686	5,441 38	293 50
North Sydney					790	12,723	678	11,235	260	3,466	40	582	3,261 01	223 66
Totals	8,237	132,223	2,174	45,439	7,721	148,791	5,084	80,136	2,672	47,512	11,244	224,018	70,673 17	987 67

Total number of messages handled........ 37,132
Total number of words handled........ 678,119
Total cost of maintenance........ 70,673 17
Total Revenue........ 987 67

*Includes returns from 1st April 1916 to 31st December, 1916.
†Includes returns from 1st April 1916 to 10th November, 1916.

TABLE No. 6.—Detailed Statement of Business handled by the One station on the East Coast owned and operated by the Marconi Wireless Telegraph Company of Canada, Limited, under contract with the Department of the Naval Service.

Name of Station.	Private Business to and from Ships.		Private Business between Stations.		Business to and from Government Ships.		Government business between Stations.		Service Messages.		Retransmitted Messages.		Cost of Maintenance.	Revenue.
	Messages.	Words.	Messages.	Words.	Messages.	Words.	Messages.	Words.	Messages.	Words.	Messages.	Words.	$ cts.	$ cts.
Pictou	89	2,469	221	16,262	177	3,975	16	389	128	2,035	72	1,220	1,750 00	....

Total number of messages handled............ 703
Total number of words handled............ 26,350
Total cost of maintenance............ $ 1,750 00
Total revenue............

TABLE No. 7.—Detailed Statement of Business handled by LePas and Port Nelson Radiotelegraph Stations owned by the Department of Railways and Canals.

Name of Station.	Private Business to and from Ships.		Private Business between Stations.		Business to and from Government Ships.		Government business between Stations.		Service Messages.		Retransmitted Messages.	
	Messages.	Words.	Messages.	Words.	Messages.	Words.	Messages.	Words.	Messages.	Words.	Messages.	Words.
LePas	28	552	616	11,991	7	71	1,772	156,996	607	18,514	....	....
Port Nelson	31	984	616	11,991	20?	15,531	1,772	156,996	608	18,528	....	....
Totals	59	1,536	1,232	23,982	214	15,602	3,544	313,992	1,215	37,042	....	....

Total number of messages handled............ 6,264
Total number of words handled............ 392,154

The cost of maintenance of these stations is borne by the Department of Railways and Canals and all revenue collected accrues to that Department.

8 GEORGE V, A. 1918

ASSISTANCE RENDERED TO SHIPS DURING THE YEAR BY THE GOVERNMENT RADIO-
TELEGRAPH SERVICE.

West Coast.

SS. *Orion.*—On the 20th June, 1916, Tofino reported by telephone to the
Estevan station that the captain of the ss. *Orion* had landed there and reported
that his vessel was disabled with a broken shaft eight miles west of Lennard
island, and required the assistance of the U.S. Government tug *Snohomish*
immediately. Cape Flattery was at once advised by wireless of the accident.
The *Snohomish* proceeded to the assistance of the disabled boat and took her in
tow.

SS. *Northwestern.*—On the 17th July, 1916, the ss. *Northwestern* advised
the Digby Island station, by wireless, that she had propellor trouble, several
blades having shaken off and that she was proceeding south. The tug *Samson*
joined the ss. *Northwestern* later and stood by her on the remainder of her trip
south. Constant wireless communication was maintained with both ships.

SS. *Redondo.*—On the 19th August, 1916, the ss. *Redondo* broke her rudder
stock, off Maud Island, Discovery passage, and was compelled to anchor off
that island and await assistance. Wireless communication was immediately
established with the ss. *Redondo* by the Cape Lazo station. The owners were
advised of the vessel's condition and they despatched a tug boat which towed the
Redondo to Seattle.

SS. *Princess Maquinna.*—On the 30th August, 1916, distress signals were
received at the Point Grey station from the ss. *Princess Maquinna*, the vessel
having run ashore during fog near Small island on her way to Vancouver. The
Princess Maquinna eventually backed off and proceeded to Vancouver escorted
by the ss. *Princess Alice.*

SS. *Kunajiri Maru.*—On the 23rd September, 1916, the ss. *Kunajiri
Maru* ran ashore in a thick fog near New Dungeness lighthouse. The Gonzales
Hill station was requested to arrange for a tug and was informed by the Seattle
station that the tug *Tyee* would leave at once. The *Tyee* and *Unalga* stood
by the *Kunajiri Maru* but their services were not required as the vessel floated
the following morning and proceeded to Port Townsend for survey.

SS. *Princess Alice.*—On the 15th October, 1916, the ss *Princess Alice* sent
a message through the Cape Lazo station, notifying her owners that she had
run aground in Mensies bay. The *Princess Alice* floated off the next day with
the assistance of the tug *Nitinat.*

SS. *Belfast.*—On the 16th October, 1916, advice was received from Hesquit,
via the Estevan Station, that the ss. *Belfast* was anchored close to the shore at
the entrance to Sydney inlet, in a dangerous position. The Ucluelet lifeboat
left to stand by and the ss. *Belfast* wired to Seattle for a tug. This information
was given to the U.S. Revenue Cutter *Unalga* by the Gonzales Hill station.

SS. *Santa Ana.*—On the 28th October, 1916, the ss. *Santa Ana* reported
to the Ketchikan station that her low pressure crank had broken and that she
was anchored off Macy island. The boat being closer to Ketchikan she maintained communication with that station, but the Digby Island station handled
messages to and from the ship. The ss. *Valdez* took the ss. *Santa Ana* in tow
early on the morning of the 31st October, 1916. When abeam of the Digby
Island station bound for Seattle, the *Santa Ana* reported all well.

Barge Donald D.—At 8.45 a.m. on the 3rd November, 1916, the ss. *Prince
John* reported by wireless to the Triangle Island station as follows: "At 11 p.m.
last night the barge *Donald D* broke away from the tug *Dola*, eight miles west

of Pine island, strong easterly gale, heavy sea, tug short of coal, please send assistance to take off crew. *Dola* going to Alert bay for coal, *Prince John* now abeam Pine island going off shore see if can find *Donald D.*"

The Triangle Island station requested the Captain of the *Prince John* to do all in his power to assist, and also got in touch with other stations to render assistance. The crew of the *Donald D*, consisting of five men and one woman, were eventually rescued by the ss. *Prince John*.

SS. *Niels Nielson.*—On the 27th November, 1916, the ss. *Niels Nielson*, bound from Seattle to Vladivostock, with a valuable cargo, reported to the Triangle Island station that she had lost her propeller and required assistance; the vessel was then 103 miles from Triangle island. The Gonzales Hill station reported the accident to the tug *Snohomish*, which vessel left Port Angeles to render assistance. The tug *Goliath* was also dispatched from cape Flattery at midnight on the 27th November. On the morning of the 29th November the Gonzales Hill station requested the ss. *Niels Nielson* to keep the station posted as to her movements, and later received advice from the vessel, *via* the Estevan station, that she expected to sight the tug *Goliath* in two hours. Messages were also sent to the tugs and the *Goliath* replied at 1.50 p.m. that she was alongside the ss. *Niels Nielson*, and expected to have a hawser aboard her in a few minutes. At 10 p.m. the *Snohomish* advised that the *Goliath* had the *Niels Nielson* in tow, about twenty miles from cape Cook, and later that she had towed her safely to Victoria, assisted part of the way by the tug *Tyee.*

SS. *Stanley N. Dollar.*—On the 12th January, 1917, the Gonzales Hill station received a message from the ss. *Princess Alice*, advising that the ss. *Stanley N. Dollar* was ashore in Active pass and required immediate assistance. The B.C. Salvage Company was advised and the ss. *Salvor* was dispatched to the scene of the accident, arriving in the vicinity in four hours' time. Unfortunately, the *Salvor* also ran ashore, at 9 p.m., on Enterprise reef and was not floated off until 7 a.m. the following morning. In the meantime the *Nitinat* had arrived and pulled the *Stanley N. Dollar* off at 7.30 a.m. on the 13th January.

SS. *Prince John.*—On the 26th January, 1917, weak signals were picked up by the Digby Island station, from the ss. *Prince John*, stating that they were ashore in Wrangell narrows, taking water fast. The Digby Island station got in touch with the ss. *Prince Albert*, which vessel proceeded to the assistance of the *Prince John*. The tug *Pioneer* pulled off the *Prince John*, and she transferred her passengers to the *Prince Albert*, and then beached for repairs.

SS. *Princess Patricia.*—On the 7th February, 1917, the *Princess Patricia* went ashore at Point Grey and the tug *Qualicum* was sent from Vancouver, to render assistance. The assistance rendered by the Point Grey station enabled the *Princess Patricia* to be floated within five hours after the first report of the accident.

SS. *Santa Ana.*—On the 18th March, 1917, a message was received from the ss. *Santa Ana*, *via* the ss. *Norwood* and ss. *Northwestern*, advising that she was ashore near Craig, Alaska, but not making water. The *Santa Ana* was ashore for several days but eventually floated off safely.

SS. *Prince Rupert.*—On the 23rd March, 1917, a distress call was received by the Digby Island station from the ss. *Prince Rupert*, advising that the boat had struck the rocks and was filling fast and requesting immediate assistance. The nearest steamer in range was the ss. *Humboldt*, northbound. At the request of the captain of the ss. *Prince Rupert* the Digby Island station asked the *Humboldt* to return at full speed, which he immediately proceeded to do. Several other boats from Prince Rupert also left to render assistance. The passengers were taken off the vessel and brought into Prince Rupert. Constant wireless communication was maintained with the vessel.

8 GEORGE V, A. 1918

East Coast and Great Lakes.

The radiotelegraph stations on the east coast and great lakes were not called upon to render any assistance to distressed vessels during the year.

NEW CONSTRUCTION, ADDITIONS AND ALTERATIONS.

West Coast.

Cape Lazo.—The old three-piece mast was found to be rotting at the base, so a large concrete footing was placed around it. New mast bands were made and the stays refitted. Preventer bands and stays were placed on the topmast, and the mast set up and painted. The tree mast was also set up and painted. All the apparatus was overhauled.

Dead Tree Point.—All the station buildings were painted, the mast was also painted and the rigging overhauled.

Estevan.—The rigging was overhauled and the mast painted. About an acre of ground was cleared and the digging of a well commenced. The tramway was improved by putting down new iron rails for the use of a gasolene car. The apparatus was overhauled and new piping in connection with the engine-cooling tanks put in. A new receiver was also installed.

Gonzales Hill.—The rigging was overhauled, and new preventer stays and strongbacks were put up. The masts were painted, a new aerial erected, and the earth system strengthened. New partitions were put up in the dwelling house, and a few minor repairs made to the dwelling and operating houses.

Pachena.—The apparatus was overhauled and put in good working order.

Point Grey.—The masts and rigging were overhauled and the masts painted. A new power-set and non-synchronous disc, to operate off the power mains, was installed and the station overhauled generally.

Triangle Island.—The masts and all apparatus was thoroughly overhauled and placed in good working order.

East Coast.

In pursuance of the policy of government ownership of radiotelegraph coast stations, an agreement was entered into with the Marconi Wireless Telegraph Company of Canada, whereby the North Sydney station has been transferred to the department for the sum of $5,365.44.

North Sydney.—In order to increase the range of the North Sydney station a second mast was erected at that point and the height of the existing mast increased to 165 feet; the operating house was also removed to a new position. The total cost of the above work was $1,827.69.

Great Lakes.

Point Edward.—Owing to the action of the Hydro-Electric Commission of Ontario changing the frequency of the power supply from 60 to 25 cycles, new transformers and motors had to be installed to supply power to the radiotelegraph transmitting apparatus. The total cost of the installation was $1,341.00.

Port Burwell.—A septic tank and drainage was put in at this station and surface well installed.. The total cost of this work was $387.94.

Headquarters.—A tubular iron mast, one hundred and forty feet in height, was erected at the Naval Stores, Wellington St., Ottawa, for the use of this branch in connection with the testing of radiotelegraph apparatus.

Radiotelegraph Act.—The following amendments to the radiotelegraph Regulations have been made since the 1st August, 1914.—

SHIP STATIONS IN TERRITORIAL WATERS.

103. *The Radiotelegraph Stations on board ships* (other than H.M. ships of war or Canadian Government vessels) *shall not be worked while such ships are within the territorial waters of Canada, unless specific permission is granted therefor* by the controlling Canadian coast stations for the locality, and then only provided such working does not interfere with the operation of any coast station established in Canada, and that the provisions of the Radiotelegraph Convention of London, 1912, and the Service Regulations, annexed thereto, are strictly observed.

WAVELENGTH TO BE USED BY SHIP STATIONS.

106. All Canadian licensed Ship Stations shall use the wavelength of 600 metres exclusively during the period of hostilities.

NATIONALITY OF OPERATORS.

No. 88 (*a*). No person shall be permitted to attend examination for any class of certificate of proficiency in radiotelegraphy—

    (i) who is not a British subject;

    (ii) who has at any time been of enemy nationality;

    (iii) whose parents were not òf British nationality at the time of his birth; .

    (iv) whose parents have at any time been of enemy nationality.

(*b*) Candidates for examination for first-class certificate of proficiency must be not less than eighteen years of age.

(*c*) This regulation shall take effect on the 15th October, 1916, and shall remain in force until the cessation of hostilities, unless sooner repealed.

SHIP STATIONS IN HARBOURS.

104. (*a*) The Radiotelegraph Stations on board ships (other than H.M. ships of war or Canadian Government vessels) *shall not be worked whilst such ships are within a harbour of the Dominion of Canada.*

(*b*) For the proper enforcement of the above, *ships of British register in Canadian harbours must completely disconnect their aerial wires from their radio apparatus,* the ends of such wires being suspended entirely clear of the radiotelegraph cabin, preferably from the main rigging, *in such a manner as to show they are properly disconnected.*

(*c*) *Ships of foreign register* in a Canadian harbour *must* (subject to the provisions of the following subsection *d*) *take down their aerial wires completely* and disconnect the same from their radiotelegraph apparatus.

8 GEORGE V, A. 1918

(*d*) Ships of foreign register remaining in a Canadian harbour for *less than thirty-six hours, may at the discretion of the competent naval authority,* be permitted to leave their aerials up, provided the same are disconnected in accordance with the provisions of subsection (*b*) of this regulation.

(*e*) Subsections (*b*), (*c*), and (*d*) of this regulation, relative to the disconnection of aerials in ships lying in Canadian harbours will not, until further notice, apply to Canadian or British vessels in Canadian harbours on the Great Lakes. Such vessels must, nevertheless, strictly observe the provisions of subsection (*a*).

Transports.—The department continues to equip transports plying to Canada with radiotelegraph apparatus, when requested to do so by the Admiralty. An efficient staff of wireless officers is maintained at Montreal, Halifax and St. John for the inspection of the wireless apparatus on all transports.

Personnel.—The personnel of the Radiotelegraph Service in the Dominion is as follows:—

	GOVERNMENT.				COMMERCIAL.			
	Head-quarters.	Coast Stations.	Land Stations.	Ship Stations.	Head-quarters.	Coast Stations.	Land Stations.	Ship Stations.
Engineers and officers in charge....	1	20	2	47	9	20	10	64
Operators................	....	40	5	30	....	40	16	5
Other employees...........	5	6	....	....	80	....	28	....
Executive officials and inspectors..	6	2	....	1	1	....	....	3
	12	68	7	78	90	60	54	72

Total personnel, 441.

I am glad to report that all members of the Radiotelegraph Service directly in the employ of this department continue to take a great interest in their work and have carried out their duties in a satisfactory and efficient manner.

I have the honour to be, sir,

Your obedient servant,

C. P. EDWARDS,

General Superintendent, Government Radiotelegraph Service.

FISHERIES PROTECTION SERVICE.

OTTAWA, April 15, 1917.

The Deputy Minister,
    Department of the Naval Service,
        Ottawa.

SIR,—I have the honour to report as follows with regard to the Fisheries Protection Service for the year ending March 31, 1917, as to the numbers of vessels and men in the service, their stations, brief descriptions of the vessels and the names of their commanding officers.

The ships of the Fisheries Protection Service still number nine, although the *Canada* has actually been commissioned under the White Ensign and has been serving in the Naval Service since shortly after the outbreak of war.

It is also pointed out that the increased requirements for coastal defence, necessitated by the continuance of the war, do not allow of these vessels being utilized very much for the duties for which they were originally commissioned, although the department makes every effort to see that the fisheries laws are strictly complied with and to have complaints made by the fishermen investigated at once.

NAMES OF VESSELS AND THEIR COMMANDING OFFICERS.

Canada.—Lieut. Commander C. J. Stuart, R.N.R.
Curlew.—W. J. Milne.
Constance.—J. E. Morris.
Petrel.—C. O. McDonald.
Gulnare.—Clement Barkhouse.
Vigilant.—P. C. Robinson.
Galiano.—Lieut. R. M. Pope, R.N.R.
Malaspina.—Holmes Newcombe.
Restless.—Charles Moore.

C.G.S. " CANADA."

Is a twin-screw steel ship, length 206 feet, beam 25 feet, draught 11 feet 2 inches, registered tonnage 411 tons, speed 16 knots.   When on fisheries protection duty she is armed with two 12-pdr. Q.F. and two 3-pdr. Hotchkiss guns. The vessel is electrically lighted throughout, and is fitted with a powerful searchlight.   Her complement is sixty officers and men, all told, and she was built by Vickers, Sons & Maxim, Limited, England, in 1904.   She is commanded by Lieut. Commander C. J. Stuart, R.N.R.

This ship is commissioned under the White Ensign and has not been engaged in fisheries protection work since the outbreak of war.

C.G.S. " CURLEW."

Is a composite single-screw vessel, length 116 feet 3 inches, beam 19 feet 8 inches, draught 11 feet, speed $10\frac{1}{2}$ knots and registered tonnage, 157.85 tons.   Her complement is twenty-two officers and men, all told, and she is commanded by Capt. W. J. Milne.

April 1, 1916, found the *Curlew* engaged in patrol duty in the northern portion of the bay of Fundy, which was continued until the beginning of May, when she proceeded to Halifax for refit.   The foremast and one of the fresh-water tanks had to be replaced, and these, with other minor repairs, kept the ship in dockyard hands until June 30, when she returned to the bay of Fundy and resumed her fisheries duties, landing stores at the life-saving station at Little Wood island, *en route.*

On July 25, the *Curlew* was able to render some assistance in re-floating the ss. *Tyne,* which vessel had gone ashore on the Old Proprietor ledge, Grand Manan. On July 31, ship went in search of the barge *Mule,* adrift in the bay of Fundy, but the barge sank before assistance arrived.

During the month of August regular duties were carried out, including a watch being kept on the fishermen operating drift-nets for salmon in St. John harbour and off the New Brunswick shore.

On September 2 a lifeboat and stores were taken to Little Wood island from Digby, and on the 6th ship went to the assistance of the ss. *J. L. Cann,* which vessel was in a dangerous position off Briar island, with a broken shaft. On September 27 the *Curlew* embarked an official of the department and proceeded to Whitehead island, inspecting positions for life-saving stations, lookouts, etc. After returning him to St. John, ship cruised to the lobster fishing-grounds off Seal island.

At the beginning of October the life-saving stations at Seal island, Baker's cove, Westport and Little Wood island, were inspected by the commanding officer, the rest of the month being occupied in regular patrol work. Grand Harbour was visited on November 5, to watch the sardine fishermen. The catch in this locality was large and the prices good. The same may be said of the catch, earlier in the season, in St. John's harbour.

The *Curlew* located and reported an uncharted rock southward off Whitehead island on November 16.

On December 20 the ship cruised St. Mary's bay in search of the U.S. schooner *W. H. Mason;* this vessel foundered in deep water at the entrance to the bay, only the top of her masts being visible.

In January a new motor life-boat was towed from St. John to Little Wood island and moored in a sheltered position in the harbour ready for use. The life-saving station at Baker's cove was then visited and the damage done to the slip inspected and reported on. The *Curlew* remained at Yarmouth, breaking ice in the channel, until January 21, when she returned to patrol duty on the New Brunswick shore.

February 15 to 17 were spent breaking ice in the harbour of St. Andrews, to allow the traffic proceeding to the public wharf. On March 7 a lifeboat was taken from Little Wood island to Bay View, and on the 30th ship proceeded in search of a wreck, but was unable to locate it owing to weather conditions.

The winter being particularly cold and stormy very little fishing was carried on.

C.G.S. "CONSTANCE."

Is a single-screw composite steamer, whose length is 115 feet 6 inches, beam 19 feet 6 inches, draught 11 feet 6 inches, and registered tonnage 125 tons. Her complement is twenty-three officers and men, all told, and she is commanded by Capt. J. E. Morris.

The *Constance* came out of dockyard hands April 11, 1916, and immediately was utilized for war service, on which service she has been kept throughout the year.

C.G.S. "PETREL."

Is a steel, single-screw ship, length 116 feet, beam 22 feet, draught 9 feet, speed 11 knots, and registered tonnage 191 tons. Her complement is twenty-four officers and men, all told, and she is commanded by Capt. C. O. McDonald.

This ship was in commission at the beginning of the fiscal year, carrying out her regular duties, which she continued to do until May 19, when she pro-

SESSIONAL PAPER No. 38

ceeded to Little Wood island and left the ship's carpenter at the life-saving station to repair the launching ways, returning later to embark the carpenter on the completion of the repairs.

On June 16 the *Petrel* proceeded to Shelburne, calling at Victoria Beach to take in tow a life-boat for Halifax, which place was reached on the 22nd. Ship was placed in dockyard hands July 6 and remained until September 10, when repairs were completed and she was once more ready for sea.

After visiting the life-saving station at Clark's Harbour and reporting on the repairs necessary there, the *Petrel* returned to Halifax September 17, and from that date has been occupied on war service, although the commanding officer has inspected and reported on several life-saving stations when in their respective vicinities.

C.G.S. " GULNARE."

Is a steel single-screw vessel, whose length is 137 feet, beam 20 feet 5 inches, draught 12 feet, registered tonnage 262 tons. Her complement is twenty-five officers and men, all told, and she is commanded by Capt. Clement Barkhouse.

As was the case last year the *Gulnare* was employed continuously on Naval Service and was unable to attend to fisheries protection duties.

C.G.S. " VIGILANT."

Is a twin-screw steel ship, whose length is 177 feet, beam 22 feet, draught 9 feet 6 inches, registered tonnage 242 tons, and speed 16 knots. She is electrically lighted throughout and fitted with a powerful searchlight. Her complement is thirty officers and men, all told, and she is commanded by Capt. P. C. Robinson.

This ship went into commission at Port Dover April 14, but did not proceed to sea until the 21st when the Consulting Naval Engineer embarked and ship proceeded on trial trip, returning to port the same evening. The *Vigilant* then proceeded on her regular routine, visiting the life-saving station on Long point on April 25, and working on the boundary.

May 22 Captain King came on board to adjust the ship's compasses, disembarking on the evening of the 23rd. Ship then cruised on the boundary until June 11, when measles broke out in the ship and in spite of disinfecting, prevented much work being carried out until the early part of July.

July 14 the *Vigilant* left for lake Ontario, the director of the Naval Service embarked at Trenton on the 17th, and the various life-saving stations along the lake Ontario shore were inspected. On the 7th the ship returned to lake Erie, and the life-saving stations along that lake were inspected, the director of the Naval Service disembarking at Port Stanley on the 22nd, when work was resumed on the boundary. Fishermen now became very active off Long point, and work was practically confined to this part of the lake for the next couple of months. Life-saving stations were visited from time to time and work on the boundary continued until September 7, when the ship proceeded to Port Dover to land nets taken off Long point.

Stormy weather kept the vessel in port, and on the 16th the ice having become too bad, arrangements were made to lay up and the crew was paid off on December 23, 1916.

During the season of navigation, the ship steamed 5,818 miles, and seized 618 nets.

C.G.S. " MALASPINA."

Is a steel single-screw vessel, whose length is 160 feet, beam 26½ feet, draught 12½ feet, speed 14½ knots, and displacement 700 tons. She is electrically lighted throughout and fitted with a powerful searchlight. Her complement is thirty-three officers and men all told, and she was built by the Dublin Dockyard Company, Dublin, Ireland, in 1913. She is commanded by Capt. Holmes Newcombe.

8 GEORGE V, A. 1918

April 1, 1916, the *Malaspina* was busy preparing for sea, taking on stores for various wireless and life-saving stations; she left Esquimalt with these supplies on the 6th and returned on the 10th, then proceeded on examination service until the 19th. The ship's boilers were then washed out and she proceeded to Vancouver on the 23rd with the admiral superintendent on board; here applicants for the motor-boat patrol were interviewed and ship returned to Esquimalt.

April 29, the vessel proceeded to Ucluelet and towed the life-boat to Esquimalt for repairs, returning May 1. Examination service was then carried out by this ship until the 23rd, during which time she was inspected by the director of the Naval Service. On May 24 the *Malaspina* took the admiral superintendent to Fulford harbour, returning the following day. Examination service was carried out during the month of June, with the exception of a day or two when the admiral superintendent was taken on short trips. July 7 the ship went into dockyard hands for overhaul, repairs being completed on the 24th, after which she coaled and on the 7th left for Vancouver, thence to Leonard island, where a scow was taken in tow to Tofino.

From August 1 to 8 the *Malaspina* was employed in laying cable from Leonard to Vancouver island, after which she returned to Ucluelet with the scow, and after obtaining water at Uchucklisit, proceeded to Estevan with stores for the wireless station. On the 10th, as the ship was returning to Esquimalt she seized the motor-boat *Greg* for infraction of the Customs laws and brought her to Esquimalt, the fish being sold the next day and the matter reported to the collector of Customs, who ordered the vessel delivered at the Marine Department's wharf at Victoria.

This was done on the 12th, the *Malaspina* afterwards cruising on the west coast and in Hecate straits until the 20th, when a leak appeared in the main boiler, necessitating return to Esquimalt, which was reached on the 25th. On the 30th the ship left for Vancouver for repairs, remaining there until September 28, then returned to Esquimalt and proceeding with the admiral superintendent to Telegraph harbour, returning to Esquimalt on October 3. From the 4th to the 23rd the ship was on examination service, then proceeded to deliver stores to the various life-saving and wireless stations; visited Prince Rupert on the 27th and commenced cruising in the Chatham straits, but was recalled to Esquimalt, where she arrived on December 3. She proceeded on examination service until the 22nd, then made a trip to Vancouver with the admiral superintendent, afterwards going into dockyard hands for refit.

On January 24 examination service was again taken up and continued until the end of the fiscal year.

C.G.S. " GALIANO."

Is a steel, single-screw vessel, length 160 feet, beam $26\frac{1}{2}$ feet, draught $12\frac{1}{2}$ feet, speed $14\frac{1}{2}$ knots, and displacement 700 tons. She is electrically-lighted throughout and fitted with a powerful searchlight. Her complement is thirty-three officers and men, all told, and she was built at Dublin, Ireland, by the Dublin Dockyard Co., in 1913. She is commanded by Lieut. R. M. Pope, R.N.R.

The *Galiano* was at Alert Bay April 1, 1916, *en route* to Cape St. James with Mr. Stephenson of the radiotelegraph branch, who was sent to report on available sites for a radiotelegraph station. The ship then proceeded to Prince Rupert, where Mr. Stephenson disembarked, after which cruising was carried on in the eastern side of the Hecate strait, and two fishing vessels ordered to report to the collector of Customs, as they had no marks of identification or papers to show. She then proceeded to Alert Bay, exchanged wireless operators and on April 22 returned to Prince Rupert for coal, afterwards cruising on the west side of Hecate strait, thence to Triangle island and Union Bay for coal, as the latter had not been obtained at Prince Rupert. The ship sailed from

Union Bay April 29, on receipt of instructions to proceed to the northern end of the Queen Charlotte islands. On May 4 returned to Prince Rupert for stores, visited Triangle island again and then proceeded to Vancouver to meet the director of the Naval Service, who embarked on the 15th, called at Victoria and Esquimalt and then continued on a tour of inspection of various life-saving stations, etc., returning to Vancouver May 31, when the director of the Naval Service disembarked and ship returned to Esquimalt, going on examination service from June 3 to 25.

On June 26, Commander Shenton embarked, by instruction of the admiral superintendent and proceeded on a tour of inspection of the radiotelegraph stations, returning to Esquimalt July 7 for examination service, which continued until August 18. Ship then went on fisheries protection duty to Barkley sound, the salmon fishing on the Swiftsure Bank being then good. On the 23rd two boats fishing cod off Race Rocks, manned by Japanese, were ordered to report to the collector of Customs, as they had no papers or marks of identification. Examination duty was then resumed until August 28, when ship went on the ways at Yarrows for cleaning and painting of hull.

September 5 ship left for Prince Rupert and Triangle, transferring wireless operators and calling at various ports. Returned to Esquimalt on the 12th, left for Vancouver and made two return trips, and on the 19th left for Pachena and Estevan, transferring operators.

The *Galiano* was in dockyard hands from October 1 to 21, and from the latter date to January 25, practically all her time was spent in examination service. She then proceeded to Prince Rupert, arriving there January 30, cruised on the eastern side of Hecate strait, thence to Dixon's Entrance, returning to Prince Rupert on February 10. Left again on the 12th for the islands on the southern part of Hecate strait, bad weather prevailing practically all the time. After coaling at Union Bay ship arrived at Esquimalt on February 24 and on the 26th went into dry dock. Refit was completed on March 21, and shortly afterwards ship went on examination service, which continued till the end of the fiscal year.

C.G.S. " RESTLESS."

Length 71 feet, beam 17 feet, draught 7 feet, is commanded by Capt. Charles Moore.

The *Restless* is required for naval work and has been so employed since August, 1914. She was docked on June 11, 1916, for repairs, which were completed on June 26, and on December 4 underwent refit of machinery and boiler, returning to duty December 18, 1916.

C.G.S. ' FISPA.'

This vessel belonging to the fisheries branch was, in November, 1916, sent to Prince Rupert, to look after the protection of fisheries in that vicinity, as the regular fisheries protection vessels were not able to give all their time to this work.

The winter was an unusually severe one and as the vessel was small it was difficult for her to do much cruising. However, the various straits and channels were patrolled as much as possible up to the middle of April, when instructions were given the commanding officer to return south, and the vessel was returned to the inspector of fisheries on April 30.

I have the honour to be, sir,
Your obedient servant,

C. E. KINSGMILL, Admiral,
Director of the Naval Service.

8 GEORGE V, A. 1918

LIFE–SAVING SERVICE.

OTTAWA, May 1, 1917.

The Deputy Minister,
    Department of the Naval Service,
        Ottawa.

SIR,—I have the honour to make the following report concerning the Life-
saving Service of Canada for the fiscal year ending 31st March, 1917.

The type of life-saving station at present in existence on the east coast and
along the shores of the Great Lakes is rapidly becoming useless, owing to the
fact that the ocean-going vessels now in use have become so large as to reduce
to a minimum the number of marine disasters. It should also be borne in mind
that the fishermen in most instances are now provided with up-to-date motor-
boats, and are therefore better able to provide assistance in a case of emergency
than many of the stations, so that it would appear desirable to gradually do
away with a number of the least useful stations.

During the year a different arrangement has been made for the inspection
of the stations on the east coast; this duty is now carried out by officers of the
Fisheries Protection Service, while cruising in the vicinity of the various stations
and has been found to work out very satisfactorily.

NOVA SCOTIA.

Bay View.—Permanent crew. Throughout the year various disabled
fishing boats have been towed in by the crew at this station. Besides this the
schooner *Sam Slick*, 80 tons, which went ashore in Digby Gut on the 22nd
December, was floated with the help of the steamer *Bear River*.

Canso.—Volunteer crew. The crew of this life-boat have rendered assistance to the following vessels during the year: 8th June, 1917, schooner *Helen &
Mary*, with 22 fishermen on board, ashore at Booth shoal; 4th August, Canadian
Government ship ashore at Starling rock; 5th September, schooner *Maton*, 20
persons on board, ashore on Middle Ground; 23rd September, *Hazel L. Ritchie*
grounded in the harbour; 25th September, schooner *Coreau*, ashore on Whit-
man rock; 25th November, American schooner *Primer*, ashore on a ledge at
Cape island.

Cheticamp.—Permanent crew. Assistance was as usual rendered in various
forms to local fishermen, but nothing of a very serious nature occurred in this
vicinity.

Clark's Harbour.—Volunteer crew. One schooner of 200 tons, with a cargo
of hard coal, was given assistance by the crew of this life-boat on the 16th
August, 1916.

Herring Cove.—Volunteer crew. This crew went to the assistance of one
small disabled motor-boat which was being carried out to sea in a heavy northwest wind.

Seal Island.—Subsidized volunteer crew. Three vessels got into trouble
in this vicinity during the year, but there were no casualties. The *Vesta* was
sunk in Lobster bay on the 23rd July; the *Harold B. Cousins* went ashore on Black
ledge on 24th July; and the *Little Elsie* was adrift to the southwest of Seal
island, with one man aboard, for 21 hours on the 14th September. The crew
went out in search of the *Vesta* and *Little Elsie*, and in the case of the *Harold
B. Cousins* assisted in floating her and getting her under way to Yarmouth.

Westport, Brier Island.—Subsidized volunteer crew. Three wrecks occurred in the vicinity of this station. November 2, the schooner *Florence E. Melanson* at Green island; December 1, the schooner *L. M. Ellis* at Dartmouth Point ledge; and on December 18 the schooner *William Mason*, off Irish bank. In the first two cases there was no loss of life, but in the last no one was saved.

Whitehead.—Volunteer crew. The schooner *J. W. Margeson* was wrecked off Whitehead on December 18, 1916. The crew was rescued, but the life-boat was damaged beyond repair.

NEW BRUNSWICK.

Cape Tormentine.—Volunteer crew. On the 22nd July the schooner *Ulva* struck a reef off Jourmain island, and the crew were brought ashore in a gasolene boat. The schooner *Wild Brier* foundered five miles west of Jourmain light on 22nd August, in a heavy squall. The crew was rescued.

Little Wood island.—Permanent crew. Several disabled motor-boats were towed in during the year. On June 7 and 8 assistance was rendered the schooner *Capsize*, and she was towed in to the breakwater. On July 23 the *Tyne* was given assistance, the life-boat standing by for two days and nights. Two men adrift in a fog off Muir ledges were brought in to safety on 26th July, and on 13th December a man blown adrift from Nova Scotia in a thick snowstorm was brought in and cared for for two days.

Richibucto.—Permanent crew. During the year assistance was rendered to the following vessels: June 16, barkentine *Rolf*, 200 tons, with cargo of salt; June 28, schooner *Stella McLean*, 50 tons; August 18 large fishing boat *St. Joseph;* October 26, schooner *Maud Weston.* Besides this various fishing boats were towed in, etc.

ONTARIO.

Point Pelee.—Permanent crew. Services of various kinds were rendered by the crew at this station during the season of navigation. On the 23rd November the schooner *Freedna* went to pieces on the east side of the point in a southwest gale. The crew was saved.

Port Hope.—Volunteer crew. On September 15, 1916, the *Henry B. Hall*, 1,800 tons, was wrecked off Port Hope. The crew was saved.

Toronto.—Permanent crew. 53 small craft were assisted by the crew of this station during the season of 1916, besides which the crew answered numerous calls for assistance in the case of drowning accidents, etc.

BRITISH COLUMBIA.

Bamfield.—Permanent crew. This crew rendered assistance in the way of towing, etc., to several motor-boats with engine trouble, etc.

Ucluelet.—Permanent crew. On November 17 the tug *V.N.& T. No. 1*, adrift off Sidney inlet, was picked up by the crew; and at various times assistance has been given to fishing boats, etc.

I have the honour to be, sir,
Your obedient servant,

C. E. KINGSMILL, Admiral,
Director of the Naval Service.

8 GEORGE V, A. 1918

LIFE-SAVING STATIONS OF CANADA.

No.	Stations.	Established.	Coxswain.	Crew.	Description of Boat.
	New Brunswick.				
1	Little Wood Is. (P).....	1910	Harry Harvey..........	8	36-ft. self-righting power boat.
2	Richibucto (P.N.)......	1907	Thos. Legoof...........	7	Race Point surf-boat, 24 ft. long
3	Point Escuminac........	1908	E. F. Flieger....••....	7	Beebe-McLellan self-bailing.
4	Cape Tormentine.......	1912	I. Allen................	7	Beebe-McLellan self-bailing.
	Nova Scotia.				
5	Baker's Cove.........	1886	R. L. Baker............	. 7	Dobbin's pattern self-righting, 28 ft. long.
6	Blanche...............	1889	Jas. C. Swaine.........	7	Beebe-McLellan surf-boat, self-bailing, 25 ft. long.
7	Clark's Harbour........	1900	Byron Swim...........	7	Beebe-McLellan self-bailing, 25 ft. long, low ends.
8	Canso.................	....	J. J. Berrigan..........	7	Dobbin's pattern surf-boat, self-bailing, 25 ft. long.
9	Devil's Island.........	1885	B. H. Henneberry......	7	Beebe-McLellan surf-boat, self-bailing, 25 ft. long.
10	Duncan Cove..........	1886	J. W. Holland..........	7	Beebe-McLellan surf-boat, self-bailing, 25 ft. long.
11	Herring Cove..........	1885	Edw. V. Dempsey......	7	Dobbin's pattern self-righting and bailing, 25 ft. long.
12	Pictou Island..........	1889	Duncan McCallum......	7	Dobbin's pattern self-righting and bailing, 25 ft. long.
13	Port Mouton..........	1889	Walter Cook....•......	7	Beebe-McLellan surf-boat, self-bailing, 25 ft. long.
14	Scattarie..............	1885	Jas. Nearing...........	7	Beebe-McLellan boat on east side.
15	Seal Island (P)........	1880	Smith G. Penny........	7	Beebe-McLellan boat on west side.
16	Whitehead.............	1890	John Phalen............	7	Dobbin's pattern surf-boat, self-bailing, 25 ft. long.
17	Cheticamp, (P.N)......	1911	L. J. Aucoin.............	7	Beebe-McLellan twin screw motor boat.
18	Bay View, Digby (P.N.)................	1911	J. W. Hayden..........	7	36 ft. self-bailing, self-righting power boat.
19	Westport, Brier Is......	....	Ralph Welch............	.....	Subsidized motor boat,
	P. E. Island.				
20	Priest Pond............	1909	Chas. Campbell........	12	Board of Trade rocket apparatus.
21	Charlottetown.........	1907	E. White..............	6	Beebe-McLellan self-bailing.
22	Souris.................	1907	Plus Cheverie..........	7	Beebe-McLellan self-bailing.
23	Cascumpeque...........	....	Joshua Hutt...........	8	Beebe-McLellan self-bailing.
24	Alberton...............	1907	S. Gallant.............	12	Board of Trade rocket apparatus.
	British Columbia.				
25	Bamfield (P)..........	{1909} {1907}	Geo. Murray...........	11	Self-righting, self-bailing, 36-ft. power boat.
26	Ucluelet (P)...........	1908	F. Tyler (act.).........	9	Self-righting, self-bailing, 36-ft. power boat.
27	Clayoquot (P).........	1908	J. McLeod.•...........	8	Doherty's improved Beebe-McLellan.
	Ontario, Great Lakes.				
28	Cobourg...............	1882	D. Rooney.............	8	Dobbin's pattern self-righting and bailing.
29	Collingwood.,.........	1885	R. H. McFarlane.......	7	Beebe-McLellan self-bailing surf-boat.
30	Goderich..............	1886	Malc. McDonald.......	7	Surf-boat.
31	Long Point (P.N)......	1902	Jas. Smith.............	9	Surf-boat.
32	Point Pelee (P.N.).....	1900	L. Wilkinson...........	7	Surf-boat.
33	Port Hope.............	1889	John McMahon....•....	7	Dobbin's pattern self-righting and bail ing.
34	Port Stanley...........	1885	W. Brown...••........	7	Beebe-McLellan surf-boat, self-bailing, 25 feet long.
35	Toronto (P.N.).........	1883	W. F. Chapman........	14	Two motor launches.
36	Consecon.............	1898	R. Bedford............	7	Dobbin's pattern self-righting and bailing.
37	Southampton...........	1907	Hector McLeod........	7	Beebe-McLellan surf-boat, self-bailing.

NOTE:—Stations marked "P" have permanent crews, always on duty; those marked "P.N." have crews always on duty during the season of navigation. The other stations simply have volunteer crews, which drill twice a month and are called out on the occurrence of a wreck.

STORES BRANCH.

DEPARTMENT OF THE NAVAL SERVICE

Ottawa, September 25, 1917.

The Deputy Minister,
   Department of the Naval Service,
      Ottawa.

SIR,—I have the honour to submit the annual report of the Stores Branch for the fiscal year ending March 31, 1917.

1. PURCHASING AND CONTRACT SECTION.

The work of this section during the past fiscal year has materially increased in keeping with the expansion and increased activities of the service. In addition, the difficulty of obtaining supplies has multiplied enormously, but in spite of many obstacles the many demands made upon it have been successfully met. Prices in all lines have advanced materially and available supplies of raw materials have decreased, necessitating substitution and continual adjustment to meet these conditions. This applies to all lines, but more particularly perhaps to provisions and clothing. It is most gratifying, however, that the Canadian manufacturers and dealers, appreciating the situation, have, with few exceptions, realized their responsibilities and privileges under the Crown and have given our requirements preference over other demands.

Demands from the dockyards, including as they did supplies for Imperial Ships and Establishments, were much in excess of previous years, both as to quantity and variety. These were dealt with to best advantage, resulting in purchases and contracts aggregrating in value $1,282,599.

In addition, purchases to the value of $289,196 were negotiated locally from the several dockyards. Purchases were also negotiated by ships and establishments direct, mainly of fresh provisions, to a total value of $431,637.

Purchases were negotiated on behalf of the Imperial Government direct, exclusive of fuel, to the value of $854,116.

Contracts for supplies of fresh provisions were maintained on both coasts and at outlying points as necessary for the convenience of ships of this service, as well as of those of the Imperial and Allied Governments. Supplies obtained under these are included in the value of purchases negotiated by ships and establishments direct, as shown above.

Contracts for supplies of fuel were also maintained on both coasts. Purchases under these aggregated $2,204,448. This includes supplies for Imperial ships and transports.

Purchases of printing and stationery were negotiated through the Government Printing and Stationery department, as usual. These totalled in value $125,817.

During the year contracts were entered into for the charter of thirteen vessels in all. Expenditure under this head totalled $292,828. In addition, five vessels were purchased outright, involving an expenditure of $552,265. Contracts were also entered into for the contruction of twelve steel vessels of the trawler type, involving an expenditure of approximately $1,800,000.

Contracts were also entered into for the erection of various buildings, etc., involving a total expenditure of approximately $39,246.

21277—7

8 ꞌGEORGE V, A. 1918

Miscellaneous purchases to the value of $276,298 were negotiated in fulfil-
ment of demands received from the Fisheries, Hydrographic, Radiotelegraph,
Fishery Protection, and other branches of the department.

The following is a summary of liability incurred during the year:—

Provisions.. ....$	746,397
Clothing..	879,985
Medical supplies...	10,775
Naval stores..	621,979
Fuel..	2,204,448
Ordnance and ammunition..............................	54,981
Stationery and printing....................................	125,817
Miscellaneous..	2,960,637
	$ 7,605,019

II. STOREKEEPING SECTION.

The growth and expansion of the service during the year have had a marked
influence on the activities of the Stores Branch.

Various new phases of Naval Supply work having arisen in the course of
the year, it has been necessary to extend the organization to cope with the new
conditions.   The original scheme of organization, however, still proves adequate
for the requirements of the service.

The first consideration of the branch is given to Ships and Establishments
of the Naval Service proper, whether Canadian or Imperial.   The work of
supplying stores and equipment to men-of-war being of paramount importance,
every effort is made to provide for all their requirements promptly, and to
render every assistance possible for their efficient maintenance.   Satisfactory
results have been obtained in this work at both Halifax and Esquimalt dockyards,
and at other ports as necessary.   Notwithstanding the present difficulty of
obtaining and transporting supplies, all Canadian and Imperial ships calling
at Canadian dockyards, transports under the Canadian and Imperial Governments, and ships of Allied Governments, have been supplied with stores of
all descriptions required for maintenance and for carrying out necessary refits.
Facilities are placed at the disposal of visiting ships on the station as for those
of the Canadian Naval Service.

During the year eighteen vessels have been added to the Naval Establishment, of which one was purchased, thirteen chartered, three transferred from
other departments, and one given to the department.   Three vessels previously
employed, one by charter, and two on loan from private individuals, were
returned in the course of the year.   In addition, a number of motor launches
were engaged in patrol work during the summer of 1916.

As in the past, service has been rendered to the various services connected
with the department.   These are the Patrol Service, the Fishery Protection
Service, the Examination Service, and the Hydrographic Surveys, having in all
a total of twenty-seven vessels (the Fishery Patrol Service consisting of a number
of smaller craft), the Tidal and Current Surveys, the Radiotelegraph Service,
the Royal Naval Canadian Volunteer Reserve, the Life Saving Service, The Fish-
breeding Service, and various other fishery establishments throughout the
country.   The supply of these services entails a very considerable amount of
work, owing to the nature of their requirements, which, though often small, are
special and altogether peculiar to themselves.   As far as possible, uniform
systems for supplying and accounting of stores are being adopted, with a view
to obtaining greater efficiency with the minimum amount of expense.

The facilities maintained at the Halifax and Esquimalt dockyards are very
complete, and provide for quick despatch at all times and under all circumstances.
This is necessarily a factor of great importance, more especially under war

SESSIONAL PAPER No. 38

conditions. The absolute necessity of supplying the requirements of ships and establishments promptly so as not to hinder in any way the operations of the service, renders it essential that a large reserve of supplies be always available, and an efficient organization maintained to carry on the work. This work at the dockyards is under the charge of the Naval Store officers, who are directly responsible for the efficiency and effectiveness of the supply systems under their charge.

The variety of the stores handled for all services is necessarily very wide, the following being a general list of descriptions: Provisions; uniforms and clothing, and materials for making these; medical supplies, surgical instruments, and hospital equipment; lumber; metals of many kinds and in every state of manufacture; hardware and tools; textiles, flags and cordage; packings and rubber goods, paints, lubricating and fuel oils; glass, leather goods, brushes, furniture and furnishings, tackle; charts, meteorological and navigation instruments; and other miscellaneous supplies of almost every description; fuel; and ordnance, ammunition, torpedoes, and torpedo stores. Standardization of all supplies is aimed at, and particular attention is given to inspection, both of which tend towards greater efficiency, economy, and the maintenance of the high standard of quality required in all naval supplies.

The reserves of the supplies of the above descriptions maintained at both dockyards are of necessity large, since a considerable margin of safety is essential, as the requirements of the service cannot from their nature be forecasted with exactitude in advance. The state of the market for many materials, too, is abnormal, and prompt deliveries of extra quantities which may be required. from contractors uncertain. As far as possible, provision is made each year for requirements based on the consumption of the previous year or two years. From time to time, however, changes in policy, additions to the fleets, or other unforeseen events occurring necessitate adjustments to meet the new conditions. In view of the great increase in the issues to ships and establishments, the value of the stock at both dockyards has been materially increased. At the commencement of the year the values were $469,618 and $351,611 at Halifax and Esquimalt dockyards; at the end of the year these values were increased to $488,150 and $534,816 respectively.

The usual procedure of annual requisitions for supplies required during the ensuing year, and supplementary requisitions for unforeseen requirements, has been followed, and very large deliveries have resulted. The total value of receipts of stores at Halifax dockyard was $805,282 and at Esquimalt $570,-496, an increase of $165,186 and $268,630 respectively.

Likewise, the issues to ships and establishments have been largely increased both in number and value. At Halifax, the increase is $82,593, and at Esquimalt $127,936, the values for the year being $592,926 and $411,270, respectively. Transactions involved number 14,050 for Halifax, and 18,444 for Esquimalt.

The Imperial authorities continue to avail themselves of the facilities at the dockyards for keeping large supplies of stores for issue to ships operating in Atlantic and Pacific waters. Every assistance is afforded in connection with the storage and accounting of these stores.

In addition to the assistance rendered to Imperial ships in the past, arrangements were made in the course of the year to supply all the requirements of clothing stores and provisions for ships based on Esquimalt. Large reserves have been provided, and all necessary arrangements completed to ensure an efficient service.

Large reserves of steaming coal are maintained at both dockyards for Canadian and Imperial requirements. The total receipts during the year at Halifax amounted to 78,575 tons, and at Esquimalt 31,711 tons. The issues at Halifax were 77,733 tons, and at Esquimalt 29,626 tons. The greater part of these

8 GEORGE V, A. 1918

quantities being of admiralty coal, the values are not included in the value of purchases. In addition, the following large quantities of Canadian coal were handled on direct issue to ships from contractors:—

At Halifax and the East coast.. 138,509 tons.
At Esquimalt and the West coast...................................... 16,545 "

Supplies of fuel oil are also maintained at both dockyards. In the year the following quantities were handled:—

At Halifax... 107,000 gallons.
At Esquimalt.. 23,943 "

Considerable quantities of old stores, chiefly in the nature of scrap, were sold by public tender from Halifax dockyard in view of the necessity for providing further storage space for other purposes, and the favourable conditions of the market for selling material of this kind. The stores, which included steel, iron, cordage, phosphor bronze, rubber, wire rope, besides two ships' boats, were classified into various grades according to quality and probable use when sold. The amount realized approximately $10,000, is highly satisfactory, and may be attributed to the care taken in the proper classification of the material.

Owing to the large number of ships added to the Naval Establishment, it has been necessary to draw up established allowances for engineers', carpenters', boatswains', and gunners' naval and ordnance stores for each ship. Particular care is given to the preparation of these allowances, so that the greatest conomy may be effected, consistent with the efficiency of the service.

All supplies of stores are made in accordance with the allowances, additional requirements being supplied only on special authority.

Ships and establishments, including the dockyards, keep accounts of all stores received and expended. These accounts are rendered to headquarters periodically for audit. In the year a large number of accounts have been audited, with satisfactory results.

The system of biennial stocktaking has been continued during the year, and good progress has been made, notwithstanding the pressure of other work. Under this system the stocks of all stores at both dockyards are reviewed in their entirety every two years. The results of the stocktaking made are very gratifying from every point of view, and testify to the efficient manner in which the staffs concerned have performed their duties, under trying conditions.

III. TRANSPORTATIONS.

The arrangement under which the department, in conjunction with the Director of Overseas Transport, is responsible for the necessary work in connection with the export of material on behalf of the Imperial Government have been continued in force and greatly expanded during the financial year 1916-17.

The Department of the Naval Service is the agent of the Admiralty in this connection, and during the fall of 1914 had arranged for the forwarding of large quantities of material on behalf of the Admiralty. Shortly after the outbreak of war the Canadian Pacific Railway Company placed at the Government's disposal, for transportation duties, the services of Mr. A. H. Harris of their staff. During the fall months of that year the transport of material forwarded by the Canadian Government to French and British ports had been performed under his direction. In December, 1914, it was realized by the department that efficiency would be promoted by co-operation and the co-ordination of our interests with those under control of Mr. Harris, who had been appointed Acting Director Overseas Transport by the Government. In February, 1915, this gentleman, at the instance of the Government, visited London and arranged with the Imperial Authorities for the initiation and conduct of a regular Store Service between Canadian and European ports.

The Admiralty then placed a small number of requisitioned ships on this service. The Director Overseas Transport was given general control of the traffic inland, by rail or otherwise, its reception and storage of shipment, the allocation of the cargo to the different ships and storage on board of the various materials so as to ensure the maximum use of the tonnage placed at our disposal by the Admiralty.

In October, 1916, the Acting Director Overseas Transport again visited England and France at the instance of the Government. He discussed with the Imperial Officers controlling the European activities of. the service, its further development and improvement with a view to obtaining closer co-operation of all interested parties. This exchange of views and the personal discussion of the problems involved has resulted in the simplification of many systems and in closer co-operation between the various services, Canadian, Imperial, and Allied, which it is confidently expected will result in increased efficiency.

Recently the growth of the tonnage to be shipped and the further extension of Government activities to commodities hitherto handled by private effort has made the provision of further cargo space imperative. The policy of requisitioning space on all liners sailing from Canadian ports has been adopted as the most convenient and efficient method of meeting the new situation. Eighty-five per cent of the cargo space on all liners was taken over by the Government at fixed rates. The remainder was placed at the disposal of the shipping companies for the accommodation of private shipments of foodstuffs or other necessary war supplies only. This arrangement has since been modified by the force of circumstances till practically all the space available is at the disposal of the Government. Arrangements have been made for the provision of space for approved shipments on account of private firms so that undue hardship may not result from the requisitioning of practically all the available ocean space.

In practice the inconvenience will be much less than anticipated, as Government supervision of trade has been extended to cover practically every branch of the Canadian activities, whether foodstuffs, raw materials, timber, or manufactured goods.

The Department of the Naval Service controls the movements of all ships, and is the medium of communication with the Admiralty on all matters of policy. All expenses in connection with the service are defrayed by the department on behalf of the Imperial Government on presentation of duly certified invoices.

Accommodation, as necessary, has been arranged for at the various ports. The facilities of the shipping companies have been at the disposal of the Transport Service, as required. Advantage has been taken of these to a large extent, and a very great debt of gratitude is owing to shipping and transportation interests for continual assistance and ready co-operation in all matters relating to the service.

Contracts have been made for the supply of bunker coal, as necessary; 230,000 tons have been purchased from Canadian firms for vessels in the service during the year ending March 31, 1917.

Arrangements have been made as necessary for the repair and fitting of ships for special purposes, and for the supply of such provisions, stores and gear as are required while the ships are in Canadian ports.

This service from a small beginning has grown to a very large undertaking. The average export movement for the year ending 31st March, 1917, amounts to more than 200,000 tons per month, or roughly eight fully loaded freight trains of material per day. The monthly total now exceeds 400,000 tons, and the sailings two per diem. This traffic originates in all parts of Canada, and the work of organizing its transportation to the ports of shipment is very great. The services rendered by the Director of Overseas Transport and his staff in this connection cannot be overestimated.

The organization has worked with the greatest regularity and despatch. Practically no delays have been experienced throughout the period of review. The movement has been rendered possible only by the ready co-operation of all transportation companies with the staff of the service in all matters.

The traffic may, for convenience, be divided into two classes: first, "General Stores"; second, "Timber Shipments."

The first includes forage, grain, sugar and miscellaneous provisions, shell and ammunition of all kinds, militia stores, Admiralty supplies, and miscellaneous raw material and manufactured articles of a great variety.

The greater part of this traffic has been handled through the port of Montreal during the season of navigation, and from Halifax and St. John during the winter months.

In view of the importance of utilizing to the utmost every ton of shipping on the service, no efforts have been spared to give each ship the promptest despatch possible.

The remarkable success of these efforts may be seen from the following statement of the average time occupied in loading store transports at the ports of Montreal and St. John, N.B., for the nine months ending March 31, 1917.

	Montreal July 1 to Nov. 30.		St. John, N.B. Dec. 1 to March 31.	
	Days.	Hours.	Days.	Hours.
Time in port	5	19	9	0
Time actually loading	4	13	6	4
Idle Time	1	6	2	20

The lost time includes stoppages on account of rain preventing work, Sundays, repairs and fitting of ships for special purposes, unloading westbound cargo and ballast, shifting bunker coal, and miscellaneous delays.

As regards the timber shipments, these have been made chiefly from Maritime Province ports. In addition a number of cargoes have been loaded on the Pacific coast and also at Montreal, Quebec, Rimouski, and the Saguenay river.

During 1916-17 shipments of timber totalling 333,000,000 were made under the jurisdiction of the Transport Service.

The organization of these shipments has required constant care and attention. The scattered ports of loading and the variation in conditions and equipment for handling the cargoes have made constant demands on the time and energies of the Director Overseas Transport and his staff.

The record is highly creditable in the difficult circumstances under which much of the work had to be performed, as will be realized from the following figures, giving the total average rates of loading timber ships for the nine months from June, 1916, to March, 1917, inclusive, at the St. Lawrence, Newfoundland, and Atlantic Coast ports: A total of eighty ships loaded, at an average rate of 183 standards, or about 360,000 ft.b.m., per weather working day during the nine months.

The accounting work in connection with the handling of these ships, it will be realized, is a large undertaking.

An arrangement has been arrived at whereby the labour for loading of the store ships at Halifax, St. John, and Montreal is supplied through the shipping companies. For each ship handled they receive an agency fee of $100. The labour is charged from the actual time-sheets of the employees engaged on the work, plus an overhead charge of 10 per cent to cover use of gear, superintendence, etc. A charge is made also to cover the time of the dock office staff engaged on transport work, checking, preparing of manifests, etc., based on the actual time worked. All payments on behalf of the ship, such as stevedoring, stores, petty repairs, etc., are defrayed in the first place by them, payment being made by the department on presentation of certified claims accompanied by original vouchers. Payments made in this manner aggregate, for the year ending March 31, 1917, $2,697,000.

In the case of ships loading at various other ports, arrangements are made locally by contract with local stevedores, or otherwise, as necessary.

All invoices covering coal are paid direct by the department, as are claims for special fittings, alterations, repairs, etc.

The following statement shows the disbursements on account of the Overseas Transport Service, April 1, 1916, to March 31, 1917:—

Bunker coal	$1,195,000
Stevedoring, ship's accounts, etc.	2,697,000
Repairs, fittings, alterations	215,000
Total	$4,107,000

The thanks of the department are due the Canadian Pacific Railway Company for the services of a number of experienced transportation officers, without which this work could not have been carried out on the same scale with the excellent results achieved, and for their ready co-operation at all times, often at considerable expense and inconvenience to their own services. To the efforts of the Director of Overseas Transport are largely due the success of the operation of the whole service. His intimate knowledge of transportation problems of every kind, his resourcefulness in times of difficulty, and his indefatigable efforts at all times for the good of the work have made its successful operation possible in the face of many handicaps. He has been greatly assisted by his principal assistant, on whom the detailed work in connection with the movement of traffic largely devolved; by his representative in Halifax, who has been largely responsible for the organization of the timber service; and by his dock superintendent, who supervised the loading of transports, and to whom is largely due the celerity with which this work has been performed; his accountant has also performed valuable work, and the staff of each of these officers have given their services to the work in a very whole-hearted manner.

To the success of the efforts of these gentlemen in furnishing a prompt and efficient means of transportation is undoubtedly due the increasing magnitude of the orders now being placed for the products of the mines, forests, fields and factories of Canada by the Imperial and Allied Governments.

GENERAL.

During the period under review the work of the branch has increased materially in all directions. New members have been added to the staff to cope with the increased work, and the employment of a number of female clerks has been resorted to, with satisfactory results, in several important lines. The honest and whole-hearted way in which the members of the staffs at the dockyards and at headquarters have carried out their duties is a source of gratifica-

8 GEORGE V, A. 1918

tion. At the dockyards, especially, the work·has been strenuous. Constant unforeseen requirements arise, and the manner in which emergencies have been met reflects credit on the Naval Store officers and their staffs. At headquarters the year's work has been carried out satisfactorily according to schedule. The Naval Store officers at Halifax and Esquimalt, and the heads of the Purchasing and Storekeeping divisions in Ottawa deserve much credit for the satisfactory way in which the work of the branch has been done. To these officers, in a great measure, is due whatever success has attended·our efforts to maintain an efficient supply and contract organization.

I am, sir, your obedient servant,

J. A. WILSON,
Director of Stores.

SUPPLEMENT

TO THE

7th ANNUAL REPORT OF THE DEPARTMENT OF THE NAVAL SERVICE,
FISHERIES BRANCH.

CONTRIBUTIONS

TO

CANADIAN BIOLOGY

BEING STUDIES FROM THE

BIOLOGICAL STATIONS OF CANADA

1917--1918

PRINTED BY ORDER OF PARLIAMENT.

OTTAWA
J. DE LABROQUERIE TACHÉ
PRINTER TO THE KING'S MOST EXCELLENT MAJESTY
1918

[No. 38a—1918.]

THE BIOLOGICAL BOARD OF CANADA

Professor E. E. PRINCE, Commissioner of Fisheries, Chairman.

Professor A. B. MACALLUM, Advisory Research Council, Ottawa, Secretary-Treasurer.

Professor L. W. BAILEY, University of New Brunswick, Fredericton, N.B.

Professor A. H. R. BULLER, University of Manitoba, Winnipeg.

Rev. Canon V. A. HUARD, Laval University, Museum of Public Instruction, Quebec, P.Q.

Professor A. P. KNIGHT, Queen's University, Kingston, Ont.

Professor J. P. McMURRICH, University of Toronto, Toronto.

Dr. A. H. MacKAY, Dalhousie University, Halifax, N.S.

Professor J. G. ADAMI, McGill University, Montreal.

CONTENTS.

PREFACE.

By Professor Edward E. Prince, *LL.D., M.A., D.Sc., F.R.S.C., Commissioner of Fisheries for Canada, Chairman of the Biological Board, Life Member of the British Science Guild, Vice-President of the International Fisheries Congress, Washington, D.C., 1907, Member of International Relations Committee, American Fisheries Society, 1917, Chairman of Food Refrigeration Committee, Canadian Research Council, Ottawa, etc.*

The staff of scientists at the Dominion Biological stations at St. Andrews, New Brunswick, and Departure Bay, Nanaimo, British Columbia, have continued their laborious investigations into fishery problems and the marine and fresh-water resources of Canada with unabated energy and zeal. The results, or rather portions of them, are contained in the sixteen reports now published.

The subjects cover a wide range, and in many cases deal with vexed questions vitally affecting our fishing industries.

It is simple justice to say that many of the researches now presented were carried on with much sacrifice on the part of the scientists engaging in them, and without any remuneration at all, or with meagre acknowledgment in the form of an inadequate honorarium.

As chairman of the Biological Board of Canada, and for twenty-five years the chief adviser and scientific fishery authority of the Government of Canada, I desire to testify to the zeal, skill, and laborious devotion of the qualified and trained specialists who completed the investigations contained in the pages of this volume of "Contributions to Canadian Biology."

The biological stations, in their laboratories, libraries, instruments, stores of chemicals, glassware, and fishing gear, provide facilities of no ordinary kind for workers trained in the science schools of our Canadian universities, but these facilities, by a rigid rule of the Biological Board, are available only to advanced students, professors, or members of university staffs, and qualified, therefore, to undertake original research and discovery. Unlike the Biological Stations in many other countries, no courses of instruction or elementary lectures are given, and no attempt at popularizing science made. To add to the knowledge, so urgently needed by our fisheries, to increase accurate information on which fishery legislation should alone be based, have been the main objects aimed at; but it is possible that some scheme of fishery education and the dissemination of popular information, regarding fishes and aquatic resources generally, may be added to the future plans of the Biological Board.

The authors of the papers now published represent the following Canadian Universities: Toronto, Queens (Kingston, Ont.), McGill, Western University (London, Ont.), Laval, Manitoba, Dalhousie (Halifax, N.S.), Acadia (Wolfville, N.S.), and New Brunswick (Fredericton); and other scientists from the United States and from Canada have also contributed.

The stations have now the advantage of resident scientific curators, viz: Dr. A. G. Huntsman at St. Andrews, N.B., and Dr. C. McLean Fraser, at Departure Bay, B.C., and a new impetus to successful work has been given by the labours of these gifted and distinguished Canadian biologists.

As in preceding volumes of the "Contributions," I have prepared brief summaries of the reports which follow, for purposes of easy reference.

8 GEORGE V, A. 1918

I. SEA-LION QUESTION IN BRITISH COLUMBIA, A REPORT BY SPECIAL COMMISSIONERS—(W. Hamar Greenwood, F. C. Newcombe, and C. McLean Fraser).

The report, with thirty-six half-tone illustrations, refers, in its opening pages, to the steps taken in the United States, and the controversies arising out of the late Professor Dyche's studies on the Californian sea-lion (*Zalophus*), which devours squid, and to the conclusions of the California Commission of 1901, which decided that Steller's sea-lion (*Eumetopias*) is largely a fish-eater. Dr. Newcombe and his son published, in 1914, a report in which it is stated that, at River's inlet, damage to nets (estimated at $1,600 in 1915), and mutilation of salmon, were the charges laid against the sea-lion; while at Barkeley sound, it was claimed they drove away schools of fish, and devoured enormous numbers of herring and halibut. It is claimed that in 1913, damage to the extent of over $3,000 was done to one British Columbia Packer's Association (Wadham's) cannery.

After a cruise to various localities on D.G.S. *Malaspina,* securing of evidence from practical men at different points, and after much correspondence and transmission of questionnaires, it was found that the sea-lion, in the opinion of most of the witnesses devoured food fishes, salmon and halibut being most frequently noticed, sockeye and coho salmon, as well as herring and shore fishes, were mentioned, but no dog- or hump-back-salmon. In one instance, dogfish and birds are mentioned as being devoured. The parties who gave information were unanimous in their view that sea-lions are food-fish destroyers, and they were equally unanimous in favour of the killing off of these animals, and of a government bounty to encourage total extermination. One prominent witness however, said: "Don't kill them off; but strike terror into them".

The bands of sea-lions appear in Barkley sound in November, and were reported to the commission as being numerous in various inlets early in December. Thirteen were killed at Bird Rocks, a principal resort and hauling ground, and on examining the food, it was found that herrings in a perfect, undamaged condition were found in all of them, as much as two gallons of these fish being mingled with other partially-digested food. Remains of flat-fish, squid, etc., showed the sea-lion to be a bottom feeder, and the finding of the vertebræ of a dogfish (*Squalus*) suggests that if sea-lions were exterminated, the dogfish might be a still greater pest than they are at present. In 1913, 11,000 sea-lions was estimated as the total number on the B.C. resorts, but there were probably considerably more.

In 1915-16, a government bounty was paid on 4,000 sea-lions killed, though 8,000 (6,000 being pups) was nearer the total number, and some rookeries were entirely destroyed.

Sea-lions can be utilized in various ways. The flesh yields oil, and guano; and the skin makes excellent leather for gloves, moccasins, and boots. The British Columbia Glove Company, and other firms, would pay 5 cents per pound for hides, if 5,000 could be supplied with certainty. It is said that sea-lions will bring about $1,000 profit to each hunter for one month's work in California. The hides, after heavy salting, are usually tanned in San Francisco. The hide may weigh 150 pounds, and the whole animal from 1,500 to 3,000 pounds.

As to the effect of the Dominion Government bounty ($2 for each muzzle), it did not prove an unqualified success, as the hunters killed sea-lions on rookeries too far distant to affect the fishing localities, such as River's inlet, etc. The appropriation was soon exhausted, and no bounty was obtainable for those men who killed sea-lions nearer at hand, as in Barkley sound.

Many scientists are not convinced of the alleged serious damage to valuable fish by sea-lions, and further study of their life-history and habits is urgent. In some localities the chief run of salmon is just after the pupping season, when the sea-lion is not feeding, according to zoologists. ˙ In the opinion of the commission, sea-lions should be reduced in number, or driven away from localities where damage can be done; but on many rookeries there is no necessity for extermination, especially as valuable products (oil, leather, and fertilizer) might be obtained by creating a sea-lion industry. In such case, a wise method would be to adopt official control of sea-lion destruction conjointly with conservation, and a certain number only to be killed each year.

The second part of the report describes, in detail, the various rookeries, and estimates the total number of sea-lions upon them.

II. LOBSTER INVESTIGATIONS, LONG BEACH POND, N.S.—

(PROF. A. P. KNIGHT).

The author, in his report on the lobster investigations at the Government pond in Nova Scotia, during the season of 1915, commences by distinguishing between the nature of the sea lagoon, or pond of 5 acres, and the pond of three-quarters of an acre enclosed by cement walls. In 1914 the latter leaked extensively, but the department repaired the leak. Later, leakage again occurred, but was repaired, and on Dr. Knight's arrival on June 26, 1915, the water was 5 feet 8 inches deep, at low water. Next month it leaked again, and the rearing boxes (10 x 10 x 2½) rested on the mud, and by August 7, two boxes were immersed 5 inches in the mud. At the United States lobster station, at Wickford, R.I., where rearing was first carried out, there is always 12 feet of water underneath the boxes at low tide, excepting at one corner, where there is 5½ feet.

Early in July a vegetable parasite threatened the young larvæ, there being 40,000 hatched in the four boxes by July 14, but the parasite was *Licmophora Lyngbyei* (in 1915), instead of the species in 1914, *Synedra investiens.* To avert loss of fry, two boxes were removed into the water of the bay, but 20,000 fry were retained in two boxes were removed into the water of the bay, but 20,000 fry were retained in two boxes in the pond. Nearly all the latter were lost, only twenty-one surviving, in the second stage, on July 30. On August 2 a further trial with over 20,000 fry had a similar disappointing result; only 146 fry, in the second stage, survived until August 17. When canvas shades were used, to shut off the sunlight, the first stage lasted nine days instead of thirteen (when unshaded), and the water was 1 degree warmer. The greater success at Wickford, where 40 per cent of the lobster fry were reared, may be due to: (1) greater depth of water under the boxes; (2) comparative absence of mud and diatoms; (3) a higher temperature, 68° to 75° instead of 58·09° to 58·9°, and these conditions are of paramount importance. If the sea-water were heated to 68° or 70°, it would require 250 pounds of coal every twenty-four hours to effect this, as 2 cubic feet of water per minute passes through each rearing box.

The adult lobsters, early in 1915, were found to be covered with growths of sea-weed, and from that cause, and the muddy water, out of 167 left in the pond, 33 appeared to have perished; but of 312 not more than 38 died from the pound-conditions in 1915, the reduced mortality being due to care in collecting, feeding, and distributing them, and in shorter detention.

The author's notes on the egg-laying of lobsters are very interesting. Half of the females extruded only a few hundred eggs, instead of many thousands, and at least 80 per cent of these eggs were unfertilized. Unfertilized eggs soon drop off, and it is easy to see why fishermen find so many she-lobsters not carrying eggs, and

8 GEORGE V, A. 1918

the eggs, indeed, are often eaten by the female if unfertilized. In one case the eggs did not adhere at all, but floated soft and jelly-like on the water.

Moulting took place, though in some places the creatures did not survive, as they were weak, and the materials for a new shell were lacking. Some lobsters were blind, but moulting restored the sight; sea-weed growths often penetrated into the eyes, and underlying tissues, which were thus destroyed.

Of 47 females impounded in midsummer, 1914, 30 had extruded eggs by the end of September, and on April 8, 1915, these 30 lobsters were all found bearing fertilized eggs, showing that 64 per cent carried fertilized eggs from June, 1914, to June, 1915, most of the eggs being extruded, however, in August. By the 7th of July, 12 had hatched and got rid of the eggs, 12 bore eggs nearly in the hatching stage, 2 had newly extruded eggs. On the 29th of July, 7 of the 12 bore new eggs, and as they had already produced new eggs, there were thus 9 which proved that annual spawning was true of these lobsters at any rate.

The conclusion reached is that some lobsters are annual, others biennial, spawners, and others do not spawn even biennially.

Apart from the primary object of the Government pond, viz., saving berried lobsters in the open fishing season and liberating them in the close season, a pond of this nature may be used to secure intercourse between the two sexes, and increase the production of fertile eggs. The author justly regards his results as very important, when the production of fertile eggs resulted on placing 15 males in the pond with 47 females, in 1914-15.

A few more Government ponds might be built along the Atlantic coast, to extend the tests made at Long Beach, and promote beneficial results, viz., the increase of egg-laying. The paucity of berried lobsters in the open sea, as compared with the far greater percentage in the enclosure is obviously explained by the close intercourse secured by impounding both sexes, as at Long Beach.

III. THE PEARLY FRESH-WATER MUSSELS OF ONTARIO

(Mr. John D. Detweiler, M.A.)

The pearl-button industry depends upon material provided by pearly shells and mussels, which occur in many Canadian rivers and lakes; hence, the economic import-ance of the research reported upon by the author. He describes his studies at the Fairport station, Iowa, where these pearly mussels have received special attention. Young mussels (glochidia) become attached to the gills and fins of fishes, for a couple of weeks, before entering on an independent existence. These infant mussels, 1,000 to 2,000 in number, may attach themselves as parasites on a single fish, and of the nine or ten species of common pearly mussels, each species has its own special host or par-ticular fish.

The mussel fishery, for button purposes, tends to reduce the supply of these shell-fish very seriously; hence artificial propagation and increase are desirable, as in the United States, where such mussel-culture has been very successful, and over 330,000,-000 glochidia were used to infect about 430,000 fish in one season. The supply of com-mon mussels was studied by the author in a number of Ontario waters, and details are given of the Grand river, river Aux Sables, Point Edward bay, and Nottawasaga. and many others. *Lampsilis luteola* and *Quadrula plicata*, and other species, have good commercial qualities; but many species are too thin to be of use. The shells are fished by wire scoops, with long handles, worked from scows, which are towed by a

SESSIONAL PAPER No. 38a

gasolene launch. After being boiled, the meat is removed from the shells and many pearls and slugs are found, some of value. The increasing violence of floods, in the rivers studied, must have been injurious to mussel beds, and the regulation of the flow of water is essential. Vegetable detritus on river beds, and small diatoms, etc., appear to form the food of these mussels, and favourable conditions for such food should be maintained.

The prohibitive steps suggested include annual close times, size limit, restriction of methods, closed reserves, and a license system, as well as the adoption extensively of mussel culture. No less important are the stocking of waters by transferring mussels, and the rearing of the best species by mussel inoculation, etc.

IV. THE SHIP-WORM (TEREDO) ON THE ATLANTIC COAST OF CANADA—(Dr. E. M. Kindle).

The destructive character of the ship-worm (*Teredo*) has long been known; but its rapidity in boring timbers is not so well known, and the author instances a beech log, at the west side of the entrance of Charlottetown harbour, Prince Edward Island. thoroughly honeycomed recently during the short period of eleven months. A half-tone illustration shows this log, and demonstrates how much more rapidly *Teredo* works than the boring shrimp (*Limnoria*) which destroys soft timber at the rate of half inch per year. Timber cut from February to May best resists *Teredo's* attacks. and in the cold winter season it is inactive. · The tunnels bored, lime-lined, do not intersect, and it is rare for *Teredo* to pass from one timber to another. At the water-line and in the false keel of vessels are the main places of attack. *Teredo* spawns from April to August in Iceland, but in Canada it is probably about July. Mud seems to deter the boring operations; but, where the bottom is sandy, injury is more prevalent. Thorough application of creosote (14 to 16 pounds impregnation to the cubic foot) is effective; but at Christiania, piles were attacked when 10 pounds to the square foot were applied. The ship-worm survives for 10 days, but not beyond two weeks when removed from the water and kept in a cool place. Freezing (temperature 6°C.) does not kill them; but they die in two hours in fresh water. A large ship-worm reaches a length of about a foot (30 cm). The prevailing European species (*T. norvegica*) ranges from the Mediterranean to southwest Norway, but within Arctic limits, Prof. G. O. Sars records it only in piles in west Finmark. *Teredo navalis* the species in Canada, shows discontinuous distribution on the Atlantic shores of North America (see Dr. Kindle's sketch map). Rare or absent in the Bay of Fundy, and scarce north-east of Halifax, it occurs abundantly all round Cape Breton and the southern shore of the gulf of St. Lawrence, including the shores of Prince Edward Island. According to Dr. Murphy it is especially destructive about Sydney harbour.

The presence or absence of the ship-worm may be due to temperature, salinity, and amount of fresh water, and probably turbidity or silt in the water. It is often associated with the boring shrimp in its range, and may overlap, but one becomes less plentiful, it may be said, as we advance into the territory of the other. A number of molluscs associated with *Teredo* in their distribution occur in warm areas, and show similar isolation and discontinuity. Off southeast Nova Scotia the 20-fathom line approaches within half a mile of the coast, and everywhere a narrow zone of shoal water inside the 100-fathom line renders it colder than the Northumberland straits, where 20 to 10 fathoms or less prevails over a large extent. A zone of shallow water, if close to and unprotected from deep water, is as effective a faunal barrier as a land barrier, a point worthy of more attention from palæontologists. . The isolation of *Teredo,* and the warm-water mollusks referred to, is recent, and the occurrence of oyster shells 40 miles southwest of Halifax, and at Cole harbour; in Chaleur bay and north, as far as Montreal, indicates that a milder climate once extended from southern New England to the waters of the St. Lawrence.

V. REARING B.C. SOCKEYE SALMON IN FRESH-WATER.

(Dr. C. McLean Fraser).

After references to well-known attempts to rear Atlantic salmon and sea-trout, especially in Scotland, without permitting them access to the sea, and pointing out that slower growth and smaller sizes were apparent when retained in fresh water, the author states that in the fall of 1912, sockeye from Harrison Lake hatchery were placed in the small rearing ponds, New Westminster, B. C. These had been hatched in the spring of 1913, and in 1915 males were found to be ripe, and after yielding milt they recovered condition. But the females did not become ripe until their fourth year (1916), when they were from 9 to 11 inches long, and their eggs were rather small, but they were artificially fertilized, and an attempt to hatch them made. Study of the scales showed that these pond-reared fish indicated a growth which can be compared to that of the river sockeye to the end of the second year, but the third year's growth showed a decrease, and the fourth year's a still further decrease in the rate. The average growth in inches each year shown by the author is as follows:—

	1st year.	2nd year.	3rd year.	4th year.	5th year.
Sockeye reared in fresh-water...	2·7	2·3	2·3	1·6	...
Sockeye from Fraser river (fifth year)	2·9	8·6	7·7	3·1	...
Sockeye two years in fresh-water.	2·6	3·2	8·2	6·1	2·4

Most of the Fraser river fish remained one year only in fresh-water after hatching, and the author gives figures for these. There is no question that the sockeye mostly die soon after spawning, but the pond-reared fish recovered after spawning, and seemed none the worse. This environment renders the fish apparently more like a fresh-water species, and indicates, in the author's opinion, a close relation to the Genus *Salmo.*

VI. AGE AND GROWTH OF POLLOCK—(Prof. J. W. Mavor).

The pollock has in recent years so greatly increased in commercial importance that information upon its age and growth is valuable. The author found that young pollocks' scales show no winter rings, indicating that during their first year they live in shallow water. They occur in 2 to 20 fathoms, and in about a dozen hauls of the drag seine interesting catches of these young pollock were made; but when about 11 cm. probably move into deeper water, so that the seine does not secure them. Two length measurements were adopted in these studies, namely, the standard length, the tip of the snout to end of backbone, and total length measurement, from snout to end ·of·outspread tail. As in the case of·the herring, one single year in the pollock will yield so abundantly that it predominates for several successive years, and the author now confirms the conclusion of Mr. Douglas Macallum in 1914, that the fish of 1909 were the most abundant year-class in 1914, 1915, and 1916. The material obtained for the studies of second-year fish showed that they range from 29 cm. to 45 cm. and were probably·large for their age. Fish in the third year, with two winter rings showing in the scales, were 362:4 cm. standard length and so on up to the seventh year, when they measured 72 cm. Macallum studied 1,250 pollock in 1914-15, and Dr. Mavor, in the course of his work, examined and obtained material from 2,387 fish.

Detailed tables are given to establish the author's results.

VII. HYDROGRAPHICAL OBSERVATIONS, BAY OF FUNDY—
(Mr. E. H. CRAIGIE, B.A.; Mr. W. H. CHASE, B.A.)

The authors give the results of two cruises in the Bay of Fundy, 1915, to confirm and extend the hydrographical observations already published. Fifteen stations were established, and third and fourth cross-sections, and one longitudinal section of the bay completed. It is noted that:—

(1) A higher temperature prevails in the deeper water layer; indeed, a cold tongue of water occupies the middle of the bay. In one instance, at Station I, a peculiar rise, in a depth of 40 to 70 fathoms, also a rise at Station IX in 20 fathoms; and (in 1914) at Station II (60 fathoms), were discovered, probably evidencing deep ·currents.

(2) The upper regions of the bay show a very constant temperature from 5 fathoms to the bottom. The first phenomenon is due, probably, to vertical rising of the water, owing to the great tides; and the second, to the more widespread and complete tidal mixing of water at the head of the bay. The air was in no case less than 2·2 degrees warmer than the surface water, and often more; but it is noted that H.M. S. *Challenger*, in a few cases only, found the water temperature higher than the air, in the adjacent Nova Scotia regions. The *Challenger* and *Helland-Hansen* results are not, therefore, confirmed on the whole. The temperature of the water tends to be higher on the Nova Scotia side than on the New Brunswick side, and the bottom temperature of the Annapolis basin is much lower, in many cases, than that of Digby ·Gut, or the inflowing river-water. The detailed results are given in three tables: (1) showing temperature records, Bay of Fundy, 1915; (2) showing temperature records, Annapolis basin and St. Mary bay; (3) specific gravity, etc., St. Mary bay.

VIII. AFFECTED SALMON, MIRAMICHI HATCHERY, NEW
BRUNSWICK—(Principal F. C. HARRISON).

In the fall of 1915, disease appeared among the live parent salmon in the South Esk hatchery pond. Of 2,400 fish nearly one-quarter showed fungus, scales eaten off, eyes blinded, and many salmon moribund. No unhealthy conditions appeared in the pond or inflowing water supply, according to the information furnished. Exact bacteriological studies were arranged, and cultures made of portions of the flesh, liver, kidney, swim-bladder, milt, and heart's blood. Diseased portions of the skin were studied in microscopic sections, and in teased fragments. The latter afforded the best results. The first stage of the disease was noticed in fish conveyed in pontoons from the fishermen's nets. The fungus was *Saprolegnia,* but it remained to be seen if it were a primary or secondary cause of the trouble, and no live salmon could be inoculated; but an experiment was made with gold-fish. In all the organs, apparently healthy, of the salmon examined, bacteria were found in great numbers, but of a few species only. Very exact technical methods were used, and ten different forms of bacilli were distinguished in the cultures made, in about a dozen media, with results tabulated by the author on page 165.

The important *Bacillus salmonis pestis,* a short thick bacillus, with rounded ends, varying in length, and occurring singly and in pairs, end to end was not found. It is actively mobile, non-sporebearing, and survives for a week, and indeed grows profusely in the temperature of ice-and-salt mixture, but is killed at 98·6° F., and is apparently a strict aerobe ,pathogenic to fish, but not to frogs, mice, etc.

It gains access through wounds, or ulceration in the fish's skin. It grows well in sea-water, and can be transmitted from dead, diseased fish, to live fish in the same water. Attempts failed to inoculate live gold-fish with the various bacilli described.

The author's conclusion is that numerous bacteria associated with the fungus, may be the cause of the disease.

IX. AFFECTED MIRAMICHI SALMON, NEW BRUNSWICK—

(By. Dr. A. G. HUNTSMAN).

The author, after noting that an epidemic of disease such as this had not been noticed in the previous year, and that the temperature was lower than in 1914, and the water temperature in the salmon hatchery pond was never higher than 65° F. after September 11 the author concludes that temperature is not a factor. The lower temperature in October doubtless restrained the spread of the disease, as no new diseased fish appeared. The fish were less crowded, there being 328 fewer impounded than in 1914. The salmon parasite (*Lepeophtheirus*) occurred in a considerable portion of the fish trapped by the fishermen, and as it injures the skin it must determine the location of the fungus (*Saprolegnia ferax*). The internal organs of the diseased salmon showed no lesions, but the bacteriological phase of the epidemic is treated in Dr. F. C. Harrison's report. Removal and destruction of all diseased and dead salmon alone can help to lessen the trouble, and steps are necessary to secure improvement in the renewal of the water supplying the pond. The most suitable temperature also should be maintained. The eggs from diseased fish were naturally of lowered vitality, and great losses, 40 to 60 per cent, resulted. *Saprolegnia* may attack eggs only of low vitality. Bacteria possibly cause the disease, but may not affect the eggs, and fry could not in this way have the disease transmitted; but it may be carried in the water used for shipping eggs and fry.

X. THE SMOKING OF HADDOCKS FOR CANADIAN MARKETS--(Miss Olive G. Patterson.)

Salt and smoked haddock are too often prepared, it is pointed, out, from fish inferior in quality or even tainted, whereas the best "finnans" can only be made from fish in the freshest condition, kept cold, and cured by strict methods. Finnan haddies in Canada are often inferior because: (1) no vertebral cut is made; (2) smoke is not sufficiently dense; (3) the fish are left from one to three days, in order to drain the blood, etc., away, whereas one hour on ice would be sufficient.

Various conditions were tested, namely, method of splitting, time in brine and smoke, quality of brine and smoke. The studies included seven separate experiments:—

(1) Perfectly fresh fish cured by usual New Brunswick methods.
(2) Salt constant, but smoke varied.
(3) Smoke constant, but brine varied.
(4) Small fish, under variations of both conditions.
(5) Preservative value and palatability of salt content.
(6) Hake experiment.
(7) Proof that dorsal incision is most desirable after the usual splitting.

Fish up to four pounds require one hour in the brine, but thirty minutes suffices to preserve excellent flavour, and smoking (beech, or old wood sawdust) for ten hours is sufficient, but fifteen to eighteen hours dries more thoroughly, for preserving. Adjacent home markets and more distant markets require appropriate variation in details.

XI. OBSERVATIONS OF HADDOCKS, ETC.—

(Prof. F. C. Harrison).

Rigid bacteriological methods were followed in the study of material obtained from haddocks, caught one or two miles from St. Andrew's station; and some other material, fresh and cured, from the market.

An examination of the intestinal content of twelve haddocks was made, and microscopically numerous small bacilli, of at least ten species, could be determined, but no cocci or spirilla were observed. The most common bacillus, a liquefying form, seemed to be related closely to *B. vulgaris*. It is especially interesting, because it was found in the flesh, as well as on the surface, of the finnan haddies, which were experimented with at the station, and also on some spoiled haddock from a fish dealer. Fragments of the flesh of cured haddock were placed in inoculation flasks, and plate cultures secured. Four of the organisms then discovered were similar to those from the intestinal content. The researches show that salting and smoking fish does not kill the organisms on fresh fish, after they are gutted; but it is undeniable that there is too much carelessness in handling fish commercially. Exposure to warm air and sunlight, before gutting and salting, increases the bacteria.

XII. BACTERIOLOGY OF SWELLED CANNED SARDINES.—(Mr. WILFRID SADLER, M.Sc., B.S.A.)

After referring to the presence of micro-organisms in various foods, including mussels, clams, canned salmon, etc., the author refers to the canned method in the New Brunswick and Maine sardine canneries, which he visited. The filled and finished cans are sterilized in boiling water for 1½ to 2 hours. Scrupulous care is exercised in the final packing processes, and questionable cans are discarded or re-processed.

Two main classes of bacteria were isolated; (1) gas-producers of eight types; (2) non-gas-producers.

No organisms were found in the cotton-seed oil used, but in the sea-water, herring intestines, etc., several strains of bacteria were discovered, but none producing gas in carbo-hydrates. After a description of the seventeen or more media used, and the methods adopted, Mr. Sadler describes the features of the swelled cans, the bulged convex appearance, the escape and forcing out of oil or sauce between the soldered edges, and a rattling sound when shaken. Gas is expelled on opening the can, and the odour may be normal, or offensive. In the former case, doubtless spices and other ingredients hide the odour of putrefaction. The contents may be soft, mingled with the oil and maceated, in contrast to the firm non-macerated white appearance of the normal contents.

The elaborate cultures and tests in the laboratory are detailed by the author, and summarized on pages 208 and 209. An experiment was made with normal cans from the Chamcook factory, and the organisms, numbers 35, 37, and 64 were used for inoculation. These organisms were, respectively: (1) a large coccus, not-motile, rod-like, short, and thick; (2) rod-like, and three times as long as broad; (3) some ranging from the coccus to short thick rods. In each case, typically swelled cans resulted.

The source of the harmful micro-organisms remains to be discovered, and the stage at which infection occurs; also effective prevention and the results of the effects, by experimental inoculation, on laboratory animals.

XIII. BACTERIAL DESTRUCTION OF COPEPODS.—(Mr. WILFRID SADLER, M.Sc., etc.)

In some marine plankton, studied at the Atlantic station, in 1916, a number of copepods, or small crustaceans, were observed by Professor Willey to be apparently in process of destruction by bacteria. It was suggested to the author, by Dr. Willey, that a study might be made of them. The copepods occur in the central cavity of the first feelers or antennæ. By the usual bacteriological methods, and by seven fish concoctions, specially prepared, three different types of bacteria were isolated, fourteen media being used in the investigation. The first type were short, rod-like, non-motile organisms, non-spore-bearing, and without capsule; the second was of the same length, but twice as broad, not much longer than broad, and similarly non-spore-bearing, and apparently capsuleless, and lastly a third type, coccus, either in pairs or occurring in masses in the form of Streptococci, non-spore bearing, and with capsule faintly apparent. The first is probably *B. neapolitanus,* a sub-type of *B. coli*; the second, rapidly motile to and fro, or on an axis, and a typical form of Para-Gærtner group; and the third non-motile, though rotatory, and showing violent agitation, a variety of liquefying *Streptococcus gracilis,* namely *Micrococcus zymogenes,* and the last-named culture probably causes the destruction of the copepods, and if this destruction be extensive, its effective upon the minute food of young fishes, and a variety of other important creatures in the sea, may be serious. No inoculations of healthy living copepods was possible in 1916.

XIV. CHECK-LIST OF MARINE INVERTEBRATES.—(Dr. E. M. KINDLE and E. J. WHITTAKER, M.A.)

The authors, in their list of over 1,000 invertebrates, occurring along the Atlantic shores of Canada, set forth the bathymetric range from between tide marks to a depth of 100 fathoms—five graduations, namely, 100, 100-50, 50-15, and 15-1, and inshore less than 1 fathom; also the minimum and maximum depths.

They embody published faunal results from 1901, the date of Dr. Whiteave's valuable and remarkable catalogue, published by the Geological Survey. To make the contribution more complete a bibliography of fifty papers and memoirs follows the check list, to which is added an alphabetical index, including synonyms.

XV. HYDROGRAPHY IN PASSAMAQUODDY BAY AND VICINITY.— (Rev. Professor ALEXANDER VACHON.)

Professor Vachon made a series of observations during a number of cruises in the *Prince* in the summer of 1915, and gives a summary with tables of his researches into the temperature, salinity, and density of the sea-water at ten successive stations in July and August, at different hours, and at different stages of the tide. These constitute the potent factors which affect the assemblages of marine organisms forming the benthos, the nekton, and the plankton, in the ocean. The investigations of the author, involving lengthy laboratory studies, are difficult to summarize, as the paper itself is very much condensed.

XVI. THE HYDROIDS OF EASTERN CANADA.—DR. C. McLEAN FRASER.)

The author is able in this paper to extend substantially the list which he published in 1913—(a list of fifty Nova Scotia species)—and now determines 112 species, sixteen for the first time in the area referred to, and one species which is regarded as new to science. The distribution is tabulated, and an interesting summary of the distribution of the Gymnoblastea, the Campanularidæ, and five other orders. A systematic list, with distribution and synonyms, is given, and the author discusses the principles of the classification of the hydroids, and combats Levinson's view that the character of the individual (zooid), not the colony (zoarium), should determine the classification, and the doubtful value of the operculum (urged by Levinson) as the sole basis for dividing the Family Sertularidæ into genera is maintained, because it is so easily injured, and thus readily altered.

I

Part I.

PRELIMINARY REPORT OF THE COMMISSION ON THE SEA-LION QUESTION, 1915.

Dr. Charles F. Newcombe, Victoria, B.C., Chairman;
Wm. Hamar Greenwood, Vancouver, B.C., Secretary; and
Dr. C. McLean Fraser, Curator of the Government Biological Station, Nanaimo, B.C.

Introduction.

In May, 1915, the Biological Board of Canada appointed an honorary commission to make an inquiry as to the effect of the bounty of two dollars per head which had been offered by the Dominion Government to aid in the reduction of the number of sea-lions in the province of British Columbia, and which applied during the year 1915 only. .

The commission, after some changes, finally consisted of Dr. C. F. Newcombe, of Victoria, chairman; W. Hamar Greenwood, B.A., of Vancouver, secretary; and Dr. C. McLean Fraser, of the Biological Station, Nanaimo.

Early in August, Prof. A. B. Macallum, of the University of Toronto, Secretary of the Biological Board of Canada, visited the west coast and met two of the commissioners at Vancouver. Authority was then given for an early commencement of the investigation, but it was left to the commissioners themselves to draw up a plan of operation which would best fulfil the purposes of the proposed inquiry. The commissioners at once decided that there should be a division of the work of the commission, Mr. Greenwood undertaking to collect all information possible by correspondence and personal interviews, the other two members more especially devoting their time to field and laboratory work, with the view of gaining more knowledge as to the life-history of the sea-lion.

In order to facilitate the statistical section, a schedule of questions was drawn up and forwarded to officials of all the fishing plants of the province, and, for the field party, application was made through the Biological Board for the use of one of the vessels belonging to the Department of Naval Service. These matters are referred to later in the report.

2. ACTION ELSEWHERE ON THE SEA-LION QUESTION.

The sea-lion question is by no means a new one. As long ago as 1898 it was very much to the fore in California. In 1899 the State Commission authorized the killing of numbers of the animals, giving the reason for so doing in the sixteenth biennial report of the State Board of Fish Commissioners of the state of California for the years 1899-1900, pp. 26-40. In this report is included, as well, much correspondence on the subject.

At the outset, in April, 1899, the commissioners called a meeting of all persons interested to consider the evidence that might be offered regarding the damage done by sea-lions. The reason given in the report for calling this meeting is as follows: "For many years the fishery interests have strenuously complained of the damage done by sea-lions in the bays and rivers of the state. This commission has had the subject under consideration for many years. During the fall of 1898 and the spring of 1899 the salmon fishermen made repeated calls upon us for relief in this behalf, claiming that the sea-lions were appearing in the bays and lower rivers in increasing numbers, and that they follow the salmon from the ocean for more than 100 miles

8 GEORGE V, A. 1918

inland. The managers of the canneries and the buyers for the San Francisco markets joined in these requests. Our patrol force corroborated the statements and alleged that the territory covered by them swarmed with these animals. Formerly the sea-lions were hunted for commercial purposes, but their hides and oil no longer find a profitable market, and the industry has failed, in consequence of which they have greatly increased in number."

Fishermen, market men, and cannery men were unanimous in asking for a reduction in number on account of the destruction by them of salmon and other food fishes. So voluminous was the evidence that such scientists as Jordan, Gilbert, and Harkness were convinced of the justice of this plea.

As a number of the larger rookeries were situated on federal lighthouse reservations, the commission wrote to the Hon. Lyman Gage, then Secretary of the Treasury, to ask permission to kill sea-lions on these reservations, giving quite fully the reasons advanced for making such a request. The request was granted on April 27, but on May 31, before any lions were killed, the permit was suspended. On June 9 a letter from the Treasury Department gave the information that the suspension was due to protests from the United States Fish Commission, the secretary of the United States Department of Agriculture, the New York Zoological Society, and various others.

The commission in reply stated its case at greater length, and called the attention of the Treasury Department to the fact that while their evidence was backed up and accepted by scientists who had studied the question at first hand, all of the opposition came from men who had no personal knowledge of the various aspects of the question. This reply was sufficient to convince the United States Commissioner of Fisheries, who therefore withdrew his opposition. However, it failed elsewhere, and consequently the Lighthouse Board refused to cancel the suspension until further evidence was deduced.

The case of the commission, of which A. T. Vogelsang was chairman, may be stated briefly as follows:—

Previous to 1884 sea-lions were killed for commercial purposes. Cheaper substitutes have been obtained for the hides, oil, and trimmings, and commercial killing is no longer profitable. Since that time the animals have greatly increased in number, and hence the amount of destruction has greatly increased. They chase the salmon for a long distance up the bays and rivers. " They are voracious and destructive to the last degree. It is estimated by the fishermen upon the rivers, and the salmon canners, that from 20 to 40 per cent of the fish entering the bays are destroyed by this means. They enter the nets of the fishermen and take the fish already gilled. They tear and destroy the nets and cause irreparable damage to the hardy and industrious fishermen. They are seen every day during the salmon run with fish in their jaws and almost no net is hauled that does not show a large percentage of fish destroyed by these animals. It is so now that the fishermen, when laying out their nets, must patrol them from end to end as they drift with the current or tide, armed with Winchester rifles, to protect the nets from the depredation of these beasts." There is little use in providing hatcheries to increase the supply of salmon if the sea-lions are allowed to kill so many of them in the sea. Captain Butwell, chief lightkeeper at Año Nuevo island, in the summer of 1899 made an examination of the stomach of a large grey sea-lion (*Eumetopias stelleri*) and found over sixty pounds of fish bones. In the following summer a deputy killed a sea-lion with a salmon in its jaws, the head of which sea-lion is now preserved at Stanford University.

The case of the opposition is presented most fully by W. T. Hornaday, as representing the New York Zoological Society. He says:—

" Judging from all the facts which have been brought forward up to this date, and from correspondence with naturalists from the Pacific coast, we feel constrained to say that, in our judgment, the evidence against the destructiveness of the fur seal is very far from being sufficient to warrant the California Fish Commission in asking the United States Government to permit the destruction on its reservations." He blames the California Commission for condemning the sea-lion on what he considers unsatisfactory evidence. His reasons are summarized as follows:—

"*First.*—We have good reason to believe that the estimated number of sea-lions on the Pacific coast· (10,000) is very greatly in excess of the actual number.

"*Second.*—The estimate of the amount of fish consumed daily by the sea-lion herds (500,000 pounds) we consider to be preposterous and absurd. This presupposes that each sea-lion consumes 50 pounds of fish per day, whereas, the full ration of an adult male sea-lion in captivity amounts to only 12 pounds or less per day.

"*Third.*—In .the absence of statistics based on detailed scientific observation of known reliability, the assumption that the sea-lions are responsible for a marked decrease in the fish supply of the Pacific coast is unwarranted.

' *Fourth.*—The people of the whole United States have proprietary rights in all the living creatures which inhabit the waters of the coast of California, as well as all other states, and particularly the sea-lion herds which breed on the public domain; and the people of California have no right, either in law or equity, to wantonly destroy the sea-lion herds until the justification of such a course has been clearly and satisfactorily proven.

"*Fifth.*—The sea-lion has been condemned by the California Fish Commission without having had the benefit of counsel or witness for the defence, a proceeding so thoroughly un-American that the findings based thereon are unworthy of serious consideration."

In view of these reasons he asked for the preservation of " the very interesting and valuable sea-lion herds of the Pacific coast."

Mr. Vogelsang, in direct reply to Mr. Hornaday, says that the fifth reason is entirely untrue, as he has shown in his correspondence that all evidence available was considered, some of this evidence from scientists of repute. He objects to the statement that sea-lions are valuable, and as far as the interest goes, they cannot be considered more interesting than other harmful animals, the coyote for instance. He indicates the weight of such remonstrance by saying: " It seems to me remarkable that your society is not aware of the fact that the fur seal does not frequent the rookeries of the California coast, and the varieties against which our activities have been chiefly directed are the barking sea-lion (*Zalophus*) and, incidentally, the grey sea-lion (*Eumetopias*)."

The commission was so confident of the correctness of their stand that they published all this correspondence in the matter and left the public to judge.

Before going further it should be stated that throughout this California report reference is made to two species of sea-lion, the barking sea-lion (*Zalophus californianus*) and the grey, or Steller's sea-lion (*Eumetopias stelleri*), but the general statements apply to both of these. There is evidence that both are found in British Columbia waters, but although *Zalophus* has been reported. it may be only an occasional visitor (see further evidence in this report). The grey sea-lion is the common one on the British Columbia coast and northward.

While the controversy was going on between the California State Commission and the Treasury Department, in the summer of 1899, Prof. L. L. Dyche, of the University of Kansas, made examination of the stomachs of several sea-lions killed

8 GEORGE V, A. 1918

in the vicinity of Monterey, finding in the cases where the contents were suitable for identification, these consisted largely of squid. No traces of salmon were found.

A reference to this work of Dyche's, which was made in an article by C. H. Merriam appearing in *Science*, May 17, 1901, has been very extensively quoted in support of the contention that sea-lions are of little detriment to the fishing industry. Without in any way questioning the results of the investigation, it may be pointed out that these results do not necessarily have much bearing on the sea-lion question in British Columbia. We have no evidence that the grey sea-lion is ever found as far south as Monterey, although it is quite possible that some individuals from the rookery at Año Nuevo or even from that at the Farallones may pay visits to that region. On the other hand, at that time the California sea-lion was found in large numbers around Santa Cruz island, a short distance north of Monterey, and at many points to the south of this. There is every likelihood, therefore, that the majority, if not all, of the animals examined by Dyche were of the California species. Colour is given to this conclusion further by the statement of the United States Commissioners, later referred to, "that the Steller sea-lion is largely a fish consumer and the California sea-lion is largely a squid eater," this statement, of course, being based on the evidence they were able to obtain at that time. It is the Steller sea-lion, almost entirely, with which we are concerned.

On account of further refusals of the Lighthouse Board in 1900 to cancel the suspension of the permit to kill sea-lions on the federal reservations, in 1901 the California commission asked for the appointment of a special commission to look into the matter thoroughly. The request was granted. Cloudsley Rutter was appointed chairman of the commission, R. E. Snodgrass was named by the California commission, and E. C. Starks by the California Academy of Science. This commission visited points along the coast from Monterey to Puget sound, making personal observations and obtaining information from those having personal knowledge of the subject. The report of the commission was submitted to the United States Fish Commission, and appeared in the report of the commissioner for 1902, pp. 116-119.

The following remarks bear on *Eumetopias.* Eighteen stomachs were examined, of which thirteen contained food. All of these had eaten fish, and five of them had also eaten squid, but the fish was relatively large in amount, up to 35 pounds, while the squid was small, six being the greatest number in any stomach. "This study indicates that the Steller sea-lion is largely a fish consumer and the California sea-lion is largely a squid eater. It seems apparent, however, that either species feeds on whatever is most convenient."

"At the mouth of the Columbia river, sea-lions were seen fishing in considerable numbers near the jetty at the mouth of the river, but none was seen to catch a fish of any kind. Gulls were frequently observed hovering about a group of sea-lions and acting as if picking up food. One such flock of gulls was seen coming gradually nearer the jetty from a group of sea-lions about a mile away; after a time it was shown that they were following a large piece of salmon flesh, which the tide brought within 20 feet of the observer. Salmon were seen and photographed that had been mutilated (presumably by sea-lions and seals) after being caught in gill nets. Such mutilated specimens were common. The fishermen stated that the seals simply pull off the gills but the sea-lions always take a bite out of the belly of the netted salmon. A number of pound nets were visited, but no sea-lions were seen in them.

"The fishermen were unanimous in their denunciation of the sea-lions. A fishing company at Chinook, Washington, states that it was damaged $1,500 in 1901 by sea-lions letting fish out of the nets, the damage to the nets not being included. The sea-lions enter the traps in the same way that the fish do, and, after eating what they wish, break their way out through the side.

"The shallow water and the large number of salmon at the mouth of the Columbia river make that point a favourite breeding ground, and there is no doubt that the sea-lions are doing much damage there."

Although permission to kill sea-lions on federal reservations was refused, the commission, by means of arming their patrols, killed a great number of sea-lions at other points along the coast. The report states: " It may be added that our activities have been exerted, nevertheless, to the destruction of a large number of these animals upon such rookeries and other places along the coast as are not subject to the control of the Treasury Department of the United States. The effect on the salmon industry is already apparent, as, since the summer of 1899, the number of sea-lions present in the bays and rivers has been much less than formerly." Apparently the number killed by the patrol was greatly augmented by the number killed by the fishermen themselves.

The destruction at that time seems to have had the desired effect, as since then no serious complaint has been made to the commission. We have this on the authority of Mr. N. B. Scofield, who was in 1898, and is now in 1916, in the employ of the California Fish commission. Sea-lions have been so reduced in numbers that in 1909 a law was passed, forbidding the killing, maiming or capturing sea-lions, in the waters of Santa Barbara channel and on the land adjacent thereto, in order to prevent the extermination of the black or California sea-lion.

As evidence that California was not alone in the demand for reduction in the number of sea-lions, it may be stated that the Oregon Legislature passed a Bill, offering a bounty of $2.50 for each sea-lion killed in the waters of the state or within one marine league of the shore. On account of faulty wording of the Bill, the money was not available, but the Fishermen's Protective Union raised a fund by private subscription to hire men to shoot the lions on their breeding grounds. In Washington, too, there has been some complaint at times but nothing definite seems to have been done.

3. PREVIOUS WORK ON THE SEA-LION QUESTION IN BRITISH COLUMBIA.

So far as is known to the present commission, the only investigations hitherto made in British Columbia are those which were conducted by the chairman and his son, in the year 1913. In the spring of that year, the chairman was requested by the British Columbia authorities in Victoria, B.C., to conduct an investigation to disclose the numbers of sea-lions that frequent and breed upon our coast, and the number and locations of the islands where they breed. This was in consequence of the many complaints made that sea-lions were seriously damaging the fisheries.

No information whatever was furnished to those in charge of this inquiry of 1913 relating to previous controversies regarding the food habits of sea-lions in California or other states, but before starting for the north, such literature as was accessible was consulted, and an examination was made of the report of the United States Commissioner of Fisheries for 1902, to which reference was made by Hornaday and others when describing the California and Steller's sea-lion. This report at once revealed the widely divergent opinions entertained by competent naturalists as to the food habits of the sea-lions, and special pains were taken in the field to procure from all sources information as to their food, and the evidence of the older Indians, who in their younger days had depended largely on sea-lions for food, and had utilized their skins and other parts in various ways, was noted.

The result of the inquiry made by these investigators is mentioned in the annual provincial report for the year 1913, published in 1914. The ground covered by it included the coast line from Boundary bay, North Latitude 49°, to the Nass river in 54° 40', at various points in which the officials of more than thirty salmon canneries and herring plants were personally interviewed, and further information was obtained from their employees, both white and Indian. Amongst these points were the lower Fraser river, Knights inlet, Alert bay, Quathiaski cove, Rivers inlet, Bella Coola, Kimsquit, Namu, Bella

Bella, Skeena river, Nass river, Masset, Skidegate, Quatsino, Ucluelet, and the important cannery known as Kildonan, at Uchucklesit, Barkley sound. As the result of inquiries at these stations it was learned that serious complaints of depredations by sea-lions were made at only two localities, viz., Rivers inlet and Barkley sound. In each of these places damage had been so great that active steps had been taken to diminish their numbers by the fishing companies affected. Indians questioned at more than forty villages were unanimous in stating that the principal food of sea-lions was fish, and that these fish consisted in the greater part of fish eaten by man, especially salmon, herring, and halibut. In not a single instance was any wish expressed that sea-lions should be protected, as no dependence is now placed on them for food, clothing, or any of the native arts or industries.

Over 1,800 miles of coast line were examined, mostly in a small gasolene sloop. Three groups of islands, forming breeding places, were noted, and a fourth indicated, and the number of individuals seen was estimated at upwards of 11,000. In addition to the rookeries, a large number of isolated rocks, used as resting places, were visited and recorded. The rookeries and hauling-out places were shown on a map accompanying the report.

Later in the season a second visit to the rookeries in Queen Charlotte sound and off cape Scott was made. A number of successful photographs were taken, islands not before visited were explored, and an estimate made of the numbers frequenting these. The joint report shows that the injury to the fisheries complained of is of two kinds. At Rivers inlet the complaint was that nets were damaged and destroyed and vast numbers of salmon were devoured or mutilated, while at two localities in Barkley sound it was stated that the principal loss was in the herring fishery, which suffered largely through the presence of great bands of sea-lions surrounding the schools of fish and driving them out from the heads of bays and inlets where the most successful fishing had always been carried on. Complaint was also made that they devoured enormous numbers of herring and halibut.

As regards the food question, little information was obtained by personal observation. Three adults were examined, two of which contained no food whatever in their stomachs, while the third was full of fish, including salmon, cod, and bass.

A second kind of sea-lion was reported by Indians of Barkley sound as occurring there, and from their description it was concluded that this was the California species, *Zalophus californianus*. It is surmised that this species and perhaps the majority of the individuals belonging to Steller's species came from the American side, as the rookeries in the state of Washington are far nearer to Barkley sound than those on the Canadian side.

4. THE CALIFORNIA SEA-LION IN BRITISH COLUMBIA WATERS.

The following notes tend to confirm the statements made by Indians of Ucluelet in 1913, that a second kind of sea-lion visits Barkley sound at times, though never in large numbers.

Dr. C. H. Townshend, Director of the New York Aquarium, permits the quotation from a letter written on November 9, 1915, of a passage relating to a period when he was the naturalist on the United States Bureau of Fisheries steamer *Albatross*:—

> "I visited Barkley sound in 1889 with the *Albatross*. The sea-lions I saw and heard barking at the time were on some rocks, I think not far from the lighthouse. They were unquestionably the California species, which is the only barking sea-lions in that region. Sea-lions do a good deal of moving about up and down the coast. They do not confine themselves to any one neighbourhood."

Dr. Townshend also sent, at the same time, a copy of the Bulletin No. 29, of the Zoological Society of New York, for April, 1908. This contains an interesting article by Dr. Townshend entitled "An Inquisitive Sea-lion," describing the behaviour of a young specimen of *Zalophus californianus,* which was attracted to the *Albatross* while at anchor one evening at Port Townshend, by the barking of a setter dog. It spent the night in the ship's dinghy, and Dr. Townshend was able to make a very successful photograph of it before it grew dark. The photograph is reproduced on page 412.

Further information of similar bearing was obtained from Prof. Trevor Kincaid, of the University of Washington. At the Alaska-Yukon-Pacific Exposition, held in Seattle in 1909, two animals were included in one of the exhibits, as fur seals. Prof. Kincaid was asked to examine them, as there was much doubt as to the correctness of this designation. Both of them were found to belong to the California species of sea-lion, and those in charge of them stated that they had been taken in the salmon traps at New Dungeness, not far from the entrance to Puget sound. After the close of the exposition the two animals were moved to the zoological collection at Woodland park, Seattle, still labelled as Alaska fur seals. A visit was made by a member of this commission to the Zoological Garden mentioned, and the caretaker was interviewed with little result. The animals in question had died soon after their arrival at Woodland park.

In December, 1915, Indians employed in hunting for the commission, stated that the second kind of sea-lions was well known in Barkley sound as the black or barking kind, but these only pass in as far as Alberni canal very seldom. The last one that was recalled had been killed off Nahmint about five years ago.

5. THE SEA-LION QUESTION AS IT AFFECTS BRITISH COLUMBIA.

At the preliminary meeting of the commission in August a decision was reached as to two main methods of seeking information on the sea-lion question. The one was to make a trip along the coast to get personal information if possible, although little was expected on account of the lateness of the season, and failing this, to get information from those who claimed to have firsthand knowledge concerning the habits and food of the sea-lions as well as the nature and extent of their depredations. The other was to obtain information by correspondence with cannery managers, fishery officers and others interested or likely to be able to furnish such.

In connection with the former of these, the Department of the Naval Service kindly put at the disposal of the commission, for three weeks, the steamer *Malaspina,* Captain Holmes Newcomb commanding. The commission is under no little obligation to Captain Newcomb, his officers and crew for the courtesy shown during the trip.

On August 30 the *Malaspina,* with Drs. Newcombe and Fraser on board, started northward. The attempt to visit all of the rookeries along the coast had to be given up through lack of time, partly due to delay by smoke and fog, and by waiting for a chance to coal at Prince Rupert. The Cape St. James rookery was not visited, nor was that on the Cape Scott group of islands; three attempts to get out to the Haycocks and Triangle islands all failed on account of foggy and heavy weather. The rookery on the Sea Otter group was visited, where there were sea-lions visible, but on account of the dangerous reefs in the vicinity, it was not possible to get close enough with so large a boat to make an estimate of the number, and the swell was too heavy to attempt it with a small boat. A small rookery at the west end of Hope island was visited, and here the only attempts made to capture sea-lions proved abortive. On two mornings in succession Indian hunters, hired for the purpose, tried to shoot and spear one or more of the herd of forty or fifty that were visible in the surf, but without

8 GEORGE V, A. 1918

success. Finally the rookery at Solander island, off cape Cook, was visited. The weather was very foggy, but after waiting for an hour and a half in the vicinity, the captain was able to bring his ship near enough the rocks to make the sea-lions plainly visible. The number was estimated to be at least 1,000, although it may have been somewhat in excess of that number. Dr. Newcombe, in his report in 1913, did not consider Solander island to be a rookery but as shown elsewhere in this report, he is now convinced that it is one.

6. INFORMATION FROM EYE-WITNESSES.

As the personal information on this trip, consequently, was somewhat limited, as much as possible was made of the evidence of eye-witnesses. These may be divided into three classes: (1) Those who were not sufficiently familiar with sea-lions to be able to distinguish them from hair seals, (2) those who claimed to have personally seen sea-lions chasing and eating some species of fish, (3) those who claimed to have seen sea-lions eating fish and had also examined the stomachs of one or more of these animals.

Of group (3) the majority were Indians, some of them old men, who, in earlier days, had made use of many portions of the sea-lions for various purposes. Besides these there were two white men, viz., Mr. F. Inrig, manager of the British Columbia Packers' cannery at Wadhams on Rivers inlet, and Mr. J. Boyd, Fisheries Overseer at Bella Bella. Group (2) included cannery men, cold storage men, active fishermen, sea captains, fishery officers, as well as others, in no way directly connected with the fishing business. The evidence of those in group (1) has not been considered.

Representatives from numerous localities from Alert bay to Prince Rupert, and all along the west coast of Vancouver island from cape Scott to Barkley sound supplied information for this area and even beyond it to the mouth of the Nass river and Hecate strait. Twenty-six in all made statements sufficiently definite to be worthy of consideration. The commission does not vouch for any of the evidence submitted, but sees no reason to doubt its accuracy. The points at least on which there was general agreement must be accepted until such times as they can either be corroborated or disproved. Already a portion of the evidence has been confirmed as shown in a later portion of the report.

7. MATERIALS USED BY SEA-LIONS AS FOOD.

There was not a dissenting voice to the assertion that sea-lions eat food fishes. Of the food fishes eaten, salmon and halibut have been most frequently noticed, and of the species of salmon, spring, sockeye and coho. Humpback and dog salmon were not reported. Besides the salmon and halibut, other food fishes, viz., herring, oolachan, red cod, ling cod, and rock cod were mentioned. Devil fish (which probably included squid also) were frequently mentioned, dogfish and birds in a single instance. It may be well to note here that lack of positive evidence is not negative evidence. These men, almost without exception, stated that they saw no signs of sea-lions chasing other than food fishes or of the remains of other than food fishes in their stomachs. Naturally so, because in the first place they would never take the trouble to learn the haunts of fish not suitable for food, and in the second place, the sea-lions would be killed almost entirely in the neighbourhood of fishing grounds of some sort, and would more likely than otherwise have eaten those very food fishes. This does not prove that the sea-lion does not eat anything else in the sea when the food fishes are not readily available. This matter is taken up again later.

S. INJURY TO THE FISHING INDUSTRY.

With regard to the injury done to the fisheries of the province, only the salmon, halibut, and herring industries need be considered. Taking first the salmon fishery, the complaints of injury were almost wholly confined to the Rivers Inlet region. Here the sockeye season is at its height just after the pupping season, during which period it has been stated by many authorities, no food is taken by the adults. When the pups are two or three weeks old, according to the Indians, they are able to swim at the surface of the water and are then taken by the adults into the neighbouring waters

while the latter satisfy their appetites, now especially voracious after the long fast. It is quite probable that the amount of the stomach content at that time (Mr. Inrig reported having seen thirty-six sockeye salmon in one lion's stomach) cannot be taken as typical for the whole year.

The sea-lion is such a powerful swimmer that it can readily overtake a salmon, which it catches and shakes until the piece comes out and the bite is swallowed. If the fish are plentiful, the bitten fish is not touched further but another is attacked in a similar manner. If the fish are scarce the part of the fish left after the first bite

8 GEORGE V, A. 1918

may be seized again by the same individual or by other individuals, as they commonly go hunting in small herds. At times they find it more convenient to take the salmon out of the gill-nets, especially when they are being hauled, as then the fish are near the surface of the water. One case was reported where sixteen salmon in succession were taken, as fast as the net was hauled to the surface, the one animal making the entire capture. It is at such times that harm is done to the gear. The lions are so powerful that if the net is taut they pass through it with ease. If it is looser they may get tangled up in the net and do much more damage to it.

The rookery in the Sea Otter group of islands is opposite the mouth of Rivers inlet, (see map, page 13), so that all schools of fish entering the inlet must pass near by. The sockeye run comes just at the time when the lions need the greatest supply of food, hence what could be more opportune for them.

Apparently in the early days of the industry the sea-lions were not so numerous. It was not until about 1911 that they appeared in large enough numbers to be especially troublesome. In 1912 and in 1913 so many fish were taken from the nets set in the inlet for some distance from the mouth that the fishermen found it useless to continue fishing in that locality. Many of the sea-lions were killed in 1914 and 1915, and the season of 1915 was a particularly good one in the inlet.

The injury done to the halibut fisheries has not been so serious, partly because the habits of the halibut require a different method of fishing. The attack made on an individual of this species can only be observed when a halibut is taken from the hook when that part of the line is near the surface, at which time the halibut is attacked in the same way the salmon is. Damage was reported from Hecate strait and from the area to the north and northwest of Vancouver island. In fishing for this species there is little chance for any damage to gear.

Damage to the herring industry was reported only from Barkley sound. Here the complaint was not so much that the numbers of the herring were being diminished as that the schools are broken up, scattered and driven seaward. As many as 300 sea-lions have been reported from the sound where they use the Bird rocks for a hauling-out place. Two plants have been in operation, one at Ucluelet, near the entrance, and the other at Uchucklesit, far up the sound. Barkley sound is a long distance from any known rookery, but as the lions do not appear here until late in the fall, the pups no longer need care, and as the adults are such powerful swimmers such distances would not mean much to them. In other localities, notably Clayoquot, Quatsino sound, and in the Nass river, herring runs are followed by sea-lions, but as yet not enough fishing has been done for any special observation to be made.

9. THE FLATTERY ROOKERY.

This Malaspina trip covered the " spheres of influence" of all of the British Columbia rookeries, but it was possible that it did more than that. Barkley sound is a long way from Solander island, where, so far as is known, the nearest British Columbia rookery exists. It is much nearer to what is generally spoken of as the Flattery rookery, off the west coast of the state of Washington. It is probable that occasional sea-lions seen in the strait of Georgia, as far north as the mouth of the Fraser river and at Entrance island, near Nanaimo, as well as others in the strait of Fuca, are from the Flattery rookery. On that account it seemed desirable to obtain more definite information concerning this rookery.

Mr. John N. Cobb, editor of the *Pacific Fisherman*, who has shown much interest in the work of the commission, obtained the assistance of the United States Revenue Service, who kindly placed the *Snohomish*, Lieut. H. W. Pope commanding, at the service of its members, for the purpose of visiting the rookery. As the State Department was also interested in the information, Mr. Cobb went along to represent that department.

SESSIONAL PAPER No. 38a

On October 25, Mr. Cobb and Drs. Newcombe and Fraser met the *Snohomish* at Port Angeles and proceeded to Neah bay, where the night was spent in order to make an early start in the morning to visit the rookery. In the morning, however, such a storm was raging outside the cape, that visiting the rookery was out of the question. The next day was no better, and hence the visit had to be abandoned. The trip was not entirely in vain notwithstanding, as from the Indians at Neah bay it was learned that the rookery in question is located on the Jagged islets, about nine miles south of the Umatilla reef, or twenty-one miles south of cape Flattery. Judging from some photographic prints of the rookery that were shown, it must be quite a large one. The Indians, too, gave the impression that it was of large size although no definite estimate could be obtained from them. From this rookery the sea-lions come out into the strait of Fuca, haul out on rocks not far from Neah bay, and even come into the bay itself after fish. The Indians here had the same story to tell concerning the eating of halibut, salmon, and herring.

10. BARKLEY SOUND INVESTIGATION.

In order to obtain more definite information as to the damage done by Steller's sea-lion than that afforded by the statements of white and Indian fishermen, certain arrangements were made with Mr. Martin, manager of the Wallace Fisheries Company at Kildonan, Barkley sound. Mr. Martin courteously afforded every facility at his disposal at the cannery, and the commissioners had such an excellent base of supply provided for them that it was unnecessary to take any camp outfit.

Two points of special interest were to be taken up. The first was with regard to the interference by sea-lions with the herring fishery in the way of keeping these fish off-shore, or by breaking up the schools; the second was with respect to the statement that they annually devour large quantities of herring.

In 1915, the sea-lions made their first appearance for the season in Barkley sound on November 1. On the morning of November 3, Dr. Fraser, being provided with a motor-boat and two men from the cannery, was able to visit their hauling-out place on Bird rocks. Small groups were seen from the entrance of Uchucklesit harbour to Bird rocks, and on the rocks there were about sixty, but these fell off into the water before it was possible to get a shot. It was an easy matter to chase small herds, up to ten or twelve, for a long distance, as they kept together well, coming to the surface often. Some shots were fired, but as no means of retrieving them were available at the time, no specimen was obtained. Some photographs, indicating their presence, were obtained, but otherwise these do not give much information. Apparently all of these lions were of the Steller species, and there were no small ones in the lot.

On the following morning, on the way from Kildonan to Port Alberni, small groups of lions were seen at intervals from the mouth of the harbour almost as far as the Canadian Northern construction headquarters. In every locality in which they were seen there was every evidence of herring schools there also.

From reports received by the chairman early in December, it was learned that sea-lions were in great abundance in nearly all of the numerous inlets branching from the larger waters, known as Barkley sound, and that they were as usual pursuing the herrings, which were then being taken for curing and for bait. As stormy weather then prevailed, causing wrecks and loss of life just outside of the sound, it was thought that a more successful hunt could be made in the more inside waters of Uchucklesit inlet. As Dr. Fraser was out of the province at the time, and Mr. Greenwood's engagements prevented him from taking part in the investigation, the consideration of the food question as far as these Barkley sound sea-lions were concerned was undertaken by Dr. Newcombe alone.

8 GEORGE V, A. 1918

It was a matter of congratulation, however, that Mr. Clyde L. Patch, Dominion taxidermist, was able to take an active part in the investigation. Hearing from the chairman that an attempt was to be made to secure a large number of sea-lions (including, it was hoped, the California species), Mr. Taverner, zoologist of the Royal Victoria Museum, Ottawa, supported by the Director of the Geological Survey, Dr. R. G. McConnell, offered to send a skilled taxidermist, with a view to saving all skeletons and skins for permanent preservation as a mounted group. Mr. Patch co-operated heartily in the work of collecting specimens, and, in spite of very adverse weather conditions, secured the desired parts of fourteen individuals, together with data as to sex and size. He also made plaster casts of various parts, to be utilized when mounting these specimens.

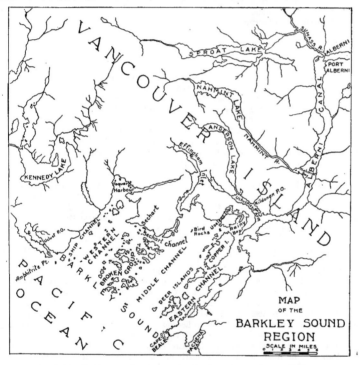

MAP OF THE
BARKLEY SOUND REGION
SCALE IN MILES

On arriving at Kildonan, a short distance inside of Uchucklesit inlet, on December 16, it was found that the herring and their pursuers were no longer there; they had been for some weeks, but had passed out into the sound. Native hunters were secured, and a small gasolene fish-boat was hired, in preference to the large craft, the loan of which was offered by Mr. Martin. The two Indians were armed with rifles and with the ordinary fur-seal spears of the west coast, in order to retrieve the bodies of any wounded individuals. Independent Indian hunters were also promised a certain sum for every sea-lion they could secure.

SESSIONAL PAPER No. 38a

The first goal was the Bird rocks, the principal resort and retiring place of sea-lions in Barkley sound, where, it was stated, a day or two earlier, some hundreds had been seen from passing vessels. On the way out two independent hunters in a small canoe furnished with gasolene were overtaken. They had just wounded a female sea-lion, and speared it while under observation.

At Bird rocks there was a large number of sea-lions, some hauled up, and a large number swimming about close to the shore. All were somewhat wild, but two were killed and hauled on board to be examined at leisure at Kildonan. The weather was dull and rainy, and hence it was impossible to secure successful photographs. After this the hunting was left to the Indians to carry on, resulting in eleven more specimens being brought in, two of which were paid for by Mr. Patch on behalf of the Geological Survey, as the chairman considered that a run of eleven or twelve specimens, all telling the same story, was sufficient for the purpose of the commission.

On opening the stomachs of the twelve specimens containing fish, it was found that all of them had herring in an unmutilated condition. Evidently they had bolted them without any mastication. The quantities amounted to from one-half to two gallons, including the pulpy mass of more or less digested food. Two contained one or two rounded stones.

The following table shows the sex, length, etc., of those examined, as noted by Mr. Patch:—

No.	Where Killed.	Sex.	Length.	Stomach Contents.
1	Bird rocks........	Male.	8 ft. 4½ in.	Small crabs, devil fish.
2	,, ...	,, ...	9 ,, 5 ,,	Stone, clam shell.
3	Off Uchucklesit	Female.............	8 ,, 3 ,,	Herring.
4	,, ...	Male..............	9 ,, 2¼ ,,	,,
5	,, ...	,, ...	6 ,, 10 ,,	,,
6	,, ...	,, ...	8 ,, 11 ,,	,,
7	,, ...	,, ...	8 ,, 2¼ ,,	,,
8	,, ...Female........		8 ,, 3½ ,,	,,
9	,, ...Male.		8 ,, 2 ,,	,,
10	,, ...	,, ...	7 ,, 3½ ,,	,,
11	,, ...	,, ...	8 ,, 8 ,,	,,
12	,, ...	,, ...	7 ,, 11 ,,	,,
13	,, ...Female........		8 ,, 3½ ,,	,,
14	,, ...Male..............		10 ,, 4½ ,,	,,

In addition to these fourteen, a male brought to Kildonan a few days previous to the arrival of Dr. Newcombe and Mr. Patch, was opened and examined by Mr. W. A. Newcombe, who reported that it had been killed amongst the herring, and that it contained a large number of these fish and their skeletons, in addition to a pulpy mass of indistinguishable material.

From the results above detailed it seemed clear that at this time of the year, at least, the main food of Stellar's sea-lion, while in Barkley sound, is one of the most important food fishes of the province, and that the contention of the white and native fishermen relating thereto was amply supported by incontestable evidence.

Some of the stomach contents were bottled up and sent to Dr. Fraser for examination, on which he reports as follows: The main portion of the material from sea-lion stomachs sent from Barkley sound consisted of herring in a more or less digested state, but the other contents are worth considering. These were (1) the dorsal fin and some vertebræ of dogfish—enough to make diagnosis definite; (2) a portion of a vertebral column of a flatfish—not enough to make identification of species possible; (3) a clavicle from some bony fish, possibly from the same flatfish; (4) a number of cephalopod beaks; (5) a clam shell that had been bored by *Thais*; (6) small stones; (7) numerous nematode parasites of the Ascaris type.

The finding of the dogfish remains is especially interesting. Only one of all the eyewitnesses examined mentioned dogfish as an article of sea-lion diet. In recent years the dogfish have been so numerous in Barkley sound during the early part of the herring season that the fishermen find it unprofitable to put out their nets since the dogfish do so much damage to them. It may be only a coincidence, but when the sea-lions come in about the first of November, the dogfish no longer interfere with the nets. The fact that sea-lions do eat dogfish indicates that it might be more than a coincidence. Without question the dogfish is a greater pest than the sea-lion at the present time. It might be a still greater pest if the sea-lion were exterminated.

The flatfish remains, as well as those of the squid and devilfish, indicate that at times the sea-lion is a bottom feeder, possibly only in shallow water. The dead clam shell and the stones were likely scooped up when the bottom feeding was being carried on.

From the variety obtained in two of the stomachs it seems as though the sea-lion is not restricted in its diet but that anything will serve, the most abundant material receiving the greatest attention.

11. INFORMATION BY CORRESPONDENCE.

While the investigation in the sea-lion haunts was being carried on, the secretary was getting information by correspondence. To facilitate and unify this, a set of questions, accompanied by a circular letter (see appendix), was sent to each British Columbia cannery manager, etc., who was likely to have knowledge of any phase of the question. To these questions a large number of replies were obtained, and these, in general, definitely confirmed the evidence already quoted, and brought out some points not previously considered.

Comparatively few endeavoured to estimate damage to gear, but the total estimates given amounted to over $1,600 for the year 1915. It was scarcely expected that any very definite figures would be given for the value of the fish lost by mutilation or for the diverted run of fish but a number of replies indicated that in the case of the salmon, the value of the fish lost by mutilation, and in the case of the herring, the value of the loss by diverted run, would be considerable. The only place where any definite change in the number of sea-lions was noted was at Rivers inlet, where there was a definite increase during 1911-12-13, and since then a noticeable decrease.

None of those directly interested in the fish business could give any definite information as to the value of sea-lions. Such information from other sources will be treated separately.

The correspondents were almost unanimously in favour of complete extermination. to ensure which they wished a Government bounty, none of them feeling able to cope with the situation themselves. That extermination might be as rapid as possible, shooting the adults and clubbing the pups on the rocks soon after they were born in June, should afford the most definite results, although poisoning and other extreme methods were also suggested. These methods would not do very well in Barkley sound where the sea-lions come in late in the fall. As a bounty mark, the muzzle seemed to satisfy the majority, although it was also suggested that the mark should be changed from year to year.

12. KILLING SEA-LIONS.

Nothing was done systematically towards the killing of sea-lions, except in Barkley sound, where it has been going on with more or less vigour for several years, until the year 1914. So much damage was done to the fisheries of Rivers inlet in 1913 (Manager Inrig estimated the loss of gear at Wadham's cannery alone at

SESSIONA . PAPER No. 38a

$3,021) that the following year several cannerymen decided to co-operate in decreasing the number. A levy of $1.50 was made for each boat fishing, and as there were 700 boats fishing, this provided a fund of $1,050. Two dollars a tail were offered for sea-lions, and in thirty-six hours enough tails were obtained to take up all the bounty, that is to say 525 were procured.

During this year again, on Barkley sound, men were supplied with guns and ammunition and sent to drive the sea-lions away from the schools of herring. They can be chased thus like herds of cattle. No effort was made to retrieve any of those shot, but a large number must have been killed.

In 1915, Wadham's cannery supplied two gasolene fish carriers, and giving twenty men to each a holiday, armed them with rifles and supplied them with between $400 and $500 worth of ammunition, sent them off to the rookery to kill sea-lions. The first trip was made in the second or third week in May, and a thousand rounds of ammunition were used. Hundreds must have been killed, but only three noses were taken home. The second hunt took place in the first week in June. This time 200 muzzles were obtained, and it was estimated that 750 altogether must have been killed. The muzzles were handed in to the fishery officer for the bounty of $2, which was placed on sea-lions last year by the Department of Fisheries, $5,750 being set aside for that purpose. This bounty was all used up early in June, many muzzles being brought in after the bounty money had all been paid out.

Of the 2,875 sea-lions for which bounty was paid, 1,160 were killed at or near the Sea Otter group at the mouth of Rivers Inlet, 1,616 on the East and West Haycocks (islands in the cape Scott group) and the few remaining at various spots along the coast. Beside the number mentioned from the Haycocks, 674 were brought in too late for bounty. (These figures were supplied by Mr. F. H. Cunningham, Chief Inspector of Fisheries, the list including the number to whom bounty was paid, the number and the location where obtained. See Appendix B).

In the two years, therefore, there is positive evidence that 4,074 sea-lions were killed, 3,549 in 1915, and 525 in 1914. According to the statements of Fisheries Overseer Saugstad at Rivers inlet, and Boyd at Bella Bella, through whom most of the bounty was applied for, there would certainly not be more than 50 per cent saved of those killed. Of the adults, there might not be more than one in ten, but among the pups there would be quite a large proportion. Approximately 75 per cent of the muzzles brought in were from pups. In the localities alone in which sea-lions were killed for bounty in 1914 and 1915, at a conservative estimate there must have been 8,000 killed, of which approximately 6,000 were pups. The number killed in Barkley sound and at isolated spots elsewhere would add materially to this number. At such a rate, extermination would not seem far off. In fact it was practical extermination of the 1915 increase on the Sea Otter and Haycock rookeries.

Comparing these numbers with the estimated number for the whole coast, 11,000, given by Dr. Newcombe as seen in 1913, it would seem that an estimate based on the numbers that may be seen at the rookeries and hauling-out places, must be too low. Even during the pupping season, all the lions will not be on the rookeries at the same time, for while the adult male and female may fast at such a time, there is no evidence that immature individuals do so, and the probability is that they feed then as they do at other times of the year. During the rest of the year, it is known that at times all the members of a herd may be away from the rookery or hauling-out place at one time, but there is no assurance that all of them are ever on the rocks at the same time. Certainly there are times when some are on the rocks and others are in the water, since that has been observed by the commissioners on different occasions. If they are not all on the rocks at the same time, an estimate based on the number seen at any one time would not take into account those in the water.

8 GEORGE V, A. 1918

Consider the case of Solander island for example. In the investigation by Dr. Newcombe in 1913, since at times there were no lions whatever visible, doubt was expressed as to its being a rookery (there is now conclusive evidence that it is), although at other times upwards of one thousand were seen there. Even when a thousand of them were on the rocks there may have been many more scattered about, actively feeding or in search of food.

Taking it for granted, therefore, that 11,000 was a fair estimate in 1913 for the number of sea-lions that could be seen at the rookeries and hauling-out places, it is evident that to this number, an addition must be made, amounting to an unknown percentage of the whole number, to get at the total number in British Columbia waters.

13. COMMERCIAL USES TO WHICH SEA-LION CARCASSES MIGHT BE PUT.

From evidence of manufacturers and sea-lion hunters the suggestion was conveyed to the commissioners that there was an economic and commercial value in sea-lion hides, whiskers, and carcasses. Under the bounty system the whole carcass of a sea-lion, with the exception of the muzzle, is disregarded, thrown into the sea, or left on the rookeries or hauling-out grounds to putrify, so far as any effort is made by the Government to utilize it. Much time was spent and many persons interviewed in obtaining definite information as to the feasibility of utilizing sea-lion carcasses for commercial purposes, with the happy result, however, of its being demonstrated that the hide of a sea-lion is eminently suitable for tanning into leather, from which durable and serviceable gloves and boots to-day are being made; that the whiskers have a value of 25 cents a piece to Orientals; and that the flesh can be rendered into oil and guano, for which a good market is ever available. While it was impossible, owing to the short time at the disposal of the commissioners, to investigate this side of the problem in an exhaustive manner, on account of the great distances from Vancouver and Victoria to San Francisco and New York, where comprehensive and accurate corroboration of the commercial uses of the carcasses of sea-lions can be obtained, yet sufficient evidence was discovered to point to the conclusion that in killing sea-lions the economic value of their entire carcasses should be taken into consideration, so that, if it were found possible and feasible, then the monetary returns from the disposal of the carcasses in the form of hides, whiskers, oil, and guano would at least equal and possibly, with care, exceed the amount of the bounty offered by the Government. It is in the mind of the commissioners that if such a consummation could be reached, a real service to industry and the country could be rendered. It is in this direction that the commissioners desire to pursue their inquiries during the coming year.

What turn that inquiry might take is indicated by the fact that Mr. W. F. Robinson, president of the Robinson Fisheries Company, manufacturers, producers, and distributors of fish oil and fish fertilizer, Anacortes, Washington, writing to the commission under date of August 11, 1915, says: "We have never yet had the carcasses of sea-lions to use in our fertilizer plant, but could do so if we had them, as we understand they grow to a very large size. Unless the expense of obtaining the sea-lions is too great, or your works are not near the source of production, we believe they could be handled to advantage."

Messrs. Anderson and Miskin, 448 Seymour street, Vancouver, in answer to an inquiry from the commission, wrote the following letter, in which it is understood that the oil from the sea-lions corresponds to seal oil:—

"Replying to your telephonic inquiry *re* our requirements of seal oil, we are buyers of the same quality as is produced in Newfoundland from the blubber of the young harps (hair seal). It is principally used in miners' lamps, and must be free of moisture. If we get the right quality, we can use 500 to

700 tons per annum. Samples are usually submitted before we purchase, or it is guaranteed to be the finest quality, and what is termed 'water white.' Straw and coloured oil, which is much cheaper, we handle a small quantity of. Oil from old harps is very much darker than what is produced from the young ones.

"There is a good market for seal oil in United Kingdom, and we have no doubt whatever that, if the stuff can be produced on the Pacific coast, it would be to our mutual advantage. If a small trial lot was sent home on consignment through us, it would enable our friends to judge of the character of the oil, and if not suited for their purposes there would be no difficulty in disposing of it in the open market. If, on the other hand, it did suit them, they would doubtless be willing to make a contract for the quantity we have already stated, under guarantee of quality equal to consignment parcel, of which sealed samples could be retained here."

As to guano obtained from fish, whales, and other sea animals, its price is in the neighbourhood of $40 a ton. It is used as a fertilizer, and also manufactured into chicken food. The demand is steady and growing. Similar guano, it is thought, could be made from the carcasses of sea-lions.

In relation to the manufacture of sea-lion hide products, the commission is indebted to R. C. Grinnell, British Columbia Glove Company, Eburne, Point Grey, for valuable information obtained during an interview on October 22. Mr. Grinnell speaks from personal knowledge as in his factory he has made gloves, boots, and moccasins from sea-lion hides. In fact, he has built up a small but substantial business in leather goods made from sea-lion hides. Naturally, therefore, he is emphatic in his declaration that sea-lions are of commercial value, especially for their hides.

In 1913 he took a hunting trip to Haycock islands and got 500 hides which, when green and salted, weighed almost 200 pounds apiece. These hides he tanned in the ordinary way and made into gloves in his factory which in the fall of that year, was situated at Coquitlam. In tanning the hide reduces about 75 per cent, and when tanned runs from an inch to a quarter of an inch in thickness. It is thin under the flippers but it is thicker on the belly than on the back. In making the hide into leather it may be split into three layers, and when thus split can be readily manipulated. From this leather, chrome-tanned leather gloves are made. From the hide of a fair-sized male, $2\frac{1}{2}$ to 3 dozen pairs of gloves may be made, but taking an average of male, female and pup, only about 25 square feet of leather can be obtained, enough to make one dozen pairs of gloves. The range of gloves made runs from the fine automobile gloves or gauntlets to the heavy loggers' mittens, the former selling at $24 a dozen pairs and the latter from $10.50 to $15. No better material can be obtained for loggers' mittens, as the hide of the sea-lion by nature is of fine fibre, tough, strong, flexible, and of close grain, enabling it to keep out water, while still retaining its pliability. The other gloves as well are very durable and serviceable. On the day following the interview, Mr. Grinnell brought into the secretary's office two pairs of gloves made from sea-lion hide, tanned in his own factory and made up in the interval. One pair was from the hide of a sea-lion pup, this selling at $1.50 or, by the dozen, $12.50; the other was from an adult, selling at $1.75 a pair, or $13.50 a dozen. The secretary bought the two pairs, and has them on exhibition in his office at present. With eight or nine men working, twenty-five to fifty pairs of gloves a day are made. More men are wanted, as the output could easily be increased. Glove business from sea-lion hides is a good business. There is a ready market in Canada for all the factory can turn out.

The moccasins that Mr. Grinnell makes from the sea-lion hides give good satisfaction. They are pliable and fit snugly to the foot. The price is $26 per dozen

8 GEORGE V, A. 1918

pairs. Boots from these hides stand water as well as rubber boots. A pair were
made for a customer, who has to wade through water and chemical liquor all the
time while at work, and even here they gave excellent satisfaction. For boot purposes,
green hides are better than dry hides, but all sea-lion hides are good.

Mr. Grinnell would be glad to consider a proposal to buy all the sea-lion hides
that could be delivered to him, and is sure if he could get the supply at a fair price
he could build up a large industry. He would be willing to pay 5 cents a pound for
green hides if he were guaranteed 5,000 hides. If he could get hides in large enough
numbers to make it worth while he could ship them to San Francisco, as he has a
standing order to ship any hides he can get at 6 or 7 cents a pound for green hides
of females and pups and 2 cents a pound for males, but he has to pay the freight.
It would take 5,000 per annum to satisfy this demand.

If the lions can be obtained, the skinning is a simple matter. A good man can
skin a lion in from fifteen to twenty-five minutes and should be able to skin three or
four an hour. He would thus make good wages if he could get steady work for the
day at 25 cents a skin.

Mr. Grinnell is of the opinion that the oil from the sea-lion alone should make it
worth while saving the carcass, and the remainder of the carcass made into guano
or chicken food should command a good price.

P. H. McMullen, representing the McMullen Hide and Fur Company, 956 Powell
street, Vancouver, said he would handle any quantity of sea-lion hides at a price similar
to that suggested by Mr. Grinnell.

14. BOUNTY PAYMENTS FOR KILLING SEA-LIONS.

By good fortune the commission interviewed A. K. Sinclair, 2940 Ontario street,
Vancouver, a sea-faring man, an old sealer and perhaps the pioneer sea-lion hunter for
profit in British Columbia. He tells the sea-lion story from a different viewpoint,
that of the hunter. In May, 1914, he was on a hunting trip for Hibbard & Stewart,
hide dealers, 958 Powell street, Vancouver, as skipper of the schooner *Tuladi,* the
agreement being that he was to receive 3 cents a pound for green salted sea-lion hides,
delivered in Vancouver.

He was at Rivers inlet on May 25, 1914, where, he states, he organized the plan
mentioned elsewhere in this report by which the canners there gave $1,050 in bounty
in an effort to diminish the depredations of the sea-lions by killing off a number of
them.

Sinclair had to wait about a week for good weather before he could get on the
Virgin rocks. From his anchorage in Schooner Retreat, every day he spied out the
land until conditions were ripe. On June 5 or 6 he made a landing on the Virgin
rocks from a dory. The sea-lions made as if they would prevent his landing, but after
killing five or six of them from the dory he and one hunter succeeded in getting on the
rocks. They left one man on the schooner and one man in the dory not far from the
rocks. It was breeding season, and all the sea-lions stayed on the rocks when the
landing was made. The lions were not frightened, they did not stampede, they seemed
indifferent to the visitors. If any sea-lions slid off the rocks on the approach of the
hunters they returned to the rocks after the hunters landed.

The hunters shot all the cows and bulls they could within that radius, and cut the
tails from all they had killed to collect the bounty. They started killing at 6 in the
morning and finished at 2 in the afternoon. At the end of the killing, 750 tails were
counted. They then turned back to Rivers inlet, declared enough tails to collect $1,050
and hoping that more bounty might be put up they did not reveal the possession of a
greater number.

SESSIONAL PAPER No. 38a ·

After Sinclair and his crew had collected the bounty they went back to the Virgin rocks and skinned some of the sea-lions for their hides. They got about 2,000 pounds, when the weather turned bad and prevented any further landings. The wind came in from the west every day about 10 a.m. and kept blowing steadily and strong until evening, when it died down. All that they got from the hides on this trip amounted to $60, but they had the $1,050 bounty money besides.

The following year, leaving Vancouver on May 12, Sinclair with two others took the 40-foot gasoline schooner *Atlintoo* up the coast to hunt for sea-lions. They got a few near Smiths inlet. On May 16 they were off Virgin rocks, but very few sea-lions were in sight. They arrived at Rivers inlet May 20, where they tried to get the canners again to put up a bounty fund, but the canners had decided to go hunting sea-lions on their own account. Sinclair describes the hunting party from the canneries as composed of sixteen or twenty men armed with "pop guns," twenty-two rifles, revolvers, and other firearms. They left Rivers inlet 2 a.m. one Sunday, went to Virgin rocks, and got back about four in the afternoon. They were not successful, as they had begun too early. Four noses were all they had. (The bounty mark had been changed from tails to noses.) Later, many other parties from Rivers inlet went out to Virgin rocks, until from much shooting the sea-lions got scared off. On June 3 Sinclair and his crew got fourteen noses after making a landing on Virgin rocks. He found the sea-lions timid, for as soon as they saw the launch they got off the rocks into the water, and even the mothers left their young when the hunters landed. "The sea-lions went off like sheep." He was dissatisfied with Virgin rocks and went to Calvert island, where he anchored, and got four noses one day, ten another, and eight another. In all he got fifty-seven noses, and landed at Rivers inlet, where he collected on them in the name of George Allen. Fifteen noses he brought to Vancouver and collected on them there.

Mr. Sinclair declares that to make a success of sea-lion hunting it is necessary to be able to land on Virgin rocks every day or every other day. He says that if there had been a bounty in 1914 he could have killed 90 per cent of those on Virgin rocks. If he had been offered $2,500 to clear the sea-lions off Virgin rocks in 1914 and protect the Rivers inlet fisheries he would have accepted it and done the job completely. The proper way to attack these animals to reduce their numbers is to get the old ones first. When females are pupping the old sea-lions never leave the rocks to feed or do anything else. The bull sea-lions are as thin as rakes after the cows are done pupping, at which time they are all very voracious. If it is desired to exterminate the sea-lions, all the rookeries should be hunted at the same time. During the pupping season they are easily fooled, since they persist in staying on the breeding grounds. Sinclair would take six or seven good shots and reach the rocks about June 1. He would hide three men on the rocks with orders to shoot only the old ones and to shoot to kill, aiming at the spot just below the ear. The old ones will not leave the rocks at this time if they are not fired at from the water, and the pups cannot, for they are not strong enough, as they are suckled by the mothers for ten days or two weeks after birth. When the adults are killed the pups can readily be clubbed, and if not they would die of starvation.

Sinclair is of the opinion that bounty should not be paid unless the hide were brought in, as the hide could be sold for more than the bounty. He would be willing to hunt sea-lions, collecting a bounty on the hide of $1 for pups, $3 for females, and $2 for bulls. He says also that bounty paid on sea-lions killed at a long distance from any locality where fishing is in operation is money thrown away. He thinks East Haycocks, Tree Nob island, Butterworth rocks, Massett, Banks island, Price island, Bonilla banks, and Aristazable island are too far away from Rivers inlet to allow sea-lions from them to be the cause of depredations to fishing.

An article appeared in the *Pacific Motor-Boat*, Seattle, Wash., in November, 1915, treating of sea-lion hunting by motor-boat in Oregon, so pertinent to the Canadian

38a—3½

8 GEORGE V, A. 1918

inquiry that, with the permission of the publisher, Mr. Miller Freeman, it is reproduced in part:—

"A rather unique industry is carried on each year in motor-boats off the
coast of Curry county, Oregon. The Rogue River reef and the Cape Blanco
reef are each year combed for sea-lions, and the work of killing them is often
hazardous and dangerous.

"The killing is not done for amusement, but for profit, the skins being
valued at from $4 to $6 each, and some other portions of the carcass being of
sufficient value to make the average for each animal killed between $5 and $6.

The annual slaughter does not take place until the young are born, usually
in July and August. This plan of leaving the pups insures a supply for the
hunters the next year and there is no danger of the disappearance of the sea-lions
from the vicinity where they are sought.

The largest rocks in the Blanco reef are off shore from three to seven miles
and the hunters must go well prepared. It is possible they might be obliged
to stay about the rocks two or three days at a time, for the ocean occasionally
becomes so rough the small boats are obliged to stay in the lee until the weather
improves.

Until late years the hunters used rowboats in which to seek the lions and
sometimes were on the rocks several days before they could return ashore at
Port Orford, the nearest town. Recently, however, gasoline boats are utilized
altogether in hunting. It is customary to go from shore to the rocks where the
sea-lions make their home, in a small open craft, and, after making a kill, the
skins are picked up from the reef by a larger craft, the gasoline schooner *Tramp,*
a 15-ton boat of Marshfield. Captain John Swing has transported the sea-lion
hides in the *Tramp* from the two reefs for the past ten years, trans-shipping
them for San Francisco at Coos Bay.

The average number of hides secured each season varies from 300 to 400,
the hunters feeling they have done a profitable season's work if they make a
clear profit of $1,000, since the season is only for a month, and the time goes
quickly while they are engaged. The hides are used by manufacturers for
belting. They are prepared by salting them heavily but not tanned until they
reach their destination at San Francisco. The skins are heavy, the hunters
finding them occasionally weighing 150 pounds when secured from an animal
of extraordinary size.

Taking the skins from the sea-lions is an occupation that calls for quick
and expert ability. A good skinner can take a hide off in from five to seven
minutes, when working at ordinary speed. Robert Forty and James Crewe
each has a record of skinning a common-sized animal in three and a half
minutes. While there is no means of weighing the sea-lions, the hunters
estimate their weight from 1,500 to over 3,000 pounds. The larger the pelt, of
course, the better the price is secured."

Thus it will be seen that in paying a bounty of $2 for each muzzle of a slain sea-
lion and disregarding the hide and carcass, there is lost an opportunity to encourage
the prevention of fisheries depredations and at the same time, by means of a business
organization centered in the government officials, make the sea-lion, through its hide
and carcass, pay the bounty and more. When further facts are obtained concerning
methods of organization, aiming at using for commercial purposes the sea-lion carcass,
the commission should be able to outline a plan that would achieve that economical
and conservative result.

SESSIONAL PAPER No. 38a

15. CONCLUSIONS AND RECOMMENDATIONS.

The commissioners are satisfied that as the numbers of sea-lions in or near Rivers inlet increased from 1911 to 1913, they were present in sufficient numbers to be a serious menace to the fishing industry, although there was no diminution in the pack until 1913. Thus the pack for 1910 was 129,398 cases, for 1911, 101,066 cases, and for 1912, it amounted to 137,697 cases; in 1913 there were only 68,096 cases put up, the smallest pack since 1901. This was the year in which it was found useless to fish farther out towards the mouth of Rivers inlet than the entrance to Draineys inlet. The fact that the fishermen had to stop all fishing in this region on account of the number of fish taken out of the nets and the amount of damage done to gear is backed up by the fact that the cannery managers of the five outer canneries in the inlet were willing to put up their own money in 1914 as a bounty that the number of sea-lions might be reduced. Coincident with the decrease in the number brought about in this way in 1914, the pack went up again, amounting to 109,052 cases. While the fluctuation from year to year is always evident, the great decrease in the pack for 1913 can scarcely be accounted for on that basis. In 1915 a bounty of two dollars per muzzle was placed on sea-lions by the Department of Fisheries. This might have been expected to help out the Rivers inlet canneries, and probably it did so as the pack 146,838 cases, slightly surpassed the previous high record of 1912. Of this pack, over 130,000 cases were sockeye, over 27 per cent of the total sockeye pack for the province for this year. Since such a pack is worth approximately $1,200,000, it is certainly worth conserving.

However, as this bounty of two dollars was an indiscriminating bounty, its success was not unqualified. It is true that many sea-lions were killed in the vicinity of Rivers inlet, but it is also true, as shown in this report, that more than twice the number were killed at points too far distant from Rivers inlet to have any effect on the fishing there, not because sea-lions, on occasion, do not travel so far, but that at, and for some time after, the pupping season, they remain in the vicinity of the rookery, and this season corresponds with the time of the sockeye run in Rivers inlet. Furthermore, it is commonly believed that the numbers in the Sea Otter rookery have greatly increased since the lions were driven from Triangle island after the erection of the lighthouse and the installation of a wireless plant there. If this is true, the killing of so many sea-lions on the East and West Haycocks in 1915 will tend to drive those uninjured away from these islands and hence it might increase the numbers in the Sea Otter rookery, thus doing harm rather than good to the Rivers inlet fishing. Since only the muzzle was required to obtain the bounty, it was possible for a very few individuals to kill a sufficient number on the rookeries in a very short time to take up all of the bounty, whether these lions were doing any harm or not, consequently, in other cases where sea-lions, likely to be doing harm, were killed, there was no bounty available. As an example, the Barkley sound fishermen had made complaints of depredations by sea-lions but as the whole available bounty was used up in June, while the sea-lions did not come into Barkley sound until the first of November, the Barkley sound fishermen received no benefit whatever from the bounty. If the skins and carcasses had been made use of, such wholesale killing in such a short period would not have been possible, and some return might have been obtained from the money expended.

The opinion is still held by eminent scientific men that it has not yet been proved that fish is an important item of the food of sea-lions. Drs. Merriam, Evermann and Hornaday have been much quoted in this regard. These men and others, during the California controversy, refused to put any faith in the statements of the fishermen regarding the sea-lion depredations. The period covered by the researches of the commission has been a limited one but even in this limited period sufficient

8 GEORGE V, A. 1918

evidence was obtained to prove that during a certain time of the year at least, food fish are eaten in large quantities by grey sea-lions. As in this instance the statements of the fishermen are definitely corroborated, there is evidently a fair basis for accepting other statements upon which there is general agreement, provided always that allowance must be made for a bias, natural to those interested in this as in any other question. It is on account of this bias that the evidence from independent witnesses is always desirable. Taking that into consideration, it is recommended that the commission should continue to study the life-history of the sea-lion, particularly during the breeding season, which corresponds to the time of the big run of sockeye at Rivers inlet. This should be accomplished with comparative ease but the habits during the remainder of the year cannot be so readily ascertained as in such investigation many difficulties will have to be overcome.

The amount of food required just after the pupping season cannot be considered as an index for the rest of the year. That taken by the sea-lions in Barkley sound in November and December would be much nearer the average. The results of feeding in captivity do not help much as opinions differ so markedly. Thus, as previously quoted, Hornaday states that 12 pounds a day or less is sufficient food for an adult male sea-lion, while Scammon says, the keeper at Woodward's Gardens, San Francisco, informed him that he fed a male and a female sea-lion, regularly, every day, fifty pounds of fresh fish. [1] In any case, the amount of food required by a sea-lion in captivity, where its movements are necessarily much restricted, might be very different to the amount required by one during the active life out in the sea, where, in many instances, the food is so plentiful that there is great temptation to eat more than actual necessity calls for.

The presence of dogfish remains in the stomach of a sea-lion caught in Barkley sound opens up a large question that should be investigated, particularly in view of the statement that the dogfish cease to bother the herring nets as soon as the sea-lions appear in the neighbourhood. While a definite comparison of the damage done to the herring fishery by the dogfish and the sea-lion is impossible, this at least can be said: while it does not pay to fish for herring when the dogfish interfere and the sea-lions are absent, it does pay to do so when the reverse is the case. If the disappearance of the dogfish is in any sense due to the presence of the sea-lion, the sooner the matter is investigated the better.

Although at the present time no other species is so much a pest as the dogfish, there are other undesirable species, and while the commission has no definite information as to the relation of any of these to the sea-lion, the possibility of the sea-lion's maintaining equilibrium in such cases is worthy of consideration.

While the commissioners recommend that sea-lions should be driven away or greatly reduced in numbers where it is evident that they are doing appreciable damage, they are not satisfied that there is any necessity for decreasing the numbers at other rookeries, except after some organized plan by which the pups could be free from injury, as in the case mentioned off the Oregon coast, in order that the industrial value of the sea-lions should be conserved, and more particularly in view of the possible friendly offices of the sea-lion that suggest further inquiry. Even in the case where it is considered necessary to diminish the number of sea-lions materially, the monetary value of the hide and carcass should be taken into consideration in any plan adopted.

CHARLES F. NEWCOMBE.

WM. HAMAR GREENWOOD.

C. McLEAN FRASER.

---

[1] Scammon, C. M. Marine Mammals of the Northwestern Coast, 1874, page 135.

SESSIONAL PAPER No. 38a

PART II.

REPORT AND CONCLUSIONS OF THE SEA-LION INVESTIGATION, 1916.

In order to ascertain the effect upon the sea-lion population of the bounty of $2 per head which was placed upon them early in the year 1915, and the desirability or otherwise of continuing it, the commission appointed by the Biological Board of Canada considered it advisable: (1) to procure the number of individuals killed in order to obtain the bounty, (2) to visit the rookeries in order to make an estimate of the number of sea-lions still remaining in the province (3) to visit all localities from which complaints had been sent of depredations by these animals, and (4) to investigate, as far as possible, the nature of the food of the sea-lions, as grave doubts had been expressed by well-known men of science as to whether food fish formed any part of their diet, some authorities even stating that their principal food consisted of animals which are enemies of fish used by man.

The lateness of the season when the commissioners were first able to commence their labours and the unsuitability of the valuable government vessel for approaching the rookeries placed at their disposal, prevented them from completing the programme thus sketched. The number of sea-lions killed was obtained with approximate accuracy; a great deal of information was procured from the various fishing stations as to the damage done by them during the fishing season and a beginning was made in the line of inquiry as to whether sea-lions do or do not eat food fish at one of the points at which complaint was made of their interference and destructive habits.

The rookeries, however, were not adequately examined, nor had the commissioners any opportunity of personally investigating the food question at Rivers inlet, one of the most important salmon fisheries on the coast and one from which the most urgent complaints of damage had emanated, and also that one in the neighbourhood of which by far the greatest number of sea-lions, pups and adults, had been slaughtered early in 1915.

It was therefore pointed out by the commissioners in their report for 1915 that it was their opinion that, with the object of completing the task originally proposed by them, their work should be resumed in 1916 early enough to be on Rivers inlet fishing ground during part of the salmon season and also in time to visit the rookeries when the sea-lions were assembled to bear their young, in order to be able to make as accurate an estimate of their numbers as possible.

The lack of facilities for communication with Rivers inlet made it difficult to decide on the most suitable time to visit this locality. The regular mail service and the telegraph and telephone communication made it an easy matter to get data as to conditions at Barkley sound, but at Rivers inlet telegraph and telephone communication is lacking and mail arrives but once a week.

From reports already received the commission was led to believe that sea-lion depredation occurred both before and after the pupping season in early June. Since it was desirable to get as full information as possible as to the numbers of sea-lions at the different rookeries, it seemed possible that this could be obtained during the trip in which the Rivers inlet question was to be considered.

For the twofold purpose especially, a 45-foot motor launch, the *Emoh*, was chartered, with Captain Massey commanding. Leaving Vancouver on June 21 and Departure Bay the following morning, a start was made for Rivers inlet, and

8 GEORGE V, A. 1918

Wadhams was reached on June 24. On this part of the trip, as well as throughout the remainder of it, advantage was taken of every opportunity to confirm or add to the information already received.

Contrary to expectations, there was no sign of any sea-lions in the inlet and no word of any being seen, singly or in herds, as they had been reported early in the season in other years. Since, therefore, there was no immediate prospect of carrying on personal investigation in Rivers inlet, the commission proceeded to make a survey of the various rookeries.

17. SURVEY OF THE ROOKERIES.

I. *The Sea Otter Group.*

In the first place attention was directed to the rookery on the Sea Otter group of islands, near the entrance to Rivers inlet. Manager Inrig offered to send out a Wadhams Cannery boat with its crew and others armed with rifles to shoot some sea-lions for inspection. The offer was accepted, and on June 25 the rookeries were visited.

On Pearl rocks, the first of the group to be visited (see fig. 2), there were about 250 sea-lions, about 50 of them being pups. As the sea was smooth, a landing was made from a row-boat, on the largest of the rocks, and a female, 7 feet 1 inch long, which had been shot, was opened and examined, but the stomach was empty. Here, as on the other rocks in this group, the pups were very young, some of them newly born, and none of them yet able to take to the water or to swim properly if they did get in.

Watch rock (see fig. 3), was next visited, but on this there were three adults. Two of these were shot and examined. They were both small males, one of them 7 feet 6 inches in length (see fig. 5) and the other 8 feet 1 inch. The stomachs were empty.

Finally the Virgin group was visited. This group consists of three larger rocky islands and other smaller ones. There were lions on all, a total number of at least 2,500, of which nearly 1,000 were pups. One male, 10 feet 4 inches long (see fig. 13), was examined, with the same result as in the other cases.

Evidently it was no use trying to learn what the sea-lion takes as food by examining the stomachs of those killed on the rookeries, and hence the members of the commission wished for no further slaughter. The boat crew were not satisfied with this, however, and many more were made to suffer. The adults all took to the water at the sound of the first volley if they had not already done so on the near approach of the boat, but they come to the surface at short intervals, rising until the head, neck and shoulders are visible, at which time they offer a target to the marksmen. The young pups are very helpless, so that they may easily be approached and many of these were clubbed to death. (It was in this way that most of them were killed for bounty the previous year.) Several photographs of pup groups were obtained on both Pearl and Virgin rocks (see figs. 6-12).

II. *The East Haycocks.*

On the following day, June 26, the rookeries to the northwest of Vancouver island, on what is sometimes known as the cape Scott group of islands, were visited. On the way from Rivers inlet, sea-lions were again seen on the islands of the Sea Otter group, but no attempt was made to get near enough to make an estimate of the number. Channel rock to the southward of Pearl rocks was showing slightly above water and on it there were about twenty-five sea-lions.

In the cape Scott group, the West Haycocks were first visited but no sea-lions were visible. The East Haycocks, however, presented the most wonderful sight of

SESSIONAL PAPER No. 38a

the whole trip. For a considerable distance above the water's edge, the rocks every-where were lined with sea-lions. The lowest estimate made as to the number was 6,000. The pups here were larger and hence, in such a number, it was difficult to distinguish them from the yearlings and small females. For that reason the num-ber of pups could not be approximated. As it was pouring rain unfortunately photo-graphy was out of the question.

No rookeries have been reported from the larger islands, Lanz and Cox, there-fore, although the shores were scanned with glasses from a distance, no closer examina-tion was made. Triangle island, which formerly was the base for a large rookery, no longer supports one. The island was not visited but by means of wireless com-munication the commission was assured that no breeding took place there in 1916.

In the open ocean for miles around Haycocks, sea-lions were seen, singly or in small groups, the last of these for the day about 14 miles away in the direction of Quatsino sound.

III. Solander Island.

The rookery at Solander island, off cape Coop, was examined the following day, June 27. The day was fine and the sea smooth. The *Emoh* was left in the offing, while two members of the commission in the boat's dinghy, rowed over to the rookery in the hope that some photographs could be obtained for there would be much commotion among the members of the herd. Such hopes were vain for so timid were these huge beasts that even the approach of this small boat struck them with terror and they began to tumble off into the water, consequently, in order to show any large portion of the number, long range photographs had to be taken (see figs. 16, 17). Three or four of the large bulls remained to be seen at shorter range, swaying from side to side and uttering most deafening roars. Some of their most faithful consorts remained with them almost to the last. One in particular seemed very loath to go (see fig. 21). He was probably the largest of the herd, and one of the largest seen at any of the rookeries, but he, too, finally took the plunge. His total length must have been over 12 feet and his weight over a ton. (Dr. Newcombe in his sea-lion report for 1913, gives the actual weight of a 12-foot sea-lion, brought into Alert bay, April 26, 1913, as 2,240 pounds.)

In the water the animals seem to have less fear, and when a score of them came up at the same time, near together (see fig. 23), and in close proximity to the small boat, to give their deep roar in unison, one felt that it was as well that they did not realize the extent of their powers.

This rookery was not a large one, so that the number, little in excess of 500, could be fairly accurately counted. Here again the pups were large enough to take to the water, and they were among the first to do so; hence the relative number could not be definitely estimated.

On June 28, while returning from Sea Otter cove to Rivers inlet, sea-lions were seen at cape Russell and other points between this and cape Scott.

IV. Cape St. James.

There remained one large rookery, that on the rocks off cape St. James, at the southern extremity of the Queen Charlotte islands, and a start was made for this on June 29. In the neighbourhood of Estevan island, engine trouble developed to such extent that it was necessary to go to Prince Rupert for repairs. This made a delay of some days.

On July 9, Butterworth rocks, to the northwest of Stephens island, were visited, as this is a well-known hauling-out place, but not a rookery. Two sea-lions were seen.

These were 150 miles from the nearest known rookery. They disappeared into the water while the boat was still at long range, but they appeared to be of good size. They could hardly be breeding adults so far away from a rookery, and there were no pups on the rocks. They were probably bachelor males, such as were seen and examined on Watch rock in the Sea Otter group.

Hecate strait was crossed on July 11, and cape St. James reached on July 13. Here again the day was fine and the sea smooth, with the exception of a certain amount of swell. Thus near approach was possible, and some photographs were obtained (see figs. 30-33), but no attempt was made to land. There were only about 1,000 sea-lions on the rocks, and the pups could not readily be distinguished from the other members of the herd. Individuals in the water were seen as far away as Scudder point, 25 miles distant from the rookery.

On the return, Rivers inlet was reached on July 17.

18. A COMPARISON OF THE ENUMERATIONS OF 1913 AND 1914.

While the rookeries are still under consideration, it is well to compare the enumeration here made with that made by Dr. C. F. Newcombe and W. A. Newcombe in 1913[1]. A table of comparison will serve as a basis for bringing out special points.

Rookery.	1913.		1916.	
	Date.	Number.	Date.	Number.
Cape St. James..............	June 12, 13....	2,000	July 13........	1,000
Sea Otter group—				
Pearl rocks......	June 21, 22. ..	1.350	June 25........	250
Watch rocks	June 22.	112	June 25........	3
Virgin rocks.....	Aug. 28, 29, Sept. 2.......	2,300	June 25........	2,500
Cape Scott group—				
Triangle island.................	July 15, 19......	300	None breeding.	
East Haycocks	Aug. 17, 25.....	3,200	June 26........	6,000
Solander island...................	July 20.... ...	None seen.	June 27..... .	500

To this should possibly be added about thirty-five, which were seen by the commissioners off Hope island, September 3 and 4, 1915, where it may be, as the Nawhitti Indians aver, there is a small rookery. This was not visited either in 1913 or 1916.

There is little difference in the total estimate in the two cases, but a comparison of the individual rookeries bears out the statement made in the earlier report that to get the extent of the whole sea lion population, the number seen on the rookeries must be increased by an unknown number representing those in the water at the same time.

Taking the cape St. James rookery in the first place, if the whole 1913 herd was on the rocks when Dr. Newcombe made the enumeration and the whole 1916 herd was on the rock when the commissioners made the enumeration, there is no accounting for the reduction of the numbers as no raids were made on the rookery for the bounty in 1915 and very few were killed that could have belonged to the herd. The discrepancy is even greater than would appear from the above figures. The 1913 enumeration was made on June 12 and 13, when, as was stated in the report, but few pups had been born. In 1916 the enumeration was made a month later, when the pups of the year would not only all be born, but all able to take to the water. To make a more correct

---

[1] Provincial Fisheries Department's Report, British Columbia, 1913, pp. R131-R145, with 16 plates.

comparison it would be necessary to add about 500 to the 1913 number for the pups that were born in that year. Unless in the meantime there was an epidemic, or an extensive migration took place, neither of which is probable, the number on the rocks on July 13, 1916, did not by any means represent the whole herd. The fact that several were seen at various points even up to 25 miles from the rookery, bears this out. It is even probable that the two bachelor males (?) seen on Butterworth rocks belonged to this herd.

In this connection mention should be made of a conversation which the commissioners had at Claxton on July 15, with a Haida Indian, Timothy Tait, belonging to the Ninstints tribe, who is recognized by the Haida as the principal owner of the cape St. James rookery. He said that he didn't think the placing of the new lighthouse on the island of cape St. James had made any difference to the rookery, to which, as usual, he had paid several visits during the year (he had killed a number of sea-lions for food). He said he and his people found scattering pups at all times of the year, although the months of June and July were the most productive.

Coming next to the Sea Otter group, the only exact comparison of the two years can be made in the case of the Pearl rocks and Watch rock, since the time of the year almost exactly coincides. The large reduction shown in 1916 was to be expected from the number of onslaughts made on this portion of the rookery in the interval. Watch rock, which was a breeding place in 1913, evidently is one no longer. The portion of the rookery on Virgin rocks shows no material difference. Apparently the number killed has not materially decreased the size of the herd, unless, since the 1913 count was made over two months later in the year, it is quite possible a smaller percentage of the whole number was on the rocks.

In the spring of 1892, when J. M. Macoun, C.M.G., was acting on the Behring Sea Commission to make an enumeration of the fur seals, he visited these rocks and some notes in his diary, which he kindly put at the disposal of the commission, helps out in this comparison. On May 12, writing of the Virgin group, he says: " The largest island was then approached, and, as the sea-lions, by which it was covered, did not take alarm, a careful estimate was made of their numbers. Making allowance for all possible kinds of error, I can safely say, there were 1,500 on the one island, and more than 2,000 in the group." As this estimate was made on May 12, no pups of the year could have been counted. Hence the number, over 2,000, must be compared with the number apart from the pups, estimated at 1,500, in 1916. If this indicates anything, it is that, instead of a natural increase, which should be considerable in fourteen years, there has been a decided decrease here as on Pearl rocks. The difference of the attitude of the sea-lion towards mankind is striking. After seeing so many exhibitions of timidity in 1916, it is hard for the commissioners to realize that, not so very long since, the sea-lion did not take alarm at the approach of a boat, even at a time distant from the pupping season.

In the cape Scott group, the reduction in number on Triangle island, noted in 1913, has continued to the ultimate conclusion, as now no lions breed on the island. At the East Haycocks, the figures would indicate a great increase in number during the three years, when, as a matter of fact, there should have been a great decrease, since 2,290, from which the muzzles were taken, were killed, besides many that were not retrieved. During the summer of 1913, Mr. Grinnell and his men hunted the sea-lions on and around the Haycocks, until they had secured 500 hides. The surprise, therefore, is not that W. A. Newcombe did not see more than he did when he visited this rookery late in August, but that he saw as many as he did, after so much hunting. The large number seen on the rocks in 1916 did not represent the whole herd, since, as has been stated, numerous lions were seen in the water and on the rocks from cape Russell to cape Scott.

Considering, finally, the Solander island rookery, it will be noted that Dr. Newcombe saw none when passing on July 20, and that others passing near the same

8 GEORGE V, A. 1918

time, notably Captains Gillam and Troup, who took special notice, at Dr. New-combe's request, saw no sign of any, hence it was supposed that it was not a breeding place. Since on June 27 the pups were large enough to take to the water, they are able evidently to feed for themselvs by July 20, and the whole herd was away from the rookery. The majority of them must have been away even on June 27, as there were not nearly so many on the rocks as there were on September 14, 1915, when it was estimated that there were upwards of 1,000 visible. At that time the lions were present both on Solander island proper and the small outlying rock (see fig. 15), while on June 27 they were entirely confined to the outlying rock.

The number that haunt Barkley sound cannot well be counted here. If they are from a British Columbia rookery, they have probably been counted in with the others, and if, which is more probable, they come from the Jagged islet rookery, off the Washington coast, they cannot properly find a place in this enumeration.

Summing up the whole matter, although the enumeration in 1913 as well as that in 1916 was as well done as it could be, by making a single visit or few visits to each rookery, there are little data for comparison of the relative numbers in the two years. The estimate on the rookeries is slightly higher in 1916 than in 1913, but that is largely because in the majority of cases the visit was made at a more opportune time. It would not be legitimate to draw the conclusion from the figures that the number of sea-lions was greater in 1916 than in 1913, especially in the face of the fact that 8,000 animals had been killed in the intervening period. The only instance where a direct comparison could be made, viz., at Pearl and Watch rocks, there was evidence of a decided diminution. While in round numbers 10,000 fairly well represents these seen on the rocks at the rookeries, there is a large number besides these, possibly even as great a number or greater, scattered over a wide area along the whole coast.

19. THE RIVERS INLET SITUATION.

Having finished the examination of the rookeries, the whole attention of the commission was turned to the Rivers inlet situation. The return from Queen Charlotte islands on July 17 should have been at the height of the season for sockeye—the special tit--bit for the sea lion—during which time the depredations are most serious. Judging from the number reported in previous years, the commission concluded that there should be no difficulty in getting several sea-lions, shot right in the fishing area, that the stomachs might be examined at a time there would be every chance of seeing the quantity and nature of the food before it would be digested to any extent.

From the outset, however, the prospects were none too promising. The season was wet and backward, the fish were running low, so that catches were very small. Although sea-lions were reported in the inlet, they were much less numerous than in preceding years, but torn nets and mutilated fish were shown to indicate that they still were doing damage.

At several canneries along the inlet there were Indians who had hunted fur seals. If any of these could be obtained to shoot and spear the sea-lions, the best results could be expected. Because of the poor season, every available man was required to fish, and it proved no easy matter to get any of them to undertake sea-lion hunting. After some delay, a Sitka Indian, Louis, agreed to try his luck, but no one with experience could be obtained to go with him. The best that could be done was to hire an Indian boy, Jimmie, as boat puller. These two were supplied with a boat from one of the canneries, a rifle, ammunition, and a spear and taken down to where some of the outermost nets in the inlet were drifting, as it was here that the most damage was reported. They were out with the nets on Wednesday and Thursday nights, July 19 and 20 (the lions did not bother in the daytime), while the *Emoh* was moored at the Goose Bay fishing camp near by. Neither sound nor sight of sea-lion was noticed on either occasion, although the fishermen still reported their presence.

The following detailed reports were obtained from the fishermen in the neighbourhood on Thursday morning:—

Boat 1397 reported seeing two sea-lions near the nets the previous night.

Boat 4867 reported being bothered the previous night by the sea-lions, but not as much as the night before.

Boat 4901 reported that sea-lions had torn the net the previous night.

Boat 4876 reported that sea-lions had been seen all afternoon the day before down by the point.

Boat 1381, manned by a Jap, reported no trouble.

Boat 1405, also manned by a Jap, reported that sea-lions were on the net the night before between 8 and 9 o'clock.

Boat 4791 reported no trouble the previous night, but some the night before.

Boat 4588 reported that fish had been taken from the net and eaten about 11 o'clock the previous night. Claimed by fisherman that he had lost 50 fish in a week, shown by the heads and tails left in the net.

Boat 1398, manned by a Jap, reported that he had seen sea-lions in the net about 10 o'clock in the morning.

Boat 4915, from the Good Hope cannery, reported disturbance by sea-lions in the net the previous night.

An independent boat reported that he had seen sea-lions in the inlet at 4 o'clock the previous afternoon.

Boat 4870, a Good Hope cannery boat, reported having seen sea-lions during the night.

Boat 4844 reported having noticed sea-lions in the inlet the previous night at 9 o'clock.

Boat 1416 reported that fish had been eaten by sea-lions on the net at 8 o'clock the previous night.

Boat 1153, manned by a Jap, reported that he had not been bothered with sea-lions.

Boat 1394, manned by a Jap, reported having seen sea-lions in the fishing area at 11 o'clock the previous night.

After the negative results of Wednesday and Thursday nights, Manager Inrig and Net Foreman Anderson (it may be mentioned here that cannery managers and men, especially those at Wadhams where the commission made its headquarters, gave every assistance in the investigation consistent with the serious demands on their time occasioned by their own interests) intimated that some of the white fishermen would be willing to give assistance. Accordingly, several of them were supplied with ammunition and a substantial reward was offered for each sea-lion brought in. Louis went out with one of these fishermen to be right at the net as Jimmie in the meantime had been discarded. Friday night proved no better than the others, although some torn nets and mutilated fish were still shown as evidence of the sea-lions' presence.

The weekly close season lasts from 6 a.m. on Saturday to 6 p.m. Sunday. The net foreman offered the use of two nets for Saturday night if permission could be obtained from Fisheries Overseer Saugstad, the idea being that if two nets, and only two, were put out Saturday evening, all the inducements for the sea-lions would be centred around these nets. Mr. Saugstad readily granted permission and arrangements were made to carry the plan into effect. Two men were assigned to each boat. S. Simonsen of Sea Otter cove, V.I., went with Louis in the one boat, while G. Bjerregard, of Holberg, V.I., and J. C. Holm, of Campbell river, V.I., manned the other. From long experience these men were thoroughly acquainted with fishing conditions in the outer part of the inlet. The commissioners, as on previous occasions, remained near by in Goose bay. Early in the morning the men were picked up but no sea-lions had been shot and there was little evidence of their presence except the remains of three sockeye and one humpback that were found in the nets. A photograph was taken of these remains (se fig. 34.) It is interesting and instructive to compare this photograph with one taken at the Canadian Fish and Cold Storage plant at Prince Rupert, September 8, 1915, which shows the way in which salmon are mutilated by hair seals (see fig. 35.)

20. LITTLE EVIDENCE OF SERIOUS DAMAGE IN 1916.

After a week of negative results there was no encouragement to stay longer and the commission prepared to depart on the following morning. As the fishermen would all be fishing again on Sunday night, they were encouraged to make a final effort to get sea-lions while the commissioners were still in the neighbourhood. The *Emoh* anchored in Goose bay for the night, and in the morning (July 24), since there were no results reported, a start was made for home at 4.30. As the fishermen were still confident that sea-lions could be captured in the inlet, they were assured that the offer of reward would hold good until the end of the season, if the stomachs were sent to the Biological station for examination. No claim has yet been made for such reward.

21. PROBABLE AMOUNT OF INJURY DONE BY THE SEA-LION.

It will be seen from the above account that the commission spared no pains to get concrete evidence on the situation at Rivers inlet. If a week of such endeavour at the height of the season could produce no positive results, there was no hope that a whole season's residence there would do so. Such being the case, the commission feels justified in stating that, as far as the 1916 season was concerned, the sea-lions were not a very decided menace to the fishing in the inlet. The *Emoh* travelled several miles up and down the inlet every day during the sojourn there, and only on one occasion was there seen a trace of a sea-lion, and at that time only one was seen. The majority of the men that fished in the outer part of the inlet were questioned, none of whom reported having seen more than four or five. The sea-lion is undoubtedly to blame for some torn nets and mutilated fish, but that he alone is to blame is open to question. On account of his bad reputation, all the blame is put on him whether he deserves it or not. It might be mentioned that nets are commonly torn at other fish centres where the men scarcely know what a sea-lion looks like. All the fishermen agree in declaring that the damage in 1916 was much less than in the previous years. If any further evidence is needed to show that the commission is more than justified in making this stand, it is supplied by a letter to the secretary from Mr. Frank Inrig, dated November 19, after the close of the fishing season. It reads as follows:—

To the Secretary of the Sea-Lion Commission,
Room 929 Birks Building, Vancouver, B.C.

DEAR SIR,—As manager of the British Columbia Packers' Canneries, Wadhams and Brunswick, at Rivers inlet, I can speak with knowledge of the depredations of the sea-lions in former years to the commercial fisheries at Rivers inlet. Up to two years ago these depredations were great, and in terms of money, costly to the canneries.

But the expenditure of a few thousand dollars on bounties by the Federal Government, two years ago, resulted in many sea-lions, both young and old, being killed at and on the rookeries in the Pacific, and besides that a thorough scare being thrown into all the sea-lions frequenting the waters adjacent to Rivers inlet. The sea-lions, always timid, became exceptionally timorous in the presence of man, and shunned rather than sought the fishing areas. This to my mind was due to the hunting of sea-lions induced by the offer of a bounty.

In the year 1916 the sea-lions were not excessively harmful. They did not bother the fishing operations at Rivers inlet to any great degree, and not at all as they did three years ago. This I attribute to the effect of the hunting under the bounty system, and also to the fact that before the season opened for fishing the sea-lions on the Sea Otter group of rookeries were pretty thoroughly scared by being shot at and in some cases killed by fishermen at Rivers inlet. I think they have lost their voraciousness and courage to appear where man is and where fishing operations are being carried on at Rivers inlet.

Now I do not think the sea-lions should be killed off as long as they remain as quiet as they did this year, for their hides may still be made use of for commercial purposes and their carcasses turned into hen food or fertilizer, but I do think that the Federal Government, through the Fisheries Overseer at Rivers inlet, might spend two hundred dollars a year on ammunition to be served out to the fishermen for them to make a scare raid on the Sea Otter group of rookeries every year before the salmon fishing begins, in order to terrorize the sea-lions and make them fearful of man. This would keep them away from the fishing operations throughout the season and protect the fish and the gear of the fishermen. Don't kill off the sea-lions, but strike terror into them.

If this communication is of any use to you, you are at liberty to do with it as you wish.

Yours faithfully,

FRANK INRIG.

Vancouver, B.C.,
November 19, 1916.

There are still large numbers of sea-lions along the British Columbia coast. On the rookeries alone over 10,000 were seen in June and July, 1916. The rookery estimate is not sufficiently accurate as an index of the whole number to show the reduction that took place by the slaughter of 8,000 sea-lions in 1914-15 and to some extent in 1913, except in the case of some of the rocks of the Sea Otter group, where extensive diminution was indicated.

The menace to the fishing industry in Rivers inlet, so much complained of in previous years, had largely disappeared in 1916.

The Steller sea-lion undoubtedly eats large quantities of food fishes at certain times of the year, but for the remainder of the year there is little or no evidence as to what he does eat. Since it has been shown that fish not used as food as well as squid and devil fish are eaten, he cannot at all times be the epicure that some people would have us believe. Although he requires animal food, it is probable that he will take any kind available in quantity sufficient to satisfy his hunger. It is even possible that in helping to keep down other injurious species he does more good than harm to the fishing industry, provided he can be kept away from the nets or other fishing gear. Reference has been made to the influence the sea-lion may have on the dogfish question and the dogfish is not the only carnivorous species that is taken as food.

8 GEORGE V, A. 1918

22. SUGGESTED CONTROL OF DESTRUCTION OF SEA-LIONS.

The economic side of the question has been discussed and it is not necessary to refer to it again except to mention two points. The first is that the price of leather is rapidly going up, thus adding force to the argument as to the value of sea-lion skins. The second is with reference to the sea-lion carcass. It has been truly said that the flesh should make good fertilizer and poultry food, but it must be remembered that up to the present, plants for producing marine animal fertilizer on this coast have not been especially noted for their financial successes. Sea-lion carcasses cannot be taken to any of the fertilizer plants now in existence and made use of at a profit. With the processes now in use, it would not pay to erect a fertilizer plant to make use of fish offal at Rivers inlet or any other fishing centre where the fishing season is so short. No line of economic research in connection with the fishing industry on this coast offers a more promising field than that to do with the elimination of waste or rather the transmutation of waste products to products of commercial value at a cost that will ensure a reasonable profit on the outlay. When cheaper methods of producing fertilizer and poultry food have been worked out, the sea-lion carcass may become an important factor.

The commissioners have no hesitation in stating that they can see no valid reason at present at any rate for adopting any plan looking toward total extermination of the Steller sea-lion. Even when its depredations were most serious it has been shown that these can be reduced to a negligible quantity in a comparatively short time. Since that is so, it should not be a difficult matter to keep the depredation at a minimum. It may be well that, as Manager Inrig has suggested, this could be done by spending $200 for ammunition each year to scare them away and terrorize them. If it could be done at Rivers inlet it should be done equally well at Barkley sound, possibly better since the lions come in there apparently in a single group about the first of November. If this were done it should be under the control of the Federal Department of Fisheries, as Mr. Inrig suggests. If the scare is not sufficient, it might be advisable to materially reduce the numbers of sea-lions at the rookery responsible for the depredation, when the menace became threatening. In either case the operation should be so controlled that the greatest commercial value could be obtained. Indiscriminate and promiscuous killing should not be tolerated.

While the number of sea-lions is as great as it is at present, it might be legitimate to allow the killing of a certain number each year as in the case of all other species of commercial value, provided that not more than the number which would represent the annual increase were taken, under conditions that would ensure conservation.

CHARLES F. NEWCOMBE,

WM. HAMAR GREENWOOD,

C. McLEAN FRASER.

23. APPENDIX A.

I. FORMAL QUESTIONS SUBMITTED TO SALMON CANNERS AND OTHERS.

SEA-LION COMMISSION.

(Appointed under Authority Biological Board of Canada.)

1. Are Sea-Lions injurious to the Fisheries of British Columbia?..................
2. Have your own fishing operations ever been injured or interfered with by them?...
3. Please state the nature of such damage this year and the estimated loss:

   Gear   ..   .. $...........
   Mutilated fish   ..   ..
   Diverted run of fish   ..   ..

4. Other years?..
5. Is the lessened run of fish (if any) attributable to Sea-Lions?..................
6. Has the Herring Fishery been interfered with this year by Sea-Lions?............
7. Have you noticed any steady increase year by year to the amount of injury caused
  by Sea-Lions?..
8. Are Sea-Lions of any commercial value?....................................
9. Do they assist your fisheries in any way?....................................

*[Methods of dealing with Sea-Lions if considered to be injurious to the
Fisheries of B.C.]*

1. Do you recommend complete extermination or merely a reduction in numbers?....
2. Could your company deal with this question in your neighbourhood without
  Government aid?..
3. If not, in what manner could the Government most effectually aid you?.........

   [A] By employing hunters under Government supervision?..............
   [B] By offering a bounty open to all willing to hunt?..................
   [C] By providing money or ammunition to be expended under the control
  of the fishing companies?...

4. Can you give information as to the existence of Rookeries or other places frequented
  by Sea-Lions in your neighbourhood?....................................
5. What is the best time for killing them?......................................
6. What is the best method?..
7. What is the best evidence on which to pay the bounty?..........................
  (At present the muzzle is taken as proof.)
8. Should the bounty be paid for pups, or adults, or both?.....................
9. What has been the effect of the bounty for killing Sea-Lions upon this year's
  fishing?...
10. Have you any remarks or suggestions to make not covered by the above list of
  questions?..
11. Have you examined the contents of Sea-Lion stomachs?......................

II. FORMAL LETTER SENT BY THE SECRETARY OF THE COMMISSION TO CANNERS AND OTHERS.

SEA-LION COMMISSION.

To the Manager,

 Dear Sir,—On behalf of the Sea-Lion Commission appointed under the authority
of the Biological Board of Canada, we invite your cordial assistance in getting information and opinions regarding the alleged depredations of these animals.

 It has been stated that sea-lions destroy fish and fishing gear and interfere with
the free prosecution of fishing operations by means of seine nets and other appliances.

38a—4

8 GEORGE V, A. 1918

It also has been suggested that the sea-lions be exterminated or so thoroughly attacked to death by man as to frighten them away from their depredatory raids, and that this be encouraged by giving a bounty of two dollars ($2) a sea-lion, such bounty to be paid on presentation of the muzzle of the animal as voucher for its extinction.

We will be glad if you will answer the questions set out in the enclosed form to the best of your knowledge and belief, and add any observations you may think fit. It has been suggested that the canneries, where any depredations from sea-lions occur, might be left to handle the problem themselves without any idea of government bounty, on the assumption that fishermen attached to the canneries would protect their own interests.

Your speedy attention to the requests made on you in this letter and enclosed form will be appreciated and will assist the sea-lion commissioners in the preparation of their report on the whole question.

APPENDIX B.

NUMBER of Sea-Lions on which bounty has been paid in British Columbia for the fiscal year 1915-1916.

Name of Claimant.	Number Paid For.	Where Killed.	Amount of Bounty paid.
			$ cts.
Andrew Spalding	24	Banks island	48 00
Henry Rudland	1	Butterworth rocks	2 00
George Jones	1	Massett	2 00
J. W. Robinson	11	Price island	22 00
John Wootten	20	Calvert island	40 00
Henry Brown	12	Bonilla banks	24 00
Wm. Leighton	1	Tree Nob island	2 00
Peter Robinson	1	Stephens island	2 00
David Parnell	2	Butterworth rocks	4 00
George Allen	15	Virgin rocks	30 00
J. Wootten	342	Sea Otter group	684 00
Jas. Robinson	2	Aristazable island	4 00
J. Wootten	49	Sea Otter group	98 00
F. S. Carpenter	1	Price island	2 00
Henry Brown	2	Bonilla banks	4 00
A. Goodman	50	Virgin rocks	100 00
L. H. Hogan	97	" "	194 00
Geo. Allen	57	" "	114 00
D. McLennan	63	" "	126 00
J. Wootten	1,174	East Haycocks	2.348 00
Dan. McCloskey	153	Pearl and Virgin rocks	506 00
F. S. Carpenter	26	Price island	52 00
Spruce Marten	2	Seymour inlet	4 00
Lake Joe	51	Virgin rocks	102 00
Jacob White	82	Sea Otter group	164 00
Chief Schwish	1	Village island	2 00
James Rush	1	Ucluelet	2 00
Wm. Taylor	2	Otter point	4 00
Dan. Quital	1	Duncan bay	2 00
Jacob White	442	East Haycocks	884 00
Albert Thompson	180	Virgin rocks	360 00
Tom George	1	Smith's inlet	2 00
Benson Keatta	1	Abousat	2 00
Wm. Fatty	1	Abousat	2 00
Joe Hayes	1	Long Beach	2 00
Joe Williams	2	" "	4 00
Joe Martin	2	Cape Cod	4 00
Abram Jeffries	1	Thormanby island	2 00
Totals	2,875		5,750 00

EXPLANATION OF FIGURES.

1. Wadhams cannery, Rivers inlet. The *Emoh* is the white boat in the right foreground.

2. The largest of the Pearl rocks.

3. Watch rock.

4. The largest of the Virgin rocks after all the adult sea-lions had taken to the water.

5. Male sea-lion killed on Watch rock.

6-12. Groups of sea-lion pups on Pearl and Virgin rocks.

13. Male sea-lion killed on one of the Virgin rocks, and two pups.
    (2-13 were taken June 25, 1916.)

14. A figure to show the position at Solander island relative to cape Cook.

15. Solander island.

16-18. The outlying rock at Solander island, taken as the sea-lions were leaving it.

19-22. Remnants of the herd, showing some of the largest males.

23. Sea-lions in the water at Solander island.
    (14-23 were taken June 27, 1916.)

24. A figure to show the relative position of cape St. James island, on which the lighthouse is situated, to the main island, Kunghit. Four groups of rocks extend in a chain southward from cape St. James.

25. A figure to show the position of the first two groups of rocks relative to cape St. James island.

26. The first group of rocks south of cape St. James island.

27. The second group.

28. The third group.

29. The fourth and final rock. It was on the second and third of these groups that the sea-lions were seen in abundance.

30-33. Views of the sea-lion herd on the rocks at cape St. James.
    (24-33 were taken July 9, 1916.)

34. The remains of three sockeye and one humpback (the largest piece being the humpback) taken from a net in Rivers inlet July 23, 1916, said to have been mutilated by sea-lions.

35. Remains of salmon taken from the nets near Prince Rupert, September 8, 1915, said to have been mutilated by hair seals.

36. Scow on which Dr. Newcombe and Mr. Patch examined sea-lions in December, 1915, near Kildonan cannery, Barkley sound.
    (Photos 1-35 by C. M. Fraser, 36 by C. F. Newcombe.)

38a—4½

Fig. 1.

Fig. 2.

Fig. 3.

Fig. 4.

Fig. 5.

Fig. 6.

Fig. 7.

Fig. 8.

Fig. 9.

Fig. 10.

Fig. 11.

Fig. 12.

Fig. 13.

Fig. 14.

Fig. 15.

Fig. 16.

Fig. 17.

Fig. 18.

Fig. 19.

Fig. 20.

Fig. 21.

Fig. 22.

Fig. 23.

Fig. 24.

Fig. 25.

Fig. 26.

Fig. 27.

Fig. 28.

Fig. 29.

Fig. 30.

Fig. 31.

Fig. 32.

Fig. 33.

Fig. 34.

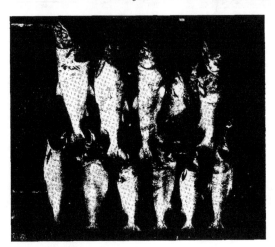

Fig. 35.

Fig. 36.

LOBSTER INVESTIGATIONS AT LONG BEACH POND, N.S.

(A. P. KNIGHT, M.A., M.D., F.R.S.C., Professor of Animal Biology, Queen's University, Kingston, Ont.)

RECOMMENDATIONS.

1. That the rearing operations hitherto conducted by the Board at Long Beach pond be discontinued.

2. That the executive committee consider the advisability of securing from the Fisheries Branch of the Department of Naval Service full control over the operation of one of the present lobster hatcheries, in which to conduct a series of experiments on the rearing of lobster fry, using warm sea-water, as suggested by Professor Macallum.

3. That the executive committee confer with the department as to the best method of collecting statistics regarding the relative numbers of male and female lobsters trapped next season, and also the percentage of females carrying fertilized eggs.

4. That several more enclosures be built at a moderate cost, by either the Board or by the Fisheries Department at different points along the maritime coast, for the purpose of determining more definitely the percentage of commercial lobsters which extrude eggs in July and August.

ACKNOWLEDGMENTS.

Acknowledgment is due the Department of Naval Service for furnishing a plentiful supply of both berried and commercial lobsters for the purpose of carrying on the experiments described in the following report; also for placing at the disposal of the Board the services of Mr. Andrew Halkett. Mr. Halkett gave us every assistance. More particularly, he kept an accurate count of the lobsters received at the pond, allotted to the various enclosures, and returned to the sea.

The Board is also indebted to the department for moving the rearing plant from the southwest end of the pond, and placing it within the cement pound.

POUND AND POND.

In the following report the reader must distinguish carefully between the natural pond of some 5 acres, and the artificial pound of about three-fourths of an acre, enclosed by cement walls and forming the northeast part of the pond.

Fig. 1.—Long Beach Pond viewed from the northeast end. In the foreground can be seen first the mess-house; beyond this, the cement pound; further away is the larger part of the pond. In the distance can be seen the engine house and plant for rearing lobsters.

8 GEORGE V, A. 1918

Last year, 1914, because of the excessive leakage of water from the pound, the Board approved of the location of an experimental rearing plant of four boxes at the southwest end of the pond, and my report upon the operations of that year has been already published.

LEAKAGE.

On December 18, 1914, the Board was notified that the leakage, which had persisted throughout the previous summer, had been stopped, and that there was at that date a depth of 6½ feet of water in the pound at low tide. During the winter of 1915, however, the leakage again developed and was again reported stopped on June 26, 1915. At this date there was said to be a depth of 5 feet 8 inches of water at low tide.

On my arrival, July 3, 1915, the pound was again leaking, not copiously, it is true, but sufficiently to show that in the course of a few days or weeks the rearing boxes, 4 feet in depth, would likely be resting in the mud. As a precaution, therefore, against possible injury to our larvæ, the boxes were reduced in depth to 2½ feet. On the assumption that there would be, as intimated, 6½ feet of water at low tide, a space of 4 feet would intervene between the bottom of our shallow boxes and the mud beneath.

At Wickford, R.I.—the original home of the plant—the depth of water below the boxes is 12 feet at low tide, excepting at one corner, where it is only 5½ feet. At Long Beach it was hoped that a depth of 4 feet might suffice to test the scheme. Last year at low tide there were only between 20 and 22 inches of water below our boxes; this year, after operating our plant for seventeen days, the boxes were resting in the mud, so great was the leakage.

Fig. 2.—West side of cement pound showing leakage of water. Over the ironrods at the upper left hand corner of the illustration can be seen the gearing of the rearing apparatus inside of the cement pound.

At the extreme low water of August 7, two of the boxes were resting 5 inches in the mud. Measurements at eleven different points around our apparatus gave the

SESSIONAL PAPER No. 38a

following depths of water, 21 inches, 22, 17, 20, 17, 19, 19, 23, 24, 26, 24, or an average of 21 inches, in which to float our apparatus. It can scarcely be expected that an apparatus, which requires at least 10 feet of water in which to operate, can be made to operate successfully in a depth of 21 inches.

FIRST HATCHING.

"Our first hatching began July 12, and in two days we had about 40,000 larvæ in the four boxes. While only an odd diatom could be found on the fry during the first day, large numbers were visible by the fifteenth. As the diatoms increased, the fry became "fuzzy" to the naked eye. Both last year and this the effect of the diatoms was largely, if not solely, mechanical. Feeding was interfered with, the animals became exhausted with the effort of swimming, sank to the bottom, and soon died.

The remarkable thing about this mortality was that last year it was caused by the diatom *Synedra investiens*, whereas this year it was caused by *Licmophora Lyngbyei*. Why the principal destructive organism should have been different in the two years is difficult to understand, unless it were due to the fact that in 1914 the sea-water reaching our boxes came through the sand, gravel, and mud of the sea-wall, whereas, in 1915 it came through an earthenware pipe from the open sea.

As soon as it became apparent that this season's fry were likely to share the same fate as those of last year, the contents of two of the boxes were transferred to St. Mary's bay, in order, if possible, to save their lives. Meanwhile the leakage steadily grew worse. On the 19th the average depth of water below the boxes was only 10 inches. As a result, good ventilation became impossible, because the water drawn in through the bottom windows gradually became muddy. It was resolved, therefore, not to use more than two boxes for rearing purposes for the remainder of the season. The other two were fitted up with shelters, or nests, for adult lobsters, so that more accurate observations could be made upon them than was possible in the compartments of the pound.

DETENTION DEVICES.

It should, perhaps, be explained that we employed five different devices, or enclosures, for impounding adults. The smallest was the crate, about 3 feet by 2 feet by 2 feet, which floated on the water, and could be used for temporary purposes only. The second was our rearing boxes, 10 feet by 10 feet by 2½ feet, with revolving paddles inside, so as to aerate the water, as described in the report of last year. The third was the compartment, 20 feet by 10 feet by the varying depth of the water at high and at low tide. The wooden slats of which it was constructed were only about 4½ feet high. As can be seen from the illustration, there were six of these compartments within the cement pound. The fourth enclosure was the pound, and the fifth, the pond, but these two latter were so large that is was impossible to use them for observation purposes. The compartments could be used for observation purposes only at low water. The real purpose of their construction was to serve as sub-divisions of the pound, in which lobsters could be kept for experimental and observational purposes.

FAILURE.

We had even worse luck this season than last. Of the 20,000 fry which we tried to rear in the two remaining boxes, beginning July 12, only twenty-one remained alive on the 30th of July, and they were all in the second stage of development. Not one had moulted a second time, and they had taken thirteen days before moulting even

38a—5½

once. Of the 20,000 to 22,000 fry which we tried to rear at a second trial, beginning August 2, only 146 were alive on August 17, and these also were all in the second stage.

In the August rearing the larvæ were shaded from the sunlight by heavy painted canvas screens lying close over the boxes; in July they were not. The effect of the shading appeared to be to reduce the first stage from thirteen days to nine days, and to lessen the number of diatoms; but the larvæ died just the same.

It is, of course, true that the warmer water in August (about one degree) may have had more to do with the shortening of the first stage than the exclusion of light. Indeed, the influence of direct sunlight upon larvæ is still an open question. To be sure, the fry, when left to themselves, swim straight into the light, but it does not follow that because they do so, the result to themselves is necessarily beneficial.

Fig. 3.—Showing the interior of the cement pound.   The six latticed compartments are for retaining lobsters so that they can be studied at close range.

Leaving out for the present the influence of light, it may well be asked: "What favourable conditions exist at Wickford, that enable the operators there to raise 40 per cent of their fry to the crawling or fourth stage, which do not exist at Long Beach pond?" And the answer is: first, too slight a depth of water under our rearing boxes, thus favouring the entrance of mud and diatoms from the bottom; secondly, the presence in the water of an unusual number of diatoms not generally found in open sea-water;* thirdly, too low a temperature of water. While the temperature at Wickford varies during the rearing season from 68° to 75°, the mean average temperature at Long Beach this season was only 58·09° for July, and 58·9° for August. The two following tables give the daily temperatures at Long Beach for July and August, respectively:—

---

* Professor McClement's Report "Diatoms and Lobster Rearing"—Contributions to Canadian Biology, 1915-16. Supp. 6th Ann. Rep. Dept. Naval Service (Fisheries), Ottawa, 1917.

SESSIONAL PAPER No. 38a

TEMPERATURES and kind of weather at Long Beach Pond, during the month of July, 1915.

Date.	Wind.	Temperature of Pound Water.			Temperature air outside.	Weather.
		Maximum.	Mean.	Minimum.		
		°	°	°	°	
July 12...	SW.	....	55·5	....	not taken.	Foggy.
" 13..	SW.	....	58·0	....	"	Fair.
" 14...	calm.	Temp. in St. Mary's Bay 56.8.	56·0	....	"	Fair.
" 15 ..	SW.	....	59·8	....	67·0	Foggy.
" 16...	S.	....	57·3	....	56·5	Foggy.
" 17...	SW.	....	58·0	....	59·8	Foggy and rainy.
" 18...	SW.	....	56·0	....	61·0	Foggy.
" 19 ..	SW.	....	58·0	....	not taken.	Fair to rainy.
" 20...	SW.	....	56·0	....	55·7	Foggy.
" 21...	NE.	....	58·5	....	not taken.	Raining.
" 22...	NE.	60 8	58·4	56 0	"	Cloudy.
" 23...	N.	62·0 / 62·0	60·2	57 / 60	63·0	Fair.
" 24. .	SW.	65·0 / 63·0	61·5	59·0 / 59·0	not taken.	Fair.
" 25...	E.	61.5 / 64·5	60·5	57·0 / 59·0	'	Fair.
" 26...	SW.	60·8 / 60·5	59·2	56·5 / 59·0	54·8	Foggy.
" 27...	SW.	59·0 / 57·0	55·8	58·0 / 55·0	58·0	Rainy and foggy.
" 28...	SW.	58·0 / 61·5	58·0	53·0 / 59·0	54·0	Foggy.
" 29...	SW.	61·0 / 58·5	57·5	55·0 / 55·5	60 0	Fair.
" 30...	S.	57·5 / 61·5	58·5	55·0 / 60·0	64·0	Foggy.
" 31...	SE.	61·5	59·1	56·7	63·0	Foggy.
Totals..			1161·8	. ...	716·8	

Mean average temperature of water = 58·09°.   Mean average temperature of air = 59·7°.

8 GEORGE V, A. 1918

TEMPERATURE and kind of weather at Long Beach Pond during the month of August, 1915.

Date.	Wind.	Temperature of Pound Water.			Temperature air outside.	Weather.
		Maximum.	Mean.	Minimum.		
		°	°	°	°	
Aug. 1...	S. Faired 10 A.M.	62·3 65·5	60·5	57·0 57·3	78·0	Foggy.
" 2...	Calm and Cloudy	64·7 63·6	61·3	58·0 59·0	72·0	Foggy.
" 3...	N. Sun shining.	61·0 64·0	58·5	55·0 54·7	54·8	Fair.
" 4...	S.	61·0	56·5	52·0	59·8	Fair.
" 5...	NE.	61·0 61·5	58·1	55·0 55·0	58·8	Cloudy.
" 6...	NE.	61·0 66·0	60·0	56·5 56·5	59·8	Fair.
" 7...	S.	65·0 63·0	60·5	57·0 57·5	66·5	Fair.
" 8...	SW. changed to N.	63·0	60·0	57·0	58·5	Foggy.
" 9..	Calm.	64·0 59·5	59·3	57·0 57·0	62·0	Foggy.
" 10...	SW.	60·0 59·5	58·0	57·5 56·0	65·0	Foggy.
" 11...	NE.	60·5 64·7	59·9	57·5 57·0	60·0	Fair.
" 12...	SW.	63·0	60·0	57·0	59·0	Fair.
" 13...	S.	61·5	58·7	56·0	61·0	Foggy.
" 14...	S.	55·5 59·5	56·5	55·0 55·0	55·5	Foggy.
" 15...	NE.	59·5 60·0	58·0	56·5 56·0	64·0	Foggy.
" 16...	SW.	61·0 60·5	58·8	56·3 57·3	63·0	Foggy.
" 17...	SW.	60·0	57·7	55·5	62·0	Foggy.
	Totals..................		1002·3	....	1059·7	

August Mean average temperature of water=58·9°   Mean average temperature of air=62·3°
July Mean average temperature of water=58·09°   Mean average temperature of air=59·7°.

On this subject the Rhode Island Commission remarks:—

The temperature of the water is of paramount importance in order to obtain the best results. Although it is possible to rear lobsters with some success in cold water, the best results will be obtained with water at a temperature of 65° to 75° F. This higher temperature results in a more rapid development of the lobsters. This more rapid development results, first, in a reduction of the expenses of operating the plant, because of the less time required, and, second, in a greater proportion of fry reared to the fourth stage, because in the shorter time there is less chance for death from cannibalism, parasites and injury.

Prof. A. B. Macallum has suggested that, in order to overcome the handicap of cold water, we should use sea-water that has been heated to 68° or 70°. This appears to be a good suggestion, unless its adoption would increase to too great an extent the cost of operating our plant. At a moderate calculation, about 2 cubic feet of water per minute enters, and, of course, leaves each rearing box. To heat this quantity of water from 58°, which is our average temperature, up to 70° will require the combustion of about 250 pounds of coal per day of twenty-four hours.

As the enlarged Wickford plant is composed of fifty-two boxes, the total consumption of coal for the rearing season of two months would amount to about 300 tons. Accordingly, to the regular expense of running a Wickford plant of fifty-two boxes, namely, wages of five men, gasoline, oil, food for the larvæ, wear and tear, there would have to be added in Canada the wages of an extra engineer and fireman, besides the cost of the 300 tons of coal.

WINTERING IN THE POUND.

Next to the leakage of water, the feature which attracted most attention at Long Beach during the early season of 1915 was the pitiable condition of the lobsters which had wintered in the pound. They were simply covered with growths of green, brown, and orange coloured algæ. The green measured from 1 to 3 inches in length, the brown from several inches to three feet, and the orange-coloured ones about one-quarter to one-half inch. These latter grew not alone on the body, but over the eyes, and rendered them blind, at least for the time being. Their gills varied in colour from grey to almost black, strongly suggesting that the function of these organs was impaired by a coating of the black mud in which they were compelled to live during the year.

The animals which had passed the winter in the pond were distinctly better. They were not so much infested with algæ, but the effects of their confinement became very apparent when they were compared with the commercial lobsters which were placed in the pond between May 10 and June 15. In the former the natural colours of the body were completely hidden by the grey mud and copious growth of weeds which they carried, whereas the latter showed the bright colours characteristic of the normal lobster. Moreover, the commercial ones were free from algal growths, and their gills exhibited the well-known flesh colour. The difference between pond and pound lobsters, on the one hand, and commercial lobsters, on the other, was comparable to the difference between the dirt and rags of a tramp and the cleanliness and dress of a gentleman.

CONFINEMENT.

The fundamental conditions for a healthy life are very much the same for lobsters as for other animals. They must have plenty of food, well-ventilated water, adequate exercise alternated with rest, and diffused sunlight. How many of these conditions can be said to be freely supplied to a lobster that passes all of its time in a crate, car, box, compartment of the pound, or even in the pound itself? One has but to think of the ill effects of confinement upon wild animals, or even upon domesticated animals, to realize how harmful it is. Human beings, whose occupation confines them much in factories, shops, or offices, and those who are confined in jails, asylums, or detention camps—all suffer more or less from their confinement. Is not the spread of tuberculosis among cattle largely due to their confinement in ill-ventilated stables? Do not zoological gardens also show instances of deterioration in health, due to the violation of the fundamental laws of biology? Lobsters can be no exception to the rule. When kept in confinement we cannot expect to find them in the same condition of health and vitality as when they live in the open sea. No wild animal flourishes so well in confinement as in the open. Liberty of movement is essential to health. It matters not whether lobsters are retained in small or large enclosures, or, for that matter, in the whole pond, the ill-effects upon the lobsters soon become apparent. In the case of the smaller crates and cars, the animals soon die. In the

8 GEORGE V, A. 1918

larger compartments of the pound, or pond, the ill-effects may not become apparent for several months, but slowly and surely the lobsters' health and vitality are under-mined and they finally succumb to the adverse conditions.

No doubt, by a long course of breeding and artificial selection, it might be pos-sible, in the case of the lobster, just as in the case of our domesticated animals, to breed a stock that would be less sensitive to the ill-effects of confinement, but, until we have bred such a strain, the nearer we can make the conditions of confinement approximate to the conditions in which the animal lives in the sea, the lower will be the mortality.

MUDDY BOTTOM.

Next to the copious growth of weeds, blinding and encumbering the lobsters which had wintered at Long Beach, perhaps the next most unfavourable condition was the mud. There is, of course, mud and mud. Every lobster fisherman knows perfectly well that during winter and early spring the largest catches are made off shore, on muddy or sandy bottom. In late spring or early summer the fishermen move their traps towards the shore, and find the best fishing on rocky bottom along the side of kelp or other kinds of sea-weed. But, while the lobster finds a congenial home on a soft sea-bottom, it does not follow that the animal, when compelled to pass the winter in Long Beach pound, necessarily finds the mud therein equally congenial. The mud of the pound has a disgusting odour, largely due to the gas, sulphuretted hydrogen. Every one who is familiar with this gas knows its characteristic odour, and the characteristic odour could be obtained anywhere in the central area of the pound by simply driving a wand down into the mud. For example, at low water on the morning of August 8 a spruce wand six-sixteenths by seven-sixteenths was pushed $5\frac{1}{2}$ feet into the mud by the mere pressure of the hand. This was at the north end of our engine house. At the south end, 3 feet were found. At the south end of our hatching boxes, 5 feet. At all points, on withdrawing the wand, the characteristic odour of sulphuretted hydrogen was experienced, and the adherent mud had all the appearance of a sulphide precipitate.

That the gas was really sulphuretted hydrogen became evident in another way. The gas-ladened mud blackened any board, oar, or boat that was painted with white lead, and which remained in contact with the mud for a few hours. Moreover, it precipitated soluble salts of silver, iron, copper, etc., and there is no doubt that the surface of the gill filaments were darkened and their function partially destroyed by sulphides or other particles of mud. In this way it is easy to understand how the gills of lobsters in the pound gradually turned, first, to a grey colour, and finally became almost black.

Dr. McGill, chief analyst of the Inland Revenue laboratory, Ottawa, made an examination of the mud, the super-natant sea-water, and the gills of an adult lobster which had died in the pound. He reports as follows: "The mud is chiefly silica, with a considerable amount of inter-mixed sulphide of iron. The gills of the lobster con-tained iron and phosphates, with a possible trace of sulphur."

Dean Goodwin, D.Sc. of the Kingston School of Mining, reports a similar finding to that of Dr. McGill.

MORTALITY.

The severe conditions under which the animals passed the winter seem to have affected their general health and caused a rather high death-rate. Of course, it is quite impossible to estimate the death-rate among lobsters in their natural habitat. In the sea, allowance must be made for those that die of hunger, or are killed by enemies. In the pond and pound the adults have no enemies, and, consequently, should show a low rate of mortality, otherwise there would be no reason for placing them in sanctuaries. We can only form an idea of the rate of mortality in sanctuaries by keeping track of those which die from year to year, and ascertaining, if possible, the cause of death. For example, of 167 lobsters left in the pond and pound last season (1914) only 134 could be found this season, thus showing a loss of 33. Of the 312 placed in the pond and pound this season (1915) all have been accounted for, the loss by death being a total of thirty-eight. But, just as thirty-three in the one case does not represent the true loss by death (because some of last year's lobsters may yet be recovered from the pond), so thirty-eight does not show the true mortality this year, that is, the mortality due to the ill-effects of detention in the pound or pond. The loss this year must be reduced to twenty, because eight of the thirty-eight were poisoned by the accidental use of red paint on the paddles in one of our hatching boxes, and ten others died in the course of transportation to the pound. The real loss, therefore, this year is only 6 per cent of the total, whereas, the loss on last year's numbers (if no more can be found in the pond) was nearly 20 per cent. The greatly decreased mortality this season is, undoubtedly, due to the great care exercised by the department in collecting, feeding, and distributing them, and the shorter detention period in the pond and pound. No one, who appreciates the facts, will advocate the retention of lobsters in either pond or pound for more than a few months at a time.

EGG-LAYING.

Egg laying at Long Beach this season had two peculiarities. The first was that about half the females extruded only a few hundred eggs in place of many thousands, and the second was that the eggs on probably 80 per cent of the mothers were unfertilized.

In explanation of the former fact (noticed last year also) we at first assumed that the mothers had been interrupted in the act of egg-laying by being dipped up in the net. Subsequent facts, however, showed that this was not the case, because, when such lobsters were confined in crates or cars for a few weeks, the number of eggs was never increased. Secondly, when (as happened on a few occasions) such a lobster died, *post mortem* examination showed that the beast had extruded all the ripe eggs in her ovaries, excepting perhaps half a dozen or so. This great reduction from the full complement of eggs had to be explained on some other grounds. As this peculiarity in egg-laying was limited, so far as the writer can remember, to females which had spent the winter in the pond or pound, the reduction in the number of eggs would seem to be due to the unfavourable conditions under which the animals had lived throughout the winter—crowding in a small compartment, lack of adequate food, excessive growth of algæ upon them, and the uncongenial mud of the bottom. In illustration of this subject, the following facts may be quoted. In one compartment of the pound were fifty females which had hatched their eggs in the summer of 1914 and been retained in the pound all winter. Whether they had extruded eggs last autumn and lost them during the winter or early spring is not known, but, at any rate, they were all found without eggs on April 8, 1915. On July 19 an examination of the 50 resulted, as follows:—

    22 had no eggs on them.
    21 had new eggs on them, but none with the full complement. Within a week 4 of these
        21 had lost the few eggs which they had.
    1 only had a full complement of eggs.
    2 had died.
    1 male only was present throughout the winter with these females.
    3 were unaccounted for.

It is probable that few if any of the eggs carried by these twenty-one females were fertilized, because there was only one male present in the enclosure to mate with the fifty females. It happened, unfortunately, at the time of this examination that the rearing apparatus absorbed all my attention, and, consequently, no examination of the eggs was made to see whether they were fertilized or not. Nor must it be supposed that the loss of eggs by four of these females out of the twenty-one was the only instance of the kind which came under our notice this season. On another

8 GEORGE V, A. 1918

occasion a female, which was known to carry a few eggs, was later found to be without any. In a third instance two females, both with eggs, were placed in a crate and a few days afterwards one of them was found to have lost her eggs.

Here, then, we have records of three different occasions on which lobsters lost their eggs a short time after extruding them. If unfertilized eggs "go bad" and drop off within a few weeks or even months after extrusion, it is easy to understand how our fishermen find not more than an average of 20 per cent (according to one member of the Shell Fish Commission of 1912-13) of the females carrying eggs. It may be, too, that mothers, when pressed by hunger, eat their eggs, whether fertilized or not fertilized. I have myself watched a female tearing off unfertilized eggs from her swimmerets, passing them forward and transferring them to her mouth with her maxillipedes. On examining her abdomen, the egg clusters could be seen ragged and torn on each side and partly removed. It could not be said in this instance that the eating of her eggs was the result of hunger, because all the lobsters in the pound this summer were well cared for and regularly fed.

The fourth instance of the loss of eggs was the most remarkable of all. In this case none of the eggs adhered to the abdomen. The first intimation we had that eggs were being laid was seeing them floating around in the current on the floor of one of our rearing boxes. These were all soft and jelly-like, and undoubtedly, diseased and unfertilized.

Fig. 4.—Mother lobsters carrying newly extruded eggs. These are attached to the paired swimming feet on the under surface of the abdomen. When carrying eggs, the mothers always bend the latter part of the abdomen and tail under the body so that the eggs are as well protected as if carried in a covered cup. In the illustration the abdomen is extended so as to expose the eggs to view.

MOULTING.

We had opportunities of witnessing several successful moults and also several failures to moult, followed by death. The act is too well known to require description. In healthful surroundings and under the stimulus of adequate food, the act cannot be a critical one for a vigorous animal, but, if conditions are not favourable, as in the pound, then the act may well be fraught with danger. There can be but little food in winter, especially, within the limited area of the compartments, and considering the leakage, the supply of fresh sea-water at low tide must also have been scanty. The slimy mud that covered their gills was an ever-present menace, so that the animals were weakened by their long confinement, and some of them, therefore, unfit to store materials in the body for the manufacture of the new shell or the excretion of waste material from the body. What more likely thing could happen than that some of them would succeed in moulting, while others would fail and die?

BLIND LOBSTERS.

On noticing the blind lobsters, the first question that occurred to me was to ask whether the sight would be restored after moulting. The question was generally answered in the affirmative, but not always. In the case of a female which had spent a year at least, and possibly more, in the pond, it was found that she was still blind. The algal growths had penetrated too deeply into the substance of the eye and had destroyed the underlying tissue. In one other case, the sight was impaired, but not lost; but, generally speaking, the process of moulting restored the sight.

NUMBERS OF EGG-BEARING FEMALES.

It is greatly to be regretted that statistics in regard to the relative numbers of egg-bearing lobsters are not available. The following table from Herrick's book is valuable so far as it goes. Facts of a like kind are given by Vinal Edwards for No Man's Land. Similar facts do not appear to be available in Canada, so far as the writer knows.

RECORD of the Total Catch of Lobsters at Woodshole, Mass., from December 1, 1893, to June 30, 1894, showing the number and size of egg-bearing females.

Length.	No. Males.	No. Females	Females with eggs.	Totals.	Length.	No. Males.	No. Females	Females with eggs.	Totals.
in.					in.				
6	3	4	....	7	10⅛	0	1	1	1
6¼	1	....	....	1	10¼	62	71	17	133
6½	3	4	....	7	10½	79	103	28	182
6¾	5	0	....	5	10⅝	1	....	....	1
7	45	47	1	93	10¾	18	18	2	36
7⅛	....	1	....	1	11	31	62	20	93
7¼	10	4	....	14	11¼	10	11	....	21
7½	66	47	....	113	11½	11	30	4	41
7¾	20	9	....	29	11¾	2	2	....	4
8	168	140	2	308	12	9	14	3	23
8⅛	....	1	....	1	12¼	1	....	....	1
8¼	44	29	....	73	12½	4	7	....	11
8½	143	115	7	258	12¾	....	1	1	1
8¾	26	27	1	53	13	4	4	....	8
9	170	166	13	336	13½	1	....	....	1
9⅛	....	1	1	1	14	1	....	....	1
9¼	32	38	4	70	14½	1	2	....	3
9½	148	169	24	317	15	....	3	....	3
9¾	27	29	3	56					
10	167	184	36	351	Totals......	1,313	1,344	168	2,657

Percentage of females which carry eggs, 12.

Percentage of females with eggs at No Man's Land, 63·7, but that was over twenty years ago, when lobsters were more abundant than now.

8 GEORGE V, A. 1918

These figures indicate that a much higher percentage of females are berried along the Massachusets coast than in St. Mary's bay or the Bay of Fundy. Inquiries made among the lobster fishermen, both last summer and this, go to show that out of every 1,000 to 2,000 adults, only from two to three are found to carry eggs. Is it not time that other statistics besides measurements of length should be collected and published in our annual reports?

In collecting statistics, the important points are: (*a*) the relative numbers of males and females caught during a season; (*b*) the percentage of females that carry mature, or ripe, eggs during the open season; (*c*) the percentage of females which extrude new eggs during July, August, and September; (*d*) and especially, the proportion of these eggs which are fertilized and unfertilized.

With such statistics before us for a few years we should soon know whether we are making good the wastage of lobsters or not. At present we do not know. In a vague way we conclude that, because millions of newly hatched fry are being planted annually in the sea, therefore, we must necessarily be increasing our lobster supply, or, at least, keeping the supply up to the numbers annually trapped by the fishermen. The fallacy of this reasoning is clearly realized by the Shell Fish Commission (1912-13) page 27: "The annual returns, though showing a very large increase in the money value, are really misleading, because, while the supply of lobsters is declining, the price has so materially advanced that the total value is greater to-day than at any previous period."

The results of all our hatching and all our egg-planting, therefore, has not sufficed to replenish our depleted waters: that they have increased the numbers is pure guess work. The same criticism precisely may fairly be made about rearing the fry. We are working away in the dark, increasing the chances of survival, no doubt, but without demonstrable proof of any increase in the numbers of animals which grow to maturity.

Can we not be a little more accurate in our methods? Let us first of all collect for a few years the statistics for which I am pleading. With these as a basis for comparison, let us erect, say, fifty enclosures, 20 feet by 20 feet, at a cost not exceeding $200 each, or $10,000 in all. Impound in these during July and August, twenty-five males and twenty-five females—all carefully chosen and fully mature, and I am confident that we shall get a very large increase in the number of eggs. And after all, the greatest aid in preventing the extinction of the lobster will be to increase the egg bearers. Mother ocean will feed the fry, if we protect the egg producers. But, if we continue to hatch, as has been done in the past, we never know what increase results from our efforts, but we do know that frequently we are feeding fish.

Much desirable information can probably be obtained by circularizing canners and fishermen and explaining clearly to them the objects which the department has in view.

In fact, Mr. W. S. Trask, a canner at Little River gladly gave me such information as he had at his disposal. From May 10 to June 15 he bought 7,151 adult lobsters from fishermen. He did not take the time (nor did the fishermen) to distinguish males from females, but he was confident from some observations which he had made a few years before, that there were generally more females than males. Out of the 7,151 adults which he had purchased, only thirty-five carried eggs, that is, 1 per cent, on the assumption that the sexes are equal in numbers. How can the lobster industry be kept up, if only one mother out of every 100 bears ripe eggs?

Probably few females are ever sterile. When eggs are not fertilized, one cause will probably be the lack of facilities for mating. This, at least, was apparently the

---

NOTE.—Mention should be made of the information collected by Mr. Halkett at Baker's Pond, C.B., showing the relative percentage of males and females there to be about 46 males to 54 females per hundred.

cause this year at Long Beach. Up to to August 2, forty-three females had extruded eggs, and careful examination of twenty-eight of these showed that only five carried fertilized eggs. The reason of this seems clear enough. With the fifty females which wintered in the pound, there was, as already stated, only one male. Whether this one male could fertilize the eggs of forty-nine females is certainly open to question.

It is true that the department placed thirty males and thirty females (commercial) in the pond or pound for experimental purposes this season, but, unfortunately, eight of the males were poisoned, several of them were undersized, and six others died from causes unknown. It will thus be seen that, if we take into account the relatively small proportion of males to females, and the unfavourable conditions in which both sexes were confined in the pound—I refer to the mud, not to feeding, which was carefully done,—it is not much wonder that many of the extruded eggs remained unfertilized, then softened and dropped off.

ANNUAL SPAWNING.

It was intimated in my report for 1914 that some females which had extruded eggs in August of that year were to be retained in the pound all winter, and might throw some light upon the subject of annual spawning. Of forty-seven females placed in the pound in midsummer, 1914, thirty had extruded eggs by the end of September. There were confined with these females, fifteen males. Leaving out of consideration ten females which were under 10 inches in length, the proportion of full-grown males to females was 15 to 37, or nearly 1 male to 2 females. The result was that on the 8th of April, 1915, when these thirty females were again examined, all bore fertilized eggs. In other words, 64 per cent of the females placed in the pound last June carried fertilized eggs to June of this year. As a matter of fact, most of the eggs were "laid" in August, but the important point is the large number of berried females which resulted from the experiment. These animals were not examined again until July 7, 1915, when the following results were found:—

12 had no eggs on them, being probably hatched off in the interval between April 8 and July 7.

12 were in the act of hatching their eggs.

2 had newly extruded eggs upon them.

1 was dead.

1 was lost off the dip net in removing it from the compartment.

2 could not at that date be accounted for, probably hidden in the mud.

—

30

The twelve which had old eggs upon them on April 8, but were without eggs on July 7, were placed in a compartment by themselves and re-examined again on July 29, when seven of them were found to be carrying newly extruded eggs.

These seven females with the two which bore new eggs on July 7 make a total of nine, which had carried eggs in 1914, and again extruded eggs in 1915. The remaining five of the twelve escaped from the enclosure in which they were confined, and, as a consequence, it became impossible to identify them from others in the pound, but so far as these nine lobsters are concerned, annual spawning is an undoubted fact.

One female, at least, of these seven, bore "bad" eggs, and one other, though the eggs appeared normal and of the usual number, nevertheless, carried unfertilized eggs, as shown by microscope examination.

MORE FERTILIZED EGGS.

The problem of problems in the lobster industry is not how to rear fry to the crawling stage, but how to increase the number of females which carry fertilized eggs.

8 GEORGE V, A. 1918

The artificial hatching of lobster eggs may be important, though many doubt it; the artificial rearing of lobster fry to the fourth or fifth stage may be important, though this remains to be proved, at any rate in Canadian waters; but the biggest of all lobster problems is how to increase the number of fertilized eggs. Unfertilized eggs are probably produced in vast numbers, if biennial spawning is the rule; in vaster numbers still, if annual spawning is the rule.

Reverting again to the 7,151 adults bought by Mr. W. S. Trask this season, among which he found only thirty-five berried females, and to Mr. J. W. Tidd's catch of 3,000 lobsters in 1913, among which he found only three berried females, we are faced with the problem of explaining how it happens that there were not about 3,500 berried females among Mr. Trask's purchases, if lobsters spawn annually, or 1,750 if lobsters spawn biennially, similarly with Mr. Tidd's catch, and with the catch of every lobster fisherman in the Maritime Provinces.

We have no knowledge of the extent to which the sexes mingle with each other in the sea. Conclusions based upon the tagging of lobsters and their subsequent liberation and capture may be misleading. Tagging does seem to indicate, however, that they are strongly local in their habits, and, if so, they may meet each other only at intervals and solely by accident. How different conditions are to-day for mating, compared with what they were in early colonial days when lobsters were so abundant along the Atlantic coast that after every storm they were found lying along the shore in windrows!

If the facilities for mating are lacking, this may be the reason why so few females carry fertilized eggs. If there is no mating, the mothers will extrude their eggs annually or biennially, as the case may be, but the eggs, being unfertilized, will "go bad" and subsequently drop off.

It must not be supposed, therefore, that the eggs found in June, July, August, and September on berried females are necessarily "good eggs." For breeding purposes they may be as useless as those of a pullet with which no cockerel has cohabited. As illustrating the truth of this statement, it is only necessary to point out that of twenty-eight females which extruded eggs in Long Beach pond this season, only five were found to carry fertilized eggs. These results are quite different from those of last year, but the conditions were different in the two years. In 1914 the mating lobsters were placed in a compartment specially located near the entrance of fresh sea-water from the intake pipe, and by the end of the season, as already stated, 64 per cent of the females carried fertilized eggs, as compared with 1 per cent reported by fishermen. In the case of the mating lobsters of this year, 1915, some of them, were placed at first in the pond and others of them in the pound. Subsequently they were transferred to two of our rearing boxes, and later again to the third compartment of the pound. Considering, too, that there were only 26 males to 109 females and that the transfer from one enclosure to another was unnatural; considering also the unfavourable conditions under which they lived in the pound, one can readily understand that copulation took place less frequently than under the more natural conditions of 1914. But after making every allowance for the conditions which militated against the extrusion and fertilization of eggs, we find that 44 out of 109 females extruded eggs in the summer of 1915, or over 40 per cent.

When it is remembered that the Shell Fish Commission estimated from their inquiries that the percentage of berried females ranged from 2 per cent to 40 per cent,[*] and that this latter percentage existed only where fishing is permitted in June and July, as in Northumberland strait, and when it is considered also that in these months some lobsters are carrying old eggs and others are carrying new ones, it will readily be seen that the 40 per cent does not represent the true proportion of newly extruded eggs at all. Let us find out, if possible, the correct proportion of hen-lobsters which carry new eggs, or of those which carry mature eggs, but not a combination of the two.

---

* These figures were obtained not from the Commission but by correspondence with only one member of the Commission.

MATING GROUNDS.

So few facts are known in regard to the mating of lobsters that special attention should be given to this subject next year. While the pound has proved to be useless this season as a suitable place in which to rear fry or retain adults, the southwest end of the pond, as stated in last year's report, could be made very useful, both as a sanctuary for beried females and as a mating ground for commercial lobsters. If the compartments at present in the pound were removed to the southwest end of the pond, and the cost of doing this need not exceed $200, there would then be ample space for both sanctuary and mating ground and better conditions than prevailed this past summer.

It cannot be stated too often that the great problem is how to increase the number of fertilized eggs. The hatchery cannot add a single fry to those which the mother will hatch out. On the contrary, the hatchery often starts them upon their ocean life, infected with diatoms, as shown by Professor Gorham. The rearing plant guards and feeds the fry for a brief three or four weeks, and then liberates them to take their chances in wind and tide and among a multiplicity of voracious enemies. In contrast with the uncertainty of hatching and rearing fry, an increase in the number of females carrying fertilized eggs would mean an incalculable increase in the number of fry, and consequently, a better chance of survival until they become adults.

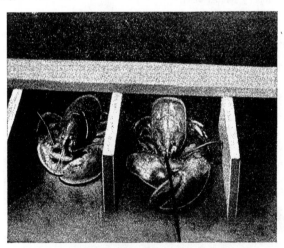

Fig. 5.—Two lobsters resting in their shelters.

To realize how greatly the number of berried lobsters may be increased, as they were actually increased in the pound in 1914 from 1 per cent to 64 per cent, we have only to consider how rapidly a farmer could increase his poultry if he bred from sixty-four hens out of a hundred, instead of from one hen. He might use a hatching apparatus (as we do for lobsters) and a rearing apparatus also, if there is such a thing for chickens, but the increase in his poultry would be slow indeed, compared with what it would be if he bred from sixty-four mothers in place of from one. If we could come anything near increasing our berried lobsters from 1 per cent to 64 per cent, we might burn down our lobster hatcheries and never notice the loss, so far as the lobster industry is concerned.

8 GEORGE V, A. 1918

Of course, there may be other causes at work, besides lack of facilities for mating, to account for the small number of berried females. If so, these causes must be studied and, if possible, removed. But, at any rate, no one can be blind enough to overlook the significance of the mating experiments of last year and this.

THE EVERYDAY LIFE OF THE LOBSTER.

While our lobster-rearing experiments at Long Beach pond, both last year and this, resulted in failure, it cannot be said that the two seasons' work was entirely barren of results. Apart from the observations which have been made on mating, and which, it is hoped, may prove even more useful to the lobster industry than any success which might have been achieved in lobster rearing, we have been able to make some contributions to our knowledge of the every day life of the lobster.

Very early in our operations of this year it was decided to use but two rearing boxes, instead of four. The other two were fitted up with shelters, or nests, for the study of adults.

Obeservations were made every day from July 20 to August 6, when the animals had to be removed. The excesive leakage from the pound left our boxes resting in the mud, and contributed not a little to bring about the death of several adults, through the lack of properly aerated water.

POSTURES.

When performing certain functions, for example, cleaning themselves, egg-laying, fighting, etc., the adults took up certain appropriate postures. One of these, which may be spoken of as the cleaning posture, was first observed among lobsters which had wintered in either pond or pound. Within a week after these animals had been placed

Fig. 6.—This illustration is from a lobster cast which has been shaped to resemble the posture of a mother lobster when hatching her eggs. The swimmerets are Visible under the abdomen and these are moved gently backwards and forwards in the water so as to assist in liberating the young from the "shell". This same posture is taken when the animal is cleaning itself.

in the rearing box, their appearance had changed very much for the better. No lady in the land could spend more time on her toilet than these lobsters did in cleaning themselves. They did not, of course, wash, massage, paint or powder their faces, nor did they curl their hair, but they did spend days and days in attempts to free themselves from the excessive growth of algæ, which covered almost every part of their body.

At first they ate voraciously; later on, much more moderately. Their only toilet instruments were the opposable thumb and finger (pincers) of their walking legs. Every part of their body which could be reached by those appendages was carefully gone over. It was no uncommon thing to see a lobster raise the first pair of walking legs over the great claws and use them in cleaning the rostrum and antennules. The antennæ (feelers) would be grasped by the pincers and drawn through between the thumb and finger, thus stripping off algæ and dirt, in much the same way as a person might strip off the excess of dirt from a string by drawing it through between his thumb and finger.

When thus cleaning themselves, the animals rest almost entirely upon the tips of their great claws and the telson which is bent at right angles to the long axis of the body. The middle region is arched slightly upward, and the walking legs are thus left almost completely free for cleaning movements.

THE HATCHING POSTURE.

This posture has often been described and does not differ from the cleaning one, excepting that the animal rests on its walking legs as well as on its great claws and telson. The movements are limited to a gentle swaying backwards and forwards of the swimming feet, evidently for the purpose of assisting the fry to liberate themselves from the egg capsule (shell).

EGG-LAYING POSTURE.

The egg-laying posture, as we saw it, was different from that described by Anderton. The general position is that of a more or less erect frog. The abdomen is bent completely under the body, and the broad tail is well spread out on each side, so as to form an almost perfect cup. The anterior part of the body is inclined at an angle of nearly

Fig. 7.—The egg-laying posture.

45°, on account of the animal resting on the tips of the great claws. The posture is such as to allow the eggs, as soon as they leave the orifice of the oviduct, to fall by gravity over the receptaculum seminis and drop easily and naturally into the abdominal cup already described. After the eggs have filled the cup, the female turns upon her back for 15 or 20 minutes and remains almost motionless, the walking legs alone swaying backwards and forwards at intervals of a minute or two. During this quiet period the egg glue is apparently hardening so as to fix the eggs to each other and to the hairs of the swimmerets.

.8 GEORGE V, A. 1918

That the egg glue requires time to harden in the water was demonstrated by the fact that one female, which was lying on her back after egg-laying, was dipped up too soon from the box and righted in position. As a result, nearly all her eggs dropped off on the board on which the observer was standing.

THE RESTING POSTURE.

This is the posture which an animal naturally adopts when left to itself in a crate, box, or other enclosure, and usually after being fed. If there are many animals

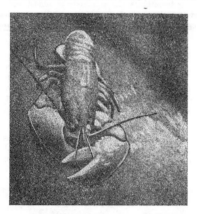

Fig. 8.—The resting posture. From a photograph of
an animal under water.

together, they will often take up this posture in one corner and lie one on top of the other. It is their usual posture in shelters.

FIGHTING POSTURE.

There is nothing new to describe about this posture. Most people who have watched lobsters when removed from the water have seen them elevate their great claws, open their scythe-like jaws, and otherwise adopt a threatening or defensive attitude. It is the regular pose of female lobsters, in defence of their eggs, and of the male lobsters towards each other. Time after time have we seen two males pass females without adopting any belligerent attitude, but as soon as they approached each other "squared off" for a fight. Though the males are generally restless, the larger ones chasing the smaller from place to place, we never actually saw one injure the other.

BIENNIAL SPAWNING.

It remains to say a few words on the subject of biennial spawning. The fact that nine lobsters spawned in 1914, and again in 1915, is beyond all question. It is also equally beyond question that out of 50 lobsters which hatched their eggs in July, 1914, and moulted in the autumn of 1914 (according to the testimony of the caretaker of the pond) twenty-two did not spawn this summer at all. If lobsters spawn biennially, then these females should have extruded new eggs in July and August of 1915, but they did not.

From the evidence which we have collected thus far at Long Beach, it is quite clear that some lobsters spawn annually, some biennially, and some do not spawn even biennially. Of course, it is only fair to point out again that the conditions in both pond and pound are unnatural, and, therefore, we need not be surprised when we meet with departures from the normal habits of the animal, whether the habit be annual or biennial spawning.

A REVIEW.

In looking over the operations of the pound for the past two years, let it be frankly acknowledged at the outset that the main purpose for which it was built has not been realized. Can it be fairly said, then, that the money spent in the purchase of the pond and the construction of the pound has been wasted? I think not.

In addition to being a sanctuary for berried females, the pound has brought about the discovery that the numbers of lobsters may be increased by bringing the sexes together. This, of course, was not the primary object for which the pound was built. So far as can be judged from public reports and from the Board's correspondence with the Fisheries Branch, the discovery was made by accident. Sixty-two commercial lobsters were sent to the pound in 1914 for the purpose of observing whether lobsters spawn annually or biennially. Long before a conclusion could be reached on the subject, it was discovered that 64 per cent. of the forty-seven females in the pound had extruded fertilized eggs—a most astonishing fact, when every fisherman in Digby County knows that only about one female in every hundred carries eggs. This opinion of the fishermen·is corroborated by Mr. Andrew Halkett. In his report upon the Baker Lobster pound, Cape Breton, 1909-10, page 16, he mentions a trip which he took with Rafuse & Son, fishermen, to seventy-five traps, containing altogether fifty-six males and sixty females. Only one of the females was berried.

Why this great difference in egg-bearing between open-sea lobsters and those in Long Beach pound? One obvious explanation is that it is due to the close intercourse between male and female lobsters in a compartment 20 feet long by 10 feet wide. The fact that 40 per cent. of the females at Long Beach this summer (1915) extruded eggs under most unfavourable conditions appears to corroborate the discovery. At any rate, the results of the two years' observations, in my judgement, amply justify the department in building a few more enclosures at different points along the maritime coast in order to test still further the extent to which egg-bearing may be artificially promoted.

Surely the expenditure of money on industrial and economic problems is one of the functions of Government. If it is not, then much of the expenditure on Experimental Agricultural Stations and on investigations into our peat and other mineral resources is unjustifiable. Far, however, from the money hitherto spent upon such scientific investigations being wasted, it is money well spent. Similarly, I trust it will be realized in a few years that the money spent upon Long Beach pond will have been amply justified either by the direct or indirect scientific results that have been achieved.

[II]

THE PEARLY FRESH-WATER MUSSELS OF ONTARIO.

By John D. Detweiler, M.A., St. Andrew's College, Toronto.

(With one figure in the text).

INTRODUCTION.

As a part of the pearly fresh-water mussel investigation, conducted by the Biological Board of Canada, a number of localities, from which promising reports had come in, were visited in August, 1916.

The investigation had a twofold object: first, to determine the abundance, species and commercial value of the mussels; and, second, to ascertain whether it would be advisable to introduce artificial propagation in any Canadian waters.

In order to facilitate the work, the Board decided to send the author to the Fairport Biological Station at Fairport, Iowa, so that he might thoroughly acquaint himself with the problem in hand.

THE UNITED STATES FISHERIES BIOLOGICAL STATION, FAIRPORT, IOWA.

This station was established in 1908, and is the centre of mussel propagation and of the investigation of problems relating thereto.

In the practical propagation of mussels the station serves as headquarters for field operations conducted throughout the Mississippi basin, including the Mississippi river and its tributaries. There may be in the field at one time from two to six field parties operating near the station or at a distance of several hundred miles. For full account see United States Bureau of Fisheries, Document 829, by Dr. Coker.

METHODS AND TECHNIQUE OF ARTIFICIAL PROPAGATION.

The methods of propagation are based upon the peculiar character of the normal course of development of the fresh-water mussels. The young mussels, with rare exceptions, when first liberated from the mother clam must become parasitic upon a fish in order to pass through the next stage of their development. To this end these young mussels—glochidia, as they are called at this stage—attach themselves to the fins or gills of a fish, if the opportunity presents itself. They already have two shells which under proper stimulus work like a small trap, and a very slight wound seems to be produced which after attachment begins at once to heal over. In this way the glochidia become more or less safely encysted and now virtually live the life of parasites, subsisting on the juices of the fish. In the course of two weeks, more or less, having completed their metamorphosis, they break away from their host, drop to the bottom and begin an independent existence.

If not over-infected, the fish seem to suffer no injurious effects. Naturally, the limit of successful infection depends on the size and nature of the fish. Careful investigation of natural and artificial infection has shown that a moderate-sized fish may carry successfully from 1,000 to 2,000 glochidia.

Mussels do not attach themselves indiscriminately, but for each species of mussel there is a limited number of species of fish that may serve as host. In some cases the number that may act as a host is apparently very exclusive. In this connection

8 GEORGE V, A. 1918

it may be mentioned that the gar, including at least the two species *L. platostomus* and *L. osseus,* has been found to be practically the only host for one of the most desirable of shells, the Yellow sand-shell *(Lampsilis anodontoides).*

In actual artificial infection of fish the operation is essentially as follows: The gravid mussels and their suitable fish hosts are placed in a vat or tub containing a requisite amount of water. The mussel is now opened, the marsupial pouch split open along its ventral border and the glochidia are squeezed out into one of the valves of the mussel, which valve also serves as a small water container. The glochidia are then poured into the tub and the water agitated, more or less, so that they will be kept in suspension. From time to time individual fish are caught and gills examined to determine the extent of infection. The optimum amount of infection varies for different sizes and species of fish and also for the condition the fish are in. It is generally accomplished within the limit of 5 to 20 minutes. Over-infection must be guarded against.

Naturally, there cannot be any definite rule as to the number of glochidia to be used with any number of fish, the person in charge must be guided by his experience. When sufficiently infected, the fish are removed to the river or pond. If develop-ment in the gills is to be watched, they may be transferred to crates anchored in the river or pond.

The gravid female clams may generally be found by looking over material where fishermen are at work. Unless the glochidia are sufficiently developed, the operation is useless, for not until then will they open and close their valves when stimulated. The fish are caught with the seine or net.

From this it will be seen that the experimental shell-fish station and the fish-cultural station go hand in hand. In fact it is a point of economy to combine the two.

Although artificial infection would appear to be a comparatively simple operation, a working knowledge of the process has only been obtained as a result of careful and laborious research. As yet only a few species of mussels are thus propagated. The search for natural hosts is still being prosecuted. Experimental work is also being carried on with the object of determining the period of parasitism, and the life history of the young mussel after parasitism, and to lead to such improvements of methods as will make the work most productive of practical results.

It is interesting to note that within a period of two years, young mussels of sufficient size to cut and finish buttons from their shells were reared at the station. These were raised from artificially infected fish, which were kept in floating crates or in earth ponds. They are not only the first mussels to be reared to such a size from artificial infection, but they are the first commercial forms known to have been grown in ponds.

RESULTS OF ARTIFICIAL PROPAGATION.

Although there is no means of definitely checking up the results of artificial pro-pagation on a large scale, where the mussels already exist, yet the extent of the confidence the United States Government has in the undertaking may be shown by the fact that during the last fiscal year, 331,451,490 glochidia, in round numbers, were liberated in the parasitic condition and 424,550 fish were employed in the opera-tions.[1] It is believed that a considerable proportion of the glochidia fall upon unfavourable ground, or fail to reach maturity from other causes. However, since a large number can be liberated at a comparatively small cost, the attempt is deemed justifiable. So far restocking, only, has been attempted, and in general fishermen report that where artificial infection has been carried on, more young shells are found

[1] Annual Report of the Commissioner of Fisheries to the Secretary of Commerce for Fiscal Year ended June 30, 1916.

than ever before. Such encouraging reports have come in from Lake Pepin, Wisconsin; White and Black rivers, Arkansas, and from Fairport, in the vicinity of the station.

THE SOJOURN AT THE STATION.

My sojourn at the station, July 25, August 3, was both highly profitable and very pleasant. Laboratory accommodation and facilities were freely offered. Valuable instruction, demonstrations and advice were gladly given by the Director and his staff. By assisting in the examination of gills for natural infection, and in carrying out artificial infection under the supervision of an experienced man, I was enabled to get a working knowledge of the operations, which would have been quite impossible to obtain otherwise.

The kindness with which I was received, the consideration shown for my wants and comfort, and the pleasure taken in facilitating the object of my visit were beyond my highest anticipations. In this connection I wish to particularly mention Mr. A. Shira, the Director; Mr. Canfield, Superintendent of Fish Culture; Prof. Clark and Dr. Howard, Scientific Assistants; Mr. Gorham, Foreman, and Mr. Southall, Shell Expert. The Station has also kindly sent me a set of classified shells, thereby facilitating classification here.

ORIGIN OF OUR LARGER MUSSEL FAUNA.

The identity of the mussel fauna of certain Canadian areas with that of the Mississippi waters at once suggests a probable common origin. Our forms no doubt migrated northward on the retreat of the ice cap which is believed to have covered northern North America during the great ice age. As this ice field retreated toward the North West, numerous lakes were formed, now represented by our modern Great Lakes, and these probably all except lake Ontario drained into the Mississippi system. Several of the old drainage courses have been discovered, among them being the ancient Lake Erie outlet, by way of the Wabash into the Mississippi river, and the glacial lake Chicago along the Chicago river. Even lake Superior appears to have had a watercourse into the Mississippi by way of the St. Croix river.[1] Numerous species of mussels no doubt found their way up these waterways into the ancient lakes, and ultimately populated the rivers now flowing into them.

THE GRAND RIVER.

As far as I have been able to ascertain, the Grand river contains more mussels of commercial value than any other Ontario waters. This river rises in the township of Melancthon, Dufferin county, within a distance of almost twenty-five miles from Georgian bay. Its source, at an elevation of approximately 1.700 feet above sea-level may be said to mark the highlands of the southwestern Ontario plateau. From its source to its outlet into lake Erie, at Port Maitland, by the river, the distance is 175 miles and the drainage area is approximately 2,500 square miles. The drainage basin is wide at its headwater area, and narrow in the lower flat country, where most of the rivers flow directly into the lake.

The river may be topographically divided into two parts—upper and lower. The upper part extends well into Waterloo County and includes the Conestogo tributary. Here, on the flat headwater table lands, the declivity is small; then for a distance becomes quite steep. At Elora, for example, there is a single drop of over 40 feet where the river enters a limestone gorge. The fall of the lower river is gradual and uniform, and generally becomes flat towards the lake. The following table will show the approximate fall of the whole river.

---

[1] Pop. Sc. Monthly XLVI No. 2, p. 217. U.S. Geol. Survey Monographs, XXXVIIa.

8 GEORGE V, A. 1918

TABLE I.—DISTANCE from Port Maitland approximate in sea level.

Place.	Mileage.	Difference	Elevation	Difference, Lake Erie Level.
Port Maitland.........................	0	7	573·94	0
Foot dam, Dunnville.................	7	0	573·94	7·06
Water above dam.................	7	22	581·00	13·00
York................................	29	5	594·00	16·00
Foot dam, Caledonia.................	34	0	610·00	8·00
Top dam, "	34	0	618·00	0
Behind dam, "	34	16	618·00	1·00
At mouth, Fairchild's...............	50	10	619·00	20·00
Cockshutt Bridge, Brantford.........	60	4	639	5
Foot lower dam, "	64	0	644·00	14·00
Behind " · "	64	3	658·17	17·00
Behind upper dam, "	67	9	675·00	5·00
Below dam. Paris	76	0	680·00	8·00
Behind dam, "	76	7	688·00	114·00
Bridge, Glenmorris	83	7	802·00	51·00
Foot dam, Galt.....................	90	0	853	9·00
Above dam, "	90	30	862·00	156·00
At Bridge, Conestogo................	120	15	1018·00	....
At Elora............................	135	Total head 5	....	Both dams 56 ft.
At Fergus..........................	140	Total head 7	....	" " 38 ft.
At Bridge, Belwood.................	147	Water level	1367·00	....

In the upper stretches of the river, including its tributaries, extending roughly to the vicinity of Paris, the stream-bed is composed of rocks and course gravel almost throughout, and flows in places over exposed limestone for considerable distances. From Paris southward the bed consists chiefly of:—

TABLE No. 2.

Vicinity—   Nature of Bed—

Paris to Brantford........... Gravel, sand.
Western Counties canal....... Gravel, sand, silt and clay.
Brantford to 12 miles below.... Gravel, sand and clay.
To Caledonia............... Fine gravel, sand and silt.
Caledonia to York.......... Gravel, exposed limestone.
York to Dunnville.......... Fine gravel, sand and silt.
Dunnville to Lake.......... Largely silt.

This section of the province, in common with all southwestern Ontario, is occupied throughout by comparatively undisturbed limestone and other Silurian and Devonian strata with overlying drift, clays, sands and more recent superficial deposits. The deep deposit of drift material naturally lends itself to erosion, and consequently the river carries considerable quantities of sand and gravel during heavy floods, scouring the channel from the headwaters to below Brantford. Below this point a large area of the river channel with the small declivity produces such a condition that light deposits may take place rather than the scouring of the bed to any extent. All the tributaries also bring down large quantities of material.

DISTRIBUTION OF MUSSELS.

Some years ago when repairs were being made on the feeder canal at Dunnville, shells were found in such abundance that they were picked up by the wagon load. This discovery led to the establishment of a small shelling industry at this point. Last year (1915) 265 tons were shipped from Dunnville, and this year approximately 260 tons.

Two or three years ago, during low water, three men picked up and shipped five or six car-loads from a point about one or one and one-half miles below York, and shipped, it is reported, to Buffalo.

From the lower dam at Brantford to the old power-house at Echo Place, there is what was at one time a barge canal, about 1¾ miles long. Where cuts were made it is about 50 feet wide and 5 or 6 feet deep. There is still in this system Mohawk lake, three-eighths of a mile wide by one-third mile long and 20 to 30 feet deep in places. Six or seven years ago, when the water was let out for repairs, this was the best place in the immediate vicinity of Brantford for clams, as to size, quantity and variety.

It is said that about ten years ago clams were abundant at a point about half way between Brantford and Paris, called Mulloy's Farm.

I am also informed by the city engineer of Brantford that large numbers of clams are to be found in the vicinity of Bow Park farm.

The fall on the Speed river, a tributary of the Grand, is well utilized, and clams of good size are found behind nearly all the dams which hold back the water over a considerable area of storage basins.[1]

SPECIES AND CHARACTERISTICS OF SHELLS.

I have twice visited the Dunnville area, and found a considerable variety of mussels of commercial value. My investigation there was much facilitated by Mr. H. Clark, who superintends the shell-fishing. In discussing the mussel fauna, only such species as are of commercial value will be considered.

In the following list common names are also given along with the scientific ones:—[2]

Scientific Name.	Common Name.
Lampsilis alata, Say	Pink heel-splitter.
Lampsilis luteola, Lam	Fat mucket.
Lampsilis recta, Lam	Black sand-shell.
Lampsilis venticosa, Barnes	Pocketbook.
Obliquaria reflexa, Raf	Three-horned warty-back.
Quadrula lachrymosa, Lea	Maple leaf.
Quadrula plicata, Say	Blue-point.
Quadrula rubiginosa, Lea	Wabash pig-toe.
Quadrula undulata, Barnes	Three-ridge.

No doubt this list does not contain all the species of commercial value found in this district. I have, in fact, picked up the Fluted-shell, *Symphynota costata*, Raf., a good many miles north of Dunnville, and it likely occurs here. I might in passing mention *Lampsilis gracilis*, Barnes, (Paper shell), a large mussel found here, but which is of no practical value on account of the thinness of its shell. Of the above species those most commonly occurring are *L. alata*, *Q. plicata*, and *Q. undulata*, *L. alata* is a good-sized heavy clam, quite a large number of the shells weighing in the neighbourhood of a pound, but its value is much reduced for button manufacture on account of its usual pink or purple colour. *Q. plicata* and *Q. undulata* are similar in appearance and comprise the chief commercial species of this area. They grow to a large size, and as a rule have a good white lustre. I have in my collection one of the former species weighing 1⅜ pounds, and of the latter, one 1¹²⁄₃₂ pounds in weight. *L. luteola* is naturally a valuable shell, as its quality is excellent, and it cuts and finishes with least waste. The area around Dunnville, however, does not appear to be particu-

---

[1] I am indebted to the Hydro-Electric Power Commission office at Brantford for valuable data, and also for reports on clam distribution on the Grand river system.

[2] For nomenclature see Synopsis of Naiades, or pearly fresh water mussels. Proceedings, U.S. National Museum, Vol. XXII, No. 1205, 1900, Charles T. Simpson.

8 GEORGE V, A. 1918

larly favourable to its development. It may perhaps be found more plentifully and of better quality farther up the river in localities more nearly approximating the condition in lakes. The other species are of good quality, but owing to their scarcity in this area, have little commercial importance.

METHODS OF THE DUNVILLE MUSSEL FISHERY.

On my visit to the fishing grounds at Dunville I found two gangs of men at work on the river above the town; one at a distance of about two miles, and the other some five and one-half miles farther on, near Morgan's island. In the former locality they had a pile of shells which would weigh about five tons. These were fished and shelled in about three and one-half days, by two men and two boys. The men did the fishing, while one boy ran the gasolene launch and the other removed the meat from the shells. The outfit for procuring the clams consists of two scows fastened rigidly together by a plank at each end. The distance between the scows is 4 or 5 feet. The men stand on the stern plank while operating the scoops. The scoop, or dip-net is a dipper-like apparatus with a handle of from 12 to 18 feet in length. The bowl consists of a wire cage about 16 inches in depth, and is attached to a triangular iron frame, 16 inches to a side. Thus the opening of the scoop is triangular and works in the manner of a dredge. To assist in the raking of the beds by this scoop, a number of iron spikes about 3 inches long are fastened to the lower part of the triangular frame, and are set about 3 inches apart. This helps to draw the scoop into the river shown and are set about 3 inches apart. This helps to draw the scoop into the river bed. A line passes from the lower end of the scoop to the forward plank and this is of such a length as to allow the handle to stand vertically against the stern plank. The whole outfit is towed by a gasolene launch. The scows, though varying in size, are about 16 feet long by 3½ feet wide and 14 inches deep. The following diagram may serve to illustrate the fishing outfit in operation:—

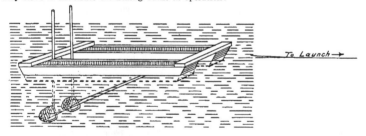

To Launch →

Fig. 1.

In order to remove the mussels from their shells they are subjected to boiling in water. This kills the animal, causes the relaxation of the powerful adductor muscles, which hold the valves together, and permits the easy removal of the muscles from their attachment on the valves. The boiling pans vary in size, but are usually about 6 feet long by 4 feet wide and 8 inches deep. .

The bed near Morgan's island is about ⅛ mile long and 50 feet wide. Here the bottom is gravelly, and although the shells are numerous and of good quality, the number of dead ones is considerably larger than farther down the river, where the bottom is muddy.

Last year the shelling was done below the town at a point a mile north of Port Maitland. Here 265 tons were taken from an area less than ¾ of a mile in length. The bed, I am told, showed no signs of depletion. This year the fishing has been done above the town, and although about 260 tons have been taken, the ground is apparently not as productive as was anticipated.

SESSIONAL PAPER No. 38a

PEARLS.

A considerable number of pearls and slugs are also found. Some are of very fair size and good quality. In Mr. Clark's opinion, pearling alone would insure a sufficient return for one's labours if followed up. The highest figure yet obtained for a pearl was $75.

RECOMMENDATIONS.

In order to develop to the fullest extent the resources of the river, three main steps are urgent; first, to insure against depletion of the present stock of clams; second, to restock and stock artificially all favourable areas, and third, to improve the river in general by stream regulation. Since the last-mentioned object is so fundamental, I shall deal with it first.

STREAM REGULATION AND SOME OF ITS ADVANTAGES.

Through the progressive removal of the natural physical conditions regulating stream-flow, the floods in the river have for some years been becoming more and more violent and destructive. This increased flood-flow has naturally reduced the volume of low water-flow proportionately. These two conditions, along with the scouring and general damage of river-bed, constitute an increasing menace to mussel life, to fisheries, and to power development along the river.

Some idea of the truth of the above statements may be deduced from a study of the following table of volume of flow at different points. The maximum flow of greatest recent flood is also included. This took place in the spring of 1912.

APPROXIMATE flow in cubic feet per second, period 1914, 1915 and 1916.

Grand River Stations.	Maximum.*	Minimum.*	Mean.	Drainage area in sq. miles.	1912. Estimated Maximum.
Belwood....	4,600	3	190	280	10,000
Conestogo..........	9,300	15	375	550	20,000
Galt	19,000	55	810	1,360	50,000
Glenmorris	23,000	70	900	1,390	....
Brantford....	26,000	100	14,000	2,000	100,000
York....	27,000	200	1,550	2,280	....

* Maximum flows are mean of two gauge heights, taken a.m. and p.m. daily.   Minimum flows in some stations consist of leakage from dams.

The danger consequent upon these conditions cannot readily be overestimated. The fact that drainage areas of the Grand River and Great Miami river flowing through Dayton, Ohio, are approximately equal, is sufficient proof. No doubt far-reaching measures for the prevention of dangerous floods will have to be taken in the future. If such measures involve water conservation, the resources of the river will be enormously increased.

In the fall of 1912 the Hydro-electric Power Commission made a reconnaissance survey of the river watershed covering the main stream from Caledonia to the headwaters; also of the larger tributaries from their confluence with the main stream to their headwaters. In this survey, the main object of which was to ascertain what locations, if any, merited examination as sites for storage reservoirs and regulating works, it was found that by the building of nine dams ranging from 30 to 65 feet, storage reservoirs ranging from 450 acres to 3,000 acres in area could be obtained; the aggregate acreage being between ten and eleven thousand. While the above figures

8 GEORGE V, A. 1918

are approximations, it is believed to be reasonably certain that the system of storage basins would have an aggregate impounding capacity of not less than five billion cubic feet.[1] It will be evident that the economic advantage accruing from such pools of dependable character cannot be lightly esteemed. In relation to mussel life there would be not only the addition of new flood areas, but also no doubt the improvement of the bed of the streams back of these areas. In these lake-approximations, or river-lakes as they have been called, admirable conditions should be afforded for the particularly valuable shell *L. luteola.* Not only does this shell work up well into buttons but it also lends itself readily to artificial propagation on a commercial basis. Although it is rare to find shells of commercial value in lakes, these river-lakes form a natural habitat for the above mentioned mussel. For example, Lake Peoria, a lake expansion in the Illinois R. forms at present probably the best mussel producing district in the United States. As the young mussels are parasitic on fish in the early stage of their life history, it would of course be necessary to construct effective fish-ways at these dams.

Further, by a study of tables 1 and 2 it will be seen that there are considerable stretches in the river where apparently suitable mussel areas obtain. If mussels are not found here in a survey, the fault will probably be due to flood conditions prohibiting their development in these areas. If such is the case, flow-regulation should overcome the unfavourable environment.   ,

FOOD, A FACTOR OF THE ENVIRONMENT.

In the discussion of favourable environments, due consideration must be given to the food problem. This is doubtless the most important factor in the environment of the mussel, and it is unfortunate that no extensive work has been done along this line. Actual records of stomach contents of fresh-water mussels are rare. Records of analysis show that among the microscopic forms, minute plants, diatomaceæ and other algæ, constitute a part of the food of the mussels. With reference to the food habits, Professor Clark and Dr. Wilson report in part, as follows: " The stomach contents of mussels taken from the main current of the St. Mary's, St. Joseph, and Maumee rivers were rather noteworthy for their paucity of organic material. Through the large mass of muddy matrix filling the stomach were usually scattered a few *Scenedesmus,* various diatoms, and an occasional *Pediastrum* or *Cosmarium.*" Dr. Petersen, a Danish ecologist and Director of the Danish Biological Station, has fully demonstrated that the fine dust-like detritus forming a thin top layer of bottom deposits constitutes a large part of the food of the oyster and other mollusks. Dr. Jensen, Petersen's colleague, concluded after investigating the source of the detritus that its origin is primarily from sea plants, broken down until it assumes the fine dust like form. It has been suggested[2] that the "large mass of muddy matrix" referred to by Clark and Wilson was probably the kind of material described by Petersen as " dust-fine detritus." Although large bivalves may not be able to avail themselves of the layer of dust-fine detritus, it is no doubt taken in by water currents. Dr. Jensen also examined the water by centrifuging, and obtained material identical with the top layer of bottom deposits. In Oneida lake the surface of the bottom deposits, in bays and quiet bodies of water, is reported to be of precisely the character described by Dr. Petersen. It would, indeed, be very interesting to establish the relationship between stomach-contents of different species of mussels and the nature of the river bed in which they do, or do not thrive. It would, no doubt, lead to valuable information with regard to the choice and the establishment of new areas for their development. It may be found that the food

---

[1] Sixth Annual Report, Hydro-Electric Power Commission of Ontario, 1916.

[2] Relation of Mollusks to Fish in Oneida Lake, by Frank Collins Baker, University of Syracuse, N.Y., July, 1916.

supply of the mussels is by no means fully dependent on the free-swimming organisms, and that the favourable localities, discussed above, are largely conducive to the development of the mussel on account of conditions favouring the deposition of the " detritus."

RESTOCKING AND STOCKING.

The restocking of areas where mussels at present exist, and where active fishing is going on, and the stocking of new areas, may be summed up under the head of artificial propagation. As the method pursued in artificial propagation has been described in a general way, we shall now consider its application to the river in question.

Of all mussels so far experimented with, *L. luteola* lends itself most readily to artificial propagation on a commercial basis. It is the species chiefly propagated at present by the United States Government. As time and opportunity prevented my making an extensive survey of Grand River, I cannot state the extent to which this species occurs therein. It is, nevertheless, very generally distributed in Ontario waters, but in order to attain to a size and abundance suitable for commercial value it apparently must have the conditions more or less as described above in " river-lakes." The specimens so far obtained from the river are not of very good quality. This is probably due to unfavourable conditions preventing its optimum development in the areas from which they come. In a commercial appraisal made of some of our shells by Mr. John B. Southall, Shell Expert at the Fairport Station, this particular shell was reported on as follows:[1] " medium size, no discoloration, brittle, third grade[2] and yielding 788, 16—line,[3] gross blanks per ton." In his remarks he further states that they were rather thin and of a steel-coloured nacre and produced blanks that would chip and cleave during the processes of button manufacture.

With regard to this mussel I would suggest a careful examination of the areas lying behind the larger dams with a view to stocking them with the valuable species. Such a survey might include the dams at Dunville, Caledonia, Brantford and Galt on the main river, and also the larger ones on the Speed tributary, where the fall is well utilized, and where clams of good size are said to be found in all such storage basins as hold back water over a considerable area. Behind the dam at Caledonia there is a stretch of practically dead water for twenty miles which might lend itself favourably to the development of this mussel. Here the river bed can be classed as permanent, inasmuch as the usual freshet velocity of the river water above is greatly reduced on reaching this point. At Brantford the old barge canal, described above, containing also Mohawk lake, might prove a very suitable locality for propagation on a small scale. For the purpose of stocking, I would strongly recommend that an attempt be made to introduce the particularly fine *luteolas* of lake Pepin, in the Mississipi, about 30 miles down the river from St. Paul, Minn. In the United States gravid mussels, for purposes of infection, have not been shipped over a much greater distance than 300 miles, but I am informed by the Director of the Fairport Station that they sent a couple of shipments of live mussels from Fairport to New York in the fall of 1916, and that the majority reached their destination in good condition. The distance from lake Pepin to Galt, Ont., would be about 835 miles by rail.

Fortunately, this species is not very exclusive in its choice of hosts, neither is its spawning period of short duration, as is the case with some other commercial mussels. All the Lampsilinæ, in fact, are gravid, more or less, during the whole year

---

[1] In the report of the appraisal the *luteolas* sent from the Canada Co. Cut and from the Grand River were combined in one report.

[2] In grading the material I sent him, the texture and lustre of the niggerhead (*Q. ebenus*) was taken as the standard.

[3] A line in button measurement is 1/40 of an inch.

but most ripe ones are found from April to July. In my survey in August I found quite a number of gravid *luteolas* but none that on microscopic examination proved to be ripe. This early and extended spawning period would be favourable to successful shipping, before the warm weather comes on. The fish that may serve as carriers belong mainly to the families Centrarchidæ and Percidæ. The species are: *P. sparoides* (speckled bass); *P. annularis* (crappie); *L. pallidus* (blue sunfish); *M. salmoides* (large-mouthed black bass); *M. dolomieu* (small-mouthed black bass); *S. vitreum* (yellow pickerel); *S. Canadense* (sand pickerel); *P. flavescens* (yellow perch) and *R. chrysops* (white bass), all well represented in our waters.

Since the artificial propagation of this mussel is past the experimental stage, I did not consider it advisable to repeat the operation here, on my return from Fairport, particularly as my time was limited and as the localities visited did not appear very favourable. It was kindly suggested at Fairport that gravid mussels be shipped over here for infecting purposes.

Lampsilis recta, though not found plentifully in the Grand river, is a very valuable shell on account of its fine quality. Mr. Southall reported it to be of large size, without discolouration, firm and of first grade, making 369, 16—line and 470, 24—line gross blanks per ton. Although the usual run of this species is coloured, those from the Dunnville area seem to be of fine quality. There are, however, some shells which show discoloration. In the fiscal year 1916, 11,288,300 larval mussels of this species were planted at Fairport. The fish which may serve as hosts for artificial propagation are: *L. pallidus* (blue sunfish) and *A. cyanellus* (green sunfish). The former of these species occurs abundantly in some parts of lake Ontario and lake Erie and their tributaries, but the latter has not been reported from Ontario, although it is supposed that it will be found in lake Erie. *P. annularis* (crappie, also called silver bass) has been found naturally infected with this mussel, but it is rare in our waters.[1]

The spawning period of this mussel is similar to that of *Lampsilis luteola* and the river appears to be adapted to this species. The shellers at Dunnville seem to prize this shell above all others.

Lampsilis ventricosa.—This shell is not used very extensively in button manufacture, but it is worked up into novelties. Large shells, however, make buttons of good lustre. Last year 447,000 glochidia were used for infection at Fairport. The species of fish that may serve as hosts in artificial propagation are: *P. annularis, L. pallidus,* and *M. salmoides* (large-mouthed black bass). At present it would not appear to be essential to increase the stock of this shell.

The *Quadrula* group is well represented in the Grand, but only two species appear in large quantities—*Q. plicata* and *Q. undulata.* These constitute at present our chief button shells, and the Canadian Pearl Button Company, of Trenton, Ont., which has the sole right to the Dunnville fishery at present, reports that the shells from the Grand compare favourably with those shipped to their plant from the United States. In the commercial appraisal of these two species from the Grand, the report is as follows :—

Species.	Common Name.	Size.	Discolouration.	Texture.	Grade.	No. of gross blanks per ton	
						16-line.	24-line.
Q. plicata[2]	Bluepoint	Large	None	Firm	3rd	142	245
Q. undulata	Three-ridge	Large	None	Firm	3rd	182	214

[1] Manual of Vertebrates of Ontario, by C. W. Nash, has been consulted for fish distribution in our waters.

[2] The *plicata* from Mud Creek, near Port Franks, were evidently grouped with those of the Grand river, for there is but a single report.

SESSIONAL PAPER No. 38a

It is noted that they had a very uneven inner surface, causing waste in cutting blanks; the tips of the shells were too thin for buttons. The colour and nacre were not as bright as the usual run of the species found in the Mississippi river; but it nevertheless makes a good button and, with proper care, the material could be worked up with profit. As the Button Company of Trenton works up tons and tons of these shells their statement as to the comparative value of the shells must also receive due consideration.

With regard to the propagation of the former species (*Q. plicata*), Dr. Howard, of Fairport, Iowa, makes the following statement:—

'Several factors favour the artificial propagation of this species upon a practical scale. It is common and at present one of the most used shells in the button industry. It seems to be a form not narrowly restricted as to hosts, and these are indicated to be among the commonest and most readily obtainable fishes. Although a river form, its habit as a dweller in stiller water and on mud bottom makes it susceptible to propagation or control under conditions readily imitable in artificial lakes or ponds. A continuous water supply is desirable; my observation has been, however, that it will survive rather adverse conditions in this respect. I have collected many live specimens from a slough which had gone dry to the extent that only mud remained. Under these conditions the majority of the pond mussels, *Anodonta corpulenta,* had died. I would cite also the finding of this species accidentally introduced in the parasitic stage into an artificial pond at Fairport, Iowa. The pond had gone dry, and I found a specimen still alive buried in mud barely moist. It is evident, I think, from these observations that the species is hardy, at least as regards some of the more common vicissitudes to which mussels are naturally subjected."[1]

In his experimental work with this species he found that *P. annularis* (crappie), *P. sparoides* (speckled bass), *P. flavescens* (yellow perch), and *L. pallidus* (blue sunfish) were successful carriers. The spawning period is short, being confined chiefly to the month of July. In the last fiscal year 147,000 glochidia of this species were set free in the parasitic stage at Fairport.

At present the safe-guarding of the beds against depletion is more urgent than experimental work in artificial propagation of this species. As experience and equipment are obtained, work on the more difficult *Quadrulas* should no doubt be proceeded with.

I have so far not obtained any data of experimental work done on *Q. undulata*. In general appearance the two forms are similar. In *plicata*, the umbones are more elevated and inflated than in *undulata*.

PROTECTION OF FRESH-WATER MUSSELS.

For the protection of the present mussel beds the following methods may be considered of sufficient importance to merit discussion.[2]

(*a*) A closed season in each year.
(*b*) Restriction as to the methods of fishing.
(*c*) Restriction as to size of mussels retained by fishermen.
(*d*) Closed regions for specified number of years.
(*e*) The imposition of licenses.

---

[1] Experiments in propagation of Fresh Water Mussels of the Quadrula group. By Dr. A. D. Howard, Bureau of Fisheries, Document No. 801.

[2] See also, Protection of Fresh Water Mussels, by R. E. Coker, Ph.D., Bureau of Fisheries, Document No. 793.

8 GEORGE V, A. 1918

(*a*) The main object to be attained by instituting a closed season for fishing is the protection of the beds during the breeding season. Incidentally, however, a second benefit naturally accompanies the one sought, for by limiting the length of the season, the extent of the fishing will likewise be diminished. Since the chief commercial shells so far shipped are *Quadrula plicata* and *undulata,* and since these species have short periods of gravidity during the summer months, the closed season restriction peculiarly applies to the Grand. But the river also supports other shells of some commercial value which have long breeding seasons, and thus the protection afforded would not be sufficiently wide-reaching. This will be particularly true in case of artificial propagation. Besides, an interruption of fishing operations during a few summer months would seriously interfere with the industry.

. (*b*) At present the shells are obtained in one way only, as described above. This method is fortunately not the one against which complaints are generally made. Although it roots up the bed it does not unnecessarily injure the mussels which are too small for commercial purposes, and these should be returned to the water.

(*c*) It is obvious that there is a limit to the size of a shell beneath which it is pure wastefulness to retain it. The fishermen and the button manufacturers lose time in handling the material and the beds are depleted at a much greater rate than they would otherwise be for the same finished product. A limit for every species is, as a rule, impracticable if for no other reason, at least for the fact that the determination of species is sometimes difficult. After a size limit has been decided upon, considerable details will have to be worked out in order to satisfactorily enforce any regulations agreed upon.

(*d*) One of the most immediate protective measures is that of closed areas. This best meets the case of the long breeding species and gives them an opportunity to restock areas, preventing for a term of years the disturbance of gravid clams some of which, when disturbed, discharge the young even though not mature. It also favours the building up of beds by allowing the young clams to establish themselves. The system on which a river or portions of it are to be closed, and the time and duration of areas closed can best be determined by studying field and biological conditions.

(*e*) By the granting of fishing permits as at present on the Grand, no doubt the number of shellers is thereby limited. It is a question, however, just how far the interests of a private person or firm are safeguarded as well as those of the fishing grounds. Although such a fishing permit was granted with a view to stimulating shell prospecting it nevertheless undoubtedly discriminates against other persons or firms. If fishing licenses were granted to resident fishers, thereby eliminating the exploiters or such persons as would not wish to follow up the industry, no doubt good results would be obtained. This would also leave to fishers the opportunity to sell to such firms as paid the best prices.

RIVER AUX SABLES.

In the brief survey of this river for shells I confined my attention chiefly to its lower stretches from which reports of abundance of shells had come in.

The east branch of the river rises a short distance north of Jaffa, in the township of Hibbert, county of Perth. The west branch has its course several miles to the west of this point and the two branches unite near the northern boundary of Stephen township. After a course of about 90 miles the river enters Lake Huron at a point 12 miles, almost due west, from the confluence of the two branches. This U-shaped river is remarkable for its meandering course and for its apparently recent geological history.

Until about 25 years ago the river outlet was not as now, but at a distance of 10 miles further south, near the village of Port Franks. It is an artificial channel one-quarter of a mile in length. Previous to this cut the river made an abrupt turn at Grand Bend when within one-quarter of a mile from the lake, and it flowed almost parallel to the lake shore to the natural outlet, below Port Franks. This deviation of its course was probably due to the sand collecting near its northwesterly banks, forcing the river southwards.

Owing to the frequently occurring floods on the lowlands, the Canada Company, which owns extensive tracks of land in the district, decided to make a cut from the northwestward flowing arm of the river to the southward arm. I shall refer to it as the "Canada Company Cut." It passes through the former lake Burwell and is 3.5 miles in length. Later on, wishing to further improve their lands, the Company put the second cut through at Grand Bend, diverting the river directly into the lake. Although the upper part of the old river channel, between Grand Bend and the lower cut is dry, it still contains a large volume of water. It approximates, in fact, to a narrow lake about 8 miles in length. In places it is a few hundred feet wide and quite deep. The greatest depth at which I took soundings was 17 feet. A fair and apparently continuous current of water flows from it into the main stream at the cut.

Previous to the construction of the artificial channels the river must have been admirably suited to the support of mussel life. Even when the second cut was put in at Grand Bend, and the water let off, I am told by an old resident, Mr. Brenner, that the bed was paved with shells for a considerable distance, many of these being of very large size.

On ascending the river for a few miles from Grand Bend we found large numbers of good-sized clam shells lying on the banks, evidently thrown up in dredging the bed after the cut had been made. In the river we also found quite a number of large mussels of commercial value, the species *Q. undulata* predominating. Other species found were *L. luteola, L. ventricosa,* the large but useless *A. grandis,* and a dead *S. costata.* These mussels were lying about on the bed of the river, in water about a foot deep. With the small amount of water flowing it is difficult to understand how such a quantity of mussels of good size could be maintained. Hand picking here would yield a fair quantity of commercial shells, but since the river is small the supply would soon be exhausted. From Grand Bend we went to Port Franks and crossing the Canada Co. Cut near its western terminus, investigated the water for clams. We found a small bed near the bridge, in shallow water, somewhat protected from the main current. Many of the shells were of large size and also represented quite a variety of species:—*L. recta, L. centricosa, L. luteola, Q. undulata, Q. rubiginosa,* and *S. costata.* In the commercial appraisal the *uteolas,* sent from this locality, were reported on in conjunction with those from the Grand so that I cannot state precisely what their grade is. We found *L. recta* 6 inches in length and of very fine quality. It was gratifying to find such a collection of shells in an artificial waterway. At Port Franks I was told that the vicinity contained "oceans of shells." As I was not yet acquainted with the river bed, I hoped for good things from it, thinking I might find a suitable area for *L. luteola.*

As stated above, this old channel constitutes a rather long narrow lake from which a small stream of water flows. The bottom of this bed is in many places densely covered with aquatic vegetation, *Chara* predominating. The shores are usually either steep or marshy. Large clams in considerable quantities were found in the shallow water along the shore, where they appear to be somewhat generally distributed. The commonest species is *Q. undulata,* although the Lampsilis group is also represented. I also found one *Q. rubignosa.* I found it to be practically impossible to determine the extent of the mussel life beyond a short distance from shore, except in very deep parts, and in the upper stretches where quite large barren areas of compact bottom obtain. The small crow-foot bar which I had made for shell prospecting, proved in general absolutely valueless here on account of the dense mat of vegetation covering a large part of the river bed. With a good motor launch and a heavy dredge one might

8 GEORGE V, A. 1918

settle the problem, but I do not consider the undertaking worth the trouble or expense. In the deeper parts of the river I was able to use the crow-foot bar but got no shells except dead ones. The river may at one time have contained large quantities of mussels but it seems too stagnant to make good clam beds possible. This condition also would promote the growth of the vegetation now so abundant.

Taking all conditions into consideration this area is of no value for mussel culture. The shells that are there are perhaps only a remnant of a once larger supply and may in time quite disappear. The L. *luteolas* found were fairly large but were badly stained and seemed unhealthy.

In order to make a careful survey of this locality I decided to further investigate the cut and work my way to the east branch of the river to prospect for shells there. The lower end of the cut is quite wide and approximates a small river, but we found no clams with the exception of the bed near the bridge mentioned above. I was able to determine that the upper part of the river's section between the cut and Grand Bend does contain the commercial shell *Q. undulata.* At one place where I went into the water to a depth of four or five feet, I found the bed to consist of fine clay mud quite thickly covered with mussels of this species. They were, however, rather smaller than usual.

This river seems to be peculiar in having a very irregular channel as to width and depth. At places it is shallow and narrow and then again it becomes wide and deep. Shells seem to be quite generally distributed. Even at Ailsa Craig, which must be over 40 miles up the river from the cut, we found the species *Q. undulata, L. ventricosa, L. luteola* and *Unio gibbosus.* They were not plentiful and of rather small size—too small to be of much value. Good beds of shells may be found on a more thorough investigation. In fact, I am inclined to think that the shells found lying in the shallow places near Grand Bend and in the Canada Company Cut may be washed down from native beds up stream from these points. Conditions in the lower stretches of the river seem to be very favourable to mussel development even with the small flow of water.

I also investigated the river near its mouth at Port Franks, but evidently there are no mussel beds of any importance there. No doubt the great quantities of sand carried down during floods do not permit their development.

It is singular that even small streams in this vicinity support mussels of commercial value. At the mouth of Mud creek, a small stream near Port Franks, I found a number of *Q. undulata* of fairly good size. *Q. rubiginosa* and small *luteolas* were also found here. Shells are reported to be plentiful further up this creek.

In the vicinity of Grand Bend and Port Franks a considerable quantity of shells should be obtainable by hand picking at low water. As the areas are not large, however, the supply would soon be exhausted. Since $20 per ton, delivered at the station, has been offered for them, some enterprising man might find his labours well repaid.

I should advise that the river above the Canada Company Cut be examined with a view to determining its resources in mussel life.

POINT EDWARD.

On my arrival at the bay at Point Edward, near Sarnia, I was again several times assured of the abundance of shells by men about the lumber yards. I obtained a row-boat from the Spanish River Lumber Company, and crossed the North bay (north of the Cleveland lumber tramway) in search of shells. The water here has an average depth of about 3·5 feet and the shells are therefore readily obtained with a dip net or by wading. The sandy bottom is free of weeds with the exception of the margins near the marshy borders. As the water was clear I could readily see the bottom. I found only small shells such as we find in any of our fresh water lakes, for example

SESSIONAL PAPER No. 38a

small worthless *luteolas*. Not having completely satisfied myself I again went over the ground thoroughly the next day in company with Captain Glass of Sarnia, finding very little, however, of any value whatever. The current flowing through the river here is very strong. It seemed foolish to look so carefully for shells large enough and in sufficient quantity to be of commercial value, but I desired to thoroughly settle the matter. Popular reports concerning shells are generally misleading. This is due to the fact that very few people understand shells from a commercial point of view. With regard to lake Smith, for example, glowing reports of shells were made. One man supporting this view was kind enough to get a boat and take me over the ground, but we found only numerous specimens of the common worthless lake clams.

NOTTAWASAGA RIVER.

Mr. Gross, button-manufacturer of Kitchener, Ont., had been informed that large quantities of mussels had been found along the river. He decided to investigate the reports and agreed to my accompanying him. A motor launch was engaged to take us up the river. Several miles up the river we discovered a bed where the mussels were very thick. We needed but to drag the crow-foot bar a short distance when a considerable number of clams would be caught. Shells were also obtained in a similar manner near the mouth of the river, just out from the Riveria hotel. In all, the following species were taken: *L. recta, L. ventricosa, U. gibbosus, S. costata,* and *S. edentulus.* In the commercial appraisal the *L. ventricosa* are reported to be small, no discoloration, hard and brittle, fourth grade, and giving 640 16-line gross blanks per ton. Many of the *ventricosa* taken were too small to be of commercial value and had to be thrown back. The shells here are very remarkable for their colour. *Ventricosa* is in fact the only species showing no discoloration. Some of the *recta* are extremely dark purple. Mr. Gross did not consider it worth while to prospect further. Only a small part of the river has thus been surveyed for shells. The prospect here is not at all promising, at any rate not until there is a demand for coloured shells. It would be interesting to determine the cause of discoloration. This is as yet unknown.

The bottom, from which most of the shells came, was gravelly and the water from 5 to 6 feet deep. There is a large flow here and the river should support considerable mussel life.

GENERAL REMARKS.

This investigation was conducted only at selected points on a few of our rivers. The results cannot, therefore, be taken as finally indicative of our mussel resources. The river Thames, for example, draining a large area between the Grand and the Aux Sables, both of which contain commercial shells, has not been touched. It is impossible to know our resources until a more extended survey is made.

A great deal of important information could no doubt be obtained quite economically if further fresh-water mussel investigations were combined with those of the district hydrographers of the Hydro-electric Power Commission of Ontario. They, I believe, cover a great many points along our rivers regularly. In the month of June of last year the staff at Brantford visited the following stations:—

Stations.	*Streams.*
Burford,	Whiteman's Creek,
Onondaga,	Fairchild's Creek,
Brantford,	Grand River,
Canning,	Nith River,
Nicholson,	Nottawasaga River,
Glenmorris,	Grand River,

38a—7½

Stations.	*Streams.*
Galt,	Grand River,
Kimberley,	Beaver River,
Hespeler,	Speed River,
Markdale,	Rocky Saugeen River,
Hornings Mills,	Pine River,
Welland Canal,	Welland River,
Owen Sound,	Sydenham River,
Meaford,	Big Head River,
York,	Grand River,
Severn,	Severn River,
Washago,	Black River,
Port Elgin,	Saugeen River,
Walkerton,	Saugeen River,
Salem,	Irwine,
Belwood, Conestogo and St. Jacobs,	Grand and Conestogo Rivers,
Carahers,	Speed River,
Kilworth, Fenshaw, Ealing, Kimberley,	Thames, three branches,
Arkona,	Aux Sables River.

In the present year a good many other stations will probably be added. With a car at their disposal the points could be readily reached and often much time saved.

The investigation might also be extended beyond the province of Ontario. The St. John river, N.B., has a large area that may possibly be suitable for mussel culture. Ten miles above Fredericton the Keswick stream enters from the north, and below this point the bed is literally choked with alluvial islands. At Sugar island, the largest of the group, the river measures 2·5 miles from bank to bank. From Fredericton to Gagetown, a distance of 34 miles, the surrounding land is very low. On the east a mere alluvial flat of great extent separates the waters of the St. John from those of the Jemseg. Some farmers here obtain annually a crop of fish and vgetables.[1] A few of the upper sinuses that branch off to the east from the river might also be suitable for clams. One would not expect to find our larger species there now, but it does not necessarily follow that they would not thrive if introduced. The greatest difficulty would probably be found in procuring the proper species of fish to act as hosts. Here it may be mentioned that in the flood areas of the Mississippi many fish, cut off from the river when the flood subsides, are caught, infected and liberated again. In this way the double purpose of restocking the river with clams and reclaiming the fish is served.

In Manitoba there seems to have been an immigration from the upper waters of the Mississippi region. I am informed that in the *Journal of Conchology* (Leeds, Eng.) IV., pp. 339-346, 1885, there is an interesting account of the Mollusca of Manitoba by R. M. Christy. In a letter received from Dr. Bryant Walker, Detroit, Mich., relative to this article, it is stated that the author (Mr. Christy) lists nineteen species of which six are unidentified. They are: *L. recta, radiata, luteola, borealis,* and *alata. Q. rubiginosa, plicata, lachrymosa,* (and *asperima*), *undulata* and *heros. Symp. complanata; Stroph. edentula.* Mussels in that region were abundant and especially in the Shell river, which runs into the Assiniboine from the east, about fifty miles above its junction with the Qu'Appelle. Hundreds of dead shells belonging to many species occurred.

---

[1] The St. John River. Dr. W. Bailey.

SESSIONAL PAPER No. 38a

Dr. Walker obtained through the Am. Mus. of Nat. Hist. of N.Y., the following species from the Assiniboine: *Lamp. recta, ventricosa, luteola,* and *alata; Sym. complanata; An. grandis* and *Quad. undulata, lachrymosa* and *rubiginosa.*

Many species of commercial mussels are thus represented in our western waters.

Finally, since the maintenance of a mussel supply depends on our fresh-water fish supply, it will be necessary to direct our attention to the greater and more important problem of fish conservation. It is obvious that the two problems go hand in hand, and a station set aside for the latter should be supplemented by a department working in the interests of the former wherever the conditions of the surrounding country demand it. Fish ponds in which the proper species of fish could be reared for the purposes of infection and experiment, might at the same time yield valuable information in the interests of fish-culture. Such information would be of the greatest importance in hastening the day when the farmer would raise his fish as naturally as he raises his poultry. In the near future fresh-water research laboratories, in which our fishery problems are scientifically worked out, will have to be established. But our inland fishery problems can never be satisfactorily solved until the still more basic problem of water conservation is seriously dealt with. Of all the problems relative to national economy none is more likely to engage our serious attention in the future than that of water conservation.

Fig. 1.—Wood bored by *Teredo navalis* at Charlottetown, P.E.I., within a
months.

IV

NOTES ON THE HABITS AND DISTRIBUTION OF TEREDO NAVALIS ON THE ATLANTIC COAST OF CANADA.[1]

By E. M. KINDLE, Ph. D., etc.

INTRODUCTION.

A specimen of the boring work of the " ship worm," *T. navalis* was recently presented to the Museum of the Canadian Geological Survey by Mr. H. E. Miller, accompanied by notes showing the dates within which the destructive work had been accomplished. Although a considerable literature exists on the destructive work of Teredo, records of its habits and work in Canadian waters are sufficiently scarce to justify recording some of the interesting facts which have been communicated to the writer by Mr. H. E. Miller. In the course of his work as an engineer in the Department of Public Works in renewing wharves, piling, and other seashore structures in Prince Edward Island, Mr. Miller has had unusual opportunities to become acquainted with the work of the Teredo. The data relating to the habits of the boring mollusc, popularly known as the ship worm, which are recorded in this paper have been supplied chiefly by Mr. Miller.

The distribution of *Teredo navalis* presents some novel features. It affords an example of discontinuous distribution which parallels that of the common oyster in Canadian waters. It is associated with the gulf of St. Lawrence colony of the Acadian fauna, but its distribution varies rather widely, as will be pointed out, from that of some of the other species of this northern Acadian colony.

HABITS.

Considerable human interest attaches to the boring work of the mollusc, *Teredo navalis*, because it is equally capable of destroying wharves, or railway bridges, or sinking ships when precautions to check its ravages are neglected. The depredations of Teredo are not confined to any particular parts of the world's coast lines. Its work is well known on the Pacific coast, where the Isopod, *Limnoria tenebrans*, is locally even more destructive.[2] In Europe the extraordinary increase in the numbers and abundance of Teredo at various widely separated periods have several times brought it into very prominent notice. During one of these periodic increases in its numbers —about 1730-32—Holland was imperilled by the threatened destruction of its sea dykes.[3]

The rapidity with which timbers are frequently destroyed by *Teredo navalis* is shown by the accompanying photograph (fig. 1) of a portion of a beech timber which was 12 inches square when placed in the water. The timber was perfectly sound when placed in the tidal zone just west of the entrance to Charlottetown harbour, Prince Edward Island. The completely honeycombed condition shown in the figure was accomplished in a period of sixteen months. This is a much more rapid rate of

---

[1] Published with the permission of the Director of the Geological Survey.

[2] Harrington, N. R., and Griffin, B. B. Notes on the distribution and habits of some Puget Sound Invertebrates. Trans., N.Y. Acad. Sci., 1897, pp. 158-9.

[3] Van Baumhauer, F. H.—The Teredo and its Depredations (translated from Archives of Holland, Vol. I). Popular Science Monthly, Vol. XIII, 1878, pp. 400-410. 545-558.

8 GEORGE V, A. 1918

destruction than has been ascribed to its ally *Limnoria lignorum,* which Murphy[1] states can, when abundant, destroy soft timber at the rate of half an inch or more every year. Stearns[2] has recorded two interesting examples of the work of Teredo. He states that "upon the seafront of San Francisco I have known piles of Oregon pine and fir over a foot in diameter rendered worthless in eighteen months." Dr. Dall is quoted by Stearns as having noted a case of the destruction of the supports of a small pier made of piles 6 to 8 inches in diameter near the entrance to Chesapeake bay in six weeks. Prof. A. E. Verrill writes that "*T. navalis* is very abundant and destructive on the southern coast of New England. At my summer home on an island near New Haven it will reduce 2-inch planks and 4-inch stakes to a honeycomb condition in one season—1st July to September—as I have often proved by experience."[3] Although only a very thin film of wood separates the innumerable burrows, they in no case intersect or cut into each other.

The time of year at which timber is cut, according to Mr. Miller, is an important factor in determining the extent to which it is subject to or immune from the ravages of the Teredo. "Trees cut during the months from October to January give much greater resistance or are less attractive to the Teredo than the trees cut from February to May. The Teredo is practically inactive during the cold of winter."

One of the peculiarities of the boring habits of Teredo is its aversion to boring from one timber to another, no matter how firmly attached and adjusted they may be. "Over a shipbuilding experience of fifty years our general foreman of works, Mr. John White, observed only two cases where worms had worked from the hull planking into the timbers of vessels.

"Spawning time appears to be about July. Vessels launched in spring and hauled out before July, and those launched in October are practically free of the Teredo; those exposed during the latter part of June and during July, if not protected, being very freely attacked."

"To a great extent the Teredo will attack unprotected vessel hulls as freely as fixed timber, particularly if remaining idle for any length of time. Constant motion through the water, however, appears to hamper the attachment of the spawn to some little extent. Such protection, however, as tarring, copper or marine painting and creosoting proves an effective measure as long as the protecting agent remains intact."

"The point of entry of the borer spawn into the timber is below half-tide mark. A peculiarity is that standing timbers show a severed condition (very much after the fashion produced by the beaver), at from one to two feet above low-water spring tide mark in localities where spring tides have a range of 9 to 11 feet. From this point down the borers work entirely within the timber, not passing the line of the bottom, where this is muddy, but not having the same objection to sand, as shown by the specimen forwarded."

"Mr. Crandall, of the Crandall Engineering Concern, Boston, Mass., has made the statement to me, that if timber could be kept covered with a film of mud, it would be kept immune through the entry of Teredo spawn being prevented. Certain it is, that all other things being equal (particularly temperature and saltiness) the Teredo is much more prevalent and destructive where the surrounding shore and bottom is sandy. In twenty years' experience this office has never observed a creosoted stick affected by the Teredo. The impregnation used is fourteen and sixteen pounds to the cubic foot."[4]

A small amount of creosote appears to be not very effective, since Stearns states that at Christiania, where the Teredo is very destructive, he was told that "all the

[1] Proc. and Trans. N.S., Inst. Nat. Sci., Vol. V, 1881, p. 365.
[2] Stearns, R. E. C.—The Teredo or Ship-worm. American Naturalist, Vol. XX, 1886, pp. 134-135.
[3] Verrill, A. E. Letter to the author, February 21, 1917.
[4] Letter from H. E. Miller, to the author.

piles had been creosoted (ten pounds to the square foot) before they were driven in, but not to much purpose."[1]

The palmento of the southern states and some of the Australian woods are said to be immune from the attacks of Teredo. The papers by Putnam[2] and Cunningham[3] contain much information on the habits of Teredo.

An Icelandic naturalist[4] has made some interesting observations and experiments on the habits and biological characteristics of *Teredo norwegica,* the species found on the southern and western coasts of Iceland. Mr. Frits Johansen has kindly furnished the following translation and summary of these from the Danish: "The propagating (spawning) season continues through the whole summer (April-August). No larvæ are found in the mantle-cavity or in the sea; but numerous very small ones (burrows 1mm. long 0·5mm. wide) are found in driftwood from Faxebugt (W. coast) at the end of July.

"The growing period is mostly limited to two years as shown by experiment: I kept some pieces of wood with Teredo taken from the false keel of a fishing boat and kept it in a shaded cool place; the animals remained alive ten days; but inside of two weeks all were dead. Kept in a temperature of 6° C. for two days they all froze stiff, but were alive when thawed out again. In fresh water they only lived two to three hours; three hours in half sea and half fresh water or in putrid sea water.

"It is mostly only on two places that ships are attacked; at the waterline and in the false keel (or if this is missing the lower part of the keel itself). That this keel part is attacked is because it is buried in the sand, when the ship is beached, and thus gets no paint or tar. The "waterline" part of the ship gets easily its protection of paint or tar scraped off when loading, anchoring, etc. Plank edges are first and most attacked.

"The Teredo avoids leaving the wood in which it bores. Hence from the false keel only a few had penetrated to the true keel, and the burrows avoided the outer surface of the false keel. Where two parts of the false keel joined, the burrows never went through the contact but stopped short of a couple of inches. But how does the Teredo know when to stop burrowing? Maybe by sound-sense? In piers at Reykjavik, where *Limnoria lignorum* Ratk. burrows together with Teredo, one frequently sees that Limnoria eats away the woodparts surrounding the Teredo burrows and the calcareous lining of the Teredo burrows are exposed. Teredo therefore protects itself by thickening its calcerous lining 3 to 4 times the usual thickness by internal secretions.

"Boats on the water at the south and southwest coast are attacked by it.

"In later years it has been very numerous and destructive in sea-going ships belonging to the southwest coast; in many cases Teredo has been imported with ships bought in England, but some ships built in Iceland or lumber put into ships in Iceland have been attacked. Ships belonging to the north and northwest coasts (beached during the winter) seem to be free of Teredo. Maybe the many English ships bought and the unusually mild winter, and the fact that the ships are on the sea all winter are the causes of its frequency at the southwest coast for the last five or six years.

"The largest Teredo I have seen measured 27·5 cm. (to the base of the siphons) siphons ca. 2·5 cm.; average size of Teredo 16-18 cm., built in 1892."

---

[1] *Ibid,* p. 135.

[2] Putnam, J. W.—The Preservation of Timber. Scientific American Supplement, Vol. X, No. 236, July 10, 1880, 3762-3763.

[3] Cunningham, J. T.—Teredo. Encyclopaedia Britannica, 9th Ed., Vol. XXIII, 1888, pp. 184-186.

[4] Saemundson, B. Zoolog. Meddel. fra Island (Zool. Notes from Iceland, p. 43, pp. 57-60). Vidmskab. Meddel. fra Naturhist. Foren. Kbhn. for Aared 1903 (Scientific papers from Natural History Society in Copenhagen for year 1903).

8 GEORGE V, A. 1918

BATHYMETRIC RANGE.

There is but little information on the depth to which Teredo can work below low tide level in Canadian waters beyond Murphy's[1] photograph of a piece of bored spruce which was submerged two years, four feet below low water at Pictou, N.S. At Woods Hole, Mass., it has been found living at a depth of 13 fathoms[2] and in New York harbour at 25 fathoms.[3] Three well-known rock and clay-boring molluscs are found in the same general region with *Teredo navalis.* These are:—

> *Petricola pholadiformis.*
> *Zirfaea crispata.*
> *Saxicava arctica.*

P. pholadiformis appears to be most common near the inter-tidal zone, but it has been dredged at a depth of 30 fathoms in St. Marys bay by Dr. A. G. Huntsman. The recorded range of *Z. crispata* is from low tide to 70 fathoms in Canadian waters. Off the Maine coast it is recorded by Verrill[4] at from 22 to 44 fathoms. At Woods Hole it also occurs at a considerable depth below low tide. *Saxicava arctica* is another rock boring shell which has a considerable range below the tide line. On the Iceland coast it is found between tide marks[5] while off the Labrador coast it is common at 10 to 50 fathoms.[6]

Honeyman reported limestone boulders bored by Saxicava which were found at a depth of 65 fathoms off the Nova Scotia coast.[7]

The rock-boring habit gives to molluscs which practise it a special geological significance, as pointed out by Barrows.[8] The rock cells of such molluscs gradually expand as the rock is entered from the small aperture on the surface drilled by the very young shell into chambers corresponding to the size of the adult molluscs which thus leave no avenue of escape for the shell even after its death. The improbability of the removal of boring shells by current action to waters deeper or shallower than the living animal occupied permits the fossil molluscan rock-boring shells to yield information which is precise within the limits of their vertical range concerning the depth of the sea in which they lived.

DISTRIBUTION.

The genus Teredo has a wide distribution around the coasts of the North Atlantic. None of its several species however belong properly to the Boreal fauna although there are outlying colonies of some species which are surrounded by the boreal fauna. *T. norvegica,* which is the prevailing indigenous species on the eastern side of the North Atlantic, affords in its European distribution an interesting example of such discontinuous distribution toward the northern limits of its range. This species ranges through the Mediterranean and up the west coast of Europe into the waters of S.W. Norway. But G. O. Sars[9] states that "the only place inside of the Arctic

---

[1] Proc. and Trans. N.S. Inst. Nat. Sci., Vol. 5, 1881, p. 376, fig. 4.
[2] Summer, F. B. Osburn, R.C., Cole, L. J. A Biological Survey of the Waters of Woods Hole and Vicinity. Bur. of Fisheries, Bull. 1913, Vol. XXXI, Part II, Sec. III, p. 702.
[3] Proc. and Trans. N.S. Inst. of Nat. Sci., Vol. V, 1881, p. 376, fig. 14.
[4] Am. Jour. Sci., Vol. 7, 1874, p. 503.
[5] Johansen, A. C. On the Mollusca between tide marks at the coasts of Iceland. Videnskabelige Middelelser fra den Naturhistoriske Foresig I. Kjobenhaon, 1902, p. 386.
[6] Mem. Bos. Soc. Nat. Hist., Vol. I, p. 282.
[7] Honeyman, Dr. D. Glacial Boulders of Our Fisheries and Invertebrates. Attached and Detached. Trans. Nova Scotian Institute of Natural Science, Vol. VIII, Part III (1888-89), p. 210.
[8] Barrows. A. L. The Geologic Significance of Fossil Rock-Boring Animals (read before the Palæontological Society of America). Bull. Pal. Soc. Amer., Vol. 28, 1917.
[9] Mollusca regions Arcticæ Norvagiæ, p. 98, Christiana, 1878.

SESSIONAL PAPER No. 38a

region where this form has been noticed is at Oexfjord in West Finmark, where my father found it boring in piles."

This Finmark colony of *Teredo norvegica* is far to the north of the northern margin of the continuous distribution zone of the species on the Norwegian coast.

B. Saumundson[1] writes as follows regarding the occurrence of Teredo in Icelandic waters: "The Icelandic name of Teredo, 'tremadkur,' was first mentioned as Icelandic by E. Olafssen in his journey through Iceland Soroe in 1772: '*Teredo navalis intra lignum* is the bad worm, which spoils the driftwood' (West Iceland). Later it is mentioned by Mohr, 1786 (Icelandic Natural History) and by Morch (Fauna Mollusc. Island), 1868, both on the authority of Olafssen, so that neither of these two men have noticed it in Iceland themselves.

The species was found living in a pier at Reykjavik by me five years ago, and definitely determined by Ad. Jensen as *T. norweviga* Spengl. ·

The species is found in driftwood all around the island. It was found by me only in standing lumber (piers) at Reykyavik (West coast)."

A Teredo listed as *T. navalis?* and *T. denticulata* is included in Mollier's[2] and Morch's[3] lists of the mollusca of Greenland. Posselt[4] refers Moller's *T. navalis* to *T. denticulata* which he records from a single locality in S. Greenland,—avigtut.

The distribution of *Teredo navalis* along the Atlantic coast of Canada and New England affords an excellent example of discontinuous distribution. The essential features of this distribution are indicated in the sketch map (fig. 2), showing the distribution of Teredo in these waters. The map includes south of the Bay of Fundy the recorded occurrences of two or three species besides *T. navalis* but it clearly shows that the coast line distribution of this species is broken by 400 miles or more of coast line along which it is either absent or very rare. This mollusc is present in great abundance around the southern shores of the gulf of St. Lawrence and the coast of Cape Breton island. But southwest of the Str. of Canso it becomes scarce. In the Bay of Fundy, *T. navalis* is either very rare or entirely absent. South of this bay, however, it again becomes common on the Maine coast and from Frenchman's bay southwest appears to be generally present along the New England coast.

Mr. H. E. Miller has furnished the following notes on the distribution of *T. navalis* on the coast of Prince Edward Island: "Teredo is present in all waters surrounding the Prince Edward Island and up the inland tidal waters as far as the salinity of the water is sufficient.

"Regarding the coast of New Brunswick to the westward of this province, I cannot speak from personal observation never having visited that coast but from what I can learn the borer is to be found along the whole coast of Miscou and Shippigan and for at least a short distance along the Chaleur Bay coasts. I understand they do not work as far up to the rivers, as in this province. This is readily understood from the fact that the rivers are practically fresh very nearly to the outlet, draining immense areas and salinated by a very small range of tide.

"At Rustico Harbour on the North side of the island, there is great activity. The locality is entirely sandy. At Tignish, on the other hand, another sandy locality, the destruction is much less, but there is a very strong current, much sand in suspension, and considerable fresh water. The same comparison is true between localities of a muddy nature. Considering two localities, one sandy and one muddy, each with a considerable constant suspension of the material forming the bottoms, the destruction appears to be greater in the sandy locality."[1] The photograph here shown in fig. 1 indicates the great activity and abundance of *T. navalis* at Charlottetown on the south coast of the island.

1 Letter to the writer.
2 Index Molluscorum Groenlandica, 1842, p. 21.
3 Middelelser au Gronland, Vol. XXIX, 1905, pp. 289-362.
4 Meddel. on Gronland, Band 23, 1898, p. 101.

8 GEORGE V, A. 1918

Dr. Martin Murphy who made a special investigation of the distribution of Teredo in Nova Scotia stated that at Sydney Harbour, Cape Breton island, Nova Scotia, *T. navalis* is " as destructive if not more so than at any of the points on our coast."[1] It is abundant along the coasts of Northumberland strait as far west at least as Shediac." How much farther northwest its range extends is not known but probably not much farther. Murphy states that the zone of Teredo's operations on the east coast of Nova Scotia begins about Musquodoboit harbour and extends from there to Whitehaven.[2] He found that it became scarce on the Atlantic coast between the strait of Canso and Halifax. From Halifax southwest along the Nova Scotia coast only traces of Teredo are found and they are neither numerous nor destructive according to Murphy. The writer has not observed Teredo on the Bay of Fundy coast of Nova Scotia and Murphy does not appear to have seen it there. Dr. A. G. Huntsman of the St. Andrews biological station informs the writer that " we obtained it once near one of the Western isles, that is very close to Frye's island, in some sunken timber, and at another time we obtained it from some floating blocks which had, quite evidently, drifted in from outside, probably from the Gulf Stream. It is very probable therefore, that Teredo is not indigenous to the Bay of Fundy, but comes in periodically in floating wood." Professor Ganong reported in 1885 that " a broad and strong tide-dam was completely undermined and destroyed by them (*T. navalis*) within the space of six years,"[3] at Frye's island which is located in the lower and wider part of the bay. This author at a later date however modified this statement by saying that the destruction of Frye's island was the combined work of Teredo and the crustacean *Limnoria lignorum*. It is possible that it was altogether the work of *L. lignorum* as suggested by Verrill. Whiteaves[4] records *T. navalis* from St. John in a ship's hull. But that this record represents exotic specimens appears certain from Professor Ganong's statement that in St. John harbour the Teredo is not only absent but " ships which enter the harbour infested by them are free from them within two days."[5] The testimony of Professor Verrill regarding the occurrence of Teredo in the Bay of Fundy is important because of his intimate knowledge of the Bay of Fundy fauna. He writes that " so far as I remember I did not find *Teredo navalis* in Bay of Fundy during the seven summers I collected there. I think I did find *T. norvegica* a few times in buoys." . . . " At Eastport, Me., I found Laminaria very abundant in piles, fish-weir stakes, etc., but found no Teredo with it there."[6]

At least three factors are probably active in excluding *T. navalis* from the Bay of Fundy. Temperature is doubtless one of these. The area in which Teredo is most abundant is, speaking broadly, essentially the same as that of the isolated colonies of oysters in the waters about the southern shore of the gulf of St. Lawrence. Although the waters in winter are much colder than those of the Bay of Fundy, during the critical period of the spawning time they are warmer. Professor E. W. McBride[7] has pointed out how the existence of the oyster in this region depends upon the warming of the water in the shoal areas where alone they can exist during the spawning season. Whiteaves[8] still earlier called attention to the special temperature conditions which afforded on the south side of the gulf of St. Lawrence a congenial environment for a northern colony of the Acadian fauna.

---

[1] Murphy, M.   On the Ravages of the Teredo Navalis and Limnoria lignorum on Piles and Submerged Timber in Nova Scotia and the means being adopted in other countries to prevent their attack.   Proc. and Trans.   Nova Scotian Inst. Nat. Sci., Vol. V, Part IV, 1882, pp. 357-376.
[2] Murphy, M.   Supplementary Notes on Destroyers of the Submerged Wood of Nova Scotia, Proc. and Trans. N.S. Inst. Sci., Vol. 8, p. 218.
[3] Ganong, W. F.   The Economic Molusca of Acadia, N.B. Nat. Hist. Soc. Bull. No. VII, 1888, p. 111.
[4] Catalogue of Marine Invertebrates of Eastern Canada, 1901, p. 151.
[5] Ganong, W. F.   Nat. Hist. Soc. N.Y. Bull 4, p. 89, 1885.
[6] Verrill, A. E.   Letter to the author, February 21, 1917.
[7] The Canadian Oyster, Can. Rec. Sci., Vol. IX, 1905, pp. 154-5.
[8] Catalogue of Marine Invertebrata of Eastern Canada, p. 15, Can. Geol. Survey, 1901.

SESSIONAL PAPER No. 38a

Another factor of importance in controlling the distribution of Teredo is salinity. There appears to be general agreement among shipping men and others familiar with the work of Teredo that any considerable amount of fresh water is fatal to it. On this point, Mr. H. E. Miller states that "where the flow of fresh water is sufficient to have any effect on salinity there is an entire absence of Teredo."[1]

The speedy destruction of *T. navalis* already alluded to which results when it is brought into St. Johns harbour on ships is doubtless due to its inability to withstand brackish water. While this factor would explain its absence from certain bays and estuaries of the Bay of Fundy, neither salinity nor temperature will afford a satisfactory explanation of the general scarcity or absence of Teredo in these waters. If temperature alone were sufficient to bar Teredo from the Bay of Fundy it is difficult to understand how *Illyanassa obsoleta*, one of its congeners in the Acadian colony of the gulf of St. Lawrence should be able to make its way into the shallow bays on the east side of the Bay of Fundy, where I have found it at most points where I have dredged. This species on the opposite side of the Bay of Fundy is rare or absent.[2] One of the peculiarities of *T. navalis* is its aversion to water containing sediments or other impurities in suspension. Various writers have noted this aversion. The waters of the Bay of Fundy are unique in their extreme turbidity; no other waters on the American coast approach them in this respect. This is due to the very high tides, and the correspondingly swift currents in the estuaries which keep the waters near the coast everywhere turbid with sediment. In the Bay of Fundy there is a tidal range of 40 to 60 feet. In Northumberland Strait where Teredo is abundant the tidal range is in the neighbourhood of 10 or 12 feet. The turbidity of the Bay of Fundy waters, particularly in the upper and narrower portion of the Bay, exceeds that of Northumberland strait in somewhat the same proportion as its tides exceed those of the strait. The high turbidity of the estuarine waters of the Bay of Fundy is believed to be chiefly responsible for the general absence or scarcity of Teredo. Barrows[3] has pointed out that a definite correlation exists between the rock boring habit and a location on the open coast. The need of protection from the waves at and near the tide line on open coasts doubtless developed rock boring as a protective measure. This normal open-coast environment which involved exposure to the surf included the normal salinity of the open sea and comparative freedom from silt. The heavily silt laden waters of the upper part of the Bay of Fundy afford the very antithesis of the open coast environment which is normal to rock boring molluscs and in this fact is to be found the explanation of the absence or scarcity of *T. navalis* as well as the rock borers *Zirfaea crispata* and *Petricola pholadiformis* in the Bay of Fundy.

ASSOCIATED SPECIES.

A small crustacean, *Limnoria lignorum,* is associated with Teredo in some parts of its range whose wood-destroying habits are similar to those of Teredo. These two species which are similar only in habits, differ sufficiently in their preference for certain environmental factors to lead them to reach their maximum numbers and development along different parts of the coast line. Their zones of habitat, however, overlap according to Murphy. This author states regarding the areas occupied by these two species that "wooden wharves or bridges along the Bay of Fundy and from there along the Atlantic coast as far as Whitehaven suffer from the Limnoria, while the location of the Teredo is farther east and north." . . . "There is no neutral ground between them. Their domains overlap for a few miles, each of the little borers becoming less abundant as we advance farther into the territory of the other."[4]

---

[1] Letter to the writer.
[2] Huntsman, Dr. A. G. Letter to the writer, February 5, 1917.
[3] Barrows, A. L. The Geologic Significance of Fossil Rock-Boring Animals, Bull. Geol. Soc. Amer., Vol. 1917.
[4] Proc. and Trans. N.S. Inst. Sci., Vol. 8, 1895, p. 218.

8 GEORGE V, A. 1918

It is interesting to note that one of the molluscs which is common in Sydney harbour, Cape Breton island, where Teredo has perhaps its maximum abundance, is the rock borer *Zirfaea crispata*. Although reported rarely in the gulf of St. Lawrence by Whiteaves I have found it rather abundant near low-tide mark at North Sydney. Along the Bay of Fundy coast of Nova Scotia, however, I have found no trace of it. Stimpson reports it to be very rare at Grand Manan. Verrill has recorded it at from 8 to 70 fathoms in the Bay of Fundy. But it does not appear to occur in the Bay of Fundy near tide mark, as it does at Sydney. Like Teredo, *Z. crispata* appears to be absent or rare along the Atlantic coast south of the Bay of Fundy. This species, like *T. navalis*, has a wide distribution. On the Pacific coast it is reported from Vancouver to San Diego, California, by Carpenter.[1] It is distributed along the European side of the Atlantic from France to northern Norway.[2] Although found in an elevated beach near Christian shoal, Greenland, Jensen states "that *Zirfaea (Pholas) crispata* no longer lives at Greenland may be regarded as a fact."[3]

Another boring shell which is associated with *T. navalis* around the shores of Prince Edward Island is *Petricola pholadiformis*. The Canadian Geological Survey Museum collections include a specimen of hard red shale with shells of this mollusc from Charlottetown, P.E.I. Concerning this shell, Dr. A. G. Huntsman[4] writes: "*Petricola pholadiformis* is abundant in the lower part of the gulf of St. Lawrence around Prince Edward Island, and occurs boring in the red sandstone there. It has been reported by Verkruzen from St. Marys bay, Nova Scotia, and I have myself dredged it there in 30 fathoms hard clay bottom. I have not found it in the Bay of Fundy proper." Dr. Huntsman's observations on this shell indicates pretty clearly the discontinuous distribution of *T. navalis* and *Z. crispata*, which eliminates them from the fauna of the upper part of the Bay of Fundy.

Teredo navalis belongs in the gulf of St. Lawrence to an isolated faunal group which is confined to Dawson's warm "Acadian bay." The subboreal or syrtensian fauna of the central and northern part of the gulf of St. Lawrence are excluded from this fauna. Concerning this fauna, Dawson[5] wrote: "It thus forms a peculiar and exceptional zoological province" . . . "It affords to the more delicate marine animals a more congenial habitat than they can find in the Bay of Fundy or even on the coast of Maine."

Among the characteristic species which comprise this Northumberland strait colony of the Acadian fauna are the following:—

> *Ostrea virginica.*
> *Venus mercenaria.*
> *Zirfaea crispata.*
> *Astarte undata.*
> *Crepidula fornicata.*
> *Crepidula plana.*
> *Ilyanassa obsoleta.*

Some of these species, as *O. virginica* and *V. mercenaria* are entirely absent from the Bay of Fundy waters. Some others, like *I. obsoleta* are entirely absent on the west coast of the Bay of Fundy but present in the warm shallow inlets on the eastern side of the bay. The Northumberland Strait colony is separated from the northeastern border of the New England zone of the Acadian fauna by the deep basin of the Bay of Fundy and the Atlantic coast waters of northern Nova Scotia. The

[1] Dall considers the Pacific Coast form to be a species distinct from *Z. crispata*.
[2] Adolf S. Jensen, Middelelser on Groenland, Vol. XXIX, 1905, p. 296.
[3] *Ibid.*
[4] Letter to the author, February 12, 1917.
[5] Dawson, J. Annual address. Can. Nat. Ser. 2, Vol. VII, 1875, p. 277-8.

reason for this isolation becomes apparent on examination of a bathymetric chart of the waters of the Maritime Provinces. The whole of Prince Edward island and Northumberland strait lie inside the 20-fathom line, and much of the broad strait has a depth of 10 fathoms or less. On the southeastern coast of Nova Scotia, however, the 20-fathom line frequently approaches to within one-half mile of the coast, and there is everywhere a narrow zone of shoal water inside the 100-fathom zone which renders it colder than the broad shallow warm waters of Northumberland strait. It illustrates well the fact that a zone of shallow water if sufficiently close to and unprotected from deep waters may serve as a faunal barrier as effectively as a land barrier. This example of an isolated colony of the northern New England shallow zone marine fauna surrounded by a sub-boreal fauna is worthy of the attention of palæontologists who are prone to predict land barriers as offering the only possible explanation of faunal differences similar to those described above.

FORMER DISTRIBUTION OF THE NORTHUMBERLAND FAUNA.

There are several bits of evidence which seem to indicate that the present isolation and limited distribution of the colony of comparatively warm-water mollusca now living in the Northumberland strait with which *T. navalis* is associated is of recent origin. *Ostrea virginica,* the most strikingly southern type of this assemblage, apears to have extended as far westward as Montreal at one time during the Pleistocene. Several years ago Sir William Dawson wrote: "I have picked up a loose specimen at Saco which has the appearance of being a fossil specimen from the Leda clay, and Mr. Paisley has sent me specimens from Chaleur bay which are said to have come from Pleistocene beds 16 feet from the surface."[1] More recently Edward Ardley[2] has reported finding *Ostrea* near Montreal, 9 feet below the surface, associated with *Mya truncata, Macoma calcarea, Astarte, Laurentiana,* and *Saxicava rugosa.* At Cole Harbour on the east coast of Nova Scotia the flukes of anchors bring up numerous dead oyster shells, where the living oyster is unknown.[3]

On the east coast of Nova Scotia, Mr. W. J. Wintemburg of the section of Archaeology of the Geological Survey, has found in an old Indian shell heap on Mahone bay, 40 miles southwest of Halifax, shells of *Ostrea virginica* and *Venus mercenaria.* Neither shell is known south-west of Halifax, on the east coast of Nova Scotia at present, but their discovery in the shell heap appears to indicate that they lived in the bay when the shell heap materials were accumulating.

It may be suggested tentatively that the beds containing *O. virginica* at Montreal are synchronous in time with the Don River interglacial beds at Toronto. It is probable that the milder climatic conditions which prevailed during the early part of the Don River interval[4] rendered the temperature of the Atlantic coastal waters of the Maritime Provinces sufficiently mild to give the oyster and its congeners continuous distribution from southern New England to the gulf of St. Lawrence.

---

[1] Dawson, J. W. Ice Age in Canada, 1893, p. 243.
[2] Ardley, Edward. "The Occurrence of Ostrea in the Pleistocene Deposits of the Vicinity of Montreal." Ottawa Naturalist, Vol. 26, 1912, p. 67.
[3] Proc. and Trans. N.S., Inst. Nat. Sci. Vol. I, 1863, p. 98.
[4] A. P. Coleman, Int. Cong. Geol., Guide Book, No. 6, 1913, pp.15-31.

Fig. 2.—Sketch map showing the discontinuous distribution of Teredo around the coasts of Nova Scotia and New Brunswick. The habitat of Teredo is shown by black border on coast line. Area where Teredo is absent or rare is shown without black border.

V

REARING SOCKEYE SALMON IN FRESH WATER.

By C. McLean Fraser, Ph.D., F.R.S.C., etc.

Curator of the Dominion Biological Station, Nanaimo, B.C.

In several instances, successful attempts have been made to rear the Atlantic salmon, *Salmo salar,* to maturity without permitting it to have access to the sea.

Yarrell[1] describes such an attempt that was made nearly a century ago as follows: "A large landed proprietor in Scotland . . . wrote as follows: 'In answer to your inquiry about salmon fry I have put into my newly formed ponds, the water was first let in about the latter end of 1830, and in April, 1831, I put in a dozen or two small salmon fry, 3 or 4 inches long, taken out of a river here, thinking it would be curious to see whether they would grow without the possibility of their getting to the sea or salt water. As the pond, between three and four acres in extent, had been newly stocked with trout, I did not allow any fishing till the summer of 1833, when we caught, with fly, several of those salmon, from two to three pounds' weight, perfectly well developed and filled up, of the best salmon colour outside, the flesh well-flavoured and well-coloured, though a little paler than that of new-run fish.' "

This attempt was successful as far as it went, but no evidence is given that any of the fish lived to maturity. It has been shown by Dahl, Hutton, and others that, in some rivers in particular, the Atlantic salmon commonly remains three years in fresh water, the length of time these were kept, without any artificial restraint. The experiment is interesting, however, since it shows that the retention idea is by no means of recent development.

Menzies[2] refers to this experiment and mentions others as follows:: " Since then various experiments in this direction have been conducted with more or less success, notably those by Sir J. Gibson Maitland, at Howietoun, where eggs deposited in the winter of 1880-1 were duly hatched and the fry reared until, when nearly four years old (i.e., the same age as grilse), they were found to be ready to spawn, and the ova of the females when fertilized by milt, were found to develop in a perfectly normal manner. In the report of the Fishery Board for Scotland for the year 1908, part II, appendix III, details are given of a male grilse kelt which, owing to an oversight, was left for a year in a small fresh-water ' catch-pit,' and which, in spite of these unnatural conditions, had again become ripe for spawning.

" Through the kindness of Mr. George Muirhead, the commissioner for the Duke of Richmond and Gordon, who sent me the scales and particulars to Mr. Calderwood, I have been able to examine the scales of a somewhat remarkable fish, which died at the Tugnet hatchery, on the Spey, in August last. The details of the life of this most interesting specimen—a male—as supplied by the keeper of the hatchery are as follows: 'Hatched in April, 1905, the parr was placed in the rearing pond in the summer of the same year, and was retained there until the date of its death in August, 1911, when it weighed 4 pounds 3 ounces. During this period it spawned twice, for the first time in January, 1910, and for the second and last time in March, 1911; on the latter occasion its weight was 5 pounds 3 ounces, 1 pound more than when it died.'

---

[1] Yarrell, Wm. A history of British fishes, Part II, 1836, p. 21.
[2] Menzies, W. J. M. The infrequency of spawning in the salmon. Salmon Fisheries I, for 1911, Fishery Board for Scotland, 1912, p. 5.

8 GEORGE V, A. 1918

"It is interesting to observe that, although this fish enjoyed steady hand feeding, it had only attained one-tenth of the weight it would, in all probability, have reached had it spent the last four years of its life in the natural manner in the sea, and the scales show that the feeding has been, as one might expect, of a regular character, and it would be impossible to estimate the age in the regular way. The absence of a spawning mark is at first sight particularly striking, although this is not so surprising when one remembers that a great deal of the erosion of scales takes place after the fish has ceased feeding and left the sea, and while it is in the river before spawning."

Masterman[3] makes reference to salmon that were bred in tanks at the Plymouth Marine laboratory. He says: "Through the courtesy of Dr. Allen, the Director of the Plymouth Marine laboratory, I was enabled to examine the scales of young salmon which were bred in the tanks, and for two successive seasons were 'stripped' of ripe ova and milt. Their scales show no trace of worn edge or of spawning mark." He gives a photograph of a scale of one of these salmon (see fig. 27).

Similar experiments have been carried on with the British "sea-trout", the migratory trout of the British coasts, the name applied to it by those who consider the "brown trout", said to be non-migratory, a different species and even by those who think the two are of the same species, developed under different conditions. Tate Regan[4] definitely states "In the British Isles there is only one species of trout." Lamond[5] gives an approving review of the arguments presented by Regan and in discussing one of these, viz., that sea trout, if prevented from going to the sea, will live and breed in fresh water, makes reference to an experiment carried out at Howietoun under the supervision of the hatchery superintendent, John Thompson, whose notes are recorded thus: "The parents were caught in a tributary of the river Forth, brought to Howietoun and spawned on November 23, 1886. There were 450 ova laid down to hatch of which some 350 hatched out successfully in February, 1887, and the fry (some 250) were shifted from the hatchery house to one of our ponds, in June of the same year and then fed the same as other fry. The young fish were again shifted into a larger pond in June, 1888, when the average size was found to be about three inches. In August, 1889, some specimen fish, about six inches in length, were taken from the pond by Dr. Day for examination and comparison with common trout, *S. fario,* and we were all agreed that it was impossible to distinguish them by the eye from *S. fario.* In April, 1890, the fish were again moved to another pond and I spawned some of the females in November of the same year, crossing the ova with milt from *S. levenensis* and *S. fontinalis.* A few fry of the former were hatched out and reared but were afterwards mixed with other fry. The remainder of the parent sea-trout were afterwards, I think, turned out into a reservoir, when about five years old. They never attained to any great size."

In all the cases mentioned, apparently the only difference observed between the fish retained in fresh water and those normally migrating is the difference in size, the retained specimens growing much more slowly than the normal migrating specimens. The scant supply of food in the fresh water as compared with the supply in the sea, which is commonly given as the reason for the slower growth in fresh water, apparently cannot be the controlling cause in all of these cases, since in some of them at least the fish may have been fed as much as they wished for. Possibly the lack of any necessity for special activity in search for food accounts for a similar lack of appetite and a sluggishness in digestion and a general condition that is not conductive to rapid growth. This would also account for any differences in external appearance and in

[3] Masterman, A. T. Report on investigations upon the salmon with special reference to age determination by study of scales, Fishery Investigations, Board of Agriculture and Fisheries, series I, Vol. I, 1913, p. 31, London.
[4] Regan, C. Tate. The Fresh Water Fishes of the British Isles, 1911.
[5] Lamond, Henry. The Sea Trout, 1916.

the color of the flesh of the fish as well. The complete fresh water life, as far as these experiments show, causes no delay in the approach of the spawning period.

In only one of these cases was the later life of the fish followed up and reported upon. This fish survived two spawning periods and lived to be 6½ years old. There is thus nothing to indicate that its life was shortened in the continued existence in fresh water, nor can it be said definitely that it was prolonged.

Regan contends that there is no structural difference between the sea trout and the brown trout, but the difference in general appearance is due to the length of time spent in fresh water. That is to say, he is of the opinion that the brown trout is simply a sea trout that has given up migrating to the sea. Lamond apparently is of much the same opinion. If this contention is correct, and it is backed up by many convincing arguments, the continued life in fresh water must have a physiological effect if not a morphological, different to that when migration to the sea takes place, because the brown trout is so different in general appearance, when grown, that it is usually considered a different species or it might even be said many different species, where local conditions produce an appearance, different from the typical.

An experiment with the sockeye salmon, *Oncorhynchus nerka,* which is being carried on at the hatchery at New Westminster, B.C., by Hatchery Officer H. W. Doak, under the jurisdiction of Lieut.-Col. F. H. Cunningham, Chief Inspector of Fisheries for British Columbia, may be of greater interest than any of these. Already it is of sufficient importance to be worth recording.

In the fall of 1912 some sockeye eggs were taken from Harrison lake to the Bon Accord hatchery, where they hatched out in the spring of 1913. The fry were put into rearing ponds near the hatchery, but later, when the hatchery was moved over to Queen's Park, New Westminster, on account of Canadian Northern Railway operations, the fish were removed to ponds on the new site, where some of them still live and thrive.

In the fall of 1915 some of the males, then in their third year, became ripe and the milt was removed. The spent fish mended perfectly and continued to live and grow. As none of the spawning fish were marked, it was not possible to tell if those spawned again in 1916, but certainly some of the males spawned in that year. None of the females showed any signs of developing a spawning condition in the third year, i.e., in 1915, but they did so the following year. When they were ripe the eggs were removed, artificially mixed with milt for fertilization, and put in the hatchery, but although they remained fresh for a long period, none of them hatched out. The rest of the eggs were spawned naturally in the gravel at the bottom of the pond, but apparently they were not fertilized, as none of them hatched out either. The eggs were 5 to 5.5 mm. in diameter, somewhat smaller than even the smallest of normal sockeye eggs.

The spawning occurred about November 1, and on the 29th of January following a number of these fish were examined. There were nine of them altogether, running from 9 to 11 inches in length (not including caudal fin rays). They were not weighed, but probably none of them would weigh over a pound, and some of them not that much. The fish that had quit feeding during the spawning period, were taking food quite readily again and appeared to be perfectly mended. The skin was bright and metallic and the scales were shed quite readily.

Scales from four of them were taken for examination. Although there is much sameness in the rate of growth indicated throughout, it is possible in almost every perfect scale to make out the winter check somewhat readily. The growth is not quite regular even during the active part of the year, the irregularity is most noticeable in the second year's growth, but it is probably on account of the general slow growth that it is more noticeable in these than in normal scales. There may have been some disturbing influences in connection with their life in ponds as small as those in which they were kept.

8 GEORGE V, A. 1918

A calculation made to get the amount of growth each year gave the following results in inches) :—

Total length.	1st year.	2nd year.	3rd year.	4th year.
11·0	2·3	3·5	3·0	2·2
9·7	3·0	3·5	1·9	1·3
9·5	2·8	3·0	2·1	1·6
9·5	2·7	3·3	2·3	1·2
Average.. 9·9	2·7	3·3	2·3	1·6

The first of these was a female, and probably all of the others were males. There is a marked difference in the growth in the third year, but it cannot be stated with certainty that the small growth in the last three but particularly in the second one was due to the spawning of these males in the third year. There was no indication of a spawning mark on any of the scales. (This agrees with Menzies' statement for the Atlantic salmon, quoted above).

The great majority of the Fraser river sockeye remain in the fresh water for one year. The average growth of 614 four-year-old sockeye, hatched out at the same time as these and caught in the summer of 1916, is as follows:—

Total length.	1st year.	2nd year.	3rd year.	4th year.
22·3	2·9	8·6	7·7	3·1

No sockeye belonging to the same year class but remaining two years in the fresh water have yet been obtained as these are usually caught when in the 5th or 6th year, but a comparison may be made with the 5-year fish that were hatched out the preceding year. The average of 56 of these is as follows:—

Total length.	1st year.	2nd year.	3rd year.	4th year.	5th year.
22·5	2·6	3·2	8·2	6·1	2·4

I have not seen any sockeye from the Fraser that had remained in fresh water for three years, and as far as I am aware, none have been reported. Dr. Gilbert has reported some from the Nass river, that remained in fresh water for three years, but has given no figure of the scales. Even if the growth rate had been calculated for these Nass river fish, no direct comparison could be made with the Fraser river fish.

As far as comparison can be made, these pond-reared fish have a growth parallel to that of other sockeye, that remain in the fresh water under normal conditions, but the comparison can be carried only to the end of the second year. There is nothing to indicate that hand feeding in the pond makes any improvement in growth over natural feeding in the streams or lakes. The growth in length in the third year is less than that in the second, and that in the fourth less than that in the third, a decrease in somewhat the same portion, although not to the same extent, as is found in those living in the sea.

There is nothing remarkable in the fact that these fish lived over the fourth winter. Five year specimens are found in all types of sockeye, six years specimens are comparatively common and seven year specimens have been reported. The outstanding feature of the whole question lies in the fact that these fish have spawned and have mended perfectly and some of the males have lived over a year after the first spawning.

A large number of sockeye, as well as all other species of Pacific salmon, certainly die soon after spawning, and there is no convincing evidence that any of them long survive the spawning process under normal conditions, but these pond reared sockeye survived and began feeding again, apparently little the worse. They were examined again on April 20 and the nine of them were still alive, of good colour, and apparently in good health. It is true that they did not go through a wearing struggle in getting to spawning beds but that cannot have made all the difference because many of the Pacific salmon, even in some cases the sockeye, spawn in streams that are reached from the sea with no special effort. The spawning effort itself should have been as severe on these as on those spawning under natural conditions or those artificially spawned. The physiological condition of the body must have become changed under the changed conditions of life, so that the fish has become, in its nature, more like a fish that normally remains in the fresh water throughout its existence. This may indicate that the genus *Oncorhynchus* is even more intimately related to the genus *Salmo* than has been suspected.

Mr. Doak has some pond-reared sockeye younger than these, and some coho at different stages as well, hence there is every chance for him to follow up the experiment far enough to get quite decided results.

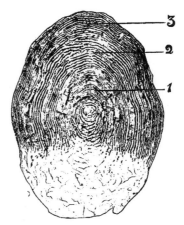

EXPLANATION OF FIGURE.

The figure is from a photograph of a scale from a 4-year-old sockeye that was reared entirely in fresh water, taken from the fish on January 29. The numbers 1, 2 and 3, indicate the limit of the first, second and third year's growth, respectively. The margin is the limit of the fourth year's growth.

VI

ON THE AGE AND GROWTH OF THE POLLOCK IN THE BAY OF FUNDY.

By Professor James W. Mavor, Ph.D., Union College, Schenectady, N.Y.

(With one Diagram.)

I.—INTRODUCTION.

The present report represents the results of studies on the age and growth of pollock caught in the Bay of Fundy during .the years 1915 and 1916. A report Mr. Douglas Macallum, prepared under the direction of the present writer, then curator of the St. Andrews Biological Station, dealing with the pollock caught in 1914, is already in the press. Mr. Macallum's report refers particularly to the older pollock of from three to six or more years growth, as determined by their scales. Besides working out the rate of growth of these pollock, he obtained indications that the most frequent year class was that of 1909. Some of the results of this report are included in the present paper for comparison with the data obtained in 1915 and 1916.

The object of the investigation has been to determine: (1) the distribution of the young pollock, (2) the rate of growth of young pollock during their first two or three years, (3) the relative frequency of the different year classes in typical commercial catches.

· The writer is indebted to the members of the staff of the Biological Station at St. Andrews in 1915 and 1916 for assistance in measuring and taking the scales from fish. He is particularly indebted to Mr. E. Horne 'Craigie for the measurements made in July, 1915, and to Dr. A. G. Huntsman, the curator of the Station, for assistance and advice in obtaining the young pollock in 1916.

II.—METHODS OF MEASURING FISH AND STUDYING SCALES.

Two measurements for length have been employed. The *standard length* is measured from the tip of the snout to the end of the vertebral column (easily determined by feeling with the fingers). The *total length* is measured from the tip of the snout to the end of the tail, the caudal fin having its normal spread. In the case of fish over 20 cm. in length the measurements are always to the nearest centimeter; in the case of the smaller fish, under 20 cm., to the nearest millimeter. The standard length was chosen at the beginning of these investigations for the following reasons: (1) It can be more accurately determined by the ordinary methods, (2) it is not affected by the position or spread of the tail or by injuring the tail, (3) it measures the actual length of the body of the fish, (4) it has been found by Hjort, in the case of herring, that a better correspondence between actual lengths and lengths as calculated from the position of the rings on the scales is obtained by taking a length V measured from the anterior end of the pectoral fin to the end of the vertebral column, than by taking the total length. The standard length differs from V by the length of the head only, while the total length differs by the length of head and tail. The total length has been recorded for comparison with the measurements of the European investigators who use this length.

In 1914 the standard length only was recorded. In 1915, for catches No. 1 and No. 2, both the standard and total lengths were recorded, and for catches No. 3 to No. 5 only the standard lengths. In 1916 for catches No. 1 to No. 40, both standard and total lengths were recorded and for catches No. 41 to No. 62, the total length only.

The scales of the fish were taken in most cases from a region marked by the end of the right pectoral fin when extended along the side of the body in a posterior

111

8 GEORGE V, A. 1918

direction. When the region had been injured either in capture or transport, the nearest uninjured region to this was used. The scales were stored in envelopes on which the length of the fish and other data were written. For microscopic study the scales were cleaned and flattened between two slides. In calculating the proportional lengths from the position of the winter rings, the positions of the outer edges of the winter rings were marked on strips of paper so placed that the edge of the paper coincided with the camera lucida image of the antero-posterior diameter of the scale in its anterior part. These strips were then placed on the apparatus devised by Hjort and the proportional lengths read off. For each fish, at least two scales were examined in this way.

III.—THE FIRST YEAR'S GROWTH.

A number of small Pollock, shown by their scales to be in their first year of growth were obtained. The greater number of these were caught in a shore seine about two fathoms in depth and twenty fathoms in length. The hauls were made in two localities and were as follows:

A.—North of Wilson's beach, Campobello island. Wilson's beach is on the western side of Campobello island and faces a stretch of tidal water lying between this island and the islands to the west of it, often called by the fishermen "The River". The Western shore of Campobello island descends somewhat abruptly, and, in consequence, the tidal current comes close to the shore. The hauls were made at about the time of low water on the morning of August 4; at which time many small pollock ranging around 35 cm. in length were seen in schools inshore. The results of these five hauls all made within a mile or two of each other, are grouped together and labelled catch No. 19. The separate hauls are given below.

Haul No. 1.—The seine was set a considerable distance from the shore so that the corks went under. The catch consisted of four pollock under 11 cm. and 1 pollock 42 cm. total length, and one flounder.

Haul No. 2.—The seine was set so that the cords just remained afloat. The catch consisted of seventeen pollock between 28 and 47 cm. total length, and no other fish.

Haul No. 3.—This was a short haul, the seine being set at about its own depth. The catch consisted of a few flounders and skulpins.

Haul No. 4.—This was a deep haul, the seine being set at about twice its own depth, the corks being completely under, on a beach covered with kelp. The catch consisted of fifteen pollock under 11 cm. total length, four skulpins, four flounders, and two sea ravens.

Haul No. 5.—This haul was made in shallow water and went foul of rocks. The catch consisted of a few flounders and a few skulpins.

B.—Bliss island. These hauls were made on the shores of a small island in the bay of Fundy, northeast of Campobello island and southwest of L'Etang harbour, where, as in the case af Wilson's beach, strong tides run. In all, six hauls were made and the catches numbered 28 to 33. Three hauls were made at low water on the evening of August 16, the seine being set in about its own depth. The hauls yielded the following small gadoids:—

Haul No. 1.—Two hake.

Haul No. 2.—Two pollock, forty-four cod, numerous hake.

Haul No. 3.—One pollock, two cod.

SESSIONAL PAPER No. 38a

Three hauls were taken at the next low water on the morning of August 17, yielding the following small gadoids:—

Haul No. 1.—Numerous hake.

Haul No. 2.—Five pollock, four cod, and four hake.

Haul No. 3.—Four hake.

The length frequencies of the twenty-seven small pollock obtained in catches 19 and 29 to 32 are given in table I.

The length frequencies of the fish caught in the seine catches 19 and 29-32 form rather even curves with a mode at 8 cm. and 9 cm. The mean standard length of these fish, as calculated from measurements made to the nearest millimeter, is 8·7 cm., and the mean total length, as calculated in the same way is 9·7 cm.

The scales of these fish show a series of rings of plates corresponding to the centres of the scales of longer pollock. The number of these rings is from 4 to 10. In no case were the rings of plates close together, indicating winter growth.

In 1913 five small pollock were caught in the shore seine at Sandy Cove, N.S. Their length frequencies were as follows:—

Total lengths............	7 cm.	8 cm.	9 cm.	Standard lengths...	7 cm.	8 cm.
Frequency....	1	1	3	Frequency	2	3

The measurements were made to the nearest millimeter, and the mean total length was 8·2 cm. and the mean standard length 7·4 cm.

Seven other small pollock were obtained, five from weirs which had been seined for herring and two caught on hook and line from the station wharf. The length frequencies of these fish are given in table 2, and show that these fish were larger than those caught in the shore seine. Their mean standard length was 12·2 cm. and their mean total length was 13·3 cm. Their scales corresponding to their larger size show a greater number of rings of plates but do not show any winter rings. So far as any importance can be attached to the occurrence of these seven fish, it would seem to indicate that the young, after they attain a certain length, about 11 cm., move into slightly deeper water where they are not caught by the shore seine.

IV—THE SECOND YEAR'S GROWTH.

Among the pollock caught in the shore seine at Wilson's beach on August 4, as described in the previous section and grouped together as catch No. 19, eighteen were between 29 and 45 cm. total length. Two of these, specimens No. 660 and No. 661, 29 and 32 cm. total length, show only a single winter ring in their scales. The lengths of these fish at the end of their first winter as calculated from the positions of the winter rings in the scales is shown in table 3.

It is to be noted that these fish are probably large for their age being caught in a shoal with large fish. They constitute, however, the only data the writer has been able to obtain on pollock in their second year's growth. It is hoped in future work to fill this unfortunate gap in the investigations.

V.—THE THIRD YEAR'S GROWTH.

In all seventy-three pollock in their third year were caught. They were all caught in the shore seine near Wilson's beach, Campobello island, and are included in catches 17 and 19.

Catch 17 was taken on the morning of August 3, 1916, when numerous schools of small pollock were seen close inshore just north of Wilson's beach, and the shore seine was set at low water. One haul yielded fifty-seven specimens ranging between 30 cm. and 47 cm. in total length. The seine was rapidly hauled in over a rocky bottom and the only other fish caught was one *Pseudopleuronectes americanus* 35 cm. in length. The scales of these pollock all show two winter rings. The length frequencies are given in table 4. The mean total length is 39·6 cm. and the mean standard length is 36·4 cm.

Catch No. 19 has already been described in a previous section. It included sixteen pollock whose scales showed two winter rings. The total lengths of these fish at the ends of their first and second winters, as calculated from their scales, are given in table No. 5. The lengths given are, in each case, the average of two measurements on different scales. The mean total lengths of two-year old fish of the catch are, at the end of the first winter, 15·4 cm. and at the end of the second winter, 31·8 cm. The mean length of the fish when caught on August 4 was 39·2 cm. The mean increase in total length during the second year, t_2, was 16·4 cm. and the mean increase during the third year up to August 4 was 7·4 cm. The length frequencies of the fish in the different years of their growth are shown in table 6. The corresponding figures for the standard lengths are: mean standard length at end of first winter, 14·1 cm.; mean standard length at end of second winter, 31·3 cm; mean standard length when caught on August 4, 35·9 cm.

VI.—THE FREQUENCY OF THE DIFFERENT YEAR CLASSES IN THE YEARS 1914, 1915 AND 1916.

From measurements made on 1,250 pollock caught in July, 1914, Mr. Douglas Macallum constructed a length frequency curve, given in the paper already referred to. This curve, as Mr. Macallum noted, shows two modes, one at 63 cm., and one at 68 cm., the former being the more prominent one. The mean length of 6-year old fish (67·8 cm.) corresponds closely with the frequency curve at 68 cm., as scale studies show, and the mean length of 5-year old fish (63· cm.) with the mode at 62 to 63 cm. The most prominent mode is at 63 cm., i.e., 5-year old fish, or the class of 1909.

The material for the study of the pollock in 1915 consisted of the measurements and scales of 652 fish obtained in five catches from Casco bay, off Campobello island, New Brunswick. The first two of these catches were made on June 22, and included 331 fish, the other three catches were made on July 16, and included 321 fish. The length frequencies of these pollock, both the actual numbers caught and the per cent in each centimeter class, are given in table 7. In catches 1 and 2, both the standard and the total lengths were measured while the catches 3 to 5, only the standard lengths were taken. The table gives the standard lengths for all five catches and, in addition, the total lengths for catches 1 and 2. From the column in the table giving the per cent of specimens in each centimeter class for the first two catches and the similar column for the last three catches, it will be seen that they agree in showing the most frequent classes at 65 and 66 cm. Since the distribution of lengths in the catches is similar and since the catches were chosen at random, it would seem fair to assume that they represent correctly the distribution in point of size of fish caught during June and July in the vicinity of Campobello island. The frequency curve for the standard lengths of catches 1 to 5 is shown in the graph where the lengths have been grouped in 2 cm. classes and the frequencies plotted in per cent. This curve has a single mode at 66 cm., corresponding to the most frequent class in the per cent column. An examination of the scales of the fish from a typical catch, catch 2, was made in the

SESSIONAL PAPER No. 38a

following manner: The envelopes, each containing the scales of a single fish, were arranged in the order of the standard lengths of the fish; the scales from every fourth envelope were examined and the number of rings counted. In this way, without examining scales from all the fish, scales from a representative sample of the catch were examined. The numbers of fish in each year class are shown in table 8. The mean standard length of the 5-year old fish of the class of 1910 was 63·9 cm., and that of the 6-year-old fish of the class of 1909 was 67·4 cm. The mode on the 1915 frequency curve is therefore seen to be due to the greater frequency of the 6-year-old fish of the class of 1909, or the same which gave rise to the most prominent mode in the 1914 frequency curve. The mean standard length of catches 1 and 2 is 67·5 cm., and the mean total length is 72·8 cm.

The material for the study of the pollock of three winters and over, in 1916, consisted of measurements of thirty-two catches made near Campobello island between July 10 and October 16. The first eleven of these catches, Nos. 2 to 18, were measured by the writer, both the standard and the total length being recorded and scale samples taken from each fish. The remaining catches were measured by Capt. Sheppard Mitchell of the Biological Station staff, and the total lengths recorded. The dates and locations of the catches and the number of pollock they contained are given in table 9.

The length frequencies of these catches have been tabulated and catches grouped according to the date of capture. Catches 2 to 12 were made betwen July 10 and 14; their standard length frequencies are given in table 10, columns I to X. From column IX it can be seen that the mode for these catches is about 66 c.m. The mode for catches 15 to 18 is seen from column XIV to be also 66 cm., although the frequencies of the 67 and 68 cm. classes are also large. Catches 2 to 18, which contain 567 fish, have been combined in columns XVI and XVII, which give the length frequencies in per cent. These columns show that the mode, in this case, is to be placed at 67 cm. The mode at 67 cm. is slightly in advance of the mode of the 1915 curve which is at 66 cm.

In the case of the remaining catches, numbers 41 to 62, the total length only was recorded. The catches are grouped according to the time of capture, July, August, first half of September, latter half of September, and October. In each of these groups the combined length frequencies of the separate catches, the per cent length frequency obtained by reducing the combined frequencies to per cent of the total number of fish concerned and the per cent frequency in classes of 2 centimeter intervals are given. The later percentages are each obtained by adding two of the percentages of the previous column. They are entered opposite the length of even number although they really correspond to a length which is the mean of the length of the two classes, the percentages of which were added, e.g. in column IV the per cent 8·0 corresponds to a length of 63·5 cm. The percentages in 2 centimeter classes are given because they make possible a more rapid inspection of the table. From table 11 it will be seen that the mode for catches 2 to 18 is 74cm., which may be taken to be the total length corresponding to 67 cm. The mode for catches 41 to 62 is at 80 cm. and it will be noted that this is approximately the mode of the separate groups of catches. The total length 80 cm., may be considered to correspond approximately to a standard length of 67/74 × 80 cm. or 72·5 cm.

During the summer of 1916, pollock were scarce around Campobello island, but they became more plentiful in the autumn. The catches 41 to 62 measured by Captain Mitchell are therefore regarded as more typical. It is these measurements which I have used in constructing the curve for 1916 in the graph. As these were measurements of the total length and the measurements for 1914 and 1915 were of the standard length the curve has been moved in the diagram so that its actual mode at 80 cm. comes at 72 cm. This has been done merely for the purposes of comparison. The form of the curve for total lengths is of course different from that for standard lengths. It is also to be considered that this curve represents fish caught later in the year than those used

8 GEORGE V, A. 1918

for the 1914 and 1915 curves, a fact which would make the corresponding modal length less than that shown.

The numbers of winter rings have been counted for the scales of the fish of catches 3, 6 and 7, and the results are shown in table 12. The table shows that these catches, which had a mode at 67 cm., were composed predominately of 6-year-old fish. This being the case, the mode at 72 cm. of the curve for catches 41 to 62 shown in fig. 1, probably corresponds to the 7-year-old fish or the fish of the 1909 year class, the same which gave rise to the modes in the 1914 and 1915 curves.

VII.—SUMMARY.

1. It has been found that young pollock showing in their scales no winter rings and therefore probably in their first year's growth occur in shallow tidal water on the western coast of the Bay of Funday.

2. Data as to the rate of growth during the first two years are given.

3. Evidence is given for believing that the 1909 class has been the most abundant during the three years 1914, 1915, and 1916.

VIII.—TABLES.

TABLE 1.—Length Frequencies of Small Pollock caught in shore seine in 1916.

A. Standard Lengths—Numbers in columns represent number of specimens in centimeter groups.

Length	7 cm.	8 cm.	9 cm.	10 cm.	11 cm.
Catch 19	3	6	8	2	–
Catch 29-32	–	3	–	4	1
Total	3	9	8	6	1

B. Total Lengths—Numbers in columns represent number of specimens in centimeter groups.

Length	7 cm.	8 cm.	9 cm.	10 cm.	11 cm.	12 cm.
Catch 19	2	4	7	5	1	–
Catch 29-32	–	1	2	–	4	1
Total	2	5	9	5	5	1

TABLE 2.—Length Frequencies of Small Pollock, Catches Nos. 21-26, five seined in herring weirs and two caught with hook and line from Station wharf August 3 to 9.

A—STANDARD LENGTHS.

Lengths	11 cm.	12 cm.	13 cm.	14 cm.	15 cm.
Frequency	3	1	1	2	–

B—TOTAL LENGTHS.

Lengths	11 cm.	12 cm.	13 cm.	14 cm.	15 cm.
Frequency	1	2	1	1	2

SESSIONAL PAPER No. 38a

TABLE 3.—Calculated Lengths of Pollock from Catch No 19, showing a Single Winter Ring.

	Standard Lengths.		Total Lengths.	
—	1st. Ring.	Length.	1st. Ring.	Length.
Specimen 660	19 cm.	27 cm.	20 cm.	29 cm.
" 661....	20	29	22	32

TABLE 4.—Length Frequencies of Pollock of Catch 17.

A. Standard Length Frequencies in Centimeter Classes.

Cm. Class.......	27	28	29	30	31	32	33	34	35	36	37	38	39	40	41	42	43	44
Frequency..	1	–	1	–	–	1	1	8	10	16	3	3	2	3	3	3	1	1

B. Total Length Frequencies in Centimeter Classes.

Cm. Class.... ...	30	31	32	33	34	35	36	37	38	39	40	41	42	43	44	45	46	47
Frequency........	1	–	1	–	–	1	1	7	11	14	5	2	2	2	4	3	2	1

TABLE 5.—Lengths of Pollock of Catch 19 at the end of each of their first two winters as calculated from their scales and their lengths when caught.

Specimen No.	Standard Length.			Total Length.		
	1st. Ring. 1915.	2nd. Ring. 1916.	Edge. 1916.	1st. Ring. 1915.	2nd. Ring. 1916.	Edge. 1916.
662	12	27	32	13	30	35
663...........	12	29	34	13	32	37
664...	14	28	33	15	32	37
665	13	31	35	14	34	38
666	14	29	35	15	32	38
667....	14	28	36	15	30	39
668..........	13	32	36	14	35	39
669.........	14	31	36	16	34	39
670	15	32	36	16	35	39
671..	17	31	36	19	33	39
672............	14	32	36	15	36	40
673	14	33	37	15	36	40
674.........	17	34	37	19	37	40
675...	13	33	38	14	36	41
676.........	13	33	37	14	36	41
677........	17	37	41	19	40	45
Mean.............	14·1	31·3	35·9	15·4	31·8	39 2

8 GEORGE V, A. 1918

TABLE 6.—Length Frequencies of Pollock of Catch No. 19, those at the end of first and second winters being calculated from their scales.

Length cm	13	14	15	16	17	18	19
Frequency	2	4	5	2	–	–	2

Length cm	30	31	32	33	34	35	36	37	38	39	40
Frequency	1	–	3	1	2	2	4	1	–	–	1

Length cm	35	36	37	38	39	40	41	42	43	44	45
Frequency	1	–	2	2	5	3	2	–	–	–	1

TABLE 7.—Length Frequencies of Pollock caught in 1915 and Comprising Catches Nos. 1 to 5.

Length in cm.	Standard Lengths.								Total Lengths.		
	No. in Catch.		% in each cm. class.	No. in Catch.			% in each cm. class.		No. in Catch.		% in each cm. class.
	1	2	1-2	3	4	5	3-5	1-5	1	2	1-2
I	II	III	IV	V	VI	VII	VIII	IX	X	XI	XII
52	1		·3					·2			
55				2			·6	·3			
56					2	1	1·0	·5			
57				1		2	1·0	·5	1		·3
58	4	1	1·5	1	1		·6	1·1			
59	2	3	1·5	2			·6	1·4			
60	2	4	1·8	3	3		1·9	1·8			
61	7	5	3·6	5		1	1·9	2·8			
62	19	10	8·8	6	9	6	6·7	7·7			
63	20	13	10·0	5	5	1	3·5	6·7			
64	24	12	10·9	8	12	2	7·1	8·9	4	1	1·5
65	27	11	11·5	10	15	13	12·2	11·7	2	3	1·5
66	19	20	11·8	9	15	7	9·9	10·7	1		·3
67	15	9	7·3	5	16	9	9·6	8·3	8	5	3·9
68	13	12	7·6	9	19	8	11·6	9·4	9	11	6·1
69	3	7	3·0	7	11	7	8·0	5·4	19	12	9·4
70	8	8	4·8	6	7	6	6·1	5·4	22	9	9·4
71	7	5	3·6	1	5	5	3·5	3·5	15	10	7·6
72	9	2	3·3	2	3	8	4·2	3·7	25	14	11·8
73	4	4	2·4	4	2	1	2·2	2·3	19	18	11·2
74	4	1	1·5	3	2	2	2·2	1·8	13	7	6·1
75	2	5	2·1	2	2	6	3·2	2·6	10	8	5·4
76	2	2	1·2	1		1	·6	·9	7	7	4·2
77	1	1	·6	1		4	1·6	1·4	5	5	3·0
78	2		·6		1	1	·6	·6	5	7	3·6
79	1		·3	1		2	·9	·6	7	4	3·3
80						2	·6	·3	8	4	3·6
81					1		·3	·2	4	1	1·5
82						1	·3	·2	4	1	1·5
83									1	4	1·5
84									2	1	·9
85									2	3	1·5
86											
87									3		·9
Total..	196	135		94	131	96					

NOTE.—Lengths are to nearest centimeter.
    Numbers refer to catch numbers.
    Date of Catches Nos. 1-2, June 22.
    Date of Catches Nos. 3-5, July 16.

SESSIONAL PAPER No. 38a

TABLE 8.—The Age Frequencies of Pollock caught in 1915, Catches 1 to 5.

Number of winter rings	4	5	6	7	8
Year class	1911	1910	1909	1908	1907
Frequency	1	13	17	2	1

TABLE 9.—Catches of Pollock examined in 1916.

Catch.	Date.	Place.	No. of Pollock.
2	July 10..	Off East Quoddy Light, Campobello Island	10
3	" 11..	do.	66
6	" 12..	do.	45
7	" 13..	do.	74
10	" 14..	do.	29
11	" 14..	do.	45
12	" 14..	do.	31
15	Aug. 2..	Wolves	68
16	" 2 .	"	168
18	" 3..	Off Casco Bay Island, Campobello Island	31
41	Sept. 4.	Off Pope's Folly, near Campobello Island	40
42	" 4..	do.	40
43	" 4..	do.	33
44	" 5..	do.	55
45	" 6..	do.	24
46	" 7..	do.	21
47	" 7.	do.	15
48	" 7..	do.	22
49	" 11..	do.	11
50	" 11 .	Off Green Island Shoal, near Campobello Island	10
51	" 20..	do.	19
52	" 28..	do.	35
53	" 28..	do.	21
54	" 28..	do.	41
55	Oct. 2..	do.	96
56	" 3 .	do.	139
57	" 4..	do.	87
58	" 5..	do.	98
59	" 6..	do.	89
60	" 7..	Off Pope's Folly, near Campobello Island	94
61	" 12..	Off Indian Island, near Campobello Island	100
62	" 16..	Off Green Island Shoal, near Campobello Island	78

TABLE 10.—Standard Length Frequencies of Catches 2 to 18.

Length in cm.	Frequency in each catch.							Catches 2–12, July 10–14.		Frequency in each catch.			Catches 15–18, August 2–3.		Catches 1–18, July 10–Aug. 3.	
	Catch 2, July 10.	Catch 3, July 11.	Catch 6, July 12.	Catch 7, July 13.	Catch 10, July 14.	Catch 11, July 14.	Catch 12, July 14.	Per cent in each cm. class.		Catch 15, Aug. 2–XI. „ 16, „ 2–XII. „ 18, „ 3–XIII.			Per cent in each cm. class.		Per cent in each cm. class.	
								1 cm.	2 cm.				1 cm.	2 cm.	1 cm.	2 cm.
I	II	III	IV	V	VI	VII	VIII	IX	X	XI	XII	XIII	XIV	XV	XVI	XVII
40							1	·3	·3						·2	2
1							1	·3	3						·2	·2
2								2					·4	·4	·2	·2
3			1					·3	·3		·4		·4		·4	
4				1				·3	·6					·4	·2	·6
5				3				1·0		1	1		·7		·9	
6				1		3		1·3	2·3	5	2		2·6	3·3	1·9	2·8
5		2		1	1	1	2	2·3		3	4		2·6		2·5	
6		1		1		3	2	2·3	4·6	4			1·5	4·1	1·9	4·4
5		3	1	3	4	3	2	5·3		1	6		2·6		4·1	
8			4	3		3	2	4·0	9·3		2	1	1·1	3·7	2·7	6·8
9		4	3	2		4	3	5·3			1		·4		3·0	
0		3	2	2		4	3	4·7	10·0		2		7·7	6·1	2·8	5·8
1	1	4	1	3	3	4	2	6·0		2	5		2·6		4·4	
2	2	5	2	6	2	4	1	7·3	13·3		1	3	1·5	4·1	4·6	9·0
8	2	2	2	4	1	5	2	6·0			8	1	3·4		4·8	
4	1		4	3	3	3	1	5·0	11·0	2	13	1	6·0	9·4	5·5	10·3
6		4	7	6	3		3	7·7		5	9	1	5·6		6·7	
6		6	3	6	4	4	1	8·0	15·7	8	18	2	10·3	15·9	9·2	15·9
6	1	3	2	5	1	2		4·7		7	16	2	9·4		6·9	
6	1	8	3	9	1	1	1	8·0	12·7	6	12	5	8·6	18·0	8·3	15·2
0		4	2	4		1		4·0		4	11	4	7·1		5·5	
9	1	5	3	2	1		2	4·7	8·7		13	1	5·3	12·4	5·0	10·5
1	1	2	1	1				1·7		6	5	3	5·3		3·4	
2		5		3	1		1	3·3	5·0		5	1	2·3	7·6	2·8	6·2
2		3		1	1			1·7		3	5	4	4·5		3·0	
1		1	1	1	1			1·3	3·0	1	5		2·3	6·8	1·8	4·8
5				2	2			1·3			7		2·6		1·9	
0		1						·3	1·6	4	3		2·6	5·2	1·4	3·3
77			1					·3		3	3		2·3		1·2	
78										1	1	1	1·1	3·4	·5	1·7
9											5		1·9		·9	
6			1					·3	·3		4		1·5	3·4	·9	1·8

SESSIONAL PAPER No. 38a

81.	·6	·2	·4	·4				·3	·3					1		
82.	·2	·4	·4	·4			1	·3	·3				1			
83.		·2		·4	1		1						1			
84.			·4													
Total.					31	168	68			31	45	20	74	45	66	10

38a—9½

8 GEORGE V, A. 1918

TABLE 11.—Total length frequencies of catches 2 to 62.

	Catches 2-12, July 10-14.			Catches 15-18, August 2-3.			Catches 41-50, September 4-11.			Catches 51-54, September 20-28.			Catches 55-58, October 31.			Catches 2-18.		Catches 41-62.	
	I	II	III	IV	V	VI	VII	VIII	IX	X	XI	XII	XIII	XIV	XV	XVI	XVII	XVIII	XIX	XX
		Combined frequency.	% in each cm. class.	% in each 2 cm. class	Combined frequency.	% in each cm. class.	% in each 2 cm. class	Combined frequency.	% in each cm. class.	% in each 2 cm. class	Combined frequency.	% in each cm. class.	% in each 2 cm. class	Combined frequency.	% in each cm. class.	% in each 2 cm. class	% in each cm. class.	% in each 2 cm. class	% in each cm. class	% in each 2 cm. class
44																				
52																				
55																				
56																				
57																				
58																				
59																				
60																				
61																				
62																				
63																				
64																				
65																				
66																				
67																				
68																				
69																				
70																				
71																				
72																				
73																				
74																				
75																				
76																				
77																				
78																				
79																				
80																				
81																				
82																				
83																				
84																				

SESSIONAL PAPER No. 38a

85		1·5			1·1			1·0	8		9	1		3·3	9		1·9		5			1
86	2·9	1·4	2·2	1·1		·16	·6	5	·43	3·4	4	·6·9	2·6	7		2·2	6	·3		
87		1·9		·2			·4	4		·9	1		2·2	6	4·1	2·4	4			
88	2·1	1·2	·9	·7	·9		·5	3	·18	·9		5·5	3·3	9	1·9	1·5	4		·3	
89		·8		1·1			·4						2·2	6		1·5	4			
90	1·5	·7	·16	·4	·4							5·2	3·0	8	1·9	·4	1			
91				·9												·0	0			
92			·2	·2							1				·4	·4	1			
Total in caches....								781			116			271			267			300

8 GEORGE V, A. 1918

TABLE 12.—Length frequencies of the Pollock of catches 3, 6 and 7, arranged according to age and catch.

Length to nearest cm.	Catch 3.			Catch 6.			Catch 7.					
	No. of winter rings.			No. of winter rings.			No. of winter rings.					
	4	5	6	4	5	6	4	5	6			
51				1								
52							1					
53							3					
54							1					
55	2						1					
56	1						1					
57	3				1		2	1				
58				4				3				
59		4		1	2			2				
60		2	1		2			2				
61	1	2	1		1		1	1	1			
62		5			2			6				
63		2			1	1		2	1			
64					1	3	1	1				
65		1	3		4	2		1	4			
66		2	2		2	1		2	3			
67		2	2			2		1	4			
68		5	5	1		2		1	8			
69		3	3		1	1		1	3			
70		2	2		2	1		1	2			
71		1	1			1						
72		3	3					1	2			
73		2	2						1			
74		1	1			1			1			
75								1	1			
76		1	1	1								
77												
78												
79												
80												
81												
82									1			
Total	7	38	27	7	20	15	11	27	32			
Mean lengths	56·9	62·9	68·6	59·9	63·8	66·3	55·9	63·3	68·4			

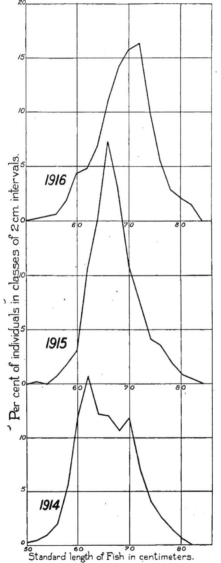

Curves showing length frequencies of Pollock caught in 1914, 1915 and 1916.

The curves for 1914 and 1915 are constructed from measurements of the standard length and are based upon measurements on 1,250 fish in the case of the 1914 curve and in the case of the 1915 curve on 652 fish. The curve for 1916 is based on measurements of the total length of 1,168 fish. In order to compare it with the curves for 1914 and 1915 the whole curve has been moved to the left so that the mode which was at 80 cm. is at 72 cm.

VII

FURTHER HYDROGRAPHIC INVESTIGATIONS IN THE BAY OF FUNDY.

By E. Horne Craigie, B.A., University of Toronto and W. H. Chase, B.A., Acadia University.

(With 25 figures and 1 map.)

During the summer of 1914 a hydrographic section of the Bay of Fundy was made, a report of which appeared in the *Contributions to Canadian Biology,* 1914-1915.[1] At the beginning of July, 1915, it was suggested that a considerable amount of dredging should be done with a view to working out the fauna of the Bay of Fundy, and the opportunity was taken to combine with this work a repetition of the hydrographic observations made in the previous year and to extend them over the greater part of the Bay. It was thus possible to collect sufficient data to give a general idea of the conditions existing in the water of this important and interesting region.

OBSERVATIONS MADE AND APPARATUS EMPLOYED.

The work was carried out during two cruises in the month of July. The first of these enabled dredging to be carried on at twenty-four stations in St. Mary bay, Nova Scotia, and observations to be taken at stations I to IV in the Bay of Fundy—the stations which were established in 1914. The work of the second cruise comprised dredging at nine stations in the Annapolis basin and the establishment of two more cross-sections and a longitudinal section of the Bay of Fundy.

In St. Mary bay and the Annapolis basin, the stations in which were numbered consecutively in Arabic numerals, temperatures and water samples were taken at the surface and at the bottom at each dredging station, largely for the sake of the connection of these conditions with the fauna found. At all the Bay of Fundy stations, observations were made at the surface, at depths of 5 and 10 fathoms, and then at 10 fathom intervals to the bottom. In the table of data the records for the bottom have been put opposite the nearest depth in tens of fathoms. The exact depth of the observation may be seen at a glance from the record of "Depth" near the top of the column for each station. The hydrographic data obtained in St. Mary bay and the Annapolis basin are tabulated here chiefly in order that they may be accessible when required, though few deducations can be made from them at present. At the Bay of Fundy stations V to XV, dredge hauls were taken; and at these and the Annapolis basin stations, surface plankton samples were also obtained.

The apparatus employed was the same as that used in 1914, and has been described in the report of the work done in that year. The temperature of the air and of the surface water were taken by means of a delicate chemical thermometer, all other temperatures were determined by reversing thermometers. The temperatures at 5 and 10 fathoms at station III, and from 10 to 40 fathoms at station IV, were determined by a Negretti-Zambra thermometer,[2] all other temperatures below the surface by a Richter thermometer.[3] The water samples were obtained by means of a Petterssen-

---

[1] Craigie, E. Horne. "A Hydrographic Section of the Bay of Fundy in 1914."
[2] Magnaghi pattern frame, Negretti and Zambra thermometer No. 170664.
[3] Laboratoire Hydrographique, Kobenhavn, Preisliste, 1914, No. 75, thermometer No. 164.

8 GEORGE V, A. 1918

Nansen water-bottle. A full description of both this water-bottle and the reversing thermometers may be found in the section on hydrographic work in the report on the " Investigation of the Bays of the Southern Coast of New Brunswick with a view to Their Use for Oyster Culture."[1]

The temperatures read on the Richter thermometer were all corrected for the expansion of the mercury column at the temperature at which the reading was made, and the corrected figures were recorded in the tables and used in constructing the temperature curves. All temperatures are in the centigrade scale.

The densities and salinities of the water samples were determined by W. H. Chase, but as he was called away by military duties, he was unfortunately prevented from completing the work.[2] Such discrepancies between density and salinity in many cases were found in the records that it was considered necessary to repeat the analysis of the samples, and Professor Vachon of Laval University was so kind as to do this during the summer of 1916. Unfortunately, Prof. Vachon found that the water samples must have altered by evaporation since they were collected, and it has accordingly been regretfully decided not to publish the data for the Bay of Fundy stations, but to confine this report to the temperature observations. The densities, salinities and chlorine contents of the samples from St. Mary bay, as determined by W. H. Chase, will be found in table III at the end of the report.

LOCATION OF OBSERVATION STATIONS.

The positions of all the stations are indicated on the accompanying map, on which the fifty and hundred fathom lines have also been inserted, giving an idea of the conformation of the bottom of the Bay. The stations were located so as to give as complete sections as possible, showing the conditions existing in the various parts of the water. In making the observations, the stations were found by the use of a log.

Stations I to IV are on a straight line drawn from East Quoddy Head, Campobello island, to Boar's Head, Petit Passage, Long island, as follows:—

```
Station   I.. .. .. .. .. .. .. .. .. ..  7 miles from East Quoddy Head.
   "      II.. .. .. .. .. .. .. .. .. ..19   "    "     "     "
   "      III.. .. .. .. .. .. .. .. ..27   "    "     "     "
   ..     IV.. .. .. .. .. .. .. .. .. ..37   "    "     "     "
```

The remaining Bay of Fundy stations are located as follows:—

```
Station   V.. .. .. .. .. .. .. .. ..   22 miles N.W. from Digby Gut.
   "      VI.. .. .. .. .. .. .. .. ..    8   "  S. from Partridge Island, St. John
                                                   Harbour.
   ..     VII.. .. .. .. .. .. .. .. .. .  14½  "  S. from Partridge Island, St. John
                                                   Harbour.
   "      VIII.. ., .. .. .. .. .. .. ..   21½  "  S. from Partridge Island, St. John
                                                   Harbour.
   ..     IX.. .. .. .. .. .. .. .. .. ..   28   "  S. from Partridge Island, St. John
                                                   Harbour.
   ..     X.. .. .. .. .. .. .. .. .. ..  11½  "  E. from Station VII.
   "      XI.. .. .. .. .. .. .. .. .. ..    5   "  S. from Quaco Head.
   "      XII.. .. .. .. .. .. .. .. .. .. 10½  "    "      "      "
   "      XIII.. .. .. .. .. .. .. .. .. .. 15½  "    "      "      "
   "      XIV.. .. .. .. .. .. .. .. .. .. 20½  "    "      "      "
   "      XV.. .. .. .. .. .. .. .. .. .. 16   "  S.E. by S. from Quaco Head.
```

The distances are measured in geographical miles.

---

[1] Mavor, Craigie, and Detweiler in " Contributions to Canadian Biology, 1914-15."
[2] The responsibility for the planning of the work, selecting the stations, etc., rests with E. Horne Craigie, as does also the recording and working up of the temperature data, while observations on density and salinity were in charge of W. H. Chase. The two workers collaborated on the draft of the earlier part of this report, and on the preparation of the accompanying map and some of the figures. Owing to Mr. Chase's departure for the front, it has been necessary to complete the report without his assistance or criticism.

'SESSIONAL PAPER No. 38a

DEDUCTIONS FROM DATA OBTAINED IN THE BAY OF FUNDY.

A.—*Temperature Curves.*

From the corrected data obtained at each station, a temperature curve has been ·drawn (figs. 1-15), and upon the basis of these curves four profiles have been constructed representing respectively the three transverse sections and one longitudinal section of the Bay of Fundy. The discrepancies in depth at some stations shown by the curves and profiles are to be explained by the state of the tide when the observations were made. The bottom conformation has been drawn as accurately as possible with the aid of charts.

If the data for stations I to IV be compared with those recorded in August, 1914,[1] it will be observed that, with the exception of the surface temperatures at stations II and IV, all the readings are considerably lower in the new observations, the bottom temperatures averaging 2.7° lower than in 1914. The range of temperatures between the surface and the bottom is thus much greater in 1915, the difference in the surface temperatures being comparatively little. These differences between the temperatures found in the two years are to be explained, no doubt, by the fact that the new observations were taken six weeks earlier in the season than the old ones, when the heating effect of the summer sun and air had had less time to penetrate to the deeper water. Thus there is to be seen a very rapid fall of temperature in the layers of water near the surface (figs. 1-4). In this connection, it must be remembered that the heat conductivity of sea water is so slight as to be practically negligible. " The heat conveyed by the sun to the uppermost water-layers cannot therefore be propagated into deep water by conduction, but only through movements of the water-waves, currents, convection ' currents,' etc."[2] The fact that the deeper water is heated so much in a period of six weeks must be attributed to the vertical mixing of the water by the great tides occurring in this region.

Another effect of this vertical mixing by the strong tidal currents was referred to in the previous report, namely, the considerable areas of the same, or nearly the same temperature occurring at many of the stations. This is most marked in the case of the stations farther up the Bay, the temperatures at stations X to XV (figs. 10-15) inclusive. being practically constant between a depth of 5 fathoms and the bottom. The fact that this uniformity becomes more marked in the upper part of the Bay bears out the theory that the tides are responsible for it, the tides being greatest at the head of the Bay, while the water there is shallower, so that the tides are likely to effect a more complete mixing of the mass of water.

Helland-Hansen, generalizing upon the basis of temperature curves for four stations distributed over the Atlantic from the Faroe-Shetland channel to the Sargasso Sea says: "From the surface downwards the temperature falls very rapidly for the first hundred metres; at 100 metres it is 4° to 6° colder than at the surface. Beyond 100 metres the temperature decreases at first much more slowly. . . : The layers in which the temperature changes very rapidly are called 'discontinuity layers' (by the Americans 'thermocline,' and by the Germans ' Sprungschicht')."[3] The curves obtained for the first four Bay of Fundy stations, i.e. those nearest the open Atlantic, (figs. 1-4) agree with these observations to an extent which seems little short of remarkable in shallow and enclosed water, especially where conditions are so peculiar as they are in the Bay of Fundy. Indeed it would hardly seem justifiable to consider the correspondence as more than a matter of chance were it not for the fact that it appears even more clearly in the curves for the same stations in August, 1914. The comparison is made particularly apt

---

[1] Craigie, E. Horne. " A Hydrographic Section of the Bay of Fundy in 1914." Contributions to Canadian Biology, 1914-1915.
[2] Helland-Hansen in " The Depths of the Ocean," by Sir John Murray and Dr. Johan Hjort, p. 226.
[3] " The Depths of the Ocean," p. 223.

8 GEORGE V, A. 1918

by the fact that Helland-Hansen's observations were made between June 24 and August 10—at practically the same time of year as our own work.

While the density and salinity records are not being included in this report, for the reasons explained above, it is perhaps worth while remarking in this connection that the observed densities also correspond rather closely with the records obtained in the part of the open Atlantic near Nova Scotia by the *Challenger* expedition in May 1873. The surface densities for the *Challenger* stations 49 and 50 are, respectively, 1.02354 and 1.02451, the bottom readings for the same stations being 1.02400 and 1.02546. The depth at station 40 was only 85 fathoms, that at station 50 was 1,250 fathoms.[1]

The surface and bottom densities found at our stations I to IV were:—

Station—	I.	II.	III.	IV.
Surface..	10242	10240	10239	10246
Bottom..	10246	10250	10252	10252

The surface densities throughout the Bay varied from 10238 (stations VI and VII) to 10248 (station XIII). The bottom densities ran from 10244 (station X) to 10252 (stations III and IV). Thus it appears that the density of the waters of the Bay of Fundy corresponds quite closely with that of the neighbouring part of the Atlantic. Once more, no doubt, the thorough mixture brought about by the tides is to be held responsible for this, as it seems improbable that evaporation in the Bay of Fundy is nearly sufficient to counterbalance the influx of fresh water.

Helland-Hansen remarks that the high surface temperature shown by his curves "is principally due to the absorption of heat rays from the sun. In places the water is heated by contact with warm air, but this source of heat is of less importance, *the temperature of the surface water being, as a rule, higher than the temperature of the air.*"[2] He makes no mention of the time of day at which his readings were made, which, of course, would greatly affect the air temperature—unless he refers to the mean air temperature of the day. All our observations, practically, were made in daylight, and in no case was the air less than 2.2° warmer than the surface water, while in most cases it was considerably more. It may be noted in passing that although three of Helland-Hansen's four stations mentioned above are farther north than the Bay of Fundy, and all four are in the open Atlantic, his lowest surface temperature (that in the Faroe-Shetland channel) is 13°C.—more than 1° higher than the highest reading obtained in the Bay of Fundy. In looking over the records of the *Challenger* observations[3] in July, 1873, it is found that at 6 a.m. on the 16th of the month the air temperature was as much as 3°F. below that of the surface water in the harbour of Madeira; but in the majority of cases the air was warmer than the surface water. On the 15th the mean air temperature was 0.1° F. less than the mean surface water temperature, and on the 26th it was 0.5° F. less, but such cases are considerably in the minority. In May, 1873, when the *Challenger* was in this part of the Atlantic, only in a few cases again did the water temperature exceed the air temperature; and in no case was the mean surface water temperature for the day higher than the mean air temperature, until the 22nd of the month, when the ship had gone south to about the 40th parallel of north latitude.

The temperature curves for stations I to IV do not show so clearly as did those of 1914 the resemblance between stations II, III, and IV, and the distinct difference from these of station I. The curve for station I shows a peculiar rise in temperature between 40 and 70 fathoms. A similar, though smaller rise occurs at the same depth

---

[1] Report on the Specific Gravity of Ocean Water, observed on board H.M.S. *Challenger* during the years 1873-76." By J. Y. Buchanan, pp. 14 and 16. Report on the Scientific Results of the Voyage of H.M.S. *Challenger*, Phys. and Chem., Vol. I.

[2] ".The Depths of the Ocean," p. 225. (The italics are due to the present writer.)

[3] " Meteorological Observations made during the voyage of H.M.S. *Challenger*, 1873-76." Report on the Scientific Results of the Voyage of H.M.S. *Challenger*, Narrative, Vol. II, 1882.

in station II and is represented in station III also, at a somewhat deeper point. This is evidently the effect of some current and its occurrence both in the Grand Manan Channel (station I) and at the two neighbouring stations in the open Bay would seem to suggest that it is tidal. It is to be regretted that there was not an opportunity to make further observations with a view to elucidating this matter.

It may be noted that in 1914 a similar, though smaller rise in temperature occurred at a depth of 60 fathoms at station II with the tide two-thirds flood, while in the present case it was one-half flood at the same station. At station I, where the irregularity is most marked, the tide was flood, while at the same station in 1914 no such irregularity was found with the tide one-third flood. Thus from the present limited data there is no indication that this condition occurs regularly at any particular state of the tide. A similar rise is to be seen at a depth of 20 fathoms at station IX (fig. 9).

B. *Profiles.*

The profile for the section from East Quoddy Head to Petit Passage (fig. 16) shows no marked disagreement with that obtained in 1914. The cold water along the slope from Grand Manan found in 1914 does not appear in the new section. As before, the temperatures tend to be a little higher on the Nova Scotia side of the bay than on the New Brunswick side.[1] The irregularities showing in the graphs, which were discussed in the previous section are not represented in the profile.

The water below 6°C. occupying most of this profile does not appear in that of the St. John to Digby section (fig. 17), and a similar position but less space is occupied by the water between 6.38° and 7°. The tendency of the water towards the Nova Scotia side to be warmer does not appear in this section.

The profile from Quaco Head to Port Lorne (fig 18), shows that the water below 7° has disappeared, and its place, though much less space, is taken by water between 7.9° and 8°. From these three profiles it is easy to picture each successive layer of cold water running up the bay and gradually diminishing in extent until it finally disappears, its place being taken by the next layer. Of course, these remarks are not to be taken as meaning that the water is believed to be actually divided into distinct layers behaving thus.

The longitudinal section from Cape Chignecto to station III (fig. 19) shows that the layers do not simply taper and fade away, but end rather suddenly, clearly suggesting that the water flows up the bay and the lower layers are continually retarded by friction with the bottom, though this appearance is probably due to tidal action. A peculiar condition appears between stations VII, X, and XII. The presence of warmer water at station VII might be attributed to warm water coming in from the Atlantic surface, passing along the south shore, and turning north about this region (see fig. 20), but the source of the cold water at station X is not so clear. It seems possible that as the warm surface water is turned north across the bay (fig. 20) the cold water below goes on up the bay and so comes to the surface. It is most unfortunate that there was not time to make a complete transverse section through station X. Presumably the condition will be due to tidal action, but just how it is produced is not evident in the present state of our knowledge.

[1] I am informed by Dr. A. G. Huntsman that observations taken during the summer of 1916, nearer the shore on each side, showed this much more markedly, so that the isotherms should really dip quite rapidly near the coast in this profile. His observations appear to indicate a current entering at the mouth of the bay and passing up the Nova Scotia side, producing a corresponding current in an outward direction on the New Brunswick side. A somewhat similar condition, with peculiar tidal changes, was demonstrated in the St. Croix River by Craigie in 1914. (Craigie, E. Horne. "Hydrographic Investigations in the St. Croix River and Fassamaquoddy Bay in 1914." Contributions to Canadian Biology, 1914-1915.)

8 GEORGE V, A. 1918

C. Horizontal Distribution of Temperature.

In the hope that more light might thereby be thrown on the subject, three maps have been constructed, showing the distribution of temperature in the surface water (fig. 20) and at depths of ten fathoms and thirty fathoms respectively (figs. 21 and 22). As pointed out above, figure 20 shows an indication of an influx of warm surface water, which passes along the south shore and then turns across the bay (see foot note on page 131). If this represents a current in this direction, however, the deeper water should be colder than on the other side, as it must come in from the cold Labrador current, and we have already seen that the results both seasons tend rather the other way. Figures 21 and 22 show no sign of such a circulation, but rather combine with the four profiles to indicate a simple tongue of cold water up the middle of the bay. The cold area on the slope of Grand Manan in the 1914 profile especially supports this. There is nothing at ten fathoms corresponding in any way to the area of colder water appearing at the surface of station X (8·46° surface temperature) and points east of it, nor does the conformation of the shore appear to suggest any satisfactory explanation. That proposed at the end of the previous section appears to be the only one at present. The isolated area of warmer water east of Grand Manan (station II) in fig. 20 does not seem to be explicable on the basis of the present data either. The probable position of the 10°C. isotherm along the north shore is indicated by a broken line, although, of course, there are not sufficient data to locate this properly.

DEDUCTIONS FROM DATA OBTAINED IN ST. MARY BAY.

From the data obtained in St. Mary bay (table II) a plan of the distribution of temperature in the surface water of that bay has been drawn (fig. 23). It shows a rather uniform arrangement with gradually increasing temperature as one passes up the bay from Petit Passage, the shape of the isotherms suggesting that there may be a current up each side with a reverse current down the middle. Immediately below Petit Passage the effects of the tremendous tidal currents through that channel are visible, producing a rather complicated arrangement of the isotherms, due apparently to several interfering cross-currents. The arrangements of the water must, of course, vary very greatly at different states of the tide and the fact that all the observations must be taken at different times makes it improbable that the diagram represents such a condition as ever exists at any one time.

It has been thought worth while also to include a diagram representing a longitudinal section of St. Mary bay (fig. 24), although it must be fully recognized that such a profile, constructed from temperature data taken at the surface and the bottom only, is of a very tentative nature. The figure shows gradual and apparently rather uniform rise of temperature as one passes up the bay, just such as might be expected, the colder area at the surface of station 15 being the only indication of the cross-currents suggested by the surface diagram (fig. 23). No doubt if temperatures at intermediate depths had been taken, more might have been seen. The relations of the cold water appearing at the bottom of stations 13 and 15 are shown by fig. 25, which represents a line carried down the bay from station 13 somewhat farther west than the line in fig. 24. It is seen that this cooler water is spread out sideways from a layer which probably approaches the surface about the mouth of the bay, and occupies almost the whole depth at station 22. It will be noted that, the bay being rather shallow throughout, the temperatures are all comparatively high.

The bottom temperatures in the Annapolis basin (stations 26-33, table II) are peculiar in being much lower in many cases (especially station 31) than any water entering from the river (station 33) or any present in Digby Gut (station 25).

SUMMARY.

This set of observations is a continuation and extension of that made in 1914. The stations have been selected in such a way as to form three transverse sections and

SESSIONAL PAPER No. 38a

one longitudinal section of the bay of Fundy, thus making it possible to get a fairly clear idea of the temperature distribution in this interesting body of water by examining the profiles constructed and the accompanying diagrams showing the horizontal distribution of temperature at the shallower-levels.

The observations made at the stations where work was carried on in 1914 show little difference in surface temperature, but markedly colder water below. The fact that a seasonal difference of only. six weeks makes such a great difference in the temperature of the deep water shows how great is the effect· of vertical mixing due to the very great tides. This effect is also seen in the large areas of very uniform temperature found in both years.

The results obtained at stations near the mouth of the bay show an interesting agreement with observations made by Helland-Hansen in the open Atlantic. The statement of this investigator that the temperature of the surface water is, as a rule, higher than the air temperature is not borne out by the Bay of Fundy observations, nor by those of the *Challenger* expedition in this region of the Atlantic.

A slight rise of temperature at an intermediate depth, seen in three stations near the mouth of the bay, gives evidence of deep currents, but no data are available from which definite information concerning these can be obtained.

There is a clear indication that the water on the Nova Scotia side of the lower part of the bay is, on the whole, warmer than on the New Brunswick side, and the plan of the surface temperatures suggests a current of warm surface water from the Atlantic flowing in along the south shore and then turning north about half way up the bay, so that its influence is not visible in the higher profiles. All the other evidence, however, indicates a simple tongue of cold water up the middle of the bay.

Several points with regard to the surface temperatures remain unexplained.

The plan of distribution of temperature in the surface water of St. Mary bay shows a rather uniform increase of temperature in the upper part of the bay, with indications of certain currents·and tidal disturbances. The ·longitudinal profile, which is based upon insufficient data, gives no suggestion of any peculiar or striking conditions.

In conclusion, it remains only to express our indebtedness to Dr. Philip Cox, who accompanied us on both cruises, and Mr. J. R. McMurrich, who joined the party on the second, as well as to Dr. A. B. Macallum, Dr. C. C. Benson, and Dr. A. G. Huntsman for valuable assistance and criticism. We are also deeply indebted to Professor Vachon, Laval University, for the trouble he took in re-titrating the water samples.

8 GEORGE V, A. 1918

TABLE I—Temperature Records for Bay of Fundy Stations in 1915.

Station	I.	II.	III.	IV.	V.	VI.	VII.	VIII.	IX.	X.	XI.	XII.	XIII.	XIV.	XV.
Date	July 14	July 14	July 13	July 13	July 31	July 22	July 22	July 22	July 22	July 28	July 28	July 28	July 27	July 27	July 29
Time	12.30 P.M.– 1.30 P.M.	9.45 A.M.– 11.00 A.M.	6.00 P.M.– 8.00 P.M.	3.45 P.M.– 4.40 P.M.	10.25 A.M.– 11.30 A.M.	9.00 A.M.– 10.30 A.M.	11.15 A.M.– 12.30 P.M.	1.30 P.M.– 3.00 P.M.	4.00 P.M.– 5.15 P.M.	8.30 A.M.– 9.15 A.M.	11.30 A.M.– 12.15 P.M.	10.00 A.M.– 11.00 A.M.	10.00 A.M.– 11.30 A.M.	8.25 A.M.– 9.30 A.M.	12.15 P.M.– 1.10 P.M.
Bottom	Sand.	Mud.	Mud.	Sand & hard.	Gravel.	Shells.	Coarse sand.	Shells.	Rock.	Coarse gravel.	Sand.	Rock.	Sand & hard.	Rock.	Sand.
Depth	81 F.	64 F.	114 F.	83 F.	55 F.	43 F.	55 F.	48 F.	47 F.	47 F.	39·5 F.	36 F.	41 F.	35 F.	34 F.
Tide	Flood.	½ Flood.	Ebb.	½ Ebb.	½ Flood.	½ Ebb.	¾ Ebb.	Flood.	½ Flood.	½ Flood.	½ Flood.	½ Flood.	½ Ebd.	½ Flood.	½ Flood.
Air Temperature	16·10°	13·90°	14·25°	16·20°	13·70°	14·66°	17·95°	15·75°	14·75°	12·93°	14·73°	14·76°	11·92°	15·39°	12°
Temperature at Surface	9·86°	11·69°	10·61°	11·38°	10·41°	100°	12·33°	12·68°	11·71°	8·46°	10·51°	9·20°	8·48°	9·96°	110°
" 5 F	8·07°	7·49°	9·7°	9·5°	7·79°	9·27°	10·15°	11·13°	8·33°	7·89°	8·93°	8·04°	8·41°	8·93°	9·64°
" 10 F	7·55°	7·47°	6·2°	8·3°	7·15°	7·96°	7·88°	7·17°	7·82°	7·90°	8·7·4°	8·03°	8·40°	8·91°	9·54°
" 20 F	2·15°	6·00°	6·12°	7·7°	6·80°	7·39°	6·70°	7·11°	7·95°	7·84°	8·41°	7·49°	8·43°	8·91°	9·51°
" 30 F	5·74°	6·4°	5·59°	6·2°	6·77°	7·30°	6·51°	6·80°	7·27°	7·82°	8·44°	7·97°	8·42°	8·93°	9·54°
" 40 F	5·73°		5·59°	5·81°	6·70°	7·03°	6·42°	6·79°		7·81°		7·93°			
" 50 F	6·26°	5·79°	5·59°	5·78°	6·71°		6·38°	6·77°	6·92°						
" 60 F	6·08°	5·63°	5·59°	5·76°											
" 70 F	5·72°														
" 75 F			5·70°	5·77°											
" 80 F	5·73°														
" 90 F			5·64°												
" 100 F			5·64°												
" 114 F			5·66°												

TABLE II.—Temperatures in St. Mary Bay and Annapolis Basin in 1915. (°Centigrade.)

Station.	1.	2.	3.	4.	5.	6.	7.	8.	9.	10.	11.
Date	July 7	July 7	July 7	July 7	July 7	July 7	July 7	July 8	July 8	July 7	July 13
Time	11.15 A.M.	10.30 A.M.	12.10 P.M.	1.45 P.M.	8.45 A.M.	2.45 P.M.	3.30 P.M.	8.10 A.M.	8.50 A.M.	4.35 P.M.	1.35 P.M.
Bottom	Mud.	Mud.	Mud.	Gravel.	Mud.	Mud.	Shell & sand.	Sand.	Sand.	Sand.	Sand.
Depth	4 F.	7 F.	14·5 F.	15·5 F.	11·5 F.	11·5 F.	9·5 F.	18 F.	18 F.	2·5 F.	17·5 F.
Tide	2/3 Ebb.	1/2 Ebb.	5/6 Ebb.	Ebb.	5/6 Flood.	1/6 Flood	1/3 Flood.	1/6 Ebb.	1/4 Ebb.	1/2 Flood.	1/6 Ebb.
Air Temperature	..	....	....	15·60°	....	15·62°	15·35°	13·85°	15·00°	14·05°	14·35°
Surface Temperature	14·80°	13·78°	13·92°	13·95°	13·95°	13·52°	12·90°	12·98°	12·79°	11·39°	11·96°
Bottom Temperature	13·40°	11·82°	11·61°	11·37°	10·54°	10·36°	10·22°	9·03°	8·68°	10·77°	9·29°

Station.	12.	13.	14.	15.	16.	17.	18.	19.	20.	21.	22.
Date	July 8	July 13	July 8	July 8	July 8	July 13	July 13	July 13	July 13	July 13	July 13
Time	10.20 A.M.	1.00 P.M.	10.55 A.M.	11.45 A.M.	12.25 P.M.	11.15 A.M.	9.45 A.M.	9.00 A.M.	10.30 A.M.	5.40 A.M.	6.55 A.M.
Bottom	Rock.	Sand.	Rock.	Rock.	Rock.	Rock.	Coarse gravel.	Rock.	Sand.	Sand.	Rock.
Depth	14·5 F.	18 F.	19·5 F.	18·5 F.	7·5 F.	26 F.	14·5 F.	6·5 F.	28 F.	23·5 F.	19·5 F.
Tide	1/2 Ebb.	1/6 Ebb.	2/3 Ebb.	5/8 Ebb.	Ebb.	5/8 Flood	2/3 Flood.	1/2 Flood.	3/4 Flood.	Ebb.	1/6 Flood.
Air Temperature	15·58°	19·38°	15·80°	15·65°	15·43°	15·67°	13·57°	13·30°	13·54°	12·35°	11·51°
Surface Temperature	12·80°	11·45°	9·57°	10·12°	10·98°	10·48°	11·43°	11·67°	10·09°	9·28°	9·63°
Bottom Temperature	8·29°	8·79°	7·81°	8·44°	10·07°	8·69°	9·39°	10·90°	8·34°	8·06°	8·09°

Station.	23.	24.	25.	26.	27.	28.	29.	30.	31.	32.	33.
Date	July 13	July 13	July 23	July 23	July 23	July 24	July 23	July 23	July 24	July 24	July 24
Time	7.40 A.M.	8.15 A.M.	2.30 P.M.	10.15 A.M.	3.30 P.M.	9.05 A.M.	11.15 A.M.	Noon.	10.00 A.M.	10.30 A.M.	11.30 A.M.
Bottom	Gravel.	Rock.	Rock.	Mud.	Mud.	Mud & shell.	Mud.	Mud.	Mud.	Sand.	Gravel.
Depth	15·5 F.	8·5 F.	38 F.	6 F.	11·5 F.	7 F.	3·5 F.	2·5 F.	7·5 F.	8 F.	9 F.
Tide	1/4 Flood.	1/3 Flood.	Ebb.	1/3 Ebb.	1/6 Ebb.	Flood.	1/2 Ebb.	2/3 Ebb.	1/6 Ebb.	1/4 Ebb.	1/3 Ebb.
Air Temp	13·96°	12·09°	16·85°	15·57°	18·50°	16·32°	17·25°	17·95°	14·63°	17·76°	18·55°
Surface Temperature	10·22°	10·93°	11·68°	11·14°	11·92°	9·41°	12·70°	12·52°	11·22°	12·31°	15·33°
Bottom Temperature	9·17°	10·29°	9·30°	9·05°	8·76°	8·54°	10·04°	11·04°	6·99°	12·19°	13·33°
15 Fathom Temperature	....	....	9·80°	....	....	....	....	....	....	....	....

8 GEORGE V, A. 1918

TABLE III.—Specific Gravity, Chlorine Content, and Salinity of Water Samples from Bottom of St. Mary Bay Stations in 1915.

Station.	Sp. Gt. at 15·56° C.	% Chlorine.	% Total Salts.	Station.	Sp. Gt. at 15·56° C.	% Chlorine.	% Total Salts.
1	10243	1·817	3·276	13	10248	1·832	3·304
2	....	(1·819)	(3·280)	14	10249	1·842	3·322
3	10248	1·825	3·291	15	10249	1·849	3·334
4	10247	1·833	3·306	16	10247	1·840	3·318
5	10247	1.832	3·304	17	10248	1·845	3·327
6	10248	1·835	3·309	18	10245	1·835	3·309
7	10248	1·835	3·309	19	10247	1·855	3·346
8	10247	1·831	3·302	20	10247	1·869	3·370
9	10248	1·842	3·322	21	10248	1·866	3·365
10	10248	1·842	3·322	22	10245	1·861	3·354
11	10246	1·841	3·319	23	10249	1·857	3·347
12	10249	1·836	3·311	24	10248	1·861	3·353

The density of each water sample was determined at room temperature by means of a delicate hydrometer, and corrected to read at 15.56° C. by Buchanan's Diagram.[1] The methods of analysis and of calculating the salinity were those of Dittmar.[1]

[1] Report on the Scientific Results of the Voyage of H.M.S. *Challenger*. Physics and Chemistry, Vol. I, 1884.

J. Y. Buchanan. "Report on the Specific Gravity of Samples of Ocean Water observed on board H.M.S. *Challenger*, during the years 1873-76." Diagram 1.

William Dittmar. "Report on Researches into the Composition of Ocean Water collected by H.M.S. *Challenger* during the years 1873-76." pp. 4 and 40.

BAY of FUND

showing

HYDROGRAPHIC & DREDGING

STATIONS of 1915.

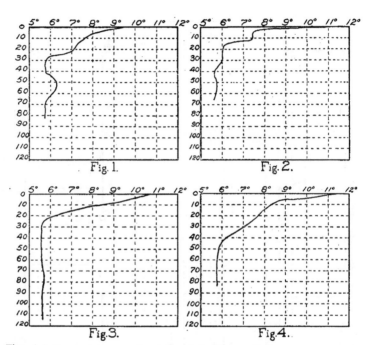

Figs. 1–4. Temperature curves for stations I. to IV. respectively.

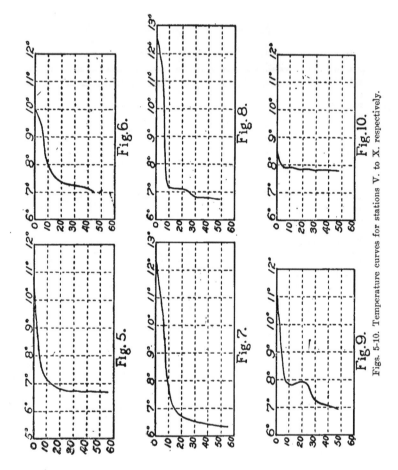

Figs. 5-10. Temperature curves for stations V. to X. respectively.

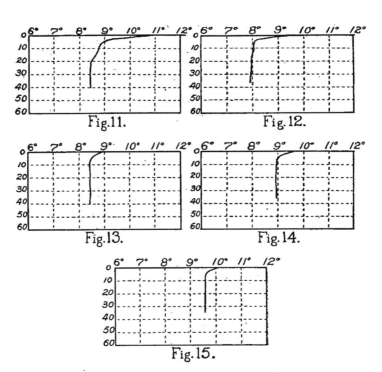

Figs. 11-15. Temperature curves for stations XI. to XV. respectively.

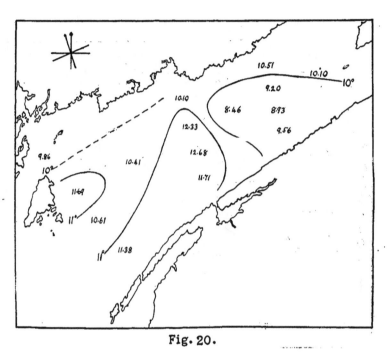

Fig. 20.

Fig. 20. The Bay of Bundy, showing temperatures of the surface water.

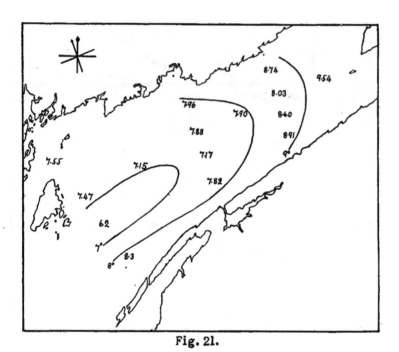

Fig. 21.

Fig. 21. The Bay of Fundy, showing temperatures of the water at a depth of 10 fathoms.

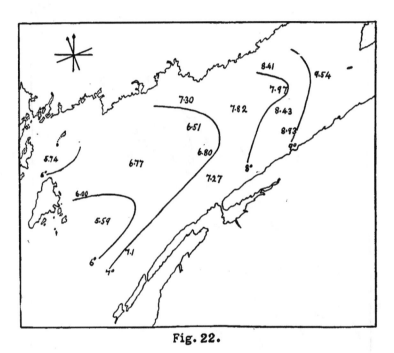

Fig. 22.

Fig. 22. The Bay of Fundy, showing temperatures of the water at a depth of 30 fathoms.

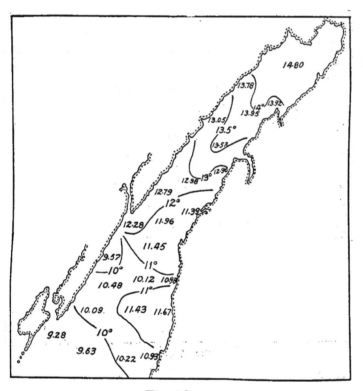

Fig. 23.

Fig. 23. St. Mary Bay, showing temperatures of the surface water.

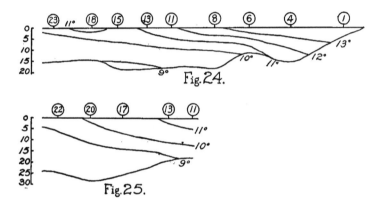

Figs. 24 and 25. Longitudinal isothermal profile of St. Mary Bay.

VIII.

EXAMINATION OF AFFECTED SALMON, MIRAMICHI HATCHERY, NEW BRUNSWICK.

By F. C. Harrison, D.Sc., F.R.S.C., etc., Principal of Macdonald College, Ste. Anne de Bellevue, P.Q.

On October 11, 1915, I received a telephone message from Dr. A. B. Macallum, Secretary-Treasurer of the Biological Board of Canada, with reference to a diseased condition of the salmon in the hatchery at South Esk, N.B. He also informed me that Dr. Huntsman, of the University of Toronto, was leaving in order to investigate the trouble, and if I thought it wise to do so I could join him and proceed to the hatchery.

I got into telephonic communication with Dr. Huntsman on his passing through Montreal, and after discussing the situation thought it best to remain at the laboratory to examine the diseased fish that Dr. Huntsman would send me in order that I might investigate the disease, for it seemed better to attempt the finding out of the trouble with all bacteriological facilities to hand, which would have been lacking at the hatchery, and which at that time it was impossible to take there.

Retaining Pond at the Miramichi Hatchery, South Esk, N.B.

On October 14, I received a copy of the letter which Dr. Macallum received from the Deputy Minister of the Department of Naval Service, reading as follows:—

The officer in charge of the Miramichi hatchery, which is located on the South Esk river, a small tributary of the Southwest Miramichi, recently reported that a disease had broken out amongst the salmon in the retaining pond in connection with the hatchery in which the parent fish are placed and retained

8 GEORGE V, A. 1918

until the spawning time comes around. It happened that the Superintendent of Fisheries was in the Maritime Provinces when this information was received, and I had him instructed to visit the pond and look into the matter.

There were on Tuesday of this week somewhat over 2,400 salmon in the pond, between 300 and 400 of which were affected. The disease takes the form of a fungus. The first indication is the removal of the scales from the back of the neck. They are evidently eaten off. Then a white fungus develops, which rapidly spreads down the head to the eyes and makes the fish blind. It subsequently appears on different parts of the body and on the extremities of the fins and tail. The fish diseased were beginning to die, which indicates that they will not last more than a week or ten days after they become affected.

An examination of the pond revealed no reason for any unhealthful conditions. Neither did there seem to be anything through which the water was flowing before it reached the pond to cause it to be unhealthful. Some fish that were in the towing pontoons which had recently been taken from the fishermen's nets to be placed in the pond, were examined, and on a few of them the first stage of the disease above referred to was in evidence.

As it seemed possible that the scales might have been removed from the fish striking the top of the pontoons, one of the fishermen's nets was visited and when lifted there were three salmon and a grilse in it. Two of the salmon were large females weighing about fifteen pounds, and they were perfectly healthy, but the third, a small male weighing 5 or 6 pounds, was apparently affected, as the scales were eaten away from the back of the head and he had an unhealthy appearance.

It would appear from the above that an epidemic has broken out amongst the fish in the river, and in view of the importance of the matter it is desirable that a capable bacteriologist should be immediately sent to the pond to thoroughly investigate the whole matter. I may add that this pond has been in operation for many years and in no instance in the past has any such trouble been experienced. The tide enters the pond, and at each high tide the water is slightly brackish.

I shall be obliged if you will give the matter immediate consideration and wire me whether the Biological Board can at once arrange to send a properly qualified man to investigate the matter. If it cannot, it may be possible for the Department to arrange with that of Agriculture to send an officer from the laboratory at the Experimental Farm here.

N.B.—Since writing the above a report has just been received from the officer in charge of the Port Arthur hatchery, in which he states that a disease, apparently of a similar nature, has broken out amongst salmon trout in the Nipigon river. This is the first time that the department has heard of any such disease there.

A few days later I received a statement from Dr. Huntsman, the main points of which are contained in his report on this outbreak of salmon disease, now being published.

On the arrival of the specimens of fish sent by Dr. Huntsman, they were immediately examined. They arrived in good condition, packed in ice, and were opened in the usual way. After examination of the organs and the flesh near the abraded spots or where the fungus was growing, pieces of the various organs were excised with a sterile knife, and cut open with a second sterile knife, and a portion of the pulp, etc., of the organ removed by means of a sterile platinum loop. In a few cases pieces of the organs were taken out, seized with the forceps and scorched in the flame, and then cut open with a sterile knife and a portion removed to sterile petri dishes. In all cases the material was mixed with beef peptone salt-water agar, and from the various fish a large number of colonies were isolated. These colonies were lettered and numbered, and besides those here described a large number of other colonies were isolated, which were compared and found similar to those mentioned by letter and number.

FISH No. 1. Appearance normal, with the exception of a few patches of diseased skin around the head. On opening, the organs appeared normal. Plates were made from milt, liver, swimming bladder, kidney, heart's blood. In all cases the material was transferred to sterile petri dishes and beef peptone salt water agar poured over. After the plates had set they were kept at 20°C. Results:—

> *Milt.*—About 60 colonies.
>
> *Liver.*—About 100 colonies.
>
> *Swimming bladder.*—Contained a quantity of liquid. Very large number of colonies, too numerous to count.
>
> *Heart's blood.*—About 300 colonies to the oese. All these colonies were very similar.
>
> *Kidneys.*—About 90 colonies.

Four species were isolated from this fish, marked A1, A2, A3, A4.

Flesh near diseased skin normal in appearance.

FISH No. 2.—External appearance normal except some bruises with traces of the fungus development near tail and head. On opening, the liver was rather pale in colour, somewhat friable, intestines empty, caeca empty. Right ovary eggs pink in colour; left ovary eggs much darker in colour, almost liver-coloured. Flesh normal and good colour. Same technique. One oese from each of the parts mentioned.

> *Ovary.*—Pink eggs. From one crushed egg 300 or 400 colonies developed. A larger number from the one crushed egg from the dark red left ovary.
>
> *Liver.*—20 colonies.
>
> *Heart's blood.*—60 colonies per oese, all practically identical.

Isolations B1, B2, B3, B4.

FISH No. 3.—Exterior appearance normal with the exception of a few small areas discoloured visible in the skin. Flesh normal in appearance. Interior organs apparently normal. Smears from the various organs showed bacteria.

> *Heart's blood.*—About 250 colonies to the oese, all similar.
>
> *Eggs.*—Innumerable colonies. Two species.
>
> *Liver.*—20—30 colonies per oese.
>
> *Kidneys.*—80—100 colonies.

Two isolations—C1, C2.

FISH No. 4.—A large fish; much gelatinous slime around the tail. Some areas of skin affected with the fungus. Flesh beneath appeared healthy. Intestines slightly congested, empty. Liver dark in colour. Eggs salmon pink in colour, apparently normal. Swimming bladder empty. Smears from the heart's blood liver and kidney showed a number of organisms:—

> *Heart's blood.*—30—40 colonies, all similar.
>
> *Liver.*—10—12, all similar.
>
> *Kidneys.*—20 colonies, all similar.
>
> *Eggs.*—About 150 per egg. This is an estimate, as a large growth had occurred in the vicinity of the crushed part of the egg.

One isolation, D1.

FISH No. 5.—Skin between the eyes and the back of the head was bruised and in places dirty white in colour. Microscopical preparations showed the presence of fungus. Flesh normal. All organs normal. Intestines empty. Smears from the milt, liver, heart's blood showed a number of organisms. Plates:—

> *Heart's blood.*—Numerous colonies.
> *Liver.*—40—50 colonies.
> *Milt.*—A few colonies.
> Three isolations—E1, E2, E3.

FISH No. 6.—Skin bruised between eyes, fungus present in this area. Flesh normal. Organs normal in appearance. Intestines empty. Eggs, salmon pink in colour. Intestines slightly congested. Smears from heart's blood, liver and egg showed bacteria present. Plates:—

> *Heart's blood.*—About 80 colonies, all similar.
> *Liver.*—30—40 colonies, all similar.
> *Eggs.*—One egg about 200 colonies, all similar.
> One isolation, F1.

FISH No. 7.—A large amount of diseased skin from which preparations of the fungus were prepared. Flesh normal. Intestines empty. Organs apparently healthy.

> *Kidneys.*—About 30 colonies, all similar.
> *Liver.*—About 50 colonies, all similar.
> *Heart's blood.*—30—40 colonies, all similar.
> One isolation, G1.

FISH No. 8.—Large amount of diseased skin from which fungus growth was easily demonstrated. Liver pale in colour. Ovary deep reddish. Intestines empty. Many whitish eggs in ovary. Spleen normal. Plates:—

> *Egg.*—About 150 colonies to the egg, large masses of bacterial growth near the crushed portion.
> *Liver.*—About 250 colonies.
> *Heart's blood.*—About 150 colonies, all similar.

A number of diseased portions of skin were cut off and examined in a variety of ways. Very good prepartions were obtained by teasing portions of the diseased skin, triturating the material with 40 per cent potassium hydrate. After removal from this reagent they were washed in water and transferred to Lugol solution, or else stained with safranin, eosin, or fluorescin, dehydrated and mounted in balsam. Such teased particles of the skin gave, as a rule, better results than sections.

These preparations show that the fungus was a *Saprolegnia,* and I presume that full particulars of this fungus have been already given by Dr. Huntsman. A very full account of the salmon disease probably caused by *Saprolegnia* is given in the report of the United States Commissioner of Fisheries for 1878, the article having been reproduced from the proceedings of the Royal Society of Edinburgh, written by A. B. Stirling. of the Anatomical Museum of the University of Dublin. A very comprehensive paper by S. Walpole and Prof. T. H. Huxley entitled "Disease among the Salmon of many Rivers in England and Wales" appears in the bulletin of the United States Fish Commission, vol. 1, 1881, and was a reprint of a pamphlet contained in the "21st Annual Report of the Inspector of Fisheries for England and Wales for the year 1881 presented to both Houses of Parliament by command of Her Majesty."

It seemed peculiar that injuries, which appeared at first to be mere abrasions, and which subsequently became infected by the fungus *Saprolegnia,* should have such a disastrous effect upon the fish as to produce sluggishness and death in the short period of time mentioned by the officer of the hatchery and by Dr. Huntsman, and it therefore seemed important to make a thorough examination of the diseased fish to see if there were other factors producing disease, and to ascertain if the fungus *Saprolegnia*, was a primary or a secondary invader. Unfortunately such investigation was hampered by the fact that no live salmon were available for inoculation, and the only means of ascertaining the pathogenicity of the organisms isolated was to attempt to infect the common gold fish.

During the course of this examination I obtained a publication of the Fishery Board of Scotland entitled "The Life-history of Salmon in Fresh water, Glasgow, 1898," containing a paper by J. Hume Patterson, Assistant Bacteriologist of the Corporation of Glasgow, on "The Cause of Salmon Diseases", and I am indebted to this paper for the methods which were subsequently used for the inoculation of the live gold fish.

Before the gold fish could be inoculated it was necessary to work out in some detail the various organisms which were isolated from the salmon. The principal biological and cultural characteristics of those were as follows:—

A. 1.

A medium sized bacillus with rounded ends, occasionally bent, which occurs singly and sometimes in short chains. Actively motile, stains well with methylene blue, and is gram negative.

Gelatine Plates:—

24 *hours,* colonies just visible to the naked eye.

48 *hours,* colonies 2 mm. in diameter, round, with a liquefying centre saucer-shaped. Centre of the colony dense with a mass of deposited bacteria.

With ⅔ objective edges of the colony seemed slightly fimbriate, and the mass within the centre might be seen moving.

3 *days,* colonies had grown to between 5 and 9 mm. in diameter, but with similar appearance to that at 48 hours.

4 *days,* geletine completely liquefied.

Gelatine Stick:—

Growth is best at the top. Line of puncture filiform.

24 *hours,* Liquefaction begins, extending to the sides of tube and about 2 mm. in depth.

48 *hours,* growth uniform, line of puncture a cloudy area 10 mm. in diameter with small outgrowths into gelatine forming a cloudy cylinder. At the surface liquefaction is stratiform to a depth of 4 mm.

3 *days,* the growth has increased, stratified liquefaction extended to a depth of 7 mm. and the cloudy area looks like a saccate cylinder.

8 *days,* liquefaction to a depth of 8 mm.

10 *days,* there is a distinct dark stratum underneath the liquefied area.

13 *days,* very slight increase.

Beef Peptone Agar, 48 hours:—

Colonies 1 - 2 mm. diameter, round, raised, entire edge, glistening white appearance. With the ⅔ objective the edges were entire, colonies dense, and grandular with a narrow clear margin.

3 *days,* colonies 2 - 5 mm. diameter, round, more massive and dense, convex, whiteish to light brown in centre.

38a—11

Sloped Beef Peptone Agar, Blood Heat (37.5):—

Little change after three days' growth.

The organism grew fairly well at blood heat.

24 hours, spread over about half the sloped surface.

48 hours, growth denser, spreading, flat, glistening, smooth, semi-opaque, whitish. No further change.

Glucose Agar Slope:—

24 hours, at room temperature, smooth, vigorous, whitish, moist and spreading. Cloudiness near the growth.

5 days, colony more cloudy, considerable gas production and the column of agar is burst apart in the middle.

Glucose Agar Stick:—24 hours. Growth vigorous over surface and pronounced cloudiness from the surface to a depth of 10 mm.

48 hours. Increase. in growth and a few gas bubbles appear on the line of puncture.

No further change occurs.

Beef Broth:—

24 hours, strong, cloudy.

3 days, much heavier. Sediment flocculent.

7 days, yellowish-green appearance in the upper layer otherwise no change.

Dunhams's Solution:—

The organism grew well in Dunham's solution, and at the end of 5 days at room temperature was tested with Ehrlich test, allowed to stand 20 minutes and the results then recorded. This organism was negative to this test. No Indol.

Milk:—

24 hours, no change.

3 days, coagulated with extrusion of slight amount of whey.

5 days, curd has become firmer, and a cheesy smell developed.

7 days, slightly more whey extruded;

No other change, although observed for some twenty days.

Litmus Milk:—

24 hours, no change.

48 hours, no change in constituency, but colour is changed to avellaneous.[1]

5 days. Colour uniform, slight digestion with separated whey, soft curd, yellowish ring around glass, smell disagreeable.

3 weeks.—Curd still undigested, whey yellowish, yellow ring, curd avellaneus, few gas bubbles on shaking.

Potato:—

24 hours. Moderate, dry, slightly raised, cream-coloured growth.

48 hours Increase of growth, dry, raised, slightly rugose, cream-yellow colour.

6 days. Abundantly raised, massive, rugose growth, cream colour at margins and pinkish on top. Odour unpleasant and slightly pungent, resembling that on milk.

3 weeks. No change.

A. 2.

Small bacillus with rounded ends, short, often in pairs, actively motile, stains well with methylene blue, and is gram negative.

---

[1] *Chromotaxia seu Nomenclator Colorum.* P. A. Saccardo.

SESSIONAL PAPER No. 38a

Gelatine Plates:—

> *24 hours.* Colonies just visible to the naked eye.
>
> *48 hours.* Colonies have attained a size of 2-3 mm. in diameter; round, saucer-shaped. In the centre a dense mass of deposited bacteria with liquefying area around. With ⅔ objective interior of the colony is glumose. Edges clearer, but less distinct than A. 1.
>
> *3 days.* In moderately seeded plates there is complete liquefaction.

Gelatine Stick:—

> *24 hours.* Growth uniform. Line of punctures a cloudy area 5 mm. in diameter along line. Liquefaction begins in 24 hours, extending to sides of tube and 3 mm. in depth.
>
> *48 hours* Increase in growth with similar appearance, and stratified liquefaction to a depth of 5 mm. Liquefaction gradually increases.
>
> *4 days.* 10 mm. deep and the remainder of the tube saccate liquefies.
>
> *6 days.* Liquefaction to a depth of 4 cm.
>
> *10 days.* Liquefaction of the gelatine in the tube complete.

Beef Peptone Agar:—

> *48 hours* at room temperature. Colonies 1-2 mm. in diameter, raised, glistening, whitish colony by reflected and greenish opalescent by transmitted light. With ⅔ objective edges entire, centre granular with a clear hyaline margin all around.
>
> *3 days.* Not much increase in size, but more in density. Colony becoming whiter and more convex, somewhat resembling a yeast colony.

Beef Peptone Agar, at 37°C.:—

> Very slight growth at *24 hours,* after which there was no further growth.

Glucose Agar Slope:—

> *24 hours.* Abundant, flat, slightly spreading, smooth, moist, whitish growth.
>
> No further change noticed until about second week, when the agar becomes brownish beneath the slope.

Glucose Agar Stick:—

> *24 hours.* Growth filiform on surface, thin and spreading. Not characteristic.
>
> *48 hours.* Gas bubble on surface and below. Afterwards no further change.

Beef Broth:—

> *24 hours,* strong clouding, which increases, with abundant sediment.
>
> No further change.

Dunham's Solution:—

> *5 days,* at room temperature; tested with Ehrlich's reagents; allowed to stand for 20 minutes and then recorded. No Indol.

Milk:—

> *24 hours.* No change.
>
> *3 days.* Coagulated with extrusion of slight amount of whey.
>
> *5 days.* Curd becomes firmer, and cheesy smell develops.
>
> Amount of whey increases up to seventh day, after which there is no further change.

38a—11½

Litmus Milk:—

24 hours. No change.

48 hours. No change in colour or consistency; on shaking numerous small gas bubbles appear and form a foam on surface.

6 days. Coagulated, moderately firm curd, liliacinus in colour. About a quarter of the tube is whey, and much darker in colour (atro-violaceus).

3 weeks. There is a reddish ring at the surface, considerable digestion, whey occupying three-quarters of the tube, isabellinus in colour. Curd flocculent, avellaneus; odour slightly cheesy.

Potato:—

24 hours. Growth moderate, filiform, slightly raised, cream-yellow colour. This increases, and in

6 days growth is moderate, raised, rugose, moist, shiny; dirty cream-yellow, darker in centre where growth is most massive.

3 weeks. No further change.

A. 3.

Medium-size bacillus with rounded ends, resembles A. 1 in appearance. Active motile, stains well with methylene blue, and is gram negative.

Gelatine Plates:—

24 hours. Just visible to the naked eye. Growth rapid.

48 hours. Colonies are 2-5 mm. in diameter, round. Liquefaction saucer-shaped, inner ring dense, caused by deposited bacilli. With $\frac{2}{3}$ objective the edges of the colonies are fimbriate centre grumose and flocculent. Masses of the bacteria can be seen in movement.

3 days. Colonies increase to 12 mm. in diameter, saucer-shaped liquefaction, whitish in centre, more transparent at the margin. To the naked eye the edges are entire, but with a microscope slightly fimbriate. There is a cheesy smell on opening the plates.

4 days. Plates are liquefied.

Gelatine Stick:—

24 hours. Resembles A. 1, but slightly less growth.

48 hours. Line of bacteria is filiform, smooth on surface. Liquefaction stratiform, 4 mm. deep. Liquefaction continues.

10 days. Liquefaction is 1 cm. deep with medium beneath darker in colour, but clear.

Agar Plates:—

48 hours. Colonies are 1-3 mm. in diameter, round, raised, yellowish-white. With $\frac{2}{3}$ objective edges are entire, dark in centre, granular, gradually becoming lighter to margin, which is clear.

3 days. Colonies are round, white, edges entire, brownish in centre. Convex.

4 days. No change.

Agar Slope, 37°C.:—

24 hours. Very slight growth, filiform.

7 days. No further change.

Glucose Agar Slope, 20°:—

A spreading, flat, white, shiny growth; agar beneath very cloudy. Cream yellow. No gas.

Glucose Agar Stick:—

Growth filiform, spreading; cream colour at centre, lighter at margins. Cloudy to half-way down the agar.

Beef Broth:—

24 hours. Clouding moderate. Sediment.
3 days. Growth heavier, slight pellicle.
5 days. Ring and pellicle.
7 days. Yellowish-green colour in upper layers.
Subsequently no change.

Dunham's Solution:—

Grown for five days at room temperature, tested with Ehrlich test, allowed to stand 20 minutes and then recorded. No Indol.

Milk:—

Fifth day. No change until the fifth day, when there is coagulation with soft curd, cheesy odor. Curd gradually becomes harder and the whey greenish in colour. Digestion takes place to about half the volume.

Litmus Milk:—

The colour is gradually bleached and in *48 hours* is avellaneus.
5 days. Coagulation takes place in 5 or 6 days, a soft, fine curd which gradually digests. Blue ring at the top; separated whey is isabellinus in colour.
3 weeks. Greenish-blue colour; whey thick, curd avellaneus, odour unpleasant.

Potato:—

24 hours. Growth moderate, raised, filiform, cream-yellow in colour.
48 hours. Growth becomes dirty and ochraceus, slightly rugose. Growth gradually changes to ferrugineus in colour.
3 weeks. No change.

A. 4.

A small bacillus, short, rather stout, with rounded ends. In appearance resembles A. 2. Actively motile, stains well with methylene blue, and is gram negative.

Gelatine Plates:—

24 hours. Just visible to the naked eye.
48 hours. Colonies punctiform (less than 1 mm.) white and glistening, with ⅔ objective they are seen to be round, with entire edges, and granular.
3 days. Colonies slightly punctiform, white, glistening, convex, capitate. With ⅔ objective edges entire and granular.
No further change.

Gelatine Stick:—

24 hours. Growth unifrom, line of bacteria filiform.
48 hours. Growth filiform to villous. Four gas bubbles on line of bacteria.
3 days. There is more growth. Line of bacteria villous to papillate.
10 days. Slight depression at the point of puncture may be noticed, but no liquefaction.
13 days. Liquified area around the line of puncture.

8 GEORGE V, A. 1918

Agar Plates:—

48 hours. Colonies are filiform, glistening, raised. With ⅔ objective the colonies are round, dense in centre, and granular, clearer at margin, edges entire.

3 days. Colonies slightly larger, opalescent, white.

No further change.

Gelatine Agar Slope at 37° C:—

Little, if any, growth observed. Continuous observation for 7 days.

Glucose Agar Slope:—

Growth moderate, moist, shiny, slightly raised, whitish.

3 weeks. Agar is brown beneath the slope.

Glucose Agar Stick:—

Growth filiform, thin surface, growth spreading. Gas bubbles along line of puncture.

No further change except the agar becomes brown beneath the surface to a depth of 1-2 cm.

Beef Broth:—

24 hours. Slight clouding and sediment.

3 days. Clouding and sediment increase slightly.

No further change.

Dunham's Solution:

Grown for five days at room temperature, tested with Ehrlich test, allowed to stand 20 minutes and then recorded. Indol positive.

Milk:—

5 days. No change visible.

6 7 days. On shaking tube a gassy foam rises to the surface.

10 days. Milk had coagulated, hard curd, whitish whey.

Litmus Milk:—

No change in appearance in *24 hours.*

48 hours. Abundant gas which rises to the surface in small bubbles. This was noticed each day up to the sixth day, and the foam was very heavy. The milk gradually coagulates and forms a blue ring down one side of the tube, remainder is a firm curd adhering to the tube. Bleached cream colour.

Potato:—

24 hours. Moderate growth, filiform, slightly moist, cream coloured.

48 hours. Becomes slightly rugose.

6 days. Growth slight, slightly raised, and a dirty yellow (melleus).

3 weeks. No further change.

B. 1.

This organism on examination was found to resemble in all respects A. 1.

B. 2.

A small size bacillus about 1½ times as long as wide, rounded end, frequently in pairs. Actively motile, stains well with methylene blue, negative with gram.

Gelatine Plates:—

24 hours. Visible to the naked eye.

48 hours. Punctiform, colony raised, glistening, whitish. ⅔ objective shows round, dense, granular colony, entire edges.

No further change.

Gelatine Stick:—

24 hours. Growth uniform, round, filiform; no liquefaction.

48 hours. Growth uniform, no liquefaction to surface.

3 days. Slight depression at the boint of bacteria. No liquefaction.

Agar plates:—

48 hours. Uniform, 1 m.m. in diameter, round, glistening, colony. With ⅔ objective round, dense, shading to lighter; granular, edges entire.

3 days. Colonies are glistening and bluish white.

No further change.

Agar slope 37° C.:—

7 days. Very slight growth, one or two small colonies appearing on the surface but otherwise no change.

Glucose Agar Slope:—

Moderate growth, spreading, flat, moist and whitish.

48 hours. A few gas bubbles appear and slight increase in growth.

3 weeks. Agar is brown underneath the slope.

Glucose Agar Stick:—

Filiform, slight growth on surface, gas bubbles along line of puncture.

No further change except for browning of the agar underneath the surface.

Beef broth:—

24 hours. Moderate growth, moderate sediment.

3 days. Growth slightly heavier.

5 days. Clearing.

No further change.

Dunham's Solution:—

Grown for five days at room temperature, tested with Ehrlich test, allowed to stand 20 minutes and then recorded. Indol positive.

Litmus Milk:—

24 hours. No change.

48 hours. A fine foam on the surface when tube is shaken. Colour liliaceous, no coagulation.

6 days. Much gas in foam form. No coagulation. Colour liliaceous. Colour gradually bleaches. Blue ring forms on surface. Bluish whey but little digestion.

Potato:—

24 hours. Filliform, dry, raised, colour niveus.

6 days. Growth becomes slightly raised and more massive.

3 weeks. No change.

B. 3.

Resembles in all respects *A. 4.*

8 GEORGE V, A. 1918

B. 4.

Resembles in all respects *A. 4.*

C. 1.

Small to medium bacillus about twice as long as broad, slightly rounded ends. Actively motile, stains somewhat unevenly with methylene blue, gram negative.

Gelatine Plates:—

24 hours. Colonies visible to the naked eye.
48 hours. Colonies punctiform, round, white, raised and glistening. ⅔ objective round, evenly dense and granular with entire edges.
No further change.

Gelatine Stick:—

Growth uniform, line of puncture filiform, 4 gas bubbles along line of puncture.
10 days. Depression at the point of puncture.
13 days. Line of bacteria has liquefied.

Agar Plates:—

48 hours. Colonies are punctiform, 1-1½ mm. in diameter, round, raised, white, glistening.
With ⅔ objective colonies are round, dense in centre, clear margins, granular, entire edges.
No further change.

Agar, 37°C.:—

24 hours. Moderate growth, flat, slightly spreading, smooth and translucent.
No further change.

Glucose Agar Slope:—

Flat, moist, spreading, whitish growth, few gas bubbles.
No further change except browning of the agar beneath surface.

Glucose Agar Stick:—

24 hours. Filiform, growth spreading on surface.
48 hours. Few gas bubbles along line of puncture.
No further change.

Beef Broth:—

24 hours. Moderate clouding, flocculent, abundant sediment.
5 days. Clearing.
No further change.

Dunham's Solution:—

Grown for five days at room temperature, tested with Ehrlich test, allowed to stand 20 minutes and then recorded. Indol positive.

Litmus Milk:—

24 hours. No change.
48 hours. Slight amount of gas, colour somewhat lighter, no coagulation.
6 days. Much gas in foam form. No. coagulation. Colour liliaceous.
Subsequently milk coagulates, blue ring, surface clear, whey on one side, curd adhering to two-thirds of the tube; bleached to a cream colour and of firm consistency.

Potato:—

Slightly raised, moderate growth, cream-yellow.

3 weeks. No further change.

D. 1.

Medium-size bacillus, with slightly rounded ends, actively motile, stains well with methylene blue, gram negative.

Gelatine Plates:—

Colonies visible to the naked eye in *24 hours.*

48 hours. Uniform, round, white, glistening colony; ⅔ objective round, granular, dense to the edge, edges entire.

3 days. Colonies become more dense. Convex.

No further change.

Gelatine Stick:—

48 hours. Line of puncture is villous. Slight softening of the gelatine on the surface.

Subsequently growth along line of puncture becomes villous to papillate, softening gradually extending along line of puncture.

Agar Plates:—

48 hours. Punctiform to 1 mm. in diameter, round, white, raised, glistening colony; ⅔ objective colonies round, dense in centre to clear margin, granular, edges entire.

3 days. Slight increase in sizes; otherwise no change.

Agar slope, 37° C.:—

No growth at this temperature.

Glucose Agar Slope:—

Moist, flat, spreading, whitish growth. Agar becomes brown beneath the growth, but no further change.

Glucose Agar Stick:—

Line of puncture filiform, spreading on surface, three or four small bubbles appear in *48 hours* and slight increase in growth; otherwise no change except browning under growth.

Beef Broth:—

24 hours. Growth moderate, sediment moderate and flocculent.

5 days. Clearing.

No further change.

Dunham's Solution:—

Grown for five days at room temperature, tested with Ehrlich test, allowed to stand 20 minutes and then recorded. Indol positive.

Litmus Milk:—

24 hours. No apparent change, but on tapping the tube small gas bubbles rise to the surface.

48 hours. Gas more pronounced. Colour liliaceous.

6 days. Foamy gas. No coagulum. Colour liliaceous.

3 weeks. Blue ring on surface cleared away along one side, remainder firm curd adhering to the tube. Bleached cream colour. .

Potato:—

Moderate growth, raised, rugose, waxy, cream yellow in colour.
E. 1., E. 2. and E. 3.
    Resemble *A. 1.*

F. 1.

Medium size bacillus with rounded ends. Actively motile.
On staining with methylene blue there are two or three dark granules in most of the organisms. Gram negative.

Gelatine plates:—

    24 hours. Just visible to the naked eye. Round, white, glistening, ⅔ object-ive brown, edges entire, granular.
    Subsequent liquefaction.

Gelatine Stick:—

    Growth uniform, line of puncture filiform, growth becomes slightly heavier and on the 6th day there is a slight liquefied depression.
    10 days. Liquefaction is infundibuliform.
    13 days. Complete liquefaction.

Agar Plates:—

Agar slope, 37°:—

    Very slight, if any, growth (7 days).

Glucose agar slope:—

    Filiform, non-spreading growth.

Glucose Stick:—

    Filiform growth, nothing on the surface.
    6 days. Slightly heavier, subsequently no change.

Beef Broth:—

    Slight clouding, flocculent sediment.
    3 days, clearing.
    No further change.

Dunham's Solution:—

    Grown for five days at room temperature, tested with Ehrlich test, allowed to stand 20 minutes, and then recorded. Very weak Indol.

Litmus Milk:—

    6 days. No change visible until 6th day, when colour becomes darker. This increases.
    6 weeks. Colour is atrocyaneus. There is progressive digestion without coagulation.

Potato:—

    Whitish growth restricted and filiform.
    3 weeks. No further change.

G. I.

Medium size moderately thick bacillus with rounded ends, very considerable variation as to size, actively motile, stains well with methylene blue, gram negative.

Gelatine plates:—

> *24 hours.* Just visible to the naked eye.
> *48 hours.* Punctiform.
> *8 days.* 1 - 5 mm. in diameter, round, saucer-shaped, liquefaction. Whitish in colour, most dense near centre. Radiating lines like the spokes of a wheel from the centre consisting of deposited bacteria. With ⅔ objective edges are entire and interior granular to grumose.
> *4 days.* Plates have liquefied.

Gelatine Stick:—

> *48 hours.* Liquefaction heavier, 6 mm. in depth. This increases and is stratiform to sacchate. In ten days tube is completely liquefied.

Agar Plates:—

Agar slope, 37°:—

> Very slight growth, in 24 hours.
> *48 hours.* More abundant growth, spreading, flat, glistening, semi-opaque.
> *3 days.* Slightly heavier.
> No further change.

Glucose agar slope:—

> Moist, white, spreading, smooth, Gas in condensation water.
> *3 weeks.* Cream-yellow colour at the base of the slope, and centre of surface growth.

Glucose Stick:—

> Filiform, slightly spreading on surface, 3 or 4 gas bubble along line of puncture.
> No further change.

Beef Broth:

> *24 hours.* Strong, cloudy, moderate sediment.
> *3 days.* Pellicle over entire surface.
> *7 days.* Yellow-cream colour in the outer layers.
> No other change.

Dunham's Solution:—

> Grown for five days at room temperature, tested with Ehrlish test, allowed to stand 20 minutes, and then recorded. Indol very strong production.

Litmus Milk:—

> *48 hours.* Colour is lighter.
> *2 days.* Alkaline digestion commences.
> *6 days.* Almost complete digestion, remaining curd, in fine particles, dirty violaceous in colour. Whey ¾ of tube. Semi-transparent and avellaneous in colour, no odour. Blue ring at surface.

Potato:—

> *24 hours.* No apparent change.
> *48 hours.* Slight growth, filiform, yellowish.
> *6 days.* Moderate growth, slightly raised, moist on the moist part of potato and dry at the top, ferruginious in colour.
> *3 weeks.* Colour is redder, otherwise no further change.

8 GEORGE V, A. 1918

H. I.

A short to medium stout bacillus, actively motile, stains well with methylene blue, is gram negative.

Gelatine Plates:—

> *24 hours.* Just visible to the naked eye.
> *4 days.* Punctiform, later liquified.

Gelatine Stick:

> Growth uniform, filiform.
> *48 hours.* Slightly liquefying, 2 mm. in depth, stratiform. Liquefaction increases and is slightly sacchate with flocculence.
> *10 days.* Liquefaction becomes infundibuliform.
> *15 days.* Whole tube is liquefied.

Agar Plate:—

> *48 hours.* Round, uniform, glistening, colony. With ⅔ objective round, edges slightly erose. Slightly granular colony.
> *3 days.* Colony becomes more massive and bluish white; otherwise no further change.

Agar Slope, 37°:—

> Very slight growth, one or two colonies. Increases along line of puncture.
> *7 days.* No further change.

Glucose Agar Slope:—

> Thin, translucent, moist, film in 24 hours. No further change.

Glucose Stick:—

> Filiform. No surface growth.

Beef Broth:—

> *24 hours.* Slight clouding, flocculent and abundant sediment.
> *3 days.* Clearing.
> *7 days.* No further change.

Dunham's Solution:—

> Grown for five days at room temperature, tested with Ehrlish test, allowed to stand 20 minutes, and then recorded. Indol very strong.

· *Litmus Milk:—*

> *24 hours.* No change.
> *48 hours.* Tubes become darker in colour, atro-violaceous. No coagulation. Subsequently there is gradual digestion. Whey first with a violet shade, throughout, which gradually concentrates as a deep blue ring on top, and curd becomes semi-transparent, isabellinus in colour, and thick but not viscous. A little undigested curd at bottom of tube. (3 weeks.)

Potato:—

> *24 hours.* Very slight growth.
> *4 days.* Growth moist, slightly raised, smooth. Colour brown, light testaceous.
> *3 weeks.* Colour changes somewhat between rosaceous and testaceous. No further change.

SESSIONAL PAPER No. 38a

SUMMARY OF CHARACTERS.

	Diam. over 1 m.	Chains.	Spores.	Capsules.	Motile.	Gram.	Broth.				Agar.		Gel. Plate.			Potato.			Milk.			Gas.	Indol.	Gas in Gluc. Agar.
							Cloudy.	Ring.	Pellicle.	Sediment.	Shiny.	Dull.	Chrom.	Round.	Liquef.	Mod.	Colour.	Grows at 37° C	Acid curd.	Rennet curd.	Casein pep.			
A 1.....	−	+	−	−	+	−	+	−	−	+	+	−	−	+	+	+	+	+	−	−	−	+	−	+
A 2.....	−	+	−	−	+	−	+	−	−	+	+	−	−	+	+	+	+	+	−	+	+	−	+	+
A 3.....	−	+	−	−	+	−	+	+	−	+	+	−	−	+	+	+	+	+	−	+	+	−	−	+
A 4.....	−	+	−	−	+	−	+	−	−	+	+	−	−	+	−	+	+	+	−	+	−	±	+	+
B 2.....	−	+	−	−	+	−	+	−	−	+	+	−	−	+	+	+	+	+	−	+	+	±	+	+
C 1.....	−	+	−	−	+	−	+	−	−	+	+	−	−	+	−	+	+	+	−	+	+	±	+	+
D 1.....	−	+	−	−	+	−	+	−	−	+	+	−	−	+	+	+	−	−	−	+	+	+	+	+
F 1.....	−	+	−	−	+	−	+	−	−	+	−	+	−	+	+	−	−	+	−	+	+	−	+	+
G 1.....	−	+	−	−	+	−	+	−	+	+	+	−	−	+	+	+	+	+	−	+	+	−	+	+
H 1	−	+	−	−	+	−	+	−	−	+	+	−	−	+	+	+	+	+	−	+	+	−	+	+
B Sal-monis pestis.	?	+	−	−	+	−	+	−	+	+	+	−	−	+	+	+	+	−	+	−	+	−	..	−

CHARACTERISTICS OF THE MICRO-ORGANISM (*Bacillus salmonis pestis* Patterson).

Morphological Characters.

A short, thick bacillus with rounded ends, varying in length, occurring singly and in pairs lying end to end. Actively motile, non-spore-bearing, does not stain with Gram's method, grows rapidly and profusely at the room temperature, but shows little or no growth at 37° C., and is killed at this temperature in about six days.

The organism exposed to a mixture of ice and salt for a week not only survived that low temperature, but grew profusely while in the mixture. Involution forms were only observed in glucose media. It appears to be a strict aerobe. Pathogenic to fish, non-pathogenic to frogs, mice, and guinea-pigs.

Cultures.—Room Temperature.

Gelatine Plates.—In about three days small, greyish, pin-point colonies appear, with a ring of liquefaction around them of a transparent greyish colour, which rapidly increases, the plate becoming completely liquefied in about 36 hours after their appearance. The dense pin-point centre and transparent area of liquefaction around is markedly characteristic of the bacillus, together with the very rapid liquefaction of the gelatine.

Gelatine Stab.—Profuse growth along needle track at the end of 18 hours, which gradually increases and rapidly liquefies the gelatine.

Carbol Gelatine, 1 per cent Stab.—Slight growth in 18 hours along needle track, which gradually liquefies the gelatine.

Carbol Gelatine, ·05 per cent Stab.—The growth is more profuse.

Carbol Gelatine, ·03 per cent, Stab.—Very profuse growth.

8 GEORGE V, A. 1918

	Room Temperature.	37° C.
Agar Streak :—	Dense, profuse, cream-coloured moist shining growth along needle track in 18 hours, with irregular margin, which gradually spreads over the surface of the agar.	Growth barely visible.
Agar Smear :—	Small pin-point cream-coloured colonies at the end of 18 hours with irregular spreading transparent margins.	" "
Agar Glucose Stab :—	Profuse cream-coloured growth along needle track for about half an inch at the end of 24 hours, spreading on the surface. The agar gradually becomes cloudy from the surface and parallel to it, and extends for about half an inch down the media. No gas production.	" "
Agar Glucose Plate :—	Cream-coloured colonies with moist shining surface and white cloudiness around each Colony.	" "
Blood Serum :—		
Bouillon :—	At the end of 18 hours the bouillon becomes cloudy throughout, with a marked skim on the surface and clinging to sides of tube, with a slight deposit at the bottom.	No perceptible growth.
Bouillon (Glucose) :—	Similar to ordinary bouillon, but growth much more profuse..	Very slight growth.
Bouillon Taurocholate Glucose :—	Slight growth, turning the media slightly red. No gas formation..........	No growth.
Litmus Milk :—	In about 48 hours there is a distinct acid reaction, which gradually increases, and in about seven days the milk becomes coagulated and gradually digested.	No perceptible change.
Peptone Water :—	Marked cloudiness throughout at the end of 18 hours. Gives no indol reaction.	Very slight cloudiness at the end of 48 hours. Gives no indol reaction.
Potato :—	Very profuse yellowish brown growth at the end of 18 hours, raised on the surface of media like blisters, with moist shining surface.	Very slight growth in 48 hours.
Agar (Anaerobically) :—	No growth...	No growth.

The organism also withstands the effect of ordinary water, sterile water and sea-water for a considerable time, as flasks of those inoculated with it and kept at the room temperature for over a month gave profuse growths when reinoculated on agar. It does not, however, survive more than a week in distilled water. It also keeps well on sub-cultures, as tubes of agar inoculated from sub-cultures about a year old gave profuse growths in about 18 hours.

The chief characteristics of the bacillus are those:—

Actively motile, non-spore-bearing bacillus.
On sub-culture it grows profusely in 18 hours at the room temperature.
On sub-culture it grows profusely when exposed to 0 deg. C. for a week.
Shows *little or no growth at 37° C.*
Is *killed at 37° C.* (98·6° F.) in about six days.
Liquefies gelatine with extreme rapidity.
Coagulates and digests milk.
Forms a cloudiness in glucose agar in the neighbourhood of the growth.
Grows well in sea water.
Strict aerobe.
Involution forms only observed on glucose media.
Does *not* stain with Gram's method.
Pathogenic to fish.
Non-pathogenic to frogs, mice, and guinea-pigs.

CONCLUSIONS.

(1) The fungus *Saprolegnia ferax* is not the cause of the salmon disease.

(2) The disease is due to the invasion of the tissues of the fish by a special bacillus (*Bacillus salmonis pestis*).

(3) The bacillus gains access through abrasion or ulceration of the skin, and the disease is apparently not contracted when the skin of the fish is in a healthy state.

(4) *Bacillus salmonis pestis* can be transmitted from dead diseased fish to other dead fish in the same water.

(5) *Bacillus salmonis pestis* can be transmitted from dead fish to living fish in the same water, and since dead fish are a suitable nidus for the growth of the bacillus, it is obviously desirable to have all dead fish removed from the river immediately they are observed, and burned, as by simply burying, the germ is left in a condition to be again carried into the stream.

(6) The fact that the bacillus grows profusely when placed in a freezing mixture of ice and salt, while a temperature of 37°C. soon destroys it, shows that the cold season is more favourable to its growth.

(7) Fish akin to salmon are more susceptible to the disease than others, as rainbow trout, river trout, and sea trout when attacked succumbed in from two to four days, while dace and gold-fish died in about 18 and 35 days, respectively.

(8) *Bacillus salmonis pestis* grows well in sea water, whereas *Saprolegnia* does not grow at all; therefore a diseased salmon entering the sea, and returning to the river apparently free from fungus, cannot be said to be free from the disease.

GOLD-FISH EXPERIMENT.

Late in November a number of gold-fish were purchased and placed in a large tank in one of our laboratories. The change of water resulted in a few dying, so to avoid any errors due to management we kept them for a month before inoculation. They were then removed from the aquarium and two fish were placed in each of eight large museum jars, and kept thus for another week. The water was changed every third day, and the fish fed every alternate day.

The inoculation was carried out in the following manner: The fish was taken out with the hand and the top of the head and part of one side near the gills gently rubbed with sandpaper until there was a slight effusion of blood, and this abraded area was then rubbed with a platinum oese of 3 mm. charged with material taken from a 24-hour-old agar slope culture. A separate piece of sandpaper was used for each fish. Several loopsful of the culture were added to the water of each jar.

In this way organisms A1, A2, A3, A4, B1, B2, C1, D1, E1, F1, G1 were inoculated in duplicate, and four fish were rubbed with sandpaper but not inoculated. The fish were observed daily, and the inoculated water was changed on the third day.

The control fish rubbed with sandpaper and not inoculated are still alive, and of the inoculated fish, one in each of the jars inoculated with A, A2, B2, C1, and D1, died 22, 30, 34, 27, 43 days after inoculation.

Bacteriological examination was made of these fish, but in no case was I able to obtain from the dead fish the organism which was inoculated. Evidently these organisms were non-pathogenic to gold-fish. One fish in each of the jars from which the dead fish were taken remains alive, and, at the time of writing (May 10) appear quite normal. Of course there is the possibility that some of the organisms isolated might be pathogenic for salmon and not for gold-fish.

Patterson states with reference to his B. *salmonis pestis* that:—

> "Dace inoculated with this bacillus died as the result of inoculation in from two to seven days. Dace, river trout, sea trout and gold fish inoculated

8 GEORGE V, A. 1918

with *Saprolegnia* remained healthy. Dace, sea trout and one gold fish inoculated with *Saprolegnia* and *B. salmonis pestis* died in various periods of time (2 to 18 days) except the gold fish which died after inoculation and showed signs of the fungus on the gill covers. No attempt was made to make cultures from the dead gold fish."

Patterson concludes that —   :

"*Saprolegnia* grows on live fish in the presence of the organism, which breaks down the superficial tissues and forms a suitable nidus for the fungus to grow on."

I had no *Saprolegnia* to try similar experiments.

The difficulty of obtaining and keeping fish for experiments in a laboratory unequipped for such work, and the difficulty because of lack of laboratory equipment to carry out experimental work at the hatchery, will have to be overcome before any decisive experiments can be undertaken.

It is, however, significant that all organs apparently healthy in the salmon examined contained bacteria in large numbers, and of comparatively few species, and I am unable to state or find in any literature or obtain information as to the bacterial content of the normal organs of fish, or how soon after death, and to what extent, these organs are invaded by bacteria. Very large numbers of bacteria were found in the eggs from a number of the fungus-infected salmon, and under normal conditions one would scarcely expect to find so many bacteria present.

All that can be stated at present is that Patterson's organism, *B. salmonis pestis,* was not found, and that the large number of bacteria present accompanying the *Saprolegnia* may have some pathogenic role, but the rules of proof (Koch's postulates) would have to be worked out where fish, the means of keeping them, and laboratory facilities are provided.

IX

REPORT ON AFFECTED SALMON IN THE MIRAMICHI RIVER, NEW BRUNSWICK.

(By A. G. HUNTSMAN, B.A., M.B., F.R.S.C., etc., Curator of the Biological Station, St. Andrew's, New Brunswick.)

In the early part of October, 1915, Mr. G. J. Desbarats, the Deputy Minister of the Naval Service, requested that the Biological Board arrange an investigation of a disease which had broken out among the salmon in the Northwest Miramichi river. I was instructed to proceed to the Miramichi hatchery, South Esk, New Brunswick, examine the conditions there, investigate the possibility of organisms other than bacteria being responsible for the disease, and arrange for the shipment of material for bacteriological examination to Principal F. C. Harrison, of Macdonald College, Ste. Anne de Bellevue, Que.

The hatchery was visited on October 11 and 12. It is located near the mouth of a small stream which empties into the Northwest branch of the Miramichi river, a few miles from Newcastle. Mr. Donald Morrison, the local inspector of fisheries, and Mr. Wm. Sheasgreen, the officer in charge of the hatchery, gave every assistance.

Down the stream from the hatchery is a pond for retaining the salmon previous to the stripping at spawning time. It consists of a portion of the stream enclosed by boards, with spaces between for the circulation of the water. The water is changed regularly by the action of the tide and by the current of the stream. The level of the water in the pond is prevented from falling too low by a dam across the stream below the pond.

A large proportion of the fish in the pond had been officially reported to be visibly affected, and I found white patches of fungus with extensive ulcerations in the centre of many of the patches in the worst cases. The head, the back, and the tail were the parts that in most instances showed evidence of the disease. In the earlier stages the affected parts were seen to be covered with a greyish thin film of fungus, which was easily rubbed off. If the fish were removed from the water these greyish patches could scarcely be seen. The fish that were in the worst condition were sluggish, came inshore into the shallow water, or floated near the surface with the fins exposed. Frequently the caudal fin was partly out of the water and the head very low, the fish floating at an angle approaching the vertical.

Mr. Sheasgreen gave the following information on October 12:—

"During the latter part of September small marks, chiefly on the head, were noticed on a large proportion of the fish in the pond. A few marked fish (those with definite wounds) had been received from the fishermen. It has been the custom whenever an opportunity presented to take these marked fish from the pond and bury them. The records show that twenty-two fish were taken out from the 18th to the 21st of September, three on the 25th, and five on the 28th. On the outbreak of the disease (the last of September) at first only dead fish were removed, but later badly infected living ones as well. Beginning with September 30, fish were received every day, never less than seven, and once as many as thirty-eight. The dead fish were all well covered with the fungus. On October 6 we began to reject some of the fish brought in by the fishermen, who by this time were noticing the fungus on some of the fish that they were catching. Of the fish brought in there were no large number badly marked previous

38a—12   169

to October 6. They all showed, if any, only slight marks, and no evident fungus. From that date on, from 15 to 30 per cent (2 to 4 out of every dozen) of the fish taken each day from three traps near the hatchery, of which records were kept, showed signs of the disease, and were rejected. The fish from a trap 2½ miles up the river showed twenty-six affected out of a total of fifty-two on October 6, twenty-two out of 40 on October 8, and three out of thirteen on October 11, apparently showing a steady improvement as if the infected fish had passed up the river. Up to nearly the 8th of October the salmon in the pond did not seem to be as active (jump as much) as in previous years, but since that date there has been a marked improvement.

"Last year (1914) there were 2,636 salmon in the pond. This year the pond has been enlarged and is from one-quarter to one-third larger than last year. The number of fish that had been placed in the pond previous to September 30 was 2,308.

"This disease has not been noticed in the salmon in any year previous to this, although salmon in the Gaspe region are reported to have had fungus disease last year."

From a comparison of the numbers of the fish and the sizes of the pond it is evident that there has been far less crowding of the fish this year than last. As to temperature, the Monthly Weather Reviews of the Meteorological Service show that at Chatham, 20 miles from the hatchery at the mouth of the Miramichi river, the mean monthly temperatures for the months of August and September, 1915, are only slightly (·6° and ·2°) above the averages for those months for the past forty years. And for the month of September both the mean temperature and the maximum temperature are lower than for the same month in 1914.

The temperature records for the water at the hatchery are incomplete. Temperatures were observed in the hatchery from August 30 to September 20. The records show a range from 50° to 68°F., with an average temperature of about 58°. Temperatures have been observed in the retaining pond from October 6 to 20, and show a range from 46° to 52°, the temperature remaining comparatively uniform during that period. Temperatures observed in the hatchery from October 14 to 20 show that on bright days the temperature in the pond is two to three degrees higher than in the hatchery, and on cloudy days about the same as in the hatchery. Judging from this, the temperature in the pond has at no time since fish were put in (September 11) been higher than 65°F. Temperature does not appear to have been a special causative factor in 1915. The gradual lowering of the temperature has doubtless helped to stop the spread of the disease, Mr. Sheasgreen stating that on October 20 no new diseased fish were appearing.

As to the place of origin of the disease, the presence of diseased fish among those caught in the traps over a considerable period of time indicates that the disease was present for some distance up and down the Northwest Miramichi river. Diseased fish were not noticed among those taken from the traps until one week after the disease had been observed in the pond. Mr. Sheasgreen states that he and his assistants buried all the fish removed from the pond. This obviates the possibility of fish from the pond having carried the infection to the fish in the river, although not the possibility of the pond having served as a source for the distribution of the infection up and down the river.

The avenue of infection appears to have been chiefly through abrasions of the skin. The principal parts seen to be affected in the early stages of the disease were: the tip of the snout, the margins of the jaws, the top of the head, and the middle line of the back, and the margins of the fins. These are the parts most liable to injury in the traps or in the cars used for transporting the salmon to the retaining pond. An examination of the fish caught in the traps and brought to the retaining pond on

SESSIONAL PAPER No. 38a

October 12, all with no visible disease, showed that the great majority had some abrasions, the commonest being on the tip of the snout, the top of the head, and the margins of the fins (particularly the caudal). There were also net marks around the middle of the head and the marks of fish lice (removal of scales) along the middle line of the back in a number of cases. These marks explain the usual distribution of the fungus, the other parts of the body—for example, the sides—being attacked only in the later stages.

The vigour of the fish declines with the spread of the fungus. Fish with well-developed but localized patches of fungus on the head or elsewhere, or with wounds raw or bleeding, appeared to be nearly as vigourous as healthy fish. But if the fungus were present over much of the surface they were sluggish, came close inshore or floated near the surface with the fins, particularly the caudal, sticking out of the water. In the last stages they dropped to the bottom of the water on their sides.

The only data with reference to the rate of spread of the disease have to do with a fish put in clean on October 4th and removed on the 12th in a sluggish condition, with the fungus covering most of the surface, but so slightly developed that it was not easily seen after the fish had been removed from the water.

The salmon-louse [*Lepeophtheirus salmonis* (Kröyer), see Wilson, 1905, p. 640] was found on a fairly large proportion of the fish taken from the traps. It occurred chiefly along the middle of the back between the fins. It appears to be responsible for the removal fo the scales and doubtless determines the location of the disease in this region.

The fungus proved to be *Saprolegnia,* several species of which are commonly found growing on dead organic matter in fresh water. Prof. J. H. Faull of the University of Toronto, to whom material was submitted, informs me that it belongs to the *ferax* group of *Saprolegnia,* but since no oospores could be seen (they are rarely found) exact identification was impossible. Several species of the *ferax* group occur on dead or diseased fishes (Hofer, 1906, p. 106.) The growth and extension of the *Saprolegnia* proceeds *pari passu* with the disease and may be taken as an evidence of the extent of the disease. Whether its relation to the disease is to any extent a causal one or whether it is merely an accompaniment, may well be disputed.

An examination of the internal organs of the diseased salmon revealed no distinct lesions. A microscopic study of the body fluids and of sections of the organs likewise revealed nothing. We may conclude that the disease is confined strictly to the skin and subjacent parts.

The bacteriological examination of the diseased fish was in the hands of Principal Harrison. However, having some material, I handed over to Dr. H. K. Detweiler of the Pathological Department, University of Toronto, portions of the skin from fish in various stages of the disease. He very kindly had sections made and stained with thionin blue in order to demonstrate, if possible, the presence of the *Bacillus salmonis pestis,* which was found by J. Hume Patterson (1903) in cases of the salmon disease occuring in Great Britain. He informs me that no positive results have been obtained. Negative results in such a case prove nothing.

The gross characters of this disease appear to be identical with those of the well known salmon disease that appeared in the form of an epidemic among the salmon in certain rivers in the north of England and Scotland in 1877. It spread in the course of a few years to the neighbouring rivers up and down the coast and has continued in an endemic state in the waters of Great Britain ever since. No means of successfully combatting it has as yet been found.

The *Saprolegnia ferax* was for many years considered to be the cause of the disease (Stirling, 1878 and 1879, and Walpole and Huxley, 1882). In 1903, however, Patterson published the results of investigations which went to show that *Saprolegnia* was not

38a—12½

8 GEORGE V, A. 1918

responsible for the disease, but a *Bacillus (B. salmonis pestis)*. The *Bacillus* alone brought about the death of fish, but not the *Saprolegnia* alone. The latter was able to grow in tissues already invaded by the *Bacillus*. The *Bacillus* grew in sea water, but the *Saprolegnia* did not. Salmon affected by the disease while in salt water would therefore not show any fungus until after arriving in fresh water. Patterson states that the cold season is more favourable for the growth of the *Bacillus* and Malloch (1910, p. 117) states that the colder the weather the worse the disease becomes. But Patterson's experiments merely show that the *Bacillus* grows better at 0° C. (32° F.) than at 37° C. (98.6° F.), whereas at room temperature (60° F. ?) the growth was very much more rapid than at 0° C.

In the case of the disease in the Miramichi river, Mr. Sheasgreen has stated that the condition of the fish in the pond improved rapidly during the latter half of October and at the same time the number of diseased fish taken in the traps decreased. The lower temperature *may* have been responsible for this, either by improving the condition of the fish or by decreasing the rate of spread of the infection.

For eradicating the disease our only hope, and that a slender one, is to systematically remove all dead and diseased fish as soon as discovered. Patterson recommends that they be burned and *not buried*, since the organisms survive in the dead fish and may be carried again into the streams. Unless due to some undiscovered temporary factor, the disease is practically certain to appear again.

Whatever organism may be most responsible for the disease, the latter being an affection of the skin, will be influenced by other organisms as well, and there will also be a number of contributing factors, the chief of which will be those that lower the general vitality of the fish. In the case of the salmon retained for spawning purposes, an effort should be made in the future to improve the conditions in the ponds, particularly with regard to renewal of the water and the attainment of the most suitable temperature, so that the fish will be affected as little as possible. If the disease reappears, experiments should be instituted to determine the conditions best adapted to prevent its spreading.

The use of the fish for spawning purposes raises the question of the possible effect of the disease on the eggs or on the next generation. The Deputy Minister informs me under date of April 6, 1916, that in three hatcheries, supplied from the Miramichi retaining pond, the loss had already reached a figure of from 42 per cent to 61 per cent of the original number of eggs. It seems probable that many infected fish had recovered, as maintained by Mr. Sheasgreen, and that these gave eggs of greatly lowered vitality. The fish stripped were all in good condition, and precautions were taken to prevent any infection reaching the eggs from the exterior of the fish or from the pond.

What would be the result if some of the infection did reach the eggs? The *Saprolegnia* is known to attack fish eggs, but it is at least probable that this occurs only when the eggs are of low vitality. Also *Saprolegnia* spores are so widely distributed as to be present in the water in the hatching troughs in any case, although those from the fish may belong to a more virulent strain.

It is improbable that the bacteria, which may have a causal relation to the disease in the salmon, will attack the salmon eggs. Plehn (1911) found that *Bacterium salmonicida*, which produces furunculosis in the brown trout (*Salmo fario*) attacked neither the eggs, the alevins, nor the fry of the trout, but did attack the yearlings. It is therefore quite unlikely that the disease can be transmitted through the fry and by that means be carried to the streams in which fry from Miramichi eggs may be planted. It is possible, however, that it might be carried in the water used for shipping the eggs or fry.

It is very desirable that during a future season other rivers should be investigated. It has been claimed that in the rivers of Great Britain the salmon disease was present in a sporadic form previous to the outbreak in 1877.

LITERATURE.

Hofer, B. Handbuch der Fischkrankheiten. Stuttgart. 1906.

Malloch, P. D. Life-History and Habits of the Salmon, etc. London. 1910.

Patterson, J. H. The Cause of Salmon Disease. Pub'n., Fishery Board for Scotland. 1903.

Plehn, M. Die Furunkulose der Salmoniden. Centralbl. f. Bakt., etc., I Abt., Originale, Bd. 60, Ht. 7, p. 609, 1911.

Stirling, A. B. Notes on the Fungus Disease affecting Salmon. Proc. Roy. Soc. Edin., vol. IX, p. 726. 1878.
Additional Observations on the Fungus Disease, etc. Proc. Roy. Soc. Edin., vol. X, p. 232. 1879.

Walpole and Huxley. On Saprolegnia in Relation to the Salmon Disease. Quart. Journ. Micr. Sc., vol. XXII. new series, p. 311. 1882.

Wilson, C. B. North American Parasitic Copepods belonging to the Family Caligidae. Part I. The Caliginae. Proc. U. S. Nat. Museum. vol. XXVIII, p. 479. 1905.

X

THE SMOKING OF "HADDOCKS" FOR CANADIAN MARKETS—AN IN-VESTIGATION CONDUCTED AT THE MARINE BIOLOGICAL STATION AT ST. ANDREW'S, N.B.

By Miss OLIVE GAIR PATTERSON, M.A., M.B., University of Toronto.

1. INTRODUCTION.

The production of finnan haddie is an industry of some importance on the coasts of the Maritime Provinces. This importance, however, is not national, in degree, as it is on the Scottish coast. There is not the demand on the market for finnan haddie "Made in Canada" that there might quite well be, if it were made to become the equivalent of the Scotch article of diet in flavour and texture. The processes used in both countries are somewhat similar, it is true, being based on the original method used in the little Scottish town of Findon on the north coast. Variations were intro-duced by the different fish-curers, which were considered expedient or profitable to them, but at times detrimental to the culinary value of the fish, upon which followed a lowering of both the market value and the demand on the market for this excellent foodstuff. The point of first importance in the Scottish industry was the improvement of the flavour of fresh fish, and, of second importance, was the preservation of the fish. These are in the reverse order in the industry as developed in this country. Many of the markets are far distant, and flavour has been sacrificed to preservation, but often inferior, second-rate or slightly tainted fish are used in producing the finnan haddie, so that the quality of the finished product is poor or, at any rate, not to be relied upon. The best of the catch is put up for exportation on ice, fresh, and until these first quality ones are used to make finnan haddie, the Canadian market will not increase its demand for them, the consumer preferring to purchase the fresh fish off ice rather than the smoked one of doubtful origin and quality. It is surely the part of wisdom to create the demand on the market by first producing a more excellent haddie, and then to encourage fish curers to reach and keep up that standard of excellence.

2. SCOTTISH METHOD.

The method of producing finnan haddies, as practised in Aberdeenshire, the most important Scottish centre of the industry, includes the processes of splitting, salting, and smoking.

"The fresh haddock is first treated by removing the head, splitting, eviscerating, and then giving an extra cut behind the backbone from the right-hand side in order to expose to view and facilitate the curing of the thick muscles of the back. This supple-mentary cut does not extend to the tail. The fish is then salted for half an hour in strong brine, and, after draining, is ready for smoking ".[1] Peat and sawdust are used in producing the smoke; the fish, which are placed on sticks in tiers one above the other, receive constant attention during their short stay of five or six hours in the dense smoke which the peat produces.

Smaller fish are cured separately, the time of both pickling and smoking being diminished so that the flesh does not become tough—on the contrary, these lightly cured small fish are a great delicacy.

The Canadian method of curing differs in some important essentials from the Scotch, besides varying in minor details.

---

[1] Excerpt from H. M. Smith's "Note. on Scotch Methods, etc." U.S. Commission of Fish and Fisheries, 1901.

3. CANADIAN METHOD.

(1) No vertebral cut is made after splitting. Bacteriological tests of the flesh under the backbone of finnan haddie only forty-eight hours old gave positive cultures of trimenthylamine-producing bacteria in many cases.[2]

(2) The smoke is produced by burning hardwood, preferably beech or birch. The smoke is, consequently, not so dense and the process has to be continued for a much longer period of time, fifteen to eighteen hours, when the fish is a rich golden brown colour, the edges almost brittle, and the flesh in the middle thick portions still moist and scarcely flavoured by the smoke.

(3) At times the fish are allowed to stand one to three days before curing, ostensibly to allow the blood to drain away, but this can be accomplished in one hour on ice, so that one fails to see the point of this lack of expeditiousness.

4. CONDITIONS ESSENTIAL FOR SUPERIOR PRODUCT.

The endeavour was made to determine, if possible, what were the optimum conditions for the production of finnan haddie *par excellence* on the coasts of the Canadian Maritime provinces. That these conditions would differ from the Scotch has been pointed out—for example, in the absence of peat as fuel, and the demands of distant markets; and under these latter circumstances a certain sacrifice of flavour to preserving property must be made, still, it is quite within the limits of possibility to so standardize the industry that these variable conditions would be altered to suit the requirements of the market for which the fish were destined.

These variable conditions are:—

    (1) Time of the fish in brine.
    (2) Quality of brine.
    (3) Quality of smoke.
    (4) Time of smoking.
    (5) Method of splitting.

5. SCIENTIFIC TESTS OF CURING METHODS.

Most of these conditions were varied in the tests described below. The record of the flavour of the different haddies when cooked was made from the opinions obtained from several individuals to whom were given samples of the various products.

Experiment 1.—The first haul of haddock were cured according to the method used by certain of the New Brunswick curers—except that here, as in each test, perfectly fresh fish and of approximately the same size were used. That the fish should be of the same size and weight is important, as a comparison otherwise would be obviously inaccurate.

Experiment 2.—The fish in this lot were smoked for varying periods of time, the salting being constant.

Experiment 3.—In this the conditions were reversed. Smoking time constant and time in the brine varied.

Experiment 4.—Small fish were used and both conditions were varied to produce a delicately flavoured lightly-cured fish.

Experiment 5.—In this the preservative value of the salt content of the fish is shown and its limit, as far as palatibility is concerned.

Experiment 6.—In this the method is applied to the hake.

Experiment 7.—Proves the advisability of the dorsal incision.

---

[2] Bacteriological examinations were made by Dr. F. C. Harrison, MacDonald College, and his report appears in the present volume of Biological Contributions.

SESSIONAL PAPER No. 38a

Experiment.	Date.	Preparation.	Salting.	Smoking.	Remarks.
No. 1..	July 20. ..	Split abdominally—eviscerated—washed clean.	25 minutes' brine of sufficient concentration to float a fish. Then allowed to drain.	18 hours over slow hardwood fire.	Colour—dark brown—edges very dry—almost brittle.
No. 2..	August 2...	Split abdominally—eviscerated.	*(a)* 30 minutes as above.	6 hours over old wood to which was added creosote.	Colour—light brown. Flesh—soft. Flavour—delicate.
			(b) 30 minutes as above.	15 hours......... "	Colour—darker. Flesh—firm. Flavour—excellent. Preserved 4 days.
No. 3..	August 4, one dozen large fish ¾ lb.	Split abdominally. Eviscerated. Kept on ice overnight—Well washed.	*(a)* 30 minutes........	18 hours	Excellent flavour. Flesh not tough nor too salty.
			(b) 2 hours..	18 hours..........	Flesh too salty but not toughened. Salt could be removed by previous soaking.
			(c) 4 hours...	18 hours	Texture too tough. Preserved 17 days at 10° C.
No. 4..	August 10, one dozen small fish ½-1 lb.	Opened dorsally given the extra cut along the vertebrae.	*(a)* 15 minutes......	*(a)* 1. 5 hours. ... 2. 10 hours.. .... 3. 15 hours......	1. Insufficiently flavoured. 2. Still moist—flavour delicious. 3. Flesh crumbly—did not hold together in cooking. Preserved nine days.
			(b) 30 minutes..	*(b)* 10 hours..........	4. Flavour not so good as when salted 15 minutes but flesh firmer and of better keeping quality.
No. 5..	August 10.	As above...... .	*(c)* 1 hour..	*(c)* 1. 10 hours... ..	Flavour—somewhat coarsened texture—otherwise good. Excessive salt removed by three washings previous to cooking—20 minutes.
				2. 15 hours... ...	Flavour—about the same as above. Preserved—8 days to 20. Texture coarsened somewhat.
No. 6..	August 18, ten small hake.	Split abdominally...	*(a)* Salted ½ hour........	About 10 hours until brown colour. Very windy day ..	Flavour—inferior to haddock but reasonably good. Texture—inferior to haddock, but reasonably good.
			(b) Salted 1 hour.	" " ..	Too salty—much too long for these fish which are thinner than the haddock.

8 GEORGE V, A. 1918

Details of Experiment 7.—Estimations of the NaCL content of the fish muscle and inner portions to determine approximately how much the flesh under the backbone absorbed within a given time. The portions were extracted with 10 vols. water for three hours with frequent stirring—10 c.c. of the boiled filtered extract were used in the estimations.

Exp. No.	Sample.	c.c. N/11 silver nitrate used.	Equivalent in grams NaCl.	Per cent in moist muscle.
83	Salted ½ hour, flesh under bone..	1·965 c.c.	0·01965	1·965
84	Salted 2 hours, flesh under bone.	2·5 c.c.	0·025	2·5
87	Salted 4 hours, flesh under bone.	8·26 c.c.	0·0826	8·26
86	Salted 4 hours, flesh from surface	11·05 c.c.	0·1105	11·05

Obviously, this table shows that it takes some four hours for the flesh under the bone to approximate that of the external portion of the flesh in salinity, and affords a strong argument for the exposure of the back muscle to the saline by making the vertebral cut.

6. CONCLUSIONS.

(1) The splitting of the fish in the usual way, but also making an additional cut along the vertebral column is the most effective method of preparation.

(2) The fish are freed from blood by allowing to remain on ice 1 to 2 hours. They should then be washed freely with fresh water.

(3) Small fish should not be salted more than 15 minutes. Larger fish up to four pounds should not be salted more than one hour if the texture of the fish· is to be preserved, and half an hour is the optimum length of time in saline for the flavour of the fish.

(4) Ten hours over a beechwood sawdust, or old-wood smoke produced a deliciously flavoured fish. Fifteen to eighteen hours browns and dries the fish and aids in its preservation by more thorough drying.

These conditions should be altered to suit the market. the more lighty cured fish being utilized in the home markets and the heavier-salted for the distant ones. The chief condition to be emphasized, however, is the utilization, for the production of finnan haddie, of first-class perfectly fresh haddock, and the keeping of it cold after it is prepared.

XI.

SOME OBSERVATIONS ON HADDOCKS AND "FINNAN HADDIES" RELATING TO THE BACTERIOLOGY OF CURED FISH.

By Principal F. C. Harrison, D.Sc., Macdonald College, P.Q.

During the month of July, 1915, the writer whilst at the Biological Station, St. Andrews, N.B., examined bacteriologically the intestinal content of twelve haddocks. The haddocks were caught about a mile to two miles from the station, were brought to the laboratory, opened, and a portion of the intestine ligatured and removed. An opening was then cut into the piece with sterilized scissors, and a heated platinum needle thrust in, and the small amount adhering to the needle was transferred to about 5 c.c. of sterilized water and thoroughly shaken.

Plates were made from the dilution, from 1 to 3 œse being used for each plate. Plates were made with :—

Haddock sea water gelatine..	12 per cent.
Beef peptone sea water gelatine..	12 "
Lactose litmus sea water gelatine..	12 "

In this manner the intestinal content of twelve fish was plated, and a large number of isolations made.

At the same time a microscopical examination of the intestinal contents was made. Smear preparations invariably showed numerous bacilli, mostly small forms, no cocci and no spirilla. The bacterial content of the twelve fish was similar. Ten different species of bacteria were isolated; of these four were liquefiers, and about 25 per cent of the total number of colonies from each fish belonged to this group. Many of the plates gave a strong odour of trimethylamine, and one or two of the pure cultures gave this odour. In the mixed cultures, however, in the plates the odour of this substance was much stronger.

The most common organism which was found in eight of the twelve fish was a small bacillus, motile, producing small depressions in gelatine plates, with numerous smaller colonies around the edge, rapidly liquefying, producing H2S, indol, and trimethylamine, gas in glucose, but not in lactose, coagulating milk with digestion, and in short appearing to be closely related to *B. vulgaris* (Hauser).

This organism has the greater interest of all those isolated because it was found subsequently in the flesh, and on the surface of smoked haddock (finnan haddie) cured at the station, and also from some spoiled haddock received from a packer.

A short account of the methods employed in securing the fish may be of interest.

The fish were caught near the biological station, and as soon as landed they were split, salted for one and a half hours in brine of sufficient density to float the fish, and smoked for eighteen hours. For six days after smoking the fish were kept in the laboratory at a temperature ranging from 60° to 70° F., and then pieces were removed from different parts of the dried fish, each piece was thoroughly scorched and dropped into flasks containing haddock sea-water peptone broth.

Other pieces of fish were obtained thus: The backbone was cut near the tail, carefully raised, and a portion of the flesh beneath was cut out with a sterilized knife, the piece seized with sterilized forceps and held in the flame until well scorched on the outside, and then dropped into a culture flask.

8 GEORGE V, A. 1918

All flasks thus inoculated were held at room temperature; twenty-four hours later all showed turbidity. Gelatine and agar plates were made from the various flasks, and the colonies which developed were isolated in the usual manner· From this source a number of organisms were secured, and of these four were similar to those previously obtained from the intestinal content of fresh haddies.

In October, 1915, a circular of inquiry was sent to a number of fish dealers and, in response to a request for spoiled fish, a box of spoiled "haddies" was received during the course of the winter. They were covered with a semi-slimy growth, giving a watersoaked appearance. At numerous places there were whitish points resembling bacterial colonies. The flesh was somewhat softened, and the fishy odour much intensified.

From gelatine plates made from this fish the writer secured the liquefying bacillus already mentioned, and large numbers of *Torulæ*.

The most significant fact, therefore, in this piece of work is the presence of liquefying bacteria belonging to the *B. vulgaris* group in the intestinal canal of fresh haddock, and the presence of this organism on and in the flesh of smoked haddocks, and smoked haddock that were spoiled.

The amount of salt and the duration of the smoking period to produce finnan haddies of good flavour are not sufficient to kill the organisms present on the fish after they are gutted, and the antiseptic action of salt and smoke is not sufficient to inhibit the slow growth of organisms.

The writer, after studying the methods of curing haddock, has been impressed with the general carelessness displayed in allowing fish to remain for many hours exposed to warm air and sunlight before gutting and salting. True, that these observations were made under summer conditions when comparatively few haddocks are cured; but the effect of such treatment results in a large increase in the number of bacteria present on the fish, and consequent quicker spoiling of the smoked article.

In winter these conditions would be better, and although the writer has never had the opportunity of studying winter conditions, he has been impressed by the great difference in flavour between fish salted and smoked at the biological station during the winter of 1915-16, and those bought from various dealers in Montreal.

From one or two experiments on the percentage of dry matter, total ash, and chlorides as NaC1 made on a few fish sent to this laboratory, the writer suggests that such determinations should be made of a series of fish for which the amount of·salt used, the salting and smoking period were known.

Further, from the bacteriological standpoint some work should be done on haddock smoked under winter conditions.

MAY, 1916.

XII

THE BACTERIOLOGY OF SWELLED CANNED SARDINES.

By WILFRID SADDLER. M.Sc.. B.S.A.

Introduction.

In a survey of the literature relating to the bacteriology of "canned fish" it is found, with a few exceptions, that the investigations recorded have been undertaken in connection with proved and alleged cases of food poisoning. Consequently the data available are largely interrelated with data on the bacteriology of canned meats, and of ordinary meats as supplied unpreserved. The exceptions of which I have knowledge are the investigations of Prescott and Underwood (1897)[1] on "Micro-organisms in the Cannery Industries"; the work of Macphail associated with Bruére (1897)[2] on "Discolouration in Canned Lobsters"; and the recent work of Obst on "A Bacteriological Study of Sardines" (1916)[3]. Prescott and Underwood working on cans of spoiled clams and lobsters isolated species of bacteria, two classed as micrococci, the other seven as bacilli. The investigators found the cans to be badly decomposed, in some cases almost entirely liquefied, much darkened in colour and of a very disagreeable odour.

Of the bacilli, six coagulated and digested milk, while none of the seven produced gas in sugar solutions. According to the descriptions given, certain of these cultures bear a close resemblance to some recorded by me among the organisms in class II on pages 211-213. Both strains of micrococci isolated by these workers failed to coagulate milk, and failed to produce gas in sugar solution. The bacteria were not named.

Macphail and Bruére[2] in their work on lobsters isolated and recorded the features of four strains of bacteria; two were cocci, and two were fine rods. Each of the four were inoculated into sterile cans of lobster, and in due course the rules of proof were satisfied. Some of the organisms I have isolated —Class I—bear a resemblance to certain of the strains described by Macphail and Bruére, but it is impossible to express a definite opinion as to their mutual identity.

Obst[3] in the report of her investigations on "A Bacteriological Study of Sardines" states that a bacillus, designated "Bacillus A", has been found in pure culture in two hundred and eighty-seven swelled sardine cans. The organism is a spore-former* hundred and eighty-seven swelled sardine cans. The organism is a spore-former* and according to Obst is possibly identical with *B. Walfischrauschbrand* (Ivar Nielsen).[4] The only reference I can find to the bacillus of Nielsen[4] fails to give full cultural details. In the fall of last year I was in communication with Mrs. Obst, but at that time her report was not available; as I have received no copy I consider it probable that it is not yet published. From the reference cited[3] which extracts a recent paper read before the Society of American Bacteriologists I am unable to compare any of my strains with the "Bacillus A". The reference does mention the thermal death point in laboratory media, but states that the organism after inoculation into cans of sardines survives bathing in boiling water for $1\frac{1}{2}$ hours. With the strains described in my report no experiments under commercial conditions have yet been conducted. For the present I am not justified in going further than to state that based on such information as is available, it is improbable that the strains isolated by me are identical with the "Bacillus A" of Obst.

The relationship of bacteria to sardines was discussed by Auche[5] (1894), but the paper is not available.

---

* In the strains I have isolated Class I, no evidence of spores has been demonstrated.

8 GEORGE V, A. 1918

The association of mussels with food poisoning is cited by Vaughan, 1892 [6] ; citing from Vaughan's paper :—

> " That chemical poisons may be transmitted from the lower animals to man in the food is shown by the history of poisoning with mussels and with fish. As early as 1827 Combe described in detail the symptoms induced by the eating of poisonous mussels, and a valuable contribution to the same subject has recently been made by Schmitdmann, who has found that non-poisonous mussels placed in the water of Wilhelmshaven soon became poisonous, and that the poisonous mussels from the harbour soon lose their harmful properties when placed in the open sea. Linder has found in the water of this bay and in the mussels living in it a great variety of protozoa, amoeba, bacteria, and other low forms of life, which are not found in the water of the open sea, nor in the non-poisonous mussel. He has also found that if the water of the bay be filtered, non-poisonous mussels placed in it do not become poisonous. He therefore concludes that poisonous mussels are those which are suffering from disease due to residence in filthy water."

In view of the close relationship to mussels of clams, a variety of shell-fish canned in both New Brunswick and Maine, U.S.A., the observations of Linder cited by Vaughan are of considerable interest. In the same paper Vaughan describes the case of one of his own patients who showed poisoning symptoms after eating freely of canned salmon. The patient under treatment recovered. Vaughan submitted the remains of the salmon to various tests and found an organism which he describes as follows :—

> " The only germ which could be found, either by direct microscopic examination or by the preparation of plate cultures, was a micrococcus, and this was present in the salmon in great numbers. This germ grew fairly well in beef-tea, but the injection of five cubic centimeters of the beef-tea culture of different ages failed to affect white rats, kittens or rabbits. However, this micrococcus when grown for 20 days in a sterilized egg, after Hueppe's method of anaerobic culture, produces a most potent proteid poison. The white of the egg becomes thin, watery, markedly alkaline, and 10 drops of this suffices to kill white rats.
>
> "Evidently in the preparation of the salmon this can was not sterilized; it was sealed, and for months, possibly longer, this germ had been growing anaerobically, and elaborating a chemical poison."

Savage, in England who has investigated many outbreaks of food poisoning, has isolated *B. enteritides* from tinned salmon. Griffiths, cited by Vaughan and Novy [8], claims to have isolated a ptomaine *saordinin* from sardines.

In view of the types of bacteria I have isolated in the present investigation, it is of importance to note that Poels [8] in Rotterdam has isolated varieties of *B. coli* from cases of food poisoning due to the eating of meat from a supposedly healthy animal. McWeeney [9] considers that meat poisoning outbreaks are due to organisms of the following groups :—

(a) The *Typho coli* group, including *B enteritides* (Gaertner).

(b) The group of putrefactive aerobes (*Proteus,* etc.).

(c) The obligate anaerobes *(B. botulinis).*

It will be seen, pages 192, 209, that of the organisms I have isolated, some strains are varieties of the *Proteus* group, and some varieties of the *B. coli* group. Vaughan and Novy [8] describe the most common form of food poisoning that caused by contamination of foods with saprophytic bacteria; such bacteria either before or after the food has been eaten, elaborating chemical poisons.

PRESENT INVESTIGATION.

The investigation herein described of the "Bacteriology of Swelled Canned Sardines" has been undertaken on behalf of the Biological Board of Canada. The work was commenced in the summer of 1916 at the Marine Biological Station, St. Andrews, N.B., and has since been continued in the laboratories at the college. To the canners the appearance of "swells," as they are termed, in the cases of canned fish sent out from the factories is a matter of considerable concern. The desirability of undertaking experimental work in the hope of eliminating any risk of cans developing the swelled condition, occurred to the principal of Macdonald College, Dr. F. C. Harrison, in the summer of 1915. At that time Dr. Harrison was engaged at the marine station, St. Andrews, in the examination of haddock attacked by a bacterial disease, and it was while conducting this investigation that the problem discussed herein came under his notice.

The matter was brought to the attention of Dr. A. B. Macallum, secretary of the Board, and in due course it was my good fortune, on the recommendation of Dr. Harrison, to be asked to take up the work. The procedure to be adopted was left entirely in my own hands. Dr. Macallum, and Dr. A. G. Huntsman, curator of the marine station at St. Andrews, have throughout given me every encouragement, and the greatest possible help in every way which seemed likely to assist in the elucidation of the problem.

On arriving at the station in July, the necessary arrangements were made by Dr. Huntsman enabling me to visit a number of the New Brunswick canning factories. Later it was made possible for us to visit several of the largest plants operating in the State of Maine. I was thus brought into close touch with the industry of canning as a commercial undertaking, had exceptional opportunities of seeing the methods of packing as generally adopted, and accumulated a store of information as a result of discussions with the canners-themselves. Factories were visited which were engaged in the canning of herring, sardines, haddock, and clams, respectively. It is hardly necessary to say that the sardines of New Brunswick and the State of Maine are small herrings. It was apparent that the canning factories were principally concerned in the packing of sardines; and while both during the summer and since returning to the college, swelled cans of sardines, herring, haddock, lobster, and shrimps have been gradually accumulating, the work has up to the present been confined entirely to sardines and possible influences affecting the same. After nine months' work, I find that I have been able to do little more than touch the fringe of the problem, considered as a whole. The report here presented therefore is principally concerned in recording the work accomplished up to the present, such conclusions as it is legitimate to draw at this early stage, and such information as to methods and media used in the laboratory as will make the work of some service to the continuance of the investigation.

Under the circumstances I do not propose to enter into a detailed description of the equipment, methods of treatment and system of packing of the fish, and general procedure of the factories engaged in the canned fish industry; such will be more appropriate when the work has progressed to a more advanced stage. The one phase of the canning process of which brief mention must be made at this point is the temperature employed in the so-called sterilization of the cans when packed and finished. As the most common size of can produced from all the factories is one weighing from 3 to 4 ounces, the temperatures given shall be those applied to cans of this size.

In the majority of the factories visited, the cans are immersed in baths of boiling water for a period of 1½-2 hours. That completes the heating process. Briefly the essentials of the treatment of the fish—which have been salted in the boats as taken from the weirs,—on arrival at the factory is as follows: immersed in a mixture of sea-water and salt for 1 to 1½ hours; spread on racks, termed flakes, in thin layers, and for 10 minutes placed in flowing steam; dried in room through which hot air is continually circulated, for 1 hour; heads discarded and the remainder of the fish arranged in the cans; oil automatically added, and tops put on, and fastened by either the "rolling" or the "pressing" process. The cans are then heated as specified above. In some factories the preliminary steaming for 10 minutes is dispensed with, and a continuous progression through a bath of cottonseed oil at a temperature of 200° C. is substituted, this occupying 2 to 3 minutes.

In one factory where the fish are fried in oil for 3 minutes or so, the final heating is done under pressure at a temperature of 225° F. for a shorter period.

It should be added that in all the sardine factories visited, the most careful supervision is exercised in the final packing of the cans in cases before shipping. Each individual can is rapidly passed through the hands of an expert "tapper" who discards cans displaying any irregularity, such being reprocessed or entirely discarded.

The project of the investigation may be logically stated thus: "Essentially to determine whether or not the swelling of the cans is due to the activities of bacteria." If on examination, and when submitted to suitable cultural methods strains of bacteria are isolated, the procedure to be as follows:—

1. Purify and obtain in pure culture.

2. Determine the morphological, biological and biochemical characteristics of the organisms.

3. Inoculate the strains obtained in pure culture into normal cans and record condition at stated intervals.

4. Treat "control" normal cans in a similar manner except for the inoculation with the culture.

5. If swelling occurs in the inoculated cans, and no change is noted in the " control " cans, the presumption is raised that the swelling is due to the organisms used for inoculation.

6. Examine the "swelled" cans and determine in culture the presence or absence of bacteria.

7. If bacteria are found, purify and compare culturally with the strains used for inoculation.

8. If on comparison the strains be found culturally identical with those used for inoculation the cause of the "swelling" has been established; and experimental proof has been obtained to warrant the statement " that the swelling of the cans is due to the activities of bacteria."

The data recorded in this report show that up to this point, the work has been successfully accomplished in so far as concerns certain strains of bacteria; and the " Postulates of Koch " have been satisfied.

While at the biological station, I not only visited the factories as already stated, but many swelled cans of sardines were secured, and a number of organisms in the cans isolated in culture. An attempt was also made to discover the source of the organisms. Samples of sea water taken from the weirs, samples of oil and tomato sauce as used in the packing, intestines of fresh herrings, and the excreta of herrings were obtained. No organisms were found in the oil; the tomato sauce in sealed receptacles as imported from Italy has still to be examined; but from the sea water, herring intestines, and herring excreta several strains of bacteria were isolated. These, with those I found in the sardine cans, I brought back on my return to the laboratory here. During the succeeding months a number of the cultures have died out, and those remaining from sea water, herring intestines, or excreta, fail to produce gas in carbohydrates.

SESSIONAL PAPER No. 38a

For the sake of convenience I have divided the strains of bacteria isolated at St. Andrews and at various times during the fall and winter into two main classes:—

Class I.—Gas-producers.

Class II.—Non-gas-producers.

For obvious reasons my attention has been principally confined to the gas producers, Class I, and it is to the descriptions of these that the cultural part of the report is chiefly directed.

Regarding the influence of those organisms included in Class II on the condition of the fish in swelled cans, I am not in a position to express any opinion. Many of them have, however, been submitted to certain preliminary tests, the results of which are recorded, pages 211-213. Beyond this I have not gone, and no comments respecting the class are made.

Concerning the gas-producers, Class I, 8 strains have been described morphologically, biologically and biochemically. The detailed descriptions are found on pages 192-207. On pages 208 and 209 a summary arranged in tabular form is shown.

The number of cultures described in Class I, and those more briefly referred to in Class II, bear no relationship to the total number of cultures isolated in the course of the work. As was to be expected, preliminary tests of a differential nature revealed the fact that many strains were in duplicate, and sometimes even in triplicate. By repeated series of tests the duplicates or triplicates were gradually eliminated. In the pages devoted to the cultures in Class II, pages 211-213, a note is added as to the comparative frequency of the respective strains. In eliminating strains from the cultures in Class I, greater precautions were taken on account of their closer relationship to the abnormal condition of the cans. Some of the final cultures described represent the individual strains, after the elimination of as many as four or five strains which had been found to have the main characteristics in common. Three cultures of Class I were finally eliminated to avoid duplication in description, just prior to the preparation of the manuscripts, these being identical with cultures, 34, 37, and 64, respectively.

To continue the statement as to the project of the investigation, initiated on page 184, it is further required, that in order to confirm the work up to the present and complete the investigation it is desirable:—

9. That many more cans shall be examined and the contents cultured.

10. That if possible the source of the responsible organisms be determined, and also the stage at which infection takes place.

11. That experiments be conducted both under laboratory conditions, and under conditions prevailing in the canning factories, with a view to determining the most satisfactory means of eliminating "swelling."

12. That possibly the pathogenicity or degree of pathogenicity of the strains proved responsible for the "swelling" be determined by inoculation into suitable laboratory animals.

Arrangements have been made by Dr. Huntsman whereby during a later season I shall have opportunities of determining if possible the source or sources of the causal organisms of the swelled condition of cans of sardines.

The future scope of the laboratory work will necessarily include examination of swelled cans of other varieties of fish, including those of which mention is made on page 183.

When visiting the canning factories last summer the manager of one of the largest of these told me that a pressing problem with which he had to contend was the frequent appearance among sardine cans of what are termed "sour flats." The condition is one of which there appears at present to be no satisfactory explanation. The product is rendered unmarketable, and the condition is one which cannot be detected until the cans are opened.

8 GEORGE V, A. 1918

MEDIA EMPLOYED.

In this investigation I have used media prepared from fish concoctions, the ordinary laboratory media, and certain special media. In the early part of the work when experimenting with methods prior to the adoption of a definite procedure, difficulty was experienced in growing some of the strains isolated. The colonies developing on some of the plates at this time were too small to be subcultured. I therefore utilized the marine resources at hand and prepared media from fresh herrings, from clams, and from seaweed, using fresh sea water instead of tap or distilled water. It was found later that the organisms which necessitated this media were those I have put in the main Class II, the non-gas-producers. After successive subculturing in the laboratory these same strains have grown moderately well on the usual standard media.

The organisms of my main Class I, the gas-producing strains, have grown well in the standard media. The growth of some strains has been more luxuriant on herring media or clam media, but the use of such has gradually been eliminated for two reasons:—

(1) the satisfactory growth obtained on standard media, and the convenience of its use;

(2) the necessity of using the standard media in order to compare the strains isolated with varieties already described in literature.

Herring Broth.—Fresh herrings obtained direct from the weirs were washed in running water and ground up, no portions discarded, through a meat grinder, mixed with sea water, 1 part ground herring to 1–2 parts sea-water, and heated for several hours in the steamer or autoclav. The mixture was allowed to cool and the fat skimmed off; again heated, and strained through cheese cloth. The strained liquid served as the standard herring extract. Varying strengths of broth were made up, good results being obtained with the following mixture:—

500 cc standard broth,

1,000 cc. sea water,

15 grams peptone.

The ingredients were heated together in the steamer, neutralized with n/20 NaOH to + 10 (phenol phthalein indicator), cleared with white of egg, tubed and sterilized in the usual way.

Herring Agar.—To 500 cc. of the standard broth, mentioned above, were added 500 cc. or 1,000 cc. sea-water, peptone at the rate of 1 per cent and agar at the rate of 1·2 per cent; the whole heated together until ingredients dissolved, neutralized to +10, cleared with white of egg, filtered, tubed and sterilized in the usual way.

Clam Agar.—Fresh clams were dug up on the bench, washed in running water, opened and ground through meat grinder; to this was added sea water at the rate of 1 part clams to 2 parts sea water, and the whole heated for several hours in steamer or autoclav. The stewed mixture was strained through cheese cloth; this filtrate constituting the standard broth. To 500 cc. of the standard broth were added 1,000 cc. sea water, peptone at the rate of 1 per cent, and agar at the rate of 1·2 per cent; the whole heated together until ingredients dissolved, neutralized to +10, cleared with white of egg, filtered, tubed and sterilized in the usual way.

I have also steamed clams in the shell in sea water, approximately weight for weight; retaining the juice which has a typical "sheen"; then after opening the clams using them as described above.

In the earlier part of the work the medium was used successfully to some considerable extent; and in comparison with standard beef peptone agar it appeared to exercise a selective action towards certain strains of bacteria obtained from various sources. This in all probability would be due to the glycogen content. While the use of this medium has for some time been discontinued, I propose to test its value for certain phases of the laboratory analyses.

Baur[10] in working at Kiel on the denitrifying bacteria used and recommends a broth of which mussels are the essential component.

Beef Peptone Agar.—Standard methods.[11]

Beef Peptone Gelatine.—Standard methods.[11]

Glucose Agar.—One per cent glucose added to agar prepared as above, immediately before tubing.

Löeffler's Blood Serum.[12]

Löeffler's Typhoid Solution [13].—This medium containing malachite green has been recommended by Löeffler for use in culturing strains of the *colon-paratyphoid-typhoid* group.

Aesculin Agar[14].—For specific reaction of organisms of the *colon-aerogenes* group; loops of a broth culture spread on plates.

MacConkey's Neutral Red Bile Salt Lactose Broth [15].—For reduction test of organisms of the *colon-aerogenes* group.

Bouillon for Voges-Proskauer Reaction.[16]

Bouillon for Methyl Red Reaction.[17]

Solution for Reduction of Nitrates to Nitrites [18].—Giltay's synthetic solution was used.

Dunham Solution for Indol Production.[19]

Glucose Broth.—One per cent glucose in Dunham solution.

Fermentation Broths.—For the fermentation reactions I have used ten test substances. It will be seen that in addition to the glucose *salicin* I have adopted the use of another glucoside *aesculin*—used in conjunction with iron citrate by Harrison and Vanderleck—as a fermentable test substance in Dunham broth. I have been using aesculin for this purpose during the last four months in connection with work on the gas producing organisms in the Ottawa river water, and find a correlation in the black reaction of the aesculin agar medium, and the production of acid and gas in aesculin used as a carbohydrate test substance.

Litmus Milk.[20]

METHODS.

On account of the comparative paucity in the literature, of descriptions of actual methods adopted in the isolation of bacteria from swelled canned fish, the procedure I have followed has largely been determined by experience as the work has progressed. This procedure has been changed as better methods suggested themselves, and in the culturing from the many cans still awaiting examination I propose further changes affecting detail, while the use of additional media which will be to the advantage of the work has suggested itself.

Isolation of Bacteria from the Cans.

The oily greasy surface characteristic of the cans with pronounced swelling necessitated the use of a disinfecting agent which would disinfect, and remove the oil, at the

8 GEORGE V, A. 1918

same time. Absolute alcohol has proved to be simple in application and quite satisfactory. The cans were first cleaned with a weaker alcohol (70 per cent to 90 per cent)
then thoroughly treated with the absolute alcohol. Can openers, forceps, and dissect-
ing scissors were immersed in alcohol and flamed immediately before use. When a
sufficiently large aperture had been made in the can, pieces of fish and a portion of
the oil or sauce were removed with forceps and pipettes and inoculated into tubes of
liquid medium.

At the commencement, it was at once obvious that direct plating from the cans
would not be at all satisfactory on account of the oily nature of the contents; liquid
media have therefore been used for the first inoculation from the cans, the procedure
having the additional advantage in that such media serve as enrichment fluids. I
first used peptone broth (Dunham), herring broth, and nutrient broth; later, the
addition to the series of glucose peptone broth proved to have advantages. As a result
of the additional knowledge provided by a study of the strains of organisms already
worked out, it will be desirable in further work to use media having differential qualities for the first inoculations; in addition to the broths already in use.

The tubes were incubated at 37° C. except during the six weeks spent at St.
Andrews, when all cultures were kept at room temperature. The broths were examined
in 18-24 hours for growth; if no growth were apparent, further incubation was
resorted to; if growth could be noted, series of plates were made. The preliminary
incubation in broth tubes had the additional advantage to those already mentioned, in
that the oil had risen to the surface leaving the sub-surface liquid comparatively free.
Finely drawn out pipettes with the finger over the end were passed through the layer
of oil, and the culture fluid drawn up. After suitable dilutions had been made, plates
were poured using herring agar, clam agar, beef peptone agar, and glucose agar; in
the more recent work glucose agar being used almost solely. The plates were incubated—temperatures as aforementioned—and when growth was sufficient, those
colonies most common were streaked on agar slopes; from these the necessary purifi-
cation by plates being made.

NOTE.—The preliminary incubation in broth tubes was in some cases, but not
always, duplicated aerobically and anaerobically.

The following apply to the main Class I:—

Microscopic examinations.—The microscopic preparations were uniformly made from
beef peptone agar slopes incubated 18 to 24 hours at 37° C.

*Gram's Stain.—The gas-producing organisms, Class I pages 192-207, display an unusual degree of resistance to decolorisation with alcohol in the Gram method of
staining. When treated by the usual method,—decolorisation with alcohol until no further colour can be washed out,—each of the eight strains recorded
would be classified as Gram positive. The shade of violet is not as deep as
that which is typical of the classic Gram positive reaction, but the result is
much nearer positive than negative. On prolonged soaking in absolute alcohol,
30 to 40 minutes, the reaction is definitely Gram negative. Films made from
a typical Gram positive lactic acid producing organism withstood the decolorisation with alcohol for 40 minutes

The organisms herein discussed should therefore be described as Gram negative, displaying an unusual degree of resistance to the decolorisation with
alcohol.

Motility.—Hanging drops for these tests were made from the water of condensation,
agar slopes; young cultures incubated at 37° C., never longer than twenty-four
hours.

Inoculation of Media.—All tubes of media used for the determination of cultural features and biochemical reactions were inoculated from young peptone broth
cultures of the particular organism. The use of peptone salt solution instead

of nutrient broth eliminated to a minimum any risk due to the presence of muscle sugar. It may be mentioned that repeated tests for the presence of muscle sugar in the peptone used gave a negative reaction based on the absence of acid and gas; the tubes being inoculated from an active strain of the *B coli* group.

Prior to the inoculations of the series, peptone broth tubes were inoculated from agar slopes, and incubated at 37° C. After 18 to 24 hours, usually about 20 hours, the whole series of media would be inoculated with the broth from a 1 cc. pipette; 2 to 3 drops of culture to each tube. Slopes of solid media were streaked with a standard 3 mm. loop platinum needle. The number of tubes involved and the amount of test substances necessitated have been considerable throughout the work, and to insure economy of expense and time, strictly quantitative estimations of the gas evolved have not been carried out other than by means of the Dunham tube. In view of the method noted above, however, the results are truly comparative throughout. Moreover, for the particular purpose of the present work the essential point to be decided regarding the fermentation of the test substances to gas is this—does a particular culture produce gas, or does it not produce gas? It is not only of considerable interest, but of much practical and classificatory value to know whether the amount of gas produced in a given time at a given temperature from a given substance is great or small. Such information can be comparatively well shown by the use of the Dunham tube.

Indol Production.—The tubes to be tested for Indol were incubated at 37° C. for 7 days; the Bohme Ehrlich test being used.

Reduction of Nitrates.—The Giltay solution was tested after 3 to 4 days incubation at 37° C., for the presence of nitrites. The sulphanilic acid and a-naphthylamin reagents were used.

Voges Proskauer Reaction.—After 48 to 72 hours incubation at 37° C. the culture tested with a strong solution of KOH. The test if positive has usually shown the typical eosin shade in the upper layers, within 2 hours at room temperature.

Methyl Red Reaction.—Determined after incubation at 37° C. for 48 to 72 hours.

CANS OF SARDINES.

General Description. Appearance of Cans and Conditions of Contents.

Owing to the varieties of "brands" of sardines produced by the canning factories, the various methods of packing adopted, and the different substances utilized for the giving of flavour and consistency to the finished product, it is not possible other than in a general way to described the conditions met with in my examinations.

Normal cans.—In outward appearance there is a complete absence of any "bulging"; the top and bottom are either quite flat or almost imperceptibly concave. On shaking, there is no "rattle" and scarcely any movement of the contents can be heard. When opened with the cutter, there is no expulsion of air or gas, with little if any exuding of the oil or other material used in the process of packing.

The contents are firm, not macerated, and often white in colour; this last, however, depending to some extent upon the materials used in the packing. The smell is mildly characteristic of the fish, qualified by the variety of oil or tomato sauce used. There is in appearance and odour a complete absence of putrefaction. The fish are saturated to a greater or lesser extent with the oil, sauce, or other flavouring agents used, but without losing their firm and solid condition. The oil or sauce will be seen as a layer over and in the interspaces between the individual fish, rather than actually within the bodies.

8 GEORGE V, A. 1918

Swelled Cans.—Outwardly the cans vary from a slight "bulged" appearance to a more pronounced swelling. The top and bottom are forced out as a result of the pressure, and present a decided convex surface. As the swelling becomes greater the oil or sauce will be forced out between the soldered parts of the can, and in pronounced cases the outside surface is greasy and wet, and possibly covered with the oil or sauce. Swelled cans, when shaken, have a characteristic "rattle" on account of the extra space within, resulting from the swelling. When the cans are opened, gas is expelled, accompanied in advanced swellings by portions of the liquid contents. In advanced cases there is a tendency for the oil or sauce to pour out over the surface of the cans.

The condition of the contents varies considerably. Usually the fish are macerated, disintegrated, and soft, and are intermixed with the oil or sauce; they have lost their entity. The odour is variable,—frequently it is not unpleasant, resembling to an accentuated degree the natural smell of normal sardines. In other instances a pronounced putrefactive odour is evident. It may be that the putrefactive odour is present at all times and is masked by the spices or other ingredients of the sauce. That is a point which can only be definitely pronounced upon after a more extended investigation.

CANS EXAMINED.

Up to the present I have examined forty cans, normal and swelled. The cans have been obtained personally or by express:

(1) direct from various canning factories in the province of New Brunswick and in the State of Maine, U.S.A.

(2) From the Health Department of a city in the Maritime Provinces.

(3) From retail grocery stores.

Many of the normal cans, representative of the various factories, proved to be sterile; from some have been isolated spore forming bacteria, inactive on **fermentable** carbohydrates,—see page 211. Culture 21 and in no instance have gas producing organisms been found.

From certain of the swelled cans I have isolated a variety of strains of gas producing bacteria, none of which show evidence of spore formation. The cans from which these strains have been isolated are representative of three of the factories engaged in canning; and for the sake of clearness these factories have been specified as *Packer A, Packer B,* and *Packer C,* respectively. Further, from swelled cans I have also isolated strains of bacteria which fail to ferment any of the carbohydrates used as test substances (pages 212-213). It remains, therefore, to be added that from some cans apparently "swelled" I have failed to isolate gas producing bacteria.

As already stated (page 185) the organisms isolated from the various sources have for the sake of convenience been arranged in two main classes:—

Class I.—Gas producers.

Class II.—Non gas-producers.

The gas-producers (see pages 192-207) have been isolated solely from swelled cans of sardines. Of the swelled cans examined the majority were obtained from sources 1 and 3 (page 190). Some were submitted by source 2. Under the circumstances it has seemed desirable to use some means of differentiation. Accordingly the swelled cans obtained: (1) from the canning factories, and (3) from retail grocery stores have been designated "Swelled cans, Series 1"; those submitted by (2) a certain City Health Department, "Swelled Cans Series II."

SESSIONAL PAPER No. 38a

Swelled Cans, Series I.

> *Can. I, Packer B.*—Obtained direct from canning factory; packed with tomato sauce; characteristic "swelled" appearance. The pressure of the gas was so great that on the can being opened part of the contents were strewn over the laboratory bench. The odour was pleasant, though pungent, and may best be described as the natural smell of normal sardines accentuated. It is of interest to note that the plates made, using herring agar, rapidly developed at room temperature a putrid smell resembling, as expressed by a laboratory colleague, that of an "oriental latrine."
>
> See Culture 32, Class I.

> *Can. II, Packer A.*—Obtained from a retail grocery store; packed in cottonseed oil; same brand as those of "Swelled Cans, Series II". This can was passed as saleable and normal by a reputable salesman, and on personal examination of his stock I retained it as suspicious. I have no knowledge as to the date of packing. In appearance the can was slightly swollen, convex, but there was no evidence of oil exuding due to pressure of gas. On opening, a perceptible amount of gas was forced out. The contents were soft and disintegrated; colour slightly darker white than normal; odour an accentuation of the normal.
>
> See Culture 34, Class I.

> *Can III, Packer A.*—Source and brand as Can II of this series. This can submitted to me by the salesman. The appearance of the can, the appearance, condition, and colour of the contents identical with description applied to Can II.
>
> See Culture 35, Class I.

> *Can IV, Packer B.*—Source and brand as Can I of this series. In this can the swelling had not progressed as far as in can I, and on opening the gas was not so profuse. The general description there applied to the contents and to the nature of the subsequent plates is equally applicable in this instance.
>
> See Culture 36, Class I.

> *Can V, Packer B.*—Source and brand as Can I of this series. The extent to which the can had swelled, and the further description used above for Can IV apply here.
>
> See Culture 37, Class I.

> *Can VI, Packer C.*—Obtained direct from canning factory; packed in tomato sauce; characteristic " swelled " appearance top and bottom convex. On opening a small amount of gas escaped. The odour was not unpleasant, and may be described as the natural smell of normal sardines accentuated. The contents of the can were not nearly so much disintegrated as noted in some previously mentioned, were somewhat dry, and a little less hard than the contents of normal cans.
>
> See Culture 64, Class I.

Swelled Cans, Series II, Packer A.

A cargo of sardines exported by packer A had been sunk in a harbour, remaining under water for six weeks. When the cargo was salvaged, a proportion of the cans were visibly swelled. The local Health Department submitted a number of these cans for examination, as a result of which the cargo was condemned. Such cans, of course, do not represent the "swelled cans" of commerce. As, however, their condition and the nature of their contents appeared somewhat similar to the swelled cans obtained from other sources, the characteristics of some of the organisms isolated have been included in this report.

8 GEORGE V, A. 1918

To differentiate from the swelled cans obtained direct from the canning factories and from retailers I have designated the salvaged cans as " Swelled cans, series II." The brand of sardines of which this cargo consisted is one of the least expensive brands on the market; cottonseed oil is used.

Can II.—On shaking, perceptible "rattle" characteristic of the swollen cans. On opening with the cutter escape of gas and pronounced putrefactive odour; contents soft and disintegrated; colour dirty white with tendency to redness in inner portions.

See Culture 24, Class I; Culture 14, Class II.

Can III.—Characteristic "rattle"; escape of gas and pronounced putrefactive odour on opening of can; contents soft and disintegrated, and of a dirty white colour.

See Culture 26, Class I; Culture 16, Class II.

ORGANISMS OF THE GAS-PRODUCING TYPE.

Culture 24.

Source: Can II, Ser. II, Packer A.

Morphology.—Microscopically: coccus forms to short thick rods twice as long as broad; average length $\cdot 8$—1 μ *Gram negative. From old agar cultures no evidence of spores.

Motility.—In hanging drop occurring singly, in twos and in chains; some individuals with rapid movement, some having slow undulating motion.

Cultural Characteristics.—

Agar slope.—36 hrs. 37° C.—growth luxuriant, raised, glistening, iridescent, yellowish-white by transmitted light.

Löeffler's Blood Serum.—24 hrs., 37 C. moderate, yellowish-white, no liquefaction.

Löeffler's Malachite Green Sol.—Green precipitate or weak coagulum at bottom of tube; this very slowly changes and within 14 days partially digested; liquid portion assuming brownish tint.

Gelatine Stab.—Room temperature; liquefaction begins in 24 hrs. crateriform; in three days liquefaction on surface and along track of needle, crateriform to infundibuliform; growth very slimy on this medium; in 7 days yellowish, cloudy stratiform extending 1 cm. from surface, remainder infundibuliform with heavy yellow flocculent sediment to bottom of tube. In 18 days liquefaction not yet complete; upper portion heavy milky even cloudiness, merging into layers of semi-transparent cloudiness, the lower portion a heavy ferric-yellow mass of precipitate.

Nutrient Broth.—24 hrs. 37°C.—heavy clouding with bluish rim; in 3 days flocculent flakes of bluish tint on sides of tube; in 5 days very heavy dense even clouding, watered silk appearance; this condition persists.

Herring Broth.—Condition similar to above; very heavy growth; in 9 days a loop of the liquid showing decided iridescent bluish sheen.

Milk.—In 24 hrs. unchanged, except that much froth on shaking; in 3 days coagulated, soft curd, some whey expressed; in 9 days yellow digested fluid 2/3 of tube, remainder white soft curd; in 14 days ropiness noted, and medium almost entirely digested with slight amount of flocculent curd at bottom of tube; in 5 weeks almost wholly turbid yellowish digested fluid with slight jelly-like yellowish iridescent flocculent curd on base of tube.

Litmus Milk.—In 24 hours much froth on shaking, violaceus for 1 cm. from surface, remainder paler; in 3 days partly coagulated soft curd, violaceus; in 9 days digestion proceeding, fluid yellowish; in 14 days blue rim at surface, medium 5/6 digested, reddish brown tint; in 5 weeks slight flocculence, curd at base of tube, remainder partially cleared and tinted dark purpureus to heliotrope.

Aesculin agar.—I loop from peptone broth culture streaked on plates. In 24 hours growth but no definite black reaction; later assumes brown to black tint, moderate growth.

Aesculin broth.—In 24 hours black reaction.

MacConkey's N.R.B. Broth.—No reduction to canary yellow in 24 hours.

Gelatine colonies.—(1st appearance) room temperature, in 72 hours liquefaction well advanced; individual colonies up to 3 mm. diameter, round, saucer-shaped, entire edges; liquefaction typical of the proteus group, centre of colony dark white spot .25 mm. diameter, remainder of colony varying from clear space to fine precipitated granules. Under the low power objective opaque centre, edges entire; medium tinted green, and distinct earthy smell.

Agar colonies.—20 hours at 37°C., growth moderate, surface colonies round, concave, glistening, raised, distinctly radiate; by transmitted light young colonies bluish, older colonies becoming whiter, more opaque and darker in centre. Sub-surface colonies small but well defined, white. Under low power objective surface colonies distinctly yellowish with entire edges; on focussing through, dense and dark; structure cannot be defined; smaller colonies dark centre, then pale yellow, and near the edges almost transparent. Sub-surface colonies well defined, edges entire, yellow to dense.

Temperature Relations:—

Thermal death point.—10 minutes' exposure in nutrient broth at 60°C.

Optimum temperature.—Cultures incubated at room temperature and at 37°C. grow well. Most satisfactory growth at 37°C.

Vitality on Culture Media.—The culture survives several months in artificial medium, agar or gelatine.

Relation to Oxygen.—The culture is a facultative anaerobe; incubated for 36 hours under anaerobic conditions moderate growth on glucose agar as discrete colonies along track of needle 1-2 mm. diameter; by transmitted light convex, dark white centres, paling to blue at edges. Growth is not so luxuriant as under aerobic conditions.

Biochemical Reactions:—

Indol production: Indol not produced.

Reduction of nitrates: Nitrates to nitrites.

Voges-Proskauer reaction: Positive.

Methyl red reaction: Alkaline.

Fermentation of Carbohydrates.—This culture does not rapidly ferment many of the carbohydrates. In 24 hours lactose is but feebly fermented to acid; saccharose, mannite and xylose are fermented to acid and gas with profuse frothing; arabinose and inulin give slight gas; while gas appears in glycerine

8 GEORGE V, A. 1918

only after a period of 72 hours. The remaining substances used are fermented moderately well in 24 hours to acid and to gas.

Glucose.	Lactose.	Saccharose.	Mannite.	Dulcite.
+ +	+ –	+ +	+ +	+ –

Adonit.	Raffinose.	Arabinose.	Xylose.	Salicin.
– –	+ +	+ +	+ +	+ +

Aesculin.	Glycerine.	Inulin.
+ +	+ +	+ +

+ = acid.
++ = acid and gas.

Culture 26

Source: Can III, Ser. II, Packer A.

Morphology.—Microscopically, rods $1\frac{1}{3}$ to $1\frac{1}{2}$ times as long as broad; average length 1·6 μ with many longer forms even in young cultures. Gram negative*; from old agar cultures no evidence of spores.

Microscopic preparations made from cultures of this organism incubated at the same and at different temperatures have shown much variation in morphology; successive plate culturing, however, has failed to show impurity.

Motility.—In hanging drop occurring singly, and in twos, sometimes side by side; longer forms noted; non-motile.

Cultural Characteristics:—

Agar. Slope.—36 hours, 37° C., moderate, along track of needle, glistening yellowish-white by transmitted light.

Löeffler's Blood Serum.—Growth slight after 72 hours. No liquefaction.

Löeffler's Malachite Green Solution.—24 hours, 37°C., coagulated as soft junket-like curd attached to sides and bottom of tube, green, with pale green liquid expressed. After 14 days no change.

Gelatine Stab.—Room temperature—in 3 days scant growth, filiform, no liquefaction; in 18 days no change apart from increased growth, no liquefaction.

Nutrient Broth.—24 hours, 37°C., moderate clouding, no pellicle, no sediment, no ring; in 3 days watered silk appearance; in 9 days no change except slight sediment at bottom of tube.

Herring Broth.—Similar to above, but much more luxuriant growth.

Milk.—In 24 hours at 37°C., no coagulation, much froth on shaking; in 3 days coagulation beginning; in 5 days firm coagulum, no gas, no digestion; in 16 days curd slightly split by gas. In 5 weeks shrinking of curd, but no digestion.

Litmus Milk.—In 24 hours violaceus, much froth on shaking, no coagulation; in 3 days liliaceous with weak coagulum; in 5 days curd slightly cracked by gas. In 5 weeks no digestion; pale lilac to isabella.

Aesculin agar.—One loop from peptone broth culture streaked on plates; no reaction.

Aesculin broth.—In 24 hours. Slight change but no black reaction; later medium darkened slowly in several days becoming black.

MacConkey's N.R.B. broth.—No reduction to canary yellow in 48 hours.

Gelatine Colonies.—(1st appearance), 72 hours at room temperature. Surface colonies yellowish white by transmitted light, $\frac{1}{2}$–$1\frac{1}{2}$ mm. diameter; a characteristic depression immediately around edge of colony could be seen on tilting the plate; no bluish appearance; no liquefaction. Under the low power objective colonies pale yellow, with paler rim, and entire edges, structure finely granular.

Agar colonies.—20 hours. 37°C. Growth slow, punctiform, scarcely visible to the eye. Examined 3 days; by transmitted light surface colonies greyish white, elliptical and round, the larger colonies 0·5 mm. diameter. Subsurface colonies similar to above; majority of the colonies immediately under the surface. Under the low power objective all colonies appeared dense, compact with edges entire to slightly serrated.

Temperature Relations:—

Thermal death point.—10 minutes exposure in nutrient broth at 60°C.

Optimum temperature.—On agar grows moderately well, room temperature and at 37°C.

Vitality on Culture Media.—The culture survives several months in artificial medium, agar or gelatine.

Relation to Oxygen.—Incubated for 36 hours under anaerobic conditions, scant growth on glucose agar, small gas bubbles in medium, clouding of condensation water. While growth is noted, the organism prefers aerobic conditions.

Biochemical reactions:—

Indol production: Indol not produced.
Reduction of nitrates: ?
Voges-Proskauer reaction: Negative.
Methyl red reaction: Slightly acid.

Fermentation of Carbohydrates.—The carbohydrates used are but feebly acted upon by this culture. In each case, however—with exception of inulin—those substances which are fermented to gas have shown the positive reaction within 24 hours at 37°C., and no further gas production has taken place even after 5 days. The Andrade indicator has changed to a clear scarlet and no reduction has taken place after prolonged incubation. The two substances most easily acted upon are glucose and saccharose.

Glucose.	Lactose.	Saccharose.	Mannite.	Dulcite.
+ +	+ +	+ +	+ +	+ −
Adonit.	Raffinose.	Arabinose.	Xylose.	Salicin.
− −	+ +	+ +	+ +	+ +
Aesculin.	Glycerine.	Inulin.		
+ +	+ −	+±		

+ = acid.
++ = acid and gas.

Culture 32.

Source:—Can. I. Ser. I. Packer B.

Morphology:—Microscopically short thick rods twice as long as broad; average length 1-6 μ staining unevenly with Kühne's methylene blue; some longer and thinner forms, but repeated replating has failed to show impurity. Gram negative*; from old agar cultures no evidence of spores.

Motility.—In hanging drop occurring singly and in twos, actively motile, progression as in semi-circles.

Cultural Characteristics:—

Agar Slope.—36 hours 37° C., luxuriant, raised, thick, along track of needle, glistening, iridescent, yellowish white transmitted light, medium slight tendency to brown.

Herring agar.—20 hours 32° C., growth abundant and heavy along track of needle, contoured, yellowish-white; spreading over slope as bluish film of discrete colonies, transmitted light, glistening, iridescent; heavy clouding condensation water.

Löeffler's Blood Serum.—24 hours 37° C., moderate, moist, spreading; no liquefaction after 7 days.

Löeffler's Malachite Green Sol.—Coagulated as soft junket like curd attached to sides and bottom of tube, green, gas bubbles, light green clear fluid expressed; after 14 days coagulum as precipitation on sides of tube, no reduction of colour.

Gelatine Stab.—Room temperature—24 hours filiform, no liquefaction; in 4 days growth abundant; in 1 week no liquefaction and no change in medium, growth equally good in stab and on surface; no liquefaction in 21 days.

Nutrient broth.—24 hours 37° C., moderate, clouding, slight pellicle easily dislodged, pale bluish rim at top, very slight tendency to flocculency; in 48 hours flocculent precipitate suspended and at bottom; in 7 days discrete particles adhering to tube at surface, even clouding, clotted sediment on shaking.

Herring broth.—Similar to above, but much heavier.

Milk.—18 hours, 37° C., much froth on shaking, no coagulation; in 72 hours coagulation beginning, frothy; in 4 days weak coagulum with whey expressed, gas bubbles, curd splitting, whey white cloudy; in 10 days condition accentuated, no liquefaction.

Litmus milk.—In 18 hours frothy, no coagulation, violaceus, merging into light violaceous near bottom of tube; in 48 hours liliaceous, frothy, no coagulation; in 72 hours still frothy, coagulation beginning; in 4 days coagulated, some whey expressed, curd split by gas holes; in 14 days bleached with red rim at top.

Aesculin agar.—1 loop from peptone broth culture streaked on plates. In 24 hours 37° C. growth brown-black reaction.

Aesculin broth.—In 24 hours, black reaction.

MacConkey's N.R.B. broth.—No reduction to canary yellow in 48 hours.

Gelatine colonies.—Room temperature (1st appearance). In 72 hours growth luxuriant and rapid; surface colonies up to ½—1 mm. diameter, white and glistening; depression around edge of colony, as if gelatine under tension—See Culture 26. Smaller colonies bluish to white, round; subsurface colonies small, bluish to bluish white. Under low power objective surface colonies dense, pale-yellow, with paler rim and entire edges, structure finely granular; subsurface colonies similar with homogenous structure, round, edges clearly defined and entire.

Agar colonies.—20 hours 37° C., growth rapid, abundant, surface colonies 1½—2 mm. diameter, concave, smooth, glistening, tendency to striate; by transmitted light ferric to yellowish-white centre, paling to blue tint at edges, smaller colonies bluish white; subsurface colonies up to ·5 mm. diameter, yellowish-white. Under low power objective surface colonies finely granular structure, ferric-yellow paling at edges, edges entire; subsurface colonies dark "mound" appearance in centre, remainder pale lemon, finely granular with tendency to grumose, edges entire.

Herring agar colonies.—Two to three times diameter of above, umbonate, radiate, concentrically ringed.

Temperature Regulations:—

Thermal death point.—Some variation has been exhibited and further tests require to be made; tests performed up to the present indicate the T.D.P. to be around 60° C., exposed for 10 minutes in nutrient broth.

Optimum temperature.—Cultures incubated at room temperature and at 37° C. grow well; most satisfactory growth at 37° C.

Vitality on culture media.—The culture survives several months on artificial medium, agar or gelatine.

Relation to Oxygen:—

The culture is a facultative anaerobe; incubated for 36 hours at 37° C. under anaerobic conditions moderate growth on slope of glucose agar; medium cracked and split by gas bubbles, much froth in tube and heavy clouding of condensation water. The organism appears to grow equally well in the presence or in the absence of oxygen.

Biochemical Reactions:—

Indol production: Indol not produced.
Reduction of nitrates: Nitrates reduced to nitrites.
Voges Proskauer reaction: Negative.
Methyl red reaction: Alkaline.

Fermentation of Carbohydrates.—The action of this culture on lactose is feeble and slow, gas not appearing until the second day; dulcite is but slightly fermented to acid and no gas is produced. Aesculin is fermented to acid and gas in 24 hours and in 9 days the Andrade indicator reduced to a lemon yellow turbid iridescent colour, while no reduction is noted in the case of salicin. All the other test substances are fermented to acid and to gas rapidly with profuse frothing and heavy turbidity within 24 hours.

Glucose.	Lactose.	Saccharose.	Mannite.	Dulcite.
+ +	+ +	+ +	+ +	+ −
Adonit.	Raffinose.	Arabinose.	Xylose.	Salicin.
− −	+ +	+ +	+ +	+ +
Aesculin.	Glycerin.	Inulin.		
+ +	+ +	+ +		

+ = acid.
++ = acid and gas.
Culture 34.

Source: Can. II., Ser. I., Packer A.

Morphology.—Microscopically varying from coccus forms to short rods; the majority 8–1 μ long and twice as long as broad, many thinner; stains unevenly with Kühne's methylene blue; Gram negative*; from old agar cultures no evidence of spores.

Motility.—In hanging drop occurring singly and in twos; actively motile.

Cultural Characteristics:—

Agar slope.—36 hours at 37° C., moderate along track of needle, glistening iridescent, bluish by transmitted light, gas bubbles in medium presumably due to fermentation of the muscle sugar in beef extract. In agar culture 2 months old distinct sliminess has been noted.

8 GEORGE V, A. 1918

Herring agar.—20 hours 32 C., growth abundant, contoured, yellowish white growth along track of needle, spreading over slope as bluish film of discrete colonies; glistening, iridescent; heavy clouding of condensation water.

Löeffler's Blood Serum.—24 hours 37° C Moderate, ferric yellow growth, no liquefaction after 7 days.

Löeffler's Malachite Green Sol.—In 24 hours 37° C. coagulated as described in culture 32; in 14 days medium assuming a greenish brown tint, no definite reduction and no liquefaction.

Gelatine stab.—Room temperature—24 hours filiform, no liquefaction, equally good on surface and in stab; in 4 days growth abundant; in 7 days no liquefaction and no change in medium; no liquefaction in 21 days.

Nutrient broth.—18 hours 37° C., clouding moderate, slight pellicle; on shaking small flakes perceptible in medium; bluish rim; slight viscid sediment; in 72 hours cloudy waves, as watered silk, some flocculent precipitation in suspension.

Herring broth.—Similar to above, but heavier.

Milk.—18 hours 37° C., much froth on shaking, no coagulation; in 48 hours, weak coagulum beginning; in 72 hours coagulated with gas and expulsion of whey, curd later splitting with gas holes.

Litmus milk.—18 hours 37° C., much froth on shaking, liliaceous, no coagulation; in 48 hours weak coagulation beginning; in 72 hours coagulated, gas, whey expressed, later bleaching to isabella and much splitting of curd by gas.

NOTE.—Milks and litmus milks incubated for 2 months have appeared to be slowly digesting; up to the present I have been unable to verify this and further tests must be made to establish the final condition of the clot.

Aesculin agar.—1 loop from peptone broth culture streaked on plate. In 24 hours at 37° C., reaction brown-black.

Aesculin broth—In 24 hours black reaction.

MacConkey's N. R. B. Broth.—In 48 hours, 37° C., slight reduction to eosin tint, but no final reduction to canary yellow.

Gelatine colonies.—Room temperature (1st appearance) surface colonies up to ½ mm. diam.; by transmitted light bluish-white, glistening, almost transparent, resembling more the description of the *B. typhosus* colonies than the typical *B. Coli* colony; flat; subsurface colonies smaller, white to yellow-white, depression around edges, see Culture 32. Under the low power objective surface colonies pale yellow, paling near rim with hedges entire; structure finely granular with clearly defined border around more dense central structure; subsurface colonies similar.

Agar colonies.—20 hours 37°C., growth moderate, not so rapid as other cultures; surface colonies 1–1½ mm. diameter, round, concave, glistening; by transmitted light bluish with pin-point dark white centre, distinctly radiate. Subsurface colonies dirty white; organism growing better just under surface. Under low power objective surface colonies dark centre, remainder of colony faintly discernible as finely granular lemon yellow, with edges entire; subsurface dark, compact, too dense for structure to be differentiated, edges entire.

Temperature Relations:—

Thermal death point.—10 minutes exposure in nutrient broth at 60°C.

Optimum temperature.—Cultures incubated at room temperature and at 37°C. grow well; most satisfactory growth at 37°C.

Vitality on Culture medium.—The culture survives several months on artificial medium, agar or gelatine.

Relation to Oxygen.—The culture is a facultative anaerobe; incubated for 36 hours at 37°C. under anaerobic conditions growth scant on slope as fine discrete colonies; heavy growth and clouding in condensation water. Slope broken and cracked by gas bubbles, these ½ cm. diameter and extending throughout the medium; much froth.

Biochemical Reactions:—

Indol production: Indol not produced.
Reduction of Nitrates: Nitrates reduced to nitrites.
Voges-Proskauer reactions: Negative.
Methyl red reaction: Alkaline.

Fermentation of Carbohydrates.—The culture has a characteristic action upon dulcite; this test substance being fermented profusely to gas in 48 hours; acid and some gas produced within 24 hours. In aesculin, gas appears within 48 hours. Inulin is fermented to gas only after 7 – 10 days incubation. The remaining test substances are fermented moderately well to acid and gas within 24 hours; but in no case on further incubation is the reaction profuse as in the fermentation of dulcite.

Glucose.	Lactose.	Saccharose.	Mannite.	Dulcite.
+ +	+ +	+ +	+ +	+ +

Adonit.	Raffinose.	Arabinose.	Xylose.	Salicin.
– –	+ +	+ +	+ +	+ +

Aesculin.	Glycerine.	Inulin.
+ +	+ –	+ +

+ = acid.
++ = acid and gas.

Culture 35.

Source: Can. III, Ser. I, Packer A.

Morphology: Microscopically large coccus forms to short thick rods; .8 μ diam. to 1 μ long; stain evenly with Kühne's methylene blue; Gram negative*; from old agar cultures no evidence of spores.

Mobility: In hanging drop appearing singly and in twos; no motility.

Cultural characteristics:—

Agar Slope.—36 hours 37° C., moderate to abundant along track of needle, glistening, iridescent, porcelain white by transmitted light.

Herring Agar Slope.—20 hours 32° C., growth abundant, yellowish white along track of needle raised edges, glistening iridescent, by transmitted light the thinner parts bluish discrete colonies.

Löeffler's Blood Serum.—24 hours 37° C., luxuriant, moist; no liquefaction after 7 days.

Löeffler's Malachite Green Solution:—24 hours 37°C. Coagulated junket like coagulum clinging to sides of tube, gas; in 72 hours reduced greenish yellow; in 14 days reduced to yellowish-brown slimy looking liquid, partially digested.

Gelatine Stab.—Room temperature, in 24 hours filiform growth equally good surface and stab, no liquefaction, slight gas—presumably from muscle sugar—growth luxuriant. No liquefaction in 21 days.

Nutrient Broth.—18 hours 37° C., clouding even, no pellicle, no sediment, bluish rim at surface; in 48 hours heavy clouding, viscid sediment at bottom on shaking; in 72 hours flocculent suspension, later sediment increasing, medium becoming clearer, and flocculency.

8 GEORGE V, A. 1918

Herring Broth.—Moderate clouding, bluish rim at surface, pellicle, viscid precipitate on shaking; in 4 days very heavy brown-black sediment, later flocculency and heavy clouding.

Milk.—In 18 hours at 37° C., frothy but no coagulation; in 72 hours coagulation commencing, gas; in 4 days gas holes in curd, frothy; in 10 days clear whey on surface of soft gassy curd. In 2 months no digestion.

Litmus Milk.—In 18 hours 37° lilaceus, much froth and gas, no coagulation; in 72 hours coagulation beginning; in 10 days tinted whey on surface of soft curd pinkish to isabella; no digestion in 2 months.

Aesculin agar.—37° C. One loop from peptone broth culture streaked on plates; in 24 hours reaction brown to black.

Aesculin broth.—37°C. Black reaction in 24 hours.

MacConkey's N.R.B. Broth.—37°. In 48 hours no reduction to canary yellow.

Gelatine Colonies.—(Room temperature) (1st appearance). Surface colonies up to ½ mm. diameter, bluish white to white, glistening, smaller colonies more distinctly blue; depression around colonies as noted Culture 32. Subsurface colonies yellowish white, small. Under low power objective the centre yellowish brown dense compact surrounded by pale border ¼ diameter of colony; edges entire, clearly defined and hyaline. The differentiation of border from centre bears a close resemblance to colony of Asiatic cholera (plate 227 Kolle & Wassermann Atlas Tafel 10), and is not unlike plate 45 of colon colony (Park & Williams, Path. Micro-organisms, 5th edition, page 110). In the large surface colonies the whole structure is more homogeneous. Subsurface colonies appear similar.

Agar colonies.—20 hours 37° C., surface colonies 1½-2 mm. diameter. Flat to umbonate, growth rapid, colony round, surface smooth, glistening, iridescent. By transmitted light ferric-yellow centre paling to bluish at edge. Subsurface colonies punctiform. Under the low power objective surface colonies are dark in centre, "mound" appearance, gradually merging to pale lemon-brown colour, structure finely granular to grumose; subsurface colonies similar.

Temperature relations:—

Thermal Death Point.—10 minutes exposure in nutrient broth at 60°C.

Optimum Temperature.—Cultures incubated at room temperature and at 37°C. grow well; better growth at 37°C.

Vitality on Culture Media.—Survives several months, in artificial media, agar or gelatine.

Relation to oxygen.—Facultative anaerobe; incubated at 37°C. for 36 hours under anaerobic conditions, moderate bluish growth by transmitted light, on glucose agar; spreading over slope as bluish film, small discrete colonies with centre more opaque. Condensation water heavily clouded; much froth; medium throughout tube riddled with gas bubbles. The organism appears to grow equally well aerobically or anaerobically.

Biochemical Reactions:

Indol production: Indol not produced.

Production of nitrates: Nitrates reduced to nitrites.

Voges-Proskauer reaction: Positive.

Methyl red reaction: Alkaline.

Fermentation of Carbohydrates.—The action of the culture on dulcite is variable but it evidently is able to ferment this alcohol to gas, some tests being positive, some negative; the alcohol adonit on the other hand is fermented to acid and profuse gas with frothing in 24 hours. The action on inulin is somewhat characteristic, fermentation to acid and gas with frothing in 24 hours; no other strain isolated has such pronounced effect on this test substance. Within 24 hours all the remaining carbohydrates are fermented to acid and profusely to gas with very pronounced frothing. In general this culture is much more active in its fermentation reactions than any of the cultures hitherto described.

Glucose.	Lactose.	Saccharose.	Mannite.	Dulcite.
+ +	+ +	+ +	+ +	+ ±
Adonit.	Raffinose.	Arabinose.	Xylose.	Salicin.
+ +	+ +	+ +	+ +	+ +
Aesculin.	Glycerine.	Inulin.		
+ +	+ +	+ +		

+ = acid.
++ = acid and gas.

Culture 36.

Source: Can IV. Ser. I. Packer B.

Morphology.—Microscopially varying from very short stumpy rods to forms twice as long as broad; the majority ·8–1 μ long, staining unevenly with Kühne's methylene blue; Gram negative*; from old agar culture no evidence of spores.

Motility.—In hanging drop occurring singly and in pairs; extremely active motility.

Cultural Characteristics:—

   Agar slope.—36 hours 37°C., moderate along track of needle, glistening iridescent, Porcelain to yellowish white by transmitted light.

   Herring Agar slope.—20 hours at 32°C., growth moderate, slightly raised, dry but glistening, some discrete colonies, by transmitted light blue to yellow.

   Löeffler's Blood Serum.—24 hours 37° C., moderate, glistening. No liquefaction after 7 days.

   Löeffler's Malachite Green Sol.—24 hours 37°C., coagulated as Culture 34, much gas; in 72 hours reduced to greenish yellow. In 14 days coagulum not further reduced but precipitation on sides and bottom of tube; ferric-yellow liquid expressed.

   Gelatine stab.—Room temperature—in 24 hours nliform growth equally good on surface and in stab; in 48 hours no liquefaction growth on surface showing, moist; in 4 days growth luxuriant; in 7 days growth becoming brown, medium slightly tinted; no liquefaction arter 21 days.

   Nutrient Broth.—18 hours 37°C., moderate even clouding, no pellicle, bluish rim at top, no sediment; in 48 hours heavy clouding watered silk appearance, later sediment noticeable; no pellicle even after 10 days.

   Herring broth.—Moderate growth, clouding flocculent suspension, bluish rim, no pellicle; in 48 hours brown viscid sediment precipitated; in 10 days ring on surface, very heavy flocculent growth, black sediment.

   Milk.—18 hours 37°C. Much gas on shaking, with froth persistent, no coagulation; in 14 days weak coagulum commencing and coagulation slowly completed when examined at the end of two months.

   Litmus Milk.—In 18 hours no coagulation, much froth on shaking with froth persisting; violaceus merging into heliotrope; no further change in 10 days; in 14 days lilaceus, no coagulation; when examined 6 weeks late coagulation complete, lilacrus.

8 GEORGE V, A. 1918

Aesculin agar.—One loop from peptone broth culture streaked on plates; in 24 hours 37° C. brown to black reaction.

Aesculin broth.—The typical black reaction not given after 7 days; change only to brown.

MacConkey's N.R.B. broth.—In 48 hours 37° C. an eosin tint but no reduction to canary yellow after 7 days.

Gelatine colonies.—Room temperature (1st appearance) in 72 hours surface colonies small, average ½ mm. diameter, glistening flat, round; by transmitted light bluish white, almost transparent; characteristic ring in gelatine as noted. Culture 32; surface colonies yellowish white, small, round. Under the low power objective surface colonies round distinctly granular and dark yellow centre, surrounded by pale border and edges entire and hyaline; on gelatine, the colonies unlike those previously described.

N.B.—On referring to the notes made when this culture was originally isolated six months ago, I find that on agar the colonies were characteristically different from the colonies of Cultures 32, 34 or 35. It is of interest to note that this individuality has been maintained throughout a period of this length, and in spite of having many times been subcultured on laboratory media.

Agar Colonies.—20 hours, 37°C. growth rapid; surface colonies 1-1½ mm. diameter; flat, glistening, iridescent; some colonies extending as thin blue protuberances over the medium; by transmitted light colonies bluish, little darker and more opaque in centre. Subsurface colonies up to ·25 mm. diameter. Under the low power objective surface colonies coarsely granular, immediate centre slightly darker and well defined; remainder same structure throughout; edges entire; subsurface colonies compact, grumose to "mound-like" structure; often the surrounding medium a light ferric colour due to precipitated granules with no definite outline.

Temperature Relations:—

Thermal Death Point.—10 minutes exposure to 60° C. in nutrient broth.

Optimum Temperature.—Growth satisfactory when incubated either at room temperature or at 37°C. Most satisfactory growth at 37°C.

Vitality on Culture Media.—The culture survives several months on artificial media, agar or gelatine.

Relation to Oxygen:—Facultative anaerobe; incubated for 36 hours at 37° C. under anaerobic conditions grows on glucose agar as pale bluish thin film along track of needle, transmitted light; spreading over slope as discrete colonies; heavy cloudy growth in condensation water; much froth in tube, gas bubbles ½ cm. diameter throughout medium. The organism grows equally well aerobically or anaerobically.

Biochemical Reactions:

Indol production	Indol not produced.
Reduction of nitrates	Nitrates reduced to nitrites.
Voges-Proskauer reaction	Positive.
Methyl red reaction	Alkaline.

Fermentation of Carbohydrates: The culture ferments lactose to acid, but gas is not produced until 72 hours after inoculation; the amount then is small and no increase is observed on further incubation; glucose, saccharose, xylose, arabinose, and mannite are fermented to acid with profuse evolution of gas within 24 hours. The action upon raffinose is feeble. The Andrade indicator is rapidly decolourized in the aesculin, assuming a lemon yellow tint, such persisting; this colour is partially due to the glucoside itself.

Glucose.	Lactose.	Saccharose.	Mannite.	Dulcite.
+ +	+ +	+ +	+ +	- -
Adonite.	Raffinose.	Arabinose.	Xylose.	Salicin.
- -	+ -	+ +	+ +	- -
Aesculin.	Glycerine.	Inulin.		
+ -	+ -	+ -		
-				

+ = acid.
+ + = acid and gas,

Culture 37.

Source: Can V. Ser. I. Packer B.

Morphology.—Microscopically rods, three times as long as broad; average length 1·6 μ. Stain evenly. Gram negative*; from old agar cultures no evidence of spores.

Motility.—In hanging drop occurring singly and in twos; motile; movement varying from revolving motion to a wavelike undulating motion.

Cultural Characteristics:—

Agar slope.—36 hours, 37° C., luxuriant along track of needle, raised, glistening, iridescent, yellowish-white by transmitted light; gas bubbles in medium presumably from muscle sugar in meat extract. At times, particularly in the older cultures, agar growth decidedly slimy, drawing out on the needle. In 7 days, medium lemon to brown.

Herring agar.—20 hours at 32°C. Along track of needle heavy, raised, compact, greyish white, glistening, spreading as thick blue-green veil, by transmitted light slightly iridescent, heavy clouding of condensation water.

Löeffler's Blood Serum.—24 hours, 37° C., luxuriant, raised, white, spreading, no liquefaction in 7 days.

Löeffler's Malachite Green Sol.—In 24 hours precipitated light green coagulum on sides of tube; in 48 hours reduction to yellow beginning in 7 days reduced to yellow and almost entirely digested.

Gelatine Stab.—Room temperature—in 24 hours liquefaction commencing; in 48 hours crateriform to extent of 3mm, continuing down the stab as infundibuliform; in 7 days liquefaction complete and medium sharply divided into layers; immediately below surface liquefaction appears the colour of turbid whey, in successive layers turbidity and cloudiness gradually disappearing; heavy yellow flaky precipitate at bottom.

Nutrient Broth.—18 hours, 37°C., heavy clouding, surface iridescent, pellicle, bluish rim easily detached on shaking—life-belt form—medium slightly flocculent; in 4 days clouding very heavy, bluish rim; later sediment.

Herring Broth.—Very similar to above but heavier growth; in 4 days heavy clouding and thick bluish white pellicle; later flocculent.

Milk.—18 hours, coagulation commencing; in 48 hours coagulated with gas and digestion well advanced; in 10 days more than half digested, whey yellowish, heavy pellicle, soft curd; in 14 days gas bubbles still persisting, digestion proceeded, ¾ tube, the soft curd adhering to the glass, digestion not proceeding directly from surface to bottom. At a later date when the organism had

8 GEORGE V, A. 1918

been in pure culture for several months, a decided ropiness was noted, milk tubes being distinctly slimy within 24 hours after inoculation. This feature appears to have developed under cultivation and has since persisted.

Litmus Milk.—In 18 hours violaceus, no coagulation; in 48 hours gas, heavy pellicle, coagulated and digestion proceeding; in 4 days a yellow digested fluid extending 2cm. below surface, remainder violaceous; in 10 days ½ digested, remainder soft gelatinous curd; in 14 days except for tint, appearance very similar to milk as noted above.

Aesculin agar.—1 loop from peptone broth culture streaked on plates. In 24 hours black reaction.

MacConkey's N.R.B. Broth.—In 24 hours heavy growth. No reduction to canary yellow. Later colour slightly changed but no definite reduction.

Gelatine Colonies.—(1st appearance.) Room temperature in 72 hours liquefaction well advanced; individual colonies up to 3mm. diameter, round, saucer-shaped, characteristic of the organisms of the proteus group; centre of colony dark white spot ·25 mm. diameter, then clear space, then semi-transparent rim. Under the low power objective opaque centre merging into myceloid filaments, then clear space, and heavily clouded borders with entire edges; medium unchanged, no characteristic smell.

Agar colonies.—20 hours at 37°C. growth rapid, surface colonies concave, 1½-2½mm. diameter; very slimy after repeated sub-culturing drawing out on needle 10-15cm.; glistening; by transmitted light distinctly radiate, whole colony bluish but slightly more opaque in centre; subsurface colonies bluish to white. Under the low power objective surface colonies brownish with dark opaque centre in some, finely to coarsely granular; some colonies same structure throughout; edges entire hyaline. Subsurface colonies distinct, grumose to mound like.

Temperature Relations:—

Thermal death point.—10 minutes exposure in nutrient broth at 60°C.

Optimum temperature.—Cultures incubated at room temperature and at 37°C. grow well. Most satisfactory growth at 37°C.

Vitality on Culture Media.—The culture survives several months in artificial medium agar or gelatine.

Relation to Oxygen.—The culture is a facultative anaerobe; incubated for 36 hours under anaerobic conditions moderate growth on glucose agar slope, bluish tint; very heavy clouding of condensation water; on the slope seen as discrete colonies varying from a thin bluish film to converse moist colonies 1 mm. diameter with ferric yellow centre paling towards edges. The medium riddled with gas bubbles ½ - 1 cm. diameter, much froth in tube. This organism appears to grow equally well aerobically or anaerobically.

Biochemical Reactions:—

Indol production: Indol produced.

Reduction of Nitrates: Nitrates reduced to nitrites.

Voges-Proskauer reaction: Positive.

Methyl red reaction: Alkaline.

Fermentation of Carbohydrates.—This culture ferments lactose feebly to acid, the Andrade indicator showing reduction in 48 hours, and no gas is produced. Raffinose, glycerine and inulin are fermented to acid with slight production of gas; the gas in glycerine not appearing until the second day. The remaining fermentable substances are acted upon rapidly, evolving gas profusely within

24 hours. It will be seen that of the two glucosides used, salicin and aesculin, the former only is fermented to gas.

In the later cultural experiments a distinct sliminess appeared in all tubes, in peptone broths with and without added sugars; a pale white rim at surface observed to be slimy after several days at 37°C.

Glucose. Lactose. Saccharose. Mannite. Dulcite.

+ +   + −   + +   + +   − −

Adonit. Raffinose. Arabinose. Xylose. Salicin.

− −   + +   + +   + +   + +

Aesculin. Glycerine. Inulin.

− +   + +   + +

+ = acid.

++ = acid and gas.

Culture 64.

Source Can. VI., Ser. I, Packer C.

From this source four strains have been isolated—64, 64a, 64b aerobically, and 64c anaerobically. The similarity of the strains in culture is such that a detailed description of each is not warranted. There are, however, certain cultural differences in 64a, 64b and 64c as compared with 64, which I have thought worthy of special mention; and these have been noted in the following description:—

Morphology.—Microscopically varying from coccus forms to short thick rods; the former ·8 μ diameter, the latter 1½ times as long as broad; Gram negative.* The culture has been recently isolated, and no evidence of spores has been obtained; this feature cannot at present be finally reported upon.

Motility.—In hanging drop occurring singly and in twos; very actively motile; meteoric flashing across the field.

Cultural Characteristics:—

Agar Slope.—24 hours, 37°C., moderate along track of needle, flat, slightly contoured, edges well defined, iridescent, by transmitted light yellowish white with bluish edges.

Löeffler's Blood Serum.—Moderate, no liquefaction; in 72 hours moderate, much less than culture 65.

Löeffler's Malachite Green Sol.—24 hours 37° C., precipitate at bottom of tube, no coagulum, liquid turbid, pea green colour; in 7 days yellowish brown turbid fluid with ferric precipitate at bottom.

Gelatine Stab.—Room temperature—24 hours, filiform, no liquefaction; in 7 days no liquefaction, growth luxuriant, surface and in stab; yellow growth in stab.

Nutrient Broth.—24 hours 37° C., even clouding abundant, 'watered silk" appearance, no pellicle, no sediment; in 7 days clouding even, no pellicle, heavy viscid yellowish white sediment at bottom of tube.

Milk.—24 hours 37°C., frothy on shaking, no coagulation; in 72 hours soft coagulum, much gas, whey expressed, curd shrinking; in 7 days white turbid whey, curd shrinking and split by gas.

Litmus milk.—In 24 hours liliaceous, much froth on shaking, no coagulation; in 72 hours soft coagulum, bleached to isabella, curd perceptibly shrinking; much gas; in 7 days completely bleached with heliotrope rim at surface, depth of 2 cm. turbid tinted whey, curd rapidly disintegrating and permeated with gas holes.

N.B.—This culture is violent in its action upon milk.

8 GEORGE V, A. 1918

Aesculin agar.—1 loop peptone broth culture streaked on plates. In 24 hours 37°C., black reaction.

Aesculin broth.—In 24 hours, 37°C., black reaction.

MacConkey's N.R.B. Broth.—In 48 hours, 37°C., reduced to canary yellow.

Gelatine Colonies.—Room temperature (1st appearance)—identical with Culture 35—64a presents some variation. In 72 hours growth rapid abundant, more luxuriant than any of foregoing cultures; surface colonies up to 1 mm. diameter, compact, white, opaque with tendency to capitate, round; the smaller colonies bluish to bluish white. Subsurface colonies small compact.

Under the low power objective surface colonies have appearance identical with the literature descriptions of the *B. coli* colony, edges entire centre dark and opaque; subsurface colonies pale yellow in colour, very finely granular, slightly darker in centre. See Culture 35.

Agar Colonies.—20 hours, 37°C., growth rapid, flat, surface colonies 1½-2½ mm. diameter, round with tendency to spread; by transmitted light distinct bluish appearance, glistening, iridescent. Subsurface colonies up to 0·25 mm. diameter bluish to white. Under the low power objective surface colonies have small well defined dark centre, remainder lemon coloured; structure coarsely granular to grumose, edges entire, hyaline and well defined; pale radiate filaments—star-like rays—emanate from the colonies into surrounding medium. Subsurface colonies dark grumose to " mound-like."

Agar Colonies 64a.—20 hours 37°C., growth rapid, surface colonies bluish from 1–2 mm. diameter, glistening, iridescent, tendency to run together, forming blue film over agar. Subsurface colonies up to 1 mm. diameter white to yellowish white; some force their way to surface and appear as yellowish-white in centre, spreading on surface to 3 mm. diameter, blue, flat, concentrically ringed, contoured, edges undulate to lobate. Under the low power objective surface colonies (majority) finely granular at centre to grumose near edge; in some instances characteristic protuberances over agar as in culture 64, edges entire; subsurface lemon yellow, edges entire.

Temperature Relations:—

Thermal Death Point.—Exposed in nutrient broth for 10 minutes at 60°C. organism survives; exposed for 10 minutes at 70°C. no subsequent growth; exact temperature not yet definitely determined.

Optimum Temperature.—Grows well at room temperature and at 37°C. More satisfactory growth at 37°C.

Vitality on Culture Media.—Not yet determined.

Relation to Oxygen:—The culture is a facultative anaerobe; incubated for 36 hours under anaerobic conditions at 37°C. the medium—glucose sugar—is split, riddled with gas bubbles and upper portions blown to top of tube, much froth; heavy cloudy condensation water permeated whole medium. The organism grows with extreme rapidity both aerobically and anaerobically.

Chemical Reactions:

Indol production: Indol not produced.

Reduction of nitrates: Nitrates reduced to nitrites.

Voges-Proskauer reactions: Positive.

Methyl red reaction: Alkaline.

Fermentation of Carbohydrates.—The culture fails to ferment dulcite and adonit to acid or gas. All other test substances used are fermented within 24 hours to acid, and profusely with much frothing to gas. In the glucose, lactose, saccharose, mannite, raffinose, and arabinose tubes the Andrade indicator is completely reduced within 24 hours, the reduction in the xylose, salicin and aesculin tubes being slower. Compared with the other cultures described herein, the rapid and violent action upon the carbohydrates is both distinctive and characteristic, as also is the rapidity with which the Andrade indicator is decolourized. The decolourized tubes when tested with methyl red show decided alkalinity. The rapid reversion to an alkaline reaction is a point of considerable interest.

64a.—The fermentation reactions are identical with those of the above culture, but a striking difference, which may be but temporary however, has been noted in the action upon the Andrade indicator. No reduction of the indicator in any tubes was noted within 24 hours; in 72 hours glucose, mannite, arabinose, xylose and salicin had changed from the scarlet tint of the acid reaction to a deep pink shade. In 7 days the glucose, arabinose, and xylose tubes only were completely reduced giving an alkaline reaction to methyl red.

I have as yet no explanation to offer regarding this apparent selective action towards the Andrade indicator; the inoculations were made at the same time, the same amount of the respective peptone broth cultures being added as the inoculum, such broth cultures being the same age, and all medium used of the same standard stock.

In this connection it may be of interest to mention that for some months I have been experimenting with Congo red as an indicator in connection with routine water analyses for the colon group; these experiments are as yet not sufficiently complete for publication; I have used this indicator in sugar broths as a confirmatory test and find that the strains 64 and 64a exhibit again, as in the Andrade indicator, a selective action.

Glucose.	Lactose.	Saccharose.	Mannite.	Dulcite.
+ +	+ +	+ +	+ +	− −
Adonit.	Raffinose.	Arabinose.	Xylose.	Salicin.
− −	+ +	+ +	+ +	+ +
Aesculin.	Glycerine.	Inulin.		
+ +	+ ±	+ +		

++ = acid and gas.

+ = acid.

8 GEORGE V, A. 1918

Gas-Producing Organisms, Summary, Morphological and Biological Features.

Culture	24	37 (b)	32	36	26	34	35	64
Morphology	Coc. to Rod	Rod	Rod	Rod	Rod	Coc. to Rod	Coc. to Rod	Coc. to Rod
Gram's Stain	−	−	−	−	−	−	−	−
Spores	−	−	−	−	−	−	−	−
Motility	+	+ Wave-like	C + Act.	+ Act.	......	+ Act.	......	+ Very act.
Agar Slope	Lux.	Lux.	Lux.	Mod.	Mod.	Mod.	Mod. to Lux.	Mod.
Blood Serum	Mod. no Liq.	Lux. no Liq.	Mod. no Liq.	Mod. no Liq.	Slt. no Liq.	Mod. no Liq.	Lux. no Liq.	Mod. no Liq.
Malachite Green Sol.	Coag. part. dig.	Reduced.	Coag. no reduc.	Coag. slgh. reduc.	Coag. no reduction.	Coag. not reduced.	Coag. reduction.	Precip. reduction.
Gelatine Stab.	Liq.	Liq.	No liq.	No liq.	No liq.	No liq.	No liq.	No liq.
Nutrient Broth	Cloud. heavy	Cloud heavy pell.	Mod. cldg. pell.	Mod. no pell.	Mod. cloud.	Mod. cloud.	Even cloud. no pel.	Abun. cloud.
Milk	Coag. 72 hrs. dig. (a)	Coag. 18 hrs. dig. slimy.	Coag. 72 hrs.	Coag. 14 days.	Coag. 72 hrs.	Coag. 48 hrs.	Coag. 72 hrs. no dig.	Coag. 72 hrs.
Aesculin Agar	Brown Black	Black	Brown Black	Brown Black	No reaction. (e)	Black	Brown to Black	Black
MacConkey's N.R.B. Broth	No reduction.	Slight reduction.	No reduction.	No reduction.	No reduction.	No reduction.	No reduction.	Reduced to canary yellow.
Thermal Death pt. C.	60°	60°	60° (d)	60°	60°	60°	60°	60° to 70° (f)
Optimum Temperature C.	37°	37°	37°	37°	37° & 21°	37°	37°	37°
Relation to Oxygen.	facul. anaer. prefers aerob.	facul. anaer.	fac. anaer.	fac. anaer.	facul. anaer. prefers aerobic	facul. anaer.	facul. anaer.	facul. anaer.
Source.	Can II, Ser. II. Packer A.	Can V, Ser. I, Packer B.	Can I, Ser. I, Packer B.	Can IV, Ser. I, Packer B.	Can III, Ser. II, Packer A.	Can II, Ser. I, Packer A.	Can III, Ser. I, Packer A.	Can VI, Ser. I, Packer C.

a. Sliminess noted as digestion proceeds. b. Sliminess appearing after successive subculturing. c. Motion as in semi-circles. d. See page 197. e. Aesculin fermented to gas, but no action on aesculin agar. f. Not yet definitely determined, see page 206.

Gas-Producing Organisms Summary, Biochemical Reactions.

Source.	Inulin.	Glycerine.	Aesculin.	Salicin.	Xylose.	Arabinose.	Raffinose.	Adonite.	Dulcite.	Mannite.	Saccharose.	Lactose.	Glucose.	Methyl Red.	Voges Pros-kauer.	Nitrate Reduction.	Indol.	Culture.
Can II. Ser. II. Packer A.	++	g++	++	++	++	++	++	--	+-	++	++	+-	++	Alk.	+	+	-	24
Can V. Ser. I. Packer B.	++	++	+-	i++	++	++	++	--	--	++	++	+-	++	Alk.	+	+	h+	37
Can I. Ser. I. Packer B.	++	++	h++	++	++	++	++	--	++	++	++	k++	++	Alk.	-	+	-	32
Can IV. Ser. I. Packer B.	+-	+-	+o-	+-	++	++	+-	--	+-	++	++	m++	++	Alk.	+	+	-	36
Can III. Ser. II. Packer B.	+-	-+	e++	-+	++	++	++	--	+-	++	++	++	++	Acid.	-	?	-	P 26
Can III. Ser. I. Packer A.	r++	+-	++	++	++	++	++	--	q++	++	++	++	++	Alk.	-	+	-	34
Can III. Ser. I. Packer A.	t++	++	++	++	++	++	++	++	+-	++	++	++	++	Alk.	+	+	-	S 35
Can VI. Ser. I. Packer C.	++	+-	++	++	++	++	++	--	--	++	++	++	++	Alk.	+	+	-	X 64

+ Acid. ++ Acid and Gas. g Gas after 72 hours. h Sliminess appearing after successive subculturing. i Note production of gas in one glucoside, not in the other. k Feebly to gas. l Reduced, lemon yellow. m Gas not produced until 72 hours. o Andrade indicator rapidly decolourised. p Carbohydrates feebly acted upon, but positive within 24 hours. q Characteristically profuse. r Reaction very slow. s Pronounced and rapid action upon carbohydrates. t Action on inulin pronounced, more so than any of the series. x The carbohydrates attacked are fermented profusely to gas within 24 hours; rapid reduction of Andrade indicator and characteristically rapid reversion to alkalinity.

8 GEORGE V, A. 1918

EXPERIMENTAL SWELLED CANS.

Having isolated strains of gas-producing bacteria from swelled cans of sardines, and having determined their cultural features and biochemical reactions, the next step was to attempt the experimental swelling of normal cans by inoculation of organisms already isolated. Up to the present I have used three cultures for this purpose—cultures 35, 37 and 64. These three cultures on the basis of their biological and biochemical reactions are sufficiently differentiated (pages 199-207) to warrant individual trials. A number of normal cans of sardines were most courteously supplied by the manager of the Chamcook factory, St. Andrews, N.B. Some of the cans were of sardines packed in cottonseed oil, olive oil having been used for the remainder. The cans had to be "punched," inoculated, and again sealed. In order to eliminate as far as possible any error of manipulation I obtained by courtesy of the chief engineer, the services of the college plumber, who undertook the soldering. To avoid trouble from escaping oil, the cans were placed on end, rather than flat on the bottom. By the usual method a layer of solder was first spread over a portion of the can; this I cleaned and sterilized with absolute alcohol, and then with a sterile awl punched a hole 3 mm. diameter. From a 1cc. pipette, 2 to 3 drops of a young peptone broth culture of the desired organism were quickly dropped in; a small square of sterilized tin heated in the flame was at once placed over the hole, and the soldering process performed. The layer of solder previously spread over the can assisted materially in making the process effective. In this manner cans were inoculated with the respective cultures; the control cans receiving exactly the same treatment minus the inoculation. The cans, each placed in the half of a large petri dish, were incubated at a temperature of 30° to 33° C. They were examined at frequent intervals, and in 4 days swelling was observed in those inoculated. In 7 days the swelling has become so pronounced that there appeared to be danger from explosions. The cans were examined.

Normal Cans.—(Punched and resoldered). These appeared perfectly normal; no oil in petri dish, no moisture on outside of can, no swelling, no "rattle" on shaking. When opened there was no escape of gas; contents firm in texture, flesh the white of the normal sardines, and comparatively dry; odour typical and mild; normal in every respect.

INOCULATED CANS.

Can 35.—Inoculated with culture 35, oil in petri dish and on surface of can; pronounced swelling, top and bottom of can, convex; on shaking, the typical "rattle" of the original "swells"; when opened escape of gas and exuding of oil. The contents were soft, moist, and disintegrated to an even greater degree than in many of the original "swells." The oil was intermixed with the macerated sardines, and gas bubbles were very evident throughout the whole. The colour was a little darker than normal. The odour was not putrefactive, but an accentuation of the typical normal swell. The conditions noted were as evident on the side immediately opposite the point of inoculation, as at the point of inoculation itself. The condition of this can and its contents was in every respect identical with the conditions found when examining the original typical "swells," but accentuated.

Can 37.—Inoculated with culture 37. The description given of can 35 is here strictly applicable; no variation could be noted.

Can 64.—Inoculated with culture 64. The swelling of this can was more pronounced, otherwise the description given of can 35 is here strictly applicable in every respect.

Isolation of Organisms.—Pieces of fish were taken from the respective cans and inoculated into series of liquid media; glucose peptone broth, peptone broth, and nutrient broth respectively. These tubes were incubated at 37°C. for 24 hours.

Pronounced clouding of the media by each inoculum was by that time evident. Plates were made on glucose agar, and after incubation at 37°C. for 24 hours, typical colonies were picked off and streaked on agar slopes. Subsequently series of inoculations were made, and the organisms isolated proved to be identical respectively with the strains with which the experimental cans were inoculated.

Cultures 35, 37 and 64 respectively have experimentally produced typical swelled cans, have been re-isolated and proved culturally identical with the original strain. The "Postulates of Koch" have been satisfied.

ORGANISMS WHICH DO NOT PRODUCE GAS.

Culture 7.

Source: Herring Excreta.

Morphology:—Spore forming rods, occurring singly, in twos and in long forms. Gram negative.

Cultural Characteristics:—

> *Nutrient broth.*—In 24 hours at 37°C., membranous pellicle, medium clear; 1 month yellow sediment, medium clear.
>
> *Milk.*—In 5 days pellicle, no change; in 1 month yellow turbid digestion extending ⅔ down tube.
>
> *Litmus Milk.*—In 24 hours no change; in 10 days pellicle, sediment, digestion with colour varying from yellow to dark purple.
>
> *Gelatine Stab.*—Room temperature, liquefaction beginning in 2 days. In 5 days napiform to a depth of 5 mm., remainder filiform; in 14 days liquefaction still proceeding with lower part of stab a discrete villous growth; medium ferric lemon.

Biochemical Reactions:—

> Indol: not produced.
> Nitrates: not reduced.
> Glucose broth: acid, even clouding, no gas.

This culture in its reactions is typical of many strains isolated from herring excreta.

Culture 21.

Source: Normal Can sardines, Packer A.

Morphology.—Extremely long thin rods, forming spores; in hanging drop occurring singly and in twos, motile, Gram positive.

Cultural Characteristics:—

> *Nutrient broth.*—In 24 hours at 37°C., slight clouding, no pellicle; in three days membranous cup-shaped pellicle, medium cloudy; later, pellicle luxuriant, thick creamy, medium yellowish brown.
>
> *Milk.*—No change up to 5 days, when weak coagulum beginning; in 9 days tubes half cogulated; in 16 days yellow digestion nearly complete, remainder of medium firm hard curd.
>
> *Litmus Milk.*—No change in 24 hours; in 3 days pellicle, upper layers of milk dark purple, remainder violaceus, no coagulation; in 9 days digested without previous coagulation to muddy looking yellowish brown liquid.
>
> *Löeffler's Blood Serum:*—Rapid liquefaction.

8 GEORGE V, A. 1918

Gelatine Stab:—Room temperature, in 24 hours crateriform liquefaction beginn‑
ing; proceeding slowly in 7 days to 5 cm. from surface of stab; in 18 days
not complete, layers of yellowish precipitate.

Biochemical Reactions:—

Indol: not produced.
Nitrates: not reduced.
Glucose broth: acid, chiefly at surface, no gas.

From the same can, and other normal cans, strains were isolated which according
to the reactions noted proved to be identical with this culture.

Culture 13.

Source: Swelled Can I, Series II, Packer A.

Morphology.—Large coccus, occurring as staphylococcus, no spores, Gram positive.

Cultural Characteristics:—

Nutrient broth.—24 hours at 37°C., moderate, cloudy; no pellicle.

Milk.—In 5 days no change; no change in 1 month.

Litmus milk.—As milk.

Gelatine Stab.—Room temperature. In 2 days no liquefaction; in 5 days scant
growth filiform to discrete; in 14 days medium faintly browned, growth in
stab discrete and ferric yellow tint; no liquefaction, growth better under
surface.

Biochemical Reactions:—

Indol: not produced.
Nitrates: ?
Glucose broth: Acid, even clouding, no gas.

Culture 28.

Source: Same Can as Culture 13.

Morphology.—Long rods many times longer than broad, oval spores formed; Gram
negative; in hanging drop appear singly; in twos and in long chains; motile
with gliding movement.

Cultural Characteristics:—

Nutrient Broth.—24 hours 37° C. Moderate, cloudy, slight pellicle; in 1 month
cloudy with flocculent yellow sediment.

Milk.—In 5 days no change; in 1 month digested completely, yellow turbid fluid.

Litmus Milk.—In 10 days dark purple fluid with no previous coagulation; un‑
changed in 1 month.

Löeffler's Blood Serum.—Rapid liquefaction.

Gelatine Stab.—Room temperature, in 2 days slight liquefaction noted; in 5 days
liquefaction progressed to depth of 2 mm., stratiform, remainder of stab dis‑
crete colonies; in 14 days liquefaction 1 cm. depth, stratiform yellowish layers.

Biochemical reactions:—

Indol: not produced.
Nitrates: not reduced.
Glucose broth: Acid, upper part, pellicle, no gas.

Cultures 13 and 28 typical of several strains isolated from such cans.

Culture 14.

Source: Swelled Can II, Series II, Packer A.

Morphology: Long rods many times longer than broad; spores. Gram positive; in hanging drop occurring singly, in twos, and in chains; appear at first immobile but prolonged examination reveals slow laboured movement, some individuals appearing to push themselves along.

Cultural Characteristics:—

Nutrient broth.—24 hours 37°C., cloudy, flocculent pellicle; in 10 days heavy clouding with some flocculency; in 1 month clouding and yellow precipitate at bottom of tube.

Milk.—In 5 days no coagulation, ring, pellicle; in 1 month coagulated, some yellow whey expressed.

Litmus milk.—In 24 hours no change; in 10 days lilac, no coagulation; in 1 month coagulation, and some whey expressed.

Gelatine Stab.—Room temperature—in 2 days moderate growth, dip in gelatine; in 5 days crateriform liquefaction and spreading growth on surface of stab; in 14 days liquefection varied from V-shaped to crateriform to depth of 1 cm., cloudy; remainder of stab discrete.

Biochemical reactions:—

Indol: not produced.
Nitrates: not reduced.
Glucose broth: acid, more particularly near the surface, no gas.

Culture.	Morphology.	Spore formation.	Motility.	Gram's stain.	Nutrient broth.	Milk.	Litmus milk.	Löeffler's blood serum.	Gelatine stab.	Indol.	Reduction of nitrates.	Glucose broth.	Source.
7	Rod.	+	?	—	Pellicle, med. clear.	Slow digest.	Digest.	....	Liquef.	—	—	+ -	Herring excreta.
21	Rod.	+	+	+	Clouding, later pellicle.	Slow coag. later dig.	Digest. slowly without previous coagln.	Rapid liquef.	Liquef. slow.	-	-	+ -	Sardines, Packer A, Normal can.
13	Coccus.	—	?	+	Moder. cloudy.	No change.	No change.	....	No liquef.	—	?	+ -	Swelled Can I, Ser. II, Packer A.
28	Rod.	+	+	—	Cloudy, later pellicle.	Slow digest.	Cleared with no coag.	Rapid liquef.	Liquef. slowly.	-	—	+ -	As Culture 13
14	Rod.	+	+ feeb	+	Cloudy.	No change.	Slow digest.	....	Liquef. after 14 days.	—	—	+ -	Swelled Can II (Ser. II) Packer A.
16	Coccus.	—	—	+	Cloudy, later precip.	Coag. slow.	Coag. slow.	....	Liquef. slowly.	—	—	+ -	Swelled Can III (Ser. II) Packer A.

8 GEORGE V, A. 1918

BRIEF SUMMARY.

1. Forty cans of sardines, "swelled," and "normal," have been submitted to a bacteriological examination.

2. Cottonseed oil, and the excreta of fresh herrings have been examined.

3. From the "swelled" cans eight strains of gas-producing bacteria have been isolated,—Cultures 24, 26, 32, 34, 35, 36, 37 and 64.

4. The eight strains have been studied morphologically, biologically, and biochemically, and have been described, pages 192-207.

   (*a*) Two strains, Cultures 24 and 37, liquefy gelatine, and fail to ferment lactose; these are tentatively placed in the *Proteus* group, *B. vulgaris* (Hauser 1885), Migula 1900.

   (*b*) The remaining six strains are lactose-fermenting types. I consider that these include typical and a-typical types of the *colon-aerogenes* group (Escherich); but for the present an individual classification is not offered.

5. The features and reactions of the gas-producing bacteria have been summarized; pages 208 and 209.

6. Experimental "swellings", typical in every respect have been produced in the laboratory on inoculation with Cultures 35, 37, and 64 respectively. The organisms subsequently isolated have been proved culturally to be identical with those used for inoculation; thus satisfying the "Postulates of Koch."

7. No bacteria have been found in the cottonseed oil.

8. Non-gas-producing bacteria have been isolated from herring excreta, from swelled cans, and from a small percentage of the normal cans examined; brief notes are presented on pages 211-213.

9. No gas producing bacteria have been isolated from normal cans of sardines.

I desire to express my indebtedness to Dr. A. B. Macallum; to Dr. A. G. Huntsman; to Dr. F. C. Harrison; to the Maine Inspectors of the "National Canners' Association of America"; and to the proprietors and managers of the various canning factories which were visited with their permission.

SESSIONAL PAPER No. 38a

REFERENCES.

1. Prescott and Underwood, 1897. "Micro-organisms and Sterilizing Processes in the Canning Industries." Technology Quarterly X, 1. P. 183-199.

2. Macphail and Bruêre, 1897. "Discolouration in Canned Lobsters." Ottawa Supp. No. 2, 29th Annual Rept., Dept. Marine and Fisheries.

3. Obst, 1916. "A Bacteriological Study of Sardines." Abs. Bact. I, 1. P. 50.

4. Nielson, Ivar. 1890. "Ein Stuck moderner Bakteriologie aus dem 12 Janrundert." Central. fur. Bakt, u Parisit, erste abt, 7. 267.

5. Auchi, F., 1894. " Comptes rendus de la Soc. de Biologie." P. 18.

6. Vaughan, V. C. "The infection of Meat and Milk." Trans. 7th Inter. Congr. Hyg. Vol. III, Sec. III. P. 118-129.

7. Savage, W. G., 1913. "Bacterial Food Poisoning and Food Infection." M.O. Rpt. Local Govt. Bd. Food Rpts., No. 18. P. 46.

8. Vaughan and Novy, 1902. "Cellular Toxins." Lea Bros., Philadelphia, P. 262.
   loc. cit. P. 209.
   loc. cit. P. 188.

9. McWeeney. "Meat Poisoning—Its Nature, Causation and Prevention." Journ. Meat and Milk Hyg. Vol. I. John Bale, London. P. 1-31.
   (NOTE.—Separate not dated, evidently about 1909.)

10. Baur, 1902. "Ueber zwei denitrificirende Bakterien aus der Ostsee." Wissensch, Meeresuntersuch. Neue folge. Sechster Band. Abt. kiel. P. 21.

11. American Public Health Association, 1915. "Standard Methods of Water Analysis." P. 77-137.

12. Besson, 1913. "Text Book of Practical Bacteriology, etc." Longmans Green, London. P. 53.

13. Besson, 1913. "Text Book of Practical Bacteriology, etc." Lengmans Green, London. P. 410.

14. Harrison and Vanderleck, 1908. "Aesculin Bile Salt Agar for Water and Milk Analysis." Trans. Roy. Soc., Can., III, Ser. II. P. 105-110.

15. Savage, 1906. "Bacterial Examination of Water Supplies." Lewis, London. P. 215.

16. "Bacterial Destruction of Copepods." Contrib. to Canadian Biol., 1917-18, Ottawa, 1918. Ref. 6, P. 227.

17. Clarke and Lubs, 1915. "Differentiation of Bacteria of the Colon-aerogenes group." Journ. Infect. Diseases. P. 17, 160-173.

18. Giltner, Cited by, 1916. "Microbiology." Wiley, N.Y. P. 355.

19. "Bacterial Destruction of Copepods." Contrib. to Canadian Biology, 1917-18.

20. *Loc cit.* P. 218.

XIII.

BACTERIAL DESTRUCTION OF COPEPODS OCCURRING IN MARINE PLANKTON.

By WILFRID SADLER, M.Sc., B.S.A., Bacteriological Labatories, Macdonald College (McGill University), Province of Quebec, Canada.

During the summer of 1916 I was investigating the bacteriological content of "Swelled Canned Fish" for the Biological Board of Canada at the Marine Station, St. Andrews, N.B.

While there Dr. Arthur Willey (Professor of Zoology, McGill University) called my attention to the condition of some of the copepods—(*Calanus finmarchicus*—upon which he was conducting researches. Under the microscope it was seen that many parts of the tissue of copepods which had died in culture flasks were completely destroyed by masses of what appeared to be bacteria. It was particularly noticed that the axial cavity in the first antennae was entirely occupied by a dense column of writhing organisms. Tubes of nutrient broth were inoculated direct from the copepods and after two days' incubation at room temperature a definite clouding of the medium was noted.

At the request and on the suggestion of Dr. Willey I have proceeded with the examination of the cultures secured, and have obtained in pure culture the organisms concerned. Three specific strains of bacteria have been isolated.

Inasmuch as the work may have some practical significance in relation to the general subject of marine biology, and is of scientific interest, this report of the detailed studies of these organisms has been prepared.

MEDIA EMPLOYED.

I began by using various media prepared from fish concoctions in addition to the ordinary laboratory media. The latter, however, proved to be more satisfactory in every way and I have therefore confined myself to their use entirely.

Beef Peptone Agar.—Standard methods [1]—Beef extract being substituted for meat.

Beef Peptone Gelatine.—Standard methods.[1]

Glucose Agar.—1% glucose added to agar prepared as above, immediately before tubing.

Sodium Indigo Sulphate Agar.—3 per cent. sodium indigo sulphate with 2 per cent. glucose added to neutral agar. tubed and sterilized in flowing stream for three successive days.

Tochtermann's Serum Agar.—[2] For digestion test.

Löeffler's Blood Serum.—[3]   „   „   „

Aesculin Agar.[4]—For specific reaction of organisms of the colon-aerogenes group. Loops of a broth culture spread on plates.

Neutral Red Bile Salt Agar.[5]—Ditto, ditto.

Bouillon for Voges-Proskauer reaction.[6]—

Bouillon for the Methyl Red Reaction.[7]—

Solution for reduction of Nitrates to Nitrites.—Giltay's synthetic solution was used, and also a peptone potassium-nitrate solution.

8 GEORGE V, A. 1918

Dunham Solution for Indol Production.—1 per cent peptone, 5 per cent NaCl dissolved in distilled water, the reaction adjusted to + 10, medium cleared with white of egg, filtered, tubed and sterilized. After 7 days' incubation at 37½°C. the cultures were tested for indol by the Bohme Ehrlich test [8] ; the development of a cherry red colour indicating the presence of indol.

Fermentation broths.—The various sugars, alcohols, glucosides used were prepared separately as 10 per cent solutions in distilled water, and sterilized for 15 minutes in flowing steam for three successive days. Immediately before inoculation these were added to tubes of broth made up as for the indol test— the use of peptone water without beef eliminates any risk of the reaction being masked by action on the muscle sugar—in such proportions as to give a final 1 per cent sugar or other carbohydrate broth. Dunham tubes were used for the collection of the gas. For acid production the acid fuchsin indicator of Andrade,[9] as adapted by Hollman, was used at the rate of 2 per cent.

In the preparation of the indicator I have noticed as reported by Andrade. and Hollman that the colour which results from the addition of the normal caustic soda is preceptibly affected by being left open to the air. By adding the caustic soda to freshly prepared acid fuchsin solution at intervals throughout the day, leaving the reagent meanwhile exposed to the air, I have found that 2½ cc. n/NaOH will decolorize to the proper shade of amber 100 cc. fuchsin solution.

Litmus Milk.—The milk freshly separated and tubed was sterilized for three successive days for 30 minutes in flowing steam. The litmus was made up separately; a 7 per cent solution of "Merck's" litmus in distilled water, heated in the steamer for 30 minutes and left over night in the incubator, filtered, sterilized for three successive days in flowing steam and added to the milk immediately before inoculation at the rate of 1½ per cent.

NOTE: It will be seen from page 224 that culture III of this paper exhibited an unusual degree of sensitiveness to the litmus. For this reason I now consider the proportion of the indicator added to be of some importance.

CULTURAL STUDIES.

Culture I.

Morphology.—Microscopically—24-hour-old agar culture at 37°C.—short rods varying up to 1-6 μ long and 1 μ broad; some larger forms; stains unevenly with Kuhne's methylene blue, and is Gram negative. No spores are formed and no capsule shown.

Motility.—Decided brownian movement; but not the violent agitation noted in culture III. No motility.

Cultural Characteristics:—

Agar Slope.—24 hours at 37°C. growth luxuriant, raised, slightly spreading, moist, glistening, porcelain-white, edges echinulate.

Glucose Agar Slope.—Gas, growth luxuriant, raised, moist, glistening, woolly appearance, haze, porcelain-white, spreading.

Tochtermann's Serum Agar Slope.—Resembling growth on glucose agar, but no woolly appearance. In 8 days growth had permeated medium as flakes; gas, heavy precipitate collected at base of slope.

Löeffler's Blood Serum.—Moderate, spreading, flat, no digestion, no discolouration. In 7 days no digestion; colour isabella, luxuriant, moist, slightly raised, iridiscent.

Sodium Indigo Sulphate Agar Slope.—Luxuriant, raised, moist, spreading, no reduction. In 8 days no reduction.

Gelatine Stab.—21°C. 24 hours, growth filiform, equal surface and stab. In 7 days as before; gas bubbles—presumably from the muscle sugar in the beef extract —in tube. In 6 weeks no liquefaction, growth brown, echinulate, medium unchanged.

Nutrient Broth.—37°C. 24 hours. Clouding abundant, medium clearing, flaky sediment at bottom, bluish rim at top. In 3 days flocculent yellowish-white rim at top, easily dislodged on shaking. Medium almost clear.

Potato.—Abundant along track of needle, glistening, contoured, isabella colour, growth slightly raised; in 3 days iridiscence perceptible and medium slightly browned.

Milk.—Coagulation in 24 to 30 hours; curd broken by gas bubbles. In 6 weeks curd contracted, no digestion.

Litmus Milk.—In 20 hours lilac, much gas, no coagulation; in 36 hours coagulation with gassy curd; in 5 days curd bleached; in 6 weeks no digestion.

Aesculin Agar.—Luxuriant, moist, black reaction.

Neutral Red Bile Salt Agar.—Luxuriant, raised, glistening, moist. Characteristic red reaction.

Peptone Broth + Aesculin.—Black reaction.

Gelatine Colonies.—(1st appearance) 5 days at 21°C. Surface colonies up to 1 mm. diameter, raised, slightly darker in centre, paling towards edges. Under the low power objective homogenous, granular, edges entire.

Agar Colonies.—24 hours at 37°C. Surface colonies up to 3 mm. diameter, raised, concave, glistening, yellowish-white at centre, paling towards edges, edges entire, colonies bluish by transmitted light. Under low power objective edges entire, finely granular, amorphous.

Temperature Relations:—

Thermal Death Point.—10 mns. exposure in nutrient broth at 60°C.

Optimum Temperature.—37°C. Cultures incubated at 37°, 21°, and 14°C. respectively.

Vitality on Culture Media.—Active cultures have been recovered from agar after 5 months at temperature of 15°-20°C.

Relation to Oxygen.—Facultative anaerobe; glucose agar.

Biochemical reactions:—

Indol production: Indol produced.
Reduction of nitrates: Nitrates reduced to nitrites.
Voges-Proskauer reaction: Negative.
Methyl red reaction: Acid.

Fermentation of Carbohydrates:—

Glucose.	Lactose.	Saccharose.	Maltose.	Mannite.	Dulcite.
+ +	+ +	+ +	+ +	+ +	+ +
Dextrine.	Salicin.	Raffinose.	Adonite.	Inulin.	Xylose.
+ +	+ +	+ +	+ +	+ +	+ +
Glycerine.					
+ +					

+ = acid.
++ = acid and gas.

38a—15½

8 GEORGE V, A. 1918

Culturally and biochemically this organism is a variation of the *B. coli* type according to the description of Escherich.[10] The variety I have isolated differs from the original description in that it is non-motile and ferments saccharose to acid and gas. The degree of importance to be attached to any one character has been discussed at considerable length in the literature during the last thirty years; owing to the fact that this organism is used as a presumptive test for faecal contamination in systematic water analysis. Of the two variations from the original type mentioned above, the presence or absence of motility may first be considered.

There has been a tendency by some workers to consider a non-motile form of *B. coli* (Escherich)[10] as *B. aerogenes* (Escherich)[11]. This position, however, is not substantiated by the researches of Escherich and Pfaundler, MacConkey, Jackson and others. Escherich and Pfaundler[12] in describing the original *B. coli* state that generally there is motility, sometimes slight; a characteristic movement as of short forward pushes; swinging in space with sometimes no change of place is also noted. The absence of definite motion as recorded by Tafel, Frankel and others is cited in the same paper. Lembke[13] considers that motility in *B. coli* is variable. McWeeney[14] in discussing what he would regard as the genuine *B. coli* remarks: "on the motility of individuals or its absence I hesitate to lay much stress." Houston[15] in using a broad classification for the true colon group adopts his "flaginac" test which leaves open the question of motility. Durham[16] considers that all members of the true colon group are probably motile; but in the same paper states: "speaking generally morphological characters are not of much value for subdivision of these bacteria."

MacConkey[17] discusses the influence of temperature and medium on motility; and while he considers the presence or absence as important he says: "it is very difficult to arrive at a conclusion with regard to this character." Ellis[18] has proved the presence of flagella in five species of the genus *Bacterium* which were hitherto held to be non-motile; and he considers that all the genus *Bacterium* when suitably cultivated can be shown to be motile. His conclusions would appear to be not sufficiently substantiated on the data given. The English Commission on the Standardization of Methods for the bacteriological examination of water[19]; and the American Commission on Standard Methods[1] each specify motility as one characteristic of the true *B. coli*; but a comparison of the two standards reveals variance as to the significance to be attached to this specific feature. Prescott and Winslow[20] consider the sugar fermentations, particularly the fermentations of glucose and lactose, are of prime importance. Savage[21] considers motility as one of the essential characters of the true *B. coli*. Migula[22] includes *B. neapolitanus* (Emmerich)[23] which is non-motile, as identical with *B. coli* (Escherich).

Thus while the consensus of opinion is undoubtedly in favour of specifying motility as a character of the true *B. coli*, there would seem to be no justification according to present classification for excluding from this type an organism preponderatingly similar and placing it with *B. aerogenes* (Escherich)[11] on account solely of the absence of motility. Harrison[28] raises the question as to whether, provided the argument *re* motility is admitted, it removes *B. neapolitanus* to a different genus from *B. coli*.

The second variation to which I have referred (page 219) is the fermentation of saccharose to acid and gas. *B. coli* (Escherich)[10] has no action upon saccharose. Theobald Smith, cited by Prescott and Winslow[20] stated in 1893 that *B. coli* could be divided into two distinct sub-types,—the one negative to saccharose or in other words the original *B. coli*, and the other fermenting this sugar to acid and gas. Durham[16] isolated saccharose—positive organisms and gave the name *B. coli communior*, since contracted to *B. communior*. Jackson[24] has classified the organisms of the lactose fermenting type and confirms the sub-type *B. communior* of Durham. The classification of Jackson has since been adopted by the laboratory section of the American Public Health Association,[1] and on this continent has received almost general approval. Using saccharose and dulcite as differential fermentation tests Jackson considers those organisms positive to lactose and dulcite as *B. coli* (Escherich)[10]; positive to lactose, saccharose and dulcite as *B. communior* (Durham)[16]; positive to lactose and saccharose but negative to dulcite as *B. ærogenes* (Escherich)[11], positive to lactose but negative to saccharose and dulcite as *B. acidi-lactici*.[24] Further subdivision according to the action on mannite and raffinose are used for further differentiation.

MacConkey uses the Voges-Proskauer reaction as one of his differential tests and finds that the true *B. coli* is always Voges-Proskauer negative, while the *B. ærogenes* type is Voges-Proskauer positive. In the same paper he revives the name *B. neapolitanus* (Emmerich)[23] and uses this nomenclature for his saccharose positive dulcite positive strains instead of the name given by Durham—*B. communior*. MacConkey obtained a pure culture labelled *B. neapolitanus* from Kral, and out of 480 coli-like organisms isolated from human and animal fæces he found that 23 per cent gave biochemical reactions identical with the Kral culture used by him as control. He states that he cannot agree with Migula in describing *B. neapolitanus* (Emmerich) as identical with *B. coli* (Escherich). As, however, the differentiation by means of carbohydrates other than glucose and lactose has been amplified since the classification by Migula, the conclusions of both Migula and MacConkey on this particular point are perfectly legitimate. Jordan[25], in designating the saccharose-positive dulcite-positive group uses *B. communior* and *B. neapolitanus* interchangeably; biochemically this as correct, but the former is motile (16), the latter non-motile[23]. Levine[26] who apparently follows MacConkey has lately studied 333 strains of lactose fermenting bacteria from various sources. He goes one step further and giving *B. neapolitanus* its original character of non-motility according to Emmerich[23], uses that nomenclature to include non-motile forms of *B. communior* (Durham). To say the least it is interesting to revive *B. neapolitanus* as a sub-type of *B. coli* (Escherich) in view of the following statement by Jordan[25a]: "According to a strict application of the rules of priority, the bacillus now known as *B. coli* should be called *B. neapolitanus*." The dates of the original publication by Emmerich [23a], and Escherich[10], of course bear out Jordan's statement.

However, according to the first descriptions of Emmerich[23] and Escherich[10] the former found a non-motile strain and the latter a motile strain of a lactose fermenting organism. Later work already referred to has separated these two strains on the basis of saccharose fermentation[28]. We thus have two features in which the respective strains differ. A propos of the stand taken by Durham and McConkey, Harrison[28] opens the question as to whether it is legitimate to name as a species, an organism differing only in the fermenting of one sugar.

It would therefore seem legitimate, on the ground of present day classification, to tentatively characterize the organism I have isolated-a non-motile, lactose, saccharose, dulcite positive, Voges-Proskauer negative strain,—as a variety of the sub-type *B. neapolitanus* of the classic *B. coli* type of Escherich. To use *B. neapolitanus* conflicts with the nomenclature *B. communior* more usually accepted for the strains giving identical reactions. If motility is considered, *B. neapolitanus* and *B. communior* are not strictly the same; but to use the single characteristic, absence or presence of motility, to separate *B. communior* and *B. neapolitanus*, and at the same time to say that a non-motile form of colon is identical with a motile form may seem inconsistent.

The difficulty can be overcome by the tentative classification of the organism I have isolated as a non-motile strain of the sub-type *B. communior* (Durham) of the type *B. coli* (Escherich); or to take the differentation further, as *B. neapolitanus*, a sub-type of *B. coli* (Escherich).

Culture II.

Morphology.—Microscopically—24-hours-old agar culture at 37°C.—rods varying up to 1·6 μ long and ·8 μ broad; some not much longer than broad; stains evenly with Kühne's methylene blue and is Gram negative. No spores; no capsules have been demonstrated.

8 GEORGE V, A. 1918

Motility.—Rapid movement, darting to and fro, many revolve as on an axis.

Cultural Characteristics:

Agar Slope.—24 hours at 37°C.—moderate, bluish by transmitted light, moist, glistening, slightly raised, later becoming by transmitted light yellowish in centre gradually merging into transparency.

Glucose Agar Slope.—Gas, growth moderate to luxuriant, glistening, slightly raised.

Tochtermann's Serum Agar Slope.—Moist, slightly raised, bluish by transmitted light, spreading discrete colonies, gas. In 8 days growth had become yellow, much water of condensation, heavy greyish-white precipitate at base of slope.

Löeffler's Blood Serum.—Moderate, filiform, moist, glistening, no liquefaction, no discolouration. In 7 days no digestion, no discolouration.

Sodium Sulphate Agar Slope.—Raised, spreading. moist, no reduction. In 8 days no reduction.

Gelatine Stab.—21°C., 24 hours, growth filiform, equal surface and stab; 7 days, tendency to echinulate. In 6 weeks no liquefaction, growth yellowish-brówn; characteristic lateral growths resembling a poplar tree against the horizon; medium unchanged.

Nutrient Broth.—37°C. 24 hours. Clouding abundant, no pellicle, no sediment, bluish rim at top. In 1 week, slight sediment; otherwise no change.

Potato.—Moderate, flat, yellowish-white along track of needle.

Milk.—In 6 weeks no change.

Litmus Milk.—Varies from no change to a tint slightly more alkaline than control; blue rim at·top.

Aesculin Agar.—Black reaction, growth less luxuriant than in Culture I.

Neutral Red Bilesalt Agar. Moderate, pink reaction.

Peptone Broth + Aesculin.—Black reaction.

Gelatine Colonies.—5 days at 21°C.—colonies up to 5 mm. diameter; under low power objective granular; edges lobular to contoured, centre dark with paling towards edges. Deep surface colonies granular centre with dark concentric rings.

Agar Colonies.—24 hours at 37°C.—surface 1 mm. diameter, raised, concave, bluish by transmitted light, round, smooth, edges entire. Under low power objective granular, edges entire.

Temperature Relations:—

Thermal death point: 10 minutes exposure in nutrient broth at 55°C.

Optimum temperature: 37°C.; cultures incubated at 37°C., 21°C. and 14°C. respectively.

Vitality on Culture Media:—

Active cultures have been recovered from agar tubes after 5 months at temperature of 15°-20°C.

Relation to Oxygen:—

Facultative anaerobe; glucose agar.

Biochemical reactions:—

Indol production: Indol not produced.
Reduction of nitrates: Nitrates reduced to nitrites.
Voges-Proskauer reaction: Positive, after 6 hours.
Methyl red reaction: Faint acidity, shortly followed by reversion to alkalinity.

SESSIONAL PAPER No. 38a

Fermentation of Carbohydrates:—

Glucose. Lactose. Saccharose. Raffinose. Maltose.

++ ⸱± − ++ − − ++

Mannite. Dulcite. Adonit. Salicin. Dextrine. Inulin.

++ − − − − ++ ++ − −

Xylose. Glycerine.

++ ++ (slowly).

+ = acid.

++ = acid·and gas.

NOTE.—The fermentation of lactose to acid is faint, and in two days reduction is noted.

The classification of this culture must be purely tentative. It will be seen that while saccharose, maltose, mannite, salicin and dextrin are fermented to acid and gas, the organism fails to ferment lactose to gas and only faintly to acid. This has persistently been the case through several months; on one occasion, however, a small bubble of gas—1 mm. diameter—appeared in a Durham tube. This I have been unable to obtain since, confirming in triplicate. MacConkey states: "It has been my experience that where an organism produces acid and gas in one medium and apparently only acid in another, under proper subcultivation the organism will produce gas in the second medium."[17] Harrison in this laboratory has frequently cited to me verbally his own experience in this matter, which bears out the statement of MacConkey. While the organism is definitely motile it differs from *B. cloacae* of Jordan[29] in that it fails after three months to liquefy gelatine, fails to ferment lactose to gas, and fails to coagulate milk after several weeks. Rogers Clarke and Evans[30] found that the group of the types they isolated from grains—Group B—fermented to acid and gas glucose, saccharose, mannite, glycerine and adonit, but like my culture failed to ferment lactose; on the other hand this group liquefied gelatine.[30] These workers consider that such group has at best only a slight connection with the *colon-ærogenes* group. Taking the classification adopted by the American Public Health Association[1] the culture would be ruled out of the *colon-ærogenes* group at once on account of its failure to produce gas from lactose; further, milk is not coagulated. Certain of the biochemical reactions would tend to suggest the *Gaertner* group. According to Besson[31] the organisms of this group are negative to lactose, saccharose, salicin, raffinose and inulin; while those carbohydrates to which the group is positive include dulcite. This organism, it will be noted, is negative to dulcite, lactose and inulin but positive to saccharose and salicin. Jordan[32] in a study of 74 strains of the *Gaertner* group cites that the reaction to dulcite and xylose is variable, but includes dextrine among the fermentable substances not attacked; thus establishing at once a similarity and a variation respectively as compared with the organism here described. In the same paper Jordan describes strains where reaction to litmus milk cannot be differentiated from the control. Savage[33] in a classification of the *Gaertner* group divides such into two sub-groups:—

a. *True-Gaertner bacilli;*

b. *Para-Gaertner bacilli;*

to which he had previously drawn attention in reports to the Local Government Board, 1906-7-8. Citing from Savage: "The bacilli of the para-Gaertner sub-group are a number of organisms, for the most part unnamed, which appear to be not very uncommon in the healthy animal and human intestine, and which are of chief interest from their close resemblance to *true-Gaertner* bacilli. . . . They can only be culturally differentiated from the *true-Gaertner* organisms by an extended series of fermentation tests while they fail to be agglutinited by immunizing animals with

8 GEORGE V, A. 1918

any of the members of the *true-Gaertner* sub-group. They are also for the most part non-pathogenic. They have not so far been found as a cause of disease in man or in animals."

Until I am able to secure for comparative cultural tests strains of this sub-group from Dr. Savage, it would not be wise to attempt a more definite classification of the organism herein discussed. In view, however, of the decided variation from the Voges-Proskauer type of the *colon-ærogenes* group as lately given by Levine,[29] and considering the many cultural features and fermentative reactions which suggest at any rate a distant relationship to the *para-Gaertner* group, it seems not undesirable to suggest that based on the cultural features and biochemical reactions this organism be considered tentatively as an atypical form of the *para-Gaertner* group according to Savage.[33]

Culture III.

Morphology.—Microscopically the organism appears as a coccus, in pairs, in masses, and as short streptococci; the average diameter from a 24-hour-old agar culture at 37° C. being ·8 μ, stained with Kühne's methylene blue. The organism is Gram positive and non-spore-forming; capsules faintly discernible.

Motility.—Tests for motility made in hanging drop of condensation water from a young agar culture. No motility. Violent agitation can be noticed, and rotation of the cells as on an axis, but the position in the drop is unchanged.

Cultural Characteristics:—

Agar Slope.—24 hours at 37° C. growth scanty, bluish by transmitted light, filiform, flat, with later a tendency to spreading.

Glucose Agar Slope.—Growth moderate, heavier than on agar, discrete colonies, flat, spreading, glistening.

Tochtermann's Serum Agar Slope.—Growth scant to moderate, bluish by transmitted light, heavy clouding of the condensation water. In 5 days slight digestion of the medium noted.

Löeffler's Blood Serum.—Growth filiform, medium channelled and slightly darker in colour. In 5 days growth glistening, yellowish, slight digestion.

Sodium Indigo Sulphate Agar Slope.—Faint growth, no reduction of colour, 24 hours. In 14 days reduced to reddish brown.

Gelatine Stab.—21° C. In two days liquefaction beginning. In 7 days stratiform liquefaction for ⅔ of tube, even clouding with yellowish flocculent precipitate at bottom. Liquefaction complete in 1 month.

Nutrient Broth.—37° C. even clouding, moderate, no pellicle, no sediment; later medium cleared.

Potato.—Barely discernible growth in 24 hours. In 3 days faint growth, flat, spreading, white, metallic lustre.

Milk.—37° C. In 36 hours weak coagulum, no gas noted. In 72 hours digestion had begun, a clear lemon coloured liquid extending for ⅓ tube. In 7 days tube half fluid, curd soft, gelatinous, bright and of a solidity resembling macaroni; easily desintegrated on shaking; after 2 months some curd still remaining, lemon yellow in colour, consistency as before.

Litmus milk.—The reaction of the organism to this medium is unusual, and it is due to the sensitiveness here discovered that I have adopted the uniform percentage of litmus, noted on page 218. If litmus be added at the rate of 1½ per cent coagulation preceded by bleaching takes place within 36 to 48 hours. Digestion then begins and proceeds slightly more rapidly than in the milk, the contents of the tube varying in colour from a lemon yellow to claret with decided fluorescence in 72 hours. In 2 months digestion is not complete, 1-2 cm. of a jelly-like claret coloured curd remaining.

If the quantity of litmus added be more than $1\frac{1}{2}$ per cent the reaction is quite different, varying according to the percentage of litmus added. There may or may not be coagulation, the colour varying from isabella to a muddy purpureus; flakes of tinted curd can later be noted. In 2 months a condition resembling broken jelly of a variety of shades of purpureus has been recorded. A note referring to this phenomenon in greater detail is being published elsewhere.

Aesculin agar.—Growth moderate, flat, dry, brown to black.

Neutral Red Bile Salt Agar.—Growth scant, no characteristic colour reaction.

Peptone Broth Aesculin.—Black in 12 hours.

Gelatine Colonies—(1st appearance).—21°C. 4 days, punctiform to pinhead colonies, depression in medium commencing; under the low power objective structure compact, finely granular, paler towards the edges; edges ciliate.

Agar Colonies.—37° C. growth slow. 24 hours colonies ·5 mm. in diameter, growth tends to be subsurface. Under the low power objective colonies round or eliptical, edges entire to undulate, internal structure granular, dark halo in surrounding medium.

Temperature Relations.—

Thermal death point. 10 minutes' exposure in nutrient broth at 60°C.

Optimum temperature. 37°C.; cultures incubated at 37°C., 21°C. and 14°C. respectively.

Vitality of Culture Media:—

Active cultures have been recovered from agar tubes after 5 months at temperature of 15°-20°C.

Relation to Oxygen.

Facultative anaerobe. Under anærobic condition on glucose agar, growth visible in 24 hrs. at 37°C.

Biochemical Reactions:—

Indol production: no indol in 7 days.
Reduction of nitrates: no reduction to nitrites.
Voges-Proskauer reaction: negative.
Methyl red reaction: acid to methyl red.

Fermentation of Carbohydrates:—

Glucose.	Lactose.	Saccharose.	Maltose.	Mannite.	Dulcite.
+	+	+	+	+	– –
Dextrin.	Salicin.	Raffinose.	Adonite.	Inulin.	Xylose.
+	+	– –	– –	– –	– –
Glycerine.					
– –					

+ = acid.
++ = acid and gas.

In accordance with the cultural results this organism is properly included among the liquefying streptococci. Winslow [34] takes the *Str. gracilis* of Escherich, Lehmann and Neumann as the "type centre" of these liquefiers. He considers that the various streptococci which peptonise gelatine more or less actively are variants of this type; intermediate between it and some of those characterized by Andrews and Horder [35].

I find, however, a closer resemblance to an organism described by MacCallum and Hastings[36] as *Micrococcus zymogenes*. This was isolated from a fatal case of acute endocarditis, and while it shows the same main characteristics as *Str. gracilis*, it

8 GEORGE V, A. 1918

liquefies serum slightly and subsequent to coagulating milk digests the clot. This organism was later found by Birge.[37] It is in the two last characteristics that I find the close resemblance to *M. zymogenes* noted above. The original description of *Str. gracilis* of Escherich cited by Winslow [34] includes non-liquefaction of blood serum and failure to coagulate milk; but summing up the variations Winslow provisionally defines his "type centre" *Str. gracilis* as follows: Small coccus, appearing in chains, ferments lactose and coagulates milk, may ferment mannite and salicin, liquefies gelatine actively.

While the organism I have described appears to have certain particular characteristics, I hesitate to depart from Winslow's view regarding the relationship of the variants in his tentative group of streptococcus liquefiers [34]. I conclude therefore that this organism which culturally and biochemically is identical with the *M. zymogenes* of MacCallum and Hastings [36] should be placed as a variety of the type *Str. gracilis*.

SUMMARY AND CONCLUSIONS.

1. Three strains of bacteria have been isolated from the destroyed tissue of copepods which had died in culture flasks.

2. Summarized, the biological features are as follows:—

—	I. Rod-form.	II. Rod-form.	III. Coccus.
Gram's Stain	−	−	+
Spores	−	−	
Capsule	−	−	+
Motility	−	+	−
Agar	Luxuriant	Moderate	Scant.
Gelatine	No liquef.	No liquef.	Liquef.
Potato	Abundant	Moderate	Scant.
Löeffler's Blood Serum	No digestion	No digestion	Slight digest.
Milk	Coagulag.	No change	Coag. and digest
Thermal death pt	60°C.	55°C.	60°C.
Optimum temperature	37°C.	37°C.	37°C.

3. Summarized, the biochemical reactions are:—

—	I.	II.	III.
Indol	+	−	−
Nitrate reduction	+	+	−
Voges-Proskauer	−	+	−
Methyl Red	Acid.	Faintly acid, later alkal.	Acid.
Glucose	++	++	+
Lactose	+−	±−	+
Saccharose	++	++	+
Raffinose	++	−−	−−
Maltose	++	++	+
Mannite	++	++	+
Lulcite	++	−−	−−
Adonite	++	−−	−−
Salicin	++	++	+
Dextrine	++	++	+
Inulin	+	−−	−−
Xylose	++	++	−−
Glycerine	++	++	−−

+ = acid.　++ = acid and gas.

SESSIONAL PAPER No. 38a

4. Based on their cultural features and biochemical reactions the organisms are classified as follows:—

Culture I.—Tentatively as a non-motile strain of the sub-type *B. communior* (Durham) of the type *B. coli* (Escherich); or to take the differentiation further, as *B. neapolitanus,* a sub-type of *B. coli* (Escherich).

Culture II.—Considered tentatively as an atypical form of the *Para-Gaertner* group after Savage.

Culture III.—Identical with *M. zymogenes* and placed as a variety of the type of liquefying streptococci, *Streptococcus gracilis.*

5. No inoculations of these cultures have been made into healthy copepods owing to distance from the sea.

6. It is not legitimate to draw any definite conclusions regarding the relationship of these organisms to the destruction of the copepods, as no inoculation experiments have been carried out, and the postulates of Koch have not yet been satisfied. According to the descriptions presented, however, the evidence is strong in favour of Culture III being a possible causal agent.

I wish to thank very cordially Dr. F. C. Harrison for his kindness in reading the proofs, and particularly for his valuable and critical assistance with regard to the classification of the *B. coli* group; and Dr. Arthur Willey for the initial suggestion that I should undertake the investigation.

REFERENCES.

1. American Public Health Association, 1915—" Standard Methods Water Analysis," 77-137.

2. Besson, 1913—" Text Book Practical Bact., etc.," (Longmans), 53.

3. Besson, 1913—" Text Book Practical Bact., etc.," (Longmans), 52.

4. Harrison and Vanderleck, 1908—" Aesculin Bile Salt Agar for Water and Milk Analysis," Trans. Roy. Soc. Can. III. Ser. II, 105-110.

5. Savage, 1906—" Bacteriological Examination of Water Supplies," London, 221.

6. Voges and Proskauer, 1898—" Zeit. fur Hyg." 28, 20.

6. Harden, 1905, 1906—" On the Voges-Proskauer Reaction for Certain Bacteria," Proc. Roy. Soc., 77, 424.

6. Levine, Max., 1916—" The Significance of the Voges-Proskauer Reaction," Jour. Bacteriology I, 153-164.

6. Clark and Lubs, 1915—" Differentiation of Bacteria of the Colon-Aerogenes Family by Indicators." Jour. Infectious Diseases, 17, 160-173.

6. Levine—" Correlation of the Voges-Proskauer and Methyl-red Reactions on the Colon-Aerogenes group." Jour. Infec. Diseases, 18, 358-367.

6. Levine—Private Communication.

7. Clarke and Lubs, 1915—" Differentiation of Bacteria of the Colon-Aerogenes Group." Jour. Infectious Diseases, 17, 160-173.

8. Bohme, 1905—Centrall. fur Bakt, Abt. I, Orig. XL, 129-133.

9. MacConkey, 1909—Journal of Hygiene, 9, p. 91.

9. Hollman, 1914—" Decolorized Acid Fuchsin as an Acid Indicator in Carbohydrate Fermentations." Journ. Infec. Dis., 15, 227-233.

10. Escherich, 1886—"Darmbak. des Sauglings, Stuttgart."

11. Migula 1886—"System der Bakt," 396.

12. Escherich and Pfaundler. 1903—"Handbuch d. Path. Mikroorg," Kolle and Wassermann. Zweiter Band, 341-342.

13. Sscherich and Pfaundler, 1903—"Handbuch d. Path. Mikroorg," Kolle and Wassermann. Zweiter Band, 406.

15. Houston, 1905—"Bacteriological Examination of Milk." Special Report, London County Council, 37.

16. Durham, Journ. Exp. Med., V., 354-388.

17. MacConkey, 1909—"Lactose Fermenting Bacilli." Journ. Hygiene, 9, 88.

18. Ellis, 1904—"Discovery of Cilia in the genus Bacterium." Centrl. fur Bakt. II, 241-251.

19. 1904—"Report of the English Commission." Jour. State Med. XII, 471.

20. 1913—Prescott and Winslow. "Elements of Water Bacteriology," Wiley, 104.

21. Savage, 1906—"Bacteriological Examination of Water." Lewis, 82-83.

22. Migula, 1900—"System der Bakterien," 734.

23. Emmerich, 1885—"Untersuch. ub. die Pilze d. Cholera asiastica." Arch. fur Hyg., Bd. 3.

Macé (full description) 1891—"Traite Pratique de Bacteriologie." Paris, 498.

24. Jackson, 1911—"Classification of the B. coli Group." Journ. Infec. Dis., 8, 241.

25. Jordan, 1916—"General Bacteriology." Saunders Co., 275.

25a. Loq. cit., 273.

26. Levine, 1916—"Preliminary Note, Classification of the Lactose Fermenting Bacteria." Journ. Bacteriology, I., 619-621.

27. MacConkey, 1905.—"Lactose fermenting Bacteria in Faeces." Journ. Hyg. 5, 333-379.

28. Harrison, 1917—Private communication.

29. Jordan, 1890—"Report Mass. State Board of Health." 836.

30. Rogers Clarke & Evans, 1915—"Charact. of Bacteria of Colon type occurring on Grains." Journ. Infec. Dis., 117, 137-159.

31. Besson, 1913—"Text Book Practical Bacteriology, etc." Longmans, 442.

32. Jordan, 1917—"Differentiation of the Paratyphoid-Enteritides Group." Journ. Infect. Diseases, 20, 456.

33. Savage, 1913—"Bacterial Food Poisoning and Food Infection." Med. Off. Report, Local Govt. Board, 1913. Food Reports, No. 18, 33.

34. Winslow. C.-E. A. and A. R., 1908—"The Systematic Relationship of the Coccaceae." Wiley, New York, 161, 169, 170.

35. Andrews & Horder, 1906—"A Study of the Streptococci pathogenic for Man." Lancet, II., 708.

36. MacCallum, W. G. & Hastings, T. W., 1899—"A case of Acute Endocarditis caused by M. Zymogenes." Journ. Exp. Med. IV., 521.

37. Birge, 1905.

37. Birge, 1905—"Some Observations on the Occurrence of M. Zymogenes." Johns Hopkins Hosp. Bull. XVI., 309.

38. Escherich Migula, 1900—"System der Bakterien," 31.

XIV

BATHYMETRIC CHECK LIST OF THE MARINE INVERTEBRATES OF EASTERN CANADA WITH AN INDEX TO WHITEAVES' CATALOGUE.[1]

(By E. M. KINDLE and E. J. WHITTAKER.)

INTRODUCTORY NOTE.

The primary object of this paper is to bring together in columnar form all of the available information relating to the depth at which the various species of marine invertebrates live which are known from the Atlantic coastal waters of Canada. The value of the segregation and graphic presentation of any group of facts relating to invertebrate environment is obvious from the standpoint of ecology. The significance of many factors in the environment of faunas becomes clearly apparent only when treated in this way. There is no factor in marine faunal environment which more readily lends itself to this kind of analysis than bathymetric data. Such data though nearly always given by marine Zoologists are generally placed obscurely in the midst of extraneous matter and almost never shown in tabular or easily comprehensible form.

Bathymetric range of fossil faunas is a factor which enters into many problems in palæontological correlation and it is very desirable that the palæontologist as well as the zoologist should have access to the recorded bathymetric data in tabular form relating to present marine faunas. There perhaps is no group of facts pertaining to recent faunas of greater significance to stratigraphic palæontologists than those relating to the bathymetric range of species. The geologic importance of knowing the present range in depth of the marine shells now living in the Gulf of St. Lawrence is clearly apparent to the geologist who attempts to use the fossil Pleistocene shells of the St. Lawrence valley in interpreting the details of its Post-glacial history. The geological and zoological importance of this class of data has induced the authors to bring together in columnar form the recorded information regarding the bathymetric range of species as recorded by Dr. Whiteaves together with the data published by later authors. In order to facilitate rapid comparative examination of the bathymetric data it has been recorded in columnar form, five columns being used. The first three of these columns correspond respectively to the intertidal or beach, the laminarian and the coralline zones. The intertidal zone extends between low and high tides; the laminarian zone reaches from low-water mark to 15 fathoms; the fourth column includes depths of from 50 to 100 fathoms which may be termed the subcoralline zone. The 100 fathom line marks the approximate margin of the continental shelf. All of the records exceeding this depth have for convenience been placed together in a single column.

The bathymetric check list has been brought up to date by the examination of the papers on the marine invertebrates of Eastern Canada which have appeared since the publication of Dr. Whiteaves' paper. Where these later contributions have furnished new bathymetric information its source is indicated by a number following the species name which refers to the bibliographic list at the end of this paper.

The authors have also undertaken in the following pages to make more easily accessible and usable the large amount of information on the marine faunas of Eastern Canada contained in Dr. Whiteaves' Catalogue of the Marine invertebrata of Eastern Canada[2] by the preparation of an index to it. Many zoologists have doubt-

---

[1] Published with the permission of the Director of the Canadian Geological Survey.
[2] Geol. Survey of Canada, 1901.

8 GEORGE V, A. 1918

less, like Professor Prince, felt that the usefulness of this catalogue "would be vastly increased by the addition of an index."[1] The importance of this volume to the zoologist is evident and its interest to the geologist dealing with the Pleistocene is almost equally great. The student of the Pleistocene fossils of eastern Canada and the New England States finds it desirable to refer constantly to this valuable work. The omission from it of an index however, has made such reference difficult and wasteful of time and caused the student of both the Pleistocene and Recent shells to make much less use of the catalogue than its value warrants. The present index to the species of this catalogue, which number more than 1,000, is intended to remove this bar to frequent and easy reference to the wealth of information concerning the Atlantic coast faunas of Canada which was brought together by Dr. Whiteaves.

In a paper having the object and scope of the present one, it does not appear desirable to attempt any revision of the nomenclature. The nomenclature adopted by Whiteaves has therefore been followed throughout and where later authors have used names different from those accepted by Whiteaves for the same forms cross references to the latter have been used. All of the names which appear in the synonymy of the Whiteaves' catalogue will be found in the general index.

BATHYMETRIC TABLES.[2]

	Min. and Max. Depth.	Inter-tidal Zone.	Fathoms.			
			1–15	15–50	50–100	100 †
PROTOZOA.						
Reticularia (Foraminifera).						
Ammodiscus incertus, d'Orbigny						
Biloculina oblonga Montfort	D.W.					x
Biloculina ringens Lamarck 35	6–313		x	x	x	x
Bolivina punctata d'Orbigny 35	I.T.–S.W.	x	x			
Bulimina aculeata d'Orbigny	D.W.					x
Bulimina elegantissima d'Orbigny	18–D.W.			x	x	x
Bulimina pyrula d'Orbigny	7–250		x	x	x	x
Cassidulina crassa d'Orbigny	30–D.W.			x	x	x
Cassidulina laevigata d'Orbigny	10–D.W.		x	x	x	x
Cornuspira foliaceus Philippi	18–250			x	· x	x
Cristellaria crepidula F. and M.						
Cristellaria lituus d'Orbigny						
Cristellaria rotulata Lamarck						x
Globigerina aequilateralis ? 11	F.					
Haplophragmium canariense d'Orbigny 35	5½–200		x	x	x	x
Haplophragmium cassis Parker	10–20		x	x		
Hippocrepina indivisa Parker	16–20			x		
Lagena apiculata Reuss	100+					x
Lagena distoma P. and J.	10–313		x	x	x	x
Lagena globosa W. and J.	16–313			x	x	x
Lagena laevis Montagu	250					x
Lagena marginata W. and B.	30			x		
Lagena melo d'Orbigny	100+					x

[2]NOTE.—The Maximum and minimum depth recorded for each species is indicated in the first column. The bathymetric range is also indicated graphically by checking each species in each of the columns in which its range falls, thus facilitating rapid comparative examination of the recorded data. Sometimes the information regarding bathymetric range is of an approximate or comparative nature and in such cases some one of the following symbols has been used for expressing range not recorded in linear units.

o—Low water mark.	S.W.—Shallow water.
D.W.—Deep water.	<3—Depths less than 3 fathoms.
F.—Free swimming.	>100—depths greater than 100 fathoms.
I.T.—Intertidal.	10—Depth in fathoms.
P.—Parasitic.	

[1] Ottawa Naturalist, vol. 15, 1912, p. 171.

BATHYMETRIC TABLES—*Continued*.

			BATHYMETRIC RANGE.			
	Min. and Max. Depth.	Inter-tidal. Zone.		Fathoms.		
			1–15	15–50	50–100	100 †

PROTOZOA—*Con.*

Reticularia (Foraminifera)—Con.

Lagena ornata Willdenow	30–100 ?			x	x ?	x ?
Lagena semistriata Willimason	30–100 ?			x	x ?	x ?
Lagena squamosa Montagu	30			x·		
Lagena striatopunctata P. and J.	30			x		
Lagena sulcata P. and J	16–50			x		
Miliolina agglutinans d'Orbigny	10–50		x	x		
Miliolina bicornis W. and J. 35	2–50		x	x		
Miliolina ferussacii d'Orbigny	35–50			x		
Miliolina oblonga Montfort 35	2–50		x	x		
Miliolina secans d'Orbigny	<50			x		
Miliolina seminulum L. 35	2–313		x	x	x	x
Miliolina subrotunda Montfort	<50			x		
Miliolina tricarinata d'Orbigny	18–50			x		
Miliolina trigonula d'Orbigny	<50					
Nodosaria (Dentalina) communis d'Orbigny	30–50			x		
Nodosaria (Glandulina) laevigata d'Orbigny	30–313			x	x	x
Nodosaria (Dentalina) pauperata d'Orbigny	313					x
Nonionina scapha F. and M.	35–D.W. ?			x	x ?	
Nonionina labradorica	15–100			x	x	x
Patellina corrugata Williamson 35	I.T.–40	x	x	x		
Polymorphina compressa d'Orbigny	10–50		x	x		
Polymorphina lactea W. and J. 35	2–313		x	x	x	x
Polystomella arctica P. and J	30–50			x		
Polystomella striatopunctata F. and M. 35	2–300		x	x	x	x
Pulvinulina karsteni Reuss	30–250			x	x	x
Reophax findens Parker	10–50		x	x		
Reophax scorpiurus Montfort	16–20			x		
Rhabdammina abyssorum M. Sars	20–D.W.			x	x	x
Rhabdammina discreta Brady						
Rotalia beccarii Linnaeus 35	2–313		x	x	x	x
Spiroplecta biformis P. and J						
Textularia agglutinans d'Orbigny						
Textularia variabilis Willdenow				x	x·	
Trochammina inflata Montfort	10–40		x	x		
Truncatulina lobatula W. and J. 35	4–D.W.		x	x	x	x ?
Uvigerina angulosa Willdenow	D.W.			x	x	
Uvigerina pygmaea d'Orbigny	30–90			x	x	
Vaginulina spinigera Brady	D.W.				x	x
Valvulina conica P. and J	D.W.				x	x
Verneuilina polystropha Reuss 35	10–20		x	x		
Virgulina squamosa d'Orbigny						

Silicoflagellata, Radiolaria and Ciliata.

Acanthonia echinoides (Clap. & Lach) 11	F					
Acanthostaurus pallidus F	F					
Amphorella subulata (Ehrb) Daday 11						
Codonella ventricosa 11						
Codonella lagenula (Clap & Lach) 11						
Cyttarocyclis denticulata var. gigantea Brandt. 11						
Distephanus aculeatus (Ehrenberg)	S.W.–313		x	x	x	x
Distephanus speculum var. regularis Lemmermann 11						
Ebria tripatrtita (Schum) Lemmermann 11						
Plagiacanthus arachnoides Clap. 11	F.					
Ptychocyclis urnula Clap. & Lach. 11						
Strombidium sulcatum C. & L. 11						
Tintinnopsis beroidea Stein 11						
Tintinnopsis campanula Ehrb. Daday 11						
Tintinnopsis davidow Daday 11						
Tintinnopsis cylindrica 11						
Tintinnopsis lobiancoi 11						
Tintinnus acuminatus (C. & L.)11						
Tintinnus obliquus (C. & L.) 11						

8 GEORGE V, A. 1918

BATHYMETRIC TABLES—*Continued.*

			BATHYMETRIC RANGE.			
	Min. and Max. Depth.	Inter-tidal. Zone.	Fathoms.			
			1–15	15–50	50–100	100 †
PORIFERA (SPONGES).						
Calcarea.						
Amphoriscus thompsoni Lambe...	60....				x	
Grantia canadensis Lambe...	22–56..			x	x	
Heteropia rodgeri Lambe...	60....				x	
Leucosolenia cancellata Verrill...	60....				x	
Sycon asperum Lambe...	56....				x	
Sycon protectum Lambe...	56–60....				x	
Demospongiae.						
Artemisina suberitoides Vosmaer...	85....				x	
Chalina oculata (Pallas)...						
Cladorhiza abyssicola M. Sars...	200....					x
Cladorhiza grandis Verrill...	D.W....					x
Cladorhiza nordenskioldii Fristedt...	200....					x
Clathria delicata Lambe...	3–6 ?..		x			
Cliona celata Grant 35......	2–19....		x	x		
Craniella cranium (Muller)...	20–30...			x		
Desmacella peachii (Bowerbank) var. groenlandica Fristedt...	130–200...					x
Desmacidon (Homaeodictya(palmata (Johnston) 35, 47...	11–20..		x	x		
Esperella lingua (Bowerbank)...	75–80...				x	
Esperella modesta Lambe...						
Eumastia sitiens O. Schmidt...	22....			x		
Gellius arcoferus Vosmaer...	75–80...				x	
Gellius flagellifer Ridley & Dendy...	38–80...			x	x	
Gellius laurentinus Lambe...	60–130...				x	x
Halichondria panicea Johnston 35...	6–22....		x	x		
Iophon chelifer Ridley & Dendy...	100....				x	
Myxilla incrustans (Johnston)...						
Phakellia ventilabrum (Johnston)...	56....				x	
Polymastia mamillaris (Muller)...	120–210..					x
Polymastia robusta Bowerbank 35...	17–85...			x	x	
Quasillina brevis (Bowerbank)...	85....				x	
Reniera mollis Lambe...	30–60...			x	x	
Reniera rufescens Lambe...						
Stylocordyla borealis (Loven)...	85–220...				x	x
Suberites ficus (Johnston)...	1–6 ?..		x			
Suberites hispidus (Bowerbank)...	212....					x
Suberites montalbidus Carter...	20–30....			x		
Tentorium semisuberites (Schmidt)...	50–250....				x	x
Thenea muricata (Bowerbank)...	220–250...					x
Trichostemma hemisphaericum M. Sars...	112....					x
COELENTERATA.						
Hydromedusæ and Scyphomeduse.			x			
Acaulis priuarius Stimpson...	5–15....		x			
Aeginopsis laurenti Brandt 16...			x			
Aglantha rosea Forbes 16...	25 F....		x			
Aglaophenopsis cornuta (Verrill)...	200....		x			x
Antennularia antennina (L)...	10–60...			x	x	
Aurelia flavidula Peron & Lesueur...	F.					
Bouganvillia superciliaris (L. Agassiz) 16, 35...	25....			x		
Bouganvillia carolinensis (McCrady) 31...	I.T.					
Calycella syringa (L) 16, 35...	25–313....			x	x	x
Campanularia amphora (Agassiz) 16, 35, 43...	I.T.–S.W.	x	x			
Campanularia caliculata Hincks = Eucopella cali-culata (Hincks) 31 = Oxopyxis caliculata 43...	o–100...		x	x	x	
Campanularia flexuosa Hincks 43...	I.T.–10...	x	x			
Campanularia groenlandica Levinsen 31,43...	I–50....		x	x		

BATHYMETRIC TABLES—*Continued.*

	Min. and Max. Depth.	Inter-tidal Zone.	1–15	15–50	50–100	100
			BATHYMETRIC RANGE.			
			Fathoms.			
COELENTERATA—*Con.*						
Hydromedusæ—Con.						
Campanularia hincksii Alder 35, 43	o–144		x	x	x	x
Campanularia integra Linnaeus 43	I–100		x	x	x	
Campanularia magnifica Fraser 31, 43	50–72				x	
Campanularia neglecta (Alder) 31, 35,.43	I.T.–16	x	x	x		x
Campanularia verticillata (L) 43	I–330		x	x	x	x
Campanularia volubilis (Pallas) 24	o–110		x	x	x	x
Catablema vesicaria (A. Agassiz) 16						
Cladocarpus pourtalesii Verrill	112–300					x
Cladocarpus speciosus Verrill	200					x
Clava leptostyla Agassiz 31, 35	I.T.–20	x	x	x		
Clytia johnstoni (Alder) 31, 43	o–110		x	x	x	x
Clytia noliformis McCready 43	I–110		x	x	x	x
Cryptolaria triserialis Fraser 31	20			x		
Cuspidella grandis Hincks	15		x			
Cyanea arctica Peron & Lesueur 16						
Dicoryne flexuosa G. O. Sars	50–125				x	x
Diphasia fallax (Johnston) 31	4–55		x	x	x	
Diphasia mirabilis Verrill = Selaginopsis mirabilis Verrill 31	50–60				x	
Diphasia rosacea (L) 31	5–50		x	x		
Diphyopsis campanulifera (Eschscholtz) 16, 35						
Eudendrium capillare Alder 35	45			x		
Eudendrium cingulatum Stimpson	20			x		
Eudendrium dispar Agassiz 31	1–20		x	x		
Eudendrium rameum (Pallas) 35	100				x	
Eudendrium ramosum (L) 31	6–100		x	x	x	
Eudendrium tenue Agassiz 31, 35	I.T.–15	x	x	x		
Filellum expansum Levinsen 31	5		x			
Filellum serpens (Hassall) 31	50			x		
Gonothyraea gracilis (Sars) 31, 43	1–110		x	x	x	x
Gonothyraea loveni (Allman) 31, 35, 43	1–55		x	x	x	
Grammaria abietina M. Sars 31	25–60			x	x	
Grammaria gracilis Stimpson						
Halecium beani (Johnston) 31, 35	5–50		x	x		
Halecium halecinum (L) 35	3–30		x	x		
Halecium minutum Brock 31	50			x		
Halecium muricatum (Ellis & Solander) 31	30–50			x		
Halecium sessile Norman	212					x
Halecium tenellum Hincks 31, 35	50			x		
Halyclystus auricula Clark 16	o–5		x			
Hydractinia echinata Johnston 31, 35, 47	I.T.–60	x	x	x	x	
Hydrallmania falcata (L) 31	o–110		x	x	x	x
Lafoea dumosa (Fleming) 31	20			x		
Lafoea fruticosa Sars 31	20			x		
Lafoea gracillima (Alder) 31	45–60			x	x	
Lafoea pygmaea Alder 31	25			x		
Lafoea robusta Verrill	120–200					x
Lafoea symmetrica Bonnevie 31	20			x		
Lucernaria quadricornis Muller	4–10		x			
Manania auricula Clark						
Ielicertum campanula Fabricius 16, 35	5		x			
Ionocaulus glacialis (M. Sars) 47 = Corymorpha pendula Agassiz 31	o–50		x	x		
Iyriothela phrygia (Fabricius)						
belia commissuralis McCready 31, 35, 43	I.T.–10	x	x			
belia dichotoma (L) 31, 35, 43	I.T.–10	x	x			
belia gelatinosa (Pallas) 35 = Obelaria gelatinosa 43	I.T.–30	x	x	x		
belia geniculata (L) 16, 31, 35, 43	o–40		x	x		
belia longissima (Pallas) 35, 43	I–80		x	x	x	
belia pyriformis Verrill 35	I.T.	x				
percularella lacerata (Johnston) 31	I.T.	x				
hialidium languidum (L. Agassiz) = Oceania languidum 35						

38a—16

BATHYMETRIC TABLES—*Continued.*

		BATHYMETRIC RANGE.				
	Min. and Max. Depth.	Inter-tidal. Zone.	Fathoms.			
			1–15	15–50	50–100	100 x
COELENTERATA—*Con.*						
Hydromedusæ—Con.						
Physalia pelagica Lamarck	F.					
Polycanna groenlandica (Peron & Lesueur)						
Ptychogastria polaris Allman 16	60.				x	
Ptychogena lactea A. Agassiz						
Sarsia princeps Haeckel 16	5.		x			
Sertularella conica Allman 31	50.			x		
Sertularia abietina (L.) = Abietinaria abietina 31, 35	51.				x	
Sertularia filicula Ellis & Solander	20			x		
Sertularia fusiformis Hincks	200.					x
Sertularia latiuscula Stimpson						
Sertularia polyzonias L. & var. gigantea Hincks = Sertularella polyzonias (Linn) 31, 35	10–60		x	x		
Sertularia producta Stimpson						
Sertularia pumila L. 31, 35	I.T.–12.	x	x			
Sertularia rugosa L.	30–D.W.			x	x	x
Sertularia tricuspidata Alder = Sertularella tricuspidata Alder 31	40–60			x	x	
Staurophora laciniata (L. Agassiz)16						
Syncoryne mirabilis (L. Agassiz) = Sarsia mirabilis (L. Agassiz) 16, 35	5.		x			
Thamnocnidia larynx (L) = Tubularia larynx 31, 35	5–25.		x	x		
Thamnocnidia tenella Agassiz = Tubularia tenella 31	o–40.		x	x		
Thecocarpus myriophyllum (L)	30–60.			x	x	
Thuiaria argentea (Ellis & Solander) 31, 35	o–110.		x	x	x	x
Thuiaria articulata (Pallas)	45.			x		
Thuiaria cupressina (L) 35	I.T.–100.	x	x	x	x	
Thuiara lonchitis Ellis & Solander 31	50.			x		
Thuiara thuja (L) 35	..					
Tiara pileata Forskal 16.						
Tiaropsis diademata (L. Agassiz) 35						
Trachyneme digitale (O. Fabricius)	15.		x			
Tubularia crocea (Agassiz) 31, 35	o–25.		x	x		
Tubularia indivisa (L)	45.			x		
Alcyonaria.						
Acanella normani Verrill	410.					x
Acanthogorgia armata Verrill	300.					x
Actinauge nexilis Verrill	200–300.					x
Actinauge verrillii McMurrich	30–300.			x	x	x
Actinernus nobilis Verrill	200–300.					x
Actinopsis whiteavesii Verrill	200.					x
Actinostola callosa Verrill	45–300.			x	x	x
Alcyonium carneum L. Agassiz 35	o–80.		x	x	x	
Alcyonium multiflorum Verrill	131–239.					x
Alcyonium rubiforme (Ehrenberg)						
Anthomastus grandiflorus Verrill	150–300.					x
Anthoptilum grandiflorum Verrill	1250.					x
Anthothela grandiflora (Sars)	D.W.					x
Balticina finmarchica (Sars)	60–100.				x	
Bolocera tuediae (Johnston)	50–100.				x	
Ceratoisis ornata Verrill	200–300.					x
Cerianthus borealis Verrill	28–200.			x	x	x
Chondractinia nodosa (Fabricius)						
Cornulariella modesta Verrill	80–220.				x	x
Cribrina stella (Verrill) 21	I.T.	x				
Desmophyllum nobile Verrill	300.					x
Edwardsia farinacea Verrill	8–90.		x	x	x	
Edwardsia sipunculoides Stimpson	0–4.		x			
Epigonactis fecunda Verrill	150–200.					x

BATHYMETRIC TABLES—*Continued.*

	Min. and Max. Depth.	Inter-tidal Zone.	Bathymetric Range. Fathoms.			
			1–15	15–50	50–100	100 x
Alcyonaria—Con.						
Epizoanthus incrustatus (Duben & Koren)........	30–300...	....	....	x	x	x
Epizoanthus paguriphilus Verrill...............	D.W.....	....	....	....	....	x
Eunepthya lutkeni (Marenzeller).................	52.......	....	....	....	x	
Flabellum angulare Moseley.....................	1250.	....	....	....	....	x
Flabellum goodei Verrill.......................	180–400...					x
Funiculina armata Verrill......	300–400...					x
Lophohelia oculifera Edwards & Haime......... ...	D.W....					x
Metridium dianthus (Ellis) 35=M. senile (Linn). 21.	o–90.....	....	x	x	x	
Paragorgia arborea (L).........	D.W....					x
Paramuricea borealis Verrill.....................	D.W....					x
Paramuricea grandis Verrill....	D.W....					x
Peachia parasitica Verrill....						
Pennatula aculeata Danielssen...................	60–300...				z	x
Pennatula (Ptilella) borealis (Sars)...............	120–350...					x
Primnoa reseda (Pallas).........................	100–200...					x
Sagartia acanella Verrill........	D.W....					
Stomphia carneola (Stimpson)=Stomphia coccinea	8–35....	....	x	x		
(O. F. Muller) Carlgren 21.................	10–12....	....	x			
Synanthus mirabilis Verrill....................	150–330...					x
Urticina crassicornis (Muller)=Urticina felina (L)						
Hadden 21......................	13–112....	....	x	x	x	x .
Virgularia lyungmani Kolliker...................	200.......	....	....	....	....	x
Ctenophora.						
Bolina alata Agassiz 36=Berœ cucumis Fabricius,						
16, 35................	F........					
Idyia roseola L. Agassiz......................	F........	....	....	x		
Mertensia ovum (Fabricius) 16, 35...............	F.–25.....	....	x			
Pleurobrachia rhododactyla L. Agassiz 16, 35.....	F.–5.....					
ECHINODERMATA.						
Crinoidea.						
Antedon eschrichtii (Muller).....................	25–100....				x	x
Antedon quadrata P. H. Carpenter.............	25–100....				x	x
Antedon tenella (Retzius)......................						
Holothurioidea.						
Caudina arenata Stimpson 6, 35..................	o–17½.....	....	x	x		
Chirodota laevis (O. Fabricius)...............	o–5.....	....	x			
Eupyrgus scaber Lutken 6.....................	2–262....	....	x	x	x	x
Lophothuria fabricii (Duben & Koren)............	I.T.–5....	x	x	x		
Myriotrochus rinkii Steenstrup..................	7–50....	....	x	x		
Orcula barthii Troschel.........................						
Pentacta calcigera Stimpson....................	8–25.....	....	x	x		
Pentacta frondosa (Jaeger)................	o–7.....	....	x			
Pentacta minuta (Fabricius)...................	25–101....	....	x	x	x	
Psolus phantapus (L).........................	o–40.....	....	x	x		
Thyone scabra Verrill........						
Thyonidium pellucidum (Fleming)...............						
Thyonidium productum (Ayres)...................	o–D.W....	....	x	x	x	x
Trochostoma ooliticum (Pourtales) = Molpadia						
oolitica Pourtales 6, 36.......	29........	....	....	....	x	
Trochostoma turgidum (Verrill).................						
Stelleroidea.						
Asterias enopla Verrill........	53–100...					x
Asterias forbesii (Desor) 35....................	2–19....	....	x	x		
Asterias polaris (Muller & Troschel)............	o–60.....	....	x	x	x	
Asterias stellionura Perrier....	82–100...				x	
Asterias vulgaris (Stimpson) Verrill 35, 47......	o–358....	....	x	x	x	x
Cribrella pectinata Verrill......................	20.......				x	

BATHYMETRIC TABLES—*Continued.*

—	Min. and Max. Depth.	Inter-tidal Zone.	Fathoms.			
			1–15	15–50	50–100	100 x

*Stelleroidea—*Con.						
Cribrella sanguinolenta (Muller) = Henricia sanguinolenta 35, 47	o–471		x	x	x	x
Crossaster papposus (O. Fabricius)	o–179		x	x	x	x
Ctenodiscus crispatus (Retzius)	5–632		x	x	x	x
Hippasteria phrygiana (Parelius)	20–224			x	x	x
Leptasterias groenlandica (Lutken)	5–100		x	x	x	
Leptasterias littoralis (Stimpson)	I.T.–23	x	x	x		
Leptasterias tenera (Stimpson)	10–40		x	x		
Leptoptychaster arcticus (M. Sars)	100				x	
Lophaster furcifer (Duben & Koren.)	234–640					x
Odinia americana Verrill	175–400					x
Pedicellaster typicus M. Sars	75–80				x	
Pontaster hebitus Sladen	85–250				x	x
Pseudarchaster intermedius var. insignis Verrill	100–1356					x
Psilaster florae Verrill	60–230				x	x
Pteraster militaris (Muller)	10–69		x	x	x	
Pteraster pulvillus M. Sars	20			x		
Solaster earlii Verrill	170–300					x
Solaster endeca (Retzius)	o–80		x	x	x	
Solaster syrtensis Verrill	101					x
Stichaster albulus (Stimpson)	o–100		x	x	x	
Tosia eximia Verrill	80–122				x	x
Tosia granularis (Retzius)	40			x		
Tremaster mirabilis Verrill	150–250					x
Ophiuroidea.						
Amphipholis elegans (Leach)	o–210		x	x	x	x
Amphiura canadensis Verrill						
Amphiura exigua Verrill						
Amphiura sundevalli (Muller & Troschel)	10–15		x			
Astronyx loveni Muller & Troschel	85				x	
Gorgonocephalus agassizii (Stimpson) 35	o–100		x	x	x	
Gorgonocephalus eucnemis (Muller & Troschel)	18–80			x	x	
Gorgonocephalus lamarckii (Muller & Troschel)	194–239					x
Ophiacantha anomala G. O. Sars	101–131					x
Ophiacantha bidentata (Retzius)	o–250		x	x	x	x
Ophiacantha granulifera Verrill	101–200					x
Ophiacantha spectabilis G. O. Sars	131					x
Ophiacantha varispina Verrill	101–200					x
Ophiactis asperula (Phillipi) 37						
Ophioglypha lymani Ljungman 37						
Ophioglypha nodosa (Lutken)	o–330		x	x	x	x
Ophioglypha robusta (Ayres)	o–220		x	x	x	x
Ophioglypha sarsii (Lutken) 37	10–250		x	x	x	x
Ophioglypha signata Verrill						
Ophioglypha stuwitzi (Lutken)						
Ophiolebes acanella Verrill	113–122					x
Ophiopholis aculeata (L)	o–100		x	x	x	
Ophioscolex glacialis Muller & Troschel	210					x
Echinoidea.						
Echinarachnius parma (Lamarck)	1–100		x	x	x	
Schizaster fragilis (Duben & Koren)	95–300				x	x
Strongylocentrotus drobachiensis Muller 35, 47	o–110		x	x	x	x
PLATYHELMINTHES.						
Turbellaria (Planarians.)						
Fovia affinis (Oersted)						
Leptoplana ellipsoides Girard	o–45		x	x		
Procerodes ulvae (Oersted) 35	I.T.	x				
Typhlocolax acutus (Girard)	o–5		x			

BATHYMETRIC TABLES—*Continued.*

	Min. and Max. Depth.	Inter-tidal. Zone.	BATHYMETRIC RANGE. Fathoms.			
			1–15	15–50	50–100	100 x
NEMERTEA.						
Enopla.						
Amphiporus agilis Verrill..........................	10–90....	....	x	x	x	
Amphiporus angulatus (Fabricius).................	o–150.....	....	x	x	x	x
Amphiporus heterosorus Verrill....................	10–200....	....	x	x	x	x
Amphiporus lactifloreus (Johnston)...............	o.......	....	x			
Amphiporus roseus (Muller)......................	o–112.....		x	x	x	x
Amphiporus (?) superbus (Girard)...............	35..	....	......	x		
Drepanophorus lankesteri Hubrecht...............	85.......	....	....	....	x	
Tetrastemma candidum (Fabricius?) M'Intosh....	I.T.–15..	x	x			
Tetrastemma serpentinum (Girard) Stimpson.....	I.T.......	x				
Tetrastemma vittatum Verrill.........,...........	o–25......	....	x	x		
Anopla.						
Cephalothrix linearis (Rathke)...................	I.T......	x				
Cerebratulus cylindricus Packard.............•...						
Cerebratulus fuscus (Fabricius)...................	I.T.–20..	x	x	x		
Cerebratulus luridus Verrill......................						
Cerebratulus medullatus Hubrecht...............	85......	....	....	....	x	
Cerebratulus melanops Coe & Kunkel 1..........						
Lineus sanguineus (Rathke)......................	I.T......	x				
Lineus socialis (Leidy).....,....................	I.T......	x				
Lineus truncatus (Hubrecht)?...................	75–80....	....	....	....	x	
Lineus viridis (Fabricius)........................	I.T......	x				
Micrura affinis (Girard).....,...................	o–100.....		x	x	x	
Micrura rubra Verrill............................	40.......	....	....	x		
CHAETOPODA.						
Polychaeta.						
Ammotrypane aulogaster Rathke 12.............	100–125..	....	....	....	....	x
Ammotrypane cylindricaudatus Hansen 12.......						
Ammotrypane fimbriata Verrill, 35.............	5–90		x	x	x	
Ampharete gracilis Malmgren.....................	10–90....		x	x	x	
Ampharete grubei Malmgren....... ,............	4.....		x			
Amphitrite cirrhata (Muller) Packard 35, 38, 44...	8–16.....		x	x		
Amphitrite groenlendica 38, 44...,...............						
Amphitrite intermedia Malmgren 17.............	76.......	....	....	....	x	
Antinoe sarsii Kinberg 12........................	60.......	....	....	....	x	
Aphrodita aculeata L. 35........................	10–106....		x	x	x	x
Arenicola piscatorum Lamarck = Arenicola marina (Linnaeus) 20, 35......................	I.T–20.....	x	x	x		
Artacama canadensis McIntosh 38.................	30.......	....	....	x		
Artacama proboscoidea Malmgren 44.............	30–50....		....	x		
Axiothea catenata Malmgren = Axiothella catenata 33..						
Brada granosa Stimpson..........................	4–6......		x			
Brada granulata Malmgren 17.....................	60–80.....		....	....	x	
Brada sublaevis Stimpson........................						
Brada villosa Rathke 13,.........................						
Chaetozone setosa Malmgren 17..................	80......	....	....	....	x	
Chaetozone setosa canadensis McIntosh 17........						
Chaetozone whiteavesi McIntosh 17...............						
Chaetozone ? 17................................						
Chone duneri Malmgren 44.......................						
Chone cf. fauveli McIntosh 44....................	5–20......		x	x		
Chone infundibuliformis Kroyer 17...	110–170...		....	....	....	x
Chone princei McIntosh 44.......................						
Chone sp. 17......,.............................	20.......		....	x		
Cirratulus cirrhatus (Fabricius) 17...............	17–40.....		x	x		
Cistenides granulata (L).,.......................	o–50......		x	x		
Cistenides hyperborea Malmgren 38 = Pectinaria hyperborea 17................................	50–220...,		....	....	x	x

8 GEORGE V, A. 1918

BATHYMETRIC TABLES—*Continued.*

—	Min. and Max. Depth.	Inter- tidal Zone.	Fathoms.			
			1–15	15–50	50–100	100 x

CHAETOPODA—*Con.*

Polychaeta—Con.

—	Min. and Max. Depth.	Inter- tidal Zone.	1–15	15–50	50–100	100 x
Clymenella torquata (Leidy)	0–60		x	x	x	
Drilonereis canadensis McIntosh 2						
Enonella bicarinata Stimpson	0		x			
Ephesia gracilis Rathke	125					x
Ephesia sp. 13						
Erentho smitti Malmgren 44	170					x
Eteone cylindrica OErsted	5		x			
Euchone lawrencii McIntosh 44						
Euchone rubrocincta 17						
Euchone tuberculosa (Kroyer) Malmgren 17	80				x	
Eumenia crassa OErsted	110–220					x
Eunice oerstedii Stimpson	20–85			x	x	
Eunice ? 2	200					x
Eunoa nodosa (Sars)	45–60			x	x	
Eunoa oerstedi Malmgren 17, 35	17–76		x	x	x	
Eunoa spinulosa Verrill						
Euphrosyne borealis OErsted	85				x	
Eupolynoe anticostiensis McIntosh 17	7–75		x	x	x	
Eupolynoe occidentalis McIntosh	100				x	
Eusyllis tubifex Gosse	51				x	
Filograna filograna Berkeley 17	40			x		
Flabelligera affinis Sars 17	7–85		x	x	x	
Glycera dibranchiata Ehlers 3	100–120					x
Glycera siphonostoma Delle Chiaje 3						
Goniada maculata OErsted 3						
Goniada norvegica Oersted 3	150					x
Grymaea spiralis Verrill	60				x	
Harmothoe imbricata (L) 17, 35, 47	0–110		x	x	x	x
Isocirrus ? sp. 33	125					x
Laenilla glabra Malmgren 17	7		x			
Laetmonice armata Verrill	50–150				x	x
Laetmonice filicornis Kinberg 17	75				x	
Laetmonice producta var, assimilis McIntosh	85				x	
Lagisca rarispina (Sars)						
Lagisca rarispina var. occidentalis M'Intosh						
Lanassa nordenskioldi Malmgren 38, 44						
Leaena abranchiata Malmgren 17	7		x			
Leanira tetragona OErsted	110–220					x
Leanira yhleni ? Malmgren	210					x
Leodice vivida (Stimpson)						
Lepidonotus squamatus (L) 17, 35, 47	I.T.–80	x	x	x	x	
Lumbricoclymene sp. 17	45			x		
Lumbriconereis cf. assimilis McIntosh 2	200					x
Lumbriconereis fragilis (Muller) 2, 17, 35	0–430		x	x	x	x
Lumbrinereis hebes Verrill 17	5–80		x	x	x	
Maldane sarsii Malmgren 17, 33	20–30			x		
Malmgrenia whiteavesii M'Intosh	110–220					x
Melinna cristata (Sars) 35	10–90		x	x	x	
Myriochele heeri McIntosh 34						
Myxicola steenstrupi Kroyer 17	40			x		
Naidonereis quadricuspida Blainville (*fide*, Verrill)						
Nemidia (?) canadensis M'Intosh						
Nemidia (?) lawrencii M'Intosh						
Nephthys caeca (Fabricius) 17, 47	3–80		x	x	x	
Nephthys canadensis M'Intosh	56–80			x	x	
Nephthys ciliata (Muller) 35	25–40			x		
Nephthys incisa Malmgren 17, 35	2–430		x	x	x	x
Nephthys lawrencii M'Intosh						
Nephthys longisetosa OErsted = Autolytus longisetosa 12	7		x			
Nephthys picta Ehlers	30–80			x	x	
Nereis abyssicola Stimpson	40			x		
Nereis denticulata Stimpson	0		x			

BATHYMETRIC TABLES—*Continued.*

	Min. and Max. Depth.	Inter- tidal. Zone.	BATHYMETRIC RANGE. Fathoms.			
			1–15	15–50	50–100	100 x

CHAETOPODA—*Ccn.*

Polychaeta—Con.

	Min. and Max. Depth.	Inter- tidal. Zone.	1–15	15–50	50–100	100 x
Nereis iris Stimpson	20			x		
Nereis (Lycoris) pelagica L. 17, 35	o–106		x	x	x	x
Nereis virens Sars 35	o–10		x			
Nevaya whiteavesi McIntosh 24						
Nicolea zostericola (OErsted) Malmgren 17	7		x			
Nicomache canadensis McIntosh 33	175					x
Nicomache lumbricalis (Fabricius)	8–D.W.		x	x	x	x
Ninoe kinbergi Ehlers 2						
Nothria conchylega (Sars) 12 = Onuphis conchylega Sars 2, 35	7–125		x	x	x	x
Nychia amondseni Malmgren = Gattyana amondseni (Malmgren) McIntosh (17)	50–75				x	
Nychia cirrhosa (Pallas) = Gattyana cirrhosa (Pallas) McIntosh 12	7–80		x	x	x	
Onuphis cf. holobrachia Marenzeller 2	75–212				x	x
Onuphis sicula De Quatrefages	75–150				x	x
Onuphis quadricuspis Sars 2						
Ophelia glabra Stimpson	D.W.					x
Ophelia limacina Rathke	5					
Ophelia radiata Della Chiaje 12	10–12		x			
Owenia (or Ammocharis) filiformis Della Chiaje	110–220					x
Pholoe minuta (Fabricius)	8		x			
Pholoe tecta Stimpson	4		x			
Phyllodoce catenula Verrill						
Phyllodoce groenlandica OErsted	5–25		x	x		
Phyllodoce mucosa OErsted 17	30–60			x	x	
Phyllodoce sp. 17	80				x	
Pista cristata (O.F.Moller) 38, 44	75–210				x	x
Polycirrus sp. 38						
Polydara concharum Verrill	10–100		x	x	x	
Polynoe gaspeensis M'Intosh	100–212					x
Potamilla neglecta Malmgren 17	45–75			x	x	
Potamilla oculifera (Leidy)	o–60		x	x	x	
Potamilla reniformis (O.F. Moller) 44						
Potamilla torelli Malmgren 34	85				x	
Praxilla gracilis Sars = Praxillella gracilis Sars 17, 33	7–112		x	x	x	x
Praxilla mulleri (Sars)	15–40			x		
Praxillella collaris (Claparede) 33						
Praxillella praetermissa (Malmgren) Verrill 33	7		x			
Praxillella sp. 17	50			x		
Prionospio steenstrupi Malmgren	45–220			x	x	x
Protula americana M'Intosh	85				x	x
Protula media Stimpson	35–50			x		
Rhynchobolus capitatus (OErsted) = Glycera capitata 3, 35	o–17		x	x		
Sabella crassicornis Sars 17	75				x	
Sabella pavonina Savigny	125					x
Sabella penicillus (L) 44	220					x
Sabella zonalis Stimpson	4		x			
Sabellides borealis Sars 17, 31, 38	60				x	
Samthya sexcirrata Sars 17	30			x		
Scalibregma inflatum Rathke	D.W.					x
Scolecolepis cirrata (Sars) var						
Scolopos armiger (O. F. Moller) 3, 17	45–80			x	x	
Scoloplos canadensis M'Intosh						
Siphonostomum asperum Stimpson	10–25		x	x		
Spinther citrinus (Stimpson)	35			x		
Spiochaetopterus typicus Sars 13,38	30–40			x		
Spirorbis borealis Daudin (?) = Spirorbis spirillum ??? 17	S.W.		x			
Spirorbis cancellatus (Fabricius) 17	7		x			
Spirorbis carinatus Montagu	D.W.					x

8 GEORGE V, A. 1918

BATHYMETRIC TABLES—*Continued.*

	Min. and Max. Depth.	Inter-tidal Zone.	BATHYMETRIC RANGE.			
			Fathoms.			
—			1–15	15–50	50–100	100 x

CHAETOPODA—*Con.*

Polychaeta—Con.

Spirorbis granulatus (Muller)	10–50		x	x		
Spirorbis lucidus (Montagu)	4–80		x	x	x	
Spirorbis quadrangularis Stimpson 35	10–17		x	x		
Spirorbis spirillum Linnaeus 17, 35	I.T.–60	x	x	x	x	
Spirorbis stimpsoni Verrill	10–80		x	x	x	
Spirorbis validus Verrill 17	7–60		x	x	x	
Spirorbis vitreus (Fabricius)	20–30			x		
Sthenelais limicola Ehlers						
Tecturella flaccida Stimpson	3–15		x			
Terebella brunnea Stimpson	I.T.	x				
Terebella figulus Dalyell 38						
Terebellides stroemii M. Sars 17, 38, 43	7–220		x	x	x	x
Thelepus cincinnatus (Fabricius) 17, 35, 38	7–200		x	x	x	x
Thelepus cincinnatus var. canadensis M'Intosh	51				x	
Trichobranchus glacialis Malmgren 38						
Trophonia aspera Stimpson 17	7–80		x	x	x	
Trophonia plumosa (Muller) = Stylarioides plumosa, Muller. 13	8–125		x	x	x	x
Vermilia serrula Stimpson	50			x		

GEPHYREA.

Chaetifera.

Sternaspis fossor Stimpson 17, 35, 47	2–90		x	x	x	

Achaeta.

Phascolion alberti Sluiter 32	700–900					x
Phascolion strombi Montagu 32, 35 47	2–1061		x	x	x	x
Phascolion strombi canadensis Gerould 32	33–206			x	x	x
Phascolion strombi fusca Gerould 32	100–1000					x
Phascolion tubicola Verrill	85				x	
Phascolosoma boreale Keferstein = P. margaritaceum (Sars) 32	30–75			x	x	
Phascolosoma caementarium (DeQuatrefages)	2–90		x	x	x	
Phascolosoma hamulatum Packard	8		x			
Priapulus caudatus ? Lamarck						
Priapulus pygmaeus Verrill	4–5		x			

BRACHIOPODA.

Articulata.

Hemithyris psittacea (Gmelin) 19	1–60		x	x	x	'
Terebratalia spitzbergensis (Davidson)	20–120			x	x	x
Terebratella labradorensis (Sowerby)	1340					x
Terebratulina septentrionalis (Couthouy)	12–220		x	x	x	x

POLYZOA.

Cheilostomata.

B ania admiranda Packard	50			x		
Becellaria ciliata (L) 28, 35	7–96		x	x	x	
Biowerbankia gracilis caudatus (Hincks) 28, 35	40			x		
Bugula cucullifera Osburn 28, 35	25			x		
Bugula murrayana (Johnston) 28, 35	7–110		x	x	x	x
Caberea ellisii (Fleming) 9, 28, 35	6–100		x	x	x	
Cellepora avicularis Hincks	45			x		
Cellepora canaliculata Busk 28, 35	40–51			x	x	
Cellepora contigua Smitt 28	45			x		
Cellepora pumicosa (L)						

BATHYMETRIC TABLES—*Continued.*

			Bathymetric Range.			
— —	Min. and Max. Depth.	Inter-tidal. Zone.	Fathoms.			
			1–15	15–50	50–100	100 x
POLYZOA=*Con.*						
Cheilostomata—Con.						
Cellularia peachii Busk 35	4–50		x	x		
Corynoporella tenuis Hincks						
Cribrilina annulata (Fabricius) 9, 28, 35	15–D.W			x	x	x
Cribrilina punctata (Hassall) 9, 35, 47	1–50		x	x		
Electra catenularia (Jameson)						
Electra pilosa (L) = Membranipora pilosa 9	0–1		x			
Escharoides sarsii Smitt 28	10–60		x	x	x	
Flustra abyssicola G. O. Sars	220					x
Flustra borealis (Packard)	50			x		
Flustra carbasea Ellis & Solander 28	7–30		x	x		
Flustra membranaceo-truncata Smitt	56				x	
Flustra securifrons (Pallas) 28	30			x		
Flustra serrulata Busk 28	7–110		x	x	x	x
Flustra solida Stimpson	25–120			x	x	x
Gemellaria loricata (L) 9, 28, 35	0–110		x	x	x	x
Gemellaria loricata var. americana (Lamouroux)	10		x			
Hippothoa divaricata Lamouroux 35	18			x		
Hippothoa expansa Dawson						
Kinetoskias arborescens Danielssen 28	75–212				x	x
Kinetoskias smittii Danielssen	194					x
Lagenipora spinulosa Hincks						
Lepralia hippopus Smitt 28	25			x		
Lepralia (Discopora) megastoma Smitt						
Lepralia pertusa (Esper)	3–36		x	x		
Lepralia spathulifera Smitt 9, 28	30			x		
Membranipora craticula Alder 28, 35	7–38		x	x		
Membranipora cymbiformis Hincks	13–20		x	x		
Membranipora dumerilii Audouin						
Membranipora flemingii Busk 28	1–20		x	x		
Membranipora lacroixii (Audouin)	30			x		
Membranipora lineata L. 9	10–50		x	x		
Membranipora monostachys Busk 47	1–6		x			
Membranipora sophiae Busk						
Membranipora sophiae var. armifera (Hincks)	56				x	
Membranipora spinifera Hincks 28	25–45			x		
Membranipora trifolium (Searles Wood) 28	25			x		
Membranipora unicornis Fleming 28, 35	8–25		x	x		
Membraniporella crassicosta Hincks 28	10–50		x	x		
Menipea ternata (Ellis & Solander) 9, 28, 35	6–110		x	x	x	x
Microporella ciliata (Pallas) 28, 35	8–25		x	x		
Monoporella spinulifera Hincks = Mucronella spinulifera 28	25			x		
Mucronella abyssicola (Norman)						
Mucronella pavonella (Alder)						
Mucronella peachii (Johnston) 35, 47	1–6		x			
Mucronella praelucida Hincks 28	25–60			x	x	
Mucronella ventricosa (Hassall) 28, 35	14–25		x	x		
Myriozoum coarctatum (Sars) 28	25–60			x	x	
Myriozoum planum (Dawson) = Schizoporella plana Dawson 28	25			x		
Myriozoum subgracile D'Orbigny	10–50		x	x		
Porella acutirostris Smitt 35						
Porella bella (Busk)						
Porella concinna (Busk) 9, 28, 35	10–60		x	x	x	
Porella elegantula (D'Orbigny)						
Porella elegantula var papposa Packard	45			x		
Porella laevis (Fleming)	56				x	
Porella minuta (Norman)						
Porella perpusilla Busk 28	80				x	
Porella proboscidea Hincks 28	20–38			x		
Porella propinqua Smitt						
Porella saccata Busk 28	25–110			x	x	x
Porella skenei (Ellis & Solander) 28	40–75			x	x	

8 GEORGE V, A. 1918

BATHYMETRIC TABLES—*Continued.*

—	Min. and Max. Depth.	Inter-tidal Zone.	Fathoms.			
			1–15	15–50	50–100	100 x
POLYZOA—*Con.*						
*Cheilostomata—*Con.						
Porella skenei var. plana Hincks	96.				x	
Porella struma (Norman) 28	40–75			x	x	
Porella surcularis (Packard) = Cellepora surcularis 28	10–110		x	x	x	x
Porina tubulosa Norman 35	S.W.		x			
Ramphonotus minax (Busk)						
Retepora elongata Smitt	56–96				x	
Rhamphostomella bilaminata Hincks	38.			x		
Rhamphostomella costata Lorenz 28	25–80			x	x	
Rhamphostomella ovata (Smitt) 28	25–45			x		
Rhamphostomella plicata Smitt						
Rhamphostomella radiatula (Hincks) 28	45.			x		
Rhamphostomella scabra (Fabricius)						
Rhamphostomella scabra var. labiata (Stimpson)						
Schizoporella auriculata (Hassall) 28, 35	8–50		x	x		
Schizoporella biaperta (Michelin) 35, 47	1–56		x	x	x	
Schizoporella cincta Hincks (var.)						
Schizoporella cruenta (Norman)	56				x	
Schizoporella hyalina (L) 9 = Hippothoa hyalina, 28	30–313			x	x	x
Schizoporella linearis (Hassall)						
Schizoporella sinuosa (Busk) 9, 35						
Scruparia clavata Hincks 9						
Scrupocellaria americana Packard	6–30		x	x		
Scrupocellaria scabra (Van Beneden) 35						
Scrupocellaria scruposa (L)						
Smittia arctica Norman 35 = S. porifera 28	17–45			x		
Smittia candida (Stimpson)	35.			x		
Smittia globifera (Packard)	30–45			x		
Smittia landsborovii (Johnston)						
Smittia producta (Packard)						
Smittia reticulatopunctata Hincks 28	45.			x		
Smittia trispinosa (Johnston) 28, 35	25–45			x		
Umbonula verrucosa (Esper)						
Cyclostomata.						
Crisia denticulata (Lamarck) 28	10–45		x	x		
Crisia eburnea (L) 9, 28, 35	o–200		x	x	x	x
Crisia eburnea var. cribaria Stimpson = C. cribaria 28, 35	18–45			x		
Diastopora obelia Johnston	30–96			x	x	
Diastopora patina (Lamarck)	7.		x			
Discofascigera lucernaria (Sars)	50–96				x	
Fasciporina flexuosa (Orbigny)						
Hornera lichenoides (L)	220.					x
Idmonea atlantica (Forbes) Johnston 9 = Tubulipora atlantica 28, 35	40–45			x		
Idmonea serpens (L) 9	30.			x		
Lichenopora clypeiformis (Orbigny)						
Lichenopora hispida (Fleming)	30–96			x	x	
Lichenopora regularis (Orbigny) 28	25.			x		
Lichenopora verrucaria (Fabricius) 28, 35	7–60		x	x	x	
Stomatopora diastoporoides (Norman) 35						
Stomatopora granulata (Milne Edwards)	50.			x		
Stomatopora penicillata (Fabricius)						
Tubulipora expansa (Packard)						
Tubulipora fimbria Lamarck	50.			x		
Tubulipora flabellaris (Fabricius) 9, 28, 35	30.			x		
Tubulipora lobulata Hassall						

BATHYMETRIC TABLES—*Continued.*

	Min. and Max. Depth.	Inter-tidal. Zone.	Fathoms.			
			1–15	15–50	50–100	100 x
Ctenosomata.						
Alcyonidium gelatinosum (L).................	96.......	....	....	....	x	
Alcyonidium mytili Dalyell 35, 47......	1–16.....	....	x	x		
Barentsia gracilis M. Sars..........						
Barentsia major Hincks 35..........	3–13.....	....	x			
Flustrella hispida (Fabricius)........						
Pedicellina nutans Dalyell 9..........						
MOLLUSCA. *a*						
Pelecypoda.						
Anomia aculeata Muller 42..........	3–100....	....	x	x	x.	
Anomia simplex d'Orbigny 35, 46........	2–8.....	....	x			
Arca (Bathyarca) glacialis Gray........						
Arca (Bathyarca) pectunculoides Scacchi.....	70–430...	....	....		x	x
Astarte banksii (Leach)..........	10–60....	....	x	x	x	
Astarte banksii var. globosa Moller......	70–80....	....	....		x	
Astarte banksii var. striata Leach........						
Astarte castanea Say 35, 42..........	5–20.....	....	x	x		
Astarte compressa (L)..........	10–50....	....	x	x		
Astarte crebricostata Forbes..........	112–313..	....	....	....	....	x
Astarte crenata Gray 46..........	15–120...	....	....	x	x	x
Astarte lactea Broderip & Sowerby						
Astarte quadrans Gould 5..........	6–40.....	....	x	x		
Astarte subaequilatera Sowerby 42..........	50.......	....	....	x		
Astarte undata Gould 35, 42, 46..........	5–100....	....	x	x	x	
Astarte undata var lutea Perkins..........	5–100..:.	....	x	x	x	
Axinopsis orbiculata var. inaequalis Verrill & Bush.						
Cardium (Cerastoderma) ciliatum Fabricius 19, 35, 42..........	10–60....					
Cardium (Laevicardium) mortoni Conrad 35.....	2–5......					
Cardium (Cerastoderma) pinnulatum Conrad 35 42, 46.......	2–80.....	....	x	x	x	
Clidiophora gouldiana Dall 46 = Pandora gouldiana 35, 42.......	0–30.....	....	x	x		
Cochlodesma leanum (Conrad) 35..........	2–19.....					
Crenella decussata (Montagu)..........	20–60....	....	....	x	x	
Crenella faba (Moller)..........	1–15.....	....	x			
Crenella glandula (Totten) 35, 42..........	0–60.....	....	x	x	x	
Crenella pectinula (Gould)..........						
Cryptodon (Axinulus) ferruginosus (Forbes).......	200–313..	....	....	....	....	x
Cryptodon gouldii Phillipi..........	10–313..	....	x	x	x	x
Cryptodon (Axinulus) inaequalis Verrill & Bush...	14–49....	....	x	x		
Cryptodon obesus Verrill = Thyasira obesa 46...						
Cryptodon planus Verrill & Bush..........	8–100....	....	x	x	x	
Cumingia tellinoides (Conrad)..........						
Cuspidaria arctica (M. Sars)..........	190 ?	....	....	....	....	x ?
Cuspidaria glacialis G. O. Sars..........	50–313..	....	....	....	x	x
Cuspidaria pellucida (Stimpson)..........	40.......	....	....	x		
Cyprina islandica (L) 42..........	6–90.....	....	x	x	x	
Cyrtodaria siliqua (Daudin)..........	15–50....	....	....	x		
Cytherea convexa Say 42, 46 = Callocardia morrhuana 35..........	I.T.–15...	x	x			
Dacrydium vitreum (Moller)..........	100–313..	....	....	....	....	x
Ensis directus (Conrad) = E. americanum Gould 35, 46..........	0–40.....	....	x	x		

a. NOTE.—Students of the geographic distribution of the Mollusca will find it instructive to compare with this list the following two papers by Dr. Wm. H. Dall:

"Checklist of the Recent Mollusks of the Northwest coast of America from the Polar sea to San Diego, California," pp. 1–44, 1916. S. West Museum, Los Angeles, Calif.

"Report on the Mollusca of the Arctic coast of America collected by the Canadian Arctic Expedition west from Bathurst Inlet." Scientific Results of the Expedition,—in the press.

8 GEORGE V, A. 1918

BATHYMETRIC TABLES—*Continued.*

	Min. and Max. Depth.	Inter-tidal Zone.	BATHYMETRIC RANGE. Fathoms.			
			1–15	15–50	50–100	100 x
MOLLUSCA—*Con.*						
Pelecypoda—Con.						
Epitonium groenlandicus Perry....................						
Kellia suborbicularis (Montagu)....................						
Kennerlia glacialis (Leach)........................	15–50....			x		
Leda minuta (Muller).............................	15–50....			x		
Leda pernula (Muller) 19.........................	50–59....				x	
Leda pernula var. jacksonii Gould................	10–20....		x	x		
Leda tenuisulcata (Couthouy) 35.................	6–110....		x	x	x	x
Limatula subauriculata (Montagu).................	38–313....			x	x	x
Liocyma fluctuosa (Gould)........................	10–50....		x	x		
Lyonsia arenosa (Moller)..........................	15–60....			x	x	
Lyonsia hyalina Conrad 35, 42, 46................	0–30....		x	x	x	
Macoma balthica (L) 42 = M. balthica fusca 35, 46	I.T.–6...	x	x			
Macoma calcarea (Gmelin) 19, 46.................	3–80....		x	x	x	
Macoma inflata Verrill & Bush....................	38–125....			x	x	x
Megayoldia thraciaeformis (Storer) 42 = Yoldia thraciaeformis 35...............................	10–200....		x	x	x	x
Mesodesma deauratum (Turton)....................						
Modiola (Brachydontes) demissa (Dillwyn) 35, 46	I.T.–7....	x	x			
Modiola modiolus (L) 19, 35, 46...................	I.T.–25...	x	x	x		
Modiolaria corrugata (Stimpson) 35, 42...........	0–100....		x	x	x	
Modiolaria discors (L) 19, 42 46 = M. laevigata 35	0–100....		x	x	x	
Modiolaria nigra (Gray) 19, 35, 46................	I.T.–40..	x	x	x		
Mulinia lateralis (Say) 35.........................	4–10....		x			
Mya arenaria L. 19, 35, 42, 46...................	I.T.–40..	x	x	x		
Mya truncata L 19...............................	I.T.–45..	x	x	x		
Mytilus edulis L. 19, 35, 42, 46..................	I.T.–19..	x	x	x		
Nucula delphinodonta Mighels 35, 42.............	5½–100..		x	x	x	
Nucula expansa Reeve............................	30......			x		
Nucula proxima Say 35, 46........................	1–17....		x	x		
Nucula proxima var. trunculus Dall...............	4–80....		x	x	x	
Nucula tenuis (Montagu) 19......................	4–100....		x	x	x	
Ostrea virginica Gmelin 35.......................	<3 *a*....		x			
Panopaea (Panomya) norvegica Spengler..........	40–50....			x		
Pecten gibbus var. borealis Say 35...............	2–15....		x			
Pecten (Camptonectes) groenlandicus Sowerby...	200–313....					x
Pecten (Chlamys) islandicus Muller 19, 35........	1–100....		x	x	x	x
Pecten (Placopecten) magellanicus (Gmelin) 19, 35, 42, 46...................................	4–20....		x	x		
Pecten (Cyclopecten) pustulosus Verrill..........	115–430..					x
Pecten (Camptonectes) vitreus (Chemnitz).......	57–400....				x	x
Periploma fragilis (Totten) 46....................	3–100....		x	x	x	
Petricola pholadiformis Lamarck 46...............	I.T.–6....	x	x			
Portlandia glacialis (Wood).......................	15–25....		x	x		
Rochefortia molleri (Morch).......................	18......			x		
Saxicava rugosa (L) 42, 46 = S. arctica 19.......	0–50....		x	x		
Serripes groenlandicus (Gmelin) 19...............	10–60....		x	x	x	
Siliqua costata (Say) 35..........................	17 ?....			x ?		
Siliqua squama (Blainville)........................						
Solenomya borealis Totten = Solemya borealis 35						
Solenomya velum Say = Solemya velum 35......	2–5....		x			
Spisula (Hemimactra) polynyma (Stimpson)......	0–10....		x			
Spisula (Hemimactra) solidissima (Dillwyn) 35, 46	0–19....	x	x	x		
Tellina (Angulus) tenera Say 35..................	0–19....		x	x		
Teredo dilatata Stimpson..........................						
Teredo navalis L. 35.............................	13–15....	x	x			
Thracia conradi Couthouy 35.....................	6–19....		x	x		
Thracia myopsis (Beck) Moller....................	10–50....		x	x		
Thracia truncata Mighels & Adams 42............	10–60....		x	x	x	
Tottenia gemma (Totten) = Gemma gemma 35..	I.T.–14..	x	x			
Turtonia minuta (Fabricius).......................	0........		x			
Venericardia borealis (Conrad) 19, 35, 42, 46......	3–50....	x	x			
Venus mercenaria L. 25...........................	0–6....		x			

a In Long Island Sound, the Oyster flourishes in 70 to 80 feet of water. J. L. Kellog. La. Gulf Biological Station Bull. No. 3. p. 11, 1905.

BATHYMETRIC TABLES—*Continued.*

				Bathymetric Range.		
	Min. and Max. Depth.	Inter-tidal. Zone.		Fathoms.		
—			1-15	15-50	50-100	100 x

MOLLUSCA—Con.

Pelecypoda—Con.

Xylophaga dorsalis Turton						
Yoldia limatula (Say) 35, 46	2-30		x	x		
Yoldia myalis (Couthouy) 19	20			x		
Yoldia sapotilla (Gould) 35, 42	4-100		x	x	x	x
Yoldiella frigida (Torell)	100-313					x
Yoldiella lucida (Loven)	40-313			x	x	x
Zirfaœa crispata L. 35	0-70		x	x	x	

Scaphopoda.

Dentalium agile M. Sars						
Dentalium entalis L. 42	20-60			x	x	
Dentalium occidentale Stimpson	50-300				x	x
Siphonodentalium affine M. Sars	35			x		
Siphonodentalium lobatum (Sowerby)						

Gasteropoda.

Acmaea rubella (Fabricius)	20-35			x		
Acmaea testudinalis (Muller) 19, 35, 42, 46	a I.T	x				
Acrybia flava (Gould)	30			x		
Admete couthouyi (Jay) 19	10-60		x	x	x	
Æolis papillosa (L) = Aeolidia papillosa 35	I.T.-20	x	x	x		
Æolis purpurea Stimpson	I.T	x				
Æolis stellata Stimpson	I.T	x				
Alderia harvardiensis (Agassiz)	I.T	x				
Alexia myosotis (Draparnaud) 35	I.T	x				
Amaura candida Moller	20-50			x		
Amauropsis islandica (Gmelin)						
Amicula vestita (Boderip & Sowerby)						
Anachis haliaeti (Jeffreys)	67-96			x		
Ancula sulphurea Stimpson	I.T	x				
Aporrhais occidentalis Beck 19, 42, 46	2-120		x	x	x	x
Astyris lunata (Say) 35	1-19		x	x		
Astyris rosacea (Gould) 35	8-60		x	x	x	
Astyris zonalis (Linsley) 35	8		x			
Bela angulosa Sars						
Bela bicarinata Couthouy	0-100		x	x	x	
Bela bicarinata var. violacea (Mighels & Adams)	0-100		x	x	x	
Bela cancellata (Mighels) 42	25			x		
Bela cancellata var. canadensis Verrill & Bush						
Bela concinnula Verrill	16-42			x		
Bela decussata (Couthouy) 42	10-100		x	x	x	
Bela exarata (Moller)	5-18		x	x		
Bela gouldii Verrill	16-41			x		
Bela harpularia (Couthouy) 35, 42	10-190		x	x	x	
Bela impressa Beck						
Bela incisula Verrill	5-110		x	x	x	x
Bela mitrula (Loven)	10-20		x	x		
Bela nobilis (Moller) 46	2-80		x	x	x	
Bela pingelii (Moller)	45			x		
Bela pleurotomaria (Couthouy) 35, 42	1-80		x	x	x	
Bela rosea Sars	2-57		x	x	x	
Bela sarsii Verrill	10-20		x	x		
Bela scalaris Moller 42	10-100		x	x	x	
Bela woodiana (Moller)	15			x		
Bittium nigrum Totten = B. alternatum 35	I.T.-5	x	x			
Buccinum ciliatum (Fabricius) 19	3-112		x	x	x	x
Buccinum cyaneum Bruguiere	45-100			x	x	
Buccinum cyaneum var. perdix (or finmarchianum) (Beck) Mörch 19						

a The young are dredged in 15 fathoms.

BATHYMETRIC TABLES—*Continued.*

—	Min. and Max. Depth.	Inter-tidal Zone.	1–15	15–50	50–100	100 x
				Bathymetric Range. Fathoms.		
Gasteropoda—Con.						
Buccinum cyaneum var. patulum Sars.............						
Buccinum donovani Gray 19......................	o–15....	......	x			
Buccinum glaciale L................	I.T......	x				
Buccinum gouldii Verrill 19......................	60 ?......				x ?	
Buccinum tenue Gray....................						
Buccinum tottenii Stimpson 19............	a 8–15.....	......	x			
Buccinum undatum L. 19 = B. undulatum Muller 35, 42, 46....................	I.T.–170.	x	x	x	x	x
Calliostoma occidentale (Mighels & Adams)......	25–40.....			x		
Capulacmaea radiata M. Sars....................	150.......					x
Cerithiopsis costulata (Moller)...................						
Cerithiopsis greenii (Adams) 35..................	3–10......		x			
Cerithiella whiteavesii Verrill....	110–200...					x
Chaetoderma nitidulum Loven..................	10–100...		x	x	x	
Cingula (Onoba) aculeus Gould 35................	I.T......	x				
Cingula arenaria Mighels & Adams....	4–25.....		x	x		
Cingula (Alvania) areolata Stimpson..............	96......				x	
Cingula carinata Mighels & Adams..............	96–200....				x	x
Cingula (Alvania) castanea (Moller)..............	1–15.....		x			
Cingula globulus (Moller).......................	60 ?				x	
Cingula (Alvania) jan-meyeni (Friele).............	20–200....			x	x	x
Cingula minuta (Totten) 35.....................	I.T.–1...	x	x			
Cingula multilineata (Stimpson)...................						
Coryphella diversa (Couthouy) 19.................	4......		x			
Coryphella mananensis (Stimpson) 35.............	20–90...			x	x	
Coryphella stimpsoni Verrill.....................	o–51...		x	x	x	
Crenella decussata Montagu..................	20–60.....			x	x	
Crenella faba Fabricius 30.						
Crenella glandula (Potten).....................	o–60......		x	x	x	
Crenella pectinula (Gould)....						
Crepidula convexa Say 35.......................	I.T.–15..	x	x			
Crepidula fornicata (L) 35, 46.................	I.T.–19...	x	x	x		
Crepidula plana Say 35, 46.....................	I.T.–45...	x	x	x		
Crucibulum striatum (Say) 35, 42, 46..............	o–30.....		x	x		
Cylichna alba (Brown) 19, 35, 46..............	2–60...		x	x	x	
Cylichna occulta (Mighels & Adams).............						
Dendronotus arborescens Muller)19, 35............	o–45.....		x	x		
Dendronotus robustus Verrill.....................	I.T.–98...	x	x	x	x	
Diaphana debilis (Gould).......................	6–50.....		x	x		
Diaphana hiemalis (Couthouy) 19.................	40..			x		
Doris planulata Stimpson......................	I.T.	x				
Doto coronata (Gmelin) 35......................	15.......		x			
Doto formosa Verrill 35....................						
Eulima stenostoma Jeffreys.......................						
Haminea solitaria (Say) 35......................	I.T......	x				
Hanleyia mendicaria (Mighels & Adams).........	35–60.....			x	x	
Ianthina fragilis Lamarck 35....................						
Issa lacera (Muller)............................	90–92.....				x	
Lacuna glacialis Moller.	96........				x	
Lacuna neritoidea Gould.........................						
Lacuna vincta (Montagu)........................	1–30.....		x	x		
Lepeta caeca (O. F. Muller) 19, 42................	17–50....		x	x		
Lepidopleurus alveolus M. Sars.................	220.......					
Lepidopleurus cancellatus Sowerby................	95.				x	
Liostomia eburnea (Stimpson)..................	25–70.....		x	x		
Litorina litorea (L) 19, 35, 42, 46..............	I.T.–6...	x				
Litorina palliata (Say) 19, 35, 42, 46.............	I.T......	x				
Litorina rudis (Maton) 19, 35, 42.............	I.T......	x				
Lunatia groenlandica (Beck) Moller..............	3–60.....		x	x	x	
Lunatia heros (Say) 42, 46 = Polynices heros 35...	I.T.–40...	x	x	x		
Lunatia heros var. triseriata (Say) 46 = Polynices triseriata 35........................	I.T.–40....	x	x	x		
Lunatia immaculata (Totten) = Polynices immaculata 35.....................................	o–25....		x	x		

a The young are dredged in 21 fathoms.

BATHYMETRIC TABLES—*Continued.*

—	Min. and Max. Depth.	Inter-tidal. Zone.	Fathoms.			
			1-15	15-50	50-100	100 x
Gasteropoda—Con.						
Lunatia nana (Moller) = Polynices nana 35..	45.......			x		
Margarita acuminata (Sowerby) Mighels & Adams	40......			x		
Margarita cinerea Couthouy 19..............	10-60....		x	x	x	
Margarita cinerea var grandis (Mörch) G. O. Sars. 42.............	10-60....		x	x	x	
Margarita helicina (Fabricius) 19, 42........	I.T.......	x				
Margarita oliviacea (Brown)...............	4-60.....		x	x	x	
Margarita umbilicalis Broderip & Sowerby......						
Margarita undulata Sowerby 42 = Margarites un-dulatus 35.........	3-50.....		x 5	x		
Marsenina glabra (Couthouy).............	15.......		x			
Melampus bidentatus Say..................	I.T......	x				
Melampus lineatus Say 35, 46.............	I.T......	x				
Menestho albula (Fabricius)...............	2-15.....		x			
Menestho striatula (Couthouy) = Couthouyella striatula 15, 35.....................	7-204....		x	x	x	x
Molleria costulata (Moller)................	4........		x			
Nassa (Ilyanassa) obsoleta Say 35, 46.......	0-6.......		x			
Nassa (Tritia) trivittata Say 35, 46.........	I.T.-60..	x	x	x	x	
Natica clausa Broderip & Sowerby 35, 42.....	19-110...			x	x	x
Neptunea decemcostata (Say) 42, 46.........	0-45.....		x	x		
Neptunea despecta var. tornata Gould........	10-60....		x	x	x	
Odostomia bisuturalis (Say) 15, 35..........						
Odostomia fusca (Adams) 35..............	3-6.....		x			
Odostomia seminuda (Adams) 35...........	2-10.....		x			
Odostomia trifida (Totten) 35..............	0.......		x			
Odostomia (Menestho) trifida bedequensis Bartsch 15......................						
Odostomia (Chrysallida) willisi Bartsch 15.....						
Onchidoris muricata (Muller)...............	3-21.....		x	x		
Onchidoris pallida (Stimpson = Lamellidoris pallida 35........................	25.......		x			
Philine cingulata G. O. Sars...............	90.......				x	
Philine finmarchica M. Sars...............	90.......				x	
Philine fragilis G. O. Sars.................	90.......				x	
Philine lima (Brown) 19..................	10-15....		x			
Philine quadrata (Searles Wood)............	180-220..					x
Polycera lessonii Orbigny..................	0-20.....		x	x		
Puncturella noachina (L) 42...............	I.T.-50..	x	x	x		
Puncturella princeps Michels 30............						
Purpura lapillus (L) 42 = Thais lapillus 35, 46.....	I.T.	x				
Ptychatractus ligatus (Mighels) 30..........	15-60....			x	x	
Retusa gouldii (Couthouy).................						
Retusa nitidula (Loven)...................	200......					x
Retusa pertenuis (Mighels) 19, 42..........	8-10.....		x			
Scalaria (Acirsa) costulata (Mighels)........						
Scalaria groenlandica Perry 42 = Boreoscala groenlandica 35....................	10-109...		x	x	x	x
Scaphander punctostriatus (Mighels) 19.......	200......					x
Scissurella crispata Fleming...............	4-790....		x	x	x	x
Sipho ossiani (Friele)....................	180......					x
Sipho pubescens Verrill)..................	88-91....				x	
Sipho pygmaeus (Gould) 42...............	0-430....		x	x	x	x
Sipho stimpsoni (Morch) 42...............	0-112....		x	x	x	x
Sipho spitzbergensis (Reeve)...............	1-60.....		x	x	x	
Sipho ventricosus (Gray)..................						
Skeneia planorbis (Fabricius) 35............	I.T......	x				
Solariella obscura (Couthouy)..............	10-60....		x	x	x	
Solariella obscura var. bella...............	10-90....		x	x	x	
Solariella varicosa (Mighels & Adams).......	1-60.....		x	x	x	
Thais lapillus (L) 46....................	0-6......		x			
Tonicella marmorea (Fabricius) 19, 42........	0-50.....		x	x		
Tornatina canaliculata (Say) 35............	3-5......		x			
Trachydermon albus (L)..................	0-50.....		x	x		
Trachydermon ruber (L) 35 = Trachydermon rubrum 19......................	°-40.....		x	x		

BATHYMETRIC TABLES—Continued.

	Min. and Max. Depth.	Inter-tidal Zone.	Fathoms.			
			1–15	15–50	50–100	100 x
Gasteropoda—Con.						
Trichotropis borealis Broderip & Sowerby 19	10–50		x	x		
Trichotropis conica (Beck) Moller 30						
Tritonofusus kroyeri (Moller) 19	3–60		x	x	x	
Tritonofusus latericeus (Moller)	20–357			x	x	x
Tritonofusus stimpsoni lirulatus Verril 35, 46	3–20		x	x		
Tritonofusus syrtensis (Packard)	30			x		
Trophon clathratus (L) 19	20–80			x	x	
Trophon clathratus var. gunneri Loven	16–60			x	x	
Trophon fabricii (Beck) Moller	38–50			x		
Trophon truncatus (Ström)	30			x		
Turbonilla (Pyrgiscus) hecuba Dall & Bartsch 30	19			x		
Turbonilla interrupta var. fulvocincta (Totten)	2–10		x			
Turbonilla (Pyrgiscus) edwardensis Bartsch 15						
Turbonilla nivea Stimpson 35	40			x		
Turbonilla (Pyrgiscus) whiteavesi Bartsch 15						
Turritella erosa Couthouy 19	10–60		x	x	x	
Turritella reticulata Mighels & Adams 19	2–15		x			
Turritellopsis acicula (Stimpson) 19	o–50		x	x		
Urosalpinx cinerea (Say) 35, 46	1–15		x			
Velutella cryptospira Middendorf	57				x	
Velutina laevigata (Pennant) 35	o–17		x	x		
Valutina (Limneria) undata (Brown) 42	15		x			
Volumitra groenlandica Beck 7						
Volutopsis norvegica (Chemnitz)						
Pteropoda.						
Clione limacina (Phipps) 19, 35	F					
Limacina gouldii (Stimpson)	F					
Cephalopoda.						
Dibranchiata.						
Chiroteuthis lacertosa Verrill	F					
Gonatus fabricii (Lichtenstein)	F					
Histioteuthis collinsii Verrill	F					
Illex illecebrosus (Lesueur) 42 = Ommastrephes illecebrosa 35	F					
Ommastrephes megapterus (Verrill)	F					
Rossia hyatti Verrill	57–100				x	
Rossia sublevis Verrill	42–101			x	x	x
Rossia (?) tenera (Verrill)	85				x	
Octopoda.						
Octopus arcticus Prosch	60–101				x	x
Octopus lentus Verrill	120–602					x
Octopus obesus Verrill	160–300					x
Octopus piscatorum Verrill	120					x
Stauroteuthis syrtensis Verrill	250					x
CRUSTACEA.						
ENTOMOSTRACA						
Phyllopoda.						
Evadne nordmanni Loven 10, 11	F					
Evadne spinifera Linnaeus 11, 27	F					
Podon intermedius 11, 27	F					
Podon finmarchichus 27	F					
Podon leuckarti G. O. Sars 10						
Podon polyphemoides Lilljeborg 11, 27	F					

BATHYMETRIC TABLES—*Continued.*

—	Min. and Max. Depth.	Inter-tidal Zone.	Bathymetric Range. Fathoms.			
			1–15	15–50	50–100	100 x
Cirripedia and Copepoda.						
Acartia clausi Giesbrecht 10, 36............•...........	F.........					
Acartia giesbrechti Dahl 10......................						
Anchorella sp. 31................................						
Argulus alosae Gould 10.........................						
Argulus fundulus Kroyer 5, 35, 40...............	P.........					
Argulus sp. indet.........................·......	P.........					
Balanus balanoides (L) 5, 18, 35, 45............	I.T......	x				
Balanus crenatus Bruguiere 5, 18, 27, 35, 45.......	I.T.–30...	x	x	x		
Balanus hameri Ascanius 5, 35, 45................	I.T.–141..	x	x	x	x	x
Balanus improvisus Darwin 45...........•........						
Balanus porcatus Da Costa 5, 18, 27, 35...........	10–150...		x	x	x	x
Calanus finmarchichus Gunner 11, 27, 35..........	F.........					
Calanus helgolandicus Claus 10...................						
Caligus curtus Muller 35, 40.....................	P.........					
Caligus rapax Milne Edwards 35, 40..............	P.........					
Centropages hamatus Lilljeborg 10, 11............	F.........					
Centropages typicus Lilljeborg 11................	F.........					
Chondracanthus cornutus Muller 5, 40............	P.........					
Chondracanthus merlucii Holten 5, 40............	P.........					
Coronula diadema (L) 5, 18......................	P.........					
Coronula regina Darwin 45......................	P.........					
Dias longiremis Lilljeborg 27....................						
Euchaeta marina Pretandrea 10..................						
Eurytemora herdmani Thompson & Scott 10, 36..	F.........					
Harpacticus chelifer Muller 11, 27, 35...........	F.........					
Irenaeus patersoni Templeton = Anomalocera pa- tersoni 10.......................................	F.........					
Isias clavipes Boeck 10..........................						
Labidocera aestiva Wheeler 10...................						
Lepas fascicularis Ellis & Solander 5 = L. fascicu- latus 8, 35.................................						
Lepas hillii Leach 5, 8, 35......................						
Lepeophtheirus salmonis Kroyer 18...............	P.........					
Lepeophtheirus hippoglossi Kroyer a	P					
Lernaea branchialis L. 5, 18, 40.................	P.........					
Microsetella atlantica Brady & Robertson........	F.........					
Nemesis robusta 31.............................	P.........					
Oithona plumifera Baird 11.....................	F.........					
Oithona similis Claus 10..........•.............						
Pandarus sinuatus Say 40.......................	P.........					
Paracalanus parvus Claus 10....................						
Peltogaster paguri Rathke 18....................	3–6.......		x			
Pseudocalanus elongatus 10, 11..................•	F.........					
Scalpellum pressum Pilsbry 8....................	224–330..					x
Scalpellum stroemii Sars 5, 8...................	35–1000..			x	x	x
Scalpellum velutinum Hock 27...................						
Temora sp. 27...........................						
Tortanus discaudatus (Thompson & Scott) 10, 11, 22, 35, 36.................................	F.........					
Ostracoda.						
Argilloecia sp.................................						
Bradycinetus sp........•.................						
Bythocythere turgida Sars......................						
Cypridina excisa Stimpson 18....................	4–5.......		x			
Cythere abyssicola Sars.........................					x	
Cythere badia ? Norman.........................					x	
Cythere canadensis Brady 35.....................					x	
Cythere concinna Jones 35.......................					x	
Cythere costata Brady...........................					x	
Cythere dawsoni Brady..........................					x	

(a) From Skin of Hippoglossus vulgaris Flem. Le Have Island, E. Coast of Nova Scotia. C. H. Young, collector. Determined by Dr. C. B. Wilson.

38a—17

BATHYMETRIC TABLES—*Continued.*

			BATHYMETRIC RANGE.			
—	Min. and Max. Depth.	Inter- tidal. Zone.	Fathoms.			
			1–15	15–50	50–100	100 x
Ostracoda—Con.						
Cythere dunelmensis Norman 35				x		
Cythere emarginata Sars 35				x		
Cythere leioderma Norman				x		
Cythere limicola Norman				x		
Cythere lutea Muller				x		
Cythere pellucida Band				x		
Cythere tuberculata Sars 35				x		
Cythere villosa Sars 35				x		
Cythere *whitei* Band				x		
Cytheridea (?) elongata Brady				x		
Cytheridea papillosa Bosquet				x		
Cytheridea punctillata Brady				x		
Cytheridea sorbyana Jones				x		
Cytherideis foveolata Brady				x		
Cytheropteron angulatum Br. & Rob				x		
Cytheropteron arcuatum Br. & Rob				x		
Cytheropteron nodosum Brady				x		
Cytheropteron vespertillo Reuss				x		
Cytherura (?) concentrica C. B. & R. (M. S.)				x		
Cytherura cristata Brady & Crosskey				x		
Cytherura (?) pumila C. B. & R. (M.S.)				x		
Cytherura sarsii Brady				x		
Cytherura (?) undata Sars (Var.)				x		
Eucythere argus Sars sp				x		
Krithe (Ilyobates) bartonensis Jones				x		
Loxoconcha sp				x		
Philomedes brenda Baird 14						
Philomedes interpuncta Baird				x		
Schlerochilus contortus Norman				x		
Xestoleberis depressa Sars 35				x		
MALACOSTRACA						
Leptostraca, and Arthrostraca.						
Acanthonotozoma serratum (Fabricius) 5, 18	5–50		x	x		
Acanthonotozoma inflatum (Kroyer) 18	8		x			
Acanthostephia malmgreni Goes	70				x	
Acanthozone cuspidata (Lepechin) 5, 18, 27	5–80		x	x	x	
Aceros phyllonyx M. Sars	50–70			x	x	
Æga psora (L) 4, 5, 18	20–150			x	x	x
Ægina longicornis Kroyer 5	I.T.–32	x	x	x		
Ægina spinosissima (Stimpson) 5 = Æquiella spinossissima 27	10		x			
Amathilla homari (J. C. Fabricius) 18						
Ampelisca eschrichtii Kroyer 18	14–110		x	x	x	x
Ampelisca macrocephala Lilljeborg 5, 18, 35	8–50		x	x		
Ampelisca typica Spence Bate						
Amphithoe podoceroides Rathke	o–8		x			
Apmhithoe punctata Say	4		x			
Amphithoe rubricata Montagu 18, 27	8		x			
Anonyx exiguus Stimpson	8–15		x			
Anonyx nugax (Phipps) 18, 35	I.T.–40	x	x	x		
Anonyx pallidus Stimpson	4–20		x	x		
Anonyx politus Stimpson	40			x		
Anonyx pumilus Lilljeborg	10–15		x			
Apherusa bispinosa 18	10–20		x	x		
Arcturus baffini Westwood 18						
Astacilla granulata (G. O. Sars) 4, 5	7–640		x	x	x	x
Byblis gaimardii (Kroyer) 5, 18	10–60		x	x	x	
Calathura brachiata (Stimpson) 4, 35	10–250		x	x	x	x
Calliopius laeviusculus (Kroyer) 5, 18	F					
Caprella linearis (L) 5, 18, 27	4–32		x	x		
Caprella longimanus Stimpson						

Bathymetric Tables—*Continued.*

	Min. and Max. Depth.	Inter-tidal Zone.	Fathoms.			
			1–15.	15–50	50–100	100 x

MALACOSTRACA—*Con.*						
*Leptostraca and Arthrostraca—*Con.						
Caprella sanguinea Gould						
Caprella stimpsonii Spence Bate = C. robusta 27..	12		x			
Centromedon pumilus 18	15		x			
Chiridotea coeca (Say) 4, 5, 35	I.T.	x				
Chiridotea tuftsii (Stimpson) 4, 5	o		x			
Cirolana borealis Lilljeborg 4	30–300			x	x	x
Cirolana concharum Stimpson 4	0–18		x	x		
Cirolana polita Stimpson 4, 5	I.T.–150	x	x	x	x	x
Dajus mysidis Kroyer 4, 18						
Dulichia porrecta Spence Bate 18						
Epelys montosus (Stimpson) = Edotea montosa 4, 5, 35	14–40		x	x		
Epimeria loricata G. O. Sars 5	85–212				x	x
Ericthonius difformis Milne-Edwards 8 = E. ruhricornis 27	8–100		x	x	x	
Eurycope robusta Harger = Eurycope cornuta Sars 4	50–400				x	x
Eusirus cuspidatus Kroyer						
Euthemisto bispinosa (Boeck) 5, 35	F					
Euthemisto compressa Goes. 11	F					
Euthemisto libellula (Mandt.) 18	F					
Gammaracanthus macrophthalmus (Stimpson)	o		x			
Gammarus locusta (L ?) J. C. Fabricius 18, 27	I.T.–21	x	x	x		
Gnathia cerina (Stimpson) 5, 18	10–220		x	x	x	x
Gyge hippolytes (Kroyer) = Bopyroides hippolytes 4	5–70		x	x	x	
Halirages bispinosus (Spence Bate)						
Halirages fulvocinctus (M. Sars) 5, 18	10–220		x	x	x	x
Haploops setosa Boeck 5	30–110		x	x	x	
Haploops tubicola Lilljeborg 5, 18	15–106		x	x	x	
Harpinia fusiformis (Stimpson)	20–220			x	x	x
Hyale littoralis (Stimpson) = Allorchestes littoralis 5, 35	I.T.	x				
Hyperoche medusarum (Kroyer) = Hyperia medusarum 18, 35	F					
Idotea marina (L) 5 = Idothea baltica 35	I.T.–30	x	x	x		
Idotea phosphorea Harger 4, 27, 35	I.T.–30	x	x	x		
Idotea robusta Kroyer = Idothea metallica 35, 45	0–91		x	x	x	
Jaera albifrons Leach = Jaera marina, 4, 18, 35	I.T.	x				
Janira alta (Stimpson) 4, 5	I.T.–487	x	x	x	x	x
Janira spinosa Harger = Tobella spinosa 4						
Lafystus sturionis Kroyer 5, 35						
Leptocheirus pinguis (Stimpson) 47 = Ptilocheirus pinguis, 5, 27	0–150		x	x	x	x
Leptochelia filum (Stimpson) 4, 18	8–20		x	x		
Leucothoe grandimanus Stimpson	30			x		
Limnoria lignorum (Rathke) 4, 35	1–3		x			
Lysianax spinifera (Stimpson)	40			x		
Lysianopsis alba Holmes 5, 18, 27	4–13		x			
Maera danae (Stimpson) 5	50			x		
Maera sp	22–30			x		
Mayerella limicola Huntsman 41	5–50		x	x		
Melita dentata (Kroyer) 5, 18, 27	7½–430		x	x	x	x
Melita goesii Hansen	70				x	
Melphidippa sp. indet.	14–220		x	x	x	x
Metopa glacialis (Kroyer)						
Mesidotea entomon Linn 18						
Mesidotea sabinii Kroyer 18						
Metopa groenlandica Hansen 5, 27	86–150				x	x
Monoculodes borealis Boeck	20			x		
Monoculodes demissus Stimpson	4		x			
Monoculodes sp. indet.	60				x	
Munna fabricii Kroyer 4	4–200		x	x	x	x

38a—17½

8 GEORGE V, A. 1918

BATHYMETRIC TABLES—*Continued.*

	Min. and Max. Depth.	Inter-tidal. Zone.	Fathoms.			
			1–15	15–50	50–100	100 x
MALACOSTRACA—*Con.*						
*Leptostraca and Arthrostraca—*Con.						
Munnopsis typica M. Sars 4, 18	5–400		x	x	x	x
Nebalia hipes (Fabricius) 18	4–220		x	x	x	x
Oediceros lynceus M. Sars = Paroediceros lynceus 5, 18	4–85		x	x	x	
Oediceros saginatus Kroyer						
Onisimus edwardsii Kroyer 18						
Orchestia agilis S. I. Smith 5, 27, 35	I.T					
Orchestia gryllus Gould	I.T	x				
Orchomene minutus (Kroyer) = Orchomenella minuta 18	10–15		x			
Paramphithoe cataphracta (Stimpson)	4–50		x	x		
Paramphithoe pulchella (Kroyer) 5, 27	25–90			x	x	
Parathemisto oblivia (Kroyer)	F					
Pardalisca cuspidata Kroyer 5	35–70			x	x	
Phoxocephalus holbolli (Kroyer) 5, 18, 35	0–200		x	x	x	x
Phryxus abdominalis (Kroyer) 4, 18, 35	5–351		x	x	x	x
Pleustes bicuspis (Kroyer) = Paramphithoe bi-cuspis 18						
Pleustes panoplus (Kroyer) 5, 18	4–85		x	x	x	
Podocerus fucicola (Stimpson)						
Podocerus nitidus (Stimpson) = Podoceropsis ni-tidus 5	30–60			x	x	
Pontogeneia inermis (Kroyer) 5, 18, 35	I.T.–15	x	x	x		
Pontoporeia femorata Kroyer 5, 18	1–60		x	x	x	
Ptilanthura tenuis Harger 4, 35	0–19		x	x		
Rhacotropis aculeatus (Lepechin) 5, 18	10–122	x	x	x	x	x
Socarnes vahli Kroyer 18						
Stegocephalus inflatus Kroyer 5, 18, 35	50–150				x	x
Stenothoe clypeata Stimpson	30			x		
Synidotea bicuspida (Owen) = S. marmorata 4, 18	12–129		x	x	x	x
Synidotea nodulosa (Kroyer) 45	6–190		x	x	x	x
Syrrhoe crenulata Goes 5	12–100		x	x	x	
Tiron acanthurus Lilljeborg	45			x		
Tryphosa horringii Boeck 18						
Unciola irrorata Say 5, 18, 27, 35	0–430		x	x	x	x
Cumacea.						
Diastylis goodsiri (Bell) 25	60–218				x	x
Diastylis luciferus (Kroyer) 5	10–77		x	x	x	
Diastylis politus S. I. Smith 5, 25, 35	7–190		x	x	x	x
Diastylis quadrispinosus G. O. Sars 5, 18, 25, 35	2–190		x	x	x	x
Diastylis rathkii (Kroyer) 18, 25	3–499		x	x	x	x
Diastylis scorpioides (Lepechin) 25	13–206		x	x	x	x
Diastylis sculptus G. O. Sars 5, 25, 35	0–190		x	x	x	x
Diastylopsis ? resima (Kroyer) 25	57				x	
Eudorella emarginata (Kroyer)	30–52			x		
Eudorella hispida G. O. Sars 35	1–4		x			
Eudorella integra S. I. Smith = Eudorellopsis in-tegra 25	29–110			x	x	x
Eudorella pusilla G. O. Sars	1–15		x			
Lamprops quadriplicata (S. I. Smith) 5, 25	7–37		x	x		
Leucon nasicoides Lilljeborg 5	42–110			x	x	x
Leucon nasicus Kroyer	50–70				x	
Petalosarsia declivis (G. O. Sars) 25	39–89			x	x	
Schizopoda.						
Meterythrops robusta S. I. Smith = Parerythrops robusta 5	33–70			x	x	
Mysis mixta Lilljeborg 5, 18	20–90			x	x	
Mysis oculata (Fabricius)	F					
Mysis stenolepis S. I. Smith = Michtheimysis ste-nolepis 35	16–21			x		
Nyctiphanes norvegica (M. Sars) 5 = Meganycti-phanes norvegica 35, 39	F					

BATHYMETRIC TABLES—*Continued.*

	Min. and Max. Depth.	Inter-tidal Zone.	BATHYMETRIC RANGE.			
—			Fathoms.			
			1–15	15–50	50–100	100 x
Decapoda.—Macrura.						
Pseudomma roseum G. O. Sars	110–210					x
Pseudomma truncatum S. O. Smith	45–70			x	x	
Rhoda inermis (Kroyer) 5 = Thysanoessa inermis 35	40–220			x	x	x
Thysanoessa (Rhoda) inermis neglecta (Kroyer)39.	300					x
Thysanoessa raschii M. Sars 39	0–300		x	x	x	x
Calocaris mcandreae Bell	190					x
Caridion gordoni (Spence Bate) 5	27–110			x	x	x
Crangon vulgaris J. C. Fabricius 27 = Crago septemspinosus 18, 35	0–50		x	x		
Eupagurus bernhardus (L) = Pagurus acadianus Benedict 5, 27, 35, 47	0–150		x	x	x	x
Eupagurus kroyeri Stimpson = Pagurus kroyeri 5, 18, 35	0–306		x	x	x	x
Eupagurus pubescens (Kroyer) 47 = Pagurus pubescens 5, 18, 35	0–150		x	x	x	x
Hetairus debilis Spence Bate	85				x	
Hetairus tenuis Spence Bate	85				x	
Hippolyte fabricii Kroyer 27 = Spirontocaris fabricii 5, 18	0–125		x	x	x	x
Hippolyte macilenta Kroyer = Spirontocaris macilenta 18	15–75		x	x		
Hippolyte projecta Spence Bate	85				x	
Homarus americanus Milne Edwards 5, 18, 27, 35.	0–20		x	x		
Lithodes maia (L) 5	250–291					x
Munidopsis curvirostra Whiteaves	35–1290			x	x	x
Nectocrangon dentatus Rathbun 18						
Nectocrangon lar (Owen)	10–60		x	x	x	
Pagurus irroratus Linnaeus 27						
Pagurus longicarpus Say 5, 35, 47	I.T.–18	x	x	x		
Pandalus borealis Kroyer 5	40–160			x	x	x
Pandalus leptocerus Smith 5	S.W.–630		x	x	x	x
Pandalus montagui Leach 5, 18, 27, 35	6–430		x	x	x	x
Parapagurus pilosimanus S. I. Smith	353–2021					x
Pontophilus norvegicus M. Sars 5	92–115			x	x	x
Sabinea sarsii S. I. Smith 5	16–150				x	x
Sabinea septemcarinata (Sabine) 5, 18	15–85			x	x	
Sclerocrangon boreas (Phipps) 5, 18	0–36		x	x		
Spirontocaris gaimardii (Milne Edwards) 5, 18	0–60		x	x	x	
Spirontocaris gaimardii var. belcheri Bell. 18	8–75		x	x	x	
Spirontocaris groenlandica (J. C. Fabricius 5 = Hippolyte groenlandica 18, 27, 35	1–72		x	x	x	
Spirontocaris polaris (Sabine) 5 = Hippolyte polaris, 18, 27	3–218		x	x	x	x
Spirontocaris pusiola (Kroyer) 5, 35	0–125		x	x	x	x
Spirontocaris spinus (Sowerby) = Hippolyte spinus 5, 18, 27	5–90		x	x	x	
Spirontocaris stoneyi Rathbun 18	7		x			
Spirontocaris turgida (Kroyer) = Hippolyte phippsi 5	7–125		x	x	x	x
Decapoda—Brachyura.						
Cancer amaenus Herbst 1 = C. irroratus Say 18, 27, 35, 47	I.T.–19	x	x	x		
Cancer borealis Stimpson 5	I.T.–21	x	x	x		
Chionoecetes opilio (O. Fabricius) 5, 18	10–101		x	x	x	x
Hyas araneus (L) 18, 27	0–106		x	x	x	x
Hyas coarctatus Leach 5, 18, 35, 47	0–106		x	x	x	-
Libinia emarginata Leach 5, 35, 47	I.T.–19	x	x	x		
Neptunus sayi Milne Edwards	85				x	

8 GEORGE V, A. 1918

BATHYMETRIC TABLES—*Continued.*

—	Min. and Max. Depth.	Inter-tidal Zone.	Fathoms.			
			1–15	15–50	50–100	100 x
ARACHNIDA.						
Pycnogonida.						
Achelia spinosa (Stimpson)...................						
Ammothea achelioides Wilson...................					x	
Nymphon brevicollum Hoek...................	85				x	
Nymphon grossipes (O. Fabricius) 35............	12–110		x	x		x
Nymphon hirtum J. C. Fabricius................	0–50		x	x		
Nymphon longitarse Kroyer.....................	16–90			x	x	
Nymphon macrum Wilson						
Nymphon stroemii Kroyer......................	35–110			x	x	x
Phoxichilidium maxillare (Stimpson).............	I.T.–55	x	x	x	x	
Pseudopallene hispida (Stimpson)...............	50–55				x	
Pycnogonum littorale (Strom)...................	I.T.–430	x	x	x	x	x
CHORDATA.						
Amaroucium glabrum Verrill 23, 26, 35...........	0–80		x	x	x	
Amaroucium pallidum Verrill = Aplidium pallidum 23, 35...........	0–471		x	x	x	x
Aplidium despectum Herdman...................	51				x	
Ascidia complanata Fabricius = Phallusia prunum 29 = Ascidiopsis prunum 26.................	I.T.–150	x	x	x	x	x
Ascidia falcigera Herdman.....................	85				x	
Boltenia bolteni (L) 30.....................	30–56			x	x	
Boltenia bolteni (L) var. rubra = Pyura ovifera 29	30–56			x	x	
Boltenia ciliata Moller = Pyura ovifera 29........	30			x		
Boltenia elegans Herdman = Pyura ovifera 29 and Boltenia ovifera 26, 47.....................	51			x		
Botrylloides aureum Sars 23, 26..................	S.W.–160		x	x	x	x
Botryllus (spec. undet.)......................	50–96				x	
Caesira canadensis 26........................	I.T.	x				
Caesira intumescens Van Name 29...............	39			x		
Caesira septentrionalis Traustedt 29.............	50			x		
Chelyosoma geometricum Stimpson = C, macleayanum 26, 29......................	6–54		x	x	x	
Ciona tenella (Stimpson) = C, intestinalis (L) 29..	5–127		x	x	x	
Dendrodoa aggregata pulchella Verrill 29.........	10–40		x	x		
Dendrodoa carnea Agassiz 26, 29 = Cynthia carnea 35...................................	S.W.–39		x	x		
Dendrodoa grossularia Van Beneden 29...........	45			x		
Didemnopsis tenerum (Verrill) 23, 26.............	10–76		x	x	x	
Eugyra glutinans (Moller) 35...................	6		x			
Eugyra pilularis Verrill 35 = Bostrichobranchus pilularis 29................................	½–120		x	x	x	x
Glandula arenicola Verrill = Tethyum molle 29...	10–150		x	x	x	x
Glandula fibrosa Stimpson = Pandocia fibrosa 29..	30–238			x	x	x
Glandula mollis Stimpson = Tethyum molle 29...	10–150		x	x	x	x
Halocynthia echinata (L) 35 = Pyura echinata 29 and Boltenia hirsuta 26......................	0–120		x	x	x	x
Halocynthia pyriformis (Rathke) = Pyura aurantium 29 and Tethyum pyriforme americanum	0–120		x	x	x	x
Halocynthia rustica (L) = Tethyum rusticum 29..	8		x			
Halocynthia tuberculum (Fabricius) = Tethyum coriaceum Alder & Hancock 29...............	10–225		x	x	x	x
Holozoa clavata (Sars) 26,29 ?.................	S.W.–150		x	x	x	x
Leptoclinum albidum Verrill = Tetradidemnum albidum 23, 26.............................	0–110		x	x	x	x
Leptoclinum albidum var. luteolum = Tetradidemnum albidum 29.....................	0–110		x	x	x	x
Leptoclinides faeroensis Bjerkan 23.............	100–1582					x
Lissoclinum aureum Verrill 23, 26...............	S.W.–100		x	x	x	x
Macroclinum pomun Sars 23....................	75				x	
Microcosmus nacreus Van Name 29..............	26–36			x		
Molgula littoralis, Verrill = Caesira citrina 29 & Caesira littoralis 26.......................	I.T.–126	x	x	x	x	x

BATHYMETRIC TABLES—*Continued.*

	Min. and Max. Depth.	Inter-tidal. Zone.	BATHYMETRIC RANGE.			
			Fathoms.			
—			1–15	15–50	50–100	100 x
CHORDATA—*Con.*						
Molgula pannosa Verrill 35 = Caesira pannosa 26, 29..	10–80....	....	x	x	x	
Molgula papillosa Verrill 35 = Caesira papillosa 26, 29..	10–100....	....	x	x	x	
Molgula producta Stimpson 35 = Caesira producta 29..	I.T.–29...	x	x	x		
Molgula retortiformis Verrill = Caesira retortiformis 26, 29..	10–125....	....	x	x	x	x
Pera crystallina (Moller) = Caesira crystallina 29.	10–30....	....	x	x		
Pelonaia arenifera Stimpson = P. corrugata 26, 29..	15........	......	x			
Phallusia obliqua (Alder) 29 = Phallusioides obliqua 26...................................	33–320....	....	......	x	x	x
Polycitor kukenthali (Gottschaldt) 23............	8–225....	....	x	x	x	x
Tethyum finmarkense Kiaer 29....................	11–67....	....	x	x	x	
Tethyum mortenseni Hartmeyer 29................	45–350....	......	......	x	x	x

BIBLIOGRAPHY, 1902-16.

Coe, W. R. and Kunkel, B. W.
> 1. On Cerebratulus melanops n. sp.
> Gulf of St. Lawrence. Biological Bulletin, Boston, 1903, Vol. IV, No. 3.

McIntosh, W. C.
> 2. On Canadian Eunicidæ dredged by Dr. Whiteaves of the Canadian Geological Survey in 1871-73.
> Notes from the Gatty Marine Laboratory. Annals of Natural History, 1903, seventh series, Vol. XII, pp. 149-164.
> On the Goniadidæ, Glyceridæ, and Ariclidæ procured by Dr. Whiteaves in the Gulf of St. Lawrence in 1872-73.
> Notes from the Gatty Marine Laboratory, Annals of Natural History, 1905, 7th series, Vol. XV, pp. 51-54.

Richardson, H.
> 4. Isopods of North America.
> Bulletin United States Nationa lMuseum, 1905, No. 54, pp. 1-727.

Rathbun, Mary.
> 5. Fauna of New England.
> Occasional Papers, Boston Society of Natural History, No. 5, 1905, pp. 1-117.

Clark, H. L.
> 6. The Apodous Holothurians.
> Smithsonian Contributions to Knowledge, 1907, Vol. XXV, pp. 1-231.

Dall, W. H.
> 7. A Review of the American Volutidæ.
> Smithsonian Miscellaneous Collections, 1907, Vol. XLVIII, pp. 341-373.

Pilsbry, H. A.
> 8. The Barnacles in the United States National Museum.
> United States National Museum Bulletin 60, 1907.

Cornish, G. A.
> 9. Report of the Marine Polyzoa of Canso, N.S.
> Contributions to Canadian Biology. 1902-5 (1907), pp. 71-81.
> (39th Report of the Department of Marine and Fisheries, Fisheries Branch.)

BIBLIOGRAPHY, 1902-16—Continued.

Scott, Thomas.

10. On Some Entomostraca from the Gulf of St. Lawrence.
Transactions Natural History Society of Glasgow, 1907, New series, Vol. VII, 1902-5, pp. 46-52.

Wright, R. Ramsay.

11. The Plankton of Eastern Nova Scotia Waters.
Further Contributions to Canadian Biology, 1902-5 (1917), pp. 1-19.
(39th Report of the Department of Marine and Fisheries, Fisheries Branch.)

McIntosh, W. C.

12. The Opheliidæ, Scalibregmidæ and Telethusæ dredged by Dr. Whiteaves in the Gulf of St. Lawrence, Canada.
Notes from the Gatty Marine Laboratory, Annals of Natural History 1908, 8th series, Vol. 1, pp. 385-387.
13. Sphærodoridæ, Chloræmidæ and Chætopteridæ dredged in the Gulf of St. Lawrence by Dr. Whiteaves.
Notes from the Gatty Marine Laboratory, Annals of Natural History 1908, 8th series, Vol. II, p. 540-541.

Sharpe, R. W.

14. A further Report on the Ostracods of the United States National Museum.
Proceedings of the U. S. Nat. Mus. 1908, Vol. XXXV, No. 1651, pp. 339-430.

Bartsch, Paul.

15. Pyramidellidæ of New England and the adjacent region.
Proc. Boston Soc. Nat. Hist. 1909, Vol. 34, No. 4. pp. 67-113.

Bigelow, H. B.

16. Cœlenterates from Labrador and Newfoundland, collected by Mr. Owen Bryant in 1908.
Proc. U. S. Nat. Mus. 1909, Vol. 37, pp. 301-320.

Moore, J. P.

17. The Polychætous Annelids dredged in 1908 by Mr. Owen Bryant off the coast of Labrador, Newfoundland and Nova Scotia.
Proc. U. S. Nat. Mus. 1909, Vol. 37, pp. 113-146.

Rathbun, M. J.

18. The Crustacea of the Labrador Coast.
Appendices II & VI to, "Labrador" by Grenfell & Others', 1909, MacMillan & Co.

Johnson, C. W.

19. The Molluscs of Labrador.
Appendix III to, "Labrador" By Grenfell & Others', 1909, MacMillan & Co.

Ashworth, J. H.

20. The Annelids of the family Arenicolidæ of North and South America including an account of Arenicola glacialis Murdoch.
Proc. U. S. Nat. Mus. 1910, Vol. 39, pp. 1-32, text figs. 1-14.

McMurrich, J. Playfair.

21. The Actiniaria of Passamaquoddy Bay with a discussion of their synonymy.
Trans. Roy. Soc. of Can. 1910, 3rd. ser. Vol. IV, sec. IV, pp. 59-83, plates 1-3.

Sharpe, R. W.

22. Notes on the Marine Copepoda and Cladocera of Woods Hole and adjacent regions including a synopsis of the genera of the Harpacticoidea.
Proc. U. S. Nat. Mus. 1910, Vol. 38, pp. 405-436.

Van Name, W. G.

23. Compound Ascidians of the coast of New England and neighbouring British provinces.
Proc. Bos. Soc. Nat. Hist. 1910, Vol. 34, No. 11, pp. 339-424.

McIntosh, W. C.

24. On Nevaya whiteavesi, a form with certain relationships to Scherocheilus. Grube. from Canada. On the Cirratulidæ dredged in the Gulf of St. Lawrence, Canada by Dr. Whiteaves.
Notes from the Gatty Marine Laboratory, St. Andrews; Annals and Magazine of Nat. Hist. 1911, Vol. 7, 8th ser. No. 38, pp. 145-173.

Calman, W. T.

25. The Crustacea of the Order Cumacea in the collection of the United States National Museum.
Proc. U. S. Nat. Mus. 1912, Vol. 41, pp. 603-676.

BIBLIOGRAPHY, 1902-16—Continued.

Huntsman, A. G.

26. Ascidians from the coasts of Canada.
Trans. Can. Inst. 1912, Vol. IX, pt. 2, No. 21, pp. 111-148.

MacDonald, D. L.

27. On a collection of Crustacea made at St. Andrews, N.B.
Contr. to Can. Biology 1906-10 (1912), pp. 83-84.

Osburn, Raymond C.

28. Bryozoa from Labrador, Newfoundland and Nova Scotia collected by Dr. Owen Bryant.
Proc. U. S. Nat. Mus. 1912, Vol. 43, pp. 275-289.

Van Name, W. G.

29. Simple Ascidians of the coasts of New England and neighbouring British provinces.
Proc. Bos. Soc. Nat. Hist. 1912, Vol. 34, No. 13, pp. 439-619.

Dall, W. H. & Bartsch, Paul.

30. New Species of Molluscs from the Atlantic & Pacific coasts of Canada.
Vict. Mem. Mus. 1913, Bull. No. 1, p. 139-144.

Fraser. C. MacLean.

31. Hydroids from Nova Scotia.
Vict. Mem. Mus. Bull. 1913, No. 1, p. 158-180.

Gerould, J. H.

32. The Sipunculids of the Eastern coast of North America.
Proc. U. S. Nat. Mus. 1913, Vol. 44, No. 1959, pp. 373-457.

McIntosh, W. C.

33. On the Maldanidæ dredged in the Gulf of St. Lawrence by Dr. Whiteaves 1871-73.
Notes from the Gatty Marine Laboratory, St. Andrews.
Annals and Magazine of Nat. Hist. 1913, 8th ser. Vol. XI, pp. 119-128.

34. On Myriochele heeri collected by Dr. Whiteaves in the Gulf of St. Lawrence 1873.
Notes from the Gatty Marine Laboratory, St. Andrews.
Annals & Magazine of Nat. Hist. 1913, 8th ser. Vol. XII, pp. 166-169.

Summer, F. B., Osburn, R. C., and Cole, L. J.

35. A Biological Survey of the Waters of Woods Hole and vicinity.
Bureau of Fisheries Bulletin 1913, Vol. XXXI, Part II. Sec. III, pp. 549-734.

Willey, A.

36. Notes on Plankton collected across the mouth of the St. Croix River opposite the Biological Station at St. Andrews, N.B.
Proceedings Zoological Society of London, 1913, Vol. 1, pp. 283-292.

Koehler, R.

37. A contribution to the study of Ophiurians of the United States National Museum.
U. S. Nat. Mus. Bull. 84, 1914, pp. 1-172.

McIntosh, W. C.

38. On the Chætopteridæ, Amphictenidæ and Ampharetidæ dredged in the Gulf of St. Larence, Canada by Dr. Whiteaves.
Notes from the Gatty Marine Laboratory.
Annals & Magazine of Nat. Hist. 1915, 8th ser. vol. 15, pp. 47-53.

Hansen, H. J.

39. The Crustacea Ephausiacea of the U. S. National Museum.
Proc. U. S. Nat. Mus. 1915, Vol. 48, pp. 59-114.

Stock, V.

40. Parasitic Copepods of the Bay of Fundy Fishes.
Contr. to Can. Biology 1911-14 (1915) pt. 1, pp. 69-71.
Supplement to the 47th Annual Report of the Dept. of Marine & Fisheries, Fisheries Branch.

Huntsman, A. G.

41. A New Caprellid from the Bay of Fundy.
Contr. to Can. Biology 1911-14 (1915), pt. 1, pp. 39-42.
(Supplement to the 47th Annual Report of the Dept. of Marine & Fisheries, Fisheries Branch.)

BIBLIOGRAPHY. 1902-16—Concluded.

Detweiler, J. D.

42. Preliminary Notes on the Mollusca of St. Andrews & vicinity New Brunswick.
Contr. to Can. Biology 1911-14 (1915), pt. 1, pp. 46-48.
(Supplement to the 47th Annual Report of the Dept. of Marine & Fisheries, Fisheries Branch.)

Nutting, C. E.

43. American Hydroids Part III, The Campanularidæ and the Bonneviellidæ.
Special Bulletin U. S. National Museum 1915.

McIntosh, W. C.

44. On the Terebellidæ & Sabellidæ dredged in the Gulf of St. Lawrence Canada by Dr Whiteaves in 1871-73.
Notes from the Gatty Marine Laboratory.
Annals & Magazine Nat. Hist. 1916, 8th ser., Vol. 17, pp. 59-63.

Pilsbry, H. A.

45. The Sessile Barnacles (Cirripedia) contained in the collection of U. S. National Museum including a monograph of the American species.
U. S. Nat. Mus. 1916, Bull. 93, pp. 1-366.

Kindle, E. M.

46. Bottom Control of Marine Faunas as illustrated by Dredging in the Bay of Fundy.
Amer. Jour. Sci,. May 1916, Vol. XLI, pp. 449-461.
47. Notes on the Bottom Environment of the Marine Invertebrates of Western Nova Scotia.
Ottawa Naturalist 1917, Vol, XXX, pp. 149-154

INDEX

The numbers at extreme right refer to the pages in Whiteaves' Catalogue of the Marine Invertebrates of Eastern Canada; numbers in the left-hand column refer to the Bathymetric tables in the preceding section of this paper.

	Bathymetric Tables.	Whiteaves' Catalogue.
Aglaophenopsis cornuta....	232	28
Akera subangulata. *See* Diaphana debilis.		
Alauna goodsiri. *See* Diastylis rathkii.		
Alcyonidium gelatinosum....	243	114
Alcyonidium hispidum. *See* Flustrella hispida.		
Alcyonidium mytili....	243	
Alcyonium arboreum. *See* Paragorgia arborea.		
Alcyonium carneum..	234	31
Alcyonium digitatum. *See* Alcyonium carneum.		
Alcyonium gelatinosum. *See* Alcyonidium gelatinosum.		
Alcyonium glomeratum. *See* Eunepthya lutkeni.		
Alcyonium lutkeni. *See* Eunepthya lutkeni.		
Alcyonium multiflorum..	234	31
Alcyonium rubiforme..	234	31
Alderia harvardiensis(Agassiz)..	245	204
Alecto dentata. *See* Antedon tenella.		
Alecto diastoporoides. *See* Stomatopora diastoporoides.		
Alecto eschrichtii. *See* Antedon eschrichtii.		
Alecto granulata. *See* Stomatopora granulata.		
Alecto sarsii. *See* Antedon tenella.		
Alexia myosotis....	245	208
Allorchestes littoralis. *See* Hyale littoralis.		
Alpheus polaris. *See* Spirontocaris polaris.		
Alvania. *See* Cingula.		
Amaroecium glabrum. *See* Amaroucium glabrum.		
Amaroecium pallidum. *See* Amaroucium pallidum.		
Amaroucium glabrum....	254	266
Amaroucium pallidum..	254	265
Amathilla homari..	250	224
Amaura candida..	245	164
Amauropsis helicoides. *See* Amauropsis islandica.		
Amauropsis islandica (Gmelin)	245	164
Amicula emersonii. *See* Amicula vestita.		
Amicula vestita..	245	155
Ammodiscus incertus..	230	10
Ammothea achelioides..	254	263
Ammothea lutkeni. *See* Eunepthya lutkeni.		
Ammotrypane aulogaster..	237	78
Ammotrypane cylindricaudatus..	237	
Ammotrypane fimbriata..	237	78
Amoroecium pallidum. *See* Amaroecium pallidum.		
Amouroucium glabrum. *See* Amaroucium glabrum.		
Amouroucium pallidum. *See* Amaroucium pallidum.		
Ampelisca eschrichtii..	250	222
Ampelisca gaimardi. *See* Byblis gaimardii.		
Ampelisca macrocephala..	250	222
Ampelisca pelagica. *See* Ampelisca macrocephala.		
Ampelisca typica..	250	222
Ampharete gracilis..	237	74
Ampharete grubei..	237	74
Amphipholis elegans..	236	59
Amphiporus agilis..	237	65
Amphiporus angulatus..	237	64
Amphiporus heterosorus..	237	65
Amphiporus lactifloreus..	237	65
Amphiporus roseus..	237	65
Amphiporus stimpsoni. *See* Amphiporus angulatus.		
Amphiporus (?) superbus..	237	65
Amphisphyra debilis. *See* Diaphana debilis.		
Amphisphyra hiemalis. *See* Diaphane hiemalis.		
Amphisphyra pellucida. *See* Diaphana debilis.		
Amphithoe crenulata. *See* Pontogenela inermis.		
Amphithoe fulvocincta. *See* Halirages fulvocinctus.		
Amphithoe inermis. *See* Pontogeneia inermis.		
Amphithoe lasvuiscula. *See* Calliopius laeviuscula.		
Amphithoe maculata. *See* Amphithoe podoceroides.		
Amphithoe panopla. *See* Pleustes panoplus.		
Amphithoe podoceroides..	250	222
Amphithoe punctata..	250	221
Amphithoe rubricata..	250	
Amphithoe sera. *See* Acanthonotozoma serratum.		
Amphithoe virescens. *See* Amphithoe punctata.		
Amphithonotus cataphractus. *See* Paramphithoe cataphracta and Pleustes panoplus.		

SESSIONAL PAPER No. 38a

	Bathymetric Tables.	Whiteaves' Catalogue.
Buccinum lapillus. *See* Purpura lapillus.		
Buccinum lunatum. *See* Astyris lunata.		
Buccinum rosaceum. *See* Astyris rosacea.		
Buccinum scalariforme. *See* Buccinum tenue.		
Buccinum sericatum. *See* Buccinum cyaneum.		
Buccinum tenebrosum. *See* Buccinum cyaneum.		
Buccinum tenue..	246	184
Buccinum tottenii..	246	182
Buccinum truncatum. *See* Trophon truncatus.		
Buccinum tubulosum. *See* Buccinum donovani.		
Buccinum undatum...	246	181
Buccinum undulatum. *See* Buccinum cyaneum and Buccinum undatum.		
Buccinum zonalis. *See* Astyris zonalis.		
Bugula cucullifera..	240	
Bugula flexilis. *See* Kinetoskias smittii.		
Bugula murrayana..	240	93
Bugula umbella. *See* Kinetoskias arborescens.		
Bulbus flavus. *See* Acrybia flava.		
Bulimina aculeata..	230	10
Bulimina elegantissima..	230	10
Bulimina pyrula..	230	10
Bulla canaliculata. *See* Tornatina canaliculata.		
Bulla corticata. *See* Cylichna alba.		
Bulla debilis. *See* Diaphana debilis.		
Bulla gouldii. *See* Retusa gouldii.		
Bulla hiemalis. *See* Diaphana hiemalis.		
Bulla hyalina. *See* Diaphana debilis.		
Bulla insculpta. *See* Haminea solitaria.		
Bulla lineolata. *See* Philine lima.		
Bulla nucleola. *See* Cylichna alba.		
Bulla obstricta. *See* Tornatina canaliculata.		
Bulla occulta. *See* Cylichna occulta.		
Bulla pellucida. *See* Diaphana debilis.		
Bulla pertenuis. *See* Retusa pertenuis.		
Bulla puncto-striata. *See* Scaphander punctostriatus.		
Bulla reinhardi. *See* Cylichna occulta.		
Bulla solitaria. *See* Haminea solitaria.		
Bulla triticea. *See* Cylichna alba.		
Bulla velutina. *See* Velutina laevigata.		
Bullina canaliculata. *See* Tornatina canaliculata.		
Bunodactis stella. *See* Cribrina stella.		
Bunodes spectabilis. *See* Cribrina stella.		
Bunodes stella. *See* Cribrina stella.		
Byblis gaimardii...	250	223
Bythocythere turgida..	249	217

C

Caberea ellisii..	240	93
Caberea hookeri. *See* Caberea ellisii.		
Caesira canadensis..	254	
Caesira citrina. *See* Molgula littoralis.		
Caesira crystallina. Pera crystallina.		
Caesira intumescens..	254	
Caesira littoralis. *See* Molgula littoralis.		
Caesira pannosa. *See* Molgula pannosa.		
Caesira papillosa. *See* Molgula papillosa.		
Caesira producta. *See* Molgula producta.		
Caesira retortiformis. *See* Molgula retortiformis.		
Caesira septentrionalis..	254	
Calanus finmarchichus..	249	
Calanus helgolandicus..	249	
Calathura brachiata..	250	242
Caligus americanus. *See* Caligus curtus.		
Caligus curtus..	249	216
Caligus rapax..	249	
Calliope laeviuscula. *See* Calliopius laeviusculus.		
Calliopius laeviusculus..	250	227
Calliostoma occidentalis. *See* Calliostoma occidentale.		
Calliostoma occidentale..	246	160
Callista convexa. *See* Cytherea convexa.		
Callocardia morrhuana. *See* Cytherea convexa.		
Calocaris mcandreae..	253	257
Calycella syringa..	232	23

38a—18

8 GEORGE V, A. 1918

	Bathymetric Tables.	Whiteaves' Catalogue.
Cirolana concharum..	251	
Cirolana polita..	251	241
Cirratulus cirrata. *See* Cirratulus cirrhatus.		
Cirratulus cirrhatus..	237	76
Cistenides granulata..	237	74
Cistenides hyperborea..	237	74
Cladocarpus cornutus. *See* Aglaophenopsis cornuta.		
Cladocarpus pourtalesii..	233	28
Cladocarpus speciosus..	233	28
Cladorhiza abyssicola..	232	17
Cladorhiza grandis.:..	232	17
Cladorhiza nordenskioldii..	232	17
Clathria delicata..	232	18
Clava leptostyla..	233	18
Clava multicornis. *See* Clava leptostyla.		
Clavelina chrystallina. *See* Pera crystallina.		
Clidiophora gouldiana..	243	144
Clio borealis. *See* Clione limacina.		
Clio limacina. *See* Clione limacina.		
Clio retusa. *See* Clione limacina.		
Cliona celata..	232	13
Clione limacina..	248	209
Clione miquelonensis. *See* Clione limacina.		
Clione papilionacea. *See* Clione limacina.		
Clymene lumbricalis. *See* Nicomache lumbricalis.		
Clymene mulleri. *See* Praxilla mulleri.		
Clymene torquata. *See* Clymenella torquata.		
Clymenella torquata..	238	75
Clytia bicophora. *See* Clytia johnstoni.		
Clytia johnstoni..	233	24
Clytia noliformis..	233	
Clytia (Orthopyxis) poterium. *See* Campanularia caliculata.		
Clytia volubilis. *See* Clythia johnstoni.		
Cochlodesma leanum..	243	146
Codonella lagenula..	231	
Codonella ventricosa..	231	
Columbella dissimilis. *See* Astyris zonalis.		
Columbella haliaeti. *See* Anachis haliaeti.		
Columbella lunata. *See* Astyris lunata		
Columbella rosacea. *See* Astyris rosacea.		
Conilera polita. *See* Cirolana polita.		
Cornulariella modesta..	234	30
Cornuspira foliacea..	230	10
Coronula diadema..	249	215
Coronula regina..	249	216
Corymorpha glacialis. *See* Monocaulus glacialis.		
Corymorpha nutans. *See* Monocaulus glacialis.		
Corymorpha pendula. *See* Monocaulus glacialis.		
Corynoporella tenuis..	241	94
Coryne gravata. *See* Syncoryne mirabilis.		
Coryne mirabilis. *See* Syncoryne mirabilis.		
Coryphella diversa..	246	205
Coryphella mananensis..	246	205
Coryphella stimpsoni..	246	205
Couthouyella striatula. *See* Menestho striatula.		
Crago septemspinosus. *See* Crangon vulgaris.		
Crangon norvegicus. *See* Pontophilus norvegicus.		
Crangon septemcarinatus. *See* Sabinea septemcarinata.		
Crangon vulgaris..	253	253
Craniella cranium..	232	12
Crassina elliptica. *See* Astarte compressa.		
Crassina latisulca. *See* Astarte undata.		
Crassina depressa. *See* Astarte crebricostata.		
Crassina striata. *See* Astarte banksii var. striata.		
Crassivenus mercenaria. *See* Venus mercenaria.		
Crenella decussata..	246	122
Crenella faba..	246	121
Crenella glandula..	246	122
Crenella pectinula..	246	121
Crepidula convexa..	246	169
Crepidula fornicata..	246	168
Crepidula plana..	246	168
Crepidula unguiformis. *See* Crepidula plana.		
Cribrella oculata. *See* Cribrella sanguinolenta.		

	Bathymetric Tables.	Whiteaves' Catalogue.
Cythere whitei..	250	217
Cytherea convexa..	243	136
Cytherea sayana. *See* Cytherea convexa.		
Cytherea sayii. *See* Cytherea convexa.		
Cytheridea (?) elongata..	250	217
Cytheridea papillosa..	250	217
Cytheridea punctillata..	250	217
Cytheridea sorbyana..	250	217
Cytherideis foveolata..	250	217
Cytheropteron angulatum..	250	217
Cytheropteron arcuatum..	250	217
Cytheropteron nodosum..	250	217
Cytheropteron vespertillo..	250	217
Cytherura (?) concentrica..	250	217
Cytherura (?) cristata..	250	217
Cytherura (?) pumila..	250	217
Cytherura (?) sarsil..	250	217
Cytherura (?) undata..	250	217
Cyttarocyclis denticulata..	231	

D

Dacrydium vitreum..	243	120
Dajus mysidis..	251	236
Defrancia exarata. *See* Bela exarata.		
Defrancia lucernaria. *See* Discofascigera lucernaria.		
Defrancia nobilis. *See* Bela nobilis.		
Defrancia pingelii. *See* Bela pingelii.		
Defrancia scalaris. *See* Bela scalaris.		
Defrancia woodiana. *See* Bela woodiana.		
Dendrodoa aggregata var. pulchella..	.254	
Dendrodoa carnea..	254	
Dendrodoa grossularia..	254	
Dendronotus arborescens..	246	206
Dendronotus robustus..	246	206
Dendronotus reynoldsii. *See* Dendronotus arborescens.		
Dendronotus velifer. *See* Dendronotus robustus.		
Dentalium abyssorum. *See* Dentalium occidentale.		
Dentalium agile..	245	152
Dentalium dentale. *See* Dentalium occidentale.		
Dentalium dentalis. *See* Dentalium occidentale.		
Dentalium entalis..	245	152
Dentalium lobatum. *See* Siphonodentalium lobatum.		
Dentalium vitreum. *See* Siphonodentalium lobatum.		
Dentalium occidentale..	245	152
Desmacella peachii var. groenlandica..	232	17
Desmacidon (Homaeodictya) palmata..	232	17
Desmophyllum nobile..	234	42
Dexamine bispinosa. *See* Halirages bispinosus.		
Diadora noachina. *See* Puncturella noachina.		
Diaphana debilis..	246	202
Diaphana hiemalis..	246	202
Diaphana nitidula. *See* Retusa nitidula.		
Diaphana pertenuis. *See* Retusa pertenuis.		
Dias longiremis..	249	
Diastopora obelia..	242	112
Diastopora patina..	242	112
Diastylis goodsiri..	252	
Diastylis luciferus..	252	244
Diastylis politus..	252	246
Diastylis quadrispinosus..	252	245
Diastylis rathkii..	252	244
Diastylopsis (?) resima..	252	
Diastylis scorpioides.	252	
Diastylis sculptus..	252	245
Dicoryne flexuosa..	233	19
Dictyocha aculeata. *See* Distephanus aculeatus.		
Didemnopsis tenerum..	254	
Diphasia fallax..	233	26
Diphasia mirabilis..	233	26
Diphasia rosacea..	233	26
Diphyopsis campanulifera..	233	
Discofascigera lucernaria..	242	113
Discopora hispida. *See* Lichenopora hispida.		

	Bathymetric Tables.	Whiteaves' Catalogue.
Discopora skenei. *See* Porella skenei.		
Discopora verrucosa. *See* Umbonula verrucosa.		
Discoporella clypeiformis. *See* Lichenopora clypeiformis.		
Discoporella hispida. *See* Lichenopora hispida.		
Dispotaea. *See* Crucibulum.		
Distephanus speculum var. regularis..	231	
Distephanus aculeatus..	231	11
Doris arborescens. *See* Dendronotus arborescens.		
Doris coronata. *See* Doto coronata.		
Doris illuminate. *See* Polycera lessonii.		
Doris pallida. *See* Onchidoris pallida.		
Doris papillosa. *See* Æolis papillosa.		
Doris planulata..	246	207
Doto coronata..	246	204
Doto formosa..	246	204
Drepanophorus lankesteri..	237	66
Drilonereis canadensis..	238	
Duasmodactyla producta. *See* Thyonidium productum.		
Dulichia porrecta..	251	220

E

Ebria tripartita..	231	
Echinarchnius atlanticus. *See* Echinarachnius parma.		
Echinarachnius parma..	236	63
Echinaster oculatus. *See* Cribrella sanguinolenta.		
Echinaster sanguinolentus. *See* Cribrella sanguinolenta.		
Echinus drobachiensis. *See* Strongylocentrotus drobachiensis.		
Echinus granularis. *See* Strongylocentrotus drobachiensis.		
Echinus granulatus. *See* Strongylocentrotus drobachiensis.		
Echinus neglectus. *See* Strongylocentrotus drobachiensis.		
Edotea montosa. *See* Epelys montosus.		
Edwardsia farinacea..	234	37
Edwardsia sipunculoides..	234	37
Electra catenularia..	241	96
Electra pilosa..	241	95
Enonella bicarinata..	238	88
Ensatella americana. *See* Ensis directus.		
Ensis americanum. *See* Ensis directus.		
Ensis directus..	243	143
Entalis striolata. *See* Dentalium entalis.		
Eolis diversa. *See* Coryphella diversa.		
Eolis mananensis. *See* Coryphella mananensis.		
Eolis purpurea. *See* Æolis purpurea.		
Eolis stellata. *See* Æolis stellata.		
Epelys montosus..	251	240
Ephesia gracilis..	238	78
Ephesia sp..	238	
Epigonactis fecunda..	234	39
Epimeria coniger. *See* Epimeria loricata.		
Epimeria cornigera. *See* Epimeria loricata.		
Epimeria loricata..	251	227
Epitonium groenlandicum..	243	
Epizoanthus americanus. *See* Epizoanthus incrustatus.		
Epizoanthus cancrisocius. *See* Epizoanthus incrustatus.		
Epizoanthus incrustatus..	235	36
Epizoanthus paguriphilus..	235	36
Erentho smitti..	238	
Erichthonius rubricornis. *See* Erichthonius difformis.		
Ericthonius difformis..	251	221
Eschara elegantula. *See* Porella elegantula.		
Eschara lævis. *See* Porella lævis.		
Eschara lobata. *See* Escharoides sarsii.		
Eschara palmata. *See* Flustra solida.		
Eschara pavonella. *See* Mucronella pavonella.		
Eschara papposa. *See* Porella elegantula var. papposa.		
Eschara rosacea. *See* Escharoides sarsii.		
Eschara sarsii. *See* Escharoides sarsii.		
Eschara scabra. *See* Rhamphostomella scabra.		
Escharella porifera. *See* Smittia arctica.		
Escharipora annulata. *See* Cribrilina annulata.		
Escharoides coccinea var. peachii. *See* Mucronella peachii.		
Escharoides sarsii..	241	102
Escharopsis lobata. *See* Escharoides sarsii.		

8 GEORGE V, A. 1918

	Bathymetric Tables.	Whiteaves' Catalogue.
Gorgonia reseda. *See* Primnoa reseda.		
Gorgonocephalus agassizii..	236	62
Gorgonocephalus eucnemis..	236	61
Gorgonocephalus lamarckii..	236	62
Grammaria abietina..	233	28
Grammaria gracilis..	233	28
Grammaria robusta. *See* Grammaria abietina.		
Grantia canadensis..	232	12
Grymaea spiralis..	238	73
Gyge hippolytes..	251	236

H

	Bathymetric Tables.	Whiteaves' Catalogue.
Halcyonium carneum. *See* Alcyonium carneum.		
Halecium beani..	233	
Halecium halecinum..	233	24
Halecium minutum..	233	
Halecium muricatum..	233	25
Halecium robustum. *See* Lafoea robusta.		
Halecium sessile..	233	25
Halecium tenellum..	233	
Halichondria incrustans. *See* Myxilla incrustans.		
Halichondria panicea..	232	15
Halichondria ventilabrum. *See* Phakellia ventilabrum.		
Haliclystus auricula. *See* Halyclystus auricula.		
Halirages bispinosus..	251	226
Halirages fulvocinctus..	251	226
Halocynthia echinata..	254	268
Halocynthia pyriformis..	254	268
Halocynthia rustica..	254	268
Halocynthia tuberculum..	254	269
Halophila borealis. *See* Flustra borealis.		
Halyclystus auricula..	233	29
Haminea solitaria..	246	201
Hanleyia mendicaria..	246	154
Haploops setosa..	251	223
Haploops tubicola..	251	222
Haplophragmium canariense..	230	10
Haplophragmium cassis..	230	10
Harmothoe imbricata..	233	84
Harpacticus chelifer..	249	
Harpinia fusiformis..	251	231
Helix haliotoides. *See* Velutina laevigata.		
Helix laevigata. *See* Velutina laevigata.		
Hemeschara struma. *See* Porella struma.		
Hemimactra solidissima. *See* Spisula (Hemimactra) solidissima.		
Hemithyris psittacea..	240	91
Henricia sanguinolenta. *See* Cribrella sanguinolenta.		
Hetairus debilis..	253	253
Hetairus gaimardii. *See* Spirontocaris gaimardii.		
Hetairus tenuis..	253	252
Heterofusus balea. *See* Limacina gouldii.		
Heterofusus retroversus. *See* Limacina gouldii.		
Heteronereis arctica. *See* Nereis (Lycoris) pelagica.		
Heteropia rodgeri..	232	12
Heteroteuthis tenera. *See* Rossia (?) tenera.		
Hippasteria plana. *See* Hippasteria phrygiana.		
Hippasteria phrygiana..	236	50
Hippocrepina indivisa..	230	10
Hippolyte aculeata. *See* Spirontocaris groenlandicus.		
Hippolyte fabricii..	253	249
Hippolyte gaimardii. *See* Spirontocaris gaimardii.		
Hippolyte gordoni. *See* Caridion gordoni.		
Hippolyte groenlandica. *See* Spirontocaris groenlandicus.		
Hippolyte macilenta..	253	249
Hippolyte phippsii. *See* Spirontocaris turgida.		
Hippolyte polaris. *See* Spirontocaris polaris.		
Hippolyte projecta..	253	250
Hippolyte pusiola. *See* Spirontocaris pusiola.		
Hippolyte securifrons. *See* Spirontocaris spinus.		
Hippolyte sowerbaei. *See* Spirontocaris spinus.		
Hippolyte sowerbyi. *See* Spirontocaris spinus.		
Hippolyte spinus. *See* Spirontocaris spinus.		
Hippolyte turgida. *See* Spirontocaris turgida		

SESSIONAL PAPER No. 38a

M

8 GEORGE V, A. 1918

	Bathymetric Tables.	Whiteaves' Catalogue.
Membranipora unicornis..	241	96
Membraniporella crassicosta..	241	98
Menestho aebula. *See* also Menestho striatula.		
Menestho albula..	247	162
Menestho striatula..	247	162
Menipea fruticosa. *See* Bugula murrayana.		
Menipea ternata..	241	92
Mercenaria mercenaria. *See* Venus mercenaria.		
Mercenaria violacea. *See* Venus mercenaria.		
Mertensia cucullus. *See* Mertensia ovum.		
Mertensia ovum..	235	42
Mesalia lacteola. *See* Turritella reticulata.		
Mesidotea entomon..	251	
Mesidotea sabinii..	251	
Mesodesma jauresii. *See* Mesodesma deauratum.		
Mesodesma deauratum..	244	140
Metaecus medusarum. *See* Hyperoche medusarum.		
Meterythrops robusta..	252	247
Metopa glacialis..	251	232
Metopa groenlandica..	251	
Metridium dianthus..	234	37
Metridium marginatum. *See* Metridium dianthus.		
Metridium senile. *See* Metridium dianthus.		
Microcosmus nacreus..	254	
Microporella ciliata..	241	98
Microsetella atlantica..	249	
Micrura affinis..	237	67
Micrura rubra..	237	67
Mictheimysis stenolepis. *See* Mysis stenolepis.		
Miliolina agglutinans..	231	10
Miliolina bicornis..	231	10
Miliolina ferussacii..	231	10
Miliolina oblonga..	231	10
Miliolina secans..	231	10
Miliolina seminulum..	231	10
Miliolina subrotunda..	231	10
Miliolina tricarinata..	231	10
Miliolina trigonula..	231	10
Millepora lichenoides. *See* Hornera lichenoides.		
Millepora reticulata. *See* Rhamphostomella scabra.		
Millepora skenei. *See* Porella skenei.		
Millepora truncata. *See* Myriozoum subgracile.		
Modiola? cicercula. *See* Crenella decussata.		
Modiola (Brachydontes) demissa..	244	120
Modiola discrepans. *See* Modiolaria discors.		
Modiola glandula. *See* Crenella glandula.		
Modiola laevigata. *See* Modiolaria discors.		
Modiola modiolus..	244	120
Modiola nexa. *See* Modiolaria nigra.		
Modiola nigra. *See* Modiolaria nigra.		
Modiola pectinula. *See* Crenella pectinula.		
Modiola plicatula. *See* Modiola (Brachydontes) demissa.		
Modiola? vitrea. *See* Dacrydium vitreum.		
Modiolaria corrugata..	244	121
Modiolaria discors..	244	120
Modiolaria discrepans. *See* Modiolaria nigra.		
Modiolaria laevigata. *See* Modiolaria discors.		
Modiolaria nigra..	244	121
Molgula littoralis..	254	270
Molgula pannosa..	255	270
Molgula papillosa..	255	270
Molgula pilularis. *See* Eugyra pilularis.		
Molgula producta..	255	270
Molgula retortiformis..	255	270
Molleria costulata..	247	157
Molpadia colitica. *See* Trochostoma coliticum.		
Molpadia turgida. *See* Trochostoma turgidum.		
Monocaulus glacialis..	233	21
Monoculodes borealis..	251	229
Monoculodes demissus..	251	229
Monoculodes nubilatus. *See* Oediceros lynceus.		
Monoculodes sp. indet..	251	229
Monoporella spinulifera..	241	103
Montacuta elevata. *See* Rochefortia molleri.		

8 GEORGE V, A. 1918

8 GEORGE V, A. 1918

	Bathymetric Tables.	Whiteaves' Catalogue.
Phyllodoce mucosa..	239	
Phyllodoce sp..	239	
Physalia arethusa. *See* Physalia pelagica.		
Physalia pelagica..	234	29
Pilidium commodum. *See* Capulacmaea radiata.		
Pilidium radiatum. *See* Capulacmaea radiata.		
Pilidium rubellum. *See* Acmaea rubella.		
Piliscus commodus. *See* Capulacmaea radiata.		
Piliscus probus. *See* Capulacmaea radiata.		
Pista cristata..	239	
Plagiacantha arachnoides..	231	
Planaria angulata. *See* Amphiporus angulatus.		
Planaria fusca. *See* Cerebratulus fuscus.		
Planaria lactiflorea. *See* Amphiporus lactifloreus.		
Planaria linearis. *See* Cephalothrix linearis.		
Planaria rosea. *See* Amphiporus roseus.		
Planaria sanguinea. *See* Lineus sanguineus.		
Planaria viridis. *See* Lineus viridis.		
Pleurobrachia pileus.		
Pleurobrachia rhododactyla..	235	42
Pleurotoma decussata. *See* Bela decussata.		
Pleurotoma violacea. *See* Bela bicarinata var. violacea..		
Pleurotomaria bicarinata. *See* Bela bicarinata.		
Plumularia falcata. *See* Hydrallmania falcata.		
Plumularia tenerrima. *See* Hydrallmania falcata.		
Pleustes bicuspis..	252	228
Pleustes panoplus..	252	228
Podocerus fucicola..	252	221
Podocerus nitidus..	252	221
Podon finmarchichus..	248	
Podon intermedius..	248	
Podon leuckarti..	248	
Podon polyphemoides..	248	
Polia obscura. *See* Lineus viridis.		
Polycanna groenlandica..	234	22
Polycera illuminata. *See* Polycera lessonii.		
Polycera lessonii..	247	206
Polycirrus sp..	239	
Polycitor kukenthali..	255	
Polydara concharum..	239	76
Polymastia mamillaris..	232	13
Polymastia robusta..	232	13
Polymorphina compressa..	231	10
Polymorphina lactea..	231	10
Polynices. *See* Lunatia.		
Polynoe gaspeensis..	239	84
Polynoe squamata. *See* Lepidonotus squamatus.		
Polystomella arctica..	231	9
Polystomella striatopunctata..	231	9
Pontaster hebitus..	236	48
Pontogeneia inermis..	252	226
Pontophilus norvegicus..	253	255
Pontoporeia femorata..	252	230
Porella acutirostris..	241	103
Porella bella..	241	103
?Porella compressa. *See* Porella surcularis.		
Porella concinna..	241	102
Porella elegantula..	241	104
Porella elegantula var. papposa..	241	104
Porella laevis..	241	105
Porella minuta..	241	103
Porella perpusilla..	241	
Porella proboscidea..	241	103
Porella propinqua..	241	105
Porella saccata..	241	
Porella skenei..	241	104
Porella skenei var. plana..	242	104
Porella struma..	242	103
Porella surcularis..	242	104
Porellina ciliata. *See* Microporella ciliata.		
Porina tubulosa..	242	98
Portlandia glacialis..	244	127
Poseidon affinis. *See* Micrura affinis.		
Potamilla neglecta..	239	72
Potamilla oculifera..	239	72

SESSIONAL .PAPER No. 38a

	Bathymetric Tables.	Whiteaves' Catalogue.
Solaster endeca..	236	51
Solaster furcifer. *See* Lophaster furcifer.		
Solaster papposus. *See* Crossaster papposus.		
Solaster syrtensis..	236	51
Solecurtus squama. *See* Siliqua squama.		
Solemya borealis. *See* Solenomya borealis.		
Solemya velum. *See* Solenomya velum.		
Solen americanus. *See* Ensis directus.		
Solen costatus. *See* Siliqua costata.		
Solen directus. *See* Ensis directus.		
Solen ensis. *See* Ensis directus.		
Solen minutus. *See* Saxicava rugosa.		
Solenomya borealis..	244	144
Solenomya velum..	244	144
Spinther citrinus..	239	87
Spiochaetopterus typicus..	239	76
Spirontocaris fabricii.		
Spirontocaris gaimardii..	253	252
Spirontocaris gaimardii belcheri..	253	
Spirontocaris groenlandica..	253	250
Spirontocaris polaris..	253	251
Spirontocaris pusiola..	253	252
Spirontocaris spinus..	253	250
Spirontocaris stoneyi..	253	
Spirontocaris turgida..	253	251
Spirialis gouldii. *See* Limacina gouldii.		
Spiroplecta biformis..	231	10
Spirorbis borealis..	239	68
Spirorbis cancellatus..	239	69
Spirorbis carinatus..	239	70
Spirorbis granulatus..	240	70
Spirorbis lucidus..	240	69
Spirorbis nautiloides. *See* Spirorbis stimpsoni.		
Spirorbis quadrangularis..	240	70
?Spirorbis spirillum Gould. *See* Spirorbis borealis.		
Spirorbis spirillum Linnaeus..	240	
Spirorbis stimpsoni..	240	71
Spirorbis validus..	240	71
Spirorbis vitreus..	240	69
Spisula (Hemimactra) polynyma..	244	139
Spisula (Hemimactra) solidissima..	244	139
Squilla lobata. *See* Caprella linearis.		
Standella lateralis. *See* Mulinia lateralis.		
Staurophora laciniata..	234	
Stauroteuthis syrtensis..	248	213
Stegocephalus inflatus..	252	232
Stenosoma irrorata. *See* Idotea marina.		
Stenothoe clypeata..	252	232
Stephanasterias albula. *See* Stichaster albulus.		
Sternaspis fossor..	240	88
Sthenelais limicola..	240	84
Sthenoteuthis megaptera. *See* Ommastrephes megapterus.		
Stichaster albulus..	236	54
Stimpsoniella emersonii. *See* Amicula vestita.		
Stomapora expansa. *See* Tubulipora expansa.		
Stomatopora diastoporoides..	242	110
Stomatopora granulata..	242	110
Stomatopora penicillata..	242	110
Stomphia carneola..	235	40
Stomphia coccinea. *See* Stomphia carneola.		
Strombidium sulcatum..	231	
Strongylocentrotus drobachiensis..	236	62
Stylarioides plumosa. *See* Trophonia plumosa.		
Stylocordyla borealis..	232	13
Suberites ficus..	232	14
Suberites hispidus..	232	14
Suberites montalbidus..	232	14
Sycon asperum..	232	12
Sycon protectum..	232	11
Synanthus mirabilis..	235	40
Synapta coriacea. *See* Chirodota laevis.		
Syncoryne gravata. *See* Syncoryne mirabilis.		
Syncoryne mirabilis..	234	19
Synidotea bicuspida..	252	240
Synidotea nodulosa..	252	239
Syrrhoe bicuspis. *See* Tiron acanthurus.		
Syrrhoe crenulata..	252	231

SESSIONAL PAPER No. 38a

8 GEORGE V, A. 1918

V

	Bathymetric Tables.	Whiteaves' Catalogue.
Vaginulina spinigera..................................	231	10
Valvulina conica...................................	231	10
Velutella cryptospira..............................	248	167
Velutina haliotoides. *See* Velutina laevigata.		
Velutina laevigata...............................	248	166
Velutina (Limneria) undata..........................	248	167
Velutina zonata. *See* Velutina (Limneria) undata.		
Venericardia borealis................................	244	135
Venus astartoides. *See* Liocyma fluctuosa.		
Venus castanea. *See* Astarte castanea.		
Venus compressa. *See* Astarte banksii.		
Venus compressa. *See* Astarte compressa.		
Venus fluctuosa. *See* Liocyma fluctuosa.		
Venus fragilis. *See* Macoma balthica.		
Venus gemma. *See* Tottenia gemma.		
Venus islandica. *See* Cyprina islandica and Serripes groenlandicus.		
Venus mercenaria....................................	244	135
Venus minuta. *See* Turtonia minuta.		
Venus montacuti. *See* Astarte banksii.		
Venus montagui. *See* Astarte banksii.		
Vermilia serrula...................................	240	71
Verneuilina polystropha............................	231	10
Vertumnus serratus. *See* Acanthonotozoma serratum.		
Virgularia finmarchica. *See* Balticina finmarchica.		
Virgularia grandiflora. *See* Anthoptilum grandiflorum.		
Virgularia lyungmani..............................	235	34
Virgulina squamosa................................	231	10
Volumitra groenlandica............................	248	
Volutopsis norvegica..............................	248	188
Volvaria alba. *See* Cylichna alba.		
Volvaria canaliculata. *See* Tornatina canaliculta.		
Vorticella bolteni. *See* Boltenia bolteni.		

W

Waldheimia cranium. *See* Terebratalia spitzbergensis.		

X

Xestoleberis depressa..............................	250	217
Xylophaga dorsalis................................	245	151

Y

Yoldia angularis. *See* Megayoldia thraciaeformis.		
Yoldia frigida. *See* Yoldiella frigida.		
Yoldia limatula....................................	245	125
Yoldia lucida. *See* Yoldiella lucida.		
Yoldia myalis.....................................	245	126
Yoldia obesa. *See* Yoldiella lucida.		
Yoldia sapotilla...................................	245	125
Yoldia thraciaeformis. *See* Megayoldia thraciaeformis.		
Yoldiella frigida.................................	245	126
Yoldiella lucida..................................	245	126

Z

Zetes spinosa. *See* Achelia spinosa.		
Zirfaea crispata..................................	245	151
Zirphaea crispata. *See* Zirfaea crispata.		
Zoanthus incrustatus. *See* Epizoanthus incrustatus.		
Zygodactyla groenlandica. *See* Polycanna groenlandica.		

XV

HYDROGRAPHY IN PASSAMAQUODDY BAY AND VICINITY, NEW BRUNSWICK.

(By Professor ALEXANDER VACHON, B.A., L.Ph., etc., Laval University, Quebec.)

The laws that regulate the distribution of the plankton in the sea furnish a problem of paramount importance in the progressive industry of fisheries. Qualitative and quantitative determinations of the plankton are made at selected hydrographic stations, since the plankton is followed by multitudes of fishes which live on it, and those fishes are followed by others which serve as food for men.

As the plankton, which regulates, to a great extent, the migrations of the fish, is itself at the mercy of the chemical, physical and mechanical conditions of the sea, it is easily understood of what economical importance a correct knowledge of those conditions will prove. We speak of the migrations of the herrings and sardines; they are the same as those of the plankton which serve as food for them. and the presence of the plankton is ruled by depth, light, temperature, salinity, pressure and density.

TEMPERATURE.

The heat of the atmosphere, emanating from the sun, penetrates the water, and is attenuated according as the depth increases. At the surface, the temperature of the water is almost as changeable as that of the air adjoining it, the variations of which find their repercussion in the contiguous liquid, although somewhat mitigated. Cold in winter, warmer in summer, the surface water expresses the alterations in the temperature of the air. Therefore, in summer, the sun's rays heat the water at the surface, and to a depth of a few meters. The difference between the temperature of the day and that of the night ceases to be perceptible at a small depth; in order to find the region which is insensible to summer and winter variations, we must go down further. At about one thousand metres, the secular variations are imperceptible. Then begins the zone where the temperature never varies; by a slow and regular progression. the temperature grows colder and colder until it is only about one or two degrees above zero. This low temperature is found even in the tropical regions, where the scorching rays of the sun beam constantly upon the surface.

Ordinarily, the water gradually becomes cooler from the surface to the bottom, because, apart from the effect of the sun's heat at the top, cold water is more dense and goes to the bottom; but, in the polar regions, and where there are cold currents. we sometimes find an area of colder water between two warmer regions, and this state of unstable equilibrium, where the water is cooler, more salt and more dense, affords very interesting information.

Light does not penetrate into the water further than two or three hundred metres from the surface, hence, no green plants are found at such depths, as light is necessary for the decomposition of carbon dioxide which is the bread of the vegetable kingdom.

When water is heated, it goes to the surface; if it be concentrated, it seeks a lower level; should it cool for some reason or other, by the atmosphere or by evaporation, it also descends. Everything influences the temperature of the superficial water, the cold, polar currents as well as the hot currents coming from the equatorial regions.

We understand why it is that the water is so cold at the bottom of the ocean, since cold water descends, and being free from the heating influence of the sun in those depths, where the light of day never reaches, and, on account of the feeble power of water to conduct heat, the temperature of the lower regions of the ocean never varies. Kelvin and Wegemann made calculations concerning the conduction of heat through water and came to the conclusion that this conduction is practically negligible. With a temperature of 30° C. at the surface and the water perfectly still, it would take one hundred years for any heat to be perceived at a depth of a hundred

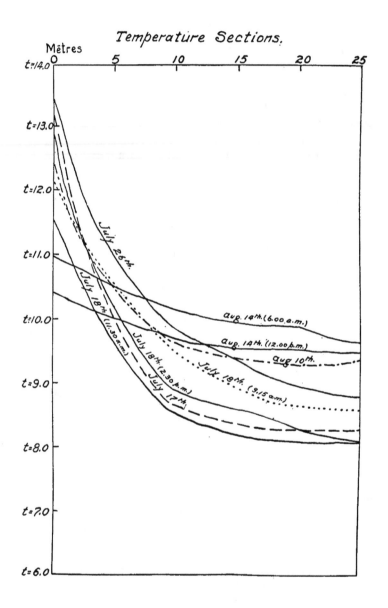

Temperature Sections.

metres. Therefore, in practice, heat propagates through the water only by the movements of the waves and currents.

Looking over our records one can see that at the same depths in different stations, the temperature gradually becomes higher as the season advances, and in the month of July, at *Prince* station 5, we found a temperature of 4°.9 C. at 100 fathoms or 182 metres.

It is an easy matter to find out the temperature of the air or of the surface water; the thermometer can be read directly as soon as the expansion or contraction of the liquid in the tube is in equilibrium with its surroundings. However, it is not thus when one has to measure the exact temperature of a layer of water situated at a depth of a few hundred or thousand feet. Between the surface and the deep layer to be examined, there may be and, as a matter of fact, there are other layers that are colder or warmer. Even if the thermometer is sent down and left long enough to indicate the temperature of the water at a measured depth, when it is brought up to be read, the mercurial column, by going through regions of different temperatures, will change in length; it will contract, if it meets colder water and will expand if it comes in contact with warmer regions, it is impossible, therefore, to thus get the temperature of the lower regions of the sea with an ordinary thermometer. Besides, the thermometer is subjected, in the lower regions, to the enormous pressure of the upper layers, that of one atmosphere for every ten metres; even if the instrument is not broken, it will be crushed; the diameter of the tube getting smaller, the mercury will indicate a higher temperature for the same expansion, and, therefore, the reading of the thermometer will be too high. It took almost two centuries to resolve these perplexing problems.

Without going into details about the different suggestions worked out to reach a solution of the problems, suffice it to say that the best of all the thermometers that have been invented so far for taking the temperature of the lower regions is the Negretti-Zambra reversing thermometer; this is the one we used in our determinations. Negretti and Zambra invented this thermometer in 1878 and it has undergone no essential changes since that time. It is noteworthy to remark here that in this type there is a narrowing of the tube just above the bulb and, when the thermometer is placed with the bulb pointing downwards, the mercury fills the tube above the narrowing to a greater or less extent according to the temperature. If the thermometer is tipped over, either by the closing of the water-bottle, as it happens with the Petterson-Nansen bottle, or while a messenger is sent down the wire, as in the case of the Ekman reversing apparatus, the mercury breaks off at the narrowing and the mercury which was above this point sinks down to the opposite end of the tube and fills it to a certain height; a scale on the tube thus gives the temperature at the time the thermometer was turned over: that is called the temperature *in situ*. The length of the broken thread of mercury varies somewhat in passing through water of higher or lower temperature and this change is calculated when the temperature of the mercury is known at the time of the reading, and this is the reason why there is always with the apparatus a second ordinary thermometer that gives the reading temperature so that the correction may be made. In order that the thermometer may be able to withstand the pressure of the water, it is placed inside a strong glass tube.

SALINITY.

Since there is no element that is absolutely insoluble, every element is found to a certain degree in sea-water. By very accurate analysis, elements which one would not expect to find have been discovered in it; common metals, such as iron, manganese and zinc, as well as precious metals, like gold and silver are found in sea-water. Those rarer metals, being present only in infinitesimal quantities, are not detected by the ordinary methods of analysis.

The water of the ocean evaporates, condenses and falls again upon the earth in the form of rain; it washes the earth, oozes through it and by the streams and rivers is carried back to where it started from. This water, coming in contact with all sorts of

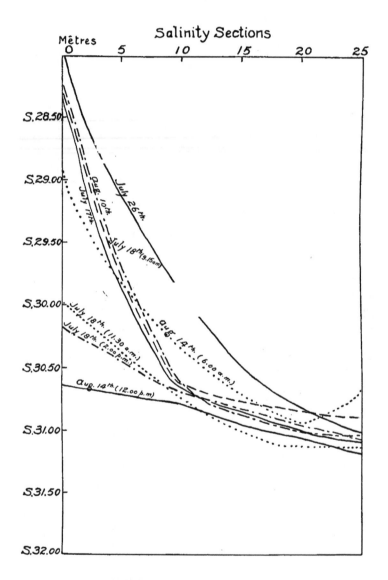

Salinity Sections

substances, takes up all that it can dissolve and carries it down into the ocean and, though the quantity of a substance which goes into solution may be comparatively small, we understand how it is that the sea contains such diverse elements.

The two predominant elements which are found in the water of the sea are chlorine and sodium. It seems logical to admit that the sea was always salt since we find in the ocean of to-day certain shells which require a definite salinity and which were quite abundant in the Cambrian seas.

Dittmar gives the following composition and percentage of the salts in sea-water:—

Sodium chloride, Na Cl..	27·213 gr. per litre.
Magnesium chloride, Mg Cl₂..	3·807 " " "
Magnesium sulphate, Mg SO₄..	1·658 " " "
Calcium sulphate, Ca SO₄..	1:260 " " "
Potassium sulphate, K₂ SO₄..	0·863 " " "
Calcium carbonate, Ca CO₃..	0·123 " " "
Magnesium bromide, Mg Br₂..	0·076 " " "
	35·000 " " "

Thoulet gives a somewhat different composition, though the amount of total salts is much the same, 35·0631 gr. per thousand grams of sea-water:—

Sodium chloride, NaCl..	27·3726 gr. per kilog.
Potassium chloride, K Cl..	0·5921 " " "
Rubidium chloride, Rb Cl..	0·0190 " " "
Calcium sulphate, Ca SO⁴..	1·3229 " " "
Magnesium sulphate, Mg SO⁴..	2·2434 " " "
Magnesium chloride, Mg Cl₂..	3·3625 " " "
Magnesium bromide, Mg Br₂..	0·0547 " " "
Calcium metaphosphate, Ca (PO₃)₂..	0·0156 " " "
Calcium bicarbonate, Ca C² O³..	0·0625 " " "
Iron bicarbonate, Fe C₂ O₃..	0·0149 " " "

From the analyses that have been made of a great many samples of sea-water, it can be stated that there are about 35 grams of salt in a thousand grams of sea-water. This amount is greater in some regions, for instance in the tropical regions and in the gulf stream, where evaporation is more intense. It is much less in other parts, especially near the continental shores where the flow of fresh water from the coast lessens the proportion of salt. For instance, in my determinations, I found as low as 15·13 gr. per thousand at *Prince* Station 18, 19·18 per thousand at Station 20, 18·35 per thousand at Station 21, 15·63 per thousand at Station 22, etc. This is easily explained by the fact that there is at those points a mixture of fresh water from the coast.

However, the average amount of salt in the ocean is about 35 gr. per thousand parts by weight. In the percentage of salts given by Dittmar and Thoulet, the acids and bases have been arbitrarily combined. Still it is very probable that in the water the salts are not found as indicated. The elements and acid radicals are found by analysis, but nothing tells us how they exist in solution. The dissolved substances mainly exist as ions, and from the freezing point and boiling point of sea-water, we calculate the ionic dissociation to be about 90 per cent; thus, only one-tenth of the total solids are present in the water as salts. It would be better, therefore, to write the composition of the solids in sea-water, as it is given by Dr. Johan Hjort:—

Na..	10·722 parts per 1000..			30·64%
Mg..	1·316 " " "			3·76%
Ca..	0·420 " " "			1·20%
K..	0·382 " " "			1·09%
Cl.	19·324 " " "			55·21%
SO₄..	2·696 " " "			7·70%
CO₃..	0·074 " " "			0·21%
Br.	0·066 " " "			0·19%
	35·000			100·00%

From the foregoing, one can readily perceive that the salinity of sea-water is not identical everywhere in the ocean; it varies in different regions and at different depths.

Prince Stations

Professor Vachon, Hydrography.

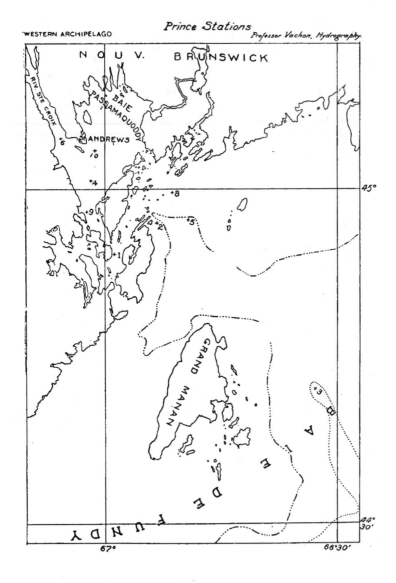

A necessary condition to make a determination of the salinity of sea-water is to secure a sample of water collected at a certain date in a certain place, at the surface or at a known depth, which is guaranteed free from mixture with different water and which has in no way evaporated.

The surface water can be collected in a bucket and hauled up. The glass bottle in which the water is to be preserved for analysis is rinsed with a portion of the sample, then filled, well stoppered and it can be kept as long as the bottle is almost completely filled and hermetically closed.

From July 14 to July 25 my samples were kept in Imperial pint bottles; after the latter date I used citrate of magnesia bottles. I took the temperature of the surface from the water in the bucket by means of a Centigrade thermometer graduated in tenths of a degree and whose accuracy I had verified beforehand.

To collect samples from below the surface, a great number of methods have been invented. At first, an ordinary stoppered bottle was sent down to a certain depth by means of a weight, and, at the desired depth, the bottle was opened and filled with water by pulling a cord attached to the stopper. In drawing it up, very little water from the surface layers could mix with the sample.

The Petterson-Nansen bottle, which we used for collecting our samples from July 14 to July 25, can isolate a sample of water at any depth. This bottle is sent down open, the lid being suspended in the upper part of the frame and held by a spring. We used the reversing thermometer attached to the frame of the bottle. We left the bottle at the desired depth for five minutes so that the thermometer could have time to accurately mark the temperature of the water *in situ*. A messenger was then sent down along the wire; this messenger unhooks the lid; the weight, which hangs below the apparatus, clasps the whole thing together and closes the bottle. This is composed of a series of metallic cylinders to insulate the water and a thermometer can be placed on the inside; this thermometer, which, however, is but slightly affected by varying temperatures as the bottle is pulled up, was not used in our determinations.

When we used the Petterson-Nansen bottle, the depth was taken in fathoms, as the meter-wheel had not arrived at the station, but, in my tables, the fathoms are expressed in metres.

From July 25, we used the Nansen reversing bottles for collecting our samples and the meter-wheel or determining the depth. The Nansen bottle has attached to it a thermometer which is tipped over with the bottle by means of a messenger. We allowed this bottle to remain at least three minutes in the water before pulling it up for a reading. A number of these bottles can be fastened along the line; a messenger is hooked below each bottle, except the lowest one; this messenger is released when the bottle is tipped over by means of a messenger sent from above; the result is that the next bottle is reversed; this releases another messenger and so on. By this apparatus, a number of samples can be taken at the same time at different depths and the bottles are not so heavy and clumsy as the Petterson-Nansen bottle.

The samples of water collected must afterwards be analysed. In such analysis the halogens are titrated with silver nitrate and the results given as grams of chlorine per thousand grams of water.

We have seen that there are many substances in sea-water, and, though the proportion of salts varies from one place to another, the relative proportion of the different elements is about the same everywhere; thus, when the quantity of chlorine has been accurately determined, we have the proportion of total salts in the sample examined. Mohr's method is used for the determination of chlorine. If a neutral or slightly alkaline solution of a chloride, bromide or iodide, in which there is a little potassium chromate comes in contact with a neutral solution of silver nitrate a white precipitate is formed as long as there is a trace of halide in solution. Thus, in sea-water, the bromine and small amount of iodine present are precipitated along with the chlorine, but the whole is calculated in grams of chlorine per thousand grams of water. As soon

8 GEORGE V, A. 1918

as the last trace of halide is precipitated, the potassium chromate indicates the end of the reaction by forming a red precipitate with the silver nitrate. If the strength of the silver nitrate has already been determined with a solution of chloride of known strength, the amount of halides in the unknown solution or in the sea-water that is analysed can be found by simple proportion. The solution of known strength which is used in hydrography for standardizing the silver nitrate solution is the sample of " normal water " which is furnished in closed glass tubes by the International Council. The amount of chlorine is marked on the tube; the sample I used contained 19.386 parts of chlorine per thousand grams. When possible, it is well to have a few bottles of the " normal water " in order to occasionally titrate the silver nitrate solution; the amount of chlorine indicated on the tube is not absolutely reliable after the tube is two-thirds empty.

As Doctor Huntsman could only obtain, last summer, and with considerable trouble, one tube of " normal water," we had to be satisfied with that.

Here I desire to express my gratitude to the Biological Board, and especially Professor Macallum, for the opportunity of taking up this study, to Dr. Huntsman, the zealous and active curator of the Biological Station at St. Andrew's, who gave so generously both of his time and of his experience to help me in every possible way in my work, and to Sir George Garneau, professor of analytical chemistry in Laval University, who helped me in the salinity determinations.

For accurate sea-water analysis, a special burette is desirable: the ordinary burette is too wide and too short for the required accuracy. The reading should be certain to a hundredth part of a c.c., which is difficult with the ordinary burette. Besides, the " drainage error " is greater than in the special one, the upper part of which is an ungraduated bulb that terminates in a fine jet. The lower part of this burette is a narrow tube graduated in hundredths of a c.c. At the present time it is most difficult, not to say impossible, to obtain one of those special burettes. Dr. Huntsman was able to get one from Dr. Mathews, of the Plymouth Marine Biological laboratory, England, but, most unfortunately, it was broken when it reached me. Two others, made to order by the Eimer and Amend Company also arrived in a broken state. We hope to be fully equipped with all the special apparatus in the near future.

DENSITY.

The density of sea-water can be taken with a pycnometer, or else with an areometer, at constant temperature; the second method is less accurate. But the densities, though they may be accurately determined by either of the methods, do not give the exact density of the water *in situ*, where it possessed a certain temperature and was compressed by a mass of water. The density of sea-water is inversely proportionate to the temperature and directly proportionate to the salinity; the lower the temperature and the higher the percentage of salts, the heavier the water. When both the temperature and the salinity of a sample of water are known, the specific gravity may easily be calculated by means of Knudsen's tables.

When I reached the Biological Station, I began my work by making salinity determinations of samples of water which had been collected a year before in St. Mary's Bay and the Annapolis Basin. The Imperial pint bottles that contained those samples were not hermetically closed; there was a deposit of salt on the covers and frequently on the outside of the bottles.

Supposing the water had evaporated, one would expect a high percentage of salts; nevertheless, the results are low, and though I give them in the tables, I can, in no way, guarantee their accuracy. There are other results obtained with samples taken at the same stations in September and October.

The other samples of water were collected on the given dates at stations chosen by Dr. Huntsman, where a study of the plankton is carried on along with the hydrography.

At *Prince* Station 1, we find a higher temperature and lower salinity at 30 metres than at 20 which showing the water at this point was in a state of unstable equilibrium, a layer of higher density being above one of lower density. As a general rule, such strange results were obtained with many of the water-samples collected later in the season. For instance, at *Prince* Station 4, the results are normal until September 15. Then we find a salinity of 31·13 ^{0}/oo at 35 metres when the salinity at 30 metres was as high as 32·57 ^{0}/oo, giving a density of 23·96 for the first and 25·10 for the second. At the same station, on October 3, we obtained a salinity of 30·73 ^{0}/oo at 20 metres when that of the surface was 31·66 ^{0}/oo. The same consideration can be made concerning Station 6, when we find on September 15 a temperature of 10·17 and a salinity of 31·67 ^{0}/oo at 35 metres whereas at 30 metres the temperature was 10·12° and the salinity 31·69 ^{0}/oo. As one can see by the tables, a number of water samples, collected at Station 6 in October, were lost, so we cannot say whether the extraordinary result mentioned is accidental. It will be seen also that at *Prince* station 6 the salinity varies greatly with the tide, especially at the surface and it is easy to understand that it should be so on account of the flow of fresh water from the Ste. Croix river, as station 6 is located in the mouth of the river, between the Biological Station and Robbinston. At station 9 on September 15 we find a zigzag of temperatures and salinities: the temperature rises somewhat from 10 to 20 metres while the salinity lowers; at 50 metres the salinity is 31·21 ^{0}/oo when we find 32·15 ^{0}/oo at 40 metres. the salinity afterwards rises normally to the bottom but the temperature rises also; however, from 50 metres down, the density increases in a normal manner. On October 3, we find at the same station (20 metres) a density of 23·88 between 24·34 at 10 and 24·40 at 30 metres. At station 16 we get a salinity of 32·63 ^{0}/oo at the surface, 32·07 ^{0}/oo at 10 metres and 31·47 ^{0}/oo at 20 metres. At 30 metres the salinity rises somewhat, but so does the temperature; there is another decrease in salinity at 40 metres. The high percentage of salts in the surface water of station 17 can be explained by the fact that the sample was collected in Yarmouth Harbour, where the depth is only 13 metres, and, therefore, the water is easily mixed.

All the bottles, except one, were broken, which contained the samples collected at Station 20; it is unfortunate as the temperatures predicted interesting figures for the salinity. From a depth of 10 metres down the temperature rises, 6·08° at 10 metres, 6·43 at 15 m., then 8·22, 10·98, 11·74, 11·93, 12·00. Perhaps the upper layers had been first cooled down to a certain depth, and that they had begun to get warmer again as the air temperature rose. But a fact worthy of attention in this particular case is that the temperature of the surface water is 15·69° when the air temperature is 11·80°. At station 21 there is also a decrease of temperature from the surface to a depth of 20 metres, but there is a rise of temperature from 30 metres to the bottom. However, at this station, as the salinity rises from the upper layers to the bottom, the increase of density is also normal. The temperatures taken at station 24 deserve special attention from the fact that there is very little difference between the surface temperature and that of the bottom, 9·37° at the surface and 9·29° at 55 metres. From 9·37° at the surface we get 9·32°, 9·31°, 9·28°; then a rise 9·29°, 9·30°; a slight fall to 9·28° and 9·29° at the bottom. These temperatures were taken at 9·20 a.m. The same day, at 5.45 in the afternoon, we have somewhat equivalent results, but the low salinity, instead of being at 50 metres, as in the forenoon when the tide was high is at 40 metres, at low tide. Two of the samples collected at station 24, September 23, 5.45 p.m. were lost; the others gave very extraordinary salinity results. The highest salinity, 32·37 ^{0}/oo is at the surface. We found 32·29 ^{0}/oo at 10 metres, 31·28 ^{0}/oo at 40 metres and 31·13 ^{0}/oo at 50 metres. A glance at the results given for stations 25 and 27 shows that at those stations also the density of the water was higher at the surface than at a certain depth. At station 25 we find a salinity of 32·47 ^{0}/oo at 10 metres and only 31·54 ^{0}/oo ten metres lower and so forth and so on.

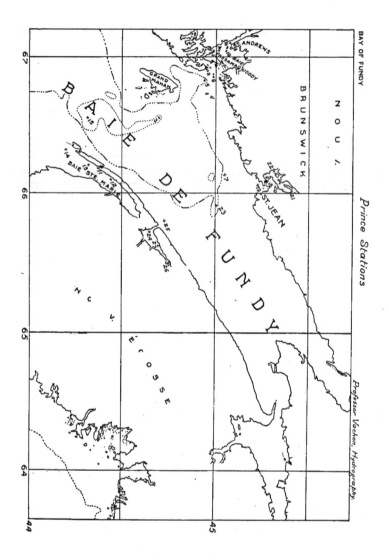

Prince Stations

Professor Vachon, Hydrography

SESSIONAL PAPER No. 38a

The following samples were collected by Mr. W. H. Chase, of Acadia University, a year before I reached the station. (The stations are indicated on a chart at the laboratory, at St. Andrews):—

Date.	Station.	Depth.	Salinity S. ‰.
July 7, 1915.	St. Mary's bay, No. 1	Bottom	29·18
" 7, 1915,	" " 2	"	31·20
" 7, 1915.	" " 3	"	31·89
" 7, 1915.	" " 4	"	30·76
" 7, 1915.	" " 5	"	30·70
" 7, 1915.	" " 6	"	31·47
" 7, 1915.	" " 7	"	31·48
" 8, 1915.	" " 8	"	30·78
" 8, 1915.	" " 9	"	30·18
" 7, 1915.	" " 10	"	30·76
" 13, 1915.	" " 11	"	30·06
" 8, 1915.	" " 12	"	31·45
" 13. 1915.	" " 13	"	30·80
" 8, 1915.	" " 14	"	29·86
" 8, 1915.	" " 15	"	30·91
" 8, 1915.	" " 16	"	30·77
" 13, 1915.	" " 17	"	30·18
" 13, 1915.	" " 18	"	29·99
" 13, 1915.	" " 19	"	29·86
" 13, 1915.	" " 20	"	30·25
" 13, 1915.	" " 21	"	30·38
" 13, 1915.	" " 22	"	30·78
" 23, 1915.	Annapolis basin, No. 25	Surface.	29·99
" 23, 1915.	" " 25	27·3 metres.	30·40
" 24, 1915.	" " 28	Surface.	30·52
" 24, 1915.	" " 28	Bottom.	30·53
" 23, 1915.	" " 29	Surface.	30·63
" 23, 1915.	" " 29	Bottom (6·3 m.).	30·74
" 23, 1915.	" " 30	" (4·6 m.).	29·79
" 24, 1915.	" " 31	Surface.	30·05
" 24, 1915.	" " 31	Bottom.	30·77
June 22, 1915.	Black Rock.	72·7 metres.	26·69
July 14, 1916.	Off Wilson's beach.	Surface.	30·88
			t°=8·8

8 GEORGE V, A. 1918

SAMPLES

"Prince" Stations. No.	Locality.	Position (vide chart).	Latitude.	Longitude.	Bottom.
1.........	Friar Roads, just south Coffin Ledge buoy.	Bald Head bears E½ N. Deer Id. Point bears N. x W½ W.	44° 54′ 27″ N.	66° 58′ 11″ W.	Hard. Rocky.
1.........	" "	" "	"	"	"
1.........	" "	" "	"	"	"
1.........	" "	" "	"	"	"
1.........	" "	" "	"	"	"
1.........	" "	" "	"	"	"
1.........	" "	" "	"	"	"
1.........	" "	" "	"	"	"
1.........	" "	" "	"	"	"
1.........	" "	" "	"	"	"
1.........	" "	" "	"	"	"
1.........	" "	" "	"	"	"
1.........	" "	" "	"	"	"
1.........	" "	" "	"	"	"
1.........	" "	" "	"	"	"
1.........	" "	" "	"	"	"
1.........	" "	" "	"	"	"
1.........	" "	" "	"	"	"
1.........	" "	" "	"	"	"
1.........	" "	" "	"	"	"
1.........	" "	" "	"	"	"
1.........	" "	" "	"	"	"
1.........	" "	" "	c	"	"
1.........	" "	" "	"	"	"
2.........	Bay of Fundy, off Head Harbour Id.	North end of Head Harbour Id. bears N.W. ¼ W. ⅜ mile. Scott Head bears S.W. x S. ½ S., 2½ miles.	44° 56′ 58″ N.	66° 53′ 0″ W.	Soft mud.

SESSIONAL PAPER No. 38a

COLLECTED.

Date.	Hour.	Depth in Metres.	Air Temperature t° C.	Tide.	Wind.	Sky.	Depth of determinations in metres.	Water Temperature t° C.	Chlorine. Cl. ‰	Salinity. S. ‰	Density. σt.	Colour of Water.
1916.												
July 25	11.50 a.m.	32·7	9·44	2½ hours of low tide.	S. W. breeze..	Cloudy.	Surface.	9·00	17·43	31·48	24·39	
„ 25	12.10 p.m.	32·7	9·44	„	„	„	20 m.	7·90	17·49	31·61	24·66	
„ 25	11.50 a.m..	32·7	9·44	„	„	„	28 „	7·40	17·5C	31·62	24·72	
Aug. 2	4.00 p.m.	32·7	9·02	2¼ hours ebb.	Calm...	„	Surface.	8·70	17·31	31·27	24 28	
„ 2	4.00 „	32·7	9·02	„	„ ...	„	10 m.	8·30	17·32	31·29	24·26	
„ 2	4.00 „	32·7	9·02	„	„ ...	„	20 „	8·25	17·36	31·36	24·42	
„ 2	4.00 „	32·7	9 02	„	„ ...	„	30 „	8·10	17·36	31·36	24·44	
„ 19	1.20 „	43 m.	12·00	½ hour to high tide.	„ ...	Clear...	Surface.	8·7	17·56	31·73	24·65	
„ 19	1.20 „	43 „	12·00	„	„ ...	„ ..	10 m.	8·25	17·63	31·86	24·81	
„ 19	1.20 „	43 „	12·00	„	„ ...	„ ..	20 „	9·31	17·62	31·83	24·76	
„ 19	1.20 „	43 „	12·00	„	„ ...	„ .	30 „	8·29	17·60	31·81	24·75	
„ 19	1.20 „	43 „	12·00	„	„ ...	„ ..	40 „	8·23	17·59	31·79	24·75	
„ 31	3.35 „	35 „	15·60	2¼ hours to low tide.	S. W. breeze.	„ ..	Surface.	9·52	17·63	31·84	24·61	
„ 31	3.35 „	35 „	15·60	„	„	„ ..	20 m.	9·10	17·67	31·93	24·72	
„ 31	3.35 „	35 „	15·60	„	„	„ ..	30 m.	9·08	17·67	31·93	24·72	
Sept. 14	3.20 „	32 „	22·63	2 hours ebb.	Calm...	„ ..	Surface.	10 30	17·30	31·25	24·01	Bluish
„ 14	3.20 „	32 „	22·63	„	„ ...	„ ..	10 m.	9·54	Sam-	ple	lost.	„
„ 14	3.20 „	32 „	22·63	„	„ ...	„ ..	20 „	9·43	17·81	32·18	24·86	„
„ 14	3.20 „	32 „	22·63	„	„ ...	„ ..	25 „	9·45	17·70	31·99	34·71	„
Oct. 3	3.45 „	35 „	13·81	High.....	Light S. W.	„ ..	Surface.	9·30	Sam-	ple	lost.	Greenish.
„ 3	3.45 „	35 „	13·81	„	„	„ ..	10 m.	9·21	„	„	„	„
„ 3	3.45 „	35 „	13·81	„	„	„ ..	20 „	9·13	17·81	32 18	24·94	„
„ 3	3.45 „	35 „	13·81	„	„	„ ..	30 „	9·15	17·69	31·96	24·74	„
„ 17	10.11 a.m..	44 „	12 45	Low	S. W. strong.	Clouds. rain.	Surface.	9·02	No	water.		„
„ 17	10.11 „	44 „	12·45	„	„	„	20 m.	8·81	„	„	.....	„
„ 17	10.11 „	44 „	12·45	„	„	„	40 „	8·78	„	„	.....	„
....	....	100 „	No determinations were made at Station No. 2.									

8 GEORGE V, A. 1918

SAMPLES

"Prince" Stations No.	Locality.		Position (vide chart.)		Latitude.	Longitude.	Bottom.
3.........	Bay of Fundy, off Grand Manan Island.		Swallow-tail light bears N. W. ¼ W., 9 miles. Southern point of Whitehead Id. bears W. x S. ¾ S. 8½ miles.		44° 42′ 5″ N...	66° 32′ 31″ W.	Soft mud..
3.........	"	"	"	"	"	"	"
3.......	"	"	"	"	"	"	"
3.........	"	"	"	"	"	"	"
3.........	"	"	"	"	"	"	"
3.........	"	"	"	"	"	"	"
3.	"	"	"	"	"	"	"
3.	"	"	"	"	"	"	"
3.	"	"	"	"	"	"	"
3.	"	"	"	"	"	"	"
3...	"	"	"	"	"	"	..
3.........	"	"	"	"	"	"	"
3.........	"	"	"	"	"	"	"
3.........	"	"	"	"	"	"	"
3.........	"	"	"	"	"	"	"
3.	"	"	"	"	"	"	"
3........ ..	"	"	"	"	"	"	"
3.........	"	"	"	"	"	"	"
3.........	"	"	"	"	"	"	"
3.........	"	"	"	"	"	"	"
3.	"	"	"	"	"	"	"
3.........	"	"	"	"	"	"	"
3........	"	"	"	"	"	"	"
3...	"	"	"	"	"	"	"
3.........	"	"	"	"	"	"	"
4.........	Passamaquoddy Bay.		Joe's point bears N. by W. ¼ W. 4½ miles. Northern p int of Pendleton Id. bears E. 3½ miles.		45° 1′ 0″ N.	67° 1′ 51″ W.	Soft mud.
4:	"	"	"	"	"	"	"
4.	"	"	"	"	"	"	"
4.	"	"	"	"	"	"	"
4.........	"	"	"	"	"	"	"
4.........	"	"	"	"	"	"	"
4.........	"	"	"	"	"	"	"
4.	"	"	"	"	"	"	"
4.........	"	"	"	"	"	"	"
4........	"	"	"	"	"	"	"
4........ ..	"	"	"	"	"	"	"
4.........	"	"	"	"	"	"	"
4.........	"	"	" ,	"	"	"	"
4.........	"	"	"	"	"	"	"
4.........	"	"	"	"	"	"	"
4.........	"	"	"	"	"	"	"
4.........	"	"	"	"	"	"	. "
....	"	"	"	"	"	"	"
... .	"	"	"	"	"	"	"
....	"	"	"	"	"	"	"

SESSIONAL PAPER No. 38a

COLLECTED—*Con.* .

Date.	Hour.	Depth in metres.	Air temperature t° C.	Tide.	Wind.	Sky.	Depth of determinations in metres.	Water temperature t° C.	Chlorine Cl. ‰	Salinity S. ‰	Density σt.	Color of Water.
1916.												
July 24	12.20 p.m.,	188 m.	14·42	½ hour to low water.	S.E..	Cloudy rain.	Surf-ace.	10·00	16·84	30·43	23·41	
" 24	12.50 "	188 m.	14·42	"	"	"	45 m.	5·90	17·87	32·29	25·46	
" 24	12.35 "	188 m.	14·42	"	"	"	90 "	4·50	18·05	32·60	25·85	
" 24	12.20 "	188 m.	14·42	"	"	"	150 "	4·90	18·06	32·62	25·84	
" 24	12.00 noon.	188 m.	14·42	"	"	"	185 "	4·90	18·06	32·62	25·84	
Aug. 25	11.54 a.m..	185 m.	13·28	2¼ hours ebb.	S.W. breeze.	Fog .	Surf-ace.	10·98	17·58	31·77	24·29	
" 25	12.54 p.m..	185 "	13·28	"	"	"	10 m.	9·87	17·66	31·91	24·60	
" 25	12.54 " ..	185 "	13·28	"	"	"	25 "	9·11	17·66	31·91	24·71	
" 25	12.54 " ..	185 "	13·28	"	"	"	50 "	7·43	17·94	32·41	25·35	
" 25	12.34 " ..	185 "	13·28	"	"	"	75 "	6·47	18·05	32·60	25·61	
" 25	12.34 " ..	185 "	13·28	"	"	"	100 "	6·10	18·19	32·85	25·88	
" 25	12.34 " ..	185 "	13·28	"	"	"	125 "	6·02	18·22	32·93	25·94	
" 25	12.15 " ..	185 "	13·28	"	"	"	150 "	5·83	18·22	32·93	25·98	
" 25	12.15 " ..	185 "	13·28	"	"	"	175 "	5·82	18·24	32·95	25·98	
Oct. 4	2·00 " ..	173 m.	15·48	1 hour flood.	Light S. W.	Hazy...	Sur-face.	11·07	Sample lost.	.....		Dark Green
" 4	2.23 " ..	173 "	15·48	"	"	" ...	10 m.	10·05	17·67	31·92	24·58	"
" 4	2.13 " ..	173 "	15·48	"	"	" ...	20 "	9·67	Sample lost.	....		"
" 4	2.13 " ..	173 "	15·48	"	"	" ...	25 "	8·71	17·93	32·39	25·16	"
" 4	2.13 " .	173 "	15·48	"	"	" ...	30 "	8·59	17·97	32·47	25·24	"
" 4	2.00 " ..	173 "	15·48	"	"	" ...	40 "	8·27	Sample lost.	.....		"
" 4	2.00 " ..	173 "	15·48	"	"	" ...	50 "	7·92	18·05	32·61	25·44	"
" 4	2.00 " ..	173 "	15·48	"	"	" ...	75 "	6·70	17·94	32·42	25·46	"
" 4	1.45 " ..	173 "	15·48	"	"	" ...	100 "	6·35	Sample lost.	.....		"
" 4	1.45 " ..	173 "	15·48	"	"	" ...	150 "	6·12	17·99	32·51	25·59	"
" 4	1.45 " ..	173 "	15·48	"	"	" ..	173 "	6·15	18·25	32·98	25·95	"
July 20	3.30 " ..	30 "	23·00	1 hour to high tide.	"	Bright..	Sur-face.	11·40	16·80	30·36	23·11	
" 20	3.30 " ..	30 "	23·00	"	"	" ..	9 m.	8·80	17·15	30·99	24·07	
" 20	3.30 " ..	30 "	23·00	"	"	" ...	18·3 "	8·30	17·23	31·13	24·22	
" 20	3.30 " ..	30 "	23·00	"	"	" ...	27·4 "	8·10	17·28	31·23	24·32	
" 27	3.30 " ..	30 "	25·00	1 hour to low tide.	S.W. breeze.	Bright..	Sur-face.	15·90	16·03	28·97	21·18	
" 27	3.30 " ..	30 "	25·00	"	"	"	10 m.	9·80	16·91	30·56	23·57	
" 27	3.30 " ..	30 "	25·00	"	"	"	15 "	8·79	17·21	31·09	24·14	
" 27	3.30 " ..	30 "	25·00	"	"	"	25 "	8·50	17·28	31·22	24·29	
Aug. 3	4.00 " .	30 "	16·30	1 hour ebb..	"	Cloudy.	Sur-face.	11·0	16·75	30·27	23·12	
" 3	4.00 "	30 "	16·30	"	"	"	10 m.	8·92	17·15	30·99	24·02	
" 3	4.00 "	30 "	16·30	"	"	"	20 "	8·91	17·15	30·99	24·02	
" 3	4.00 " ..	30 "	16·30	"	"	"	30 "	8·85	17·20	31·07	24·21	
Aug. 10	5.30 p.m.	29 m.	21·70	Half flood.	Calm.	Clear.	Sur-face.	13·22	16·71	30·19	22·67	
" 10	"	"	"	"	"	"	10 m.	9·30	17·12	30·94	23·91	
" 10	"	"	"	"	"	"	20 m.	9·19	17·20	31·08	24·04	
" 10	"	"	"	"	"	"	25 m.	9·01	17·21	31·09	24·09	
" 17	5.00 p.m.	33 m.	17·80	Half ebb.	Light S.E.	Hazy.	Sur-face.	10·95	16·92	30·58	23·36	
" 17	"	"	"	"	"	"	10 m.	9·80	17·12	30·94	23·84	
" 17	"	"	"	"	"	"	20 m.	9·43	17·33	31·32	24·19	
" 17	"	"	"	"	"	"	30 m.	9·10	17·46	31·55	24·40	

8 GEORGE V, A. 1918

SAMPLES

"Prince" Stations. No.	Locality.	Position (vide chart).		Latitude.	Longitude.	Bottom.
	Passamaquoddy Bay.	Joe's Point bears N. by W. ¼ W. 4½ miles, Northern point of Pendleton Id. bears E. 3½ miles.		45° 1′ 0″ N.	67° 1′ 51″ W.	Soft mud.
4.........	" "	"	"	"	"	"
4....	" "	"	"	"	"	"
4.........	" "	"	"	"	"	"
4.........	" "	"	"	"	"	"
4.........	" "	"	"	"	"	"
4..... ...	" "	"	"	"	"	"
4.........	" "	"	"	"	"	"
4........	" "	"	"	"	"	"
4.........	" "	"	"	"	"	"
4.........	" "	"	"	"	"	"
4.........	" "	"	"	"	"	"
4..	" "	"	"	"	"	"
4...	" "	"	"	"	"	"
4...... .	" "	"	"	"	"	"
4.........	" "	"	"	"	"	"
4.........	" "	"	"	"	"	"
4.........	" "	"	"	"	"	"
4.........	" "	"	"	"	"	"
4.........	" "	"	"	"	"	"
4..... ..	" "	"	"	"	"	"
4.........	" "	"	"	"	"	"
4..... ..	" "	"	"	"	"	"
4.........	" "	"	"	"	"	"
4.........	" "	"	"	"	"	"
4.........	" "	Bay of Fundy, between Head Harbour and the Southern Wolves.	Head Harbour Lt. bears N.W. by W. ½ W., 3⅝ miles- Swallow Tail Lt. bears a little W. of S. 11½ miles.	44° 56′ 48″ N.6	6° 48′ 41″ W.	"
5.........	" "	"	"	"	"	"
5....	" "	"	"	"	"	"
5.........	" "	"	"	"	"	"
5.........	" "	"	"	"	"	"
5...	" "	"	"	"	"	"
5.........	" "	"	"	"	"	"
5..... ...	" "	"	"	"	"	"
5... ...	" "	"	"	"	"	"
5........	" "	"	"	"	"	"
5.........	" "	"	"	"	"	"
5	" "	"	"	"	"	"
5.........	" "	"	"	"	"	"
5.........	" "	"	"	"	"	"

SESSIONAL PAPER No. 38a

COLLECTED—*Con.*

Date.	Hour.	Depth in Metres.	Air Temperature t° C.	Tide.	Wind.	Sky.	Depth of Determinations in metres.	Water Temperature t° C.	Chlorine. Cl °/∞	Salinity. S. °/∞	Density. σt.	Colour of Water.
1916.												
Aug. 16	1.35 p.m.	120 m.	12·00	¾ hour to high tide.	S.W. breeze choppy.	Hazy.	Surface.	9.60	17.40	31.45	24.27	
,, 25	4.45 p.m.	28 m.	14·31	1½ hour flood	Calm.	Foggy.	Surface.	12·48	no sample		of water.	
,, 25	,,	,,	,,	,,	,,	,,	15 m.	9·50	,,	,,	,,	
,, 25	,,	,,	,,	,,	,,	,,	25 m.	9·57	,,	,,	,,	
,, 31	12.50 p.m.	31 m.	14·91	½ hour to high tide.	,,	Clear.	Surface.	14·91	17·03	30·77	22·73	
,, 31	,,	,,	,,	,,	,,	,,	20 m.	10·07	17·48	31·59	24·30	
,, 31	,,	,,	,,	,,	,,	,,	30 m.	10·01	17·49	31·61	24·33	
Sept. 15	5.00 p.m.	36 m.	13·88	½ ebb.	S.E., light breeze.	Hazy.	Surface.	10·95	17·25	31·17	23·82	Grayish.
,, 15	5.15 p.m.	,,	,,	,,	,,	,,	10 m.	10·26	17·42	31·48	24·19	,,
,, 15	5.00 p.m.	,,	,,	,,	,,	,,	20 m.	10·07	18·02	32·56	25·07	,,
,, 15	,,	,,	,,	,,	,,	,,	30 m.	9·98	18·03	32·57	25·10	,,
,, 15	,,	,,	,,	,,	,,	,,	35 m.	9·98	17·23	31·13	23·96	,,
Oct. 3	10.20 a.m.	31 m.	13·20	Low.	Calm.	Clear.	Surface.	10·60	17 52	31·66	24·28	,, ·
,, 3	,,	,,	,,	,,	,,	,,	10 m.	9·96	sample lost.			,,
,, 3	,,	,,	,,	,,	,,	,,	20 m.	9 83	17·01	30·73	23·71	,,
,, 3	,,	,,	,,	,,	,,	,,	30 m.	9·82	17·60	31·81	24·56	,,
,, 16	12.53 p.m.	30 m.	12·41	2½ hours to high water.	Moderate S.W.	Cloudy.	Surface.	9·35	sample lost.			,,
,, 16	,,	,,	,,	,,	,,	,,	20 m.	9·14	,,	,,		,,
,, 16	,,	,,	,,	,,	,,	,,	30 m.	8·98	,,	,,		,,
,, 21	2.07 p.m.	27 m.	13·38	½ hour flood.	Strong S.W.	Cloudy, rain.	Surface.	9·32	no water sample.			,,
,, 21	,,	,,	,,	,,	,,	,,	10 m.	9·18	,,	,,	,,	,,
,, 21	,,	,,	,,	,,	,,	,,	20 m.	9·08	,,	,,	,,	,,
,, 21	,,	,,	,,	,,	,,	,,	26 m.	8·88	,,	,,	,,	,,
,, 27	9.16 a.m.	30 m.		6 21	½ hour flood.	Moder. N.W.	Clear.	Surface.	8·51	,,	,,	,,	Gre'nish.
,, 27	,,	,,	,,	,,	,,	,,	20 m.	8·81	,,	,,	,,	,,
,, 27	,,	,,	,,	,,	,,	,,	30 m.	8·80	,,	,,	,,	,,
July 25	9.00 a.m.	90 m.	12·80	High.	S.W. breeze.	Clear.	Surface.	8·50	17·42	31·47	24·28	
,,	,,	,,	,,	,,	,,	,,	28 m.	·40	17·48	31·59	24·70	
,,	,,	,,	,,	,,	,,	,,	45 ...	·90	17·61	31·82	24·97	
,,	,,	,,	,,	,,	,,	,,	65 m.	·40	17·61	31·82	25·03	
,, 25	,,	,,	,,	,,	,,	,,	85 m.	7·90	17·69	31·96	25·21	
,, 16	1.25 p. m.	,,	,,	,,	,,	,,	10 m.	9·02	17·49	31·60	24·49	
,, 16	1.30 p.m.	,,	,,	,,	,,	,,	25 m.	8·33	17·54	31·70	24·66	
,, 16	1.35 p.m.	,,	,,	,,	,,	,,	50 m.	8·31	17·62	31·84	24·80	
,, 16	,,	,,	,,	,,	,,	,,	75 m.	7·92	17·62	31·84	24·85	
,, 16	,,	,,	,,	,,	,,	,,	100 m.	6·64	17·87	32.29	25·37	
,, 16	,,	,,	,,	,,	,,	,,	110 m.	6·40	17·92	32·38	25·45	
Sept. 18	11.09 a.m.	100 m.	13·12	Low tide.	Calm.	Clear.	Surface.	11.30	16.70	30.18	22·99	Gray.
,, 18	11·24 a.m.	,,	,,	,,	,,	,,	10 m.	10 08	16.92	30.58	23.53	,,
,, 18	,,	,,	,,	,,	,,	,,	20 m.	9.74	17.02	30.75	23.76	,,

SAMPLES

"Prince" Stations. No.	Locality.	Position (vide chart).	Latitude.	Longitude.	Bottom.
5.........	Bay of Fundy, between Head Harbour and the Southern Wolves.	Head Harbour Lt. bears N.W. by W. ½ W., 3⅜ miles. Swallow tail Lt. bears a little W. of S. 11½ miles.	44° 56′ 48″ N.	66° 48′ 41″ W.	Soft mud.
5........	" "	" "	"	"	"
5...	" "	" "	"	"	"
5...	" "	" "	"	"	"
5..	" "	" "	"	"	"
5........	" "	" "	"	"	"
5........	" "	" "	"	"	"
5........	" "	" "	"	"	"
5......	" "	" "	"	"	"
5........	" "	" "	"	"	"
5.... ..	" '	" "	"	"	"
5........	" "	" "	"	"	"
5........	" "	" "	"	"	"
5........	" "	" "	"	"	"
5........	" "	" "	"	"	"
6........	Ste. Croix River, between Biological Station and Robbinston.	Biological Station bears E. ¾ S., ₇⁄₁₀ of a mile. Little Dochet Id. bears N. by W. ½ W., 2¾ miles.	45° 4′ 49″ N.	67° 5′ 53″ W.	Fairly hard mud.
6........	" "	" "	"	"	"
6........	" "	" "	"	"	"
6........	" "	" "	"	"	"
6........	" "	" "	"	"	"
6........	" "	" "	"	"	"
6........	" "	" "	"	"	"
6........	" "	" "	"	"	"
6.......	" "	" "	"	"	"
6........	" "	" "	"	"	"
6........	" "	" "	"	"	"
6...	" "	" "	"	"	"
6........	" "	" "	"	"	"
6........	" "	" "	"	"	"
6	" "	" "	"	"	"
6...... .	" "	" "	"	"	"
6........	" "	" "	"	"	"
6........	" "	" "	"	"	"
6........	" "	" "	"	"	"
6	" "	" "	"	"	"
6...... .	" "	" "	"	"	"
6........	" "	" "	"	"	"
6........	" "	" "	"	"	"

SESSIONAL PAPER No. 38a

COLLECTED—*Con.*

Date.	Hour.	Depth in metres.	Air temperature t° C.	Tide.	Wind.	Sky.	Depth of determinations in metres.	Temperature t° C.	Chlorine. Cl. ‰	Salinity. S. ‰	Density. σt	Colour of water.
1916.												
Sept. 18	11·13 a.m.	120 m.	12·00	¾ hour to high tide.	S.W. breeze choppy.	Hazy.	25 m.	9.55	17.17	31.02	23.95	Gray.
" 18	"	"	"	"	"	"	30 m.	9.51	17.71	32.00	24.72	
" 18	"	"	"	"	"	"	40 m.	9.32	17.72	32.02	24.75	"
" 18	11.00 a.m.	"	"	"	"	"	50 m.	9.08	17.84	32.23	24.98	"
" 18	"	"	"	"	"	"	75 m.	8.26	18.02	32.56	25.36	"
" 18	"	"	"	"	"	"	100 m.	7.61	18.04	32.60	25.47	"
Oct. 1	9.04 a.m.	99¾ m.	10·4	Half ebb.	Light W.	Hazy.	Surface.	9.62	17.40	31.45	24.27	Gre'n- ish.
" 4	9.18 a.m.	"	"	"	"	"	10 m.	9.48	17.53	31.68	24.47	"
" 4	9.06 a.m.	"	"	"	"	"	20 m.	9.43	17.77	32.10	24.81	"
" 4	"	"	"	"	"	"	30 m.	9.36	17.78	32.13	24.84	"
" 4	"	"	10·40	"	"	"	40 m.	9.21	17.78	32.13	24.85	"
" 4	8.51 a.m.	"	"	"	"	"	50 m.	9.07	17.82	32.20	24.95	
" 4	"	"	"	"	"	"	75 m.	8.85	17.82	32.20	24.97	"
" 4	"	"	"	"	"	"	99 m.	7.98	17.99	32.50	25.34	"
July 17	5.10 p.m.	31 m.	15·30	4 hours ebb.	S.W.	Cloudy.	Surface.	13.15	15.69	28.36	21.27	"
" 17	"	"	"	"	"	"	9.10 m	8.80	16.92	50.58	23.75	
" 17	4.50 p.m.	"	"	3 hrs. 40 m. ebb.	"	"	18.30 m.	8.30	17.12	30.94	24·07	
" 17	4.10 p.m.	"	"	3 hours ebb.	"	"	27.40 m.	8.30	17.22	31.10	24.21	
" 18	9.15 a.m.	"	"	1 hour flood.	Calm.	Foggy.	Surface.	12.10	15.68	28.33	21.45	
" 18	"	"	"	"	"	"	9.10 m	9.60	16.92	30.57	23·61	
" 18	9.00 a.m.	"	"	45 min. flood	"	"	18.30 m.	8.70	17.05	30.81	23.95	
" 18	8.45 a.m.	"	"	½ hour flood.	"	"	25.60 m.	8.60	17.08	30.87	24.00	
" 18	11.30 a.m.	"	"	3 hours flood	"	"	Surface.	11.50	16.60	29.99	22.82	
" 18	"	"	"	"	"	"	9.10 m	8.60	16.96	30.65	23.83	
" 18	11.15 a.m.	"	"	"	"	"	18.30 m.	8.10	17.22	31.11	24.24	
" 18	11.30 a.m.	"	"	"	"	"	27.40 m.	8.10	17.23	31.14	24.25	
" 18	2.55 p.m.	"	"	High tide.	"	"	Surface.	12.80	16.70	30.17	22.73	
" 18	"	"	,	"	"	"	9.10 m	8.95	16.96	30.64	23.76	
" 18	2.00 p.m.	31	16·30	"	" ..	"	27·40 m.	8·10	17·20	31.08	24·22	
" 26	4.30 p.m.	31	21·00	Low tide circ.	" ..	Cloudy.	Surface.	13·40	15·34	27·72	20·71	
" 26	4.30 "	31	21·00	"	" ..	" ..	10 m.	9·84	16·55	29·90	23·04	
" 26	4.30 "	31	21·00	"	" ..	" ..	15 m.	9·40	16·87	30·48	23·55	
" 26	4.30 "	31	21·00	"	" ..	" ..	25 m.	8·80	17·10	30·90	23·99	
Aug. 10	11.45 a.m.	30	18·50	½ flood	N. W. breeze.	Clear..	Surface.	12·65	15·65	28·28	21·33	
" 10	11.45 "	30	18·50	"	"	" ...	10 m.	9·60	16·93	30·59	23·62	
" 10	11.45 "	30	18·50	"	"	" ...	20 m.	9·30	17·14	30·98	23·96	
" 10	11.45 "	30	18·50	"	"	" ...	25 m.	9·37	17·17	31·02	23·98	
" 14	6.00 a.m.	28	11·90	Low tide...	Strong N. W.	Cloudy.	Surface.	10·95	16·01	28·94	22·10	

8 GEORGE V, A. 1918

SAMPLES

"Prince" Stations. No.	Locality.		Position (vide chart).		Latitude.	Longitude.	Bottom.
6	Ste. Croix River between Biological Station and Robbinston.		Biological Station bears E. ⅔ S., ₇⁄₁₀ of a mile Little Dochet Id. bears N. by W. ¼ W. 2¾ miles.		45° 4′ 49″ N.	67° 5′ 53″ W	Fairly hard mud.
6	"	"	"	"	"	"	"
5	"	"	"	"	"	"	"
6	"	"	"	"	"	"	"
6	"	"	"	"	"	"	"
6	"	"	"	"	"	"	"
6	"	"	"	"	"	"	"
6	"	"	"	"	"	"	"
6	"	"	"	"	"	"	"
6	"	"	"	"	"	"	"
6	"	"	"	"	"	"	"
6	"	"	"	"	"	"	"
6	"	"	"	"	"	"	"
6	"	"	"	"	"	"	"
6	"	"	"	"	"	"	"
6	"	"	"	"	"	"	"
6	"	"	"	"	"	"	"
6	"	"	"	"	"	"	"
6	"	"	"	"	"	"	"
6	"	"	"	"	"	"	"
6	"	"	"	"	"	"	"
6	"	"	"	"	"	"	"
6	"	"	"	"	"	"	"
6	"	"	"	"	"	"	"
6	"	"	"	"	"	"	"
6	"	"	"	"	"	"	"
6	"	"	"	"	"	"	"
6	"	"	"	"	"	"	"
6	"	"	"	"	"	"	"
6	"	"	"	"	"	"	"
6	"	"	"	"	"	"	"
6	"	"	"	"	"	"	"
6	"	"	"	"	"	"	"
6	"	"	"	"	"	"	"
6	"	"	"	"	"	"	"
6	"	"	"	"	"	"	"
6	"	"	"	"	"	"	"
6	"	"	"	"	"	"	"

SESSIONAL PAPER No. 38a

COLLECTED—*Con.*

Date.	Hour.	Depth in Metres.	Air Temperature t° C.	Tide.	Wind.	Sky.	Depth of determinations in metres.	Water Temperature t° C.	Chlorine. Cl. %∘	Salinity. S%∘	Density. σt.	Colour of Water.
1916.												
Aug; 14	6.00 a.m..	28 m.	11·90	Low tide circ.	Strong..	Cloudy.	18·30 m.	10·95	16·01	28·94	22·10	
,, 14	6.00 ,,	28 ,,	11·90	,, ...	,,	,, ...	10 m.	.9·13	16·78	30 33	23·33	
,, 14	6.00 ,,	28 ,,	11·90	,, ...	,,	,, ...	20 m.	9·91	16·98	30·69	23·65	
,, 14	6.00 ,,	28 ,,	11·90	,, ...	,,	,, ...	25 m.	9·68	17·12	30·93	23·86	
,, 14	12.00 p.m..	33 ,,	12·20	High tide...	,,	,, ...	Sur-face.	10·40	16·96	30·64	23·51	
,, 14	12.00 ,,	33 ,,	12·20	,, ...	,,	,, ...	10 m.	9·70	17·03	30·77	23·75	
,, 14	12.00 ,,	33 ,,	12·20	,, ...	,,	,, ...	20 m.	9·55	17·18	31·03	23·97	
,, 14	12.00 ,,	33 ,,	12·20	,, ...	,,	,, ...	25 m.	9·50	17·24	31·15	24·05	
,, 14	12.00 ,,	33 ,,	12·20	,, ...	,,	,, ...	30 m.	9·48	17·24	31·15	24·06	
,, 18	8.30 a.m..	29 ,,	13·80	½ hour to low tide.	South breeze.	Hazy ..	Sur-face.	11·75	16·07	29·04	23·19	
,, 18	8.30 ,,	29 ,,	13·80	,,	,,	,,	10 m.	10·38	16·83	30·40	23·34	
,, 18	8.30 ,,	29 ,,	13·80	,,	,,	,,	20 m.	10·09	17·13	30 95	23·82	
,, 18	8.30 ,,	29 ,,	13·80	,,	,,	,,	25 m.	10·06	17·15	30·98	23·83	
,, 22	1.10 p.m..	28 ,,	22·38	Low tide...	Calm...	,,	25 m.	14·22	15·62	28·22	20·96	
,, 22	1.10 p.m..	28 ,,	22·38	,, ...	,, ...	..	Sur-face.	10·51	17·03	30·78	23·59	
,, 22	1.10 p.m..	28 ,,	22·38	,, ...	,, ...	..	10 m.	9·83	17·24	31·16	24·01	
,, 22	1 10 p.m..	28 ,,	22·38	,, ...	,, ...	,,	20 m.	9·78	17·30	31·26	24·11	
,, 23	8.20 a.m..	32 ,,	14·90	High tide...	S.E. breeze.	,,	25 m.	12·29	16·93	30·59	23·10	
,, 23	8.20 a.m..	32 ,,	14·90	,, ...	,,	,,	Sur-face.	10·60	17·17	31·02	23·79	
,, 23	8.20 a.m..	32 ,,	14·90	,, ...	,,	,,	10 m.	10·29	17·21	31·10	23·88	
,, 23	7.58 a.m,.	32 ,,	14·90	,, ...	,,	,,	15 m.	9·78	17·39	31·43	24·22	
,, 23	7.58 a.m..	32 ,,	14·90	,, ...	,,	,,	20 m.	9·69	17·43	31·49	24·30	
,, 23	7.58 a.m..	32 ,,	14·90	,, ...	,,	,,	25 m.	9·68	17·43	31·49	24·31	
,, 31	9.45 a.m..	28 ,,	15·20	2 hours flood	Calm...	Sun-shine.	30 m.	12·52	16·14	29·17	22 00	
,, 31	9.45 a.m..	28 ,,	15·20	,,	,, ...	,,	Sur-face.	10·28	17·32	31·29	24·03	
,, 31	9.45 a.m..	28 ,,	15·20	,,	,, ...	,,	20 m.	10·26	17·34	31·34	24·07	
Sept. 15	12.03 p.m..	36 ,,	16·80	? hrs to high tide.	Light S.E. breeze.	Clear ..	27 m.	11·73	16·70	30·17	22·92	Gray .
,, 15	12.03 p.m..	36 ,,	16·80	,,	,,	,, ...	Sur-face.	10·31	17·26	31·19	23·88	,,
,, 15	12.03 p.m..	36 ,,	16·80	,,	,,	,, ...	10 m	10·21	17·54	31·69	24·32	,,
,, 15	12.03 ,,	36 ,,	16·80	,,	,,	,,	20 m.	10·17	17·53	31·67	24·34	,,
Oct. 2	11.30 a.m..	31 ,,	12·95	½ flood......	North .	,,	35 m	10·52	17·01	30·73	23·56	Gre'n-ish.
,, 2	11.50 ,,	31 ,,	12·95	,,	,,	,,	Sur-face.	10·18	17·03	30·77	23·65	Gray .
,, 2	11.30 ,,	31 ,,	12·95	,,	,,	,,	10 m.	10·12	17·31	31·27	24·06	,,
,, 2	11.30 ,,	31 ,,	12·95	,,	,,	,,	20 ,,	10·11	17·45	31·54	24·25	,,
,, 9	7.50 ,,	33 ,,	11·72	2 hours to high tide.	N.-E. breeze.	Cloudy rain.	30 ,,	10·31	No water sample.			Gray-ish.
,, 9	7.50 ,,	33 ,,	11·72	,,	,,	,,	Sur-face.	10·04	,,	,,		,,
,, 9	7 50 ,,	33 ,,	11·72	,,	,,	,,	20 m.	10 01	,,	,,		,,
,, 16	4.11 p.m..	35 ,,	14·21	1 hour ebb..	Moder-ate N.·W.	partly cloudy.	30 ,,	9·42	Sample lost.			Gre'n-ish.
,, 16	4.11 ,,	35 ,,	14·21	,,	,,	,,	Sur-face.	9·16	,,	,,		,,
,, 16	4.11 ,,	35 ,,	14·21	,,	,,	,,	20 m.	9·12	,,	,,		,,
,, 21	9.37 a.m..	31 ,,	13·91	2¼ hours ebb.	Fresh S.-W.	Misty. Clouds.	30 ,,	9·47	No water sample.			Gray-ish.
,, 21	9.37 ,,	31 ,,	13·91	,,	,,	,,	Sur-face.	9·06	,,	,,		,,
,, 21	9.37 ,,	31 ,,	13·91	,,	,,	,,	10 m.	8·90	.·	,,		,,
,, 21	9.37 ,,	31 ,,	13·91	,,	,,	,,	20 ,,	8·88	,,	,,		,,

38a—21½

8 GEORGE V, A. 1918

SAMPLES

"Prince" Stations No.	Locality.	Position (vide chart.)		Latitude.	Longitude.	Bottom.
6........	Ste Croix River between Biological station and Robbinston.	Biological station bears E ⅔ S. ₁₀/₁₀ of a mile. Little Dochet Id. bears N. by W. ½ W. 2⅜ miles.		45° 4' 49" N...	67° 5' 53" W..	Fairly hard mud.
6........	" "	"	"	"	"	"
6........	" "	"	"	"	"	"
6........	" "	"	"	"	"	"
7........	" "	"	"	"	"	"
7........	" "	"	"	"	"	"
8........	Bay of Fundy, east of White Horse Id., just south of Letite Passage.	Head Harbour Lt. bears S.-W. by W., 2⅝ miles. Green's Point Lt. bears N. by W. 2⅜ miles.		44° 59' 47" N..	66° 51' 24" W.	Sand and mud.
8........	" "	"	"	"	"	"
8.......	" "	"	"	"	"	"
8........	" "	"	"	"	"	"
9........	Passamaquoddy Bay, off Clam Cove Head.	Forest Id. bears S.-W. ¾ mile. Southern end of Clam Cove Head bears S. S.-E. ¼ miles.		44° 58' 39" N..	67° 2' 7" W...	Sand, mud and shells.
9...	" "	"	"	"	"	"
9........	" "	"	"	"	"	"
9........	" "	"	"	"	"	"
9...	" "	"	"	"	"	"
9...	" "	"	"	"	"	"
9........	" "	"	"	"	"	"
9........	" "	"	"	"	"	"
9........	" "	"	"	"	"	"
9........	" "	"	"	"	"	"
9...	" "	"	"	"	"	"
9........	" "	"	"	"	"	"
9	" "	"	"	"	"	"
9........	" "	"	"	"	"	"
9........	" "	"	"	"	"	"
9...	" "	"	"	"	"	"
9........	" "	"	"	"	"	"
9........	" "	"	"	"	"	"
9........	" "	"	"	"	"	"
9........	" "	"	"	"	"	"
9........	" "	"	"	"	"	"
9...	" "	"	"	"	"	"
9........	" "	"	"	"	"	"
9........	" "	"	"	"	"	"
9........	" "	"	"	"	"	"

SESSIONAL PAPER No. 38a

COLLECTED—*Con.*

Date.	Hour.	Depth in metres.	Air temperature t° C.	Tide.	Wind.	Sky.	Depth of determinations in metres.	Water temperature t° C.	Chlorine Cl. ‰.	Salinity S. ‰.	Density σt.	Colour of water.
1916.												
Oct. 27	10.25 ,, .	34 ,,	7·38	1¼ hours to high tide.	Moderate. N.-W.	Clear...	Surface.	8·90	No water sample.			Gre'nish Gray.
,, 27	10.25 ,, .	34 ,,	7·38	,,	,,	,, ...	20 m.	8·82	,,	,,		,,
,, 27	10.25 ,, .	34 ,,	7·38	,,	,,	,, ...	30 ,,	8·82	,,	,,		,,
......	... .	84 ,,	...	.	.	......	...	.	.	....	....	....
......	... .	84 ,,	...	.	.	......	...	.	.	....	....	....
July 14	5.00 p.m..	73 ,,	12·15	......	......	......	9 m.	7·62	17·33	31·32	24·47	... .
......	......	....	....	...	...	......	......	....	....	....	....	....
......	......	....	....	...	...	......	......	....	....	....	....	....
......	......	....	....	...	...	......	....	....	..	......	...	....
Aug. 3	3.00 p.m..	73 m.	15·05	High.	S.-W. breeze.	Cloudy .	Surface.	9·50	17·06	30·82	23·81	......
,, 3	3.00 ,, .	73 ,,	15·05	,, ...	,,	,,	10 m.	9·10	17·11	30·92	23·95	......
,, 3	3.00 ,, .	73 ,,	15·05	,, ...	,,	,,	20 ,,	8·95	17·18	31·04	24·08	......
,, 3	3.00 ,, .	73 ,,	15·05	,, ...	,,	,,	30 ,,	8·60	17·26	31·19	24·23	......
,, 3	3.00 ,, .	73 ,,	15·05	,, ...	,,	,,	40 ,,	8·42	17·32	31·29	24·33	....
,, 10	12.45 ,, .	72 ,,	22·20	Low tide ..	very slight S. breeze.	Clear...	Surface.	12·62	16·18	29·24	22·16	......
,, 10	12.45 ,, .	72 ,,	22·20	,, ...	,,	,,	10 m.	10·02	16·99	30·71	23·62	......
,, 10	12.45 ,, .	72 ,,	22·20	,, ...	,,	,,	20 ,,	9·20	17·23	31·13	24·09	......
,, 10	12.45 ,, .	72 ,,	22·20	,, ...	,,	,,	30 ,,	9·12	17·25	31·16	24·13	......
,, 10	12.45 ,, .	72 ,,	22·20	,, ...	,,	,,	40 ,,	9·12	17·25	31 16	24·13	......
,, 17	3.50 ,, .	72 ,,	18·30	1½ hour ebb.	Calm...	,,	Surface.	10·05	17·36	31·36	24·14	...
,, 17	3.50 ,, .	72 ,,	18·30	,,	,,	,,	10 m.	9·57	17·36	31·36	24·14	......
Aug. 17	4.00 p.m.	72 m.	18·30	1½ hr. ebb.	Calm.	Clear.	20 m.	9·48	17·38	31·40	24·24	
,, 17	4.00 ,,	72 ,,	18·30	,,	,,	,,	30 m.	9·02	17·47	31·57	24·46	
,, 17	4.00 ,,	72 ,,	18·30	,,	,,	,,	40 m.	9·01	17·47	31·57	24·46	
Aug. 31	2.00 ,,	78 m.	16·68	¾ hr. ebb.	S.W. breeze.	,,	Surface.	12·21	17·06	30·82	23·34	
,, 31	2.00 ,,	78 ,,	16·68	,,	,,	,,	20 m.	10·16	17·45	31·54	24·25	
,, 31	2.00 ,,	78 ,,	16·68	,,	,,	,,	75 m.	9·81	17·53	31·67	24·46	
Sept. 15	3.26 ,,	76 m.	14·80	½ hr. ebb.	S.E. breeze.	Hazy.	Surface.	10·42	17·24	31·16	23·89	Gray.
,, 15	3.26 ,,	76 ,,	14·80	,,	,,	,,	10 m.	10·11	17·58	31·75	24·44	,,
,, 15	3.26 ,,	76 ,,	14·80	,,	,,	,,	20 m.	10·12	17·57	31·74	24·44	,,
,, 15	3.26 ,,	76 ,,	14·80	,,	,,	,,	30 m.	10·11	17·59	31·78	24·45	,,
,, 15	2.51 ,,	76 ,,	14·80	,,	,,	,,	40 m.	10·02	17·79	32·15	24·75	,,
,, 15	2.51 ,,	76 ,,	14·80	,,	,,	,,	50 m.	9·85	17 27	31·21	24·05	,,
,, 15	3.15 ,,	76 ,,	14·80	,,	,,	,,	60 m.	9·92	17·42	31·47	24·25	,,
,, 15	3.15 ,,	76 ,,	14·80	,,	,,	,,	70 m.	9·92	17·62	31·84	24·53	,,
,, 15	3.15 ,,	76 ,,	14·80	,,	,,	,,	75 m.	9·93	17·80	32·16	24·78	,,
Oct. 3	11.49 a.m.	75 m.	14·56	1 hr. flood.	S.W. light breeze.	Clear.	Surface.	10·61	17·40	31·45	24·12	Gre'nish.

8 GEORGE V, A. 1918

SAMPLES

" Prince " Stations. No.	Locality.	Position (vide chart).	Latitude.	Longitude.	Bottom.
9...	Passamaquoddy Bay, off Clam Cove Head.	Forest ld. bears S.W. ¾ mile. Southern end of Clam Cove Head bears S.S.E. ¾ mile.	44° 58′ 39″ N.	67° 2′ 7″ W.	Sand, mud and shells.
9........	″	″	″	″	″	″
9........	″	″	″	″	″	″
9........	″	″	″	″	″	″
9	″	″	″	″	″	″
9...	″	″	″	″	″	″
9	″	″	″	″	″	″
9........	″	″	″	″	″	″
9........	″	″	″	″	″	″
10........	Passamaquoddy Bay, near Eastern entrance to St. Andrew's Harbour.	Navy Bar Lt. bears N.W. by N. ½ N., ⅜ mile. Tongue Shoal Lt. bears E. by N. ¾ N., ¾ mile.	45° 3′ 14″ N.	67° 1′ 45″ W.	Mud and rocks.
10.	″	″	″	″	″	″
10........	″	″	″	″	″	″
10........	″	″	″	″	″	″
10	″	″	″	′	″	″
10 ......•	″	″	″	′	″	″
10........	″	″	″	′	″	″
10........	″	″	″	″	″	″
10........	″	″	″	″	″	″
10......••	″	″	″	″	″	″
10........	″	″	″	″	″	″
10........	″	″	″	″	″	″
10......•..	″	″	″	″	″	″
10.......	″	″	″	″	″	″
10.... ..	″	″	″	″	″	″
10..	″	″	″	″	″	″
10..... .	″	″	″	″	″	″
10.. . ..	″	″	″	″	″	″
10........	″	″	″	″	″	″
10.	″	″	″	″	″	″
10...... .	″	″	″	″	″	″
10.......	″	″	″	″	″	″
10..	″	″	″	″	″	″
10	″	″	″	″	″	″
10.... .	″	″	″	″	″	″
10........	″	″	″	″	″	″
10.... ...	″	″	″	″	″	″

SESSIONAL PAPER No. 38a

COLLECTED—*Con.*

Date.	Hour.	Depth in Metres.	Air Temperature t° C.	Tide.	Wind.	Sky.	Depth in determinations metres.	Water Temperature t° C.	Chlorine. Cl °/₀₀	Salinity. S. °/₀₀	Density. σt.	Colour of Water.
1916.												
Oct. 3	11.49 a.m.	75 m.	14·56	1 hr. flood.	S. W. light breeze.	Clear.	10 m.	16·20	17·52	31·65	24·34	Gray.
" 3	11.49 "	75 "	14·56	"	"	"	20 m.	10·12	17·19	31·07	23·88	"
" 3	11.49 "	75 "	14·56	"	"	"	30 m.	9·98	17·54	31·70	24·40	"
" 3	11.35 "	75 "	14·56	"	"	"	40 m.	9·85	sample lost.			
Oct. 3	11.35 "	75 m.	14·56	1 hr. flood.	S.W. light breeze.	"	50 m.	9·83	17·64	31·88	24·58	Gre'nish.
" 3	11.35 "	75 "	14·56	"	"	"	75 m.	9·68	17·71	32·00	24·70	Gray.
Oct. 17	8.32 "	76 m.	11·61	1½ hr. to low tide.	Strong S.W.	Cloudy; rain.	Surface.	9·10	No water.			
" 17	8.32 "	76 "	11·61	"	"	"	20 m.	9·01		"		
" 17	8.32 "	76 "	11·61	"	"	"	75 m.	8·91		"		
Aug. 3	5.00 p.m.	20 m.	....	2¼ hrs. ebb tide.	S.W. breeze.	Cloudy.	Surface.	10·70	16·77	30·30	23·21	
" 3	5.00 "	20 "	...	"	"	"	10 m.	8·95	17·13	30·96	23·99	
" 3	5.00 "	20 "	...	"	"	"	20 m. (bottom.)	8·75	17·18	31·04	24·09	
Aug. 17	6.10 "	18 m.	15·12	2 hrs. to low tide.	....	Slight haze.	Surface.	11·75	17·07	30·84	23·43	
" 17	6.10 "	18 "	15·12	"	"	"	10 m.	10·18	17·18	31·04	23·89	
" 17	6.10 "	18 "	15·12	"	"	"	15 m.	10·19	17·23	31·13	23·94	
Aug. 24	3.45 "	16 m.	17·28	Low tide.	Light E.	Rain.	Surface.	13·70	No water.			
" 24	3.45 "	16 "	17·28	"	"	"	10 m.	9·72		"		
" 24	3.45 "	16 "	17·24	"	"	"	15 m.	9·61		"		
Aug. 31	11.25 a.m.	21 m.	16·89	2 hrs. to high tide.	Calm.	Clear.	Surface.	12·20	17·18	31·05	23·51	
" 31	11.25 "	21 "	16·89	"	"	"	15 m.	10·19	17·43	31·49	24·22	
" 31	11.25 "	21 "	16·89	"	"	"	20 m.	10·09	17·48	31·59	24·30	
Sept. 15	10.41 "	20 m.	16·58	2½ hrs. flood.	Light S.E. breeze.	"	Surface.	11·42	17·41	31·46	23·97	Gray.
" 15	10.41 "	20 "	16·58	"	"	"	10 m.	10·24	17·46	31·55	24·25	"
Oct. 3	9.05 "	17 m.	10.98	1 hr. to low tide.	N.W. moderate.	"	Surf.	10·51	17·36	31·36	24·06	"
" 3	9.05 "	17 "	10.98	"	"	"	10 m.	10·38	17·52	31·66	24·30	"
" 3	9.05 "	17 "	10.98	"	"	"	15 m.	9·72	17·53	31·67	24·42	"
" 9	9.33 "	22 "	10.90	High tide.	N.E.	cloudy.	Surf.	10·20	no water.			"
" 9	9.33 "	22 "	10.90	"	"	"	10 m.	9·83		"		"
" 9	9.33 "	22 "	10.90	"	"	"	20 m.	9·85		"		"
" 16	11.09 "	19 "	11.12	2 hrs. flood.	S.W. moderate.	"	Surf.	9·24	17·64	31·88	24·64	Gre'nish Gray.
" 16	11.09 "	19 "	11.12	"	"	"	13 m.	9·12	17·70	31·99	24·77	"
" 16	11.09 "	19 "	11.12	"	"	"	18 m.	9·12	17·69	31·96	24·76	"
" 21	12.52 p.m.	18 "	13.45	1 hr. to low tide.	Strong S.W.	clouds, rain.	Surf.	9.30	no water.			Grayish.
" 21	12.52 "	18 "	13.45	"	"	"	10 m.	8·95		"		"
" 21	12.52 "	18 "	13·45	"	"	"	17 m.	8·86		"		"
" 27	8.08 a.m.	19 "	4.62	2½ hrs. flood.	Moderate.	partly cloudy.	Surf.	8·64		"		Gre'nish Gray.

8 GEORGE V, A. 1918

SAMPLES

"Prince" Station No.	Locality.	Position (vide chart.)	Latitude.	Longitude.	Bottom.
10.......	Passamaquoddy Bay, near Eastern entrance to St. Andrews Harbour.	Navy Bar Lt. bears N.W. by N¼ N. ⅜ mile. Tongue Shoal Lt bears E. by N. ¾ N., ⅞ mile.	45° 3′ 14″ N.	67° 1′ 45″ W.	Mud and rocks.
10........	" "	" "	"	"	"
10........	" "	" "	"	"	"
11........	Petite Passage.........	In a direct line between Tiverton and East Ferry about midway.	44° 23′ 52″ N.	66° 12′ 34″ W.	Hard sand and rocks.
11	"	" "	"	"	"
11........	"	" "	"	"	"
11........	"	" "	"	"	"
11	"	" "	"	"	"
11........	"	" "	"	"	"
11........	"	" "	"	"	"
12.... ...	St. Mary's Bay, off Little River.	One mile S.E. from Little River wharf.	44° 26′ 17″ N.	66° 6′ 33″ W.	Fine sand.
12.. ...	" "	" "	"	"	"
12.......	" "	" "	"	"	"
12	" "	" "	"	"	"
12........	" "	" "	"	"	"
12........	" "	" "	"	"	"
12.......	" "	" "	"	"	"
13........	St. Mary's Bay, below Southern end of Petite Passage.	South Point of Digby neck bears N.E. ½ N. 2¼ miles. Church Pt. bears E. by S. ¼ S. 4¼ miles.	44° 20′ 7″ N.	66° 13′ 24″ W.	"
13..	" "	" "	"	"	"
13........	" "	" "	"	"	"
13........	" "	" "	"	"	"
13........	" "	" "	"	"	"
13	" "	" "	"	"	"
15	Bay of Fundy, off Brier Island.	8¾ miles N.-W. by W. from north end of Grande Passage. Run N. N.W. 4 miles, then run W. ½ N., 5¾ miles.	44° 19′ 30″ N..	66° 32′ 28″ W.	Fine sand..
15........	" "	" "	" ..	"	" ..
15........	" "	" "	" ..	"	" ..
15........	" "	" "	" ..	" ..	" ..
15........	" "	" "	" ..	"	" ..
15........	" "	" "	" ..	"	" ..
15........	" "	" "	" ..	"	" ..
15........	" "	" "	" ..	"	" ..
15..	" "	" "	" ..	"	" ..
15........	" "	" "	" ..	"	" ..

SESSIONAL PAPER No. 38a

COLLECTED—*Con.*

Date.	Hour.	Depth of Metres.	Air temperature t° C.	Tide.	Wind.	Sky.	Depth of determinations in metres.	Water temperature t° C.	Chlorine Cl. ‰	Salinity S. ‰	Density σt.	Colour of Water.
1916.												
Oct. 27	8.08 a.m.	19 m.	4.62	hrs. flood.	N.W.	cloudy.	13 m.	8 92	no	water.		Gray.
" 27	8.08 "	19 "	4.62	"	"	"	18 m.	8·87		"		"
Sept. 2	7.55 "	30 "	13.02	Low tide.	South breeze.	cloudy.	Surf.	9·00	17·91	32·37	25·08	
" 2	7.55 "	30 "	13.02	"	"	"	10 m.	8·91	17·94	32·41	25·14	
" 2	7.55 "	30 "	13.02	"	"	"	20 m.	8·91	17·89	32·32	25·07	
" 2	7.55 "	30 "	13.02	"	"	"	25 m.	8.42	17·89	32·32	25.13	
" 2	1.15 p.m.	35 "	15.28	High tide.	Strong south.	cloudy	Surf.	10·57	17·73	32·03	24·59	Blu-ish.
" 2	1.15 "	35 "	15.28	"	"	"	10 m.	10·32	17·79	32·15	24·70	"
" 2	1.15 "	35 "	15.28	"	"	"	20 m.	10·21	17·81	32·18	24·75	"
" 2	1.15 "	35 "	15.28	"	"	"	30 m.	10·13	17·79	32·15	24·75	"
" 4	8.50 a.m.	24 "	13.38	Low tide.	S.W.N. breeze.	clear.	Surf.	12·92	17·70	31·98	24·10	"
" 4	8.50 "	24 "	13.38	"	. "	"	10 m.	12·92	17·70	31·99	24·10	"
" 4	8.50 "	24 "	13.38	"	"	"	20 m.	11·51	17·76	32·09	24·46	"
" 4	3.10 p.m.	31 "	12.20	High tide.	S.W. breeze.	cloudy.	Surf.	12·58	17·67	31·93	24·13	Gray-ish.
" 4	3.10 "	31 "	12.20	"	"	..	10 m.	12·51	17·68	31·95	24·15	".
" 4	3.10 "	31 "	12.20	"	"	"	20 m.	11·12	17·73	32·03	24·49	"
" 4	3.10 "	31 "	12.20	"	"	"	30 m.	11·04	17·77	32·10	24·55	"
" 5	10.27 a.m.	50 "	11.90	Low tide.	N.E. breeze.	"	Surf.	11·08	17·74	32·05	24 51	Gray-ish.
" 5	10.41 "	50 "	11.90	"	"	"	10 m.	10·14	17·83	32·21	24·79	"
" 5	10.41 "	50 "	11.90	"	"	"	20 m.	9·82	17·85	32·26	24·86	"
" 5	10.27 "	50 "	11.90	"	"	"	30 m.	9·60	17·86	32·28	24·93	"
" 5	10.27 "	50 "	11.90	"	"	"	40 m.	9·18	17·91	32·36	25·05	"
" 5	10.27 "	50 "	11.90	"	"	"	48 m.	9·09	17·93	32·40	25 12	"
Sept. 6	11.45 a.m.	203 m.	14·80	Low tide...	Calm ...	Cloudy.	Sur-face.	9·17	17·98	32·48	25·15	Dark blue.
" 6	12.15 p.m.	203 "	14·80	" ...	" ...	"	10 m.	8·58	18·00	32·52	25·25	"
" 6	12.15 "	203 "	14·80	" ...	" ...	"	20 "	8·40	18·01	32·54	25·31	"
" 6	12.15 "	203 "	14·80	" ...	" ...	"	25 "	8·31	18·02	32·55	25·33	"
" 6	12.15 "	203 "	14·80	" ...	" ...	"	50 "	8·15	18·03	32·56	25·37	"
" 6	12.10 "	203 "	14·80	" ...	" ...	"	75 "	7·78	18·05	32·61	25·46	"
" 6	12.00 noon.	203 "	14·80	" ...	" ...	"	100 "	7·49	18·10	32·71	25·53	"
" 6	11.45 a.m.	203 "	14·80	" ...	" ...	"	125 "	6·28	18·19	32·87	25·85	"
" 6	11.45 "	203 "	14·80	" ...	" ...	"	150 "	5·88	18·22	32·91	25·97	"
" 6	11.45 "	203 "	14·80	" ...	" ...	"	175 "	5·57	18·24	32·9C	26·03	"
" 6	11.45 "	203 "	14·80	" ...	" ...	"	200 "	5·55	18·12	32·74	25·57	"

SAMPLES

"Prince" Stations No.	Locality.	Position (vide chart.)	Latitude.	Longitude.	Bottom.
16	Gulf of Maine, outside Yarmouth Harbour.	Beside Yarmouth, N.-W. Fairway buoy.	43° 48′ 48″ N.	66° 15′ 54″ W.	Hard rocks and gravel
16	" "	" "	"	"	"
16	" "	" "	"	"	"
16	" "	" "	"	"	"
16	" "	" "	"	"	"
16	" "	" "	"	"	"
16	" "	" "	"	"	"
16	" "	" "	"	"	"
16	" "	" "	"	"	"
16	" "	" "	"	"	"
16	" "	" "	"	"	"
17	Yarmouth Harbour	¼ mile outside Bunker Id. red light. Abreast lower end of Ship's Stern.	43° 48′ 13″ N.	66° 8′ 42″ W.	Soft mud
17	" "	" "	"	"	"
17	" "	" "	"	"	"
17	" "	" "	"	"	"
17	" "	" "	"	"	"
17	" "	" "	"	"	"
18	St. John River, between Fairville and Indiantown.	About 100 yds. off east corner of Lovett's Pt. toward Marble Cove Pt.	45° 16′ 38″ N.	66° 5′ 53″ W.	Rocks and sawdust.
18	" "	" "	"	"	"
18	" "	" "	"	"	"
18	" "	" "	"	"	"
18	" "	" "	"	"	"
19	Bay of Fundy, off St. John Harbour.	Partridge Id. bell boat bears N.E. by N. ¾ N. 2½ miles. Eastern end of Meogenes Id. bears N.-W. by N. 2⅜ miles.	45° 12′ 11″ N.	66° 3′ 40″ W.	Soft mud
19	" "	" "	"	"	"
19	" "	" "	"	"	"
20	Kennebecasis Bay, at western end of Long Id.	Milkish Head bears N. by W. ½ W. ½ mile. Outside point of Long Id. bears N.-E. by E. ¼ E. by 1¼ miles.	45° 20′ 57″ N.	66° 4′ 8″ W.	"
20	" "	" "	"	"	"
20	" "	" "	"	"	"
20	" "	" "	"	"	"
20	Kennebecasis Bay, at Western end of Long Id.	Milkish head bears N. by W. ½ W. ½ mile. Outside point of Long Id. bears N. E. by E. ¼ E. 1¼ miles.	45° 12′ 57″ N.	66° 4′ 8″ W.	"
20	" "	" "	"	"	"
20	" "	" "	"	"	"
20	" "	" "	"	"	"
20	" "	" "	"	"	"
21	Kennebecasis Bay, at eastern end of Long Id.	Outside point of Long Id. bears S.W. by S. ¼ S., 1 mile. Northern end of Long Id. bears N,N.W.	45° 24′ 44″ N.	66° 1′ 43″ W.	"
21	" "	" "	"	"	"
21	" "	" "	"	"	"
21	" "	" "	"	"	"
21	" "	" "	"	"	"
21	" "	" "	"	"	"
21	" "	" "	"	"	"

SESSIONAL PAPER No. 38a

COLLECTED—*Con.*

Date.	Hour.	Depth in metres.	Air temperature t° C.	Tide.	Wind.	Sky.	Depth of determinations in metres.	Water temperature t° C.	Chlorine Cl. °/oo	Salinity S. °/oo	Density σt,	Colour of water.
1916. Sept. 7	12.40 p.m.	41 m.	16·68	Low tide...	Calm...	Foggy..	Surface.	10·03	17·85	32·25	24·84	,,
" 7	12.50 "	41 "	16·68	" ...	" ...	" ..	10 m.	9·82	17·60	31·81	24·53	,,
" 7	12.50 "	41 "	16·68	" ...	" ...	" ..	20 "	9·78	17·39	31·42	34·24	,,
" 7	12.50 "	41 "	16·68	"	" ...	" ..	30 "	9·72	16·22	29·32	22·59	,,
" 7	12.50 "	41 "	16·68	" ...	" ...	" ..	40 "	9·69	17·21	31·09	23·99	,,
" 9	7.45 a.m.	47 "	12·52	½ hour to high tide.	" ...	Fog and rain.	Surface.	9·40	18.06	32·63	25·23	Grayish.
" 9	8.04 "	47 "	12·52	"	" ...	"	10 m.	9·21	17·75	32·07	24·83	,,
" 9	8.04 "	47 "	12·52	"	" ...	"	20 "	9·12	17·42	31·47	24·37	,,
" 9	7.45 "	47 "	12·52	"	" ...	"	30 "	9·20	17·59	31·78	24·61	,,
" 9	7.45 "	47 "	12·52	"	" ...	"	40 "	9·18	17·58	31·76	24·58	,,
" 9	7.45 "	47 "	12·52	"	" ...	"	45 "	9·18	17·89	32·33	25·02	,,
" 8	6.20 "	15 "	13·70	High tide..	South...	Thick Fog.	Surface.	11·22	17·25	31·17	23·77	,,
" 8	6.20 "	15 "	13·70	"	" ...	"	10 m.	10·83	17·54	31·69	24·27	,,
" 8	6.20 "	15 "	13·70	"	" ...	"	15 "	10·82	Water sampl e lost.			,,
" 8	1.20 p.m.	13 "	14·25	Low tide...	S.-W. breeze.	Foggy.	Surface.	12·70	17·78	32·12	24·25	,,
" 8	1.20 "	13 "	14·25	" ...	"	" ..	10 m.	11·78	17·53	31·68	24·09	,,
" 8	1.20 "	13 "	14·25	"	"	" ...	13 "	11·56	17·54	31·69	24·15	,,
" 21	4.13 "	35 "	16·35	....	Light S.-W.	Smoky.	Surface.	14·86	Water sampl e lost.			Bro'n.
" 21	4.13 "	35 "	16·35	....	"	"	10 m.	13·19	S·36	15·13	10·55	"
" 21	4.13 "	35 "	16·35	....	"	"	20 "	11·91	Water sampl e lost.			"
" 21	4.13 "	35 "	16·35	....	"	"	30 "	11·55	14·36	25·96	19·71	"
" 21	4.25 "	35 "	16·35	....	"	"	34 "	9·28	14·55	26·30	20·31	"
" 19	10.39 a.m.	19 ,,	12·25	½ hr. to low tide.	"	Cloudy.	Surface.	11·78	Water sampl e lost.			Green
" 19	10.39 "	19 ,	12·26	"	"	"	10 m.	10·62	17·03	30·78	23·57	"
" 19	10.39 "	19 "	12·26	"	"	"	19 m.	10·59	Water sampl e lost.			"
" 19	4.00 p.m.	55 "	11·80	1 hour river flood.	Light N.-W. breeze.	Clear..	Surface.	15·69	"		"	Bro'n.
" 19	4.20 "	55 "	11·80	"	"	" ...	5 m.	12·93	"		"	"
" 19	4.10 "	55 "	11·80	"	"	"	10 "	6·08	"		"	"
" 19	4.20 "	55 "	11·80	"	"	" ...	15 "	6·43	"		"	"
Sept. 19	4.10 p.m.	55 m.	11·80	1 hr. river flood.	Light N.W. breeze.	clear.	20 m.	8·22	10·61	19·18	14·92	Bro'n.
" 19	3.55 "	55 "	11·80	"	"	"	30 m.	10·98	water sampl e lost.			"
" 19	3.55 "	55 "	11·80	"	"	"	40 m.	11·74	"			"
" 19	3.55 "	55 "	11·80	"	"	"	44 m.	11·93	"			"
" 19	4.40 "	55 "	11·80	"	"	"	55 m.	12·00	"			"
" 20	3.40 "	48 "	16·10		N.W. breeze.	"	Surface.	7·20	10·15	18·35	14·38	"
" 20	3.50 "	48 "	16·10	....	"	"	10 m.	6·11	11·13	20·13	15·86	"
" 20	3.50 "	48 "	16·10	....	"	"	20 m.	10·18	11·53	20·85	15·95	"
" 20	3.40 "	48 "	16·10	....	"	"	30 m.	11·15	11·69	21·14	16·03	"
" 20	3.40 "	48 "	16·10	....	"	"	40 m.	11·21	water sampl e lost.			"
" 20	3.40 "	48 "	16·10	....	"	"	45 m.	16·10	"			Bro'n.
" 21	2.48 "	11 "	17·54	....	S.S.E. breeze.	Hazy.	Surface.	13·67	8·64	15·63	11·4	"

8 GEORGE V, A. 1918

SAMPLES

"Prince" Stations No.	Locality.	Position (vide chart.)	Latitude.	Longitude.	Bottom.
22........	St. John River, near mouth of Kennebecasis Bay.	West end of Milkish Id. bears E.N.E. Point on south side of mouth of Kennebecasis Bay bears S.S.E.	45° 18′ 30″ N.	66° 9′ 32″ W.	Soft mud.
22...	" "	" "	"	"	" .
22........	" "	" "	"	"	"
23........	Bay of Fundy, between St. John and Digby.	15 miles south of Partridge Id. bell boat. 20 miles north of Prim point.	45° 0′ 18″ N.	65° 56′ 10″ W.	Sand and gravel.
23.......	" "	" "	"	"	"
23...	" "	" "	"	"	"
23...	" "	" "	"	"	"
23...	" "	" "	"	"	"
23...	" "	" "	"	"	"
23....	" "	· " "	"	"	"
23...	" "	" "	"	"	"
23......	" " ·	" "	"	"	"
24.......	Lower end of Annapolis Basin.	Port Wade pier bears E.N. E. Outside point of Victoria Beach bears N. ½ W.	44° 39′ 15″ N.	65° 44′ 22″ W.	Fine sand.
24...... .	" "	" "	"	"	"
24.... ..	" "	" "	"	"	"
24	" "	" "	"	"	"
24.......	" "	" "	"	"	"
24.......	" "	" "	"	"	"
24........	" "	" "	"	"	"
24	" "	" "	"	"	"
24	" "	" "	"	"	"
24.	" "	" "	"	"	"
24.......	" "	" "	"	"	"
24.......	" "	" "	"	"	"
24......•	" "	" "	"	"	"
25........	Bay of Fundy, off Digby Gut.	¾ mile N.W. ½ N. from Fairway Buoy, 1¾ mile N. by E. ½ E., from Point Prim.			
25.......	" "	" "	44° 43′ 17″ N.	65° 47′ 18″ W.	Sand and shells.
25........	" "	" "	"	"	"
25	" "	" "	"	"	"
25	" "	" "	"	"	"
25........	" "	" "	"	"	"
25...	" "	" "	"	"	"
25........	" "	" "	"	"	"
25... . .	" "	" "	"	"	"
25...	" "	" "	"	"	"
25.......	" "	" "	"	"	"
25......	" "	" "	"	"	"
25........	" "	" "	"	"	"
25.......	" "	" "	"	"	"
25......•	" "	" "	"	"	"
25........	" "	" "	"	"	"
25.... ...	" "	" "	"	"	"

COLLECTED—*Con.*

Date.	Hour.	Depth in metres.	Air temperature t° C.	Tide.	Wind.	Sky.	Depth of determinations in metres.	Water temperature t° C.	Chlorine Cl. ‰	Salinity S. ‰	Density σt.	Colour of water.
1916.												
Sept. 21	2.43 p.m.	11 m.	17·54	....	S.E. breeze.	Hazy.	5 m.	11·70	water	sampl	e lost.	"
" 21	2.43 "	11 m.	17·54	....	"	"	10 m.	.....	.....	...	..	.....
Sept. 22	12.43 p.m.	95 m.	17·74	1½ hr. to low tide.	Calm.	Clear.	Surface.	10·30	17·36	31·37	24·09	Blue.
" 22	1.07 "	95 "	17·74	"	"	"	10 m.	9·56	17·74	32·06	24·76	"
" 22	1.07 "	95 "	17·74	"	.	"	20 m.	8·83	17·85	32·23	25·04	"
" 22	12.56 "	95 "	17·74	"	"	"	25 m.	8·73	17·89	32·32	25·09	"
" 22	12.56 "	95 "	17·74	"	"	"	30 m.	8·57	17·93	32·40	25·18	"
" 22	12.56 "	95 "	17·74	"	"	"	40 m.	8·38	17·95	32·44	25·24	"
" 22	12.43 "	95 "	17·74	"	"	"	50 m.	8·12	17·96	32·46	25·28	"
" 22	12.43 "	95 "	17·74	"	"	"	75 m.	7·93	18·01	32·55	25·38	"
" 22	12.43 "	95 "	17·74	"	"	"	95 m.	7·90	18·03	32·58	25·42	"
" 23	9.19 a.m.	58 "	12·83	High tide.	Light S.E. breeze.	cloudy.	Surface.	9·37	17·86	32 28	24·95	Gre'n- ish.
" 23	9.43 "	58 "	12·83	"	"	"	10 m.	9·32	water	sampl	e lost.	Gray.
" 23	9.33 "	58 "	12·83	"	"	"	20 m.	9·31	17·94	32·41	25·07	"
" 23	9.33 "	58 "	12·83	"	"	"	25 m.	9·28	17·03	32·39	25·07	"
" 23	9.33 "	58 "	12·83	"	"	"	30 m.	9·29	17·93	32·39	25·07	"
" 23	9.19 "	53 "	12·83	,	"	"	40 m.	9·30	17·96	32·45	25·10	"
" 23	9.19 · "	53 "	12·83	"	"	"	50 m.	9 28	17·33	31·32	24·22	"
" 23	9.19 "	53 "	12·83	"	"	"	55 m.	9·29	17·80	32·33	25·01	"
" 23	5.52 p.m.	55 "	15·58	Low tide.	S.W. breeze.	clear.	Surface.	10·48	17·91	32 37	24·84	Gray- ish.
" 23	5.49 "	55 "	15·58	"	"	"	10 m.	10·37	17·87	32·29	24·80	"
" 23	5.49 "	55 "	15·58	"	"	"	20 m.	10·30	water	sampl	e lost.	"
" 23	5.37 "	55 "	15·58	"	"	"	30 m.	10·22		"		"
" 23	5.37 "	55 "	15·58	"	"	"	40 m.	10·18	17·31	31·28	24·05	"
" 23	5.37 "	55 "	15·58	"	"	"	50 m.	9·86	17·23	31·13	24·00	"
Sept. 23	2.16 p.m.	74 m.	15·95	½ hour to low tide.	S.E. breeze.	Cloudy.	Surface.	9·30	17·95	32·44	25·10	Gre'n- ish.
" 23	2.45 "	74 "	15·95	"	"	"	10 m.	9·08	17·97	32·47	25·16	Gray.
" 23	2.33 "	74 "	15·95	"	"	"	20 m.	9·08	17·45	31·54	24·42	"
" 23	2.33 "	74 "	15·95	"	"	"	25 m.	9·07	17·57	31·75	24·58	"
" 23	2.33 "	74 "	15·95	"	"	"	30 m.	9·09	17·96	32·46	25·13	"
" 23	2.18 "	74 "	15·95	"	"	"	40 m.	9·02	17·92	32·38	25·09	"
" 23	2.18 "	74 "	15·95	"	"	"	50 m.	9·02	17·98	32·48	25·17	"
" 23	2.18 "	74 "	15·95	"	"	"	73 m.	9·03	17·95	32·43	25·14	"
Sept. 27	12.18 "	75 "	12 19	High tide.	S.W. breeze.	Hazy.	Surface.	9·21	Water	sampl	e lost.	Gre'n- ish.
" 27	12.31 "	75 "	12·19	"	"	"	10 m.	9.17	"	"	"	Blue.
" 27	12.18 "	75 "	12·19	"	"	"	20 m.	9·18	"	"	"	"
" 27	12.18 "	75 "	12·19	"	"	"	25 m.	9·13	17·40	31·45	24·34	"
" 27	12.18 "	75 "	12·19	"	"	"	30 m.	9·16	17·40	31·44	24·34	"
" 27	12.02 "	75 "	12·19	"	"	"	40 m.	9·14	17·85	32·25	24·98	"
" 27	12.02 "	75 "	12·19	"	"	"	50 m.	9·13	17·62	31·84	24·65	"
" 27	12.02 "	75 "	12·19	"	"	"	74 m.	9·13	Water	sampl	e lost.	"

8 GEORGE V, A. 1918

SAMPLES

"Prince" Stations No.	Locality.	Position (vide chart.)	Latitude.	Longitude.	Bottom.
26........	Basin in River, inside Annapolis Royal.	Lighthouse in bend above Granville ferry bears N. by W. ½ W. First point on south side above basin bears E.	44° 44′ 55″ N.	65° 29′ 52″ W.	Very soft mud.
26.......	" "	" "	"	"	"
26.........	" "	" "	"	"	"
26........	" "	" "	"	"	"
26....	" "	" "	"	"	"
26........	" "	" "	"	"	"
27	Annapolis River, northern passage, around Goat Island.	Lighthouse on Shaffner's Point bears N.E, ½ E Western side of Goat Id. bears S.E. by S. ½ S.			
27........	" "	" "	44° 42′ 21″ N.	65° 37′ 29″ W.	Soft mud.
27.......	" "	" "	"	"	"
27..	" "	"	" "	"	"	"
27.......	" "	" "	"	"	"
		3 miles.....	....	....	....
	Briar Island to Yarmouth.	5 "	....	....	... .
		8 "	....	....	....
		11 "	....	... .	... .
		14 "	....	... .	.. ..
		17 "	... .	. . ..	....
		20 "	....	....	....
		23 " .. .	... .	....	....
		26 "	....	....	....

SESSIONAL PAPER No. 38a

COLLECTED—*Con.*

Date.	Hour.	Depth in metres.	Air temperature t° C.	Tide.	Wind.	Sky.	Depth of determinations in metres.	Water temperature t° C.	Chlorine Cl. °/₀₀	Salinity S. °/₀₀	Density σt.	Colour of water.
1916.												
Sept. 25	10.19 a.m.	24 m.	13·40	High tide.	Quite heavy N.W. breeze.	Haze.	Sur-face,	14·05	16·14	29·17	21·71	Mud-dy.
" 25	10.19 "	24 "	13·40	"	"	"	10 m.	13·99	16·81	30·38	22·64	"
" 25	10.19 "	24 "	13·40	"	"	"	20 m.	13·72	16·95	30·63	22·90	"
Sept. 25	4.28 p.m.	22 "	14·71	Low tide.	Heavy N.W. breeze.	"	Sur-face.	14·45	16 39	29·61	21·97	"
" 25	4.28 "	22 "	14·71	"	"	"	10 m.	14·18	16·41	29·65	22·05	"
" 25	4.28 "	22 "	14·71	"	"	"	20 m.	14·00	16·72	30·21	22·52	"
Sept. 26	10.54 a.m.	30 "	10 28	High tide.	Heavy N.W. breeze.	Partly cloudy.	Sur-face.	11 62	17·69	31·96	24 35	Gre'n-ish.
" 26	10.54 "	30 "	10·28	"	"	"	10 m.	11 62	17·36	31·36	23·88	Gray.
" 26	10.54 "	30 "	10·28	"	"	"	20 m.	11·18	17·77	32·10	24·52	"
" 26	10.54 "	30 "	10·28	"	"	"	25 m.	11·17	17·79	32·15	24·55	"
Sept. 7	9.12 "	....	....	....	South.	Foggy.	Sur-face.	10·10	No water sample.			
" 7	9.33 "	....	11·70	....	"	"	"	10·00	17·76	32·09	24·71	
" 7	9.56 "	....	11·40	....	"	"	"	10·40	17·73	32·03	24·60	
" 7	10.16 "	....	11·80	....	"	"	"	10·80	17·69	31 96	24·49	
" 7	10 39 "	....	11·60	....	"	"	"	11·10	17 69	31·97	24·43	
" 7	11.02 "	....	11·80	....	"	"	"	11·20	Sample of water lost.			
" 7	11.22 "	....	11·50	....	"	"	"	9·95	17·51	31·64	24·36	
" 7	11.44 "	..	11·70	....	"	"	"	10·45	17·34	31·34	24·04	
" 7	12.10 p.m.	....	12·30	....	"	"	"	10·20	17·70	31 99	24·59	

Date.	Hour.	Locality.	Temperature.
1916.			
September 1	11.30 a.m.	Head Harbour to Petit Passage, 23 miles	10·90
" 1	11.45 a.m.	" " $25\frac{5}{8}$ "	10·95
" 1	12.00 p.m.	" " $27\frac{5}{8}$ "	9·20
" 1	12.15 p.m.	" " $29\frac{5}{8}$ "	9·05
" 1	12.30 p.m.	" " $31\frac{5}{8}$ "	10·85
" 1	12.45 p.m.	" " $33\frac{5}{8}$ "	9·90
" 1	1.00 p.m.	" " $35\frac{5}{8}$ "	9·80
" 1	1.15 p.m.	" " $37\frac{3}{8}$ "	9·85
" 1	1.30 p.m.	" " 39 "	9·55
" 1	1.45 p.m.	" " $40\frac{7}{8}$ "	10·00
" 1	2.00 p.m.	" " $42\frac{1}{8}$ "	9·75
" 1	2.15 p.m.	" " $43\frac{1}{2}$ "	9·10
" 1	2.30 p.m.	" " $45\frac{1}{2}$ "	9·00
" 1	2.45 p.m.	" " $47\frac{1}{8}$ "	9·20

WESTERN ARCHIPELAGO

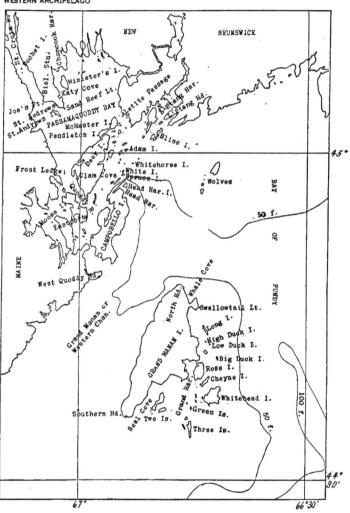

XVI.

HYDROIDS OF EASTERN CANADA.

By C. McLean Fraser, Ph.D., Curator of the Pacific Biological Station,
Departure Bay, B.C.

INTRODUCTION.

Since the early days of the Geological Survey explorations, lists of hydroids have appeared in connection with those of other invertebrata. As in these instances the hydroids that appeared accidentally in the general collection were examined in connection with this general material or sent away for examination, there were seldom many species in the list.· Verrill identified many of the species and collected in the Bay of Fundy and the gulf of St. Lawrence and his reports, although somewhat scattered were the most valuable previous to 1901, when Whiteaves, in his "Catalogue of the Marine Invertebrata of Eastern Canada," gave a comprehensive list including all the species that had been reported to that time. Since 1901 two lists have been published: the one by Stafford, in his "Fauna of the Atlantic Coast," which appeared in "Contributions to Canadian Biology," 1912, and the other my own list of the "Hydroids of Nova Scotia" in 1913. Certain references have also been made to Eastern Canadian distribution in the second and third parts of Nutting's monograph, published in 1904 and 1915, respectively.

In the meantime, collecting has been continued in connection with the Atlantic station, now at St. Andrews, N.B. The material accumulated was sent to me by Dr. A. G. Huntsman, with the request that I make an examination of it. It was of much interest to find it a most comprehensive collection, as shown by the fact that from it 79 species have been determined, while Whiteaves' list included but 58. Stafford's 69, six of which have neither name nor description, and my Nova Scotia list 50.

In some instances there is some doubt as to the validity of certain species. Stimpson named some species without giving figure or adequate description and A. Agassiz did the same. Some of these difficulties were straightened out by contemporaries, but with others there is still some confusion. Taking all together, 112 species have been determined with reasonable assurance, although in two or three cases, mentioned in the text, there is still some possibility of synonymy. The six unnamed species of Stafford's are not included in this number. In listing the hydroids in this latest collection, it is as well to include all, to bring the whole list from the eastern coasts of Canada to date.

Some Newfoundland locations are given but these are all on the gulf of St. Lawrence side. No attempt has been made to include the species reported north of the strait of Belle Isle.

Of the 112 species, 16 are reported for the first time in this area, but only one of these, *Bimeria brevis*, is described as new to science. The others are: *Dicoryne conferta, Garveia grœnlandica, Eudendrium album, Eudendrium annulatum, Tubularia spectabilis, Campanularia gigantea, Clytia cylindrica, Clytia edwardsi, Obelia articulata, Opercularella pumila, Stegopoma plicatile, Hebella pocillum, Sertularia cornicina, Antennularia americana, Plumularia setaceoides.*

The purpose of the paper is to give a complete list of species of hydroids that have been reported from the waters along the eastern coasts of Canada, with the distribution of each in this area, to give a synonymy which will include that given with the original description and one or more others where good descriptions or figures appear and all the references in connection with points in this area and to give an account of any new or important point noted.

38a—22½

8 GEORGE V, A. 1918

GEOGRAPHIC DISTRIBUTION.

For the consideration of the question of distribution, the waters of Eastern Canada can be conveniently divided into three regions: (1) The Bay of Fundy and its approaches, (2) the Gulf of St. Lawrence, (3) the east or southeast coast of Nova Scotia.

In the Bay of Fundy the waters around the island of Grand Manan have been much used as a collecting ground ever since Stimpson found a sufficient number of species to make it worth while to write up "The Marine Invertebrates of Grand Manan." Then, as now, it was recognized that on account of the exposed position and the difference in tides, the channels between the numerous small islands must be continually supplied with enough food for countless forms of great variety. . The archipelago between Passamaquoddy bay and the Bay of Fundy proper provides a large area where the conditions are somewhat similar although the salinity becomes noticeably less in the inner waters. The whole area is suitable for hydroid growth. Even at the mouth of the St. Croix river there is a sufficient interchange on account of the high tides to permit of the existence of some species. Most of the collecting has been done in shallow water and near shore, hence although 87 species have been obtained, the probability is that many others exist in areas as yet untouched.

Apart from the Passamaquoddy archipelago, one other point must be mentioned and this at the other side of the Bay of Fundy. St. Mary bay, near Brier island, Nova Scotia, must be a very satisfactory locality for hydroids. All the material sent from there, apparently was obtained during one trip, July 29-30, 1913, and yet from this material alone 30 species of hydroids were obtained. When that many were picked up in indiscriminate collecting, the locality must offer fine opportunities for one looking especially for hydroids.

The Gulf of St. Lawrence has been touched at only a few points, Malpeque, Gaspé, Seven islands, Anticosti, Bay of Islands, Newfoundland, and some individual dredging trips. It is quite possible that in the gulf there is no single restricted area that offers such a variety of conditions as that at the entrance to Passamaquoddy bay, yet along the whole coast there is variety in plenty and in the vast area of the gulf itself there are great differences in depth and in the nature of the bottom. While the 65 species already obtained may be representative, they must only serve as a sample of what is to be found there.

What is true of the Gulf of St. Lawrence is equally true of the Nova Scotia coast. The near shore waters have been touched only in the vicinity of Canso at the extreme east and at Barrington passage at the extreme south. The coast waters intervening are studded with small islands among which are innumerable channels with suitable conditions for a good food supply, in which no collecting has ever been done. The small amount of deep water dredging done by the United States Fish Commission gives some idea of the richness of the fauna in deep water. Of the 65 species from this area, five were found on sargassum from the gulf stream. These were *Syncoryne mirabilis, Clytia noliformis. Otclia hyalina, Sertularia cornicina* and *Plumularia setaceoides,* but the first two have also been reported from inshore.

In making a comparison of the hydroids found in these three areas, it will be noticed that of the 27 gymnoblastic species 25 have been found in the Bay of Fundy, 11 in the Gulf of St. Lawrence, and 15 off the Nova Scotia coast. The gymnoblastic forms are always an uncertain quantity, particularly in general collecting. So many of them are so delicate that they are soon past recognition unless they are preserved when taken from the water. It is quite possible, therefore, that the Bay of Fundy predominance is due to better preservation of material. Of the 26 species of Campanularians, 21 were found in the Bay of Fundy, 17 from the Gulf of St. Lawrence and 17 from the Nova Scotia coast, almost exactly the same proportion as the whole number of species. Of the 7 species of the Campanulinidæ, 3 were found in the Bay

SESSIONAL PAPER No. 38a

of Fundy, 5 in the Gulf of St. Lawrence, and 2 off the Nova Scotia coast. These are small forms and easily overlooked. Of the 9 species of the Halecidæ, 8 were from the Bay of Fundy, 7 from the Gulf of St. Lawrence, and 4 from the Nova Scotia coast. There is no apparent reason why the Nova Scotia coast should be lacking but there is a similar lack in the Gulf of St. Lawrence in the Lafœidæ and Hebellidæ as out of the 11 species recorded, there are 7 from the Bay of Fundy, 3 from the Gulf of St. Lawrence and 9 from the Nova Scotia coast. In the Sertularidæ the gulf of St. Lawrence leads, as out of the 24 species, 19 are from the Bay of Fundy, 21 from the Gulf of St. Lawrence, and 14 from the Nova Scotia coast. As usual in temperate regions, the Plumularidæ are poorly represented. Out of the 8 species reported, 4 are from the Bay of Fundy, 1 from the Gulf of St. Lawrence and 4 from the Nova Scotia coast, only one species being reported from more than one place. Taking the coast as a whole, the gymnoblastic species and the Campanularidæ are well represented while the Halecidæ and the Sertularidæ are proportionately low in numbers.

With the distribution here recorded additional evidence is obtained regarding the conclusion that, for a large number of species, the distribution takes place southward along the continental shores from a central circumpolar area. Of the 112 species, 65 have been reported from the Arctic regions, 72 from the west of Europe, and 57 from the west coast of North America. Furthermore, it indicates that along these coasts there is no very definite break in the continuity at any one point, although, of course, some of them extend farther southward than others. Of the 77 species that have been reported from the east coast of the United States as well, 62 of them or 80 per cent occur in the Arctic regions, Western Europe, or the west coast of North America, and 21 of them appear in the list of 51 species obtained at Beaufort, N.C., in 1911.

A table shows the distribution of each species in these regions and another shows the distribution of the Gymnoblastea and the main families of the Calyptoblastea.

8 GEORGE V, A. 1918

DISTRIBUTION TABLE FOR SPECIES.

—	Bay of Fundy.	Gulf of St. Lawrence.	Atlantic Coast of Nova Scotia.	East Coast of United States.	Arctic regions.	West Coast of Europe.	Pacific Coast of North America.
Cordylophora lacustris	x	x	....	x	....	x	
Clava leptostyla	x	x	x	x	....	x	x
Monobrachium parasitum	..	x			x	....	x
Syncoryne mirabilis	x	x	x	x	x	....	x
Dicoryne conferta	x					x	
flexuosa	x	....	x				
Bimeria brevis	x						
Garveia grœnlandica	....	x			x	....	x
Bougainvillia carolinensis	x	x	x	x			
Eudendrium album	x	....		x		x	
annulatum	x				x	x	
capillare	x		x	x	x	x	x
cingulatum	..	x					
dispar	x	x	x	x			
rameum	x		x		x	x	x
ramosum	x	x	x	x	....	x	x
tenue	x	....	x	x			
Hydractinia echinata	x	x	x	x	x	x	
Myriothela phrygia	x	....			x	x	
Acaulis primarius	x		....	x	x		
Corymorpha pendula	x	x	x	x			
Tubularia couthouyi	x			x			
crocea	x	....	x	x		....	x
indivisa	x	....	x	....	x	x	x
larynx	x	x	x	x	x	x	x
spectabilis	x			x			
tenella	x	....		x	x		
Campanularia amphora	x		x	x			
flexuosa	x	x	x	x	x	x	
gelatinosa	....	x		x	x	x	x
gigantea	x	x	....	x		x	
grœnlandica	x		x		x	x	x
hincksi	....		x	x	x	x	x
integra	x	x		x	x	x	x
magnifica	....	....	x				
neglecta	x.	x	x	x	....	x	
speciosa	....	x			x	....	x
verticillata	x	x	x	x	x	x	x
volubilis	x	x	x	x	x	x	x
Clytia cylindrica	x	....		x			x
edwardsi	x			x			x
johnstoni	x	x	x	x	x	x	x
noliformis	x	x	x	x	....		x
Eucopella caliculata	x	x	x	x	x	x	x
Gonothyræa gracilis	x	....	x	x	x	x	x
loveni	x	x	x	x	x	x	
Obelia articulata	x	....	....	x			
commissuralis	x	x	x	x	....	....	x
dichotoma	x	x	x	x	x	x	x
flabellata	x	x	....	x	x	x	x
geniculata	x	x	x	x	x	x	x
hyalina	....	....	x	x	x	x	....
longissima	x	x		x	x	x	x
Calycella syringa	x	x	x	x	x	x	x
Cuspidella costata	....	x		x		x	
grandis	....	x	....		x	x	x
Opercularella lacerata	x	....	x	x	x	x	x
pumila	x	....		x			
Stegopoma plicatile	....	x			x	x	x
Tetrapoma quadridentatum	....	x			x		
Halecium articulosum	x			x		x	x
beani	x	x	x	x	x	x	
curvicaule	x	....				x	x
gracile	x	x		x			
halecinum	x	x	....	x	x	x	x
minutum	x	x	x	....		x	
muricatum	x	x	x	....		x	x
sessile	....	x	....	....		x	
tenellum	x	x	x	x	x	x	y

SESSIONAL PAPER No. 38a

DISTRIBUTION TABLE FOR SPECIES—*Concluded.*

	Bay of Fundy.	Gulf of St. Law-rence.	Atlan-tic Coast of Nova Scotia.	East Coast of United States.	Arctic regions.	West Coast of Europe.	Pacific Coast of North America.
Hebella calcarata			x	x			
pocillum	x		x	x	x	x	x
Cryptolaria triserialis			x				
Filellum serpens	x		x	x	x	x	x
Grammaria abietina	x	x	x		x	x	x
gracilis	x						
Lafœa dumosa	x	x	x	x	x	x	x
fruticosa	x		x		x	x	x
gracillima	x	x	x	x	x	x	x
pygmæa			x			x	
symmetrica			x			x	
Abietinaria abietina	x	x	x				x
filicula	x	x		x	x	x	x
Diphasia fallax	x	x	x	x	x	x	
rosacea	x	x	x	x	x	x	
tamarisca	x		x		x	x	
Hydrallmania falcata	x	x	x	x	x	x	
Selaginopsis mirabilis		x	x	x	x	x	x
Sertularella conica			x	x			x
fusiformis		x				x	x
polyzonias	x	x	x	x	x	x	x
rugosa	x	x		x	x	x	x
tricuspidata	x	x	x	x	x	x	x
Sertularia cornicina			x	x			
pumila	x	x	x	x	x	x	x
Thuiaria argentea	x	x	x	x	x	x	x
cupressina	x	x	x	x	x	x	
fabricii	x	x		x	x	x	x
immersa	x	x				x	
latiuscula	x	x					
lonchitis	x	x	x	x	x	x	
robusta		x			x		x
similis	x	x					x
tenera	x	x			x	x	x
thuja	x	x		x	x	x	x
Aglaophenopsis cornuta			x		x		
Antennularia americana	x			x			
antennina	x			x	x	x	
Cladocarpus pourtalesi			x	x		x	
speciosus			x				
Plumularia setaceoides			x	x			
Schizotricha gracillima	x			x		x	
Thecocarpus myriophyllum	x	x		x		x	

SUMMARY OF DISTRIBUTION.

	Total.	Bay of Fundy.	Gulf of St Law-rence.	Atlan-tic Coast of Nova Scotia.	East Coast of United States.	Arctic regions.	West Coast of Europe.	Pacific Coast of North America.
Gymnoblastea	27	25	11	15	17	11	12	10
Campanularidæ	26	21	17	17	23	16	18	18
Campanulinidæ	7	3	5	2	4	5	5	4
Halecidæ	9	8	7	4	5	6	7	4
Hebellidæ and Lafœidæ	11	7	3	9	5	6	8	6
Sertularidæ	24	19	21	14	17	19	18	15
Plumularidæ	8	4	1	4	6	2	4	

8 GEORGE V, A. 1918

It is interesting to compare this list with the list of those that have been found in the Vancouver island region. Although this region is somewhat farther north than the Bay of Fundy or the greater part of the gulf of St. Lawrence, it is not subject to the same cold currents, hence the conditions are to some extent comparable.

In my 1914 paper, 136 species were listed and since then 4 more have been added to the list, making 140 in all. Of these 48 appear as well on the eastern Canadian list. On the west coast, of the families represented, the Sertularidæ is the most numerous, with 41 species, 29 per cent of the whole number, the Campanularidæ next with 34 or 24 per cent. The Gymnoblastea is represented by 25 species, 18 per cent, and the Halecidæ with 16 or 11 per cent. This is not the order on the east coast. The gymnoblastic species are more numerous than the species of any calyptoblastic family, there being 27 or 24 per cent of the whole number. The Campanularidæ with 26 or 23 per cent beats the Sertularidæ with 24 or 21 per cent and the Halecidæ has only 9 representatives or 8 per cent. The Plumularidæ, a large family, is represented by only 8 species in each case, and as none of these are common there can scarcely be a circumpolar centre for this family. A table will show this comparison more readily:—

	Total.	Gym.	Campa-nula-ridæ.	Campa-nuli-nidæ.	Hale-cidæ.	Hebel-lidæ and Lafo-eidæ.	Sertu-laridæ.	Plumu-laridæ.
Eastern Canada....................	112	27	26	7	9	11	24	8
Vancouver Island region...........	140	25	34	8	16	8	41	8

· SYSTEMATIC DISCUSSION.

With regard to nomenclature nothing need be said in connection with any of the families with the exception of the Sertularidæ. This family may well be considered on account of the treatment it has received in Levinsen's paper of 1913.[1] It is true that in this paper he introduces no opinions that were not found in his paper of 1893[2], but he goes into a much more elaborate defence of these opinions and hence the latter paper has received much more attention than the former.

In the classification of the Sertularidæ, as given in these papers, Levinsen casts all other characters aside and bases his entire taxonomic faith on the opercular apparatus as a basis for generic distinction. Naturally this throws the synonymy of the Sertularidæ, not by any means in a settled state, into greater confusion. Broch and Kramp have subscribed to his views but elsewhere they have found little favour when considered in their entirety although certain points have been accepted by a number of authors.

A lengthy discussion of the system, as expounded in the 1913 paper, will not be attempted here but a few general remarks on the soundness of the arguments deduced seems advisable.

The argument may be stated as follows: There are individual (zooidal) characters and colonial (zoarial) characters. In general the individual characters are better suited for taxonomy than colonial characters therefore all colonial characters should be excluded. Among the individual characters, some relate to the trophosome, some to the gonosome. Those relating to the trophosome are more suitable for taxonomy than those relating to the gonosome, therefore the gonosome characters should

---

[1] Systematic Studies in the Sertularidæ.

[2] Medusæ, Ctenophores and Hydroids of the West Coast of Greenland.

be excluded. Among the individual trophosome characters the nature of the opercular apparatus is a good character, therefore all other characters should be excluded and the opercular apparatus must form the one and only basis for the whole system of classification.

Let us examine the argument piece by piece. In the first place, without trying to settle the relative value of individual and colonial characters, are the colonial characters of such little value that they should be neglected entirely in classification? In connection with this, Levinsen drew an analogy in his earlier paper (p. 184) and was so well satisfied with it that he quoted it in his later paper (p. 255). It is this: "A zoological system based on that kind of characters may be compared to a botanical, in which the chief stress was laid on the inflorescences and not on the structure of the flowers. In both cases, the genus would contain a number of heterogeneous species. It can hardly be deemed doubtful that constant differences in the structure of the single individuals in question, of the hydrothecæ or hydranths, ought to be preferred as systematic characters, and that colonial characters ought only to be used when structural diversities were not to be found."

The analogy is somewhat unfortunate as in many cases the inflorescence is characteristic not only for the genus but even for the family. What more constant character would it be possible to get than the head of the Compositæ, the loose raceme of the Ranunculaceæ or the compound umbel of the Umbelliferæ? In the great majority of cases each species has a typically characteristic habitus and whatever in addition may be used as a basis for first diagnosis, as soon as the plant becomes familiar, it will be recognized by its inflorescence rather than by any single characteristic of the flower itself. So too in the case of the hydroids, each species has its own typical habitus by which it is recognized and if the genus has not so much the worse for the genus or the validity of it. The fact that the habitus of the young colony may be somewhat different to that of the colony at a later period and depends to a certain extent on environment, rather increases than decreases the value of this as a distinctive character when the life history is known. In any case even if the colonial characters, taken as a whole, are not of so much value as the individual characters, there is no reason that they should be discarded.

Turning to the next part of the argument, the characters of the gonosome are neglected because they are less important than the characters of the trophosome. Are the characters of the gonosome of so little account? Turning again to the floral analogy, how much of any system of classification would be left if all the references to the nature of the gynœcium and andrœcium and their relations to other parts of the flower were left out? In all other families of hydroids the characters of the gonosome are used extensively for taxonomy, why should they not be used in the Sertularidæ?

Finally, going back to the floral analogy once more, is it possible to find a single family of plants of any size that is divided into genera on the basis of a single character of the floral envelopes? In the hydroids as well, although one character in a family may be prominent, it is seldom that the paucity of characters is so marked as to make it necessary to rely on one character of the trophosome alone as the determining factor throughout.

Some of the points as they appear in Levinsen's paper may well be considered. After showing that the different species of *Selaginopsis* do not fit in in with the generic idea when based on the nature of the opercular apparatus, the following statement is made: "The fact that there is no constant relation between the structure of the zooids and the colonial form, or to express it in another way, that they are incommensurable values defined by different laws, must have the logical sequence, that one of them cannot be substituted for the other, and, therefore, a genus ought never to be instituted solely on the basis of a difference in the colonial form, when otherwise the zooids present distinct structural diversities " (p. 259). To state that the conclusion that "there is no constant relation between the structure of the zooids and the colonial form" is a

8 GEORGE V, A. 1918

fact, upon such little basis, makes it necessary to materially discount any argument based on the statement. The resultant assertion depends for its value on the significance of the word " distinct." According to the remainder of the paper it might better have read " when otherwise the zooids present differences in the opercular apparatus " but with such an interpretation every other taxonomist will not necessarily agree. Some of them may even have the temerity still to believe that there may be some correlation between colonial and individual characters.

Levinsen entirely neglects the systematic value of the characters of the gonosome and hence in the genera in which he has introduced the most radical changes are to be found the widest diversity in these characters. In the genus *Sertularia* " the gonothecæ present a very different habitus, being either smooth, ringed or provided with two or more spines " (p. 298), and in the genus *Odontotheca* " the gonothecæ present a very variable habitus, being either smooth, ringed or provided with two spines " (p. 308). No system of classification based on colonial characters could present more " distinct structural diversities " than this.

With regard to the nature of the opercular apparatus almost anyone will admit that it is a good character, but even if it were the most suitable single character for diagnosis, it would not signify that the whole classification must depend on it, since there are other good characters. Levinsen says, " It seems reasonable to ascribe systematic significance also to the operculum, a structure that must be regarded as the complement of the protective cases, and, so to speak, as the end result of the same effort which led to the formation of the hydrothecæ and gonothecæ " (p. 288), and yet in this classification all of the hydrotheca with the exception of the opercular apparatus receives no consideration and the gonotheca is left out entirely. Farther on in the same paragraph he says the operculum " has in common with other structures of systematic significance, a rich development of characteristic modifications which give excellent generic characters," but in his classification he has eliminated the consideration of " other structures of systematic significance."

It seems a very satisfactory character in one respect as any cases of disagreement can be blamed on regeneration or injury but the very fact that regeneration is so very apt to take place and that the apparatus is so delicate as to be so susceptible to injury, makes its value for diagnosis of doubtful significance. After one has spent as much time and observation on the operculum as Levinsen did before writing this paper it might be possible to judge the nature of the operculum correctly from the appearance of the rest of the apparatus even when the operculum has been torn away but one with less experience will certainly have serious doubts at times when the operculum is not present and it is not always possible to have an unlimited supply of material to examine for hydrothecæ perfect in this respect. When Levinsen finds it necessary to disagree with the interpretation put upon the nature of the opercular apparatus by so many careful hydroid observers, e.g., with Nutting in the case of *Sertularia pumila*, it is evident that the adoption of a system based on such a character instead of bringing about a desirable degree of unanimity will tend to make the disagreement much more pronounced.

There can be little natural about a system of classification that makes it necessary to combine the genera *Abietinaria* and *Diphasia* into a single genus to make it fit in with the classification when the differences are so evident that they are immediately separated into the same two parts but called groups instead of genera for appearance, sake.

Levinsen objects to certain genera because there are intergrading forms but his classification leaves just as large a crop of these as is to be found in any other system. There will always be these intergrading forms but nothing is to be gained by crying down one system on this account when no improvement is made in a proposed substitute. When an attempt is made to fit in a system of classification of the Sertularidæ depending on the nature of the opercular apparatus with the general classification of the hydroids in use, we have, to use Levinsen's words, "incommensurables defined by different laws, so that we must have the logical sequence, that one of them cannot be substituted for the other."

While, therefore, the care with which Levinsen did this work on the opercular apparatus is fully recognized and while the value to systematists of this exhaustive examination is in no way under-estimated, it is impossible to do otherwise than conclude as many others have done, that although the nature of the opercular apparatus is a good character and is of much value in classification, it cannot be used satisfactorily as the sole basis on which to divide the Sertularidæ into genera. The time may come when there will be more general agreement on the method of classifying this family but it will be at a time when all the main variable features of each species will be taken into consideration.

As this paper is on distribution rather than on taxonomy, it is not desirable to discuss in detail this or any other system of classification. By adhering to the nomenclature used throughout in previous papers for the Sertularidæ as for the other families, there will at least be no difficulty in following the references to the various species considered.

Sub-order *GYMNOBLASTEA.*

Family *CLAVIDÆ.*

Genus CORDYLOPHORA.

CORDYLOPHORA LACUSTRIS Allman.

Cordylophora lacustris ALLMAN, Ann. and Mag. Nat. Hist., 1st ser. viii., 1844,
p. 330.
HINCKS, Br. Hydroid Zoophytes, 1868, p. 16.
STAFFORD, Fauna Atlantic Coast, 1912, p. 72.

Distribution.—St. Andrews, Gaspé, Seven islands (Stafford).

Although this is a fresh- or brackish-water form, since it has been reported it is well to include it in the list.

Genus CLAVA.

CLAVA LEPTOSTYLA Agassiz.

Clava multicornis STIMPSON, Marine Invert. Grand Manan, 1853, p. 16.

Clava leptostyla AGASSIZ, Cont. Nat. Hist. U.S., vol. iv, 1862, p. 218.
HINCKS, British Hydroid Zoophytes, 1868' p. 6.
NUTTING, Hyd. Woods Hole. 1901, p. 321.
HARGITT, Am. Nat. 1901, p. 305.
WHITEAVES, Mar. Invert. East. Can., 1901, p. 18.
STAFFORD, Fauna Atlantic Coast, 1912, p. 72.
FRASER, Hyd. Nova Scotia, 1913, p. 159.

Distribution.—Salmon Bay (Packard); Long island point to Labrador (Verrill); St. Andrews, Canso, Seven islands (Stafford); Canso (Fraser); St. Andrews.

Family *LARIDÆ.*

Genus MONOBRACHIUM.

MONOBRACHIUM PARASITUM *Mereschkowsky.*

Monobrachium parasitum MERESCHOWSKY, Hyd. from White Sea. 1877. p. 226.
LEVINSEN, Medusæ, Ctenophorer, etc., 1893, p. 151.
parasiticum BONNEVIE, Norske Nordhavs-Ex., 1899. p. 151.
parasitum STAFFORD, Fauna Atlantic Coast. 1912. p. 73.

Distribution.—Gaspé (Stafford).

Family *DICORYNIDÆ.*

Genus DICORYNE.

DICORYNE CONFERTA (Alder).

Eudendrium confertum ALDER, Trans. Tynes. Nat. F.C., iii, 1857, p. 103.
Dicoryne conferta HINCKS, Br. Hyd. Zooph., 1868, p. 105.
ALLMAN, Gymnoblastic Hyd., 1871, p. 293.

Distribution.—Off Minister's island.

DICORYNE FLEXUOSA G. O. Sars.

Dicoryne flexuosa SARS, Bidrag til Kundskaben om Norges Hydroider, 1873, p. 96.
VERRILL, Am. Jour. Sci. and Art, 3rd. ser., vol. xvi, 1878, p. 375.
WHITEAVES, Mar. Invert. East. Can., 1901, p. 19.
STAFFORD, Fauna Atlantic Coast, 1912, p. 72.

Distribution.—Off Nova Scotia, 50 to 125 fathoms (Verrill); St. Andrews (Stafford).

Family *SYNCORYNIDÆ.*

Genus SYNCORYNE.

SYNCORYNE MIRABILIS (Agassiz).

Coryne mirabilis AGASSIZ, Cont. Nat. Hist. U.S., vol. iv, 1862, p. 185.
Syncoryne mirabilis NUTTING, Hydroids of Woods Hole, 1901, p. 328.
HARGITT, Am. Nat., 1901, p. 328.
WHITEAVES, Mar. Invert. East. Can., 1901, p. 19.
Dicoryne mirabilis STAFFORD, Fauna Atlantic Coast, 1912, p. 72.

Distribution.—Belles Amours, strait of Belle Isle (Packard); bay of Fundy (Verrill); Seven islands (Stafford); Katy cove; on sargassum in the Gulf Stream east of Nova Scotia.

Family *BIMERIDÆ.*

Genus BIMERIA.

BIMERIA BREVIS new species.

(Fig. 2).

Trophosome.—Stem simple, growing from a creeping hydrorhiza; in many cases it forms a long pedicel for a single hydranth but in others it may give off several hydranths, each on a pedicel of its own, and occasionally these pedicels may be branched. The greatest length observed was 8 mm. In the branched specimens, the branches do not come off at regular intervals, either vertically or laterally; each makes quite an acute angle with the stem. The perisarc is quite thick and wrinkled but no definite annuli are formed; the portion around the body of the hydranth is closely wrinkled or creased; hydranth small with 11-12 tentacles.

Gonosome.—Absent.

Distribution.—On *Tubularia crocea* from Katy cove.

The habitus of this species is much similar to that of *Bimeria humilis* Allman[3], but the stem is relatively much stouter, the hydranths are much smaller and the perisarc is much more wrinkled. In any case one should scarcely expect to find a species that was obtained in the warm, shallow water of the Tortugas to occur in the cold water of the bay of Fundy. It bears less resemblance to *Bimeria vestita* Wright as it is a shorter but coarser species.

---

[3] Allman, G. J. Gulf Stream Hydroids, 1877, p. 9.

Genus GARVEIA.

GARVEIA GRŒNLANDICA Levinsen.

Garveia grœnlandica LEVINSEN, Meduser, Ctenophorer, etc., 1893, p. 155.
　　　　　　　　　FRASER, Vancouver island hydroids, 1914, p. 117.
Distribution.—Bay of islands, Newfoundland, 50 to 60 fathoms.

Family *BOUGAINVILLIDÆ*.

Génus BOUGAINVILLIA.

BOUGAINVILLIA CAROLINENSIS (McCrady).

Hippocrene carolinensis MCCRADY, Gymno. of Charleston Har., 1857, p. 62.
Margelis carolinensis AGASSIZ, Cont. Nat. Hist. U.S., vol. iv, 1862, p. 344.
　　　　　　　　　A. AGASSIZ, N. A. Acalephæ, 1865, p. 156.
Bougainvillia carolinensis NUTTING, Hyd. Woods Hole, 1901, p. 330.
　　　　　　　　　STAFFORD, Fauna Atlantic Coast, 1912, p. 72.
　　　　　　　　　FRASER, New England Hydroids, 1912, p. 41.
　　　　　　　　　FRASER, Hyd. of Nova Scotia, 1913, p. 159.

Distribution.—St. Andrews, Seven islands (Stafford); Canso (Fraser); Katy cove, Joe's point.

The specimens of this species collected at Katy cove were small as compared with those described from Woods Hole. None of them were more than an inch in length but the medusa buds were well developed.

Family *EUDENDRIDÆ*.

Genus EUDENDRIUM.

EUDENDRIUM ALBUM Nutting.

Eudendrium album NUTTING, Ann. and Mag. Nat. Hist., 1898, p. 362.
　　　　　　　　　Hyd. Woods Hole, 1901, p. 334.
　　　　　　　　HARGITT, Biol. Bull., 1908, p. 97.
　　　　　　　　FRASER, Hyd. of Beaufort, 1912, p. 348.

Distribution.—Off Deer point, Campobello island, and at many points between this and Dochet island up the St. Croix river, off Brier island, Nova Scotia, 33 to 39 fathoms.

EUDENDRIUM ANNULATUM Norman.

Eudendrium annulatum NORMAN, Ann. and Mag. Nat. Hist., 1864, p. 83.
　　　　　　　　　HINCKS, Br. Hyd. Zooph., 1868, p. 83.
　　　　　　　　JÄDERHOLM, Northern and Arctic Invert., 1909, p. 51.

Distribution.—Brier island, 25 fathoms.

EUDENDRIUM CAPILLARE Alder.

Eudendrium capillare ALDER, Cat. Zooph. Northumberland and Durham, 1857, p. 15.
　　　　　　　　　HINCKS, Br. Hyd. Zooph., 1868, p. 84.
　　　　　　　　ALLMAN, Gymno. Hyd. 1871, p. 335.
　　　　　　　　NUTTING, Woods Hole Hyd., 1901, p. 334.
　　　　　　　　WHITEAVES, Marine Invert. East Can., 1901, p. 20.
　　　　　　　　FRASER, Hyd. of Beaufort, 1912, p. 348.
　　　　　　　　STAFFORD, Fauna Atlantic Coast, 1912, p. 72.

Distribution.—Le Have bank, 45 fathoms (Smith and Harger); St. Andrews (Stafford); Weir stakes at St. Andrew's island; off L'Etang head, 12 fathoms.

EUDENDRIUM CINGULATUM Stimpson.

Eudendrium cingulatum STIMPSON, Marine invert. Grand Manan, 1854, p. 9.

WHITEAVES, Marine Invert. East. Can., 1901, p. 20.

Distribution.—Off Duck Island, Grand Manan (Stimpson).

Stimpson's description of this species is very meagre but it seems to agree very well with that for *E. annulatum* Norman and very probably it is the same species. If it is the name *E. annulatum* should be retained as it has priority. A. Agassiz considered it to be the same as *Bougainvillia supercilaris* Agassiz (See N. A. Acalephæ, 1865, p. 153).

EUDENDRIUM DISPAR Agassiz.

Eudendrium dispar AGASSIZ, Cont. Nat. Hist. U.S., vol. iv, 1862, p. 285.

NUTTING, Hyd. Woods Hole, 1901, p. 332.

HARGITT, Am. Nat., 1901, p. 309.

WHITEAVES, Mar. Invert. East. Can., 1901, p. 20.

STAFFORD, Fauna Atlantic Coast, 1912, p. 72.

FRASER, Hyd. Nova Scotia, 1913, p. 160.

Distribution.—Vineyard sound to bay of Fundy (Verrill); St. Andrews, Seven islands (Stafford); Barrington passage (Fraser); Off Head Harbour Island. Off McMaster island, weir stakes, St. Andrews island, Joe's point, reef off St. Andrews, 10 fathoms.

EUDENDRIUM RAMEUM (Pallas).

Tubularia ramea PALLAS, Elench. Zooph., 1766, p. 83.

Eudendrium rameum HINCKS, Br. Hyd. Zooph., 1868, p. 80.

WHITEAVES, Mar. Invert. East Can., 1901, p. 19.

JÄDERHOLM, Northern and Arctic Invert., 1909, p. 50.

Distribution.—30 miles southeast of Halifax in 100 fathoms (Verrill); near Two islands, Grand Manan, 5-10 fathoms, off L'Etang head, off Joe's point, Weir stakes, St. Andrews island.

EUDENDRIUM RAMOSUM (Linnæus).

Tubularia ramosa LINNAEUS. Syst. Nat., 1758, p. 804.

Eudendrium ramosum HINCKS, Br. Hyd. Zooph., 1868, p. 82.

NUTTING, Hyd. Woods Hole, 1901, p. 332.

HARGITT, Am. Nat, 1901, p. 309.

WHITEAVES, Mar. Invert. East. Can., 1901, p. 19.

STAFFORD, Fauna Atlantic Coast, 1912, p. 72.

FRASER, Hyd. Nova Scotia, 1913, p. 160.

Distribution.—Bay of Fundy, 8 to 100 fathoms (Verrill); 8 miles southeast of Bonaventure island (Whiteaves); Métis and Murray bay (Dawson); St. Andrews. Gaspé, Seven islands (Stafford); Chedabucto bay, 45 fathoms (Fraser); many localities from Two islands to St. Andrews point, Brier island.

EUDENDRIUM TENUE A. Agassiz.

Eudendrium tenue A. AGASSIZ, N.A. Acalephæ, 1865, p. 160.

NUTTING, Hyd. Woods Hole, 1901, p. 333.

WHITEAVES, Mar. Invert. East. Can., 1901, p. 20.

STAFFORD, Fauna Atlantic Coast, 1912, p. 72.

FRASER, Hyd. Nova Scotia, 1913, p. 160.

Distribution.—Buzzards bay to Bay of Fundy, low water to 15 fathoms (Verrill); St. Andrews (Stafford); Canso (Fraser); many points from St. Andrews to L'Etang head, off Brier island.

Family *HYDRACTINIDÆ*.

Genus HYDRACTINIA.

HYDRACTINIA ECHINATA (Fleming).

Alcyonium echinatum FLEMING, Br. Animals, 1828, p. 517.
Hydractinia echinata HINCKS, Br. Hyd. Zooph., 1868, p. 23.
　　polyclina AGASSIZ, Cont. Nat. Hist., U.S., 1862, p. 227.
　　　　NUTTING, Hyd. Woods Hole, 1901, p. 335.
　　echinata WHITEAVES, Mar. Invert. East. Can., 1901, p. 21.
　　　　HARGITT, Am. Nat., 1901, p. 310.
　　　　STAFFORD, Fauna Atlantic Coast, 1912, p. 73.
　　　　FRASER, Hyd. Beaufort, 1912, p. 352.
　　　　FRASER, Hyd. Nova Scotia, 1913, p. 161.
Distribution.—New Jersey to Labrador (Verrill); St. Andrews, Malpeque, Gaspé, Seven islands (Stafford); Grand Manan (A. Agassiz); Canso (Fraser); High Duck island.

Family *MYRIOTHELIDÆ*.

Genus MYRIOTHELA.

MYRIOTHELA PHRYGIA (Fabricius).

Lucernaria phrygia FABRICIUS, Fauna Grœnlandica, 1780, p. 343.
Myriothela phrygia HINCKS, Br. Hyd. Zooph., 1868, p. 77.
　　　　WHITEAVES, Mar. Invert. East. Can., 1901. p. 20.
Distribution.—"Grand Manan, bay of Fundy, W. Stimpson" (L. Agassiz).

Family *PENNARIDÆ*.

Genus ACAULIS.

ACAULIS PRIMARIUS Stimpson.

Acaulis primarius STIMPSON, Mar. Invert. Grand Manan, 1854, p. 10.
　　　　WHITEAVES, Mar. Invert. East. Can., 1901, p. 21.
Distribution.—Grand Manan, 5 to 15 fathoms (Stimpson).

Family *CORYMORPHIDÆ*.

Genus CORYMORPHA.

CORYMORPHA PENDULA Agassiz.

Corymorpha nutans STIMPSON, Mar. Invert. Grand Manan, 1854, p. 9.
　　pendula AGASSIZ, Cont. Nat. Hist. U. S., vol. iv, 1862, p. 227.
　　　　NUTTING, Hyd. Woods Hole, 1901, p. 337.
　　　　HARGITT, Am. Nat., 1901, p. 312.
Monocaulis glacialis WHITEAVES, Mar. Invert. East. Can., 1901, p. 21.
　　　　STAFFORD, Fauna Atlantic Coast, 1912, p. 73.
Corymorpha pendula FRASER, Hyd. Nova Scotia, 1913, p. 161.
Distribution.—West Quoddy head. Welsh pool, Low Duck island, 4 to 15 fathoms, (Stimpson); bay of Fundy, Murray bay (Verrill); Rodger's island, Oak bay, Charlotte county (Ganong); St. Andrews (Stafford); Chedabucto bay (Fraser); St. Andrews, Wolves island, Harbour island, 25 fathoms.

Family *TUBULARIDÆ.*
Genus TUBULARIA.

TUBULARIA COUTHOUYI Agassiz.

Tubularia couthouyi AGASSIZ, Cont. Nat. Hist. U. S., 1862, p. 266.
A. AGASSIZ, N. A. Acalephæ, 1865, p. 196.
NUTTING, Hyd. Woods Hole, 1901, p. 338.

Distribution.—Grand Manan (A. Agassiz).

TUBULARIA CROCEA (Agassiz).

Parypha crocea AGASSIZ, Cont. Nat. Hist., U. S., 1862, p. 249.
Tubularia crocea NUTTING, Hyd. Woods Hole, 1901, p. 340.
HARGITT, Am. Nat., 1901, p. 315.
FRASER, New England Hydroids, 1912, p. 42.
FRASER, Hyd. Nova Scotia, 1913, p. 162.

Distribution.—Canso (Fraser); Katy cove, St. Andrews, L'Etang head, Weir stakes. St. Andrews island.

TUBULARIA INDIVISA Linnæus.

Tubularia indivisa LINNÆUS, Syst. Nat. 1767, p. 1301.
STIMPSON, Mar. Invert. Grand Manan, 1853, p. 9.
HINCKS, Br. Hyd. Zooph., 1868, p. 115.
WHITEAVES, Mar. Inv. East. Can., 1901, p. 21.
STAFFORD, Fauna Atlantic Coast, 1912, p. 72.

Distribution.—Grand Manan (Stimpson); Sable island (Dawson); Le Have bank (Smith and Harger); St. Andrews (Stafford); St. Andrews, Joe's point, off Deer island, off L'Etang head.

TUBULARIA LARYNX Ellis and Solander.

Tubularia larynx ELLIS AND SOLANDER, Nat. Hist. of Zooph., 1786, p. 31.
STIMPSON, Mar. Invert. Grand Manan, 1854, p. 9.
HINCKS, Br. Hyd. Zooph., 1868, p. 118.
NUTTING, Hyd. Woods Hole, 1901, p. 338.
WHITEAVES, Mar. Invert. East Can., 1901, p. 20.
Thamnocnidia larynx STAFFORD, Fauna Atlantic Coast, 1912, p. 72.
Tubularia larynx FRASER, Hyd. Nova Scotia, 1913, p. 162.

Distribution.—Grand Manan (Stimpson); Orphan bank (Whiteaves); Gaspé bay (Dawson); St. Andrews, Malpeque, Gaspé (Stafford); Barrington passage (Fraser); York harbour, Newfoundland.

TUBULARIA SPECTABILIS (Agassiz).

Thamnocnidia spectabilis AGASSIZ, Cont. Nat. Hist. U. S., vol. iv, 1862, p. 271.
Tubularia spectabilis NUTTING, Hyd. Woods Hole, 1901, p 339.
Distribution.—Minister's bay, east point of Bliss island.

TUBULARIA TENELLA (Agassiz).

Thamnocnidia tenella AGASSIZ, Cont. Nat. Hist. U.S., vol. iv, 1862, p. 275.
Tubularia tenella NUTTING, Hyd. Woods Hole, 1901, p. 339.
HARGITT, Am. Nat., 1901, p. 314.
WHITEAVES, Mar. Invert. East. Can., 1901, p. 20.
FRASER, Hyd. Nova Scotia, 1913, p. 162.

Distribution.—Bay of Fundy, low water to 40 fathoms (Verrill); St. Andrews, Canso, Gaspé, Seven islands (Stafford); Canso (Fraser); Niger reef, weir stakes, St. Andrews island.

Sub-order *CALYPTOBLASTEA.*

Family *CAMPANULARIDÆ.*

Genus CAMPANULARIA.

CAMPANULARIA AMPHORA (Agassiz).

Laomedea amphora AGASSIZ, Cont. Nat. Hist. U. S., vol. iv, 1862, p. 311.
Campanularia amphora NUTTING, Hyd. Woods Hole, 1901, p. 347.
    HARGITT, Am. Nat., 1901, p. 384.
    FRASER, Hyd. Nova Scotia, 1913, p. 163.
    NUTTING, Am. Hyd., pt. iii, 1915, p. 50.'

Distribution.—Grand Manan (A. Agassiz); Canso (Fraser); Grand Manan (Nutting).

CAMPANULARIA FLEXUOSA (Hincks).

Laomedea flexuosa HINCKS, Ann. and Mag. Nat. Hist., 1861, p. 260.
Campanularia flexuosa HINCKS, Br. Hyd. Zooph., 1868, p. 168.
    NUTTING, Hyd. Woods Hole, 1901, p. 348.
    WHITEAVES, Mar. Invert. East. Can., 1901, p. 22.
    STAFFORD, Fauna Atlantic Coast, 1912, p. 73.
    FRASER, Hyd. Nova Scotia, 1913, p. 163.
    NUTTING, Am. Hyd., iii, 1915, p. 45.

Distribution.—Bay of Fundy to gulf of St. Lawrence (Verrill); St. Andrews, Canso, Gaspé, Seven islands (Stafford); Canso (Fraser); Niger reef, weir stakes, St. Andrews island.

CAMPANULARIA GELATINOSA (Pallas).

Sertularia gelatinosa PALLAS, Elench. Zooph., 1766, p. 116.
Laomedea gelatinosa STIMPSON, Mar. Invert. Grand Manan, 1854, p. 8.
Obelia gelatinosa HINCKS, Br. Hyd. Zooph., 1868, p. 151.
    NUTTING, Hyd. Woods Hole, 1901, p. 351.
    WHITEAVES, Mar. Invert. East. Can., 1901, p. 23.
Campanularia gelatinosa FRASER, Hyd. of Vancouver island, 1914, p. 135.
Obelaria gelatinosa NUTTING, Am. Hyd., iii, 1915, p. 88.

Distribution.—Métis (Dawson); Near Caribou island (Packard).
This species is discussed at length in the Vancouver island paper.

CAMPANULARIA GIGANTEA Hincks.

Campanularia gigantea HINCKS, Ann. and Mag., Nat. Hist., 1866, p. 297.
    Br. Hyd. Zooph., 1868, p. 174.
    NUTTING, Am. Hyd., iii, 1915, p. 44.

Distribution.—Bay of Islands, Newfoundland, 50 to 60 fathoms, off Long island, 15 to 35 fathoms, St. Croix river, 5 to 10 fathoms.

CAMPANULARIA GRŒNLANDICA Levinsen.

Campanularia grœnlandica LEVINSEN, Medusæ, Ctenophorer, etc., 1893, p. 26.
    FRASER, Hyd. Nova Scotia, 1913, p. 163.
    FRASER. Hyd. of Vancouver island region, 1914, p. 136.
    NUTTING, Am. Hyd., iii, 1915, p. 38.

Distribution.—Canso banks, 50 fathoms (Fraser); Quoddy river, east of Spruce island, 17 fathoms, between White and Spruce islands, off Head Harbour island, 25 fathoms, off Deer point, Campobello island, off Brier island, 22 fathoms.

38a—23

CAMPANULARIA HINCKSI Alder.

Campanularia hincksi ALDER, Trans. Tynes. F. C., iii, 1857, p. 162.
     HINCKS, Br. Hyd. Zooph., 1868, p. 162.
     NUTTING, Hyd. Woods Hole, 1901, p. 345.
     WHITEAVES, Mar. Invert. East. Can., 1901 p. 22.
     NUTTING, Am. Hyd., iii, 1915, p. 87.

Distribution.—Le Have bank, 45 fathoms (Smith and Harger).

CAMPANULARIA INTEGRA MacGillivray.

Campanularia integra MACGILLIVRAY, Ann. and Mag. Nat. Hist., 1842, p. 465.
     HINCKS, Br. Hyd. Zooph., 1868, p. 163.
     STAFFORD, Fauna Atlantic Coast, 1912, p. 73.
     NUTTING, Am. Hyd., iii, 1915, p. 33.

Distribution.—Seven islands (Stafford); Spruce island, Brier island, 33 to 39 fathoms.

CAMPANULARIA MAGNIFICA, Fraser.

Campanularia magnifica FRASER, Hyd. Nova Scotia, 1913, p. 164.
     NUTTING, Am. Hyd., iii, 1915, p. 47.

Distribution.—Canso banks, 50 fathoms (Fraser); Off Newfoundland (Nutting).

CAMPANULARIA NEGLECTA (Alder).

Laomedea neglecta ALDER, Trans. Tynes. F. C., iii, 1857, p. 33.

Campanularia neglecta HINCKS, Br. Hyd. Zooph., 1868, p. 171.
     NUTTING, Hyd. Woods Hole, 1901, p. 346.
     STAFFORD, Fauna Atlantic Coast, 1912, p. 73.
     FRASER, Hyd. Nova Scotia, 1913, p. 165.
     NUTTING, Am. Hyd., iii, 1915, p. 46.

Distribution.—St. Andrews, Seven islands (Stafford); Canso (Fraser); throughout the area from Grand Manan to the St. Croix river, off Brier island.

CAMPANULARIA SPECIOSA Clark.

Campanularia speciosa CLARK, Alaskan Hydroids, 1876, p. 171.
     LEVINSEN, Medusæ, etc., 1893, p. 167.
     STAFFORD, Fauna Atlantic Coast, 1912, p. 73.
     FRASER, Hyd. V. I. region 1914, p. 139.
     NUTTING, Am. Hyd., iii, 1915, p. 48.

Distribution.—Gaspé, Seven islands (Stafford).

The hydroids reported by Stafford as belonging to this species, in all probability, belong to the species *C. magnifica*. In the Vancouver island paper attention has been called to the fact that similar mistakes have been made elsewhere owing to similarity of the trophosome. The gonangia in the two species bear no resemblance to each other.

CAMPANULARIA VERTICILLATA (Linnæus).

Sertularia verticillata LINNÆUS, Syst. Nat., 1758, p. 811.

Campanularia verticillata HINCKS, Br. Hyd. Zooph., 1868, p. 167.
     NUTTING, Hyd. Woods Hole, 1901, p. 347.
     WHITEAVES, Mar. Invert. East. Can., 1901, p. 22.
     STAFFORD, Fauna Atlantic Coast, 1912, p. 73.
     FRASER, Hyd. Nova Scotia, 1913, p. 165.
     NUTTING, Am. Hyd. iii, 1915, p. 29.

SESSIONAL PAPER No. 38a

Distribution.—Le Have banks, 45 fathoms (Smith and Harger); gulf of St. Lawrence (Packard); gulf of St. Lawrence, 20 to 50 fathoms (Whiteaves); St. Andrews, Gaspé, Seven islands (Stafford); Chedabucto bay, 50 fathoms (Fraser); Nova Scotia (Nutting); at several points in the area between Sand Reef light, L'Etang head and the north end of Campobello island.

CAMPANULARIA VOLUBILIS (Linnæus).

Sertularia volubilis LINNÆUS, Syst. Nat., 1767, p. 1311.

Campanularia volubilis HINCKS, Br. Hyd. Zooph., 1868, p. 160.
      NUTTING, Hyd. Woods Hole, 1901, p. 345.
      WHITEAVES, Mar. Invert. East. Can., 1901, p. 22.
      STAFFORD, Fauna Atlantic Coast, 1912, p. 73
      FRASER, Hyd. Nova Scotia, 1913, p. 165.
      NUTTING, Am. Hyd., iii, 1915, p. 31.

Distribution.—Bay of Fundy, low water to 60 fathoms (Verrill); gulf of St. Lawrence, off Cap des Rosiers lighthouse in 7 fathoms (Whiteaves); St. Andrews, Gaspé, Seven islands (Stafford); Barrington passage, 5 fathoms, Canso banks, 50 fathoms (Fraser); at various points from the south end of Grand Manan to the head of Passamaquoddy bay, Brier island, 33 to 39 fathoms.

Genus CLYTIA.

CLYTIA CYLINDRICA Agassiz.

Clytia cylindrica AGASSIZ, Cont. Nat. Hist. U.S., iv, 1862, p. 306.
Platypyxis cylindrica A. AGASSIZ, N. A. Acelephæ, 1865, p. 80.
Clytia cylindrica FRASER, Hyd. Beaufort, 1912, p. 358.
      FRASER, Grampus Hyd., 1915, p. 308.
      NUTTING, Am. Hyd., iii, 1915, p. 58.
Distribution.—Chamcook har., 5 fathoms, off Bliss island.

CLYTIA EDWARDSI (Nutting).

Campanularia edwardsi NUTTING, Hyd. Woods Hole, 1901, p. 346.
Clytia edwardsi FRASER, West Coast Hyd., 1911, p. 34.
      FRASER, New England Hyd., 1912, p. 44.
      FRASER, Hyd. V. I. region, 1914, p. 143.
      NUTTING, Am. Hyd., iii, 1915, p. 60.
Distribution.—St. Andrews Pt.

CLYTIA JOHNSTONI (Alder).
(Fig. 3).

Campanularia johnstoni ALDER, Ann. and Mag. Nat. Hist., 1856, p. 359.
Clytia johnstoni HINCKS, Br. Hyd. Zooph., 1868, p. 143.
Clytia bicophora AGASSIZ, Cont. Nat. Hist. U.S., iv, 1862, p. 304.
      NUTTING, Hyd. Woods Hole, 1901, p. 343.
Clytia grayi NUTTING, Hyd. Woods Hole, 1901, p. 344.
Clytia bicophora HARGITT, Am. Nat. 1901, p. 381.
Clytia johnstoni WHITEAVES, Mar. Invert., East. Can., 1901, p. 24.
      STAFFORD, Fauna Atlantic Coast, 1912, p. 73.
      FRASER, Hyd. Nova Scotia, 1915, p. 165.
      NUTTING, Am. Hyd., iii, 1915, p. 54.
Clytia bicophora NUTTING, Am. Hyd., iii, 1915, p. 56.

38a—23½

8 GEORGE V, A. 1918

Distribution.—Bay of Fundy, low water to 40 fathoms (Verrill); Le Have bank, 45 fathoms (Smith and Harger); Orphan bank (Whiteaves); St. Andrews (Stafford); Barrington passage, shallow water, Canso, low water (Fraser); Grand Manan (A. Agassiz); at various points from the south end of Grand Manan to the head of Passamaqoddy bay, off Brier island, 22 fathoms.

Since Agassiz described specimens from the New England coast and the Bay of Fundy as belonging to a new species *Clytia bicophora,* few authers have considered the species distinct from *Clytia johnstoni.* Nutting, in his Woods Hole paper, and later in his monograph, treats it so, but in his later paper he has included his earlier species, *Clytia grayi,* with *Clytia johnstoni.* He states that *Clytia bicophora* is a much more delicate and smaller species, the hydrothecæ of *C. johnstoni* being on the average twice as long and wide as those of *C. bicophora,*" and later, " The diagnostic marks of *Clytia bicophora* are the comparatively small size of the hydrothecæ, the presence of a simple instead of a complex diaphragm, and the tenuity of the hydrothecal walls." He speaks of the diaphragm of *C. johnston* as being " strong, thicker than usual, and the basal chamber well shown." The hydrotheca of *C. johnstoni* is said to have 16 teeth, that of *C. bicophora,* 12 to 14.

In the material under consideration there were specimens of this species, or of these species, from 18 localities, ranging from the southern end of Grand Manan island, through Passamaquoddy bay and up the St. Croix river, the very region from which Agassiz obtained some of his specimens. There were also some from St. Mary bay on the Nova Scotia side of the Bay of Fundy. For comparison I have specimens from Canso, N.S., and Woods Hole, Mass., together with specimens of *Clytia johnstoni* from the coast of Devon, England, obtained from the British museum.

First considering the size of the hydrothecæ, Nutting gives no measurements. the figures are not all drawn to the same scale of magnification and the scale is not given in any instance, hence it is impossible to be sure what size he considers suitable for each species. It is possible to find in one locality a variation as great as he gives as the distinction and sometimes not far from that much variation in the one colony. The average size of the English specimens is much the same as that of the Canso and Woods Hole specimens and scarcely any of those found in the bay of Fundy were smaller than these, the majority being larger and some of them being much larger. Those from St. Mary bay were larger and most of those from Passamaquoddy bay and vicinity are also; those well in from the direct waters of the bay of Fundy are. in general, larger than those more nearly out in the open. Thus, those from the vicinity of Deer island and at the mouth of the St. Croix river are larger on the average than those obtained from Grand Manan, the Wolves and Bliss island.

Some measurements will show this: The length of the hydrothecæ in the Devon, Canso, and Woods Hole specimens, varies from 0·5 to 0·65mm., St. Mary bay, 0·55 to 0·65, Grand Manan, 0·45 to 0·8, Bliss island, 0·5 to 0·75, Deer island, 0·6 to 1·0, mouth of the St. Croix river, 0·75 to 1·05. The length varies from 1·5 to 2 times the breadth. The largest specimens answer well to the type on which Nutting based the species. *C. grayi.* It is scarcely probable that Nutting described *C. bicophora* from specimens with hydrothecæ half the length of the smallest of these. It is more likely that there is a variation in size in the British specimens as there is in the bay of Fundy specimens and possibly Nutting has examined some of the larger ones while I have some of the smaller ones.

With regard to the thickness of the diaphragm, it is quite natural that the larger specimens have thicker diaphragms than the smaller but I find that when the smaller ones are examined under higher magnification, so that they appear equal in size to the larger, there is no constant difference in the appearance of the diaphragm. This is borne out by Nutting's figures. In fig. 3, pl. XII, where the drawing of the hydrotheca of *C. bicophora* is shown as large as that of *C. johnstoni* in the preceding plate. the diaphragm is shown even more plainly than in the drawing of *C. johnstoni.* The same is true in the case of the basal chamber.

The tenuity of the hydrothecal walls may vary much in the same species and the collapsible appearance is often due to the length of time the hydroids are in stale water before they are examined or before they are preserved.

Finally as to the number of teeth in the margin of the hydrothecæ, the number may vary from 12 to 16 in the hydrothecæ of the same colony and they appear to be just as liable to be numerous in the small hydrothecæ as in the large ones.

While the chasm is a great one between the small specimens and the very large ones, when only those are seen, it becomes entirely bridged when all graduations are brought into view also. The conclusion that all specimens recorded as *C. bicophora, C. grayi* and *C. johnstoni* should be all included in the one species *C. johnstoni* (Alder) to me seems unavoidable.

CLYTIA NOLIFORMIS (McCrady).

Campanularia noliformis McCRADY. Gymno. Charleston har., 1857, p. 92.
Clytia noliformis NUTTING, Hyd. Woods Hole. 1901, p. 343.
      FRASER, Hyd. Beaufort, 1912, p. 359.
      STAFFORD, Fauna Atlantic coast, 1912, p. 73.
      NUTTING, Am. Hyd., iii, 1915, p. 57.

Distribution.—Canso, Gaspé, Seven islands (Stafford); Briar island, 33 to 39 fathoms, on sargassum in Gulf Stream, east of Nova Scotia.

Genus EUCOPELLA.

EUCOPELLA CALICULATA (Hincks).

Campanularia caliculata HINCKS, Ann. and Mag. Nat. Hist., 1853, p. 178.
Clytia (Orthopyxis) poterium AGASSIZ, Cont. Nat. Hist. U. S., 1862, p. 297.
Orthopyxis poterium A. AGASSIZ, N. A. Acalephæ, 1865, p. 223.
Orthopyxis caliculata VERRILL, Mar. Invert. Vineyard sound, 1873, p. 408.
Campanularia poterium NUTTING, Hyd. Woods Hole, 1901, p. 344.
Campanularia caliculata HARGITT, Am. Nat. 1901, p. 383.
      WHITEAVES, Mar. Invert. Eastern Canada, 1901, p. 23.
      STAFFORD, Fauna Atlantic coast, 1912, p. 73.
Eucopella caliculata FRASER, Hyd. Nova Scotia, 1913, p. 166.
      FRASER, Hyd. V. I. region, 1914, p. 147.
Orthopyxis caliculata BALE, Proc. Roy. Soc. Vict., 1914, p. 72.
      NUTTING, Am. Hyd., iii, 1915, p. 64.

Distribution.—Bay of Fundy, low water to 30 fathoms, gulf of St. Lawrence at the Mingan islands, 6 fathoms (Verrill); Henley harbour, strait of Belle Isle, 20 to 30 fathoms (Packard); Seven islands (Stafford); Canso, 20 fathoms (Fraser); Sea Coal bay, N.S. (A. Agassiz).

In my previous papers where this species was recorded the name *Eucopella caliculata* has been used but now Bale and Nutting intimate that *Eucopella* must be discarded for *Orthopyxis*. It seems to be putting a big stretch on the law of priority when it is made to cover a name that was first applied to a subgenus and later a genus but admittedly never defined. It is all very well to speak of the "elaborate description" given by Agassiz for *Clytia (Orthopyxis) poterium*, but it was not sufficiently elaborate to give recognition to the fact that the species had already been described. In any case the description was not complete enough to convince Hincks of the necessity for the new genus for, while recognizing the identity of *Clytia poterium* with his own *Campanularia caliculata* in his 1868 work, he retains the name *Campanularia*.

Little stress can be laid on the fact that A. Agassiz used the name *Orthopyxis* in 1865 as there he simply refers to his father's collections without farther remarks.

8 GEORGE V, A. 1918

A stronger argument for retaining *Orthopyxis* appears in the fact that Verrill used *Orthopyxis caliculata* in all the references to the species in his paper in 1873, giving a description of the species but not of the genus on page 408, but as he returns to *Campanularia caliculata* in 1874 and again in 1879, the argument loses its strength. Nutting has evidently overlooked these references of Verrill's for he says: "I cannot find any author has used the name *Orthopyxis* since 1865."

The name *Eucopella* has a different status for when von Lendenfeld introduced it in 1885 he defined the genus and other definitions given since then do not conflict with his definition. Since the genus *Orthopyxis* had not been previously defined, Bale and Nutting are really substituting a new genus for *Eucopella,* although retaining all the characteristics of that genus, for although a name is given that had been used previously, they do not know and never can know that Agassiz had any such characteristics in mind when he applied the subgeneric name *Orthopyxis* to his species *poterium*.

Genus GONOTHYRÆA.

GONOTHYRÆA GRACILIS (Sars).

Laomedea gracilis SARS, Beretn. om zool. Reise, etc., 1851, p. 18.

Gonothyræa gracilis ALLMAN, Ann. and Mag. Nat. Hist., 1864, p. 374.
    HINCKS, Br. Hyd. Zooph., 1868, p. 183.
    FRASER, Hyd. Beaufort, 1912, p. 361.
    FRASER, Hyd. Nova Scotia, 1913, p. 166.
    NUTTING, Am. Hyd., iii, 1915, p. 70.

Distribution.—Canso, Barrington passage, low water (Fraser); off High Duck island, between Two and Three islands, off Swallowtail light, 30 to 40 fathoms off Bliss island, off St. Andrews point, off Joe's point, off Dochet island.

GONOTHYRÆA LOVENI (Allman).

Laomedea loveni ALLMAN, Ann. and Mag. Nat. Hist., 1859, p. 138.

Gonothyræa loveni ALLMAN, Ann. and Mag. Nat. Hist., 1864, p. 374.
    NUTTING, Hyd. Woods Hole, 1901, p. 352.
    STAFFORD, Fauna Atlantic Coast, 1912, p. 73.
    FRASER, Hyd. Nova Scotia, 1913, p. 166.
    NUTTING, Am. Hyd., iii, 1915, p. 69.

Distribution.—St. Andrews, Gaspé, Malpeque, Seven islands (Stafford); Chedacbucto bay, 20 fathoms (Fraser); Nigger reef, off Joe's point, off Head Harbour island, Cumming's cove, 5 to 40 fathoms.

Stafford mentions a species of *Gonothyræa* which occurs at Malpeque, between the clustered stems of *Tubularia*: "Its hydrotheca has about 24 long, narrow, rigid, sharp teeth, separated by broad, rounded spaces below and continuing as thickened lines down the hydrotheca." It is unfortunate that he did not describe this species more fully and give figures of it, since, as far as I am aware, there has been no species of *Gonothyræa* described with hydrothecæ like these. *Gonothyræa gracilis* (Sars) has hydrothecæ with long, slender, sharp, teeth but each hydrotheca has only 10 to 12 of them. Twenty-four is an unusually large number of teeth to be found on the hydrothecal margin of any hydroid species. The thickened longitudinal lines have not been mentioned in connection with other species of this genus.

Genus OBELIA.

OBELIA ARTICULATA (A. Agassiz).
(Fig. 1.)

Eucope articulata A. Agassiz, N. A. Acalephæ, 1865, p. 89.

Trophosome.—Largest colonies reaching a height of 7 cm., most of them much less than this; stem usually simple, although in some of the large colonies there is a slight indication of fasciculation; main stem continuous throughout and distinctly heavier than any of the branches; branches short and slender; main stem and branches with two to four annulations above the point where the branch or pedicel comes off; branches similarly annulated at their origin. Hydrothecate pedicels arising from each axil and one or two from each node, usually annulated throughout; hydrothecæ much deeper than wide; margin with 12 to 14 low, rounded teeth.

Gonosome.—Gonangia much elongated, with a distinct collar, borne on pedicels that are annulated throughout. They appear in the axils of the pedicels and smaller branches and at times are very numerous.

Distribution.—St. Croix river, reef near Biological station, off Joe's point, off St. Andrews point, St. Andrews island,, Chamcook harbour, Minister's island, Wolves island, off Swallowtail light, Grand Manan.

I have no doubt that this species which is common in the vicinity of the Biological station is the same as A. Agassiz described as *Eucope articulata* but his description is not very complete, hence I have included a full description at this time. The species resembles *Obelia dichotoma* in its mode of branching, *O. longissima* in the nature and arrangement of the hydrothecæ and O. *commissuralis* in the nature and arrangement of the gonangia. It is so much like these species in these respects that unless one 'gets a complete fertile colony it is somewhat difficult at times to be sure that it is not one of these species. It is quite possible that some of the records given for these other species should have been given for *O. articulata.*

OBELIA COMMISSURALIS McCrady.

Obelia commissuralis McCRADY, Gymno. Charleston har., 1857, p. 95.
           NUTTING, Hyd. Woods Hole, 1901, p. 350.
           HARGITT, Am. Nat., 1901, p. 382.
           WHITEAVES, Mar. Invert. East. Can., 1901, p. 23.
           FRASER, Hyd. Nova Scotia, 1913, p. 167.
           NUTTING, Am. Hyd., iii, 1915, p. 83.

Distribution.—Grand Manan (Verrill); Canso, low water (Fraser); Grand Manan (A. Agassiz); Seven islands.

OBELIA DICHOTOMA (Linnæus).

Sertularia dichotoma Linnæus, Syst. Nat., 1758, p. 812.
Obelia dichotoma HINCKS, Br. Hyd. Zooph., 1868, p. 156.
           NUTTING, Hyd. Woods Hole, 1901, p. 350.
           WHITEAVES, Mar. Invert. East. Can., 1901, p. 23.
Obelia pyriformis WHITEAVES, Mar. Invert. East. Can., 1901, p. 23.
Obelia dichotoma STAFFORD, Fauna Atlantic Coast. 1912, p. 73.
           FRASER, Hyd. Nova Scotia, 1913, p. 167.
           NUTTING, Am. Hyd., iii, 1915, p. 80.

Distribution.—Nova Scotia, Métis (Dawson); St. Andrews, Gaspé, Seven islands (Stafford); Canso, low water (Fraser); Grand Manan (A. Agassiz); Joe's point, east of Spruce island 17 fathoms, Brier island, 33 to 39 fathoms.

OBELIA FLABELLATA (Hincks).

Campanularia flabellata HINCKS. Ann. and Mag. Nat. Hist., 1866, p. 297.
Obelia flabellata HINCKS, Br. Hyd. Zooph., 1868, p. 157.
           NUTTING, Hyd. Woods Hole, 1901, p. 350.
           STAFFORD, Fauna Atlantic Coast, 1912, p. 73.
           NUTTING, Am. Hyd. iii, 1915, p. 84.

Distribution.—St. Andrews, Seven islands (Stafford); between White and Spruce islands.

OBELIA GENICULATA (Linnæus).

Sertularia geniculata LINNÆUS, Syst. Nat., 1767, p. 1312.
Obelia geniculata HINCKS, Br. Hyd. Zooph., 1868, p. 149.
        NUTTING, Hyd. Woods Hole, 1901, p. 350.
        WHITEAVES, Mar. Invert. East. Can., 1901, p. 23.
        STAFFORD, Fauna Atlantic Coast, 1912, p. 73.
        FRASER, Hyd. Nova Scotia, 1913, p. 167.
        FRASER, Grampus Hydroids, 1915, p. 73.
        NUTTING, Am. Hyd., iii, 1915, p. 73.

Distribution.—Bay of Fundy and northward, low water to 40 fathoms (Verrill);
gulf of St. Lawrence (Dawson); St. Andrews, Gaspé, Seven islands (Stafford); Barrington passage, 3 fathoms, Canso, low water (Fraser); High Duck island, Horse
island, Whale cove, off Swallowtail light, Wolves, north of Green island. Bliss island,
Deer island, off Joe's point, St. Andrews.

OBELIA HYALINA Clarke.

Obelia hyalina CLARKE, Bull. Mus. Comp. Zool., 1879, p. 241.
        FRASER, Hyd. Beaufort, 1912, p. 363.
        NUTTING, Am. Hyd., iii, 1915, p. 76.

Distribution.—On sargassum in the gulf stream, east of Nova Scotia.

OBELIA LONGISSIMA (Pallas).

Sertularia longissima PALLAS, Elench. Zooph., 1766, p. 119.
Obelia longissima HINCKS, Br. Hyd. Zooph., 1868, p. 154.
        NUTTING, Hyd. Woods Hole, 1901, p. 351.
        WHITEAVES, Mar. Invert. East. Can., 1901, p. 23.
        STAFFORD, Fauna Atlantic Coast, 1912, p. 73.
        NUTTING, Am. Hyd., iii, 1915, p. 85.

Distribution.—Bay of Fundy (Verrill); St. Andrews, Seven islands (Stafford);
off Bliss island, Indian Head bay, off Joe's point, St. Andrews.

Family *CAMPANULINIDÆ.*

Genus CALYCELLA.

CALYCELLA SYRINGA (Linnæus).

Sertularia syringa LINNÆUS, Syst. Nat., 1767, p. 1311.
Campanularia syringa STIMPSON, Mar. Invert. Grand Manan, 1854, p. 8.
Calycella syringa HINCKS, Br. Hyd. Zooph., 1868, p. 206.
        NUTTING, Hyd. Woods Hole, 1901, p. 355.
        WHITEAVES, Mar. Invert. East. Can., 1901, p. 23.
        STAFFORD, Fauna Atlantic Coast, 1912, p. 73.
        FRASER, Hyd. Nova Scotia, 1913, p. 168.
        FRASER, Hyd. V. I. region, 1914, p. 156.

Distribution.—Off Duck island, 25 fathoms (Stimpson); Le Have bank, 45
fathoms (Smith and Harger); gulf of St. Lawrence, on the Orphan bank and about
half-way between East cape, Anticosti, and the Bird rocks, in 313 fathoms (Whiteaves); St. Andrews, Malapeque, Gaspé, Seven islands (Stafford); Barrington passage,
shallow water, Canso banks, 50 fathoms (Fraser); at almost all points where collecting was done in the bay of Fundy.

In my 1914 paper reasons are given for believing that *Calycella pygmæa* is not
distinct from *Calycella syringa*

Genus CUSPIDELLA.

CUSPIDELLA COSTATA Hincks.

Cuspidella costata HINCKS, Br. Hyd. Zooph., 1868, p. 210.
　　　　　　STAFFORD, Fauna Atlantic Coast, 1912, p. 73.
Distribution.—Gaspé (Stafford).

CUSPIDELLA GRANDIS Hincks.

Cuspidella grandis HINCKS, Br. Hyd. Zooph., 1868, p. 210.
　　　　　　WHITEAVES, Mar. Invert. East. Can., 1901, p. 24.
Distribution.—Orphan bank (Whiteaves); Coteau harbour, Long island, Labrador (Packard).

Genus *OPERCULARELLA*.

OPERCULARELLA LACERATA (Johnston).

Campanularia lacerata JOHNSTON, Br. Zooph., 1847, p. 120.
Opercularella lacerata HINCKS, Br. Hyd. Zooph., 1868, p. 194.
　　　　　　NUTTING, Hyd. Woods Hole, 1901, p. 354.
　　　　　　STAFFORD, Fauna Atlantic Coast, 1912, p. 73.
　　　　　　FRASER, Hyd. Nova Scotia, 1913, p. 168.
Distribution.—St. Andrews (Stafford); Fox island, Chedabucto bay, low tide (Fraser); Niger reef, weir stakes, St. Andrews island, Brier island, 33 to 39 fathoms.

OPERCULARELLA PUMILA Clark.

Opercularella pumila CLARK, New England Hydroids, 1876, p. 61.
　　　　　　nana HARTLAUB, Die Hydromedusen Helgolands, 1897, p. 502.
　　　　　　pumilla HARGITT, Hyd. Woods Hole, 1909, p. 375.
Distribution.—Weir stakes, St. Andrews island.

The description and figures given by Hartlaub for *Opercularella nana* agree perfectly with the creeping form of *Opercularella pumila* as described by Clark. Clark found but empty gonangia but Hartlaub found and described the complete gonosome. There is no question but that the species is distinct from *O. lacerata* (Johnston). In the specimens found in the Bay of Fundy, the hydrothecæ are only about half as long (·25) in *O. pumila* as they are in *O. lacerata* (·45 mm) and the gonangia are of an entirely different shape. In *O. lacerata* they are rounded or truncate at the distal end, while in *O. pumila* the distal portion is drawn out to become much more tubular.

All of the material obtained at St. Andrews I. was of the creeping type but it was well supplied with gonangia.

Genus STEGOPOMA.

STEGOPOMA PLICATILE (Sars).

Lafœa plicatile SARS, Forhandl., 1863, p. 31.
Stegopoma plicatile LEVINSEN, Medusæ, Ctenophorer, etc., 1893, p. 36.
　　　　　　BROCH, Coelentérés du Fond, 1912, p. 11.
　　　　　　FRASER, Hyd. V. I. region, 1914, p. 161.
Distribution.—Bay of Islands, Newfoundland.

Genus TETRAPOMA.

TETRAPOMA QUADRIDENTATUM (Hincks).

Calycella quadridentata HINCKS, Ann. and Mag. Nat. Hist., 1874, p. 149.
Tetrapoma quadridentatum LEVINSEN, Medusar, Ctenophorer, etc., 1893, p. 180.
Calycella quadridentata STAFFORD, Fauna Atlantic Coast, 1912, p. 73.
Distribution.—Gaspé (Stafford).

Family *HALECIDÆ*.

Genus HALECIUM.

HALECIUM ARTICULOSUM Clark.

Halecium articulosum CLARK, New England Hyd., 1876, p. 63.
NUTTING, Hyd. Woods Hole, 1901, p. 358.
STAFFORD, Fauna Atlantic Coast, 1912, p. 73.
FRASER, Hyd. V.I. region, 1914, p. 164.

Distribution.—St. Andrews (Stafford); Wolves, between White and Spruce islands, southwest of Deer island, off Sandreef light, 15 fathoms, off Harbour island, 25 fathoms, off Joe's point 10 fathoms, reef near Biological station.

HALECIUM BEANI (Johnston).

Thoa beani JOHNSTON, Br. Zooph., 1847, p. 120.
Halecium beani HINCKS, Br. Hyd. Zooph., 1868, p. 224.
NUTTING, Hyd. Woods Hole, 1901, p. 358.
STAFFORD, Fauna Atlantic Coast, 1912, p. 73.
FRASER, Hyd. Nova Scotia, 1913, p. 168.

Distribution.—St. Andrews, Seven Islands (Stafford); Barrington passage, 5f., Canso banks, 50f. (Fraser); at many points from the south end of Grand Manan to the head of Passamaquody bay.

HALECIUM CURVICAULE Lorenz.

Halecium curvicaule LORENZ, Polypomedusen von Jan Mayen, 1886, p. 3.
BROCH, Hyd. Arkt. Meere, 1909, p. 150.

Distribution.—Off Joe's point, off Deer island, off Brier island, 33-39f.

HALECIUM GRACILE Verrill.

Halecium gracile VERRILL, Invert. An. Vineyard sd., 1873, p. 729.
NUTTING, Hyd. Woods Hole, 1901, p. 358.
WHITEAVES, Mar. Invert. E. Can., 1901, p. 24.
STAFFORD, Fauna Atlantic Coast, 1912, p. 73.

Distribution.—St. Andrews, Seven islands (Stafford); reef near Biological Station St. Andrews, 5 to 10 fathoms.

HALECIUM HALECINUM (Linnæus).

Sertularia halecina LINNÆUS, Syst. Nat., 1767, p. 1308.
Halecium halecinum HINCKS, Br. Hyd. Zooph., 1868, p. 221.
NUTTING, Hyd. Woods Hole, 1901, p. 357.
WHITEAVES, Mar. Invert. E. Can., 1901, p. 24.
STAFFORD, Fauna Atlantic Coast, 1912, p. 73.

Distribution.—Chateau bay, strait of Bell Isle, 30 fathoms, Bay of Funday (Packard); Bay of Fundy (Dawson); Bay of Fundy (Whiteaves); St. Andrews (Stafford); St. Andrews, off Deer island.

HALECIUM MINUTUM Broch.

Halecium minutum BROCH, Nordmeer gesammelten hydroiden, 1903, p. 4.
FRASER, Hyd. Nova Scotia, 1913, p. 168.

Distribution.—Canso banks, 50 fathoms (Fraser); Brier island, 22 fathoms, Bay of Islands, Newfoundland. 50 to 60 fathoms.

HALECIUM MURICATUM (Ellis and Solander).

Sertularia muricatum ELLIS AND SOLANDER, Nat. Hist. Zooph., 1786, p. 59.
Halecium muricatum HINCKS, Br. Hyd. Zooph., 1868, p. 223.
WHITEAVES, Mar. Invert. E. Can., 1901, p. 25.
STAFFORD, Fauna Atlantic Coast, 1912, p. 73.
FRASER, Hyd. Nova Scotia, 1913, p. 169.

Distribution.—15 miles south southeast of Bonaventure island, 50 fathoms (Whiteaves); off Caribou island, 30 to 50 fathoms, Square island, Labrador (Packard); St. Andrews, Canso, Gaspé (Stafford); Canso banks, 50 fathoms (Fraser); Quoddy river, 23 to 47 fathoms, Head Harbour island, Deer island, between Big Duck and Cheyne island, off Spruce island, 11 to 35 fathoms, between Two and Three islands, off Brier island, 33 to 39 fathoms.

HALECIUM SESSILE Norman.

Halecium sessile NORMAN, Hyd. Hebrides, 1866, p. 196.
HINCKS, Br. Hyd. Zooph., 1868, p. 229.
WHITEAVES, Mar. Invert. E. Can., 1901, p. 25.

Distribution.—Between East cape, Anticosti and Bird rocks, 12 fathoms (Whiteaves).

HALECIUM TENELLUM Hincks.

Halecium tenellum HINCKS, Ann. and Mag. Nat. Hist., 1861, p. 252.
HINCKS, British Hyd. Zooph., 1868, p. 226.
NUTTING, Hyd. Woods Hole, 1901, p. 357.
STAFFORD, Fauna Atlantic Coast, 1912, p. 73.
FRASER, Hyd. Nova Scotia, 1913, p. 169.

Distribution.—St. Andrews, Gaspé, Seven islands (Stafford); Canso banks, 50 fathoms (Fraser); common from the north end of Campobello island to the head of Passamaquoddy bay, Brier island, Seven islands, bay of Islands, Newfoundland.

Family *HEBELLIDÆ*.

Genus HEBELLA.

HEBELLA CALCARATA (A. Agassiz).

Lafœa calcarata A. AGASSIZ, N. A. Acalephæ, 1865, p. 122.
HARGITT, Am. Nat., 1901, p. 387.
Hebella calcarata NUTTING, Hyd. Woods Hole, 1901, p. 353.
FRASER, Hyd. Beaufort, 1912, p. 371.
STAFFORD, Fauna Atlantic Coast, 1912, p. 73.

Distribution.—Canso (Stafford).

HEBELLA (?) *pocillum* Hincks.

Lafœa pocillum HINCKS, Br. Hyd. Zooph., 1868, p. 204.
Distribution.—St. Andrews.

There was no gonosome present on the St. Andrews specimens to settle the question definitely as to whether this species is a *Lafœa* or an *Hebella* but as there is a distinct diaphragm in the hydrotheca, it agrees with *Hebella* in that respect and is so placed.

8 GEORGE V, A. 1918

Family *LAFŒIDÆ*.

Genus CRYPTOLARIA.

CRYPTOLARIA TRISERIALIS Fraser.

Cryptolaria triserialis FRASER, Hyd. Nova Scotia, 1913, p. 170.

Distribution.—Off Durell island, Chedabucto bay, 20 fathoms (Fraser).

Genus FILELLUM.

FILELLUM SERPENS (Hassall).

Campanularia serpens HASSALL, Trans. Micro. Soc., 1852, p. 163.

Filellum serpens HINCKS, Br. Hyd. Zooph., 1868, p. 214.

Reticularia serpens VERRILL, Check-list, 1879, p. 79.

Filellum serpens FRASER, Beaufort Hydroids, 1912, p. 369.
       FRASER, Hyd. Nova Scotia, 1913, p. 171.

Distribution.—Canso banks, 50 fathoms (Fraser); common from the north end of Campobello island to the head of Passamaquoddy bay and up the mouth of the St. Croix river, Brier island, 22 fathoms.

Genus GRAMMARIA.

GRAMMARIA ABIETINA (Sars).

Campanularia abietina SARS, Nyt. Mag. for Naturv., 1851, p. 139.

Grammaria robusta STIMPSON, Mar. Invert. Grand Manan, 1854, p. 9.

Grammaria abietina SARS, Norske Hydroider, 1863, p. 34.

Salacia abietina, HINCKS, Br. Hyd. Zooph., 1868, p. 212.

Lafœa abietina BONNEVIE, Norske, Nordhavs-Ex., 1899, p. 64.

Grammaria abietina WHITEAVES, Mar. Invert. E. Can., 1901, p. 28.
       STAFFORD, Fauna Atlantic Coast, 1912, p. 73.
       FRASER, Hyd. Nova Scotia, 1913, p. 171.
       FRASER, Hyd. V. I. region, 1914, p. 173.

Distribution.—Grand Manan (Stimpson); Le Have bank, 60 fathoms (Smith and Harger); gulf of St. Lawrence, Trinity bay, 25 fathoms, and elsewhere (Whiteaves); Gaspé, Seven islands (Stafford); Chedabucto bay, 20 fathoms (Fraser); bay of Islands, Newfoundland, 50 to 60 fathoms.

GRAMMARIA GRACILIS Stimpson.

Grammaria gracilis STIMPSON, Mar. Invert. Grand Manan, 1854, p. 9.
       WHITEAVES, Mar. Invert. E. Can., 1901, p. 28.

Distribution.—Grand Manan (Stimpson).

Genus LAFŒA.

LAFŒA DUMOSA (Fleming).

Sertularia dumosa FLEMING, Edin. Phil. Jour., 1828, p. 83.

Lafœa dumosa HINCKS, Br. Hyd. Zooph., 1868, p. 200.
       NUTTING, Hyd. Woods Hole, 1901, p. 355.
       WHITEAVES, Mar. Invert. E. Can., 1901, p. 24.

Lafœa robusta WHITEAVES. Mar. Invert. E. Can., 1901, p. 24.
      STAFFORD, Fauna Atlantic Coast, 1912, p. 73.
Lafœa dumosa FRASER, Hyd. Nova Scotia, 1913, p. 171.
      FRASER, Hyd. V. I. Region, 1914, p. 174.

Distribution.—Nova Scotia (Agassiz); between Anticosti and Gaspé, 120 to 200 fathoms (Whiteaves); St. Andrews, Gaspé, Seven islands (Stafford); Chedabucto bay, 20 fathoms (Fraser); common in all the Passamaquoddy bay area, Brier island, 22 fathoms.

LAFŒA FRUTICOSA Sars.

Lafœa fruticosa SARS, Norske Hydroider, 1863, p. 30.
      HINCKS, Br. Hyd. Zooph., 1868, p. 202.
      BONNEVIE, Norske Nordhavs-Ex., 1899, p. 64.
      VERRILL, Check-list, 1879, p. 17.
      STAFFORD, Fauna Atlantic Coast, 1912, p. 172.
      FRASER, Hyd. Nova Scotia, 1913, p. 172.

Distribution.—Seven islands (Stafford); Chedabucto bay, 20 fathoms (Fraser); Chamcook harbour, 5 fathoms.

LAFŒA GRACILLIMA (Alder).

Campanularia gracillima ALDER, Trans. Tynes Nat. F. C., 1857, p. 39.
Lafœa gracillima BONNEVIE, Norske Nordhavs-Ex., 1899, p. 64.
      NUTTING, Hyd. Woods Hole, 1901, p. 356.
      WHITEAVES, Mar. Invert. E. Can., 1901, p. 24.
      STAFFORD, Fauna Atlantic Coast, 1912, p. 73.
      FRASER, Hyd. Nova Scotia, 1913, p. 172.
      FRASER, Hyd. V. I. region, 1914, p. 175.

Distribution.—Bay of Fundy (Verrill); Le Have bank, 45 to 60 fathoms (Smith and Harger); Gaspé, Seven islands (Stafford); Canso banks, 50 fathoms (Fraser); Brier island, Seven islands, bay of Islands, Newfoundland, 50 to 60 fathoms.

LAFŒA PYGMÆA Hincks.

Lafœa pygmœa HINCKS, Br. Hyd. Zooph., 1868, p. 205.
Hebella pygmœa NUTTING, Hyd. Woods Hole, 1901, p. 353.
      BROCH, Nordmeer ges. Hyd., 1903, p. 5.
      FRASER, Hyd. Nova Scotia, 1913, p. 172.

Distribution.—Chedabucto bay, 25 fathoms (Fraser).

LAFŒA SYMMETRICA Bonnevie.

Lafœa symmetrica BONNEVIE, Norske Nordhavs-Ex, 1899, p. 64.
      BILLARD, Ex. Sc. "Travailleur" et du "Talisman," 1907, p. 176.
      FRASER, Hyd. Nova Scotia, 1913, p. 172.

Distribution.—Chedabucto bay, 25 fathoms (Fraser).

Family SERTULARIDÆ.

Genus ABIETINARIA.

ABIETINARIA ABIETINA (Linnæus).

Sertularia abietina LINNÆUS, Syst. Nat., 1758, p. 808.
      HINCKS, Br. Hyd. Zooph., 1868, p. 266.
      WHITEAVES, Mar. Invert. E. Can., 1901, p. 25.

8 GEORGE V, A. 1918

Sertularella abietina NUTTING, Hyd. Woods Hole, 1901, p. 361.

Abietinaria abietina NUTTING, Am. Hyd. ii, 1904, p. 114.

STAFFORD, Fauna Atlantic Coast, 1912, p. 73.

FRASER, Hyd. Nova Scotia, 1913, p. 173.

Distribution.—Off Nova Scotia, 51 fathoms (Allman); Mingan island, gulf of St. Lawrence and Labrador (Packard); gulf and river St. Lawrence (Dawson and Whiteaves); St. Andrews, Gaspé, Canso, Seven islands (Stafford); Canso banks, 50 fathoms (Fraser); St. George's bank, Newfoundland (A. Agassiz); off Swallowtail light, southwest of Deer island, Head harbour, McMaster island, off Joe's point, Seven islands.

ABIETINARIA FILICULA (Ellis and Solander.)

Sertularia filicula ELLIS AND SOLANDER, Nat. Hist. Zooph., 1786, p. 57.

STIMPSON, Mar. Invert. Grand Manan, 1854, p. 8.

HINCKS, Br. Hyd. Zooph., 1868, p. 264.

WHITEAVES, Mar. Invert. E. Can., 1901, p. 25.

Abietinaria filicula NUTTING, Am. Hyd. ii, 1904, p. 123.

Distribution.—Grand Manan, 20 fathoms (Stimpson); Labrador (Packard).

NOTE.—Stafford reports specimens of an *Abietinaria* species from Seven Islands, Quebec, but as all the information he gives concerning it is that it " most resembles *A. gigantea* Clark," it is impossible to place it.

Genus DIPHASIA.

DIPHASIA FALLAX (Johnston.)

Sertularia fallax JOHNSTON, Br. Zooph., 1847, p. 73.

STIMPSON, Mar. Invert. Grand Manan, 1854, p. 8.

Diphasia fallax HINCKS, Br. Hyd. Zooph., 1868, p. 249.

NUTTING, Hyd. Woods Hole, 1901, p. 361.

HARGITT, Am. Nat., 1901, p. 391.

WHITEAVES, Mar. Invert. E. Can., 1901, p. 26.

NUTTING, Am. Hyd. ii, 1904, p. 114.

STAFFORD, Fauna Atlantic Coast, 1912, p. 73.

FRASER, Hyd. Nova Scotia, 1913, p. 173.

Distribution.—Grand Manan (Stimpson); Bay of Fundy, 20 to 55 fathoms (Verrill); St. Andrews (Stafford); Barrington passage. 4 fathoms (Fraser); common throughout the Passamaquoddy bay area, Brier island. 22 fathoms.

DIAPHASIA ROSACEA (Linnæus).

Sertularia rosacea LINNÆUS, Syst. Nat., 1758, p. 807.

Diphasia rosacea HINCKS, Br. Hyd. Zooph., 1868, p. 245.

NUTTING, Hyd. Woods Hole, 1901, p. 361.

WHITEAVES, Mar. Invert. E. Can., 1901, p. 26.

NUTTING, Am. Hyd., ii, 1904, p. 107.

STAFFORD, Fauna Atlantic Coast, 1912, p. 74.

FRASER, Hyd. Nova Scotia, 1913, p. 174.

Distribution.—Strait of Belle Isle, 50 fathoms (Packard); St. Andrews (Stafford); Barrington passage (Fraser); off Deer island, 15 fathoms, off Frost ledges, Quoddy river, between White and Spruce islands, between Two and Three islands, Brier island, 33 to 39 fathoms.

DIPHASIA TAMARISCA (Linnæus).

Sertularia tamarisca LINNÆUS, Syst. Nat., 1758, p. 808.
Sertularia producta STIMPSON, Mar. Invert. Grand Manan, 1854, p. 8.
Diphasia tamarisca HINCKS, Br. Hyd. Zooph., 1868, p. 273.
Sertularia producta WHITEAVES, Mar. Invert. E. Can., 1901, p. 27.
Diphasia tamarisca NUTTING, Am. Hyd., ii, 1904, p. 108.
Distribution.—Grand Manan (Stimpson); Sea coal bay, N.S. (Verrill).

Nutting, apparently with good reason, has concluded that *Sertularia producta* Stimpson is synonymous with *Diphasia tamarisca* (Linnæus) and hence it is included here under that name.

Genus HYDRALLMANIA.

HYDRALLMANIA FALCATA (Linnæus).

Sertularia falcata LINNÆUS, Syst. Nat., 1758, p. 810.
Plumularia falcata STIMPSON, Mar. Invert. Grand Manan, 1854, p. 8.
Hydrallmania falcata HINCKS, Br. Hyd. Zooph., 1868, p. 273.
               NUTTING, Hyd. Woods Hole, 1901, p. 364.
               HARGITT, Am. Nat., 1901, p. 392.
               WHITEAVES, Mar. Invert. E. Can., 1901, p. 27.
               NUTTING, Am. Hyd., ii, 1904, p. 124.
               STAFFORD, Fauna Atlantic Coast, 1912, p. 74.
               FRASER, Hyd. Nova Scotia, 1913, p. 174.

Distribution.—Grand Manan, 25 to 35 fathoms (Stimpson); bay of Fundy, low water to 110 fathoms, Anticosti, Mingan islands (Verrill); Le Have bank, 60 fathoms, Chebucto head, Halifax harbour, 20 fathoms (Smith and Harger); Sable island, Gaspé, Métis (Dawson); gulf of St. Lawrence (Whiteaves); Grand Manan (A. Agassiz); St. Andrews, Gaspé, Seven islands (Stafford); Barrington passage (Fraser); one of the comonest species of large size in the collection.

Genus SELAGINOPSIS.

SELAGINOPSIS MIRABILIS (Verrill).

Diphasia mirabilis VERRILL, Amer. Jour. Sci. Arts, 1872, p. 9.
               WHITEAVES, Mar. Invert. E. Can., 1901, p. 26.
Selaginopsis mirabilis NUTTING, Am. Hyd., ii, 1904, p. 128.
               STAFFORD, Fauna Atlantic Coast, 1912, p. 74.
               FRASER, Hyd. Nova Scotia, 1913, p. 174.

Distribution.—Le Have bank, 60 fathoms (Smith and Harger); Gaspé, Seven islands (Stafford); Canso banks, 50 fathoms (Fraser).

Genus SERTULARELLA.

SERTULARELLA CONICA Allman.

Sertularella conica ALLMAN, Hyd. Gulf Stream, 1877, p. 21.
               NUTTING, Am. Hyd., ii, 1904, p. 79.
               FRASER, Hyd. Nova Scotia, 1913, p. 174.
Distribution.—Canso banks, 50 fathoms (Fraser).

SERTULARELLA FUSIFORMIS (Hincks).

Sertularia fusiformis HINCKS, Ann. and Mag. Nat. Hist., 1861, p. 253.
　　HINCKS, Br. Hyd. Zooph., 1868, p. 243.
　　WHITEAVES, Mar. Invert. E. Can., 1901, p. 26.

Sertularella fusiformis NUTTING. Am. Hyd., ii, 1904, p. 89.

Distribution.—Gulf of St. Lawrence, between Anticosti and Gaspé, 200 fathoms
(Whiteaves).

SERTULARELLA POLYZONIAS (Linnæus).

Sertularia polyzonias LINNÆUS. Syst. Nat., 1758, p. 813.
　　STIMPSON, Mar. Invert. Grand Manan, 1854, p. 9.

Sertularella polyzonias HINCKS, Br. Hyd. Zooph., 1868, p. 235.
　　NUTTING, Hyd. Woods Hole, 1901, p. 362.
　　WHITEAVES, Mar. Invert. E. Can., 1901, p. 25.
　　NUTTING. Am. Hyd., ii, 1904, p. 90.
　　STAFFORD, Fauna Atlantic Coast, 1912, p. 73.
　　FRASER, Hyd. Nova Scotia, 1913, p. 175.

Distribution.—Grand Manan, 10 to 40 fathoms (Stimpson); Le Have bank, 60
fathoms (Smith and Harger); Caribou island, (Packard); gulf of St. Lawrence
(Whiteaves); St. Andrews, Gaspé,Seven islands (Stafford); Chedabucto bay, 10 to 20
fathoms (Fraser); common throughout the Passamaquoddy bay area, Seven islands.

SERTULARELLA RUGOSA (Linnæus).

Sertularia rugosa LINNÆUS, Syst. Nat., 1758, p. 809.
　　STIMPSON, Mar. Invert. Grand Manan, 1854, p. 9.

Sertularella rugosa HINCKS, Br. Hyd. Zooph., 1868, p. 259.

Sertularia rugosa WHITEAVES, Mar. Invert. E. Can., 1901, p. 25.

Sertularella rugosa NUTTING, Am. Hyd., ii, 1904, p. 82.
　　STAFFORD, Fauna Atlantic Coast, 1912, p. 73.

Distribution.—Grand Manan, deep water (Stimpson); Square island, Labrador,
30 fathoms (Packard); Seven islands (Stafford); High Duck island, between White
and Spruce islands, Cumming's cove, West Quoddy head, Dochet island.

SERTULARELLA TRICUSPIDATA (Alder).

Sertularia tricuspidata ALDER, Ann. and Mag. Nat. Hist., 1856, p. 356.

Sertularella tricuspidata HINCKS. Br. Hyd. Zooph., 1868, p. 239.
　　NUTTING, Hyd. Woods Hole, 1901, p. 362.
　　WHITEAVES, Mar. Invert. E. Can., 1901, p. 26.
　　NUTTING, Am. Hyd., ii, 1904, p. 71.
　　STAFFORD, Fauna Atlantic Coast, 1912, p. 73.
　　FRASER, Hyd. Nova Scotia, 1913, p. 175.

Distribution.—Bay of Fundy, 50 to 55 fathoms (Verrill); Le Have bank, 45 to
60 fathoms (Smith and Harger); gulf of St. Lawrence (Whiteaves); strait of Belle
Isle, 40 fathoms (Packard); St. Andrews, Gaspé, Seven islands (Stafford); Canso
banks, 50 fathoms (Fraser); very common everywhere in the Passamaquoddy bay
area at all depths, Brier island, 33 to 39 fathoms.

Genus SERTULARIA.

SERTULARIA CORNICINA (McCrady).

Dynamena cornicina McCRADY. Gymno. Charleston Har., 1858, p. 204.
Sertularia cornicina NUTTING. Hyd. Woods Hole, 1901, p. 359.
    NUTTING. Am. Hyd., ii, 1904, p. 58.
    FRASER. Hyd. Beaufort. 1912, p. 374.
Distribution.—On sargassum in the Gulf Stream, east of Nova Scotia.

SERTULARIA PUMILA Linnæus.

Sertularia pumila LINNÆUS, Syst. Nat., 1758, p. 807.
    HINCKS, Br. Hyd. Zooph., 1868, p. 260.
    NUTTING. Hyd. Woods Hole, 1901, p. 359.
    WHITEAVES, Mar. Invert. E. Can., 1901, p. 25.
    STAFFORD, Fauna Atlantic Coast, 1912, p. 73.
    FRASER, Hyd. Nova Scotia, 1913, p. 175.

Distribution.—Nova Scotia and Métis (Dawson); strait of Belle Isle, between tides (Packard); St. Andrews, Canso, Seven islands (Stafford); Canso, low water (Fraser); Grand Manan (A. Agassiz); High Duck island, Wolves, Indian Head bar, Souris, P.E.I., York harbour, bay of Islands, Newfoundland, Seven islands.

Genus THUIARIA.

THUIARIA ARGENTEA (Linnæus).

Sertularia argentea LINNÆUS. Syst. Nat., 1758, p. 809.
    STIMPSON, Mar. Invert. Grand Manan, 1854, p. 8.
    HINCKS, Br. Hyd. Zooph., 1868, p. 268.
Thuiaria argentea NUTTING, Hyd. Woods Hole. 1901, p. 364.
    WHITEAVES, Mar. Invert. E. Can., 1901, p. 27.
    NUTTING, Am. Hyd., ii, 1904, p. 71.
    STAFFORD. Fauna Atlantic Coast, 1912, p. 73.
    FRASER, Hyd. Nova Scotia, 1913, p. 176.

Distribution.—Grand Manan, 4 to 6 fathoms (Stimpson); Bay of Fundy, Nova Scotia coast, gulf of St. Lawrence, low water to 110 fathoms (Verrill); Northumberland strait, gulf of St. Lawrence (Whiteaves); Gaspé bay (Dawson); Caribou island, 8 fathoms (Packard); St. Andrews, Gaspé (Stafford); Barrington passage, 5 fathoms, Canso banks, 50 fathoms (Fraser); off Deer island, off Grand Manan, bay of Islands, Newfoundland, 50 to 60 fathoms.

THUIARIA CUPRESSINA (Linnæus).

Sertularia cupressina LINNÆUS, Syst. Nat., 1758, p. 808.
    HINCKS, Br. Hyd. Zooph., 1868, p. 270.
Thuiaria cupressina NUTTING, Hyd. Woods Hole, 1901, p. 363.
    WHITEAVES, Mar. Invert. E. Can., 1901, p. 27.
    NUTTING, Am. Hyd., ii, 1904, p. 72.
    STAFFORD, Fauna Atlantic Coast, 1912, p. 73.

Distribution.—Off Nova Scotia, 51 fathoms (Allman); Bay of Fundy, low water to 100 fathoms (Verrill); Northumberland strait, gulf of St. Lawrence (Whiteaves); Henley harbour, strait of Belle Isle. 7 fathoms (Packard); St. Andrews (Stafford); St. Croix river, off Joe's point. McMaster island, Quoddy river, off Deer island, Whale cove, 20 to 30 fathoms, Brier island, 33 to 39 fathoms.

8 GEORGE V, A. 1918

THUIARIA FABRICII (Levinsen).

Sertularia fastigiata FABRICIUS, Fauna Grœnlandica, 1780, p. 458.
Sertularia fabricii LEVINSEN, Vid. Middel. Naturh. Foren., 1892, p. 48.
Thuiaria fabricii NUTTING, Am. Hyd., ii, p. 1904, p. 71.
          STAFFORD, Fauna Atlantic Coast, 1912, p. 73.
Distribution.—Gaspé, Islands (Stafford); St. Andrews.

THUIRIA IMMERSA Nutting.

Thuiaria immersa NUTTING, Am. Hyd., ii, 1904, p. 66.
          STAFFORD, Fauna Atlantic Coast, 1912, p. 73.
Distribution.—Seven islands (Stafford); St. Croix river, Grand Manan, between Mohawk and Adam island, 35 fathoms, between Green and Three islands, McMaster island, off Deer island, off Brier island, 22 fathoms.

THUIARIA LATIUSCULA (Stimpson).

Sertularia latiuscula STIMPSON, Mar. Invert. Grand Manan, 1854, p. 8.
          WHITEAVES, Mar. Invert. E. Can., 1901, p. 26.
Thuiaria latiuscula NUTTING, Am. Hyd., ii, 1904, p. 69.
          STAFFORD, Fauna Atlantic Coast, 1912, p. 73.
Distribution.—Grand Manan (Stimpson); Gaspé, Seven islands (Stafford); St. Andrews.

THUIARIA LONCHITIS (Ellis and Solander).

Sertularia lonchitis ELLIS AND SOLANDER, Nat. Hist. Zooph., 1786, p. 42.
Thuiaria articulata WHITEAVES, Mar. Invert. E. Can., 1901, p. 27.
Thuiaria lonchits NUTTING, Am. Hyd., ii, 1904, p. 66.
          FRASER, Hyd. Nova Scotia, 1913, p. 176.
Distribution.—Le Have bank, 45 fathoms (Smith and Harger); gulf of St. Lawrence (Whiteveaves); Canso banks, 50 fathoms (Fraser); St. Andrews.

THUIARIA ROBUSTA Clark.

Thuiaria robusta CLARK, Alaskan Hyd., 1876, p. 227.
          NUTTING, Am. Hyd., ii, 1904, p. 64.
          STAFFORD, Fauna Atlantic Coast, 1912, p. 73.
Distribution.—Gaspé, Seven islands (Stafford).

THUIARIA SIMILIS (Clark).

Sertularia similis CLARK, Alaskan Hyd., 1876, p. 219.
Thuiaria similis NUTTING, Am. Hyd., ii, 1904, p. 69.
          FRASER, West Coast Hyd., 1911, p. 77.
          STAFFORD, Fauna Atlantic Coast, 1912, p. 73.
          FRASER, Hyd. V. I. region, 1914, p. 199.
Distribution.—Gaspé (Stafford); St. Croix river, Quoddy river, West Quoddy head, Head Harbour island, 25 fathoms, Whale cove, Brier island, 22 fathoms, Seven islands.

THUIARIA TENERA (Sars).

Sertularia tenera SARS, Bidrag til Kundskaben etc., 1873, p. 20.
Thuiaria tenera NUTTING, Am. Hyd., ii, 1904, p. 70.
          STAFFORD, Fauna Atlantic Coast, 1912, p. 73.
Distribution.—Gaspé, Seven islands (Stafford); St. Andrews, Brier island.

THUIARIA THUJA (Linnæus).

Sertularia thuja LINNÆUS, Syst. Nat., 1758, p. 809.

Thuiaria thuja HINCKS, Br. Hyd. Zooph., 1868, p. 275.

NUTTING, Hyd. Woods Hole, 1901, p. 364.

WHITEAVES, Mar. Invert. E. Can., 1901, p. 26.

NUTTING. Am. Hyd., ii, 1904, p. 62.

STAFFORD, Fauna Atlantic Coast, 1912, p. 73.

Distribution.—Mingan islands (Packard); gulf of St. Lawrence (Whiteaves); Seven islands (Stafford); McMaster island, 30 fathoms.

NOTE.—Stafford refers to four species of *Thuiaria* from Gaspé, none of which he describes sufficiently to place, but apparently one of them is a *Synthecium* and is probably new and the others may be also.

Family *PLUMULARIDÆ*.

Genus AGLAOPHENOPSIS.

AGLAOPHENOPSIS CORNUTA (Verrill).

Cladocarpus cornutus VERRILL, Am. Jour. Sci. Arts, 1879, p. 310.

Aglaophenopsis cornuta NUTTING. Am. Hyd., i, 1900, p. 120.

WHITEAVES. Mar. Invert. E. Can., 1901, p. 28.

Distribution.—Off Sable island, on Banquereau, 200 fathoms (Verrill).

Genus ANTENNULARIA.

ANTENNULARIA AMERICANA Nutting.

Antennularia americana NUTTING. Am. Hyd., i, 1900, p. 69.

NUTTING, Hyd. Woods Hole, 1901, p. 368.

Distribution.—St. Andrews.

ANTENNULARIA ANTENNINA (Linnæus).

Sertularia antennina LINNÆUS, Syst. Nat., 1767, p. 1310.

Antennularia antennina HINCKS, Br. Hyd. Zooph., 1868, p. 280.

NUTTING, Am. Hyd., 1900, p. 69.

NUTTING, Hyd. Woods Hole, 1901, p. 367.

WHITEAVES, Mar. Invert. E. Can., 1901, p. 28.

STAFFORD. Fauna Atlantic Coast, 1912, p. 74.

Distribution.—Bay of Fundy, 10 to 60 fathoms (Verrill); St. Andrews (Stafford); channel off White Horse island.

Genus CLADOCARPUS.

CLADOCARPUS POURTALESI, Verrill.

Cladocarpus pourtalesi VERRILL, Am. Jour. Sci. Arts, 1879, p. 309.

NUTTING, Am. Hyd., i, 1900, p. 116.

WHITEAVES, Mar. Invert. E. Can., 1901, p. 28.

Distribution.—Southwest of cape Sable, 112 to 115 fathoms, Banquereau, off Sable sland, 300 fathoms (Verrill).

CLADOCARPUS SPECIOSUS Verrill.

Cladocarpus speciosus VERRILL, Amer. Jour. Sci. Arts., 1879, p. 311.

NUTTING, Am. Hyd., i, 1900, p. 116.

WHITEAVES, Mar. Invert. E. Can., 1901, p. 28.

Distribution.—Banquereau, off Sable island, 200 fathoms (Verrill),

Genus PLUMULARIA.

PLUMULARIA SETACEOIDES Bale.

Plumularia setaceoides BALE, Hyd. S. Australia, 1881, p. 28.
  FRASER, Hyd. Beaufort, 1912, p. 382.

Distribution.—On sargassum, Gulf Stream, east of Nova Scotia.

Genus SCHIZOTRICHA.

SCHIZOTRICHA GRACILLIMA (Sars).

Plumularia gracillima SARS, Vid. Selsk. Forh., 1873, p. 86.

Plumularia verrilli CLARK, Trans. Conn. Acad. Sci., 1876, p. 64.
  VERRILL, Prelim. Check-list, 1879, p. 18.

Schizotricha gracillima NUTTING, Am. Hyd., i, 1900, p. 80.
  NUTTING, Hyd. Woods Hole, 1901, p. 366.
  STAFFORD, Fauna Atlantic Coast, 1912, p. 74.

Distribution.—Grand Manan (Stafford).

Genus THECOCARPUS.

THECOCARPUS MYRIOPHYLLUM (Linnaeus).

Sertularia myriophyllum LINNÆUS, Syst. Nat., 1767, p. 1309.

Aglaophenia myriophyllum HINCKS, Br. Hyd. Zooph., 1868, p. 290.

Thecocarpus myriophyllum NUTTING, Am. Hyd., i, 1900, p. 107.
  WHITEAVES, Mar. Invert. E. Can., 1901, p. 28.

Distribution.—Le Have bank, 60 fathoms (Smith and Harger); off cape Gaspé, 60 fathoms (Whiteaves); Mingan islands (A. Agassiz).

BIBLIOGRAPHY.

(Only those papers referred to in the synonymy or in the text are listed).

Agassiz, L.—

  1862. Contributions to the natural history of the United States of America, vol. iv, p. 1-372. Boston.

Agassiz, A.—

  1865. North American Acalephæ. Illustrated Catalogue of the Museum of Comparative Zoology at Harvard College, no. 2, p. 1-234. Cambridge.

Alder, J.—

  1856. A notice of some new genera and species of British hydroid zoophytes. Annals and Magazine of Natural History, 2nd ser., vol. xviii, London.

  1857. A catalogue of the zoophytes of Northumberland and Durham. Transactions of the Tyneside Naturalists' Field Club, vol. iii, p. 1-70. Newcastle-upon-Tyne.

SESSIONAL PAPER No. 38a

Allman, G. J.—

 1844. Synopsis of the genera and species of zoophytes inhabiting the fresh
   waters of Ireland. Annals and Magazine of Natural History, 1st. ser.,
   vol. xiii, p. 328. London.
 1864. On the construction and limitation of genera among the hydroida.
   Ibid., 3rd. ser., vol. xiii.
 1871. A monograph of the gymnoblastic or tubularian hydroids. Published
   for the Ray Society, in 2 parts, 450 p., 23 pl. London.
 1877. Report of the Hydroida collected during the exploration of the Gulf
   Stream by L. F. de Pourtales. Memoirs of the Museum of Comparative
   Zoology at Harvard College, vol. v, no. 2, p. 1-64. Cambridge.

Bale. W. M.—

 1881. On the Hydroida of southeastern Australia, with descriptions of supposed new species and notes on the genus Aglaophenia. Journal of the
   Microscopical Society, Victoria, vol. ii, p. 1-34. Melbourne.
 1914. Further notes on Australian hydroids. III, Proceedings of the Royal
   Society of Victoria, vol. xxvii, n.s., pt. 1, p. 72-93. Melbourne.

Billard, A.—

 1907. Hydroides, in: Expeditiones Scientifiques du "Travailleur" et du
   "Talisman," t. viii, p. 159-241. Paris.

Bonnevie, K.—

 1899. Den norske Nordhavsexpedition, 1876-78, vol. vi, pt. 26. Zoologi Hydroida, p. 1-103. Christiania.

Broch, H.—

 1903. Die von dem Norwegischen Fischereidampfer "Michael Sars," in den
   Jahren, 1900-1902, in dem Nordmeer gesammelten Hydroiden. Bergens
   Museum Aarbog, no. 9, p. 1-14. Christiania.
 1909. Die Hydroiden der Arktischen Meere. Fauna Arctica, bd. v, Jena.
 1912. Coelentérés du Fond. Campagne Arctique de 1907. Brussels.

Clark, S. F.—

 1876. Description of new and rare hydroids from the New England coast.
   Transactions of the Connecticut Academy of Sciences, vol. iii, July,
   1875, p. 58-66. New Haven.
 1876. Report of the hydroids on the coast of Alaska and the Aleutian islands,
   collected by W. H. Dall, from 1871 to 1874. Proceedings of the Academy
   of Natural Sciences of Philadelphia, p. 205-238.
 1879. Report on the Hydroida collected during the exploration of the Gulf
   Stream and gulf of Mexico by Alexander Agassiz, 1877-78. Bulletin of
   the Museum of Comparative Zoology of Harvard College, vol. v, p.
   239-250. Cambridge.

Ellis, J. and Solander, D.—

 1786. The natural history of many curious and uncommon zoophytes collected from various parts of the globe. 208 p. London.

Fabricius, O.—

 1780. Fauna Groenlandica. Hauniae et Lipsiae.

Fleming, J.—

 1828. A history of British Animals. Edinburgh Philosophical Journal.

8 GEORGE V, A. 1918

Fraser, C. M.—

  1911. The hydroids of the west coast of North America. Bulletin from the
     Laboratories of Natural History, State University of Iowa, p. 1-91.
     Iowa City.
  1912. Notes on New England hydroids. Ibid., p. 39-48.
  1912. Some hydroids of Beaufort, North Carolina. Bulletin of the Bureau
     of Fisheries, vol. xxx, 1910, p. 339-387. Washington.
  1913. Hydroids from Nova Scotia, Canada Geological Survey, Victoria
     Memorial Museum. Bulletin No. 1, pt. xvi, p. 157-186. Ottawa.
  1914. Some hydroids of the Vancouver island region. Transactions of the
     Royal Society of Canada, 3rd ser., vol. viii, p. 99-216. Ottawa.
  1915. Pelagic hydroids, in: Exploration of the coast water between Nova
     Scotia and Chesapeake bay, July and August, 1913, by the United States
     Fisheries schooner "Grampus." Oceanography and Plankton. Bulletin
     of the Museum of Comparative Zoology at Harvard College, vol. lix, No.
     4, p. 306-314. Cambridge.

Hargitt, C. W.—

  1901. The Hydromedusæ. In three parts. American Naturalist, vol. xxxv, No.
     412, p. 301-315; No. 413, p. 379-395; No. 415, p. 575-595, New York.
  1908. A few cœlenterates of Woods Hole. Biological Bulletin of the Marine
     Biological Laboratory at Woods Hole, Mass., vol. xiv, No. 2, p. 95-120.
     Lancaster, Pa.

Hartlaub, C.—

  1897. Die Hydromedusen Helgolands. Wissenschaftlichen Meeresuntersu-
     chungen, n.f., bd. ii, hft. 3., p. 449-514. Keil und Leipzig.

Hassall, A.—

  1852. Description of three species of marine zoophytes. Transactions of the
     Royal Microscopical Society, vol. iii. London.

Hincks, T.—

  1853. Further notes on British zoophytes, with description of new species.
     Annals and Magazine of Natural History, 2nd ser., vol. xi. London.
  1861. A catalogue of the zoophytes of South Devon and South Cornwall,
     Ibid., 3rd ser., vol. viii.
  1866. On new British hydroids. Ibid., 3rd ser., vol. xviii.
  1868. A history of the British hydroid zoophytes. 2 vols. London.

Jäderholm, E.—

  1909. Northern and Arctic invertebrates in the collection of the Swedish
     State Museum. iv. Hydroiden. Kongelige Svenska Vetenskaps Akade-
     miens Handlingar, bd. 45, No. 1, p. 1-124. Stockholm.

Johnston, G.—

  1847. History of British zoophytes, ed. ii, in two volumes. London.

Levinsen, G. M. R.—

  1892. Om Fornyelsen af Ernæringsindividerne hos Hydroiderne. Videnska-
     belige Meddelelser fra den naturhistoriske Foreningi Kjøbenhavn,
     p. 12-31.
  1893. Meduser, Ctenophorer og Hydroider fra Grönlands Vestkyst tilligemed
     Bemærkninger on Hydroidernes Systematik. Ibid., p. 143-220.
  1913. Systematic Studies on the Sertularidæ. Ibid., p. 251-323,

Linnæus, C.—
  1758. Systema naturæ, 10th ed. Lipsiæ.
  1767. Ibid., 12th ed. Holmiæ.

von Lorenz, L.—
  1886. Polypomedusen von Jan Mayen, in: Die international Polarforschung,
    1882-83. Die Österreichische Polarstation, Jan Mayen. bd. iii. Wien.

McCrady, J.—
  1858. Gymnophthalmata of Charleston harbour. Proceedings of the Elliot
    Society of Natural History, vol. 1 for 1853-1858, p. 103-221. Read Apr.
    15, 1857. Charleston.

MacGillivray, J.—
  1842. Catalogue of the marine zoophytes of the neighbourhood of Aberdeen.
    Annals and Magazine of Natural History, 1st ser., vol. ix. London.

Mereschkowsky, M. C.—
  1877. On a new genus of hydroids from the White sea with short description
    of other new hydroids. Annals and Magazine of Natural History, 4th
    ser., vol. xx, p. 220-229. London.

Norman, A. M.—
  1864. On underscribed British Hydrozoa, Actinozoa and Polyzoa. Annals
    and Magazine of Natural History, 3rd ser., vol. xiii, London.
  1866. Report of the committee appointed for the purpose of exploring the
    coasts of the Hebrides by means of the dredge. Part i. On the Crus-
    tacea, Echinodernata, Polyzoa, Actinozoa and Hydrozoa. Report of the
    British Association for the Advancement of Science, 1866, p. 193-206.
    London.

Nutting, C. C.—
  1898. On three new species of hydroids and one new to Britain. Annals and
    Magazine of Natural History, 7th ser., vol. v, p. 362-366. London.
  1900. American hydroids. Pt. I. The Plumularidæ. Special Bulletin,
    United States National Museum, 152, p. Washington.
  1901. The hydroids of the Woods Hole region. United States Fish Commis-
    sion Bulletin for 1899, vol. xix, p. 325-386. Washington.
  1904. American hydroids. Pt. II. The Sertularidæ. Special Bulletin,
    United States National Museum, 152, p. Washington.
  1915. Ibid. Pt. III. The Campanularidæ and the Bonneviellidæ. 118 p.

Pallas, P.S.—
  1766. Elenchus Zoophytorum. Haag.

Sars, M.—
  1851. Beretning om en i Sommern 1849 foretagen Zoologisk Reise i Lofoten
    og Finmarken. Nyt Magazine for Naturvidenskaberne, bd. vi. Chris-
    tiania.
  1857. Bidrag til kundskaben om Middlehavets Littoral fauna. Ibid., vol. x.
  1863. Bemerkninger over fire norske Hydroider. Videnskabs-Sels-kabets
    Forhandlinger for 1862. Christiania.

Sars, G. O.—
  1873. Bidrag til kundskaben om Norges Hydroider. Ibid., for 1872,

8 GEORGE V, A. 1918

Stafford, J.—

   1912. On the fauna of the Atlantic coast of Canada. Contributions to Canadian Biology, being studies from the biological stations of Canada, 1906-1910. p. 69-78 (Hydroids, p. 72-74). Ottawa.

Stimpson, W.—

   1854. Synopsis of the marine invertebrata of Grand Manan. Smithsonian contributions to knowledge. vol. vi. Washington.

Verrill, A. E.—

   1872. Radiata from the coast of North Carolina. American Journal of Science and Arts. 3rd. ser., vol. v.

   1874-1879. Brief contributions to zoology from the Museum of Yale College. Results of recent dredging expeditions on the coast of New England. American Journal of Science and Arts, vol. vii, 1874, p. 38-138, p. 405-414, p. 500-505; vol. ix, 1875, p. 411-415; vol. x. 1875, p. 36-43; vol. xvi, 1878, p. 371-378; vol. xvii, 1879, p. 309-315.

   1879. Preliminary check-list of the marine invertebrates of Atlantic coast from cape Cod to the gulf of St. Lawrence. Prepared for the United States Commission of Fish and Fisheries.

Verrill, A. E. and Smith, S. I.—

   1874. Report of the Invertebrate animals of Vineyard sound and adjacent waters. Report of the Commissioner of Fisheries for 1871 and 1872, p. 295-747. Washington.

Whiteaves, J. F.—

   1901. Catalogue of the marine invertebrates of Eastern Canada. Geological Survey of Canada. p. 18-28. Ottawa.

EXPLANATION OF FIGURES.

(All drawings except 1*a* and 2*a* magnified 25 diameters.)

Plate I.

1. *Obelia articulata.*
   a. Colony, natural size.
   b. Portion of colony to show nature and arrangement of hydrothecæ and gonangia.

2. *Bimeria brevis.*
   a. Colonies, natural size.
   b. Branched colony.
   c. Unbranched individuals.

Plate II.

3. *Clytia johnstoni,* hydrothecæ.
   a. From the Devon Coast.
   b. From St. Mary's bay, N.S.
   c. From the coast of Grand Manan.
   d. From Bliss island.
   e. From Deer island.
   f. From the St. Croix river.

Drawings by Clara A. Fraser.

PLATE I

C. McLean Fraser.

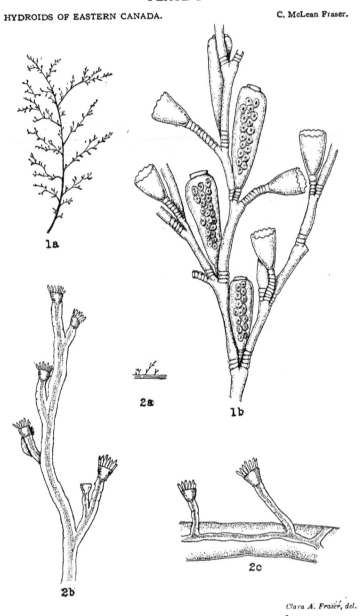

1a

2a

1b

2b

2c

Clara A. Fraser, del.

PLATE II

C. McLean Fraser.

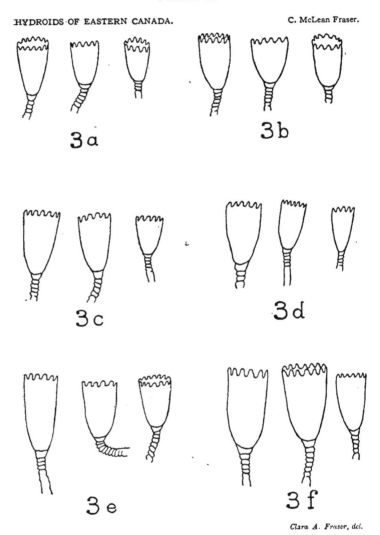

3a

3b

3c

3d

3e

3f

Clara A. Fraser, del.

CPSIA information can be obtained
at www.ICGtesting.com
Printed in the USA
BVHW07*1000180918
527708BV00025B/205/P